THE INTERNATIONAL RUGBY CHAMPIONSHIP

1883~1983

THE INTERNATIONAL RUGBY CHAMPIONSHIP 1883~1983

TERRY GODWIN

WILLOW BOOKS
Collins
Grafton Street, London
1984

Willow Books
William Collins PLC
London · Glasgow · Sydney · Auckland
Toronto · Johannesburg

First published in Great Britain 1984
© Terry Godwin 1984

Godwin, Terry
The international championship 1883–1983
1. Rugby football – Tournaments – History
I. Title
796.33'375   GV945.5

ISBN 0 00 218060 X

Filmset in Apollo by
MS Filmsetting Limited, Frome, Somerset
Printed and bound in Great Britain by
William Collins PLC, Glasgow

CONTENTS

ACKNOWLEDGEMENTS AND BIBLIOGRAPHY

Being well-acquainted with the pitfalls and frustrations of research into rugby football, and knowing to some extent the well-trodden paths of others similarly occupied, determined the fact-finding strategy for *The International Rugby Championship*. It was simply to establish one chief base, and venture further afield only if that source proved inadequate. That the choice became the National Library of Wales at Aberystwyth, which is in a manner of speaking, right on my own doorstep, was extremely fortunate for not only did it prove a treasure-house but the helpfulness and guidance of the staff was a great bonus. Where Aberystwyth was lacking, the British Museum Library, the Colindale Newspaper Library and above all, the National Library of Ireland in Dublin, filled the gaps. The source of most of the material understandably was newspapers, magazines and books. Space does not permit a complete list but the principal sources were:

NEWSPAPERS: *The Times*, the *Morning Post*, the *Daily Telegraph*, *The Guardian*, the *Daily Mail*, *The Observer*, the *South Wales Evening Post*, the *Western Mail*, the *Irish Times*, the *Irish Independent*, the *Limerick Leader*, the *Scotsman*, the *Glasgow Herald*, *The Sportsman*, the *Sporting Life* and *L'Equipe*.

MAGAZINES: *The Field*, the *Tatler*, *The Illustrated London News*, the *Illustrated Sporting and Dramatic News*, *The Sketch*, *Country Life*, the *Irish Sketch*, *Irish Life*, *Rugby World*, *Welsh Rugby*.

BOOKS AND PERIODICALS: *Rothman's Rugby Yearbook*, *Playfair Rugby Annual*, *John Wisden's Rugby Football Almanack*, *The Rugby Football Annual*, *The History of Scottish Rugby* (Sandy Thorburn, Johnston & Bacon), *History of Welsh International Rugby* (John Billot, Ron Jones Publications), *The Men In Green* (Sean Diffley, Pelham Books), *The Book of English International Rugby* (John Griffiths, Collins Willow), *Fields of Praise* (David Smith and Gareth Williams, University of Wales Press), *The World of Rugby* (John Reason and Carwyn James, BBC), *Welsh Rugby* (Clem Thomas and Geoffrey Nicholson, Collins), *The Men in Scarlet* (J.B.G. Thomas, Pelham), *A Touch of Glory* (Alun Richards, Michael Joseph).

Another major source of information was the magnificent cuttings book loaned to me by Cyril Lowe before his death and which I was allowed to retain for an extended period by his daughter, Mrs Cox.

I am also grateful for the enormous help I received from, among many others, Glyn James, honorary secretary of the Leicestershire Society of Referees, Jeff Rees and Tommy Kemp of the Hampshire Society of Referees, Denzil Lloyd of the Welsh Society of Referees, Brian Kempson of the Welsh Rugby Union, Bob Fitzgerald of the Irish Rugby Union and various members of the Rugby Football Union, the Scottish Rugby Union and French Rugby Federation.

Others who provided valuable information and guidance were Henri Garcia, Editor of *L'Equipe*; Graham Norton, from Maidstone; the indefatigable trio of rugby researchers, Tim Auty (who was particularly helpful with the picture research), Sandy Thorburn and John Griffiths; also Vivian Jenkins, Bill McMurtrie, Alf Wright and the late Carwyn James. I single out, too, John McInerney, fund-raiser extraordinaire employed by the Irish Rugby Union, and his wife, Gwenda, whose kindness and lunch-boxes sustained me during the visits to Lansdowne Road.

John Dorman, my literary agent, merits mention for his faith that the book would be completed on schedule and for convincing Tim Jollands and Louise Haines at Collins Willow of the same. Lastly, my biggest debt is to my family, particularly my wife Patti and my daughter Lisa, who not only tolerated my long absences from home, but were uncomplaining and assiduous assistants in research and in the reading of the proofs.

TERRY GODWIN
20 October 1983

PICTURE ACKNOWLEDGEMENTS

The author and publishers would like to thank the following for permission to reproduce the illustrations included in this book:

Agence Presse Sports – pages 126, 224, 248, 258, 274, 280, 282, 296, 301, 308, 315, 321 and 394

Timothy Auty Collection – pages 10, 17, 19, 21, 23, 24, 28, 30, 36, 38, 43, 49, 51, 58, 61, 68, 78, 94, 96, 110, 115, 155, 160, 175, 185, 190, 201, 209, 228, 244 and 251

BBC Hulton Picture Library – pages 12, 89, 103, 166 and 206

Central Press – pages 168 and 339

Colorsport – pages 331, 337, 348, 357, 366, 370, 378, 387, 398, 407, 418 and 426

Daily Graphic – page 120

Illustrated London News Picture Library – pages 3, 7, 72, 82, 130, 142 and 197

Rugby Football Today by E.H.D. Sewell (published 1931) – page 149

Syndication International – page 411

Western Mail, Cardiff – pages 9, 214 and 271

At the time of going to press, it proved difficult to determine the copyright holders of a number of the early photographs – interested parties should contact the publishers.

ABBREVIATIONS

The following abbreviations are used to denote rugby clubs:

Acads	Academicals
C.	College
CASG	Club Athlétique des Sports Généraux
H.	Hospital
OB	Old Boys
Ol	Olympique
PUC	Paris Universite Club
RCF	Racing Club de France
S.	Stade
SC	Sporting Club
SU	Sporting Union
TOEC	Toulouse Olympique Employés Club
U.	University
US	United Services
Wands	Wanderers

Symbols used:
* for a Captain
() indicates final appearance

PREFACE

The first rugby football international was played between Scotland and England at Raeburn Place, Edinburgh, on 27 March 1871. Ireland entered the lists, against England in 1875 and Scotland in 1877, while Wales did not begin competing until 1883 when they played England at Blackheath. Wales's next international was against Ireland in 1882 and their first match against Scotland took place at Raeburn Place on Monday, 8 January 1883. This last event completed the cycle of matches between the countries for the first time, and with England playing and beating all three other countries for the first time, the 1882–83 season is now generally accepted as the starting-point for the International Championship, even though Wales did not play Ireland that season.

All the countries played each other in 1884, but a spate of disputes and disagreements curtailed 6 of the 14 Championships up to 1898. From that point the four Home Unions learned to live with each other and even if they were not always in agreement, at least they honoured fixtures which by this time had become important events in the sporting calendar. Indeed rugby football had become one of the major crowd-pulling sports of the era, competing with all winter games in popularity, including Association Football.

The game by this time had spread throughout the British Empire, as it was then, and though reciprocal tours with Australia, New Zealand and South Africa had been established, the next major influence in the Championship was to come from much nearer home. France disproved the view, at least at club level, that rugby could be played by the English-speaking nations only and by 1906 the fledglings deemed that their game had advanced sufficiently to challenge England.

France, in fact, had already played New Zealand on 1 January 1906 before they met England at Parc des Princes in Paris on 22 March. Although France lost both matches by substantial margins, England were happy enough to invite the French to play at Richmond in 1907. Wales forged a French connection the following year and then Ireland entertained them in Dublin in 1909. Scotland had been approached for a fixture several times, but it was not until 1910 that the first Scotland-France match took place. So, in 1910, the Four Nations' Championship became the Five Nations' Championship.

The Championship was suspended during the First World War between 1915–19, and the status quo was maintained until 1931 when France were banned from the competition because of professionalism within their club game. Efforts were made to re-establish friendly relations and seemed to have been successful when the Second World War started and prevented France from rejoining the Championship. In 1947 France returned and have participated ever since. The Championship has been interrupted on only one occasion since France's re-entry – in 1972 when because of the violence in Ulster, Scotland and Wales did not honour their fixtures with Ireland.

INTRODUCTION

The International Championship has never been formally or officially recognised. The annual series of matches between England, France, Ireland, Scotland and Wales are, according to the game's governors, merely traditional contests with no prize for the winning teams or reward for the participants other than the honour of playing for one's country. It therefore follows that there is no Championship table, there are no Championship winners, no Wooden Spoonists, no winners of the Triple Crown or the Grand Slam. The International Championship, or as it is sometimes described, the Five Nations' Championship, is practically meaningless.

Fortunately, today's administrators are somewhat different from their predecessors in their approach and attitude to the question of an official Championship. Certainly they cannot approve a Championship as it was never officially inaugurated or endorsed when international rugby was first played and the original rules drawn up.

Today's administrators accede to the inevitable that most people in the game believe in a Championship and that there is absolutely no reason why that belief should be undermined by reminding everyone of archaic omissions, whether they were intended or not. It probably is quite convenient to leave the 'administration' of the Championship – the compiling of tables and the allocation of points for winning and so forth – to those who write about the game. If those writers evocatively employ other meaningless terms, such as the Triple Crown or Grand Slam, to colour their match previews it is reasonable to assume the game's administrators derive considerable benefits in terms of the number of tickets sold as a direct result of the (free) publicity.

If this proves the point that the Championship, and such theoretical trophies as the Triple Crown, are a desirable – and indeed necessary – product of the game's journalists, it leaves two questions only: how and when did the Championship begin?

My rugby researches have led me along many fruitless paths, but none have been as unrewarding as the search for the first mention of the Championship, the first publication of a Championship table and the authorship of one of the most emotive terms in rugby, the Triple Crown. Notwithstanding official attitudes of the time, one might have expected references of some sort soon after 1883, when the countries participated in what could have been construed as a Championship. Regrettably, the first allusion to it which I was able to discover was in the *South Wales Daily News* of 3 March 1893, ten years after the Championship had begun. Previewing the Wales v Ireland match the *News* wrote of the 'dreadful Wooden Spoon' being Ireland's fate if they lost. In 1894 *The Field* stated that Ireland, 'stands in the proud position of being Champion of the nations.' On 18 March 1895 the *South Wales Daily News* referred to both the Championship and the Wooden Spoon and on 14 March 1896 *The Times* proclaimed: 'Ireland have only to win to become the international Champions of the season.' Two days later *The Times* published a Championship table:

	Matches won	Matches drawn	Matches lost
Ireland	2	1	0
Scotland	1	1	1
England	1	0	2
Wales	1	0	2

The first mention, however, that I was able to unearth with regard to the Triple Crown was that of the *South Wales Daily News* on 20 March 1899: 'Ireland this year have repeated the performance of 1894 by winning the Triple Crown'. Thereafter there were many references to the existence of the

Championship, the Triple Crown and the Wooden Spoon. In 1914 *The Times* wrote of, 'the honour of the Rugby International Championship,' having gone to England, publishing at the foot of the column . . . 'How the international tournament has ended will be seen in the following summary of results.' Interestingly, few newspapers or magazines made more than passing reference to France, who started playing against all four home countries in 1910. France were rarely acknowledged in a published table; it was as if they did not play. If this was one of the many anomalies in the publication of tables, another was the insistence by some rugby annuals to totally ignore the results of seasons in which for one reason or another the Championship had not been completed. Such inconsistency has continued even today, and is largely the reason why an attempt has been made in this book to produce a much more representative table for each year of the Championship. These tables allocate precisely the finishing position of each country. Where, for instance, teams finish level on points for wins and draws, the higher position goes to the team which has scored most aggregate points. If the teams are still level using this criterion, the team which scores most tries is given preference. Interestingly, every Championship position in each table since 1883 has worked out satisfactorily employing this method, which, of course, could be supplemented further. Another consequence of adhering to a standard formula for table positions is to be seen in the number of Championships countries have won. Countries no longer 'share' a title and certainly a quintuple tie, as in 1973, would not occur again. Having ventured a new approach to the compilation of tables, one might also humbly submit the introduction of another term to add to Triple Crown and Grand Slam. The Triple Crown is 'awarded' to any one of the four home countries to beat the other three. The Grand Slam is given to any country, France included, which defeats the other four. The other nominal trophy could be a Small Slam, an award to the country which wins any three out of the four matches, save of course when the Triple Crown is the prize.

A problem not as easily overcome was that of allocating clubs to players during their respective appearances. Many players quite frequently switched clubs during their international careers, and particularly in the early years of the Championship, newspapers and magazines differed widely in the clubs they assigned to players. There were several occasions, too, when different scorers were attributed. In both cases, this book has attempted to remove the inaccuracies by either verification from individual sources, or when that method failed, by concurrence with the findings of other rugby historians. It is hoped that another advantage to the reader will be the recording of each player's number of appearances in the teams. The final appearance of each player is indicated when the figure is parenthesized.

The idea of providing match reports was resisted as much due to the varying accounts which often appeared early in the Championship as to the wish to recount unusual or little-known points of interest. Many such anecdotes have been shortened because of lack of space, a problem which also meant the regrettable omission of a list of referees and an index.

SWANSEA England beat Wales 2 goals, 4 tries to nil
EDINBURGH Scotland beat Wales 3 goals to 1 goal
MANCHESTER England beat Ireland 1 goal, 3 tries to 1 try
BELFAST Scotland beat Ireland 1 goal, 1 try to nil
EDINBURGH England beat Scotland 2 tries to 1 try
NB Wales did not play Ireland

CHAMPIONSHIP TABLE
England – Championship, Triple Crown

Pos	Country	P	W	D	L	Tries F	A	Pts
1	England	3	3	0	0	12	2	6
2	Scotland	3	2	0	1	6	3	4
3	Ireland	2	0	0	2	1	6	0
4	Wales	2	0	0	2	1	9	0

This is generally accepted as the first Championship, because one country, England, met and beat the other three for the first time and Scotland played Wales for the first time. With Ireland and Wales yet to find their international form, the critical match in 1883 – and for the subsequent four years – was between England and Scotland. Whoever won that match won the Championship, while the Irish and Welsh had to content themselves with a private battle to determine who could avoid the Wooden Spoon. England were clearly the dominant side in 1883 and by scoring 12 tries they established a fairly high standard: only Scotland, with 16 tries in 1887, beat the English try total in the run-up years to 1891, when points-scoring (and points values) became uniform and the accepted method of arriving at a result.

Although Scotland had introduced three threequarters as early as 1881, England did not try this method until their first match of 1883 (played in November 1882), against Wales.

Experimentation in playing formations was very common in those days: although contemporary accounts did not indicate whether England's six-try rout of Wales was a consequence of playing three threequarters. The headlines for the match naturally centred on Gregory Wade's three tries – the Championship's first hat-trick. Harry Tristram also made his international début for England in 1883 – a fact worth noting because many years later the Oxford University full-back was given the supreme accolade of being described as the best-ever by Billy Bancroft, the Welsh player whom many rated similarly. Scotland were not without their stars: Bill Maclagan, Charles Reid and Don Wauchope were praised long after their international days had finished.

Wales had come a long way since their humiliation by England in 1881, and they were continually seeking improvements to counter the greater skills and experience of the English and Scots. In 1883, for instance, they played eight forwards to England's nine. They also discarded the use of two full-backs, which meant that Charles Lewis, of Llandovery, had the distinction of becoming the first proper Wales full-back. Whatever weakness there was in early Irish rugby, their hierarchy certainly could not have been accused of being out of touch with their players. Most of the officers and indeed the first presidents of the IRU were players. Some, like George Scriven in 1883, captained Ireland while holding the office of president.

WALES v ENGLAND   1/1

16 December 1882
St Helen's, Swansea
England (2G, 4T) Wales nil

England T: Wade (3), Bolton, Henderson, Thomson. C: Evanson (2).

The match had many 'firsts': it was the first international staged in Wales; it was the first international refereed by a Welshman (A. Herbert); it produced the Championship's first hat-trick of tries (by Oxford's Gregory Wade); Arthur Evanson and Arthur Taylor became the first players to have brothers who had already played international rugby (Wyndham Evanson 1875–79, Henry Taylor 1879–82 – both for England). Herbert Fuller, the only Cambridge player in the England side, distinguished himself in another respect: he went on to win six blues (1878–83), a record which still holds today. Despite the severity of the defeat Wales did not savagely wield the axe: only J. Clare and E. Treharne were not selected again and Tom Clapp and Bob Gould went on to play, respectively, 12 and 9 more Championship matches.

WALES   *C.P. Lewis 1 (Llandovery College), D.H. Bowen 1 (Llanelli); W.B. Norton 1 (Cardiff), J. Clare (1) (Cardiff), D. Gwynn 1 (Swansea); C.H. Newman 1 (Newport), E. Treharne (1) (Pontypridd); T. Baker Jones 1 (Newport), T.J.S. Clapp 1 (Nantyglo), J.H. Judson 1 (Llanelli), F.J. Purdon 1 (Swansea), G.L. Morris 1 (Swansea), A. Cattell 1 (Llanelli), G.F. Harding 1 (Newport), R. Gould 1 (Newport).

ENGLAND   A.S. Taylor 1 (Blackheath); W.N. Bolton 1 (Blackheath), A.M. Evanson 1 (Oxford U.), C.G. Wade 1 (Oxford U.); A. Rotherham 1 (Oxford U.), J.H. Payne 1 (Broughton); *E.T. Gurdon 1 (Richmond), H. Vassall (1) (Oxford U.), G.T. Thomson 1 (Halifax), W.M. Tatham 1 (Oxford U.), H.G. Fuller 1 (Cambridge U.), G. Standing 1 (Blackheath), R.S.F. Henderson 1 (Blackheath), C.S. Wooldridge 1 (Oxford U.), R.S. Kindersley 1 (Oxford U.).
NB England played three threequarters for the first time.

Referee A. Herbert (Wales)

SCOTLAND v WALES   1/2

8 January 1883
Raeburn Place, Edinburgh
Scotland (3G) Wales (1G)

Scotland T: Macfarlan (2), Don Wauchope. C: Maclagan (3).
Wales T: Judson. C: Lewis.

The first match between Scotland and Wales was played on a Monday. When J.G. Walker twisted his knee (15 minutes), he became the first player to leave the field because of injury in a Championship match. Some sources stated that R.H. Bridie played for Wales. In fact Bridie, a Scot by birth who played only once for Wales (against Ireland in 1882), was replaced by W.B. Norton of Cardiff. Wales, who had arrived one player short, drafted Dr A. Griffin (Edinburgh University) into the forwards. Griffin's nationality has been the subject of some debate. However, it is certain that when A. and J.G. Walker took the field for Scotland they became the first brothers to play for the same side in a Championship match. Wales provided a pointer to the future by playing one full-back (Charles Lewis, the captain) for the first time.

SCOTLAND   D.W. Kidston 1 (Glasgow Acads); W.E. Maclagan 1 (London Scottish), D.J. Macfarlan 1 (London Scottish); A.R. Don Wauchope 1 (Cambridge U.), W.S. Brown 1 (Edinburgh Inst FP); T. Ainslie 1 (Edinburgh Inst FP), J.B. Brown 1 (Glasgow Acads), *D.Y. Cassels 1 (W. of Scotland), J. Jamieson 1 (W. of Scotland) J.G. Mowat 1 (Glasgow Acads), C. Reid 1 (Edinburgh Acads), D. Somerville 1 (Edinburgh Inst FP), A. Walker 1 (W. of Scotland), J.G. Walker (1) (W. of Scotland), W.A. Walls 1 (Glasgow Acads).

WALES   *C.P. Lewis 2 (Llandovery College); C.H. Newman 2 (Newport), W.B. Norton 2 (Cardiff); W.F. Evans (1) (Rhymney), G.F. Harding (2) (Newport); J.H. Judson (2) (Llanelli), T.J.S. Clapp 2 (Nantyglo), R. Gould 2 (Newport), T. Baker Jones 2 (Newport), H.S. Lyne 1 (Newport), F.J. Purdon (2) (Swansea), G.L. Morris 2 (Swansea), A. Cattell (2) (Llanelli), J.A. Jones (1) (Cardiff), Dr A. Griffin (1) (Edinburgh U.).

Referee G. Rowland Hill (England)

Gregory Wade, the Oxford University and England back

ENGLAND   A.S. Taylor 2 (Blackheath); W.N. Bolton 2 (Blackheath), A.M. Evanson 2 (Oxford U.), C.G. Wade 2 (Oxford U.); J.H. Payne 2 (Broughton), H.T. Twynam 1 (Richmond); W.M. Tatham 2 (Oxford U.), G. Standing (2) (Blackheath), C.S. Wooldridge 2 (Oxford U.), B.B. Middleton (1) (Birkenhead Park), H.G. Fuller 2 (Cambridge U.), R.M. Pattisson 1 (Cambridge U.), G.T. Thomson 2 (Halifax), *E.T. Gurdon 2 (Richmond), E.J. Moore 1 (Oxford U.).

IRELAND   J.W.R Morrow 1 (Queen's C. Belfast); R.E. McLean 1 (NIFC), R.H. Scovell 1 (Kingstown); W.W. Fletcher (1) (Kingstown), J.P. Warren (1) (Kingstown); S.A.M. Bruce 1 (NIFC), A.J. Forrest (1) (Wanderers), J.W. Taylor 1 (NIFC), A. Millar (1) (Kingstown), D.F. Moore 1 (Wanderers), H. King 1 (Dublin U.), J.A. Macdonald 1 (Methodist C. Belfast), R.W. Hughes 1 (NIFC), *G. Scriven 1 (Dublin U.), F.S. Heuston 1 (Kingstown).

Referee A.S. Pattison (Scotland)

ENGLAND v IRELAND   1/3

5 February 1883
Whalley Range, Manchester
England (1G, 3T) Ireland (1T)

England   T: Bolton, Tatham, Twynam, Wade. C: Evanson.
Ireland   T: Forrest.

Ireland played for most of the match with only 14 players — R.W. Hughes, the NIFC forward, having failed to recover fully from sea-sickness suffered on a wretched sea crossing the day before. Further insult was heaped on the luckless Irish because the IRU refused to allow the team travelling expenses. For four Irish players — Fletcher, Warren, Forrest and Millar — it was their only Championship appearance and four others, George Scriven (the captain), Taylor, King and Heuston played only once more. England, despite having scored ten tries in two matches, also made four changes for the Scotland match, dropping Arthur Taylor, Harry Twynam, Bernard Middleton and George Standing.

IRELAND v SCOTLAND   1/4

17 February 1883
Ormeau, Belfast
Scotland (1G, 1T) Ireland nil

Scotland   T: Reid, Somerville. C: Maclagan.

A miserable first Championship for Ireland was reflected in this match, played in a quagmire, at the NIFC Ground at Ormeau. Injuries decimated the Irish team. At one time they were down to ten players and only their defensive resolution kept the score within reasonable limits. The already well-established Scottish practice of capping schoolboys was continued with the playing of M.F. Reid, 18, a Loretto pupil, in place of D.J. Macfarlan. Ninian Finlay, Scotland's youngest ever player (17 years 36 days on his début in 1875), gained nine caps but did not play in a Championship match. Ireland's captain, George Scriven, was to be at the centre of the game's greatest controversy of the early years. He refereed the England-Scotland match of 1884, in which Law disputes led to a cessation of matches between the countries.

IRELAND   J.W.R. Morrow 2 (Queen's C. Belfast); W.W. Pike (1) (Kingstown), R.E. McLean 2 (NIFC); S.R. Collier (1) (Queen's C. Belfast), A.M. Whitestone (1) (Dublin U.); S.A.M. Bruce 2 (NIFC), F.S. Heuston (2) (Kingstown), R.W. Hughes 2 (NIFC), H. King (2) (Dublin U.), J.A. Macdonald 2 (Methodist C. Belfast), D.F. Moore 2 (Wanderers), R. Nelson 1 (Queen's C. Belfast), *G. Scriven (2) (Dublin U.), J.W. Taylor (2) (NIFC), W.A. Wallis (1) (Wanderers).

SCOTLAND   J.P. Veitch 1 (Royal HSFP); W.E. Maclagan 2 (London Scottish), M.F. Reid 1 (Loretto); P.W. Smeaton 1 (Edinburgh Acads), G.R. Aitchison (1) (Edinburgh Wands); T. Ainslie 2 (Edinburgh Inst FP), J.B. Brown 2 (Glasgow Acads), *D.Y. Cassels 2 (W. of Scotland), J. Jamieson 2 (W. of Scotland), D. McCowan 1 (W. of Scotland), W.A. Peterkin 1 (Edinburgh U.), C. Reid 2 (Edinburgh Acads), D. Somerville 2 (Edinburgh Inst FP), A. Walker 2 (W. of Scotland), W.A. Walls 2 (Glasgow Acads).

Referee H.C. Kelly (Ireland)

land), D. McCowan 2 (W. of Scotland), J.G. Mowat (2) (Glasgow Acads), C. Reid 3 (Edinburgh Acads), D. Somerville 3 (Edinburgh Inst FP), J. Jamieson 3 (W. of Scotland), A. Walker (3) (W. of Scotland), W. A. Walls 3 (Glasgow Acads).

ENGLAND   H.B. Tristram 1 (Oxford U.); W.N. Bolton 3 (Blackheath), A.M. Evanson 3 (Oxford U.), C.G. Wade 3 (Oxford U.); A. Rotherham 2 (Oxford U.), J.H. Payne 3 (Broughton); H.G. Fuller 3 (Cambridge U.), C. Gurdon 1 (Richmond), *E.T. Gurdon 3 (Richmond), R.S.F. Henderson 2 (Blackheath), E.J. Moore (2) (Oxford U.), R.M. Pattisson (2) (Cambridge U.), W.M. Tatham 3 (Oxford U.), G.T. Thomson 3 (Halifax), C.S. Wooldridge 3 (Oxford U.).

Referee H.C. Kelly (Ireland)

SCOTLAND v ENGLAND   1/5

3 March 1883
Raeburn Place, Edinburgh
England (2T) Scotland (1T)

Scotland   T: Reid.
England   T: Rotherham, Bolton.

England gained their first win in Scotland and so won what has become accepted as the inaugural Championship and the first Triple Crown triumph. Wilfred Bolton achieved the distinction of scoring a try in each of the three matches, out of 12 scored overall. England could also have triumphed in the matter of tactics, having deployed six backs against Scotland's five. One of England's scores was greeted with derision by a section of the crowd, which was deplored by the president of the Scottish Rugby Union at the after-match dinner.

SCOTLAND   D.W. Kidston (2) (Glasgow Acads); W.E. Maclagan 3 (London Scottish), M.F. Reid (2) (Loretto); P.W. Smeaton (2) (Edinburgh Acads), W. S. Brown (2) (Edinburgh Inst FP); T. Ainslie 3 (Edinburgh Inst FP), J.B. Brown 3 (Glasgow Acads), *D.Y. Cassels (3) (W. of Scot-

1884

LEEDS England beat Wales 1 goal, 2 tries to 1 goal
NEWPORT Scotland beat Wales 1 try, 1 dropped goal to nil
DUBLIN England beat Ireland 1 goal to nil
EDINBURGH Scotland beat Ireland 2 goals, 2 tries to 1 try
BLACKHEATH England beat Scotland 1 goal to 1 try
CARDIFF Wales beat Ireland 2 tries, 1 dropped goal to nil

CHAMPIONSHIP TABLE
England – Championship, Triple Crown

Pos	Country	P	W	D	L	Tries F	A	Pts
1	England (1)	3	3	0	0	5	2	6
2	Scotland (2)	3	2	0	1	6	2	4
3	Wales (4)	3	1	0	2	3	4	2
4	Ireland (3)	3	0	0	3	1	7	0

England won the Championship again, but 1884 was better known as the year of the Great Dispute. The controversy centred on England's winning try against Scotland at Blackheath and not only caused the cancellation of their fixture for 1885, but the formation of the International Board was a direct result. In essence Scotland's complaint was that England had scored from an illegal act: a knocking back by one of their own players which they, the Scots, interpreted as a knock *on*. They argued that knocking *on* implied knocking the ball with the hand in any direction and play should have been stopped before the English player (Richard Kindersley) gained possession and ran through for a try. That the incident led to much bitterness and dispute was without question, for England refused to be moved from their view that the Law was precise and clear and that they had won fairly. The Scots were told to take it or leave it.

Adjudication was suggested by Scotland, but England did not agree. It was left to Ireland and Wales to produce a formula for reconciliation: the formation of a body (the International Board) for the settlement of future disputes. At first England supported the proposal but at the inauguration of the International Board in 1886 they were conspicuous in their absence. The issue had by now become a wider one: England felt their position as chief lawmakers and governors of the game was at stake. The International Board flexed its muscles by informing England that all internationals would now be conducted under their rules, and that no one would play England unless they concurred and joined the Board. It was red rag to a bulldog if not a bull, and England played no Championship games in 1888 or 1889. Good sense took some time to prevail and the matter went to arbitration, the International Board nominating Lord Kingsburgh, the Lord Justice Clerk, and the RFU putting forward Major Marindin, president of the Football Association. These two gentlemen gave judgement in April 1890, which was binding on all parties, but from a distance looked to be heavily biased in England's favour. The International Board's insistence that all internationals be played and administered under their Laws was accepted under a new constitution, but England were to have six members on the new committee with Ireland, Scotland and Wales having only two each. The power therefore still rested with the game's founders.

ENGLAND v WALES 2/6

5 January 1884
Cardigan Fields, Leeds
England (1G, 2T) Wales (1G)

England T: Rotherham, Twynam, Wade. C: Bolton.
Wales T: Allen. C: Lewis.

The first international to be staged in Yorkshire was the scene for Wales's first try against England, scored by a North Walian, Charlie Allen. It was converted by Charles Lewis, who was the first vice-president to be elected to the Welsh Rugby Union at their foundation in Neath in 1881. Charles Chapman won his only cap, supposedly playing because Arthur Evanson had retired (Evanson, in fact, played once more, against Scotland two months later), while in the Welsh team H.J. Simpson was selected when Frank Purdon withdrew on the morning of the match. The crowd of 2000 was disappointingly small.

ENGLAND H.B. Tristram 2 (Oxford U.); C.G. Wade 4 (Oxford U.), C.E. Chapman (1) (Cambridge U.), W.N. Bolton 4 (Blackheath); A. Rotherham 3 (Oxford U.), H.T. Twynam 2 (Richmond); J.T. Hunt (1) (Manchester), C.S. Wooldridge 4 (Blackheath), C.J.B. Marriott 1 (Cambridge U.), H.G. Fuller (4) (Cambridge U.), E.L. Strong 1 (Oxford U.), W.M. Tatham 4 (Oxford U.), R.S.F. Henderson 3 (Blackheath), C. Gurdon 2 (Richmond), *E.T. Gurdon 4 (Richmond).

WALES C.P. Lewis 3 (Llandovery College); C.P. Allen 1 (Oxford U.), W.B. Norton 3 (Cardiff), C.G. Taylor 1 (Ruabon); *C.H. Newman 3 (Newport), W.H. Gwynn 1 (Swansea); W.D. Phillips 1 (Cardiff), J.S. Smith 1 (Cardiff), H.J. Simpson 1 (Cardiff), T.J.S. Clapp 3 (Newport), R. Gould 3 (Newport), H.S. Lyne 2 (Newport), F.L. Margrave 1 (Llanelli), F.G. Andrews 1 (Swansea), G.L. Morris 3 (Swansea).

Referee J.A. Gardner (Scotland)

WALES v SCOTLAND 2/7

12 January 1884
Rodney Parade, Newport
Scotland (1T, 1DG) Wales nil

Scotland T: Ainslie. DG: Asher.

As was normal in the early years of the Championship, both scores were the subject of dispute in a match which was postponed from the previous week. Harry Gwynn, the Wales half-back, had the chance to score but having crossed the Scottish line, looked for support only to drop the ball when he found none. Gwynn, who became secretary of the WRU in 1893, was also a controversial figure off the field and was renowned for provocative proposals at committee meetings of the WRU and the International Board. All the officials at the match were, incidentally, men of high office: James McLaren, the referee, was president of the RFU, and the umpires, J.A. Gardner and Richard Mullock, were respectively the secretaries of the Scottish and Welsh Rugby Unions.

WALES C.P. Lewis (4) (Llandovery College); C.P. Allen (2) (Beaumaris), W.B. Norton 4 (Cardiff), C.G. Taylor 2 (Ruabon); *C.H. Newman 4 (Newport), W.H. Gwynn 2 (Swansea); H.J. Simpson 2 (Cardiff), W.D. Phillips 2 (Cardiff), R. Gould 4 (Newport), H.S. Lyne 3 (Newport), T. Baker Jones 3 (Newport), T.J.S. Clapp 4 (Newport), F.L. Margrave (2) (Llanelli), G.L. Morris (4) (Swansea), F.G. Andrews (2) (Swansea).

SCOTLAND J.P. Veitch 2 (Royal HSFP); *W.E. Maclagan 4 (London Scottish), D.J. Macfarlan 2 (London Scottish), G.C. Lindsay 1 (Fettesian-Lorettonians); A.R. Don Wauchope 2 (Fettesian-Lorettonians), A.G.G. Asher 1 (Oxford U.); T. Ainslie 4 (Edinburgh Inst FP), J.B. Brown 4 (Glasgow Acads), J. Jamieson 4 (W. of Scotland), R. Maitland 1 (Edinburgh Inst FP), W.A. Peterkin 2 (Edinburgh U.),C. Reid 4 (Edinburgh Acads), D. Somerville (4) (Edinburgh Inst FP), J. Tod 1 (Watsonians), W.A. Walls 4 (Glasgow Acads).

Referee J.S. McLaren (England)

IRELAND v ENGLAND 2/8

4 February 1884
Lansdowne Road, Dublin
England (1G) Ireland nil

England T: Bolton. C: Sample.

Ireland introduced eight players new to international rugby but it was an injury, a broken leg, to one of their more seasoned players, S.A.M. Bruce, early in the second half which effectively ruled out their chances.

IRELAND J.W.R. Morrow 3 (Queen's C. Belfast); R.E. McLean 3 (NIFC), R.H. Scovell (2) (Dublin U.), D.J. Ross 1 (Belfast Albion); M. Johnston 1 (Dublin U.), W.W. Higgins 1 (NIFC); S.A.M. Bruce (3) (NIFC), F.H. Levis (1) (Wanderers), H.M. Brabazon 1 (Dublin U.), D.F. Moore 3 (Wanderers), J.B.W. Buchanan 1 (Dublin U.), *J.A. Macdonald 3 (Methodist C. Belfast), R.W. Hughes 3 (NIFC). W.G. Rutherford 1 (Tipperary), O.S. Stokes (1) (Cork Bankers).

ENGLAND C.H. Sample 1 (Cambridge U.); W.N. Bolton 5 (Blackheath), H.J. Wigglesworth (1) (Thornes), H. Fallas (1) (Wakefield Trinity); J.H. Payne 4 (Broughton), H.T. Twynam 3 (Richmond); W.M. Tatham 5 (Oxford U.), A. Wood (1) (Halifax), C.S. Wooldridge 5 (Blackheath), A. Teggin 1 (Broughton Rangers), H. Bell (1) (New Brighton), E.L. Strong 2 (Oxford U.), G.T. Thomson 4 (Halifax), *E.T. Gurdon 5 (Richmond), C.J.B. Marriott 2 (Cambridge U.).

Referee J.S. Laing (Scotland)

SCOTLAND v IRELAND 2/9

16 February 1884
Raeburn Place, Edinburgh
Scotland (2G, 2T) Ireland (1T)

Scotland T: Peterkin, Tod, Don Wauchope, Asher. C: Berry (2).
Ireland T: McIntosh.

Selection problems bedevilled Ireland. Only six of the side originally chosen for this match turned out. The eventual side showed eight

changes from the side beaten by England at Lansdowne Road 12 days earlier (this match being played on a Thursday). The SRU erected a grandstand and nearly 6000 spectators came to watch. Some of them were somewhat disgruntled that kick-off was half-an-hour late.

SCOTLAND J.P. Veitch 3 (Royal HSFP); *W.E. Maclagan 5 (London Scottish), E.T. Roland 1 (Edinburgh Wands), D.F. Macfarlan 3 (London Scottish); A.R. Don Wauchope 3 (Fettesian-Lorettonians), A.G.G. Asher 2 (Oxford U.); T. Ainslie 5 (Edinburgh Inst FP), C.W. Berry 1 (Fettesian-Lorettonians), J.B. Brown 5 (Glasgow Acads), J. Jamieson 5 (W. of Scotland), D. McCowan 3 (W. of Scotland), W.A. Peterkin 3 (Edinburgh U.), C. Reid 5 (Edinburgh Acads), J. Tod 2 (Watsonians), W.A. Walls 5 (Glasgow Acads).

IRELAND J.M. O'Sullivan 1 (Limerick); R.E. McLean 4 (NIFC), G.H. Wheeler 1 (Queen's C. Belfast), L.M. McIntosh (1) (Dublin U.); M. Johnston 2 (Dublin U.), W.W. Higgins (2) (NIFC); J.B.W. Buchanan (2) (Dublin U.), A. Gordon (1) (Dublin U.), T.H.M. Hobbs 1 (Dublin U.), R.W. Hughes 4 (NIFC), J. Johnston 1 (NIFC), W. Kelly (1) (Wanderers), *J.A. Macdonald (4) (Methodist C. Belfast), J.F. Maguire (1) (Cork), W.G. Rutherford 2 (Lansdowne).

Referee G. Rowland Hill (England)

Scotland's A.R. Don Wauchope, one of the most gifted backs in the early years of the Championship

ENGLAND v SCOTLAND   2/10

1 March 1884
Rectory Field, Blackheath
England (1G) Scotland (1T)

England   T: Kindersley. C: Bolton.
Scotland   T: Jamieson.

The first international to be played at the Rectory Field, Blackheath, was important in that an incident at it led to the formation of the International Board: Scotland disputed England's try (which emanated from the celebrated 'knock-back' by Scotland's C.W. Berry) and, after 10 minutes' on-field discussion, the referee awarded the match-winning conversion near the posts. The referee, George Scriven, who had captained Ireland against England and Scotland the previous season, did not officiate at another international but he became a leading figure in Irish rugby. Ironically, the RFU made a great deal of effort to 'sell' this match: they suggested clubs 'abandon' their fixtures that day, they pre-sold match tickets and erected stands. The exercise was rewarded with an 8000 attendance.

ENGLAND   H.B. Tristram 3 (Oxford U.); W.N. Bolton 6 (Blackheath), A.M. Evanson (4) (Richmond), C.G. Wade 5 (Oxford U.); A. Rotherham 4 (Oxford U.), H.T. Twynam (4) (Richmond); C. Gurdon 3 (Richmond), *E.T. Gurdon 6 (Richmond), R.S.F. Henderson 4 (Blackheath), R.S. Kindersley 2 (Oxford U.), C.J.B. Marriott 3 (Cambridge U.), E.L. Strong (3) (Oxford U.), W.M. Tatham (6) (Oxford U.), G.T. Thomson 5 (Halifax), C.S. Wooldridge 6 (Blackheath).

SCOTLAND   J.P. Veitch 4 (Royal HSFP); *W.E. Maclagan 6 (London Scottish), E.T. Roland (2) (Edinburgh Wands), D.J. Macfarlan 4 (London Scottish); A.G.G. Asher 3 (Fettesian-Lorettonians), A.R. Don Wauchope 4 (Fettesian-Lorettonians); T. Ainslie 6 (Edinburgh Inst FP), J.B. Brown 6 (Glasgow Acads), C.W. Berry 2 (Fettesian-Lorettonians), J. Jamieson 6 (W. of Scotland), D. McCowan (4) (W. of Scotland), W.A. Peterkin 4 (Edinburgh U.), C. Reid 6 (Edinburgh Acads), J. Tod 3 (Watsonians), W.A. Walls 6 (Glasgow Acads).

Referee G. Scriven (Ireland)

WALES v IRELAND   1/11

12 April 1884
Cardiff Arms Park
Wales (2T, 1DG) Ireland nil

Wales   T: Norton, Clapp. DG: Stadden.

Ireland arrived two players short and, after negotiations, their complement was made up by the inclusion of two leading Welsh players, Frank Purdon* and H.M. Jordan. Purdon had already played four times for Wales, including once against Ireland in 1882, but was never selected again after appearing for Ireland. Jordan fared better. He made his Wales début against England in 1885 and made his third and final appearance in 1889 against Scotland. No record exists as to the Irish players who did not turn up – but arguably the phrase 'One Cap Wonders' could have stemmed from this Irish team which had no fewer than ten players for whom this was their one and only appearance.

WALES   T.M. Barlow (1) (Cardiff); C.G. Taylor 3 (Ruabon), F.E. Hancock 1 (Cardiff), W.B. Norton (5) (Cardiff); W.H. Stadden 1 (Cardiff), W.H. Gwynn 3 (Swansea); T.J.S. Clapp 5 (Newport), R. Gould 5 (Newport), H.S. Lyne 4 (Newport), S. Goldsworthy 1 (Swansea), J.T. Hinton 1 (Cardiff), *H.J. Simpson (3) (Cardiff), W.D. Phillips (3) (Cardiff), W.R.B. Broderick (1) (Llanelli), J.S. Smith 2 (Cardiff).

IRELAND   J.W.R. Morrow 4 (Queen's C. Belfast); E.H. Greene 1 (Dublin U.), J. Pedlow (1) (Bessbrook); R.G. Warren 1 (Lansdowne), H.F. Spunner (1) (Wanderers); A.J. Hamilton (1) (Lansdowne), H.G. Cook (1) (Lansdowne), *D.F. Moore (4) (Wanderers), F.W. Moore 1 Wanderers), J.M. Kennedy (1) (Wanderers), W.S. Collis (1) (Wanderers), J. Fitzgerald (1) (Wanderers), R.O.N. Hall (1) (Dublin U.), L. W. Moyers (1) (Dublin U.), W.E. Johnstone (1) (Dublin U.).

Referee Not known

*Ned Van Esbeck, noted Irish rugby historian, is convinced that J. McDaniel (Newport) played and not Purdon. Confirmation came from relatives of McDaniel, who later became an official with Bath RFC. For further information, see *100 Years of Irish Rugby* by Ned Van Esbeck (Gill & McMillan).

1885

SWANSEA England beat Wales 1 goal, 4 tries to 1 goal, 1 try
GLASGOW Scotland and Wales drew, no score
MANCHESTER England beat Ireland 2 tries to 1 try
EDINBURGH Scotland beat Ireland 1 goal, 2 tries to nil
NB Ireland v Wales and England v Scotland were not played

CHAMPIONSHIP TABLE
England – Championship, Triple Crown

Pos	Country	P	W	D	L	Tries F	A	Pts
1	England (1)	2	2	0	0	7	3	4
2	Scotland (2)	2	1	1	0	3	0	3
3	Wales (3)	2	0	1	1	2	5	1
4	Ireland (4)	2	0	0	2	1	5	0

The arguments over the England-Scotland match of 1884 had not receded, and with Ireland and Wales also in dispute and refusing to play each other, the 1885 Championship was settled with each country playing two matches. The season also had a unique event – an abandoned match, between Ireland and Scotland at Ormeau, Belfast, on 21 February. If pedancy had ruled in the England-Scotland match, absurdity was the order of the day in the abandoned match.

A storm of such ferocity had blown up during it, that after 25 minutes further play was out of the question. At the time Scotland were ahead by a try scored by J. Jamieson. *The Field* wrote: 'There appeared to be a complication over a try claimed by Jamieson, but as the match remains null and void, it is of little moment.' How wrong they were. Scotland told Ireland they would claim the victory unless the Irish agreed to a replay – in Scotland. The Irish, perhaps surprisingly in view of the uneasy relations, agreed and the second match took place a fortnight later. Scotland won this, without dispute, but England, having beaten Wales and Ireland, took the title. England had now won eight Championship matches in a row.

Arthur Gould, rugby football's first superstar

WALES v ENGLAND 3/12

3 January 1885
St Helen's, Swansea
England (1G, 4T) Wales (1G, 1T)

Wales T: Jordan (2). C: Taylor.
England T: Hawcridge, Kindersley, Ryalls, Teggin, Wade. C: Payne.

Charles Lewis, who had played at full-back for Wales against England the year before, refereed. It was the first international for Arthur Gould, who was to become the outstanding personality of British rugby in the years before the turn of the century. The match attracted 5000 spectators. Some accounts credited Arthur Gould with the Welsh conversion.

WALES   A.J. Gould 1 (Newport); H.M. Jordan 1 (Newport), F.E. Hancock 2 (Cardiff), C.G. Taylor 4 (Ruabon); *C.H. Newman 5 (Newport), W.H. Gwynn 4 (Swansea); R. Gould 6 (Newport), T.J.S. Clapp 6 (Newport), H.S. Lyne (5) (Newport), T. Baker Jones 4 (Newport), S. Goldsworthy 2 (Swansea), L.C. Thomas 1 (Cardiff), J. Rowlands (1) (Lampeter), J.S. Smith (3) (Cardiff), E.S. Richards 1 (Swansea).

ENGLAND   H.B. Tristram 4 (Oxford U.); C.G. Wade 6 (Oxford U.), A.E. Stoddart 1 (Blackheath), J.J. Hawcridge 1 (Bradford); J.H. Payne 5 (Broughton), A. Rotherham 5 (Oxford U.); *E.T. Gurdon 7 (Richmond), R.S. Kindersley (3) (Exeter), E.D. Court (1) (Blackheath), H.J. Ryalls 1 (New Brighton), F. Moss 1 (Broughton), A.T. Kemble 1 (Liverpool), R.S.F. Henderson (5) (Blackheath), A. Teggin 2 (Broughton Rangers), G. Harrison 1 (Hull).

Referee C.P. Lewis (Wales)

SCOTLAND v WALES   3/13

10 January 1885
Hamilton Crescent, Glasgow
Drawn, no score

There were brothers, one back, one forward, on each side: George and Richard Maitland playing for Scotland and Arthur and Bob Gould for Wales. Another interesting selection was that of Llandovery College schoolboy, William Henry Thomas, who played in the Welsh pack at the age of 19. A relatively small crowd of 2000 paid to watch. *The Field* was critical of Welsh play: 'The Welsh method of stopping rushes by lying on the ball is hardly to be commended.'

SCOTLAND   P.R. Harrower 1 (London Scottish); *W.E. Maclagan 7 (London Scottish), A.E. Stephen 1 (W. of Scotland), G. Maitland 1 (Edinburgh Inst FP); A.R. Don Wauchope 5 (Fettesian-Lorettonians), A.G.G. Asher 4 (Fettesian-Lorettonians); T. Ainslie 7 (Edinburgh Inst FP), C.W. Berry 3 (Fettesian-Lorettonians), J. Jamie-

son 7 (W. of Scotland), R. Maitland (2) (Edinburgh Inst FP), J.G. Mitchell 1 (W. of Scotland), W.A. Peterkin 5 (Edinburgh U.), C. Reid 7 (Edinburgh Acads), G.H. Robb (1) (Glasgow Acads), J. Tod 4 (Watsonians).

WALES   A.J. Gould 2 (Newport); C.G. Taylor 5 (Ruabon), F.E. Hancock 3 (Cardiff), H.M. Jordan 2 (Newport); *C.H. Newman 6 (Newport), W.H. Gwynn (5) (Swansea); E.P. Alexander 1 (Brecon), A.F. Hill 1 (Cardiff), L.C. Thomas (2) (Cardiff), W.H. Thomas 1 (Llandovery College), S. Goldsworthy (3) (Swansea), D. Morgan 1 (Swansea), T.J.S. Clapp 7 (Newport), R. Gould 7 (Newport), T. Baker Jones (5) (Newport).

Referee G. Rowland Hill (England)

ENGLAND v IRELAND   3/14

7 February 1885
Whalley Range, Manchester
England (2T) Ireland (1T)

England   T: Bolton, Hawcridge.
Ireland   T: Greene.

England clearly were not satisfied with this side, for eleven were dropped and seven of them did not play internationally again. Ireland were still

Charles Gurdon, the Richmond forward, who like his elder brother, Edward Temple, never experienced defeat while playing for England

struggling to produce a winning combination and once again they looked to newcomers, seven in all. Two Irish players, F.W. Moore and T.C. Allen, were drafted in only at the last moment because H.M. Brabazon and J. Johnston 'failed to put in an appearance'. The match, watched by 6000, was refereed by Horace Lyne, who had played for Wales against England a month earlier.

ENGLAND   C.H. Sample 2 (Cambridge U.); J.J. Hawcridge (2) (Bradford), A.E. Stoddart 2 (Blackheath), W.N. Bolton 7 (Blackheath); A. Rotherham 6 (Oxford U.), J.H. Payne (6) (Broughton); C.H. Horley (1) (Swinton), C. Gurdon 4 (Richmond), C.S. Wooldridge (7) (Blackheath), G.T. Thomson (6) (Halifax), G. Harrison (2) (Hull), H.J. Ryalls (2) (New Brighton), F. Moss 2 (Broughton), *E.T. Gurdon 8 (Richmond), A.T. Kemble 2 (Liverpool).

IRELAND   G.H. Wheeler (2) (Queen's C. Belfast); R.E. McLean (5) (NIFC), J.P. Ross 1 (Lansdowne), E.H. Greene 2 (Dublin U.); E.C. Crawford (1) (Dublin U.), R.G. Warren 2 (Lansdowne); H.J. Neill 1 (NIFC), T.H.M. Hobbs (2) (Dublin U.), T.R. Lyle 1 (Dublin U.), F.W. Moore 2 (Wanderers), R.M. Bradshaw 1 (Wanderers), R.W. Hughes 5 (NIFC), *W.G. Rutherford 3 (Tipperary), T.C. Allen (1) (NIFC), T. Shanahan 1 (Lansdowne).

Referee H.S. Lyne (Wales)

unless Ireland agreed to a replay in Edinburgh, where Scotland duly triumphed against an Irish side wearing white jerseys. Both matches were refereed by H.C. Kelly, the NIFC forward and former Irish captain who had won six caps in pre-Championship matches. There was a crowd of 8000.

SCOTLAND   J.P. Veitch 5 (Royal HSFP); *W.E. Maclagan 8 (London Scottish), G. Maitland (2) (Edinburgh Inst FP), H.L. Evans (1) (Edinburgh U.); A.R. Don Wauchope 6 (Fettesian-Lorettonians), P.H. Don Wauchope 1 (Fettesian-Lorettonians); T. Ainslie (8) (Edinburgh Inst FP), J.B. Brown 7 (Glasgow Acads), T.W. Irvine 1 (Edinburgh Acads), J. Jamieson (8) (W. of Scotland), J.G. Mitchell (2) (W. of Scotland), W.A. Peterkin (6) (Edinburgh U.), C. Reid 8 (Edinburgh Acads), J.G. Tait (1) (Cambridge U.), J. Tod 5 (Watsonians).

IRELAND   J.W.R. Morrow 5 (Belfast Albion); J.P. Ross 2 (Lansdowne), D.J. Ross 2 (Belfast Academy), E.H. Greene 3 (Dublin U.); R.G. Warren 3 (Lansdowne), D.V. Hunter (1) (Dublin U.); R.M. Bradshaw (2) (Wanderers), *A.J. Forrest (2) (Wanderers), W. Hogg (1) (Dublin U.), J. Johnston 2 (Belfast Academy), T.R. Lyle 2 (Dublin U.), F.W. Moore 3 (Wanderers), H.J. Neill 2 (NIFC), T. Shanahan 2 (Lansdowne), J.A. Thompson (1) (Queen's C. Belfast).

Referee H.C. Kelly (Ireland)

SCOTLAND v IRELAND   3/15

7 March 1885
Raeburn Place, Edinburgh
Scotland (1G, 2T) Ireland nil

Scotland   T: Reid, Peterkin, A. R. Don Wauchope. C: Veitch.

This match stands out as one of the curiosities of the Championship, for it was played in Scotland after the abandonment of the original fixture at Ormeau, Belfast, on 21 February. The first match lasted only 25 minutes, by which time a storm had waterlogged the pitch and a fierce gale and sleet made further play impossible. Scotland at the time were leading by a try scored by J. Jamieson. Afterwards it was agreed that the match would stand as a win to Scotland,

1886

BLACKHEATH England beat Wales 2 tries, 1 goal from mark to 1 goal
CARDIFF Scotland beat Wales 2 goals, 1 try to nil
DUBLIN England beat Ireland 1 try to nil
EDINBURGH Scotland beat Ireland 3 goals, 2 tries, 1 dropped goal to nil
EDINBURGH Scotland drew England, no score
NB Ireland did not play Wales

CHAMPIONSHIP TABLE
Scotland – Championship

Pos	Country	P	W	D	L	Tries F	A	Pts
1	Scotland (2)	3	2	1	0	8	0	5
2	England (1)	3	2	1	0	3	1	5
3	Wales (3)	2	0	0	2	1	5	0
4	Ireland (4)	2	0	0	2	0	6	0

1886 was the year when scoring by points was introduced, Wales played four threequarters for the first time, and referees were provided with whistles and umpires with sticks. Points values varied in each country until 1890, when England joined the International Board and uniformity was achieved. The Board changed the points values for the 1891 season, and this is the accepted starting point of scoring by points in the Championship. It was also Scotland's turn to win the Championship, relegating England to second place because of a superior try count. Ireland – who still refused to play Wales – finished bottom for the third year in a row.

Off the field, activity was concentrated in a meeting in Dublin on the morning of the Ireland v England match on 6 February. Representatives from each of the Unions tried to reach a settlement over the England-Scotland dispute. Scotland were encouraged to accept that England had won. They did, 'but only out of regard for the interests of rugby football.' The Scots also insisted on the formation of the International Board, and all the representatives agreed to this: 'with some reservations on the part of the English delegates as to its scope of action'.

Edward Temple Gurdon, who captained England in nine matches 1882–86

ENGLAND v WALES 4/16

2 January 1886
Rectory Field, Blackheath
England (2T, 1GM) Wales (1G)

England T: Wade, Wilkinson. GM: Stoddart.
Wales T: Stadden. C: Taylor.

Wales had a comparatively inexperienced side, including five new caps, but 'their collaring was excellent'. The Welsh pack was also praised: 'in the forward play the Welshmen on the whole had the best of it' said *The Field*.

ENGLAND A.S. Taylor 3 (Blackheath); C.G. Wade 7 (Richmond), A.R. Robertshaw 1 (Bradford), A.E. Stoddart 3 (Blackheath); A. Rotherham 7 (Richmond), F. Bonsor 1 (Bradford); C. Gurdon 5 (Richmond), W.G. Clibborn 1 (Richmond), *C.J.B. Marriott 4 (Blackheath), G.L. Jeffery 1 (Blackheath), R.E. Inglis 1 (Blackheath), P.F. Hancock 1 (Blackheath), E. Wilkinson 1 (Bradford), F. Moss (3) (Broughton), C.H. Elliot (1) (Sunderland).

WALES D.H. Bowen 2 (Llanelli); C.G. Taylor 6 (Ruabon), A.J. Gould 3 (Newport), W.M. Douglas 1 (Cardiff); *C.H. Newman 7 (Newport), W.H. Stadden 2 (Cardiff); A.F. Hill 2 (Cardiff), D.H. Lewis 1 (Cardiff), G.A. Young 1 (Cardiff), W. Bowen 1 (Swansea), D. Morgan 2 (Swansea), E.P. Alexander 2 (Cambridge U.), R. Gould 8 (Newport), W.H. Thomas 2 (Llandovery College), E. Roberts 1 (Llanelli).

Referee D.F. Moore (Ireland)

WALES v SCOTLAND 4/17

9 January 1886
Cardiff Arms Park
Scotland (2G, 1T) Wales nil

Scotland T: Clay, Tod, A.R. Don Wauchope. C: Macleod (2).

This was the first match in which an international side fielded four threequarters but Wales's innovation was deemed unsuccessful and the idea was shelved.

WALES D.H. Bowen 3 (Llanelli); W.M. Douglas 2 (Cardiff), *F.E. Hancock (4) (Cardiff), A.J. Gould 4 (Newport), C.G. Taylor 7 (Blackheath); Revd A. A. Matthews (1) (Lampeter), W.H. Stadden 3 (Cardiff); A.F. Hill 3 (Cardiff), G.A. Young (2) (Cardiff), D.H. Lewis (2) (Cardiff), T.J.S. Clapp 8 (Newport), W. Bowen 2 (Swansea), D. Morgan 3 (Swansea), W.H. Thomas 3 (Cambridge U.), E.P. Alexander 3 (Cambridge U.).

SCOTLAND F. McIndoe 1 (Glasgow Acads); W.F. Holms 1 (London Scottish), D.J. Macfarlan 5 (RIE College) R.H. Morrison 1 (Edinburgh U.); A.R. Don Wauchope 7 (Fettesian-Lorettonians), P.H. Don Wauchope 2 (Fettesian-Lorettonians); *J.B. Brown 8 (Glasgow Acads), A.T. Clay 1 (Edinburgh Acads), J. French 1 (Glasgow Acads), T.W. Irvine 2 (Edinburgh Acads), W.M. Macleod 1 (Edinburgh Wands), C.J.B. Milne 1 (W. of Scotland), C. Reid 9 (Edinburgh Acads), J. Tod 6 (Watsonians), W.A. Walls 7 (Glasgow Acads).

Referee D.F. Moore (Ireland)

IRELAND v ENGLAND 4/18

6 February 1886
Lansdowne Road, Dublin
England (1T) Ireland nil

England T: Wilkinson.

With this victory England established their longest winning sequence of ten matches, which they equalled again in 1922–25. A crowd of 7000, said to be a record for Dublin, watched Ireland battle in vain. 'The Irish forwards,' declared *The Field*, 'made the serious mistake of trying to play the tight scrummage game against opponents averaging a couple of stone heavier all round.'

IRELAND J.W.R. Morrow 6 (Lisburn); D.J. Ross 3 (Belfast Academy), J.P. Ross 3 (NIFC), E.H. Greene (4) (Wanderers); *M. Johnston (3) (Wanderers), R.G. Warren 4 (Lansdowne); J. Chambers 1 (Dublin U.), T. Shanahan 3 (Lansdowne), V.C. le Fanu 1 (Cambridge U.), T.R. Lyle 3 (Dublin U.), H.M. Brabazon (2) (Dublin U.), J. Johnston 3 (Belfast Albion), R.W. Hughes (6) (NIFC),, W.G. Rutherford 4 (Tipperary), R.H. Massey-Westropp (1) (Limerick).

ENGLAND A.S. Taylor (4) (Blackheath); C.G. Wade (8) (Richmond), A.R. Robertshaw 2 (Bradford), A.E. Stoddart 4 (Blackheath); A. Rotherham 8 (Richmond), F. Bonsor 2 (Bradford); C. Gurdon 6 (Richmond), W.G. Clibborn 2 (Richmond), R.E. Inglis 2 (Blackheath), G.L. Jeffery 2 (Blackheath), A. Teggin 3 (Broughton Rangers), P.F. Hancock 2 (Blackheath), E. Wilkinson 2 (Bradford), *C.J.B. Marriott 5 (Blackheath), N. Spurling 1 (Blackheath).

Referee R. Mullock (Wales)

SCOTLAND v IRELAND   4/19

20 February 1886
Raeburn Place, Edinburgh
Scotland (3G, 2T, 1DG) Ireland nil

Scotland T: Don Wauchope (2), Morrison (2), Macfarlan. C: Macfarlan (3). DG: Asher.

Ireland's ninth Championship defeat in a row, their longest losing sequence. It could have surprised no one that eight of the team were not invited to play again. According to *The Field*: 'The Irish, dressed in green jerseys, instead of the white and green sash of yore . . . did not even approximate international strength and from start to finish they were completely outclassed.' *The Field* also took the trouble to check the attendance via the receipts. There were 3200 . . . 'of this number a goodly proportion belonged to the fair sex, and, en passant, it may be noticed that their presence is a characteristic of Edinburgh rugby gatherings.'

SCOTLAND F. McIndoe (2) (Glasgow Acads); A.E. Stephen (2) (W. of Scotland), D.J. Macfarlan 6 (London Scottish), R.H. Morrison 2 (Edinburgh U.); A.R. Don Wauchope 8 (Fettesian-Lorettonians), A.G.G. Asher 5 (Edinburgh Wands); *J.B. Brown 9 (Glasgow Acads), A.T. Clay 2 (Edinburgh Acads), T.W. Irvine 3 (Edinburgh Acads), D.A. Macleod 1 (Glasgow U.), W.M. Macleod (2) (Fettesian-Lorettonians), C.J.B. Milne 2 (W. of Scotland), C. Reid 10 (Edinburgh Acads), J. Tod 7 (Watsonians), W.A. Walls 8 (Glasgow Acads).

IRELAND J.W.R. Morrow 7 (Lisburn); *J.P. Ross (4) (Lansdowne), D.J. Ross (4) (Belfast Academy), M.J. Carpendale 1 (Monkstown); R.W. Herrick (1) (Dublin U.), J.F. Ross (1) (NIFC); J. Chambers 2 (Dublin U.), J. McMordie (1) (Queen's C. Belfast), F.H. Miller (1) (Wanderers), F.W. Moore (4) (Wanderers), V.C. le Fanu 2 (Cambridge U.), H.J. Neill 3 (NIFC), R. Nelson (2) (Queen's C. Belfast), F.O. Stoker 1 (Wanderers), J. Waites 1 (Bective Rangers).

Referee G. Rowland Hill (England)

SCOTLAND v ENGLAND   3/20

13 March 1886
Raeburn Place, Edinburgh
Drawn, no score

The first drawn match between England and Scotland. The match had been postponed from the previous week and England were handicapped by an early injury to Fred Bonsor, who was a passenger for most of the match. Mounted policemen and 36 constables were in attendance. In those days selectors had little compunction about dropping players – both captains played their last games, as did 11 others, 7 Scots and 4 Englishmen.

SCOTLAND J.P. Veitch (6) (Royal HSFP); R.H. Morrison (3) (Edinburgh U.), G.R. Wilson 1 (Royal HSFP), W.F. Holms 2 (RIE College); A.G.G. Asher (6) (Fettesian-Lorettonians), A.R. Don Wauchope 9 (Fettesian-Lorettonians); *J.B. Brown (10) (Glasgow Acads), C. Reid 11 (Edinburgh Acads), W.A. Walls (9) (Glasgow Acads), T.W. Irvine 4 (Edinburgh Acads), A.T. Clay 3 (Edinburgh Acads), C.J.B. Milne (3) (W. of Scotland), M.C. McEwan 1 (Edinburgh Acads), D.A. Macleod (2) (Glasgow U.), J. Tod (8) (Watsonians).

ENGLAND C.H. Sample (3) (Cambridge U.); A.E. Stoddart 5 (Blackheath), A.R. Robertshaw 3 (Bradford), E.R. Brutton (1) (Cambridge U.); A. Rotherham 9 (Richmond), F. Bonsor 3 (Bradford); *E.T. Gurdon (9) (Richmond), C. Gurdon (7) (Richmond), R.E. Inglis (3) (Blackheath), E. Wilkinson 3 (Bradford), W.G. Clibborn 3 (Richmond), N. Spurling 2 (Blackheath), C.J.B. Marriott 6 (Blackheath), G.L. Jeffery 3 (Cambridge U.), A. Teggin 4 (Broughton Rangers).

Referee H.G. Cook (Ireland)

1887

LLANELLI Wales drew England, no score
DUBLIN Ireland beat England 2 goals to nil
BELFAST Scotland beat Ireland 1 goal, 2 tries, 1 goal from mark to nil
EDINBURGH Scotland beat Wales 4 goals, 8 tries to nil
MANCHESTER England drew Scotland, 1 try each
BIRKENHEAD Wales beat Ireland 1 try, 1 dropped goal to 3 tries

CHAMPIONSHIP TABLE
Scotland – Championship

Pos	Country	P	W	D	L	Tries F	A	Pts
1	Scotland (1)	3	2	1	0	16	1	5
2	Wales (3)	3	1	1	1	1	15	3
3	Ireland (4)	3	1	0	2	4	5	2
4	England (2)	3	0	2	1	1	3	2

England, by losing to Ireland for the first time, and drawing with Wales and Scotland, became Wooden Spoonists for the first time. Wales showed marked improvement by finishing second and Scotland reaped a rich harvest of 16 tries in winning the Championship. Ireland, who had not won a Championship match before, had the added bonus of totalling five tries, four more than England.

In the early years of the Championship, the game was quite basic but was developing fast. Generally speaking, the forwards scrummaged and dribbled and the scoring came from the threequarters, usually following a scrum. The number of attacking ploys was necessarily limited, possibly because formations and alignments, though often changed, had not yet fully developed from two full-backs, two threequarters, two half-backs and nine forwards.

When the ball emerged from the scrum, it was taken by the nearest half-back, whose job was to feed one of the threequarters. The threequarter seemed to have a dual purpose: to run at or past his opposite number, and if successful to then avoid being sandwich-tackled by the other defenders. The emphasis was on running and beating the opposition, with no likelihood of support. Defenders in turn had one primary task: to take out the man with the ball. Quite often they received more praise than an attacker who was quick and elusive.

Very few accounts described the line-out or the techniques involved. It seems certain that the line-out was utilised simply for what it was – to restart the game after the ball had gone in to touch. Line-out play became a skilled operation similar to what we know today only after the visits of the New Zealanders and South Africans in 1905–06. It must also be remembered that forwards were not yet specialized: there was no such thing as a prop, hooker, lock or flanker and scrums probably were more of a prolonged maul with forwards positioned only according to what moment they arrived at the point of the stoppage.

WALES v ENGLAND 5/21

8 January 1887
Stradey Park, Llanelli
Drawn, no score

The last international for Charles Newman, the Newport back and Wales captain, who was the only remaining member of the team which played England in Wales's first-ever international in 1881. Newman would have won an eleventh cap for he was chosen to play against Ireland at Birkenhead on 12 March, but an injury ruled him out. Strictly speaking, this match was not played at Stradey Park. The

Llanelli pitch was frozen over and the England players refused to play on it. The adjacent cricket grounds, however, were in better condition and the match was played there. Members of the crowd who had purchased seats in the temporary stand were not at all happy that they had to vacate their prime position and stand to watch proceedings on the makeshift playing area.

WALES   D.H. Bowen (4) (Llanelli); C.G. Taylor 8 (Blackheath), A.J. Gould 5 (Newport), W.M. Douglas 3 (Cardiff); *C.H. Newman (8) (Newport), O.J. Evans 1 (Cardiff); E.P. Alexander 4 (Cambridge U.), W.H. Thomas 4 (Cambridge U.), D. Morgan 4 (Swansea), W. Bowen 3 (Swansea), A.F. Bland 1 (Cardiff), A.J. Hybart (1) (Cardiff), T.J.S. Clapp 9 (Newport), R. Gould 9 (Newport), T.W. Lockwood 1 (Newport).

ENGLAND   S. Roberts 1 (Swinton); J. le Fleming (1) (Blackheath), A.R. Robertshaw 4 (Bradford), R.E. Lockwood 1 (Dewsbury); *A. Rotherham 10 (Richmond), F. Bonsor 4 (Bradford); J.L. Hickson 1 (Bradford), R.L. Seddon 1 (Broughton Rangers), G.L. Jeffery 4 (Blackheath), H.C. Baker (1) (Clifton), W.G. Clibborn 4 (Richmond), E. Wilkinson 4 (Bradford), N. Spurling (3) (Blackheath), J.H. Dewhurst 1 (Cambridge U.), C.R. Cleveland 1 (Oxford U.).

Referee G. Rowland Hill (England)

IRELAND v ENGLAND   5/22

5 February 1887
Lansdowne Road, Dublin
Ireland (2G) England nil

Ireland   T: Montgomery, Tillie. C: Rambaut (2).

After losing every previous match against England in the Championship, Ireland had cause to celebrate. The win, in fact, was far more convincing than the score indicates. Five of England's side did not play another Championship match. The tale goes that John Macaulay, the Limerick forward, had to get married in order that he could play in the match. Having exhausted his annual leave, the only reason Macaulay could devise for further leave of absence was asking permission to wed. Macaulay, who played only one other international,

against Scotland later in the month, is credited as one of the founders of Garryowen, the club which gave its name to the famous up-and-under kicks which future Irish sides used so effectively in the Championship.

IRELAND   D.B. Walkington 1 (NIFC); C.R. Tillie 1 (Dublin U.), D.F. Rambaut 1 (Dublin U.), R. Montgomery 1 (Cambridge U.); J.H. McLaughlin 1 (Derry), *R.G. Warren 5 (Lansdowne); J. Chambers 3 (Dublin U.), J.S. Dick 1 (Queen's C. Cork), V.C. le Fanu 3 (Cambridge U.), T.R. Lyle 4 (Dublin U.), E.J. Walsh 1 (Lansdowne), J. Johnston 4 (Belfast Albion), R. Stevenson 1 (Lisburn), H.J. Neill 4 (NIFC), J. Macaulay 1 (Limerick).

ENGLAND   S. Roberts (2) (Swinton); W.N. Bolton 8 (Blackheath), A.R. St L. Fagan (1) (United Hospitals), R.E. Lockwood 2 (Dewsbury); *A. Rotherham 11 (Richmond), M.T. Scott 1 (Cambridge U.); J.L. Hickson 2 (Bradford), R.L. Seddon 2 (Broughton Rangers), G.L. Jeffery 5 (Blackheath), A. Teggin 5 (Broughton Rangers), W.G. Clibborn 5 (Richmond), A.T. Kemble (3) (Liverpool), F.E. Pease (1) (Hartlepool Rovers), J.H. Dewhurst 2 (Cambridge U.), C.J.B. Marriott (7) (Blackheath).

Referee W.D. Phillips (Wales)

IRELAND v SCOTLAND   5/23

19 February 1887
Ormeau, Belfast
Scotland (1G, 2T, 1GM) Ireland nil

Scotland   T: Maclagan, McEwan, Morton. C: Berry. GM: Berry.

Scotland opened their campaign as defending Champions with five players new to the Championship. Bill Maclagan scored his first try for Scotland.

IRELAND   J.M. O'Sullivan (2) (Cork); R. Montgomery 2 (Cambridge U.), D.F. Rambaut 2 (Dublin U.), C.R. Tillie 2 (Dublin U.); *R.G. Warren 6 (Lansdowne), J.H. McLaughlin 2 (Derry); J. Chambers 4 (Dublin U.), J.S. Dick 2 (Queen's C. Cork), J. Johnston 5 (Belfast Albion), T.R. Lyle (5) (Dublin U.), J. Macaulay (2) (Limerick), C.M. Moore 1 (Dublin U.), H.J. Neill 5 (NIFC), R. Stevenson 2 (Lisburn), E.J. Walsh 2 (Lansdowne).

The team which gained Ireland their first victory in the Championship on 5 February 1887. Back row: W.L. Stokes (President), J.S. Dick, C.R. Tillie, T.R. Lyle, H.J. Neill, V.C. le Fanu, R. Stevenson. Middle row: D.F. Rambaut, D.B. Walkington, J. Chambers, R.G. Warren, E.J. Walsh, J.H. McLaughlin, J. Johnston. Seated: John Macaulay, R. Montgomery

SCOTLAND W.F. Holms 3 (London Scottish); A.N. Woodrow 1 (Glasgow Acads), W.E. Maclagan 9 (London Scottish), D.J. Macfarlan 7 (London Scottish); P.H. Don Wauchope 3 (Fettesian-Lorettonians), C.E. Orr 1 (W. of Scotland); C.W. Berry 4 (Edinburgh Wands), A.T. Clay 4 (Edinburgh Acads), J. French 2 (Glasgow Acads), T.W. Irvine 5 (Edinburgh Acads), H.T. Ker 1 (Glasgow Acads), M.C. McEwan 2 (Edinburgh Acads), R.G. Macmillan 1 (W. of Scotland), D.S. Morton 1 (W. of Scotland), *C. Reid 12 (Edinburgh Acads).

Referee G. Rowland Hill (England)

SCOTLAND v WALES   5/24

26 February 1887
Raeburn Place, Edinburgh
Scotland (4G, 8T) Wales nil

Scotland T: Lindsay (5), Don Wauchope, Orr, Reid, Macmillan, McEwan, Maclagan, Morton. C: Berry (2), Woodrow (2).

George Lindsay, the London Scottish back, set a Championship record by scoring five tries and helped Scotland to a record twelve tries. The match was postponed from January when Lindsay was not even selected to play. An injury to D.J. Macfarlan in the intervening period gave Lindsay his chance. Wales had their excuses: Billy Douglas played on after being injured in the opening ten minutes and they were down to fourteen players for the whole of the second half after losing Jem Evans.

SCOTLAND A.W. Cameron 1 (Watsonians); W.E. Maclagan 10 (London Scottish), G.C. Lindsay 2 (London Scottish), A.N. Woodrow 2 (Glasgow Acads); P.H. Don Wauchope 4 (Edinburgh Wands), C.E. Orr 2 (W. of Scotland); C.W. Berry 5 (Edinburgh Wands), A.T. Clay 5 (Edinburgh Acads), J. French 3 (Glasgow Acads), T.W. Irvine 6 (Edinburgh Acads), H.T. Ker 2 (Glasgow Acads), M.C. McEwan 3 (Edinburgh Acads), R.G. Macmillan 2 (W. of Scotland), D.S. Morton 2 (W. of Scotland), *C. Reid 13 (Edinburgh Acads).

WALES H. Hughes 1 (Cardiff); D. Gwynn 2 (Swansea), A.J. Gould 6 (Newport), W.M. Douglas (4) (Cardiff); G.E. Bowen 1 (Swansea), O.J. Evans 2 (Cardiff); W. Bowen 4 (Swansea), E.S. Richards (2) (Swansea), D. Morgan 5 (Swansea), A.F. Bland 2 (Cardiff), W.E.O. Williams 1 (Cardiff), W.H. Thomas 5 (Cambridge U.), *R. Gould (10) (Newport), T.W. Lockwood 2 (Newport), T.J.S. Clapp 10 (Newport).

Referee F.I. Currey (England)

ENGLAND v SCOTLAND   4/25

5 March 1887
Whalley Range, Manchester
England (1T) Scotland (1T)

England   T: Jeffery.
Scotland   T: Morton.

Scotland won their second Championship even though held to a draw by England in a match mostly played in thick fog. It was England's last Championship match for two seasons, because the other home unions refused to play them until a four-nation International Board was formed. The interval was too long for most of the England team: 12 of them did not play again in a Championship match, including the captain, Alan Rotherham, then England's most capped player with 12 appearances. Another who played his last game for England was Robert Seddon, who drowned in an Australian river during the 1888 British team's tour of Australia and New Zealand. Andrew Stoddart took over the tour captaincy from Seddon and then led England when they resumed playing in the Championship in 1890.

ENGLAND   H.B. Tristram (5) (Richmond); W.N. Bolton (9) (Blackheath), A.R. Robertshaw (5) (Bradford), R.E. Lockwood 3 (Dewsbury); *A. Rotherham (12) (Richmond), F. Bonsor (5) (Bradford); C.R. Cleveland (2) (Oxford U.), J.H. Dewhurst 3 (Richmond), W.G. Clibborn (6) (Richmond), H.H. Springman (1) (Liverpool), E. Wilkinson (5) (Bradford), R.L. Seddon (3) (Broughton Rangers), A. Teggin (6) (Broughton Rangers), J.L. Hickson 3 (Bradford), G.L. Jeffery (6) (Blackheath).

SCOTLAND   W.F. Holms 4 (London Scottish); W.E. Maclagan 11 (London Scottish), G.C. Lindsay (3) (London Scottish), A.N. Woodrow (3) (Glasgow Acads); C.E. Orr 3 (W. of Scotland), P.H. Don Wauchope (5) (Edinburgh Wands); C.W. Berry 6 (Edinburgh Wands), A.T. Clay 6 (Edinburgh Acads), J. French (4) (Glasgow Acads), H.T. Ker 3 (Glasgow Acads), T.W. Irvine 7 (Edinburgh Acads), R.G. Macmillan 3 (W. of Scotland), M.C. McEwan 4 (Edinburgh Acads), D.S. Morton 3 (W. of Scotland), *C. Reid 14 (Edinburgh Acads).

Referee T.R. Lyle (Ireland)

WALES v IRELAND   2/26

12 March 1887
Birkenhead Park
Wales (1T, 1DG) Ireland (3T)

Wales   T: Morgan. DG: Gould.
Ireland   T: Montgomery (3).

A result which underlined the peculiarity of early scoring. Wales won because a goal, regardless of its type, was equal to three tries. Had the game been played, for example, in 1892 (when a try was valued at two points and a dropped goal four) the result would have been a draw. Any score values after 1894 would have meant a win for Ireland. A surprisingly large crowd of 5000 watched the match, staged at Birkenhead to minimise the travelling costs of the Irish Rugby Union, who at the time were feeling the pinch. The absence of Charles Newman allowed Llanelli's Jack Lewis to win his only cap. It was the only Championship match for Neath fullback, S.S. Clark, although he had played for Wales five years previously, also against Ireland. It was the final appearance for Charles Taylor, who was the first Welsh international to be killed in the First World War, in 1915.

WALES   S.S. Clark (1) (Neath); C.G. Taylor (9) (Blackheath), A.J. Gould 7 (Newport), G.E. Bowen 2 (Swansea); J.C. Lewis (1) (Llanelli), W.H. Stadden 4 (Cardiff); A.F. Bland 3 (Cardiff), W.E.O. Williams 2 (Cardiff), E.P. Alexander (5) (Brecon), *T.J.S. Clapp 11 (Newport), T.W. Lockwood (3) (Newport), W. Bowen 5 (Swansea), E. Roberts (2) (Llanelli), D. Morgan 6 (Swansea), W.H. Towers (1) (Swansea).

IRELAND   D.B. Walkington 2 (NIFC); D.F. Rambaut 3 (Dublin U.), M.J. Carpendale 2 (Monkstown), R. Montgomery 3 (Queen's C. Belfast); *R.G. Warren 7 (Lansdowne), P.J. O'Connor (1) (Lansdowne); E.J. Walsh 3 (Lansdowne), V.C. le Fanu 4 (Lansdowne), J. Chambers (5) (Dublin U.), T. Taggart (1) (Dublin U.), H.J. Neill 6 (NIFC), J. Johnston (6) (Belfast Academy), W. Davison (1) (Belfast Academy), R. Stevenson 3 (Lisburn), J.S. Dick (3) (Queen's C. Cork).

Referee J.A. Gardner (Scotland)

1888

NEWPORT Wales beat Scotland 1 try to nil
DUBLIN Ireland beat Wales 1 goal, 1 try, 1 dropped goal to nil
EDINBURGH Scotland beat Ireland 1 goal to nil
NB England did not play Ireland, Scotland or Wales

CHAMPIONSHIP TABLE
Ireland – Championship

Pos	Country	P	W	D	L	Tries F	A	Pts
1	Ireland (3)	2	1	0	1	2	1	2
2	Scotland (1)	2	1	0	1	1	1	2
3	Wales (2)	2	1	0	1	1	2	2

At their meeting of 4 February, the newly-formed International Board once again invited England to join. The offer was declined and consequently England played no matches this season or the following.

The 1888 Championship was therefore a desultory affair, with Ireland, Scotland and Wales winning a match apiece, and Ireland taking their first title by virtue of scoring two tries, one more than Scotland. Wales's victory, however, was significant; it was their first over Scotland. Ireland beat Wales for the first time and the early imbalances in the Championship were, with a few exceptions, being evened out.

WALES v SCOTLAND   6/27

4 February 1888
Rodney Parade, Newport
Wales (1T) Scotland nil

Wales   T: Pryce-Jenkins.

Wales gained their first victory over Scotland thanks to a début try from Tom Pryce-Jenkins, the London Welsh back. Scotland grounded the ball five times over the Welsh line but were not allowed a score on any occasion.

WALES   E.J. Roberts 1 (Llanelli); G.E. Bowen 3 (Swansea), A.J. Gould 8 (Newport), T.J. Pryce-Jenkins 1 (London Welsh); O.J. Evans 3 (Cardiff), W.H. Stadden 5 (Cardiff); *T.J.S. Clapp 12 (Newport), R.W. Powell 1 (Newport), W.H. Thomas 6 (London Welsh), A.F. Bland 4 (Cardiff), A.F. Hill 4 (Cardiff), Q.D. Kedzlie 1 (Cardiff), J. Meredith 1 (Swansea), T. Williams 1 (Swansea), W.H. Howells 1 (Swansea).

'Buller' Stadden, who scored the try which gave Wales their first Championship victory over England in February 1890

SCOTLAND   H.F.T. Chambers 1 (Edinburgh U.); W.E. Maclagan 12 (London Scottish), H.J. Stevenson 1 (Edinburgh Acads), M.M. Duncan (1) (Cambridge U.); C.E. Orr 4 (W. of Scotland), C.F.P. Fraser 1 (Glasgow U.); C.W. Berry 7 (Fettesian-Lorettonians), A.T. Clay (7) (Edinburgh Acads), A. Duke 1 (Royal HSFP), T.W. Irvine 8 (Edinburgh Acads), M.C. McEwan 5 (Edinburgh Acads), D.S. Morton 4 (W. of Scotland), *C. Reid 15 (Edinburgh Acads), L.E. Stevenson (1) (Edinburgh U.), T.B. White 1 (Edinburgh Acads).

Referee J. Chambers (Ireland)

IRELAND v WALES 3/28

3 March 1888
Lansdowne Road, Dublin
Ireland (1G, 1T, 1DG) Wales nil

Ireland   T: Warren, Shanahan. C: Rambaut. DG: Carpendale.

The sea crossing to Ireland, which could be very rough, was often used as an excuse for visiting teams' below par performances, and this match was no exception. For eight of the Welsh team, including the renowned Tom Clapp, it was their last appearance in the Championship. Ireland's victories over Wales – of which this was the first of eight in their first twenty matches — were very important in those days for Ireland rarely won against England or Scotland. Nicknames, which now abound in the game, seemed to have started around about this time. Some were less than flattering. D.F. Rambaut, the Dublin University back, for instance, was known as 'the fat little fellow'.

IRELAND   D.B. Walkington 3 (NIFC); M.J. Carpendale 3 (Monkstown), D.F. Rambaut (4) (Dublin U.), C.R. Tillie 3 (Dublin U.); R.G. Warren 8 (Lansdowne), J.H. McLaughlin 3 (Derry); *H.J. Neill 7 (NIFC), E.W. Stoker 1 (Wanderers), F.O. Stoker 2 (Wanderers), W.G. Rutherford (5) (Tipperary), T. Shanahan 4 (Lansdowne), C.M. Moore 2 (Dublin U.), J. Moffatt 1 (Belfast Academy), R.H. Mayne 1 (Belfast Academy), W. Ekin 1 (Queen's C. Belfast).

WALES   E.J. Roberts 2 (Llanelli); T.J. Pryce-Jenkins (2) (London Welsh), G.E. Bowen (4) (Swansea), C.S. Arthur 1 (Cardiff); O.J. Evans (4) (Cardiff), C.J. Thomas 1 (Newport); *T.J.S. Clapp (13) (Newport), R.W. Powell (2) (Newport), A.F. Hill 5 (Cardiff), Q.D. Kedzlie (2) (Cardiff), A.F. Bland 5 (Cardiff), W.H. Thomas 7 (London Welsh), W.H. Howells (2) (Swansea), T. Williams (2) (Swansea), J. Meredith 2 (Swansea).

Referee G. Rowland Hill (England)

SCOTLAND v IRELAND 6/29

10 March 1888
Raeburn Place, Edinburgh
Scotland (1G) Ireland nil

Scotland   T: Macfarlan. C: Berry.

Although Ireland lost to Scotland for the sixth successive time, their superior scoring in the match with Wales enabled them to win the Championship for the first time. Three of Scotland's leading players, A.R. Don Wauchope, C.W. Berry and Charles Reid, made their last appearances.

SCOTLAND   H.F.T. Chambers 2 (Edinburgh U.); W.E. Maclagan 13 (London Scottish); H.J. Stevenson 2 (Edinburgh Acads), D.J. Macfarlan (8) (London Scottish); *A.R. Don Wauchope (10) (Fettesian-Lorettonians), C.E. Orr 5 (W. of Scotland); C.W. Berry (8) (Edinburgh Wands), A. Duke 2 (Royal HSFP), T.W. Irvine 9 (Edinburgh Acads), H.T. Ker 4 (Glasgow Acads), M.C. McEwan 6 (Edinburgh Acads), A.G. Malcolm (1) (Glasgow U.), D.S. Morton 5 (W. of Scotland), C. Reid (16) (Edinburgh Acads), T.B. White 2 (Edinburgh Acads).

IRELAND   J.W.R. Morrow (8) (Lisburn); C.R. Tillie (4) (Dublin U.), A. Walpole (1) (Dublin U.), M.J. Carpendale (4) (Monkstown); R.G. Warren 9 (Lansdowne), J.H. McLaughlin (4) (Derry); W. Ekin (2) (Queen's C. Belfast), V.C. le Fanu 5 (Lansdowne), R.H. Mayne (2) (Belfast Albion), J. Moffatt 2 (Belfast Albion), C.M. Moore (3) (Dublin U.), W.A. Morton (1) (Dublin U.), *H.J. Neill (8) (NIFC), T. Shanahan (5) (Lansdowne), E.W. Stoker (2) (Wanderers).

Referee J. McLaren (England)

1889

EDINBURGH Scotland beat Wales 2 tries to nil
BELFAST Scotland beat Ireland 1 dropped goal to nil
SWANSEA Ireland beat Wales 2 tries to nil
NB England did not play Ireland, Scotland or Wales

CHAMPIONSHIP TABLE
Scotland – Championship

Pos	Country	P	W	D	L	Tries F	A	Pts
1	Scotland (2)	2	2	0	0	2	0	4
2	Ireland (1)	2	1	0	1	2	0	2
3	Wales (3)	2	0	0	2	0	4	0

This was an important year in the development of the game, for the International Board critically examined most aspects of it. The Board displayed a positive approach by seeking to establish, among other things, a mutually acceptable scoring system, laying down uniform dimensions for the ball and playing pitches, recommending a standard type of kit, and defining the powers of the referee. It now remained for England to return to the Championship.

Scotland had a good year, winning both matches to take the title for a third time. Wales failed to score a try and finished bottom of the table for the second successive season, the only time they have suffered that indignity.

Jim Hannan, regarded as one of the great tacticians of Welsh forward play 1889–90

SCOTLAND v WALES 7/30

2 February 1889
Raeburn Place, Edinburgh
Scotland (2T) Wales nil

Scotland T: Orr, Ker.

Wales had to reorganise their side after players from Cardiff and Llanelli withdrew, apparently because they wanted to play against each other in a club match. The WRU asked Cardiff to supply the replacements for the Edinburgh international and as a result of losing six players, Cardiff called off their match with Llanelli. Understandably Llanelli were annoyed and temporarily broke off fixtures. Once again, Wales experimented with four threequarters.

SCOTLAND   H.F.T. Chambers 3 (Edinburgh U.); W.F. Holms 5 (Edinburgh Wands), H.J. Stevenson 3 (Edinburgh Acads), J. Marsh 1 (Edinburgh Inst FP); C.E. Orr 6 (W. of Scotland), C.F.P. Fraser (2) (Glasgow U.); W. Auld 1 (W. of Scotland), J.D. Boswell 1 (W. of Scotland), A.

Duke 3 (Royal HSFP), H.T. Ker 5 (Glasgow Acads), M.C. McEwan 7 (Edinburgh Acads), W.A. Macdonald 1 (Glasgow U.), A. Methuen 1 (Cambridge U.), *D.S. Morton 6 (W. of Scotland), T.B. White (3) (Edinburgh Acads).

WALES   H. Hughes (2) (Cardiff); R.M. Garrett 1 (Penarth), J.E. Webb (1) (Newport), E.H. Bishop (1) (Swansea), H.M. Jordan (3) (London Welsh); C.J. Thomas 2 (Newport), R. Evans (1) (Cardiff), S.H. Nicholls 1 (Cardiff), *A.F. Hill 6 (Cardiff), W.E.O. Williams 3 (Cardiff), D.W. Evans 1 (Cardiff), T. Harding 1 (Newport), J. Hannan 1 (Newport), R.L. Thomas 1 (London Welsh), W. Bowen 6 (Swansea).

Referee A. McAllister (Ireland)

IRELAND v SCOTLAND   7/31

16 February 1889
Ormeau, Belfast
Scotland (1DG) Ireland nil

Scotland   DG: Stevenson.

Scotland won the last Championship in which only three countries competed.

IRELAND   L.J. Holmes 1 (Lisburn); R.A. Yeates 1 (Dublin U.), T.B. Pedlow 1 (Queen's C. Belfast), D.C. Woods (1) (Bessbrook); J. Stevenson (1) (Lisburn), *R.G. Warren 10 (Lansdowne); H.W. Andrews 1 (NIFC), T.M. Donovan (1) (Queen's C. Cork), E.G. Forrest 1 (Wanderers), J.S. Jameson 1 (Lansdowne), J. Moffatt 3 (Belfast Albion), L.C. Nash 1 (Queen's C. Cork), C.R.R. Stack (1) (Dublin U.), R. Stevenson 4 (Lisburn), F.O. Stoker 3 (Wanderers).

SCOTLAND   H.F.T. Chambers (4) (Edinburgh U.); W.F. Holms (6) (London Scottish), H.J. Stevenson 4 (Edinburgh Acads), J. Marsh (2) (Edinburgh Inst FP); C.E. Orr 7 (W. of Scotland), D.G. Anderson 1 (London Scottish); A.I. Aitken (1) (Edinburgh Inst FP), J.D. Boswell 2 (W. of Scotland), A. Duke 4 (Royal HSFP), T.W. Irvine (10) (Edinburgh Acads), M.C. McEwan 8 (Edinburgh Acads), J.G. McKendrick (1) (W. of Scotland), A. Methuen 2 (Cambridge U.), *D.S. Morton 7 (W. of Scotland), J.E. Orr 1 (W. of Scotland).

Referee W.D. Phillips (Wales)

WALES v IRELAND   4/32

2 March 1889
St Helen's, Swansea
Ireland (2T) Wales nil

Ireland   T: McDonnell, Cotton.

A.R. Don Wauchope, the referee in this match, had a busy day. In the morning he chaired a meeting of the International Board which out-voted, by four votes to two, a proposal to adopt the 'Welsh rules' which had been tried for 12 months 'and had effected a very great improvement in the game of football'. Arguing for the Welsh rules, Alex Duncan, of Cardiff, claimed: 'they were a great advance on the old rules – they did away with rough play and killed offside'. A Welsh proposal that: 'a match shall be decided by a majority of points' was adopted, and, in the absence of England, was employed by the other three countries for 1890 only. The match was the Championship début of Norman Biggs, who had become Wales's youngest ever player, at 17 years 4 months, when he first appeared, against the Maoris in December 1888. It was Ireland's first win in Wales. The Irish try scorers were both making their débuts.

WALES   E.J. Roberts (3) (Llanelli); A.C. Davies (1) (London Welsh), *A.J. Gould 9 (Newport), T. Morgan (1) (Llanelli), N. Biggs 1 (Cardiff); C.J. Thomas 3 (Newport), G. Griffiths (1) (Llanelli); W. Bowen 7 (Swansea), D. Morgan (7) (Swansea), S.H. Nicholls 2 (Cardiff), D.W. Evans 2 (Cardiff), T. Harding (2) (Newport), J. Hannan 2 (Newport), R.L. Thomas 2 (London Welsh), D. Griffiths (1) (Llanelli).

IRELAND   L.J. Holmes (2) (Lisburn); R.A. Yeates (2) (Dublin U.), R.W. Dunlop 1 (Dublin U.), T.B. Pedlow (2) (Queen's C. Belfast); *R.G. Warren 11 (Lansdowne), A.C. McDonnell 1 (Dublin U.); V.C. le Fanu 6 (Lansdowne), J.S. Jameson 2 (Lansdowne), E.G. Forrest 2 (Wanderers), J. Cotton (1) (Wanderers), J. Waites 2 (Bective Rangers), H.W. Andrews (2) (NIFC), J.N. Lytle 1 (NIFC), R. Stevenson 5 (Lisburn), H.A. Richey 1 (Dublin U.).

Referee A.R. Don Wauchope (Scotland)

1890

CARDIFF Scotland beat Wales 1 goal, 2 tries to 1 try
DEWSBURY Wales beat England 1 try to nil
EDINBURGH Scotland beat Ireland 1 try, 1 dropped goal to nil
DUBLIN Ireland drew Wales, 1 goal each
EDINBURGH England beat Scotland 1 goal, 1 try to nil
BLACKHEATH England beat Ireland 3 tries to nil

CHAMPIONSHIP TABLE
England – Championship

Pos	Country	P	W	D	L	Tries F	A	Pts
1	England (4)	3	2	0	1	5	1	4
2	Scotland (1)	3	2	0	1	4	3	4
3	Wales (3)	3	1	1	1	3	4	3
4	Ireland (2)	3	0	1	2	1	5	1

England resumed competing in the Championship and despite losing their first match since the break, to Wales at Dewsbury, showed that nothing really had changed when they finished up winning the title. The statistics of the Championship in the first turbulent eight years makes an interesting comparison:

	P	W	D	L
England	17	12	3	2
Scotland	21	14	3	4
Ireland	19	3	1	15
Wales	19	4	3	12

Ireland and Wales took an unusually long time to wear down the lead that England and Scotland established, but by winning 10 of the next 19 Championships between them, the Irish and the Welsh finally dispelled the myth that the Championship was a two-horse race.

WALES v SCOTLAND 8/33

1 February 1890
Cardiff Arms Park
Scotland (1G, 2T) Wales (1T)

Wales T: Gould.
Scotland T: Anderson, Boswell, Maclagan. C: McEwan.

The first appearance of Billy Bancroft, the Swansea full-back, who established a sequence of 33 Championship matches for Wales in an 11-

Jack Valentine, who won four caps for England 1890–96

year career. Bancroft started playing for the side only after the withdrawal through injury of Newport's Tom England, the original choice.

WALES   W.J. Bancroft 1 (Swansea); C.J. Thomas 4 (Newport), A.J. Gould 10 (Newport), R.M. Garrett 2 (Penarth), P. Lloyd 1 (Llanelli); E. James 1 (Swansea), W.H. Stadden 6 (Cardiff); *A.F. Hill 7 (Cardiff), W.E.O. Williams 4 (Cardiff), A.F. Bland 6 (Cardiff), W. Bowen 8 (Swansea), J. Meredith 3 (Swansea), W. Rice-Evans 1 (Swansea), J. Hannan 3 (Newport), S. Thomas 1 (Llanelli).

SCOTLAND   G. MacGregor 1 (Cambridge U.); *W.E. Maclagan 14 (London Scottish), H.J. Stevenson 5 (Edinburgh Acads), G.R. Wilson 2 (Royal HSFP); C.E. Orr 8 (W. of Scotland), D.G. Anderson 2 (London Scottish); W. Auld (2) (W. of Scotland), J.D. Boswell 3 (W. of Scotland), A. Dalgleish 1 (Gala), A. Duke 5 (Royal HSFP), F.W.J. Goodhue 1 (London Scottish), M.C. McEwan 9 (Edinburgh Acads), I. MacIntyre 1 (Edinburgh Wands), R.G. Macmillan 4 (W. of Scotland), J.E. Orr 2 (W. of Scotland).

Referee A. McAllister (Ireland)

forwards, bounced the ball a few feet infield, regathered and nipped past two defenders for a try. In 1906 bouncing the ball from touch was outlawed.

ENGLAND   W.G. Mitchell 1 (Richmond); P.H. Morrison 1 (Cambridge U.), *A.E. Stoddart 6 (Blackheath), J. Valentine 1 (Swinton); J.F. Wright (1) (Bradford), F.H. Fox 1 (Marlborough Nomads); S.M.J. Woods 1 (Cambridge U.), J.H. Dewhurst (4) (Richmond), R.T.D. Budworth 1 (Blackheath), F. Evershed 1 (Burton), J.L. Hickson 4 (Bradford), A. Robinson 1 (Blackheath), J.H. Rogers 1 (Moseley), P.F. Hancock (3) (Blackheath), F.W. Lowrie (1) (Batley).

WALES   W.J. Bancroft 2 (Swansea); P. Lloyd 2 (Llanelli), *A.J. Gould 11 (Newport), R.M. Garrett 3 (Penarth), D. Gwynn 3 (Swansea); C.J. Thomas 5 (Newport), W.H. Stadden (7) (Cardiff); W.E.O. Williams (5) (Cardiff), A.F. Bland 7 (Cardiff), D.W. Evans 3 (Cardiff), J. Hannan 4 (Newport), W.H. Thomas 8 (London Welsh), S. Thomas 2 (Llanelli), W. Bowen 9 (Swansea), J. Meredith (4) (Swansea).

Referee R.D. Rainie (Scotland)

ENGLAND v WALES   6/34

15 February 1890
Crown Flatt, Dewsbury
Wales (1T) England nil

Wales   T: Stadden.

England's re-entry into the Championship was conspicuous in that it provided Wales with their first victory in the series between the countries. Wales may have been fortunate that one of England's outstanding players, Fred Bonsor, did not play for although the Bradford half-back might not have torn them to shreds as did Leslie Stokes in the first match between the countries in 1881, reports suggested he would have given them a much more difficult time than did J.F. Wright. There was speculation at the time that Bonsor had withdrawn to allow Wright, with whom he played at Bradford, to win his first cap. In the event neither Bonsor nor Wright were selected again. Wales's winning points came from a line-out. Buller Stadden effected a long throw and on the retreat of the England

A diminutive 5ft 5in, Billy Bancroft was acknowledged as a great full-back

SCOTLAND v IRELAND   8/35

22 February 1890
Raeburn Place, Edinburgh
Scotland (1T, 1DG) Ireland nil

Scotland   T: J.E. Orr. DG: Boswell.

Ireland must have been near despair as to when they would beat Scotland. This was their eighth consecutive defeat and, apart from the try they scored in 1884, they had failed to register any score against the Scots.

SCOTLAND   G. MacGregor 2 (Cambridge U.); W.E. Maclagan 15 (London Scottish), H.J. Stevenson 6 (Edinburgh Acads), G.R. Wilson 3 (Royal HSFP); C.E. Orr 9 (W. of Scotland), D.G. Anderson 3 (London Scottish); J.D. Boswell 4 (W. of Scotland), A. Duke (6) (Royal HSFP), F.W.J. Goodhue 2 (London Scottish), H.T. Ker 6 (Glasgow Acads), *M.C. McEwan 10 (Edinburgh Acads), I. MacIntyre 2 (Edinburgh Wands), R.G. Macmillan 5 (W. of Scotland), D.S. Morton 8 (W. of Scotland), J.E. Orr 3 (W. of Scotland).

IRELAND   H.P. Gifford (1) (Wanderers); R.W. Dunlop 2 (Dublin U.), R.W. Johnston 1 (Dublin U.), T. Edwards 1 (Lansdowne); *R.G. Warren 12 (Lansdowne), A.C. McDonnell 2 (Dublin U.); W.J.N. Davis 1 (Bessbrook), E.F. Doran 1 (Lansdowne), E.G. Forrest 3 (Wanderers), J. Moffatt 4 (Belfast Albion), J. Waites 3 (Bective Rangers), R. Stevenson 6 (Dungannon), J. Roche 1 (Wanderers), H.A. Richey (2) (Dublin U.), J.H. O'Conor 1 (Bective Rangers).

Referee H.L. Ashmore (England)

IRELAND v WALES   5/36

1 March 1890
Lansdowne Road, Dublin
Ireland (1G) Wales (1G)

Ireland   T: Dunlop. C: Roche.
Wales   T: Charlie Thomas. C: Bancroft.

Nine of the players from this match found themselves in Dublin Court the next day, charged with 'riotous' behaviour following the after-match dinner. Small fines were imposed. The local press either did not possess details or tactfully chose not to report them for only brief references were published. The names of the 'culprits' were not revealed. In the match itself Ireland were odds-on to score a third successive win over Wales when five minutes from time Charlie Thomas scored a try. It was the first appearance for Tom Graham, Tyneside-born Newport forward, who was to be a cornerstone of the Welsh pack for six seasons.

IRELAND   D.B. Walkington 4 (NIFC); R.W. Dunlop 3 (Dunlop U.), R.W. Johnston 2 (Dublin U.), T. Edwards 2 (Lansdowne); *R.G. Warren 13 (Lansdowne), A.C. McDonnell 3 (Dublin U.); J. Moffatt 5 (Belfast Academy), H.T. Galbraith (1) (Belfast Academy), J. Waites 4 (Bective Rangers), J.H. O'Conor 2 (Bective Rangers), R. Stevenson 7 (Dungannon), J. Roche 2 (Wanderers), W.J.N. Davis 2 (Bessbrook), E.F. Doran (2) (Lansdowne), L.C. Nash 2 (Queen's C. Cork).

WALES   W.J. Bancroft 3 (Swansea); R.M. Garrett 4 (Penarth), *A.J. Gould 12 (Newport), G. Thomas 1 (Newport), D. Gwynn 4 (Swansea); C.J. Thomas 6 (Newport), H.M. Ingledew 1 (Cardiff); A.F. Hill 8 (Cardiff), D.W. Evans 4 (Cardiff), A.F. Bland (8) (Cardiff), J. Hannan 5 (Newport), T.C. Graham 1 (Newport), W. Bowen 10 (Swansea), W.H. Thomas 9 (London Welsh), R.L. Thomas 3 (London Welsh).

Referee F. Burnand (England)

SCOTLAND v ENGLAND   5/37

1 March 1890
Raeburn Place, Edinburgh
England (1G, 1T) Scotland nil

England   T: Evershed, Dyson. C: Jowett.

Bill Maclagan, the Scottish captain, reluctantly agreed to play in this resumption of the fixture with England after a three-year break. Maclagan, a sciatica sufferer, did not play to his usual high standards and it is hardly surprising he never played again for Scotland, though he did captain the first British team to tour South Africa, in 1891. Maclagan was unquestionably one of the outstanding backs in Scottish rugby at the time. In 16 Championship appearances, he was on the losing side only three times, all against England. He was captain eight times.

SCOTLAND G. MacGregor 3 (Cambridge U.); *W.E. Maclagan (16) (London Scottish), H.J. Stevenson 7 (Edinburgh Acads), G.R. Wilson 4 (Royal HSFP); C.E. Orr 10 (W. of Scotland), D.G. Anderson 4 (London Scottish); J.D. Boswell 5 (W. of Scotland), A. Dalgleish 2 (Gala), F.W.J. Goodhue 3 (London Scottish), H.T. Ker (7) (Glasgow Acads), I. MacIntyre 3 (Edinburgh Wands), R.G. Macmillan 6 (W. of Scotland), D.S. Morton (9) (W. of Scotland), J.E. Orr 4 (W. of Scotland), M.C. McEwan 11 (Edinburgh Acads).

ENGLAND W.G. Mitchell 2 (Richmond); P.H. Morrison 2 (Cambridge U.), R.L. Aston 1 (Cambridge U.), J.W. Dyson 1 (Huddersfield); M.T. Scott 2 (Northern), F.H. Fox (2) (Wellington); S.M.J. Woods 2 (Cambridge U.), D. Jowett 1 (Heckmondwike), J.L. Hickson 5 (Bradford), F. Evershed 2 (Burton), J.T. Toothill 1 (Bradford), A. Robinson 2 (Blackheath), H. Bedford 1 (Morley), E. Holmes 1 (Manningham), J.H. Rogers 2 (Moseley).

Referee J. Chambers (Ireland)

(Moseley), D. Jowett 2 (Heckmondwike), H. Bedford (2) (Morley), E. Holmes (2) (Manningham), A. Robinson (3) (Blackheath).

IRELAND D.B. Walkington 5 (Dublin U.); R.W. Dunlop 4 (Dublin U.), R.W. Johnston (3) (Dublin U.), T. Edwards 3 (Lansdowne); B.B. Tuke 1 (Bective Rangers), *R.G. Warren (14) (Lansdowne); J.N. Lytle 2 (NIFC), E.G. Forrest 4 (Wanderers), J. Waites 5 (Bective Rangers), J.H. O'Conor 3 (Bective Rangers), R. Stevenson 8 (Dungannon), J. Roche 3 (Wanderers), V.C. le Fanu 7 (Lansdowne), L.C. Nash 3 (Queen's C. Cork), W.J.N. Davis 3 (Bessbrook).

Referee A.R. Don Wauchope (Scotland)

ENGLAND v IRELAND   6/38

15 March 1890
Rectory Field, Blackheath
England (3T) Ireland nil

England   T: Rogers, Morrison, Stoddart.

By scoring three tries England narrowly beat Scotland to win the Championship. For seven England players, however, it was their last international, including their most experienced forward, J.L. Hickson. Ireland, with only a draw to their credit finished with the Wooden Spoon, which was a disappointment for their captain, R.G. Warren, in his fourteenth and final Championship match.

ENGLAND W.G. Mitchell 3 (Richmond); P.H. Morrison 3 (Cambridge U.), R.L. Aston (2) (Cambridge U.), *A.E. Stoddart 7 (Blackheath); M.T. Scott (3) (Northern), F.W. Spence (1) (Birkenhead Park); F. Evershed 3 (Burton), J.L. Hickson (6) (Bradford), S.M.J. Woods 3 (Cambridge U.), J.T. Toothill 2 (Bradford), J.H. Rogers 3

1891

NEWPORT England beat Wales 7-3 · DUBLIN England beat Ireland 9-0
EDINBURGH Scotland beat Wales 15-0 · BELFAST Scotland beat Ireland 14-0
RICHMOND Scotland beat England 9-3 · LLANELLI Wales beat Ireland 6-4

CHAMPIONSHIP TABLE
Scotland – Championship, Triple Crown

Pos	Country	P	W	D	L	F	A	Pts	Tries F	A
1	Scotland (2)	3	3	0	0	38	3	6	14	1
2	England (1)	3	2	0	1	19	12	4	9	3
3	Wales (3)	3	1	0	2	9	26	2	2	11
4	Ireland (4)	3	0	0	3	4	29	0	1	11

This was the year when the International Board introduced the penalty kick for offside, three years after the RFU had deemed it necessary (the penalty kick was introduced in 1882 but no goal could be scored from it). It was also decided that henceforth umpires would be known as touch-judges, which meant a diminution of their powers to the point that all they were required to do was to mark the spot where the ball left the field of play. That status remained unaltered until 1982 when in representative matches the touch-judges were allowed to report incidents of foul play and misconduct to the referee.

Other Law alterations included permission to pick up a dead ball and the fixing of the dead-ball line at 25 yards maximum.

All this may have been of little consequence to Scotland, who though they had won three Championships, celebrated 1891 with their first Triple Crown, by beating England, who were also bidding for it, at Richmond in March. It is interesting to note that reports on the size of the crowd at this match varied widely between 12,000 and 20,000. Only the reporters of one publication, *The Field*, were punctilious enough to check attendance figures, which they did occasionally by referring to official gate receipts.

WALES v ENGLAND 7/39

3 January 1891
Rodney Parade, Newport
England 7 (2G, 1T) Wales 3 (1G)

Wales   T: Pearson. C: Bancroft.
England   T: Christopherson (2), Budworth. C: Alderson.

The choice of captain in the early days of the Championship was occasionally left to the players to decide, in the changing room before kick-off. Fred Alderson, of Hartlepool Rovers, was given the England captaincy, unusually in his first match and he continued to captain them until his sixth and final appearance when Andrew Stoddart took over. Wales were without the mercurial Arthur Gould for this season. Gould had gone to the West Indies to join his brother Bob, in building bridges and other civil engineering work.

WALES   W.J. Bancroft 4 (Swansea); T.W. Pearson 1 (Cardiff), C.S. Arthur (2) (Cardiff), D. Gwynn 5 (Swansea), P. Lloyd 3 (Llanelli); C.J. Thomas 7 (Newport), H.M. Ingledew 2 (Cardiff); *W. Bowen 11 (Swansea), W. Rice-Evans 2 (Swansea), J. Hannan 6 (Newport), H. Packer 1 (Newport), P. Bennett 1 (Cardiff Harlequins), E.V. Pegge (1) (Neath), R.L. Thomas 4 (London Welsh), D.W. Evans (5) (Cardiff).

ENGLAND   W.G. Mitchell 4 (Richmond); R.E. Lockwood 4 (Heckmondwike), *F.H.R. Alderson 1 (Hartlepool Rovers), P. Christopherson 1 (Blackheath); W.R.M. Leake 1 (Harlequins), J. Berry 1 (Tyldesley); S.M.J. Woods 4 (Cambridge U.), R.P. Wilson 1 (Liverpool OB), R.T.D. Budworth 2 (Blackheath), T. Kent 1 (Salford), W.E.

Bromet 1 (Tadcaster), E.G.H. North 1 (Oxford U.), D. Jowett 3 (Heckmondwike), J.T. Toothill 3 (Bradford), J. Richards 1 (Bradford).

Referee R.D. Rainie (Scotland)

IRELAND v ENGLAND 7/40

7 February 1891
Lansdowne Road, Dublin
England 9 (2G, 3T) Ireland 0

England   T: Lockwood (2), Wilson (2), Toothill. C: Lockwood (2).

This was one of Ireland's three defeats during the season; they had no answer to the speed of the English backs. It was the début of Charles Rooke, the Dublin University forward, who later in his international career had some claims to being the first specialized flank-forward. Sammy Lee, the NIFC back, also made his first appearance. Lee was best known for his initial firmly-held objection to the introduction of the four threequarter system, but he was an outstanding player, a clever attacker and resolute defender.

IRELAND   *D.B. Walkington 6 (NIFC); R.W. Dunlop 5 (NIFC), S. Lee 1 (NIFC), R. Montgomery 4 (NIFC); A.C. McDonnell (4) (Dublin U.), B.B. Tuke 2 (Bective Rangers); J.N. Lytle 3 (NIFC), E.G. Forrest 5 (Wanderers), J. Waites (6) (Bective Rangers), J.H. O'Conor 4 (Bective Rangers), C.V. Rooke 1 (Dublin U.), J. Roche 4 (Wanderers), V.C. le Fanu 8 (Lansdowne), L.C. Nash 4 (Queen's C. Cork), W.J.N. Davis 4 (Bessbrook).

ENGLAND   W.G. Mitchell 5 (Richmond); P.H. Morrison (4) (Cambridge U.), *F.H.R. Alderson 2 (Hartlepool Rovers), R.E. Lockwood 5 (Heckmondwike); W.R.M. Leake 2 (Harlequins), J. Berry 2 (Tyldesley); S.M.J. Woods 5 (Cambridge U.), R.P. Wilson 2 (Liverpool OB), D. Jowett 4 (Heckmondwike), J. Richards 2 (Bradford), E.G.H. North 2 (Oxford U.), W.E. Bromet 2 (Tadcaster), J.T. Toothill 4 (Bradford), T. Kent 2 (Salford), L.J. Percival 1 (Oxford U.).

Referee W.M. Douglas (Wales)

George Neilson, the West of Scotland forward, one of four brothers to play for Scotland 1891–1900

SCOTLAND v WALES 9/41

7 February 1891
Raeburn Place, Edinburgh
Scotland 15 (1G, 6T, 2DG) Wales 0

Scotland   T: C.E. Orr, J.E. Orr, Goodhue, Clauss (2), Leggatt, Boswell. C: McEwan. DG: W. Neilson, Stevenson.

Scotland introduced four new players of which three, Clauss, Leggatt and W. Neilson, placed their names on the scoresheet. There were two pairs of brothers on the Scottish side, the Orrs and the Neilsons, and remarkably, three of the four scored.

SCOTLAND   H.J. Stevenson 8 (Edinburgh Acads); W. Neilson 1 (Merchiston), G. MacGregor 4 (Cambridge U.), P.R. Clauss 1 (Oxford U.); C.E. Orr 11 (W. of Scotland), D.G. Anderson 5 (London Scottish); J.D. Boswell 6 (W. of Scotland), A. Dalgleish 3 (Gala), F.W.J. Goodhue 4 (London Scottish), H.T.O. Leggatt 1 (Watsonians), *M.C. McEwan 12 (Edinburgh Acads), I. MacIntyre 4 (Edinburgh Wands), R.G. Macmillan 7 (London Scottish), G.T. Neilson 1 (W. of Scotland), J.E. Orr 5 (W. of Scotland).

WALES   W.J. Bancroft 5 (Swansea); R.M. Garrett 5 (Penarth), D. Gwynn (6) (Swansea), G. Thomas (2) (Newport), W. McCutcheon 1 (Swansea); R.B. Sweet-Escott 1 (Cardiff), H.M. Ingledew (3) (Cardiff); *W.H. Thomas 10 (Llanelli), R.L. Thomas 5 (Llanelli), T.C. Graham 2 (Newport), P. Bennett 2 (Cardiff Harlequins), W. Bowen (12) (Swansea), W. Rice-Evans (3) (Swansea), D.J. Daniel 1 (Llanelli), S.H. Nicholls (3) (Cardiff).

Referee H.L. Ashmore (England)

IRELAND v SCOTLAND   9/42

21 February 1891
Ballynafeigh, Belfast
Scotland 14 (3G, 2T, 1DG) Ireland 0

Scotland   T: Wotherspoon (3), Clauss, MacGregor. C: Boswell (3). DG: McEwan.

To score three tries in an international was a rare enough event, to score a hat-trick in his first match, as W. Wotherspoon did, made him a celebrated figure throughout the rugby world. The most conspicuous figure on the Irish side was probably their full-back, D.B. Walkington, who according to one source, wore a monocle while playing, removing it when he was required to make a tackle! Six of Ireland's side came from Bective Rangers, who were to win the Leinster Senior Cup in 1892.

IRELAND   *D.B. Walkington 7 (NIFC); H.G. Wells 1 (Bective Rangers), S. Lee 2 (NIFC), R.W. Dunlop 6 (NIFC), B.B. Tuke 3 (Bective Rangers), E.D. Cameron 1 (Bective Rangers); G. Collopy 1 (Bective Rangers), W.J.N. Davis 5 (Bessbrook), E.F. Frazer 1 (Bective Rangers), J.N. Lytle 4 (NIFC), J. Moffatt (6) (Belfast Albion), L.C. Nash 5 (Queen's C. Cork), J.H. O'Conor 5 (Bective Rangers), J. Roche 5 (Wanderers), R.D. Stokes 1 (Queen's C. Cork).

SCOTLAND   H.J. Stevenson 9 (Edinburgh Acads); P.R. Clauss 2 (Oxford U.), G. MacGregor 5 (Cambridge U.), G.R. Wilson (5) (Royal HSFP); C.E. Orr 12 (W. of Scotland), W. Wotherspoon 1 (Cambridge U.); J.D. Boswell 7 (W. of Scotland), A. Dalgleish 4 (Gala), W.R. Gibson 1 (Royal HSFP), F.W.J. Goodhue 5 (London Scottish), H.T.O. Leggatt 2 (Watsonians), *M.C. McEwan 13 (Edinburgh Acads), I. MacIntyre 5 (Edinburgh Wands), G.T. Neilson 2 (W. of Scotland), J.E. Orr 6 (W. of Scotland).

Referee G. Rowland Hill (England)

ENGLAND v SCOTLAND   6/43

7 March 1891
Athletic Ground, Richmond
Scotland 9 (2G, 1DG) England 3 (1G)

England   T: Lockwood. C: Alderson.
Scotland   T: W. Neilson, J.E. Orr. C: MacGregor (2). DG: Clauss.

W. Neilson, brought into the Scottish side for W. Wotherspoon, scorer of three tries against Ireland a fortnight earlier, scored one of the two tries which gave Scotland their first Triple Crown and denied England their third. A large crowd, variously reported as between 12,000 and 15,000, watched the match. England's disappointment was reflected in later selection: ten of their team did not play again, including seven members of the pack.

ENGLAND   W.G. Mitchell 6 (Richmond); P. Christopherson (2) (Blackheath), *F.H.R. Alderson 3 (Hartlepool Rovers), R.E. Lockwood 6 (Heckmondwike); W.R.M. Leake (3) (Harlequins), J. Berry (3) (Tyldesley); J.H. Rogers (4) (Moseley), E.G.H. North (3) (Oxford U.), R.P. Wilson (3) (Liverpool OB), R.T.D. Budworth (3) (Blackheath), S.M.J. Woods 6 (Cambridge U.), J. Richards (3) (Bradford), T. Kent 3 (Salford), D. Jowett (5) (Heckmondwike), E. Bonham-Carter (1) (Oxford U.).

SCOTLAND   H.J. Stevenson 10 (Edinburgh Acads); P.R. Clauss 3 (Oxford U.), G. MacGregor 6 (Cambridge U.), W. Neilson 2 (Merchiston); C.E. Orr 13 (W. of Scotland), D.G. Anderson 6 (London Scottish); J.D. Boswell 8 (W. of Scotland), W.R. Gibson 2 (Royal HSFP), F.W.J. Goodhue 6 (London Scottish), H.T.O. Leggatt 3 (Watsonians), *M.C. McEwan 14 (Edinburgh Acads), I. MacIntyre (6) (Edinburgh Wands), R.G. Macmillan 8 (London Scottish), G.T. Neilson 3 (W. of Scotland), J.E. Orr 7 (W. of Scotland).

Referee J. Chambers (Ireland)

J.H. O'Connor who made 16 Championship appearances 1890–96

the east and west sides of the ground. No attendance figures were reported, but according to the *South Wales Daily News*, 'an immense concourse of people assembled on the park; in fact it was the largest that had ever been witnessed at a football match in the tin plate town'. Ireland were given a warm welcome and sections of the crowd cried out, 'Home Rule for Ireland' as the team took the field. It was the first time that the James brothers, David and Evan, played together for Wales; Wales had selection problems more common to Ireland in those days: two Llanelli players, Percy Lloyd and Stephen Thomas being late replacements for Newport players George Thomas and Jim Hannan.

WALES   W.J. Bancroft 6 (Swansea); R.M. Garrett 6 (Penarth), C.J. Thomas (8) (Newport), P. Lloyd (4) (Llanelli), T.W. Pearson 2 (Cardiff); D. James 1 (Swansea), E. James 2 (Swansea); *W.H. Thomas (11) (Llanelli), R.L. Thomas 6 (Llanelli), S. Thomas (3) (Llanelli), C.B. Nicholl 1 (Llanelli), T.C. Graham 3 (Newport), J. Samuel (1) (Swansea), D. Samuel 1 (Swansea), J. Deacon 1 (Swansea).

IRELAND   D.B. Walkington (8) (NIFC); R.W. Dunlop 7 (NIFC), S. Lee 3 (NIFC), H.G. Wells 2 (Bective Rangers); E.D. Cameron (2) (Bective Rangers), R. Pedlow (1) (Bessbrook); *R. Stevenson 9 (Dungannon), J. Roche 6 (Wanderers), F.O. Stoker (4) (Wanderers), J.S. Jameson 3 (Lansdowne), L.C. Nash (6) (Queen's C. Cork), R.D. Stokes (2) (Queen's C. Cork), T. Fogarty (1) (Garryowen), C.V. Rooke 2 (Dublin U.), W.J.N. Davis 6 (Bessbrook).

Referee A. Rowsell (England)

WALES v IRELAND   6/44

7 March 1891
Stradey Park, Llanelli
Wales 6 (1G, 1DG) Ireland 4 (1T, 1DG)

Wales   T: David Samuel. C: Bancroft. DG: Bancroft.
Ireland   T: Lee. DG: Walkington.

This was the first Championship match held at Stradey Park (see Wales v England 1887) and the Llanelli officials erected temporary stands on

1892

BLACKHEATH England beat Wales 17-0 · SWANSEA Scotland beat Wales 7-2
MANCHESTER England beat Ireland 7-0 · EDINBURGH Scotland beat Ireland 2-0
DUBLIN Ireland beat Wales 9-0 · EDINBURGH England beat Scotland 5-0

CHAMPIONSHIP TABLE
England – Championship, Triple Crown

									Tries	
Pos	Country	P	W	D	L	F	A	Pts	F	A
1	England (2)	3	3	0	0	29	0	6	7	0
2	Scotland (1)	3	2	0	1	9	7	4	3	2
3	Ireland (4)	3	1	0	2	9	9	2	3	3
4	Wales (3)	3	0	0	3	2	33	0	1	9

England won the title and the Triple Crown without conceding a point, which is the only time this has been achieved. During the season England used 25 players of which only eight appeared in all three matches.

The referee was at the centre of some unruly crowd behaviour in the Wales v Scotland match and although Wales apologised for the incident they urged the RFU to: 'appoint competent men to act as referees in international matches'.

Wales were also anxious for a change in score values. But at their July meeting the International Board rejected their proposal that the value of the try be upgraded from two to three points, that the penalty goal become three points and any other goal four points. If there was no change in the scoring, at least one other link with the past was severed – mauls-in-goal were abolished.

ENGLAND v WALES   8/45

2 January 1892
Rectory Field, Blackheath
England 17 (3G, 1T) Wales 0

England T: Alderson, Evershed, Hubbard, Nichol. C: Lockwood (2), Alderson.

This was the first of three defeats for Wales during this season, but curiously the side, which included newcomers Wallace Watts and Arthur Boucher, formed the nucleus of the team which swept all before them in winning the Triple Crown the following season.

ENGLAND W.B. Thomson 1 (Blackheath); R.E. Lockwood 7 (Heckmondwike), *F.H.R. Alderson 4 (Hartlepool Rovers), G.C. Hubbard 1 (Blackheath); C. Emmott (1) (Bradford), A. Briggs 1 (Bradford); F. Evershed 4 (Blackheath), J. Pyke (1) (St Helen's Recreation), E. Bullough 1 (Wigan), T. Kent 4 (Salford), J.T. Toothill 5 (Bradford), A. Allport 1 (Blackheath), W.E. Bromet 3 (Tadcaster), W. Yiend 1 (Hartlepool Rovers), W. Nichol 1 (Brighouse Rangers).

WALES W.J. Bancroft 7 (Swansea); R.M. Garrett (7) (Penarth), *A.J. Gould 13 (Newport), W. McCutcheon 2 (Swansea), T.W. Pearson 3 (Cardiff); H.P. Phillips 1 (Newport), G.R. Rowles (1) (Penarth); R.L. Thomas (7) (Llanelli), C.B. Nicholl 2 (Llanelli), F. Mills 1 (Swansea), J. Deacon 2 (Swansea), T.C. Graham 4 (Newport), A.W. Boucher 1 (Newport), W.H. Watts 1 (Newport), J. Hannan 7 (Newport).

Referee M.C. McEwan (Scotland)

WALES v SCOTLAND   10/46

6 February 1892
St Helen's, Swansea
Scotland 7 (1G, 1T) Wales 2 (1T)

Wales   T: Hannan.
Scotland   T: Boswell, Campbell. C: Boswell.

In one of the most unpleasant incidents concerning a referee of a game in Wales, some members of the crowd attacked Jack Hodgson, a London Society official, at the end of the match. Apparently upset by some of Hodgson's decisions, the assailants by-passed police and the referee had to be rescued by Welsh players, one of whom, Arthur Gould, was struck on the chin. The match was also conspicuous in that three pairs of brothers played: Evan and David James for Wales, and C.E. and J.E. Orr and W. and G.T. Neilson for Scotland. This was the last appearance for two seasons of Tom Pearson, the Cardiff wing, which was extraordinary because during 1892–93 Pearson was a scoring sensation with a record 40 tries for his club.

WALES   W.J. Bancroft 8 (Swansea); T.W. Pearson 4 (Cardiff), *A.J. Gould 14 (Newport), W. McCutcheon 3 (Swansea), J. Conway-Rees 1 (Llanelli); D. James 2 (Swansea), E. James 3 (Swansea); C.B. Nicholl 3 (Llanelli), W.H. Watts 2 (Newport), J. Hannan 8 (Newport), T.C. Graham 5 (Newport), A.W. Boucher 2 (Newport), F. Mills 2 (Swansea), J. Deacon 3 (Swansea), P. Bennett 3 (Cardiff Harlequins).

SCOTLAND   H.J. Stevenson 11 (Edinburgh Acads); W. Neilson 3 (Cambridge U.), G.T. Campbell 1 (London Scottish), P.R. Clauss 4 (Oxford U.); *C.E. Orr 14 (W. of Scotland), D.G. Anderson 7 (London Scottish); J.D. Boswell 9 (W. of Scotland), A. Dalgleish 5 (Gala), W.R. Gibson 3 (Royal HSFP), F.W.J. Goodhue 7 (London Scottish), H.T.O. Leggatt 4 (Watsonians), R.G. Macmillan 9 (London Scottish), J.N. Millar 1 (W. of Scotland), G.T. Neilson 4 (W. of Scotland), J.E. Orr 8 (W. of Scotland).

Referee J.R. Hodgson (England)

ENGLAND v IRELAND   8/47

6 February 1892
Whalley Range, Manchester
England 7 (1G, 1T) Ireland 0

England   T: Evershed, Percival. C: Woods.

That the power of English rugby emanated chiefly from Yorkshire and Lancashire was confirmed in this match, in which only four players were not from that great breeding ground.

ENGLAND   S. Houghton 1 (Runcorn); R.E. Lockwood 8 (Heckmondwike), J.H. Marsh (1) (Swinton), G.C. Hubbard (2) (Blackheath); E.W. Taylor 1 (Rockcliff), A. Briggs 2 (Bradford); *S.M.J. Woods 7 (Wellington), L.J. Percival 2 (Oxford U.), A. Ashworth (1) (Oldham), T. Kent 5 (Salford), W.E. Bromet 4 (Tadcaster), J.T. Toothill 6 (Bradford), E. Bullough 2 (Wigan), F. Evershed 5 (Blackheath), W. Yiend 2 (Hartlepool Rovers).

IRELAND   T. Peel 1 (Limerick); R.W. Dunlop 8 (Dublin U.), S. Lee 4 (NIFC), W. Gardiner 1 (NIFC); T. Thornhill 1 (Wanderers), B.B. Tuke 4 (Bective Rangers); *V.C. le Fanu 9 (Lansdowne), T.J. Johnston 1 (Queen's U. Belfast), E.J. Walsh 4 (Lansdowne), A.K. Wallis 1 (Wanderers), J.S. Jameson 4 (Lansdowne), R.E. Smith (1) (Lansdowne), J.H. O'Conor 6 (Bective Rangers), W.J.N. Davis 7 (Bessbrook), C.V. Rooke 3 (Dublin U.).

Referee J.A. Smith (Scotland)

SCOTLAND v IRELAND   10/48

20 February 1892
Raeburn Place, Edinburgh
Scotland 2 (1T) Ireland 0

Scotland   T: Millar.

Scotland scored their tenth consecutive victory over Ireland, their longest winning sequence against any country in the Championship. The match was finished in a snow-storm.

SCOTLAND   H.J. Stevenson 12 (Edinburgh Acads); G.T. Campbell 2 (London Scottish), W. Neilson 4 (Cambridge U.), J.C. Woodburn (1)

(Kelvinside Acads); *C.E. Orr 15 (W. of Scotland), W. Wotherspoon 2 (Cambridge U.); J.D. Boswell 10 (W. of Scotland), W.R. Gibson 4 (Royal HSFP), F.W.J. Goodhue 8 (London Scottish), N.F. Henderson (1) (London Scottish), H.T.O. Leggatt 5 (Watsonians), W.A. Macdonald 2 (Glasgow U.), R.G. Macmillan 10 (London Scottish), J.N. Millar 2 (W. of Scotland), J.E. Orr 9 (W. of Scotland).

IRELAND   T. Peel 2 (Bective Rangers); R.W. Dunlop 9 (Dublin U.), S. Lee 5 (NIFC), W. Gardiner 2 (NIFC), T. Thornhill 2 (Wanderers), F.E. Davies 1 (Lansdowne); A.D. Clinch 1 (Dublin U.), G. Collopy (2) (Bective Rangers), W.J.N. Davis 8 (Edinburgh U.), E.F. Frazer (2) (Bective Rangers), T.J. Johnston 2 (Queen's C. Belfast), *V.C. le Fanu 10 (Lansdowne), C.V. Rooke 4 (Dublin U.), A.K. Wallis 2 (Wanderers), E.J. Walsh 5 (Lansdowne).

Referee H.L. Ashmore (England)

IRELAND v WALES   7/49

5 March 1892
Lansdowne Road, Dublin
Ireland 9 (1G, 2T) Wales 0

Ireland   T: Walsh (2), Davies. C: Roche.

During one period of intense Irish pressure, the crowd took up the chant: 'Go on Ireland, give them some Guinness stout.' It was an appropriate finale for Victor le Fanu, the Irish captain, playing his eleventh and last Championship match. Le Fanu, son of the novelist, Sheridan le Fanu, had other claims to fame: he was the first Irish international to play in the University Match, in 1884 and 1885. It was the first time Wales lost all three Championship matches; the next occasion was in 1937.

IRELAND   T. Peel (3) (Limerick); T. Edwards 4 (Lansdowne), S. Lee 6 (NIFC), R. Montgomery (5) (NIFC); T. Thornhill 3 (Wanderers), F.E. Davies 2 (Lansdowne); *V.C. le Fanu (11) (Lansdowne), E.J. Walsh 6 (Lansdowne), J.S. Jameson 5 (Lansdowne), C.V. Rooke 5 (Dublin U.), A.K. Wallis 3 (Wanderers), J. Roche (7) (Wanderers), J.H. O'Conor 7 (Bective Rangers), R. Stevenson 10 (Dungannon), T.J. Johnston 3 (Queen's C. Belfast).

WALES   W.J. Bancroft 9 (Swansea); A. Gould 1 (Newport), *A.J. Gould 15 (Newport), F.E. Nichols (1) (Cardiff Harlequins), N. Biggs 2 (Cardiff); E. James 4 (Swansea), D. James 3 (Swansea); W.H. Watts 3 (Newport), J. Hannan 9 (Newport), H.T. Day 1 (Newport), A.W. Boucher 3 (Newport), P. Bennett (4) (Cardiff Harlequins), C.B. Nicholl 4 (Llanelli), J. Deacon (4) (Swansea), F. Mills 3 (Swansea).

Referee E.B. Holmes (England)

SCOTLAND v ENGLAND   7/50

5 March 1892
Raeburn Place, Edinburgh
England 5 (1G) Scotland 0

England   T: Bromet. C: Lockwood.

England won the Triple Crown for the third time and without a point being scored against them. Scotland, who were also bidding for the Triple Crown, were according to some reports unfairly treated by the referee, who disallowed two scores and frequently permitted the English to harass in offside positions. It was the last international for Scotland's captain, C.E. Orr.

SCOTLAND   H.J. Stevenson 13 (Edinburgh Acads); P.R. Clauss 5 (Oxford U.), W. Neilson 5 (Cambridge U.), G.T. Campbell 3 (London Scottish); *C.E. Orr (16) (W. of Scotland), D.G. Anderson (8) (London Scottish); J.D. Boswell 11 (W. of Scotland), W.R. Gibson 5 (Royal HSFP), F.W.J. Goodhue (9) (London Scottish), W.A. Macdonald (3) (Glasgow U.), M.C. McEwan (15) (Edinburgh Acads), R.G. Macmillan 11 (London Scottish), J.N. Millar 3 (W. of Scotland), G.T. Neilson 5 (W. of Scotland), J.E. Orr 10 (W. of Scotland).

ENGLAND   T. Coop (1) (Leigh); R.E. Lockwood 9 (Heckmondwike), *F.H.R. Alderson 5 (Hartlepool Rovers), J.W. Dyson 2 (Huddersfield); A. Briggs (3) (Bradford), H. Varley (1) (Liversedge); S.M.J. Woods 8 (Wellington), T. Kent (6) (Salford), W. Yiend 3 (Hartlepool Rovers), E. Bullough (3) (Wigan), F. Evershed 6 (Blackheath), H. Bradshaw 1 (Bramley), W.E. Bromet 5 (Tadcaster) W. Nichol (2) (Brighouse Rangers), J.T. Toothill 7 (Bradford).

Referee R.G. Warren (Ireland)

1893

CARDIFF Wales beat England 12-11 · DUBLIN England beat Ireland 4-0
EDINBURGH Wales beat Scotland 9-0 · BELFAST Ireland drew Scotland 0-0
LEEDS Scotland beat England 8-0 · LLANELLI Wales beat Ireland 2-0

CHAMPIONSHIP TABLE
Wales – Championship, Triple Crown

| | | | | | | | | | Tries | |
Pos	Country	P	W	D	L	F	A	Pts	F	A
1	Wales (4)	3	3	0	0	23	11	6	8	4
2	Scotland (2)	3	1	1	1	8	9	3	0	3
3	England (1)	3	1	0	2	15	20	2	6	3
4	Ireland (3)	3	0	1	2	0	6	1	0	4

Wales won the Championship and the Triple Crown for the first time. The eleven years it had taken them was the longest period without similar success in their history. Equally significant was that the Championship's first penalty goal was produced during this season, drop kicked by Billy Bancroft in the Wales v England match at Cardiff in January.

Considering the importance of this kick – which incidentally won the match for Wales – it is curious that no record exists as to the nature of the offence which led to the referee, M.C. McEwan, a former Scottish international, awarding the penalty. Bancroft drop-kicked another penalty against Scotland in Wales's next match. The habit quickly caught on for in the Triple Crown deciding match, Charlie Rooke attempted a similar kick for Ireland, narrowly failing from the halfway line. The penalty goal had arrived.

Had Rooke succeeded, of course, Wales would have been beaten but as one report stated the Irish fate was, once again, 'the dreaded Wooden Spoon'. The crowds attending international games were rapidly growing and often temporary stands were built to accommodate them. One such stand in the Wales v Ireland match at Stradey Park collapsed before kick-off, but fortunately no one was injured. To complete the momentous nature of this match: it was the last time a side, in this instance Ireland, played with three threequarters.

Regarding administrative decisions, the RFU followed Wales's lead in abolishing appeals to the referee. The RFU, however, had more serious problems of their own: their AGM in June outvoted a proposal that players be paid for 'broken time', a decision which led to the mass withdrawal from the Union of many of their leading clubs and, eventually, the creation of a separate sport, Rugby League. In contrast to such upheavals, Scotland decided to follow the other Unions and award caps to their players. The awards were to be back-dated to the 1892 season. Previously Scottish players purchased their own caps.

WALES v ENGLAND 9/51

7 January 1893
Cardiff Arms Park
Wales 12 (1G, 2T, 1PG) England 11 (1G, 3T)

Wales T: Gould (2), Biggs. C: Bancroft. PG: Bancroft.
England T: Marshall (3), Lohden. C: Stoddart.

Over 500 braziers and tons of straw were employed to combat a severe frost and enabled 15,000 to watch this match. Wales at the time valued the try at three points, but in international matches it was worth two. Under their own scoring system Wales would have drawn only, 14-14, instead of winning by a point. Any confusion over points-values ended the following season when the International Board upgraded the try to three points, downgraded the conversion to two, and left unaltered the values of the penalty goal (three), dropped goal (four) and goal from mark (four). Interestingly Wales's winning margin came from a penalty goal taken as a dropped kick, by Billy Bancroft. According to some reports the Welsh captain, Arthur Gould, ordered Bancroft to place kick the penalty and that he was very angry when Bancroft refused. Other reports suggested there was no debate: Gould simply turned away, hardly deigning to look as Bancroft drop-kicked.

WALES   W.J. Bancroft 10 (Swansea); N. Biggs 3 (Cardiff), *A.J. Gould 16 (Newport), J. Conway-Rees 2 (Llanelli), W. McCutcheon 4 (Swansea); H.P. Phillips 2 (Newport), F.C. Parfitt 1 (Newport); T.C. Graham 6 (Newport), J. Hannan 10 (Newport), W.H. Watts 4 (Newport), H.T. Day 2 (Newport), A.W. Boucher 4 (Newport), A.F. Hill 9 (Cardiff), C.B. Nicholl 5 (Llanelli), F. Mills 4 (Swansea).

ENGLAND   E. Field 1 (Cambridge U.); R.E. Lockwood 10 (Heckmondwike), F.H.R. Alderson (6) (Hartlepool Rovers), A.E. Stoddart 8 (Blackheath); H. Marshall (1) (Blackheath), R.F.C. de Winton (1) (Blackheath); J.H. Greenwell 1 (Rockcliff), W.E. Bromet 6 (Richmond), H. Bradshaw 2 (Bramley), T. Broadley 1 (Bingley), J.T. Toothill 8 (Bradford), F. Evershed 7 (Blackheath), S.M.J. Woods 9 (Wellington), P. Maud 1 (Blackheath), F.C. Lohden (1) (Blackheath).

Referee D.S. Morton (Scotland)

IRELAND v ENGLAND   9/52

4 February 1893
Lansdowne Road, Dublin
England 4 (2T) Ireland 0

England   T: Bradshaw, Taylor.

Although Ireland failed to score a point in this, or their two other Championship matches, their play suggested that with a little more experience and technical expertise they would soon climb out from the lower reaches of the table, the fate which usually dogged them in the early days of the Championship. A crowd of 6000 attended.

IRELAND   S. Gardiner 1 (Belfast Albion); T. Edwards (5) (Lansdowne), *S. Lee 7 (NIFC), W. Gardiner 3 (NIFC); T. Thornhill (4) (Wanderers), F.E. Davies 3 (Lansdowne); R. Johnston 1 (Wanderers), T.J. Johnston 4 (Queen's C. Belfast), E.J.

Walsh (7) (Lansdowne), A.K. Wallis 4 (Wanderers), H. Lindsay 1 (Dublin U.), M.S. Egan 1 (Garryowen), J.H. O'Conor 8 (Bective Rangers), R. Stevenson 11 (Dungannon), C.V. Rooke 6 (Dublin U.).

ENGLAND   E. Field (2) (Cambridge U.); J.W. Dyson 3 (Huddersfield), R.E. Lockwood 11 (Heckmondwike), T. Nicholson (1) (Rockcliff); H. Duckett 1 (Bradford), E.W. Taylor 2 (Rockcliff); F. Evershed 8 (Burton), J.H. Greenwell (2) (Rockcliff), *S.M.J. Woods 10 (Wellington), J.T. Toothill 9 (Bradford), W.E. Bromet 7 (Richmond), W. Yiend 4 (Hartlepool Rovers), H. Bradshaw 3 (Bramley), A. Allport 2 (Blackheath), P. Maud (2) (Blackheath).

Referee A.R. Don Wauchope (Scotland)

SCOTLAND v WALES   11/53

4 February 1893
Raeburn Place, Edinburgh
Wales 9 (3T, 1PG) Scotland 0

Wales   T: Bert Gould, Biggs, McCutcheon. C: Bancroft.

Wales scored their first victory in Scotland, due to the success of their now well-established policy of playing four threequarters. Billy Bancroft scored his penalty goal through a drop kick, the second occasion he employed this method in the Championship. A.W. Cameron, the Watsonians full-back, won his second cap, six years after playing his first game for Scotland. Newport supplied nine players to the Welsh team. It was a day for celebration for one of them, Arthur Gould. He made his seventeenth Championship appearance, beating the 16 caps of Scotland's W.E. Maclagan (1883–90) and C. E. Orr (1887–92).

SCOTLAND   A.W. Cameron 2 (Watsonians); D.D. Robertson (1) (Cambridge U.), G. MacGregor 7 (London Scottish), J.J. Gowans 1 (Cambridge U.); R.C. Greig 1 (Glasgow Acads), W. Wotherspoon 3 (W. of Scotland); W.B. Cownie 1 (Watsonians), A. Dalgleish 6 (Gala), W.R. Gibson 6 (Royal HSFP), T.L. Hendry 1 (Clydesdale), H.T.O. Leggatt 6 (Watsonians), *R.G. Macmillan 12 (London Scottish), H.F. Menzies 1 (W. of Scotland), J.N. Millar 4 (W. of Scotland), G.T. Neilson 6 (W. of Scotland).

WALES   W.J. Bancroft 11 (Swansea); N. Biggs 4 (Cardiff), *A.J. Gould 17 (Newport), A Gould 2 (Newport), W. McCutcheon 5 (Swansea); H.P. Phillips 3 (Newport), F.C. Parfitt 2 (Newport); H.T. Day 3 (Newport), T.C. Graham 7 (Newport), J. Hannan 11 (Newport), W.H. Watts 5 (Newport), A.W. Boucher 5 (Newport), F. Mills 5 (Swansea), A.F. Hill 10 (Cardiff), C.B. Nicholl 6 (Llanelli).

Referee W.H. Humphreys (England)

IRELAND v SCOTLAND   11/54

20 February 1893
Ballynafeigh, Belfast
Ireland 0 Scotland 0

Once again conditions in Belfast were appalling: the Ballynafeigh pitch resembled a bog by the finish of this dour struggle. It was the second match in a row in which Scotland failed to score.

IRELAND   S. Gardiner (2) (Belfast Albion); W. Gardiner 4 (NIFC), *S. Lee 8 (NIFC), L.H. Gwynn 1 (Dublin U.); W.S. Brown 1 (Dublin U.), F.E. Davies 4 (Lansdowne); E.G. Forrest 6 (Wanderers), H. Forrest 1 (Wanderers), T.J. Johnston 5 (Queen's C. Belfast), J.S. Jameson (6) (Lansdowne), H. Lindsay 2 (Dublin U.), B. O'Brien 1 (Derry), J.H. O'Conor 9 (Bective Rangers), C.V. Rooke 7 (Dublin U.), R. Stevenson 12 (Dungannon).

SCOTLAND   H.J. Stevenson 14 (Edinburgh Acads); G.T. Campbell 4 (London Scottish), G. MacGregor 8 (London Scottish), W. Neilson 6 (Cambridge U.); J.W. Simpson 1 (Royal HSFP), W.P. Donaldson 1 (Oxford U.); J.M. Bishop (1) (Glasgow Acads), *J.D. Boswell 12 (W. of Scotland), W.B. Cownie 2 (Watsonians), D. Fisher (1) (W. of Scotland), J.R. Ford (1) (Gala), W.R. Gibson 7 (Royal HSFP), T.L. Hendry 2 (Clydesdale), H.F. Menzies 2 (W. of Scotland), J.E. Orr 11 (W. of Scotland).

Referee G. Rowland Hill (England)

A group photograph of the players in the England-Scotland match on 4 March 1893. Usually Championship teams were photographed separately

ENGLAND v SCOTLAND 8/55

4 March 1893
Headingley, Leeds
Scotland 8 (2DG) England 0

Scotland DG: Boswell, Campbell.

This was the only occasion when dropped goals have decided the outcome of an England v Scotland match. Scotland would have scored a third but the referee ruled that an attempt by Neilson, which had seemingly gone over off an upright, had not crossed the bar. It was the last international for eight England players.

ENGLAND W.G. Mitchell (7) (Richmond); J.W. Dyson (4) (Huddersfield), *A.E. Stoddart (9) (Blackheath), F.P. Jones (1) (New Brighton); H. Duckett (2) (Bradford), C.M. Wells 1 (Cambridge U.); F. Evershed (9) (Burton), F. Soane 1 (Bath), W. Yiend (5) (Hartlepool Rovers), J.T. Toothill 10 (Bradford), H. Bradshaw 4 (Bramley), L.J. Percival (3) (Rugby), W.E. Bromet 8 (Richmond), T. Broadley 2 (Bingley), J.J. Robinson 1 (Cambridge U.).

SCOTLAND H.J. Stevenson (15) (Edinburgh Acads); G.T. Campbell 5 (London Scottish), G. MacGregor 9 (London Scottish), W. Neilson 7 (Cambridge U.); J.W. Simpson 2 (Royal HSFP), W. Wotherspoon 4 (W. of Scotland); *J.D. Boswell 13 (W. of Scotland), W.B. Cownie 3 (Watsonians), R.S. Davidson (1) (Royal HSFP), W.R. Gibson 8 (Royal HSFP), T.L. Hendry 3 (Clydesdale), H.T.O. Leggatt 7 (Watsonians), R.G. Macmillan 13 (London Scottish), J.E. Orr (12) (W. of Scotland), T.M. Scott 1 (Melrose).

Referee W. Wilkins (Wales)

WALES v IRELAND 8/56

11 March 1893
Stradey Park, Llanelli
Wales 2 (1T) Ireland 0

Wales T: Bert Gould.

Wales, playing four threequarters, won the Triple Crown for the first time. It was the last occasion that an international side, Ireland, played three threequarters, despite the fact that their captain, Sammy Lee, was not in the least impressed by Wales's innovation. It was ironic, a lovely Irish twist, that Lee was dropped as Ireland's captain next season: he was kept in the side, as one of four newly-created three-quarters, and thus helped Ireland win the Triple Crown and the Championship, poignantly against Wales, in Belfast.

Irish team selection, during this period, seemed a perilous exercise for their selectors and very frustrating for compilers of team-sheets. 'The composition of the Irish team' warned Old Stager, in the *South Wales Daily News*, . . . 'all is uncertainty as is usual and warned by experience of other years I shall accept no list of the fifteen as thoroughly authentic until I see the team on the ground.' Old Stager, on this occasion had been forewarned. A 'friend' in Dublin, when asked about the Irish line-up, replied: 'arrangements here are all confusion, and there is no knowing what kind of team we shall send you.'

WALES W.J. Bancroft 12 (Swansea); N. Biggs 5 (Cardiff), *A.J. Gould 18 (Newport), A. Gould (3) (Newport), W. McCutcheon 6 (Swansea); H.P. Phillips 4 (Newport), F.C. Parfitt 3 (Newport); T.C. Graham 8 (Newport), W. H. Watts 6 (Newport), J. Hannan 12 (Newport), A.W. Boucher 6 (Newport), D. Samuel (2) (Swansea), F. Mills 6 (Swansea), A.F. Hill 11 (Cardiff), C.B. Nicholl 7 (Llanelli).

IRELAND W. Sparrow 1 (Dublin U.); R.W. Dunlop 10 (NIFC), *S. Lee 9 (NIFC), W. Gardiner 5 (NIFC); F.E. Davies (5) (Lansdowne), W.S. Brown 2 (Dublin U.); R. Stevenson (13) (Dungannon), C.V. Rooke 8 (Dublin U.), H. Lindsay 3 (Dublin U.), A.D. Clinch 2 (Dublin U.), B. O'Brien 2 (Dublin U.), A.K. Wallis (5) (Wanderers), H. Forrest (2) (Wanderers), R. Johnston (2) (Wanderers), R.W. Hamilton (1) (Wanderers).

Referee W.H. Humphreys (England)

1894

BIRKENHEAD England beat Wales 24-3 · BLACKHEATH Ireland beat England 7-5
NEWPORT Wales beat Scotland 7-0 · DUBLIN Ireland beat Scotland 5-0
EDINBURGH Scotland beat England 6-0 · BELFAST Ireland beat Wales 3-0

CHAMPIONSHIP TABLE
Ireland – Championship, Triple Crown

Pos	Country	P	W	D	L	F	A	Pts	Tries F	Tries A
1	Ireland (4)	3	3	0	0	15	5	6	2	1
2	England (3)	3	1	0	2	29	16	2	5	4
3	Wales (1)	3	1	0	2	10	27	2	2	4
4	Scotland (2)	3	1	0	2	6	12	2	2	2

Ireland's usual fate in the Championship had not gone unnoticed in the sections of the Press which regularly reported rugby football: 'Generally the Ireland-Wales match has been to decide,' remarked the *South Wales Daily Post*, 'which team should be the recipient of the ignominious Wooden Spoon ... times have changed, however. Today Erin's sons are striving to mark an epoch in the history of football by attaining the pinnacle of fame, the head of the Championship table.' And when Ireland responded to that interest by winning their first Triple Crown, *The Field* marked the occasion by writing: 'Ireland stands in the proud position of being Champion of the nations'.

Although the try was now worth three points and a conversion two, Ireland's points total in winning the title was a miserly fifteen, the lowest ever. Indeed the first season in which all four countries employed four threequarters did not produce any significant increase in try-scoring.

By now, the game was widely reported, and no doubt responding to readers' interest some newspapers made a point of producing lengthy biographies of the players of the day. The importance of physical attributes was also recognized. For example, when Fred Hutchinson, the Neath forward, made his début against Ireland, he was described as a strapping 6 foot,

and 13 stone, and, possibly more interesting, that he had begun his playing career (with Maesteg) at 14, coincidentally the same age that Arthur Gould embarked on his illustrious career with Newport.

Today's forwards might be amused to know that D.W. Nicholl, who won his only cap as a replacement for his brother Charlie, also against Ireland, was described as 'the giant of the Welsh

William McCutcheon, the Swansea back, who at 5ft 10¾in, 12 st 4 lbs, was one of the heftier backs to appear for Wales before 1900

XV ... particularly strong in the line-out'. He was 6 feet 3 inches and 13 stone 6 pounds. Sandy Thorburn, the eminent Scottish rugby historian, pointed out that in the 1896 edition of *Rugby Football*, it was stated that the ideal weight for a forward was 13 stone with a height of 5 feet 10 inches. Considering that in the late 1960s there was a prevalent view that flank-forwards had to be at least 6 feet 2 inches and 14 stone – for which John Taylor and Dai Morris were whimpering apologies – it suggests that rugby experts have not learnt very much.

Thorburn was understandably fascinated with height and weight comparisons of different eras. He examined two Scotland teams 100 years apart: in 1876 the average weight of the backs was 10 stone 10 pounds and the forwards 11 stone 13 pounds. In 1976 it was 12 stone 2 pounds and 14 stone 3 pounds. Presuming that the selected sides were typical of their particular era, arguably the figures kill off the popularly-held view that the players of old were giants, rugged, lofty and square-shouldered. Perhaps they simply posed better for team photographs!

ENGLAND v WALES 10/57

6 January 1894
Birkenhead Park
England 24 (4G, 1GM) Wales 3 (1T)

England T: Bradshaw, Morfitt, Lockwood, Taylor. C: Lockwood (3), Taylor. GM: Taylor.
Wales T: Parfitt.

The Birkenhead club took the precaution of covering the Upper Park pitch with straw and positioning small braziers on the areas worst affected by a severe frost. They also erected special stands to accommodate a crowd of 10,000. The *South Wales Daily Post* captured the atmosphere of the occasion: 'on arriving at the Mersey town, to find it thronged with sportsmen, to hear conversations and ejaculations in the Welsh language and various dialects of the English counties ... the ''Taff'' rubbed shoulders with the burly Northumbrian, the smart Cockney confabbed with the Lancashire lad, the Somerset farmer discoursed with the enthusiastic Yorkshireman. They were all drawn together by the great British magnet.' The attendance, in fact, was 7000. On the

morning of the match a meeting of the International Board decided that, 'henceforth the scoring in international matches shall be same as in ordinary matches in England and Wales.'

ENGLAND J.F. Byrne 1 (Moseley); F. Firth 1 (Halifax), C.A. Hooper 1 (Middlesex Wands), S. Morfitt 1 (West Hartlepool), *R.E. Lockwood 12 (Heckmondwike); C.M. Wells 2 (Harlequins), E.W. Taylor 3 (Rockcliff); F. Soane 2 (Bath), J. Hall 1 (North Durham), J.T. Toothill 11 (Bradford), H. Speed 1 (Castleford), W.E. Tucker 1 (Cambridge U.), H. Bradshaw 5 (Bramley), T. Broadley 3 (Bingley), A. Allport 3 (Blackheath).

WALES W.J. Bancroft 13 (Swansea); N. Biggs 6 (Cardiff), *A.J. Gould 19 (Newport), J. Conway-Rees (3) (Llanelli), W. McCutcheon (7) (Swansea); H.P. Phillips 5 (Newport), F.C. Parfitt 4 (Newport); F. Mills 7 (Swansea), A.F. Hill 12 (Cardiff), D.J. Daniel 2 (Llanelli), C.B. Nicholl 8 (Llanelli), W.H. Watts 7 (Newport), A.W. Boucher 7 (Newport), T.C. Graham 9 (Newport), J. Hannan 13 (Newport).

Referee J.A. Smith (Scotland)

ENGLAND v IRELAND 10/58

3 February 1894
Rectory Field, Blackheath
Ireland 7 (1T, 1DG) England 5 (1G)

England T: Lockwood. C: Taylor.
Ireland T: John Lytle. DG: Forrest.

George Walmsley, the Bective Rangers forward, became another serious casualty of the Championship when he broke a leg. Walmsley never played international rugby again. Despite the fact that Sammy Lee, Ireland's most experienced back was prejudiced against the four three-quarter system, the Irish adopted it for the first time in this match. Tommy Crean made his début; the big, powerful Wanderers' forward played on the 1896 British tour of South Africa, and stayed there to serve as a surgeon-captain in the Boer War. Crean won a VC in the hostilities, remarkably as did another Wanderers' international forward, Bob Johnston, who had settled in South Africa after the 1896 tour. Yet another Wanderers' player to win a VC was Frank Harvey, in the First World War.

ENGLAND   J.F. Byrne 2 (Moseley); F. Firth 2 (Halifax), C.A. Hooper 2 (Middlesex Wands), S. Morfitt 2 (West Hartlepool), *R.E. Lockwood (13) (Heckmondwike); R. Wood (1) (Liversedge), E.W. Taylor 4 (Rockcliff); F. Soane 3 (Bath), J.T. Toothill (12) (Bradford), W.E. Tucker 2 (Cambridge U.), H. Bradshaw 6 (Bramley), A. Allport 4 (Blackheath), T. Broadley 4 (Bingley), J. Hall 2 (North Durham), H. Speed 2 (Castleford).

IRELAND   W. Sparrow (2) (Dublin U.); H.G. Wells 3 (Bective Rangers), S. Lee 10 (NIFC), W. Gardiner 6 (NIFC), L.H. Gwynn 2 (Dublin U.); W.S. Brown 3 (Dublin U.), B.B. Tuke 5 (Bective Rangers); J.N. Lytle 5 (NIFC), J.H. Lytle 1 (NIFC), G. Walmsley (1) (Bective Rangers), J.H. O'Conor 10 (Bective Rangers), H. Lindsay 4 (Dublin U.), *E.G. Forrest 7 (Wanderers), T.J. Crean 1 (Wanderers), C.V. Rooke 9 (Dublin U.).

Referee W.M. Douglas (Wales)

WALES   W.J. Bancroft 14 (Swansea); T.W. Pearson 5 (Cardiff), D. Fitzgerald 1 (Cardiff), *A.J. Gould 20 (Newport), W.L. Thomas 1 (Newport); H.P. Phillips (6) (Newport), F.C. Parfitt 5 (Newport); F. Mills 8 (Swansea), A.F. Hill 13 (Cardiff), D.J. Daniel 3 (Llanelli), C.B. Nicholl 9 (Llanelli), W.H. Watts 8 (Newport), F.H. Day 4 (Newport), T.C. Graham 10 (Newport), J. Hannan 14 (Newport).

SCOTLAND   J. Rogerson (1) (Kelvinside Acads); G.T. Campbell 6 (London Scottish), G. MacGregor 10 (London Scottish), J.J. Gowans 2 (Cambridge U.), H.T.S. Gedge 1 (London Scottish); W. Wotherspoon 5 (W. of Scotland), J.W. Simpson 3 (Royal HSFP); W.B. Cownie 4 (Watsonians), A. Dalgleish 7 (Gala), W.R. Gibson 9 (Royal HSFP), W.M.C. McEwan 1 (Edinburgh Acads), *R.G. Macmillan 14 (London Scottish), H.F. Menzies 3 (W. of Scotland), G.T. Neilson 7 (W. of Scotland), H.B. Wright (1) (Watsonians).

Referee E.B. Holmes (England)

WALES v SCOTLAND   12/59

3 February 1894
Rodney Parade, Newport
Wales 7 (1T, 1DG) Scotland 0

Wales   T: Fitzgerald. DG: Fitzgerald.

England and Ireland had adopted the Welsh system of four threequarters, but Scotland were still expressing reservations, if not total caution. In this match they really did split hairs: they played four half-backs and called them threequarters. After the defeat by England a month earlier, criticism of Welsh selection was rife. The *South Wales Daily Post* leapt to the committee's defence: 'After the severe whipping experienced by the Welsh fifteen at Birkenhead, the members of the selection committee of the WRU were besieged with letters containing suggestions, criticisms and condemnation, but fortunately, for the best interests of Welsh football, they did not allow themselves to become bewildered or fluttered by the varied opinions of enthusiasts.' After Scotland had been beaten, the *Daily Post* crowed: 'hope has risen Phoenix-like from the ashes of the aspirations so roughly extinguished early in the new year.' A crowd of 20,000 saw them do it.

IRELAND v SCOTLAND   12/60

24 February 1894
Lansdowne Road, Dublin
Ireland 5 (1G) Scotland 0

Ireland   T: Wells. C: John Lytle.

On their twelfth attempt Ireland managed to beat Scotland in the Championship, so ending their longest sequence without a victory against any opposition. Everyone celebrated in Dublin – except H.G. Wells, the Irish try scorer. He was dropped.

IRELAND   P.J. Grant 1 (Bective Rangers); W. Gardiner 7 (NIFC), S. Lee 11 (NIFC), L.H. Gwynn 3 (Dublin U.), H.G. Wells (4) (Bective Rangers); W.S. Brown 4 (Dublin U.), B.B. Tuke 6 (Bective Rangers); A.T.W. Bond 1 (Derry), T.J. Crean 2 (Wanderers), *E.G. Forrest 8 (Wanderers), H. Lindsay 5 (Dublin U.), J.H. Lytle 2 (NIFC), J.N. Lytle 6 (NIFC), J.H. O'Conor 11 (Bective Rangers), C.V. Rooke 10 (Dublin).

SCOTLAND   A.W. Cameron (3) (Watsonians); G.T. Campbell 7 (London Scottish), G. MacGregor 11 (London Scottish), W. Wotherspoon 6 (W. of Scotland), H.T.S. Gedge 2 (Edinburgh Wands); J.W. Simpson 4 (Royal

HSFP), W.P. Donaldson 2 (Oxford U.); A.H. Anderson (1) (Glasgow Acads), *J.D. Boswell 14 (W. of Scotland), W.B. Cownie 5 (Watsonians), A. Dalgleish (8) (Gala), W.R. Gibson 10 (Royal HSFP), H.T.O. Leggatt 8 (Watsonians), R.G. Macmillan 15 (London Scottish), G.T. Neilson 8 (W. of Scotland).

Referee H.L. Ashmore (England)

SCOTLAND v ENGLAND   9/61

17 March 1894
Raeburn Place, Edinburgh
Scotland 6 (2T) England 0

Scotland   T: Boswell (2).

England's first defeat in five visits to Scotland; the latter fielded a complete back division comprising current or ex-London Scottish players, and two schoolboys, W.M.C. McEwan and Gordon Neilson. J.D. Boswell, who scored both Scottish tries, never played in another Championship match. The same fate befell nine of England's side, with only two forwards, Tom Broadley and Harry Speed surviving.

SCOTLAND   G. MacGregor 12 (London Scottish); G.T. Campbell 8 (London Scottish), W. Neilson 8 (Cambridge U.), H.T.S. Gedge 3 (Edinburgh Wands), J.J. Gowans 3 (Cambridge U.); W. Wotherspoon (7) (W. of Scotland), J.W. Simpson 5 (Royal HSFP); *J.D. Boswell (15) (W. of Scotland), W.B. Cownie 6 (Watsonians), W.R. Gibson 11 (Royal HSFP), H.T.O. Leggatt (9) (Watsonians), W.M.C. McEwan 2 (Edinburgh Acads), R.G. Macmillan 16 (London Scottish), H.F. Menzies (4) (W. of Scotland), W.G. Neilson (1) (Merchiston Castle).

ENGLAND   J.F. Byrne 3 (Moseley); C.A. Hooper (3) (Middlesex Wands), W.J. Jackson (1) (Halifax), S. Morfitt 3 (West Hartlepool), F. Firth (3) (Halifax); E.W. Taylor 5 (Rockcliff), C.M. Wells 3 (Harlequins); A. Allport (5) (Blackheath), J. Hall (3) (North Durham), A.E. Elliott (1) (St Thomas's H.), T. Broadley 5 (Bingley), H. Bradshaw (7) (Bramley), F. Soane (4) (Bath), H. Speed 3 (Castleford), W. Walton (7) (Castleford).

Referee W. Wilkins (Wales)

IRELAND v WALES   9/62

19 March 1894
Ballynafeigh, Belfast
Ireland 3 (1PG) Wales 0

Ireland   PG: John Lytle.

The match was played at the Ulster Cricket Club ground at Ballynafeigh, which was considered most unsatisfactory by Welsh officials who, on the morning of the match, held a special meeting to discuss the matter. The outcome was a protest sent to the International Board and future matches at Ballynafeigh were staged at the nearby Balmoral Showgrounds. Ireland were unperturbed: John Lytle's penalty goal gave them their first Triple Crown and Championship. It was personally satisfying too for Harry Lindsay, who had been capped the year before after being dropped from the Dublin University side, and for W.S. Brown, Scottish-born and Fettes-schooled, whose inclusion in the Irish team had been greeted with some misgivings. There was a 5000 attendance. Cardiff supplied all four Wales threequarters.

IRELAND   P.J. Grant (2) (Bective Rangers); R.W. Dunlop (11) (NIFC), S. Lee 12 (NIFC), W. Gardiner 8 (NIFC), L.H. Gwynn 4 (Dublin U.); B.B. Tuke 7 (Bective Rangers), W.S. Brown (5) (Dublin U.); *E.G. Forrest 9 (Wanderers), T.J. Crean 3 (Wanderers), C.V. Rooke 11 (Dublin U.), H. Lindsay 6 (Dublin U.), J.H. O'Conor 12 (Bective Rangers), A.T.W. Bond (2) (Derry), J.N. Lytle (7) (NIFC), J.H. Lytle 3 (NIFC).

WALES   W.J. Bancroft 15 (Swansea); N. Biggs (7) (Cardiff), D. Fitzgerald (2) (Cardiff), J.E. Elliott 1 (Cardiff), T.W. Pearson 6 (Cardiff); R.B. Sweet-Escott 2 (Cardiff), F.C. Parfitt 6 (Newport); *A.F. Hill (14) (Cardiff), J. Hannan 15 (Newport), W.H. Watts 9 (Newport), H.T. Day (5) (Newport), F. Mills 9 (Swansea), D.J. Daniel 4 (Llanelli), D.W. Nicholls (1) (Llanelli), F. Hutchinson 1 (Neath).

Referee R.D. Rainie (Scotland)

1895

SWANSEA England beat Wales 14-6 · EDINBURGH Scotland beat Wales 5-4
DUBLIN England beat Ireland 6-3 · EDINBURGH Scotland beat Ireland 6-0
RICHMOND Scotland beat England 6-3 · CARDIFF Wales beat Ireland 5-3

CHAMPIONSHIP TABLE
Scotland – Championship, Triple Crown

									Tries	
Pos	Country	P	W	D	L	F	A	Pts	F	A
1	Scotland (4)	3	3	0	0	17	7	6	4	0
2	England (2)	3	2	0	1	23	15	4	6	4
3	Wales (3)	3	1	0	2	15	22	2	3	6
4	Ireland (1)	3	0	0	3	6	17	0	2	5

Scotland won the Triple Crown, and therefore the Championship, by beating England with two penalty goals against a penalty goal. The scoring, of course, was significant. It was the first time that the penalty goal was the only form of scoring by both sides.

Other events of the season, though, concerned the game's administrators in a year when the Northern Union was formed by the clubs who had broken away from the Rugby Football Union during the Broken Time Dispute of 1893. It was against this background that William Cail, the RFU treasurer, set about his task of recodifying the Laws, with the principal aim of excluding professionalism in any form. It is safe to suggest that rugby football became the game it is today because of Cail's self-imposed Law recodification. It took Cail nearly 30 years to make public his views on the matter, which he did at the AGM of the RFU in his final year as treasurer in 1924. That speech was revealing, to say the least: 'I would like to point out what was occurring in the Rugby football world immediately before I took the office of treasurer, that is, during the two years I was president. The Committee of this Union were constantly hearing of illegal payments and of players on returning to their dressing-rooms finding in the pockets of their ordinary clothes money which was not there when they undressed – largely among the big clubs of Lancashire and Yorkshire. They could not find anything tangible, until a direct charge was made to the Union by Cumberland against one of the leading Yorkshire clubs, of inducing one of their players to leave for a money consideration. Our Committee at once appointed a commission to hold an inquiry, consisting of the late F.I. Currey, a past president, A.M. Crook, who has since been president, and myself. Before the inquiry we were warned, both privately and through letters to the press, that if the club were punished all the chief clubs in Yorkshire and Lancashire would secede from our Union – a serious thing seeing that a large proportion of our International players were drawn from these counties.

The inquiry was held at Preston, the club was suspended, and the suspension confirmed by the Committee, who were determined to face all consequences to keep our game pure, to be played for love of it and not for personal gain. Then followed two large general meetings, to one of which two special trains were run from Yorkshire, in order to try to carry a resolution that men should be paid for "broken time" – that is when playing football instead of working. At both of these meetings the good rally by amateur clubs saved the Union from professionalism. To show the effect of the leading Lancashire and Yorkshire clubs leaving us and forming the Northern Union, I may mention that in 1893, when the split took place, there were 481 clubs in membership, in 1896 the number was 383, and in 1903 had fallen as low as 244. Since then the number has increased, especially after the opening of the Twickenham ground. This past season (1924) 445 clubs have paid their subscriptions, and some 40 odd are in arrears, so today we have more members than ever before.'

WALES v ENGLAND   11/63

5 January 1895
St Helen's, Swansea
England 14 (1G, 3T) Wales 6 (2T)

Wales   T: Elsey, Graham.
England   T: Carey, Leslie-Jones, Thomson, Woods. C: Mitchell.

In terms of international experience, Wales had a decided edge with Billy Bancroft, Tom Pearson, Arthur Gould, Tom Graham, Arthur Boucher, Wallace Watts, Jim Hannan, Charles Nicholl and Frank Mills totalling over 100 caps between them. In contrast, England fielded ten new caps in a side which won convincingly.

WALES   W.J. Bancroft 16 (Swansea); T.W. Pearson 7 (Cardiff), O. Badger 1 (Llanelli), *A.J. Gould 21 (Newport), W. L. Thomas 2 (Newport); S. Biggs 1 (Cardiff), B. Davies 1 (Llanelli); T.C. Graham 11 (Newport), A.W. Boucher 8 (Newport), W.H. Watts 10 (Newport), J. Hannan 16 (Newport), T.H. Jackson (1) (Swansea), C.B. Nicholl 10 (Llanelli), W.J. Elsey (1) (Cardiff), F. Mills 10 (Cardiff).

ENGLAND   H. Ward (1) (Bradford); J.H.C. Fegan 1 (Blackheath), F.A. Leslie-Jones 1 (Oxford U.), E.M. Baker 1 (Oxford U.), W.B. Thomson 2 (Blackheath); R.H.B. Cattell 1 (Moseley), E.W. Taylor 6 (Rockcliff); *S.M.J. Woods 11 (Blackheath), F.O. Poole 1 (Oxford U.), W.E. Bromet 9 (Richmond), F. Mitchell 1 (Cambridge U.), W.E. Tucker 3 (Cambridge U.), C. Thomas 1 (Barnstaple), G.M. Carey 1 (Oxford U.), H.W. Finlinson 1 (Blackheath).

Referee J.A. Smith (Scotland)

SCOTLAND v WALES   13/64

26 January 1895
Raeburn Place, Edinburgh
Scotland 5 (1G) Wales 4 (1GM)

Scotland   T: Gowans. C: H.O. Smith.
Wales   GM: Bancroft.

Wales considered the frozen pitch unplayable, but consented to go ahead after Scotland were coerced into agreeing that the playing area be shortened by some 20 yards to avoid a particularly dangerous patch near one end. This area

The Scottish XV which defeated England on 9 March 1895 to win the Triple Crown and the Championship

was taped off, and there was some debate regarding a 'score' near the tape by Frank Mills. The referee, however, ruled against what would have been a winning Welsh try.

SCOTLAND A.R. Smith 1 (Oxford U.); J.J. Gowans 4 (London Scottish), G.T. Campbell 9 (London Scottish), W. Neilson 9 (London Scottish), R. Welsh 1 (Watsonians); J.W. Simpson 6 (Royal HSFP), M. Elliot 1 (Hawick); W.B. Cownie 7 (Watsonians), J.H. Dods 1 (Edinburgh Acads), *W.R. Gibson 12 (Royal HSFP), W.M.C. McEwan 3 (Edinburgh Acads), R.G. Macmillan 17 (London Scottish), G.T. Neilson 9 (W. of Scotland), T.M. Scott 2 (Hawick), H.O. Smith 1 (Watsonians).

WALES W.J. Bancroft 17 (Swansea); T.W. Pearson 8 (Cardiff), *A.J. Gould 22 (Newport), O. Badger 2 (Llanelli), E. Lloyd (1) (Llanelli); F.C. Parfitt 7 (Newport), S. Biggs 2 (Cardiff); T.C. Graham (12) (Newport), A.W. Boucher 9 (Newport), J. Hannan 17 (Newport), H. Packer 2 (Newport), T. Pook (1) (Newport), F. Mills 11 (Cardiff), C.B. Nicholl 11 (Llanelli), E. George 1 (Pontypridd).

Referee E.B. Holmes (England)

IRELAND v ENGLAND 11/65

2 February 1895
Lansdowne Road, Dublin
England 6 (2T) Ireland 3 (1T)

Ireland T: Louis Magee.
England T: Fegan, Thomas.

The brothers, Louis and Jim Magee, made their début appearances for Ireland. Jim played only twice but Louis made 27 appearances and established a reputation as one of Ireland's finest half-backs. Another member of the family, brother-in-law Tommy Little, won seven caps (1898–1901).

IRELAND G.R. Symes (1) (Monkstown); W. Gardiner 9 (NIFC), S. Lee 13 (NIFC), T.H. Stevenson 1 (Queen's U. Belfast), J.T. Magee 1 (Bective Rangers); L.M. Magee 1 (Bective Rangers), B.B. Tuke 8 (Bective Rangers); T.J. Johnston (6) (Queen's U. Belfast), H. Lindsay 7 (Armagh), A.A. Brunker 1 (Lansdowne), *J.H. O'Conor 13 (Bective Rangers), H.C. McCoull 1 (Belfast Albion), A.D. Clinch 3 (Wanderers), T.J. Crean 4 (Wanderers), C.V. Rooke 12 (Monkstown).

ENGLAND J.F. Byrne 4 (Moseley); W.B. Thomson 3 (Blackheath), E.M. Baker 2 (Oxford U.), F.A. Leslie-Jones (2) (Oxford U.), J.H.C. Fegan 2 (Blackheath); R.H.B. Cattell 2 (Moseley), E.W. Taylor 7 (Rockcliff); G.M. Carey 2 (Oxford U.), *S.M.J. Woods 12 (Blackheath), H.W. Finlinson 2 (Blackheath), W.E. Bromet 10 (Richmond), W.E. Tucker 4 (Cambridge U.), F. Mitchell 2 (Cambridge U.), F.O. Poole 2 (Oxford U.), C. Thomas 2 (Barnstaple).

Referee D.G. Findlay (Scotland)

SCOTLAND v IRELAND 13/66

2 March 1895
Raeburn Place, Edinburgh
Scotland 6 (2T) Ireland 0

Scotland T: Welsh, Campbell.

This match should have been played in January, but was postponed twice before Scotland won the second leg of their Triple Crown. Ireland may have had selection problems: they called up W.J.N. Davis, who was currently playing for Edinburgh University, after a gap of three years. Davis never played for Ireland again. Another player who made his last international appearance was Paul Clauss, scorer of several important tries in six matches for Scotland.

SCOTLAND A.R. Smith 2 (Oxford U.); J.J. Gowans 5 (London Scottish), G.T. Campbell 10 (London Scottish), W. Neilson 10 (London Scottish), R. Welsh 2 (Watsonians); J.W. Simpson 7 (Royal HSFP), P.R. Clauss (6) (Birkenhead Park); W.B. Cownie 8 (Watsonians), J.H. Dods 2 (Edinburgh Acads), W.R. Gibson 13 (Royal HSFP), T.L. Hendry (4) (Clydesdale), *R.G. Macmillan 18 (London Scottish), J.N. Millar 5 (W. of Scotland), G.T. Neilson 10 (W. of Scotland), T.M. Scott 3 (Hawick).

IRELAND J. Fulton 1 (NIFC); W. Gardiner 10 (NIFC), J.T. Magee (2) (Bective Rangers), A. Montgomery (1) (NIFC), J. O'Connor (1) (Garryowen); L.M. Magee 2 (Bective Rangers), B.B. Tuke (9) (Bective Rangers); A.D. Clinch 4 (Wanderers), T.J. Crean 5 (Wanderers), W.J.N. Davis (9) (Edinburgh U.), M.S. Egan (2) (Garryowen), H.C. McCoull 2 (Belfast Albion), E.H. McIlwaine 1 (NIFC), W. O'Sullivan (1) (Queen's C. Cork), *C.V. Rooke 13 (Monkstown).

Referee H.L. Ashmore (England)

ENGLAND v SCOTLAND   10/67

9 March 1895
Athletic Ground, Richmond
Scotland 6 (1T, 1PG) England 3 (1PG)

England   PG: Byrne.
Scotland   T: G.T. Neilson. PG: G.T. Neilson.

This was the first occasion when each side scored with a penalty goal, although it was not until the thirty-fifth encounter between the sides, in 1925, that Scotland added another. England's second penalty against Scotland took an even longer time in arriving – the forty-sixth meeting in 1936. Indeed, the propensity for penalty goals did not disfigure Calcutta Cup matches until 1955: from then only two Scotland-England matches were penalty-free.

ENGLAND   J.F. Byrne 5 (Moseley); W.B. Thomson (4) (Blackheath), E.M. Baker 3 (Oxford U.), T.H. Dobson (1) (Bradford), J.H.C. Fegan (3) (Blackheath); R.H.B. Cattell 3 (Moseley), E.W. Taylor 8 (Rockcliff); G.M. Carey 3 (Oxford U.), *S.M.J. Woods (13) (Blackheath), H.W. Finlinson 3 (Blackheath), W.E. Bromet 11 (Richmond), W.E. Tucker (5) (Cambridge U.), F. Mitchell 3 (Cambridge U.), F.O. Poole (3) (Oxford U.), C. Thomas 3 (Barnstaple).

SCOTLAND   A.R. Smith 3 (Oxford U.); R. Welsh 3 (Watsonians), W. Neilson 11 (London Scottish), J.I. Gowans 6 (London Scottish), G.T. Campbell 11 (London Scottish); J.W. Simpson 8 (Royal HSFP), W.P. Donaldson 3 (W. of Scotland); W.B. Cownie (9) (Watsonians), J.H. Dods 3 (Edinburgh Acads), W.R. Gibson (14) (Royal HSFP), W.M.C. McEwan 4 (Edinburgh Acads), *R.G. McMillan 19 (London Scottish), J.N. Millar (6) (W. of Scotland), G.T. Neilson 11 (W. of Scotland), T.M. Scott 4 (Hawick).

Referee W. Wilkins (Wales)

WALES v IRELAND   10/68

16 March 1895
Cardiff Arms Park
Wales 5 (1G) Ireland 3 (1T)

Wales   T: Pearson. C: Bancroft.
Ireland   T: Crean.

Ireland were handicapped by the absence of J.H. O'Conor and B. Tuke; O'Conor was considered to be one of the best forwards in the game at the time. Three of the Welsh team were English-born: Ralph Sweet-Escott (Somerset), Harry Packer (Berkshire) and Wallace Watts (Gloucestershire). A fourth, Tom Pearson, was born in Bombay – and it was Pearson who won the match with what was reported as one of Wales's greatest ever tries.

WALES   W.J. Bancroft 18 (Swansea); T.W. Pearson 9 (Cardiff), O. Badger 3 (Llanelli), *A.J. Gould 23 (Newport), W.L. Thomas (3) (Newport); D. Morgan 1 (Llanelli), R.B. Sweet-Escott (3) (Cardiff); A.W. Boucher 10 (Newport), W.H. Watts 11 (Newport), J. Hannan (18) (Newport), H. Packer 3 (Newport), F. Mills 12 (Cardiff), C.B. Nicholl 12 (Llanelli), E. George 2 (Pontypridd), A.M. Jenkin 1 (Swansea).

IRELAND   J. Fulton 2 (NIFC); W. Gardiner 11 (NIFC), S. Lee 14 (NIFC), T.H. Stevenson 2 (Belfast Albion), A.P. Gwynn (1) (Dublin U.); M.G. Delaney (1) (Bective Rangers), L.M. Magee 3 (Bective Rangers); C.V. Rooke 14 (Monkstown), T.J. Crean 6 (Wanderers), *E.G. Forrest 10 (Wanderers), A.D. Clinch 5 (Wanderers), J.H. Lytle 4 (Lansdowne), A.A. Brunker (2) (Lansdowne), H.C. McCoull 3 (Belfast Albion), E.H. McIlwaine (2) (NIFC).

Referee E.B. Holmes (England)

BLACKHEATH England beat Wales 25-0 · CARDIFF Wales beat Scotland 6-0
LEEDS Ireland beat England 10-4 · DUBLIN Ireland drew Scotland 0-0
DUBLIN Ireland beat Wales 8-4 · GLASGOW Scotland beat England 11-0

CHAMPIONSHIP TABLE
Ireland – Championship

Pos	Country	P	W	D	L	F	A	Pts	Tries F	A
1	Ireland (4)	3	2	1	0	18	8	5	4	0
2	Scotland (1)	3	1	1	1	11	6	3	3	2
3	England (2)	3	1	0	2	29	21	2	7	5
4	Wales (3)	3	1	0	2	10	33	2	2	9

After losing all three matches in 1895, Ireland turned the form book upside down by deservedly winning the Championship. But for being held to a 0-0 draw by Scotland, at Lansdowne Road, they would also have won the Triple Crown. Once weak opposition for the other countries to score tries against, Ireland's try-line remained inviolate. The only scores against their resolute defence were two dropped goals. England had a curious season: they finished third, ahead of Wales, having scored more points and more tries than any of the three other countries. The full impact of the loss of players because of the Broken Time dispute had yet to be felt. Scotland, Champions the season before, finished second, thanks to their victory over England, their fourth in succession.

The International Board was flexing its muscle, too. They decided that henceforth the referee should be the sole judge in all matters of fact and, in September, threatened Wales with the loss of all international fixtures because of the Arthur Gould affair. At the June AGM of the Welsh Rugby Union, Walter Rees, of Neath, was appointed secretary, which is worthy of notice here as Rees held the post until 1948, one of the longest periods of office in the game.

ENGLAND v WALES 12/69

4 January 1896
Rectory Field, Blackheath
England 25 (2G, 5T) Wales 0

England   T: Cattell (2), Fookes (2), Morfitt (2), Mitchell. C: Taylor, Valentine.

This was England's first international since the breakaway of the Northern Union clubs in 1895. Wales were without Owen Badger, when after the first 15 minutes, the Llanelli centre broke a collar-bone in a tackle. Clearly this was a more important factor than England missing their northern players. The reality of the situation was soon to show itself: England lost their next two matches and managed only three more wins up to 1900. The diminutive Badger never played for Wales again. Like several of the England team he was soon lured north where he was paid to play for Swinton. Stan Houghton, the England full-back, was another defector: he was picked to play against Ireland on 1 February but 'went north' before he could win a third cap four years after he had won his first.

ENGLAND   S. Houghton (2) (Birkenhead Wanderers); S. Morfitt 4 (West Hartlepool), J. Valentine 2 (Swinton), E.M. Baker 4 (Oxford U.), E.F. Fookes 1 (Sowerby Bridge); R.H.B. Cattell 4 (Blackheath), *E.W. Taylor 9 (Rockcliff); G.M. Carey 4 (Blackheath), J. Pinch 1 (Lancaster), F. Mitchell 4 (Cambridge U.), L.F. Giblin 1 (Cambridge U.), W. Whiteley (1) (Bramley), J. Rhodes 1 (Castleford), J.W. Ward 1 (Castleford), A. Starks 1 (Castleford).

WALES   W.J. Bancroft 19 (Swansea); F.H. Dauncey 1 (Newport), *A.J. Gould 24 (Newport), O.

Badger (4) (Llanelli), C. Bowen 1 (Llanelli); B. Davies (2) (Llanelli), D. Morgan (2) (Llanelli); H. Packer 4 (Newport), W.H. Watts (12) (Newport), A.W. Boucher 11 (Newport), A.M. Jenkin (2) (Swansea), E. George (3) (Pontypridd), F. Mills (13) (Cardiff), C.B. Nicholl 13 (Llanelli), S.H. Ramsey 1 (Treorchy).

Referee D.G. Findlay (Scotland)

WALES v SCOTLAND   14/70

25 January 1896
Cardiff Arms Park
Wales 6 (2T) Scotland 0

Wales   T: Bowen, Gould.

Two of the finest players to emerge during the early years of the Championship made their first appearance: Mark Morrison, the Scottish forward, and Gwyn Nicholls, often described as the Prince of Welsh threequarter play.

WALES   W.J. Bancroft 20 (Swansea); C. Bowen 2 (Llanelli) E.G. Nicholls 1 (Cardiff), *A.J. Gould 25 (Newport), F.H. Dauncey 2 (Newport); S. Biggs 3 (Cardiff), F.C. Parfitt 8 (Newport); H. Packer 5 (Newport), J. Evans 1 (Llanelli), W. Morris 1 (Llanelli), C.B. Nicholl 14 (Llanelli), W. Cope (1) (Blackheath), W. Davies (1) (Cardiff), D. Evans 1 (Penygraig), F. Hutchinson 2 (Neath).

SCOTLAND   A.R. Smith 4 (Oxford U.); G.T. Campbell 12 (London Scottish), A.B. Timms 1 (Edinburgh Wands), T. Scott 1 (Langholm), R. Welsh (4) (Watsonians); J.W. Simpson 9 (Royal HSFP), D. Patterson (1) (Hawick); A. Balfour 1 (Watsonians), J.H. Couper 1 (W. of Scotland), J.H. Dods 4 (London Scottish), W.M.C. McEwan 5 (Edinburgh Acads), M.C. Morrison 1 (Royal HSFP), *G.T. Neilson 12 (W. of Scotland), T.M. Scott 5 (Hawick), H.O. Smith 2 (Watsonians).

Referee G.H. Barnett (England)

ENGLAND v IRELAND   12/71

1 February 1896
Meanwood Road, Leeds
Ireland 10 (2G) England 4 (1DG)

England   DG: Byrne.
Ireland   T: Sealy, Stevenson. C: Bulger.

This win set Ireland up for their second Championship title in three years. Ernest Bromet, one of the stalwarts of the English pack since 1891, made his twelfth and final Championship appearance.

ENGLAND   J.F. Byrne 6 (Moseley); S. Morfitt 5 (West Hartlepool), J. Valentine 3 (Swinton), E.M. Baker 5 (Oxford U.), E.F. Fookes 2 (Sowerby Bridge); R.H.B. Cattell 5 (Blackheath), *E.W. Taylor 10 (Rockcliff); G.M. Carey (5) (Blackheath), J. Pinch 2 (Lancaster), A. Starks (2) (Castleford), L.F. Giblin 2 (Cambridge U.), W.E. Bromet (12) (Richmond), J.W. Ward 2 (Castleford), F. Mitchell 5 (Cambridge U.), J. Rhodes 2 (Castleford).

IRELAND   J. Fulton 3 (NIFC); W. Gardiner 12 (NIFC), *S. Lee 15 (NIFC), T.H. Stevenson 3 (Edinburgh U.), L.Q. Bulger 1 (Dublin U.); L.M. Magee 4 (Bective Rangers), G.G. Allen 1 (Derry); J.H. O'Conor 14 (Bective Rangers), J.H. Lytle 5 (NIFC), W.G. Byron 1 (NIFC), H. Lindsay 8 (Wanderers), J. Sealy 1 (Dublin U.), A.D. Clinch 6 (Wanderers), T.J. Crean 7 (Wanderers), C.V. Rooke 15 (Monkstown).

Referee D.G. Findlay (Scotland)

IRELAND v SCOTLAND   14/72

15 February 1896
Lansdowne Road, Dublin
Ireland 0 Scotland 0

At the end of the season, Ireland probably reflected that this draw prevented their winning a second Triple Crown. According to one account, either side could have won had Bulger and Smith not been off target with penalty kicks.

IRELAND   G.H. McAllan 1 (Dungannon); W. Gardiner 13 (NIFC), *S. Lee 16 (NIFC), T.H. Stevenson 4 (Edinburgh U.), L.O. Bulger 2 (Dublin U.); L.M. Magee 5 (Bective Rangers), G.G. Allen 2 (Derry); W.G. Byron 2 (NIFC), A.D. Clinch 7 (Wanderers), T.J. Crean 8 (Wanderers), H. Lindsay 9 (Armagh), J.H. Lytle 6 (NIFC), J.H. O'Conor 15 (Bective Rangers), C.V. Rooke 16 (Monkstown), J. Sealy 2 (Dublin U.).

SCOTLAND   A.R. Smith 5 (Oxford U.); W. Neilson 12 (London Scottish), G.T. Campbell 13 (London Scottish), J.J. Gowans 7 (London Scottish), C.J.N. Fleming 1 (Edinburgh Wands); J.W. Simpson 10 (Royal HSFP), W.P. Donaldson 4 (W. of Scotland); A. Balfour 2 (Watsonians), J.H. Couper 2 (W. of Scotland), J.H. Dods 5 (London Scottish), W.M.C. McEwan 6 (Edinburgh Acads), M.C. Morrison 2 (Royal HSFP), *G.T. Neilson 13 (W. of Scotland), H.O. Smith 3 (Watsonians), G.O. Turnbull 1 (W. of Scotland).

Referee E.B. Holmes (England)

IRELAND v WALES   11/73

14 March 1896
Lansdowne Road, Dublin
Ireland 8 (1G, 1T) Wales 4 (1DG)

Ireland   T: Crean, Lytle. C: Bulger.
Wales   DG: Gould.

This win brought Ireland the Championship and saw the end of one great career and the beginning of another – the last appearance for Wales of the Llanelli forward Charlie Nicholl and the début of the Newport half-back Llewellyn Lloyd. Larry O. Bulger, the Lansdowne back, who rejoiced in the nickname of 'Fat Cupid', was one of Ireland's outstanding players, an elusive runner and a devastating tackler. Tommy Crean, the Wanderers' forward, celebrated his ninth and last appearance with this second try against Wales. Ireland also saw the last of another outstanding forward, J.H. O'Conor, who won the first of his 16 caps in 1890.

IRELAND   G.H. McAllan (2) (Dungannon); W. Gardiner 14 (NIFC), *S. Lee 17 (NIFC), T.H. Stevenson 5 (Edinburgh U.), L.O. Bulger 3 (Lansdowne); L.M. Magee 6 (Bective Rangers), G.G. Allen 3 (Derry); C.V. Rooke 17 (Monks-

town), T.J. Crean (9) (Wanderers), A.D. Clinch 8 (Wanderers), J. Sealy 3 (Dublin U.), H. Lindsay 10 (Armagh), W.G. Byron 3 (NIFC), J.H. Lytle 7 (NIFC), J.H. O'Conor (16) (Bective Rangers).

WALES   W.J. Bancroft 21 (Swansea); C. Bowen 3 (Llanelli), E.G. Nicholls 2 (Cardiff), *A.J. Gould 26 (Newport), F.H. Dauncey (3) (Newport); G.Ll. Lloyd 1 (Newport), F.C. Parfitt (9) (Newport); H. Packer 6 (Newport), A.W. Boucher 12 (Newport), J. Evans 2 (Llanelli), W. Morris 2 (Llanelli), C.B. Nicholl (15) (Llanelli), D. Evans 2 (Penygraig), F. Hutchinson (3) (Neath), F. Miller 1 (Mountain Ash).

Referee E.B. Holmes (England)

SCOTLAND v ENGLAND   11/74

14 March 1896
Old Hampden Park, Glasgow
Scotland 11 (1G, 2T) England 0

Scotland   T: Fleming, Gedge, Gowans. C: Scott.

Scotland's fourth successive win over England, their longest winning sequence against their Calcutta Cup rivals, was watched by a crowd of 16,000. G. MacGregor (13 caps) and G.T. Neilson (14) made their last appearances for Scotland; likewise eight members of the England side.

SCOTLAND   G. MacGregor (13) (London Scottish); H.T.S. Gedge 4 (London Scottish), G.T. Campbell 14 (London Scottish), C.J.N. Fleming 2 (Edinburgh Wands), J.J. Gowans (8) (London Scottish); M. Elliot 2 (Hawick), W.P. Donaldson 5 (W. of Scotland); A. Balfour 3 (Watsonians), J.H. Dods 6 (London Scottish), W.M.C. McEwan 7 (Edinburgh Acads), M.C. Morrison 3 (Royal HSFP), *G.T. Neilson (14) (W. of Scotland), T.M. Scott 6 (Hawick), H.O. Smith 4 (Watsonians), G.O. Turnbull 2 (W. of Scotland).

ENGLAND   R.W. Poole (1) (Hartlepool Rovers); E.F. Fookes 3 (Sowerby Bridge), J. Valentine (4) (Swinton), E.M. Baker 6 (Oxford U.), S. Morfitt (6) (West Hartlepool); R.H.B. Cattell 6 (Blackheath), C.M. Wells 4 (Harlequins); G.E. Hughes (1) (Barrow), J.H. Barron 1 (Bingley), E. Knowles 1 (Millom), H. Speed (4) (Castleford), J. Rhodes 3 (Castleford), *F. Mitchell (6) (Blackheath), J.W. Ward (3) (Castleford), T. Broadley (6) (Bingley).

Referee W.M. Douglas (Wales)

NEWPORT Wales beat England 11-0 · DUBLIN Ireland beat England 13-9
EDINBURGH Scotland beat Ireland 8-3 · MANCHESTER England beat Scotland 12-3
NB Wales did not play either Ireland or Scotland

CHAMPIONSHIP TABLE
England – Championship

Pos	Country	P	W	D	L	F	A	Pts	Tries F	Tries A
1	England (3)	3	1	0	2	21	27	2	3	7
2	Ireland (1)	2	1	0	1	16	17	2	4	2
3	Wales (4)	1	1	0	0	11	0	2	3	0
4	Scotland (2)	2	1	0	1	11	15	2	2	3

Because of the intransigence of Scotland and Ireland over the Arthur Gould affair, Wales played neither country in 1897. Consequently the Championship was nothing more than a token affair, with all four countries finishing level with two points apiece. Based on the qualification of scoring the most points, England took the title, a particularly doubtful distinction considering that they lost both their opening matches and conceded more tries and more points than any of the other three countries.

A.S. Laidlaw, the first Scottish cap to turn professional

WALES v ENGLAND 13/75

9 January 1897
Rodney Parade, Newport
Wales 11 (1G, 2T) England 0

Wales   T: Pearson, Boucher, Jones. C: Bancroft.

Arthur Gould, rugby football's first superstar, played his twenty-seventh and final match for Wales. The handsome, engaging Gould had become a household name throughout Britain as much due to his personality and good looks as his brilliant centre play. Paradoxically, it was this fame which ended his career, for in the euphoria of the announcement of his retirement, earlier in the season, a testimonial fund was spontaneously set up. The WRU endorsed and supported the fund and Gould was duly presented with the title deeds of a house by the president of the WRU, Sir John Llewellyn. The other Unions were furious: Gould, they said, had been professionalised. Scotland and Ireland refused to play Wales in the latter part of 1897 and the International Board, in 1898, threatened even more drastic action if Wales continued to use Gould. The WRU stood their ground, knowing full well they risked complete international isolation. Gould, however, precluded a disastrous rift by confirming his earlier intention to retire. Wales, though still fuming over the affair, had obtained a way out without backing down from their view that a testimonial in no way could be described as an act of professionalism. The attitude of the other Unions, particularly the RFU, was understandable at the time. Yet the curiosity of the Gould affair was that he was allowed to continue in the game as a selector and a referee.

WALES   W.J. Bancroft 22 (Swansea); C. Bowen (4) (Llanelli), E.G. Nicholls 3 (Cardiff), *A.J. Gould (27) (Newport), T.W. Pearson 10 (Newport); S. Biggs 4 (Cardiff), D. Jones (1) (Aberavon); H. Packer (7) (Newport), A.W. Boucher (13) (Newport), W. Morris (3) (Llanelli), J. Evans (3) (Llanelli), R. Hellings 1 (Llwynypia), F.H. Cornish 1 (Cardiff), D. Evans 3 (Penygraig), J. Rhapps (1) (Penygraig).

ENGLAND   J.F. Byrne 7 (Moseley); E.F. Fookes 4 (Sowerby Bridge), E.M. Baker (7) (Oxford U.), F.A. Byrne (1) (Moseley), T. Fletcher (1) (Seaton); C.M. Wells 5 (Harlequins), *E.W. Taylor 11 (Rockcliff); F. Jacob 1 (Cambridge U.), J.H. Barron 2 (Bingley), P.J. Ebdon 1 (Wellington), R.F. Oakes 1 (Hartlepool Rovers), W.B. Stoddart 1 (Liverpool), F.M. Stout 1 (Gloucester), W. Ashford 1 (Richmond), R.H. Mangles 1 (Richmond).

Referee J.T. Magee (Ireland)

IRELAND v ENGLAND   13/76

6 February 1897
Lansdowne Road, Dublin
Ireland 13 (3T 1GM) England 9 (1T, 2PG)

Ireland   T: Gardiner (2), Bulger. GM: Bulger.
England   T: Robinson. PG: Byrne (2).

The formidable Ryan brothers, Mike and Jack, from Tipperary, made their début appearances in this match. Both were enormously strong and competitive, with a penchant for field events and Gaelic football. Their rugged play on the rugby field served Ireland well though some critics of the day were not over-enthusiastic: 'more brawn than brain', said one, 'they were of the same stamp as the Welsh forwards, Harry Day and Dick Hellings . . . but more deliberately aggressive than the Welshmen, with rather less concern for the consequences of their unrestrained exercise of strength'. Larry Bulger's seven points was the highest scored by a member of the Irish team in the Championship to date.

IRELAND   J. Fulton 4 (NIFC); L.Q. Bulger 4 (Dublin U.), T.H. Stevenson 6 (Edinburgh U.), S. Lee 18 (NIFC), W. Gardiner 15 (NIFC); L.M. Magee 7 (Bective Rangers), G.G. Allen 4 (Liverpool); J.E. McIlwaine 1 (NIFC), J.H. Lytle 8 (NIFC), W.G. Byron 4 (NIFC), M. Ryan 1 (Rockwell College), J. Ryan 1 (Rockwell College), A.D. Clinch 9 (Wanderers), *E.G. Forrest 11 (Wanderers), C.V. Rooke 18 (Monkstown).

ENGLAND   J.F. Byrne 8 (Moseley); G.C. Robinson 1 (Percy Park), W.L. Bunting 1 (Richmond), J.T. Taylor 1 (Castleford), E.F. Fookes 5 (Sowerby Bridge); S. Northmore (1) (Millom), *E.W. Taylor 12 (Rockcliff); F. Jacob 2 (Cambridge U.), J.H. Barron (3) (Bingley), P.J. Ebdon (2) (Wellington), R.F. Oakes 2 (Hartlepool Rovers), W.B. Stoddart 2 (Liverpool), F.M. Stout 2 (Gloucester), W. Ashford 2 (Richmond), R.H. Mangles (2) (Richmond).

Referee D.G. Findlay (Scotland)

SCOTLAND v IRELAND   15/77

20 February 1897
Powerhall, Edinburgh
Scotland 8 (1G, 1PG) Ireland 3 (1T)

Scotland   T: Turnbull. C: T.M. Scott. PG: T.M. Scott.
Ireland   T: Bulger.

Ireland chose this match to end the international careers of three of their most distinguished forwards, E.G. Forrest, A.D. Clinch and Charles Rooke, who had gained 41 caps between them. Forrest was a shrewd tactician with a flair for dropping goals; Clinch, (father of the great Jammie Clinch) was a strong, determined competitor; and Rooke, apart from being one of the cleverest dribblers in the game, was credited as being one of the originators of flank-forward play. Despite the victory, Scotland finished bottom of the table.

SCOTLAND   A.R. Smith 6 (Oxford U.); G.T. Campbell 15 (London Scottish), W. Neilson 13 (London Scottish), C.J.N. Fleming (3) (Edinburgh Wands), T. Scott 2 (Hawick); M. Elliot 3 (Hawick), R.C. Greig (2) (Glasgow Acads); J.H. Dods 7 (Edinburgh Acads), A.S. Laidlaw (1) (Hawick), W.M.C. McEwan 8 (Edinburgh Acads), *R.G. Macmillan 20 (London Scottish), M.C. Morrison 4 (Royal HSFP), T.M. Scott 7 (Hawick), R.C. Stevenson 1 (London Scottish), G.O. Turnbull 3 (London Scottish).

The Scottish XV which defeated Ireland 8-3 on 20 February 1897

IRELAND   P.E. O'Brien-Butler 1 (Monkstown); W. Gardiner 16 (NIFC), L.Q. Bulger 5 (Dublin U.), T.H. Stevenson (7) (Belfast Albion), L.H. Gwynn 5 (Dublin U.); L.M. Magee 8 (Bective Rangers), G.G. Allen 5 (Derry); W.G. Byron 5 (NIFC), A.D. Clinch (10) (Wanderers), *E.G. Forrest (12) (Wanderers), J.H. Lytle 9 (NIFC), J.E. McIlwaine 2 (NIFC), C.V. Rooke (19) (Monkstown), M. Ryan 2 (Rockwell College), J. Sealy 4 (Dublin U.).

Referee E.B. Holmes (England)

ENGLAND v SCOTLAND   12/78

13 March 1897
Fallowfield, Manchester
England 12 (1G, 1T, 1DG) Scotland 3 (1T)

England   T: Fookes, Robinson. C: Byrne. DG: Byrne.
Scotland   T: Bucher.

The last international staged in the north of England was played at Manchester Athletic Club's headquarters at Fallowfield. It was one of the rare occasions when the Calcutta Cup presentation ceremony did not take place at the after-match function: Scotland did not bring the trophy with them, either because it was an item overlooked or because of misplaced confidence in their team. Consolation for England was the winning of the Championship, by virtue of superior scoring. R.G. Macmillan who had played in 14 winning Scottish sides, made his last appearance.

ENGLAND   J.F. Byrne 9 (Moseley); E.F. Fookes 6 (Sowerby Bridge), W.L. Bunting 2 (Richmond), O.G. Mackie 1 (Cambridge U.), G.C. Robinson 2 (Percy Park); *E.W. Taylor 13 (Rockcliff), C.M. Wells (6) (Harlequins); H.W. Dudgeon 1 (Richmond), F. Jacob 3 (Cambridge U.), L.F. Giblin (3) (Cambridge U.), Jas Davidson 1 (Aspatria), E. Knowles (2) (Millom), J. Pinch (3) (Lancaster), W.B. Stoddart (3) (Liverpool), R.F. Oakes 3 (Hartlepool Rovers).

SCOTLAND   A.R. Smith 7 (Oxford U.); A.M. Bucher (1) (Edinburgh Acads), W. Neilson (14) (London Scottish), T. Scott 3 (Hawick), A.W. Robertson (1) (Edinburgh Acads); M. Elliot 4 (Hawick), J.W. Simpson 11 (Royal HSFP); A. Balfour (4) (Cambridge U.), J.H. Dods (8) (Edinburgh Acads), W.M.C. McEwan 9 (Edinburgh Acads), *R.G. McMillan (21) (London Scottish), M.C. Morrison 5 (Royal HSFP), T.M. Scott 8 (Hawick), R.C. Stevenson 2 (London Scottish), G.O. Turnbull 4 (London Scottish).

Referee J.T. Magee (Ireland)

RICHMOND Ireland beat England 9-6 · BELFAST Scotland beat Ireland 8-0
EDINBURGH Scotland drew England 3-3 · LIMERICK Wales beat Ireland 11-3
BLACKHEATH England beat Wales 14-7
NB Wales v Scotland not played

CHAMPIONSHIP TABLE
Scotland – Championship

Pos	Country	P	W	D	L	F	A	Pts	Tries F	A
1	England (1)	3	1	1	1	23	19	3	6	4
2	Scotland (4)	2	1	1	0	11	3	3	3	1
3	Wales (3)	2	1	0	1	18	17	2	3	4
4	Ireland (2)	3	1	0	2	12	25	2	2	5

Scotland once again refused to play Wales which left the door open for England to win a second title in succession on superior scoring. Strangely, Scotland had not cut off all ties with Wales; when the Welsh objected to the appointment of David Graham Finlay for their match with Ireland in Limerick, the SRU produced another Scottish referee, Adam Turnbull, who was accepted by Wales without hesitation. England, meanwhile, delayed a decision about whether they should play Wales. The season was nearly finished when the RFU climbed down and honoured the fixture, victory in which ironically won them the Championship.

ENGLAND v IRELAND 14/79

5 February 1898
Athletic Ground, Richmond
Ireland 9 (2T, 1PG) England 6 (1T, 1PG)

England T: Robinson. PG: Byrne.
Ireland T: Lindsay, Magee. PG: Bulger.

Sammy Lee's illustrious career for Ireland came to an end when he broke a collar-bone in the second half. He had played 19 times. Lee was described, by a Welsh critic, as one of the game's finest centres, surpassed only in all-round ability by George Stephenson, another Ulsterman who was to be such a dominant personality in Irish rugby between 1920–30. Lee was a product of the North of Ireland club, that later gave Irish rugby two other marvellous backs, Jack Kyle and Mike Gibson. It was Ireland's third consecutive win in England.

ENGLAND *J.F. Byrne 10 (Moseley); E.F. Fookes 7 (Sowerby Bridge), W.L. Bunting 3 (Richmond), O.G. Mackie (2) (Cambridge U.), G.C. Robinson 3 (Percy Park); P.G. Jacob (1) (Blackheath), H. Myers (1) (Keighley); F. Jacob 4 (Richmond), R. Pierce 1 (Liverpool), F. Shaw (1) (Cleckheaton), R.F. Oakes 4 (Hartlepool Rovers), H.W. Dudgeon 2 (Richmond), F.M. Stout 3 (Gloucester), J.H. Blacklock 1 (Aspatria), C.E. Wilson (1) (Blackheath).

IRELAND P.E. O'Brien-Butler 2 (Monkstown); F.C. Purser 1 (Dublin U.), *S. Lee (19) (NIFC), L.H. Gwynn 6 (Monkstown), L.Q. Bulger 6 (Lansdowne); L.M. Magee 9 (Bective Rangers), G.G. Allen 6 (Derry); W.G. Byron 6 (NIFC), J.E. McIlwaine 3 (NIFC), J.G. Franks 1 (Dublin U.), M. Ryan 3 (Rockwell College), J. Ryan 2 (Rockwell College), J.H. Lytle 10 (NIFC), H. Lindsay 11 (Armagh), J.L. Davis 1 (Monkstown).

Referee D.G. Findlay (Scotland)

IRELAND v SCOTLAND — 16/80

19 February 1898
Balmoral Showgrounds, Belfast
Scotland 8 (1G, 1T) Ireland 0

Scotland T: Tom Scott (2). C: T.M. Scott.

After finishing with the Wooden Spoon the previous season, Scotland began their 1898 campaign with eight new caps, while Ireland relied on a comparatively experienced side. The issue was settled by two smartly taken tries by the Hawick wing, Tom Scott. It was Scotland's thirteenth win in the first sixteen Championship matches between the countries; Ireland had experienced but one success, in their Triple Crown year of 1894.

IRELAND P.E. O'Brien-Butler 3 (Monkstown); F.C. Purser 2 (Dublin U.), F.F.S. Smithwick 1 (Monkstown), L.H. Gwynn (7) (Monkstown), L.Q. Bulger 7 (Lansdowne); *G.G. Allen 7 (Derry), L.M. Magee 10 (Bective Rangers); W.G. Byron 7 (NIFC), J.L. Davis (2) (Monkstown), J.G. Franks 2 (Dublin U.), H. Lindsay 12 (Armagh), J.H. Lytle 11 (NIFC), J.E. McIlwaine 4 (NIFC), J. Ryan 3 (Rockwell College), M. Ryan 4 (Rockwell College).

SCOTLAND J.M. Reid 1 (Edinburgh Acads); *A.R. Smith 8 (Oxford U.), E. Spencer (1) (Clydesdale), R.T. Neilson 1 (W. of Scotland), T. Scott 4 (Hawick); M. Elliot 5 (Hawick), J.T. Mabon 1 (Jedforest); J.M. Dykes 1 (Clydesdale), G.C. Kerr 1 (Durham), W.M.C. McEwan 10 (Edinburgh Acads), A. MacKinnon 1 (London Scottish), M.C. Morrison 6 (Royal HSFP), R. Scott 1 (Hawick), T.M. Scott 9 (Hawick), H.O. Smith 5 (Watsonians).

Referee E.T. Gurdon (England)

SCOTLAND v ENGLAND — 13/81

12 March 1898
Powderhall, Edinburgh
Scotland 3 (1T) England 3 (1T)

Scotland T: McEwan.
England T: Royds.

Percy Stout, making his début, joined his brother Frank, in an England team which won the Championship by virtue of a larger points total from three matches. Scotland did not play Wales, so were therefore deprived of their chance of winning a third title.

SCOTLAND J.M. Reid 2 (Edinburgh Acads); *A.R. Smith 9 (Oxford U.), T.A. Nelson (1) (Oxford U.), R.T. Neilson 2 (W. of Scotland), T. Scott 5 (Hawick); M. Elliot (6) (Hawick), J.T. Mabon 2 (Jedforest); J.M. Dykes 2 (Clydesdale), G.C. Kerr 2 (Durham), W.M.C. McEwan 11 (Edinburgh Acads), A. MacKinnon 2 (London Scottish), M.C. Morrison 7 (Royal HSFP), T.M. Scott 10 (Hawick), H.O. Smith 6 (Watsonians), R.C. Stevenson 3 (London Scottish).

ENGLAND *J.F. Byrne 11 (Moseley); W.N. Pilkington (1) (Cambridge U.), W.L. Bunting 4 (Richmond), P.M.R. Royds 1 (Blackheath), P.W. Stout 1 (Gloucester); G.T. Unwin (1) (Blackheath), A. Rotherham 1 (Richmond); F. Jacob 5 (Richmond), J.F. Shaw 1 (RNEC Keyham), H.E. Ramsden 1 (Bingley), R.F. Oakes 5 (Hartlepool Rovers), H.W. Dudgeon 3 (Richmond), F.M. Stout 4 (Gloucester), W. Ashford 3 (Richmond), Jas Davidson 2 (Aspatria).

Referee J. Dodds (Ireland)

IRELAND v WALES   12/82

18 March 1898
Limerick
Wales 11 (1G, 1T, 1PG) Ireland 3 (1PG)

Ireland   PG: Bulger.
Wales   T: Dobson, Huzzey. C: Bancroft. PG: Bancroft.

Wales were rather unhappy about the appointment of the Scottish referee, David Graham Findlay, for this match, and formally objected to that effect. Their short list of three alternatives did not include the eventual choice, Adam Turnbull, another Scot who at length won tireless praise from Welsh officials. For this, the first international to be staged in Munster, the two teams travelled together by train from Dublin and were met at Limerick station by: 'foghorns and a vast, welcoming crowd'. George Boots made his début and Billy Bancroft became captain of Wales for the first time. Seven members of the Irish team played their last Championship match, including such well-established players as W. Gardiner, the captain, Larry Bulger and Harry Lindsay.

IRELAND   J. Fulton 5 (NIFC); F.C. Purser (3) (Dublin U.), F.F.S. Smithwick (2) (Monkstown), *W. Gardiner (17) (NIFC), L.Q. Bulger (8) (Lansdowne); L.M. Magee 11 (Bective Rangers), A. Barr 1 (Methodist C. Belfast); W.G. Byron 8 (NIFC), J.E. McIlwaine 5 (NIFC), J.G. Franks (3) (Dublin U.), M. Ryan 5 (Rockwell College), J. Ryan 4 (Rockwell College), T.J. Little 1 (Bective Rangers), H. Lindsay (13) (Armagh), T. McCarthy (1) (Cork).

WALES   *W.J. Bancroft 23 (Swansea); T.W. Pearson 11 (Newport), E.G. Nicholls 4 (Cardiff), W. Jones 1 (Cardiff), H.V.P. Huzzey 1 (Cardiff); S. Biggs 5 (Cardiff), J.E. Elliott 2 (Cardiff); R. Hellings 2 (Llwynypia), W.H. Alexander 1 (Llwynypia), D.J. Daniel 5 (Llanelli), H. Davies 1 (Swansea), G. Boots 1 (Newport), T. Dobson 1 (Cardiff), F.H. Cornish 2 (Cardiff), J. Booth (1) (Pontymister).

Referee A.J. Turnbull (Scotland)

ENGLAND v WALES   14/83

2 April 1898
Rectory Field, Blackheath
England 14 (1G, 3T) Wales 7 (1T, 1DG)

England   T: Fookes (2), Frank Stout, Percy Stout. C: Byrne.
Wales   T: Huzzey. DG: Huzzey.

Arguments over the Arthur Gould affair were so prolonged that this match was postponed until 2 April. An unusual feature was the scoring of tries by brothers, Frank and Percy Stout. It was England's only victory of the season, but it enabled them to win the Championship for the second year in a row. However, they had to wait until 1910 for their next title success and another win over Wales.

ENGLAND   *J.F. Byrne 12 (Moseley); E.F. Fookes 8 (Sowerby Bridge), P.M.R. Royds 2 (Blackheath), W.L. Bunting 5 (Richmond), P.W. Stout 2 (Gloucester); R.O'H. Livesay 1 (Blackheath), A. Rotherham 2 (Richmond); H.E. Ramsden (2) (Bingley), J.F. Shaw (2) (RNEC Keyham), H.W. Dudgeon 4 (Richmond), F.M. Stout 5 (Gloucester), R.F. Oakes 6 (Hartlepool Rovers), W. Ashford (4) (Exeter), F. Jacob 6 (Richmond), Jas Davidson 3 (Aspatria).

WALES   *W.J. Bancroft 24 (Swansea); H.V.P. Huzzey 2 (Cardiff), E.G. Nicholls 5 (Cardiff), W. Jones (2) (Cardiff), T.W. Pearson 12 (Newport); S. Biggs 6 (Cardiff), J.E. Elliott (3) (Cardiff); T. Dobson 2 (Cardiff), F.H. Cornish 3 (Cardiff), W.H. Alexander 2 (Llwynypia), R. Hellings 3 (Llwynypia), D.J. Daniel 6 (Llanelli), H. Davies 2 (Swansea), G. Boots 2 (Newport), D. Evans (4) (Penygraig).

Referee J.T. Magee (Ireland)

1899

SWANSEA Wales beat England 26-3 · DUBLIN Ireland beat England 6-0
EDINBURGH Ireland beat Scotland 9-3 · EDINBURGH Scotland beat Wales 21-10
BLACKHEATH Scotland beat England 5-0 · CARDIFF Ireland beat Wales 3-0

CHAMPIONSHIP TABLE
Ireland – Championship, Triple Crown

Pos	Country	P	W	D	L	F	A	Pts	Tries F	A
1	Ireland (4)	3	3	0	0	18	3	6	5	0
2	Scotland (2)	3	2	0	1	29	19	4	4	5
3	Wales (3)	3	1	0	2	36	27	2	8	5
4	England (1)	3	0	0	3	3	37	0	1	8

After winning two matches away, in Edinburgh and Cardiff, Ireland took the Triple Crown and the Championship. As in 1896 the strength of the Irish team lay in their defence: the only points they conceded were via a penalty against Scotland and that penalty was unprecedented for it was awarded because a player was tackled without the ball. Another singular feature of 1899 was the Scotland v Wales match. Because of bad weather it was postponed four times before finally being played on 4 March at Inverleith. Considering that Scotland had refused to play Wales in the previous two seasons, the delays must have been very frustrating for the Welsh, who had set their eyes on the Championship after giving England a hiding in their opening match.

England's misfortune did not end at Swansea: they went on to lose to Ireland and Scotland and to finish bottom of the Championship for the first time, scoring three points, their lowest ever total in a season. Indeed, 1899 was only the beginning of England's 'Dark Ages'. They scraped together just 7 victories in 33 Championship matches before they won the title again in 1910: irrefutable evidence of the damage inflicted by the loss of clubs and players to the Northern Union, now established as the Rugby League.

WALES v ENGLAND   15/84

7 January 1899
St Helen's, Swansea
Wales 26 (4G, 2T) England 3 (1T)

Wales   T: Llewellyn (4), Huzzey (2). C: Bancroft (4).
England   T: Robinson.

On his first appearance for Wales, Willie Llewellyn scored four tries, a Welsh record equalled since only by Reggie Gibbs (against France in 1908) and Maurice Richards (against England in 1969). England's heaviest defeat of the season was watched by a Welsh record crowd in excess of 20,000 with receipts of £1500.

WALES   *W.J. Bancroft 25 (Swansea); H.V.P. Huzzey 3 (Cardiff), E.G. Nicholls 6 (Cardiff), R.T. Skrimshire 1 (Newport), W.M. Llewellyn 1 (Llwynypia); E. James (5) (Swansea), D. James (4) (Swansea); J. Blake 1 (Cardiff), T. Dobson 3 (Cardiff), W.H. Alexander 3 (Llwynypia), F. Scrine 1 (Swansea), D.J. Daniel 7 (Llanelli), A. Brice 1 (Aberavon), J.J. Hodges 1 (Newport), W. Parker 1 (Swansea).

ENGLAND   H.T. Gamlin 1 (Devonport Albion); G.C. Robinson 4 (Percy Park), P.W. Stout 3 (Gloucester), P.M.R. Royds (3) (Blackheath), R. Forrest 1 (Wellington); R.O'H. Livesay (2) (Blackheath), *A. Rotherham 3 (Richmond); F. Jacob 7 (Richmond), G.R. Gibson 1 (Northern), J. Daniell 1 (Cambridge U.), R.F. Oakes 7 (Hartlepool Rovers), H.W. Dudgeon 5 (Richmond), W. Mortimer (1) (Marlborough Nomads), C.H. Harper (1) (Oxford U.), Jos Davidson 1 (Aspatria).

Referee A.J. Turnbull (Scotland)

IRELAND v ENGLAND 15/85

4 February 1899
Lansdowne Road, Dublin
Ireland 6 (1T, 1PG) England 0

Ireland T: Allen. PG: Magee.

Severely beaten by Wales in their opening match, England went down in a fourth successive defeat by Ireland. Good defence allowed a respectable margin. For seven members of the English team it spelled the end of their international careers, including their two most experienced players, Fred Byrne and Ernest Taylor, winners of 27 caps between them.

IRELAND J. Fulton 6 (NIFC); I.G. Davidson 1 (NIFC), J.B. Allison 1 (Campbell C. Belfast), G.R.A. Harman 1 (Dublin U.), W.H. Brown (1) (Dublin U.); *L.M. Magee 12 (Bective Rangers), G.G. Allen 8 (Derry); M. Ryan 6 (Rockwell College), J. Ryan 5 (Rockwell College), W.G. Byron 9 (NIFC), J.E. McIlwaine 6 (NIFC), T.M.W. McGown 1 (NIFC), T. Ahearn (1) (Queen's C. Cork), J. Sealy 5 (Dublin U.), H.C. McCoull (4) (Belfast Albion).

ENGLAND J.F. Byrne (13) (Moseley); E.F. Fookes 9 (Sowerby Bridge), J.T. Taylor 2 (Castleford), S. Anderson (1) (Rockcliff), P.W. Stout 4 (Gloucester); E.W. Taylor (14) (Rockcliff), *A. Rotherham 4 (Richmond); H.W. Dudgeon 6 (Richmond), C. Thomas (4) (Barnstaple), A.J.L. Darby (1) (Cambridge U.), F. Jacob (8) (Richmond), J.H. Blacklock (2) (Aspatria), Jas Davidson 4 (Aspatria), F.M. Stout 6 (Gloucester), J.H. Shooter 1 (Morley).

Referee D.G. Findlay (Scotland)

SCOTLAND v IRELAND 17/86

18 February 1899
Inverleith, Edinburgh
Ireland 9 (3T) Scotland 3 (1PG)

Scotland PG: Donaldson.
Ireland T: Campbell, Reid, Sealy.

In the first international to be held at the SRU's new ground at Inverleith, Ireland gained their first victory on Scottish soil, their ninth attempt. It was believed to be the first occasion in the Championship that a penalty was awarded for a tackle on a player without the ball: D.B. Monypenny grub kicked past O'Brien-Butler, Ireland's full-back, chased the ball over the goal-line and was about to ground for a try when he was brought down from behind. Today it would have meant a penalty try; then Donaldson drop-kicked the penalty.

SCOTLAND J.M. Reid (3) (Edinburgh Acads); G.T. Campbell 16 (London Scottish), D.B. Monypenny 1 (London Scottish), R.T. Neilson 3 (W. of Scotland), T. Scott 6 (Langholm); *W.P. Donaldson (6) (W. of Scotland), J.T. Mabon 3 (Jedforest); J.H. Couper (3) (W. of Scotland), L. Harvey (1) (Greenock Wands), G.C. Kerr 3 (Durham), W.M.C. McEwan 12 (Edinburgh Acads), A. MacKinnon 3 (London Scottish), M.C. Morrison 8 (Royal HSFP), H.O. Smith 7 (Watsonians), R.C. Stevenson 4 (Northumberland).

IRELAND P.E. O'Brien-Butler 4 (Monkstown); G.P. Doran 1 (Lansdowne), J.B. Allison 2 (Campbell C. Belfast), C. Reid 1 (NIFC), E.F. Campbell 1 (Monkstown); *L.M. Magee 13 (Bective Rangers), A. Barr 2 (Methodist C. Belfast); W.G. Byron 10 (NIFC), T.J. Little 2 (Bective Rangers), J.H. Lytle (12) (NIFC), T.M.W. McGown 2 (NIFC), A.W.D. Meares 1 (Dublin U.), J. Ryan 6 (Rockwell College), M. Ryan 7 (Rockwell College), J. Sealy 6 (Dublin U.).

Referee E.T. Gurdon (England)

SCOTLAND v WALES 15/87

4 March 1899
Inverleith, Edinburgh
Scotland 21 (3T, 2DG, 1GM) Wales 10 (2G)

Scotland T: Gedge, Smith, Monypenny. DG: Gedge, Lamond. GM: Thomson.
Wales T: Llewelyn Lloyd, Llewellyn. C: Bancroft (2).

This match went down as the most postponed Championship encounter ever – it was played after four postponements due to inclement weather.

SCOTLAND H. Rottenburg 1 (London Scottish); H.T.S. Gedge 5 (London Scottish), D.B. Monypenny 2 (London Scottish), G.A.W. Lamond 1 (Kelvinside Acads), T. Scott 7 (Langholm); R.T. Neilson 4 (W. of Scotland), J.W. Simpson 12 (Royal HSFP); J.M. Dykes 3 (London Scottish), G.C. Kerr 4 (Edinburgh Wands), W.M.C. McEwan 13 (Edinburgh Acads), A. MacKinnon 4 (London Scottish), *M.C. Morrison 9 (Royal HSFP), H.O. Smith 8 (Watsonians), R.C. Stevenson 5 (London Scottish), W.J. Thomson 1 (W. of Scotland).

WALES   *W.J. Bancroft 26 (Swansea); H.V.P. Huzzey 4 (Cardiff), E.G. Nicholls 7 (Cardiff), R.T. Skrimshire 2 (Newport), W.M. Llewellyn 2 (Llwynypia); S. Biggs 7 (Cardiff), G.Ll. Lloyd 2 (Newport), J. Blake 2 (Cardiff), T. Dobson (4) (Cardiff), W.H. Alexander 4 (Llwynypia), F. Scrine 2 (Swansea), A. Brice 2 (Aberavon), J.J. Hodges 2 (Newport), W. Parker (2) (Swansea), R. Hellings 4 (Llwynypia).

Referee M.G. Delaney (Ireland)

ENGLAND v SCOTLAND   14/88

11 March 1899
Rectory Field, Blackheath
Scotland 5 (1G) England 0

Scotland   T: Gillespie. C: Thomson.

This was the first and only match of the Davidson brothers together, James and Joseph. Seven other England players did not play again. Scotland were less brutal in their selection: only four of their side were not called on again. It was Scotland's fourth victory in seven visits to England, who thus lost all three matches and collected the Wooden Spoon for the first time.

ENGLAND   H.T. Gamlin 2 (Devonport Albion); E.F. Fookes (10) (Sowerby Bridge), P.W. Stout (5) (Gloucester), W.L. Bunting 6 (Richmond), J.C. Matters (1) (RNEC Keyham); R.O. Schwarz 1 (Richmond), *A. Rotherham (5) (Richmond); H.W. Dudgeon (7) (Richmond), R.F. Oakes (8) (Hartlepool Rovers), Jas Davidson (5) (Aspatria), Jos Davidson (2) (Aspatria), F.M. Stout 7 (Gloucester), R.F.A. Hobbs 1 (Blackheath), J.H. Shooter 2 (Morley), A.O. Dowson (1) (Moseley).

SCOTLAND   H. Rottenburg 2 (London Scottish); H.T.S. Gedge (6) (London Scottish), D.B. Monypenny (3) (London Scottish), G.A.W. Lamond 2 (Kelvinside Acads), T. Scott 8 (Langholm); J.I.

Gillespie 1 (Edinburgh Acads), J.W. Simpson (13) (Royal HSFP); J.M. Dykes 4 (London Scottish), G.C. Kerr 5 (Edinburgh Wands), W.M.C. McEwan 14 (Edinburgh Acads), A. MacKinnon 5 (London Scottish), *M.C. Morrison 10 (Royal HSFP), H.O. Smith 9 (Watsonians), R.C. Stevenson (6) (London Scottish), W.J. Thomson 2 (W. of Scotland).

Referee J.T. Magee (Ireland)

WALES v IRELAND   13/89

18 March 1899
Cardiff Arms Park
Ireland 3 (1T) Wales 0

Ireland   T: Doran.

A record 40,000 crowd watched Ireland win the Triple Crown through a try by Gerry 'Blücher' Doran, one of three brothers from the Lansdowne Club who played for Ireland. Eddie Doran was capped twice in 1890 and Bertie Doran made eight appearances, 1900–02. The crowd scenes at the match were remarkable. The pitch had to be cleared before play could commence, half-time lasted a quarter of an hour while overflowing spectators were again pushed back, and several times during the second half play was held up because of more overspilling from the jam-packed touch-lines.

WALES   *W.J. Bancroft 27 (Swansea); H.V.P. Huzzey (5) (Cardiff), E.G. Nicholls 8 (Cardiff), R.T. Skrimshire (3) (Newport), W.M. Llewellyn 3 (Llwynypia); S. Biggs 8 (Cardiff), G.Ll. Lloyd 3 (Newport); W.H. Alexander 5 (Llwynypia), R. Hellings 5 (Llwynypia), J. Blake 3 (Cardiff), F.H. Cornish (4) (Cardiff), D.J. Daniel (8) (Llanelli), G. Boots 3 (Newport), J.J. Hodges 3 (Newport), A. Brice 3 (Aberavon).

IRELAND   P.E. O'Brien-Butler 5 (Monkstown); G.P. Doran 2 (Lansdowne), G.R.A. Harman (2) (Dublin U.), C. Reid 2 (NIFC), E.F. Campbell 2 (Monkstown); *L.M. Magee 14 (Bective Rangers), G.G. Allen (9) (Derry); W.G. Byron (11) (NIFC), J.E. McIlwaine (7) (NIFC), C.C.H. Moriarty (1) (Monkstown), M. Ryan 8 (Rockwell College), J. Ryan 7 (Rockwell College), J. Sealy 7 (Dublin U.), A.W.D. Meares 2 (Dublin U.), T.J. Little 3 (Bective Rangers).

Referee A.J. Turnbull (Scotland)

1900

GLOUCESTER Wales beat England 13-3 · SWANSEA Wales beat Scotland 12-3
RICHMOND England beat Ireland 15-4 · DUBLIN Ireland drew Scotland 0-0
EDINBURGH Scotland drew England 0-0 · BELFAST Wales beat Ireland 3-0

CHAMPIONSHIP TABLE
Wales – Championship, Triple Crown

Pos	Country	P	W	D	L	F	A	Pts	Tries F	Tries A
1	Wales (3)	3	3	0	0	28	6	6	7	2
2	England (4)	3	1	1	1	18	17	3	4	2
3	Scotland (2)	3	0	2	1	3	12	2	1	4
4	Ireland (1)	3	0	1	2	4	18	1	0	4

Wales won the Championship and the Triple Crown heralding what has been described as the greatest period in their history – the 'Golden Age'. Wales enjoyed two other periods when they reached the peak of their power and reputation, 1950–58 and 1964–79, when supremely gifted sides produced never-to-be-forgotten performances. However, in comparison the Golden Age was sensational. Although the drama, skill and excitement are now only on record, it can be in no way diminished.

It can quite reasonably be argued that modern sides must be superior, for there is much evidence to show that the game has progressed and that teams have improved tactically, are fitter and possibly quicker. However, statistics support the view that the Golden Age was the greatest era: from 1900–11 Wales played 38 Championship matches, winning 31 and drawing 1, which has been unequalled. They also won six titles, six Triple Crowns and for twelve

The England XV, with 13 new caps, which lost to Wales on 6 January 1900. Back row: W. Cobby, F.J. Bell, J. Baxter, A.T. Brettargh, H.T. Gamlin. Middle row: S. Reynolds, C.T. Scott, R.H.B. Cattell, R.W. Bell, E.T. Nicholson, J.W. Jarman, A. Cockerham. Seated: G.W. Gordon-Smith, G.H. Marsden, S.F. Coopper

years were never below the top two in the table. No other period can compare. In terms of scoring points too, the teams of the Golden Age stand comparison with any: they averaged 46 points a season, peaking at 88 points in 1910 – which is the second highest ever in the Championship.

The final evidence, however, is contained in the try-scoring. During the period they scored 132 tries at an average of 11 a season, culminating in two amazing final years, 1910 and 1911, when 8 matches produced 166 points and 39 tries. The players who oiled this great scoring machine were more often than not legends in their own playing time: forwards like Jehoida Hodges (22 caps, 1899–1906), George Travers (21, 1903–11), Arthur Brice (18, 1899–1904), George Boots (16, 1898–1904), Ivor Morgan (11, 1909–12) and Dick Hellings (9, 1897–1901). Behind them were the 'immortals', players such as Dickie Owen (31, 1901–12), Gwyn Nicholls (22, 1896–1906), Rhys Gabe (21, 1901–08), Willie Llewellyn (19, 1899–1905), Teddy Morgan (13, 1902–07), Tommy Vile (7, 1908–21) and Percy Bush (6, 1906–10). It was a period, it must be remembered, when players left Wales in droves to join the newly-formed professional Rugby League, causing the WRU to adopt (in 1900) stringent new Laws regarding professionalism and the transfer of players. It is relevant also that in 1900 England were at a low ebb, with only 244 clubs in membership. Their dearth of players was reflected in results – they won only one Championship, in 1910, and finished Wooden Spoonists five times as Wales dominated the Championship. For Scotland 1900 was hardly worth recalling – they scored an all-time low of three points.

ENGLAND v WALES 16/90

6 January 1900
Kingsholm, Gloucester
Wales 13 (2G, 1PG) England 3 (1T)

England T: Nicholson.
Wales T: Hellings, Trew. C: Bancroft (2). PG: Bancroft.

The only international ever played at Kingsholm. England played 13 new caps, a record by any country in the Championship until 1947 when Scotland and England played 14 newcomers, in the resumption of the Championship after an eight-year gap because of the War.

ENGLAND H.T. Gamlin 3 (Devonport Albion); E.T. Nicholson 1 (Birkenhead Park), A.T. Brettargh 1 (Liverpool OB), G.W. Gordon-Smith 1 (Blackheath), S.F. Coopper 1 (Blackheath); G.H. Marsden 1 (Morley), *R.H.B. Cattell (7) (Moseley); F.J. Bell (1) (Northern), R.W. Bell 1 (Cambridge U.), W. Cobby (1) (Hull), A. Cockerham (1) (Bradford Olicana), J. Baxter 1 (Birkenhead Park), J.W. Jarman (1) (Bristol), S. Reynolds 1 (Richmond), C.T. Scott 1 (Cambridge U.).

WALES *W.J. Bancroft 28 (Swansea); W.M. Llewellyn 4 (Llwynypia), D. Rees 1 (Swansea), G. Davies 1 (Swansea), W.J. Trew 1 (Swansea); L.A. Phillips 1 (Newport), G.Ll. Lloyd 4 (Newport); R. Hellings 6 (Llwynypia), A. Brice 4 (Aberavon), F. Miller 2 (Mountain Ash), W.H. Williams 1 (Pontymister), R. Thomas 1 (Swansea), G. Boots 4 (Newport), J. Blake 4 (Cardiff), J.J. Hodges 4 (Newport).

Referee A.J. Turnbull (Scotland)

WALES v SCOTLAND 16/91

27 January 1900
St Helen's, Swansea
Wales 12 (4T) Scotland 3 (1T)

Wales T: Llewellyn (2), Nicholls, Williams.
Scotland T: Dykes.

This victory by Wales could be termed the turning-point in their matches with Scotland. Wales had won only 4 of the previous 15 encounters, but from 1900 the balance tilted sharply as Scotland scraped together 3 wins in the next 15 matches up to the outbreak of the First World War.

WALES *W.J. Bancroft 29 (Swansea); W.M. Llewellyn 5 (Llwynypia), E.G. Nicholls 9 (Cardiff), G. Davies 2 (Swansea), W.J. Trew 2 (Swansea); L.A. Phillips 2 (Newport), G.Ll. Lloyd 5 (Newport); A. Brice 5 (Aberavon), F. Miller 3 (Mountain Ash), G. Boots 5 (Newport), J.J. Hodges 5 (Newport), J. Blake 5 (Cardiff), G. Dobson (1) (Cardiff), W.H. Williams 2 (Pontymister), R. Thomas 2 (Swansea).

SCOTLAND   H. Rottenburg 3 (London Scottish); T. Scott 9 (Langholm), A.B. Timms 2 (Edinburgh U.), W.H. Morrison (1) (Edinburgh Acads), J.E. Crabbie 1 (Edinburgh Acads); J.I. Gillespie 2 (Edinburgh Acads), F.H. Fasson 1 (London Scottish); D.R. Bedell-Sivright 1 (Cambridge U.), J.M. Dykes 5 (London Scottish), F.W. Henderson 1 (London Scottish), G.C. Kerr 6 (Edinburgh Wands), W.M.C. McEwan 15 (Edinburgh Acads), *M.C. Morrison 11 (Royal HSFP), T.M. Scott 11 (Hawick), W.J. Thomson (3) (W. of Scotland).

Referee A. Hartley (England)

ENGLAND v IRELAND   16/92

3 February 1900
Athletic Ground, Richmond
England 15 (1G, 2T, 1DG) Ireland 4 (1DG)

England   T: Robinson (2), Gordon-Smith. C: Alexander. DG: Gordon-Smith.
Ireland   DG: Allison.

Hugh Ferris, who made the first of four international appearances for Ireland in this match, later had the distinction of being capped by South Africa against Britain at Newlands in 1903, in the match when the Springboks adopted green as their national colours for the first time.

ENGLAND   H.T. Gamlin 4 (Blackheath); G.C. Robinson 5 (Percy Park), J.T. Taylor 3 (Castleford), G.W. Gordon-Smith 2 (Blackheath), E.T. Nicholson (2) (Birkenhead Park); G.H. Marsden 2 (Morley), J.C. Marquis 1 (Birkenhead Park); *J. Daniell 2 (Cambridge U.), R.W. Bell 2 (Cambridge U.), S. Reynolds 2 (Richmond), J. Baxter 2 (Birkenhead Park), C.T. Scott 2 (Cambridge U.), J.H. Shooter 3 (Morley), A.F. Todd 1 (Blackheath), H. Alexander 1 (Birkenhead Park).

IRELAND   P.E. O'Brien-Butler (6) (Monkstown); G.P. Doran 3 (Lansdowne), C. Reid 3 (NIFC), J.B. Allison 3 (Queen's U. Belfast), E.F. Campbell 3 (Monkstown); *L.M. Magee 15 (Bective Rangers), J.H. Ferris 1 (Queen's U. Belfast); M. Ryan 9 (Rockwell College), J.J. Coffey 1 (Lansdowne), J. Sealy 8 (Dublin U.), C.E. Allen 1 (Derry), F. Gardiner 1 (NIFC), A.W.D. Meares 3 (Wanderers), S.T. Irwin 1 (Queen's U. Belfast), P.C. Nicholson 1 (Dublin U.).

Referee D.G. Findlay (Scotland)

IRELAND v SCOTLAND   18/93

24 February 1900
Lansdowne Road, Dublin
Ireland 0 Scotland 0

A very harsh winter with severe frost and much snow had threatened to disrupt the Championship: Ireland's game against England three weeks earlier had gone ahead only after volunteers had cleared the Richmond pitch of snow; this match was delayed for a week because of frost. It was a bleak time for Ireland too: their only points in the season came from a dropped goal against England.

IRELAND   C.A. Boyd 1 (Dublin U.); G.P. Doran 4 (Lansdowne), B.R.W. Doran 1 (Lansdowne), J.B. Allison 4 (Queen's C. Belfast), I.G. Davidson 2 (NIFC); *L.M. Magee 16 (Bective Rangers), J.H. Ferris 2 (Queen's U. Belfast); C.E. Allen 2 (Liverpool), F. Gardiner 2 (NIFC), S.T. Irwin 2 (Queen's U. Belfast), T.J. Little 4 (Bective Rangers), P.C. Nicholson 2 (Dublin U.), J. Ryan 8 (Rockwell College), M. Ryan 10 (Rockwell College), J. Sealy (9) (Dublin U.).

SCOTLAND   H. Rottenburg 4 (London Scottish); T. Scott 10 (Langholm), A.R. Smith 10 (London Scottish), A.B. Timms 3 (Edinburgh U.), W.H. Welsh 1 (Edinburgh U.); R.T. Neilson 5 (W. of Scotland), J.T. Mabon (4) (Jedforest); J.A. Campbell (1) (Cambridge U.), J.M. Dykes 6 (London Scottish), J.R.C. Greenlees 1 (Cambridge U.), F.W. Henderson (2) (London Scottish), G.C. Kerr 7 (Edinburgh Wands), R. Scott 2 (Hawick), *T.M. Scott (12) (Hawick), W.P. Scott 1 (W. of Scotland).

Referee Dr Badger (England)

SCOTLAND v ENGLAND   15/94

10 March 1900
Inverleith, Edinburgh
Scotland 0 England 0

Scotland and England found themselves in the unusual position of battling it out for second place in the Championship behind Triple Crown winning Wales. The second half was late in

IRELAND v ENGLAND 17/97

9 February 1901
Lansdowne Road, Dublin
Ireland 10 (2G) England 6 (1T, 1PG)

Ireland T: Davidson, Gardiner. C: Irwin (2).
England T: Robinson. PG: Alexander.

England, who had won only two out of their previous thirteen Championship matches, still could not find the winning formula. It was Ireland's only win of the season.

IRELAND J. Fulton 8 (NIFC); I.G. Davidson 4 (NIFC), J.B. Allison 6 (Queen's U. Belfast), B.R.W. Doran 3 (Lansdowne), A.E. Freear 1 (Lansdowne); *L.M. Magee 18 (Bective Rangers), A. Barr 3 (Methodist C. Belfast); M. Ryan 12 (Rockwell College), J. Ryan 10 (Rockwell College), C.E. Allen 4 (Derry), S.T. Irwin 4 (Queen's U. Belfast), F. Gardiner 3 (NIFC), T.J. Little 6 (Bective Rangers), A.G. Heron (1) (Queen's U. Belfast), P. Healey 1 (Limerick).

ENGLAND J.W. Sagar (2) (Cambridge U.); G.C. Robinson 7 (Percy Park), *W.L. Bunting 8 (Moseley), J.T. Taylor 5 (West Hartlepool), E.W. Elliot 2 (Sunderland); R.O. Schwarz (3) (Richmond), E.J. Walton 2 (Castleford); C. Hall 1 (Gloucester), R.D. Wood 1 (Liverpool OB), C.T. Scott (4) (Blackheath), S. Reynolds (4) (Richmond), E.W. Roberts 2 (RNEC Keyham), N.C. Fletcher 2 (OMT), A. O'Neill 2 (Torquay Athletic), H. Alexander 4 (Birkenhead Park).

Referee D.G. Findlay (Scotland)

SCOTLAND v WALES 17/98

9 February 1901
Inverleith, Edinburgh
Scotland 18 (3G, 1T) Wales 8 (1G, 1T)

Scotland T: Gillespie (2), Turnbull, Flett. C: Gillespie (2), Flett.
Wales T: Llewellyn Lloyd, Boots. C: Bancroft.

The Scottish gamble of playing eight new caps and basing their side on Edinburgh University, which supplied seven players, paid off handsomely. With only a few changes, this excellent Scottish side went on to win the Championship in three of the next four seasons.

SCOTLAND A.W. Duncan 1 (Edinburgh U.); W.H. Welsh 3 (Edinburgh U.), A.B. Timms 4 (Edinburgh U.), P. Turnbull 1 (Edinburgh Acads), A.N. Fell 1 (Edinburgh U.); J.I. Gillespie 4 (Edinburgh Acads), F.H. Fasson 2 (Edinburgh U.); D.R. Bedell-Sivright 2 (Cambridge U.), J.A. Bell 1 (Clydesdale), J.M. Dykes 7 (Glasgow HSFP), A.B. Flett 1 (Edinburgh U.), A. Frew 1 (Edinburgh U.), *M.C. Morrison 13 (Royal HSFP), J. Ross 1 (London Scottish), R.S. Stronach 1 (Glasgow Acads).

WALES *W.J. Bancroft 32 (Swansea); W.M. Llewellyn 8 (London Welsh), E.G. Nicholls 12 (Cardiff), G. Davies 5 (Swansea), W.J. Trew 5 (Swansea); L.A. Phillips (4) (Newport), G.Ll. Lloyd 7 (Newport); R. Hellings (9) (Llwynypia), W.H. Alexander 6 (Llwynypia), A. Brice 8 (Aberavon), F. Miller 6 (Mountain Ash), G. Boots 8 (Newport), J.J. Hodges 8 (Newport), H. Davies 3 (Swansea), J. Blake 8 (Cardiff).

Referee R.W. Jeffares (Ireland)

SCOTLAND v IRELAND 19/99

23 February 1901
Inverleith, Edinburgh
Scotland 9 (3T) Ireland 5 (1G)

Scotland T: Gillespie, Welsh (2).
Ireland T: Doran. C: Irvine.

The playing strength of Edinburgh University was underlined in this match: they supplied five backs and two forwards to Scotland, and one back, J.B. Allison, to Ireland. The Irish did well to put a check on the Scottish scoring machine.

SCOTLAND A.W. Duncan 2 (Edinburgh U.); W.H. Welsh 4 (Edinburgh U.), A.B. Timms 5 (Edinburgh U.), P. Turnbull 2 (Edinburgh Acads), A.N. Fell 2 (Edinburgh U.); J.I. Gillespie 5 (Edinburgh Acads), F.H. Fasson 3 (Edinburgh U.); D.R. Bedell-Sivright 3 (Fettesian-Lorettonians), J.A. Bell 2 (Clydesdale), F.P. Dods (1) (Edinburgh Acads), J.M. Dykes 8 (Glasgow HSFP), A.B. Flett 2 (Edinburgh U.), A. Frew 2 (Edinburgh U.), *M.C. Morrison 14 (Royal HSFP), J. Ross 2 (London Scottish).

IRELAND C.A. Boyd 2 (Wanderers); A.E. Freear 2 (Lansdowne), B.R.W. Doran 4 (Lansdowne), J.B. Allison 7 (Edinburgh U.), I.G. Davidson 5 (NIFC); *L.M. Magee 19 (Bective Rangers), A. Barr (4) (Methodist C. Belfast); C.E. Allen 5 (Derry), T.A. Harvey 2 (Dublin U.), P. Healey 2 (Limerick), H.A.S. Irvine (1) (Belfast Collegians), T.J. Little (7) (Bective Rangers), T.M.W. Mc-Gown (3) (NIFC), J. Ryan 11 (Rockwell College), M. Ryan 13 (Rockwell College).

Referee G. Harnett (England)

ENGLAND v SCOTLAND   16/100

9 March 1901
Rectory Field, Blackheath
Scotland 18 (3G, 1T) England 3 (1T)

England T: Robinson.
Scotland T: Gillespie, Welsh, Timms, Fell. C: Gillespie (3).

This was England's biggest margin of defeat by Scotland in a home match. It ensured that Scotland won the Triple Crown for a third time, and that England finished at the foot of the table for the second time in three seasons. It was the last Championship for eight England players, including George Robinson, the Percy Park wing, who achieved the most remarkable scoring sequence of any player. Altogether Robinson scored eight tries in eight Championship matches, failing to score in only one of them: against Scotland in 1900. It was an auspicious day for Edinburgh University. They provided six of the Scottish side. J.I. Gillespie's three conversions and one try, his fourth of the season, brought his total points for the season to 22, a record for the Championship.

ENGLAND H.T. Gamlin 6 (Blackheath); G.C. Robinson (8) (Percy Park), *W.L. Bunting (9) (Richmond), N.S. Cox (1) (Sunderland), E.W. Elliot 3 (Sunderland); P.D. Kendall 1 (Birkenhead Park), B. Oughtred 1 (Hartlepool Rovers); C. Hall (2) (Gloucester), H.T.F. Weston (1) (Northampton), B.C. Hartley 1 (Blackheath), A. O'Neill (3) (Torquay Athletic), N.C. Fletcher 3 (OMT), C.S. Edgar (1) (Birkenhead Park), G.R. Gibson (2) (Northern), H. Alexander 5 (Birkenhead Park).

SCOTLAND A.W. Duncan 3 (Edinburgh U.); W.H. Welsh 5 (Edinburgh U.), A.B. Timms 6 (Edinburgh U.), P. Turnbull 3 (Edinburgh Acads), A.N. Fell 3 (Edinburgh U.); J.I. Gillespie 6 (Edinburgh Acads), R.M. Neill 1 (Edinburgh Acads); D.R. Bedell-Sivright 4 (Fettesian-Lorettonians), J.A. Bell 3 (Clydesdale), J.M. Dykes 9 (Glasgow HSFP), A.B. Flett 3 (Edinburgh U.), A. Frew (3) (Edinburgh U.), *M.C. Morrison 15 (Royal HSFP), J. Ross 3 (London Scottish), R.S. Stronach 2 (Glasgow Acads).

Referee R.W. Jeffares (Ireland)

WALES v IRELAND   15/101

16 March 1901
St Helen's, Swansea
Wales 10 (2G) Ireland 9 (3T)

Wales T: Alexander (2). C: Bancroft (2).
Ireland T: Jim Ryan, Freear, Davidson.

The thirty-third and last Championship appearance of Billy Bancroft, the Swansea full-back, and the début appearances of Rhys Gabe, Dick Jones and Dicky Owen. The Irish, having outscored the Welsh in the number of tries, were disappointed – and critical of the referee, George Harnett, for being too slow.

WALES *W.J. Bancroft (33) (Swansea); W.M. Llewellyn 9 (London Welsh), E.G. Nicholls 13 (Cardiff), G. Davies 6 (Swansea), R.T. Gabe 1 (Llanelli); Dick Jones 1 (Swansea), R.M. Owen 1 (Swansea); A. Brice 9 (Aberavon), F. Miller (7) (Mountain Ash), F. Scrine (3) (Swansea), H. Davies (4) (Swansea), G. Boots 9 (Newport), J. Blake (9) (Cardiff), W.H. Alexander (7) (Llwynypia), Bob Jones (1) (Llwynypia).

IRELAND C.A. Boyd (3) (Wanderers); A.E. Freear (3) (Lansdowne), B.R.W. Doran 5 (Lansdowne), J.B. Allison 8 (Edinburgh U.), I.G. Davidson 6 (NIFC); *L.M. Magee 20 (Bective Rangers), J.H. Ferris (4) (Queen's U. Belfast); M. Ryan 14 (Rockwell College), J. Ryan 12 (Rockwell College), C.E. Allen 6 (Derry), F. Gardiner 4 (NIFC), T.A. Harvey 3 (Dublin U.), P. Healey 3 (Limerick), J.J. Coffey 2 (Lansdowne), S.T. Irwin 5 (Queen's U. Belfast).

Referee G. Harnett (England)

1902

BLACKHEATH Wales beat England 9-8 · CARDIFF Wales beat Scotland 14-5
LEICESTER England beat Ireland 6-3 · BELFAST Ireland beat Scotland 5-0
DUBLIN Wales beat Ireland 15-0 · EDINBURGH England beat Scotland 6-3

CHAMPIONSHIP TABLE
Wales – Championship, Triple Crown

									Tries	
Pos	Country	P	W	D	L	F	A	Pts	F	A
1	Wales (2)	3	3	0	0	38	13	6	9	3
2	England (4)	3	2	0	1	20	15	4	6	4
3	Ireland (3)	3	1	0	2	8	21	2	2	5
4	Scotland (1)	3	0	0	3	8	25	0	2	7

Wales won the Championship and the Triple Crown after taking a gamble with seven new caps in their opening match against England, and then retaining what amounted to the same side throughout the season. Wales, in fact, made two changes only and both because of injury. Thus a precedent was established, for up to this point in the Championship most countries, even when they were winning, changed personnel with seemingly little regard for team building or spirit. The mystery of 1902 was Scotland's disappointing performance: Champions in 1901, they lost all three matches. England, too, defied all expectations by finishing runners-up after their dismal performance the previous season.

ENGLAND v WALES 18/102

11 January 1902
Rectory Field, Blackheath
Wales 9 (2T, 1PG) England 8 (1G, 1T)

England T: Dobson, Robinson. C: Alexander.
Wales T: Gabe, Osborne. PG: Strand-Jones.

John Robinson, the Headingley forward, made his second appearance for England, nine years after his début, against Scotland in 1893. It was the longest gap between caps of any player in the Championship. Johnny Williams, the Old Millhillans scrum-half, also bridged a nine-year break in his playing career (1956–65). Robinson earned the distinction by a little over a month, his first cap being won on 4 March 1893 while Williams's last appearance before being chosen again was on 14 April 1956. It will be noted that Gwyn Nicholls, who had won his previous 13 caps from Cardiff, had now joined Newport. Teddy Morgan, one of the outstanding wings in Wales during their Golden Age, made his début.

It was Wales's first victory at Blackheath, which was the venue (at Richardson's Field) of their first ever international, in 1881, when they conceded 13 tries to England.

ENGLAND   H.T. Gamlin 7 (Devonport Albion); S.F. Coopper 2 (Blackheath), J.E. Raphael 1 (Oxford U.), J.T. Taylor 6 (West Hartlepool), P.L. Nicholas (1) (Exeter); P.D. Kendall 2 (Birkenhead Park), B. Oughtred 2 (Hartlepool Rovers); S.G. Williams 1 (Devonport Albion), L.R. Tosswill 1 (Exeter), T.H. Willcocks (1) (Plymouth Albion), J. Jewitt (1) (Hartlepool Rovers), J.J. Robinson 2 (Headingley), D.D. Dobson 1 (Oxford U.), G. Fraser 1 (Richmond), *H. Alexander 6 (Birkenhead Park).

WALES   J. Strand-Jones 1 (Llanelli); W.M. Llewellyn 10 (Llwynypia), *E.G. Nicholls 14 (Newport), R.T. Gabe 2 (Llanelli), E.T. Morgan 1 (London Welsh); Dick Jones 2 (Swansea), R.M. Owen 2 (Swansea); A. Brice 10 (Aberavon), J.J. Hodges 9 (Newport), G. Boots 10 (Newport), W. Joseph 1 (Swansea), D. Jones 1 (Treherbert), W.T. Osborne 1 (Mountain Ash), A.F. Harding 1 (Cardiff), D. Walters (1) (Llanelli).

Referee R.W. Jeffares (Ireland)

WALES v SCOTLAND   18/103

1 February 1902
Cardiff Arms Park
Wales 14 (1G, 3T) Scotland 5 (1G)

Wales   T: Llewellyn (2), Gabe (2). C: Strand-Jones.
Scotland   T: Welsh. C: Gillespie.

Arguably one of the most gifted all-round sides in the history of Scottish rugby had no answer to a fluent Welsh side. Scotland's captain, Mark Morrison, shouldered the blame, for after winning the toss, he decided to play against the wind. Scotland found themselves 14 points in arrears by half-time and afterwards Morrison declared: 'we were too tired to fight back'.

WALES   J. Strand-Jones 2 (Llanelli); W.M. Llewellyn 11 (Llwynypia), *E.G. Nicholls 15 (Newport), R.T. Gabe 3 (London Welsh), E.T. Morgan 2 (London Welsh); G.Ll. Lloyd 8 (Newport), R.M. Owen 3 (Swansea); A. Brice 11 (Aberavon), J.J. Hodges 10 (Newport), G. Boots 11 (Newport), W. Joseph 2 (Swansea), D. Jones 2 (Treherbert), A.F. Harding 2 (Cardiff), W.T. Osborne 2 (Mountain Ash), H. Jones 1 (Penygraig).

SCOTLAND   A.W. Duncan 4 (Edinburgh U.); W.H. Welsh 6 (Edinburgh U.), A.B. Timms 7 (Edinburgh U.), P. Turnbull 4 (Edinburgh Acads), A.N. Fell 4 (Edinburgh U.); J.I. Gillespie 7 (Edinburgh Acads), F.H. Fasson 4 (Edinburgh U.); D.R. Bedell-Sivright 5 (Cambridge U.), J.V. Bedell-Sivright (1) (Cambridge U.), J.A. Bell 4 (Clydesdale), A.B. Flett 4 (Edinburgh U.), J.R.C. Greenlees 2 (Cambridge U.), W.E. Kyle 1 (Hawick), *M.C. Morrison 16 (Royal HSFP), J. Ross 4 (London Scottish).

Referee P. Gilliard (England)

ENGLAND v IRELAND   18/104

8 February 1902
Welford Road, Leicester
England 6 (2T) Ireland 3 (1T)

England   T: Coopper, Williams.
Ireland   T: F. Gardiner.

The first appearance of George Hamlet, the Old Wesley forward who became a legendary figure in Irish rugby. Hamlet made 27 Championship appearances.

ENGLAND   H.T. Gamlin 8 (Devonport Albion): S.F. Coopper 3 (Blackheath), J.E. Raphael 2 (Oxford U.), J.T. Taylor 7 (West Hartlepool), R. Forrest 3 (Blackheath); B. Oughtred 3 (Hartlepool Rovers), E.J. Walton 3 (Castleford); S.G. Williams 2 (Devonport Albion), L.R. Tosswill 2 (Exeter), *J. Daniell 4 (Richmond), P.F. Hardwick 1 (Percy Park), J.J. Robinson 3 (Headingley), D.D. Dobson 2 (Oxford U.), G. Fraser 2 (Richmond), H. Alexander (7) (Birkenhead Park).

IRELAND   *J. Fulton 9 (NIFC); I.G. Davidson 7 (NIFC), J.B. Allison 9 (Edinburgh U.), B.R.W. Doran 6 (Lansdowne), C.C. Fitzgerald 1 (Glasgow U.); L.M. Magee 21 (Bective Rangers), H.H. Corley 1 (Dublin U.); J.J. Coffey 3 (Lansdowne), G.T. Hamlet 1 (Old Wesley), F. Gardiner 5 (NIFC), S.T. Irwin 6 (Queen's U. Belfast), A. Tedford 1 (Malone), P. Healey 4 (Limerick), J. Ryan 13 (Rockwell College), T.A. Harvey 4 (Dublin U.).

Referee R. Welsh (Scotland)

IRELAND v SCOTLAND   20/105

22 February 1902
Balmoral Showgrounds, Belfast
Ireland 5 (1G) Scotland 0

Ireland   T: Gerry Doran. C: Corley.

Ireland gained their second home win over Scotland, with exactly the same score as in the first, in 1894. It was to prove Ireland's only victory of the season and one of Scotland's three losses.

IRELAND   *J. Fulton 10 (NIFC); I.G. Davidson 8 (NIFC), J.B. Allison 10 (Edinburgh U.), B.R.W. Doran 7 (Lansdowne), G.P. Doran 5 (Lansdowne); L.M. Magee 22 (Bective Rangers), H.H. Corley 2 (Dublin U.); J.J. Coffey 4 (Lansdowne), F. Gardiner 6 (NIFC), G.T. Hamlet 2 (Old Wesley), T.A. Harvey 5 (Dublin U.), P. Healey 5 (Limerick), J.C. Pringle 1 (NIFC), A. Tedford 2 (Malone), S.T. Irwin 7 (Queen's U. Belfast).

SCOTLAND   A.W. Duncan 5 (Edinburgh U.); W.H. Welsh 7 (Edinburgh U.), A.S. Drybrough 1 (Edinburgh Wands), P. Turnbull 5 (Edinburgh Acads), J.E. Crabbie 2 (Oxford U.); J.I. Gillespie 8 (Edinburgh Acads), R.M. Neill (2) (Edinburgh Acads); W.P. Scott 3 (W. of Scotland), *M.C. Morrison 17 (Royal HSFP), W.E. Kyle 2 (Hawick), J.R.C. Greenlees 3 (Cambridge U.), A.B. Flett (5) (Edinburgh U.), H.H. Bullmore (1) (Edinburgh U.), J.A. Bell 5 (Clydesdale), D.R. Bedell-Sivright 6 (Cambridge U.).

Referee A. Hill (England)

IRELAND v WALES   16/106

8 March 1902
Lansdowne Road, Dublin
Wales 15 (1G, 2T, 1DG) Ireland 0

Wales T: Nicholls, Llewellyn, Llewellyn Lloyd. C: Brice. DG: Nicholls.

This was Ireland's worst defeat at home since the start of the Championship and the third time a Wales win over Ireland had brought them the Triple Crown. Also it was the first occasion when an international was by ticket only.

IRELAND   J. Fulton 11 (NIFC); G.P. Doran 6 (Lansdowne), B.R.W. Doran (8) (Lansdowne), J.B. Allison 11 (Edinburgh U.), I.G. Davidson (9) (NIFC); *L.M. Magee 23 (Bective Rangers), H.H. Corley 3 (Wanderers); F. Gardiner 7 (NIFC), J.J. Coffey 5 (Lansdowne), A. Tedford 3 (Malone), S.T. Irwin 8 (Queen's U. Belfast), T.A. Harvey 6 (Dublin U.), P. Healey 6 (Limerick), J.C. Pringle (2) (NIFC), G.T. Hamlet 3 (Old Wesley).

WALES   J. Strand-Jones 3 (Llanelli); W.M. Llewellyn 12 (Llwynypia), *E.G. Nicholls 16 (Newport), R.T. Gabe 4 (London Welsh), E.T. Morgan 3 (London Welsh); G.Ll. Lloyd 9 (New-

port), R.M. Owen 4 (Swansea); A. Brice 12 (Aberavon), W. Joseph 3 (Swansea), J.J. Hodges 11 (Newport), G. Boots 12 (Newport), A.F. Harding 3 (Cardiff), W.T. Osborne 3 (Mountain Ash), H. Jones (2) (Penygraig) D. Jones 3 (Treherbert).

Referee J.C. Findlay (Scotland)

SCOTLAND v ENGLAND   17/107

15 March 1902
Inverleith, Edinburgh
England 6 (2T) Scotland 3 (1T)

Scotland T: Fell.
England T: Williams, Taylor.

England had played five matches without a win against Scotland and their triumph meant that the Scots ended up with the Wooden Spoon for the first time since the previous English victory in 1897. Seven of the Scottish team did not play for their country again, which was an occupational hazard usually associated with England players of the time.

SCOTLAND   A.W. Duncan (6) (Edinburgh U.); A.N. Fell 5 (Edinburgh U.), P. Turnbull (6) (Edinburgh Acads), A.B. Timms 8 (Edinburgh U.), W.H. Welsh (8) (Edinburgh U.); F.H. Fasson (5) (Edinburgh U.), E.D. Simson 1 (Edinburgh U.); D.R. Bedell-Sivright 7 (Cambridge U.), J.A. Bell (6) (Clydesdale), J.M. Dykes (10) (Glasgow HSFP), J.R.C. Greenlees 4 (Cambridge U.), W.E. Kyle 3 (Hawick), *M.C. Morrison 18 (Royal HSFP), W.P. Scott 4 (W. of Scotland), H.O. Smith (11) (Watsonians).

ENGLAND   H.T. Gamlin 9 (Devonport Albion); T. Simpson 1 (Rockcliff), J.T. Taylor 8 (West Hartlepool), J.E. Raphael 3 (Oxford U.), R. Forrest 4 (Blackheath); B. Oughtred 4 (Hartlepool Rovers), E.J. Walton (4) (Castleford); S.G. Williams 3 (Devonport Albion), L.R. Tosswill (3) (Exeter), *J. Daniell 5 (Richmond), P.F. Hardwick 2 (Percy Park), J.J. Robinson (4) (Headingley), D.D. Dobson 3 (Oxford U.), G. Fraser 3 (Richmond), B.C. Hartley (2) (Blackheath).

Referee F.M. Hamilton (Ireland)

1903

SWANSEA Wales beat England 21-5 · EDINBURGH Scotland beat Wales 6-0
DUBLIN Ireland beat England 6-0 · EDINBURGH Scotland beat Ireland 3-0
CARDIFF Wales beat Ireland 18-0 · RICHMOND Scotland beat England 10-6

CHAMPIONSHIP TABLE
Scotland – Championship, Triple Crown

Pos	Country	P	W	D	L	F	A	Pts	Tries F	A
1	Scotland (4)	3	3	0	0	19	6	6	4	2
2	Wales (1)	3	2	0	1	39	11	4	11	2
3	Ireland (3)	3	1	0	2	6	21	2	1	7
4	England (2)	3	0	0	3	11	37	0	3	8

Scotland, who had finished bottom of the Championship in 1902 after winning the Triple Crown the year before, won all three matches to take the title again. Only England managed to score against the Scots – two tries – but Scotland's 19 points' total was a rather modest return in a period which generally showed a marked improvement in scoring by all sides. Only twice between 1900 and 1983, in fact, was the title won by a side (Wales in 1936 and 1939) who scored fewer points than Scotland's 1903 total. That England's runners-up position in 1902 had been fortuity rather than an accurate reflection of their talent was confirmed by their results, three defeats and the Wooden Spoon again. Wales were second, even though they scored more points than any other side and 20 more than Scotland, the Champions.

The England XV which was defeated 6-0 by Ireland at Lansdowne Road

WALES v ENGLAND   19/108

10 January 1903
St Helen's, Swansea
Wales 21 (3G, 2T) England 5 (1G)

Wales T: Hodges (3), Owen, Pearson. C: Strand-Jones (3).
England T: Dobson. C: Taylor.

Jehoida Hodges earned himself a place in Championship history by becoming the only forward to score three tries. It was a fortuitous hat-trick: Hodges scored after being brought out of the pack to play on the wing as a replacement for Tom Pearson, who had been taken off injured after a heavy tackle by the redoubtable Harry Gamlin. Pearson, who had already scored a try, was only in the side by chance anyway: he had retired at the end of the 1902 season, but was persuaded to return to club rugby by Newport. With Gwyn Nicholls unavailable because of injury, Wales recalled Pearson to captain the side. It was his thirteenth and final match.

WALES J. Strand-Jones 4 (Llanelli); W.F. Jowett (1) (Swansea), D. Rees 2 (Swansea), R.T. Gabe 5 (Llanelli), *T.W. Pearson (13) (Newport); G.Ll. Lloyd 10 (Newport), R.M. Owen 5 (Swansea); G. Boots 13 (Newport), J.J. Hodges 12 (Newport), A. Brice 13 (Aberavon), W. Joseph 4 (Swansea), A.F. Harding 4 (London Welsh), D. Jones 4 (Treherbert), W.T. Osborne 4 (Mountain Ash), G. Travers 1 (Pill Harriers).

ENGLAND H.T. Gamlin 10 (Devonport Albion); J.H. Miles (1) (Leicester), J.T. Taylor 9 (West Hartlepool), R.H. Spooner (1) (Liverpool), T. Simpson 2 (Rockcliff); F.C. Hulme 1 (Birkenhead Park), *B. Oughtred 5 (Hartlepool Rovers); R.F.A. Hobbs (2) (Blackheath), P.F. Hardwick 3 (Percy Park), R. Bradley (1) (West Hartlepool), R.D. Wood 2 (Liverpool OB), D.D. Dobson 4 (Newton Abbot), G. Fraser 4 (Richmond), J. Duthie (1) (West Hartlepool), V.H. Cartwright 1 (Oxford U.).

Referee R. Welsh (Scotland)

SCOTLAND v WALES   19/109

7 February 1903
Inverleith, Edinburgh
Scotland 6 (1T, 1PG) Wales 0

Scotland T: Kyle. PG: Timms.

Of the penalty goals scored through a dropped kick during this Championship, A.B. Timms's must be the most remarkable, for he took the kick from close to the halfway line. Timms had the advantage of a fierce wind, but conditions were also unpleasantly rain-swept. In fact the pitch was waterlogged before the start of the match and the surplus water had to be swept away by bands of workmen.

SCOTLAND W.T. Forrest 1 (Hawick); A.N. Fell 6 (Edinburgh U.), A.B. Timms 9 (Edinburgh U.), H.J. Orr 1 (London Scottish), J.E. Crabbie 3 (Oxford U.); E.D. Simson 2 (Edinburgh U.), J. Knox 1 (Kelvinside Acads); D.R. Bedell-Sivright 8 (Cambridge U.), A.G. Cairns 1 (Watsonians), J.R.C. Greenlees 5 (Kelvinside Acads), N. Kennedy 1 (W. of Scotland), W.E. Kyle 4 (Hawick), *M.C. Morrison 19 (Royal HSFP), W.P. Scott 5 (W. of Scotland), L. West 1 (Edinburgh U.).

WALES J. Strand-Jones (5) (Llanelli); W. Arnold (1) (Swansea), R.T. Gabe 6 (Llanelli), D. Rees 3 (Swansea), W.J. Trew 6 (Swansea); *G.Ll. Lloyd 11 (Newport), R.M. Owen 6 (Swansea); J.J. Hodges 13 (Newport), G. Boots 14 (Newport), A. Brice 14 (Aberavon), A.F. Harding 5 (London Welsh), W. Joseph 5 (Swansea), D. Jones 5 (Treherbert), W.T. Osborne 5 (Mountain Ash), G. Travers 2 (Pill Harriers).

Referee A. Martelli (Ireland)

IRELAND v ENGLAND 19/110

14 February 1903
Lansdowne Road, Dublin
Ireland 6 (1T, 1PG) England 0

Ireland   T: Ryan. PG: Corley.

This defeat determined that England would finish with the Wooden Spoon. It was Ireland's fourth win in a row against England at Lansdowne Road. The trip, however, was marred by tragedy. According to John Griffiths, in *The Book of English International Rugby 1871–1982* (Collins Willow): 'Three of the RFU party which travelled for this match are believed to have contracted typhoid fever while in Dublin. Forrest, who played against Scotland later (on 21 March), died of the disease in April, as did R.S. Whalley, a former president of the Union. Oughtred, the captain, made a good recovery and became a successful naval architect.'

IRELAND   J. Fulton 12 (NIFC); C.C. Fitzgerald 2 (Dungannon), G.A.D. Harvey 1 (Wanderers), D.R. Taylor (1) (Queen's U. Belfast), H.J. Anderson 1 (Old Wesley); L.M. Magee 24 (Bective Rangers), *H.H. Corley 4 (Dublin U.); J.J. Coffey 6 (Lansdowne), F. Gardiner 8 (NIFC), T.A. Harvey 7 (Dublin U.), P. Healey 7 (Garryowen), G.T. Hamlet 4 (Old Wesley), M. Ryan 15 (Rockwell College), A. Tedford 4 (Malone), R.S. Smyth 1 (Dublin U.).

ENGLAND   H.T. Gamlin 11 (Devonport Albion); T. Simpson 3 (Rockcliff), J.T. Taylor 10 (West Hartlepool), A.T. Brettargh 2 (Liverpool OB), R. Forrest 5 (Blackheath); *B. Oughtred (6) (Hartlepool Rovers), F.C. Hulme 2 (Birkenhead Park); S.G. Williams 4 (Devonport Albion), R.D. Wood (3) (Liverpool OB), W.G. Heppell (1) (Devonport Albion), P.F. Hardwick 4 (Percy Park), B.A. Hill 1 (Blackheath), D.D. Dobson 5 (Newton Abbot), G. Fraser (5) (Richmond), V.H. Cartwright 2 (Oxford U.).

Referee J.C. Findlay (Scotland)

SCOTLAND v IRELAND 21/111

28 February 1903
Inverleith, Edinburgh
Scotland 3 (1T) Ireland 0

Scotland   T: Crabbie.

One Irish newspaper account described the sea crossing to Scotland as 'rough and dreadful', implying that this more than any great Scottish skill led to the defeat. Scotland, on their way towards winning a fourth Triple Crown, introduced one player new to the Championship, Charles France, who was a one-cap replacement for A.B. Timms, injured at practice earlier in the week.

SCOTLAND   W.T. Forrest 2 (Hawick); J.E. Crabbie 4 (Oxford U.), H.J. Orr 2 (London Scottish), A.S. Drybrough (2) (Edinburgh Wands), C. France (1) (Kelvinside Acads); E.D. Simson 3 (Edinburgh U.), J. Knox 2 (Kelvinside Acads); D.R. Bedell-Sivright 9 (Cambridge U.), A.G. Cairns 2 (Watsonians), J.R.C. Greenlees 6 (Kelvinside Acads), N. Kennedy 2 (W. of Scotland), W.E. Kyle 5 (Hawick), *M.C. Morrison 20 (Royal HSFP), W.P. Scott 6 (W. of Scotland), L. West 2 (Edinburgh U.).

IRELAND   J. Fulton 13 (NIFC); H.J. Anderson 2 (Old Wesley), J.B. Allison (12) (Edinburgh U.), G.A.D. Harvey 2 (Wanderers), C.C. Fitzgerald (3) (Dungannon); L.M. Magee 25 (Bective Rangers), *H.H. Corley 5 (Wanderers); C.E. Allen 7 (Derry), J.J. Coffey 7 (Lansdowne), G.T. Hamlet 5 (Old Wesley), P. Healey 8 (Limerick), S.T. Irwin (9) (NIFC), R.S. Smyth 2 (Dublin U.), A. Tedford 5 (Malone), Jos Wallace 1 (Wanderers).

Referee F.H.R. Alderson (England)

WALES v IRELAND   17/112

14 March 1903
Cardiff Arms Park
Wales 18 (6T) Ireland 0

Wales   T: Llewellyn (2), Gabe, Morgan (2), Brice.

This six-try rout of Ireland was refereed by Percy Cole, who became the first paid secretary of the Rugby Football Union the following year. Cole remarked: 'It was a thundering good mud-lark, especially for the referee . . . you can't ask me to criticise, I don't know one man from another.' Wales played the second half with 14 men, having lost the services of the redoubtable George Boots, who had broken his collar-bone after five minutes and had played out the remainder of the half without realising the seriousness of the injury. Boots was one of the outstanding forwards of the era. He won 16 caps between 1898 and 1904, and played 365 games in a 25-year career with Newport, for whom he still played 16 years after losing his place in the Wales team. The match receipts were £2000, a record for the time.

WALES   H.B. Winfield 1 (Cardiff); W.M. Llewellyn 13 (London Welsh), *E.G. Nicholls 17 (Cardiff), R.T. Gabe 7 (Llanelli), E.T. Morgan 4 (London Welsh); G.Ll. Lloyd (12) (Newport), R.M. Owen 7 (Swansea); A. Brice 15 (Aberavon), G. Boots 15 (Newport), J.J. Hodges 14 (Newport), G. Travers 3 (Pill Harriers), D. Jones 6 (Treherbert), W. Joseph 6 (Swansea), A.F. Harding 6 (London Welsh), W.T. Osborne (6) (Mountain Ash).

IRELAND   J. Fulton 14 (NIFC); G. Bradshaw (1) (Belfast Collegians), C. Reid (4) (NIFC), J.C. Parke 1 (Dublin U.), G.P. Doran 7 (Lansdowne); L.M. Magee 26 (Bective Rangers), *H.H. Corley 6 (Wanderers); J.J. Coffey 8 (Lansdowne), P. Healey 9 (Garryowen), G.T. Hamlet 6 (Old Wesley), Jos Wallace 2 (Wanderers), F. Gardiner 9 (NIFC), C.E. Allen 8 (Derry), T.A. Harvey (8) (Monkstown), A. Tedford 6 (Malone).

Referee P. Cole (England)

ENGLAND v SCOTLAND   18/113

21 March 1903
Athletic Ground, Richmond
Scotland 10 (2T, 1DG) England 6 (2T)

England   T: Dobson, Forrest.
Scotland   T: Dallas, Simson. DG: Timms.

John Dewar Dallas scored on this his only appearance for Scotland. Dallas was later to earn notoriety as the referee of the first Wales v New Zealand match in 1905 when he refused to allow the Bob Deans try. It is believed that Dallas did not play again for Scotland because at that time they favoured big, grafting scrummagers rather than fast, loose players such as Dallas. It is curious how Dallas's speed, or supposed lack of it, was to be at the centre of the argument that raged, and still continues to rage today, over the Deans try: that the referee had not been able to keep up with play and was therefore too far away to see Deans ground over the scoreline and then see him being pulled back by Welsh players before the breathless (inferred) referee arrived. A picture of an old dodderer was suggested. Dallas in 1905 was 27. In contrast, the referee of this match, W.M. Douglas of Wales, was 39.

ENGLAND   H.T. Gamlin 12 (Devonport Albion); T. Simpson 4 (Rockcliff), A.T. Brettargh 3 (Liverpool OB), E.I.M. Barrett (1) (Lennox), R. Forrest (6) (Blackheath); W.V. Butcher 1 (Streatham & Croydon), *P.D. Kendall (3) (Birkenhead Park); S.G. Williams 5 (Devonport Albion), R. Pierce (2) (Liverpool), N.C. Fletcher (4) (OMT), P.F. Hardwick 5 (Percy Park), B.A. Hill 2 (Blackheath), D.D. Dobson (6) (Newton Abbot), F.M. Stout 8 (Richmond), V.H. Cartwright 3 (Oxford U.).

SCOTLAND   W.T. Forrest 3 (Hawick); A.N. Fell (7) (Edinburgh U.), H.J. Orr 3 (London Scottish), A.B. Timms 10 (Edinburgh U.), J.S. Macdonald 1 (Edinburgh U.); E.D. Simson 4 (Edinburgh U.), J. Knox (3) (Kelvinside Acads); A.G. Cairns 3 (Watsonians), J.D. Dallas (1) (Watsonians), *J.R.C. Greenlees (7) (Kelvinside Acads), N. Kennedy (3) (W. of Scotland), W.E. Kyle 6 (Hawick), J. Ross (5) (London Scottish), W.P. Scott 7 (W. of Scotland), L. West 3 (Edinburgh U.).

Referee W.M. Douglas (Wales)

1904

LEICESTER England drew Wales 14-14 · SWANSEA Wales beat Scotland 21-3
BLACKHEATH England beat Ireland 19-0 · DUBLIN Scotland beat Ireland 19-3
BELFAST Ireland beat Wales 14-12 · EDINBURGH Scotland beat England 6-3

CHAMPIONSHIP TABLE
Scotland – Championship, Triple Crown

Pos	Country	P	W	D	L	F	A	Pts	Tries F	A
1	Scotland (1)	3	2	0	1	28	27	4	8	6
2	Wales (2)	3	1	1	1	47	31	3	10	8
3	England (4)	3	1	1	1	36	20	3	9	4
4	Ireland (3)	3	1	0	2	17	50	2	5	14

The points' aggregate soared to a record 128 points in 1904, a total for a four-nation competition which has since been surpassed on two other occasions only, in 1908 (142) and 1938 (176). The scoring of tries had now become every country's preoccupation and the total of 32 from 6 matches has been bettered only by the 35 scored in 1938. Scotland scored eight tries to win the title for a second successive year but Wales, once again, outscored the Champions in the number of tries (10) and points (47). The

'Our International' by Harry Furniss and published in *The Illustrated London News*, 1904

season was one which Ireland wanted to forget. Not only did they finish bottom, but they conceded 14 tries and 50 points, the highest totals scored against any side since the adoption of modern scoring values.

England, by this time, had concluded arrangements to travel to Paris to play France for a first time. They did so on 22 March, five days after their final Championship match, against Scotland. England won this non-Championship pot-boiler, 35-8. France's initiation into international rugby had been three months earlier against New Zealand.

ENGLAND v WALES 20/114

9 January 1904
Welford Road, Leicester
England 14 (1G, 2T, 1PG) Wales 14 (2G, 1GM)

England   T: Elliot (2), Brettargh. C: Stout. PG: Gamlin.
Wales   T: Llewellyn, Morgan. C: Winfield (2). GM: Winfield.

Crawford Findlay, the Scottish referee, did not endear himself to the Welsh, not only because he ruled a forward pass in a move which would have brought a match-winning try near no-side. Dicky Owen, the Welsh scrum-half, had become frustrated at being so frequently penalized by Findlay that ultimately he gave up feeding the Welsh scrum, giving the ball instead to one of the English half-backs. J.G. Milton, the England forward, enjoyed a double distinction: he made his début appearance while still at school and he was the son of a former England international, W.H. Milton, who had played in two pre-Championship matches 1874–75. Another interesting selection was that of Sam Ramsey, the Scottish-born Treorchy forward. Ramsey returned eight years after winning his first cap.

ENGLAND   H.T. Gamlin 13 (Devonport Albion); E.J. Vivyan 2 (Devonport Albion), E.W. Dillon 1 (Blackheath), A.T. Brettargh 4 (Liverpool OB), E.W. Elliot (4) (Sunderland), P.S. Hancock 1 (Richmond), W.V. Butcher 2 (Bristol); V.H. Cartwright 4 (Oxford U.), G.H. Keeton 1 (Richmond), C.J. Newbold 1 (Cambridge U.), P.F. Hardwick 6 (Percy Park), J.G. Milton 1 (Bedford GS), N.H. Moore 1 (Bristol), *F.M. Stout 9 (Richmond), B.A. Hill 3 (Blackheath).

WALES   H.B. Winfield 2 (Cardiff); W.M. Llewellyn 14 (Newport), *E.G. Nicholls 18 (Cardiff), R.T. Gabe 8 (Cardiff), E.T. Morgan 5 (London Welsh); Dick Jones 3 (Swansea), R.M. Owen 8 (Swansea); A.F. Harding 7 (London Welsh), G. Boots (16) (Newport), J.J. Hodges 15 (Newport), A. Brice 16 (Cardiff), D.J. Thomas 1 (Swansea), W. Joseph 7 (Swansea), J. Evans (1) (Blaina), S.H. Ramsey (2) (Treorchy).

Referee J.C. Findlay (Scotland)

ENGLAND v IRELAND 20/115

13 February 1904
Rectory Field, Blackheath
England 19 (2G, 3T) Ireland 0

England   T: Moore (2), Vivyan (2), Simpson. C: Vivyan (2).

England accumulated 33 points in their first two matches, but still finished the season with only one victory. The selection of Jim Wallace made the Irish pack very much a fraternal affair, for he played alongside not only his brother, Joe, but the Ryan brothers, Mick and Jack. It was Jack Ryan's fourteenth and final appearance for Ireland. E.J. Vivyan's ten points were the highest scored by an English player in the Championship to date.

ENGLAND   H.T. Gamlin 14 (Devonport Albion); E.J. Vivyan 3 (Devonport Albion), E.W. Dillon 2 (Blackheath), A.T. Brettargh 5 (Liverpool OB), T. Simpson 5 (Rockcliff); P.S. Hancock 2 (Richmond), W.V. Butcher 3 (Bristol); *J. Daniell 6 (Richmond), G.H. Keeton 2 (Richmond), C.J. Newbold 2 (Cambridge U.), P.F. Hardwick 7 (Percy Park), J.G. Milton 2 (Bedford GS), N.H. Moore 2 (Bristol), F.M. Stout 10 (Richmond), B.A. Hill 4 (Blackheath).

IRELAND   J. Fulton 15 (NIFC); C.G. Robb 1 (Queen's U. Belfast), H.H. Corley 7 (Wanderers), J.C. Parke 2 (Dublin U.), G.P. Doran (8) (Lansdowne); T.T.H. Robinson 1 (Wanderers), F.A. Kennedy 1 (Wanderers); *C.E. Allen 9 (Derry), F. Gardiner 10 (NIFC), M. Ryan 16 (Rockwell College), J. Ryan (14) (Rockwell College), R.S. Smyth (3) (Dublin U.), A. Tedford 7 (Malone), Jas Wallace 1 (Wanderers), Jos Wallace 3 (Wanderers).

Referee T. Williams (Wales)

WALES v SCOTLAND 20/116

6 February 1904
St Helen's, Swansea
Wales 21 (3G, 1T, 1PG) Scotland 3 (1T)

Wales T: Gabe, Jones, Morgan, Brice. C: Winfield (3). PG: Winfield.
Scotland T: Orr.

The referee, F.W. Nicolls, could well have been the centre of attention during this match. Clad in 'a close-fitting cap and a long overcoat, and rather prominent white boots', Nicolls had cause to rebuke Bedell-Sivright, the Scottish forward, for 'roughing up' Winfield and Owen. Nicolls remained something of a mysterious figure, however, possibly because different versions of his name appeared. The correct spelling is given in the minutes of a Leicestershire Society meeting later in the year, which Nicolls signed when he became chairman of what is one of the oldest referee's societies. It was the fifth and final appearance of G.O. Turnbull, the West of Scotland forward, who had been recalled after an absence of seven years.

WALES   H.B. Winfield 3 (Cardiff); *W.M. Llewellyn 15 (Newport), C.C. Pritchard 1 (Newport), R.T. Gabe 9 (Cardiff), E.T. Morgan 6 (London Welsh); Dick Jones 4 (Swansea), R.M. Owen 9 (Swansea); A.F. Harding 8 (London Welsh), J.J. Hodges 16 (Newport), E. Thomas 1 (Newport), A. Brice 17 (Cardiff), W. Neill 1 (Cardiff), W. Joseph 8 (Swansea), D.H. Davies (1) (Neath), H. Watkins 1 (Llanelli).

SCOTLAND   W.T. Forrest 4 (Hawick); H.J. Orr 4 (London Scottish), G.E. Crabbie (1) (Edinburgh Acads), L.M. MacLeod 1 (Cambridge U.), J.S. Macdonald 2 (Edinburgh U.); E.D. Simson 5 (Edinburgh U.), A.A. Bisset (1) (RIE College); D.R. Bedell-Sivright 10 (W. of Scotland), L.H.I. Bell 2 (Edinburgh Acads), A.G. Cairns 4 (Watsonians), W.E. Kyle 7 (Hawick), *M.C. Morrison 21 (Royal HSFP), E.J. Ross (1) (London Scottish), W.P. Scott 8 (W. of Scotland), G.O. Turnbull (5) (Edinburgh Wands).

Referee F.W. Nicolls (England)

IRELAND v SCOTLAND 22/117

27 February 1904
Lansdowne Road, Dublin
Scotland 19 (2G, 3T) Ireland 3 (1T)

Ireland T: Moffatt.
Scotland T: Bedell-Sivright (2), Timms, Macdonald, Simson. C: Macdonald (2).

This was the second time that Scotland scored five tries in Ireland, and they have scored more points on only one other occasion, when they won 20-6 in 1962. Five Irish players made their last Championship appearances, including J. Fulton, the NIFC full-back whose career had started in 1895, and Mick Ryan, a regular since 1897.

IRELAND   J. Fulton (16) (NIFC); J.E. Moffatt 1 (Old Wesley), J.C. Parke 3 (Dublin U.), *H.H. Corley (8) (Wanderers), C.G. Robb 2 (Queen's U. Belfast); T.T.H. Robinson 2 (Dublin U.), E.D. Caddell 1 (Dublin U.); C.E. Allen 10 (Derry), F. Gardiner 11 (NIFC), G.T. Hamlet 7 (Old Wesley), P. Healey (10) (Limerick), M. Ryan (17) (Rockwell College), A. Tedford 8 (Malone), Jas Wallace (2) (Wands), Jos Wallace 4 (Wands).

SCOTLAND   W.T. Forrest 5 (Hawick); H.J. Orr (5) (London Scottish), A.B. Timms 11 (Cardiff), L.M. MacLeod 2 (Cambridge U.), J.S. Macdonald 3 (Edinburgh U.); E.D. Simson 6 (Edinburgh U.), J.I. Gillespie 9 (Edinburgh Acads); D.R. Bedell-Sivright 11 (W. of Scotland), L.H.I. Bell (3) (Edinburgh Acads), A.G. Cairns 5 (Watsonians), W.E. Kyle 8 (Hawick), W.M. Milne 1 (Glasgow Acads), *M.C. Morrison 22 (Royal HSFP), W.P. Scott 9 (W. of Scotland), J.B. Waters 1 (Cambridge U.).

Referee W. Williams (England)

IRELAND v WALES   18/118

2 March 1904
Balmoral Showgrounds, Belfast
Ireland 14 (1G, 3T) Wales 12 (4T)

Ireland   T: Tedford (2), Jos Wallace, Thrift. C: Parke.
Wales   T: Morgan (2), Gabe, Cliff Pritchard.

Crawford Findlay, the Scottish referee, who had upset Wales by some of his decisions in the match with England earlier in the season, added to his unpopularity by wrongly allowing an Irish try, because of a forward pass, and denying a winning score for Wales by Dick Jones. Findlay did not officiate at a Wales match again – but Ireland were happy enough to allow him to referee their match with New Zealand in 1905 and France in 1911. Harry Thrift, scorer of one of the Irish tries on his début appearance, became secretary of the International Board when he retired in 1909 after winning 17 caps. Concomitant with Thrift's first cap was Louis Magee's twenty-seventh and last, which made him the most capped Irishman to date. Magee was one of the outstanding backs of the Championship before the First World War. He, as much as anyone, transformed Ireland from a side of no-hopers into a force that every other side respected.

IRELAND   M.F. Landers 1 (Cork Constitution); H.B. Thrift 1 (Dublin U.), J.C. Parke 4 (Dublin U.), G.A.D. Harvey 3 (Wanderers), C.G. Robb 3 (Queen's U. Belfast); L.M. Magee (27) (Bective Rangers), F.A. Kennedy (2) (Wanderers); *C.E. Allen 11 (Derry), A. Tedford 9 (Malone), R.W. Edwards (1) (Malone), H.J. Knox 1 (Dublin U.), F. Gardiner 12 (NIFC), H.J. Millar 1 (Monkstown), G.T. Hamlet 8 (Old Wesley), Jos Wallace 5 (Wanderers).

WALES   H.B. Winfield 4 (Cardiff); *W.M. Llewellyn 16 (Newport), C.C. Pritchard 2 (Newport), R.T. Gabe 10 (Cardiff), E.T. Morgan 7 (London Welsh); Dick Jones 5 (Swansea), R.M. Owen 10 (Swansea); A Brice (18) (Cardiff), W. Neill 2 (Cardiff), E. Thomas 2 (Newport), C.M. Pritchard 1 (Newport), H. Watkins 2 (Llanelli), A.F. Harding 9 (London Welsh), S. Bevan (1) (Swansea), H. Jones (1) (Neath).

Referee J.C. Findlay (Scotland)

SCOTLAND v ENGLAND   19/119

19 March 1904
Inverleith, Edinburgh
Scotland 6 (2T) England 3 (1T)

Scotland   T: Crabbie, Macdonald.
England   T: Vivyan.

This well-deserved win over England meant that Scotland won the Championship for the third time in four seasons. It was a fitting finale for one of Scotland's great players, Mark Morrison, whose 23-cap career encompassed a period (1896–1904) when great headway was made in the game's development. Morrison, who led the 1903 British team to South Africa, was 27 when his international career ended. Another notable player for whom it was his last international, was Harry Gamlin, England's most capped player to date. Gamlin, often termed the 'Octopus' because of his all-embracing tackles, was the rock on which many attacking moves foundered. Several players needed treatment after a bone-jarring tackle from the Somerset-born Gamlin, who was 26 when his 15-cap career ended. The referee for the match was Sammy Lee, the former Ireland captain, and an old adversary of Morrison.

SCOTLAND   W.T. Forrest 6 (Hawick); J.E. Crabbie 5 (Edinburgh Acads), L.M. MacLeod 3 (Cambridge U.), A.B. Timms 12 (Cardiff), J.S. Macdonald 4 (Edinburgh U.); J.I. Gillespie (10) (Edinburgh Acads), E.D. Simson 7 (Edinburgh U.); D.R. Bedell-Sivright 12 (W. of Scotland), A.G. Cairns 6 (Watsonians), H.N. Fletcher 1 (Edinburgh U.), W.E. Kyle 9 (Hawick), W.M. Milne 2 (Glasgow Acads), *M.C. Morrison (23) (Royal HSFP), W.P. Scott 10 (W. of Scotland), J.B. Waters (2) (Cambridge U.).

ENGLAND   H.T. Gamlin (15) (Devonport Albion); E.J. Vivyan (4) (Devonport Albion), A.T. Brettargh 6 (Liverpool OB), E.W. Dillon 3 (Harlequins), T. Simpson 6 (Rockcliff); P.S. Hancock (3) (Richmond), W.V. Butcher 4 (Bristol); *J. Daniell (7) (Richmond), G.H. Keeton (3) (Richmond), C.J. Newbold 3 (Cambridge U.), P.F. Hardwick (8) (Percy Park), J.G. Milton 3 (Bedford GS), N.H. Moore (3) (Bristol), F.M. Stout 11 (Richmond), V.H. Cartwright 5 (Oxford U.).

Referee S. Lee (Ireland)

1905

CARDIFF Wales beat England 25-0 · EDINBURGH Wales beat Scotland 6-3
CORK Ireland beat England 17-3 · EDINBURGH Ireland beat Scotland 11-5
SWANSEA Wales beat Ireland 10-3 · RICHMOND Scotland beat England 8-0

CHAMPIONSHIP TABLE
Wales – Championship, Triple Crown

Pos	Country	P	W	D	L	F	A	Pts	Tries F	A
1	Wales (2)	3	3	0	0	41	6	6	11	2
2	Ireland (4)	3	2	0	1	31	18	4	9	4
3	Scotland (1)	3	1	0	2	16	17	2	4	5
4	England (3)	3	0	0	3	3	50	0	1	14

Wales finally accomplished what they had been threatening for four years – they won the Triple Crown and the Championship. The deciding match was at Swansea where Ireland, having beaten England and Scotland also, were positioned to take the titles for the first time since 1899. A try by Robinson gave Ireland the lead but Wales made a great recovery to triumph deservedly. With hindsight, the 1905 side was one of the best in Welsh rugby history, not only for scoring 11 tries and achieving a 41-6 points balance, but for the fluent way they played, embodying the closest yet to 15-man rugby.

Nine months after beating Ireland, virtually the same Welsh side beat the touring All Blacks in their legendary encounter at Cardiff Arms Park. The fact that the best side in Britain had beaten the best from overseas may have been an indication of the greatness of the Wales side of 1905: more to the point was that Wales, like the other Championship sides, were not fooled by the result. The British game, by and large, was many years behind in development, the style of play demonstrated by the All Blacks.

WALES v ENGLAND   21/120

14 January 1905
Cardiff Arms Park
Wales 25 (2G, 5T) England 0

Wales T: Morgan (2), Gabe, Harding, Dick Jones, Llewellyn, Watkins. C: Davies (2).

This was England's biggest losing points margin in any Championship match until it was equalled by the 12-37 defeat by France in 1972. It was also the greatest number of tries registered against England until Wales scored eight on the same ground in 1922. England had now lost seven matches to Wales in a row.

WALES   G. Davies 7 (Swansea); *W.M. Llewellyn 17 (Newport), D. Rees 4 (Swansea), R.T. Gabe 11 (Cardiff), E.T. Morgan 8 (London Welsh); Dick Jones 6 (Swansea), R.M. Owen 11 (Swansea); W. Joseph 9 (Swansea), G. Travers 4 (Pill Harriers), W. Neill 3 (Cardiff), A.F. Harding 10 (London Welsh), D. Jones 7 (Treherbert), J.J. Hodges 17 (Newport), H. Watkins 3 (Llanelli), C.M. Pritchard 2 (Newport).

ENGLAND   S.H. Irvin (1) (Devonport Albion); F.H. Palmer (1) (Richmond), E.W. Dillon (4) (Blackheath), J.E. Raphael 4 (Oxford U.), S.F. Coopper 4 (Blackheath); F.C. Hulme 3 (Birkenhead Park), W.V. Butcher 5 (Bristol); *F.M. Stout 12 (Richmond), C.J. Newbold 4 (Blackheath), J.L. Mathias 1 (Bristol), W.L.Y. Rogers 1 (Blackheath), B.A. Hill 5 (Blackheath), T.A. Gibson 1 (Northern), W.T.C. Cave (1) (Blackheath), V.H. Cartwright 6 (Oxford U.).

Referee J. Lefevre (Ireland)

SCOTLAND v WALES 21/121

4 February 1905
Inverleith, Edinburgh
Wales 6 (2T) Scotland 3 (1T)

Scotland T: Little.
Wales T: Llewellyn (2).

Wales gained their first victory at Inverleith thanks to two well-taken tries by Willie Llewellyn, and were thus firmly on their way to winning the Championship for the third time since 1900. Scotland were led for the first time by W.P. Scott, who had the unenviable task of taking over from the formidable Mark Morrison. When Morrison gave up playing international rugby in 1904, he had guided Scotland to three Championship wins and two Triple Crowns.

The story goes that Scott, leading one of Scotland's famous foot-rushes, booted Rhys Gabe in the backside when the Wales centre dived in to try to check the drive. Schoolmaster Gabe may have saved a score, but for six months he could not sit down properly, even having to take his classes at school standing up.

SCOTLAND W.T. Forrest 7 (Hawick); J.S. Macdonald (5) (Edinburgh U.), J.L. Forbes 1 (Watsonians), L.M. MacLeod 4 (Cambridge U.), J.E. Crabbie (6) (Oxford U.); P. Munro 1 (Oxford U.), E.D. Simson 8 (Edinburgh U.); A.G. Cairns 7 (Watsonians), H.N. Fletcher (2) (Edinburgh U.), W.E. Kyle 10 (Hawick), A.W. Little (1) (Hawick), W.M. Milne 3 (Glasgow Acads), A. Ross 1 (Royal HSFP), *W.P. Scott 11 (W. of Scotland), R.S. Stronach 3 (Glasgow Acads).

WALES G. Davies 8 (Swansea); *W.M. Llewellyn 18 (Newport), D. Rees (5) (Swansea), R.T. Gabe 12 (Cardiff), E.T. Morgan 9 (London Welsh); W.J. Trew 7 (Swansea), R.M. Owen 12 (Swansea); W. Joseph 10 (Swansea), G. Travers 5 (Pill Harriers), W. Neill 4 (Cardiff), A.F. Harding 11 (London Welsh), D. Jones 8 (Treherbert), C.M. Pritchard 3 (Newport), J.J. Hodges 18 (Newport), H. Watkins 4 (Llanelli).

Referee H. Kennedy (Ireland)

IRELAND v ENGLAND 21/122

11 February 1905
Mardyke, Cork
Ireland 17 (1G, 4T) England 3 (1T)

Ireland T: Moffatt (2), Allen, Maclear, Wallace. C: Maclear.
England T: Coopper.

Basil Maclear, rejected by England for being 'not good enough', played instead for Ireland by the qualification of living in Cork. It was in his adopted city that Maclear made his Irish début, ironically against England, and by all accounts played a marvellous match, making two tries and scoring one. 'He was,' wrote Sean Diffley in *The Men in Green* (Pelham), 'a most fastidious looking character who often wore spotlessly white gloves on the field of play. This eccentricity, however, did not conceal some very fine football ability. He was very fast and dashing, possessed a good swerve and was a noted tackler.' Maclear was one of eight Irish international players to be killed in the First World War.

IRELAND M.F. Landers 2 (Cork Constitution); J.E. Moffatt 2 (Old Wesley), B. Maclear 1 (Cork County), G.A.D. Harvey 4 (Wanderers), H.B. Thrift 2 (Dublin U.); T.T.H. Robinson 3 (Dublin U.), E.D. Caddell 2 (Dublin U.); *C.E. Allen 12 (Derry), J.J. Coffey 9 (Lansdowne), A. Tedford 10 (Malone), H.G. Wilson 1 (Malone), G.T. Hamlet 9 (Old Wesley), H.J. Knox 2 (Dublin U.), Jos Wallace 6 (Wanderers), H.J. Millar 2 (Monkstown).

ENGLAND C.F. Stanger-Leathes (1) (Northern); S.F. Coopper 5 (Blackheath), A.T. Brettargh 7 (Liverpool OB), H.E. Shewring 1 (Bristol), T. Simpson 7 (Rockcliff); F.C. Hulme (4) (Birkenhead Park), W.V. Butcher 6 (Bristol); *F.M. Stout 13 (Richmond), C.J. Newbold 5 (Blackheath), J.L. Mathias 2 (Bristol), W.L.Y. Rogers (2) (Blackheath), W.M. Grylls (1) (Redruth), G. Vickery (1) (Aberavon), J. Green 1 (Skipton), V.H. Cartwright 7 (Oxford U.).

Referee R. Welsh (Scotland)

SCOTLAND v IRELAND   23/123

25 February 1905
Inverleith, Edinburgh
Ireland 11 (1G, 2T) Scotland 5 (1G)

Scotland   T: Timms. C: Forrest.
Ireland   T: Tedford, Wallace, Moffatt. C: Maclear.

This was Ireland's second victory in 12 visits to Scotland. Scotland, who had axed three players after their defeat by Wales earlier in the month, ended the Championship careers of another five.

SCOTLAND   W.T. Forrest (8) (Hawick); W.T. Ritchie 1 (Cambridge U.), L.M. MacLeod (5) (Cambridge U.), A.B. Timms 13 (Cardiff), R.H. McCowat (1) (Glasgow Acads); E.D. Simson 9 (Edinburgh U.), P. Munro 2 (Oxford U.); A.G. Cairns 8 (Watsonians), M.R. Dickson (1) (Edinburgh U.), W.E. Kyle 11 (Hawick), W.M. Milne (4) (Glasgow Acads), A. Ross 2 (Royal HSFP), *W.P. Scott 12 (W. of Scotland), R.S. Stronach 4 (Glasgow Acads), L. West 4 (Carlisle).

Teddy Morgan, the London Welsh threequarter who scored 3 of Wales's 11 tries in 1905

IRELAND   M.F. Landers 3 (Cork Constitution); J.E. Moffatt 3 (Old Wesley), B. Maclear 2 (Cork County), G.A.D. Harvey (5) (Wanderers), H. Thrift 3 (Dublin U.); T.T.H. Robinson 4 (Dublin U.), E.D. Caddell 3 (Dublin U.); *C.E. Allen 13 (Derry), J.J. Coffey 10 (Lansdowne), G.T. Hamlet 10 (Old Wesley), H.J. Knox 3 (Dublin U.), H.J. Millar 3 (Monkstown), A. Tedford 11 (Malone), Jos Wallace 7 (Wanderers), H.G. Wilson 2 (Malone).

Referee P. Cole (England)

WALES v IRELAND   19/124

11 March 1905
St Helen's, Swansea
Wales 10 (2G) Ireland 3 (1T)

Wales   T: Wyndham Jones, Morgan. C: Davies (2).
Ireland   T: Robinson.

With both sides having beaten England and Scotland, for the first time this Wales-Ireland match had the added incentive of the Triple Crown. Wales won thus providing Willie Llewellyn, along with George Davies and Wyndham Jones, a fitting climax to their Championship careers. George Davies had scored the only try in Wales's 1900 Triple Crown victory over Ireland.

WALES   G. Davies (9) (Swansea); *W.M. Llewellyn (19) (Newport), E.G. Nicholls 19 (Cardiff), R.T. Gabe 13 (Cardiff), E.T. Morgan 10 (London Welsh); W. Jones (1) (Mountain Ash), R.M. Owen 13 (Swansea); W. Joseph 11 (Swansea), G. Travers 6 (Pill Harriers), W. Neill 5 (Cardiff), A.F. Harding 12 (London Welsh), J.F. Williams 1 (London Welsh), J.J. Hodges 19 (Newport), D. Jones 9 (Treherbert), H. Watkins 5 (Llanelli).

IRELAND   M.F. Landers (4) (Cork Constitution); H.B. Thrift 4 (Dublin U.), J.C. Parke 5 (Dublin U.), B. Maclear 3 (Monkstown), J.E. Moffatt (4) (Old Wesley); T.T.H. Robinson 5 (Dublin U.), E.D. Caddell 4 (Dublin U.); *C.E. Allen 14 (Derry), J.J. Coffey 11 (Lansdowne), G.T. Hamlet 11 (Old Wesley), H.G. Wilson 3 (Malone), A. Tedford 12 (Malone), H.J. Knox 4 (Dublin U.), H.J. Millar (4) (Monkstown), Jos Wallace 8 (Wanderers).

Referee W. Williams (England)

ENGLAND v SCOTLAND   20/125

18 March 1905
Athletic Ground, Richmond
Scotland 8 (1G, 1T) England 0

Scotland   T: Simson, Stronach. C: Scott.

The international début of Adrian Stoop was hardly an auspicious occasion for England. Even though England employed him sparingly for the next four years, the Harlequin established himself as one of the great architects of back play. Some even credited him with the idea that each half-back should have his own identity and clearly defined functions; in other words that one should work the scrummage and the other should develop the play. Altogether he played in 12 Championship games and was on the winning side in half of those: hardly the statistics associated with a wonder player, but Stoop's greatness chiefly lay in his ability to show others what could be done. Scotland, whose only win of the season this was, did not select four members of their side again, including the captain, A.B. Timms, who had won 14 caps, and G.A.W. Lamond, who had been recalled six years after winning his first cap.

ENGLAND   J.T. Taylor (11) (West Hartlepool); S.F. Coopper 6 (Blackheath), A.T. Brettargh (8) (Liverpool OB), J.E. Raphael 5 (Oxford U.), T. Simpson 8 (Rockcliff); A.D. Stoop 1 (Oxford U.), W.V. Butcher (7) (Bristol); *F.M. Stout (14) (Richmond), J.G. Milton 4 (Camborne School of Mines), C.J. Newbold (6) (Blackheath), C.E.L. Hammond 1 (Harlequins), J.L. Mathias (3) (Bristol), S.H. Osborne (1) (Harlequins), T.A. Gibson (2) (Northern), V.H. Cartwright 8 (Oxford U.).

SCOTLAND   D.G. Schulze 1 (London Scottish); W.T. Ritchie (2) (Cambridge U.), G.A.W. Lamond (3) (Bristol), *A.B. Timms (14) (Cardiff), T. Elliot (1) (Gala); E.D. Simson 10 (Edinburgh U.), P. Munro 3 (Oxford U.); A.G. Cairns 9 (Watsonians), W.E. Kyle 12 (Hawick), J.C. MacCallum 1 (Watsonians), H.G. Monteith 1 (Cambridge U.), A. Ross 3 (Royal HSFP), W.P. Scott 13 (W. of Scotland), R.S. Stronach (5) (Glasgow Acads), L. West 5 (Carlisle).

Referee D.H. Bowen (Wales)

RICHMOND Wales beat England 16-3 · CARDIFF Wales beat Scotland 9-3
LEICESTER Ireland beat England 16-6 · DUBLIN Scotland beat Ireland 13-6
BELFAST Ireland beat Wales 11-6 · EDINBURGH England beat Scotland 9-3
Non-Championship match: PARIS England beat France 35-8

CHAMPIONSHIP TABLE
Ireland – Championship

								Tries	
Pos Country	P	W	D	L	F	A	Pts	F	A
1 Ireland (2)	3	2	0	1	33	25	4	9	6
2 Wales (1)	3	2	0	1	31	17	4	9	4
3 Scotland (3)	3	1	0	2	19	24	2	3	8
4 England (4)	3	1	0	2	18	35	2	6	9

The Championship was more of a footnote than the main chapter of the 1906 season, because it took place after the most momentous event in the history of British rugby – the First All Blacks tour. The New Zealanders arrived in September 1905 and by the time they left to play France in Paris on 1 January 1906, the shock waves had been felt throughout Britain. It was not merely that the All Blacks had lost just one match on a fabulous tour – against Wales – but they had shown a form of rugby, in concept and execution, the like of which no one had seen before. It was as if a new game had been invented, which of course it was, when compared with the way the game had developed in Britain. In summary, the New Zealand game consisted of teamwork beyond comparison, fitness, inventiveness in tactical play, and most important, specialist forward play all the way through from prop to flanker.

That British teams could not cope with the All Black steamroller is hardly surprising. That the international teams, or nearly all of them, set about adapting and adopting the new methods and approach, was surprising for at the time there was probably not a more conservative sport in Britain than rugby. Change had been gradual, with the game meandering rather than developing and more squabbling over the minutiae of the Laws than discussion as to how the game could be improved. Some of the tactics and deployments were introduced for the 1906 Championship: Wales, for instance, adopted a seven-man pack for the England game; appointed a specialist hooker; tried to effect a solid, fluent scrummaging technique; and attempted planned moves behind the scrum, which may not all have been rooted in All Black rugby style, but at least expressed an eagerness to adapt. The consequence: England, who had not shown themselves as being so flexible, were completely overpowered at Richmond. Ireland, too, changed their line-up, played seven forwards and a 'flyer', and also beat England, 16-6 at Leicester. Wales struggled to beat Scotland and then, with an erratic return to their former style of playing, went down without a whimper to Ireland in Belfast.

That the All Blacks had changed the British game was unquestionable: that it was ready for yet another shock, in the shape of the First Springboks, who came touring later in 1906, it was not. The South Africans, different again from the New Zealanders, set new standards in fitness, physique, blistering pace fore and aft and straight, hard running. The combination left Ireland and Wales beaten and disillusioned; England thankful and lucky with a draw; and Scotland, who beat them, the only country with any pride at all.

Other changes had taken place by now. Bouncing the ball in from touch and the Field Goal had been abolished. The value of a goal from a mark was three points, from four, which was, incidentally, the last change in scoring values for 42 years. In the Championship itself, England lost their sixth match in succession, their longest losing sequence until 1971–73 when they lost seven in a row.

ENGLAND v WALES   22/126

13 January 1906
Athletic Ground, Richmond
Wales 16 (2G, 2T) England 3 (1T)

England   T: Hudson.
Wales   T: Hodges, Maddocks, Morgan, Charlie Pritchard. C: Winfield (2).

Wales fielded seven backs, a rover in Cliff Pritchard, and seven forwards. Equally important to the game's development was the introduction of a pack with players in allotted positions, notably in the front row where they had a distinguishable hooker in George Travers and two props. Pritchard's role was curious and reports criticized him for cluttering up the midfield. England, who had come in to this match after five-try drubbing by New Zealand, displayed nothing new, except ten players whose first international this was.

ENGLAND   E.J. Jackett 1 (Falmouth); A. Hudson 1 (Gloucester), H.E. Shewring 2 (Bristol), J.E. Raphael 6 (OMT), A.E. Hind (1) (Leicester); D.R. Gent 1 (Gloucester), R.A. Jago 1 (Devonport Albion); H.A. Hodges 1 (Nottingham), A.L. Kewney 1 (Rockcliff), *V.H. Cartwright 9 (Nottingham), C.E.L. Hammond 2 (Harlequins), T.S. Kelly 1 (Exeter), E.W. Roberts 3 (RNEC Keyham), W.A. Mills 1 (Devonport Albion), G.E.B. Dobbs 1 (Devonport Albion).

WALES   H.B. Winfield 5 (Cardiff); H.T. Maddocks 1 (London Welsh), *E.G. Nicholls 20 (Cardiff), R.T. Gabe 14 (Cardiff), E.T. Morgan 11 (London Welsh); P.F. Bush 1 (Cardiff), R.M. Owen 14 (Swansea); C.C. Pritchard 3 (Pontypool); W. Joseph 12 (Swansea), G. Travers 7 (Pill Harriers), H. Watkins (6) (Llanelli), A.F. Harding 13 (London Welsh), D. Jones 10 (Treherbert), J.J. Hodges 20 (Newport), C.M. Pritchard 4 (Newport).

Referee A. Jardine (Scotland)

WALES v SCOTLAND   22/127

3 February 1906
Cardiff Arms Park
Wales 9 (3T) Scotland 3 (1PG)

Wales   T: Hodges, Cliff Pritchard, Maddocks.
Scotland   PG: MacLeod.

The Welsh experiment of playing seven forwards, first tried against England in January, with George Travers as a specialized hooker, was deemed not a success, despite their victory. They played two outside-halves, Billy Trew and Reggie Gibbs, and media criticism of Trew's performance seemed carping, considering that the Swansea player was one of the most gifted backs ever to play for Wales: 'easily the finest rugby player I ever saw', wrote the highly-respected Dai Gent in 1932; while Rhys Gabe declared him: 'the most complete footballer who ever played for Wales'.

WALES   H.B. Winfield 6 (Cardiff); H.T. Maddocks 2 (London Welsh), *E.G. Nicholls 21 (Cardiff), C.C. Pritchard (4) (Pontypool), E.T. Morgan 12 (London Welsh); W.J. Trew 8 (Swansea), R.A. Gibbs 1 (Cardiff); R.M. Owen 15 (Swansea); W. Joseph 13 (Swansea), G. Travers 8 (Pill Harriers), D. Jones (11) (Treherbert), A.F. Harding 14 (London Welsh), J.F. Williams (2) (London Welsh), C.M. Pritchard 5 (Newport), J.J. Hodges 21 (Newport).

SCOTLAND   J.G. Scoular 1 (Cambridge U.); W.C. Church (1) (Glasgow Acads), T. Sloan 1 (Glasgow Acads), K.G. MacLeod 1 (Cambridge U.), A.B.H.L. Purves 1 (London Scottish); E.D. Simson 11 (Edinburgh U.), P. Munro 4 (Oxford U.); D.R. Bedell-Sivright 13 (Edinburgh U.), A.G. Cairns 10 (Watsonians), W.E. Kyle 13 (Hawick), J.C. MacCallum 2 (Watsonians), H.G. Monteith 2 (Cambridge U.), W.L. Russell 1 (Glasgow Acads), W.P. Scott 14 (W. of Scotland), *L. West 6 (Hartlepool Rovers).

Referee J.W. Allen (Ireland)

ENGLAND v IRELAND 22/128

10 February 1906
Welford Road, Leicester
Ireland 16 (2G, 2T) England 6 (2T)

England T: Jago, Mills.
Ireland T: Tedford (2), Maclear, Purdon. C: Gardiner, Maclear.

Ireland played seven forwards and used Basil Maclear as a rover. That the experiment was successful was reflected in the quality of victory. It was Ireland's highest score against England for an away match until 1964 when they scored 18 points. Five England players, including the three newcomers in the backs, did not play again.

ENGLAND E.J. Jackett 2 (Falmouth); A. Hudson 2 (Gloucester), C.H. Milton (1) (Camborne School of Mines), J.R.P. Sandford (1) (Marlbrough Nomads), J.E. Hutchinson (1) (Durham City); D.R. Gent 2 (Gloucester), R.A. Jago 2 (Devonport Albion); C.E.L. Hammond 3 (Harlequins), *V.H. Cartwright 10 (Nottingham), H.A. Hodges (2) (Nottingham), T.S. Kelly 2 (Exeter), W.A. Mills 2 (Devonport Albion), A.L. Kewney 2 (Rockcliff), E.W. Roberts 4 (RNEC Keyham), G.E.B. Dobbs (2) (Devonport Albion).

IRELAND G.J. Henebrey 1 (Garryowen); J.C. Parke 6 (Dublin U.), H.B. Thrift 5 (Dublin U.), F. Casement 1 (Dublin U.), H.J. Anderson 3 (Old Wesley); B. Maclear 4 (Monkstown); E.D. Cad-dell 5 (Dublin U.), W.B. Purdon 1 (Queen's U. Belfast); F. Gardiner 13 (NIFC), *C.E. Allen 15 (Derry), A. Tedford 13 (Malone), J.J. Coffey 12 (Lansdowne), H.G. Wilson 4 (Malone), H.J. Knox 5 (Lansdowne), M. White 1 (Queen's C. Cork).

Referee A. Llewellyn (Wales)

IRELAND v SCOTLAND 24/129

24 February 1906
Lansdowne Road, Dublin
Scotland 13 (2G, 1GM) Ireland 6 (2T)

Ireland T: Parke, Robb.
Scotland T: Bedell-Sivright, Munro. C: MacCallum (2). GM: MacLeod.

M.W. Walter, the London Scottish back, made his first appearance for Scotland after turning down a chance to play for England against Ireland on 10 February. Ireland, pleased with the performance of the seven-man pack using Basil Maclear as a rover in the win over England in that match, repeated the experimental lineup. Its failure against Scotland was heavily criticized, and Ireland reverted to eight forwards for the next match, against Wales.

IRELAND G.J. Henebrey 2 (Garryowen); C.G. Robb (4) (Queen's U. Belfast), J.C. Parke 7 (Dublin U.), F. Casement 2 (Dublin U.), H.J. Anderson (4) (Old Wesley); B. Maclear 5 (Monkstown); W.B. Purdon 2 (Queen's U. Bel-

Ireland convert a try in the England-Ireland match on 10 February 1906

fast), E.D. Caddell 6 (Dublin U.); *C.E. Allen 16 (Derry), J.J. Coffey 13 (Lansdowne), F. Gardiner 14 (NIFC), H.J. Knox 6 (Lansdowne), A. Tedford 14 (Malone), M. White 2 (Queen's C. Cork), H.G. Wilson 5 (Malone).

SCOTLAND   J.G. Scoular 2 (Cambridge U.); K.G. MacLeod 2 (Cambridge U.), J.L. Forbes 2 (Watsonians), M.W. Walter 1 (London Scottish), A.B.H.L. Purves 2 (London Scottish); E.D. Simson 12 (Edinburgh U.), P. Munro 5 (Oxford U.); D.R. Bedell-Sivright 14 (Edinburgh U.), A.G. Cairns 11 (Watsonians), K.E. Kyle 14 (Hawick), J.C. MacCallum 3 (Watsonians), H.G. Monteith 3 (London Scottish), W.L. Russell 2 (Glasgow Acads), W.P. Scott 15 (W. of Scotland), *L. West 7 (London Scottish).

Referee V.H. Cartwright (England)

IRELAND v WALES   20/130

10 March 1906
Balmoral Showgrounds, Belfast
Ireland 11 (1G, 2T) Wales 6 (2T)

Ireland T: Thrift, Wallace, Maclear. C: Gardiner.
Wales T: Morgan, Gabe.

Wales were thwarted in their attempt to win another Triple Crown by a remarkable performance by Ireland, who were reduced to 13 players towards the end after the loss of Ernie Caddell with a broken leg and Willie Purdon with torn knee ligaments. The Welsh defeat had its repercussions: long-standing personalities such as Teddy Morgan, Gwyn Nicholls, the captain, Will Joseph and Jehoida Hodges, did not play again in the Championship and two other members of the pack were not selected again.

IRELAND   G.J. Henebrey 3 (Garryowen); B. Maclear 6 (Monkstown), J.C. Parke 8 (Dublin U.), F. Casement (3) (Dublin U.), H.B. Thrift 6 (Dublin U.); E.D. Caddell 7 (Dublin U.), W.B. Purdon (3) (Queen's U. Belfast); F. Gardiner 15 (NIFC), *C.E. Allen 17 (Derry), H.J. Knox 7 (Lansdowne), J.J. Coffey 14 (Lansdowne), A. Tedford 15 (Malone), H.G. Wilson 6 (Malone), M. White 3 (Queen's C. Cork), Jos Wallace (9) (Wanderers).

WALES   H.B. Winfield 7 (Cardiff); E.T. Morgan (13) (London Welsh), *E.G. Nicholls (22) (Cardiff), R.T. Gabe 15 (Cardiff), H.T. Maddocks 3 (London Welsh); R.A. Gibbs 2 (Cardiff), R.M. Owen 16 (Swansea); W. Joseph (14) (Swansea), G. Travers 9 (Pill Harriers), J. Powell (1) (Cardiff), D. Westacott (1) (Cardiff), J.J. Hodges (22) (Newport), C.M. Pritchard 6 (Newport), T. Evans 1 (Llanelli), A.F. Harding 15 (London Welsh).

Referee Dr J.W. Simpson (Scotland)

SCOTLAND v ENGLAND   21/131

17 March 1906
Inverleith, Edinburgh
England 9 (3T) Scotland 3 (1T)

Scotland T: Purves.
England T: Mills, Raphael, Simpson.

This was a contest for the Wooden Spoon, but though England outscored Scotland, they finished bottom because of overall inferior scoring. Adrian Stoop's influence was not yet bearing fruit.

SCOTLAND   J.G. Scoular (3) (Cambridge U.); K.G. MacLeod 3 (Cambridge U.), J.L. Forbes (3) (Watsonians), M.W. Walter 2 (London Scottish), A.B.H.L. Purves 3 (London Scottish); E.D. Simson 13 (Edinburgh U.), P. Munro 6 (Oxford U.); D.R. Bedell-Sivright 15 (Edinburgh U.), A.G. Cairns (12) (Watsonians), W.E. Kyle 15 (Hawick), J.C. MacCallum 4 (Watsonians), H.G. Monteith 4 (London Scottish), W.L. Russell (3) (Glasgow Acads), W.P. Scott 16 (W. of Scotland), *L. West (8) (London Scottish).

ENGLAND   E.J. Jackett 3 (Falmouth); J.E. Raphael (7) (OMT), H.E. Shewring 3 (Bristol), J.G.G. Birkett 1 (Harlequins), T. Simpson (9) (Rockcliff); J. Peters 1 (Plymouth), A.D. Stoop 2 (Harlequins); C.H. Shaw 1 (Moseley), A.L. Kewney 3 (Rockcliff), *V.H. Cartwright (11) (Nottingham), C.E.L. Hammond 4 (Harlequins), T.S. Kelly 3 (Exeter), J. Green 2 (Skipton), W.A. Mills 3 (Devonport Albion), R. Dibble 1 (Bridgwater Albion).

Referee J.W. Allen (Ireland)

SWANSEA Wales beat England 22-0 · EDINBURGH Scotland beat Wales 6-3
DUBLIN Ireland beat England 17-9 · EDINBURGH Scotland beat Ireland 15-3
CARDIFF Wales beat Ireland 29-0 · BLACKHEATH Scotland beat England 8-3
Non-Championship match: RICHMOND England beat France 41-13

CHAMPIONSHIP TABLE
Scotland – Championship, Triple Crown

Pos	Country	P	W	D	L	F	A	Pts	Tries F	A
1	Scotland (3)	3	3	0	0	29	9	6	7	1
2	Wales (2)	3	2	0	1	54	6	4	12	2
3	Ireland (1)	3	1	0	2	20	53	2	4	11
4	England (4)	3	0	0	3	12	47	0	3	12

Wales scored 54 points and 12 tries, yet still had to be content with being runners-up to Scotland, who won the Triple Crown for the fifth time. This put Scotland one ahead of Wales in taking the revered trophy, two ahead of England and three in front of Ireland. It was a bleak Championship for Ireland, whose defence conceded a record 53 points, and for England, Wooden Spoonists for a third year in succession. Another mark of the decline in England's fortunes: Wales, for the first time, led them in the number of victories, 11-10.

WALES v ENGLAND   23/132

12 January 1907
St Helen's, Swansea
Wales 22 (2G, 4T) England 0

Wales T: Maddocks (2), Williams (2), Brown, Gibbs. C: Gibbs (2).

After the humiliations suffered in the early matches against England, Wales had the satisfaction that this overwhelming victory placed them ahead in the Championship series between the countries, 11-10. Wales's idea of a rover had by now dissolved: instead they fielded an extra back, Reggie Gibbs. A week earlier England had scored nine tries against a French team playing its first game in Britain; but none of that scoring power was in evidence against Wales nor did reports hint of the genius to come of Adrian Stoop. But it is interesting to speculate what Stoop might have thought of the Welsh line-up in this his first match against them and how much if anything it influenced his own thinking and planning of midfield play in later years.

WALES D.B. Davies (1) (Llanelli); J.L. Williams 1 (Cardiff), R.T. Gabe 16 (Cardiff), J. Evans 1 (Pontypool), H.T. Maddocks 4 (London Welsh); R.A. Gibbs 3 (Cardiff); W.J. Trew 9 (Swansea), *R.M. Owen 17 (Swansea); W. Neill 6 (Cardiff), G. Travers 10 (Pill Harriers), J. Brown 1 (Cardiff), T. Evans 2 (Llanelli), J. Watts 1 (Llanelli), C.M. Pritchard 7 (Newport), W. Dowell 1 (Newport).

ENGLAND E.J. Jackett 4 (Falmouth); S.F. Cooper (7) (Blackheath), H.E. Shewring 4 (Bristol), J.G.G. Birkett 2 (Harlequins), F.S. Scott (1) (Bristol); A.D. Stoop 3 (Harlequins), R.A. Jago 3 (Devonport Albion); C.H. Shaw 2 (Moseley), L.A.N. Slocock 1 (Liverpool), T.S. Kelly 4 (Exeter), W.A. Mills 4 (Devonport Albion), J. Green 3 (Skipton), W.M.B. Nanson (1) (Carlisle), *B.A. Hill (6) (Blackheath), F.J.V. Hopley 1 (Blackheath).

Referee J.I. Gillespie (Scotland)

SCOTLAND v WALES   23/133

2 February 1907
Inverleith, Edinburgh
Scotland 6 (2T) Wales 3 (1PG)

Scotland   T: Purves, Monteith.
Wales   PG: Winfield.

David MacGregor, the Pontypridd back and captain, was one of the first players with dual qualifications to be faced with the problem for whom he should play. Born in Pontypridd of a Scottish father and educated at Watson's College in Edinburgh, MacGregor returned to Wales to establish himself in the Pontypridd side. Wales picked him as a reserve for this match having seen him play well for Watsonians against Newport in December. They could hardly have been surprised when MacGregor decided to play for Scotland instead, blood loyalty being rewarded with further caps against Ireland and England and, of course, the honour of playing in a Triple Crown winning side.

SCOTLAND   T. Sloan 2 (Glasgow Acads); K.G. MacLeod 4 (Cambridge U.), D.G. MacGregor 1 (Pontypridd), M.W. Walter 3 (London Scottish), A.B.H.L. Purves 4 (London Scottish); E.D. Simson 14 (London Scottish), *L.L. Greig 1 (US Portsmouth); D.R. Bedell-Sivright 16 (Edinburgh U.), G.M. Frew 1 (Glasgow HSFP), I.C. Geddes 1 (London Scottish), J.C. MacCallum 5 (Watsonians), H.G. Monteith 5 (London Scottish), G.A. Sanderson 1 (Royal HSFP), W.P. Scott 17 (W. of Scotland), L.M. Spiers 1 (Watsonians).

WALES   H.B. Winfield 8 (Cardiff); J.L. Williams 2 (Cardiff), R.T. Gabe 17 (Cardiff), J. Evans 2 (Pontypool), H.T. Maddocks 5 (London Welsh); R.A. Gibbs 4 (Cardiff); *W.J. Trew 10 (Swansea), R.M. Owen 18 (Swansea); J. Webb 1 (Abertillery), G. Travers 11 (Pill Harriers), J. Watts 2 (Llanelli), T. Evans 3 (Llanelli), C.M. Pritchard 8 (Newport), W. Dowell 2 (Newport), J. Brown 2 (Cardiff).

Referee J. Lefevre (Ireland)

IRELAND v ENGLAND   23/134

9 February 1907
Lansdowne Road, Dublin
Ireland 17 (1G, 3T, 1GM) England 9 (2T, 1PG)

Ireland   T: Caddell (2), Tedford, Thrift. C: Parke. GM: Parke.
England   T: Imrie, Slocock. PG: Pickering.

After their six-try slaughtering from Wales in January, England rang the changes in their team. It still did not prevent Ireland running in four tries and scoring their sixth success in a row at home.

IRELAND   C. Thompson 1 (NIFC); H.B. Thrift 7 (Dublin U.), J.C. Parke 9 (Dublin U.), T.J. Greeves 1 (NIFC), B. Maclear 7 (Monkstown); E.D. Caddell 8 (Wanderers), T.T.H. Robinson 6 (Wanderers); *A. Tedford 16 (Malone), G.T. Hamlet 12 (Old Wesley), J.J. Coffey 15 (Lansdowne), H.G. Wilson 7 (Malone), J.A. Sweeney 1 (Blackrock College), R.E. Forbes (1) (Malone), W.St J. Cogan 1 (Queen's C. Cork), M. White 4 (Queen's C. Cork).

ENGLAND   E.J. Jackett 5 (Falmouth); W.C. Wilson 1 (Richmond), H.E. Shewring 5 (Bristol), A.S. Pickering (1) (Harrogate), H.M. Imrie (1) (Durham City); J. Peters 2 (Plymouth), R.A. Jago (4) (Devonport Albion); C.H. Shaw 3 (Moseley), L.A.N. Slocock 2 (Liverpool), T.S. Kelly 5 (Exeter), W.A. Mills 5 (Devonport Albion), *J. Green 4 (Skipton), J.G. Milton (5) (Camborne School of Mines), G. Leather (1) (Liverpool), S.G. Williams 6 (Devonport Albion).

Referee J.T. Tulloch (Scotland)

SCOTLAND v IRELAND 25/135

23 February 1907
Inverleith, Edinburgh
Scotland 15 (3G) Ireland 3 (1PG)

Scotland T: Sanderson, Purves, Frew. C: Mac-
Leod, Geddes (2).
Ireland PG: Parke.

The honour of kicking Ireland's first penalty
goal against Scotland fell to Jim Parke, the Dublin University centre, who was to distinguish
himself in many other sports. A more typical
Irish hero was Basil Maclear, whose bone-
shaking hand-off of Darkie Bedell-Sivright ren-
dered the large, formidable Scottish forward
unconscious, needing a touch-line recovery:
precursor perhaps of the more famous clash
between Haydn Mainwaring and Avril Malan in
the Barbarians v South Africa match of 1961.

SCOTLAND D.G. Schulze 2 (London Scottish);
A.B.H.L. Purves 5 (London Scottish), M.W.
Walter 4 (London Scottish), D.G. MacGregor 2
(Pontypridd), K.G. MacLeod 5 (Cambridge U.);
E.D. Simson 15 (London Scottish), *P. Munro 7
(London Scottish); D.R. Bedell-Sivright 17
(Edinburgh U.), G.M. Frew 2 (Glasgow HSFP),
I.C. Geddes 2 (London Scottish), J.C. MacCallum
6 (Watsonians), H.G. Monteith 6 (London Scot-
tish), G.A. Sanderson 2 (Royal HSFP), W.P. Scott
18 (W. of Scotland), L.M. Spiers 2 (Watsonians).

IRELAND C. Thompson 2 (Belfast Collegians);
H.B. Thrift 8 (Dublin U.), J.C. Parke 10 (Dublin
U.), T.J. Greeves 2 (NIFC), B. Maclear 8 (Monks-
town); T.T.H. Robinson 7 (Wanderers), E.D.
Caddell 9 (Wanderers); *C.E. Allen 18 (Derry),
W.St J. Cogan (2) (Queen's C. Cork), F. Gardiner
16 (NIFC), G.T. Hamlet 13 (Old Wesley), H.S.
Sugars (1) (Royal HSFP), J.A. Sweeney 2 (Black-
rock College), A. Tedford 17 (Malone), H.G.
Wilson 8 (Malone).

Referee A.O. Jones (England)

WALES v IRELAND 21/136

9 March 1907
Cardiff Arms Park
Wales 29 (2G, 4T, 1DG, 1PG) Ireland 0

Wales T: Williams (3), Jones, Gabe, Bush. C:
Winfield (2). DG: Bush. PG: Winfield.

This was Wales's biggest winning points margin
against Ireland in the Championship, and it was
achieved against a back-drop of controversy in
the Principality. Billy Trew, Wales's captain,
was selected but refused to play in protest
against the WRU suspension of his Swansea
club-mate, Fred Scrine, for improper language
to a referee. Percy Bush, of Cardiff, took Trew's
place, and produced a remarkable performance:
he scored a try and a dropped goal, and featured
in four other tries. Bush kept his place for the
next match, against England, and Trew, his
point made, returned in the centre. The Irish
considered changes were necessary: Basil Maclear, their highly-talented centre, and the captain, Charlie Allen were discarded.

WALES H.B. Winfield 9 (Cardiff); D.P. Jones (1)
(Pontypool), J. Evans (3) (Pontypool), *R.T.
Gabe 18 (Cardiff), J.L. Williams 3 (Cardiff); P.F.
Bush 2 (Cardiff), R.J. David (1) (Cardiff); G.
Travers 12 (Pill Harriers), W. Neill 7 (Cardiff), J.
Brown 3 (Cardiff), T. Evans 4 (Llanelli), J. Watts
3 (Llanelli), W. Dowell 3 (Newport), C.M. Prit-
chard 9 (Newport), A.F. Harding 16 (London
Welsh).

IRELAND W.P. Hinton 1 (Old Wesley); B. Mac-
lear (9) (Monkstown), T.J. Greeves 3 (NIFC), J.C.
Parke 11 (Dublin U.), H.B. Thrift 9 (Dublin U.);
F.M.W. Harvey 1 (Wanderers), T.T.H. Robinson
(8) (Wanderers); *C.E. Allen (19) (Derry), A.
Tedford 18 (Malone), H.G. Wilson 9 (Malone),
J.A. Sweeney (3) (Blackrock College), F. Gar-
diner 17 (NIFC), G.T. Hamlet 14 (Old Wesley),
M. White (5) (Queen's C. Cork), H.J. Knox 8
(Lansdowne).

Referee F.W. Marsh (England)

ENGLAND v SCOTLAND   22/137

16 March 1907
Rectory Field, Blackheath
Scotland 8 (1G, 1T) England 3 (1T)

England   T: Peters.
Scotland   T: Purves, Simson. C: Geddes.

Scotland, who in November had scored a two tries to nil victory over South Africa, made the season one of the most memorable in their history by going on to win the Triple Crown. It was an auspicious season, too, for A.B.H.L. Purves; he scored a try in all three matches. While the Scots had plenty to celebrate England were in despair: this was their third defeat of the year and the sixth time in nine seasons that they finished bottom of the table. Eight of their players bade farewell to international rugby, while Scotland also changed the old order somewhat by ending the Championship careers of the London Scottish half-back E.D. Simson and West of Scotland forward W.P. Scott, who had won 35 caps between them.

ENGLAND   E.J. Jackett 6 (Falmouth); W.C. Wilson (2) (Richmond), H.E. Shewring (6) (Bristol), J.G.G. Birkett 3 (Harlequins), A.W. Newton (1) (Blackheath); J. Peters 3 (Plymouth), S.P. Start (1) (US Portsmouth); C.H. Shaw (4) (Moseley), L.A.N. Slocock 3 (Liverpool), T.S. Kelly 6 (Exeter), W.A. Mills 6 (Devonport Albion), J. Green (5) (Skipton), *E.W. Roberts (5) (RNEC Keyham), G.D. Roberts 1 (Oxford U.), S.G. Williams (7) (Devonport Albion).

SCOTLAND   D.G. Schulze 3 (London Scottish); A.B.H.L. Purves 6 (London Scottish), T. Sloan 3 (Glasgow Acads), D.G. MacGregor (3) (Pontypridd), K.G. Macleod 6 (Cambridge U.); *P. Munro 8 (London Scottish), E.D. Simson (16) (London Scottish); D.R. Bedell-Sivright 18 (Edinburgh U.), G.M. Frew 3 (Glasgow HSFP), I.C. Geddes 3 (London Scottish), J.C. MacCallum 7 (Watsonians), G.A. Sanderson 3 (Royal HSFP), J.M.B. Scott 1 (Edinburgh Acads), W.P. Scott (19) (W. of Scotland), L.M. Spiers 3 (Watsonians).

Referee T.D. Schofield (Wales)

1908

BRISTOL Wales beat England 28-18 · SWANSEA Wales beat Scotland 6-5
RICHMOND England beat Ireland 13-3 · DUBLIN Ireland beat Scotland 16-11
BELFAST Wales beat Ireland 11-5 · EDINBURGH Scotland beat England 16-10
Non-Championship matches:
PARIS England beat France 19-0 · CARDIFF Wales beat France 36-4

CHAMPIONSHIP TABLE
Wales – Championship, Triple Crown

| | | | | | | | | | Tries | |
Pos	Country	P	W	D	L	F	A	Pts	F	A
1	Wales (2)	3	3	0	0	45	28	6	10	6
2	England (4)	3	1	0	2	41	47	2	9	7
3	Scotland (1)	3	1	0	2	32	32	2	5	8
4	Ireland (3)	3	1	0	2	24	35	2	5	8

Another milestone in the history of the Championship was the scoring of 142 points, a record aggregate for a four-nation tournament which has been bettered only once, when 176 points were scored in 1938. Four tries, sometimes five, were now commonplace in each game. The increase in try-scoring produced a corresponding rise in the number of conversions: the age of the specialized place-kicker had dawned. However, penalty goals had not yet become an overriding obsession with either kickers or referees, possibly because referees were often interpreting the game within its spirit rather than responding to the letter of the Law.

It must also be remembered that at the time the Laws were riddled with ambiguity, and interpretations varied from area to area. Not until 1911 did the International Board seek to end some of the anomalies, when they issued a missive to players and referees: 'with a view to securing uniformity of Rulings', (c.f. 1925 Championship introduction).

ENGLAND v WALES 24/138

18 January 1908
Ashton Gate, Bristol
Wales 28 (3G, 2T, 1DG, 1PG) England 18 (3G, 1T)

England T: Birkett (2), Lapage, Williamson. C: Wood (2), Roberts.
Wales T: Gabe (2), Bush, Gibbs, Trew. C: Winfield (2), Bush. DG: Bush. PG: Winfield.

R.H. Williamson, of Oxford University, is credited by some as England's first specialized scrum-half. With Adrian Stoop unavailable because of injury, Williamson had the curious experience of playing with five different partners in his three Championship matches and against Australia and France. In this match, played mostly in fog on Bristol City football ground, Williamson was opposed by a Welsh player making his début appearance, Tommy Vile. Both scrum-halves earned praise but Vile eventually won a far greater reputation even though his career was also comparatively short.

ENGLAND A.E. Wood 1 (Gloucester); D. Lambert 1 (Harlequins), *J.G.G. Birkett 4 (Harlequins), W.N. Lapage 1 (US Portsmouth), A. Hudson 3 (Gloucester); J. Peters (4) (Plymouth), R.H. Williamson 1 (Oxford U.); R. Gilbert 1 (Devonport Albion), F. Boylen 1 (Hartlepool Rovers), C.E.L. Hammond 5 (Harlequins), G.D. Roberts (2) (Harlequins), L.A.N. Slocock 4 (Liverpool), R. Dibble 2 (Bridgwater Albion), W.A. Mills (7) (Devonport Albion), H. Havelock 1 (Hartlepool Rovers).

WALES   H.B. Winfield 10 (Cardiff); J.L. Williams 4 (Cardiff), R.T. Gabe 19 (Cardiff), W.J. Trew 11 (Swansea), R.A. Gibbs 5 (Cardiff); P.F. Bush 3 (Cardiff), T.H. Vile 1 (Newport); J. Webb 2 (Abertillery), G. Travers 13 (Pill Harriers), W. Neill 8 (Cardiff), J. Brown 4 (Cardiff), J. Watts 4 (Llanelli), C.M. Pritchard 10 (Newport), W. Dowell 4 (Pontypool), *A.F. Harding 17 (London Welsh).

Referee J.T. Tulloch (Scotland)

WALES v SCOTLAND   24/139

1 February 1908
St Helen's, Swansea
Wales 6 (2T) Scotland 5 (1G)

Wales   T: Trew, Williams.
Scotland   T: Purves. C: Geddes.

Scottish players complained that they had been deprived of a match-winning try by Geddes in the last minute. According to one of his colleagues, the Scot grounded a foot over the line, but was dragged back. The referee, W. Williams of England, ruled that Geddes had not crossed the line and ordered a scrum instead.

WALES   H.B. Winfield 11 (Cardiff); J.L. Williams 5 (Cardiff); R.T. Gabe 20 (Cardiff), W.J. Trew 12 (Swansea), R.A. Gibbs 6 (Cardiff); P.F. Bush 4 (Cardiff), T.H. Vile 2 (Newport); G. Hayward 1 (Swansea), *G. Travers 14 (Pill Harriers), W. Neill 9 (Cardiff), J. Brown 5 (Cardiff), W. Dowell 5 (Pontypool), A.F. Harding (18) (London Welsh), J. Watts 5 (Llanelli), J. Webb 3 (Abertillery).

SCOTLAND   D.G. Schulze 4 (RN College Dartmouth); H. Martin 1 (Oxford U.), T. Sloan 4 (London Scottish), M.W. Walter 5 (London Scottish), A.B.H.L. Purves 7 (London Scottish); *L.L. Greig 2 (US Portsmouth), G. Cunningham 1 (Oxford U.); D.R. Bedell-Sivright 19 (Edinburgh U.), J.A. Brown 1 (Glasgow Acads), G.M. Frew 4 (Glasgow HSFP), I.C. Geddes 4 (London Scottish), G.C. Gowlland 1 (London Scottish), J.C. MacCallum 8 (Watsonians), J.M.B. Scott 2 (Edinburgh Acads), L.M. Spiers 4 (Watsonians).

Referee W. Williams (England)

The England XV which defeated Ireland on 8 February 1908. Back row: R. Gilbert, H. Havelock, R. Dibble, F.J.V. Hopley, L.A.N. Slocock, H.H. Vassall, F. Boylen. Middle row: A. Hudson, T.S. Kelly, C.E.L. Hammond, J.G.G. Birkett, W.N. Lapage. Seated: R.H. Williamson, G.V. Portus, A.E. Wood

ENGLAND v IRELAND   24/140

8 February 1908
Athletic Ground, Richmond
England 13 (2G, 1T) Ireland 3 (1PG)

England   Hudson (2), Williamson. C: Wood (2).
Ireland   PG: Parke.

Despite this victory England were not satisfied with their side, dropping six of them, including the captain, C.E.L. Hammond. Another to be discarded, after only one appearance, was H.H. Vassall, regarded as one of the finest centres in Britain.

ENGLAND   A.E. Wood (2) (Gloucester); A. Hudson 4 (Gloucester), J.G.G. Birkett 5 (Harlequins), H.H. Vassall (1) (Oxford U.), W.N. Lapage 2 (US Portsmouth); G.V. Portus (1) (Blackheath), R.H. Williamson 2 (Oxford U.); R. Gilbert 2 (Devonport Albion), F. Boylen 2 (Hartlepool Rovers), *C.E.L. Hammond (6) (Harlequins), F.J.V. Hopley (2) (Blackheath), L.A.N. Slocock 5 (Liverpool), R. Dibble 3 (Bridgwater Albion), T.S. Kelly 7 (Exeter), H. Havelock (2) (Hartlepool Rovers).

IRELAND   W.P. Hinton 2 (Old Wesley); *H.B. Thrift 10 (Dublin U.), J.C. Parke 12 (Monkstown), G.G.P. Beckett 1 (Dublin U.), C. Thompson 3 (Belfast Collegians); H.R. Aston 1 (Dublin U.), F.N.B. Smartt 1 (Dublin U.); G.T. Hamlet 15 (Old Wesley), T. Smyth 1 (Malone), A. Tedford 19 (Malone), E.McG. Morphy (1) (Dublin U.), H.G. Wilson 10 (Malone), B.A.H. Solomons 1 (Dublin U.), T.G. Harpur 1 (Dublin U.), C. Adams 1 (Old Wesley).

Referee T.D. Schofield (Wales)

IRELAND v SCOTLAND   26/141

29 February 1908
Lansdowne Road, Dublin
Ireland 16 (2G, 2T) Scotland 11 (1G, 1T, 1PG)

Ireland   T: Thrift (2), Thompson, Beckett. C: Parke, Hinton.
Scotland   T: MacLeod, Martin. C: MacLeod. PG: MacLeod.

Scotland's attempt to win a third successive match in Ireland foundered because of injuries to M.W. Walter, who broke a collar-bone after only five minutes, and K.G. MacLeod near noside. It was the last Championship appearance of Darkie Bedell-Sivright, who was first capped against Wales in 1900 and went on to accumulate 20 caps for Scotland. 'Strong in the line-out, a magnificent dribbler and a murderous tackler, he had many critics of his uncompromising desire and ability to be first onto the ball,' was how Sandy Thorburn, the Scottish rugby historian described Bedell-Sivright, who led the British team's tour to New Zealand in 1904 and died of blood poisoning on 5 September 1915 during the Dardanelles Campaign. He was 35.

IRELAND   W.P. Hinton 3 (Old Wesley); *H.B. Thrift 11 (Dublin U.), J.C. Parke 13 (Monkstown), G.G.P. Beckett 2 (Dublin U.), C. Thompson 4 (Belfast Collegians); F.N.B. Smartt 2 (Dublin U.), E.D. Caddell 10 (Wanderers); F. Gardiner 18 (NIFC), G.T. Hamlet 16 (Old Wesley), T.G. Harpur 2 (Dublin U.), H.J. Knox (9) (Lansdowne), T. Smyth 2 (Malone), B.A.H. Solomons 2 (Dublin U.), A. Tedford 20 (Malone), H.G. Wilson 11 (Malone).

SCOTLAND   D.G. Schulze 5 (London Scottish); H. Martin 2 (Oxford U.), K.G. MacLeod 7 (Cambridge U.), M.W. Walter 6 (London Scottish), A.B.H.L. Purves 8 (London Scottish); *L.L. Greig (3) (US Portsmouth), G. Cunningham 2 (Oxford U.); D.R. Bedell-Sivright (20) (Edinburgh U.), J.A. Brown (2) (Glasgow Acads), G.M. Frew 5 (Glasgow HSFP), J.C. MacCallum 9 (Watsonians), G.A. Sanderson (4) (Royal HSFP), J.M.B. Scott 3 (Edinburgh Acads), L.M. Spiers 5 (Watsonians), J.S. Wilson 1 (London Scottish).

Referee W. Williams (England)

IRELAND v WALES   22/142

14 March 1908
Balmoral Showgrounds, Belfast
Wales 11 (1G, 2T) Ireland 5 (1G)

Ireland   T: Aston. C: Parke.
Wales   T: Williams (2), Gibbs. C: Winfield.

The twelfth and final appearance of Bert Winfield, one of the outstanding full-backs of his time. He was killed in a car accident in September 1919. The man of the match, however, in Wales's fifth Triple Crown success, was Swansea's Dicky Owen, who was carried off shoulder-high, by several of his team-mates at the end. It was the final Championship appearances of Ernie Caddell, the talented Wanderers half-back, and of Alf Tedford, who had won the first of 21 consecutive caps in 1902.

IRELAND   W.P. Hinton 4 (Old Wesley); C. Thompson 5 (Belfast Collegians), *J.C. Parke 14 (Monkstown), G.G.P. Beckett (3) (Dublin U.), H.B. Thrift 12 (Dublin U.); E.D. Caddell (11) (Wanderers), H.R. Aston (2) (Dublin U.); J.J. Coffey 16 (Lansdowne), F. Gardiner 19 (NIFC), G.T. Hamlet 17 (Old Wesley), H.G. Wilson 12 (Malone), A. Tedford (21) (Malone), T. Smyth 3 (Malone), T.G. Harpur (3) (Dublin U.), B.A.H. Solomons 3 (Dublin U.).

WALES   *H.B. Winfield (12) (Cardiff); R.A. Gibbs 7 (Cardiff), W.J. Trew 13 (Swansea), R.T. Gabe (21) (Cardiff), J.L. Williams 6 (Cardiff); Dick Jones 7 (Swansea), R.M. Owen 19 (Swansea); W. Neill (10) (Cardiff), G. Travers 15 (Pill Harriers), W. Dowell (6) (Pontypool), J. Watts 6 (Llanelli), T. Evans 5 (Llanelli), J. Webb 4 (Abertillery), G. Hayward 2 (Swansea), R. Thomas 1 (Mountain Ash).

Referee J.D. Dallas (Scotland)

SCOTLAND v ENGLAND   23/143

21 March 1908
Inverleith, Edinburgh
Scotland 16 (1G, 1T, 2DG) England 10 (2G)

Scotland   T: MacLeod (2). C: Geddes. DG: Purves, Schulze.
England   T: Birkett, Slocock. C: Lambert (2).

The age of high scoring in the Championship had arrived, and this concept typified a more positive approach by all sides. A score of four tries a match was now a common event and supplemented by a marked increase in dropped goals and penalty goals, the points average for each match soared to over 20. The price of failure, however, was still high: England discarded ten of the players who played for their country before a record 20,000 crowd at Inverleith. J. Davey, the Redruth half-back, who made his England début, was one of 15 Cornishmen – the County Championship winning side – to represent Britain in the Olympic Games at White City in the summer of 1908, when they were beaten 3-32 by Australia, the only other team competing.

SCOTLAND   D.G. Schulze 6 (London Scottish); H. Martin 3 (Oxford U.), K.G. MacLeod (8) (Cambridge U.), C.M. Gilray 1 (London Scottish), A.B.H.L. Purves (9) (London Scottish); J. Robertson (1) (Clydesdale), A.L. Wade (1) (London Scottish); G.M. Frew 6 (Glasgow HSFP), *I.C. Geddes (5) (London Scottish), W.E. Kyle 16 (Hawick), J.C. MacCallum 10 (Watsonians), H.G. Monteith (7) (London Scottish), L. Robertson 1 (London Scottish), J.M.B. Scott 4 (Edinburgh Acads), L.M. Spiers 6 (Watsonians).

ENGLAND   G.H.D'O. Lyon (1) (US Portsmouth); D. Lambert 2 (Harlequins), J.G.G. Birkett 6 (Harlequins), W.N. Lapage (3) (US Portsmouth), A. Hudson 5 (Gloucester); J. Davey 1 (Redruth), R.H. Williamson (3) (Oxford U.); R. Gilbert (3) (Devonport Albion), F. Boylen (3) (Hartlepool Rovers), W.L. Oldham (1) (Coventry), F.B. Watson 1 (US Portsmouth), *L.A.N. Slocock (6) (Liverpool), R. Dibble 4 (Bridgwater Albion), T.S. Kelly (8) (Exeter), T. Woods (1) (Bridgwater Albion).

Referee H.H. Corley (Ireland)

CARDIFF Wales beat England 8-0 · EDINBURGH Wales beat Scotland 5-3
DUBLIN England beat Ireland 11-5 · EDINBURGH Scotland beat Ireland 9-3
SWANSEA Wales beat Ireland 18-5 · RICHMOND Scotland beat England 18-8
Non-Championship matches: LEICESTER England beat France 22-0
PARIS Wales beat France 47-5 · DUBLIN Ireland beat France 19-8

CHAMPIONSHIP TABLE
Wales – Championship, Triple Crown

| | | | | | | | | Tries | |
Pos	Country	P	W	D	L	F	A	Pts	F	A
1	Wales (1)	3	3	0	0	31	8	6	7	1
2	Scotland (3)	3	2	0	1	30	16	4	7	3
3	England (2)	3	1	0	2	19	31	2	5	7
4	Ireland (4)	3	0	0	3	13	38	0	2	10

Another serious rift in relations between the countries nearly overturned the 1909 Championship. Scotland, by now quite militant in their attitude against professionalism, levelled charges against England for supporting professionalism simply because they had endorsed expenses for the visiting Australian players following on from a similar arrangement made with the First All Blacks in 1905. Scotland cancelled their match with Australia and threatened to call off the game against England. Exactly how the dispute was settled is not clear but the England-Scotland match was played at Richmond, and not as scheduled at Twickenham, for the opening of the new RFU headquarters had been postponed because of a delay in the construction of a stand.

This was the background against which the RFU, at their AGM in May 1909, introduced the following addition to their byelaws relating to professionalism: 'that in no case that a Referee be paid more than a reasonable and actual out of pocket expenses, which must be detailed, and that any application for or offer of more than such expenses be reported by the person receiving the application or offer to the Rugby Union.'

WALES v ENGLAND   25/144

16 January 1909
Cardiff Arms Park
Wales 8 (1G, 1T) England 0

Wales   T: Hopkins, Williams. C: Bancroft.

Wales introduced six new caps, including Jack Bancroft and Phil Waller. Bancroft, like his brother Billy before him, had an outstanding career for Wales, for whom he appeared 17 times in the Championship. Waller played on five occasions, establishing his reputation as a top-class specialized hooker after he had finished with Wales, on tour with the British team in South Africa in 1910. Waller stayed on in the Republic after the tour and was killed in 1917 in the First World War while serving with a South African Heavy Artillery Regiment. England's long period without victory against Wales since 1898 had now extended to 11 matches.

WALES   J. Bancroft 1 (Swansea); J.L. Williams 7 (Cardiff), J.P. Jones 1 (Newport), *W.J. Trew 14 (Swansea), P.L. Hopkins 1 (Swansea); Dick Jones 8 (Swansea), R.M. Owen 20 (Swansea); T. Evans 6 (Llanelli), G. Travers 16 (Pill Harriers), P.D. Waller 1 (Newport), J. Brown (6) (Cardiff), J. Webb 5 (Abertillery), J. Blackmore (1) (Abertillery), G. Hayward (3) (Swansea), I. Morgan 1 (Swansea).

ENGLAND   E.J. Jackett 7 (Leicester); E.R. Mobbs 1 (Northampton), F.N. Tarr 1 (Oxford U.), E.W. Assinder (1) (Old Edwardians), B.B. Bennetts (1) (Penzance); J. Davey (2) (Redruth), T.G. Wedge (1) (St Ives); A.D.W. Morris (1) (US Portsmouth), *R. Dibble 5 (Bridgwater Albion), A.L. Kewney 4

(Rockcliff), W.A. Johns 1 (Gloucester), E.D. Ibbitson 1 (Headingley), F.G. Handford 1 (Manchester), H. Archer 1 (Guy's H.), J.G. Cooper (1) (Moseley).

Referee J.D. Dallas (Scotland)

SCOTLAND v WALES   25/145

6 February 1909
Inverleith, Edinburgh
Wales 5 (1G) Scotland 3 (1PG)

Scotland PG: Cunningham.
Wales T: Trew. C: Bancroft.

As in the previous year, Scotland had a chance to win the match in the last minutes, only for Cunningham to miss a penalty kick. Wales would have had cause to feel hard done by: the kick was awarded by Rupert Jeffares, the Irish referee, because Jack Bancroft lay on top of the ball without playing it. What the referee failed to realise was that Bancroft could make no move to obey the letter of the law – he was unconscious, having been kicked in the head while diving to stop a foot-rush by the Scottish forwards.

SCOTLAND   D.G. Schulze 7 (London Scottish); H. Martin 4 (Edinburgh Acads), A.W. Angus 1 (Watsonians), C.M. Gilray 2 (London Scottish), J.T. Simson 1 (Watsonians); G. Cunningham 3 (Oxford U.), J.M. Tennent 1 (W. of Scotland); G.M. Frew 7 (Glasgow HSFP), G.C. Gowlland 2 (London Scottish), W.E. Kyle 17 (Hawick), J.C. MacCallum 11 (Watsonians), J.M. Mackenzie 1 (Edinburgh U.), A. Ross 4 (Royal HSFP), *J.M.B. Scott 5 (Edinburgh Acads), J.S. Wilson (2) (London Scottish).

WALES   J. Bancroft 2 (Swansea); A.M. Baker 1 (Newport), J.P. Jones 2 (Newport), *W.J. Trew 15 (Swansea), J.L. Williams 8 (Cardiff); Dick Jones 9 (Swansea), R.M. Owen 21 (Swansea); J. Webb 6 (Abertillery), G. Travers 17 (Pill Harriers), T. Evans 7 (Llanelli), J. Watts 7 (Llanelli), R. Thomas (2) (Mountain Ash), P.D. Waller 2 (Newport), E. Thomas 3 (Newport), I. Morgan 2 (Swansea).

Referee R.W. Jeffares (Ireland)

IRELAND v ENGLAND   25/146

13 February 1909
Lansdowne Road, Dublin
England 11 (1G, 2T) Ireland 5 (1G)

Ireland   T: Parke. C: Pinion.
England   T: Palmer (2), Mobbs. C: Palmer.

Ronnie Poulton, scorer of five tries in Oxford's 35-3 annihilation of Cambridge two months earlier, made his Championship début. Described variously as a 'genius', the 'greatest figure that ever played', and 'a man apart', Poulton left a lasting impression on all who saw him. A deceptively elusive centre, his ability to change pace flummoxed most defences. Clearly Poulton was a creator of scores rather than a try-scorer: apart from tries against South Africa and Ireland, he produced try-scoring skill in only one other match, his fifteenth and final one, when he scored four against France at Stade Colombes in 1914. He was to live barely a year after that. He was 25 when killed by a sniper's bullet in Belgium on 5 May 1915.

IRELAND   W.P. Hinton 5 (Old Wesley); H.B. Thrift 13 (Wanderers), J.C. Parke 15 (Monkstown), C. Thompson 6 (Belfast Collegians), E.C. Deane (1) (Monkstown); F.N.B. Smartt (3) (Dublin U.), G. Pinion 1 (Belfast Collegians); G.T. Hamlet 18 (Old Wesley), T. Smyth 4 (Malone), O.J.S. Piper 1 (Cork Constitution), *F. Gardiner 20 (NIFC), C. Adams 2 (Old Wesley), B.A.H. Solomons 4 (Dublin U.), H.G. Wilson 13 (Malone), M.G. Garry 1 (Bective Rangers).

ENGLAND   E.J. Jackett 8 (Leicester); A.C. Palmer 1 (The London H.), C.C.G. Wright 1 (Cambridge U.), R.W. Poulton 1 (Oxford U.), E.R. Mobbs 2 (Northampton); F. Hutchinson 1 (Headingley), H.J.H. Sibree 1 (Harlequins); H.J.S. Morton 1 (Cambridge U.), *R. Dibble 6 (Bridgwater Albion), A.L. Kewney 5 (Rockcliff), W.A. Johns 2 (Gloucester), E.D. Ibbitson 2 (Headingley), F.G. Handford 2 (Manchester), H. Archer (2) (Guy's H.), A.J. Wilson (1) (Camborne School of Mines).

Referee J.D. Dallas (Scotland)

SCOTLAND v IRELAND 27/147

27 February 1909
Inverleith, Edinburgh
Scotland 9 (3T) Ireland 3 (1PG)

Scotland T: Lindsay-Watson, McGregor, Kyle.
Ireland PG: Parke.

Fred Gardiner, the NIFC forward, was pressed into service as half-back for Ireland in his twenty-first and last Championship match. Gardiner was not new to the position: in the famous victory over Wales in 1906, Gardiner was brought out of the pack to replace W.B. Purdon. It was Scotland's eleventh victory in thirteen home matches against Ireland.

SCOTLAND D.G. Schulze 8 (London Scottish); R.H. Lindsay-Watson (1) (Hawick), T. Sloan (5) (London Scottish), J. Pearson 1 (Watsonians), J.T. Simson 2 (Watsonians); J.R. McGregor (1) (Edinburgh U.), J.M. Tennent 2 (W. of Scotland); G.M. Frew 8 (Glasgow HSFP), W.E. Kyle 18 (Hawick), W.G. Lely (1) (London Scottish), J.C. MacCallum 12 (Watsonians), J.M. Mackenzie 2 (Edinburgh U.), A. Ross (5) (Royal HSFP), *J.M.B. Scott 6 (Edinburgh Acads), C.D. Stuart 1 (W. of Scotland).

IRELAND W.P. Hinton 6 (Old Wesley); H.B. Thrift 14 (Dublin U.), J.C. Parke 16 (Monkstown), C. Thompson 7 (Belfast Collegians), R.M. McGrath (1) (Cork Constitution); G. Pinion 2 (Belfast Collegians), *F. Gardiner (21) (NIFC); J.C. Blackham 1 (Queen's C. Cork), M.G. Garry 2 (Bective Rangers), T. Halpin 1 (Garryowen), G.T. Hamlet 19 (Old Wesley), O.J.S. Piper 2 (Cork Constitution), T. Smyth 5 (Malone), B.A.H. Solomons 5 (Dublin U.), H.G. Wilson 14 (Malone).

Referee V.H. Cartwright (England)

Jim Watts, the Llanelli forward, who was one of the bulwarks of the Welsh pack 1907–09

WALES v IRELAND 23/148

13 March 1909
St Helen's Swansea
Wales 18 (3G, 1T) Ireland 5 (1G)

Wales T: Jack Jones, Hopkins, Watts, Trew. C: Bancroft (3).
Ireland T: Thompson. C: Parke.

Wales became the first country to win the Triple Crown in successive seasons. It was a disappointing note on which to leave the Championship for Jim Parke, Ireland's veteran threequarter. In 17 Championship matches since 1903, in which he scored 30 points, he had been consistency itself, reliable in defence and occasionally a scintillating attacker. Parke, like England's Stanley Harris q.v., was one of the most versatile sportsmen of the age: an outstanding athlete, scratch golfer and a lawn tennis player good enough to compete in the Davis Cup. Parke was not the only Irish player to play his last Championship: also discarded were Harry Thrift, Greeves, Pinion and Henebrey, all backs.

WALES   J. Bancroft 3 (Swansea); J.L. Williams 9 (Cardiff), J.P. Jones 3 (Newport), *W.J. Trew 16 (Swansea), P.L. Hopkins 2 (Swansea); Dick Jones 10 (Swansea), R.M. Owen 22 (Swansea); J. Webb 7 (Abertillery), G. Travers 18 (Pill Harriers), P.D. Waller 3 (Newport), E. Thomas 4 (Newport), T. Evans 8 (Llanelli), J. Watts (8) (Llanelli), R. Thomas 1 (Pontypool), I. Morgan 3 (Swansea).

IRELAND   G.J. Henebrey (4) (Garryowen); H.B. Thrift (15) (Wanderers), J.C. Parke (17) (Monkstown), T.J. Greeves (4) (NIFC), C. Thompson 8 (Belfast Collegians); G. Pinion (3) (Belfast Collegians), F.M. McCormac 1 (Wanderers); T. Halpin 2 (Garryowen), O.J.S. Piper 3 (Cork Constitution), M.G. Garry 3 (Bective Rangers), *G.T. Hamlet 20 (Old Wesley), T. Smyth 6 (Malone), H.G. Wilson 15 (Malone), B.A.H. Solomons 6 (Dublin U.), J.C. Blackham 2 (Queen's C. Cork).

Referee F.C. Potter-Irwin (England)

ENGLAND   E.J. Jackett (9) (Leicester); A.C. Palmer (2) (The London H.), C.C.G. Wright (2) (Cambridge U.), R.W. Poulton 2 (Oxford U.), E.R. Mobbs 3 (Northampton); F. Hutchinson (2) (Headingley), H.J.H. Sibree (2) (Harlequins); H.J.S. Morton 2 (Cambridge U.), *R. Dibble 7 (Bridgwater Albion), A.L. Kewney 6 (Leicester), W.A. Johns 3 (Gloucester), E.D. Ibbitson (3) (Headingley), F.G. Handford (3) (Manchester), H.C. Harrison 1 (Royal Marines), F.B. Watson (2) (US Portsmouth).

SCOTLAND   D.G. Schulze 9 (London Scottish); H. Martin (5) (Oxford U.), J. Pearson 2 (Watsonians), C.M. Gilray 3 (Oxford U.), J.T. Simson 3 (Watsonians); J.M. Tennent 3 (W. of Scotland), *G. Cunningham 4 (Oxford U.); G.M. Frew 9 (Glasgow HSFP), G.C. Gowlland 3 (London Scottish), J. Reid-Kerr (1) (Greenock Wanderers), W.E. Kyle 19 (Hawick), J.C. MacCallum 13 (Watsonians), J.M. Mackenzie 3 (Edinburgh U.), A.R. Moodie 1 (St Andrew's U.), J.M.B. Scott 7 (Edinburgh Acads).

Referee E.G. Nicholls (Wales)

ENGLAND v SCOTLAND   24/149

20 March 1909
Athletic Ground, Richmond
Scotland 18 (3G, 1T) England 8 (1G, 1T)

England   T: Mobbs, Watson. C: Palmer.
Scotland   T: Tennent (2), Gilray, Simson. C: Cunningham (3).

Another rebuff for England with their sixth successive home defeat against Scotland, their worst ever sequence. In fact England's home record against the Scots was as remarkable as it was appalling: in 12 matches since the first encounter at Blackheath in 1884, England had won only twice – hardly the fare to put before the Prince of Wales who was among a 20,000 crowd to see Scotland's latest victory. It was also the last of England's itinerant matches: from now on they would be playing at their magnificent new stadium at Twickenham. Scotland were to encounter far less charity there – they were to win only 4 times in 31 visits. The referee of this last match at Richmond was interesting, the former Wales' captain, Gwyn Nicholls. It was the only Championship match which he refereed.

1910

SWANSEA Wales beat France 49-14 · TWICKENHAM England beat Wales 11-6
EDINBURGH Scotland beat France 27-0 · CARDIFF Wales beat Scotland 14-0
TWICKENHAM England drew Ireland 0-0 · BELFAST Scotland beat Ireland 14-0
PARIS England beat France 11-3 · DUBLIN Wales beat Ireland 19-3
EDINBURGH England beat Scotland 14-5 · PARIS Ireland beat France 8-3

CHAMPIONSHIP TABLE
England – Championship

									Tries	
Pos	Country	P	W	D	L	F	A	Pts	F	A
1	England (3)	4	3	1	0	36	14	7	9	4
2	Wales (1)	4	3	0	1	88	28	6	21	5
3	Scotland (2)	4	2	0	2	46	28	4	12	8
4	Ireland (4)	4	1	1	2	11	36	3	3	10
5	France (0)	4	0	0	4	20	95	0	4	22

With the inclusion of France, the Championship now became a competition between five countries; France's precocious talent had been tested against England since 1906, against Wales since 1908 and Ireland from 1909. Scotland had been somewhat backward in establishing a French connection, and although the SRU had been formally approached for a match by the French as far back as 1907, it was not until 22 January 1910 that the first Scotland-France match took place at Inverleith. Understandably, this first Championship for France was a chastening experience. They conceded 22 tries and 95 points, which was to prove the worst total ever against any side. However, the fragile French defence presented the other countries with opportunities to improve their scoring aggregates. Wales did best of all in 1910, creating two

The Scottish XV beaten by Wales. Back row: J. Pearson, J.M. Tennent, A.W. Angus, G.C. Gowlland, C.D. Stuart, W.R. Sutherland. Middle row: J.C. MacCallum, D.G. Schulze, W.E. Kyle, G.M. Frew, J.M.B. Scott, L.M. Spiers, J.M. Mackenzie. Seated: J.T. Simson, E. Milroy

Championship records with 88 points and 21 tries. This points total stood until 1976, when Wales raised it to a new level, 102. The try total remains unsurpassed.

Despite their high scoring Wales finished second, behind an England side which closed an 11-year gap since winning the Championship, which was England's longest period without a title win until the 1980 side punctuated a 16-year sequence. An injury to Jim Tennent, the Scotland outside-half, in the match with Wales was reckoned to have been caused by bad studs. Consequently the injury brought into focus the damage that studs could cause, and new regulations were thereafter introduced governing the size and form of boot studs.

WALES v FRANCE   1/150

1 January 1910
St Helen's Swansea
Wales 49 (8G, 2T, 1PG) France 14 (1G, 1T, 2PG)

Wales T: Gibbs (3), Morgan (2), Maddocks (2), Trew, Jack Jones, Gronow. C: Bancroft (8). PG: Bancroft.
France T: Lafitte, Mauriat. C: Menrath. PG: Menrath (2).

The first Championship match between Wales and France produced a cluster of records. The total of 63 points was the biggest aggregate of any international match although equalled in 1975 when South Africa beat France 38-25 at Bloëmfontein; it was Wales's highest score against any opposition; Wales's total of 10 tries was their highest in the Championship; Jack Bancroft's total of 19 points was an individual record until equalled by Keith Jarrett in 1967; and Bancroft's 8 conversions have never been bettered.

WALES   J. Bancroft 4 (Swansea); H.T. Maddocks (6) (London Welsh), J.P. Jones 4 (Newport), *W.J. Trew 17 (Swansea), R.A. Gibbs 8 (Cardiff); Dick Jones 11 (Swansea), R.M. Owen 23 (Swansea); T. Evans 9 (Llanelli), J. Pullman (1) (Neath), J. Webb 8 (Abertillery), I. Morgan 4 (Swansea), B. Gronow 1 (Bridgend), P.D. Waller (4) (Newport), C.M. Pritchard 11 (Newport), E. Thomas (5) (Newport).

FRANCE   A. Menrath (1) (SCUF); M. Bruneau 1 (S. Bordelais), H. Houblain (1) (SCUF), M. Burgun 1 (RCF), *G. Lane 1 (RCF); C. Martin 1 (FC Lyon), J. Maysonnie (1) (S. Toulouse); P. Mauriat 1 (FC Lyon), A. Masse 1 (S. Bordelais), M. Hourdebaigt 1 (S. Bordelais), P. Guillemin 1 (RCF), R. Lafitte 1 (SCUF), G. Thevenot 1 (SCUF), M. Boudreau 1 (SCUF), J. Anduran (1) (SCUF).

Referee W. Williams (England)

ENGLAND v WALES   26/151

15 January 1910
Twickenham
England 11 (1G, 1T, 1PG) Wales 6 (2T)

England T: Chapman, Solomon. C: Chapman. PG: Chapman.
Wales T: Gibbs, Webb.

The first international to be held at Twickenham is best remembered for a sensational score in the first minute by F.E. Chapman. England played nine new caps, six in the pack, one of whom was Charles 'Cherry' Pillman. The Blackheath forward won 17 caps, breaking his leg on his last appearance, against Scotland in 1914. Pillman was one of the first recognized roving flank-forwards and one of the 'true rugby geniuses' of his era. He was reckoned to have won a Test match singlehanded: for the British Lions in South Africa in the summer of 1910 when he was picked at fly-half, moved around between centre, wing and full-back, led an occasional forward rush, made both tries and converted one! England's previous win over Wales had been in 1898. Adrian Stoop returned to captain England after a three-year absence. Before this defeat, Wales had won eight Championship matches in succession.

ENGLAND   W.R. Johnston 1 (Bristol); F.E. Chapman 1 (Westoe), J.G.G. Birkett 7 (Harlequins), B. Solomon (1) (Redruth), R.W. Poulton 3 (Oxford U.); *A.D. Stoop 4 (Harlequins), D.R. Gent 3 (Gloucester); H.J.S. Morton 3 (Blackheath), W.A. Johns 4 (Gloucester), L. Haigh 1 (Manchester), D.F. Smith 1 (Richmond), E.L. Chambers 1 (Bedford), H. Berry 1 (Gloucester), L.E. Barrington-Ward 1 (Edinburgh U.), C.H. Pillman 1 (Blackheath).

WALES   J. Bancroft 5 (Swansea); R.A. Gibbs 9 (Cardiff), J.P. Jones 5 (Newport), *W.J. Trew 18 (Swansea), P.L. Hopkins (3) (Swansea); Dick Jones (12) (Swansea), R.M. Owen 24 (Swansea); J. Webb 9 (Abertillery), J. Pugsley 1 (Cardiff), T. Evans 10 (Llanelli), B. Gronow 2 (Bridgend), C.M. Pritchard (12) (Newport), H. Jarman 1 (Newport), D.J. Thomas 2 (Swansea), I. Morgan 5 (Swansea).

Referee J.D. Dallas (Scotland)

SCOTLAND v FRANCE   1/152

22 January 1910
Inverleith, Edinburgh
Scotland 27 (3G, 4T) France 0

Scotland   T: Tennent (3), Robertson (2), Angus, Gowlland. C: MacCallum (3).

Scotland did not award caps for this their first match against France, but out of deference to their visitors, who wore light blue, the Scots took the field with white jerseys. France, with seven players new to Championship rugby, conceded seven tries, a total equalled only once since in matches between the countries, in 1925. Scotland's 27 points also has been surpassed only once, when they won 31-3 in 1912.

SCOTLAND   F.G. Buchanan 1 (Oxford U.); I.P.M. Robertson (1) (Watsonians), A.W. Angus 2 (Watsonians), J. Pearson 3 (Watsonians), J.T. Simson 4 (Watsonians); *G. Cunningham 5 (Oxford U.), J.M. Tennent 4 (W. of Scotland); G.M. Frew 10 (Glasgow HSFP), G.C. Gowlland 4 (London Scottish), J.C. MacCallum 14 (Watsonians), A.R. Moodie 2 (St Andrew's U.), J.M.B. Scott 8 (Edinburgh Acads), L.M. Spiers 7 (Watsonians), R.C. Stevenson 1 (St Andrew's U.), C.D. Stuart 2 (W. of Scotland).

FRANCE   J. Combe 1 (S. Français); E. Lesieur 1 (S. Français), J. Dedet 1 (S. Français), M. Burgun 2 (RCF), C. Vareilles 1 (S. Français); C. Martin (2) (FC Lyon), A. Theuriet 1 (SCUF); M. Boudreau (2) (SCUF), J. Cadenat 1 (SCUF), *M. Communeau 1 (S. Français), P. Guilleman 2 (RCF), M. Hourdebaigt 2 (S. Bordelais), R. Lafitte (2) (SCUF), A. Masse 2 (S. Bordelais), P. Mauriat 2 (FC Lyon).

Referee G.A. Harris (Ireland)

WALES v SCOTLAND   26/153

5 February 1910
Cardiff Arms Park
Wales 14 (1G, 3T) Scotland 0

Wales   T: Pugsley, Spiller, Baker, Ivor Morgan. C: Bancroft.

Billy Spiller, who won a place in cricket history by becoming the first player to score a first-class hundred for Glamorgan, scored a try on his first appearance for Wales. Scotland played with 14 men for most of the second half, having lost Jim Tennent with an elbow injury. Tennent's injury was caused by boot studs, and was a contributory factor in the introduction of regulations regarding the size and shape of studs. Six of Scotland's players came from Watsonians.

WALES   J. Bancroft 6 (Swansea); R.A. Gibbs 10 (Cardiff), W. Spiller 1 (Cardiff), *W.J. Trew 19 (Swansea), A.M. Baker (2) (Newport); P.F. Bush 5 (Cardiff), W.L. Morgan (1) (Cardiff); J. Webb 10 (Abertillery), J. Pugsley 2 (Cardiff), B. Gronow 3 (Bridgend), T. Evans 11 (Llanelli), H. Jarman 2 (Newport), E. Jenkins 1 (Newport), D.J. Thomas 3 (Swansea), I. Morgan 6 (Swansea).

SCOTLAND   D.G. Schulze 10 (London Scottish); W.R. Sutherland 1 (Hawick), A.W. Angus 3 (Watsonians), J. Pearson 4 (Watsonians), J.T. Simson 5 (Watsonians); J.M. Tennent 5 (W. of Scotland), E. Milroy 1 (Watsonians); *G.M. Frew 11 (Glasgow HSFP), G.C. Gowlland 5 (London Scottish), W.E. Kyle (20) (Hawick), J.C. MacCallum 15 (Watsonians), J.M. Mackenzie 4 (Edinburgh U.), J.M.B. Scott 9 (Edinburgh Acads), L.M. Spiers 8 (Watsonians), C.D. Stuart 3 (W. of Scotland).

Referee G.H.B. Kennedy (Ireland)

ENGLAND v IRELAND   26/154

12 February 1910
Twickenham
England 0 Ireland 0

The début of Dicky Lloyd and Harry Read, Ireland's first specialized half-back pairing. According to Sean Diffley, Lloyd was: 'a completely equipped halfback, worthy of being bracketed with such all-time great Irish halves as Louis Magee and Jack Kyle'. In any event credit is due to Lloyd for determining the role of the fly-half in Irish rugby, for before he concentrated on that position only, it was common for half-backs to alternate. Altogether Lloyd and Read played 12 times together between 1910–13. Ireland gave first caps to seven players in this match: only W.F. Riordan, of Cork Constitution, was not called on again.

ENGLAND   W.R. Johnston 2 (Bristol); F.E. Chapman 2 (Westoe), J.G.G. Birkett 8 (Harlequins), L.W. Hayward (1) (Cheltenham), E.R. Mobbs 4 (Northampton); *A.D. Stoop 5 (Harlequins), D.R. Gent (4) (Gloucester); H.J.S. Morton (4) (Blackheath), W.A. Johns 5 (Gloucester), L. Haigh 2 (Manchester), D.F. Smith (2) (Richmond), E.L. Chambers (2) (Bedford), H. Berry 2 (Gloucester), L.E. Barrington-Ward 2 (Edinburgh U.), C.H. Pillman 2 (Blackheath).

IRELAND   W.P. Hinton 7 (Old Wesley); C. Thompson 9 (Belfast Collegians), A.S. Taylor 1 (Queen's U. Belfast), A.R. Foster 1 (Queen's U. Belfast), J.P. Quinn 1 (Dublin U.); R.A. Lloyd 1 (Dublin U.), H.M. Read 1 (Dublin U.); O.J.S. Piper 4 (Cork Constitution), J.C. Blackham 3 (Queen's C. Cork), *G.T. Hamlet 21 (Old Wesley), T. Halpin 3 (Garryowen), T. Smyth 7 (Malone), W.F. Riordan (1) (Cork Constitution), B.A.H. Solomons 7 (Wanderers), G. McIldowie 1 (Malone).

Referee T.D. Schofield (Wales)

IRELAND v SCOTLAND   28/155

26 February 1910
Balmoral Showgrounds, Belfast
Scotland 14 (1G, 3T) Ireland 0

Scotland T: Dobson, Walter (2), Stuart. C: MacCallum.

This scoreline was an exact reversal of Scotland's fate in their first match of the season, against Wales in Cardiff three weeks earlier. It was a punishing experience for Ireland's comparatively new side which had done well, under George Hamlet's captaincy to hold England to a draw at Twickenham a fortnight earlier.

IRELAND   W.P. Hinton 8 (Old Wesley); J.P. Quinn 2 (Dublin U.), C. Thompson 10 (Belfast Collegians), A.R. Foster 2 (Queen's U. Belfast), A.S. Taylor 2 (Queen's U. Belfast); R.A. Lloyd 2 (Dublin U.), H.M. Read 2 (Dublin U.); J.C. Blackham 4 (Wanderers), T. Halpin 4 (Garryowen), *G.T. Hamlet 22 (Old Wesley), G. McIldowie 2 (Malone), H. Moore 1 (Queen's U. Belfast), O.J.S. Piper 5 (Cork Constitution), T. Smyth 8 (Newport), B.A.H. Solomons 8 (Wanderers).

SCOTLAND   D.G. Schulze 11 (Northampton); D.G. Macpherson 1 (The London H.), M.W. Walter (7) (London Scottish), J. Pearson 5 (Watsonians), J.D. Dobson (1) (Glasgow Acads); *G. Cunningham 6 (Oxford U.), A.B. Lindsay 1 (The London H.); C.H. Abercrombie 1 (US Portsmouth), G.M. Frew 12 (Glasgow HSFP), G.C. Gowlland 6 (London Scottish), J.C. MacCallum 16 (Watsonians), J.M. Mackenzie 5 (Edinburgh U.), J.M.B. Scott 10 (Edinburgh Acads), R.C. Stevenson 2 (St Andrew's U.), C.D. Stuart 4 (W. of Scotland).

Referee V.H. Cartwright (England)

FRANCE v ENGLAND 1/156

3 March 1910
Parc des Princes, Paris
England 11 (1G, 2T) France 3 (1T)

France T: Communeau.
England T: Hudson (2), Berry. C: Chapman.

England introduced eight new caps in this first Championship match in France, which though a comfortable win was the last international for six players, including the captain, Edgar Mobbs. (England had played France four times previously in matches which were not recognized as part of the Championship.)

FRANCE J. Combe 2 (S. Français); E. Lesieur 2 (S. Français), G. Lane 2 (RCF), C. Vareilles (2) (S. Français), M. Bruneau 2 (S. Bordelais); J. Dedet 2 (S. Français), G. Laterrade 1 (S. Tarbes); R. de Malmann 1 (RCF), J. Cadenat 2 (SCUF), *M. Communeau 2 (S. Français), P. Guillemin 3 (RCF), A. Masse 3 (S. Bordelais), M. Hourdebaigt 3 (S. Bordelais), G. Thevenot 2 (SCUF), P. Mauriat 3 (FC Lyon).

ENGLAND C.S. Williams (1) (Manchester); F.E. Chapman 3 (Westoe), A.A. Adams (1) (The London H.), *E.R. Mobbs (5) (Northampton), A. Hudson (6) (Gloucester); H. Coverdale 1 (Blackheath), A.L.H. Gotley 1 (Oxford U.); N.A. Wodehouse 1 (US Portsmouth), W.A. Johns (6) (Gloucester), R.H.M. Hands 1 (Oxford U.), E.S. Scorfield (1) (Percy Park), J.A.S. Ritson 1 (Northern), H. Berry 3 (Gloucester), L.E. Barrington-Ward 3 (Edinburgh U.), C.H. Pillman 3 (Blackheath).

Referee G. Bowden (Scotland)

IRELAND v WALES 24/157

12 March 1910
Lansdowne Road, Dublin
Wales 19 (5T, 1DG) Ireland 3 (1T)

Ireland T: McIldowie.
Wales T: Williams (3), Gibbs, Dyke. DG: Bush.

The Welsh selectors certainly knew what they were doing in recalling Johnny Williams, the Cardiff wing, for his first cap of the season: for the second time he scored a hat-trick of tries against Ireland, bringing his total to eight in four matches against them. It was Wales's biggest total of tries against Ireland in Ireland. Percy Bush bade farewell to international rugby having been on the winning side on each of his six appearances.

IRELAND W.P. Hinton 9 (Old Wesley); C.T. O'Callaghan 1 (Carlow), A.S. Taylor 3 (Queen's C. Belfast), R.K. Lyle 1 (Dublin U.), *C. Thompson 11 (Belfast Collegians); A.N. McClinton 1 (NIFC), F.M. McCormac 2 (Wanderers); H.G. Wilson (16) (Malone), T. Smyth 9 (Newport), G. McIldowie (3) (Malone), W.S. Smyth 1 (Belfast Collegians), O.J.S. Piper 6 (Cork Constitution), B.A.H. Solomons (9) (Wanderers), J.C. Blackham (5) (Wanderers), T. Halpin 5 (Garryowen).

WALES J. Bancroft 7 (Swansea); *R.A. Gibbs 11 (Cardiff), L.M. Dyke 1 (Cardiff), W. Spiller 2 (Cardiff), J.L. Williams 10 (Cardiff); P.F. Bush (6) (Cardiff), T.H. Vile 3 (Newport); J. Webb 11 (Abertillery), J. Pugsley 3 (Cardiff), B. Gronow (4) (Bridgend), T. Evans 12 (Llanelli), H. Jarman 3 (Newport), E. Jenkins (2) (Newport), D.J. Thomas 4 (Swansea), I. Morgan 7 (Swansea).

Referee J.D. Dallas (Scotland)

SCOTLAND v ENGLAND   25/158

19 March 1910
Inverleith, Edinburgh
England 14 (1G, 3T) Scotland 5 (1G)

Scotland   T: Macpherson. C: MacCallum.
England   T: Birkett (2), Berry, Ritson. C: Chapman.

After 12 years in the doldrums England at last had something to celebrate: a decisive victory over Scotland which won them the Championship. It was the first occasion on which the Stoop brothers, Adrian and Frank, played together for England.

SCOTLAND   D.G. Schulze 12 (London Scottish); W.R. Sutherland 2 (Hawick), J. Pearson 6 (Watsonians), A.W. Angus 4 (Watsonians), D.G. Macpherson (2) (The London H.); *G. Cunningham 7 (Oxford U.), J.M. Tennent (6) (W. of Scotland); C.H. Abercrombie 2 (US Portsmouth), G.C. Gowlland (7) (London Scottish), J.C. MacCallum 17 (Watsonians), J.M. Mackenzie 6 (Edinburgh U.), J.M.B. Scott 11 (Edinburgh Acads), L.M. Spiers (9) (Watsonians), R.C. Stevenson 3 (St Andrew's U.), C.D. Stuart 5 (W. of Scotland).

ENGLAND   W.R. Johnston 3 (Bristol); F.E. Chapman 4 (Westoe), *J.G.G. Birkett 9 (Harlequins), F.M. Stoop 1 (Harlequins), P.W. Lawrie 1 (Leicester); A.D. Stoop 6 (Harlequins), A.L.H. Gotley 2 (Oxford U.); G.R. Hind 1 (Guy's H.), J.A.S. Ritson 2 (Northern), L. Haigh 3 (Manchester), R. Dibble 8 (Bridgwater Albion), R.H.M. Hands (2) (Oxford U.), H. Berry (4) (Gloucester), L.E. Barrington-Ward (4) (Edinburgh U.), C.H. Pillman 4 (Blackheath).

Referee G.H.B. Kennedy (Ireland)

FRANCE v IRELAND   1/159

28 March 1910
Parc des Princes, Paris
Ireland 8 (1G, 1T) France 3 (1T)

France   T: Guillemin.
Ireland   T: Thompson, Smyth. C: McClinton.

Charles Thompson and Jack Coffey, stalwarts of Irish rugby since the turn of the century, made their last Championship appearances in this 'rough' game, watched by a crowd of 10,000 and played on a Monday.

FRANCE   J. Combe 3 (S. Français); J. de Muison (1) (S. Français), M. Burgun 3 (RCF), R. Roujas (1) (S. Tarbes), E. Lesieur 3 (S. Français); G. Laterrade 2 (S. Tarbes), J. Dedet 3 (S. Français); R. de Malmann (2) (RCF), P. Guillemin 4 (RCF), P. Mauriat 4 (FC Lyon), G. Thevenot (3) (SCUF), M. Legrain 1 (S. Français), A. Masse (4) (S. Bordelais), M. Hourdebaigt (4) (S. Bordelais), *M. Communeau 3 (S. Français).

IRELAND   W.P. Hinton 10 (Old Wesley); C. Thompson (12) (Belfast Collegians), A.R. Foster 3 (Derry), R.K. Lyle (2) (Dublin U.), C.T. O'Callaghan 2 (Carlow); A.N. McClinton (2) (NIFC), F.M. McCormac (3) (Wanderers); J.J. Coffey (17) (Lansdowne), W. Tyrrell 1 (Queen's U. Belfast), O.J.S. Piper (7) (Cork Constitution), W.J. Beatty 1 (Richmond), T. Smyth 10 (Newport), *G.T. Hamlet 23 (Old Wesley), W.S. Smyth 2 (Belfast Collegians), C. Adams 3 (Old Wesley).

Referee V.H. Cartwright (England)

PARIS France beat Scotland 16-15 · SWANSEA Wales beat England 15-11
TWICKENHAM England beat France 37-0 · EDINBURGH Wales beat Scotland 32-10
DUBLIN Ireland beat England 3-0 · EDINBURGH Ireland beat Scotland 16-10
PARIS Wales beat France 15-0 · CARDIFF Wales beat Ireland 16-0
TWICKENHAM England beat Scotland 13-8 · CORK Ireland beat France 25-5

CHAMPIONSHIP TABLE
Wales – Championship, Triple Crown, Grand Slam

Pos	Country	P	W	D	L	F	A	Pts	Tries F	A
1	Wales (2)	4	4	0	0	78	21	8	18	5
2	Ireland (4)	4	3	0	1	44	31	6	10	6
3	England (1)	4	2	0	2	61	26	4	13	7
4	France (5)	4	1	0	3	21	92	2	5	18
5	Scotland (3)	4	0	0	4	43	77	0	9	19

Scoring 18 tries Wales won the Grand Slam, the first time it had been achieved within the confines of the Championship proper, although Wales had beaten all four countries twice before, in 1908 and 1909. Included in the Welsh success, of course, was their seventh Triple Crown. They had to wait until 1948 before they won another. Arguably, the 1911 Championship was the greatest ever, with 55 tries and 247 points scored. The try total has never been surpassed, and the points' aggregate stood as a record for 61 years, improved upon only after the try had been upgraded to four points, in 1972.

Scotland will remember the season with little but regret: they lost all four matches for the first time, and conceded a record number of tries, 19, as well as 77 points. Administratively, there were important changes with regard to England's representation on the International Board. The RFU's voting strength was marginally reduced from six to four, although the other Unions still had two votes each only.

FRANCE v SCOTLAND   2/160

2 January 1911
Stade Colombes, Paris
France 16 (2G, 2T) Scotland 15 (1G, 2T, 1DG)

France   T: Laterrade, Failliot (2), Peyroutou. C: Descamps (2).
Scotland   T: MacCallum, Munro, Abercrombie. C: Turner. DG: Pearson.

This was Scotland's first match in France and France's first victory in international rugby. Compared with French try-scoring wings of latter years, the hero of the day was atypical: Pierre Failliot was 6 foot tall and weighed 14 stone, with pace and strength which was to severely test the defences of all the home countries before he was discarded by France in 1913. Curiously France have never exceeded their four-try total against Scotland, although they equalled it in 1924, 1955, 1965 and 1977.

FRANCE   J. Combe (4) (S. Français); P. Failliot 1 (RCF), M. Burgun 4 (RCF), A. Franquenelle 1 (SC Vaugirard), G. Lane 3 (RCF); G. Laterrade 3 (S. Tarbes), G. Peyroutou 1 (CA Périgueux); J. Bavozet 1 (FC Lyon), *M. Communeau 4 (S. Français), P. Descamps (1) (RCF), F. Forgues 1 (A. Bayonne), P. Guillemin 5 (RCF), M. Legrain 2 (S. Français), P. Mauriat 5 (FC Lyon), P. Mounicq 1 (S. Toulouse).

SCOTLAND   H.B. Tod (1) (Gala); W.R. Sutherland 3 (Hawick), T.E.B. Young (1) (Durham), F.G. Buchanan 2 (Kelvinside Acads), J. Pearson 7 (Watsonians); *P. Munro 9 (London Scottish), F.L. Osler 1 (Edinburgh U.); C.H. Abercrombie 3 (US Portsmouth), R. Fraser 1 (Cambridge U.),

J.C. MacCallum 18 (Watsonians), A.R. Moodie (3) (St Andrew's U.), J.M.B. Scott 12 (Edinburgh Acads), A.M. Stevenson (1) (Glasgow U.), R.C. Stevenson 4 (St Andrew's U.), F.H. Turner 1 (Oxford U.).

Referee A.O. Jones (England)

WALES v ENGLAND   27/161

21 January 1911
St Helen's, Swansea
Wales 15 (4T, 1PG) England 11 (1G, 2T)

Wales   T: Gibbs, Morgan, Spiller, Pugsley. PG: Birt.
England   T: Roberts, Kewney, Scholfield. C: Lambert.

This was Harry Jarman's last appearance for Wales, who had been rated as one of Britain's finest forwards during the 1910 tour of South Africa. Jarman died a hero's death a few years later, throwing himself in front of a runaway coal truck which was careering towards a group of playing children. England fielded six players new to the Championship in this match, and two of them, Roberts and Scholfield, scored tries.

WALES   J. Bancroft 8 (Swansea); J.L. Williams 11 (Cardiff), W. Spiller 3 (Cardiff), F.W. Birt 1 (Newport), R.A. Gibbs 12 (Cardiff); *W.J. Trew 20 (Swansea), R.M. Owen 25 (Swansea); J. Webb 12 (Abertillery), J. Pugsley 4 (Cardiff), A.P. Coldrick 1 (Newport), H. Jarman (4) (Pontypool), W. Perry (1) (Neath), T. Evans 13 (Llanelli), D.J. Thomas 5 (Swansea), I. Morgan 8 (Swansea).

ENGLAND   S.H. Williams 1 (Newport); D. Lambert 3 (Harlequins), *J.G.G. Birkett 10 (Harlequins), J.A. Scholfield (1) (Cambridge U.), A.D. Roberts 1 (Northern); A.D. Stoop 7 (Harlequins), A.L.H. Gotley 3 (Blackheath); L.G. Brown 1 (Oxford U.), N.A. Wodehouse 2 (US Portsmouth), R. Dibble 9 (Bridgwater Albion), L. Haigh 4 (Manchester), W.E. Mann 1 (US Portsmouth), A.L. Kewney 7 (Leicester), J.A. King 1 (Headingley), C.H. Pillman 5 (Blackheath).

Referee J.I. Gillespie (Scotland)

Marcel Communeau, who captained France in their first Championship victory against Scotland on 2 January 1911

ENGLAND v FRANCE   2/162

28 January 1911
Twickenham
England 37 (5G, 2T, 2PG) France 0

England   T: Lambert (2), Pillman (2), Mann, Adrian Stoop, Wodehouse. C: Lambert (5). PG: Lambert (2).

Douglas Lambert's 22 points were a record for a Championship match. It was also England's biggest winning margin against any country, and their biggest Championship score against France. The French team's first visit to Twickenham might have produced a more respectable score but for injuries which restricted the performances of their half-backs, Guy Laterrade and Georges Peyroutou, and their full-back François Dutour.

ENGLAND   S.H. Williams 2 (Newport); D. Lambert 4 (Harlequins), *J.G.G. Birkett 11 (Harlequins), F.M. Stoop 2 (Harlequins), A.D. Roberts 2 (Northern); A.D. Stoop 8 (Harlequins), A.L.H. Gotley 4 (Blackheath); L.G. Brown 2 (Oxford U.), N.A. Wodehouse 3 (US Portsmouth), R. Dibble 10 (Bridgwater Albion), L. Haigh 5 (Manchester), W.E. Mann 2 (US Portsmouth), A.L. Kewney 8 (Leicester), J.A. King 2 (Headingley), C.H. Pillman 6 (Blackheath).

FRANCE   F. Dutour 1 (S. Toulouse); E. Lesieur 4 (S. Français), M. Burgun 5 (RCF), T. Varvier 1 (RCF), G. Charpentier 1 (S. Français); G. Peyroutou (2) (CA Périgueux), G. Laterrade 4 (S. Tarbes); R. Duval 1 (S. Français), J. Bavozet 2 (FC Lyon), *M. Communeau 5 (S. Français), P. Mauriat 6 (FC Lyon), P. Mounicq 2 (S. Toulouse), M. Legrain 3 (S. Français), P. Guillemin 6 (RCF), F. Forgues 2 (A. Bayonne).

Referee E.A. Johns (Wales)

SCOTLAND v WALES   27/163

4 February 1911
Inverleith, Edinburgh
Wales 32 (2G, 6T, 1DG) Scotland 10 (2T, 1DG)

Scotland   T: Turner, Scott. DG: Munro.
Wales   T: Gibbs (3), Spiller (2), Williams (2), Rhys Thomas. C: Dyke (2). DG: Spiller.

This was the highest number of tries Wales scored in any match against Scotland, beating the five they registered in 1947 and 1972. Scotland were handicapped by an injury to J.M. Macdonald, who went off soon after half-time. The luckless Edinburgh Wanderer never played for Scotland again, a fate he shared with D.G. Schulze, F.G. Buchanan and F.L. Osler. Cardiff RFC had plenty to celebrate – all of Wales's points, save a try by Pontypool's Rhys Thomas, were scored by their players.

SCOTLAND   D.G. Schulze (13) (London Scottish); D.M. Grant 1 (Elstow School), A.W. Angus 5 (Watsonians), F.G. Buchanan (3) (Kelvinside Acads), J.M. Macdonald (1) (Edinburgh Wands); *P. Munro 10 (London Scottish), F.L. Osler (2) (Edinburgh U.); C.H. Abercrombie 4 (US Portsmouth), R. Fraser 2 (Cambridge U.), J.M. Mackenzie 7 (Edinburgh U.), L. Robertson 2 (London Scottish), A.R. Ross 1 (Edinburgh U.), J.M.B. Scott 13 (Edinburgh Acads), R.C. Stevenson 5 (St Andrew's U.), F.H. Turner 2 (Oxford U.).

WALES   F.W. Birt 2 (Newport); R.A. Gibbs 13 (Cardiff), W. Spiller 4 (Cardiff), L.M. Dyke 2 (Cardiff), J.L. Williams 12 (Cardiff); *W.J. Trew 21 (Swansea), R.M. Owen 26 (Swansea); J. Webb 13 (Abertillery), G. Travers 19 (Newport), A.P. Coldrick 2 (Newport), R. Thomas 2 (Pontypool), D.J. Thomas 6 (Swansea), T. Evans 14 (Llanelli), J. Birch 1 (Neath), J. Pugsley 5 (Cardiff).

Referee J.G. Davidson (Ireland)

IRELAND v ENGLAND   27/164

11 February 1911
Lansdowne Road, Dublin
Ireland 3 (1T) England 0

Ireland   T: Tommy Smyth.

Frank Stoop was one of four not called on by England again, the Harlequin centre clearly being blamed for a poor clearing kick which led to Tommy Smyth scoring the winning try for Ireland.

IRELAND   W.P. Hinton 11 (Old Wesley); C.T. O'Callaghan 3 (Carlow), A.R. Foster 4 (Queen's U. Belfast), J.P. Quinn 3 (Dublin U.), A.R.V. Jackson 1 (Wanderers); R.A. Lloyd 3 (Dublin U.), H.M. Read 3 (Dublin U.); T. Smyth 11 (Malone), *G.T. Hamlet 24 (Old Wesley), M.R. Heffernan 1 (Cork Constitution), S.B.B. Campbell 1 (Derry), T. Halpin 6 (Garryowen), C. Adams 4 (Old Wesley), M.G. Garry 4 (Bective Rangers), P.J. Smyth 1 (Belfast Collegians).

ENGLAND   S.H. Williams 3 (Newport); D. Lambert (5) (Harlequins), *J.G.G. Birkett 12 (Harlequins), F.M. Stoop (3) (Harlequins), A.D. Roberts 3 (Northern); A.D. Stoop 9 (Harlequins), A.L.H. Gotley 5 (Blackheath); L.G. Brown 3 (Oxford U.), N.A. Wodehouse 4 (US Portsmouth), G.R. Hind (2) (Guy's H.), L. Haigh 6 (Manchester), W.E. Mann (3) (US Portsmouth), A.L. Kewney 9 (Leicester), J.A. King 3 (Headingley), C.H. Pillman 7 (Blackheath).

Referee J.D. Dallas (Scotland)

SCOTLAND v IRELAND   29/165

25 February 1911
Inverleith, Edinburgh
Ireland 16 (2G, 2T) Scotland 10 (2T, 1DG)

Scotland   T: Simson, Angus. DG: Munro.
Ireland   T: O'Callaghan, Foster, Adams, Quinn. C: Hinton, Lloyd.

This was Ireland's biggest score against Scotland in Scotland until they registered a 20-8 victory in 1932. Seven of the Scottish team, including their captain, Pat Munro, did not play in another Championship match.

SCOTLAND   A. Greig (1) (Glasgow HSFP); J.T. Simson (6) (Watsonians), A.W. Angus 6 (Watsonians), C. Ogilvy 1 (Hawick), D.M. Grant (2) (Elstow School); *P. Munro (11) (London Scottish), A.B. Lindsay (2) (The London H.); R. Fraser 3 (Cambridge U.), G.M. Frew 13 (Glasgow HSFP), J.C. MacCallum 19 (Watsonians), J.M. Mackenzie (8) (Edinburgh U.), J.M.B. Scott 14 (Edinburgh Acads), R.C. Stevenson (6) (St Andrew's U.), C.D. Stuart 6 (W. of Scotland), F.H. Turner 3 (Oxford U.).

IRELAND   W.P. Hinton 12 (Old Wesley); C.T. O'Callaghan 4 (Carlow), A.R. Foster 5 (Queen's U. Belfast), A.R.V. Jackson 2 (Wanderers), J.P. Quinn 4 (Dublin U.); R.A. Lloyd 4 (Dublin U.), H.M. Read 4 (Dublin U.); C. Adams 5 (Old Wesley), S.B.B. Campbell 2 (Derry), M.G. Garry 5 (Bective Rangers), T. Halpin 7 (Garryowen), *G.T. Hamlet 25 (Old Wesley), M.R. Heffernan 2 (Cork Constitution), P.J. Smyth 2 (Belfast Collegians), T. Smyth 12 (Malone).

Referee V.H. Cartwright (England)

FRANCE v WALES   2/166

28 February 1911
Parc des Princes, Paris
Wales 15 (3G) France 0

Wales   T: Morgan, Williams, Owen. C: Bancroft (3).

Played on Shrove Tuesday, Wales's first Championship match in France produced their biggest winning margin in France. It was equalled in 1975 when Wales won 25-10. Johnny Williams, of Cardiff, was appointed captain instead of Billy Trew because of his knowledge of French.

FRANCE   T. Varvier 2 (RCF); J. Dedet 4 (S. Français), C. du Souich 1 (SCUF), P. Failliot 2 (RCF), G. Lane 4 (RCF); A. Theuriet 2 (SCUF), *R. Duval 2 (S. Français); P. Mauriat 7 (FC Lyon), J. Bavozet (3) (FC Lyon), G. Dufour (1) (S. Tarbes), P. Guillemin (7) (RCF), P. Mounicq 3 (S. Toulouse), J. Cadenat 3 (SCUF), F. Forgues 3 (A. Bayonne), M. Legrain 4 (S. Français).

WALES   J. Bancroft 9 (Swansea); R.A. Gibbs 14 (Cardiff), W. Spiller 5 (Cardiff), L.M. Dyke 3 (Cardiff), *J.L. Williams 13 (Cardiff); W.J. Trew 22 (Swansea), R.M. Owen 27 (Swansea); J. Webb 14 (Abertillery), G. Travers 20 (Newport), J. Pugsley 6 (Cardiff), T. Evans 15 (Llanelli), J. Birch (2) (Neath), R. Thomas 3 (Pontypool), D.J. Thomas 7 (Swansea), I. Morgan 9 (Swansea).

Referee W. Williams (England)

WALES v IRELAND   25/167

11 March 1911
Cardiff Arms Park
Wales 16 (2G, 1T, 1PG) Ireland 0

Wales   T: Tom Evans, Webb, Gibbs. C: Bancroft (2). PG: Bancroft.

The fact that Wales and Ireland, once again, were jointly positioned to win the Triple Crown drew a then record crowd of over 40,000 to Arms Park. Thousands were locked out and despite the attempts of the police, some of whom were mounted, hundreds broke through the gates and climbed walls. Several gatecrashers were injured after falling from the top of the stand. Victory brought Wales not only the Triple Crown, but their first Championship Grand Slam (they beat all four countries in 1908 and 1909 before France formally became part of the Championship). It was a fitting climax for the two Welsh wings, Johnny Williams and Reggie Gibbs, both outstanding try scorers. Williams was on the winning side in 13 out of 14 matches, scoring 15 tries, and Gibbs ran in 13 tries in his 15 matches, 12 of which Wales won.

WALES   J. Bancroft 10 (Swansea); R.A. Gibbs (15) (Cardiff), W. Spiller 6 (Cardiff), L.M. Dyke (4) (Cardiff), J.L. Williams (14) (Cardiff); *W.J. Trew 23 (Swansea), R.M. Owen 28 (Swansea); A.P. Coldrick 3 (Newport), G. Travers (21) (Newport), J. Webb 15 (Abertillery), T. Evans (16) (Llanelli), J. Pugsley (7) (Cardiff), W.G. Evans (1) (Brynmawr), D.J. Thomas 8 (Swansea), I. Morgan 10 (Swansea).

IRELAND   W.P. Hinton 13 (Old Wesley); C.T. O'Callaghan 5 (Carlow), A.R. Foster 6 (Derry), A.R.V. Jackson 3 (Wanderers), J.P. Quinn 5 (Dublin U.); R.A. Lloyd 5 (Dublin U.), H.M. Read 5 (Dublin U.); *G.T. Hamlet 26 (Old Wesley), C. Adams 6 (Old Wesley), T. Smyth 13 (Malone), H. Moore 2 (Queen's U. Belfast), T. Halpin 8

(Garryowen), M.G. Garry (6) (Bective Rangers), M.R. Heffernan 3 (Cork Constitution), S.B.B. Campbell 3 (Derry).

Referee F.C. Potter-Irwin (England)

ENGLAND v SCOTLAND   26/168

18 March 1911
Twickenham
England 13 (2G, 1T) Scotland 8 (1G, 1T)

England   T: Birkett, Lawrie, Wodehouse. C: Lagden (2).
Scotland   T: Simson, Sutherland. C: Cunningham.

Scotland's first match at Twickenham brought to an end their remarkable run of nine wins from ten visits to grounds in England. It was also their fourth defeat of the season, which meant they were relegated to the status of Wooden Spoonists for the first time since 1902.

ENGLAND   S.H. Williams (4) (Newport); A.D. Roberts 4 (Northern), J.G.G. Birkett 13 (Harlequins), R.W. Poulton 4 (Oxford U.), P.W. Lawrie (2) (Leicester); A.D. Stoop 10 (Harlequins), *A.L.H. Gotley (6) (Blackheath); L.G. Brown 4 (Oxford U.), N.A. Wodehouse 5 (US Portsmouth), R. Dibble 11 (Bridgwater Albion), L. Haigh (7) (Manchester), R.O. Lagden (1) (Oxford U.), A.L. Kewney 10 (Leicester), J.A. King 4 (Headingley), C.H. Pillman 8 (Blackheath).

SCOTLAND   C. Ogilvy 2 (Hawick); W.R. Sutherland 4 (Hawick), G. Cunningham (8) (London Scottish), R.F. Simson (1) (London Scottish), S.S.L. Steyn 1 (London Scottish); E. Milroy 2 (Watsonians), J.Y.M. Henderson (1) (Watsonians); D.M. Bain 1 (Oxford U.), J. Dobson 1 (Glasgow Acads), R. Fraser (4) (Cambridge U.), G.M. Frew (14) (Glasgow HSFP), W.R. Hutchison (1) (Glasgow HSFP), *J.C. MacCallum 20 (Watsonians), C.D. Stuart (7) (W. of Scotland), F.H. Turner 4 (Oxford U.).

Referee T.D. Schofield (Wales)

IRELAND v FRANCE   2/169

25 March 1911
Mardyke, Cork
Ireland 25 (3G, 2T, 1DG) France 5 (1G)

Ireland   T: Quinn, O'Callaghan, Jackson (2), Heffernan. C: Lloyd (3). DG: Lloyd.
France   T: Failliot. C: Dutour.

The last Championship appearance of George Hamlet, the most revered forward in Irish rugby history before the First World War, and whose international career began against England at Leicester in 1902. A crowd of 10,000 watched France lead 5-0 at half-time in the city of Cork's second international match. It was Ireland's highest score against France, a record which stood until 1975 when it was equalled by a 25-6 win at Lansdowne Road. This was the last international refereed by Scotland's James Crawford Findlay. Like his younger brother, David Graham Findlay, who handled seven Championship matches between 1895–1900, Crawford Findlay became President of the Scottish Rugby Union.

IRELAND   F.M.W. Harvey (2) (Wanderers); C.T. O'Callaghan 6 (Carlow), A.R. Foster 7 (Derry), A.R.V. Jackson 4 (Wanderers), J.P. Quinn 6 (Dublin U.); R.A. Lloyd 6 (Dublin U.), H.M. Read 6 (Dublin U.); C. Adams 7 (Old Wesley), S.B.B. Campbell 4 (Derry), R.I. Graham (1) (Dublin U.), *G.T. Hamlet (27) (Old Wesley), M.R. Heffernan (4) (Cork Constitution), T. Halpin 9 (Garryowen), H. Moore 3 (Queen's U. Belfast), P.J. Smyth (3) (Belfast Collegians).

FRANCE   F. Dutour 2 (S. Toulouse); E. Lesieur 5 (S. Français), G. Borchard (1) (RCF), J. Dedet 5 (S. Français), P. Failliot 3 (RCF); G. Laterrade (5) (S. Tarbes), R. Duval (3) (S. Français); R. Monnier 1 (SBUC), P. Mauriat 8 (FC Lyon), J. Cadenat 4 (SCUF), C. du Souich (2) (SCUF), M. Legrain 5 (S. Français), R. Paoli 1 (S. Français), *M. Communeau 6 (S. Français), P. Mounicq 4 (S. Toulouse).

Referee J.C. Findlay (Scotland)

PARIS Ireland beat France 11-6 · EDINBURGH Scotland beat France 31-3
TWICKENHAM England beat Wales 8-0 · SWANSEA Wales beat Scotland 21-6
TWICKENHAM England beat Ireland 15-0 · DUBLIN Ireland beat Scotland 10-8
BELFAST Ireland beat Wales 12-5 · EDINBURGH Scotland beat England 8-3
NEWPORT Wales beat France 14-8 · PARIS England beat France 18-8

CHAMPIONSHIP TABLE
England – Championship

									Tries	
Pos	Country	P	W	D	L	F	A	Pts	F	A
1	England (3)	4	3	0	1	44	16	6	12	4
2	Ireland (2)	4	3	0	1	33	34	6	6	10
3	Scotland (5)	4	2	0	2	53	37	4	12	6
4	Wales (1)	4	2	0	2	40	34	4	8	8
5	France (4)	4	0	0	4	25	74	0	7	17

It was England's turn to win the Championship, although they finished with the same number of points as Ireland. The only defeat the Irish suffered was at Twickenham, and it was the margin, 0-15, which determined they should be in second position for the second year running. Scotland clearly were determined to avenge their defeat in Paris the previous season: their 31-3 win over France was the biggest score of the season. The Scots also had the satisfaction of depriving the English of the Grand Slam, Triple Crown and Calcutta Cup all in one go — an 8-3 victory at Inverleith. The Scots also featured in another of the Championship's scoring quirks. They scored more points than anyone, 53, and equalled England's 12 tries, but still ended in third position, ahead of Wales.

FRANCE v IRELAND   3/170

1 January 1912
Parc des Princes, Paris
Ireland 11 (1G, 2T) France 6 (2T)

France   T: Paoli, Dufau.
Ireland   T: Taylor, Foster, Lloyd. C: Taylor.

An attendance of 20,000, which is an indication of the popularity of rugby in France at the time, watched this match, played on a Monday. France introduced six players new to the Championship. Two of the Irish players, Edwards and Taylor, were killed in the First World War, as were eight of the French team, Conil de Beyssac, Boyau, Burgun, Dufau, Ihingoue, Lane, Larribeau and Varvie.

FRANCE   T. Varvier (3) (RCF); P. Failliot 4 (RCF), G. Lane 5 (RCF), D. Ihingoue 1 (BEC), J. Dufau 1 (Biarritz Ol); L. Larribeau 1 (CA Périgueux), M. Burgun 6 (RCF); P. Mounicq 5 (S. Toulouse), J. Conil de Beyssac 1 (SBUC), M. Boyau 1 (SBUC), R. Paoli 2 (S. Français), F. Forgues 4 (A. Bayonne), *P. Mauriat 9 (FC Lyon), M. Communeau 7 (S. Français), J. Domercq 1 (A. Bayonne).

IRELAND   W.P. Hinton 14 (Old Wesley); C.V. McIvor 1 (Dublin U.), A.S. Taylor (4) (Queen's U. Belfast), A.R. Foster 8 (Derry), C.T. O'Callaghan (7) (Carlow); *R.A. Lloyd 7 (Dublin U.), H.M. Read 7 (Dublin U.); S.B.B. Campbell 5 (Derry), W.J. Beatty 2 (NIFC), W.V. Edwards 1 (Malone), T. Halpin 10 (Garryowen), R. Hemphill 1 (Dublin U.), H. Moore 4 (Queen's U. Belfast), G.V. McConnell 1 (Edinburgh U.), R.d'A. Patterson 1 (Wanderers).

Referee A.O. Jones (England)

SCOTLAND v FRANCE   3/171

20 January 1912
Inverleith, Edinburgh
Scotland 31 (5G, 1T, 1PG) France 3 (1T)

Scotland   T: Gunn, Sutherland (2), Pearson, Will, Turner. C: Turner (5). PG: Pearson.
France   T: Communeau.

Scotland exacted a handsome revenge for their defeat in France the previous season: it was their biggest score and highest number of conversions against France, and the 28-point winning margin was their largest against any country. France reacted accordingly: they dropped five of their team.

SCOTLAND   W.M. Dickson 1 (Blackheath); W.R. Sutherland 5 (Hawick), A.W. Angus 7 (Watsonians), J. Pearson 8 (Watsonians), J.G. Will 1 (Cambridge U.); A.W. Gunn 1 (Royal HSFP), J. Hume 1 (Royal HSFP); D.M. Bain 2 (Oxford U.), J. Dobson 2 (Glasgow Acads), C.C.P. Hill 1 (St Andrew's U.), D.D. Howie 1 (Kirkcaldy), *J.C. MacCallum 21 (Watsonians), W.D.C.L. Purves 1 (Cambridge U.), R.D. Robertson (1) (London Scottish), F.H. Turner 5 (Oxford U.).

FRANCE   F. Dutour 3 (S. Toulouse); P. Failliot 5 (RCF), D. Ihingoue (2) (BEC), J. Dufau 2 (Biarritz Ol), M. Burgun 7 (RCF); *J. Dedet 6 (S. Français), L. Larribeau 2 (CA Périgueux); M. Boyau 2 (SBUC), M. Communeau 8 (VC Beauvais), J. Conil de Beyssac 2 (SBUC), J. Domercq (2) (A. Bayonne), P. Mauriat 10 (FC Lyon), R. Monnier (2) (SBUC), R. Paoli (3) (S. Français), E. Vallot (1) (SCUF).

Referee J.J. Coffey (Ireland)

ENGLAND v WALES   28/172

20 January 1912
Twickenham
England 8 (1G, 1T) Wales 0

England   T: Brougham, Pym. C: Chapman.

Wales, winners of the Grand Slam in 1911, toppled at the first hurdle in their 1912 campaign. Each side introduced six players new to the Championship.

ENGLAND   W.R. Johnston 4 (Bristol); F.E. Chapman 5 (Westoe), R.W. Poulton 5 (Harlequins), J.G.G. Birkett 14 (Harlequins), H. Brougham 1 (Harlequins); A.D. Stoop 11 (Harlequins), J.A. Pym 1 (Blackheath); A.H. MacIlwaine 1 (US Portsmouth), J.H. Eddison 1 (Headingley), R.C. Stafford 1 (Bedford), J.A. King 5 (Headingley), D. Holland 1 (Devonport Albion), *R. Dibble 12 (Newport), N.A. Wodehouse 6 (US Portsmouth), C.H. Pillman 9 (Blackheath).

WALES   J. Bancroft 11 (Swansea); E.J. Davies 1 (Cardiff), W. Spiller 7 (Cardiff), F.W. Birt 3 (Newport), J.P. Jones 6 (Pontypool); J.M.C. Lewis 1 (Cardiff), *R.M. Owen 29 (Swansea); J. Webb 16 (Abertillery), H. Davies 1 (Neath), G. Stephens 1 (Neath), R. Thomas 4 (Pontypool), A.P. Coldrick 4 (Newport), L. Trump 1 (Newport), H. Uzzell 1 (Newport), D.J. Thomas (9) (Swansea).

Referee J.T. Tulloch (Scotland)

WALES v SCOTLAND   28/173

3 February 1912
St Helen's, Swansea
Wales 21 (2G, 1T, 2DG) Scotland 6 (2T)

Wales   T: Hirst, Morgan, Plummer. C: Bancroft (2). DG: Trew, Birt.
Scotland   T: Will, Milroy.

A gang of snow clearers had to be employed to enable the match to take place, after a heavy snowfall during the morning. It was the last international for three of Wales's long-serving players, Dicky Owen, Jim Webb and Ivor Morgan, while in contrast, George Hirst and Reggie Plummer celebrated their first caps with one try apiece. Thus the fruitful half-back partnership of Billy Trew and Owen came to an end: they were selected twice more as a pair but chose instead to play for their club, Swansea. Many believed that Ivor Morgan was the most important cog in the development of forward play during the era, and was regarded as the first genuine loose forward produced by Wales.

WALES   J. Bancroft 12 (Swansea); R.C.S. Plummer 1 (Newport), F.W. Birt 4 (Newport), W.

Davies 1 (Aberavon), G.L. Hirst 1 (Newport); W.J. Trew 24 (Swansea), *R.M. Owen (30) (Swansea); G. Stephens 2 (Neath), H. Davies (2) (Neath), J. Webb (17) (Abertillery), A.P. Coldrick 5 (Newport), H. Uzzell 2 (Newport), L. Trump 2 (Newport), R. Thomas 5 (Pontypool), I. Morgan (11) (Swansea).

SCOTLAND   W.M. Dickson 2 (Blackheath); W.R. Sutherland 6 (Hawick), A.W. Angus 8 (Watsonians), J. Pearson 9 (Watsonians), J.G. Will 2 (Cambridge U.); A.W. Gunn 2 (Royal HSFP), E. Milroy 3 (Watsonians); D.M. Bain 3 (Oxford U.), J. Dobson 3 (Glasgow Acads), D.D. Howie 2 (Kirkcaldy), *J.C. MacCallum 22 (Watsonians), W.D.C.L. Purves 2 (London Scottish), L. Robertson 3 (London Scottish), J.M.B. Scott 15 (Edinburgh Acads), F.H. Turner 6 (Liverpool).

Referee F.C. Potter-Irwin (England)

ENGLAND v IRELAND 28/174

10 February 1912
Twickenham
England 15 (5T) Ireland 0

England   T: Roberts (2), Birkett, Brougham, Poulton.

Adrian Stoop and Cherry Pillman, the architects of the win over Wales the previous month, were not available, but England were in no way weakened and romped home against an Irish side which was experienced at half-back but largely untried at forward.

ENGLAND   W.R. Johnston 5 (Bristol); A.D. Roberts 5 (Northern), R.W. Poulton 6 (Harlequins), J.G.G. Birkett 15 (Harlequins), H. Brougham 2 (Harlequins); H. Coverdale 2 (Blackheath), J.A. Pym 2 (Blackheath); A.H. MacIlwaine 2 (US Portsmouth), J.H. Eddison 2 (Headingley), R.C. Stafford 2 (Bedford), J.A. King 6 (Headingley), D. Holland 2 (Devonport Albion), *R. Dibble 13 (Newport), N.A. Wodehouse 7 (US Portsmouth), A.L. Kewney 11 (Rockcliff).

IRELAND   W.P. Hinton 15 (Old Wesley); C.V. McIvor 2 (Dublin U.), M. Abraham 1 (Bective Rangers), *A.R. Foster 9 (Queen's U. Belfast), J.P. Quinn 7 (Dublin U.); R.A. Lloyd 8 (Dublin U.), H.M. Read 8 (Dublin U.); S.B.B. Campbell 6 (Derry), G.V. Killeen 1 (Garryowen), T. Smyth

(14) (Malone), W.V. Edwards (2) (Malone), H. Moore 5 (Queen's U. Belfast), T. Halpin 11 (Garryowen), R. Hemphill 2 (Dublin U.), G.V. McConnell 2 (Edinburgh U.).

Referee T.D. Schofield (Wales)

IRELAND v SCOTLAND 30/175

24 February 1912
Lansdowne Road, Dublin
Ireland 10 (1T, 1DG, 1PG) Scotland 8 (1G, 1T)

Ireland   T: Foster. DG: Lloyd. PG: Lloyd.
Scotland   T: Turner, Will. C: MacCallum.

Scotland, who had lost only one of their first nine matches in Ireland, were now finding success hard to achieve at Lansdowne Road. Despite the fact that Scotland had scored ten tries in the season so far, they dropped three of their backs after this match.

IRELAND   R.A. Wright (1) (Monkstown); J.P. Quinn 8 (Dublin U.), A.R. Foster 10 (Derry), M. Abraham 2 (Bective Rangers), C.V. McIvor 3 (Dublin U.); *R.A. Lloyd 9 (Dublin U.), H.M. Read 9 (Dublin U.); C. Adams 8 (Old Wesley), G.S. Brown 1 (Monkstown), S.B.B. Campbell 7 (Derry), T. Halpin (12) (Garryowen), R. Hemphill 3 (Dublin U.), G.V. Killeen 2 (Garryowen), H. Moore 6 (Queen's U. Belfast), R.d'A. Patterson 2 (Wanderers).

SCOTLAND   C. Ogilvy (3) (Hawick); S.S.L. Steyn (2) (Oxford U.), A.W. Angus 9 (Watsonians), C.M. Gilray (4) (London Scottish), J.G. Will 3 (Cambridge U.); A.W. Gunn 3 (Royal HSFP), E. Milroy 4 (Watsonians); J. Dobson 4 (Glasgow Acads), C.C.P. Hill (2) (St Andrew's U.), D.D. Howie 3 (Kirkcaldy), *J.C. MacCallum 23 (Watsonians), W.D.C.L. Purves 3 (London Scottish), L. Robertson 4 (London Scottish), J.M.B. Scott 16 (Edinburgh Acads), F.H. Turner 7 (Liverpool).

Referee F.C. Potter-Irwin (England)

England's XV which played Scotland on 16 March 1912

IRELAND v WALES   26/176

9 March 1912
Balmoral Showgrounds, Belfast
Ireland 12 (1G, 1T, 1DG) Wales 5 (1G)

Ireland   T: McIvor, Brown. C: Lloyd. DG: Lloyd.
Wales   T: Davies. C: Bancroft.

One of the most inexperienced Welsh sides since the turn of the century, which included seven new caps, were no match for Ireland, even though they were leading 5-0 at half-time. The team was not without courage: Tom Williams, of Swansea, broke an arm in the second half but returned to the field after he had had the arm bandaged.

IRELAND   W.P. Hinton (16) (Old Wesley); J.P. Quinn 9 (Dublin U.), A.R. Foster 11 (Derry), M. Abraham 3 (Bective Rangers), C.V. McIvor 4 (Dublin U.); H.M. Read 10 (Dublin U.), *R.A. Lloyd 10 (Dublin U.); G.S. Brown (2) (Monkstown), G.V. Killeen 3 (Garryowen), R. Hemphill (4) (Dublin U.), W.J. Beatty (3) (NIFC), H. Moore (7) (Queen's U. Belfast), S.B.B. Campbell 8 (Derry), C. Adams 9 (Old Wesley), R.d'A. Patterson 3 (Wanderers).

WALES   *J. Bancroft 13 (Swansea); R.C.S. Plummer 2 (Newport), F.W. Birt 5 (Newport), W. Davies (2) (Aberavon), B. Lewis 1 (Swansea); W.J. Martin 1 (Newport), T.H. Vile 4 (Newport); G. Stephens 3 (Neath), G.E. Merry 1 (Pill Harriers), H. Hiams 1 (Swansea), T. Williams 1 (Swansea), L. Trump 3 (Newport), H. Uzzell 3 (Newport), F. Hawkins 1 (Pontypridd), W. Jenkins 1 (Cardiff).

Referee J.D. Dallas (Scotland)

SCOTLAND v ENGLAND   27/177

16 March 1912
Inverleith, Edinburgh
Scotland 8 (1G, 1T) England 3 (1T)

Scotland   T: Sutherland, Usher. C: MacCallum.
England   T: Holland.

England's chances of winning the Triple Crown were effectively ruled out in the first half when they lost J.A. King, the Headingley forward, with two broken ribs. So Adrian Stoop, their renowned architect of back play, finished his Championship career as he had started it – with a defeat at the hands of the Scots. This was the only match of the season in which George Will, Scotland's wing discovery from Cambridge University, failed to score a try.

SCOTLAND   W.M. Dickson 3 (Blackheath); W.R. Sutherland 7 (Hawick), W. Burnet (1) (Hawick), A.W. Angus 10 (Watsonians), J.G. Will 4 (Cambridge U.); J.L. Boyd (1) (US Portsmouth), E. Milroy 5 (Watsonians); D.M. Bain 4 (Oxford U.), J. Dobson (5) (Glasgow Acads), D.D. Howie 4 (Kirkcaldy), *J.C. MacCallum (24) (Watsonians), L. Robertson 5 (London Scottish), J.M.B. Scott 17 (Edinburgh Acads), F.H. Turner 8 (Liverpool), C.M. Usher 1 (London Scottish).

ENGLAND   W.R. Johnston 6 (Bristol); A.D. Roberts 6 (Northern), R.W. Poulton 7 (Harlequins), J.G.G. Birkett 16 (Harlequins), H. Brougham 3 (Harlequins); A.D. Stoop (12) (Harlequins), J.A. Pym 3 (Blackheath); A.H. MacIlwaine 3 (US Portsmouth), J.H. Eddison 3 (Headingley), R.C. Stafford 3 (Bedford), J.A. King 7 (Headingley), D. Holland (3) (Devonport Albion), *R. Dibble (14) (Newport), N.A. Wodehouse 8 (US Portsmouth), A.L. Kewney (12) (Rockcliff).

Referee F. Gardiner (Ireland)

WALES v FRANCE   3/178

25 March 1912
Rodney Parade, Newport
Wales 14 (1G, 3T) France 8 (1G, 1T)

Wales   T: Davies (2), Plummer, Jones. C: Thomas.
France   T: Lesieur, Larribeau. C: Boyau.

A Monday match, Wales nearly paid for the mistake of underestimating France, who led at half-time 8-6. Playing for Wales was not yet paramount for some players: Billy Trew and Dicky Owen preferred to tour Devon with their club, Swansea. It was the last Championship match for eight of the Welsh team.

WALES   H. Thomas (1) (Llanelli); R.C.S. Plummer 3 (Newport), J.P. Jones 7 (Pontypool), W. Spiller 8 (Cardiff), E.J. Davies (2) (Cardiff); W.J. Martin (2) (Newport), T.H. Vile 5 (Newport); G. Stephens 4 (Neath), G.E. Merry (2) (Pill Har-

riers), H. Hiams (2) (Swansea), F. Hawkins (2) (Pontypridd), W. Jenkins 2 (Cardiff), A.P. Coldrick (6) (Newport), L. Trump (4) (Newport), H. Uzzell 4 (Newport).

FRANCE   F. Dutour 4 (S. Toulouse); E. Lesieur (6) (S. Français), *G. Lane 6 (RCF), J. Sentilles 1 (S. Tarbes), J. Dufau 3 (Biarritz Ol); L. Larribeau 3 (CA Périgueux), G. Charpentier 2 (S. Français); F. Forgues 5 (A. Bayonne), M. Communeau 9 (VC Beauvais). M. Monniot 1 (RCF), J. Pascarel 1 (TOEC), A. Forestier (1) (SCUF), J. Cadenat 5 (SCUF), P. Thil 1 (S. Nantes), M. Boyau 3 (S. Bordelais).

Referee A.O. Jones (England)

FRANCE v ENGLAND   3/179

8 April 1912
Parc des Princes, Paris
England 18 (1G, 3T, 1DG) France 8 (1G, 1T)

France   T: Dufau, Failliot. C: Boyau.
England   T: Birkett, Brougham, Eddison, Roberts. C: Pillman. DG: Coverdale.

England regained the title they last won in 1910 with this convincing victory in France on Easter Monday. It was the last Championship match for J.G.G. Birkett, who had won 17 caps since 1906, and for six other members of the side.

FRANCE   F. Dutour 5 (S. Toulouse); P. Failliot 6 (RCF), *G. Lane 7 (RCF), J. Sentilles 2 (S. Tarbes), J. Dufau (4) (Biarritz Ol); G. Charpentier (3) (S. Français), L. Larribeau 4 (CA Périgueux); P. Thil 2 (S. Nantes), J. Pascarel 2 (TOEC), M. Monniot (2) (RCF), P. Mounicq 6 (S. Toulouse), J. Cadenat 6 (SCUF), M. Boyau 4 (S. Bordelais), M. Communeau 10 (VC Beauvais), F. Forgues 6 (A. Bayonne).

ENGLAND   W.R. Johnston 7 (Bristol); A.D. Roberts 7 (Northern), M.E. Neale (1) (Blackheath), J.G.G. Birkett (17) (Harlequins), H. Brougham (4) (Harlequins); H. Coverdale 3 (Blackheath), J.A. Pym (4) (Blackheath); A.H. MacIlwaine 4 (US Portsmouth), J.H. Eddison (4) (Headingley), R.C. Stafford (4) (Bedford), W.B. Hynes (1) (US Portsmouth), J.E. Greenwood 1 (Cambridge U.), J.A.S. Ritson 3 (Northern), *N.A. Wodehouse 9 (US Portsmouth), C.H. Pillman 10 (Blackheath).

Referee T.D. Schofield (Wales)

1913

PARIS Scotland beat France 21-3 · CARDIFF England beat Wales 12-0
TWICKENHAM England beat France 20-0 · EDINBURGH Wales beat Scotland 8-0
DUBLIN England beat Ireland 15-4 · EDINBURGH Scotland beat Ireland 29-14
PARIS Wales beat France 11-8 · SWANSEA Wales beat Ireland 16-13
TWICKENHAM England beat Scotland 3-0 · CORK Ireland beat France 24-0

CHAMPIONSHIP TABLE
England – Championship, Triple Crown, Grand Slam

Pos	Country	P	W	D	L	F	A	Pts	Tries F	A
1	England (1)	4	4	0	0	50	4	8	13	0
2	Wales (4)	4	3	0	1	35	33	6	8	6
3	Scotland (3)	4	2	0	2	50	28	4	12	6
4	Ireland (2)	4	1	0	3	55	60	2	10	14
5	France (5)	4	0	0	4	11	76	0	3	20

The International Board was moved to rebuke the French authorities for the behaviour of the crowd at the France v Scotland match at Parc des Princes on 1 January. A recurrence of the trouble would lead, the International Board threatened, to a cessation of international matches with France. No doubt this was intended more as a warning to the French supporters, rather than a reprimand to the French officials, who were quite unprepared for the trouble caused. Scotland's reaction was somewhat stronger; they refused to play France in 1914. Their argument, the SRU explained, was not with the French team or the French authorities, but they refused to accept a situation in which a referee's decisions were questioned and his safety threatened by spectators. France's opinion of this rather high-handed dismissal was not made public, but they ensured that extra police were on duty for their next home match, against Wales. This time the referee, M.A. Miles, of England, was cheered by the crowd when he refused to allow the game to continue until squads of Gardes de Republique, who had formed up behind the Welsh goal-line near the final whistle, had withdrawn.

FRANCE v SCOTLAND 4/180

1 January 1913
Parc des Princes, Paris
Scotland 21 (3G, 2T) France 3 (1T)

France T: Sébedio.
Scotland T: Stewart (3), Gordon (2). C: Turner (3).

With Stade Colombes unplayable because of flooding, this match was transferred to Parc des Princes. Strict refereeing by John Baxter and his frequent awarding of penalties against France upset the crowd, who reacted with such hostility that players and police had to escort the referee from the ground at no-side. Scotland reacted by refusing to play France in 1914 and the RFU said they would no longer supply referees for matches in France. The match was important in one other respect: it was Scotland's biggest score against France in France.

FRANCE F. Dutour (6) (S. Toulouse); L. Larribeau 5 (CA Périgueux), *G. Lane (8) (RCF), J. Sentilles (3) (S. Tarbes), P. Jauréguy 1 (S. Toulouse); M. Burgun 8 (RCF), M. Hedembaigt 1 (A. Bayonne); F. Forgues 7 (A. Bayonne), M. Legrain 6 (S. Français), M. Leuvielle 1 (SBUC), P. Mauriat 11 (FC Lyon), P. Mounicq 7 (S. Toulouse), J. Pascarel 3 (TOEC), J. Sébedio 1 (S. Tarbes), P. Thil 3 (S. Nantes).

SCOTLAND W.M. Dickson 4 (Oxford U.); W.R. Sutherland 8 (Hawick), R.E. Gordon 1 (US Portsmouth), A.W. Angus 11 (Watsonians), W.A. Stewart 1 (The London H.); A.W. Gunn (4) (Royal HSFP), E. Milroy 6 (Watsonians); C.H. Abercrombie 5 (US Portsmouth), D.M. Bain 5

(Oxford U.), P.C.B. Blair 1 (Cambridge U.), D.D. Howie 5 (Kirkcaldy), G.A. Ledingham (1) (Aberdeen GSFP), J.B. Macdougall 1 (Greenock Wands), *F.H. Turner 9 (Liverpool), C.M. Usher 2 (London Scottish).

Referee J.W. Baxter (England)

WALES v ENGLAND 29/181

18 January 1913
Cardiff Arms Park
England 12 (1G, 1T, 1DG) Wales 0

England T: Coates, Pillman. C: Greenwood. DG: Poulton.

This was England's first victory in Wales since 1895 and it put them on course for the Grand Slam. In those days England thought little about blooding newcomers in the hotbed of Welsh rugby – seven obtained first caps at Cardiff, including one Cyril Nelson Lowe, who was to prove himself as arguably the greatest wing ever to play for England. Lowe scored 18 tries in his England career (1913–23) which is a record that still stands. Another England newcomer was W.J.A. Davies, described as one of the greatest half-backs who ever lived. Wales, their Golden Age assuredly behind them, took the defeat badly: eight of the side never played again.

WALES R.F. Williams 1 (Cardiff); R.C.S. Plummer (4) (Newport), F.W. Birt (6) (Newport), W. Spiller (9) (Cardiff), W.P. Geen 1 (Newport); H.W. Thomas (1) (Swansea), *T.H. Vile 6 (Newport); G. Stephens 5 (Neath), F. Perrett 1 (Neath), B. Hollindale (1) (Swansea), H. Wetter (1) (Newport), P. Jones 1 (Newport), R. Thomas (6) (Pontypool), F. Andrews 1 (Pontypool), J. Morgan (1) (Llanelli).

ENGLAND W.R. Johnston 8 (Bristol); C.N. Lowe 1 (Cambridge U.), F.E. Steinthal 1 (Ilkley), R.W. Poulton 8 (Harlequins), V.H.M. Coates 1 (Bath); W.J.A. Davies 1 (US Portsmouth), W.I. Cheesman 1 (OMT); J.A.S. Ritson 4 (Northern), J.A. King 8 (Headingley), J.E. Greenwood 2 (Cambridge U.), G. Ward 1 (Leicester), L.G. Brown 5 (Oxford U.), *N.A. Wodehouse 10 (US Portsmouth), S. Smart 1 (Gloucester), C.H. Pillman 11 (Blackheath).

Referee S.H. Crawford (Ireland)

ENGLAND v FRANCE 4/182

25 January 1913
Twickenham
England 20 (1G, 5T) France 0

England T: Coates (3), Pillman (2), Poulton. C: Greenwood.

This was England's third international of the month, which had started with a defeat by South Africa on 4 January. The six-try rout brought England's total number of tries in four Championship matches against the French to 20. One Frenchman, Jean Caujolle, earned ceaseless praise: 'Caujolle ... played a very great game' wrote E.H.D. Sewell, 'his touch-finding under pressure was very fine, and he is, by a good deal, the best full-back French football has produced.' Sewell, however, was critical of the forwards: 'Their game suffers from each forward having a fixed position in the scrum. The two outside rear rank men were frequently not pushing an ounce of their weight.'

ENGLAND W.R. Johnston 9 (Bristol); C.N. Lowe 2 (Cambridge U.), F.E. Steinthal (2) (Ilkley), R.W. Poulton 9 (Harlequins), V.H.M. Coates 2 (Bath); W.J.A. Davies 2 (US Portsmouth), W.I. Cheesman 2 (OMT); J.A.S. Ritson 5 (Northern), J.A. King 9 (Headingley), J.E. Greenwood 3 (Cambridge U.), G. Ward 2 (Leicester), L.G. Brown 6 (Oxford U.), *N.A. Wodehouse 11 (US Portsmouth), S. Smart 2 (Gloucester), C.H. Pillman 12 (Blackheath).

FRANCE J. Caujolle 1 (S. Tarbes); G. André 1 (RCF), J. Dedet 7 (S. Français), M. Burgun 9 (RCF), P. Failliot 7 (RCF); M. Bruneau (3) (S. Bordelais), A. Theuriet (3) (SCUF); G. Favre 1 (FC Lyon), J. Pascarel 4 (TOEC), P. Thil 4 (S. Nantes), P. Mounicq (8) (S. Toulouse), *M. Leuvielle 2 (S. Bordelais), M. Legrain 7 (RCF), M. Communeau (11) (S. Français), J. Sébedio 2 (S. Tarbes).

Referee J. Games (Wales)

SCOTLAND v WALES   29/183

1 February 1913
Inverleith, Edinburgh
Wales 8 (1G, 1T) Scotland 0

Wales   T: Clem Lewis, Tuan Jones: C: Clem Lewis.

Wales fielded one of their most inexperienced XVs. Fourteen players mustered 31 caps only between them and they relied heavily on the experienced Billy Trew, the captain, who was making his twenty-fifth Championship appearance. Scotland, likewise, had only a few players fully acquainted with the demands of international rugby.

SCOTLAND   W.M. Dickson 5 (Oxford U.); W.A. Stewart 2 (The London H.), R.E. Gordon 2 (US Portsmouth), A.W. Angus 12 (Watsonians), W.R. Sutherland 9 (Hawick); J.H. Bruce-Lockhart 1 (London Scottish), E. Milroy 7 (Watsonians); C.H. Abercrombie (6) (US Portsmouth), D.M. Bain 6 (Oxford U.), P.C.B. Blair 2 (Cambridge U.), D.D. Howie (6) (Kirkcaldy), L. Robertson 6 (London Scottish), J.M.B. Scott 18 (Edinburgh Acads), *F.H. Turner 10 (Liverpool), C.M. Usher 3 (London Scottish).

WALES   R.F. Williams 2 (Cardiff); G.L. Hirst 2 (Newport), T. Jones (1) (Pontypool), *W.J. Trew 25 (Swansea), H. Lewis 1 (Swansea); J.M.C. Lewis 2 (Cardiff), R. Lloyd 1 (Pontypool); Revd J.A. Davies 1 (Swansea), R. Richards 1 (Aberavon), F. Perrett 2 (Neath), G. Stephens 6 (Neath), W. Jenkins 3 (Cardiff), F. Andrews 2 (Pontypool), P. Jones 2 (Newport), H. Uzzell 5 (Newport).

Referee S.H. Crawford (Ireland)

IRELAND v ENGLAND   29/184

8 February 1913
Lansdowne Road, Dublin
England 15 (4T, 1PG) Ireland 4 (1DG)

Ireland   DG: Lloyd.
England   T: Coates (2), Pillman, Ritson. PG: Greenwood.

Dicky Lloyd and Harry Read played together for Ireland for the eleventh time but in a side which contained seven new caps their experience counted for little. The only consolation for Ireland was that Lloyd's dropped goal was the only score registered against England in a season in which they won the Grand Slam. Not everyone was pleased with England. On 22 February *London Opinion* published a poem by P.G. Wodehouse bemoaning the fact that Cyril Lowe rarely, if ever, received a pass while playing for England. Cartoonists of the day, too, accused the England backs of 'starving' the little Cambridge wing. Vince Coates had scored six tries in his first three matches for England.

IRELAND   G. Young (1) (UC Cork); J.P. Quinn 10 (Dublin U.), G.W. Holmes 1 (Dublin U.), J.B. Minch 1 (Bective Rangers), C.V. McIvor 5 (Dublin U.); *R.A. Lloyd 11 (Dublin U.), H.M. Read 11 (Dublin U.); S.B.B. Campbell 9 (Derry), E.W. Jeffares 1 (Wanderers), G.V. Killeen 4 (Garryowen), R.d'A. Patterson 4 (Wanderers), W. Tyrrell 2 (Queen's U. Belfast), F.G. Schute 1 (Dublin U.), J.E. Finlay 1 (Queen's U. Belfast), P. Stokes 1 (Garryowen).

ENGLAND   W.R. Johnston 10 (Bristol); C.N. Lowe 3 (Cambridge U.), A.J. Dingle 1 (Hartlepool Rovers), R.W. Poulton 10 (Harlequins), V.H.M. Coates 3 (Bath); W.J.A. Davies 3 (US Portsmouth), W.I. Cheesman (3) (OMT); J.A.S. Ritson 6 (Northern), J.A. King 10 (Headingley), J.E. Greenwood 4 (Cambridge U.), A.E. Kitching (1) (Blackheath), L.G. Brown 7 (Oxford U.), *N.A. Wodehouse 12 (US Portsmouth), S. Smart 3 (Gloucester), C.H. Pillman 13 (Blackheath).

Referee J.R.C. Greenlees (Scotland)

SCOTLAND v IRELAND 31/185

22 February 1913
Inverleith, Edinburgh
Scotland 29 (4G, 3T) Ireland 14 (2G, 1DG)

Scotland T: Stewart (4), Usher, Bowie, Purves.
C: Turner (4).
Ireland T: Schute, Stokes. C: Lloyd (2). DG:
Lloyd.

This was the last Championship match for Harry
Read, the Dublin University scrum-half, thus
bringing to an end the famous half-back partnership with Dicky Lloyd. Read and Lloyd came
together in 1910 and played 12 matches with
Read at scrum-half and Lloyd outside him, the
first consistently specialized half-back pairing
in the Championship. The break-up coincided
with Scotland's biggest score against Ireland;
the seven tries were also their biggest total
against Ireland. W.A. Stewart's four tries was
the best individual effort since George Lindsay's
five against Wales in 1887, and since equalled
only by Ian Smith, against France and Wales in
1925.

SCOTLAND W.M. Dickson (6) (Oxford U.); W.R.
Sutherland 10 (Hawick), R.E. Gordon (3) (US
Portsmouth), J. Pearson 10 (Watsonians), W.A.
Stewart 3 (The London H.); T.C. Bowie 1
(Watsonians), E. Milroy 8 (Watsonians); D.M.
Bain 7 (Oxford U.), P.C.B. Blair 3 (Cambridge
U.), G.H.H.P. Maxwell 1 (Edinburgh Acads),
W.D.C.L. Purves 4 (London Scottish), L. Robert-
son 7 (London Scottish), J.M.B. Scott 19 (Edin-
burgh Acads), *F.H. Turner 11 (Liverpool), C.M.
Usher 4 (London Scottish).

IRELAND J.W. McConnell (1) (Lansdowne);
C.V. McIvor 6 (Dublin U.), G.W. Holmes (2)
(Dublin U.), J.B. Minch 2 (Bective Rangers), F.
Bennett (1) (Belfast Collegians); *R.A. Lloyd 12
(Liverpool), H.M. Read (12) (Dublin U.); S.B.B.
Campbell 10 (Edinburgh U.), J.E. Finlay 2
(Queen's U. Belfast), E.W. Jeffares (2) (Wan-
derers), G.V. Killeen 5 (Garryowen), R.d'A.
Patterson 5 (Wanderers), F.G. Schute (2) (Dublin
U.), P. Stokes 2 (Garryowen), W. Tyrrell 3
(Queen's U. Belfast).

Referee J.W. Baxter (England)

FRANCE v WALES 4/186

27 February 1913
Parc des Princes, Paris
Wales 11 (1G, 2T) France 8 (1G, 1T)

France T: Failliot, André. C: Struxiano.
Wales T: Clem Lewis, Davies, Williams. C:
Clem Lewis.

Billy Trew, of Swansea, made his twenty-sixth
and final Championship appearance, 22 of
which were on the winning side. Trew was
regarded as one of the finest footballers of his
generation, a speedy, graceful runner, accurate
passer and good kicker. His versatility, too,
served Wales well. Normally a fly-half, he also
contributed much to Welsh attacking flair at
centre and wing. The match, which was played
on a Thursday, was also the last appearance for
France of Pierre Failliot, the Racing Club wing,
whose speed and aggressive running drew as
much praise from those who played against him
as he did from the Press.

FRANCE J. Semmartin 1 (SCUF); G. André 2
(RCF), A. Franquenelle 2 (SC Vaugirard), P.
Jauréguy 2 (S. Toulouse), P. Failliot (8) (RCF); P.

Ferdinand Forgues, though not chosen to play, leads out the
French team at Twickenham on 25 January 1913

Struxiano 1 (S. Toulouse), C. Bioussa 1 (S. Toulouse); F. Forgues 8 (A. Bayonne), P. Thil (5) (S. Nantes), M. Boyau 5 (S. Bordelais), *M. Leuvielle 3 (S. Bordelais), P. Mauriat 12 (FC Lyon), G. Favre (2) (FC Lyon), G. Podevin 1 (S. Français), M. Legrain 8 (S. Français).

WALES   G.I. Gethin (1) (Neath); M. Lewis (1) (Llwynypia), J.P. Jones 8 (Pontypool), *W.J. Trew (26) (Swansea), H. Lewis 2 (Swansea); J.M.C. Lewis 3 (Cardiff), R. Lloyd 2 (Pontypool); Revd J.A. Davies 2 (Swansea), T. Williams 2 (Swansea), F. Perrett 3 (Neath), T.C. Lloyd 1 (Neath), G. Stephens 7 (Neath), R. Richards 2 (Aberavon), H. Uzzell 6 (Newport), P. Jones 3 (Newport).

Referee J.F.H. Miles (England)

WALES v IRELAND   27/187

8 March 1913
St Helen's, Swansea
Wales 16 (2G, 1T, 1PG) Ireland 13 (2G, 1PG)

Wales   T: Bryn Lewis (2), Jones. C: Bancroft (2). PG: Bancroft.
Ireland   T: Quinn, Stewart. C: Lloyd (2). PG: Lloyd.

A.L. Stewart, scorer of one of Ireland's tries, was one of eight Irish internationals to be killed in the First World War. Wales, with three victories out of four, now had even more reason to regret losing to England in the first match of the season at Cardiff.

WALES   J. Bancroft 14 (Swansea); B. Lewis (2) (Swansea), W.P. Geen (2) (Newport), *J.P. Jones 9 (Pontypool), H. Lewis 3 (Swansea); J.M.C. Lewis 4 (Cardiff), R. Lloyd 3 (Pontypool); Revd J.A. Davies 3 (Swansea), F. Andrews (3) (Pontypool), W. Jenkins (4) (Cardiff), F. Perrett (4) (Neath), G. Stephens (8) (Neath), T.C. Lloyd 2 (Neath), R. Richards (3) (Aberavon), H. Uzzell 7 (Newport).

IRELAND   A.W.P. Todd 1 (Dublin U.); G.H. Wood 1 (Dublin U.), A.R.V. Jackson 5 (Wanderers), A.L. Stewart 1 (NIFC), J.P. Quinn 11 (Dublin U.); *R.A. Lloyd 13 (Liverpool), S.E. Polden 1 (Clontarf); C. Adams 10 (Old Wesley), J.J. Clune 1 (Blackrock College), J.E. Finlay 3 (Queen's U. Belfast), W. Tyrrell 4 (Queen's U.

Belfast), G.V. Killeen 6 (Garryowen), G.V. McConnell 3 (Derry), R.d'A. Patterson 6 (Wanderers), P. O'Connell 1 (Derry).

Referee J.G. Cunningham (Scotland)

ENGLAND v SCOTLAND   28/188

15 March 1913
Twickenham
England 3 (1T) Scotland 0

England   T: Brown.

Deprived of the Grand Slam by a Scottish victory the year before, England narrowly achieved their ambition for the first time without argument. The outstanding feature of England's play throughout the season was their defence – which was beaten only once, by a dropped goal from Dicky Lloyd in the Irish match.

ENGLAND   W.R. Johnston 11 (Bristol); C.N. Lowe 4 (Cambridge U.), F.N. Tarr (2) (Leicester), R.W. Poulton 11 (Harlequins), V.H.M. Coates (4) (Bath); W.J.A. Davies 4 (US Portsmouth), F.E. Oakley 1 (US Portsmouth); J.A.S. Ritson (7) (Northern), J.A. King (11) (Headingley), J.E. Greenwood 5 (Cambridge U.), L.G. Brown 8 (Oxford U.), *N.A. Wodehouse (13) (US Portsmouth), S. Smart 4 (Gloucester), G. Ward 3 (Leicester), C.H. Pillman 14 (Blackheath).

SCOTLAND   W.M. Wallace 1 (Cambridge U.); J.B. Sweet 1 (Glasgow HSFP), J. Pearson (11) (Watsonians), E.G. Loudoun-Shand (1) (Oxford U.), W.R. Sutherland 11 (Hawick); T.C. Bowie 2 (Watsonians), E. Milroy 9 (Watsonians); D.M. Bain 8 (Oxford U.), P.C.B. Blair (4) (Cambridge U.), G.H.H.P. Maxwell 2 (Edinburgh Acads), W.D.C.L. Purves (5) (London Scottish), L. Robertson (8) (London Scottish), J.M.B. Scott (20) (Edinburgh Acads), *F.H. Turner 12 (Oxford U.), C.M. Usher 5 (London Scottish).

Referee T.D. Schofield (Wales)

IRELAND v FRANCE   4/189

24 March 1913
Mardyke, Cork
Ireland 24 (3G, 3T) France 0

Ireland T: Quinn (3), Tyrrell (2), Patterson. C: Lloyd (3).

A morning kick-off on Easter Monday, when it was 'too hot' for rugby, brought a record-equalling performance by J.P. Quinn. His three tries equalled R. Montgomery's hat-trick against Wales in 1887. Ireland's six tries were their highest in an international, a record which stood until equalled by the 1953 side against Scotland. It was also Ireland's biggest winning points margin against France: a fact which may have influenced the French selectors for 12 of their team never played again in an international. There was a crowd of 8000.

IRELAND A.W.P. Todd 2 (Dublin U.); C.V. McIvor (7) (Dublin U.) A.L. Stewart 2 (NIFC), A.R.V. Jackson 6 (Wanderers), J.P. Quinn 12 (Dublin U.); S.E. Polden 2 (Clontarf), *R.A. Lloyd 14 (Liverpool); P. O'Connell 2 (Bective Rangers), G.V. Killeen 7 (Garryowen), G.V. McConnell (4) (Derry), S.B.B. Campbell (11) (Derry), R.d'A. Patterson (7) (Wanderers), W. Tyrrell 5 (Queen's U. Belfast), C. Adams 11 (Old Wesley), J.J. Clune 2 (Blackrock College).

FRANCE J. Semmartin (2) (SCUF); G. André 3 (RCF), A. Franquenelle (3) (SC Vaugirard), J. Dedet (8) (S. Français), P. Jauréguy (3) (S. Toulouse); P. Struxiano 2 (S. Toulouse), C. Bioussa 2 (S. Toulouse); P. Mauriat (13) (FC Lyon), J. Pascarel (5) (TOEC), P. Tavernier (1) (S. Toulouse), G. Podevin (2) (S. Français), J. Cadenat (7) (SCUF), *M. Boyau (6) (SBUC), M. Legrain 9 (S. Français), A. Eutrope (1) (SCUF).

Referee J.F.H. Miles (England)

1914

PARIS Ireland beat France 8-6 · TWICKENHAM England beat Wales 10-9
CARDIFF Wales beat Scotland 24-5 · TWICKENHAM England beat Ireland 17-12
DUBLIN Ireland beat Scotland 6-0 · SWANSEA Wales beat France 31-0
BELFAST Wales beat Ireland 11-3 · EDINBURGH England beat Scotland 16-15
PARIS England beat France 39-13 · NB Scotland did not play France

CHAMPIONSHIP TABLE
England – Championship, Triple Crown, Grand Slam

									Tries	
Pos	Country	P	W	D	L	F	A	Pts	F	A
1	England (1)	4	4	0	0	82	49	8	20	9
2	Wales (2)	4	3	0	1	75	18	6	14	4
3	Ireland (4)	4	2	0	2	29	34	4	7	10
4	Scotland (3)	3	0	0	3	20	46	0	4	9
5	France (5)	3	0	0	3	19	78	0	5	18

England won the Grand Slam for the second year in a row and took the Championship for the third time in succession, which equalled their 1883–85 title-winning sequence. The greatness of this England side is emphasized by the fact that it scored 20 tries, one less than Wales's Championship best of 1910, and it aggregated 82 points, the highest ever by England. Even the high-scoring 1980 Grand Slam England side did not match that total. Wales, too, had a fine season and contemporary accounts declared they were unlucky to lose 9-10 at Twickenham. However, the Welsh totalled 14 tries and accumulated 75 points to finish second, ahead of an Ireland side which was in the process of being rebuilt. Scotland, who had refused to play France because of crowd troubles in Paris the year before, lost all three matches they played. They were, however, involved in a seven-try spectacular with England at Inverleith, losing by one point to the Champions. The result of France's five-year apprenticeship in the Championship made fairly dismal reading: they had lost 18 of 19 matches played, and had conceded 415 points and 105 tries, 9 tries coming in the final match of the 1914 season, against England

at Stade Colombes on 13 April. This was also the last match before the outbreak of the First World War.

Rugby suffered more than most sports. In total 111 internationals were killed, including those of New Zealand and South Africa. It is often overlooked that the club game in Britain was also devastated. A chilling example of the cost in lives to an individual club is that of London Scottish: on the last day of the 1914 season they fielded four sides, of those 60 players 45 were killed.

FRANCE v IRELAND   5/190

1 January 1914
Parc des Princes, Paris
Ireland 8 (1G, 1T) France 6 (2T)

France   T: Lacoste, André.
Ireland   T: Quinn, Wood. C: Lloyd.

This match was played on a Thursday. It was the début of Willie Collopy, whose father, George, won two caps against Scotland in 1891 and 1892. Willie, one of Ireland's outstanding forwards to have played either before or after the First World War, made 19 Championship appearances, and on seven of those occasions his younger brother, Dick, was in the same team.

FRANCE   R. Lasserre 1 (A. Bayonne); G. André 4 (RCF), G. Pierrot 1 (S. Pau), F. Poydebasque 1 (A. Bayonne), J. Lacoste 1 (S. Tarbes); L. Larribeau 6 (CA Périgueux), C. Bioussa (3) (S. Toulouse); *F. Forgues 9 (A. Bayonne), J. Conil de Beyssac 3 (SBUC), M. Legrain 10 (S. Français), M-F. Lubin-

Lebrère 1 (S. Toulouse), J-M. Arnal 1 (RCF), F. Faure 1 (S. Tarbes), P. Lavaud 1 (AS Carcassonne), J. Sébedio 3 (S. Tarbes).

IRELAND   A.W.P. Todd (3) (Dublin U.); J.P. Quinn 13 (Dublin U.), G.H. Wood (2) (Dublin U.), A.R.V. Jackson 7 (Wanderers), A.L. Stewart (3) (NIFC); *R.A. Lloyd 15 (Liverpool), S.E. Polden 3 (Clontarf); J.J. Clune 3 (Blackrock College), W.P. Collopy 1 (Bective Rangers), J.C.A. Dowse 1 (Monkstown), C. Adams 12 (Old Wesley), P. O'Connell 3 (Bective Rangers), P. Stokes 3 (Garryowen), W. Tyrrell 6 (Queen's U. Belfast), J.S. Parr 1 (Wanderers).

Referee E.W. Calver (England)

ENGLAND v WALES   30/191

17 January 1914
Twickenham
England 10 (2G) Wales 9 (1G, 1DG)

England   T: Brown, Pillman. C: Chapman (2).
Wales   T: Willie Watts. C: Bancroft. DG: Hirst.

Wales, attempting to rebuild their side, introduced five new players. For experience they relied entirely on Jack Bancroft, the Swansea full-back, who was their only player who had reached double figures in the number of appearances. England also experimented: the Leicester half-backs Wood and Taylor were among six new caps. The winning scores, however, came from the veterans of the side, Brown, Pillman and Chapman.

ENGLAND   W.R. Johnston 12 (Bristol); C.N. Lowe 5 (Cambridge U.), F.E. Chapman 6 (Hartlepool Rovers), *R.W. Poulton 12 (Liverpool), J.H.D. Watson 1 (Blackheath); F.M. Taylor (1) (Leicester), G.W. Wood (1) (Leicester); A.G. Bull (1) (Northampton), A.F. Maynard 1 (Cambridge U.), J.E. Greenwood 6 (Cambridge U.), L.G. Brown 9 (The London H.), J. Brunton 1 (North Durham), S. Smart 5 (Gloucester), G. Ward 4 (Leicester), C.H. Pillman 15 (Blackheath).

WALES   J. Bancroft 15 (Swansea); H. Lewis (4) (Swansea), W.H. Evans 1 (Llwynypia), W. Watts (1) (Llanelli), G.L. Hirst 3 (Newport); J.M.C. Lewis 5 (Cardiff), R. Lloyd 4 (Pontypool); *Revd J.A. Davies 4 (Llanelli), D. Watts 1 (Maesteg), J. Bedwelty Jones 1 (Abertillery), T.C. Lloyd 3 (Neath), P. Jones 4 (Pontypool), T. Williams 3 (Swansea), E. Morgan 1 (Swansea), H. Uzzell 8 (Newport).

Referee J.R.C. Greenlees (Scotland)

WALES v SCOTLAND   30/192

7 February 1914
Cardiff Arms Park
Wales 24 (2G, 1T, 2DG, 1PG) Scotland 5 (1G)

Wales   T: Ivor Davies, Wetter, Hirst. C: Bancroft (2). DG: Hirst, Lewis. PG: Bancroft.
Scotland   T: Stewart. C: Laing.

By all accounts a very rough match. 'The dirtier side won' was how Scotland's captain, David Bain, described it after having six stitches for a head wound. Bain was not the only Scottish casualty: W.R. Sutherland was a limping passenger for most of the second half. It was Scotland's tenth successive defeat in the Principality, their worst sequence, home or away, against Wales.

WALES   J. Bancroft 16 (Swansea); G.L. Hirst 4 (Newport), J. Wetter 1 (Newport), W.H. Evans 2 (Llwynypia), I.T. Davies 1 (Llanelli); J.M.C. Lewis 6 (Cardiff), R. Lloyd 5 (Pontypool); *Revd J.A. Davies 5 (Llanelli), D. Watts 2 (Maesteg), J. Bedwelty Jones 2 (Abertillery), T.C. Lloyd 4 (Neath), P. Jones 5 (Pontypool), T. Williams 4 (Swansea), E. Morgan 2 (Swansea), H. Uzzell 9 (Newport).

SCOTLAND   W.M. Wallace 2 (London Scottish); J.G. Will 5 (Cambridge U.), W.R. Sutherland (12) (Hawick), R.M. Scobie 1 (London Scottish), W.A. Stewart (4) (The London H.); A.S. Hamilton 1 (Headingley), A.T. Sloan 1 (Edinburgh Acads); *D.M. Bain 9 (Oxford U.), G.H.H.P. Maxwell 3 (Edinburgh Acads), A.R. Ross 2 (Edinburgh U.), A.M. Stewart (1) (Edinburgh Acads), A.W. Symington 1 (Cambridge U.), A. Wemyss 1 (Gala), D.G. Donald 1 (Oxford U.), A.D. Laing 1 (Royal HSFP).

Referee V. Drennon (Ireland)

ENGLAND v IRELAND   30/193

14 February 1914
Twickenham
England 17 (1G, 4T) Ireland 12 (1G, 1T, 1DG)

England T: Lowe (2), Davies, Pillman, Roberts.
C: Chapman.
Ireland T: Jackson, Quinn. C: Lloyd. DG:
Lloyd.

This match became front page news in Britain,
not only because of the attendance of George V
and Prime Minister Asquith, but because the
visit of the Irish coincided with the high debate
in Parliament over Home Rule for Ireland. Tom
Schofield, the Welsh referee, who for years had
been a vociferous critic of rough play in the
Principality, introduced a novel method of
getting the scrummages straight: he simply
kicked the backsides of the rearmost player.

ENGLAND W.R. Johnston 13 (Bristol); C.N.
Lowe 6 (Cambridge U.), F.E. Chapman (7) (Hart-
lepool Rovers), *R.W. Poulton 13 (Liverpool),
A.D. Roberts (8) (Northern); W.J.A. Davies 5
(US Portsmouth), F.E. Oakley 2 (US Ports-
mouth); H.C. Harrison 2 (US Portsmouth), A.F.
Maynard 2 (Cambridge U.), A.L. Harrison 1 (US
Portsmouth), L.G. Brown 10 (The London H.), J.
Brunton 2 (North Durham), S. Smart 6 (Glouces-
ter), G. Ward 5 (Leicester), C.H. Pillman 16
(Blackheath).

IRELAND F.P. Montgomery 1 (Queen's U. Bel-
fast); A.R. Foster 12 (Derry), A.R.V. Jackson 8
(Wanderers), J.B. Minch 3 (Bective Rangers),
J.P. Quinn 14 (Dublin U.); *R.A. Lloyd 16
(Liverpool), V. McNamara 1 (UC Cork); W.
Tyrrell 7 (Queen's U. Belfast), W.P. Collopy 2
(Bective Rangers), C. Adams 13 (Old Wesley),
J.J. Clune 4 (Blackrock College), G.V. Killeen 8
(Garryowen), P. O'Connell 4 (Bective Rangers),
J.S. Parr 2 (Wanderers), J. Taylor 1 (Belfast
Collegians).

Referee T.D. Schofield (Wales)

IRELAND v SCOTLAND   32/194

28 February 1914
Lansdowne Road, Dublin
Ireland 6 (2T) Scotland 0

Ireland T: Quinn, McNamara.

Although Ireland won this last of the pre-First
World War Championship matches with Scotland, the series had decisively favoured the
Scots. This was largely due to the fact that
Scotland won the first ten matches and Ireland
began to show winning form only from 1899.
This early lead, 21-8, was significant too in that
it gave Scotland an advantage they have never
surrendered. Ireland had to wait until 1983 to
draw level with 42 wins, which ended the last
match-winning advantage Scotland held over
any country.

IRELAND F.P. Montgomery 2 (Queen's U. Bel-
fast); *J.P. Quinn (15) (Dublin U.), A.R.V. Jack-
son 9 (Wanderers), J.B. Minch (4) (Bective
Rangers), A.R. Foster 13 (Derry); H.W. Jack 1
(UC Cork), V. McNamara 2 (UC Cork); C. Adams
(14) (Old Wesley), W.P. Collopy 3 (Bective
Rangers), J.C.A. Dowse 2 (Monkstown), G.V.
Killeen 9 (Garryowen), P. O'Connell 5 (Bective
Rangers), J.S. Parr 3 (Wanderers), J. Taylor 2
(Belfast Collegians), W. Tyrrell 8 (Queen's U.
Belfast).

The English XV which beat Ireland on 14 February 1914

SCOTLAND   W.M. Wallace 3 (Cambridge U.); J.B. Sweet (2) (Glasgow HSFP), R.M. Scobie 2 (RMA Sandhurst), J.R. Warren (1) (Glasgow Acads), J.G. Will 6 (Cambridge U.); T.C. Bowie 3 (Watsonians), *E. Milroy 10 (Watsonians); D.M. Bain (10) (Oxford U.), D.G. Donald (2) (Oxford U.), A.D. Laing 2 (Royal HSFP), J.B. Macdougall 2 (Greenock Wanderers), G.H.H.P. Maxwell 4 (Edinburgh Acads), A.R. Ross 3 (Edinburgh U.), F.H. Turner 13 (Liverpool), A. Wemyss 2 (Gala).

Referee J.W. Baxter (England)

WALES v FRANCE   5/195

2 March 1914
St Helen's, Swansea
Wales 31 (5G, 2T) France 0

Wales   T: Wetter (2), Uzzell (2), Hirst, Revd Alban Davies, Evans. C: Bancroft (5).

On only two other occasions have Wales bettered this score against France: 49-14 in 1910 and 35-3 in 1931. The French were completely bewildered by the speed of the Welsh backs and the power of their forwards. For six Frenchmen it was a last appearance in the Championship. Jack Bancroft's career ended too – but on a high note for he converted five of Wales's seven tries.

WALES   J. Bancroft (17) (Swansea); G.L. Hirst 5 (Newport), J. Wetter 2 (Newport), W.H. Evans 3 (Llwynypia), I.T. Davies 2 (Llanelli); J.M.C. Lewis 7 (Cardiff), R. Lloyd 6 (Pontypool); *Revd J.A. Davies 6 (Llanelli), D. Watts 3 (Maesteg), J. Bedwelty Jones 3 (Abertillery), T.C. Lloyd 5 (Neath), P. Jones 6 (Pontypool), T. Williams 5 (Swansea), E. Morgan 3 (Swansea), H. Uzzell 10 (Newport).

FRANCE   J. Caujolle 2 (S. Tarbes); G. André 5 (RCF), J. Lacoste 2 (S. Tarbes), A. Besset 1 (SCUF), G. Pierrot 2 (S. Pau), M. Hedembaigt (2) (A. Bayonne), F. Poydesbasque (2) (A. Bayonne); *M. Leuvielle 4 (S. Bordelais), M. Legrain (11) (S. Bordelais), J. Conil de Beyssac 4 (S. Bordelais), F. Faure 2 (S. Tarbes), R. Desvouges (1) (S. Français), J-M. Arnal (2) (RCF), P. Lavaud (2) (AS Carcassonne), R. Lasserre 2 (A. Bayonne).

Referee J.F.H. Miles (England)

IRELAND v WALES   28/196

14 March 1914
Balmoral Showgrounds, Belfast
Wales 11 (1G, 2T) Ireland 3 (1T)

Ireland   T: Foster.
Wales   T: Bedwelty Jones, Evans, Wetter. C: Lewis.

This was one of several occasions when a selected side, having posed for the team photograph before kick-off, had to be changed at the last moment. The Irish captain, Dicky Lloyd, strained a tendon while warming up on the pitch; his place was taken by Harry Jack and the captaincy went to A.R. Foster, the most experienced man in the side. Many apocryphal tales have been told of this match, which was a bruising, no-quarter struggle. One was of the confrontation the night before of two opposing forwards who threatened mayhem against each other the next day. Honours in that particular contest apparently were even. Other rough incidents in the match attracted much publicity, though the referee turned the proverbial blind eye to all.

IRELAND   F.P. Montgomery (3) (Queen's U. Belfast); J.T. Brett (1) (Monkstown), M. Abraham (4) (Bective Rangers), A.R.V. Jackson (10) (Wanderers), *A.R. Foster 14 (Derry); H.W. Jack 2 (UC Cork), V. McNamara (3) (UC Cork); W.P. Collopy 4 (Bective Rangers), J.S. Parr (4) (Wanderers), P. O'Connell (6) (Bective Rangers), W. Tyrrell (9) (Queen's U. Belfast), G.V. Killeen (10) (Garryowen), J.C.A. Dowse (3) (Monkstown), J. Taylor (3) (Belfast Collegians), J.J. Clune (5) (Blackrock College).

WALES   R.F. Williams (3) (Cardiff); G.L. Hirst (6) (Newport), J. Wetter 3 (Newport), W.H. Evans (4) (Llwynypia), I.T. Davies (3) (Llanelli); J.M.C. Lewis 8 (Cardiff), R. Lloyd (7) (Pontypool); *Revd J.A. Davies (7) (Llanelli), D. Watts (4) (Maesteg), J. Bedwelty Jones (4) (Abertillery), T.C. Lloyd (6) (Neath), P. Jones (7) (Pontypool), T. Williams (6) (Swansea), E. Morgan (4) (Swansea), H. Uzzell 11 (Newport).

Referee J.T. Tulloch (Scotland)

SCOTLAND v ENGLAND   29/197

21 March 1914
Inverleith, Edinburgh
England 16 (2G, 2T) Scotland 15 (1G, 2T, 1DG)

Scotland   T: Will (2), Huggan. C: Turner. DG: Bowie.
England   T: Lowe (3), Poulton. C: Harrison (2).

Only those close to the game were aware of a private battle arranged beforehand between Cyril Lowe and George Will, great friends and playing colleagues at Cambridge University, but facing each other at Inverleith. 'We had a bet that the other one wouldn't get a try,' Lowe said. 'As it turned out, we were both wrong: we were a bit better at scoring than we were predicting or defending.' Lowe scored three tries, Will two. The match was marred by the broken leg suffered by Cherry Pillman, the great Blackheath forward. He never played again. Even more tragic was that 11 of the players in the match were killed during the First World War.

SCOTLAND   W.M. Wallace (4) (Cambridge U.); J.L. Huggan (1) (London Scottish), R.M. Scobie (3) (US Portsmouth), A.W. Angus 13 (Watsonians), J.G. Will (7) (Cambridge U.); T.C. Bowie (4) (Watsonians), *E. Milroy (11) (Watsonians); A.D. Laing 3 (Royal HSFP), G.H.H.P. Maxwell 5 (Edinburgh Acads), I.M. Pender (1) (London Scottish), A.R. Ross (4) (Edinburgh U.), A.W. Symington (2) (Cambridge U.), F.H. Turner (14) (Liverpool), C.M. Usher 6 (London Scottish), E.T. Young (1) (Glasgow Acads).

ENGLAND   W.R. Johnston 14 (Bristol); C.N. Lowe 7 (Cambridge U.), J.H.D. Watson 2 (Blackheath), *R.W. Poulton 14 (Liverpool), A.J. Dingle 2 (Hartlepool Rovers); W.J.A. Davies 6 (US Portsmouth), F.E. Oakley 3 (US Portsmouth); H.C. Harrison 3 (US Portsmouth), A.F. Maynard (3) (Cambridge U.), J.E. Greenwood 7 (Cambridge U.), L.G. Brown 11 (Blackheath), J. Brunton (3) (North Durham), S. Smart 7 (Gloucester), G. Ward (6) (Leicester), C.H. Pillman (17) (Blackheath).

Referee T.D. Schofield (Wales)

FRANCE v ENGLAND   5/198

13 April 1914
Stade Colombes, Paris
England 39 (6G, 3T) France 13 (2G, 1T)

France   T: André, Capmau, Lubin-Lebrère. C: Besset (2).
England   T: Poulton (4), Lowe (3), Davies, Watson. C: Greenwood (6).

The last international before the outbreak of War produced a clutch of records. England's nine tries were the most scored by them in a Championship match; it was their ninth win in a row; Cyril Lowe became the only player to score a hat-trick of tries in successive internationals; and John Greenwood's six conversions were England's best until equalled by G.W. Parker against Ireland in 1938. *The Sportsman* wrote of England's 'brilliant victory' but castigated the French for failing to stay: 'their forwards ... being outclassed towards the end'. One French newspaper summed up: 'L'equipe d'Angleterre, robuste, solide et suffisamment rapide en avants.' It also effusively praised Cyril Lowe ... 'le petit Lowe, rapide, adroit, inteligent brilla.'

FRANCE   J. Caujolle (3) (S. Tarbes); J. Lacoste (3) (S. Tarbes), G. Pierrot (3) (S. Pau), A. Besset (2) (SCUF), G. André (6) (RCF); M. Burgun (10) (Castres Ol), L. Larribeau (7) (Biarritz Ol); E. Iguinitz (1) (A. Bayonne), F. Faure (3) (S. Tarbes), M-F. Lubin-Lebrère 2 (S. Toulouse), *M. Leuvielle (5) (S. Bordelais), J. Conil de Beyssac (5) (S. Bordelais), A. Capmau (1) (S. Toulouse), P. Bascou (1) (A. Bayonne), F. Forgues (10) (A. Bayonne).

ENGLAND   W.R. Johnston (15) (Bristol); C.N. Lowe 8 (Cambridge U.), J.H.D. Watson (3) (Blackheath), *R.W. Poulton (15) (Liverpool), A.J. Dingle (3) (Hartlepool Rovers); W.J.A. Davies 7 (US Portsmouth), F.E. Oakeley (4) (US Portsmouth); H.C. Harrison (4) (US Portsmouth), A.R.V. Sykes (1) (Blackheath), J.E. Greenwood 8 (Cambridge U.), L.G. Brown 12 (Blackheath), A.L. Harrison (2) (US Portsmouth), S. Smart 8 (Gloucester), F.le S. Stone (1) (Blackheath), R.L. Pillman (1) (Blackheath).

Referee J. Games (Wales)

1920

PARIS Scotland beat France 5-0 · SWANSEA Wales beat England 19-5
TWICKENHAM England beat France 8-3 · EDINBURGH Scotland beat Wales 9-5
DUBLIN England beat Ireland 14-11 · PARIS Wales beat France 6-5
EDINBURGH Scotland beat Ireland 19-0 · CARDIFF Wales beat Ireland 28-4
TWICKENHAM England beat Scotland 13-4 · DUBLIN France beat Ireland 15-7

CHAMPIONSHIP TABLE
Wales – Championship

									Tries	
Pos	Country	P	W	D	L	F	A	Pts	F	A
1	Wales (2)	4	3	0	1	58	23	6	11	3
2	England (1)	4	3	0	1	40	37	6	9	5
3	Scotland (4)	4	3	0	1	37	18	6	6	4
4	France (5)	4	1	0	3	23	26	2	7	5
5	Ireland (3)	4	0	0	4	22	76	0	3	19

Wales won the first Championship staged since 1914 with England in second place on points difference. The War had exacted a great toll among rugby players, at both international and club level, and all the Championship contenders had to effect extensive rebuilding of their sides. Ireland found great difficulty in producing a team of quality, and by the end of the campaign had lost all four matches for the first time, conceding a record 76 points and 19 tries.

Great interest was centred on France and there was much speculation as to how they would fare after their initiation into Championship competition 1910–14. 'France was the surprise of the year,' wrote Ernest Ward, a leading rugby critic of the time, 'With some luck she might have won all her matches. French "Rugger" has come on tremendously; the forward play has improved and behind the scrummage the halves and threequarters have got a nice idea of getting off and backing up.' In terms of results, however, France achieved little. The season extended their losing run to 17 matches, which is the longest losing sequence in the Championship. The rot was stopped only in the last match of the season, against Ireland. Administratively, however, France came of age in 1920. In Paris on 11 October their affairs, which had been the responsibility of the Union des Sociétés Françaises des Sports Athlétique, were formally transferred to the much-less-of-a-mouthful Fédération Française de Rugby – the French Rugby Union.

FRANCE v SCOTLAND   5/199

1 January 1920
Parc des Princes, Paris
Scotland 5 (1G) France 0

Scotland   T: Crole. C: Kennedy.

This was the last Championship match to be held at the old Parc des Princes, and marked the renewal of fixtures between Scotland and France after the unfortunate break of 1913. The referee had then needed protection from the crowd, unhappy with his decisions. This time, Frank Potter-Irwin, was carried shoulder high to the pavilion after the match. As a tactful gesture, the French Rugby Federation presented Potter-Irwin with a medal as a souvenir of the occasion. Charles Usher might have deserved a medal as well: the London Scottish forward interrupted his Paris honeymoon so that he could comply with his selection in the match against France. The Scottish selectors, however, were more considerate of Usher's position when they picked their teams for a trial match a fortnight later. They did not ask him to play, for by this time Usher had already been pencilled in as captain for the next Championship match, against Wales on 7 February.

Another interesting selection for the French match was that of J. Hume at scrum-half; Hume had gained his first cap in 1912. France fielded only four players with previous Championship experience, Lasserre, Struxiano, Sébedio and Lubin-Lebrère but the occasion was more notable for the first appearance of André Jauréguy, one of the outstanding French backs to play up to the split of 1931.

FRANCE   A. Chilo 1 (RCF); A. Jauréguy 1 (RCF), R. Lasserre 3 (A. Bayonne), R. Crabos 1 (RCF), P. Serre 1 (US Perpignan); E. Billac 1 (A. Bayonne), *P. Struxiano 3 (S. Toulouse); J. Sébedio 4 (AS Béziers), P. Pons 1 (S. Toulouse), M-F. Lubin-Lebrère 3 (S. Toulouse), A. Cassayet 1 (S. Tarbes), L. Puech 1 (S. Toulouse), R. Thierry 1 (RCF), J. Laurent 1 (A. Bayonne), R. Marchand 1 (S. Poitiers).

SCOTLAND   G.L. Pattullo 1 (Panmure); A.T. Sloan 2 (Edinburgh Acads), Dr E.C. Fahmy 1 (Abertillery), *A.W. Angus 14 (Watsonians), G.B. Crole 1 (Oxford U.); A.S. Hamilton (2) (Headingley), J. Hume 2 (Royal HSFP); D.D. Duncan 1 (Oxford U.), R.A. Gallie 1 (Glasgow Acads), F. Kennedy 1 (Stewart's FP), A.D. Laing 4 (Royal HSFP), W.A.K. Murray 1 (London Scottish), G. Thom 1 (Kirkcaldy), A. Wemyss 3 (Edinburgh Wands), C.M. Usher 7 (London Scottish).

Referee F.C. Potter-Irwin (England)

WALES v ENGLAND   31/200

17 January 1920
St Helen's, Swansea
Wales 19 (1G, 1T, 2DG, 1PG) England 5 (1G)

Wales   T: Powell, Shea. C: Shea. DG: Shea (2). PG: Shea.
England   T: Day. C: Day.

Jerry Shea, the Newport centre, set a Championship record by scoring 16 points on his début. It was another occasion when a selected player, W.M. Lowry, was photographed with the rest of the team just before kick-off but did not play. The incident was blandly reported: 'The teams were photographed as announced; but when a few minutes later, Greenwood led his men out to the tune "Hearts of Oak", it was noticed that Lowry was no longer with the team, and that H.L.V. Day, of the Army, had taken his place.'

The report went on to explain that the Selection Committee's decision to replace Lowry was based on the fact that he had given an 'indifferent exhibition' the week before and because of the 'rather spongy surface' of St Helen's. Charles Grave, cartoonist of the *Illustrated Sporting & Dramatic News*, did not let the incident pass without comment: 'As Lowry was denied his cap at the last moment,' Graves's caption read: 'perhaps the RU will spend some money on a new hat for him. You can get lovely bowlers in Swansea for 4/6.' Graves was wrong: Lowry *had* been presented with his cap before the game, which might make the Birkenhead Park wing the only player to have been capped without playing. Lowry made his one appearance for England, in the next match against France.

WALES   J. Rees 1 (Swansea); W.J. Powell 1 (Cardiff), J. Shea 1 (Newport), A. Jenkins 1 (Llanelli), B.E. Evans 1 (Llanelli); B. Beynon 1 (Swansea), J. Wetter 4 (Newport); J. Williams 1 (Blaina), *H. Uzzell 12 (Newport), J. Whitfield 1 (Newport), S. Morris 1 (Cross Keys), G. Oliver 1 (Pontypool), T. Parker 1 (Swansea), C.W. Jones 1 (Bridgend), J. Jones 1 (Aberavon).

ENGLAND   B.S. Cumberlege 1 (Blackheath); C.N. Lowe 9 (Blackheath), E.D.G. Hammett 1 (Newport), J.A. Krige (1) (Guy's H.), H.L.V. Day 1 (Leicester); H. Coverdale (4) (Blackheath), C.A. Kershaw 1 (US Portsmouth); S. Smart 9 (Gloucester), J.R. Morgan (1) (Hawick), W.H.G. Wright 1 (Plymouth Albion), G. Holford 1 (Gloucester), L.P.B. Merriam 1 (Blackheath), F.W. Mellish 1 (Blackheath), *J.E. Greenwood 9 (Cambridge U.), W.W. Wakefield 1 (Harlequins).

Referee J.T. Tulloch (Scotland)

ENGLAND v FRANCE   6/201

31 January 1920
Twickenham
England 8 (1G, 1PG) France 3 (1T)

England   T: Davies. C: Greenwood. PG: Greenwood.
France   T: Crabos.

Cyril Lowe and John Greenwood, with ten caps apiece, were very much the senior players in this the resumption of matches with France. The visitors earned high praise: 'The French put up a singularly fine fight ... (their side) was unquestionably the best France has sent to this country.' Cambre was singled out for a fine individual performance and Paul Serre also made his mark: '[he] hurled Lowry in to touch five times. Once the spectators booed the Frenchman, but it was uncalled for as it was a fair tackle. Serre grabbed the Cheshire man by the back of his jersey and literally threw him into touch.' Interestingly neither Serre nor Lowry played in an international again.

ENGLAND   H. Millett (1) (Guy's H.); C.N. Lowe 10 (Blackheath), E.D.G. Hammett 2 (Newport), A.M. Smallwood 1 (Cambridge U.), W.M. Lowry (1) (Birkenhead Park); W.J.A. Davies 8 (US Portsmouth), C.A. Kershaw 2 (US Portsmouth); F. Taylor 1 (Leicester), G.S. Conway 1 (Cambridge U.), W.H.G. Wright (2) (Plymouth Albion), G. Holford (2) (Gloucester), L.P.B. Merriam (2) (Blackheath), F.W. Mellish 2 (Blackheath), *J.E. Greenwood 10 (Cambridge U.), W.W. Wakefield 2 (Harlequins).

FRANCE   G. Cambre 1 (FC Oloron); A. Jauréguy 2 (RCF), B. Lavigne 1 (US Dax), R. Crabos 2 (RCF), P. Serre (2) (US Perpignan); E. Billac 2 (A. Bayonne), *P Struxiano 4 (S. Toulouse); M-F. Lubin-Lebrère 4 (S. Toulouse), P. Pons 2 (S. Toulouse), E. Soulié 1 (CASG), L. Puech 2 (S. Toulouse), A. Cassayet 2 (S. Tarbes), R. Thierry 2 (RCF), J. Laurent 2 (A. Bayonne), A. Guichemerre 1 (US Dax).

Referee W.A. Robertson (Scotland)

SCOTLAND v WALES   31/202

7 February 1920
Inverleith, Edinburgh
Scotland 9 (1T, 2PG) Wales 5 (1G)

Scotland   T: Sloan. PG: Kennedy (2).
Wales   T: Jenkins. C: Jenkins.

After seven successive defeats by Wales, Scotland found the formula for victory. Both sides suffered injuries and Wales finished with 13 players, having lost their captain, Harry Uzzell, and Jim Jones. It was Ben Beynon's last appearance, the Swansea fly-half, who changed codes and became a professional footballer with Swansea Town. Charles Usher took over from A.W. Angus as Scotland's captain, possibly as a reward for cutting short his Paris honeymoon to play for his country against France in January. Scotland included two players, Dr E.C. Fahmy and Neil Macpherson, who were playing with Welsh clubs.

SCOTLAND   G.L. Pattullo 2 (Panmure); E.B. Mackay 1 (Glasgow Acads), A.W. Angus 15 (Watsonians), Dr E.C. Fahmy 2 (Abertillery), G.B. Crole 2 (Oxford U.); A.T. Sloan 3 (Edinburgh Acads), J.A.R. Selby 1 (Watsonians); D.D. Duncan 2 (Oxford U.), R.A. Gallie 2 (Glasgow Acads), F. Kennedy 2 (Stewart's FP), A.D. Laing 5 (Royal HSFP), N.C. Macpherson 1 (Newport), G.H.H.P. Maxwell 6 (RAF), G. Thom 2 (Kirkcaldy), *C.M. Usher 8 (London Scottish).

WALES   J. Rees 2 (Swansea); W.J. Powell 2 (Cardiff), J. Shea 2 (Newport), A. Jenkins 2 (Llanelli), B. Williams 1 (Llanelli); B. Beynon (2) (Swansea), J. Wetter 5 (Newport); J. Williams 2 (Blaina), S. Morris 2 (Cross Keys), *H. Uzzell 13 (Newport), J. Whitfield 2 (Newport), G. Oliver 2 (Pontypool), T. Parker 2 (Swansea), J. Jones 2 (Aberavon), C.W. Jones 2 (Bridgend).

Referee S.H. Crawford (Ireland)

IRELAND v ENGLAND   31/203

14 February 1920
Lansdowne Road, Dublin
England 14 (1G, 3T) Ireland 11 (1G, 1T, 1PG)

Ireland   T: Dickson, Lloyd. C: Lloyd. PG: Lloyd.
England   T: Lowe, Mellish, Myers, Wakefield. C: Greenwood.

Edward Myers, the Bradford centre, scored a try in his first match for England. Myers is the only 'American' to have played for England; he was born in New York, of Yorkshire parents, on 23 September 1895. The Irish team was unusual in that it contained three players from the Cardiff club: J.E. Finlay, T.H. Wallace and C.H. Bryant, and one player, W.S. Smyth, who had last been capped in 1910.

IRELAND   W.E. Crawford 1 (Lansdowne); J.A.N. Dickson 1 (Dublin U.), W.J. Cullen (1) (Manchester), T.H. Wallace 1 (Cardiff), C.H. Bryant 1

(Cardiff); *R.A. Lloyd 17 (Liverpool), A.K. Horan 1 (Blackheath); N. Butler (1) (Garryowen), H.H. Coulter 1 (Queen's U. Belfast), W.S. Smyth (3) (Belfast Collegians), J.E. Finlay 4 (Cardiff), R.Y. Crichton 1 (Dublin U.), W.D. Doherty 1 (Guy's H.), P. Stokes 4 (Garryowen), W.J. Roche 1 (UC Cork).

ENGLAND   B.S. Cumberlege 2 (Blackheath); C.N. Lowe 11 (Blackheath), E. Myers 1 (Bradford), A.M. Smallwood 2 (Cambridge U.), S.W. Harris 1 (Blackheath); W.J.A. Davies 9 (US Portsmouth), C.A. Kershaw 3 (US Portsmouth); F. Taylor (2) (Leicester), G.S. Conway 2 (Cambridge U.), S. Smart 10 (Gloucester), A.H. MacIlwaine (5) (The Army), A.T. Voyce 1 (Gloucester), F.W. Mellish 3 (Blackheath), *J.E. Greenwood 11 (Cambridge U.), W.W. Wakefield 3 (Harlequins).

Referee W.A. Robertson (Scotland)

FRANCE v WALES 6/204

17 February 1920
Stade Colombes, Paris
Wales 6 (2T) France 5 (1G)

France   T: Jauréguy. C: Struxiano.
Wales   T: Bryn Williams, Powell.

The second Championship match to be staged at Stade Colombes brought France their seventeenth successive defeat, the longest sequence in the Championship. Referees seem always to have been at the centre of controversy in matches in France then – and this match was no exception. Colonel Craven, of England, awarded what would have been a match-winning try by France but then changed the decision after consultation with the Welsh touch-judge. At

The French team line-up before their match against Wales at Stade Colombes, Paris, where their sequence of defeats was extended to 17 matches, a record for the Championship

one time, too, the referee was so dissatisfied with scrummage feed that he put the ball in himself.

FRANCE   G. Cambre 2 (FC Oloron); A. Jauréguy 3 (RCF), B. Lavigne (2) (US Dax), R. Crabos 3 (RCF), A. Chilo 2 (RCF); E. Billac 3 (A. Bayonne), *P. Struxiano 5 (S. Toulouse); M. Biraben 1 (S. Toulouse), P. Pons 3 (S. Toulouse), M-F. Lubin-Lebrère 5 (S. Toulouse), A. Cassayet 3 (S. Tarbes), R. Thierry (3) (RCF), J. Laurent (3) (A. Bayonne), R. Marchand (2) (S. Poitiers), G. Constant (1) (US Perpignan).

WALES   J. Rees 3 (Swansea); W.J. Powell 3 (Cardiff), J.P. Jones 10 (Pontypool), A. Jenkins 3 (Llanelli), B. Williams 2 (Llanelli); J. Wetter 6 (Newport), F. Reeves 1 (Cross Keys); J. Williams 3 (Blaina), S. Morris 3 (Cross Keys), W. Morris 1 (Abertillery), *H. Uzzell 14 (Newport), J. Whitfield 3 (Newport), G. Oliver 3 (Pontypool), R. Huxtable 1 (Swansea), C.W. Jones (3) (Bridgend).

Referee Colonel W.S.D. Craven (England)

SCOTLAND v IRELAND   33/205

28 February 1920
Inverleith, Edinburgh
Scotland 19 (2G, 2T, 1PG) Ireland 0

Scotland   T: Crole (2), Angus, Browning. C: Kennedy (2). PG: Kennedy.

Scotland's biggest winning margin in any match against Ireland helped them to their thirteenth victory in 16 home Championship matches against Ireland. The Irish had to endure two more defeats before, in 1926, the pendulum swung in their favour in the number of victories over the Scots.

SCOTLAND   G.L. Pattullo 3 (Panmure); A. Browning 1 (Glasgow HSFP), A.W. Angus 16 (Watsonians), A.T. Sloan 4 (Edinburgh Acads), G.B. Crole 3 (Oxford U.); Dr E.C. Fahmy 3 (Abertillery), J.A.R. Selby (2) (Watsonians); D.D. Duncan 3 (Oxford U.), R.A. Gallie 3 (Glasgow Acads), F. Kennedy 3 (Stewart's FP), A.D. Laing 6 (Royal HSFP), N.C. Macpherson 2 (Newport), W.A.K. Murray 2 (London Scottish), *C.M. Usher 9 (London Scottish), G. Thom 3 (Kirkcaldy).

IRELAND   W.E. Crawford 2 (Lansdowne); C.H. Bryant (2) (Cardiff), T.H. Wallace 2 (Cardiff), P.J. Roddy 1 (Bective Rangers), B.A.T. McFarland 1 (Londonderry); W. Duggan 1 (UC Cork), J.B. O'Neill (1) (Queen's U. Belfast); H.H. Coulter 2 (Queen's U. Belfast), A.W. Courtney 1 (UC Dublin), R.Y. Crichton 2 (Dublin U.), *W.D. Doherty 2 (Guy's H.), J.E. Finlay 5 (Cardiff), A.H. Price 1 (Dublin U.), W.J. Roche 2 (UC Cork), P. Stokes 5 (Garryowen).

Referee J.W. Baxter (England)

WALES v IRELAND   29/206

13 March 1920
Cardiff Arms Park
Wales 28 (3G, 3T, 1DG) Ireland 4 (1DG)

Wales   T: Bryn Williams (3), Jenkins, Whitfield, Parker. C: Jenkins (2), Wetter. DG: Jenkins.
Ireland   DG: McFarland.

This was Wales's highest score against Ireland since beating them 29-0 in 1907, which was remarkable in view of the nearly waterlogged condition of the Arms Park. Wales's six tries equalled their record against Ireland, set in 1903 and equalled again in 1907. The victory enabled Wales to win the Championship for the first time since 1911. Ireland finished with the Wooden Spoon which they last received in 1909.

WALES   J. Rees 4 (Swansea); W.J. Powell (4) (Cardiff), J.P. Jones 11 (Pontypool), A. Jenkins 4 (Llanelli), B. Williams (3) (Llanelli); J. Wetter 7 (Newport), F. Reeves 2 (Cross Keys); J. Williams 4 (Blaina), S. Morris 4 (Cross Keys), G. Oliver (4) (Pontypool), *H. Uzzell (15) (Newport), J. Whitfield 4 (Newport), R. Huxtable (2) (Swansea), T. Parker 3 (Swansea), E. Morgan 1 (Llanelli).

IRELAND   W.E. Crawford 3 (Lansdowne); J.A.N. Dickson 2 (Dublin U.), *T.H. Wallace (3) (Cardiff), W. Duggan (2) (UC Cork), B.A.T. McFarland 2 (Derry); W.A. Cunningham 1 (Lansdowne), A.K. Horan (2) (Blackheath); M.J. Bradley 1 (Dolphin), H.H. Coulter (3) (Queen's U. Belfast), A.W. Courtney 2 (VC Dublin), J.E. Finlay (6) (Cardiff), R.Y. Crichton 3 (Dublin U.), W.D. Doherty 3 (Guy's H.), P. Stokes 6 (Garryowen), H.N. Potterton (1) (Wanderers).

Referee F.C. Potter-Irwin (England)

ENGLAND v SCOTLAND 30/207

20 March 1920
Twickenham
England 13 (2G, 1T) Scotland 4 (1DG)

England T: Harris, Kershaw, Lowe. C: Greenwood (2).
Scotland DG: Bruce-Lockhart.

One of England's tries was scored by Stanley Harris on his second and final appearance. A very fine wing, Harris has claims to being the greatest all-rounder in the history of modern sport. Having turned down an invitation to run in the Olympics for Britain, he danced his way to the final of the World Ballroom Championships, won the South African amateur light-heavyweight boxing title in 1921, won a Wimbledon mixed-doubles title, represented South Africa in the Davis Cup and played polo for England. He was playing club rugby in Johannesburg when he was selected to tour with Ronnie Cove-Smith's British Lions in South Africa in 1924. Harris, holder of the CBE, was badly wounded during the First World War and was a Japanese prisoner-of-war in the Second. He died in Cape Town in 1973.

ENGLAND B.S. Cumberlege 3 (Blackheath); C.N. Lowe 12 (Blackheath), E. Myers 2 (Bradford), E.D.G. Hammett 3 (Newport), S.W. Harris 2 (Blackheath); W.J.A. Davies 10 (US Portsmouth), C.A. Kershaw 4 (US Portsmouth); T. Woods 1 (US Portsmouth), G.S. Conway 3 (Cambridge U.), S. Smart (11) (Gloucester), A.F. Blakiston 1 (Northampton), A.T. Voyce 2 (Gloucester), F.W. Mellish 4 (Blackheath), *J.E. Greenwood (12) (Cambridge U.), W.W. Wakefield 4 (Harlequins).

SCOTLAND G.L. Pattullo (4) (Panmure); A.T. Sloan 5 (Edinburgh Acads), A.W. Angus (17) (Watsonians), J.H. Bruce-Lockhart (2) (London Scottish), G.B. Crole (4) (Oxford U.); Dr E.C. Fahmy (4) (Abertillery), C.S. Nimmo (1) (Watsonians); D.D. Duncan (4) (Oxford U.), R.A. Gallie 4 (Glasgow Acads), F. Kennedy 4 (Stewart's FP), N.C. Macpherson 3 (Newport), G.H.H.P. Maxwell 7 (London Scottish), G. Thom (4) (Kirkcaldy), A. Wemyss 4 (Edinburgh Wands), *C.M. Usher 10 (London Scottish).

Referee T.D. Schofield (Wales)

IRELAND v FRANCE 6/208

3 April 1920
Lansdowne Road, Dublin
France 15 (5T) Ireland 7 (1T, 1DG)

Ireland T: Price. DG: Lloyd.
France T: Gayraud, Got (2), Jauréguy (2).

France ended Ireland's run of five Championship wins by chalking up their first win in Ireland, and only their second Championship win since beating Scotland in 1911. The match signalled the close of one great career and the start of another: for Dicky Lloyd it was his eighteenth and final Championship match and for George Stephenson the first of 40 appearances. Lloyd was a forerunner of the breed of unerringly accurate touch-kickers, he was a superb drop and place kicker, and whether scrum-half or fly-half, he was a master footballer to compare with Jack Kyle and Louis Magee. Stephenson was considered one of the most talented centres of any era, and, until Kyle came along, he held the record for the most international appearances. Raoul Got, who scored two début tries for France, must have been a character; according to one report he 'wore a tight-fitting black skull cap which made him look rather like a pierrot'.

IRELAND W.E. Crawford 4 (Lansdowne); J.A.N. Dickson (3) (Dublin U.), G.V. Stephenson 1 (Queen's U. Belfast), P.J. Roddy (2) (Bective Rangers), B.A.T. McFarland 3 (Derry); *R.A. Lloyd (18) (Liverpool), S.E. Polden (4) (Clontarf); M.J. Bradley 2 (Dolphin), D. Browne (1) (Blackrock College), A.W. Courtney 3 (UC Dublin), A.H. Price (2) (Dublin U.), R.Y. Crichton 4 (Dublin U.), J.T. Smyth (1) (Queen's U. Belfast), W.J. Roche (3) (UC Cork), P. Stokes 7 (Garryowen).

FRANCE G. Cambre (3) (FC Oloron); A. Jauréguy 4 (RCF), F. Borde 1 (RCF), R. Crabos 4 (RCF), R. Got 1 (US Perpignan); E. Billac 4 (A. Bayonne), *P. Struxiano (6) (S. Toulouse); J. Larrieu 1 (S. Tarbes), P. Moureu 1 (AS Béziers), J. Sébedio 5 (S. Tarbes), L. Puech 3 (S. Toulouse), E. Soulié 2 (CASG), M. Biraben 2 (US Dax), W. Gayraud (1) (S. Toulouse), M-F. Lubin-Lebrère 6 (S. Toulouse).

Referee J.M. Tennant (Scotland)

1921

TWICKENHAM England beat Wales 18-3 · EDINBURGH France beat Scotland 3-0
SWANSEA Scotland beat Wales 14-8 · TWICKENHAM England beat Ireland 15-0
CARDIFF Wales beat France 12-4 · DUBLIN Ireland beat Scotland 9-8
BELFAST Wales beat Ireland 6-0 · EDINBURGH England beat Scotland 18-0
PARIS England beat France 10-6 · PARIS France beat Ireland 20-10

CHAMPIONSHIP TABLE
England – Championship, Triple Crown, Grand Slam

								Tries	
Pos	Country	P	W	D	L	F	A	Pts	F	A
1	England (2)	4	4	0	0	61	9	8	13	1
2	France (4)	4	2	0	2	33	32	4	5	6
3	Wales (1)	4	2	0	2	29	36	4	4	7
4	Scotland (3)	4	1	0	3	22	38	2	5	8
5	Ireland (5)	4	1	0	3	19	49	2	5	10

The RFU's Jubilee year was appropriately celebrated by England, in impressive fashion, winning their third Grand Slam. The formation of this excellent England side had begun in 1920 and they fulfilled all hopes and ambitions to charge through the Championship like a threshing machine. A measure of their omnipotence was that they conceded nine points only. France had reason to be proud with regard to points, too. For the first time they scored more than they conceded, 33-32. The French also finished second, their highest position to date. Ireland fared only marginally better than the previous season, in that they scored one victory, while Wales and Scotland produced middle-of-the-road teams and performances. The RFU and WRU had by now agreed that all their international sides would be numbered.

Ernest Ward, writing in *The Rugby Football Annual*, left little doubt as to his view of 1921: 'What we like to remember about this England fifteen that won the famous victories over Wales and Ireland at Twickenham and Scotland at Inverleith, was not only the skill of our men, but the splendid straightness of our players. They played hard; but all was fair and wholesome.'

ENGLAND v WALES   32/209

15 January 1921
Twickenham
England 18 (1G, 3T, 1DG) Wales 3 (1T)

England   T: Smallwood (2), Kershaw, Lowe. C: Hammett. DG: Davies.
Wales   T: Ring.

Whatever the shortcomings of early players, they were certainly not lacking in courage. Three Welsh players were badly hurt, but lasted the match: Jack Jones broke a collar-bone, Tom Johnson injured his arm and Jack Wetter suffered a torn knee cartilage.

ENGLAND   B.S. Cumberlege 4 (Blackheath); C.N. Lowe 13 (Blackheath), E.D.G. Hammett 4 (Newport), E. Myers 3 (Bradford), A.M. Smallwood 3 (Leicester); *W.J.A. Davies 11 (US Portsmouth), C.A. Kershaw 5 (US Portsmouth); R. Edwards 1 (Newport), E.R. Gardner 1 (Devonport Services), L.G. Brown 13 (Blackheath), F.W. Mellish 5 (Blackheath), T. Woods 2 (Devonport Services), A.F. Blakiston 2 (Northampton), A.T. Voyce 3 (Gloucester), W.W. Wakefield 5 (Harlequins).

WALES   J. Rees 5 (Swansea); J. Ring (1) (Aberavon), J.P. Jones (12) (Pontypool), J. Shea (3) (Newport), T. Johnson 1 (Cardiff); *J. Wetter 8 (Newport), F. Reeves (3) (Cross Keys); L. Attewell 1 (Newport), J. Whitfield 5 (Newport), T. Parker 4 (Swansea), S. Winmill 1 (Cross Keys), D. Edwards (1) (Glynneath), W. Hodder 1 (Pontypool), E. Morgan 2 (Llanelli), D. Marsden-Jones (1) (Cardiff).

Referee J.C. Sturrock (Scotland)

The players leaving the field in the Wales v Scotland match during one of several pitch invasions by spectators

SCOTLAND v FRANCE   6/210

22 January 1921
Inverleith
France 3 (1T) Scotland 0

France   T: Billac.

France gained a famous victory, their first in Scotland, thanks to a try by Eugene Billac. It was the first of only two occasions that Scotland failed to score in a home match with France, the other being in 1954.

SCOTLAND   H.H. Forsayth 1 (Oxford U.); I.J. Kilgour (1) (RMA Sandhurst), A.E. Thomson 1 (US Portsmouth), A.L. Gracie 1 (Harlequins), J.H. Carmichael 1 (Watsonians); A.T. Sloan 6 (Edinburgh Acads), *J. Hume 3 (Royal HSFP); J.M. Bannerman 1 (Glasgow HSFP), R.S. Cumming 1 (Aberdeen U.), R.A. Gallie 5 (Glasgow Acads), A.D. Laing (7) (Royal HSFP), J.B. Macdougall 3 (Wakefield), N.C. Macpherson 4 (Newport), W.A.K. Murray (3) (Kelvinside Acads), G.H.H.P. Maxwell 8 (London Scottish).

FRANCE   J. Clément 1 (RCF); R. Got 2 (US Perpignan), *R. Crabos 5 (RCF), F. Borde 2 (RCF), J. Lobies 1 (RCF); E. Billac 5 (A. Bayonne), R. Piteu 1 (S. Pau); M. Biraben 3 (US Dax), J. Boubée 1 (S. Tarbes), G. Coscoll 1 (AS Béziers), R. Lasserre 4 (A. Bayonne), M-F. Lubin-Lebrère 7 (S. Toulouse), P. Pons 4 (S. Toulouse), F. Vaquer 1 (US Perpignan), E. Soulié 3 (CASG).

Referee W.P. Hinton (Ireland)

WALES v SCOTLAND   32/211

5 February 1921
St Helen's, Swansea
Scotland 14 (1G, 2T, 1PG) Wales 8 (2DG)

Wales   DG: Jenkins (2).
Scotland   T: Thomson, Buchanan, Sloan. C: Maxwell. PG: Maxwell.

This was the only occasion a Championship match came perilously close to being abandoned because of crowd problems. With 50,000 spectators filling the ground, there were continual overspills at the touchlines and in-goal areas. At one time the players had to retire to the changing-rooms, as mounted police tried to clear the ground. After several stoppages the referee, John Baxter – who had suffered more than his fair share of difficulties in the 1913 France v Scotland match – called the captains together to consider whether the match should continue. At one point Scotland were ready to march off on their own. Eventually, the much interrupted contest ended with Scotland scoring their first victory in Wales for 29 years.

WALES   J. Rees 6 (Swansea); F. Evans (1) (Llanelli), A. Jenkins 5 (Llanelli), P. Baker Jones (1) (Newport), M.G. Thomas 1 (St Bart's H.); W. Bowen 1 (Swansea), *T.H. Vile (7) (Newport); J. Williams 5 (Blaina), S. Winmill 2 (Cross Keys), T. Roberts 1 (Risca), W. Hodder 2 (Pontypool), L. Attewell 2 (Newport), T. Parker 5 (Swansea), J. Jones 3 (Aberavon), E. Morgan 3 (Llanelli).

SCOTLAND   H.H. Forsayth 2 (Oxford U.); A.T. Sloan 7 (Edinburgh Acads), A.L. Gracie 2 (Harlequins), A.E. Thomson 2 (US Portsmouth), J.H. Carmichael 2 (Watsonians); R.L.H. Donald 1 (Glasgow HSFP), *J. Hume 4 (Royal HSFP); J.M. Bannerman 2 (Glasgow HSFP), J.C.R. Buchanan 1 (Stewart's FP), R.S. Cumming (2) (Aberdeen U.), G. Douglas (1) (Jedforest), R.A. Gallie 6 (Glasgow Acads), G.H.H.P. Maxwell 9 (London Scottish), J.N. Shaw 1 (Edinburgh Acads), C.M. Usher 11 (Edinburgh Wands).

Referee J.W. Baxter (England)

ENGLAND v IRELAND 32/212

12 February 1921
Twickenham
England 15 (1G, 2T, 1DG) Ireland 0

England   T: Blakiston, Brown, Lowe. C: Cumberlege. DG: Lowe.

The sixth and final appearance of Frank Mellish, the Blackheath forward. Mellish, who won the MC in the First World War, went to South Africa later that year when he won the first two of his six caps for South Africa, against New Zealand.

ENGLAND   B.S. Cumberlege 5 (Blackheath); C.N. Lowe 14 (Blackheath), E.D.G. Hammett 5 (Newport), E. Myers 4 (Bradford), A.M. Smallwood 4 (Leicester); *W.J.A. Davies 12 (US Portsmouth), C.A. Kershaw 6 (US Portsmouth); R. Edwards 2 (Newport), E.R. Gardner 2 (Devonport Services), L.G. Brown 14 (Blackheath), F.W. Mellish (6) (Blackheath), T. Woods 3 (Devonport Services), A.F. Blakiston 3 (Northampton), A.T. Voyce 4 (Gloucester), W.W. Wakefield 6 (Harlequins).

IRELAND   W.E. Crawford 5 (Lansdowne); D.J. Cussen 1 (Dublin U.), G.V. Stephenson 2 (Queen's U. Belfast), A.R. Foster 15 (Derry), H.S.T. Cormac 1 (Clontarf); W.A. Cunningham 2 (Lansdowne), T. Mayne 1 (NIFC); J.J. Bermingham 1 (Blackrock College), W.P. Collopy 5 (Bective Rangers), A.W. Courtney 4 (UC Dublin), *W.D. Doherty 4 (Guy's H.), P. Stokes 8 (Garryowen), T.A. McClelland 1 (Queen's U. Belfast), C.F.G.T. Hallaran 1 (US Portsmouth), N.M. Purcell 1 (Lansdowne).

Referee T.D. Schofield (Wales)

WALES v FRANCE 7/213

26 February 1921
Cardiff Arms Park
Wales 12 (2T, 2PG) France 4 (1DG)

Wales   T: Jack Williams, Hodder. PG: Jenkins (2).
France   DG: Lasserre.

Wales had become accustomed to scoring tries at will at home, particularly against France. On this occasion the French defence was of a very high standard and limited Wales to just two tries. France's dropped goal was scored unusually by a forward, René Lasserre.

WALES   B.O. Male 1 (Cross Keys); T. Johnson 2 (Cardiff), G. Davies 1 (Llanelli), A. Jenkins 6 (Llanelli), M.G. Thomas 2 (St Bart's H.); W. Bowen 2 (Swansea), T. Williams (1) (Swansea); L. Attewell (3) (Newport), T. Roberts 2 (Risca), J. Williams 6 (Blaina), S. Winmill 3 (Cross Keys), *T. Parker 6 (Swansea), W. Hodder (3) (Pontypool), E. Morgan (4) (Llanelli), J. Jones 4 (Aberavon).

FRANCE   J. Clément 2 (RCF); R. Got 3 (US Perpignan), *R. Crabos 6 (RCF), J. Lobies 2 (RCF), F. Borde 3 (RCF); E. Billac 6 (A. Bayonne), R. Piteu 2 (S. Pau); R. Lasserre 5 (A. Bayonne), F. Vaquer 2 (US Perpignan), J. Larrieu 2 (S. Tarbes), A. Cassayet 4 (S. Tarbes), P. Moureu 2 (AS Béziers), G. Coscoll (2) (AS Béziers), P. Pons 5 (S. Toulouse), M. Biraben 4 (US Dax).

Referee P.M.R. Royds (England)

IRELAND v SCOTLAND 34/214

26 February 1921
Lansdowne Road, Dublin
Ireland 9 (3T) Scotland 8 (1G, 1T)

Ireland   T: Cussen, Stephenson, Cunningham.
Scotland   T: Hume, Sloan. C: Maxwell.

Ireland scored their third successive home win over Scotland, the one area of success in their early Championship forays against the Scots.

IRELAND W.E. Crawford 6 (Lansdowne); H.S.T. Cormac 2 (Clontarf), G.V. Stephenson 3 (Queen's U. Belfast), A.R. Foster 16 (Derry), D.J. Cussen 2 (Dublin U.); W.A. Cunningham 3 (Lansdowne), T. Mayne 2 (NIFC); J.J. Bermingham 2 (Blackrock College), W.P. Collopy 6 (Bective Rangers), A.W. Courtney 5 (UC Dublin), *W.D. Doherty 5 (Cambridge U.), C.F.G.T. Hallaran 2 (US Portsmouth), T.A. McClelland 2 (Queen's U. Belfast), P. Stokes 9 (Blackrock College), N.M. Purcell 2 (Lansdowne).

SCOTLAND H.H. Forsayth 3 (Oxford U.); J.W.S. McCrow (1) (Edinburgh Acads), A.L. Gracie 3 (Harlequins), A.T. Sloan 8 (Edinburgh Acads), J.H. Carmichael (3) (Watsonians); R.L.H. Donald 2 (Glasgow HSFP), *J. Hume 5 (Royal HSFP); J.M. Bannerman 3 (Glasgow HSFP), J.C.R. Buchanan 2 (Stewart's FP), R.A. Gallie 7 (Glasgow Acads), J.B. Macdougall 4 (Wakefield), G.H.H.P. Maxwell 10 (London Scottish), G.M. Murray 1 (Glasgow Acads), J.L. Stewart (1) (Edinburgh Acads), J.N. Shaw (2) (Edinburgh Acads).

Referee J.W. Baxter (England)

IRELAND v WALES 30/215

---

12 March 1921
Balmoral Showgrounds, Belfast
Wales 6 (1T, 1PG) Ireland 0

Wales T: Melbourne Thomas. PG: Johnson.

Wales's fourth successive victory over Ireland condemned the latter to bottom place in the Championship. It was also the last international for A.R. Foster, the Derry centre who won 17 caps in an 11-year career. Six Welshmen, including five of the pack, did not play again in the Championship.

IRELAND W.E. Crawford 7 (Lansdowne); D.J. Cussen 3 (Dublin U.), A.R. Foster (17) (Derry), G.V. Stephenson 4 (Queen's U. Belfast), H.S.T. Cormac (3) (Clontarf); W.A. Cunningham 4 (Lansdowne), H.W. Jack (3) (UC Cork); J.J. Bermingham 3 (Blackrock College), W.P. Collopy 7 (Bective Rangers), A.W. Courtney 6 (UC Dublin), *W.D. Doherty 6 (Cambridge U.), C.F.G.T. Hallaran 3 (US Portsmouth), T.A. McClelland 3 (Queen's U. Belfast), J.K.S.

Thompson 1 (Dublin U.), N.M. Purcell 3 (Lansdowne).

WALES J. Rees 7 (Swansea); T. Johnson 3 (Cardiff), G. Davies 2 (Llanelli), D. Davies 1 (Bridgend), M.G. Thomas 3 (St Bart's H.); J.M.C. Lewis 9 (Cardiff), A. Brown (1) (Newport); J. Williams (7) (Blaina), W. Morris (2) (Abertillery), J. Prosser (1) (Cardiff), S. Winmill (4) (Cross Keys), *T. Parker 7 (Swansea), A. Baker 1 (Neath), T. Roberts 3 (Risca), J. Jones (5) (Aberavon).

Referee J.M. Tennant (Scotland)

SCOTLAND v ENGLAND 31/216

---

19 March 1921
Inverleith, Edinburgh
England 18 (3G, 1T) Scotland 0

England T: Brown, Edwards, King, Woods. C: Hammett (3).

England registered their biggest victory margin in Scotland to obtain the Triple Crown for the sixth time. Newspaper accounts wrote glowingly of the performance. One rugby writer, E.R. Ward, wrote: 'This simply was an exacting task of the genius of the England Fifteen. It had prospered amazingly under the fair circumstances of the Welsh match; it had succeeded in the heavy going of the Irish match; it succeeded at Inverleith in something like half a hurricane, one of those days when anything might happen.'

SCOTLAND H.H. Forsayth 4 (Oxford U.); A.T. Sloan (9) (Edinburgh Acads), A.E. Thomson (3) (US Portsmouth), C.J.G. Mackenzie (1) (US Portsmouth), A.L. Gracie 4 (Harlequins); R.L.H. Donald (3) (Glasgow HSFP), *J. Hume 6 (Royal HSFP); J.M. Bannerman 4 (Glasgow HSFP), J.C.R. Buchanan 3 (Stewart's FP), R.A. Gallie (8) (Glasgow Acads), F. Kennedy (5) (Stewart's FP), J.B. Macdougall (5) (Wakefield), N.C. Macpherson 5 (Newport), C.M. Usher 12 (Edinburgh Wands), G.H.H.P. Maxwell 11 (London Scottish).

ENGLAND B.S. Cumberlege 6 (Blackheath); C.N. Lowe 15 (Blackheath), A.M. Smallwood 5 (Leicester), E.D.G. Hammett 6 (Newport), Q.E.M.A.

King (1) (Blackheath); *W.J.A. Davies 13 (US Portsmouth), C.A. Kershaw 7 (US Portsmouth); R. Edwards 3 (Newport), E.R. Gardner 3 (Devonport Services), L.G. Brown 15 (Blackheath), T. Woods 4 (Devonport Services), R. Cove-Smith 1 (Cambridge U.), A.F. Blakiston 4 (Northampton), A.T. Voyce 5 (Gloucester), W.W. Wakefield 7 (Harlequins).

Referee S.H. Crawford (Ireland)

FRANCE v ENGLAND 7/217

28 March 1921
Stade Colombes, Paris
England 10 (2G)   France 6 (2PG)

France   PG: Crabos (2).
England   T: Blakiston, Lowe. C: Hammett (2).

Until this match, England had conceded three points only, but two penalty goals from René Crabos not only wrecked an otherwise splendid defensive record but threatened their Grand Slam prospects.

FRANCE   J. Clément 3 (RCF); J. Lobies (3) (RCF), F. Borde 4 (RCF), *R. Crabos 7 (RCF), E. Cayrefourcq (1) (S. Tarbes); A. Bousquet 1 (AS Béziers), R. Piteu 3 (S. Pau); P. Moureu 3 (AS Béziers), C-A. Gonnet 1 (SC Albi), M. Biraben 5 (US Dax), A. Cassayet 5 (St Gaudens), L. Puech 4 (S. Toulouse), J. Boubée 2 (S. Tarbes), A. Guichemerre 2 (US Dax), E. Soulié 4 (CASG).

ENGLAND   B.S. Cumberlege 7 (Blackheath); C.N. Lowe 16 (Blackheath), L.J. Corbett 1 (Bristol), E.D.G. Hammett 7 (Newport), A.M. Smallwood 6 (Leicester); *W.J.A. Davies 14 (US Portsmouth), C.A. Kershaw 8 (US Portsmouth); R. Edwards 4 (Newport), T. Woods (5) (Pontypool), L.G. Brown 16 (Blackheath), W.W. Wakefield 8 (Harlequins), R. Cove-Smith 2 (Cambridge U.), G.S. Conway 4 (Cambridge U.), A.T. Voyce 6 (Gloucester), A.F. Blakiston 5 (Northampton).

Referee J.C. Sturrock (Scotland)

FRANCE v IRELAND 7/218

9 April 1921
Stade Colombes, Paris
France 20 (4G) Ireland 10 (2G)

France   T: Piteu (2), Cassayet, Boubée. C: Crabos (4).
Ireland   T: Stokes (2). C: Wallis (2).

This defeat spelled the end of their international careers for six Irish players, four of them in the pack, including the captain, W.D. Doherty. There was some doubt, if not dispute, concerning the last French try by Jean Boubée. According to *The Times*: 'It appeared that the Irishmen were under some misapprehension connected with the last score, for they were standing still as the try was scored.' Jock Cunningham, of Scotland, who made his début as an international referee, did not officiate at another. An injury to Jean Clément, the usual French choice for full-back, meant that René Lasserre, one of the forwards, was selected to play out of position.

FRANCE   R. Lasserre 6 (A. Bayonne); J. Baquet (1) (S. Toulouse), H. Jeangrand (1) (S. Tarbes), *R. Crabos 8 (RCF), M. de Laborderie 1 (RCF); A. Bousquet (2) (AS Béziers), R. Piteu 4 (S. Pau); E. Soulié 5 (CASG), C-A. Gonnet 2 (SC Albi), M. Biraben 6 (US Dax), L. Puech (5) (S. Toulouse), P. Moureu 4 (AS Béziers), J. Boubée 3 (S. Tarbes), A. Cassayet 6 (St Gaudens), A. Guichemerre 3 (US Dax).

IRELAND   W.E. Crawford 8 (Lansdowne); D.J. Cussen 4 (Dublin U.), G.V. Stephenson 5 (Queen's U. Belfast), T.G. Wallis 1 (Wanderers), C.T. Davidson (1) (NIFC); W.A. Cunningham 5 (Lansdowne), T. Mayne (3) (NIFC); J.J. Bermingham (4) (Blackrock College), W.P. Collopy 8 (Bective Rangers), A.W. Courtney (7) (UC Dublin), *W.D. Doherty (7) (Cambridge U.), R.Y. Crichton 5 (Dublin U.), T.A. McClelland 4 (Queen's U. Belfast), N.M. Purcell (4) (Lansdowne), P. Stokes 10 (Garryowen).

Referee J.G. Cunningham (Scotland)

PARIS France drew Scotland 3-3 · CARDIFF Wales beat England 28-6
EDINBURGH Scotland drew Wales 9-9 · DUBLIN England beat Ireland 12-3
TWICKENHAM England drew France 11-11 · EDINBURGH Scotland beat Ireland 6-3
SWANSEA Wales beat Ireland 11-5 · TWICKENHAM England beat Scotland 11-5
PARIS Wales beat France 11-3 · DUBLIN Ireland beat France 8-3

CHAMPIONSHIP TABLE
Wales – Championship

Pos	Country	P	W	D	L	F	A	Pts	Tries F	A
1	Wales (3)	4	3	1	0	59	23	7	15	6
2	England (1)	4	2	1	1	40	47	5	10	13
3	Scotland (4)	4	1	2	1	23	26	4	6	6
4	France (2)	4	0	2	2	20	33	2	6	6
5	Ireland (5)	4	1	0	3	19	32	2	4	10

The most notable feature of the 1922 Championship was three drawn matches, the highest ever number until repeated in 1962. Wales ruled supreme, completing a fabulous run of success in the Championship which had started in 1902. Of the 16 Championships held since then, the Welsh had won six and were runners up seven times; of 56 matches played, 42 were won and 2 drawn; and the icing on their cake was the scoring of eight tries against England, the most ever registered against rugby football's founding nation.

Concerning the Laws of the game, it had now become a penalty offence to delay feeding the scrummage and a player who had made a 'fair catch' (the original description for a mark) was now required to take the kick himself.

FRANCE v SCOTLAND 7/219

2 January 1922
Stade Colombes, Paris
France 3 (1T) Scotland 3 (1T)

France T: Jauréguy.
Scotland T: Browning.

The début of Eric Liddell, whose speed around the field won him seven Scottish caps before he gave up rugby to concentrate on athletics. Liddell's rise to Olympic Games fame was the subject of a highly-acclaimed film of the early 1980s, *Chariots of Fire*. It was the final appearance of J. Hume, the Royal HSFP scrum-half. Hume had a curious career, begun as far back as 1912, yet ending up with only seven caps; four of which were gained against France.

FRANCE J. Clément 4 (Valence Sp); A. Jauréguy 5 (S. Toulouse), F. Borde 5 (S. Toulouse), *R. Crabos 9 (St Sever), R. Got 4 (US Perpignan); J. Pascot 1 (US Perpignan), R. Piteu 5 (S. Pau); R. Lasserre 7 (US Cognac), J. Sébedio 6 (AS Carcassonne), F. Cahuc (1) (St Girons), P. Moureu 5 (AS Béziers), A. Cassayet 7 (St Gaudens), M. Biraben 7 (US Dax), M-F. Lubin-Lebrère 8 (S. Toulouse), P. Pons (6) (S. Toulouse).

SCOTLAND W.C. Johnston (1) (Glasgow HSFP); A. Browning 2 (Glasgow HSFP); G.P.S. Macpherson 1 (Oxford U.), A.L. Gracie 5 (Harlequins), E.H. Liddell 1 (Edinburgh U.); J.C. Dykes 1 (Glasgow Acads), J. Hume (7) (Royal HSFP); A. Wemyss 5 (Edinburgh Wands), D.M. Bertram 1 (Watsonians), A.K. Stevenson 1 (Glasgow Acads), D.S. Davies 1 (Hawick), J.M.

Bannerman 5 (Glasgow HSFP), J.R. Lawrie 1 (Melrose), G.H.H.P. Maxwell 12 (London Scottish), *C.M. Usher 13 (Edinburgh Wands).

Referee H.C. Harrison (England)

WALES v ENGLAND 33/220

21 January 1922
Cardiff Arms Park
Wales 28 (2G, 6T) England 6 (2T)

Wales T: Bowen, Delahay, Islwyn Evans, Hiddlestone, Parker, Palmer, Richards, Whitfield. C: Rees (2).
England T: Day, Lowe.

Wales's eight tries were the most scored against England in any match. It spelled the end of international rugby for four of England's players, including Barry Cumberlege, who had created their second try by running out of defence. The Blackheath full-back played in eight matches only for England but was regarded as one of the most gifted players of his day: 'Cumberlege belongs to the Tristram breed. He was a dead field, a huge kick, and a mighty tackle ... here and there he would take his courage into his hands and run up to the attacking line: but he was splendidly safe ... his errors could be numbered on the fingers of one hand.' The match was interesting in two other respects: it was the first time that both sides in an international were numbered, and that Wales played two specialized flank-forwards.

WALES   J. Rees 8 (Swansea); C. Richards 1 (Pontypool), B.E. Evans 2 (Llanelli), I. Evans 1 (Swansea), F. Palmer 1 (Swansea); W. Bowen 3 (Swansea), W.J. Delahay 1 (Bridgend); *T. Parker 8 (Swansea), J. Whitfield 6 (Newport), T. Jones 1 (Newport), S. Morris 5 (Cross Keys), T. Roberts 4 (Risca), Revd J.G. Stephens 1 (Llanelli), D. Hiddlestone 1 (Neath), W. Cummins 1 (Treorchy).

ENGLAND   B.S. Cumberlege (8) (Blackheath); C.N. Lowe 17 (Blackheath), E.D.G. Hammett (8) (Blackheath), E. Myers 5 (Bradford), H.L.V. Day 2 (Leicester); V.G. Davies (1) Harlequins), C.A. Kershaw 9 (US Portsmouth); R. Edwards 5 (Newport), E.R. Gardner 4 (Devonport Services), J.S. Tucker 1 (Bristol), W.W. Wakefield 9

(Harlequins), A.F. Blakiston 6 (Blackheath), A.T. Voyce 7 (Gloucester), G.S. Conway 5 (Cambridge U.), *L.G. Brown (17) (Blackheath).

Referee J.M. Tennant (Scotland)

SCOTLAND v WALES 33/221

4 February 1922
Inverleith, Edinburgh
Scotland 9 (2T, 1PG) Wales 9 (1G, 1DG)

Scotland Browning (2). PG: Browning.
Wales T: Bowen. C: Samuel. DG. Islwyn Evans.

This was only the second draw between the countries in 33 meetings since 1883, Wales being saved by a 20-yard dropped goal from Islwyn Evans two minutes from no-side.

SCOTLAND   H.H. Forsayth 5 (Oxford U.); A. Browning 3 (Glasgow HSFP), R.C. Warren 1 (Glasgow Acads), A.L. Gracie 6 (Harlequins), E.H. Liddell 2 (Edinburgh U.); G.P.S. Macpherson 2 (Oxford U.), W.E. Bryce 1 (Selkirk); A. Wemyss 6 (Edinburgh Wands), D.M. Bertram 2 (Watsonians), W.G. Dobson 1 (Heriot's FP), D.S. Davies 2 (Hawick), J.M. Bannerman 6 (Glasgow HSFP), J.R. Lawrie 2 (Melrose), *C.M. Usher 14 (Edinburgh Wands), J.C.R. Buchanan 4 (Stewart's FP).

WALES   F. Samuel 1 (Mountain Ash); F. Palmer 2 (Swansea), I. Evans 2 (Swansea), B.E. Evans 3 (Llanelli), C. Richards 2 (Pontypool); W. Bowen 4 (Swansea), W.J. Delahay 2 (Bridgend); *T. Parker 9 (Swansea), J. Whitfield 7 (Newport), T. Jones 2 (Newport), S. Morris 6 (Cross Keys), T. Roberts 5 (Risca), Revd J.G. Stephens 2 (Llanelli), W. Cummins 2 (Treorchy), D. Hiddlestone 2 (Neath).

Referee R.A. Lloyd (Ireland)

IRELAND v ENGLAND 33/222

11 February 1922
Lansdowne Road, Dublin
England 12 (4T) Ireland 3 (1T)

Ireland T: Wallis.
England T: Lowe, Gardner, Maxwell-Hyslop, Smallwood.

One newspaper account of this match was particularly scathing of the Irish team: 'the Irish pack carried several passengers and badly trained men, and the stand-off half-back and centre threequarter backs were a dead failure in attack'. Wavell Wakefield, then a mere fledgling with ten caps, was praised however: 'it was his greatest game to date ... he seemed faster than ever and what is more possessed of the "devil" without which no forward can be called "great". Some of the older members of the Irish crowd must have thought sadly of the days of the brothers Ryan, who, like Wakefield, spared no man who stood in their way.'

IRELAND W.E. Crawford 9 (Lansdowne); T.G. Wallis 2 (Wanderers), D.B. Sullivan 1 (UC Dublin), G.V. Stephenson 6 (Queen's U. Belfast), D.J. Cussen 5 (Dublin U.); J.R. Wheeler 1 (Queen's U. Belfast), W.A. Cunningham 6 (Lansdowne); *W.P. Collopy 9 (Bective Rangers), R.H. Owens 1 (Dublin U.), T.A. McClelland 5 (Queen's U. Belfast), S. McVicker 1 (Queen's U. Belfast), M.J. Bradley 3 (Dolphin), J.K.S. Thompson 2 (Dublin U.), C.F.G.T. Hallaran 4 (US Portsmouth), R.Y. Crichton 6 (Dublin U.).

ENGLAND R.C.W. Pickles 1 (Bristol); C.N. Lowe 18 (Blackheath), E. Myers 6 (Bradford), M.S. Bradby 1 (US Portsmouth), A.M. Smallwood 7 (Leicester); *W.J.A. Davies 15 (US Portsmouth), C.A. Kershaw 10 (US Portsmouth); R. Cove-Smith 3 (Cambridge U.), E.R. Gardner 5 (Devonport Services), J.E. Maxwell-Hyslop 1 (Oxford U.), R.F.H. Duncan 1 (Guy's H.), W.W. Wakefield 10 (Harlequins), H.L. Price 1 (Oxford U.), A.T. Voyce 8 (Gloucester), G.S. Conway 6 (Cambridge U.).

Referee J.M. Tennant (Scotland)

SCOTLAND v IRELAND 35/223

25 February 1922
Inverleith, Edinburgh
Scotland 6 (2T) Ireland 3 (1T)

Scotland T: Bryce, Liddell.
Ireland T: Clarke.

Inverleith was renowned for being a ground where the wind often was strong and veering, and in this match it lived up to its reputation, for both sides had problems. It was the first appearance of Harry Stephenson, who joined his brother, George, in Ireland's back division. George gained a reputation as a highly-talented centre and rather overshadowed Harry, a wing who played in 12 internationals.

SCOTLAND H.H. Forsayth 6 (Oxford U.); A. Browning 4 (Glasgow HSFP), R.C. Warren 2 (Glasgow Acads), A.L. Gracie 7 (Harlequins), E.H. Liddell 3 (Edinburgh U.); G.P.S. Macpherson 3 (Oxford U.), W.E. Bryce 2 (Selkirk); A. Wemyss (7) (Edinburgh Wands), D.M. Bertram 3 (Watsonians), W.G. Dobson 2 (Heriot's FP), D.S. Davies 3 (Hawick), J.M. Bannerman 7 (Glasgow HSFP), J.R. Lawrie 3 (Melrose), *C.M. Usher 15 (Edinburgh Wands), J.C.R. Buchanan 5 (Stewart's FP).

IRELAND W.E. Crawford 10 (Lansdowne); H.W.V. Stephenson 1 (US Portsmouth), G.V. Stephenson 7 (Queen's U. Belfast), D.B. Sullivan 2 (UC Dublin), T.G. Wallis 3 (Wanderers); J.R. Wheeler 2 (Queen's U. Belfast), J.A.B. Clarke 1 (Bective Rangers), *W.P. Collopy 10 (Bective Rangers), M.J. Bradley 4 (Dolphin), I. Popham 1 (Cork Constitution), C.F.G.T. Hallaran 5 (US Portsmouth), S. McVicker 2 (Queen's U. Belfast), R.H. Owens (2) (Dublin U.), J.D. Egan (1) (Bective Rangers), J.K.S. Thompson 3 (Dublin U.).

Referee T.D. Schofield (Wales)

ENGLAND v FRANCE   8/224

25 February 1922
Twickenham
England 11 (1G, 2PG) France 11 (1G, 2T)

England   T: Voyce. C: Day. PG: Day (2).
France   T: Cassayet, Got, Lasserre. C: Crabos.

England, unbeaten in the Championship at Twickenham, came very close to ending the ground's impregnability. A try by Tommy Voyce, converted by Harold Day, near no-side enabled England to draw.

ENGLAND   R.C.W. Pickles (2) (Bristol); C.N. Lowe 19 (Blackheath), E. Myers 7 (Bradford), M.S. Bradby (2) (US Portsmouth), H.L.V. Day 3 (Leicester); *W.J.A. Davies 16 (US Portsmouth), C.A. Kershaw 11 (US Portsmouth); R. Cove-Smith 4 (Cambridge U.), E.R. Gardner 6 (Devonport Services), R. Edwards 6 (Newport), R.F.H. Duncan 2 (Guy's H.), W.W. Wakefield 11 (Cambridge U.), A.T. Voyce 9 (Gloucester), J.E. Maxwell-Hyslop 2 (Oxford U.), G.S. Conway 7 (Cambridge U.).

FRANCE   J. Clément 5 (Valence Sp); A. Laffond (1) (A. Bayonne), R. Ramis 1 (US Perpignan), *R. Crabos 10 (St Sever), R. Got 5 (US Perpignan); J. Pascot 2 (US Perpignan), R. Piteu 6 (S. Pau); R. Lasserre 8 (US Cognac), A. Cassayet 8 (St Gaudens), J. Boubée 4 (Biarritz Ol), J. Sébedio 7 (AS Carcassonne), M-F. Lubin-Lebrère 9 (S. Toulouse), M. Biraben 8 (US Dax), E. Soulié 6 (CASG), C-A. Gonnet 3 (SC Albi).

Referee J.M. Tennant (Scotland)

WALES v IRELAND   31/225

11 March 1922
St Helen's, Swansea
Wales 11 (1G, 2T) Ireland 5 (1G)

Wales   T: Whitfield (2), Islwyn Evans. C: Samuel.
Ireland   T: Stokes. C: Wallis.

This was Wales's fifth successive win over Ireland, which equalled their best ever winning sequence against the Irish. It was also Wales's ninth home win in a row against Ireland, their best ever winning sequence against them. It meant that Wales won the Championship and Ireland finished with the Wooden Spoon.

WALES   F. Samuel 2 (Mountain Ash); F. Palmer (3) (Swansea), I. Evans 3 (Swansea), B.E. Evans 4 (Llanelli), C. Richards 3 (Pontypool); W. Bowen 5 (Swansea), W.J. Delahay 3 (Bridgend); *T. Parker 10 (Swansea), J. Whitfield 8 (Newport), T. Jones 3 (Newport), S. Morris 7 (Cross Keys), T. Roberts 6 (Risca), Revd J.G. Stephens 3 (Llanelli), W. Cummins 3 (Treorchy), D. Hiddlestone 3 (Neath).

IRELAND   B.A.T. McFarland (4) (Derry); D.B. Sullivan 3 (UC Dublin), T.G. Wallis 4 (Wanderers), G.V. Stephenson 8 (Queen's U. Belfast), H.W.V. Stephenson 2 (US Portsmouth); J.R. Wheeler 3 (Queen's U. Belfast), J.A.B. Clarke 2 (Bective Rangers); J.C. Gillespie 1 (Dublin U.), M.J. Bradley 5 (Dolphin), C.F.G.T. Hallaran 6 (US Portsmouth), *W.P. Collopy 11 (Bective Rangers), S. McVicker 3 (Queen's U. Belfast), T.A. McClelland 6 (Queen's U. Belfast), P. Stokes 11 (Garryowen), I. Popham 2 (Cork Constitution).

Referee J.C. Sturrock (Scotland)

ENGLAND v SCOTLAND   32/226

18 March 1922
Twickenham
England 11 (1G, 2T) Scotland 5 (1G)

England   T: Lowe (2), Davies. C: Conway.
Scotland   T: Dykes. C: Bertram.

After drawing against France and Wales and beating Ireland, Scotland were hoping to maintain their unbeaten record on this visit to Twickenham, but: 'a crowd of quite 40,000 – fairly evenly divided between those who love the bagpipes and those who merely respect their properties – watched England recover from an apparently hopeless situation to win an exciting struggle.' Penalty goals were still scarce in the Championship but, curiously, few accounts revealed why the kicks had been awarded. In this match Maxwell failed with a late penalty and the offence was recorded as 'feet up'.

ENGLAND   J.A. Middleton (1) (Richmond); C.N. Lowe 20 (Blackheath), E. Myers 8 (Bradford), A.M. Smallwood 8 (Leicester), I.J. Pitman (1) (Oxford U.); *W.J.A. Davies 17 (US Portsmouth), C.A. Kershaw 12 (US Portsmouth); P.B.R.W. William-Powlett (1) (US Portsmouth), H.L. Price 2 (Oxford U.), R.F.H. Duncan (3) (Guy's H.), R. Cove-Smith 5 (Cambridge U.), W.W. Wakefield 12 (Harlequins), A.T. Voyce 10 (Gloucester), J.E. Maxwell-Hyslop (3) (Oxford U.), G.S. Conway 8 (Cambridge U.).

SCOTLAND   H.H. Forsayth (7) (Oxford U.); J.M. Tolmie (1) (Glasgow HSFP), A.L. Gracie 8 (Harlequins), G.P.S. Macpherson 4 (Oxford U.), E.B. Mackay (2) (Glasgow Acads); J.C. Dykes 2 (Glasgow Acads), W.E. Bryce 3 (Selkirk); J.C.R. Buchanan 6 (Stewart's FP), D.M. Bertram 4 (Watsonians), W.G. Dobson (3) (Heriot's FP), D.S. Davies 4 (Hawick), J.M. Bannerman 8 (Glasgow HSFP), J.R. Lawrie 4 (Melrose), G.H.H.P. Maxwell (13) (Edinburgh Acads), *C.M. Usher (16) (Edinburgh Wands).

Referee R.A. Lloyd (Ireland)

FRANCE v WALES   8/227

23 March 1922
Stade Colombes, Paris
Wales 11 (1G, 2T) France 3 (1T)

France   T: Jauréguy.
Wales   T: Whitfield, Cummins, Islwyn Evans. C: Jenkins.

A Thursday match, the Welsh selectors took the unusual step of dropping two of the players chosen, Frank Palmer (Swansea) and Harold Davies (Newport), bringing in Cliff Richards and Islwyn Evans shortly before kick-off. The selectors believed that the newcomers would perform better on a hard, sun-baked pitch.

FRANCE   J. Clément 6 (Valence Sp); A. Jauréguy 6 (S. Toulouse), F. Borde 6 (S. Toulouse), *R. Crabos 11 (St Sever), R. Got 6 (US Perpignan); E. Billac 7 (A. Bayonne), R. Piteu 7 (S. Pau); R. Lasserre 9 (US Cognac), F. Vaquer (3) (US Perpignan), J. Boubée 5 (Biarritz Ol), P. Moureu 6 (AS Béziers), A. Cassayet 9 (St Gaudens), M-F. Lubin-Lebrère 10 (S. Toulouse), E. Soulié 7 (CASG), C-A. Gonnet 4 (SC Albi).

WALES   F. Samuel (3) (Mountain Ash); C. Richards 4 (Pontypool), A. Jenkins 7 (Llanelli), I. Evans (4) (Swansea), B.E. Evans (5) (Llanelli); W. Bowen (6) (Swansea), W.J. Delahay 4 (Bridgend); *T. Parker 11 (Swansea), J. Whitfield 9 (Newport), T. Jones 4 (Newport), S. Morris 8 (Cross Keys), T. Roberts 7 (Risca), Revd J.G. Stephens (4) (Llanelli), D. Hiddlestone (4) (Neath), W. Cummins (4) (Treorchy).

Referee R.W. Harland (Ireland)

IRELAND v FRANCE   8/228

8 April 1922
Lansdowne Road, Dublin
Ireland 8 (1G, 1PG) France 3 (1T)

Ireland   T: George Stephenson. C: Wallis. PG: Wallis.
France   T: Pascot.

This was a battle to avoid the Wooden Spoon, but that dubious honour fell on Ireland, despite their victory, for France had scored just one point more overall. The defeat meant that Ireland had now suffered three successive seasons at the bottom of the Championship.

IRELAND   W.J. Stewart 1 (Preston Grasshoppers); T.G. Wallis (5) (Wanderers), D.B. Sullivan (4) (UC Dublin), G.V. Stephenson 9 (Queen's U. Belfast), H.W.V. Stephenson 3 (US Portsmouth); J.A.B. Clarke 3 (Bective Rangers), J.R. Wheeler 4 (Queen's U. Belfast); M.J. Bradley 6 (Dolphin), W.P. Collopy 12 (Bective Rangers), J.C. Gillespie (2) (Dublin U.), T.A. McClelland 7 (Queen's U. Belfast), S. McVicker (4) (Queen's U. Belfast), I. Popham 3 (Cork Constitution), P. Stokes (12) (Garryowen), *J.K.S. Thompson 4 (Dublin U.).

FRANCE   J. Clément 7 (Valence Sp); R. Got 7 (US Perpignan), R. Ramis 2 (US Perpignan), *R. Crabos 12 (RCF), M. de Laborderie 2 (RCF); J. Pascot 3 (US Perpignan), R. Piteu 8 (S. Pau); R. Lasserre 10 (US Cognac), N. Sicart (1) (US Perpignan), J. Etchepare (1) (A. Bayonne), P. Moureu 7 (AS Béziers), J. Bernon 1 (FC Lourdes), M. Biraben (9) (US Dax), E. Soulié (8) (CASG), L. Beguet 1 (RCF).

Referee J.M. Tennant (Scotland)

1923

TWICKENHAM England beat Wales 7-3 · EDINBURGH Scotland beat France 16-3
CARDIFF Scotland beat Wales 11-8 · LEICESTER England beat Ireland 23-5
DUBLIN Scotland beat Ireland 13-3 · SWANSEA Wales beat France 16-8
DUBLIN Ireland beat Wales 5-4 · EDINBURGH England beat Scotland 8-6
PARIS England beat France 12-3 · PARIS France beat Ireland 14-8

CHAMPIONSHIP TABLE
England – Championship, Triple Crown, Grand Slam

									Tries	
Pos	Country	P	W	D	L	F	A	Pts	F	A
1	England (2)	4	4	0	0	50	17	8	10	4
2	Scotland (3)	4	3	0	1	46	22	6	12	4
3	Wales (1)	4	1	0	3	31	31	2	5	7
4	France (4)	4	1	0	3	28	52	2	6	11
5	Ireland (5)	4	1	0	3	21	54	2	5	12

England won the Grand Slam while Ireland finished bottom of the Championship for the fourth season in a row. 'It is certainly open to question,' John Wisden's *Rugby Football Almanack* remarked, 'whether they [England] had a better all-round team than Scotland, who overcame France, Wales and Ireland, and had nothing the worst of the play in the struggle with England.' That assessment missed the point in that England had beaten Scotland in Scotland for the third successive time, a feat few teams had achieved. In fact, England repeated the exploit only once again, between 1952–56.

The year, of course, was an important one in the history of the game. Apocryphal legend or not, it was 100 years since William Webb Ellis picked up the ball and ran at Rugby School ... hence the fitting venue to stage a centenary festival. The School organized the festival, and its high point was a match between England and Wales against Scotland and Ireland, played on 1 November. Wisden declared: 'naturally, sentiment demanded the playing of the game in (sic) Rugby School Close so that it had to be decided before the privileged few ... but it was a pity the public could not have had the opportunity of seeing such a game.' A private affair or not, the match attracted enormous publicity – which was undoubtedly good for the game at the time – and many of the foremost players and administrators of the past attended in honour of the occasion, including Fred Stokes, England's first captain, then 73, and Harry Vassall, one of the leading figures in Oxford and England rugby when the Championship began. England and Wales won the match 21-16.

There was one important amendment to the Law regarding the scrummage: it was declared illegal for more than three players to make up the front row.

SCOTLAND v FRANCE   8/229

20 January 1923
Inverleith, Edinburgh
Scotland 16 (2G, 2T) France 3 (1GM)

Scotland T: McLaren (2), Bryce, Liddell. C: Drysdale (2).
France GM: Beguet.

The French suffered a series of match-stopping injuries but no report considered this the cause of their downfall by so substantial a margin. They failed to match the Scots at forward, and they failed tactically, not appreciating the value of a strong wind in the second half. Drysdale and Gracie were singled out for exceptional contributions. 'Gracie, as usual, kicked splendidly,' said one report, '[he] ran with fine speed and determination; was utterly unselfish and, in defence, as strong as anybody on the field.'

SCOTLAND   D. Drysdale 1 (Heriot's FP); A.C. Wallace 1 (Oxford U.), E. McLaren 1 (Royal HSFP), *A.L. Gracie 9 (Harlequins), E.H. Liddell 4 (Edinburgh U.); S.B. McQueen 1 (Waterloo), W.E. Bryce 4 (Selkirk); D.S. Kerr 1 (Heriot's FP), D.M. Bertram 5 (Watsonians), A.K. Stevenson 2 (Glasgow Acads), L.M. Stuart 1 (Glasgow HSFP), J.M. Bannerman 9 (Glasgow HSFP), J.R. Lawrie 5 (Melrose), J.C.R. Buchanan 7 (Stewart's FP), D.S. Davies 5 (Hawick).

FRANCE   J. Clément 8 (Valence Sp); M. Lalande 1 (RCF), *R. Crabos 13 (RCF), F. Borde 7 (S. Toulouse), A. Jauréguy 7 (S. Toulouse); J. Pascot 4 (US Perpignan), C. Dupont 1 (FC Lourdes); J. Bernon (2) (FC Lourdes), J. Bayard 1 (S. Toulouse), L. Beguet 2 (RCF), P. Moureu 8 (AS Béziers), A. Cassayet 10 (St Gaudens), J. Larrieu 3 (S. Tarbes), A. Guichemerre (4) (US Dax), J. Sébedio (8) (S. Tarbes).

Referee T.H. Vile (Wales)

ENGLAND v WALES   34/230

20 January 1923
Twickenham
England 7 (1T, 1DG) Wales 3 (1T)

England   T: Price. DG: Smallwood.
Wales   T: Michael.

F.G. Gilbert, the Devonport Services full-back, was 39 when he made his début in this match and is generally recognized as the oldest player to appear for England in a Championship match. In fact it was very much a veteran occasion for England players: Reg Edwards was 36, W.J.A. Davies was 33, Cyril Lowe was 32 and Cecil Kershaw was 28. One critic, Ubique, was full of praise for Edwards in particular, and for the English forwards in general: 'where all played so superbly it may be a little invidious to single out anyone for special mention, but of Edwards it can with justice be said that he played the game of his life. He was the best forward on the field.'

ENGLAND   F.G. Gilbert 1 (Devonport Services); C.N. Lowe 21 (Blackheath), E. Myers 9 (Bradford), L.J. Corbett 2 (Bristol), A.M. Smallwood 9 (Leicester); *W.J.A. Davies 18 (US Portsmouth), C.A. Kershaw 13 (US Portsmouth); E.R. Gardner 7 (Devonport Services), R. Edwards 7 (Newport), W.G.E. Luddington 1 (Devonport Services), W.W. Wakefield 13 (Cambridge U.), R. Cove-Smith 6 (OMT), H.L. Price 3 (Leicester), A.T. Voyce 11 (Gloucester), G.S. Conway 9 (Rugby).

WALES   J. Rees 9 (Swansea); T. Johnson 4 (Cardiff), R.A. Cornish 1 (Cardiff), A. Jenkins 8 (Llanelli), W.R. Harding 1 (Swansea); *J.M.C. Lewis 10 (Cardiff), W.J. Delahay 5 (Bridgend); T. Parker 12 (Swansea), T. Roberts 8 (Newport), D.G. Davies 1 (Cardiff), G. Thomas 1 (Llanelli), A. Baker 2 (Neath), S. Morris 9 (Cross Keys), G. Michael 1 (Swansea), J. Thompson (1) (Cross Keys).

Referee J.M.B. Scott (Scotland)

WALES v SCOTLAND   34/231

3 February 1923
Cardiff Arms Park
Scotland 11 (1G, 2T) Wales 8 (1G, 1PG)

Wales   T: Lewis. C: Albert Jenkins. PG: Albert Jenkins.
Scotland   T: Liddell, Stuart, Gracie. C: Drysdale.

A crowd of 40,000 produced record receipts of nearly £6000 for the Welsh Rugby Union, but the match is best remembered for a magnificent try which won the game for Scotland. Archie Gracie, the scorer, had the distinction of being carried off in triumph by Welsh supporters, though Gracie was more concerned at the time for the health of a small boy whom he had accidentally kicked as he grounded the ball near the dead-ball line. The boy lost a few teeth and Scotland gained their first victory at Cardiff since 1890.

WALES   B.O. Male 2 (Pontypool); T. Johnson 5 (Cardiff), R.A. Cornish 2 (Cardiff), A. Jenkins 9 (Llanelli), W.R. Harding 2 (Swansea); *J.M.C. Lewis (11) (Cardiff), W.J. Delahay 6 (Bridgend); A. Baker 3 (Neath), S. Morris 10 (Cross Keys), D.G. Davies (2) (Cardiff), T. Parker 13 (Swansea), G. Michael 2 (Swansea), G. Thomas 2 (Llanelli), L. Jenkins 1 (Aberavon), T. Roberts (9) (Newport).

SCOTLAND   D. Drysdale 2 (Heriot's FP); A. Browning 5 (Glasgow HSFP), E. McLaren 2 (Royal HSFP), *A.L. Gracie 10 (Harlequins), E.H. Liddell 5 (Edinburgh U.); S.B. McQueen 2 (Waterloo), W.E. Bryce 5 (Selkirk); D.S. Kerr 2 (Heriot's FP), D.M. Bertram 6 (Watsonians), A.K. Stevenson 3 (Glasgow Acads), L.M. Stuart 2 (Glasgow HSFP), J.M. Bannerman 10 (Glasgow HSFP), J.R. Lawrie 6 (Melrose), D.S. Davies 6 (Hawick), J.C.R. Buchanan 8 (Stewart's FP).

Referee J.W. Baxter (England)

ENGLAND v IRELAND   34/232

10 February 1923
Welford Road, Leicester
England 23 (2G, 3T, 1DG) Ireland 5 (1G)

England   T: Lowe, Corbett, Price, Smallwood, Voyce. C: Conway (2). DG: Davies.
Ireland   T: McClelland. C: Crawford.

This match was by way of an experiment to reintroduce international rugby to the provinces, but was regarded as a failure because fewer than 20,000 attended. Every home match thereafter was staged at Twickenham. The wide margin of the win was totally unexpected: 'The Irish team,' wrote Ubique, 'had come over with the reputation of being a lively lot, fast, young, and dashing, and about the best side that had represented Ireland since the war. Ireland were not only beaten in every single department of the game, but England actually ran up the largest number of points they have ever done against them.'

ENGLAND   F.G. Gilbert (2) (Devonport Services); C.N. Lowe 22 (Blackheath), E. Myers 10 (Bradford), L.J. Corbett 3 (Bristol), A.M. Smallwood 10 (Leicester); *W.J.A. Davies 19 (US Portsmouth), C.A. Kershaw 14 (US Portsmouth); E.R. Gardner 8 (Devonport Services), F.W. Sanders 1 (Plymouth Albion), W.G.E. Luddington 2 (Devonport Services), W.W. Wakefield 14 (Cambridge U.), R. Cove-Smith 7 (OMT), H.L. Price (4) (Leicester), A.T. Voyce 12 (Gloucester), G.S. Conway 10 (Rugby).

IRELAND   W.E. Crawford 11 (Lansdowne); D.J. Cussen 6 (Dublin U.), G.V. Stephenson 10 (Queen's U. Belfast), F. Jackson (1) (NIFC), R.O. McClenahan 1 (Instonians); W.H. Hall 1 (Instonians), J.B. Gardiner 1 (NIFC); R.D. Gray 1 (Old Wesley), T.A. McClelland 8 (Queen's U. Belfast), *J.K.S. Thompson 5 (Dublin U.), M.J. Bradley 7 (Dolphin), R. Collopy 1 (Bective Rangers), D.McC. Cunningham 1 (NIFC), C.F.G.T. Hallaran 7 (US Portsmouth), J.H. Mahoney (1) (Dolphin).

Referee T.H. Vile (Newport)

IRELAND v SCOTLAND   36/233

24 February 1923
Lansdowne Road, Dublin
Scotland 13 (2G, 1T) Ireland 3 (1T)

Ireland   T: Cussen.
Scotland   T: Liddell, McQueen, Browning. C: Browning (2).

This was Scotland's ninth victory in eighteen visits to Ireland, in which period the home side won only six times. Badly mauled by England a fortnight earlier, Ireland showed considerable improvement. 'The great satisfaction,' reported Wisden, 'was the improvement in the home forwards. No equals of the Scottish scrummagers were these, and they tired before the end, but they played with much spirit and no little skill against an exceptionally formidable pack.' Ernie Crawford, the Lansdowne full-back, also came in for praise: '[he] saved his side time and again. In what is now a long career, he has rarely or never given a finer exhibition of full-back play.'

It was Denis Cussen's second try for Ireland. Cussen, 21, was one of the Championship's fastest men, which was hardly surprising as he was the Irish sprint champion with a best time of 9.8 seconds for 100 yards.

IRELAND   W.E. Crawford 12 (Lansdowne); D.J. Cussen 7 (Dublin U.), G.V. Stephenson 11 (Queen's U. Belfast), J.B. Gardiner 2 (NIFC), R.O. McClenahan 2 (Instonians); W.H. Hall 2 (Instonians), W.A. Cunningham 7 (Lansdowne); M.J. Bradley 8 (Dolphin), R. Collopy 2 (Bective Rangers), W.P. Collopy 13 (Bective Rangers), D.McC. Cunningham 2 (NIFC), P.E.F. Dunn (1) (Bective Rangers), R.D. Gray 2 (Old Wesley), *J.K.S. Thompson 6 (Dublin U.), T.A. McClelland 9 (Queen's U. Belfast).

SCOTLAND D. Drysdale 3 (Heriot's FP); A Browning 6 (Glasgow HSFP), E. McLaren 3 (London Scottish), *A.L. Gracie 11 (Harlequins), E.H. Liddell 6 (Edinburgh U.); S.B. McQueen 3 (Waterloo), W.E. Bryce 6 (Selkirk); N.C. Macpherson 6 (Newport), D.M. Bertram 7 (Watsonians), J.C.R. Buchanan 9 (Stewart's FP), L.M. Stuart 3 (Glasgow HSFP), J.M. Bannerman 11 (Glasgow HSFP), J.R. Lawrie 7 (Melrose), D.S. Davies 7 (Hawick), R.S. Simpson (1) (Glasgow Acads).

Referee T.H. Vile (Wales)

WALES v FRANCE 9/234

24 February 1923
St Helen's, Swansea
Wales 16 (2G, 1T, 1PG) France 8 (1G, 1T)

Wales T: Harding, Melbourne Thomas, Baker. C: Albert Jenkins (2). PG: Rees.
France T: Lalande, Lasserre. C: Larrieu.

Jack McGowan, the Irish referee, frustrated by his inability to convey to French players the possible consequences of their rough, unlawful play, was forced to consult with a French official on the touchline, and instruct him to issue the necessary warning to René Lasserre, the French captain.

WALES J. Rees 10 (Swansea); T. Johnson 6 (Cardiff), M.G. Thomas 4 (St Bart's H.), A. Jenkins 10 (Llanelli), W.R. Harding 3 (Swansea); D.E. John 1 (Llanelli), W.J. Delahay 7 (Bridgend); *T. Parker (14) (Swansea), G. Michael (3) (Swansea), A. Baker 4 (Neath), G. Thomas 3 (Llanelli), S. Morris 11 (Cross Keys), L. Jenkins (2) (Aberavon), D. Pascoe 1 (Bridgend), M. Williams (1) (Newport).

FRANCE J. Clément 9 (Valence Sp); M. Lalande 2 (RCF), H. Behotéguy 1 (RCF), R. Ramis (3) (US Perpignan), A. Jauréguy 8 (S. Toulouse); C. Lacazedieu 1 (US Dax), C. Dupont 2 (FC Lourdes); J. Bayard 2 (S. Toulouse), J. Larrieu 4 (S. Toulouse), L. Beguet 3 (RCF), P. Moureu 9 (AS Béziers), A. Cassayet 11 (St Gaudens), *R. Lasserre 11 (US Cognac), J. Etcheberry 1 (SA Rochefort), J. Castets 1 (RC Toulon).

Referee J.B. McGowan (Ireland)

IRELAND v WALES 32/235

10 March 1923
Lansdowne Road
Ireland 5 (1G) Wales 4 (1DG)

Ireland T: Cussen. C: Crawford.
Wales DG: Powell.

Despite this victory Ireland finished with the Wooden Spoon for the fourth year running. Wales were far from pleased with their side: nine of them, including seven of the forwards, did not play again in the Championship. It was the first time since 1899 that Wales failed to score a try against Ireland. Another player who made his last appearance was Billy Cunningham, the Lansdowne stand-off half, who shortly after emigrated to South Africa. It was while he was living in the Republic that Cunningham was asked to join the British touring team for the Third Test in which he scored a try.

IRELAND W.E. Crawford 13 (Lansdowne); D.J. Cussen 8 (Dublin U.), G.V. Stephenson 12 (Queen's U. Belfast), J.B. Gardiner 3 (NIFC), R.O. McClenahan (3) (Instonians); W.A. Cunningham

Caricature of W.J.A. Davies, Welsh-born English fly-half who played between 1913–23

(8) (Lansdowne), W.H. Hall 3 (Instonians); M.J. Bradley 9 (Dolphin), R. Collopy 3 (Bective Rangers), W.P. Collopy 14 (Bective Rangers), D.McC. Cunningham 3 (NIFC), T.A. McClelland 10 (Queen's U. Belfast), *J.K.S. Thompson 7 (Dublin U.), J.D. Clinch 1 (Dublin U.), R.Y. Crichton 7 (Dublin U.).

WALES   J. Rees 11 (Swansea); W.R. Harding 4 (Swansea), *A. Jenkins 11 (Llanelli), T. Collins (1) (Mountain Ash), J. Powell (1) (Cardiff); D.E. John 2 (Llanelli), W.J. Delahay 8 (Bridgend); S. Davies (1) (Treherbert), G. Thomas (4) (Llanelli), A. Baker (5) (Neath), S. Morris 12 (Cross Keys), D. Pascoe (2) (Bridgend), J.H. Davies (1) (Aberavon), T.L. Richards (1) (Maesteg), W.J. Radford (1) (Newport).

Referee J.M. Tennant (Scotland)

SCOTLAND v ENGLAND   33/236

2 April 1923
Inverleith, Edinburgh
England 8 (1G, 1T) Scotland 6 (2T)

Scotland   T: Gracie, McLaren.
England   T: Smallwood, Voyce. C: Luddington.

England's third consecutive win over Scotland in Scotland was watched by a large crowd of 30,000 which included the young Duke of York. The victory also gave England the Triple Crown. It was the seventh and final appearance of Neil Macpherson, who later in the year was suspended *sine die* by the SRU for accepting the gift of a gold watch from his club, Newport. The watch had been awarded to mark Newport's unbeaten season 1922–23. The SRU also banned all Scotsmen from playing against Macpherson or any other member of the Newport club who had accepted a similar gift. A sum of nearly £500 was raised by the public and the WRU gave permission for the money to purchase watches for each player to the value of £21. Only the intervention of the International Board prevented a serious rift developing. Eventually the ban was lifted.

SCOTLAND   D. Drysdale 4 (Heriot's FP); A. Browning (7) (Glasgow HSFP), E. McLaren 4 (London Scottish), *A.L. Gracie 12 (Harlequins), E.H. Liddell (7) (Edinburgh U.); S.B. McQueen

(4) (Waterloo), W.E. Bryce 7 (Selkirk); N.C. Macpherson (7) (Newport), D.M. Bertram 8 (Watsonians), A.K. Stevenson (4) (Glasgow Acads), L.M. Stuart 4 (Glasgow HSFP), J.M. Bannerman 12 (Glasgow HSFP), J.R. Lawrie 8 (Melrose), J.C.R. Buchanan 10 (Stewart's FP), D.S. Davies 8 (Hawick).

ENGLAND   T.E. Holliday 1 (Aspatria); C.N. Lowe 23 (Blackheath), E. Myers 11 (Bradford), H.M. Locke 1 (Birkenhead Park), A.M. Smallwood 11 (Leicester); *W.J.A. Davies 20 (US Portsmouth), C.A. Kershaw 15 (US Portsmouth); E.R. Gardner 9 (Devonport Services), F.W. Sanders 2 (Plymouth Albion), W.G.E. Luddington 3 (Devonport Services), R. Cove-Smith 8 (OMT), W.W. Wakefield 15 (Cambridge U.), A.F. Blakiston 7 (Northampton), A.T. Voyce 13 (Gloucester), G.S. Conway 11 (Rugby).

Referee T.H. Vile (Wales)

FRANCE v ENGLAND   9/237

2 April 1923
Stade Colombes, Paris
England 12 (1G, 1T, 1DG) France 3 (1PG)

France   PG: Beguet.
England   T: Conway, Wakefield. C: Luddington. DG: Davies.

There were several instances of players being selected to play and being replaced at the last moment, but none as unusual as that of Jean Clément, who arrived at Stade Colombes and requested he should stand down because he said he was not feeling on form. The reluctant Clément's place went to Christian Magnanou, a team-mate from Racing Club. The match, played on Easter Monday, was watched by a French record crowd of 35,000. France were handicapped by an injury to André Behotéguy, which allowed Tommy Voyce to come out of the English forwards to play as an extra three-quarter. It was the English forwards who won the day, however, with tries by Conway and Wakefield enabling England to win the Grand Slam. It was the last Championship match for three of England's greatest players: Cyril Lowe, W.J.A. Davies and Cecil Kershaw. Lowe had played in 21 winning England sides, Davies 20.

FRANCE   C. Magnanou 1 (RCF); A. Jauréguy 9 (S. Toulouse), A. Behotéguy 1 (A. Bayonne), R. Salinie (1) (US Perpignan), M. Lousteau (1) (US Dax); E. Billac (8) (A. Bayonne), R. Piteu 9 (S. Pau); P. Moureu 10 (AS Béziers), J. Bayard 3 (S. Toulouse), L. Beguet 4 (RCF), J. Castets 2 (RC Toulon), A. Cassayet 12 (St Gaudens), J. Larrieu 5 (S. Tarbes), *R. Lasserre 12 (US Cognac), J. Boubée 6 (Biarritz Ol).

ENGLAND   T.E. Holliday 2 (Aspatria); C.N. Lowe (24) (Blackheath), E. Myers 12 (Bradford), H.M. Locke 2 (Birkenhead Park), A.M. Small-wood 12 (Leicester); *W.J.A. Davies (21) (US Portsmouth), C.A. Kershaw (16) (US Portsmouth); E.R. Gardner (10) (Devonport Services), F.W. Sanders (3) (Plymouth Albion), W.G.E. Luddington 4 (Devonport Services), W.W. Wakefield 16 (Cambridge U.), R. Cove-Smith 9 (OMT), A.F. Blakiston 8 (Northampton), A.T. Voyce 14 (Gloucester), G.S. Conway 12 (Rugby).

Referee T.H. Vile (Wales)

IRELAND   W.E. Crawford 14 (Lansdowne); D.J. Cussen 9 (Dublin U.), G.V. Stephenson 13 (Queen's U. Belfast), J.B. Gardiner 4 (NIFC), A.C. Douglas 1 (Instonians); W.H. Hall 4 (Instonians), J.A.B. Clarke 4 (Bective Rangers); M.J. Bradley 10 (Dolphin), W.P. Collopy 15 (Bective Rangers), R. Collopy 4 (Bective Rangers), R.Y. Crichton 8 (Dublin U.), C.F.G.T. Hallaran 8 (US Portsmouth), T.A. McClelland 11 (Queen's U. Belfast), I. Popham (4) (Cork Constitution), *J.K.S. Thompson (8) (Dublin U.).

Referee P.M.R. Royds (England)

FRANCE v IRELAND   9/238

14 April 1923
Stade Colombes, Paris
France 14 (1G, 3T)   Ireland 8 (1G, 1T)

France   T: Jauréguy (2), Beguet, Moureu. C: Beguet.
Ireland   T: Douglas, McClelland. C: Crawford.

As in the previous season Ireland were condemned to conclude another disappointing season with the Wooden Spoon because they failed to score more points against France. Twice in the match, Ireland led, but the French forwards possessed greater stamina and: 'their habit of spreading fan-wise over the ground cramped the efforts of the Irish backs considerably.'

FRANCE   J. Clément (10) (Valence Sp); A. Jauréguy 10 (S. Toulouse), F. Borde 8 (S. Toulouse), *R. Crabos 14 (St Sever), M. Lalande (3) (RCF); C. Lacazedieu 2 (US Dax), C. Dupont 3 (FC Lourdes); J. Boubée 7 (Biarritz Ol), J. Etcheberry 2 (SA Rochefort), H. Fargues (1) (US Dax), J. Castets (3) (RC Toulon), A. Cassayet 13 (St Gaudens), L. Beguet 5 (RCF), J. Larrieu (6) (S. Tarbes), P. Moureu 11 (AS Béziers).

1924

PARIS Scotland beat France 12-10 · SWANSEA England beat Wales 17-9
DUBLIN Ireland beat France 6-0 · EDINBURGH Scotland beat Wales 35-10
BELFAST England beat Ireland 14-3 · TWICKENHAM England beat France 19-7
EDINBURGH Scotland beat Ireland 13-8 · CARDIFF Ireland beat Wales 13-10
TWICKENHAM England beat Scotland 19-0 · PARIS Wales beat France 10-6

CHAMPIONSHIP TABLE
England – Championship, Triple Crown, Grand Slam

| | | | | | | | | | Tries | |
Pos	Country	P	W	D	L	F	A	Pts	F	A
1	England (1)	4	4	0	0	69	19	8	17	5
2	Scotland (2)	4	3	0	1	60	47	6	12	11
3	Ireland (5)	4	2	0	2	30	37	4	8	9
4	Wales (3)	4	1	0	3	39	71	2	9	18
5	France (4)	4	0	0	4	23	47	0	7	10

For the second time, England won the Grand Slam for the second season in a row, the only country to achieve this distinction. England scored 17 of the 53 tries, a total beaten only once in the history of the Championship when 55 were scored in the fabulous 1911 season. 1924 was arguably Wales's poorest season; although they avoided the indignity of the Wooden Spoon, they lost for the fourth time in succession, equalling their worst ever sequence, and they conceded 18 tries and 71 points. There was an understandable outcry in the Principality against the Welsh Rugby Union, who set up a sub-committee in March to 'consider whether the present method of selecting international players can be improved'. In June, at the Union's AGM, the sub-committee's recommendation for the creation of five selectors won approval: the Big Five was born. The first Big Five were chosen on 1 September 1924 and comprised Tom Schofield, James Jarrett, R.P. Thomas, D.B. Jones and Ifor Thomas. The first team they chose was severely beaten by New Zealand (29 November 1924) and despite substantial changes in personnel for the 1925 Championship, Wales managed only one victory.

This was also the year of the Ossie Male and Neil Macpherson affairs, each in its own way emphasizing the wide gulf in opinion and attitude not only between individual Unions but between officials and players.

The Ossie Male incident was, by present day standards, quite extraordinary. It was controversial even then, though it was responsible for changing many aspects of Welsh rugby, and was one of the reasons why a Big Five selection panel was set up. Briefly, Male was suspended during a train journey from Cardiff to Paddington, which was the initial stage of the journey that Male and his fellow Welsh players were making for the match in France – because he played for his club the previous week. At that time players who were selected for an international match were required to stand down from all games for six days beforehand. Male was sent home when the train reached Paddington and the committee members responsible for the decision were villified for it for a fortnight afterwards. Changes in the hierarchy were demanded – and were made.

The Neil Macpherson affair arose later in 1924, in November, when the Scottish Rugby Union announced that they had suspended Macpherson *sine die* for accepting a gift of a gold watch which had been presented to him and his other playing colleagues at Newport as a memento of their unbeaten season the year before. The gift was not in question. Its value, however, was. The Scots took great exception to the International Board's ruling that no gift should exceed the value of £2. Macpherson's watch cost £21. What made the SRU particularly angry was that the WRU had approved the gifts paid for, incidentally, by Newport supporters.

The SRU had also threatened to ban any Scottish player who played with or against any member of the Newport club, but this threat, plus the suspension of Macpherson, was lifted after the intervention of the International Board. The players kept their watches; the International Board simply ensured that such a presentation would not occur again. Macpherson, though, never played for Scotland again.

FRANCE v SCOTLAND 9/239

1 January 1924
Stade Pershing, Paris
France 12 (4T) Scotland 10 (1T, 1DG, 1PG)

France T: Jauréguy, Piquiral, Galau, Moureu.
Scotland T: Wallace. DG: Waddell. PG: Davies.

The match was played on a heavy ground at Stade Pershing, where it was transferred after the Seine had flooded Stade Colombes. It was a replica of the relocated match of 1913, which had been switched to Parc des Princes because Colombes was similarly awash. Wisden paid high tribute to France: 'So far from the game taking the course expected, the French pack thoroughly outplayed their opponents. To the general surprise, they not only had the more powerful scrummagers, but they heeled skilfully and at times in the loose fairly raced the Scotsmen off their feet. The excellence of the home side did not end there, for the forwards on occasions handled a wet ball in capital style.' The product of that supremacy was four tries against Scotland's one, a haul achieved only once before (in 1911) and only three times since.

FRANCE E. Besset (1) (FC Grenoble); A. Jauréguy 11 (S. Français), A. Behoteguy 2 (A. Bayonne), *R. Crabos 15 (St Sever), L. Cluchague 1 (Biarritz Ol); H. Galau 1 (S. Toulouse), C. Dupont 4 (RC Rouen); L. Lepatey 1 (SC Mazemet), C-A. Gonnet 5 (RCF), L. Beguet 6 (RCF), P. Moureu 12 (AS Béziers), A. Cassayet 14 (St Gaudens), R. Lasserre 13 (FC Grenoble), J. Etcheberry 3 (US Cognac), E. Piquiral 1 (RCF).

SCOTLAND D. Drysdale 5 (Heriot's FP); A.C. Wallace 2 (Oxford U.), A.L. Gracie (13) (Harlequins), E. McLaren (5) (London Scottish), C.E.W.C. Mackintosh (1) (London Scottish); H. Waddell 1 (Glasgow Acads), W.E. Bryce 8 (Selkirk); D.S. Kerr 3 (Heriot's FP), A. Ross 1

(Kilmarnock), R.A. Howie 1 (Kirkcaldy), L.M. Stuart 5 (Glasgow HSFP), J.M. Bannerman 13 (Glasgow HSFP), *J.C.R. Buchanan 11 (Stewart's FP), K.G.P. Hendrie 1 (Heriot's FP), D.S. Davies 9 (Hawick).

Referee E. Roberts (Wales)

WALES v ENGLAND 35/240

19 January 1924
St Helen's, Swansea
England 17 (1G, 4T) Wales 9 (3T)

Wales T: Johnson, Tom Jones, Owen.
England T: Catcheside (2), Jacob, Locke, Myers. C: Conway.

The 27-year-old Tommy Voyce played for most of the second half with a broken rib, and was an inspiration to an England side which won in Wales for the first time since 1913. Wales had gambled on six new caps in the pack, but despite the defeat only one of them, Ifor Thomas, did not play again. It was the last international, however, for four of the backs, including Joe Rees, the full-back and captain.

WALES *J. Rees (12) (Swansea); T. Johnson 7 (Cardiff), R.A. Cornish 3 (Cardiff), D.H. Davies (1) (Aberavon), M.G. Thomas (5) (St Bart's H.); A. Owen (1) (Swansea), E. Watkins 1 (Neath); S. Morris 13 (Cross Keys), I. Thomas (1) (Bryncethin), T. Jones 5 (Newport), W.J. Ould 1 (Cardiff), C. Pugh 1 (Maesteg), A.C. Evans 1 (Pontypool), I. Morris 1 (Swansea), I. Jones 1 (Llanelli).

ENGLAND B.S. Chantrill 1 (Bristol); H.C. Catcheside 1 (Percy Park), L.J. Corbett 4 (Bristol), H.M. Locke 3 (Birkenhead Park), H.P. Jacob 1 (Oxford U.); E. Myers 13 (Bradford), A.T. Young 1 (Cambridge U.); R. Edwards 8 (Newport), A. Robson 1 (Northern), R. Cove-Smith 10 (OMT), W.G.E. Luddington 5 (Devonport Services), G.S. Conway 13 (Rugby), A.F. Blakiston 9 (Liverpool), A.T. Voyce 15 (Gloucester), *W.W. Wakefield 17 (Leicester).

Referee A.W. Angus (Scotland)

IRELAND v FRANCE   10/241

26 January 1924
Lansdowne Road, Dublin
Ireland 6 (2T) France 0

Ireland   T: George Stephenson, Atkins.

René Crabos, the French captain, broke his left leg in two places and was carried off on a stretcher. Kept in hospital overnight, Crabos was taken by St John's Ambulance to Kingstown Pier (now Dun Laoghaire) to rejoin his departing team-mates. Crabos, who had played 16 times in the Championship, never played again. It was also René Lasserre's last game, he had won the first of his 14 caps in 1914. Crabos, who was not 25 until 7 February, had been one of the outstanding personalities of French rugby. He was multi-talented, and found time to spare from his rugby activities to participate in athletics, football, lawn tennis and pelota. He played his first game of rugby at 13, represented the French Army and France at 20 and captained both by the time he was 21. France had won four Championship matches since the War — and Crabos played a prominent role in each one.

IRELAND   *W.E. Crawford 15 (Lansdowne); H.W.V. Stephenson 4 (US Portsmouth), G.V. Stephenson 14 (Queen's U. Belfast), J.B. Gardiner 5 (NIFC), A.P. Atkins (1) (Bective Rangers); J.C. McDowell (1) (Instonians), W.H. Hall 5 (Instonians); J.D. Clinch 2 (Dublin U.), W.R.F. Collis 1 (Harlequins), W.P. Collopy 16 (Bective Rangers), R. Collopy 5 (Bective Rangers), R.Y. Crichton 9 (Dublin U.), C.F.G.T. Hallaran 9 (US Portsmouth), T.A. McClelland 12 (Queen's U. Belfast), J. McVicker 1 (Belfast Collegians).

FRANCE   L. Pardo 1 (S. Hendaye); R. Got 8 (US Perpignan), *R. Crabos (16) (RCF), A. Behotéguy 3 (A. Bayonne), M. Besson 1 (CASG); H. Galau 2 (S. Toulouse), C. Dupont 5 (RC Rouen); R. Lasserre (14) (FC Grenoble), J. Etcheberry 4 (US Cognac), E. Ribère 1 (US Perpignan), E. Piquiral 2 (RCF), P. Moureu 13 (AS Béziers), J. Danion (1) (RC Toulon), L. Beguet 7 (RCF), L. Lepatey 2 (SC Mazamet).

Referee A.A. Lawrie (Scotland)

SCOTLAND v WALES   35/242

2 February 1924
Inverleith, Edinburgh
Scotland 35 (4G, 4T, 1PG) Wales 10 (2G)

Scotland   T: Smith (3), Bryce, Bertram, Wallace, Waddell, Macpherson. C: Drysdale (4). PG: Drysdale.
Wales   T: Griffiths, Ivor Jones. C: Male (2).

This defeat provoked one of the classic rugby remarks, made by a Welsh player on a coach trip the day after the match as they viewed the Forth Bridge: 'Take a good look boys . . . this is the last time we will see it at the expense of the WRU.' For six of the Welsh team it was a poignantly accurate prediction. Scotland had scored 12 tries against Wales in 1887, before uniform scoring was adopted, so their eight tries in this match represents their biggest try total against any country. It was the most Wales have conceded to any country. Five of the Scottish tries were scored by the threequarters, all of whom played together at Oxford University.

SCOTLAND   D. Drysdale 6 (Heriot's FP); I.S. Smith 1 (Oxford U.), G.P.S. Macpherson 5 (Oxford U.), G.G. Aitken 1 (Oxford U.), A.C. Wallace 3 (Oxford U.); H. Waddell 2 (Glasgow Acads), W.E. Bryce 9 (Selkirk); A. Ross (2) (Kilmarnock), D.M. Bertram 9 (Watsonians), R.A. Howie 2 (Kirkcaldy), *J.C.R. Buchanan 12 (Stewart's FP), J.M. Bannerman 14 (Glasgow HSFP), J.R. Lawrie 9 (Leicester), K.G.P. Hendrie 2 (Heriot's FP), A.C. Gillies 1 (Watsonians).

WALES   B.O. Male 3 (Cardiff); H.J. Davies (1) (Newport), J.E. Evans (1) (Llanelli), M.A. Rosser 1 (Penarth), T. Johnson 8 (Cardiff); V.M. Griffiths 1 (Newport), E. Watkins 2 (Neath); *J. Whitfield 10 (Newport), S. Morris 14 (Cross Keys), I. Morris (2) (Swansea), T. Jones (6) (Newport), C. Pugh 2 (Maesteg), I. Jones 2 (Llanelli), W.J. Ould (2) (Cardiff), D.G. Francis (1) (Llanelli).

Referee J.B. McGowan (Ireland)

IRELAND v ENGLAND   35/243

9 February 1924
Ravenhill, Belfast
England 14 (1G, 3T) Ireland 3 (IT)

Ireland   T: Douglas.
England   T: Catcheside (2), Corbett, Hamilton-Wickes. C: Conway.

This was the only match England played in Ulster and it featured the first appearance of Richard Hamilton-Wickes, scorer of a 'sensational' try in the 1923 University Match. Hamilton-Wickes more than fulfilled English expectations: he brought off several important tackles and scored a very good try.

IRELAND   *W.E. Crawford 16 (Lansdowne); H.W.V. Stephenson 5 (US Portsmouth), G.V. Stephenson 15 (Queen's U. Belfast), J.B. Gardiner 6 (NIFC), A.C. Douglas 2 (Instonians); J.R. Wheeler (5) (Queen's U. Belfast), J.A.B. Clarke 5 (Bective Rangers); W.P. Collopy 17 (Bective Rangers), R.Y. Crichton 10 (Dublin U.), R. Collopy 6 (Bective Rangers), J. McVicker 2 (Belfast Collegians), I.M.B. Stuart 1 (Dublin U.), J.D. Clinch 3 (Dublin U.), C.F.G.T. Hallaran 10 (US Portsmouth), T.A. McClelland 13 (Queen's U. Belfast).

ENGLAND   B.S. Chantrill 2 (Bristol); H.C. Catcheside 2 (Percy Park), L.J. Corbett 5 (Bristol), H.P. Jacob 2 (Oxford U.), R.H. Hamilton-Wickes 1 (Harlequins); E. Myers 14 (Bradford), A.T. Young 2 (Cambridge U.); C.K.T. Faithfull 1 (Harlequins), A. Robson 2 (Northern), R. Cove-Smith 11 (OMT), W.G.E. Luddington 6 (Devonport Services), G.S. Conway 14 (Rugby), A.F. Blakiston 10 (Liverpool), A.T. Voyce 16 (Gloucester), *W.W. Wakefield 18 (Leicester).

Referee T.H. Vile (Wales)

ENGLAND v FRANCE   10/244

23 February 1924
Twickenham
England 19 (2G, 3T) France 7 (1T, 1DG)

England   T: Jacob (3), Catcheside, Young. C: Conway (2).
France   T: Ballarin. DG: Behotéguy.

Not since 1914 had an English side displayed such scoring power as this one. Including this, their third match, they had totalled 50 points and scored 14 tries. During that time too they had made only two changes.

ENGLAND   B.S. Chantrill 3 (Bristol); H.C. Catcheside 3 (Percy Park), L.J. Corbett 6 (Bristol), H.M. Locke 4 (Birkenhead Park), H.P. Jacob 3 (Oxford U.); E. Myers 15 (Bradford), A.T. Young 3 (Cambridge U.); R. Edwards 9 (Newport), A. Robson 3 (Northern), R. Cove-Smith 12 (OMT), W.G.E. Luddington 7 (Devonport Services), G.S. Conway 15 (Rugby), A.F. Blakiston 11 (Liverpool), A.T. Voyce 17 (Gloucester), *W.W. Wakefield 19 (Leicester).

FRANCE   L. Pardo (2) (S. Hendaye); J. Ballarin 1 (S. Tarbes), *F. Borde 9 (S. Toulouse), A. Behotéguy 4 (A. Bayonne), R. Got 9 (US Perpignan); H. Galau 3 (S. Toulouse), R. Piteu 10 (TOEC); L. Beguet (8) (RCF), C-A. Gonnet 6 (RCF), L. Lepatey (3) (SC Mazamet), A. Cassayet 15 (RC Narbonne), P. Moureu 14 (AS Béziers), E. Piquiral 3 (RCF), F. Clauzel 1 (AS Béziers), J. Etcheberry 5 (US Cognac).

Referee A.E. Freethy (Wales)

SCOTLAND v IRELAND   37/245

23 February 1924
Inverleith, Edinburgh
Scotland 13 (2G, 1T) Ireland 8 (1G, 1T)

Scotland   T: Waddell (2), Bertram. C: Drysdale (2).
Ireland   T: George Stephenson (2). C: George Stephenson.

Scotland's fourth win in a row at home against Ireland — their best sequence since winning eight home matches between 1884–97. Several accounts questioned some of the selection decisions by Scotland, particularly in playing various players out of position. The Irish pack was considered a great disappointment after giving a good account of itself in the earlier match against England.

SCOTLAND   D. Drysdale 7 (Heriot's FP); I.S. Smith 2 (Oxford U,), G.G. Aitken 2 (Oxford U.), J.C. Dykes 3 (Glasgow Acads), R.K. Millar (1) (London Scottish); H. Waddell 3 (Glasgow Acads), W.E. Bryce 10 (Selkirk); R.G. Henderson 1 (Newcastle Northern), D.M. Bertram 10 (Watsonians), R.A. Howie 3 (Kirkcaldy), *J.C.R. Buchanan 13 (Stewart's FP), J.M. Bannerman 15 (Glasgow HSFP), J.R. Lawrie 10 (Leicester), K.G.P. Hendrie (3) (Heriot's FP), A.C. Gillies 2 (Watsonians).

IRELAND   W.J. Stewart 2 (Queen's U. Belfast); H.W.V. Stephenson 6 (US Portsmouth), G.V. Stephenson 16 (Queen's U. Belfast), J.B. Gardiner 7 (NIFC), A.C. Douglas 3 (Instonians); W.H. Hall (6) (Instonians), J.A.B. Clarke 6 (Bective Rangers); J.D. Clinch 4 (Dublin U.), *W.P. Collopy 18 (Bective Rangers), R. Collopy 7 (Bective Rangers), R.Y. Crichton 11 (Dublin U.), C.F.G.T. Hallaran 11 (US Portsmouth), T.A. McClelland 14 (Queen's U. Belfast), I.M.B. Stuart (2) (Dublin U.), J. McVicker 3 (Belfast Collegians).

Referee T.H. Vile (Wales)

WALES v IRELAND   33/246

8 March 1924
Cardiff Arms Park
Ireland 13 (2G, 1T) Wales 10 (2T, 1DG)

Wales   T: Richards, Pugh. DG: Watkins.
Ireland   T: Tom Hewitt, Frank Hewitt, George Stephenson. C: Crawford (2).

This victory by Ireland stopped a run of nine successive home wins by Wales against them. It was also Wales's fourth successive defeat, which equalled their longest losing Championship run of 1883–84 and 1888–90. It was a special day for Frank Hewitt, making his début for Ireland at stand-off half; he was 17 years 5 months and 5 days old, which made him

Frank Hewitt, Ireland's youngest ever international

Ireland's youngest ever international. The celebration was completed when Frank and his brother, Tom, who was not yet 19 and was also making his Ireland début, scored a try apiece.

WALES   B.O. Male 4 (Cardiff); C. Richards (5) (Pontypool), *J. Wetter (9) (Newport), T. Evans (1) (Swansea), W.R. Harding 5 (Swansea); V.M. Griffiths 2 (Newport), E. Watkins 3 (Neath); D. Parker 1 (Swansea), G. Hathway 1 (Newport), J. Whitfield (11) (Newport), A.C. Evans 2 (Pontypool), R. Randell 1 (Aberavon), W.J. Jones (1) (Llanelli), J. Gore 1 (Blaina), C. Pugh 3 (Maesteg).

IRELAND   *W.E. Crawford 17 (Lansdowne); T.R. Hewitt 1 (Queen's U. Belfast), G.V. Stephenson 17 (Queen's U. Belfast), J.B. Gardiner 8 (NIFC), H.W.V. Stephenson 7 (US Portsmouth); F.S. Hewitt 1 (Instonians), J.A.B. Clarke (7) (Bective Rangers); C.F.G.T. Hallaran 12 (US Portsmouth), W.P. Collopy (19) (Bective Rangers), R. Collopy 8 (Bective Rangers), R.Y. Crichton 12 (Queen's U. Belfast), T.A. McClelland (15) (Queen's U. Belfast), J. McVicker 4 (Belfast Collegians), J.D. Clinch 5 (Dublin U.), W.R.F. Collis 2 (Wanderers).

Referee J.L. Tulloch (Scotland)

ENGLAND v SCOTLAND   34/247

15 March 1924
Twickenham
England 19 (3G, 1DG) Scotland 0

England   T: Catcheside, Myers, Wakefield. C: Conway (3). DG: Myers.

England's seventh win in a row against Scotland gave them their sixth Championship in eight years and their fourteenth overall; it was also their fifth Grand Slam success. Four of the Scottish pack never played again. Carston Catchside had the distinction of scoring a try in each of his first four matches for England.

ENGLAND   B.S. Chantrill (4) (Bristol); H.C. Catcheside 4 (Percy Park), L.J. Corbett 7 (Bristol), H.M. Locke 5 (Birkenhead Park), H.P. Jacob 4 (Oxford U.); E. Myers 16 (Bradford), A.T. Young 4 (Cambridge U.); R. Edwards (10) (Newport), A. Robson 4 (Northern), R. Cove-Smith 13 (OMT), W.G.E. Luddington 8 (Devonport Services), G.S. Conway 16 (Rugby), A.F. Blakiston 12 (Liverpool), A.T. Voyce 18 (Gloucester), *W.W. Wakefield 20 (Leicester).

SCOTLAND   D. Drysdale 8 (Heriot's FP); I.S. Smith 3 (Oxford U.), G.P.S. Macpherson 6 (Oxford U.), G.G. Aitken 3 (Oxford U.), A.C. Wallace 4 (Oxford U.); H. Waddell 4 (Glasgow Acads), W.E. Bryce (11) (Selkirk); D.S. Davies 10 (Hawick), D.M. Bertram (11) (Watsonians), R.A. Howie 4 (Kirkcaldy), R.G. Henderson (2) (Newcastle Northern), J.M. Bannerman 16 (Glasgow HSFP), J.R. Lawrie (11) (Leicester), *J.C.R. Buchanan 14 (Stewart's FP), A.C. Gillies 3 (Watsonians).

Referee T.H. Vile (Wales)

FRANCE v WALES   10/248

27 March 1924
Stade Colombes, Paris
Wales 10 (2T, 1DG) France 6 (2T)

France   T: Behotéguy, Lubin-Lebrère.
Wales   T: Finch, Rickards. DG: Griffiths.

Although Wales gained some consolation from beating France, the 1924 season went down as one of their worst, having conceded a record 18 tries in 4 matches. While on his way to Paris, Welsh officials suspended Ossie Male, who had been selected to play at full-back, because he had broken the rule of playing for his club within a week of the international (see above). With no other full-back aboard the train, which Male left at Paddington, Wales switched Melville Rosser to full-back and brought Joe Jones into a rearranged back division.

FRANCE   E. Bonnes (1) (RC Narbonne); R. Got (10) (US Perpignan), A. Behotéguy 5 (A. Bayonne); A. Dupouy (1) (SA Bordelais), A. Jauréguy 12 (S. Toulouse); H. Galau (4) (S. Toulouse), C. Dupont 6 (RC Rouen); A. Bioussa 1 (S. Toulouse), M-F. Lubin-Lebrère 11 (S. Toulouse), J. Bayard (4) (S. Toulouse), E. Piquiral 4 (RCF), F. Clauzel 2 (AS Béziers), P. Moureu 15 (AS Béziers), J. Etcheberry 6 (US Cognac), *A. Cassayet 16 (RC Narbonne).

WALES   M.A. Rosser (2) (Penarth); E. Finch 1 (Llanelli), A.R. Stock 1 (Newport), J. Jones (1) (Swansea), *W.R. Harding 6 (Swansea); V.M. Griffiths (3) (Newport), E. Watkins (4) (Neath); D. Parker 2 (Swansea), G. Hathway (2) (Newport), S. Morris 15 (Cross Keys), A.R. Rickards (1) (Cardiff), R. Randell (2) (Aberavon), J. Gore 2 (Blaina), A.C. Evans (3) (Pontypool), C. Pugh 4 (Maesteg).

Referee R.A. Roberts (England)

1925

PARIS Ireland beat France 9-3 · TWICKENHAM England beat Wales 12-6
EDINBURGH Scotland beat France 25-4 · SWANSEA Scotland beat Wales 24-14
TWICKENHAM England drew Ireland 6-6 · DUBLIN Scotland beat Ireland 14-8
CARDIFF Wales beat France 11-5 · BELFAST Ireland beat Wales 19-3
MURRAYFIELD Scotland beat England 14-11 · PARIS England beat France 13-11

CHAMPIONSHIP TABLE
Scotland – Championship, Triple Crown, Grand Slam

								Tries	
Pos	Country	P	W	D	L	F	A	Pts	F	A
1	Scotland (2)	4	4	0	0	77	37	8	17	6
2	Ireland (3)	4	2	1	1	42	26	5	9	6
3	England (1)	4	2	1	1	42	37	5	9	9
4	Wales (4)	4	1	0	3	34	60	2	9	14
5	France (5)	4	0	0	4	23	58	0	5	14

It was fitting that in the season during which they opened their new ground at Murrayfield, Scotland should have won all four matches and the Championship. In the process they established two records, a total of 77 points and 17 tries. That this was Scotland's only Grand Slam might be regarded as strange: considering the influence their players have exerted in the game; the number of their players included in British teams before and since; and the obsessively strict adherence to the Laws by their officials and administrators. It must also be remembered that this was Scotland's first title win since 1907, which was an incredibly long time in the doldrums until compared with the even longer wait for Championship success between 1939 and 1973. No country has a divine right to win Grand Slams, Triple Crowns or Championships but a Championship in which some always win (or nearly always), and others always lose (or nearly always), can hardly be good for the game. The season was significant in another respect: it signalled the end of England's Golden Era. In the 11 Championships since 1910 they had won the title 7 times, were runners-up twice and scored 135 tries. They had won 35 and drawn 3 of 44 Championship matches and their record included a 13-match sequence without defeat which no other country has ever matched. Wales, too, struggled. For the second year in a row they finished above only France.

FRANCE v IRELAND   11/249

1 January 1925
Stade Colombes, Paris
Ireland 9 (2T, 1PG) France 3 (1T)

France   T: Ribère.
Ireland   T: Sugden, George Stephenson. PG: Crawford.

François Borde, the French captain, was so badly injured after 20 minutes that it was feared he might 'lose the use of his left arm'. With only 14 players, France employed 'rough and unfair tactics' and large sections of the 25,000 crowd became very hostile to the referee and the Irish players. The referee, J. McGill, of Scotland, further incensed the crowd by ordering a retake of an Ernie Crawford penalty kick when the French team charged. The Irish captain, whose first kick missed, made no mistake with the retake. The luckless Borde, unlike his predecessor René Crabos in 1924, recovered from his injury to play once more, against England in 1926. This match had an unusual beginning: the kick-off was taken by the French aviator, D'Oisy, who became famous after flying solo from Paris to Tokyo. Marcel-Frederic Lubin-Lebrère, who won his first cap against Ireland in 1914, played his last Championship match. The match was played on a Thursday.

FRANCE   A. Chilo (3) (RCF); A. Jauréguy 13 (S. Français), *F. Borde 10 (S. Toulouse), M. Baillette 1 (US Perpignan), M. Besson 2 (CASG); Y. du Manoir 1 (RCF), R. Piteu 11 (TOEC); A. Bioussa 2 (S. Toulouse), E. Ribère 2 (US Perpignan), G. Gerintes 1 (CASG), M-F. Lubin-Lebrère (12) (S. Toulouse), A. Cassayet 17 (RC Narbonne), A. Maury 1 (S. Toulouse), J. Marcet 1 (SC Albi), C. Montade 1 (US Perpignan).

IRELAND   *W.E. Crawford 18 (Lansdowne); H.W.V. Stephenson 8 (US Portsmouth), G.V. Stephenson 18 (Queen's U. Belfast), J.B. Gardiner 9 (NIFC), T.R. Hewitt 2 (Queen's U. Belfast); F.S. Hewitt 2 (Instonians), M. Sugden 1 (Dublin U.); M.J. Bradley 11 (Dolphin), R. Collopy 9 (Bective Rangers), W.R.F. Collis 3 (Harlequins), J.D. Clinch 6 (Dublin U.), D. McC. Cunningham 4 (NIFC), R.D. Gray 3 (Old Wesley), C.F.G.T. Hallaran 13 (US Portsmouth), J. McVicker 5 (Belfast Collegians).

Referee J. McGill (Scotland)

ENGLAND v WALES   36/250

17 January 1925
Twickenham
England 12 (3T, 1PG) Wales 6 (2T)

England   T: Hamilton-Wickes, Kittermaster, Voyce. PG: Armstrong.
Wales   T: Thomas, James.

This was England's tenth successive Championship victory, which equalled a similar run between 1883–86 but has not yet been matched by any other country. England also achieved nine wins in a row 1912–14.

ENGLAND   J.W. Brough (1) (Silloth); R.H. Hamilton-Wickes 2 (Harlequins), H.M. Locke 6 (Birkenhead Park), L.J. Corbett 8 (Bristol), J.C. Gibbs 1 (Harlequins); H.J. Kittermaster 1 (Oxford U.), E.J. Massey 1 (Leicester); W.G.E. Luddington 9 (Devonport Services), J.S. Tucker 2 (Bristol), R. Armstrong (1) (Northern), R. Cove-Smith 14 (OMT), *W.W. Wakefield 21 (Harlequins), A.F. Blakiston 13 (Liverpool), A.T. Voyce 19 (Gloucester), H.G. Periton 1 (Waterloo).

WALES   *T. Johnson 9 (Cardiff); W.P. James 1 (Aberavon), Evan Williams 1 (Aberavon), R.A. Cornish 4 (Cardiff), C. Thomas 1 (Bridgend); W.J. Hopkins 1 (Aberavon), W.J. Delahay 9 (Cardiff); S. Morris 16 (Cross Keys), C. Williams (1) (Llanelli), B. Phillips 1 (Aberavon), C. Pugh 5 (Maesteg), I. Richards 1 (Cardiff), J. Gore (3) (Blaina), W.I. Jones 1 (Cambridge U.), D. Parker 3 (Swansea).

Referee A.A. Lawrie (Scotland)

SCOTLAND v FRANCE   10/251

24 January 1925
Inverleith, Edinburgh
Scotland 25 (2G, 5T) France 4 (1DG)

Scotland   T: Smith (4), Wallace (2), Gillies. C: Gillies, Drysdale.
France   DG: du Manoir.

The last international at Inverleith, by now too small a venue to cater for the huge numbers who wanted to watch Scotland, was played during a partial eclipse of the sun. Crowds of 20,000 to 30,000 had packed into Inverleith, but three times that number swelled Murrayfield – and the coffers of the SRU. If the celestial interruption was not enough to mark the occasion, Scotland ensured its place in posterity by scoring seven tries, a total achieved only once before, in their first match in 1910 when the French were hardly serious opposition. The principal executioner in this match was Ian Smith, who scored four scintillating tries.

SCOTLAND   D. Drysdale 9 (Heriot's FP); I.S. Smith 4 (Oxford U.), *G.P.S. Macpherson 7 (Oxford U.), G.G. Aitken 4 (Oxford U.), A.C. Wallace 5 (Oxford U.); J.C. Dykes 4 (Glasgow Acads), J.B. Nelson 1 (Glasgow Acads); J.C.R. Buchanan 15 (Exeter), J. Gilchrist (1) (Glasgow Acads), W.H. Stevenson (1) (Glasgow Acads), D.J. MacMyn 1 (Cambridge U.), J.M. Bannerman 17 (Glasgow HSFP), J.W. Scott 1 (Stewart's FP), J.R. Paterson 1 (Birkenhead Park), A.C. Gillies 4 (Carlisle).

FRANCE   J. Ducousso 1 (S. Tarbes); F. Raymond 1 (S. Toulouse), J. Ballarin (2) (S. Tarbes), M. Baillette 2 (US Perpignan), J. Halet 1 (AC Strasbourg); Y. du Manoir 2 (RCF), C. Dupont 7 (Havre AC); C. Montade 2 (US Perpignan), J. Marcet 2 (SC Albi), A. Maury 2 (S. Toulouse), A.

Cassayet 18 (RC Narbonne), A. Laurent 1 (Biarritz Ol), A. Bioussa 3 (S. Toulouse), E. Ribère 3 (US Perpignan), *J. Boubée (8) (SU Agen).

Referee Dr E. de Courcy Wheeler (Ireland)

WALES v SCOTLAND   36/252

7 February 1925
St Helen's, Swansea
Scotland 24 (1G, 5T, 1DG) Wales 14 (1G, 2T, 1PG)

Wales   T: Hopkins, Jones, Cornish. C: Parker. PG: Parker.
Scotland   T: Smith (4), Wallace (2). C: Drysdale. PG: Drysdale.

Scotland's six tries were the most they have ever scored in Wales, and for the second match in succession Ian Smith scored four tries, thus equalling for a second time the Scottish record set by W.A. Stewart against Ireland in 1913 for most tries in an international. Even though Smith failed to register a try in either of the two remaining Championship matches, his eight tries equalled the season record held by Cyril Lowe and helped him to create a career record of 24 tries. As in the previous season's defeat by Scotland – when Smith scored three out of eight tries – Wales savagely axed their team, dropping six players for the next game against France. Five of these were never capped again. Scotland lent another touch of distinction to the match: they had a Lord in their forwards, J.M. Bannerman, and a knight as a touch-judge, Sir Robert C. Mackenzie.

WALES   T. Johnson 10 (Cardiff); W.P. James (2) (Aberavon), Evan Williams (2) (Aberavon), R.A. Cornish 5 (Cardiff), C. Thomas (2) (Bridgend); W.J. Hopkins (2) (Aberavon), W.J. Delahay 10 (Cardiff); C. Pugh (6) Maesteg), *S. Morris 17 (Cross Keys), R.C. Herrera 1 (Cross Keys), B. Phillips 2 (Aberavon), W.I. Jones 2 (Llanelli), D. Parker 4 (Swansea), I. Richards 2 (Cardiff), S. Lawrence 1 (Bridgend).

SCOTLAND   D. Drysdale 10 (Heriot's FP); I.S. Smith 5 (Oxford U.), *G.P.S. Macpherson 8 (Oxford U.), G.G. Aitken 5 (Oxford U.), A.C. Wallace 6 (Oxford U.); J.C. Dykes 5 (Glasgow Acads), J.B. Nelson 2 (Glasgow Acads); D.S.

Davies 11 (Hawick), J.C.H. Ireland 1 (Glasgow HSFP), R.A. Howie 5 (Kirkcaldy), D.J. MacMyn 2 (Cambridge U.), J.M. Bannerman 18 (Glasgow HSFP), J.W. Scott 2 (Stewart's FP), A.C. Gillies 5 (Carlisle), J.R. Paterson 2 (Birkenhead Park).

Referee J.W. Baxter (England)

ENGLAND v IRELAND   36/253

14 February 1925
Twickenham
England 6 (2T) Ireland 6 (2T)

England   T: Smallwood (2).
Ireland   T: Tom Hewitt, Harry Stephenson.

Although held to a draw, England established a sequence of 13 Championship matches without defeat, the longest by any country. A.M. Smallwood clearly enjoyed playing against Ireland – this was the third time he scored a try against them out of seven overall.

ENGLAND   T.E. Holliday 3 (Aspatria); R.H. Hamilton-Wickes 3 (Harlequins), L.J. Corbett 9 (Bristol), H.M. Locke 7 (Birkenhead Park), A.M. Smallwood 13 (Leicester); H.J. Kittermaster 2 (Oxford U.), E.J. Massey 2 (Leicester); W.G.E. Luddington 10 (Devonport Services), J.S. Tucker 3 (Bristol), R.R.F. MacLennan 1 (OMT), R. Cove-Smith 15 (OMT), *W.W. Wakefield 22 (Harlequins), A.F. Blakiston 14 (Liverpool), A.T. Voyce 20 (Gloucester), R.G. Lawson (1) (Workington).

IRELAND   *W.E. Crawford 19 (Lansdowne); H.W.V. Stephenson 9 (US Portsmouth), J.B. Gardiner 10 (NIFC), T.R. Hewitt 3 (Queen's U. Belfast), G.V. Stephenson 19 (Queen's U. Belfast); F.S. Hewitt 3 (Instonians), M. Sugden 2 (Dublin U.); R.Y. Crichton 13 (Dublin U.), W.R.F. Collis 4 (Wanderers), R. Collopy 10 (Bective Rangers), J. McVicker 6 (Belfast Collegians), D.McC. Cunningham 5 (NIFC), W.F. Browne 1 (US Portsmouth), J.D. Clinch 7 (Dublin U.), G.R. Beamish 1 (Coleraine).

Referee T.H. Vile (Wales)

IRELAND v SCOTLAND   38/254

28 February 1925
Lansdowne Road, Dublin
Scotland 14 (2G, 1DG) Ireland 8 (1G, 1PG)

Ireland T: Harry Stephenson. C: Crawford.
PG: Crawford.
Scotland T: Wallace, MacMyn. C: Drysdale,
Dykes. DG: Waddell.

This was Scotland's fourth successive victory
over Ireland and their twenty-sixth overall in 38
Championship matches played between the
countries. However, Scotland were to win only
5 of the next 27 meetings, which amounts to one
of the most remarkable changes of fortune in the
history of the Championship.

IRELAND *W.E. Crawford 20 (Lansdowne);
H.W.V. Stephenson 10 (US Portsmouth), G.V.
Stephenson 20 (Queen's U. Belfast), J.B. Gar-
diner 11 (NIFC), T.R. Hewitt 4 (Queen's U.
Belfast); F.S. Hewitt 4 (Instonians), M. Sugden 3
(Dublin U.); G.R. Beamish 2 (Coleraine), W.F.
Browne 2 (US Portsmouth), J.D. Clinch 8 (Dublin
U.), W.R.F. Collis 5 (Wanderers), R. Collopy 11
(Bective Rangers), R.Y. Crichton (14) (Dublin
U.), M.J. Bradley 12 (Dolphin), J. McVicker 7
(Belfast Collegians).

SCOTLAND *D. Drysdale 11 (Heriot's FP); I.S.
Smith 6 (Oxford U.), J.C. Dykes 6 (Glasgow
Acads), G.G. Aitken 6 (Oxford U.), A.C. Wallace
7 (Oxford U.); H. Waddell 5 (Glasgow Acads),
J.B. Nelson 3 (Glasgow Acads); D.S. Davies 12
(Hawick), J.C.H. Ireland 2 (Glasgow HSFP), R.A.
Howie 6 (Kirkcaldy), D.J. MacMyn 3 (Cam-
bridge U.), J.M. Bannerman 19 (Glasgow
HSFP), J.W. Scott 3 (Stewart's FP), J.R. Paterson
3 (Birkenhead Park), J.C.R. Buchanan (16)
(Exeter).

Referee A.E. Freethy (Wales)

WALES v FRANCE   11/255

28 February 1925
Cardiff Arms Park
Wales 11 (1G, 2T) France 5 (1G)

Wales T: Finch (2), Delahay. C: Parker.
France T: de Laborderie. C: Ducousso.

With Welsh rugby in the doldrums – this was
only their third win in three seasons – it was not
surprising that home attendances dwindled. A
crowd of only 27,000 paid to witness the
eleventh successive win over France.

WALES T. Johnson (11) (Cardiff); E. Finch 2
(Llanelli), G. Davies (3) (Llanelli), *R.A. Cornish
6 (Cardiff), W.R. Harding 7 (Swansea); Eddie
Williams (1) (Neath), W.J. Delahay 11 (Cardiff);
S. Morris (18) (Cross Keys), R.C. Herrera 2 (Cross
Keys), D. Parker 5 (Swansea), I. Richards (3)
(Cardiff), W.I. Jones 3 (Llanelli), W. Lewis (1)
(Llanelli), E. Beynon 1 (Swansea), B. Phillips 3
(Aberavon).

FRANCE J. Ducousso 2 (S. Tarbes); J. Halet (2)
(AS Strasbourg), M. de Laborderie 3 (RCF), C.
Magnanou 2 (A. Bayonne), R. Bringeon (1)
(Biarritz Ol); Y. du Manoir 3 (RCF), *R. Piteu 12
(TOEC); A. Maury 3 (S. Toulouse), J. Marcet 3
(SC Albi), C. Montade 3 (US Perpignan), R.
Levasseur 1 (S. Français), A. Laurent 2 (Biarritz
Ol), E. Barthe 1 (S. Bordelais), A. Cassayet 19 (RC
Narbonne), F. Clauzel (3) (AS Béziers).

Referee R.W. Harland (Ireland)

IRELAND v WALES   34/256

14 March 1925
Ravenhill, Belfast
Ireland 19 (2G, 2T, 1PG) Wales 3 (1T)

Ireland T: Millin, George Stephenson,
Browne, Harry Stephenson. C: George Stephen-
son (2). PG: George Stephenson.
Wales T: Turnbull.

Ireland's third successive win over Wales, a
sequence they have equalled only once (1966–
68), coincided with their biggest score to date

against the Welsh. They scored 19 points again in 1927 but had to wait until 1979, when they registered 21 points, to improve the total. The victory meant that Ireland finished in second place in the Championship, their highest position since 1912, when they were runners-up to England.

IRELAND *W.E. Crawford 21 (Lansdowne); H.W.V. Stephenson 11 (US Portsmouth), T.J. Millin (1) (Dublin U.), J.B. Gardner (12) (NIFC), G.V. Stephenson 21 (Queen's U. Belfast); E.O'D. Davy 1 (UC Dublin), M. Sugden 4 (Dublin U.); G.R. Beamish 3 (Coleraine), M.J. Bradley 13 (Dolphin), W.F. Browne 3 (US Portsmouth), S.J. Cagney 1 (London Irish), R. Collopy (12) (Bective Rangers), D.McC. Cunningham (6) (NIFC), J. McVicker 8 (Belfast Collegians), R.S. Flood (1) (Dublin U.).

WALES   D.N. Rocyn-Jones (1) (St Mary's H.); W.R. Harding 8 (Swansea), B.R. Turnbull 1 (Cardiff), D. Davies (2) (Bridgend), E. Finch 3 (Llanelli); W.J. Delahay 12 (Cardiff), A. John 1 (Llanelli); D. Parker 6 (Swansea), *W.I. Jones (4) (Llanelli), S. Lawrence 2 (Bridgend), R.C. Herrera 3 (Cross Keys), J. Brown (1) (Cardiff), S. Hinam 1 (Cardiff), B. Phillips 4 (Aberavon), E. Beynon (2) (Swansea).

Referee J.W. Baxter (England)

SCOTLAND v ENGLAND   35/257

21 March 1925
Murrayfield
Scotland 14 (2G, 1DG) England 11 (1G, 1T, 1PG)

Scotland   T: Nelson, Wallace. C: Drysdale, Gillies. DG: Waddell.
England   T: Hamilton-Wickes, Wakefield. C: Luddington. PG: Luddington.

The opening of the Scottish Rugby Union's new ground at Murrayfield coincided with Scotland's sixth Triple Crown and first and only Grand Slam. A record crowd for the Championship, 80,000, saw them achieve it. It was A.M. Smallwood's fourteenth and final match for England and it was the first time that he played for a side which was defeated. The only other blemish on the Leicester wing's record was a draw the previous month against Ireland. Ian Smith's sensational try-scoring during this season, tended to obscure the feat of A.C. Wallace, who scored a try in all four matches.

Wavell Wakefield's England team which lost 11-14 to Scotland on 21 March 1925

SCOTLAND   D. Drysdale 12 (Heriot's FP); I.S. Smith 7 (Oxford U.), *G.P.S. Macpherson 9 (Oxford U.), G.G. Aitken 7 (Oxford U.), A.C. Wallace 8 (Oxford U.); H. Waddell 6 (Glasgow Acads), J.B. Nelson 4 (Glasgow Acads); D.S. Davies 13 (Hawick), J.C.H. Ireland 3 (Glasgow HSFP), R.A. Howie (7) (Kirkcaldy), D.J. MacMyn 4 (London Scottish), J.M. Bannerman 20 (Glasgow HSFP), J.W. Scott 4 (Stewart's FP), J.R. Paterson 4 (Birkenhead Park), A.C. Gillies 6 (Carlisle).

ENGLAND   T.E. Holliday 4 (Aspatria); R.H. Hamilton-Wickes 4 (Harlequins), L.J. Corbett 10 (Bristol), H.M. Locke 8 (Birkenhead Park), A.M. Smallwood (14) (Leicester); E. Myers 17 (Bradford), E.J. Massey (3) (Leicester); W.G.E. Luddington 11 (Devonport Services), J.S. Tucker 4 (Bristol), R.R.F. MacLennan 2 (OMT), R. Cove-Smith 16 (OMT), *W.W. Wakefield 23 (Harlequins), A.F. Blakiston 15 (Liverpool), A.T. Voyce 21 (Gloucester), D.C. Cumming 1 (Cambridge U.).

Referee A.E. Freethy (Wales)

Barthe (2) (S. Bordelais), A. Bioussa 4 (S. Toulouse), E. Piquiral 5 (RCF).

ENGLAND   T.E. Holliday 5 (Aspatria); R.H. Hamilton-Wickes 5 (Harlequins), L.J. Corbett 11 (Bristol), H.M. Locke 9 (Birkenhead Park), S.G.U. Considine (1) (Bath); E. Myers (18) (Bradford), A.T. Young 5 (Cambridge U.); W.G.E. Luddington 12 (Devonport Services), J.S. Tucker 5 (Bristol), R.R.F. MacLennan (3) (OMT), R. Cove-Smith 17 (OMT), *W.W. Wakefield 24 (Harlequins), A.F. Blakiston (16) (Liverpool), A.T. Voyce 22 (Gloucester), D.C. Cumming (2) (Cambridge U.).

Referee A.E. Freethy (Wales)

FRANCE v ENGLAND   11/258

13 April 1925
Stade Colombes, Paris
England 13 (2G, 1GM) France 11 (1G, 2T)

France   T: Barthe, Besson, Cluchague. C: Ducousso.
England   T: Hamilton-Wickes, Wakefield. C: Luddington (2). GM: Luddington.

This was the last Championship appearance of Pierre Moureu, a regular in the French pack since 1920, as well as five of his colleagues. Five England players, too, never played again, including A.F. Blakiston, a ubiquitous forward, who had won 16 caps since 1920. Wavell Wakefield's try was his fifth for England.

FRANCE   J. Ducousso (3) (S. Tarbes); M. Besson 3 (CASG), C. Magnanou 3 (A. Bayonne), M. de Laborderie (4) (RCF), L. Cluchague (2) (Biarritz Ol); Y. du Manoir 4 (RCF), *R. Piteu 13 (TOEC); A. Maury 4 (S. Toulouse), J. Marcet 4 (SC Albi), P. Moureu (16) (AS Béziers), A. Laurent 3 (Biarritz Ol), R. Levasseur (2) (S. Français), E.

PARIS Scotland beat France 20-6 · CARDIFF Wales drew England 3-3
BELFAST Ireland beat France 11-0 · MURRAYFIELD Scotland beat Wales 8-5
DUBLIN Ireland beat England 19-15 · TWICKENHAM England beat France 11-0
MURRAYFIELD Ireland beat Scotland 3-0 · SWANSEA Wales beat Ireland 11-8
TWICKENHAM Scotland beat England 17-9 · PARIS Wales beat France 7-5

CHAMPIONSHIP TABLE
Scotland – Championship

									Tries	
Pos	Country	P	W	D	L	F	A	Pts	F	A
1	Scotland (1)	4	3	0	1	45	23	6	9	6
2	Ireland (2)	4	3	0	1	41	26	6	8	6
3	Wales (4)	4	2	1	1	26	24	5	6	4
4	England (3)	4	1	1	2	38	39	3	10	8
5	France (5)	4	0	0	4	11	49	0	2	11

Scotland not only won the title for the second successive season, but notched up their longest sequence of matches without defeat, six, since an eight-match run of 1885–87. Ireland, once again, finished runners-up, which seemed the destiny of a side which had talent and ambition but usually found one side too good for them. Wales won two matches, in itself an achievement, while England at least kept France pinned to the foot of the table. It was France's third season without a victory and their 11 points' aggregate equalled their lowest ever total of 1913.

Nothing held back the development of the game, however. Wales passed a law prohibiting players under their jurisdiction from advancing beyond the front row of the scrummage until the ball had been heeled. The International Board also decided that all international matches be 40 minutes each way with a five-minute interval and that time-keeping be vested exclusively with the referees – 30 years after referees had been empowered to be 'sole judges of fact'.

FRANCE v SCOTLAND 11/259

2 January 1926
Stade Colombes, Paris
Scotland 20 (1G, 4T, 1PG) France 6 (1T 1PG)

France T: Piquiral. PG: Gonnet.
Scotland T: Wallace (3), MacMyn, Bannerman. C: Drysdale. PG: Gillies.

Scotland had scored more points and won by a bigger margin in France only once when then won 21-3 in 1913. France had some excuse for the heaviness of their defeat: Bioussa and Ribère were injured and had to receive treatment.

FRANCE L. Destarac 1 (S. Tarbes); M. Besson 4 (CASG), C. Magnanou 4 (A. Bayonne), M. Chapuy (1) (S. Français), A. Jauréguy 14 (S. Français); Y. du Manoir 5 (RCF), R. Llary (1) (AS Carcassonne); J. Etcheberry 7 (CS Vienne), C-A. Gonnet 7 (RCF), A. Maury 5 (S. Toulouse), A. Puig 1 (AC Perpignan), *A. Cassayet 20 (RC Narbonne), E. Ribère 4 (US Perpignan), A. Bioussa 5 (S. Toulouse), E. Piquiral 6 (RCF).

SCOTLAND *D. Drysdale 13 (Oxford U.); I.S. Smith 8 (Edinburgh U.), R.M. Kinnear 1 (Heriot's FP), J.C. Dykes 7 (Glasgow Acads), A.C. Wallace (9) (Oxford U.); H. Waddell 7 (Glasgow Acads), J.B. Nelson 5 (Glasgow Acads); D.S. Davies 14 (Hawick), J.C.H. Ireland 4 (Glasgow HSFP), W.V. Berkley 1 (Oxford U.), D.J. MacMyn 5 (London Scottish), J.M. Bannerman 21 (Glasgow HSFP), J.W. Scott 5 (Stewart's FP), A.C. Gillies 7 (Watsonians), J.R. Paterson 5 (Birkenhead Park).

Referee W.M. Llewellyn (Wales)

WALES v ENGLAND 37/260

16 January 1926
Cardiff Arms Park
Wales 3 (1T) England 3 (1T)

Wales T: Andrews.
England T: Wakefield.

George Andrews, the Newport wing, scored a try on his début appearance for Wales and went on to score two more in his short, five-match Championship career. One of the Arms Park entrances was stormed by a section of the locked-out crowd and those that eluded arrest managed to watch the game from the back of the stand.

WALES D.B. Evans (1) (Swansea); G.E. Andrews 1 (Newport), A.R. Stock 2 (Newport), R.A. Cornish 7 (Cardiff), *W.R. Harding 9 (Swansea); Bobby Jones 1 (Northampton), W.J. Delahay 13 (Cardiff); T.W. Lewis 1 (Cardiff), J.H. John 1 (Swansea), T. Hopkins 1 (Swansea), D.M. Jenkins 1 (Treorchy), R.C. Herrera 4 (Cross Keys), S. Hinam 2 (Cardiff), B. Phillips (5) (Aberavon), D. Jones 1 (Newport).

ENGLAND H.C. Catcheside 5 (Percy Park); H.C. Burton (1) (Richmond), A.R. Aslett 1 (Richmond), T.E.S. Francis 1 (Cambridge U.), R.H. Hamilton-Wickes 6 (Harlequins); H.J. Kittermaster 3 (Harlequins), J.R.B. Worton 1 (Harlequins); R.J. Hanvey 1 (Aspatria), J.S. Tucker 6 (Bristol), E. Stanbury 1 (Plymouth Albion), A. Robson (5) (Northern), W.G.E. Luddington (13) (Devonport Services), H.G. Periton 2 (Waterloo), A.T. Voyce 23 (Gloucester), *W.W. Wakefield 25 (Harlequins).

Referee W.H. Acton (Ireland)

IRELAND v FRANCE 12/261

23 January 1926
Ravenhill, Belfast
Ireland 11 (1G, 1T, 1PG) France 0

Ireland T: Stephenson (2). C: Hewitt. PG: Stephenson.

This was France's ninth successive Championship defeat, their previous victory being against Ireland in 1923.

IRELAND *W.E. Crawford 22 (Lansdowne); D.J. Cussen 10 (Dublin U.), T.R. Hewitt 5 (Queen's U. Belfast), G.V. Stephenson 22 (Queen's U. Belfast), R.L. Hamilton (1) (NIFC); M. Sugden 5 (Dublin U.), E.O'D. Davy 2 (UC Dublin); M.J. Bradley 14 (Dolphin), W.R.F. Collis (6) (Harlequins), S.J. Cagney 2 (London Irish), J.L. Farrell 1 (Bective Rangers), C.F.G.T. Hallaran 14 (Wanderers), J. McVicker 9 (Belfast Collegians), J.McF. Neill (1) (Instonians), R.D. Gray (4) (Old Wesley).

FRANCE L. Destarac 2 (S. Tarbes); C. Dulaurans 1 (S. Toulouse), V. Graule 1 (US Perpignan), R. Graciet 1 (SA Bordelais), J. Revillon 1 (RCF); J. Pascot (5) (US Perpignan), B. Berges (1) (S. Toulouse); A. Maury 6 (S. Toulouse), C-A. Gonnet 8 (RCF), J. Marcet 5 (SC Albi), *A. Cassayet 21 (RC Narbonne), E. Piquiral 7 (RCF), E. Ribère 5 (US Perpignan), J. Etcheberry 8 (CS Vienne), A. Bioussa 6 (S. Toulouse).

Referee A.A. Lawrie (Scotland)

SCOTLAND v WALES 37/262

6 February 1926
Murrayfield
Scotland 8 (1G, 1PG) Wales 5 (1G)

Scotland T: Waddell. C: Drysdale. PG: Gillies.
Wales T: Herrera. C: Everson.

Despite the outcome, Wales's first match at Murrayfield was in many ways a conspicuous success for Wick Powell. The London Welsh scrum-half was picked on the wing as a gamble to contain the Scottish scoring machine, Ian Smith, who had scored seven tries in his previous two matches against the Welsh. Smith did not score and for evermore in the Principality, Powell was lauded for a skill not usually associated with a scrum-half. It was Scotland's sixth Championship victory in a row, their best ever winning sequence.

SCOTLAND *D. Drysdale 14 (Heriot's FP); I.S. Smith 9 (Edinburgh U.), R.M. Kinnear 2 (Heriot's FP), J.C. Dykes 8 (Glasgow Acads),

W.M. Simmers 1 (Glasgow Acads); H. Waddell 8 (Glasgow Acads), J.B. Nelson 6 (Glasgow Acads); D.S. Davies 15 (Hawick), J.C.H. Ireland 5 (Glasgow HSFP), G.M. Murray (2) (Glasgow Acads), D.J. MacMyn 6 (London Scottish), J.M. Bannerman 22 (Glasgow HSFP), J.W. Scott 6 (Stewart's FP), A.C. Gillies 8 (Watsonians), J.R. Paterson 6 (Birkenhead Park).

WALES W.A. Everson (1) (Newport); G.E. Andrews 2 (Newport), A.R. Stock (3) (Newport), *R.A. Cornish 8 (Cardiff), W.C. Powell 1 (London Welsh); Bobby Jones 2 (Northampton), W.J. Delahay 14 (Cardiff); D.M. Jenkins 2 (Treorchy), J.H. John 2 (Swansea), T. Hopkins 2 (Swansea), S. Hinam 3 (Cardiff), R.C. Herrera 5 (Cross Keys), D. Jones 2 (Newport), S. Lawrence 3 (Bridgend), E. Watkins 1 (Blaina).

Referee D. Helliwell (England)

IRELAND v ENGLAND 37/263

13 February 1926
Lansdowne Road, Dublin
Ireland 19 (2G, 2T, 1PG) England 15 (3G)

Ireland T: Cussen (2), Frank Hewitt, Stephenson. C: Stephenson (2). PG: Stephenson.
England Haslett, Periton, Young. C: Francis (3).

This was Ireland's first win against England since 1911, the nine-match sequence being their longest without a victory against the English. George Stephenson, Ireland's most prolific accumulator of points, brought his career total to 51 with his 10 points in this match. He had scored 11 tries.

IRELAND *W.E. Crawford 23 (Lansdowne); D.J. Cussen 11 (Dublin U.), G.V. Stephenson 23 (NIFC), F.S. Hewitt 5 (Instonians), T.R. Hewitt 6 (Queen's U. Belfast); E.O'D. Davy 3 (UC Dublin), M. Sugden 6 (Dublin U.); M.J. Bradley 15 (Dolphin), C.T. Payne 1 (NIFC), A.McM. Buchanan 1 (Dublin U.), J. McVicker 10 (Belfast Collegians), J.L. Farrell 2 (Bective Rangers), C.F.G.T. Hallaran (15) (Wanderers), J.D. Clinch 9 (Wanderers), S.J. Cagney 3 (London Irish).

ENGLAND H.C. Catcheside 6 (Percy Park); R.H. Hamilton-Wickes 7 (Harlequins), A.R. Aslett 2

(Richmond), T.E.S. Francis 2 (Cambridge U.), Sir T.G. Devitt 1 (Cambridge U.); H.J. Kittermaster 4 (Harlequins), A.T. Young 6 (Blackheath); E. Stanbury 2 (Plymouth Albion), J.S. Tucker 7 (Bristol), R.J. Hanvey 2 (Aspatria), *W.W. Wakefield 26 (Harlequins), L.W. Haslett 1 (Birkenhead Park), H.G. Periton 3 (Waterloo), A.T. Voyce 24 (Gloucester), W.E. Tucker 1 (Cambridge U.).

Referee W.J. Llewellyn (Wales)

SCOTLAND v IRELAND 39/264

27 February 1926
Murrayfield
Ireland 3 (1T) Scotland 0

Ireland T: Gage.

This was Scotland's only defeat of the season and Ireland, who also won three matches, were relegated to being runners-up because they totalled fewer points

SCOTLAND *D. Drysdale 15 (Oxford U.); I.S. Smith 10 (Edinburgh U.), J.C. Dykes 9 (Glasgow Acads), R.M. Kinnear (3) (Heriot's FP), W.M. Simmers 2 (Glasgow Acads); H. Waddell 9 (Glasgow Acads), J.B. Nelson 7 (Glasgow Acads); D.S. Davies 16 (Hawick), J.C.H. Ireland 6 (Glasgow HSFP), D.S. Kerr 4 (Heriot's FP), D.J. MacMyn 7 (London Scottish), J.M. Bannerman 23 (Glasgow HSFP), J. Graham 1 (Kelso), J.R. Paterson 7 (Birkenhead Park), J.W. Scott 7 (Stewart's FP).

IRELAND *W.E. Crawford 24 (Lansdowne); D.J. Cussen 12 (Dublin U.), G.V. Stephenson 24 (NIFC), T.R. Hewitt 7 (Queen's U. Belfast), J.H. Gage 1 (Queen's U. Belfast); E.O'D. Davy 4 (UC Dublin), M. Sugden 7 (Dublin U.); M.J. Bradley 16 (Dolphin), W.F. Browne 4 (US Portsmouth), A.McM. Buchanan 2 (Dublin U.), S.J. Cagney 4 (London Irish), J.D. Clinch 10 (Wanderers), J.L. Farrell 3 (Bective Rangers), J. McVicker 11 (Belfast Collegians), C.J. Hanrahan 1 (Dolphin).

Referee B.S. Cumberlege (England)

The Scottish XV which defeated Wales 8-5 at Murrayfield on 6 February 1926

ENGLAND v FRANCE   12/265

27 February 1926
Twickenham
England 11 (1G, 2T) France 0

England   T: Aslett (2), Kittermaster. C: Francis.

Reports wrote very unkindly of the English pack in a match between sides who finished ultimately at the foot of the Championship. The French selectors were not happy either, axing five, including Piteu, their long-serving scrum-half and Borde, one of their more talented midfield men.

ENGLAND   T.E. Holliday 6 (Aspatria); Sir T.G. Devitt 2 (Cambridge U.), A.R. Aslett 3 (Richmond), T.E.S. Francis 3 (Blackheath), J.C. Gibbs 2 (Harlequins); H.J. Kittermaster 5 (Harlequins), A.T. Young 7 (Blackheath); C.K.T. Faithfull 2 (Harlequins), J.S. Tucker 8 (Bristol), R.J. Hanvey 3 (Aspatria), *W.W. Wakefield 27 (Harlequins), L.W. Haslett (2) (Birkenhead Park), H.G. Periton 4 (Waterloo), A.T. Voyce 25 (Gloucester), J.W.G. Webb 1 (Northampton).

FRANCE   L. Destarac 3 (S. Tarbes); J. Revillon 2 (RCF), A. Behotéguy 6 (US Cognac), F. Borde (11) (S. Toulouse), A. Jauréguy 15 (S. Français); V. Graule 2 (US Perpignan), R. Piteu (14) (TOEC); A. Maury (7) (S. Toulouse), C-A. Gonnet 9 (RCF), J. Marcet (6) (SC Albi), *A. Cassayet 22 (RC Narbonne), A. Puig (2) (US Perpignan), A. Bioussa 7 (S. Toulouse), J. Etcheberry 9 (CS Vienne), E. Piquiral 8 (RCF).

Referee A.E. Freethy (Wales)

WALES v IRELAND   35/266

13 March 1926
St Helen's, Swansea
Wales 11 (1G, 2T) Ireland 8 (1G, 1PG)

Wales   T: Harding, Hopkins, Herrera. C: Rees.
Ireland   T: Hanrahan. C: Stephenson. PG: Stephenson.

This defeat cost Ireland the Triple Crown and what would have been their first Grand Slam. In the last minute Tom Hewitt attempted a match-winning dropped goal only for it to swing wide. A dropped goal was then worth four points.

WALES   T.E. Rees 1 (London Welsh); C.F. Rowlands (1) (Aberavon), R.A. Cornish 9 (Cardiff), W.J. Delahay 15 (Cardiff), *W.R. Harding 10 (Swansea); W.H. Lewis 1 (London Welsh), W.C. Powell 2 (London Welsh); R.C. Herrera 6 (Cross Keys), J.H. John 3 (Swansea), D.M. Jenkins 3 (Treorchy), S. Hinam 4 (Cardiff), D. Jones 3 (Newport), T. Hopkins 3 (Swansea), S. Lawrence 4 (Bridgend), E. Watkins 2 (Blaina).

IRELAND   *W.E. Crawford 25 (Lansdowne); D.J. Cussen 13 (Dublin U.), G.V. Stephenson 25 (Queen's U. Belfast), T.R. Hewitt (8) (Queen's U. Belfast), J.H. Gage 2 (Queen's U. Belfast); E.O'D. Davy 5 (UC Dublin), M. Sugden 8 (Dublin U.); M.J. Bradley 17 (Dolphin), A.McM. Buchanan 3 (Dublin U.), W.F. Browne 5 (US Portsmouth), S.J. Cagney 5 (London Irish), J. McVicker 12 (Belfast Collegians), J.L. Farrell 4 (Bective Rangers), J.D. Clinch 11 (Wanderers), C.J. Hanrahan 2 (Dolphin).

Referee B.S. Cumberlege (England)

ENGLAND v SCOTLAND   36/267

20 March 1926
Twickenham
Scotland 17 (2G, 1T, 1DG) England 9 (3T)

England   T: Tucker, Voyce, Webb.
Scotland   T: Smith (2), Waddell. C: Waddell (2). DG: Dykes.

Scotland's first victory at Twickenham was comprehensive and well deserved. It spelled the end of Championship rugby for seven English players, including the great Tommy Voyce, the Gloucester flank-forward. Voyce, who was two months short of his twenty-ninth birthday, had played in 26 Championship matches for England and was on the winning side 19 times.

ENGLAND   T.E. Holliday (7) (Aspatria); R.H. Hamilton-Wickes 8 (Harlequins), A.R. Aslett 4 (Richmond), T.E.S. Francis (4) (Blackheath), H.L.V. Day (4) (Leicester); H.J. Kittermaster (6) (Harlequins), A.T. Young 8 (Blackheath); C.K.T. Faithfull (3) (Harlequins), J.S. Tucker 9 (Bristol),

R.J. Hanvey (4) (Aspatria), *W.W. Wakefield 28 (Harlequins), E. Stanbury 3 (Plymouth Albion), H.G. Periton 5 (Waterloo), A.T. Voyce (26) (Gloucester), J.W.G. Webb 2 (Northampton).

SCOTLAND   *D. Drysdale 16 (Oxford U.); I.S. Smith 11 (Edinburgh U.), J.C. Dykes 10 (Glasgow Acads), W.M. Simmers 3 (Glasgow Acads), G.M. Boyd (1) (Glasgow HSFP); H. Waddell 10 (Glasgow Acads), J.B. Nelson 8 (Glasgow Acads); D.S. Davies 17 (Hawick), J.C.H. Ireland 7 (Glasgow HSFP), D.S. Kerr 5 (Heriot's FP), D.J. MacMyn 8 (London Scottish), J.M. Bannerman 24 (Glasgow HSFP), J.W. Scott 8 (Stewart's FP), J.R. Paterson 8 (Birkenhead Park), J. Graham 2 (Kelso).

Referee W.H. Acton (Ireland)

FRANCE v WALES   12/268

5 April 1926
Stade Colombes, Paris
Wales 7 (1T, 1DG) France 5 (1G)

France   T: Gerintes. C: Gonnet.
Wales   T: Watkins. DG: Cornish.

This was Wales's sixth successive win in France, their longest winning sequence there. French newspapers lamented the home side's ill fortune at not being able to improve on a half-time lead.

FRANCE   L. Destarac 4 (S. Tarbes); M. Besson 5 (CASG), M. Baillette 3 (US Perpignan), R. Graciet 2 (S. Bordelais), *A. Jauréguy 16 (S. Français); V. Graule 3 (US Perpignan), H. Laffont (1) (RC Narbonne); A. Cassayet 23 (RC Narbonne), E. Ribère 6 (US Perpignan), C. Montade (4) (US Perpignan), J. Sayrou 1 (US Perpignan), G. Gerintes (2) (CASG), E. Piquiral 9 (RCF), A. Laurent (4) (Biarritz Ol), C-A. Gonnet 10 (RCF).

WALES   T.E. Rees 2 (London Welsh); E. Finch 4 (Llanelli), *W.J. Delahay 16 (Cardiff), R.A. Cornish (10) (Cardiff), W.R. Harding 11 (Swansea); Bobby Jones (3) (Northampton), W.C. Powell 3 (London Welsh); R.C. Herrera 7 (Cross Keys), J.H. John 4 (Swansea), D.M. Jenkins (4) (Treorchy), S. Hinam (5) (Cardiff), D. Jones 4 (Newport), T. Hopkins (4) (Swansea), S. Lawrence 5 (Bridgend), E. Watkins (3) (Blaina).

Referee R.W. Harland (Ireland)

PARIS Ireland beat France 8-3 · TWICKENHAM England beat Wales 11-9
MURRAYFIELD Scotland beat France 23-6 · CARDIFF Scotland beat Wales 5-0
TWICKENHAM England beat Ireland 8-6 · DUBLIN Ireland beat Scotland 6-0
SWANSEA Wales beat France 25-7 · DUBLIN Ireland beat Wales 19-9
MURRAYFIELD Scotland beat England 21-13 · PARIS France beat England 3-0

CHAMPIONSHIP TABLE
Scotland – Championship

									Tries	
Pos	Country	P	W	D	L	F	A	Pts	F	A
1	Scotland (1)	4	3	0	1	49	25	6	10	6
2	Ireland (2)	4	3	0	1	39	20	6	8	4
3	England (4)	4	2	0	2	32	39	4	5	9
4	Wales (3)	4	1	0	3	43	42	2	10	7
5	France (5)	4	1	0	3	19	56	2	5	12

For the third season in succession, Scotland won the Championship and Ireland were runners-up; it was Scotland's first hat-trick. Despite beating England for the first time, France finished bottom of the table for the fourth year in a row, equalling the longest Championship sequence for Wooden Spoons by Ireland in 1920–23. These were sad days indeed for France for until that precious win against England in the last match of the Championship they had lost 14 successive matches, their worst losing sequence since the 17 defeats of 1911–20.

That any tries were scored at this time was remarkable, for tactically the game had become defensive and tight. The scrummage formation had now settled into 3-2-3, with the blind-side flanker (wing-forward as he was then known) aiming to smother the scrum-half, the open-side flanker the scourge of the fly-half, and the No. 8 (then known as the lock-forward) acting as a defensive sweeper behind his own backs. For a back to score a try against such measured defence required great speed, ingenuity or luck – or a mixture of all three. Fortunately for the game, there were plenty of players with the ability to score tries – as proved by the statistics of the 1920–31 period which produced an average of 38 tries a season. Only in one other period, 1910–14, when 245 tries were scored at an average of 49 a season, were there more tries recorded. However, that glut was largely due to each country reaping a rich harvest against the fragile defence of the newcomers, France.

FRANCE v IRELAND 13/269

1 January 1927
Stade Colombes, Paris
Ireland 8 (1G, 1PG) France 3 (1T)

France T: Ribère.
Ireland T: Davy. C: Stephenson. PG: Stephenson.

Irish newspaper correspondents reported on the 'menacing attitude of spectators' against some of the decisions of the Scottish referee, R.L. Scott. The match became 'very rough' and the referee and touch-judges occasionally had to 'restore order'. France had now suffered 13 successive defeats in the Championship.

FRANCE   M. Piquemal 1 (S. Tarbes); *A. Jauréguy 17 (S. Français), M. Besson (6) (CASG), M. Baillette 4 (US Quillan), E. Vellat 1 (FC Grenoble); Y. du Manoir 6 (RCF), E. Bader 1 (SS Primevères); E. Ribère 7 (US Quillan), E. Piquiral 10 (FC Lyon), A. Prevost 1 (SC Albi), J. Etcheberry 10 (CS Vienne), A. Cassayet 24 (RC Narbonne), C-A. Gonnet 11 (RCF), R. Hutin 1 (CASG), R. Bousquet 1 (SC Albi).

IRELAND   *W.E. Crawford 26 (Lansdowne); D.J. Cussen 14 (Dublin U.), G.V. Stephenson 26

(Queen's U. Belfast), J.M. Atkinson (1) (NIFC), J.B. Ganly 1 (Monkstown); E.O'D. Davy 6 (UC Dublin), P.F. Murray 1 (Wanderers); M.J. Bradley 18 (Dolphin), S.J. Cagney 6 (London Irish), W.F. Browne 6 (US Portsmouth), J.D. Clinch 12 (Wanderers), J.L. Farrell 5 (Bective Rangers), J. McVicker 13 (Belfast Collegians), C.T. Payne 2 (NIFC), N.G. Ross 1 (Malone).

Referee R.L. Scott (Scotland)

ENGLAND v WALES 38/270

15 January 1927
Twickenham
England 11 (1G, 1GM, 1PG) Wales 9 (2T, 1PG)

England T: Corbett. C: Stanbury. GM: Corbett. PG: Stanbury.
Wales T: Andrews, Harding. PG: Male.

Wales played for all but the first quarter of an hour with 14 men, having lost Dai Jones, the Newport forward, with a shoulder injury. England introduced five players new to the Championship, and one of them, H.C.C. Laird, the Harlequins stand-off, became their youngest ever player, at 18 years 134 days. Wales's only consolation was that they scored two tries to one.

ENGLAND K.A. Sellar 1 (US Portsmouth); R.H. Hamilton-Wickes (9) (Harlequins), *L.J. Corbett 12 (Bristol), H.M. Locke 10 (Birkenhead Park), J.C. Gibbs 3 (Harlequins); H.C.C. Laird 1 (Harlequins), J.R.B. Worton (2) (Harlequins); K.J. Stark 1 (Old Alleynians), J.S. Tucker 10 (Bristol), T.J. Coulson 1 (Coventry), R. Cove-Smith 18 (OMT), J. Hanley 1 (Plymouth Albion), E. Stanbury 4 (Plymouth Albion), G.S. Conway (17) (Hartlepool Rovers), H.G. Periton 6 (Waterloo).

WALES B.O. Male 5 (Cardiff); G.E. Andrews 3 (Newport), *B.R. Turnbull 2 (Cardiff), J. Roberts 1 (Cardiff), W.R. Harding 12 (Swansea); W.H. Lewis 2 (London Welsh), W.C. Powell 4 (London Welsh); R.C. Herrera (8) (Newport), J.H. John 5 (Swansea), D. Jones (5) (Newport), S. Lawrence (6) (Bridgend), T.W. Lewis 2 (Cardiff), H. Phillips 1 (Newport), W. Williams 1 (Crumlin), W. Thomas 1 (Llanelli).

Referee R.L. Scott (Scotland)

SCOTLAND v FRANCE 12/271

22 January 1927
Murrayfield
Scotland 23 (4G, 1PG) France 6 (2T)

Scotland T: Waddell (2), Smith (2). C: Gillies (3), Drysdale. PG: Gillies.
France T: Piquiral, Hutin.

France's first match at Murrayfield was another benefit day for Ian Smith, who followed up his previous season's four tries against France with another brace. The Scots, at this time, were enjoying one of their most successful periods in the Championship. In contrast, France were suffering badly and all their earlier promise dissolved in a string of defeats which inevitably left them with the Wooden Spoon.

SCOTLAND D. Drysdale 17 (Heriot's FP); I.S. Smith 12 (Edinburgh U.), *G.P.S. Macpherson 10 (Edinburgh Acads), J.C. Dykes 11 (Glasgow Acads), W.M. Simmers 4 (Glasgow Acads); H. Waddell 11 (Glasgow Acads), J.B. Nelson 9 (Glasgow Acads); D.S. Davies 18 (Hawick), J.C.H. Ireland 8 (Glasgow HSFP), J.W. Allan 1 (Melrose), J.M. Bannerman 25 (Glasgow HSFP), J.W. Scott 9 (Stewart's FP), J. Graham 3 (Kelso), J.R. Paterson 9 (Birkenhead Park), A.C. Gillies 9 (Watsonians).

FRANCE M. Piquemal 2 (S. Tarbes); J. Revillon (3) (CASG), R. Graciet 3 (S. Bordelais), V. Graule 4 (US Perpignan), R. Houdet 1 (S. Français); *Y. du Manoir (7) (RCF), E. Bader (2) (SS Primevères); C-A. Gonnet 12 (RCF), R. Hutin 2 (CASG), J. Etcheberry 11 (CS Vienne), R. Bousquet 2 (SC Albi), A. Cassayet 25 (RC Narbonne), A. Prevost 2 (SC Albi), E. Piquiral 11 (FC Lyon), E. Ribère 8 (US Quillan).

Referee B.S. Cumberlege (England)

WALES v SCOTLAND   38/272

5 February 1927
Cardiff Arms Park
Scotland 5 (1G) Wales 0

Scotland   T: Kerr. C: Gillies.

Scotland scored their fifth consecutive win over Wales, their best winning sequence against the Welsh. It was also their fourth win in a row in Wales, their longest run of success in the Principality. Wales's previous victory over Scotland was in 1914.

WALES   *B.O. Male 6 (Cardiff); J.D. Bartlett 1 (Llanelli), B.R. Turnbull 3 (Cardiff), J. Roberts 2 (Cardiff), W.R. Harding 13 (Swansea); G. Richards (1) (Cardiff), W.J. Delahay (17) (Cardiff); W. Williams 2 (Crumlin), J.H. John 6 (Swansea), H. Phillips 2 (Newport), T.W. Lewis (3) (Cardiff), T. Arthur 1 (Neath), E.M. Jenkins 1 (Aberavon), W. Thomas 2 (Llanelli), I. Jones 3 (Llanelli).

SCOTLAND   D. Drysdale 18 (Heriot's FP); E.G. Taylor (1) (Oxford U.), *G.P.S. Macpherson 11 (Edinburgh Acads), J.C. Dykes 12 (Glasgow Acads), W.M. Simmers 5 (Glasgow Acads); H. Waddell 12 (Glasgow Acads), J.B. Nelson 10 (Glasgow Acads); D.S. Davies 19 (Hawick), J.C.H. Ireland 9 (Glasgow HSFP), D.S. Kerr 6 (Heriot's FP), J.W. Scott 10 (Stewart's FP), J.M. Bannerman 26 (Glasgow HSFP), J. Graham 4 (Kelso), A.C. Gillies 10 (Watsonians), J.R. Paterson 10 (Birkenhead Park).

Referee W.H. Jackson (England)

ENGLAND v IRELAND   38/273

12 February 1927
Twickenham
England 8 (1G, 1T) Ireland 6 (1T, 1PG)

England   T: Gibbs, Laird. C: Stanbury.
Ireland   T: Hugh McVicker. PG: Stephenson.

England introduced three new players to their pack, Law, Eyres and Davies, but despite this victory all three joined the ranks of one-cap wonders.

ENGLAND   K.A. Sellar 2 (US Portsmouth); H.C. Catcheside 7 (Percy Park), *L.J. Corbett 13 (Bristol), H.M. Locke 11 (Birkenhead Park), J.C. Gibbs 4 (Harlequins); H.C.C. Laird 2 (Harlequins), A.T. Young 9 (Blackheath); D.E. Law (1) (Birkenhead Park), J.S. Tucker 11 (Bristol), K.J. Stark 2 (Old Alleynians), E. Stanbury 5 (Plymouth Albion), R. Cove-Smith 19 (OMT), H.G. Periton 7 (Waterloo), P.H. Davies (1) (Sale), W.C.T. Eyres (1) (Richmond).

IRELAND   *W.E. Crawford 27 (Lansdowne); D.J. Cussen (15) (St Mary's H.), G.V. Stephenson 27 (NIFC), F.S. Hewitt 6 (Instonians), J.B. Ganly 2 (Monkstown); E.O'D. Davy 7 (Lansdowne), M. Sugden 9 (Wanderers); C.J. Hanrahan 3 (Dolphin), C.T. Payne 3 (NIFC), J. McVicker 14 (Belfast Collegians), J.L. Farrell 6 (Bective Rangers), H. McVicker 1 (Richmond), W.F. Browne 7 (US Portsmouth), T.O. Pike 1 (Lansdowne), N.G. Ross (2) (Malone).

Referee T.H. Vile (Wales)

IRELAND v SCOTLAND   40/274

26 February 1927
Lansdowne Road, Dublin
Ireland 6 (2T) Scotland 0

Ireland   T: Pike, Ganly.

This match, supposedly celebrating the opening of the new East Stand, was all but ruined by rain, heavy and continuous, and a fierce, biting wind. Players were quickly numbed with cold and so muddied as to be unrecognizable to friend, foe or spectator. The crowd, standing in the rain or unprotected in the new stand which had yet to be roofed, underwent all manner of misery. The referee, Barry Cumberlege, suffered a deadened arm by the end and the Scottish touch-judge — 'who with amazing hardihood, turned out in a lavender suit, sans hat or overcoat' — spent much of his time clearing the mud from the eyes and mouths of players. The East Stand survived until the end of the 1983 season when it was replaced by the Triple Crown Stand.

IRELAND   *W.E. Crawford 28 (Lansdowne); J.B. Ganly 3 (Monkstown), F.S. Hewitt 7 (Instonians), G.V. Stephenson 28 (NIFC), J.H. Gage 3

(Queen's U. Belfast); E.O'D. Davy 8 (Lansdowne), M. Sugden 10 (Wanderers); A.McM. Buchanan 4 (Dublin U.), W.F. Browne 8 (US Portsmouth), T.O. Pike 2 (Lansdowne), H. McVicker 2 (Richmond), J.L. Farrell 7 (Bective Rangers), J. McVicker 15 (Belfast Collegians), C.J. Hanrahan 4 (Dolphin), C.T. Payne 4 (NIFC).

SCOTLAND   D. Drysdale 19 (Heriot's FP); I.S. Smith 13 (Edinburgh U.), *G.P.S. Macpherson 12 (Edinburgh Acads), J.C. Dykes 13 (Glasgow Acads), W.M. Simmers 6 (Glasgow Acads); H. Waddell 13 (Glasgow Acads), J.B. Nelson 11 (Glasgow Acads); D.S. Davies (20) (Hawick), J.C.H. Ireland 10 (Glasgow HSFP), D.S. Kerr 7 (Heriot's FP), J.W. Scott 11 (Stewart's FP), J.M. Bannerman 27 (Glasgow HSFP), J. Graham 5 (Kelso), J.R. Paterson 11 (Birkenhead Park), A.C. Gillies 11 (Watsonians).

Referee B.S. Cumberlege (England)

WALES v FRANCE　　　　13/275

26 February 1927
St Helen's, Swansea
Wales 25 (2G, 5T) France 7 (1T, 1DG)

Wales   T: Roberts (2), Harding (2), Thomas, Andrews, Morgan. C: Male (2).
France   T: Prevost. DG: Verger.

Wales extended their winning sequence to 13 in the first 13 Championship matches with France, their longest run of success against any country. The man who suffered most during this miserable period for France was their captain, Aimé Cassayet. In 26 Championship matches he was on the losing side 22 times. Cassayet participated in only two French victories in his seven-year international career – against Ireland in 1921 and 1923. Sadly, Cassayet became seriously ill soon after this match and died, aged 28, three months later.

WALES   B.O. Male 7 (Cardiff); G.E. Andrews 4 (Newport), W.G. Morgan 1 (Cambridge U.), J. Roberts 3 (Cardiff), W.R. Harding 14 (Swansea); W.H. Lewis 3 (London Welsh), *W.C. Powell 5 (London Welsh); H. Phillips 3 (Newport), J.H. John 7 (Swansea), W. Williams 3 (Crumlin), J. Burns 1 (Cardiff), T. Arthur 2 (Neath), E.M. Jenkins 2 (Aberavon), W. Thomas 3 (Llanelli), I. Jones 4 (Llanelli).

FRANCE   L. Destarac 5 (S. Tarbes); R. Houdet 2 (S. Français), M. Baillette 5 (US Quillan), V. Graule (5) (US Perpignan), F. Raymond 2 (S. Toulouse); A. Verger 1 (S. Français), P. Carbonne (1) (US Perpignan); E. Piquiral 12 (FC Lyon), E. Ribère 9 (US Quillan), A. Prevost (3) (SC Albi), R. Bousquet 3 (SC Albi), *A. Cassayet (26) (RC Narbonne), J. Etcheberry (12) (CS Vienne), C-A. Gonnet 13 (RCF), R. Hutin (3) (CASG).

Referee W.H. Jackson (England)

IRELAND v WALES　　　　36/276

12 March 1927
Lansdowne Road, Dublin
Ireland 19 (2G, 2T, 1PG) Wales 9 (1G, 1DG)

Ireland   T: Stephenson (2), Ganly (2). C: Stephenson (2). PG: Stephenson.
Wales   T: Morgan. C: Powell. DG: Lewis.

This win meant that Ireland finished runners-up in the Championship for the third season in a row, denied victory by Scotland's higher points-scoring for the second successive year. The win, which equalled Ireland's highest score against Wales set in 1925, was all the more remarkable for the fact that they lost a forward, Alan Buchanan, through injury before half-time.

IRELAND   *W.E. Crawford (29) (Lansdowne); J.H. Gage (4) (Queen's U. Belfast), G.V. Stephenson 29 (NIFC), F.S. Hewitt (8) (Instonians), J.B. Ganly 4 (Monkstown); E.O'D. Davy 9 (Lansdowne), M. Sugden 11 (Wanderers); T.O. Pike 3 (Lansdowne), W.F. Browne 9 (US Portsmouth), H. McVicker 3 (Richmond), J.L. Farrell 8 (Bective Rangers), J. McVicker 16 (Belfast Collegians), C.J. Hanrahan 5 (Dolphin), A.McM. Buchanan (5) (Dublin U.), M.J. Bradley (19) (Dolphin).

WALES   B.O. Male 8 (Cardiff); G.E. Andrews (5) (Newport), W.G. Morgan 2 (Cambridge U.), J. Roberts 4 (Cardiff), W.R. Harding 15 (Swansea); W.H. Lewis 4 (Maesteg), *W.C. Powell 6 (London Welsh); T. Arthur 3 (Neath), J.H. John (8) (Swansea), J. Burns (2) (Cardiff), E.M. Jenkins 3 (Aberavon), H. Phillips 4 (Newport), W. Williams (4) (Crumlin), W. Thomas 4 (Llanelli), I. Jones 5 (Llanelli).

Referee B.S. Cumberlege (England)

SCOTLAND v ENGLAND 37/277

19 March 1927
Murrayfield
Scotland 21 (1G, 4T, 1DG) England 13 (2G, 1PG)

Scotland T: Smith (2), Dykes, Macpherson, Scott. C: Gillies. DG: Waddell.
England T: Gibbs, Laird. C: Stanbury, Stark. PG: Stark.

This was Scotland's third victory in a row over England, and their biggest score against them to date. The match aggregate of 34 points was also the highest to date in an England-Scotland match, a total since beaten on six occasions only.

SCOTLAND *D. Drysdale 20 (Heriot's FP); I.S. Smith 14 (Edinburgh U.), G.P.S. Macpherson 13 (Edinburgh Acads), J.C. Dykes 14 (Glasgow Acads), W.M. Simmers 7 (Glasgow Acads); H. Waddell 14 (Glasgow Acads), J.B. Nelson 12 (Glasgow Acads); J.W. Scott 12 (Stewart's FP), J.C.H. Ireland (11) (Glasgow HSFP), D.S. Kerr 8 (Heriot's FP), D.J. MacMyn 9 (London Scottish), J.M. Bannerman 28 (Glasgow HSFP), J. Graham 6 (Kelso), J.R. Paterson 12 (Birkenhead Park), A.C. Gillies (12) (Watsonians).

ENGLAND K.A. Sellar 3 (US Portsmouth); H.C. Catcheside (8) (Percy Park), *L.J. Corbett 14 (Bristol), H.M. Locke (12) (Birkenhead Park),

Wavell Wakefield takes the field for the final time in an England jersey, against France on 2 April 1927

J.C. Gibbs 5 (Harlequins); H.C.C. Laird 3 (Harlequins), A.T. Young 10 (Blackheath); E. Stanbury 6 (Plymouth Albion), J.S. Tucker 12 (Bristol), K.J. Stark 3 (Old Alleynians), W.E. Pratten 1 (Blackheath), R. Cove-Smith 20 (OMT), J. Hanley 2 (Plymouth Albion), H.G. Periton 8 (Waterloo), W.W. Wakefield 29 (Harlequins).

Referee N.M. Purcell (Ireland)

FRANCE v ENGLAND 13/278

2 April 1927
Stade Colombes, Paris
France 3 (1T) England 0

France T: Vellat.

After eleven wins and one draw, this was England's first defeat by France in the Championship and it ended France's run of 15 successive Championship defeats. Eight England players never played in the Championship again, including the captain, Len Corbett, and Wavell Wakefield, England's leading cap winner. Wakefield has been variously described as England's best captain and finest exponent of forward play. In his seven years with England, he was on a winning side 20 times in 30 appearances, participating in three Championship successes, three Triple Crowns and three Grand Slams.

FRANCE L. Destarac (6) (S. Tarbes); E. Vellat (2) (FC Grenoble), A. Behotéguy 7 (A. Bayonne), G. Gérald 1 (RCF), *A. Jauréguy 18 (S. Français); A. Verger 2 (S. Français), C. Dupont 8 (S. Bordelais); A. Loury 1 (RCF), C-A. Gonnet (14) (RCF), J. Morère 1 (S. Toulouse), J. Galia 1 (US Quillan), R. Bousquet 4 (SC Albi), E. Ribère 10 (US Quillan), A. Cazenave 1 (S. Pau), E. Piquiral 13 (RCF).

ENGLAND J.N.S. Wallen (1) (Waterloo); W. Alexander (1) (Northern), *L.J. Corbett (15) (Bristol), R.A. Buckingham (1) (Leicester), J.C. Gibbs (6) (Harlequins); C.C. Bishop (1) (Blackheath), A.T. Young 11 (Blackheath); K.J. Stark 4 (Old Alleynians), J.S. Tucker 13 (Bristol), E. Stanbury 7 (Plymouth Albion), R. Cove-Smith 21 (OMT), W.E. Pratten (2) (Blackheath), H.G. Periton 9 (Waterloo), J. Hanley 3 (Plymouth Albion), W.W. Wakefield (30) (Harlequins).

Referee A.E. Freethy (Wales)

1928

PARIS Scotland beat France 15-6 · SWANSEA England beat Wales 10-8
BELFAST Ireland beat France 12-8 · MURRAYFIELD Wales beat Scotland 13-0
DUBLIN England beat Ireland 7-6 · TWICKENHAM England beat France 18-8
MURRAYFIELD Ireland beat Scotland 13-5 · CARDIFF Ireland beat Wales 13-10
TWICKENHAM England beat Scotland 6-0 · PARIS France beat Wales 8-3

CHAMPIONSHIP TABLE
England – Championship, Triple Crown, Grand Slam

									Tries	
Pos	Country	P	W	D	L	F	A	Pts	F	A
1	England (3)	4	4	0	0	41	22	8	9	6
2	Ireland (2)	4	3	0	1	44	30	6	12	6
3	Wales (4)	4	1	0	3	34	31	2	8	7
4	France (5)	4	1	0	3	30	48	2	8	14
5	Scotland (1)	4	1	0	3	20	38	2	6	10

England won the Grand Slam for the sixth time, overcoming their critical hurdles in Cardiff and Dublin by narrow margins. Ireland, in fact, outscored England 2-1 in tries in a season in which Ireland produced a record 12, a total they were to equal only once again, in 1953. It was an important season, too, for France. After 13 consecutive defeats, they managed to beat Wales for the first time, a victory that enabled them to vacate their customary position at the foot of the table; the Wooden Spoon went to Scotland for the first time since 1911. The relatively high scoring of the 1920s, when the Championship average was 38 tries a season, was consistent with the quality possession now obtained from the set-pieces, particularly the line-out. Jumpers had become specialized and it had become common practice for the wings, rather than the scrum-halves, to throw in to them.

Until this season, largely because of the increased popularity of the game, many newspapers and magazines published feature articles and comments by leading players and officials. These articles generally provided a behind-the-scenes account: they conveyed the players' views to the public and were an interesting and valuable insight. The authorities, however, disapproved of the practice, and by 1928 the Four Home Unions had decreed it should cease.

FRANCE v SCOTLAND 13/279

2 January 1928
Stade Colombes, Paris
Scotland 15 (5T) France 6 (2T)

France T: Haget, Camel.
Scotland T: Simmers, Paterson, Dykes, Douty, Scott.

The thirteenth Championship match between France and Scotland was marred by tragedy. Yves du Manoir, who had captained France against Scotland at Murrayfield the previous year, but was dropped for this match, was killed when an Army aeroplane he was flying crashed shortly before kick-off. As a tribute to du Manoir, who also captained Racing Club de France, it was decided to rename Colombes Stadium, which was owned by Racing, the Stade Yves du Manoir. It was the third time in seven visits to France that Scotland scored five tries.

FRANCE M. Magnol 1 (S. Toulouse); *A. Jauréguy 19 (S. Français), G. Gérald 2 (RCF), J. Coulon (1) (FC Grenoble), C. Dulaurans 2 (S. Toulouse); H. Haget (1) (CASG), G. Daudignon (1) (S. Français); A. Loury 2 (RCF), F. Camicas 1 (S. Tarbes), J. Morère (2) (O Marseille), J. Galia 2 (US Quillan), A. Camel 1 (S. Toulouse), A. Cazenave (2) (S. Pau), E. Ribère 11 (US Quillan), G. Branca 1 (S. Français).

SCOTLAND   *D. Drysdale 21 (Heriot's FP); G.P.S. Macpherson 14 (Edinburgh Acads), R.F. Kelly 1 (Watsonians), J.C. Dykes 15 (Glasgow HSFP), W.M. Simmers 8 (Glasgow Acads); H.D. Greenlees 1 (Leicester), P.S. Douty 1 (London Scottish); W.B. Welsh 1 (Hawick), W.N. Roughead 1 (London Scottish), W.G. Ferguson 1 (Royal HSFP), D.J. MacMyn (10) (London Scottish), J.M. Bannerman 29 (Glasgow HSFP), J. Graham 7 (Kelso), J.R. Paterson 13 (Birkenhead Park), J.W. Scott 13 (Stewart's FP).

Referee R. McGrath (Ireland)

WALES v ENGLAND   39/280

21 January 1928
St Helen's, Swansea
England 10 (2G) Wales 8 (1G, 1T)

Wales   T: Bartlett, Dai John. C: Jones.
England   T: Taylor, Laird. C: Richardson (2).

Wales completely outplayed England and should have won. But a stumble/slip by Rowe Harding facilitated a try for Taylor in the first half, and a much debated offside decision against Tom Hollingdale prevented a winning try in the second half. Harding did not play again for Wales.

WALES   T.E. Rees (3) (London Welsh); J.D. Bartlett 2 (London Welsh), B.R. Turnbull 4 (Cardiff), J. Roberts 5 (Cardiff), *W.R. Harding (16) (Swansea); D.E. John 3 (Llanelli), A. John 2 (Llanelli); F.A. Bowdler 1 (Cross Keys), C. Pritchard 1 (Pontypool), H. Phillips 5 (Newport), E.M. Jenkins 4 (Aberavon), A. Skym 1 (Llanelli), Iorwerth Jones 1 (Llanelli), Ivor Jones 6 (Llanelli), T. Hollingdale 1 (Neath).

ENGLAND   K.A. Sellar 4 (US Portsmouth); W.J. Taylor 1 (Blackheath), C.D. Aarvold 1 (Cambridge U.), J.V. Richardson 1 (Birkenhead Park), Sir T.G. Devitt (3) (Blackheath); H.C.C. Laird 4 (Harlequins), A.T. Young 12 (Blackheath); E. Stanbury 8 (Plymouth Albion), J.S. Tucker 14 (Bristol), *R. Cove-Smith 22 (OMT), D. Turquand-Young 1 (Richmond), K.J. Stark 5 (Old Alleynians), T.M. Lawson (1) (Workington), J. Hanley 4 (Plymouth Albion), T.J. Coulson (2) (Coventry).

Referee R.W. Harland (Ireland)

IRELAND v FRANCE   14/281

28 January 1928
Ravenhill, Belfast
Ireland 12 (4T) France 8 (1G, 1T)

Ireland   T: Ganly (2), Arigho (2).
France   T: Ribère, Henri Behotéguy. C: André Behotéguy.

This was Ireland's fourth win in a row at home against France, their longest winning home sequence against their visitors.

'Never mind the ball, get on with the game. . . .' Action during the Wales-England match on 21 January 1928. The well-collared Welsh player is Llanelli scrum-half, Arthur John

IRELAND   W.J. Stewart 3 (NIFC); J.B. Ganly 5 (Monkstown), R.V.M. Odbert (1) (RAF), *G.V. Stephenson 30 (Queen's U. Belfast), J.E. Arigho 1 (Lansdowne); E.O'D. Davy 10 (Lansdowne), M. Sugden 12 (Wanderers); G.R. Beamish 4 (RAF), T. Bramwell (1) (NIFC), J.D. Clinch 13 (Wanderers), J.L. Farrell 9 (Bective Rangers), C.J. Hanrahan 6 (Dolphin), H. McVicker (4) (The Army), C.T. Payne 5 (NIFC), T.O. Pike 4 (Lansdowne).

FRANCE   L. Pellisier 1 (RCF); J. Jardel 1 (S. Bordelais), *A. Behotéguy 8 (US Cognac), H. Behotéguy 2 (US Cognac), F. Raymond (3) (S. Toulouse); A. Verger 3 (S. Français), C. Lacazedieu 3 (US Dax); E. Ribère 12 (US Perpignan), J. Galia 3 (US Quillan), R. Bonamy (1) (S. Bordelais), H. Lacaze 1 (CA Périgueux), A. Camel 2 (S. Toulouse), J. Duhau 1 (S. Français), F. Camicas 2 (S. Tarbes), A. Loury (3) (RCF).

Referee C. Anderson (Scotland)

SCOTLAND v WALES   39/282

4 February 1928
Murrayfield
Wales 13 (2G, 1T) Scotland 0

Wales   T: Albert Jenkins, Dai John, Roberts. C: Male (2).

Wales's first win at Murrayfield, which also ended an eight-match losing sequence against Scotland since 1920. Only in the opening matches with Scotland, 1883–92, when Wales won just once, had they fared worse. From this point onwards it was Scotland who found victories hard to come by.

SCOTLAND   D. Drysdale 22 (London Scottish); J. Goodfellow 1 (Langholm), G.P.S. Macpherson 15 (Edinburgh Acads), R.F. Kelly 2 (Watsonians), W.M. Simmers 9 (Glasgow Acads); H.D. Greenlees 2 (Leicester), P.S. Douty (2) (London Scottish); J.H. Ferguson (1) (Gala), W.N. Roughead 2 (London Scottish), W.G. Ferguson 2 (Royal HSFP), J.W. Scott 14 (Stewart's FP), *J.M. Bannerman 30 (Glasgow HSFP), J. Graham 8 (Kelso), W.B. Welsh 2 (Hawick), J.R. Paterson 14 (Birkenhead Park).

WALES   *B.O. Male 9 (Cardiff); J.D. Bartlett (3) (London Welsh), J. Roberts 6 (Cardiff), A. Jenkins 12 (Llanelli), W.C. Powell 7 (London Welsh); D.E. John 4 (Llanelli), A. John 3 (Llanelli); F.A. Bowdler 2 (Cross Keys), C. Pritchard 2 (Pontypool), H. Phillips 6 (Newport), E.M. Jenkins 5 (Aberavon), A. Skym 2 (Llanelli), Iorwerth Jones 2 (Llanelli), T. Hollingdale 2 (Neath), Ivor Jones 7 (Llanelli).

Referee R.W. Harland (Ireland)

IRELAND v ENGLAND   39/283

11 February 1928
Lansdowne Road, Dublin
England 7 (1T, 1DG) Ireland 6 (2T)

Ireland   T: Arigho, Sugden.
England   T: Richardson. DG: Richardson.

This victory meant that England had won ten and drawn one of the last twelve matches against Ireland, a run which included five wins out of six matches at Lansdowne Road. Ireland could take comfort from the fact that they outscored their visitors in tries and that the match was the hardest, and closest, England endured on their way to winning the Grand Slam. It was the last appearance of Harry Stephenson, who made many important contributions to Irish threequarter play but inevitably was known as 'the other Stephenson' for it was his brother, George, who usually caught the crowd's attention and the headlines.

IRELAND   W.J. Stewart 4 (NIFC); H.W.V. Stephenson (12) (US Portsmouth), J.B. Ganly 6 (Monkstown), *G.V. Stephenson 31 (NIFC), J.E. Arigho 2 (Lansdowne); E.O'D. Davy 11 (Lansdowne), M. Sugden 13 (Wanderers); C.J. Hanrahan 7 (Dolphin), C.T. Payne 6 (NIFC), T.O. Pike 5 (Lansdowne), J.L. Farrell 10 (Bective Rangers), S.J. Cagney 7 (London Irish), W.F. Browne 10 (US Portsmouth), J.D. Clinch 14 (Wanderers), G.R. Beamish 5 (Leicester).

ENGLAND   K.A. Sellar 5 (US Portsmouth); W.J. Taylor 2 (Blackheath), C.D. Aarvold 2 (Cambridge U.), J.V. Richardson 2 (Birkenhead Park), G.V. Palmer 1 (Richmond); H.C.C. Laird 5 (Harlequins), A.T. Young 13 (Blackheath); E. Stanbury 9 (Plymouth Albion), J.S. Tucker 15

(Bristol), R.H.W. Sparks 1 (Plymouth Albion), K.J. Stark 6 (Old Alleynians), *R. Cove-Smith 23 (OMT), J. Hanley 5 (Plymouth Albion), H.G. Periton 10 (Waterloo), F.D. Prentice 1 (Leicester).

Referee A.E. Freethy (Wales)

ENGLAND v FRANCE   14/284

25 February 1928
Twickenham
England 18 (3G, 1T) France 8 (1G, 1T)

England   T: Periton (2), Palmer (2). C: Richardson (3).
France   T: Galia, Jauréguy. C: Verger.

Having lost to Scotland and Ireland, France plunged to defeat at Twickenham, where they were still seeking a first victory. The French were capable of attractive rugby and had the ability to score tries. Their chief problem was defence: they had now conceded 27 tries in 7 matches in England. It proved to be the final Championship match for their most experienced forward, Etienne Piquiral, who had made the first of 14 appearances in 1924.

ENGLAND   K.A. Sellar (6) (US Portsmouth); W.J. Taylor 3 (Blackheath), C.D. Aarvold 3 (Cambridge U.), J.V. Richardson 3 (Birkenhead Park), G.V. Palmer 2 (Richmond); H.C.C. Laird 6 (Harlequins), A.T. Young 14 (Blackheath); E. Stanbury 10 (Plymouth Albion), J.S. Tucker 16 (Bristol), R.H.W. Sparks 2 (Plymouth Albion), K.J. Stark 7 (Old Alleynians), *R. Cove-Smith 24 (OMT), J. Hanley 6 (Plymouth Albion), H.G. Periton 11 (Waterloo), F.D. Prentice 2 (Leicester).

FRANCE   L. Pellissier 2 (RCF); J. Jardel (2) (S. Bordelais), H. Behotéguy 3 (US Cognac), A. Behotéguy 9 (US Cognac), *A. Jauréguy 20 (S. Français); A. Verger 4 (S. Français), L. Serin 1 (AS Béziers); J. Hauc 1 (RC Toulon), F. Camicas 3 (S. Tarbes), J. Sayrou 2 (US Perpignan), J. Galia 4 (US Quillan), A. Camel 3 (S. Toulouse), E. Ribère 13 (US Quillan), A. Bioussa 8 (S. Toulouse), E. Piquiral (14) (FC Lyon).

Referee A.E. Freethy (Wales)

SCOTLAND v IRELAND   41/285

25 February 1928
Murrayfield
Ireland 13 (2G, 1T) Scotland 5 (1G)

Scotland   T: Kerr. C: Drysdale.
Ireland   T: Ganly, Davy, Stephenson. C: Stephenson (2).

The last appearance for Ireland of W.F. 'Horsey' Browne, who became famous for calming his fellow forwards when the going got rough against France in 1927. He died in 1931 aged 28.

SCOTLAND   *D. Drysdale 23 (London Scottish); J. Goodfellow 2 (Langholm), J.W.G. Hume 1 (Oxford U.), J.C. Dykes 16 (Glasgow Acads), W.M. Simmers 10 (Glasgow Acads); H. Lind 1 (Dunfermline), J.B. Nelson 13 (Glasgow Acads); J.W. Allan 2 (Melrose), W.N. Roughead 3 (London Scottish), D.S. Kerr 9 (Heriot's FP), W.G. Ferguson 3 (Royal HSFP), J.M. Bannerman 31 (Glasgow HSFP), J. Graham 9 (Kelso), J.R. Paterson 15 (Birkenhead Park), W.B. Welsh 3 (Hawick).

IRELAND   W.J. Stewart 5 (NIFC); R.M. Byers 1 (NIFC), *G.V. Stephenson 32 (NIFC), J.B. Ganly 7 (Monkstown), A.C. Douglas (4) (Instonians); E.O'D. Davy 12 (Lansdowne), M. Sugden 14 (Wanderers); T.O. Pike 6 (Lansdowne), S.J. Cagney 8 (London Irish), W.F. Browne (11) (US Portsmouth), C.T. Payne 7 (NIFC), C.J. Hanrahan 8 (Dolphin), J.L. Farrell 11 (Bective Rangers), G.R. Beamish 6 (Leicester), J.D. Clinch 15 (Wanderers).

Referee B.S. Cumberlege (England)

WALES v IRELAND   37/286

10 March 1928
Cardiff Arms Park
Ireland 13 (2G, 1T) Wales 10 (2G)

Wales   T: Dai John, Albert Jenkins. C: Ivor Jones (2).
Ireland   T: Arigho (2), Ganly. C: Stephenson (2).

Wales employed seven players from Llanelli but

after a rampaging display by the Irish forwards, four of them, including the captain Albert Jenkins and both half-backs, were axed, never again to play for their country.

WALES   B.O. Male 10 (Cardiff); W.C. Powell 8 (London Welsh), J. Roberts 7 (Cardiff), *A. Jenkins (13) (Llanelli), E. Finch (5) (Llanelli); D.E. John (5) (Llanelli), A. John (4) (Llanelli); H. Phillips 7 (Newport), C. Pritchard 3 (Pontypool), F.A. Bowdler 3 (Cross Keys), E.M. Jenkins 6 (Aberavon), A. Skym 3 (Llanelli), Iorwerth Jones 3 (Llanelli), T. Hollingdale 3 (Neath), Ivor Jones 8 (Llanelli).

IRELAND   W.J. Stewart 6 (NIFC); J.E. Arigho 3 (Lansdowne), J.B. Ganly 8 (Monkstown), *G.V. Stephenson 33 (NIFC), R.M. Byers 2 (NIFC); E.O'D. Davy 13 (Lansdowne), M. Sugden 15 (Wanderers); G.R. Beamish 7 (Leicester), J.L. Farrell 12 (Bective Rangers), J.P. Mullane 1 (Bohemians), J. McVicker 17 (Belfast Collegians), C.T. Payne 8 (NIFC), T.O. Pike (7) (Lansdowne), J.D. Clinch 16 (Wanderers), S.J. Cagney 9 (London Irish).

Referee T.H.H. Warren (Scotland)

ENGLAND v SCOTLAND   38/287

17 March 1928
Twickenham
England 6 (2T) Scotland 0

England   T: Hanley, Laird.

After three successive defeats, England beat Scotland to notch up their sixth Grand Slam. Scotland, Champions in 1927, found themselves bottom of the table. Good though this England side was, six of them never played in another Championship match.

ENGLAND   T.W. Brown 1 (Bristol); W.J. Taylor (4) (Blackheath), C.D. Aarvold 4 (Cambridge U.), J.V. Richardson (4) (Birkenhead Park), G.V. Palmer (3) (Richmond); H.C.C. Laird 7 (Harlequins), A.T. Young 15 (Blackheath); R.H.W. Sparks 3 (Plymouth Albion), J.S. Tucker 17 (Bristol), E. Stanbury 11 (Plymouth Albion), K.J. Stark (8) (Old Alleynians), *R. Cove-Smith 25 (OMT), J. Hanley (7) (Plymouth Albion), H.G. Periton 12 (Waterloo), F.D. Prentice (3) (Leicester).

SCOTLAND   *D. Drysdale 24 (London Scottish); J. Goodfellow (3) (Langholm), G.P.S. Macpherson 16 (Edinburgh Acads), W.M. Simmers 11 (Glasgow Acads), R.F. Kelly (3) (Watsonians); A.H. Brown 1 (Heriot's FP), J.B. Nelson 14 (Glasgow Acads); L.M. Stuart 6 (Glasgow HSFP), W.N. Roughead 4 (London Scottish), D.S. Kerr (10) (Heriot's FP), W.G. Ferguson (4) (Royal HSFP), J.M. Bannerman 32 (Glasgow HSFP), J. Graham 10 (Kelso), J.R. Paterson 16 (Birkenhead Park), J.W. Scott 15 (Stewart's FP).

Referee T.H. Vile (Wales)

FRANCE v WALES   14/288

9 April 1928
Stade Colombes, Paris
France 8 (1G, 1T) Wales 3 (1T)

France   T: Houdet (2). C: André Behotéguy.
Wales   T: Powell.

After beating France in the first 13 Championship matches, Wales lost to them for the first time. For threequarters of the game the French were without André Camel, who had injured his shoulder, so the victory was even more meritorious. Five of the Welsh team, including the captain Ossie Male, never played another Championship match.

FRANCE   L. Pellissier (3) (RCF); *A. Jauréguy 21 (S. Français), A. Behotéguy 10 (US Cognac), H. Behotéguy (4) (US Cognac), R. Houdet 3 (S. Français); A. Verger (5) (S. Français), C. Dupont 9 (S. Bordelais); H. Lacaze 2 (CA Périgueux), F. Camicas 4 (S. Tarbes), J. Sayrou 3 (US Perpignan), R. Majérus 1 (S. Français), A. Camel 4 (S. Toulouse), E. Ribère 14 (US Quillan), A. Bioussa 9 (S. Toulouse), J. Galia 5 (US Quillan).

WALES   *B.O. Male (11) (Cardiff); G. Davies 1 (Cardiff), B.R. Turnbull 5 (Cardiff), R. Jones (1) (Swansea), J. Roberts 8 (Cardiff); W.H. Lewis (5) (Maesteg), W.C. Powell 9 (London Welsh); F.A. Bowdler 4 (Cross Keys), C. Pritchard 4 (Pontypool), H. Phillips (8) (Newport), E.M. Jenkins 7 (Aberavon), A. Skym 4 (Llanelli), Iorwerth Jones (4) (Llanelli), Ivor Jones 9 (Llanelli), T. Hollingdale 4 (Neath).

Referee R.W. Harland (Ireland)

1929

PARIS Ireland beat France 6-0 · TWICKENHAM England beat Wales 8-3
MURRAYFIELD Scotland beat France 6-3 · SWANSEA Wales beat Scotland 14-7
TWICKENHAM Ireland beat England 6-5 · DUBLIN Scotland beat Ireland 16-7
CARDIFF Wales beat France 8-3 · BELFAST Ireland drew Wales 5-5
MURRAYFIELD Scotland beat England 12-6 · PARIS England beat France 16-6

CHAMPIONSHIP TABLE
Scotland – Championship

								Tries	
Pos	Country	P	W	D	L	F	A	Pts	F	A
1	Scotland (5)	4	3	0	1	41	30	6	9	8
2	Wales (3)	4	2	1	1	30	23	5	8	4
3	Ireland (2)	4	2	1	1	24	26	5	6	6
4	England (1)	4	2	0	2	35	27	4	9	9
5	France (4)	4	0	0	4	12	36	0	4	9

For the fifth time in six seasons France ended up with the Wooden Spoon. During that time they had lost 21 out of 24 Championship matches, and though at times they had played very well, they had yet to develop the discipline required for consistent success. In comparison, the thistle was flourishing: Scotland's title was their fourth in five seasons. There were no half-measures with the Scots at that time: generally speaking, they either won the title or finished bottom. Irish rugby was like the curate's egg, and they usually found one side to lose against, which denied them more than one Championship. Welsh rugby historians have tended to glide over the period 1922–30 because there was little to commend in either performance or results. However, 1929 was a better year for the Welsh than most during that period: their runners-up position was their highest placing since their last title win in 1922. England were still playing fairly well, and followed up their 1928 Grand Slam with victories against Wales and France.

The season revealed a further hardening of attitude over articles on the game in the Press. The RFU added committee members to the list of those not allowed to write and be paid for it.

FRANCE v IRELAND   15/289

30 December 1928
Yves du Manoir Stadium, Paris
Ireland 6 (2T) France 0

Ireland   T: Davy, Stephenson.

Ireland scored their sixth Championship win in a row against France, their highest consecutive number of wins against any country. It was also their third successive victory in France, equalling their best ever sequence of 1910–14.

FRANCE   M. Piquemal 3 (S. Tarbes); *A. Jauréguy 22 (S. Français), G. Gérald 3 (RCF), G. Caussarieu (1) (S. Pau), R. Houdet 4 (S. Français); R. Sarrade (1) (S. Pau), C. Dupont (10) (FC Lourdes); A. Bioussa 10 (S. Toulouse), G. Branca 2 (S. Français), B.H. Lacaze 3 (CA Périgueux), F. Camicas 5 (S. Tarbes), J. Hauc 2 (RC Toulon), E. Ribère 5 (US Quillan) J. Galia 6 (US Quillan), R. Majérus 2 (S. Français).

IRELAND   W.J. Stewart 7 (Preston Grasshoppers); J.E. Arigho 4 (Lansdowne), P.F. Murray 2 (Wanderers), *G.V. Stephenson 34 (Queen's U. Belfast), J.B. Ganly 9 (Monkstown); E.O'D. Davy 14 (Lansdowne), M. Sugden 16 (Wanderers); G.R. Beamish 8 (Leicester), S.J. Cagney 10 (London Irish), J.D. Clinch 17 (Wanderers), M.J. Dunne 1 (Lansdowne), J.L. Farrell 13 (Bective Rangers), J.P. Mullane (2) (Limerick Bohemians), C.J. Hanrahan 9 (Dolphin), C.T. Payne 9 (NIFC).

Referee B.S. Cumberlege (England)

ENGLAND v WALES 40/290

19 January 1929
Twickenham
England 8 (IG, 1T) Wales 3 (1T)

England T: Wilkinson (2). C: Wilson.
Wales T: Morley.

England's stranglehold over Wales continued with an eighth successive home victory, which was their longest winning sequence against them.

ENGLAND T.W. Brown 2 (Bristol); R.W. Smeddle 1 (Cambridge U.), C.D. Aarvold 5 (Cambridge U.), G.M. Sladen 1 (US Portsmouth), G.S. Wilson 1 (Tyldesley); H.C.C. Laird 8 (Harlequins), H. Whitley (1) (Northern); E. Stanbury 12 (Plymouth Albion), J.S. Tucker 18 (Bristol), R.T. Foulds 1 (Waterloo), R.H.W. Sparks 4 (Plymouth Albion), *R. Cove-Smith 26 (KCH), H. Wilkinson 1 (Halifax), H.G. Periton 13 (Waterloo), J.W.R. Swayne (1) (Bridgwater Albion).

WALES J. Bassett 1 (Penarth); G. Davies 2 (Cardiff), J. Roberts 9 (Cardiff), W.G. Morgan 3 (Swansea), J.C. Morley 1 (Newport); W. Roberts (1) (Cardiff), W.C. Powell 10 (London Welsh); D.R. Jenkins (1) (Swansea), C. Pritchard 5 (Pontypool), F.A. Bowdler 5 (Cross Keys), T. Arthur 4 (Neath), H. Jones 1 (Neath), R. Jones (1) (London Welsh), *I. Jones 10 (Llanelli), W. Thomas 5 (Swansea).

Referee R.W. Harland (Ireland)

SCOTLAND v FRANCE 14/291

19 January 1929
Murrayfield
Scotland 6 (1T, 1PG) France 3 (1T)

Scotland T: Paterson. PG: Brown.
France T: Behotéguy.

This was Scotland's fifth win in a row against France, their best ever winning sequence against them. The French team wore numbered jerseys – but it was of little use to spectators because the match programme did not record the fact. Dan Drysdale, an outstanding full-back and then 27, made his twenty-fifth and final appearance for Scotland.

SCOTLAND *D. Drysdale (25) (London Scottish); I.S. Smith 15 (Edinburgh U.), G.G. Aitken (8) (London Scottish), J.C. Dykes 17 (Glasgow Acads), W.M. Simmers 12 (Glasgow Acads); A.H. Brown 2 (Heriot's FP), J.B. Nelson 15 (Glasgow Acads); J.W. Allan 3 (Melrose), H.S. Mackintosh 1 (W. of Scotland), R.T. Smith 1 (Kelso), J.A. Beattie 1 (Hawick), J.M. Bannerman 33 (Glasgow HSFP), K.M. Wright 1 (London Scottish), J.R. Paterson 17 (Birkenhead Park), W.V. Berkley 2 (London Scottish).

FRANCE M. Magnol 2 (S. Toulouse); *A. Jauréguy 23 (S. Français), A. Behotéguy 11 (US Cognac), G. Gérald 4 (RCF), R. Houdet 5 (S. Français); C. Magnanou 5 (A. Bayonne), C. Lacazedieu (4) (US Dax); J. Hauc (3) (RC Toulon), F. Camicas 6 (S. Tarbes), J. Sayrou 4 (US Perpignan), A. Camel 5 (S. Toulouse), R. Majérus 3 (S. Français), A. Bioussa 11 (S. Toulouse), J. Augé 1 (US Dax), G. Branca (3) (S. Français).

Referee B.S. Cumberlege (England)

WALES v SCOTLAND 40/292

2 February 1929
St Helen's, Swansea
Wales 14 (1G, 3T) Scotland 7 (1DG, 1PG)

Wales T: Roberts (2), Morgan, Peacock. C: Ivor Jones.
Scotland DG: Dykes. PG: Brown.

Although beaten by England in the opening match of the season, Wales gave a far better performance against Scotland, a defeat which denied the latter the Grand Slam for a second time in their history. The Scots had won on their previous four visits to Wales.

WALES J. Bassett 2 (Penarth); J. Roberts 10 (Cardiff), H.M. Bowcott 1 (Cardiff), *W.G. Morgan 4 (Swansea), J.C. Morley 2 (Newport); F.L. Williams 1 (Cardiff), W.C. Powell 11 (London Welsh); F.A. Bowdler 6 (Cross Keys), C. Pritchard 6 (Pontypool), R. Barrell 1 (Cardiff), T. Arthur 5 (Neath), H. Jones (2) (Neath), H. Peacock 1 (Newport), A.E. Broughton (1) (Treorchy), I. Jones 11 (Llanelli).

SCOTLAND   T.G. Aitchison 1 (Edinburgh U.); I.S. Smith 16 (Edinburgh U.), J.C. Dykes 18 (Glasgow Acads), W.M. Simmers 13 (Glasgow Acads), T.G. Brown (1) (Heriot's FP); A.H. Brown (3) (Heriot's FP), J.B. Nelson 16 (Glasgow Acads); J.W. Allan 4 (Melrose), H.S. Mackintosh 2 (Glasgow U.), R.T. Smith 2 (Kelso), J.A. Beattie 2 (Hawick), *J.M. Bannerman 34 (Glasgow HSFP), K.M. Wright 2 (London Scottish), W.V. Berkley 3 (London Scottish), J.R. Paterson 18 (Birkenhead Park).

Referee D. Helliwell (England)

ENGLAND v IRELAND   40/293

9 February 1929
Twickenham
Ireland 6 (2T) England 5 (1G)

England   T: Smeddle. C: Wilson.
Ireland   T: Davy, Sugden.

This was Ireland's first victory in England since 1906 and their first at Twickenham. As in so many England-Ireland clashes of the period, supremacy was fought for fiercely, the margin was usually close, and the winning side required either luck or great skill. The latter was the case this time, for Mark Sugden, that 'wee leprechaun' of a scrum-half, broke intuitively to the blind-side of a scrum near the English line and with, as Sean Diffley described it, 'a veritable Donnybrook Fair of dummies', jinked over for the winning try.

ENGLAND   T.W. Brown 3 (Bristol); R.W. Smeddle 2 (Cambridge U), C.D. Aarvold 6 (Cambridge U.), G.M. Sladen 2 (US Portsmouth), G.S. Wilson (2) (Tyldesley); H.C.C. Laird (9) (Harlequins), A.T. Young (16) (Blackheath); E. Stanbury 13 (Plymouth Albion), J.S. Tucker 19 (Bristol), R.H.W. Sparks 5 (Plymouth Albion), D. Turquand-Young 2 (Richmond), *R. Cove-Smith (27) (KCH), H. Wilkinson 2 (Halifax), H.G. Periton 14 (Waterloo), R.T. Foulds (2) (Waterloo).

IRELAND   W.J. Stewart 8 (Preston Grasshoppers); R.M. Byers 3 (NIFC), P.F. Murray 3 (Wanderers), *G.V. Stephenson 35 (NIFC), J.E. Arigho 5 (Lansdowne); E.O'D. Davy 15 (Lansdowne), M. Sugden 17 (Wanderers); C.J. Hanrahan 10 (Dolphin), H.C. Browne 1 (US Portsmouth), S.J. Cagney 11 (London Irish), J.L. Farrell 14 (Bective Rangers), M.J. Dunne 2 (Lansdowne), C.T. Payne 10 (NIFC), J.D. Clinch 18 (Wanderers), G.R. Beamish 9 (Leicester).

Referee   A.E. Freethy (Wales)

IRELAND v SCOTLAND   42/294

23 February 1929
Lansdowne Road, Dublin
Scotland 16 (2G, 2T) Ireland 7 (1T, 1DG)

Ireland   T: Arigho. DG: Davy.
Scotland   T: Macpherson, Bannerman, Ian Smith, Simmers. C: Dykes, Allan.

Having beaten France and England, Ireland had high hopes of another victory to put them at the top of the table. The interest in the same swelled Lansdowne Road to capacity and over 40,000 crammed in to see the game, which caused concern because of overspilling onto the in-goal area. Barry Cumberlege had problems in deciding whether players had actually grounded for tries among the spectators. In the event, Scotland's pack dominated and there was no dispute as to the merit of their victory, their third in four visits to Lansdowne Road.

IRELAND   W.J. Stewart 9 (Preston Grasshoppers); R.M. Byers 4 (NIFC), P.F. Murray 4 (Wanderers), J.B. Ganly 10 (Monkstown), J.E. Arigho 6 (Lansdowne); *E.O'D. Davy 16 (Lansdowne), M. Sugden 18 (Wanderers); G.R. Beamish 10 (Leicester), H.C. Browne 2 (US Portsmouth), S.J. Cagney 12 (London Irish), J.D. Clinch 19 (Wanderers), M.J. Dunne 3 (Lansdowne), J.L. Farrell 15 (Bective Rangers), J.S. Synge (1) (Lansdowne), C.J. Hanrahan 11 (Dolphin).

SCOTLAND   T.G. Aitchison 2 (Gala); I.S. Smith 17 (Edinburgh U), G.P.S. Macpherson 17 (Edinburgh Acads), J.C. Dykes (19) (Glasgow Acads), W.M. Simmers 14 (Glasgow Acads); H.D. Greenlees 3 (Leicester), J.B. Nelson 17 (Glasgow Acads); R.T. Smith 3 (Kelso), H.S. Mackintosh 3 (Glasgow U.), J.W. Allan 5 (Melrose), W.V. Berkley (4) (London Scottish), *J.M. Bannerman 35 (Oxford U.), J.R. Paterson 19 (Birkenhead Park), W.B. Welsh 4 (Hawick), K.M. Wright 3 (London Scottish).

Referee B.S. Cumberlege (England)

WALES v FRANCE 15/295

25 February 1929
Cardiff Arms Park
Wales 8 (1G, 1T) France 3 (1T)

Wales T: Arthur, Barrell. C: Parker.
France T: André Camel

Louis Magnol, the Toulouse full-back, performed so many heroic feats in defence that at the end of the match spectators carried him, shoulder-high, from the pitch. The quality of the French tackling meant that for the first time Wales failed to score double figures against France in Wales.

WALES J. Bassett 3 (Penarth); J. Roberts 11 (Cardiff), H.M. Bowcott 2 (Cardiff), *W.G. Morgan 5 (Swansea), J.C. Morley 3 (Newport); F.L. Williams 2 (Cardiff), W.C. Powell 12 (London Welsh); R. Barrell 2 (Cardiff), C. Pritchard 7 (Pontypool), T. Arthur 6 (Neath), F.A. Bowdler 7 (Cross Keys), E.M. Jenkins 8 (Aberavon), D. Parker 7 (Swansea), I. Jones 12 (Llanelli), H. Peacock 2 (Newport).

FRANCE M. Magnol 3 (S. Toulouse); A. Domec (1) (S. Toulouse), *A. Behotéguy 12 (US Cognac), G. Gérald 5 (RCF), C. Dulaurans (3) (S. Toulouse);

C. Magnanou 6 (A. Bayonne), L. Serin 2 (AS Béziers); A. Camel 6 (S. Toulouse), R. Bousquet 5 (RC Toulon), J. Sayrou 5 (US Perpignan), M. Camel 1 (S. Toulouse), H. Lacaze (4) (CA Périgueux), A. Bioussa 12 (S. Toulouse), F. Camicas 7 (S. Tarbes), J. Augé (2) (US Dax).

Referee H.E.B. Wilkins (England)

IRELAND v WALES 38/296

9 March 1929
Ravenhill, Belfast
Ireland 5 (1G) Wales 5 (1G)

Ireland T: Davy. C: Stephenson.
Wales T: Williams. C: Parker.

This was the first draw between the sides since 1890. Ireland had now extended their unbeaten home run against Wales to four matches, one fewer than their best ever sequence of 1888–96. The result, in effect, left the Championship open to Scotland, to pip Wales and Ireland for the title.

IRELAND W.J. Stewart (10) (Preston Grasshoppers); R.M. Byers (5) (NIFC), *G.V. Stephenson 36 (NIFC), M.P. Crowe 1 (Lansdowne), J.E. Arigho 7 (Lansdowne); E.O'D. Davy 17

The English XV which Scotland defeated 12-6 at Murrayfield on 16 March 1929 to clinch the Championship

(Lansdowne), M. Sugden 19 (Wanderers); H.C. Browne (3) (US Portsmouth), C.T. Payne 11 (NIFC), J.L. Farrell 16 (Bective Rangers), M. Deering (1) (Bective Rangers), C.J. Hanrahan 12 (Dolphin), S.J. Cagney (13) (London Irish), J.D. Clinch 20 (Wanderers), G.R. Beamish 11 (Leicester).

WALES   J. Bassett 4 (Penarth); J. Roberts (12) (Cardiff), H.M. Bowcott 3 (Cardiff), *W.G. Morgan 6 (Swansea), J.C. Morley 4 (Newport); F.L. Williams 3 (Cardiff), W.C. Powell 13 (London Welsh); F.A. Bowdler 8 (Cross Keys), C. Pritchard (8) (Pontypool), D. Parker 8 (Swansea), T. Arthur 7 (Neath), R. Barrell 3 (Cardiff), H. Peacock 3 (Newport), A. Lemon 1 (Neath), I. Jones 13 (Llanelli).

Referee J. McGill (Scotland)

ENGLAND v SCOTLAND   39/297

16 March 1929
Murrayfield
Scotland 12 (4T) England 6 (2T)

Scotland   T: Ian Smith (2), Brown, Nelson.
England   T: Meikle, Novis.

A brace of tries by the high-scoring Ian Smith set the seal on Scotland winning the Championship, but it was the Scottish forwards, with a storming finish, who deserved the plaudits. It was a poignant end to the career of Lord Bannerman, who had been one of the mainstays of the Scottish pack since 1921. Although described as a veteran, Lord Bannerman was just 27 when he played his thirty-sixth and final match. The attendance was in excess of 80,000.

SCOTLAND   T.G. Aitchison (3) (Gala); I.S. Smith 18 (Edinburgh U.), G.P.S. Macpherson 18 (Edinburgh Acads), W.M. Simmers 15 (Glasgow Acads), C.H.C. Brown (1) (Dunfermline); H.D. Greenlees 4 (Leicester), J.B. Nelson 18 (Glasgow Acads); R.T. Smith 4 (Kelso), H.S. Mackintosh 4 (Glasgow U.), J.W. Allan 6 (Melrose), J.W. Scott 16 (Bradford), *J.M. Bannerman (36) (Oxford U.), J.R. Paterson (20) (Birkenhead Park), W.B. Welsh 5 (Hawick), K.M. Wright (4) (London Scottish).

ENGLAND   T.W. Brown 4 (Bristol); R.W. Smeddle 3 (Cambridge U.), A.R. Aslett 5 (Rich-

mond), G.M. Sladen (3) (US Portsmouth), A.L. Novis 1 (The Army); S.S.C. Meikle (1) (Waterloo), E.E. Richards 1 (Plymouth Albion); E. Stanbury 14 (Plymouth Albion), R.H.W. Sparks 6 (Plymouth Albion), J.W.G. Webb (3) (Northampton), T.W. Harris 1 (Northampton), H. Rew 1 (The Army), H. Wilkinson 3 (Halifax), *H.G. Periton 15 (Waterloo), D. Turquand-Young 3 (Richmond).

Referee Dr J.R. Wheeler (Ireland)

FRANCE v ENGLAND   15/298

1 April 1929
Stade Colombes, Paris
England 16 (2G, 2T) France 6 (2T)

France   T: Houdet, Ribère.
England   T: Aarvold (2), Gummer, Periton. C: Stanbury (2).

England, who had lost to France for the first time on their previous visit there in 1927, fashioned four tries and a convincing victory. France were thus condemned to Wooden Spoon status once again, and all the evidence suggests that this was one of their poorest teams since entering the Championship in 1910.

FRANCE   M. Magnol (4) (S. Toulouse); *A. Jauréguy (24) (S. Français), A. Behotéguy 13 (US Cognac), G. Gérald 6 (RCF), R. Houdet 6 (S. Français); R. Graciet (4) (S. Bordelais), L. Serin 3 (AS Béziers); J. Sayrou (6) (US Perpignan), F. Camicas (8) (S. Tarbes), R. Bousquet 6 (SC Albi), A. Camel 7 (S. Toulouse), J. Galia 7 (US Quillan), A. Bioussa 13 (S. Toulouse), E. Ribère 16 (US Quillan), M. Camel (2) (S. Toulouse).

ENGLAND   T.W. Brown 5 (Bristol); C.D. Aarvold 7 (Headingley), A.R. Aslett (6) (Richmond), A. L. Novis 2 (Blackheath), J.S.R. Reeve 1 (Harlequins); R.S. Spong 1 (Old Millhillians), E.E. Richards (2) (Plymouth Albion); E. Stanbury (15) (Plymouth Albion), J.S. Tucker 20 (Bristol), H. Rew 2 (Blackheath), S.A. Martindale (1) (Kendal), D. Turquand-Young (4) (Richmond), *H.G. Periton 16 (Waterloo), E. Coley 1 (Northampton), C.H.A. Gummer (1) (Plymouth Albion).

Referee A.E. Freethy (Wales)

1930

PARIS France beat Scotland 7-3 · CARDIFF England beat Wales 11-3
BELFAST France beat Ireland 5-0 · MURRAYFIELD Scotland beat Wales 12-9
DUBLIN Ireland beat England 4-3 · TWICKENHAM England beat France 11-5
MURRAYFIELD Ireland beat Scotland 14-11 · SWANSEA Wales beat Ireland 12-7
TWICKENHAM England drew Scotland 0-0 · PARIS Wales beat France 11-0

CHAMPIONSHIP TABLE
England – Championship

									Tries	
Pos	Country	P	W	D	L	F	A	Pts	F	A
1	England (4)	4	2	1	1	25	12	5	6	2
2	Wales (2)	4	2	0	2	35	30	4	6	4
3	Ireland (3)	4	2	0	2	25	31	4	4	8
4	France (5)	4	2	0	2	17	25	4	3	5
5	Scotland (1)	4	1	1	2	26	30	3	6	6

The most far-reaching event of 1930 was the decision that all matches would now be played under the Laws as framed and altered by the International Board. However, the Board conspicuously ignored protests from some areas that near-foot hooking was contrary to the Laws.

The Championship got off to an exciting, stimulating start with France winning their first two matches against Scotland and Ireland, and then running out of steam. The French had not won two matches since 1921, but Le Coq's crowing was muted after they were beaten at Twickenham and by Wales in Paris. England ultimately won the title, but with only two points separating the top from the bottom side, Scotland, it was a close-run thing. That the Championship was one of the closest ever probably explained the poor returns in terms of tries and points-scoring. The number of tries, 25, and the total of points, 128, were the lowest since the tournament had become a Five-Nation affair in 1910 and substantially reduced the averages for a period which was otherwise rich in tries and points.

FRANCE v SCOTLAND   15/299

1 January 1930
Stade Colombes, Paris
France 7 (1T, 1DG) Scotland 3 (1T)

France   T: Bioussa. DG: Magnanou.
Scotland   T: Simmers.

Scotland were bidding to win a third match in a row in France but had to give second best to outstanding loose forward play. Eugene Ribère was particularly effective and the French captain received able support from André Camel and Alex Bioussa, who scored the French try. In the Scottish team, F.H. Waters made his début appearance 26 years after his father, J.B. Waters, played twice for Scotland. J.W. Scott, a top-class scrummaging forward since 1925, made his seventeenth and final appearance.

FRANCE   M. Piquemal 4 (S. Tarbes); R. Samatan 1 (SU Agen), M. Baillette 6 (US Quillan), G. Gérald 7 (RCF), R. Houdet 7 (S. Français); C. Magnanou 7 (A. Bayonne), L. Serin 4 (AS Béziers); A. Ambert 1 (S. Toulouse), C. Bigot 1 (US Quillan), J. Choy 1 (RC Narbonne), R. Majérus 4 (S. Français), A. Camel 8 (TOEC), *E. Ribère 17 (US Quillan), A. Bioussa 14 (S. Toulouse), J. Galia 8 (US Quillan).

SCOTLAND   R.W. Langrish 1 (London Scottish); I.S. Smith 19 (London Scottish), *G.P.S. Macpherson 19 (Edinburgh Acads), J.W.G. Hume (2) (Edinburgh Wands), W.M. Simmers 16 (Glasgow Acads); W.D. Emslie 1 (Royal HSFP), J.B. Nelson 19 (Glasgow Acads); J.W. Allan 7 (Melrose), H.S. Mackintosh 5 (Glasgow U.), R.T. Smith 5 (Kelso), J.W. Scott (17) (Waterloo), J.

Stewart (1) (Glasgow HSFP), W.B. Welsh 6 (Hawick), F.H. Waters 1 (Cambridge U.), R. Rowand 1 (Glasgow HSFP).

Referee D. Helliwell (England)

WALES v ENGLAND   41/300

18 January 1930
Cardiff Arms Park
England 11 (1G, 1T, 1PG) Wales 3 (1T)

Wales   T: Jones-Davies.
England   T: Reeve (2). C: Black. PG: Black.

The withdrawal of the Exeter hooker, Henry Rew, on the morning of the match meant that England had to fly Sam Tucker over from Bristol. Tucker arrived at the ground minutes before the start of the match, and played so well that he kept his place for the three remaining Championship matches, actually captaining England against France and Scotland, with Rew returning, as Tucker's prop, in both matches. England's victory was their fourth in succession over Wales, which matched their best sequence of 1883–85. Equally significant, it was England's third win in four visits to Wales. Thirteen players, nine Englishmen, four Welsh, made their first international appearances.

WALES   J. Bassett 5 (Penarth); J.C. Morley 5 (Newport), *H.M. Bowcott 4 (Cardiff), T.E. Jones-Davies 1 (London Welsh), A. Hickman 1 (Neath); F.L. Williams 4 (Cardiff), D.E.A. Roberts (1) (London Welsh); T. Arthur 8 (Neath), F.A. Bowdler 9 (Cross Keys), A. Skym 5 (Cardiff), D. Parker (9) (Swansea), E.M. Jenkins 9 (Aberavon), W.T. Thomas (1) (Abertillery), I. Jones 14 (Llanelli), T. Hollingdale (5) (Neath).

ENGLAND   J.G. Askew 1 (Cambridge U.); A.L. Novis 3 (Blackheath), F.W.S. Malir 1 (Otley), M. Robson 1 (Oxford U.), J.S.R. Reeve 2 (Harlequins); R.S. Spong 2 (Old Millhillians), W. H. Sobey 1 (Old Millhillians); D.A. Kendrew 1 (Woodford), J.S. Tucker 21 (Bristol), A.H. Bateson 1 (Otley), B.H. Black 1 (Oxford U.), J.W. Forrest 1 (US Portsmouth), W.E. Tucker 2 (Blackheath), *H.G. Periton 17 (Waterloo), P.D. Howard 1 (Oxford U.).

Referee R.W. Jeffares (Ireland)

IRELAND v FRANCE   16/301

25 January 1930
Ravenhill, Belfast
France 5 (1G) Ireland 0

France   T. Samatan. C: Ambert.

The first time Ireland failed to score against France – and also the only time they did not score against the French in any home match. It was the eleventh and final Champtionship appearance of Jim Ganly, the little Monkstown wing, who was best known as scorer of one of Ireland's two tries in the famous match against Scotland in 1927.

IRELAND   E.W.F. de Vere Hunt 1 (The Army); J.B. Ganly (11) (Monkstown), *G.V. Stephenson 37 (Queen's U. Belfast), P.F. Murray 5 (Wanderers), J.E. Arigho 8 (Lansdowne); E.O'D. Davy 18 (Lansdowne), M. Sugden 20 (Wanderers), G.R. Beamish 12 (Leicester), M.J. Dunne 4 (Lansdowne), C. Carroll (1) (Bective Rangers), C.T. Payne 12 (NIFC), C.J. Hanrahan 13 (Dolphin), J. L. Farrell 17 (Bective Rangers), J. McVicker (18) (Belfast Collegians), J.D. Clinch 21 (Wanderers).

FRANCE   M. Piquemal 5 (S. Tarbes); R. Samatan 2 (SU Agen), M. Baillette 7 (US Quillan), G. Gérald 8 (RCF), J. Taillantou 1 (S. Pau), C. Magnanou 8 (A. Bayonne), L. Serin 5 (AS Béziers); A. Ambert 2 (S. Toulouse), J. Duhau 2 (SA Bordeaux), J. Choy 2 (RC Narbonne), A. Camel 9 (TOEC), R. Majérus 5 (S. Français), *E. Ribère 18 (US Quillan), A. Bioussa 15 (S. Toulouse), J. Galia 9 (US Quillan).

Referee B.S. Cumberlege (England)

SCOTLAND v WALES   41/302

1 February 1930
Murrayfield
Scotland 12 (1G, 1T, 1DG) Wales 9 (1G, 1DG)

Scotland   T: Simmers (2). C: Waters. DG: Waddell.
Wales   T: Graham Jones. C: Ivor Jones. DG: Graham Jones.

Over 60,000 spectators, the largest pre-war crowd at a Championship match, watched Herbert Waddell win the match for Scotland with a last-minute dropped goal. It was, coincidentally, the last appearance for Waddell and the Welsh captain, Ivor Jones. Each had made 15 Championship appearances. It was an auspicious day too for R.C. Warren, the Glasgow Academicals full-back; he returned to the Scottish side eight years after earning his previous cap.

SCOTLAND   R.C. Warren 3 (Glasgow Acads); I.S. Smith 20 (London Scottish), *G.P.S. Macpherson 20 (Edinburgh Acads), T.M. Hart 1 (Glasgow U.), W.M. Simmers 17 (Glasgow Acads); H. Waddell (15) (Glasgow Acads), J.B. Nelson 20 (Glasgow Acads); R.T. Smith 6 (Kelso), H.S. Mackintosh 6 (Glasgow Acads), R.A. Foster 1 (Hawick), J.A. Beattie 3 (Hawick), F.H. Waters 2 (London Scottish), W.C.C. Agnew 1 (Stewart's FP), R. Rowand 2 (Glasgow HSFP), W.B. Welsh 7 (Hawick).

WALES   J. Bassett 6 (Penarth); G. Davies (3) (Cardiff), B.R. Turnbull (6) (Cardiff), G. Jones 1 (Cardiff), R.W. Boon 1 (Cardiff); F.L. Williams 5 (Cardiff), W.C. Powell 14 (London Welsh); T. Arthur 9 (Neath), H.C. Day 1 (Newport), E.M. Jenkins 10 (Aberavon), A. Skym 6 (Cardiff), D. Thomas 1 (Swansea), A. Lemon 2 (Neath), H. Peacock 4 (Newport), *I. Jones (15) (Llanelli).

Referee Dr J.R. Wheeler (Ireland)

IRELAND v ENGLAND   41/303

8 February 1930
Lansdowne Road, Dublin
Ireland 4 (1DG) England 3 (1T)

Ireland   DG: Murray.
England   T: Novis.

Having won at Cardiff the previous month, England travelled to Dublin with understandable confidence. But the Irish pack gave a storming performance, which coupled with fine tackling by their backs and a dropped goal from Paul Murray, produced England's only defeat of the season.

IRELAND   F.W. Williamson 1 (Dolphin); *G.V. Stephenson 38 (The London H.), E.O'D. Davy 19 (Lansdowne), M.P. Crowe 2 (Lansdowne), J.E. Arigho 9 (Lansdowne); P.F. Murray 6 (Wanderers), M. Sugden 21 (Wanderers); H.O'H. O'Neill 1 (Queen's U. Belfast), C.J. Hanrahan 14 (Dolphin), C.T. Payne 13 (NIFC), M.J. Dunne 5 (Lansdowne), J.L. Farrell 18 (Bective Rangers), N.F. Murphy 1 (Cork Constitution), J.D. Clinch 22 (Wanderers), W.J. McCormick (1) (Wanderers).

ENGLAND   J.G. Askew 2 (Cambridge U.); A.L. Novis 4 (Blackheath), F.W.S. Malir 2 (Otley), M. Robson 2 (Oxford U.), J.S.R. Reeve 3 (Harlequins); R.S. Spong 3 (Old Millhillians), A. Key 1 (Old Cranleighans); D.A. Kendrew 2 (Woodford), J.S. Tucker 22 (Bristol), A.H. Bateson 2 (Otley), B.H. Black 2 (Oxford U.), J.W. Forrest 2 (US Portsmouth), W.E. Tucker (3) (Blackheath), *H.G. Periton 18 (Waterloo), P.D. Howard 2 (Old Millhillians).

Referee A.E. Freethy (Wales)

ENGLAND v FRANCE   16/304

22 February 1930
Twickenham
England 11 (1G, 2T) France 5 (1G)

England   T: Periton, Reeve, Robson. C: Black.
France   T: Serin. C: Ambert.

France had shown marked improvement on the previous poor season by starting their 1930 Championship campaign with victories over Scotland and Ireland. The Twickenham bogey still applied, however, and although they opened the scoring, their title hopes dissolved under sustained pressure from a resourceful, hard-working English pack, inspiringly led for the first time by the Bristol hooker, Sam Tucker.

ENGLAND   J.G. Askew (3) (Cambridge U.); J.S.R. Reeve 4 (Harlequins), A.L. Novis 5 (Blackheath), M. Robson 3 (Oxford U.), H.P. Jacob (5) (Blackheath); R.S. Spong 4 (Old Millhillians), W.H. Sobey 2 (Old Millhillians); H. Rew 3 (Exeter), *J.S. Tucker 23 (Bristol), A.H. Bateson 3 (Otley), J.W. Forrest 3 (US Portsmouth), B.H. Black 3 (Oxford U.), H. Wilkinson (4) (Halifax), H.G. Periton 19 (Waterloo), P.D. Howard 3 (Old Millhillians).

FRANCE   M. Piquemal 6 (S. Tarbes); R. Houdet (8) (S. Français), G. Gérald 9 (RCF), M. Baillette 8 (US Quillan), R. Samatan 3 (SU Agen); C. Magnanou 9 (A. Bayonne), L. Serin 6 (AS Béziers); A. Ambert 3 (S. Toulouse), C. Bigot 2 (US Quillan), J. Choy 3 (RC Narbonne), R. Majérus 6 (S. Français), A. Camel 10 (S. Toulouse), *E. Ribère 19 (US Quillan), A. Bioussa 16 (S. Toulouse), J. Galia 10 (US Quillan).

Referee A.E. Freethy (Wales)

SCOTLAND v IRELAND   43/305

22 February 1930
Murrayfield
Ireland 14 (1G, 3T) Scotland 11 (1G, 2T)

Scotland   T: Ford, Macpherson, Waters. C: Waters.
Ireland   T: Davy (3), Crowe. C: Murray.

Eugene O'D. Davy scored three first-half tries to equal the Irish individual try record established by J.P. Quinn against France in 1913 and by R. Montgomery against Wales in 1887.

SCOTLAND   R.C. Warren 4 (Glasgow Acads); I.S. Smith 21 (London Scottish), *G.P.S. Macpherson 21 (Edinburgh Acads), W.M. Simmers 18 (Glasgow Acads), D.St C. Ford 1 (US Portsmouth); T.M. Hart (2) (Glasgow U.), J.B. Nelson 21 (Glasgow Acads); H.S. Mackintosh 7 (Glasgow U.), W.N. Roughead 5 (London Scottish), R.T. Smith (7) (Kelso), W.C.C. Agnew (2) (Stewart's FP), L.M. Stuart 7 (Glasgow HSFP), W.B. Welsh 8 (Hawick), F.H. Waters 3 (London Scottish), J. Graham 11 (Kelso).

IRELAND   F.W. Williamson 2 (Dolphin); J.E. Arigho 10 (Lansdowne), M.P. Crowe 3 (Lansdowne), E.O'D. Davy 20 (Lansdowne), *G.V. Stephenson 39 (The London H.); P.F. Murray 7 (Wanderers), M. Sugden 22 (Wanderers); H.O'H. O'Neill 2 (Queen's U. Belfast), T.C. Casey 1 (Young Munster), C.J. Hanrahan 15 (Dolphin), C.T. Payne 14 (NIFC), M.J. Dunne 6 (Lansdowne), J.L. Farrell 19 (Bective Rangers), G.R. Beamish 13 (Leicester), J. D. Clinch 23 (Dublin U.).

Referee B.S. Cumberlege (England)

WALES v IRELAND   39/306

8 March 1930
St Helen's, Swansea
Wales 12 (3T, 1PG) Ireland 7 (1DG, 1PG)

Wales   T: Skym, Arthur, Jones/Peacock jointly. PG: Bassett.
Ireland   DG: Davy. PG: Murray.

It was not the first time that Ireland had the prize of the Triple Crown snatched from them by Wales, who showed vastly improved form after losing to England and Scotland. No one was more disappointed than George Stephenson, Ireland's captain and the Championship's most capped player, who was making his fortieth and final appearance. First capped in 1920, against France, Stephenson had played in an Ireland side which had finished bottom of the table four seasons in a row (1920–23) and had then become a prominent figure in their rise to challenge the title during the next seven seasons. But the luck was against the Irish, and Stephenson – Ireland did not once win the Championship or the Triple Crown.

WALES   *J. Bassett 7 (Penarth); J.C. Morley 6 (Newport), T.E. Jones-Davies 2 (London Welsh), W.G. Morgan 7 (Guy's H.), H. Jones 1 (Swansea); F.L. Williams 6 (Cardiff), W.C. Powell 15 (London Welsh); T. Arthur 10 (Neath), H.C. Day 2 (Newport), E.M. Jenkins 11 (Aberavon), A. Skym 7 (Cardiff), D. Thomas 2 (Swansea), A. Lemon 3 (Neath), H. Peacock 5 (Newport), N. Fender 1 (Cardiff).

IRELAND   F.W. Williamson (3) (Dolphin); *G.V. Stephenson (40) (The London H.), E.O'D. Davy 21 (Lansdowne), M.P. Crowe 4 (Lansdowne), J.E. Arigho 11 (Lansdowne); P.F. Murray 8 (Wanderers), M. Sugden 23 (Wanderers); H.O'H. O'Neill 3 (Queen's U. Belfast), C.J. Hanrahan 16 (Dolphin), C.T. Payne (15) (NIFC), M.J. Dunne 7 (Lansdowne), J.L. Farrell 20 (Bective Rangers), N.F. Murphy 2 (Cork Constitution), J.D. Clinch 24 (Wanderers), G.R. Beamish 14 (Leicester).

Referee D. Helliwell (England)

ENGLAND v SCOTLAND   40/307

15 March 1930
Twickenham
England 0 Scotland 0

In one of the most closely contested matches in the history of the Championship, this 0-0 draw was sufficient to win England the title. It was only the second time in 21 matches that England had failed to register a point against Scotland, whose eight most recent visits to Twickenham had given them one victory only. The England side was very young and inexperienced. One of three new caps was J.C. Hubbard, whose father, G.C. Hubbard, played twice for England in 1892.

ENGLAND   J.C. Hubbard (1) (Harlequins); C.C. Tanner 1 (Gloucester), M. Robson (4) (Oxford U.) F.W.S. Malir (3) (Otley), J.S.R. Reeve 5 (Harlequins); R.S. Spong 5 (Old Millhillians), W.H. Sobey 3 (Old Millhillians); H. Rew 4 (Exeter), *J.S. Tucker 24 (Bristol), A.H. Bateson (4) (Otley), J.W. Forrest 4 (US Portsmouth), B.H. Black 4 (Oxford U.), H.G. Periton (20) (Waterloo), P.W.P. Brook 1 (Cambridge U.), P.D. Howard 4 (Old Millhillians).

SCOTLAND   R.C. Warren (5) (Glasgow Acads); W.M. Simmers 19 (Glasgow Acads), *G.P.S. Macpherson 22 (Edinburgh Acads), J.E. Hutton 1 (Harlequins), D.St C. Ford 2 (US Portsmouth); H.D. Greenlees (5) (Leicester), J.B. Nelson 22 (Glasgow Acads); H.S. Mackintosh 8 (W. of Scotland), W. N. Roughead 6 (London Scottish), J.W. Allan 8 (Melrose), W.B. Welsh 9 (Hawick), L.M. Stuart (8) (Glasgow HSFP), A. H. Polson (1) (Gala), F.H. Waters 4 (London Scottish), J. Graham 12 (Kelso).

Referee R.W. Jeffares (Ireland)

FRANCE v WALES   16/308

21 April 1930
Stade Colombes, Paris
Wales 11 (1T, 2DG) France 0

Wales   T: Skym. DG: Morgan, Powell.

With victories over Scotland and Ireland in the bag, France faced Wales in an unprecedented position of being able to win the Championship. The proximity of the prize dictated France's game, which was punctuated with brutal fist and boot exchanges the like of which had rarely been seen in the Championship. One Welsh player, Hubert Day, needed nine stitches after being punched in the mouth. On another occasion, Cyril Rutherford, the highly-respected secretary of the French Rugby Federation, ran on to the field to point out to the referee, D. Helliwell, that a French player had provoked an incident which led to a Welsh player retaliating with his fist. French officials were so upset by this and other incidents that they formally reprimanded several players; and one of their forwards was told he would never play internationally again. In the event, nine of the French team were not chosen again.

FRANCE   L. Piquemal (7) (S. Tarbes); J. Taillantou (2) (S. Pau), G. Gérald 10 (RCF), A. Behotéguy (14) (US Cognac), R. Samatan 4 (SU Agen); C. Magnanou (10) (A. Bayonne), L. Serin 7 (AS Béziers); J. Choy 4 (RC Narbonne), A. Ambert (4) (S. Toulouse), R. Bousquet (7) (SC Albi), R. Majérus (7) (S. Français), A. Camel (11) (S. Toulouse), *E. Ribère 20 (US Quillan), A. Bioussa (17) (S. Toulouse), J. Galia 11 (US Quillan).

WALES   T. Scourfield (1) (Torquay); H. Jones (2) (Neath), *W.G. Morgan (8) (Guy's H.), E.C. Davey 1 (Swansea), R.W. Boon 2 (Cardiff); F.L. Williams 7 (Cardiff), W.C. Powell 16 (London Welsh); E. Jones 1 (Llanelli), H.C. Day 3 (Newport), T. Arthur 11 (Neath), A. Skym 8 (Cardiff), E.M. Jenkins 12 (Aberavon), A. Lemon 4 (Neath), N. Fender 2 (Cardiff), H. Peacock (6) (Newport).

Referee D. Helliwell (England)

1931

PARIS France beat Ireland 3-0 · TWICKENHAM England drew Wales 11-11
MURRAYFIELD Scotland beat France 6-4 · CARDIFF Wales beat Scotland 13-8
TWICKENHAM Ireland beat England 6-5 · DUBLIN Ireland beat Scotland 8-5
SWANSEA Wales beat France 35-3 · BELFAST Wales beat Ireland 15-3
MURRAYFIELD Scotland beat England 28-19 · PARIS France beat England 14-3

CHAMPIONSHIP TABLE
Wales – Championship

									Tries	
Pos	Country	P	W	D	L	F	A	Pts	F	A
1	Wales (2)	4	3	1	0	74	25	7	15	5
2	Scotland (5)	4	2	0	2	47	44	4	9	9
3	France (4)	4	2	0	2	24	44	4	4	10
4	Ireland (3)	4	2	0	2	17	28	4	4	6
5	England (1)	4	0	1	3	38	59	1	9	11

This was the last season of French participation in the Championship, for 16 years, caused by a dispute which had its roots in professionalism. For many years the Four Home Unions had been perturbed by rumours that French players were being paid to play (though it must be stressed the practice involved French clubs and was not at international level). The French Fédération seemed powerless to eradicate or curb such payments, and it was this impotence that eventually determined the Four Home Unions' action. In February 1931, therefore, they handed France the final warnings: unless their game was restored to complete amateurism, links at all levels would be severed at the end of the season. At the time of the announcement, France had already played and beaten Ireland. It says much for the character of French officials that they were able to fulfil the remaining international commitments with such a threat hanging over them. Equally, they realized that unless they asserted control over the clubs, not only was French international rugby in jeopardy but so too their own raison d'être. Even if this created an uneasy atmosphere in the Championship, it was played to a conclusion and ended with Wales in celebration of their first title win for eight years, which had been their longest run without winning since the ten-year wait of 1883–93.

Welsh rugby, however, was not without problems; not the least of their concerns was the fact that they were the only Home Union not yet possessing their own ground: Cardiff Arms Park was leased, St Helen's, Swansea, was on loan. The WRU therefore resolved to find a ground of their own. That the purchase of their own ground and the establishment of a national headquarters took 40 years to achieve was an indication of the difficulty that faced the WRU.

With events and problems of such magnitude besieging the Championship, it was almost overlooked that England also had plenty to fret about. Their Wooden Spoon status was their first since 1907 and 59 points were scored against them. There may have been worse England sides before 1931 and since; none of them, until the 1970 side, let the floodgates open so wide.

FRANCE v IRELAND   17/309

1 January 1931
Stade Colombes, Paris
France 3 (1T)   Ireland 0

France   T: Ribère.

This was the first time that Ireland failed to score in nine visits to France. Try-scoring, however, was the speciality of Eugene Ribère – this was the fourth that he had scored against Ireland.

FRANCE   M. Savy 1 (AS Montferrand); R. Samatan 5 (SU Agen), M. Baillette 9 (RC Toulon), G. Gérald 11 (RCF), L. Augras 1 (SU Agen); L. Servole 1 (RC Toulon), L. Serin 8 (AS Béziers); J. Duhau 3 (SA Bordeaux), M. Porra (1) (FC Lyon), J. Choy (5) (RC Narbonne), A. Clady 1 (FC Lézignan), M. Rodrigo 1 (SA Bordeaux), *E. Ribère 21 (US Quillan), C. Bigot 3 (FC Lézignan), E. Camo 1 (CA Villeneuve).

IRELAND   J.T. Egan 1 (Cork Constitution); E.J. Lightfoot 1 (Lansdowne), P.F. Murray 9 (Wanderers), M.P. Crowe 5 (Lansdowne), J.E. Arigho 12 (Lansdowne); E.O'D. Davy 22 (Lansdowne), *M. Sugden 24 (Wanderers); G.R. Beamish 15 (London Irish), J.D. Clinch 25 (Wanderers), J.L. Farrell 21 (Bective Rangers), C.J. Hanrahan 17 (Dolphin), N.F. Murphy 3 (Cork Constitution), J. Russell 1 (UC Cork), J.A.E. Siggins 1 (Belfast Collegians), H.H.C. Withers 1 (The Army).

Referee T.H. Vile (Wales)

ENGLAND   L.L. Bedford 1 (Headingley); J.S.R. Reeve 6 (Harlequins), D.W. Burland 1 (Bristol), M.A. McCanlis 1 (Gloucester), C.D. Aarvold 8 (Headingley); T.J.M. Barrington 1 (Bristol), E.B. Pope 1 (Blackheath); H. Rew 5 (Exeter), *J.S. Tucker (25) (Bristol), M.S. Bonaventura (1) (Blackheath), J.W. Forrest 5 (US Portsmouth), B.H. Black 5 (Blackheath), D. H. Swayne (1) (Oxford U.), R.F. Davey (1) (Leytonstone), P.D. Howard 5 (Old Millhillians).

WALES   *J. Bassett 8 (Penarth); J. C. Morley 7 (Newport), E.C. Davey 2 (Swansea), T.E. Jones-Davies 3 (London Welsh), R.W. Boon 3 (Cardiff); H.M. Bowcott 5 (Cardiff), W.C. Powell 17 (London Welsh); A. Skym 9 (Cardiff), H.C. Day 4 (Newport), T. Arthur 12 (Neath), T. Day 1 (Swansea), E.M. Jenkins 13 (Aberavon), A. Lemon 5 (Neath), N. Fender 3 (Cardiff), W. Thomas 6 (Swansea).

Referee Dr J.R. Wheeler (Ireland)

ENGLAND v WALES   42/310

17 January 1931
Twickenham
England 11 (1G, 2PG) Wales 11 (1G, 1T, 1GM)

England   T: Burland. C: Burland. PG: Black (2).
Wales   T: Jones-Davies, Morley. C: Bassett. GM: Powell.

This draw meant that Wales had now played nine matches without a win against England. Even worse, they had still to win at Twickenham, where England had now run up eight victories and a draw. Welsh newspaper accounts made much of a Don Burland conversion. Both touch-judges deemed the kick had missed but at half-time the referee, Dr Wheeler, confirmed he had decided otherwise by informing officials of the fact and ordering that the scoreboard be altered.

Goals from a mark were rare events, even in the 1930s. Wick Powell's may have been unique: he decided to take it as a placed kick, rather than drop-kicking it which would have been usual. In the event, England players did not charge, as they were entitled to do, which suggests they had been sufficiently confused by Powell's action to have decided that he had been awarded a penalty kick.

SCOTLAND v FRANCE   16/311

24 January 1931
Murrayfield
Scotland 6 (2PG) France 4 (1DG)

Scotland   PG: Allan (2).
France   DG: Servole.

Scotland, playing in white, scored their fifth successive home victory over France but could not add to the 16 tries they had scored in the previous four. It was the first time that a Scotland-France encounter had been settled by penalty goals.

SCOTLAND   R.W. Langrish 2 (London Scottish); I.S. Smith 22 (London Scottish), J. E. Hutton (2) (Harlequins), A. W. Wilson 1 (Dunfermline), W. M. Simmers 20 (Glasgow Acads); H. Lind 2 (Dunfermline), J. B. Nelson 23 (Glasgow Acads); J. W. Allan 9 (Melrose), *W.N. Roughead 7 (London Scottish), H. S. Mackintosh 9 (W. of Scotland), J.A. Beattie 4 (Hawick), D.A. McLaren (1) (Durham), J.S. Wilson 1 (St Andrew's U), W.B. Welsh 10 (Hawick), A.W. Walker 1 (Cambridge U).

FRANCE   M. Savy 2 (AS Montferrand); L. Augras 2 (SU Agen), G. Gérald 12 (RCF), M. Baillette 10 (RC Toulon), R. Samatan 6 (SU Agen); L.

Servole 2 (RC Toulon), M. Rousie (1) (CA Ville-neuve); R. Scohy 1 (BEC) J. Duhau 4 (SA Bordeaux), A. Duclos (1) (FC Lourdes), A. Clady 2 (FC Lézignan), J. Galia 12 (CA Villeneuve), C. Bigot (4) (FC Lézignan), *E. Ribère 22 (US Quil-lan), E. Camo 2 (CA Villeneuve).

Referee R.W. Jeffares (Ireland)

WALES v SCOTLAND 42/312

7 February 1931
Cardiff Arms Park
Wales 13 (2G, 1T) Scotland 8 (1G, 1T)

Wales T: Morley, Thomas, Boon. C: Bassett (2).
Scotland T: Crichton-Miller (2). C: Allan.

Watcyn Thomas played for much of the game with a broken collar-bone and his bravery was rewarded when the Llanelli forward scored a try. An earlier example of such devotion to duty was in 1900 when Dick Hellings continued to play with a broken arm against England at Gloucester – and the Llwynypia forward also scored a try. Before the match there was a minute's silence in respect of the memory of James Aikman Smith, who had died while on his way to Cardiff. Aikman Smith was one of the most remarkable administrators in the history of the game: an implacable opponent of profession-alism, a meticulously careful treasurer of the Scottish RFU and a vociferous voice on the International Board, he represented Scottish interests for 44 years.

WALES *J. Bassett 9 (Penarth); J.C. Morley 8 (Newport), E.C. Davey 3 (Swansea), T.E. Jones-Davies (4) (London Welsh), R.W. Boon 4 (Car-diff); H.M. Bowcott 6 (Cardiff), W.C. Powell 18 (London Welsh); A. Skym 10 (Cardiff), H.C. Day (5) (Newport), T. Day 2 (Swansea), T. Arthur 13 (Neath), E. M. Jenkins 14 (Aberavon), A. Lemon 6 (Neath), W. Thomas 7 (Swansea), N. Fender 4 (Cardiff).

SCOTLAND R.W. Langrish 3 (London Scottish); I.S. Smith 23 (London Scottish), G.P.S. Mac-pherson 23 (Edinburgh Acads) W.M. Simmers 21 (Glasgow Acads), G. Wood 1 (Gala); H. Lind 3 (Dunfermline), J.B. Nelson 24 (Glasgow Acads); J.W. Allan 10 (Melrose), *W.M. Roughead 8 (London Scottish), H.S. Mackintosh 10 (W. of

Scotland), A.W. Walker 2 (Cambridge U.), J.A. Beattie 5 (Hawick), W.B. Welsh 11 (Hawick), J.S. Wilson 2 (St Andrew's U.), D. Crichton-Miller 1 (Gloucester).

Referee J.G. Bott (England)

ENGLAND v IRELAND 42/313

14 February 1931
Twickenham
Ireland 6 (1T, 1PG) England 5 (1G)

England T: Black. C: Black.
Ireland T: McMahon. PG: Murray.

An Irish team competing at Twickenham with-out the indefatigable George Stephenson, who had retired the previous season, was unusual in itself. However, the Irish approach to the task was not different: fiery bustle from their for-wards, panache at half-back and tireless tack-ling from the backs. The result was another Irish win at headquarters, by the same score as in 1929. And, as then, the consequence of defeat was the dropping of the half-backs as well as three others by England.

ENGLAND L.L. Bedford (2) (Headingley); J.S.R. Reeve 7 (Harlequins), D.W. Burland 2 (Bristol), M.A. McCanlis (2) (Gloucester), A.C. Harrison 1 (Hartlepool Rovers); T.J.M. Barrington (2) (Bris-tol), G.J. Dean (1) (Harlequins); P.C. Horden 1 (Blackheath), R.H.W. Sparks 7 (Plymouth Al-bion), G.G. Gregory 1 (Taunton), J.W. Forrest 6 (US Portsmouth), B.H. Black 6 (Blackheath), *P.D. Howard 6 (Old Millhillians), P.E. Dunkley 1 (Harlequins), E.H. Harding (1) (Devonport Services).

IRELAND J.T. Egan (2) (Cork Constitution); E.J. Lightfoot 2 (Lansdowne), E.O'D. Davy 23 (Lans-downe), L.B. McMahon 1 (UC Dublin), J.E. Arigho 13 (Lansdowne); P.F. Murray 10 (Wan-derers), *M. Sugden 25 (Wanderers); J.A.E. Siggins 2 (Belfast Collegians), H.H.C. Withers 2 (NIFC), V.J. Pike 1 (Lansdowne), J.L. Farrell 22 (Bective Rangers), J. Russell 2 (UC Cork), N.F. Murphy 4 (Cork Constitution), J.D. Clinch 26 (Wanderers), G.R. Beamish 16 (London Irish).

Referee A.E. Freethy (Wales)

G.P.S. Macpherson's team which registered Scotland's biggest ever score against England 28-19, on 21 March 1931

IRELAND v SCOTLAND — 44/314

28 February 1931
Lansdowne Road, Dublin
Ireland 8 (1G, 1T) Scotland 5 (1G)

Ireland   T: Sugden, Pike. C: Murray.
Scotland   T: Mackintosh. C: Allan.

J.B. Nelson, rated as one of Scotland's finest pre-war scrum-halves, made his final Championship appearance. Nelson, who won the first of his 25 caps in 1925, had the distinction of playing in four Championship winning sides, and was famed for his strength and aggressive running. On this occasion, however, Nelson was bested by Mark Sugden, whose clever, stylish play, in which the dummy often featured, kept the pressure on Scotland. Like many great players Sugden started his rugby career in another position – centre – and was one of several Irish internationals born in England.

IRELAND   J.C. Entrican (1) (Queen's U. Belfast); E.J. Lightfoot 3 (Lansdowne), E.O'D. Davy 24 (Lansdowne), M.P. Crowe 6 (Lansdowne), J.E. Arigho 14 (Lansdowne); P.F. Murray 11 (Wanderers), *M. Sugden 26 (Wanderers); H.H.C. Withers 3 (NIFC), J.A.E. Siggins 3 (Belfast Collegians), J. Russell 3 (UC Cork), N.F. Murphy 5 (Cork Constitution), V.J. Pike 2 (Lansdowne), J.L. Farrell 23 (Bective Rangers), G.R. Beamish 17 (London Irish), J.D. Clinch 27 (Wanderers).

SCOTLAND   R.W. Langrish (4) (London Scottish); I.S. Smith 24 (London Scottish), W.M. Simmers 22 (Glasgow Acads), A.W. Wilson 2 (Dunfermline), G. Wood 2 (Gala); H. Lind 4 (Dunfermline), J.B. Nelson (25) (Glasgow Acads); J.W. Allan 11 (Melrose), *W.N. Roughead 9 (London Scottish), H.S. Mackintosh 11 (W. of Scotland), A.W. Walker 3 (Cambridge U.), J.A. Beattie 6 (Hawick), W.B. Welsh 12 (Hawick), D. Crichton-Miller 2 (Gloucester), J.S. Wilson 3 (St Andrew's U.).

Referee B.S. Cumberlege (England)

WALES v FRANCE — 17/315

28 February 1931
St Helen's, Swansea
Wales 35 (5G, 2T, 1DG) France 3 (1T)

Wales T: Ralph (2), Davey, Fender, Lang, Williams, Arthur. C: Bassett (5). DG: Powell.
France T: Petit.

Wales extended their winning sequence over France in Wales to a record nine with this victory, which was also their biggest score against France since the first meeting in Wales in 1910, when they won 49-14. It was also the third time Wales had run in seven tries against France (1914 and 1927 being the previous occasions). Wales's best try haul was the ten they scored in the first Championship meeting in 1910.

WALES *J. Bassett 10 (Penarth); J.C. Morley 9 (Newport), E.C. Davey 4 (Swansea), F.L. Williams 8 (Cardiff), R.W. Boon 5 (Cardiff); A.R. Ralph 1 (Newport), W.C. Powell 19 (London Welsh); A. Skym 11 (Cardiff), T. Day 3 (Swansea), D.R. James 1 (Treorchy), T. Arthur 14 (Neath), E.M. Jenkins 15 (Aberavon), A. Lemon 7 (Neath), N. Fender 5 (Cardiff), J. Lang 1 (Llanelli).

FRANCE M. Savy 3 (AS Montferrand); R. Samatan 7 (SU Agen), P. Clément (1) (RCF), M. Vigerie (1) (SU Agen), L. Augras (3) (SU Agen); L. Servole 3 (RC Toulon), L. Serin 9 (AS Béziers); M. Rodrigo (2) (SA Mauléon), C. Petit (1) (SU Lorrain), P. Barrère (1) (RC Toulon), J. Duhau (5) (SA Bordeaux), R. Scohy 2 (Bordeaux EC), J. Galia 13 (CA Villeneuve), *E. Ribère 23 (US Quillan), E. Camo 3 (CA Villeneuve).

Referee R.W. Harland (Ireland)

IRELAND v WALES — 40/316

14 March 1931
Ravenhill, Belfast
Wales 15 (1G, 2T, 1DG) Ireland 3 (1T)

Ireland T: Siggins.
Wales T: Morley (2), Davey. C: Bassett. DG: Ralph.

Ireland-Wales matches were always bruising affairs and there were other vital factors which made this match more fiercely contested than most: Wales stood to win the Championship and Ireland were bidding for the Triple Crown. Both sides suffered injuries, but Ireland were further handicapped when Crowe went off in the second half with concussion. It meant the end of an era for several distinguished Irish players: Joe Arigho, Mark Sugden, Jimmy Farrell and Jammie Clinch. These players were the heart and soul of Irish rugby at the time, although none of them ever played in a side which won the Championship or the Triple Crown.

IRELAND D.P. Morris 1 (Bective Rangers); E.J. Lightfoot 4 (Lansdowne), E.O'D. Davy 25 (Lansdowne), M.P. Crowe 7 (Lansdowne), J.E. Arigho (15) (Lansdowne), P. F. Murray 12 (Wanderers), *M. Sugden (27) (Wanderers); H.H.C. Withers (4) (NIFC), J. Russell 4 (UC Cork), J.A.E. Siggins 4 (Belfast Collegians), V.J. Pike 3 (Lansdowne), J. L. Farrell (24) (Bective Rangers), N.F. Murphy 6 (Cork Constitution), J.D. Clinch (28) (Wanderers), G.R. Beamish 18 (London Irish).

WALES *J. Bassett 11 (Penarth); J.C. Morley 10 (Newport), E.C. Davey 5 (Swansea), F.L. Williams 9 (Cardiff), R.W. Boon 6 (Cardiff); A.R. Ralph 2 (Newport), W.C. Powell 20 (London Welsh); A. Skym 12 (Cardiff), D.R. James (2) (Treorchy), T. Day 4 (Swansea), T. Arthur 15 (Neath), E.M. Jenkins 16 (Aberavon), A. Lemon 8 (Neath), J. Lang 2 (Llanelli), N. Fender (6) (Cardiff).

Referee M.A. Allan (Scotland)

SCOTLAND v ENGLAND 41/317

21 March 1931
Murrayfield
Scotland 28 (5G, 1T) England 19 (2G, 2T, 1PG)

Scotland T: Mackintosh (2), Smith (2), Ford, Logan. C: Allan (5).
England T: Tallent (2), Reeve (2). C: Black (2). PG: Black.

Scotland ran up their biggest score against England, home or away, and their greatest number of tries, six, and conversions, five, against their old enemy. The match total of ten tries and seven conversions has never been surpassed and the 47 points match total has only once been bettered, in 1980 when England won 30-18.

SCOTLAND A.W. Wilson (3) (Dunfermline); I.S. Smith 25 (London Scottish), *G.P.S. Macpherson 24 (Edinburgh Acads), D.St C. Ford 3 (US Portsmouth), W.M. Simmers 23 (Glasgow Acads); H. Lind 5 (Dunfermline), W.R. Logan 1 (Edinburgh U.); J.W. Allan 12 (Melrose), W.N. Roughead 10 (London Scottish), H.S. Mackintosh 12 (W. of Scotland), A.W. Walker 4 (Cambridge U.), J.A. Beattie 7 (Hawick), W.B. Welsh 13 (Hawick), D. Crichton-Miller (3) (Gloucester), J.S. Wilson 4 (St Andrew's U.).

ENGLAND E.C.P. Whiteley 1 (Old Alleynians); J.S.R. Reeve (8) (Harlequins), J. A. Tallent 1 (Cambridge U.), *C.D. Aarvold 9 (Headingley), A. C. Harrison (2) (Hartlepool Rovers); T.C. Knowles (1) (Birkenhead Park), E.B. Pope 2 (Blackheath); H. Rew 6 (Exeter), R.H.W. Sparks 8 (Plymouth Albion), G.G. Gregory 2 (Taunton), J.W. Forrest 7 (US Portsmouth), B.H. Black 7 (Blackheath), P.C. Hordern 2 (Blackheath), P.E. Dunkley 2 (Harlequins), P.D. Howard 7 (Old Millhillians).

Referee Dr J. R. Wheeler (Ireland)

FRANCE v ENGLAND 17/318

6 April 1931
Stade Colombes, Paris
France 14 (2T, 2DG) England 13 (2G, 1T)

France T: Clady, Galia. DG: Baillette, Gérald.
England T: Burland, Smeddle, Tallent. C: Black (2).

A dropped goal by Géo Gérald, playing in his thirteenth and final Championship match, gave France their second victory over England in 17 matches. This Easter Monday clash, however, was to be France's last Championship match until 1947, for their administrators had been unable to convince the Four Home Unions that French rugby affairs were being run properly. England thus finished without a victory for the first time since 1907, which was also the previous occasion that they had 'won' the Wooden Spoon.

FRANCE M. Savy (4) (AS Montferrand); R. Samatan (8) (SU Agen), G. Gérald (13) (RCF), M. Baillette (11) (RC Toulon), P. Guelorguet (1) (RCF); L. Servole (4) (RC Toulon), L. Serin (10) (AS Béziers); R. Scohy (3) (Bordeaux EC), R. Namur (1) (RC Toulon), H. Buisson (1) (AS Béziers), E. Camo (4) (CA Villeneuve), A. Clady (3) (FC Lézignan), R. Triviaux (1) (US Cognac), *E. Ribère (24) (US Quillan), J. Galia (14) (CA Villeneuve).

ENGLAND E.C.P. Whiteley (2) (Old Alleynians); R.W. Smeddle (4) (Cambridge U.), D. W. Burland 3 (Bristol), J.A. Tallent 2 (Cambridge U.), *C.D. Aarvold 10 (Headingley); R.S. Spong 6 (Old Millhillians), E.B. Pope (3) (Blackheath); H. Rew 7 (Exeter), R.H.W. Sparks (9) (Plymouth Albion), G.G. Gregory 3 (Taunton), J. W. Forrest 8 (US Portsmouth), B.H. Black 8 (Blackheath), P.W.P. Brook 2 (Harlequins), P.C. Hordern 3 (Blackheath), P. D. Howard (8) (Old Millhillians).

Referee A.E. Freethy (Wales)

1932

SWANSEA Wales beat England 12-5 · MURRAYFIELD Wales beat Scotland 6-0
DUBLIN England beat Ireland 11-8 · MURRAYFIELD Ireland beat Scotland 20-8
CARDIFF Ireland beat Wales 12-10 · TWICKENHAM England beat Scotland 16-3

CHAMPIONSHIP TABLE
Ireland – Championship

| | | | | | | | | Tries | |
Pos Country	P	W	D	L	F	A	Pts	F	A
1 Ireland (4)	3	2	0	1	40	29	4	9	5
2 England (5)	3	2	0	1	32	23	4	6	3
3 Wales (1)	3	2	0	1	28	17	4	4	5
4 Scotland (2)	3	0	0	3	11	42	0	3	9

After a long, exasperating 20-year interval Ireland won the Championship. Ireland endured only one period longer without a title win, 22 years from 1952–74, but the fact that they had come close to winning four times between 1925–28, merited a change of luck. In the course of outpointing the other two chief contenders, England and Wales, Ireland achieved two landmarks: a fourth successive victory over the Scots in Scotland and their four tries at Cardiff were the most they have ever scored in Wales. The one hiccup in what would otherwise have been a perfect season was losing to England at Lansdowne Road, their only home match. Wales had some consolation after being deprived by Ireland of the Triple Crown – their earlier victories over England and Scotland meant they had extended a sequence without defeat to eight matches, a run bettered only once when they were unbeaten for nine matches in a row, 1970–73. England were particularly pleased about their win over the Irish: it ended a run of six matches without a win.

With France excluded, the number of points and tries in the Championship understandably dipped dramatically. One view, however, was that it was mainly a result of the visit of Benny Osler's Third Springboks earlier in the season; they had beaten all four countries. Osler, an astute tactical kicker, was said to have greatly influenced the way the game was played in Britain; and that the home countries as a result adopted a tight, defensive style which curbed try-scoring. That theory is inconclusive, particularly when examining the number of highly talented attacking players in Britain from 1932 to 1939. It is unlikely that they changed their style of playing because of Osler. If they did, was it voluntary, or were they advised to do so and, if so, by whom? There were no coaches in those days to whom blame can be apportioned, and team captains usually had such a short term of office that their influence had to be limited.

There is no doubt, however, that try-scoring was at a premium from 1932–39. The high and low years were 1938, when 35 tries were scored, and 1939 when the total dropped to 10. The average for the eight-year period was eighteen a season. This was the worst return of any period in the history of the Championship when only four sides competed. To blame one man, poor Osler, seems absurd. More likely, the answer lay in the absence of France. Without France's notoriously frail defence to practise against, the other countries were deprived of the opportunities to flex their try-scoring muscles.

WALES v ENGLAND 43/319

16 January 1932
St Helen's, Swansea
Wales 12 (1G, 1DG, 1PG) England 5 (1G)

Wales T: Boon. C: Bassett. DG: Boon. PG: Bassett.
England T: Coley. C: Barr.

Both sides in this match had been beaten by South Africa the previous month, which may have accounted for the fact that a relatively small crowd of 30,000 turned up to watch Wales beat England in Swansea for the first time since 1922. England responded by dropping five players, including the Old Millhillian half-backs, Roger Spong and Wilf Sobey. By all accounts Spong had been given a desperately hard time by the Welsh breakaway forwards, particularly Arthur Lemon.

WALES   *J. Bassett 12 (Penarth); J.C. Morley 11 (Newport), E.C. Davey 6 (Swansea), F.L. Williams 10 (Cardiff), R.W. Boon 7 (Cardiff); A.R. Ralph 3 (Newport), W.C. Powell 21 (London Welsh); T. Day 5 (Swansea), F.A. Bowdler 10 (Cross Keys), A. Skym 13 (Cardiff), D. Thomas 3 (Swansea), E. M. Jenkins 17 (Aberavon), W. Davies 1 (Swansea), A. Lemon 9 (Neath), W. Thomas 8 (Swansea).

ENGLAND   R.J. Barr 1 (Leicester); C.C. Tanner 2 (Gloucester), R.A. Gerrard 1 (Bath), J.A. Tallent 3 (Cambridge U.), *C.D. Aarvold 11 (Blackheath); R.S. Spong (7) (Old Millhillians), W.H. Sobey 4 (Old Millhillians); G.G. Gregory 4 (Bristol), D.J. Norman (1) (Leicester), N.L. Evans 1 (RNEC Keyham), C.S.H. Webb 1 (Devonport Services), R.G.S. Hobbs 1 (Richmond), L.E. Saxby (1) (Gloucester), J.McD. Hodgson 1 (Northern), E. Coley (2) (Northampton).

Referee F.J.C. Moffat (Scotland)

SCOTLAND v WALES   43/320

---

6 February 1932
Murrayfield
Wales 6 (1T, 1PG) Scotland 0

Wales   T: Boon. PG: Bassett.

After running South Africa to 3-6 only three weeks previously, Scotland were entitled to some measure of confidence in their ability to loosen the Welsh hold in recent matches between the countries. But Wales, supported by an estimated 12,000 of their countrymen, held their lead firmly and confidently. It was one of those rare occasions when Wales wore lettered jerseys – perhaps because the Scottish Rugby Union held the numbering of players with such disdain!

SCOTLAND   T.H.B. Lawther (1) (Old Millhillians); I.S. Smith 26 (London Scottish), D.St C. Ford 4 (US Portsmouth), *W.M. Simmers 24 (Glasgow Acads), G. Wood 3 (Gala); H. Lind 6 (Dunfermline), W.R. Logan 2 (Edinburgh U.); J.W. Allan 13 (Melrose), W.N. Roughead (11) (London Scottish), H.S. Mackintosh 13 (W. of Scotland), M.S. Stewart 1 (Stewart's FP), J.A. Beattie 8 (Hawick), J. Graham (13) (Kelso), W.B. Welsh 14 (Hawick), F.H. Waters 5 (London Scottish).

WALES   *J. Bassett 13 (Penarth); J.C. Morley 12 (Newport), E.C. Davey 7 (Swansea), F.L. Williams 11 (Cardiff), R.W. Boon 8 (Cardiff); A.R. Ralph 4 (Newport), W.C. Powell 22 (London Welsh); A. Skym 14 (Cardiff), F.A. Bowdler 11 (Cross Keys), T. Day 6 (Swansea), D. Thomas 4 (Swansea), E.M. Jenkins 18 (Aberavon), W. Davies 2 (Swansea), A. Lemon 10 (Neath), W. Thomas 9 (Swansea).

Referee T. Bell (Ireland)

IRELAND v ENGLAND   43/321

---

13 February 1932
Lansdowne Road, Dublin
England 11 (1G, 2PG) Ireland 8 (1G, 1PG)

Ireland   T: Waide. C: Murray. PG: Murray.
England   T: Burland. C: Burland. PG: Burland (2).

England ended a run of three Irish victories with this triumph at Lansdowne Road, which compensated somewhat for the defeat by Wales at Cardiff the previous month. Although England discarded three players after the match, the performance of their new half-backs, Elliot and Gadney, had been encouraging; they were to play together six times until 1934. The recall of D.W. Burland, the Bristol centre, also worked well. He contributed all England's points with a try, conversion and two penalty goals.

IRELAND   D.P. Morris 2 (Bective Rangers); E.J. Lightfoot 5 (Lansdowne), P.F. Murray 13 (Wanderers), E.W.F. de Vere Hunt 2 (Rosslyn Park), S.L. Waide 1 (NIFC); E.O'D. Davy 26 (Lansdowne), M.D. Sheehan (1) (London Irish); V.J. Pike 4 (Lansdowne), T.C. Casey (2) (Young Munster), J.L. Farrell 25 (Bective Rangers), M.J. Dunne 8 (Lansdowne), J.A.E. Siggins 5 (Belfast

Collegians), N.F. Murphy 7 (Cork Constitution), W.McC. Ross 1 (Queen's U. Belfast), *G.R. Beamish 19 (Leicester).

ENGLAND   R.J. Barr (2) (Leicester); C.C. Tanner 3 (Gloucester), D.W. Burland 4 (Bristol), R.A. Gerrard 2 (Bath), *C.D. Aarvold 12 (Blackheath); W. Elliot 1 (US Portsmouth), B.C. Gadney 1 (Leicester); G.G. Gregory 5 (Bristol), R.S. Roberts (1) (Coventry), N.L. Evans 2 (RNEC Keyham), R.G.S. Hobbs 2 (Richmond), C.S.H. Webb 2 (Devonport Services), A. Vaughan-Jones 1 (US Portsmouth), J.McD. Hodgson 2 (Northern), T.W. Harris (2) (Northampton).

Referee W. Burnett (Scotland)

SCOTLAND v IRELAND   45/322

27 February 1932
Murrayfield
Ireland 20 (4G) Scotland 8 (1G, 1T)

Scotland   T: Wood, Simmers. C: Allan.
Ireland   T: Lightfoot (2), Hunt, Waide. C: Murray (4)

Paul Murray, a gifted scrum-half unfortunate to be at the peak of his career at the same time as Mark Sugden, was a place-kicker of some quality – as proved by his four conversions in this match. Scotland had injury problems but these were not used as an explanation for Ireland's fourth victory in a row at Murrayfield.

SCOTLAND   A.H.M. Hutton (1) (Dunfermline); I.S. Smith 27 (London Scottish), G. Wood. 4 (Gala), D.St C. Ford (5) (US Portsmouth), *W.M. Simmers 25 (Glasgow Acads); W.D. Emslie (2) (Royal HSFP), W.R. Logan 3 (Edinburgh U.); J.W. Allan 14 (Melrose), H.S. Mackintosh 14 (W. of Scotland), R.A. Foster 2 (Hawick), M.S. Stewart 2 (Stewart's FP), J.A. Beattie 9 (Hawick), A.W. Walker (5) (Birkenhead Park), W.B. Welsh 15 Hawick), F.H. Waters (6) (London Scottish).

IRELAND   E.C. Ridgeway 1 (Wanderers); S.L. Waide 2 (NIFC), E.W.F. de Vere Hunt 3 (Rosslyn Park), M.P. Crowe 8 (Lansdowne), E.J. Lightfoot 6 (Lansdowne); E. O'D. Davy 27 (Lansdowne), P.F. Murray 14 (Wanderers); *G.R. Beamish 20 (Leicester), M.J. Dunne 9 (Lansdowne), J.L. Farrell 26 (Bective Rangers), N.F. Murphy 8 (Cork Constitution), V.J. Pike 5 (Lansdowne),

W.McC. Ross 2 (Queen's U. Belfast), C.J. Hanrahan 18 (Dolphin), J.A.E. Siggins 6 (Belfast Collegians).

Referee   B.S. Cumberlege (England)

WALES v IRELAND   41/323

---

12 March 1932
Cardiff Arms Park
Ireland 12 (4T) Wales 10 (2T, 1DG)

Wales   T: Davey, Ralph. DG: Ralph.
Ireland   T: Ross (2), Lightfoot, Waide.

Wales had never been a happy hunting ground for Ireland – they had won only 4 times in 20 visits – but this victory was particularly important for it won them the Championship and

Wilf Wooller and Claude Davey, two of Wales's outstanding players of the 1930s

deprived Wales, for a change, of winning the Triple Crown. The latter was usually Ireland's fate, for Ireland had been frustrated on five occasions, 1905, 1911, 1926, 1930 and 1931. Ireland's four tries represented their biggest haul ever in Wales. In fact they have never scored more than four tries against the Welsh, although they equalled the total on three occasions in Ireland. The match was also significant in the number of well-known players on both sides who played their last Championship matches: Jack Bassett, Jack Morley and Ned Jenkins of Wales and Jimmy Farrell and Charlie Hanrahan of Ireland.

WALES   *J. Bassett (14) (Penarth); J.C. Morley (13) (Newport), E.C. Davey 8 (Swansea), F.L. Williams 12 (Cardiff), R.W. Boon 9 (Cardiff); A.R. Ralph (5) (Newport), W.C. Powell 23 (London Welsh); A. Skym 15 (Cardiff), F.A. Bowdler 12 (Cross Keys), T. Day 7 (Swansea), D. Thomas 5 (Swansea), E.M. Jenkins (19) (Aberavon), W. Davies (3) (Swansea), W. Thomas 10 (Swansea), A. Lemon 11 (Neath).

IRELAND   E.C. Ridgeway 2 (Wanderers); E.J. Lightfoot 7 (Lansdowne), M.P. Crowe 9 (Lansdowne), E.W.F. de Vere Hunt 4 (Rosslyn Park), S.L. Waide 3 (NIFC); E.O'D. Davy 28 (Lansdowne), P.F. Murray 15 (Wanderers); J.L. Farrell (27) (Bective Rangers), C.J. Hanrahan (19) (Dolphin), V.J. Pike 6 (Lansdowne), M.J. Dunne 10 (Lansdowne), J.A.E. Siggins 7 (Belfast Collegians), W.McC. Ross 3 (Queen's U. Belfast), N.F. Murphy 9 (Cork Constitution), *G.R. Beamish 21 (Leicester).

Referee E. Holmes (England)

ENGLAND v SCOTLAND   42/324

---

19 March 1932
Twickenham
England 16 (2G, 2T) Scotland 3 (1T)

England   T: Aarvold (2), Black, Tanner. C: Burland (2).
Scotland   T: Smith.

This was England's first victory over Scotland since 1928 and was distinctive in that Carl Aarvold scored two excellent tries and Burland had a particularly fine game in the centre. The Scots took the cue: they discarded ten of their players, including their superbly gifted centre, G.P.S. Macpherson, and Simmers, their long-serving wing. In fact Ian Smith was the only member of the backs to campaign again in 1933.

ENGLAND   T.W. Brown 6 (Bristol); C.C. Tanner (4) (Gloucester), D.W. Burland 5 (Bristol), R.A. Gerrard 3 (Bath), *C.D. Aarvold 13 (Blackheath); W. Elliot 2 (US Portsmouth), B.C. Gadney 2 (Leicester); R.J. Longland 1 (Northampton), G.G. Gregory 6 (Bristol), N.L. Evans 3 (RNEC Keyham), C.S.H. Webb 3 (Devonport Services), R.G.S. Hobbs (3) (Richmond), A. Vaughan-Jones 2 (US Portsmouth), J.McD. Hodgson 3 (Northern), B.H. Black 9 (Blackheath).

SCOTLAND   A.S. Dykes (1) (Glasgow Acads); I.S. Smith 28 (London Scottish), *G.P.S. Macpherson (25) (Edinburgh Acads), G. Wood (5) (Gala), W.M. Simmers (26) (Glasgow Acads); H. Lind 7 (Dunfermline), J.P. McArthur (1) (Waterloo); R.A. Foster (3) (Hawick), H.S. Mackintosh (15) (W. of Scotland), R. Rowand 3 (Glasgow HSFP), F.A. Wright (1) (Edinburgh Acads), J.A. Beattie 10 (Hawick), W.B. Welsh 16 (Hawick), J.S. Wilson (5) (St. Andrew's U.), G.F. Ritchie (1) (Dundee HSFP).

Referee Dr J.R. Wheeler (Ireland)

1933

TWICKENHAM Wales beat England 7-3 · SWANSEA Scotland beat Wales 11-3
TWICKENHAM England beat Ireland 17-6 · BELFAST Ireland beat Wales 10-5
MURRAYFIELD Scotland beat England 3-0 · DUBLIN Scotland beat Ireland 8-6

CHAMPIONSHIP TABLE
Scotland – Championship, Triple Crown

									Tries	
Pos	Country	P	W	D	L	F	A	Pts	F	A
1	Scotland (4)	3	3	0	0	22	9	6	3	3
2	Ireland (1)	3	1	0	2	22	30	2	4	6
3	England (2)	3	1	0	2	20	16	2	6	3
4	Wales (3)	3	1	0	2	15	24	2	3	4

The 1933 season was used as a trial period for an International Board recommendation that the first forwards at a stoppage point would be the first forwards down in the scrummage. It was a controversial experiment at a time when most sides, at both international and club level, were committed to specialization – which the Board, rather strangely considered detrimental to the game. Suffice to say, the idea was still-born and forgotten within two seasons.

The Championship itself was a one-horse race. Scotland were unquestionably the best side, deserving of the Triple Crown. It was a personal triumph in his last season for Ian Smith, or the Flying Scot as he was known. Smith was appointed captain after Scotland had lost every match the season before.

ENGLAND v WALES 44/325

21 January 1933
Twickenham
Wales 7 (1T, 1DG) England 3 (1T)

England T: Elliot.
Wales T: Boon. DG: Boon.

This was a match etched deep in Welsh rugby folklore, for it was Wales's first victory at Twickenham, in ten visits since 1910. The modest, self-effacing Ronnie Boon became an overnight hero in the Principality because of his contribution to the score with a try and a dropped goal. Fifty years later Boon put his role in perspective: the Welsh forwards, inspiringly led by Watcyn Thomas, deserved all the credit, he argued. Few are as magnanimous as the dapper little wing for whom the dropped kick was but one embellishment of a whole range of attacking skills. Englishmen will recall the match as the last Championship appearance of their high-quality wing, Carl Aarvold. A less remembered fact was that Wales had played seven new caps, including two striblings who were destined to become giants of Welsh rugby before the War, Wilf Wooller and Vivian Jenkins.

ENGLAND   T.W. Brown 7 (Bristol); L.A. Booth 1 (Headingley), D.W. Burland 6 (Bristol), R.A. Gerrard 4 (Bath), *C.D. Aarvold (14) (Blackheath); W. Elliot 3 (US Portsmouth), A. Key (2) (Old Cranleighans); R.J. Longland 2 (Northampton), G.G. Gregory 7 (Bristol), N.L. Evans 4 (US Portsmouth), C.S.H. Webb 4 (Devonport Services), A.D.S. Roncoroni 1 (Richmond), R. Bolton 1 (Wakefield), A. Vaughan-Jones (3) (US Portsmouth), B.H. Black (10) (Blackheath).

WALES   V.G.J. Jenkins 1 (Bridgend); R.W. Boon 10 (Cardiff), E.C. Davey 9 (Swansea), W. Wooller 1 (Rydal School), A.H. Jones 1 (Cardiff); H.M. Bowcott 7 (London Welsh), M.J. Turnbull 1 (Cardiff); E. Jones 2 (Llanelli), B. Evans 1 (Llanelli), A. Skym 16 (Cardiff), R.B. Jones 1 (Cambridge U.), D. Thomas 6 (Swansea), T. Arthur 16 (Neath), I. Isaacs 1 (Cardiff), *W. Thomas 11 (Swansea).

Referee T. Bell (Ireland)

WALES v SCOTLAND   44/326

4 February 1933
St Helen's, Swansea
Scotland 11 (1G, 1T, 1PG) Wales 3 (1T)

Wales   T: Arthur.
Scotland   T: Smith, Jackson. C: Fyfe. PG: Fyfe.

Scotland played eight new caps to take this the first leg of their first Triple Crown for eight years. The Welsh selectors had problems: when Maurice Turnbull, the designated scrum-half, withdrew because of injury, they suggested his partner Harry Bowcott stand down so that the Swansea half-backs Ron Morris and Bryn Evans could play.

WALES   G. Bayliss (1) (Pontypool); A. Hickman (2) (Neath), E.C. Davey 10 (Swansea), W. Wooller 2 (Colwyn Bay), A.H. Jones (2) (Cardiff); R.R. Morris 1 (Swansea), B. Evans (1) (Swansea); E. Jones 3 (Llanelli), B. Evans 2 (Llanelli), A. Skym 17 (Cardiff), R. B. Jones (2) (Cambridge U.), D. Thomas 7 (Swansea), T. Arthur (17) (Cardiff), I. Isaacs (2) (Cardiff), *W. Thomas 12 (Swansea).

SCOTLAND   D.I. Brown 1 (Cambridge U.); *I.S. Smith 29 (London Scottish), H.D.B. Lorraine 1 (Oxford U.), H. Lind 8 (Dunfermline), K.C. Fyfe 1 (Cambridge U.); K.L.T. Jackson 1 (Oxford U.), W.R. Logan 4 (Edinburgh Wands); J.A. Waters 1 (Selkirk), J.M. Ritchie 1 (Watsonians), J.R. Thom 1 (Watsonians), J.A. Beattie 11 (Hawick), M.S. Stewart 3 (Stewart's FP), W.B. Welsh 17 (Hawick), J.M. Henderson 1 (Edinburgh Acads), R. Rowand 4 (Glasgow HSFP).

Referee J.G. Bott (England)

ENGLAND v IRELAND   44/327

11 February 1933
Twickenham
England 17 (1G, 4T) Ireland 6 (1T, 1PG)

England   T: Novis (2), Booth, Gadney, Sadler. C: Kendrew.
Ireland   T: Hunt. PG: Murray.

England's scoring power, so often held in check by successive Irish defences, was given full vent in this match. It was ten years since they last scored five tries against the Irish, whose pack, for once, did not dictate the course of events.

ENGLAND   T.W. Brown 8 (Bristol); L.A. Booth 2 (Headingley), D.W. Burland 7 (Bristol), R.A. Gerrard 5 (Bath), *A.L. Novis 6 (Blackheath); W. Elliot 4 (US Portsmouth), B.C. Gadney 3 (Leicester); N.L. Evans (5) (US Portsmouth), G.G. Gregory 8 (Bristol), D.A. Kendrew 3 (Leicester), A.D.S. Roncoroni 2 (Richmond), C.S.H. Webb 5 (Devonport Services), E.H. Sadler 1 (The Army), W.H. Weston 1 (Northampton), C.L. Troop 1 (The Army).

IRELAND   R.H. Pratt 1 (Dublin U.); E.J. Lightfoot 8 (Lansdowne), L.B. McMahon 2 (UC Dublin), E.W.F. de Vere Hunt (5) (Wanderers), S.L. Waide 4 (NIFC); *E.O'D. Davy 29 (Lansdowne), P.F. Murray 16 (Wanderers); M.J. Dunne 11 (Lansdowne), V.J. Pike 7 (Lansdowne), H.O'H. O'Neill 4 (UC Cork), J.A.E. Siggins 8 (Belfast Collegians), J. Russell 5 (UC Cork), N.F. Murphy (10) (Cork Constitution), W.McC. Ross 4 (Queen's U. Belfast), G.R. Beamish 22 (Leicester).

Referee M.A. Allan (Scotland)

IRELAND v WALES   42/328

11 March 1933
Ravenhill, Belfast
Ireland 10 (1T, 1DG, 1PG) Wales 5 (1G)

Ireland   T: Barnes. DG: Davy. PG: Siggins.
Wales   T: Bowcott. C: Jenkins.

This defeat led to one of the largest team reshuffles in Welsh rugby history, with 11 players discarded, including some of the most famous players of the time, Frank Williams, Ronnie Boon, Harry Bowcott, Arthur Bowdler, Arthur Lemon and Watcyn Thomas. Some vindictiveness on the part of the selectors was in evidence. Against their wishes, Watcyn Thomas, the captain, played Bob Barrell at prop and Lemon at flanker, which were their accustomed positions, instead of the other way around which, for reasons best known to themselves, the selectors had decreed. In the event Watcyn Thomas was dropped at a time when he was one of the outstanding forwards in the Championship.

IRELAND   R.H. Pratt 2 (Dublin U.); E.J. Lightfoot 9 (Lansdowne), M.P. Crowe 10 (Lansdowne), R.J. Barnes (1) (Dublin U.), S.L. Waide (5) (NIFC); E.O'D. Davy 30 (Lansdowne), P.F. Murray 17 (Wanderers); M.J. Dunne 12 (Lansdowne), V.J. Pike 8 (Lansdowne), H.O'H. O'Neill 5 (UC Cork), J. Russell 6 (UC Cork), J.A.E. Siggins 9 (Belfast Collegians), C.E.St J. Beamish 1 (NIFC), *G.R. Beamish 23 (Leicester), W.McC. Ross 5 (Queen's U. Belfast).

WALES   V.G.J. Jenkins 2 (Bridgend); W. Wooller 3 (Colwyn Bay), F.L. Williams (13) (Cardiff), G. Jones (2) (Cardiff), R.W. Boon (11) (Cardiff); H.M. Bowcott (8) (London Welsh), M.J. Turnbull (2) (Cardiff); E. Jones 4 (Llanelli), F.A. Bowdler (13) (Cross Keys), R. Barrell (4) (Cardiff), A. Skym 18 (Cardiff), W.J. Moore (1) Bridgend), L. Rees (1) (Cardiff), *W. Thomas (13) (Swansea), A. Lemon (12) (Neath).

Referee M.A. Allan (Scotland)

SCOTLAND v ENGLAND   43/329

18 March 1933
Murrayfield
Scotland 3 (1T) England 0

Scotland   T: Fyfe.

The last occasion on which England failed to register a score against Scotland, who having introduced eight new caps against Wales the previous month were rewarded for their faith in the same side. In contrast, six England players never appeared again in the Championship.

SCOTLAND   D.I. Brown 2 (Cambridge U.); *I.S. Smith 30 (London Scottish), H.D.B. Lorraine 2 (Oxford U.), H. Lind 9 (Dunfermline), K.C. Fyfe 2 (Cambridge U.); K.L.T. Jackson 2 (Oxford U.), W.R. Logan 5 (Edinburgh Wands); J.A. Waters 2 (Selkirk), J.R. Thom 2 (Watsonians), J.M. Ritchie 2 (Watsonians), W.B. Welsh 18 (Hawick), J.M. Henderson 2 (Edinburgh Acads), M.S. Stewart 4 (Stewart's FP), J.A. Beattie 12 (Hawick), R. Rowand 5 (Glasgow HSFP).

ENGLAND   T.W. Brown (9) (Bristol); L.A. Booth 3 (Headingley), D.W. Burland (8) (Bristol), R.A. Gerrard 6 (Bath), *A.L. Novis (7) (Blackheath); W. Elliot 5 (US Portsmouth), B.C. Gadney 4 (Leicester); D.A. Kendrew 4 (Leicester), G.G.

Gregory 9 (Bristol), R.J. Longland 3 (Northampton), C.S.H. Webb 6 (Devonport Services), A.D.S. Roncoroni (3) (Richmond), W.H. Weston 2 (Northampton), E.H. Sadler (2) (The Army), C.L. Troop (2) (The Army).

Referee Dr J.R. Wheeler (Ireland)

IRELAND v SCOTLAND   46/330

1 April 1933
Lansdowne Road, Dublin
Scotland 8 (2DG) Ireland 6 (2T)

Ireland   T: Crowe, Murray.
Scotland   DG: Jackson, Lind.

Ian Smith celebrated his thirty-first and final match for Scotland by leading his country to a thoroughly deserved Triple Crown success. Smith, first capped in 1924, came to the Scottish captaincy late in his career, but obviously made a very good job of it because he led a side which had been Wooden Spoonists the previous season to win the Championship. It was unusual for the title to hang on the result of an Ireland-Scotland match: in this case it became the last match of the season because heavy snow enforced a postponement from the scheduled date, 25 February.

IRELAND   R.H. Pratt 3 (Dublin U.); J.J. O'Connor 1 (UC Cork), P.B. Coote (1) (Leicester), M.P. Crowe 11 (Lansdowne), E.J. Lightfoot (10) (Lansdowne); *E.O'D. Davy 31 (Lansdowne), P.F. Murray (18) (Wanderers); G.R. Beamish (24) (Leicester), M.J. Dunne 13 (Lansdowne), H.O'H. O'Neill (6) (UC Cork), J. Russell 7 (UC Cork), J.A.E. Siggins 10 (Belfast Collegians), C.E.St J. Beamish 2 (Harlequins), W.McC. Ross 6 (Queen's U. Belfast), V.J. Pike 9 (Lansdowne).

SCOTLAND   D.I. Brown (3) (Cambridge U.); *I.S. Smith (31) (London Scottish), H.D.B. Lorraine (3) (Oxford U.), H. Lind 10 (Dunfermline), P.M.S. Gedge (1) (Edinburgh Wands); K.L.T. Jackson 3 (Oxford U.), W.R. Logan 6 (Edinburgh Wands); J.A. Waters 3 (Selkirk), J.R. Thom (3) (Watsonians), J.M. Ritchie 3 (Watsonians), J.A. Beattie 13 (Hawick), M.S. Stewart 5 (Stewart's FP), W.B. Welsh (19) (Hawick), J.M. Henderson (3) (Edinburgh Acads), R. Rowand 6 (Glasgow HSFP).

Referee B.S. Cumberlege (England)

1934

CARDIFF England beat Wales 9-0 · MURRAYFIELD Wales beat Scotland 13-6
DUBLIN England beat Ireland 13-3 · MURRAYFIELD Scotland beat Ireland 16-9
SWANSEA Wales beat Ireland 13-0 · TWICKENHAM England beat Scotland 6-3

CHAMPIONSHIP TABLE
England – Championship, Triple Crown

Pos	Country	P	W	D	L	F	A	Pts	Tries F	A
1	England (3)	3	3	0	0	28	6	6	8	2
2	Wales (4)	3	2	0	1	26	15	4	6	4
3	Scotland (1)	3	1	0	2	25	28	2	5	8
4	Ireland (2)	3	0	0	3	12	42	0	4	9

As with Scotland the previous year, there were no serious challengers to England's supremacy, for although they did much reshuffling within the team they won the Triple Crown convincingly. Wales, bottom in 1933, showed substantial improvement by beating Scotland and Ireland, and finishing runners-up. These were the days when the fast breakaway forwards were in their prime. Their chief duty was to hound the fly-half and inside centre. These so-called 'spoiling' tactics disrupted many attacking ploys. Often overlooked, however, was that a by-product of the disruption was an increase in broken play possession. The speed of service from set-pieces became increasingly important, much more variety was needed of both half-backs, and the scrum-half's strength and ability to break inside the defensive shield opened up new vistas for the attacking side. Therefore the 1930s were not entirely negative play. Another development in the game was the drop out from halfway after an unconverted try, which was not as important in the 15-man game as it was to become in that highly popular offshoot, seven-a-side rugby.

WALES v ENGLAND

45/331

20 January 1934
Cardiff Arms Park
England 9 (3T) Wales 0

England T: Meikle (2), Warr.

Wales played 13 new caps on a day which celebrated the opening of the new north stand. The stand, with 5242 seats, cost £20,000 which was substantially offset by an attendance of 50,000 and receipts of £9000, both records. The Welsh selectors were severely criticized in their choice – not only because of their inexperience but because nine of the players played most of their rugby outside Wales – and consequently five became one-cap wonders.

WALES   B. Howells (1) (Llanelli); B.T.V. Cowey 1 (The Welsh Regt., Newport), E.C. Davey 11 (Sale), J.I. Rees 1 (Edinburgh Wands), G.R. Rees-Jones 1 (London Welsh); C.W. Jones 1 (Cambridge U.), D.D. Evans (1) (Cardiff U.); C.R. Davies (1) (Bedford), *J.R. Evans (1) (Newport), G. Hughes 1 (Penarth), H. Truman 1 (Llanelli), D. Thomas 8 (Swansea), G. Prosser 1 (Neath), A.M. Rees 1 (London Welsh), K.W.J. Jones (1) (London Welsh).

ENGLAND   H.G. Owen-Smith 1 (Oxford U.); A.L. Warr 1 (Oxford U.), P. Cranmer 1 (Oxford U.), R.A. Gerrard 7 (Bath), G.W.C. Meikle 1 (Waterloo); W. Elliot 6 (US Portsmouth), B.C. Gadney 5 (Leicester); H. Rew 8 (Blackheath), G.G. Gregory 10 (Bristol), R.J. Longland 4 (Northampton), J.C. Wright (1) (Metropolitan Police), J. Dicks 1 (Northampton), J.McD. Hodgson 4 (Northern), H.A. Fry 1 (Liverpool), P.C. Hordern (4) (Gloucester).

Referee F.W. Haslett (Ireland)

SCOTLAND v WALES 45/332

3 February 1934
Murrayfield
Wales 13 (2G, 1T) Scotland 6 (1T, 1PG)

Scotland   T: Logan. PG: Ritchie.
Wales   T: Cowey (2), Rees. C: Jenkins.

For the second match in succession against Wales, Scotland introduced eight new caps, but unlike at Swansea the infusion of fresh blood did not come off. Cliff Jones, making his second appearance for Wales, apparently had an excellent game. Yet not one account mentioned him in any context.

SCOTLAND   K.W. Marshall 1 (Edinburgh Acads); R.W. Shaw 1 (Glasgow HSFP), R.C.S. Dick 1 (Cambridge U.), *H. Lind 11 (Dunfermline), J. Park (1) (Royal HSFP); K.L.T. Jackson (4) (Oxford U.), W.R. Logan 7 (Edinburgh Wands); W.A. Burnet 1 (W. of Scotland), L.B. Lambie 1 (Glasgow HSFP), J.M. Ritchie 4 (Watsonians), J.D. Lowe (1) (Heriot's FP), M.S. Stewart 6 (Stewart's FP), D.A. Thom 1 (London Scottish) R. Rowand (7) (Glasgow HSFP) J.A. Waters 4 (Selkirk).

WALES   V.G.J. Jenkins 3 (Bridgend); B.T.V. Cowey 2 (Newport), *E.C. Davey 12 (Swansea), J.I. Rees 2 (Swansea), G.R. Rees-Jones 2 (London Welsh); C.W. Jones 2 (Cambridge U.), A. Jones 1 (Llanelli); T. Day 8 (Swansea), I. Evans 1 (London Welsh), D.R. Prosser 1 (Neath), G. Hughes 2 (Penarth), W. Ward 1 (Cross Keys), G. Prosser 2 (Neath), A. Fear 1 (Newport), J. Lang 3 (Llanelli).

Referee H.L.V. Day (England)

IRELAND v ENGLAND 45/333

10 February 1934
Lansdowne Road, Dublin
England 13 (2G, 1T) Ireland 3 (1T)

Ireland   T: Morgan.
England   T: Fry (2), Meikle. C: Gregory (2).

Ireland introduced five newcomers to the Championship in this match and at the end of the match axed two of their veterans, Eugene

O'D. Davy and Morgan Crowe. Davy won 32 caps for Ireland, alternating between centre and fly-half, and his strength and speed on the burst, plus tremendous tackling, earned him the accolade of Ireland's finest pre-war fly-half. He was not without natural cunning either. Once, playing for Lansdowne against Cardiff, he tap kicked a penalty as the Welsh players retreated expecting a kick at goal, and ran over for a try in the corner. It was not cricket, nor indeed rugby, said Cardiff (who actually admired the ruse as they admitted later). Subsequently the International Board thwarted the innovation, and changed the Laws so that it was obligatory for the ball to travel a minimum of ten yards.

IRELAND   R.H. Pratt 4 (Dublin U.); J.J. O'Connor 2 (UC Cork), M.P. Crowe (12) (Lansdowne), J.V. Reardon 1 (Cork Constitution), L.B. McMahon 3 (UC Dublin); E.O'D. Davy (32) (Lansdowne), G.J. Morgan 1 (Clontarf); C.R.A. Graves 1 (Wanderers), V.J. Pike 10 (Lansdowne), S. Walker 1 (Instonians), J. Russell 8 (UC Cork), M.J. Dunne 14 (Lansdowne), W.McC. Ross 7 (Queen's U. Belfast), M.E. Bardon (1) (Bohemians), *J.A.E. Siggins 11 (Belfast Collegians).

ENGLAND   H.G. Owen-Smith 2 (Oxford U.); A.L. Warr (2) (Oxford U.), P. Cranmer 2 (Oxford U.), R.A. Gerrard 8 (Bath), G.W.C. Meikle 2 (Waterloo); W. Elliot (7) (US Portsmouth), *B.C. Gadney 6 (Leicester); R.J. Longland 5 (Northampton), G.G. Gregory 11 (Bristol), H. Rew 9 (Blackheath), J.W. Forrest 9 (US Portsmouth), J. Dicks 2 (Northampton), W.H. Weston 3 (Northampton), H.A. Fry 2 (Liverpool), J.McD. Hodgson 5 (Northern).

Referee M.A. Allan (Scotland

SCOTLAND v IRELAND 47/334

24 February 1934
Murrayfield
Scotland 16 (2G, 1T, 1PG) Ireland 9 (3T)

Scotland   T: Dick (2), Crawford. C: Shaw (2). PG: Allan.
Ireland   T: Russell (2), O'Connor.

Scotland had last beaten Ireland in a home match in 1924, at Inverleith, so this was their first victory over the Irish at Murrayfield. The sides matched each other try for try so the issue was settled by place kicks. It was Scotland's only victory of the season, and Ireland's second out of three defeats.

SCOTLAND   K.W. Marshall 2 (Edinburgh Acads); R.W. Shaw 2 (Glasgow HSFP), R.C.S. Dick 2 (Cambridge U.), H. Lind 12 (Dunfermline), J.A. Crawford (1) (London Scottish); J.L. Cotter 1 (Hillhead HSFP), W.R. Logan 8 (Edinburgh Wands); J.W. Allan 15 (Melrose), G.S. Cottington 1 (Kelso), J.M. Ritchie 5 (Watsonians), J.A. Beattie 14 (Hawick), *M.S. Stewart 7 (Stewart's FP), L.B. Lambie 2 (Glasgow HSFP), J.G. Watherston 1 (Edinburgh Wands), J.A. Waters 5 (Selkirk).

IRELAND   R.H. Pratt (5) (Dublin U.); D. Lane 1 (UC Cork), N.H. Lambert 1 (Lansdowne), J.V. Reardon (2) (Cork Constitution), J.J. O'Connor 3 (UC Cork); J.L. Reid 1 (Richmond), G.J. Morgan 2 (Clontarf); V.J. Pike 11 (Lansdowne), W.McC. Ross (8) (Queen's U. Belfast), C.R.A. Graves 2 (Wanderers), S. Walker 2 (Instonians), *J.A.E. Siggins 12 (Belfast Collegians), C.E.St J. Beamish 3 (Leicester), J. Russell 9 (UC Cork), M.J. Dunne 15 (Lansdowne).

Referee B.S. Cumberlege (England)

WALES v IRELAND 43/335

10 March 1934
St Helen's, Swansea
Wales 13 (2G, 1T) Ireland 0

Wales   T: Fear, Cowey, Jenkins. C: Jenkins (2).

Vivian Jenkins became the first Wales full-back to score a try in the Championship, and it was 33 years before another, Keith Jarrett, emulated him against England at Cardiff in 1967. This was Victor Pike's twelfth and final appearance for Ireland, to end one of the most distinguished dynasties in Irish rugby. Pike was one of five brothers from Tipperary, all massive forwards, who played for Leinster. Three of them became Bishops and two, Victor and Ted, played for Ireland. This match set in motion a period of total domination of Ireland by Wales in Wales. In 22 matches 1922–83 the Irish won only three times.

Action from England's Triple Crown deciding match against Scotland at Twickenham on 17 March 1934. K.C. Fyfe, Scotland's left wing, is under pressure close to his own line

WALES V.G.J. Jenkins 4 (Bridgend); B.T.V. Cowey 3 (Newport), *E.C. Davey 13 (Swansea), J.I. Rees 3 (Swansea), A. Bassett 1 (Aberavon); C.W. Jones 3 (Cambridge U.), A. Jones (2) (Llanelli); T. Day 9 (Swansea), I. Evans (2) (London Welsh), D.R. Prosser (2) (Neath), G. Hughes (3) (Penarth), W. Ward (2) (Cross Keys), G. Prosser (3) (Neath), J. Lang 4 (Llanelli), A. Fear 2 (Newport).

IRELAND D.J. Langan (1) (Clontarf); D. Lane 2 (UC Cork), N.H. Lambert (2) (Lansdowne), A.H. Bailey 1 (Lansdowne), J.J. O'Connor 4 (UC Cork); J.L. Reid (2) (Richmond), G.J. Morgan 3 (Clontarf); N.F. McGrath (1) (London Irish), V.J. Pike (12) (Aldershot Services), J. Megaw 1 (Instonians), *J.A.E. Siggins 13 (Belfast Collegians), J. Russell 10 (UC Cork), C.R.A. Graves 3 (Wanderers), C.E.St J. Beamish 4 (Leicester), M.J. Dunne (16) (Lansdowne).

Referee W. Burnett (Scotland)

ENGLAND v SCOTLAND 44/336

17 March 1934
Twickenham
England 6 (2T) Scotland 3 (1T)

England T: Booth, Meikle.
Scotland T: Shaw.

Having won at Cardiff Arms Park and Lansdowne Road, England came home to Twickenham to win the Triple Crown and the Championship. Success was one thing, selection another. Six England players, including four of what was described as a very good pack, were not required again for the Championship.

ENGLAND H.G. Owen-Smith 3 (St Mary's H.); L.A. Booth 4 (Headingley), P. Cranmer 3 (Oxford U.), R.A. Gerrard 9 (Bath), G.W.C. Meikle (3) (Waterloo); C.F. Slow (1) (Leicester), *B.C. Gadney 7 (Leicester); H. Rew (10) (Blackheath), G.G. Gregory (12) (Bristol), R.J. Longland 6 (Northampton), J.W. Forrest (10) (US Portsmouth), J. Dicks 3 (Northampton), W.H. Weston 4 (Northampton), H.A. Fry (3) (Liverpool), D.A. Kendrew 5 (Leicester).

SCOTLAND K.W. Marshall 3 (Edinburgh Acads); R.W. Shaw 3 (Glasgow HSFP), R.C.S. Dick 3 (Cambridge U.), H. Lind 13 (Dunfermline), K.C. Fyfe 3 (Cambridge U.); J.L. Cotter (2) (Hillhead HSFP), W.R. Logan 9 (Edinburgh Wands); J.W. Allan (16) (Melrose), G.S. Cottington 2 (Kelso), J.M. Ritchie (6) (Watsonians), J.A. Beattie 15 (Hawick), *M.S. Stewart (8) (Stewart's FP), L.B. Lambie 3 (Glasgow HSFP), J.G. Watherston (2) (Edinburgh Wands), J.A. Waters 6 (Selkirk).

Referee F.W. Haslett (Ireland)

1935

TWICKENHAM England drew Wales 3-3 · CARDIFF Wales beat Scotland 10-6
TWICKENHAM England beat Ireland 14-3 · DUBLIN Ireland beat Scotland 12-5
BELFAST Ireland beat Wales 9-3 · MURRAYFIELD Scotland beat England 10-7

CHAMPIONSHIP TABLE
Ireland – Championship

Pos	Country	P	W	D	L	F	A	Pts	Tries F	A
1	Ireland (4)	3	2	0	1	24	22	4	6	2
2	England (1)	3	1	1	1	24	16	3	2	4
3	Wales (2)	3	1	1	1	16	18	3	3	3
4	Scotland (3)	3	1	0	2	21	29	2	5	7

Ireland could not have thought much of their title prospects after being decisively beaten by England at Twickenham. However, by defeating Scotland and Wales, Ireland leap-frogged to their first title win since 1932. In effect the Irish had the Scots to thank for it, because England would have been Champions had they been able to overthrow their Murrayfield jinx. They battled well but Scotland prevailed for a sixth home victory in a row over England.

ENGLAND v WALES   46/337

19 January 1935
Twickenham
England 3 (1PG) Wales 3 (1T)

England PG: Boughton.
Wales T: Wooller.

A penalty goal by Boughton saved England from defeat, but it was the first time in 21 matches since 1909 that they had not registered a try against Wales. In those days England-Wales matches were tough, keenly contested but rarely dirty. This one seemed to be an exception with both sets of forwards involved in rough-

housing. Although England had won the Triple Crown the previous season, they capped nine newcomers in this match.

ENGLAND   H.J. Boughton 1 (Gloucester); L.A. Booth 5 (Headingley), P. Cranmer 4 (Oxford U.), J. Heaton 1 (Liverpool U.), R. Leyland 1 (Waterloo); P.L. Candler 1 (Cambridge U.), J.L. Giles 1 (Coventry); *D.A. Kendrew 6 (Leicester), E.S. Nicholson 1 (Oxford U.), R.J. Longland 7 (Northampton), J. Dicks 4 (Northampton), A.J. Clarke 1 (Coventry), A.G. Cridlan 1 (Blackheath), W.H. Weston 5 (Northampton), D.T. Kemp (1) (Blackheath).

WALES   V.G.J. Jenkins 5 (Bridgend); B.T.V. Cowey (4) (Newport), *E.C. Davey 14 (Swansea), W. Wooller 4 (Cambridge U.), A. Bassett 2 (Aberavon); C.W. Jones 4 (Cambridge U.), W.C. Powell 24 (Northampton); E. Jones (5) (Llanelli), S.C. Murphy 1 (Cross Keys), T. Day 10 (Swansea), D. Thomas 9 (Swansea), H. Truman (2) (Llanelli), A. M. Rees 2 (Cambridge U.), A. Skym (19) (Cardiff), J. Lang 5 (Llanelli).

Referee F.W. Haslett (Ireland)

WALES v SCOTLAND   46/338

2 February 1935
Cardiff Arms Park
Wales 10 (2T, 1DG) Scotland 6 (2T)

Wales T: Jones, Wooller. DG: Jenkins.
Scotland T: Thom, Shaw.

Cliff Jones seems to have been at the centre of the action: he scored a scintillating try, created another for Wilf Wooller and then had to leave the field with a bad arm injury. The winning score came two minutes from time when Vivian

Jenkins dropped a goal. The Scottish team was largely untried in the international field. Only Jock Beattie, making his sixteenth appearance, and Logan, the scrum-half, were versed in the cut-and-thrust of it all.

WALES   V.G.J. Jenkins 6 (Bridgend); A. Bassett 3 (Aberavon), W. Wooller 5 (Cambridge U.), *E.C. Davey 15 (Swansea), J.I. Rees 4 (Swansea); C.W. Jones 5 (Cambridge U.), W.C. Powell 25 (Northampton); T.J. Rees 1 (Newport), S.C. Murphy 2 (Cross Keys), T. Day 11 (Swansea), D. Thomas 10 (Swansea), T. Williams 1 (Cross Keys), A.M. Rees 3 (Cambridge U.), A. Fear 3 (Newport), J. Lang 6 (Llanelli).

SCOTLAND   K.W. Marshall 4 (Edinburgh Acads); W.G.S. Johnston 1 (Cambridge U.), R.C.S. Dick 4 (Guy's H.), R.W. Shaw 4 (Glasgow HSFP), *K.C. Fyfe 4 (Cambridge U.); C.F. Grieve 1 (Oxford U.), W.R. Logan 10 (Edinburgh Wands); R.O. Murray 1 (Cambridge U.), G.S. Cottington 3 (Kelso), R.M. Grieve 1 (Kelso), J.A. Beattie 16 (Hawick), W.A. Burnet 2 (W. of Scotland), D.A. Thom 2 (London Scottish), L.B. Lambie 4 (Glasgow HSFP), J.A. Waters 7 (Selkirk).

Referee F.W. Haslett (Ireland)

ENGLAND v IRELAND   46/339

9 February 1935
Twickenham
England 14 (1G, 3PG) Ireland 3 (1T)

England   T: Giles. C: Boughton. PG: Boughton (3).
Ireland   T: O'Connor.

This relatively inexperienced Ireland side – in which only the captain, Jack Siggins, had won caps in double figures – was far better than the scoreline suggests. In fact they improved to such an extent that they went on to win the Championship ahead of their conquerors.

ENGLAND   H.J. Boughton 2 (Gloucester); L.A. Booth 6 (Headingley), J. Heaton 2 (Liverpool U.), R. Leyland 2 (Waterloo), P. Cranmer 5 (Oxford U.); J.A. Tallent (4) (Blackheath), J.L. Giles 2 (Coventry); *D.A. Kendrew 7 (Leicester), E.S. Nicholson 2 (Oxford U.), R.J. Longland 8 (Northampton), J. Dicks 5 (Northampton), A.J. Clarke 2 (Coventry), A.G. Cridlan 2 (Blackheath), W.H. Weston 6 (Northampton), A.T. Payne 1 (Bristol).

IRELAND   D.P. Morris 3 (Bective Rangers); D. Lane 3 (UC Cork), P. Crowe 1 (Blackrock College), E.C. Ridgway 3 (Wanderers), J.J. O'Connor 5 (UC Dublin); A. H. Bailey 2 (UC Dublin), G.J. Morgan 4 (Clontarf); C.E.St J. Beamish 5 (Leicester), C.R.A. Graves 4 (Wanderers), S. Walker 3 (Instonians), S.J. Deering 1 (Bective Rangers), J. Russell 11 (UC Cork), H.J.M. Sayers 1 (Aldershot Services), P.J. Lawlor 1 (Bective Rangers), *J.A.E. Siggins 14 (Belfast Collegians).

Referee M.A. Allan (Scotland)

IRELAND v SCOTLAND   48/340

23 February 1935
Lansdowne Road, Dublin
Ireland 12 (4T) Scotland 5 (1G)

Ireland   T: O'Connor, Lawlor, Bailey, Ridgeway.
Scotland   T: Shaw. C: Fyfe.

Irish goal-kicking had let them down against Scotland the previous season, and the art was conspicuously lacking again; Ridgeway, Sayers and Siggins all tried and failed. Fortunately Ireland scored enough tries for it not to be crucial in a match which set them up to win the Championship.

IRELAND   D.P. Morris 4 (Bective Rangers); J.J. O'Connor 6 (UC Dublin), E.C. Ridgeway 4 (Wanderers), A.H. Bailey 3 (UC Dublin), D. Lane (4) (UC Cork); V.A. Hewitt 1 (Instonians), G.J. Morgan 5 (Clontarf); S.J. Deering 2 (Bective Rangers), J. Russell 12 (UC Cork), P.J. Lawlor 2 (Bective Rangers), C.R.A. Graves 5 (Wanderers), S. Walker 4 (Instonians), *J.A.E. Siggins 15 (Belfast Collegians), H.J.M. Sayers 2 (Aldershot Services), C.E.St J. Beamish 6 (Leicester).

SCOTLAND   K.W. Marshall 5 (Edinburgh Acads); W.G.S. Johnston 2 (Cambridge U.), R.C.S. Dick 5 (Guy's H.), H. Lind 14 (London Scottish), K.C. Fyfe 5 (Cambridge U.); *R.W. Shaw 5 (Glasgow HSFP), W.R. Logan 11 (Edinburgh Wands); A.S.B. McNeil (1) (Watsonians), G.S. Cottington 4 (Kelso), R.M. Grieve 2 (Kelso), J.A. Beattie 17 (Hawick), W.A. Burnet 3 (W. of Scotland), D.A. Thom 3 (London Scottish), L.B. Lambie 5 (Glasgow HSFP), J.A. Waters 8 (Selkirk).

Referee J. Hughes (England)

Jack Siggins, the Belfast Collegians forward, who captained Ireland in nine Championship matches 1934–36

IRELAND v WALES   44/341

9 March 1935
Ravenhill, Belfast
Ireland 9 (1T, 2PG) Wales 3 (1PG)

Ireland   T: Doyle. PG: Siggins, Bailey.
Wales   PG: James.

This victory earned Ireland the Championship, and it was thoroughly deserved for they played for a large part of the match without Joe O'Connor, who had broken a collar-bone in a collision with Wilf Wooller. Wales failed to score a try against Ireland for the first time in 12 successive matches and this, added to a general inefficiency, led to last appearances for five players, including Wick Powell, a hero on many occasions in his 26-cap career.

IRELAND   D.P. Morris (5) (Bective Rangers); J.J. O'Connor 7 (UC Dublin), A.H. Bailey 4 (UC Dublin), E.C. Ridgeway (5) (Wanderers), J. L. Doyle (1) (Bective Rangers); V.A. Hewitt 2 (Instonians), G.J. Morgan 6 (Clontarf); C.E.St J. Beamish 7 (Leicester), C.R.A. Graves 6 (Wanderers), S. Walker 5 (Instonians), J. Russell 13 (UC Cork), S.J. Deering 3 (Bective Rangers), H.J.M. Sayers 3 (Aldershot Services), P.J. Lawlor 3 (Bective Rangers), *J.A.E. Siggins 16 (Belfast Collegians).

WALES   T.O. James 1 (Aberavon); G.R. Rees-Jones 3 (Oxford U.), *E.C. Davey 16 (Swansea), W. Wooller 6 (Cambridge U.), A. Bassett 4 (Aberavon); C.W. Jones 6 (Cambridge U.), W.C. Powell (26) (Northampton); T.J. Rees 2 (Newport), S.C. Murphy (3) (Cross Keys), T. Day (12) (Swansea), D. Thomas (11) (Swansea), T. Williams 2 (Cross Keys), A.M. Rees 4 (Cambridge U.), J. Lang 7 (Llanelli), A. Fear (4) (Newport).

Referee M. A. Allan (Scotland)

SCOTLAND v ENGLAND   45/342

16 March 1935
Murrayfield
Scotland 10 (2G) England 7 (1T, 1DG)

Scotland   T: Fyfe, Lambie. C: Fyfe (2).
England   T: Booth. DG: Cranmer.

This was Scotland's sixth successive win over England at Murrayfield, their best ever sequence there. Although England created many chances, the contest was decided by the harmony and skill of the Scottish halves, Logan and Shaw. Nevertheless it was Scotland's only victory of the season and they finished bottom of the Championship.

SCOTLAND   K.W. Marshall 6 (Edinburgh Acads); J.E. Forrest (1) (Glasgow Acads), R.C.S. Dick 6 (Guy's H.), W.C.W. Murdoch 1 (Hillhead HSFP), K.C. Fyfe 6 (Cambridge U.); *R.W. Shaw 6 (Glasgow HSFP), W.R. Logan 12 (Edinburgh Wands); R.O. Murray (2) (Cambridge U.), P.W. Tait (1) (Royal HSFP), R.M. Grieve 3 (Kelso), J.A. Beattie 18 (Hawick), W.A. Burnet 4 (W. of Scotland), D.A. Thom (4) (London Scottish), L.B. Lambie (6) (Glasgow HSFP), J.A. Waters 9 (Selkirk).

ENGLAND   H.J. Boughton (3) (Gloucester); L.A. Booth (7) (Headingley), P. Cranmer 6 (Richmond), J. Heaton 3 (Liverpool U.), R. Leyland (3) (Waterloo); J. R. Auty (1) (Headingley), *B.C. Gadney 8 (Leicester); J. Dicks 6 (Northampton), E.S. Nicholson 3 (Oxford U.), R.J. Longland 9 (Northampton), A.J. Clarke 3 (Coventry), C.S.H. Webb 7 (Devonport Services), W.H. Weston 7 (Northampton), A.G. Cridlan (3) (Blackheath), A.T. Payne (2) (Bristol).

Referee R.W. Jeffares (Ireland)

SWANSEA Wales drew England 0-0 · MURRAYFIELD Wales beat Scotland 13-3
DUBLIN Ireland beat England 6-3 · MURRAYFIELD Ireland beat Scotland 10-4
CARDIFF Wales beat Ireland 3-0 · TWICKENHAM England beat Scotland 9-8

CHAMPIONSHIP TABLE
Wales – Championship

Pos	Country	P	W	D	L	F	A	Pts	Tries F	A
1	Wales (3)	3	2	1	0	16	3	5	3	1
2	Ireland (1)	3	2	0	1	16	10	4	4	1
3	England (2)	3	1	1	12	14	3	4	3	
4	Scotland (4)	3	0	0	3	15	32	0	2	8

Wales won the Championship even though their 16 points from three matches was the lowest ever title-winning total, save for Ireland's 15 points in 1894. Ireland were second, having established a four-match winning sequence which they have bettered only once, when they won five in a row 1968–69. The RFU, for reasons best known to themselves, proposed to the International Board that the value of a dropped goal be changed from four to three points. The proposal must have had its roots in domestic club rugby for the dropped goal was somewhat of a rarity in international matches and on a few occasions only could this method of scoring have been said to have affected the outcome of a match. In any event the International Board rejected the proposal when they considered it in 1937, though, of course, the value of the kick was changed in 1949.

WALES v ENGLAND 47/343

18 January 1936
St Helen's, Swansea
Wales 0 England 0

The second time a Wales-England fixture produced no score, the previous occasion being in 1887 at Llanelli. Of more concern to Wales, it was their second home match running in which they failed to score against England. Clearly, the inability to score was a disappointment to the respective supporters, particularly as both sides had shown no such ineffectiveness in victories over New Zealand the previous month.

WALES   V.G.J. Jenkins 7 (London Welsh); G.R. Rees-Jones (4) (Oxford U.), *J.I. Rees 5 (Swansea), W. Wooller 7 (Cambridge U.), B.E.W. McCall 1 (The Welch Regt., Newport); C.W. Jones 7 (Cambridge U.), H. Tanner 1 (Swansea); T.J. Rees 3 (Newport), B. Evans 3 (Llanelli), T. Williams 3 (Cross Keys), H. Thomas 1 (Neath), G. Williams 1 (Aberavon), A.M. Rees 5 (London Welsh), E. Long 1 (Swansea), J. Lang 8 (Llanelli).

ENGLAND   H.G. Owen-Smith 4 (St Mary's H.); A. Obolensky 1 (Oxford U.), R.A. Gerrard 10 (Bath), P. Cranmer 7 (Richmond), H.S. Sever 1 (Sale); P.L. Candler 2 (St Bart's H.), *B.C. Gadney 9 (Leicester); D.A. Kendrew 8 (Leicester), E.S. Nicholson (4) (Leicester), R.J. Longland 10 (Northampton), C.S.H. Webb 8 (Devonport Services), A.J. Clarke 4 (Coventry), W.H. Weston 8 (Northampton), E.A. Hamilton-Hill 1 (Harlequins), P.E. Dunkley 3 (Harlequins).

Referee F.W. Haslett (Ireland)

SCOTLAND v WALES 47/344

1 February 1936
Murrayfield
Wales 13 (2G, 1T) Scotland 3 (1T)

Scotland T: Murray.
Wales T: Wooller, Davey, Jones. C: Jenkins (2).

Murrayfield held few terrors for Wales, who won for the fourth time in five visits to Scotland's headquarters. The match's highlight was another sparkling try from Cliff Jones.

SCOTLAND K.W. Marshall 7 (Edinburgh Acads); W.C.W. Murdoch 2 (Hillhead HSFP), *R.C.S. Dick 7 (Guy's H.), H.M. Murray 1 (Glasgow U.), K.C. Fyfe 7 (Cambridge U.); R.W. Shaw 7 (Glasgow HSFP), W.R. Logan 13 (Edinburgh Wands); R.M. Grieve 4 (Kelso), W.A.H. Druitt 1 (London Scottish), J.A. Waters 10 (Selkirk), J.A. Beattie 19 (Hawick), W.A. Burnet 5 (W. of Scotland), M.McG. Cooper 1 (Oxford U.), G.D. Shaw 1 (Sale), P.L. Duff 1 (Glasgow Acads).

WALES V.G.J. Jenkins 8 (London Welsh); B.E.W. McCall 2 (Newport), W. Wooller 8 (Cambridge U.), *E.C. Davey 17 (Swansea), J.I. Rees 6 (Swansea); C.W. Jones 8 (Cambridge U.), H. Tanner 2 (Swansea); T.J. Rees 4 (Newport), B. Evans 4 (Llanelli), T. Williams 4 (Cross Keys), H. Thomas 2 (Neath), G. Williams 2 (Aberavon), A.M. Rees 6 (London Welsh), E. Long 2 (Swansea), J. Lang 9 (Llanelli).

Referee C.H. Gadney (England)

IRELAND v ENGLAND 47/345

8 February 1936
Lansdowne Road, Dublin
Ireland 6 (2T) England 3 (1T)

Ireland T: Bailey, Boyle.
England T: Sever.

England were seeking their fifth successive victory over Ireland, but were denied it, as much due to their own inability to make more of their chances as to the tenacity of their defence.

Irish newspaper previews made much of the first – and only – appearance at Lansdowne Road of Prince Alexander Obolensky, who had inspired the rugby public with two tries against New Zealand a month earlier. 'Obo' suffered the fate of so many wings before him and was starved of opportunities to show his distinctive gangling style of running.

IRELAND G.L. Malcolmson 1 (NIFC); F.G. Moran 1 (Clontarf), A.H. Bailey 5 (UC Dublin), L.B. McMahon 4 (Blackrock College), C.V. Boyle 1 (Dublin U.); V.A. Hewitt 3 (Instonians), G.J. Morgan 7 (Clontarf); S. Walker 6 (Instonians), C.R.A. Graves 7 (Wanderers), C.E.St J. Beamish 8 (NIFC), S.J. Deering 4 (Bective Rangers), J. Russell 14 (UC Cork), H.J.M. Sayers 4 (Lansdowne), R. Alexander 1 (NIFC), *J.A.E. Siggins 17 (Belfast Collegians).

ENGLAND H.G. Owen-Smith 5 (St Mary's H.); A. Obolensky 2 (Oxford U.), R.A. Gerrard 11 (Bath), P. Cranmer 8 (Richmond), H.S. Sever 2 (Sale); P.L. Candler 3 (St Bart's H.), *B.C. Gadney 10 (Leicester); R.J. Longland 11 (Northampton), D.A. Kendrew (9) (Leicester), H.F. Wheatley 1 (Coventry), A.J. Clarke (5) (Coventry), C.S.H. Webb 9 (Devonport Services), E.A. Hamilton-Hill (2) (Harlequins), J. McD. Hodgson (6) (Northern), P.E. Dunkley 4 (Harlequins).

Referee M.A. Allan (Scotland)

SCOTLAND v IRELAND 49/346

22 February 1936
Murrayfield
Ireland 10 (2T, 1DG) Scotland 4 (1DG)

Scotland DG: Murdoch.
Ireland T: Walker, McMahon. DG: Hewitt.

The burgeoning talent of Larry McMahon, the Blackrock College centre, was one of the features of Ireland's fifth victory in six visits to Murrayfield. A fine passer, McMahon was also an intuitive opportunist, as he proved in this match: seizing on two loose passes by Scotland he made a try for himself and another for Walker.

SCOTLAND J.M. Kerr 1 (Heriot's FP); W.C.W. Murdoch 3 (Hillhead HSFP), *R.C.S. Dick 8 (Guy's H.), H.M. Murray (2) (Glasgow U.), R.J.E. Whitworth (1) (London Scottish); R.W. Shaw 8

(Glasgow HSFP), W.R. Logan 14 (Edinburgh Wands); R.M. Grieve 5 (Kelso), W.A.H. Druitt 2 (London Scottish), J.A. Waters 11 (Selkirk), J.A. Beattie 20 (Hawick), W.A. Burnet 6 (W. of Scotland), M.McG. Cooper (2) (Oxford U.), V.G. Weston 1 (Kelvinside Acads), P.L. Duff 2 (Glasgow Acads).

IRELAND G.L. Malcolmson 2 (NIFC); J.J. O'Connor 8 (UC Cork), A.H. Bailey 6 (UC Dublin), L.B. McMahon 5 (Blackrock College), C.V. Boyle 2 (Dublin U.); V.A. Hewitt 4 (Instonians), G.J. Morgan 8 (Clontarf); R. Alexander 2 (NIFC), S. Walker 7 (Instonians), C.E.St J. Beamish 9 (NIFC), H.J.M. Sayers 5 (Lansdowne), S.J. Deering 5 (Bective Rangers), *J.A.E. Siggins 18 (Belfast Collegians), J. Russell 15 (UC Cork), C.R.A. Graves 8 (Wanderers).

Referee J.W. Faull (Wales)

WALES v IRELAND 45/347

14 March 1936
Cardiff Arms Park
Wales 3 (1PG) Ireland 0

Wales PG: Jenkins.

As in 1931, everything hung on the clash between Wales and Ireland: a win for Wales meant the Championship, for Ireland it meant the Triple Crown. This heightened the attraction of the match to such an extent that many thousands more than could be accommodated tried to gain access to the Arms Park. When hundreds rushed the gates, the Cardiff City Fire Brigade dispersed them with hoses. More seriously, many spectators were injured inside the ground when overspilling on the terracing caused panic and many were trampled on in the resultant stampede. Ireland were a much more experienced side but the issue was settled by a penalty goal kicked by Vivian Jenkins after an Irish player was penalized for not playing the ball after a tackle. Towards the end Ireland still could have won when Vic Hewitt attempted a dropped goal which narrowly missed.

WALES V.G.J. Jenkins 9 (London Welsh); *J.I. Rees 7 (Swansea), W.T.H. Davies 1 (Swansea), W. Wooller 9 (Cambridge U.), B.E.W. McCall (3) (Newport); C.W. Jones 9 (Cambridge U.), H. Tanner 3 (Swansea); T.J. Rees 5 (Newport), B.

Evans 5 (Llanelli), T. Williams 5 (Cross Keys), H. Thomas 3 (Neath), G. Williams (3) (Aberavon), A.M. Rees 7 (London Welsh), J. Lang 10 (Llanelli), E. Long 3 (Swansea).

IRELAND G.L. Malcolmson 3 (NIFC); C.V. Boyle 3 (Dublin U.), A.H. Bailey 7 (UC Dublin), L.B. McMahon 6 (UC Dublin), J.J. O'Connor 9 (UC Cork); V.A. Hewitt (5) (Instonians), G.J. Morgan 9 (Clontarf); S. Walker 8 (Instonians), C.R.A. Graves 9 (Wanderers), C.E.St J. Beamish 10 (NIFC), J. Russell 16 (UC Cork), S.J. Deering 6 (Bective Rangers), H.J.M. Sayers 6 (Lansdowne), R. Alexander 3 (NIFC), *J.A.E. Siggins 19 (Belfast Collegians).

Referee C.H. Gadney (England)

ENGLAND v SCOTLAND 46/348

21 March 1936
Twickenham
England 9 (3T) Scotland 8 (1G, 1PG)

England T: Bolton, Candler, Cranmer.
Scotland T: Shaw. C: Fyfe. PG: Fyfe.

This bottom-of-the-table clash ended with England winning their only match of the season and Scotland beaten in all three.

ENGLAND H.G. Owen-Smith 6 (St Mary's H.); A. Obolensky (3) (Oxford U.), R.A. Gerrard (12) (Bath), P. Cranmer 9 (Richmond), H.S. Sever 3 (Sale); P.L. Candler 4 (St Bart's H.), *B.C. Gadney 11 (Leicester); R.J. Longland 12 (Northampton), H.B. Toft 1 (Waterloo), J. Dicks 7 (Northampton), C.S.H. Webb (10) (Devonport Services), P.E. Dunkley (5) (Harlequins), R. Bolton 2 (Harlequins), W.H. Weston 9 (Northampton), P.W.P. Brook (3) (Harlequins).

SCOTLAND J.M. Kerr 2 (Heriot's FP); R.W. Shaw 9 (Glasgow HSFP), H. Lind (15) (London Scottish), R.C.S. Dick 9 (Guy's H.), K.C. Fyfe 8 (Sale); C.F. Grieve (2) (Oxford U.), W.R. Logan 15 (Edinburgh Wands); R.M. Grieve (6) (Kelso), G.S. Cottington (5) (Headingley), W.A.H. Druitt (3) (London Scottish), *J.A. Beattie (21) (Hawick), W.A. Burnet (7) (W. of Scotland), R.W. Barrie (1) (Hawick), V.G. Weston (2) (Kelvinside Acads), J.A. Waters 12 (Selkirk).

Referee T.H. Phillips (Wales)

1937

TWICKENHAM England beat Wales 4-3 · SWANSEA Scotland beat Wales 13-6
TWICKENHAM England beat Ireland 9-8 · DUBLIN Ireland beat Scotland 11-4
MURRAYFIELD England beat Scotland 6-3 · BELFAST Ireland beat Wales 5-3

CHAMPIONSHIP TABLE
England – Championship

									Tries	
Pos	Country	P	W	D	L	F	A	Pts	F	A
1	England (3)	3	3	0	0	19	14	5	4	3
2	Ireland (2)	3	2	0	1	24	16	4	6	2
3	Scotland (4)	3	1	0	2	20	23	2	3	7
4	Wales (1)	3	0	0	3	12	22	0	3	4

The fiftieth Championship was won by England with Wales Wooden Spoonists, an almost complete reversal of the outcome of 1936. The Championship was anomalous in that both Ireland, the runners-up, and third-placed Scotland scored more points than the Champions.

Of the 50 Championships played, England had won 18, Scotland 14, Wales 11, Ireland 7 and France none. But in the subsequent 39 Championships, the balance of power shifted totally with Wales winning 16 times, France 9, Ireland 6, England 6 and Scotland only 2. Allowing that several early Championships were only partly completed, that England did not compete in 1888 and 1889 and France played in only 16 up to their banishment in 1931, the change in fortunes has been remarkable. Ireland, the 'Steady Eddies', might be absolved in that after 1937 they featured nearly as often as they did before. The significant roles in this great turn around concern Wales and France, who between them won 25 of the 39 titles post-1937, and England and Scotland, who totalled only 8 during the same period. In basic terms an explanation for the *volte-face* is that Wales and France have improved and England and Scotland have not. A detailed study might indicate something totally different: it would be fascinating and illuminating and, at the very least, provide England and Scotland with something to debate.

ENGLAND v WALES 48/349

16 January 1937
Twickenham
England 4 (1DG) Wales 3 (1T)

England DG: Sever.
Wales T: Wooller.

Once again, England used the Welsh match as an opportunity to blood new players – seven in all, including five in the pack. Wales were less audacious; they introduced three newcomers. Curiously two of the men facing each other in an international for the first time, Robin Prescott and Bill Clement, were to contribute far more to the game off-the-field than they did in this match. Each became secretary of their respective Unions.

ENGLAND *H.G. Owen-Smith 7 (St Mary's H.); A.G. Butler 1 (Harlequins), P.L. Candler 5 (St Bart's H.), P. Cranmer 10 (Richmond),H.S. Sever 4 (Sale); T.A. Kemp 1 (Cambridge U.), J.L. Giles 3 (Coventry); R.E. Prescott 1 (Harlequins), H.B. Toft 2 (Waterloo), R.J. Longland 13 (Northampton), T.F. Huskisson 1 (OMT), A. Wheatley 1 (Coventry), D.A. Campbell 1 (Cambridge U.), W.H. Weston 10 (Northampton), D.L.K. Milman 1 (Bedford).

WALES V.G.J. Jenkins 10 (London Welsh); W.H. Clement 1 (Llanelli) W. Wooller 10 (Cardiff), *E.C. Davey 18 (London Welsh), J.I. Rees 8 (Swansea); W.T.H. Davies 2 (Swansea), H. Tanner 4 (Swansea); T.J. Rees 6 (Newport), B. Evans (6) (Llanelli), E. Evans 1 (Llanelli), D.L. Thomas (1) (Neath), H. Thomas 4 (Neath), A.M. Rees 8 (London Welsh), E. Long 4 (Swansea), J. Lang (11) (Swansea).

Referee R.A. Beattie (Scotland)

England's new captain, Tuppy Owen-Smith, gives advice at a training session at the HAC Ground in the City of London before the opening match of the 1937 season, against Wales

WALES v SCOTLAND 48/350

6 February 1937
St Helen's, Swansea
Scotland 13 (2G, 1T) Wales 6 (2T)

Wales T: Wooller (2).
Scotland T: Wilson Shaw, Dick (2). C: Duncan Shaw (2).

Edinburgh Wanderers had the rare distinction of providing each team's captain for a Championship match. The Scottish selectors of the day could hardly have been accused of inconsistency: for the third time since 1933 they brought in eight new players to face Wales, a practice begun in 1901 when it was rare for players' international careers to extend beyond half-a-dozen caps. It proved to be Scotland's last victory in Wales until 1962.

WALES T.O. James (2) (Aberavon); W.H. Hopkin (1) (Newport), *J.I. Rees 9 (Edinburgh Wands), W. Wooller 11 (Cardiff), W.H. Clement 2 (Llanelli); R.R. Morris (2) (Bristol), H. Tanner 5 (Swansea); T. Williams 6 (Cross Keys), W.H. Travers 1 (Newport), T.J. Rees (7) (Newport), H. Rees 1 (Cardiff), H. Thomas 5 (Neath), E. Long 5 (Swansea), A.M. Rees 9 (London Welsh), E. Watkins 1 (Cardiff).

SCOTLAND J.M. Kerr 3 (Heriot's FP); W.G.S. Johnston 3 (Richmond), R.C.S. Dick 10 (Guy's H.), D.J. Macrae 1 (St Andrew's U.), R.W. Shaw 10 (Glasgow HSFP); W.A. Ross 1 (Hillhead HSFP), *W.R. Logan 16 (Edinburgh Wands); M.M. Henderson 1 (Dunfermline), G.L. Gray 1 (Gala), W.M. Inglis 1 (Cambridge U.), G.B. Horsburgh 1 (London Scottish), C.L. Melville 1 (The Army), W.B. Young 1 (Cambridge U.), G.D. Shaw 2 (Gala), J.A. Waters 13 (Selkirk).

Referee C.H. Gadney (England)

ENGLAND v IRELAND 48/351

13 February 1937
Twickenham
England 9 (2T, 1PG) Ireland 8 (1G, 1T)

England T: Butler, Sever. PG: Cranmer.
Ireland T: Moran (2). C: Bailey.

England, who edged out Wales by a single point in January, were involved in another photo-finish. H.S. Sever, whose dropped goal had won the Welsh match, did the trick against Ireland with a try. The difference, though, in a match in which both sides scored two tries was that Peter Cranmer's penalty goal was worth one more point than A.H. Bailey's conversion.

ENGLAND   *H.G. Owen-Smith 8 (St Mary's H.); A.G. Butler (2) (Harlequins), P. Cranmer 11 (Richmond), P.L. Candler 6 (St Bart's H.), H.S. Sever 5 (Sale); T.A. Kemp 2 (Cambridge U.), J.L. Giles 4 (Coventry); R.E. Prescott 2 (Harlequins), H.B. Toft 3 (Waterloo), R.J. Longland 14 (Northampton), T.F. Huskisson 2 (OMT), A. Wheatley 2 (Coventry), D.A. Campbell (2) (Cambridge U.), W.H. Weston 11 (Northampton), J. Dicks (8) (Northampton).

IRELAND   G.L. Malcolmson 4 (NIFC); F.G. Moran 2 (Clontarf), L.B. McMahon 7 (Blackrock College), A.H. Bailey 8 (UC Dublin), C.V. Boyle 4 (Dublin U.); G.E. Cromey 1 (Queen's U. Belfast), *G.J. Morgan 10 (Clontarf); S. Walker 9 (Instonians), T.S. Corken 1 (Belfast Collegians), C.R.A. Graves 10 (Wanderers), J. Russell 17 (UC Cork), S.J. Deering 7 (Bective Rangers), P.J. Lawlor 4 (Bective Rangers), R. Alexander 4 (NIFC), J.A.E. Siggins 20 (Belfast Collegians).

Referee J.W. Faull (Wales)

IRELAND v SCOTLAND   50/352

27 February 1937
Lansdowne Road, Dublin
Ireland 11 (1G, 2T) Scotland 4 (1DG)

Ireland   T: Alexander, McMahon, Moran.
C: Bailey.
Scotland   DG: Wilson Shaw.

The fiftieth Championship match between Ireland and Scotland was played on a bitterly cold day in Dublin where a keen wind and occasional snow tested both sides. An injury to Wilson Shaw severely handicapped Scotland, who made several handling errors which led to two of Ireland's three tries. Despite their victory Ireland dispensed with the services of Jack Russell and Sam Deering, two of the stalwarts of their pack.

IRELAND   G.L. Malcolmson 5 (NIFC); C.V. Boyle 5 (Dublin U.), A.H. Bailey 9 (UC Dublin), L.B. McMahon 8 (Blackrock College), F.G. Moran 3

(Clontarf); G.E. Cromey 2 (Queen's U. Belfast), *G.J. Morgan 11 (Clontarf); C.R.A. Graves 11 (Wanderers), T.S. Corken 2 (Belfast Collegians), S. Walker 10 (Instonians), S.J. Deering (8) (Bective Rangers), J. Russell (18) (UC Cork), P.J. Lawlor 5 (Bective Rangers), R. Alexander 5 (NIFC), J.A.E. Siggins 21 (Belfast Collegians).

SCOTLAND   J.M. Kerr (4) (Heriot's FP); W.G.S. Johnston 4 (Richmond), D.J. Macrae 2 (St Andrew's U.), I. Shaw (1) (Glasgow HSFP), R.W. Shaw 11 (Glasgow HSFP); R.B. Bruce-Lockhart 1 (Cambridge U.), *W.R. Logan 17 (Edinburgh Wands); M.M. Henderson 2 (Dunfermline), G.L. Gray 2 (Gala), W.M. Inglis 2 (Cambridge U.), G.B. Horsburgh 2 (London Scottish), C.L. Melville 2 (The Army), W.B. Young 2 (Cambridge U.), G.D. Shaw 3 (Gala), J.A. Waters 14 (Selkirk).

Referee C.H. Gadney (England)

ENGLAND v SCOTLAND   47/353

20 March 1937
Murrayfield
England 6 (2T) Scotland 3 (1PG)

Scotland   PG: Duncan Shaw.
England   T: Sever, Unwin.

After six successive defeats at Murrayfield, England wrung out their first ever victory there, which earned them a Triple Crown and the Championship. It was the last Championship match for nine members of the Scottish team, including their two most experienced players, Logan and Waters.

SCOTLAND   K.W. Marshall (8) (Edinburgh Acads); W.G.S. Johnston (5) (Richmond), R.W. Shaw 12 (Glasgow HSFP), D.J. Macrae 3 (St Andrew's U.), R.H. Dryden (1) (Watsonians); W.A. Ross (2) (Hillhead HSFP), *W.R. Logan (18) (Edinburgh Wands); M.M. Henderson (3) (Dunfermline), G.L. Gray (3) (Gala), W.M. Inglis 3 (Cambridge U.), G.B. Horsburgh 3 (London Scottish), C.L. Melville (3) (Black Watch Regt.), W.B. Young 3 (Cambridge U.), G.D. Shaw 4 (Sale), J.A. Waters (15) (Selkirk).

ENGLAND   *H.G. Owen-Smith (9) (St Mary's H.); E.J. Unwin 1 (Rosslyn Park), P.L. Candler 7 (St Bart's H.), P. Cranmer 12 (Richmond), H.S. Sever 6 (Sale); F.J. Reynolds 1 (Old Cranleighans), B.C.

Gadney 12 (Leicester); H.F. Wheatley 2 (Coventry), H.B. Toft 4 (Waterloo), R.J. Longland 15 (Northampton), T.F. Huskisson 3 (OMT), A. Wheatley 3 (Coventry), J.G. Cook (1) (Bedford), W.H. Weston 12 (Northampton), R. Bolton 3 (Harlequins).

Referee S. Donaldson (Ireland)

IRELAND v WALES   46/354

3 April 1937
Ravenhill, Belfast
Ireland 5 (1G) Wales 3 (1PG)

Ireland   T: Bailey. C: Walker.
Wales   PG: Legge.

This match should have been played on 13 March but was postponed because of heavy snow. Defeat not only relegated Wales, Champions the previous year, to bottom place in the table, but meant they had lost every match in the season for the first time since 1892.

IRELAND   G.L. Malcolmson (6) (NIFC); F.G. Moran 4 (Clontarf), L.B. McMahon 9 (UC Dublin), A.H. Bailey 10 (UC Dublin), C.V. Boyle 6 (Dublin U.); G.E. Cromey 3 (Queen's U. Belfast), *G.J. Morgan 12 (Clontarf); E. Ryan 1 (Dolphin), T.S. Corken (3) (Belfast Collegians), S. Walker 11 (Instonians), C.J. Reidy (1) (London Irish), R.B. Mayne 1 (Queen's U. Belfast), P.J. Lawlor (6) (Bective Rangers), R. Alexander 6 (Royal Ulster Constabulary), J.A.E. Siggins (22) (Belfast Collegians).

WALES   W.G. Legge 1 (Newport); J.I. Rees 10 (Swansea), E.C. Davey 19 (London Welsh), *W. Wooller 12 (Cardiff), W.H. Clement 3 (Llanelli); W.T.H. Davies 3 (Swansea), H. Tanner 6 (Swansea); T. Williams (7) (Cross Keys), W.H. Travers 2 (Newport), I. Bennett (1) (Aberavon), H. Thomas (6) (Neath), H. Rees 2 (Cardiff), A.R. Taylor 1 (Cross Keys), E. Watkins 2 (Cardiff), A.M. Rees 10 (London Welsh).

Referee M.A. Allan (Scotland)

1938

CARDIFF Wales beat England 14-8 · MURRAYFIELD Scotland beat Wales 8-6
DUBLIN England beat Ireland 36-14 · MURRAYFIELD Scotland beat Ireland 23-14
SWANSEA Wales beat Ireland 11-5 · TWICKENHAM Scotland beat England 21-16

CHAMPIONSHIP TABLE
Scotland – Championship, Triple Crown

Pos	Country	P	W	D	L	F	A	Pts	Tries F	A
1	Scotland (3)	3	3	0	0	52	36	6	10	7
2	Wales (4)	3	2	0	1	31	21	4	6	4
3	England (1)	3	1	0	2	60	49	2	10	11
4	Ireland (2)	3	0	0	3	33	70	0	9	13

A points' total of 176 and 35 tries were records for a six-match Championship, the previous best being 142 points in 1908 and 32 tries in 1904. Apart from providing further evidence against the notion that the 1930s were tactically the most barren in the history of the Championship, it emphasized just how many players of flair were playing at the time. The greatest of these were undoubtedly Scotland's Wilson Shaw and Cliff Jones, of Wales, who fought a fine duel at Murrayfield in a match which effectively settled the Championship. Scotland won it and went on to win the Triple Crown. Wales shrugged off the defeat to beat Ireland and become runners-up.

Ray Longland and Peter Cranmer, notable contributors to pre-war English rugby

Ireland lost all three matches but their aggregate of 33 points was higher than that scored by any of the title-winning sides of the previous five seasons. England, too, scored prolifically: their 60 points put them at the top of the scoring table, though third only in the Championship.

There was a significant change this season to the Law regarding penalty kicks. The offending side now had to retire ten yards from the place of the offence, which had the effect of making penalty kicks a much more productive form of scoring. Hitherto the player taking the kick had to retreat because the opposition were allowed to form a line of demarcation at the place of the offence. Understandably the new Law increased the kicker's options – though it was to be some years before highly-specialized place kickers began to dominate the game.

WALES v ENGLAND 49/355

15 January 1938
Cardiff Arms Park
Wales 14 (1G, 1T, 2PG) England 8 (1G, 1T)

Wales T: McCarley, Idwal Rees. C: Jenkins. PG: Jenkins (2).
England T: Candler, Sever. C: Freakes.

Wales capped a new No. 8 from Aberavon, Walter Vickery, whose father, George, also an Aberavon player, played once for England, against Ireland, in 1905. Another Welsh newcomer, Alan McCarley, had the distinction of scoring a try. The most outstanding Welsh contribution, however, came from Cliff Jones, who endorsed the view that he was the outstanding fly-half of the era. Indeed contemporary critics who have been fortunate enough to compare him with his successors rated Jones the best ever to wear the Welsh No. 10 jersey. There can be no better biographical sketch of him than that by David Smith and Gareth Williams in *Fields of Praise* (University of Wales Press): '. . . in his balance, his handling, his eye for an opening, his shattering speed off the mark, his killer instinct, his game blazed with the authentic light of genius.'

WALES V.G.J. Jenkins 11 (London Welsh); W.H. Clement 4 (Llanelli), J.I. Rees 11 (Swansea), E.C. Davey 20 (London Welsh), A. Bassett 5 (Cardiff); *C.W. Jones 10 (Cardiff), H. Tanner 7 (Swansea); H. Rees 3 (Cardiff), W. Travers 3 (Newport), M.E. Morgan 1 (Swansea), F.L. Morgan 1 (Llanelli), E. Watkins 3 (Cardiff), A.M. Rees 11 (London Welsh), A. McCarley 1 (Neath), W. Vickery 1 (Aberavon).

ENGLAND H.D. Freakes 1 (Harlequins); E.J. Unwin 2 (Rosslyn Park), *P. Cranmer 13 (Moseley), B.E. Nicholson 1 (Harlequins), H.S. Sever 7 (Sale); P.L. Candler 8 (St Bart's H.), B.C. Gadney (13) (Headingley); R.J. Longland 16 (Northampton), H.B. Toft 5 (Waterloo), H.F. Wheatley 3 (Coventry), A. Wheatley 4 (Coventry), T.F. Huskisson 4 (OMT), W.H. Weston 13 (Northampton), R. Bolton 4 (Harlequins), D.L.K. Milman 2 (Bedford).

Referee R.A. Beattie (Scotland)

SCOTLAND v WALES 49/356

5 February 1938
Murrayfield
Scotland 8 (1G, 1PG) Wales 6 (2T)

Scotland T: Crawford. C: Crawford PG: Crawford.
Wales T: McCarley (2).

Another nail-biting finish with Scotland winning through a penalty goal two minutes from time. Controversy surrounded the penalty award, given by England's Cyril Gadney, because a Welsh forward was lying on the ball in a maul near the goal-line. Apparently the forward (Harry Rees) was semi-concussed and could not move. Rees was also pinned on top of another concussed Welsh player, Haydn Tanner, with the ball trapped between them. Gadney, one of the most experienced referees in

British rugby at the time, was officiating at his third Scotland-Wales match and had been in charge of two other Wales games. After this match he refereed another six internationals – none involving Wales.

SCOTLAND G. Roberts 1 (Watsonians); A.H. Drummond 1 (Kelvinside Acads), R.C.S. Dick 11 (Guy's H.), D.J. Macrae 4 (St Andrew's U.), J.G.S. Forrest 1 (Cambridge U.); *R.W. Shaw 13 (Glasgow HSFP), T.F. Dorward 1 (Gala); J.B. Borthwick 1 (Stewart's FP), J.D.H. Hastie 1 (Melrose), W.M. Inglis 4 (The Army), G.B. Horsburgh 4 (London Scottish), A. Roy 1 (Waterloo), W.B. Young 4 (Cambridge U.), W.H. Crawford 1 (US Portsmouth), P.L. Duff 3 (Glasgow Acads).

WALES V.G.J. Jenkins 12 (London Welsh); W.H. Clement 5 (Llanelli), J.I. Rees 12 (Swansea), W. Wooller 13 (Cardiff), A. Bassett (6) (Cardiff); *C.W. Jones 11 (Cardiff), H. Tanner 8 (Swansea); M.E. Morgan 2 (Swansea), W.H. Travers 4 (Newport), H. Rees 4 (Cardiff), E. Watkins 4 (Cardiff), F.L. Morgan 2 (Llanelli), A.M. Rees (12) (London Welsh), A. McCarley 2 (Neath), W. Vickery 2 (Aberavon).

Referee C.H. Gadney (England)

IRELAND v ENGLAND 49/357

12 February 1938
Lansdowne Road, Dublin
England 36 (6G, 1T, 1PG) Ireland 14 (1G, 3T)

Ireland T: Bailey, Cromey, Daly, Mayne. C: Crowe.
England T: Giles, Bolton, Marshall, Nicholson, Prescott, Reynolds, Unwin. C: Parker (6). PG: Parker.

This was Ireland's heaviest defeat ever in a Championship match and was the exception to the rule that matches with England were always close affairs. It would not have been anywhere near as one-sided but for the phenomenal place-kicking of G.W. Parker, who on his début appearance, contributed 15 points to England's total with 6 conversions and a penalty goal. Another débutant, R.M. Marshall, a young forward from Oxford University, ran 50 yards for a try; it was not long before critics were calling Marshall the 'new Wakefield'. Ireland refused to be panicked by the massacre – only Crowe, Daly and Megaw were dropped from the side.

IRELAND   P. Crowe (2) (Blackrock College); M.J. Daly (1) (Harlequins), A.H. Bailey 11 (UC Dublin), L.B. McMahon 10 (Blackrock College), V.J. Lyttle 1 (Belfast Collegians); G.E. Cromey 4 (Queen's U. Belfast), *G.J. Morgan 13 (Old Belvedere); E. Ryan 2 (Dolphin), C.R.A. Graves 12 (Wanderers), D.B. O'Loughlin 1 (UC Cork), R.B. Mayne 2 (Queen's U. Belfast), S. Walker 12 (Instonians), R. Alexander 7 (NIFC), J. Megaw (2) (Instonians), J.W.S. Irwin 1 (NIFC).

ENGLAND   G.W. Parker 1 (Gloucester); E.J. Unwin 3 (Rosslyn Park), B.E. Nicholson (2) (Harlequins), *P. Cranmer 14 (Moseley), H.S. Sever 8 (Sale); F. J. Reynolds 2 (Old Cranleighans), J.L. Giles 5 (Coventry); R. J. Longland 17 (Northampton), H.B. Toft 6 (Waterloo), R.E. Prescott 3 (Harlequins), R.M. Marshall 1 (Oxford U.), T.F. Huskisson 5 (OMT), W.H. Weston 14 (Northampton), R. Bolton (5) (Harlequins), D.L.K. Milman 3 (Bedford).

Referee J.C.H. Ireland (Scotland)

SCOTLAND v IRELAND   51/358

26 February 1938
Murrayfield
Scotland 23 (2G, 2T, 1DG, 1PG) Ireland 14 (1G, 3T)

Scotland   T: Forrest (2), Macrae, Drummond. C: Crawford (2). DG: Dorward. PG: Drummond.
Ireland   T: Cromey, O'Loughlin, Moran, Morgan. C: Walker.

This was an extraordinary result, not only because it was Scotland's second biggest score against Ireland, but because it was their one victory in a 13-match streak of Irish success, 1935–54. Wilson Shaw was at his masterful best. The Irish backs were often cruelly exposed, and as a consequence, three of them were dropped, never to play again.

SCOTLAND   G. Roberts 2 (Watsonians); A.H. Drummond (2) (Kelvinside Acads), R.C.S. Dick 12 (Guy's H.), D.J. Macrae 5 (St Andrew's U.), J.G.S. Forrest 2 (Cambridge U.); *R.W. Shaw 14

(Glasgow HSFP), T.F. Dorward 2 (Gala); J.B. Borthwick (2) (Stewart's FP), J.D.H. Hastie 2 (Melrose), W.M. Inglis 5 (The Army), G.B. Horsburgh 5 (London Scottish), A. Roy 2 (Waterloo), W.B. Young 5 (Cambridge U.), W.H. Crawford 2 (US Portsmouth), P.L. Duff 4 (Glasgow Acads).

IRELAND   R.G. Craig 1 (Queen's U. Belfast); F.G. Moran 5 (Clontarf), A.H. Bailey (12) (UC Dublin), L.B. McMahon (11) (Blackrock College), J.J. O'Connor (10) (Blackrock College); G.E. Cromey 5 (Queen's U. Belfast), *G.J. Morgan 14 (Old Belvedere); E. Ryan (3) (Dolphin), C.R.A. Graves 13 (Wanderers), H. Kennedy 1 (Bradford), D.B. O'Loughlin 2 (UC Cork), D. Tierney 1 (UC Cork), R. Alexander 8 (NIFC), J.W.S. Irwin 2 (NIFC), S. Walker 13 (Instonians).

Referee C.H. Gadney (England)

WALES v IRELAND   47/359

12 March 1938
St Helen's, Swansea
Wales 11 (1G, 1T, 1PG) Ireland 5 (1G)

Wales   T: Taylor, Clement. C: Legge. PG: Wooller.
Ireland   T: Moran. C: McKibbin.

Having failed to score in their previous two visits to Wales Ireland had the satisfaction of registering an excellent try, by Fred Moran. It was still not enough to stop Wales chalking up their third successive home victory over Ireland, who finished the season having been beaten in every match for the first time since 1934. The Irish defence was badly mauled during the season, giving away 70 points, the worst concession by any side when four sides competed for the Championship.

WALES   W.G. Legge (2) (Newport); J.I. Rees (13) (Swansea), E.C. Davey (21) (London Welsh), W. Wooller 14 (Cardiff), W. H. Clement (6) (Llanelli); *C.W. Jones (12) (Cardiff), H. Tanner 9 (Swansea); M.E. Morgan 3 (Swansea), W.H. Travers 5 (Newport), H. Rees (5) (Cardiff), E. Watkins 5 (Cardiff), F.L. Morgan 3 (Llanelli), A.R. Taylor 2 (Cross Keys), W. Vickery 3 (Aberavon), A. McCarley (3) (Neath).

IRELAND   R.G. Craig (2) (Queen's U. Belfast); F.G. Moran 6 (Clontarf), H.R. McKibbin 1 (Queen's U. Belfast), J.D. Torrens 1 (Bohemians), C.V. Boyle 7 (Dublin U.); G.E. Cromey 6 (Queen's U. Belfast), G.J. Morgan 15 (Old Belvedere); H. Kennedy (2) (Bradford), C.R.A. Graves (14) (Wanderers), C.E.St J. Beamish (11) (Leicester), D. Tierney 2 (UC Cork), R.B. Mayne 3 (Queen's U. Belfast), D.B. O'Loughlin 3 (UC Cork), H.J.M. Sayers 7 (Lansdowne), S. Walker (14) (Instonians).

Referee J.C.H. Ireland (Scotland)

ENGLAND v SCOTLAND   48/360

---

19 March 1938
Twickenham
Scotland 21 (5T, 2PG) England 16 (1T, 1DG, 3PG)

England   T: Unwin. DG: Reynolds. PG: Parker (3).
Scotland   T: Renwick (2), Shaw (2), Dick. PG: Crawford (2).

Scotland's total of five tries was the highest number they scored in England in the Championship, and in complete reversal to events of 1937, the victory won them the Triple Crown and the Championship. Scotland's 52 points' aggregate was also significant: it represented the biggest total by a side winning the competition when four sides competed only, though it was interesting that England scored 60 points and finished in third place. Similarly Wales, in 1907, totalled 54 points, but still did not win the title.

Regarding individual players, this match confirmed for many that Wilson Shaw was one of the greatest fly-halves of the pre-war Championship. Not only did Shaw score two brilliant tries but he created another; some would place Shaw in the top half-dozen fly-halves of all time. G.W. Parker's short, explosive career ended after this match. In 2 appearances, for England, his kicking had produced 24 points, a phenomenon which no one had seen in the pre-war Championship.

ENGLAND   G.W. Parker (2) (Blackheath); E.J. Unwin (4) (Rosslyn Park), P.L. Candler (9) (St Bart's H.), P. Cranmer (15) (Moseley), H.S. Sever (9) (Sale); F.J. Reynolds (3) (Old Cranleighans), J.L. Giles (6) (Coventry); R.J. Longland (18) (Northampton), *H.B. Toft 7 (Waterloo), H.F. Wheatley 4 (Coventry), R.M. Marshall 2 (Oxford U.), A. Wheatley (5) (Coventry), W.H. Weston (15) (Northampton), A.A. Brown (1) (Exeter), D.L.K. Milman (4) (Bedford).

SCOTLAND   G. Roberts 3 (Watsonians); W.N. Renwick 1 (London Scottish), R.C.S. Dick (13) (Guy's H.), D.J. Macrae 6 (St Andrew's U.), J.G.S. Forrest (3) (Cambridge U.); *R.W. Shaw 15 (Glasgow HSFP), T.F. Dorward 3 (Gala); W.F. Blackadder (1) (W. of Scotland), J.D.H. Hastie (3) (Melrose), W.M. Inglis (6) (The Army), G.B. Horsburgh 6 (London Scottish), A. Roy 3 (Waterloo), W.B. Young 6 (Cambridge U.), W.H. Crawford 3 (US Portsmouth), P.L. Duff 5 (Glasgow Acads).

Referee I. David (Wales)

1939

TWICKENHAM England beat Wales 3-0 · CARDIFF Wales beat Scotland 11-3
TWICKENHAM Ireland beat England 5-0 · DUBLIN Ireland beat Scotland 12-3
BELFAST Wales beat Ireland 7-0 · MURRAYFIELD England beat Scotland 9-6

CHAMPIONSHIP TABLE
Wales – Championship

| | | | | | | | | | Tries | |
Pos	Country	P	W	D	L	F	A	Pts	F	A
1	Wales (2)	3	2	0	1	18	6	4	3	1
2	Ireland (4)	3	2	0	1	17	10	4	3	2
3	England (3)	3	2	0	1	12	11	4	1	3
3	Scotland (1)	3	0	0	3	12	32	0	3	4

Wales, Ireland and England each won two matches but Wales took the Championship with a marginally higher score aggregate. The ten tries of 1939, however, was an all-time low, consistent perhaps with the general feeling of depression as the war clouds gathered over Europe.

It has been suggested that the imminence of war was one of the reasons why the Four Home Unions decided in 1939 to accept France back into the fold, rather more as a public expression of unity and friendliness than ready acceptance that the French had reformed with regard to professionalism. The Four Home Unions paved the way for France's re-entry at a meeting held in Edinburgh the day before the Scotland v England match on 17 March. Although the letter sent to the French Federation, following this meeting, was in no way an open invitation – indeed it conveyed the same doubts that led to France's isolation in 1931 – it served the purpose of obtaining assurances from France, which were implicit to re-entry. The French Federation met in May and duly gave assurances, including a promise to abandon their club championship, which, of course, never happened. The resumption of friendly relations was finally agreed at a Four Home Unions meeting in London on 7 July: they would restart at the beginning of the 1939–40 season. The War prevented it, and it was not until 1947 that the prodigals returned to add Gallican spice to the Saxon-Celtic-Gaelic trinity and the Five Nations Championship was resurrected.

Although the Championship was abandoned during the War years, matches took place periodically under that most curious of pseudonyms, an unofficial international. Most of these matches involved active servicemen. Even professional rugby league players were allowed to participate and France was not left out either. The latter played a Great Britain side at the Paris Velodrome in 1940, a British Army side and a British Empire side in 1945 and Wales (twice), Ireland and the Kiwis (the New Zealand Army side) in 1946.

ENGLAND v WALES 50/361

21 January 1939
Twickenham
England 3 (1T) Wales 0

England T: Teden.

In 1937 England had introduced seven new players in the match against Wales and ended the season winning the Triple Crown. The formula was repeated for this match, this time with eight newcomers, and the 'gamble' came off thanks to a try by one of them, Teden. Of the 50 Championship matches played before the outbreak of war, England had won 25, Wales 19 and 6 were drawn. England's superiority had begun in 1923 for of the 17 matches played since then Wales had managed only 3 victories.

ENGLAND H.D. Freakes 2 (Oxford U.); R.H. Guest 1 (Liverpool U.), J. Heaton 4 (Waterloo), G.E. Hancock 1 (Birkenhead Park), R.S.L. Carr 1

Vivian Jenkins, who played full-back for Wales 13 times 1933–39

(Old Cranleighans); G.A. Walker 1 (Blackheath), P. Cooke 1 (Richmond); R.E. Prescott 4 (Harlequins), *H.B. Toft 8 (Waterloo), D.E. Teden 1 (Richmond), T.F. Huskisson 6 (OMT), H.F. Wheatley 5 (Coventry), J.K. Watkins 1 (US Portsmouth), J.T.W. Berry 1 (Leicester), R.M. Marshall 3 (Oxford U.).

WALES   V.G.J. Jenkins (13) (London Welsh); F.J.V. Ford (1) (The Welch Regt.), D.I. Davies (1) (London Welsh), *W. Wooller 15 (Cardiff), S. Williams 1 (Aberavon); W.T.H. Davies 4 (Swansea), H. Tanner 10 (Swansea); M.E. Morgan (4) (Swansea), W.H. Travers 6 (Newport), W.E.N. Davis 1 (Cardiff), E. Watkins 6 (Cardiff), F.L. Morgan (4) (Llanelli), A.R. Taylor (3) (Cross Keys), C. Challinor (1) (Neath), W. Vickery (4) (Aberavon).

Referee J.C.H. Ireland (Scotland)

WALES v SCOTLAND   50/362

4 February 1939
Cardiff Arms Park
Wales 11 (1G, 1T, 1PG) Scotland 3 (1PG)

Wales   T: Mickey Davies, Travers. C: Wooller. PG: Wooller.
Scotland   PG: Crawford.

The fiftieth Championship match between Scotland and Wales was also their last meeting before the outbreak of war. Each side had scored 24 victories with two matches drawn. G.H. Gallie, the Edinburgh Academical, won his only cap, 19 years almost to the day after his father, R.A. Gallie, had played for Scotland against Wales.

WALES   H. Davies 1 (Swansea); E.L. Jones (1) (Llanelli), M.J. Davies 1 (Oxford U.), *W. Wooller 16 (Cardiff), S. Williams 2 (Aberavon);

W.T.H. Davies 5 (Swansea), H. Tanner 11 (Swansea); L. Davies 1 (Swansea), W. H. Travers 7 (Newport), W.E.N. Davies 2 (Cardiff), E. Watkins (7) (Cardiff), R.E. Price 1 (Weston-super-Mare), E. Evans 2 (Llanelli), E. Long 6 (Swansea), L. Manfield 1 (Otley).

SCOTLAND G. Roberts 4 (Watsonians); J.B. Craig (1) (Heriot's FP), D.J. Macrae 7 (St Andrew's U.), J.R.S. Innes 1 (Aberdeen U.), W.N. Renwick (2) (Edinburgh Wands); *R.W. Shaw 16 (Glasgow HSFP), W.R.C. Brydon (1) (Heriot's FP); G.H. Gallie (1) (Edinburgh Acads), R.W.F. Sampson 1 (London Scottish), W. Purdie 1 (Jedforest), G.B. Horsburgh 7 (London Scottish), A. Roy 4 (Waterloo), W.B. Young 7 (King's College H.), W.H. Crawford 4 (United Services), P.L. Duff (6) (Glasgow Acads).

Referee A.S. Bean (England)

ENGLAND v IRELAND 50/363

11 February 1939
Twickenham
Ireland 5 (1G) England 0

Ireland T: Irwin. C: McKibbin.

The fiftieth Championship encounter between England and Ireland was conspicuous for the fact that it was the first time since 1911 that England failed to score in the match with Ireland. As England had managed only three points against Wales the previous month, it made a vivid contrast to the spate of high scores of the 1938 season, when England had accumulated 50 points by the same stage. The selectors dealt with the problem in time-honoured fashion — out went three players, the two half-backs and the full-back. England had won 30 of the matches, Ireland 18 and 2 were drawn.

ENGLAND H.D. Freakes (3) (Oxford U.); R.H. Guest 2 (Waterloo), J. Heaton 5 (Waterloo), G.E. Hancock 2 (Birkenhead Park), R.S.L. Carr 2 (Old Cranleighans); G.A. Walker (2) (Blackheath), P. Cooke (2) (Richmond); R.E. Prescott 5 (Harlequins), *H.B. Toft 9 (Waterloo), D.E. Teden 2 (Richmond), T.F. Huskisson 7 (OMT), H.F. Wheatley 6 (Coventry), J.K. Watkins 2 (US Portsmouth), J.T.W. Berry 2 (Leicester), R.M. Marshall 4 (Oxford U.).

IRELAND C.J. Murphy 1 (Lansdowne); F.G. Moran 7 (Clontarf), H.R. McKibbin 2 (Instonians), J.D. Torrens 2 (Bohemians), V.J. Lyttle 2 (Belfast Collegians); G.E. Cromey 7 (Belfast Collegians), *G.J. Morgan 16 (Old Belvedere); J.G. Ryan 1 (UC Dublin), C. Teehan 1 (UC Cork), D. Tierney (3) (UC Cork), D.B. O'Loughlin 4 (Garryowen), R.B. Mayne 4 (Malone), H.J.M. Sayers (Lansdowne), R. Alexander 9 (NIFC), J.W.S. Irwin 3 (NIFC).

Referee J.C.H. Ireland (Scotland)

IRELAND v SCOTLAND 52/364

25 February 1939
Lansdowne Road, Dublin
Ireland 12 (2T, 1PG, 1GM) Scotland 3 (1T)

Ireland T: Moran, Torrens. PG: McKibbin. GM: Sayers.
Scotland T: Innes.

This was the first of nine successive victories achieved by Ireland over Scotland. At this point, however, after 52 Championship matches Scotland still had the advantage, with 30 wins to Ireland's 19 with 3 drawn.

IRELAND C.J. Murphy 2 (Lansdowne); V.J. Lyttle (3) (Bradford), J.D. Torrens 3 (Bohemians), H.R. McKibbin 3 (Instonians), F.G. Moran 8 (Clontarf); G.E. Cromey 8 (Queen's U. Belfast), *G.J. Morgan 17 (Old Belvedere); T.A. Headon 1 (UC Dublin), C. Teehan 2 (UC Cork), H.J.M. Sayers 9 (Lansdowne), J.G. Ryan 2 (UC Dublin), D.B. O'Loughlin 5 (Garryowen), R.B. Mayne 5 (Malone), R. Alexander 10 (Royal Ulster Constabulary), J.W.S. Irwin 4 (NIFC).

SCOTLAND W.M. Penman (1) (RAF); J.R.S. Innes 2 (Aberdeen U.), D.J. Macrae 8 (St Andrew's U.), *R.W. Shaw 17 (Glasgow HSFP), K.C. Fyfe (9) (London Scottish); R.B. Bruce-Lockhart 2 (Cambridge U.), T.F. Dorward 4 (Gala); I.C. Henderson 1 (Edinburgh Acads), I.N. Graham 1 (Edinburgh Acads), W. Purdie 2 (Jedforest), G.B. Horsburgh 8 (London Scottish), A. Roy 5 (Waterloo), G.D. Shaw (5) (Sale), W.B. Young 8 (Kings Collage H.), D.K.A. Mackenzie 1 (Edinburgh Wands).

Referee C.H. Gadney (England)

IRELAND v WALES 48/365

11 March 1939
Ravenhill, Belfast
Wales 7 (1T, 1DG) Ireland 0

Wales T: Willie Davies. DG: Willie Davies.

For the seventh time Ireland were frustrated by Wales in their bid to win the Triple Crown, which they had last won in 1899. The deciding score was a dropped goal near the end by Willie Davies, which was the last dropped goal valued at four points to be scored in the Championship. A try a few moments later by the same player scotched the last faint hopes Ireland had of retrieving the situation. Because of the outbreak of war this was the last international for 25 players. Con Murphy, the Lansdowne full-back, was the only Irish player to bridge the gap: he played twice again in 1947. Howard Davies, Haydn Tanner, Bill Travers and Les Manfield returned to help Wales rebuild eight years later. Of the 48 Championship matches played up to 1939 Ireland had won 18, Wales 28 and 2 were drawn.

IRELAND C.J. Murphy 3 (Lansdowne); F.G. Moran (9) (Clontarf), H.R. McKibbin (4) (Instonians), J.D. Torrens (4) (Bohemians), C.V. Boyle (8) (Lansdowne); G.E. Cromey (9) (Belfast Collegians), *G.J. Morgan (18) (Old Belvedere); T.A. Headon (2) (UC Dublin), C. Teehan (3) (UC Cork), J.G. Ryan (3) (UC Dublin), R.B. Mayne (6) (Malone), D.B. O'Loughlin (6) (Garryowen), R. Alexander (11) (Royal Ulster Constabulary), H.J.M. Sayers (10) (Aldershot Services), J.W.S. Irwin (5) (NIFC).

WALES H. Davies 2 (Swansea); C. Matthews (1) (Bridgend), M.J. Davies (2) (Oxford U.), *W. Wooller (17) (Cardiff), S. Williams (3) (Aberavon); W.T.H. Davies (6) (Swansea), H. Tanner 12 (Swansea); W.E.N. Davis (3) (Cardiff), W.H. Travers 8 (Newport), V.J. Law (1) (Newport), L. Davies (2) (Swansea), R.E. Price (2) (Weston-super-Mare), E. Evans (3) (Llanelli), E. Long (7) (Swansea), L. Manfield 2 (Otley).

Referee J.C.H. Ireland (Scotland)

SCOTLAND v ENGLAND 49/366

18 March 1939
Murrayfield
England 9 (3PG) Scotland 6 (2T)

Scotland T: Murdoch, Shaw.
England PG: Heaton (3).

This was the last Championship match before the Second World War ended major rugby activity for eight years. Surprisingly, 7 of the 30 players involved bridged that gap to renew their Championship careers. For Scotland it was the end of a dismal season: three defeats and the Wooden Spoon. In the 49 Championship matches played by the countries up to the outbreak of war, England had won 22, Scotland 21 and 5 were drawn.

SCOTLAND G. Roberts (5) (Watsonians); J.R.S. Innes 3 (Aberdeen U.), D.J. Macrae (9) (St Andrew's U.), *R.W. Shaw (18) (Glasgow HSFP), W.C.W. Murdoch 4 (Hillhead HSFP); R.B. Bruce-Lockhart (3) (London Scottish), T.F. Dorward (5) (Gala); I.C. Henderson 2 (Edinburgh Acads), I.N. Graham (2) (Edinburgh Acads), W. Purdie (3) (Jedforest), G.B. Horsburgh (9) (London Scottish), A. Roy (6) (Waterloo), W.B. Young 9 (King's College H.), W.H. Crawford (5) (US Portsmouth), D.K.A. Mackenzie (2) (Edinburgh Wands).

ENGLAND E.J. Parsons (1) (RAF); R.H. Guest 3 (Waterloo), J. Heaton 6 (Waterloo), G.E. Hancock (3) (Birkenhead Park), R.S.L. Carr (3) (Old Cranleighans); T.A. Kemp 3 (St Mary's H.), J. Ellis (1) (Wakefield); D.E. Teden (3) (Richmond), *H.B. Toft (10) (Waterloo), R.E. Prescott (6) (Harlequins), H.F. Wheatley (7) (Coventry), T.F. Huskisson (8) (OMT), J. K. Watkins (3) (US Portsmouth), J.T.W. Berry (3) (Leicester), R.M. Marshall (5) (Oxford U.).

Referee I. David (Wales)

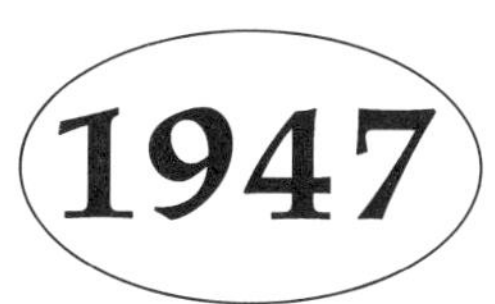

PARIS France beat Scotland 8-3 · CARDIFF England beat Wales 9-6
DUBLIN France beat Ireland 12-8 · MURRAYFIELD Wales beat Scotland 22-8
DUBLIN Ireland beat England 22-0 · MURRAYFIELD Ireland beat Scotland 3-0
TWICKENHAM England beat Scotland 24-5 · PARIS Wales beat France 3-0
SWANSEA Wales beat Ireland 6-0 · TWICKENHAM England beat France 6-3

CHAMPIONSHIP TABLE
England – Championship

Pos	Country	P	W	D	L	F	A	Pts	Tries F	A
1	England (3)	4	3	0	1	39	36	6	7	8
2	Wales (1)	4	3	0	1	37	17	6	8	2
3	Ireland (2)	4	2	0	2	33	18	4	7	5
4	France (0)	4	2	0	2	23	20	4	6	3
5	Scotland (4)	4	0	0	4	16	57	0	2	12

England won the first Championship to take place since the War, with a slightly superior scoring aggregate to that of Wales. Both had won three matches and whereas Wales's defeat, against England, was a narrow one, 6-9 at Twickenham, England's loss was by a surprisingly big margin of 22-0 in Dublin. Ireland certainly would have been close contenders for the title but for defeat in France in their first match. Ireland looked a good side against England, narrowly beating Scotland and then giving Wales a tough match in Swansea.

Scotland, Wooden Spoonists in the previous Championship, in 1939, went to the bottom again. This time they lost all four matches, for the first time since 1911. When England defeated them easily, 24-5, at Twickenham, the Scots had lost seven matches in a row, which was then their worst sequence since the Championship started.

France, back in the Championship for the first time since they were banned in 1931, began with surprising confidence and a much more mature approach than anyone could have expected. Having opened the season with victories over Scotland and Ireland, they lost by only 0-3 against Wales, at Colombes, and then 3-6 to England at Twickenham. They scored only six fewer points than England overall, but more significant, for the first time they scored more tries than they conceded, 6-3. It was an encouraging re-entry, to say the least.

FRANCE v SCOTLAND 17/367

1 January 1947
Stade Colombes, Paris
France 8 (1G, 1T) Scotland 3 (1PG)

France   T: Lassegue, Terreau. C: Prat.
Scotland   PG: Geddes.

This match proclaimed the resumption of the Championship after eight years, and France's re-entry. Scotland had not played in Paris since 1930, when they also lost. More significantly, it was the first time that the Scots had failed to score a try in France where they had often previously reaped a rich harvest of tries. Only one player, I.C. Henderson, had played before in the Championship.

FRANCE   A. Alvarez 1 (US Tyrosse); E. Pebeyre 1 (CA Brive), *L. Junquas 1 (A. Bayonne), M. Sorondo 1 (US Montauban), J. Lassegue 1 (S. Toulouse); M. Terreau 1 (US Bressane), Y. Bergougnan 1 (S. Toulouse); E. Buzy 1 (FC Lourdes), M. Jol 1 (Biarritz Ol), J. Princlary 1 (CA Brive), A. Moga 1 (CA Bègles), R. Soro 1 (US Romans), J. Prat 1 (FC Lourdes), J. Matheu 1 (Castres Ol), G. Basquet 1 (SU Agen).

SCOTLAND   *K.I. Geddes 1 (London Scottish); T.G.H. Jackson 1 (The Army), C.R. Bruce 1 (Glasgow Acads), C.W. Drummond 1 (Melrose),

W.D. MacLennan 1 (US Portsmouth); I.J.M. Lumsden 1 (Bath), A.W. Black 1 (Edinburgh U.); A.G.M. Watt 1 (Edinburgh Acads), I.C. Henderson 3 (Edinburgh Acads), T.P.L. McGlashan 1 (Royal HSFP), J.M. Hunter (1) (London Scottish), G.L. Cawkwell (1) (Oxford U.), W.I.D. Elliot 1 (Edinburgh Acads), J.H. Orr 1 (Edinburgh City Police), D.W. Deas 1 (Heriot's FP).

Referee C.H. Gadney (England)

WALES v ENGLAND 51/368

18 January 1947
Cardiff Arms Park
England 9 (1G, 1DG) Wales 6 (2T)

Wales T: Stephens, Evans.
England T: White. C: Gray. DG: Hall.

Dicky Guest, who had played in three Championship matches before the War in 1939, was the only capped player in the England side for this the resumption of Wales-England matches after an eight-year gap. Wales, likewise, fielded new players, 13 in all, with only Haydn Tanner, the captain, and Howard Davies previously capped.

WALES H. Davies 3 (Llanelli); K.J. Jones 1 (Newport), J. Matthews 1 (Cardiff), W.B. Cleaver 1 (Cardiff), L. Williams 1 (Llanelli); B.L. Williams 1 (Cardiff), *H. Tanner 13 (Cardiff); D. Jones 1 (Swansea), R.E. Blakemore (1) (Newport), G.W. Bevan (1) (Llanelli), S. Williams 1 (Llanelli), G. Parsons (1) (Newport), O. Williams 1 (Llanelli), G.W. Evans 1 (Cardiff), J.R.G. Stephens 1 (Neath).

ENGLAND A. Gray 1 (Otley); R.H. Guest 4 (Waterloo), N.O. Bennett 1 (St Mary's H.), E.K. Scott 1 (St Mary's H.), D.W. Swarbrick 1 (Oxford U.); N.M. Hall 1 (St Mary's H.), W.K.T. Moore 1 (Devonport Services); G.A. Kelly 1 (Bedford), A.P. Henderson 1 (Cambridge U.), H.W. Walker 1 (Coventry), *J. Mycock 1 (Sale), S.V. Perry 1 (Cambridge U.), M.R. Steele-Bodger 1 (Cambridge U.), D.F. White 1 (Northampton), B.H. Travers 1 (Oxford U.).

Referee R.A. Beattie (Scotland)

IRELAND v FRANCE 18/369

25 January 1947
Lansdowne Road, Dublin
France 12 (4T) Ireland 8 (1G, 1PG)

Ireland T: McKay. C: Mullan. PG: Mullan.
France T: Lassegue (2), Prat, Sorondo.

After being treated rather uncharitably in their early encounters with Ireland, France confirmed they had learned a great deal. This was their third win in a row over Ireland. Considering Ireland lost only two other matches in the period 1947–49, it was a victory of some note. Moreover France had only once scored more tries in Ireland – five in 1920 – and they repeated the four-try haul on only one other occasion, 1963.

IRELAND *C.J. Murphy 4 (Lansdowne); B.T. Quinn (1) (Old Belvedere), K. Quinn 1 (Old Belvedere), J. Harper 1 (Instonians), B. Mullan 1 (Clontarf); J. W. Kyle 1 (Queen's U. Belfast), R. Carroll 1 (Lansdowne); M.R. Neely 1 (Belfast Collegians), K.D. Mullen 1 (Old Belvedere), J.C. Daly 1 (London Irish), C.P. Callan 1 (Lansdowne), E. Keeffe 1 (Sunday's Well), D. Hingerty 1 (UC Dublin), R.D. Agar 1 (Malone), J.W. McKay 1 (Queen's U. Belfast).

FRANCE A. Alvarez 2 (US Tyrosse); E. Pebeyre 2 (CA Brive), *L. Junquas 2 (A. Bayonne), M. Sorondo 2 (US Montauban), J. Lassegue 2 (S. Toulouse); M. Terreau 2 (US Bressane), Y. Bergougnon 2 (S. Toulouse); E. Buzy 2 (FC Lourdes), M. Jol 2 (Biarritz Ol), J. Princlary 2 (CA Brive), R. Soro 2 (US Romans), A. Moga 2 (CA Bègles), J. Prat 2 (FC Lourdes), J. Matheu 2 (Castres Ol), G. Basquet 2 (SU Agen).

Referee J.B.G. Whittaker (England)

SCOTLAND v WALES 51/370

1 February 1947
Murrayfield
Wales 22 (2G, 3T, 1PG) Scotland 8 (1G, 1PG)

Scotland T: Elliot. C: Geddes. PG: Geddes.
Wales T: Ken Jones (2), Bleddyn Williams,

Cleaver, Les Williams. C: Tamplin (2). PG Tamplin.

By this victory, their highest score in Scotland since 1911, Wales moved ahead in their series of Championship matches against Scotland, 25-24, a lead which they have remorselessly increased since. The match was something of a reunion for R.W.F. Sampson, of Scotland, and Haydn Tanner and Howard Davies, of Wales, who were the only players to survive from the previous meeting between the countries eight years earlier.

SCOTLAND *K.I. Geddes 2 (London Scottish); T.G.H. Jackson 2 (The Army), C.W. Drummond 2 (Melrose), C.R. Bruce 2 (Glasgow Acads), D.D. Mackenzie 1 (Edinburgh U.); I.J.M. Lumsden 2 (Bath), A.W. Black 2 (Edinburgh U.); I.C. Henderson 4 (Edinburgh Acads), R.W.F. Sampson (4) (London Scottish), R. Aitken (1) (Royal Navy), F.H. Coutts 1 (Melrose), D.W. Deas (2) (Heriot's FP), W.I.D. Elliot 2 (Edinburgh Acads), J.H. Orr (2) (Edinburgh City Police), A.G.M. Watt 2 (Edinburgh Acads).

WALES H. Davies 4 (Llanelli); K.J. Jones 2 (Newport), B.L. Williams 2 (Cardiff), W.B. Cleaver 2 (Cardiff), L. Williams 2 (Llanelli); G. Davies 1 (Pontypridd), *H. Tanner 14 (Cardiff); W.J. Evans (1) (Pontypool), W. Gore 1 (Newbridge), C. Davies 1 (Cardiff), W.E. Tamplin 1 (Cardiff), S. Williams 2 (Llanelli), O. Williams 2 (Llanelli), G.W. Evans 2 (Cardiff), J.R.G. Stephens 2 (Neath).

Referee Captain M.J. Dowling (Ireland)

IRELAND v ENGLAND 51/371

8 February 1947
Lansdowne Road, Dublin
Ireland 22 (2G, 3T, 1PG) England 0

Ireland T: O'Hanlon (2), Mullan (2), McKay. C: Mullan (2). PG:Mullan.

This match was a rout; not only Ireland's highest score to date against England, they ran in a record five tries and established their biggest ever winning margin against the English. The Irish forwards were irresistible and Ernie Strathdee, making his début, was outstanding at scrum-half. Surprisingly England's selectors did not panic: although they made

changes for their next match, against Scotland, only one player who had suffered a baptism of fire at Lansdowne Road never played again. However, M.P. Donnelly, the Oxford centre, became a Test cricketer for New Zealand.

IRELAND *C.J. Murphy (5) (Lansdowne); B. O'Hanlon 1 (Dolphin), J.D.E. Monteith 1 (Queen's U. Belfast), J. Harper 2 (Instonians), B. Mullan 2 (Clontarf); J.W. Kyle 2 (Queen's U. Belfast), E. Strathdee 1 (Queen's U. Belfast); M.R. Neely 2 (Belfast Collegians), K.D. Mullen 2 (Old Belvedere), J.C. Daly 2 (London Irish), C.P. Callan 2 (Lansdowne), E. Keeffe 2 (Sunday's Well), D. Hingerty 2 (UC Dublin), J.M. McKay 2 (Queen's U. Belfast), R.D. Agar 2 (Malone).

ENGLAND A. Gray 2 (Otley); R.H. Guest 5 (Waterloo), J. Heaton 7 (Waterloo), M.P. Donnelly (1) (Oxford U.), D.W. Swarbrick 2 (Oxford U.); N.M. Hall 2 (St Mary's H.), W.K.T. Moore 2 (Devonport Services); H.W. Walker 2 (Coventry), A.P. Henderson 2 (Cambridge U.), G.A. Kelly 2 (Bedford), *J. Mycock 2 (Sale), S.V. Perry 2 (Cambridge U.), M.R. Steele-Bodger 2 (Cambridge U.), D.F. White 2 (Northampton), B.H. Travers 2 (Oxford U.).

Referee M.A. Allan (Scotland)

SCOTLAND v IRELAND 53/372

22 February 1947
Murrayfield
Ireland 3 (1T) Scotland 0

Ireland T: Mullan.

This was Scotland's fifth defeat in their last six matches with Ireland and also the first time since 1926 that they had failed to score against their visitors.

SCOTLAND K.I. Geddes 3 (London Scottish); W.D. Maclennan (2) (US Portsmouth), C.W. Drummond 3 (Melrose), C.R. Bruce 3 (Glasgow Acads), D.D. Mackenzie 2 (Edinburgh U.); *W.H. Munro 1 (Glasgow HSFP), E. Anderson 1 (Stewart's FP); T.P.L. McGlashan 2 (Royal HSFP), A.T. Fisher 1 (Waterloo), H.H. Campbell 1 (London Scottish), F.H. Coutts 2 (Melrose), A.G.M. Watt 3 (Edinburgh Acads), D.D. Valentine 1 (Hawick), D.I. McLean 1 (Royal HSFP), J.B. Lees 1 (Gala).

IRELAND   J.A.D. Higgins 1 (Ulster Civil Service); B. O'Hanlon 2 (Dolphin), *J.D.E. Monteith 2 (Queen's U. Belfast), J. Harper (3) (Instonians), B. Mullan 3 (Clontarf); J.W. Kyle 3 (Queen's U. Belfast), E. Strathdee 2 (Queen's U. Belfast); M.R. Neely 3 (Belfast Collegians), K.D. Mullen 3 (Old Belvedere), J.C. Daly 3 (London Irish), C.P. Callan 3 (Lansdowne), E. Keeffe 3 (Sunday's Well), J.W. McKay 3 (Queen's U. Belfast), D. Hingerty 3 (UC Dublin), R.D. Agar 3 (Malone).

Referee C.H. Gadney (England)

ENGLAND v SCOTLAND   50/373

15 March 1947
Twickenham
England 24 (4G, 1DG) Scotland 5 (1G)

England T: Bennett, Guest, Henderson, Holmes. C: Heaton (4). DG: Hall.
Scotland T: Jackson. C: Geddes.

Jack Heaton's four conversions were a record for England against Scotland until equalled by Nim Hall in 1953 and they helped England to win this fiftieth Championship match between the countries with their highest score to date against Scotland. A frozen pitch may have provided optimum conditions, but it also resulted in a spate of injuries. At one stage four players, two from each side, were in the changing rooms receiving treatment. Arriving at the match had also been an ordeal. The severe winter conditions delayed the train bringing the Scottish team so that their journey took 20 hours; Mickey Steele-Bodger, a student in Edinburgh at the time, and sustained by a tin of Ovaltine tablets and an orange only, arrived at 4 a.m. on match day; and D.I. McLean, unable to travel with the Scottish team, suffered a 24-hour slow train with no restaurant or sleeping berths. Seven of the Scots were not asked to endure such deprivations again.

ENGLAND   A. Gray (3) (Otley); C.B. Holmes 1 (Manchester), N.O. Bennett 2 (St Mary's H.), *J. Heaton 8 (Waterloo), R.H. Guest 6 (Waterloo); N.M. Hall 3 (St Mary's H.), J.O. Newton-Thompson 1 (Oxford U.); H.W. Walker 3 (Coventry), A.P. Henderson 3 (Cambridge U.), G.A. Kelly 3 (Bedford), J.T. George 1 (Falmouth), J. Mycock 3 (Sale), M.R. Steele-Bodger 3

(Edinburgh U.), D.F. White 3 (Northampton), R.H.G. Weighill 1 (Harlequins).

SCOTLAND   K.I. Geddes (4) (London Scottish); T.G.H. Jackson 3 (London Scottish), C.W. Drummond 4 (Melrose), W.H. Munro (2) (Glasgow HSFP), D.D. Mackenzie 3 (Edinburgh U.); *C.R. Bruce 4 (Glasgow Acads), E. Anderson (2) (Stewart's FP); T.P.L. McGlashan 3 (Royal HSFP), A.T. Fisher (2) (Waterloo), H.H. Campbell 2 (London Scottish), F.H. Coutts (3) (Melrose), I.C. Henderson 5 (Edinburgh Acads), D.D. Valentine (2) (Hawick), W.I.D. Elliot 3 (Edinburgh Acads), D.I. McLean (2) (Royal HSFP).

Referee I. David (Wales)

FRANCE v WALES   18/374

22 March 1947
Stade Colombes, Paris
Wales 3 (1PG) France 0

Wales PG: Tamplin.

This was Wales's seventeenth win in eighteen Championship matches against France; but it was the first time they had failed to score a try against the French. One of two newcomers in the Welsh side was Bob Evans, the Newport policeman, an inspiring leader of the Monmouthshire side which had beaten the impressive Kiwi touring side of 1946. An absentee from the side originally selected was George Parsons, Evans's club-mate. As in the Ossie Male affair the drama took place on the Paddington Express. After Parsons boarded the train he was confronted with an allegation that he had been improperly negotiating with a rugby league club. Parsons strongly denied the accusation but, like Male, he was sent home. Parsons, who had made his début against England two months earlier, was never selected for Wales again. Within a year he switched codes and became a rugby league player.

FRANCE   A. Alvarez 3 (US Tyrosse); E. Pebeyre 3 (CA Brive), *L. Junquas 3 (A. Bayonne), M. Sorondo 3 (US Montauban), J. Lassegue 3 (S. Toulouse); M. Terreau 3 (US Bressane), Y. Bergougnan 3 (S. Toulouse); J. Princlary (3) (CA Brive), M. Jol 3 (Biarritz Ol), E. Buzy 3 (FC Lourdes), A. Moga 3 (CA Bègles), R. Soro 3 (US

Romans), J. Matheu 3 (Castres Ol), J. Prat 3 (FC Lourdes), G. Basquet 3 (SU Agen).

WALES   H. Davies 5 (Llanelli); K.J. Jones 3 (Newport), B.L. Williams 3 (Cardiff), L. Williams 3 (Llanelli), P. Rees 1 (Llanelli); W.B. Cleaver 3 (Cardiff), *H. Tanner 15 (Cardiff); D. Jones 2 (Swansea), W. Gore 2 (Newbridge), C. Davies 2 (Cardiff), W.E. Tamplin 2 (Cardiff), S. Williams 3 (Llanelli), R.T. Evans 1 (Newport), G.W. Evans 3 (Cardiff), J.R.G. Stephens 3 (Neath).

Referee A.S. Bean (England)

WALES v IRELAND   49/375

29 March 1947
St Helen's, Swansea
Wales 6 (1T, 1PG) Ireland 0

Wales   T: Bob Evans. PG: Tamplin.

A frozen ground had postponed this match from 8 March. Ireland, bidding for the Triple Crown, arrived late because of traffic difficulties and kick-off was delayed by half-an-hour. The Irish problems did not end there. Jackie Kyle, their brilliant fly-half, was subdued by a pre-planned defensive blanket, in which the Cardiff flanker Gwyn Evans played a prominent part. The Irish forwards, too, failed to get the better of their Welsh counterparts on a sticky, muddy pitch.

WALES   H. Davies (6) (Llanelli); K.J. Jones 4 (Newport), B.L. Williams 4 (Cardiff), L. Williams 4 (Llanelli), P. Rees (2) (Llanelli); W.B. Cleaver 4 (Cardiff), *H. Tanner 16 (Cardiff); D. Jones 3 (Swansea), W. Gore (3) (Newbridge), C. Davies 3 (Cardiff), W.E. Tamplin 3 (Cardiff), S. Williams 4 (Llanelli), R.T. Evans 2 (Newport), G.W. Evans 4 (Cardiff), J.R.G. Stephens 4 (Neath).

IRELAND   J.A.D. Higgins 2 (Ulster Civil Service); B. O'Hanlon 3 (Dolphin), *J.D.E. Monteith (3) (Queen's U. Belfast), M.F. Lane 1 (UC Cork), B. Mullan 4 (Clontarf); J.W. Kyle 4 (Queen's U. Belfast), E. Strathdee 3 (Queen's U. Belfast); M.R. Neely (4) (Belfast Collegians), K.D. Mullen 4 (Old Belvedere), J.C. Daly 4 (London Irish), C.P. Callan 4 (Lansdowne), E. Keeffe 4 (Sunday's Well), D. Hingerty (4) (UC Dublin), J.W. McKay 4 (Queen's U. Belfast), R.D. Agar 4 (Malone).

Referee J.B.G. Whittaker (England)

ENGLAND v FRANCE   18/376

19 April 1947
Twickenham
England 6 (2T) France 3 (1PG)

England   T: Guest, Roberts.
France   PG: Prat.

The last Championship appearance of Jack Heaton, the Waterloo centre and England captain. Heaton had a strange international career: he won three caps in 1935, was forgotten for four years and came back to win another three. Recalled again in 1947, after eight years, Heaton won three more caps, the last two as captain. Among the new caps was Vic Roberts, an uncompromising tearaway flanker from Penryn. Roberts should have been capped a month earlier, against Scotland, having been told that he was in the side when Mickey Steele-Bodger failed to arrive late on Friday night (q.v.). Much to Roberts's chagrin, Steele-Bodger did arrive in the early hours of the morning and insisted he play, despite the fact that he was told that he had been replaced by Roberts. Steele-Bodger was allowed to play and won the cap. Curiously, every member of the French side, except Henri Dutrain, was earning their fourth cap.

ENGLAND   S.C. Newman 1 (Oxford U.); D.W. Swarbrick 3 (Oxford U.), N.O. Bennett 3 (St Mary's H.), *J. Heaton (9) (Waterloo), R.H. Guest 7 (Waterloo); N.M. Hall 4 (St Mary's H.), J.O. Newton-Thompson (2) (Oxford U.); G.A. Gibbs 1 (Bristol), A.P. Henderson 4 (Cambridge U.), H.W. Walker 4 (Coventry), J.T. George 2 (Falmouth), J. Mycock (4) (Sale), V.G. Roberts 1 (Penryn), M.R. Steele-Bodger 4 (Edinburgh U.), R.H.G. Weighill 2 (Harlequins).

FRANCE   A. Alvarez 4 (US Tyrosse); E. Pebeyre (4) (CA Brive), *L. Junquas 4 (A. Bayonne), M. Sorondo 4 (US Montauban), H. Dutrain 1 (S. Toulouse); M. Terreau 4 (US Bressane) Y. Bergougnan 4 (S. Toulouse); L. Caron 1 (FC Lyon), M. Jol 4 (Biarritz Ol), E. Buzy 4 (FC Lourdes), A. Moga 4 (CA Bègles), R. Soro 4 (US Romans), J. Matheu 4 (Castres Ol), J. Prat 4 (FC Lourdes), G. Basquet 4 (SU Agen).

Referee T. Jones (Wales)

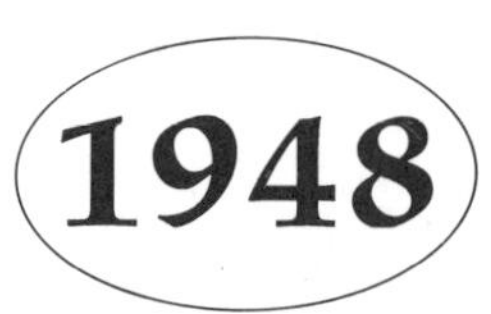

1948

PARIS Ireland beat France 13-6 · TWICKENHAM England drew Wales 3-3
MURRAYFIELD Scotland beat France 9-8 · CARDIFF Wales beat Scotland 14-0
TWICKENHAM Ireland beat England 11-10 · SWANSEA France beat Wales 11-3
DUBLIN Ireland beat Scotland 6-0 · BELFAST Ireland beat Wales 6-3
MURRAYFIELD Scotland beat England 6-3 · PARIS France beat England 15-0

CHAMPIONSHIP TABLE
Ireland – Championship, Triple Crown, Grand Slam

									Tries	
Pos	Country	P	W	D	L	F	A	Pts	F	A
1	Ireland (3)	4	4	0	0	36	19	8	10	5
2	France (4)	4	2	0	2	40	25	4	9	4
3	Scotland (5)	4	2	0	2	15	31	4	3	6
4	Wales (2)	4	1	1	2	23	20	3	5	5
5	England (1)	4	0	1	3	16	35	1	2	9

If you mention Grand Slam to an Irish rugby fan, he will either answer promptly '1948' or he will embark on a long, tortuous explanation as to the number of times cruel fate robbed them of the honour. It is one of the incongruities of the Championship that in the 100 years since it first started, Ireland – and Scotland for that matter – have beaten all four countries only once. Undoubtedly, fate or luck was on Ireland's side in 1948 when they beat everyone but they certainly did not sweep all before them. In fact, only one side, England, have won a Slam scoring fewer points, 34 in 1957, than the 36 Ireland mustered in 1948. The problem which plagued Ireland in 1948 was their goal-kickers, or rather the lack of them. They scored ten tries but only three were converted and they scored no dropped goals or penalties. Clearly this was a disadvantage in each match and accounted for the narrow margins of victory. Ireland won the Championship again in 1949, losing one match (to France) but scored only five tries – 26 points came from kicks and they were Champions without dispute.

Another interesting comparison with Ireland's success in 1948, was that of France. They won two matches and lost two, to finish runners-up for the first time since 1921. The French, however, contrived to make nine tries, one fewer than Ireland, and yet had a better points total, 40. The French scoring in 1948 was by far their best in their 19 seasons in the Championship. It was significant too that of their overall 15 victories, 8 of them had been in the last 4 Championships. The day of Le Coq had dawned. If there was any doubt remaining that they were among the most powerful competitors in the Championship, it was banished between 1949–83 when they scored 75 victories, won 9 titles and finished runners-up on 12 occasions.

In the year in which the RFU surrendered their 58-year domination of the International Board, and their representation was reduced to two votes in line with the other member countries, England found themselves bottom of the table, without even one victory to cheer them.

FRANCE v IRELAND 19/377

1 January 1948
Stade Colombes, Paris
Ireland 13 (2G, 1T) France 6 (2T)

France T: Basquet, Soro.
Ireland T: Reid, McCarthy, Mullan. C: Mullan (2).

This match was played on a Thursday. It was Ireland's first win over France since 1929, and at the same venue. On only one other occasion have Ireland scored three tries in France: on their second visit in 1912. Ernie Strathdee, captain of Ireland in this match, was dropped for the next, against Scotland.

FRANCE   L. Rouffia (1) (US Romans); P. Jeanjean (1) (RC Toulon), M. Terreau 5 (US Bressane), M. Sorondo (5) (US Montauban), M. Pomathios 1 (SU Agen); A. Alvarez 5 (US Tyrosse), G. Dufau 1 (RCF); E. Buzy 5 (FC Lourdes), L. Martin 1 (S. Pau), L. Caron 2 (Castres Ol), R. Soro 5 (US Romans), A. Moga 5 (CA Bègles), J. Prat 5 (FC Lourdes), J. Matheu 5 (Castres Ol), *G. Basquet 5 (SU Agen).

IRELAND   J.A.D. Higgins 3 (Lansdowne); B. O'Hanlon 4 (Dolphin), W.D. McKee 1 (NIFC), P.J. Reid 1 (Garryowen), B. Mullan 5 (Clontarf); J.W. Kyle 5 (Queen's U. Belfast), *E. Strathdee 4 (Queen's U. Belfast); J.C. Corcoran (1) (London Irish), K.D. Mullen 5 (Old Belvedere), A.A. McConnell 1 (Belfast Collegians), C.P. Callan 5 (Lansdowne), E. Keeffe (5) (Sunday's Well), J.S. McCarthy 1 (Dolphin), J.W. McKay 5 (Queen's U. Belfast), R.D. Agar 5 (Malone).

Referee T.N. Pearce (England)

ENGLAND v WALES   52/378

17 January 1948
Twickenham
England 3 (1PG) Wales 3 (1T)

England   PG: Newman.
Wales   T: Ken Jones.

Ken Jones, the Newport wing, probably felt lucky to be passed the ball let alone score a try, for ten of his colleagues were from Cardiff, a record club representation in the Championship. Sid Newman, the Oxford University full-back, had mixed fortunes. He kicked England's penalty goal – a monster from 50 yards – but he had to retire 15 minutes from no-side with a broken wrist. Tommy Kemp, the Richmond fly-half, played his last game; he was first capped against Wales in 1937. The attendance was 73,000.

ENGLAND   S.C. Newman (2) (Oxford U.); R.H. Guest 8 (Waterloo), N.O. Bennett 4 (US Portsmouth), E.K. Scott 2 (Redruth), D.W. Swarbrick 4 (Oxford U.); *T.A. Kemp (4) (Richmond), R.J.P. Madge 1 (Exeter); H.W. Walker 5 (Coventry), J.H. Keeling (1) (Guy's H.), G.A. Kelly (4) (Bedford), S.V. Perry 3 (Cambridge U.), H.F. Luya 1 (Headingley), M.R. Steele-Bodger 5

(Edinburgh U.), B.H. Travers 3 (Oxford U.), D.B. Vaughan 1 (Devonport Services).

WALES   R.F. Trott 1 (Cardiff); K.J. Jones 5 (Newport), W.B. Cleaver 5 (Cardiff), B.L. Williams 5 (Cardiff), J. Matthews 2 (Cardiff); G. Davies 2 (Pontypridd), *H. Tanner 17 (Cardiff); L. Anthony 1 (Neath), M. James 1 (Cardiff), C. Davies 4 (Cardiff), W.E. Tamplin 4 (Cardiff), D. Jones (1) (Llanelli), O. Williams 3 (Llanelli), G.W. Evans 5 (Cardiff), L. Manfield 3 (Cardiff).

Referee R.A. Beattie (Scotland)

SCOTLAND v FRANCE   18/379

24 January 1948
Murrayfield
Scotland 9 (1T, 2PG) France 8 (1G, 1PG)

Scotland   T: Jackson. PG: Murdoch (2).
France   T: Lacaussade. C: Alvarez. PG: Prat.

Scotland called up two veteran players, W.C.W. Murdoch and J.S.R. Innes, to open their 1948 campaign. Murdoch, first capped 13 years earlier, against England, rewarded the faith placed in him by winning the match with the second of two penalty goals. Innes, who won his first three caps in 1939, was another astute choice. It was Innes who seized on a kick ahead to put Jackson over for a try. Roger Lacaussade, who scored the French try directly under the noses of defenders trying to snatch up a dropped goal attempt that was miles wide, was not given another chance to prove his opportunism.

SCOTLAND   W.C.W. Murdoch 5 (Hillhead HSFP); T.G.H. Jackson 4 (London Scottish), *J.R.S. Innes 4 (Aberdeen GSFP), C.W. Drummond 5 (Melrose), D.D. Mackenzie 4 (Edinburgh U.); D.P. Hepburn 1 (Woodford), W.D. Allardice 1 (Aberdeen GSFP); R.M. Bruce 1 (Gordonians), G.G. Lyall 1 (Gala), W.P. Black 1 (Glasgow HSFP), L.R. Currie 1 (Dunfermline), J.C. Dawson 1 (Glasgow Acads), W.I.D. Elliot 4 (Edinburgh Acads), J.B. Lees 2 (Gala), A.G.M. Watt 4 (Edinburgh Acads).

FRANCE   A. Alvarez 6 (US Tyrosse); M. Pomathios 2 (SU Agen), L. Junquas 5 (A. Bayonne), P. Dizabo 1 (US Tyrosse), R. Lacaussade (1) (S. Bordelais); L. Bordenave 1 (RC Toulon), Y. Bergougnan 5 (S. Toulouse); E. Buzy 6 (FC

Lourdes), L. Martin 2 (S. Pau), P. Aristouy 1 (S. Pau), R. Soro 6 (US Romans), A. Moga 6 (CA Bègles), J. Prat 6 (FC Lourdes), J. Matheu 6 (Cástres Ol), *G. Basquet 6 (SU Agen).

Referee A.S. Bean (England)

WALES v SCOTLAND   52/380

7 February 1948
Cardiff Arms Park
Wales 14 (1G, 2T, 1PG) Scotland 0

Wales T: Bleddyn Williams, Matthews, Ken Jones. C: Tamplin. PG: Tamplin.

This inaugurated a sequence of seven successive post-war victories by Wales over Scotland at Cardiff. The Scots played in a strong wind in the first-half but their veteran full-back, Murdoch, failed to give them an advantage by missing five penalty kicks.

WALES R.F. Trott 2 (Cardiff); K.J. Jones 6 (Newport), B.L. Williams 6 (Cardiff), W.B. Cleaver 6 (Cardiff), J. Matthews 3 (Cardiff); G. Davies 3 (Pontypridd), *H. Tanner 18 (Cardiff); L. Anthony 2 (Neath), M. James 2 (Cardiff), C. Davies 5 (Cardiff), W.E. Tamplin 5 (Cardiff), S. Williams 5 (Llanelli), O. Williams 4 (Llanelli), G.W. Evans 6 (Cardiff), L. Manfield 4 (Cardiff).

SCOTLAND W.C.W. Murdoch 6 (Hillhead HSFP); T.G.H. Jackson 5 (London Scottish), *J.R.S. Innes 5 (Aberdeen GSFP), A. Cameron 1 (Glasgow HSFP), D.D. Mackenzie 5 (Edinburgh U.); D.P. Hepburn 2 (Woodford), W.D. Allardice 2 (Aberdeen GSFP); R.M. Bruce 2 (Gordonians), G.G. Lyall 2 (Gala), L.R. Currie 2 (Dunfermline),

The nonpareil Jean Prat, an outstanding back-row forward and also one of the Championship's most prolific scorers

J.C. Dawson 2 (Glasgow Acads), W.P. Black 2 (Glasgow HSFP), W.I.D. Elliot 5 (Edinburgh Acads), J.B. Lees 3 (Gala), A.G.M. Watt (5) (Edinburgh Acads).

Referee T.N. Pearce (England)

ENGLAND v IRELAND   52/381

14 February 1948
Twickenham
Ireland 11 (1G, 2T) England 10 (2G)

England   T: Guest (2). C: Uren (2).
Ireland   T: Kyle, McKay, McKee. C: Mullan.

This was Ireland's third win in a row over England and two of the victories had taken place at Twickenham. The Irish forwards' aggressive play in the loose, added to Karl Mullen's quick hooking, put England in retreat for most of the match. Against the run of play, Dicky Guest scored a marvellous 60-yard try after intercepting a pass inside his own 25. Uren converted to produce a closer match than their play merited.

ENGLAND   R. Uren 1 (Waterloo); R.H. Guest 9 (Waterloo), N.O. Bennett 5 (US Portsmouth), *E.K. Scott 3 (Redruth), C.B. Holmes 2 (Manchester); I. Preece 1 (Coventry), R.J.P. Madge 2 (Exeter); H.W. Walker 6 (Coventry), A.P. Henderson 5 (Cambridge U.), G.A. Gibbs (2) (Bristol), S.V. Perry 4 (Cambridge U.), H.F. Luya 2 (Headingley), D.F. White 4 (Northampton), M.R. Steele-Bodger 6 (Edinburgh U.), D.B. Vaughan 2 (Devonport Services).

IRELAND   J. Mattsson (1) (Wanderers); B. O'Hanlon 5 (Dolphin), W.D. McKee 2 (NIFC), P.J. Reid 2 (Garryowen), B. Mullan 6 (Clontarf); J.W. Kyle 6 (Queen's U. Belfast), H. de Lacy 1 (Harlequins); A.A. McConnell 2 (Belfast Collegians), *K.D. Mullen 6 (Old Belvedere), J.C. Daly 5 (London Irish), C.P. Callan 6 (Lansdowne), J.E. Nelson 1 (Malone), J.W. McKay 6 (Queen's U. Belfast), J.S. McCarthy 2 (Dolphin), D.J. O'Brien 1 (London Irish).

Referee T. Jones (Wales)

WALES v FRANCE   19/382

21 February 1948
St Helen's, Swansea
France 11 (1G, 2T) Wales 3 (1PG)

Wales   PG: Ossie Williams.
France   T: Basquet, Terreau, Pomathios. C: Alvarez.

After nine successive defeats, France gained their first victory in Wales, and the 3-0 tally in tries reflected their overall superiority. It was a salutary warning to Wales, who had averaged five tries a match against France in the previous encounters in Wales. There was also crowd trouble. Spectators, some with forged tickets, frequently spilled over the touchlines. One actually ran onto the field threatening a French player after a bout of fisticuffs. He was unceremoniously despatched by one of the Welsh forwards.

WALES   R.F. Trott 3 (Cardiff); K.J. Jones 7 (Newport), B.L. Williams 7 (Cardiff), W.B. Cleaver 7 (Cardiff), J. Matthews 4 (Cardiff); G. Davies 4 (Pontypridd), *H. Tanner 19 (Cardiff); L. Anthony (3) (Neath), M. James 3 (Cardiff), C. Davies 6 (Cardiff), W.E. Tamplin (6) (Cardiff), S. Williams (6) (Llanelli), O. Williams 5 (Llanelli), G.W. Evans 7 (Cardiff), L. Manfield 5 (Cardiff).

FRANCE   A. Alvarez 7 (US Tyrosse); M. Pomathios 3 (SU Agen), M. Terreau 6 (US Bressane), L. Junquas (6) (A. Bayonne), J. Lassegue 4 (S. Toulouse); L. Bordenave 2 (RC Toulon), Y. Bergougnan 6 (S. Toulouse); E. Buzy 7 (FC Lourdes), L. Martin 3 (S. Pau), L. Caron 3 (Castres Ol), R. Soro 7 (US Romans), A. Moga 7 (CA Bègles), J. Matheu 7 (Castres Ol), J. Prat 7 (FC Lourdes), *G. Basquet 7 (SU Agen).

Referee A.S. Bean (England)

IRELAND v SCOTLAND   54/383

28 February 1948
Lansdowne Road, Dublin
Ireland 6 (2T) Scotland 0

Ireland   T: Mullan, Kyle.

This was Scotland's fourth defeat in a row at Lansdowne Road. The Scots' initial lead in the series was now gradually being eroded and this, Ireland's twentieth victory, put them only ten in arrears.

SCOTLAND   W.C.W. Murdoch 7 (Hillhead HSFP); T.G.H. Jackson 6 (London Scottish), C.W. Drummond 6 (Melrose), *J.R.S. Innes 6 (Aberdeen GSFP), D.D. Mackenzie (6) (Edinburgh U.); D.P. Hepburn 3 (Woodford), W.D. Allardice 3 (Aberdeen GSFP); I.C. Henderson 6 (Edinburgh Acads), G.G. Lyall 3 (Gala), S. Coltman 1 (Hawick), L.R. Currie 3 (Dunfermline), H.H. Campbell 3 (London Scottish), W.I.D. Elliot 6 (Edinburgh Acads), R.M. Bruce (3) (Gordonians), W.P. Black 3 (Glasgow HSFP).

IRELAND   J.A.D. Higgins 4 (Ulster Civil Service); B. Mullan 7 (Clontarf), M. O'Flanagan (1) (Lansdowne), W.D. McKee 3 (NIFC), B. O'Hanlon 6 (Dolphin); J.W. Kyle 7 (Queen's U. Belfast), H. de Lacy (2) (Harlequins); A.A. McConnell 3 (Belfast Collegians), *K.D. Mullen 7 (Old Belvedere), J.C. Daly 6 (London Irish), C.P. Callan 7 (Lansdowne), J.E. Nelson 2 (Malone), J.S. McCarthy 3 (Dolphin), J.W. McKay 7 (Queen's U. Belfast), D.J. O'Brien 2 (London Irish).

Referee C.H. Gadney (England)

IRELAND v WALES   50/384

13 March 1948
Ravenhill, Belfast
Ireland 6 (2T) Wales 3 (1T)

Ireland   T: Mullan, Daly.
Wales   T: Bleddyn Williams.

Amid scenes of great jubilation, Ireland won the Triple Crown for the first time since 1899. The crowd carried players shoulder-high off the pitch, and Chris Daly, from Cobh, County Cork, but playing with London Irish, had his jersey torn to shreds by souvenir-hunters. Daly, a 'perpetual-motion' prop, earned his hero status by scoring the winning try, bursting through from a line-out onto a loose ball. The Irish captain, Karl Mullen, was not forgotten either: for years to come he was deservedly given credit for welding a rumbustious, fiery gang of forwards into a formidable unit, who hunted together and supported each other with a discipline and dedication which was to characterize Irish rugby thereafter. Mullen was a brilliant hooker, possibly Ireland's first specialized craftsman in this position. It was principally his leadership that made him one of Ireland's all-time greats. It is often overlooked in this, the fiftieth Championship match between the countries, that four of this Grand Slam Irish team never played internationally again, including the match-winner, Daly.

IRELAND   J.A.D. Higgins (5) (Ulster Civil Service); B. O'Hanlon 7 (Dolphin), W.D. McKee 4 (NIFC), P.J. Reid (3) (Garryowen), B. Mullan (8) (Clontarf); J.W. Kyle 8 (Queen's U. Belfast), E. Strathdee 5 (Queen's U. Belfast); A.A. McConnell 4 (Belfast Collegians), *K.D. Mullen 8 (Old Belvedere), J.C. Daly (7) (London Irish), C.P. Callan 8 (Lansdowne), J.E. Nelson 3 (Malone), J.W. McKay 8 (Queen's U. Belfast), J.S. McCarthy 4 (Dolphin), D.J. O'Brien 3 (London Irish).

WALES   R.F. Trott 4 (Cardiff); K.J. Jones 8 (Newport), B.L. Williams 8 (Cardiff), W.B. Cleaver 8 (Cardiff), L. Williams 5 (Cardiff); G. Davies 5 (Pontypridd), *H. Tanner 20 (Cardiff); E. Davies (1) (Aberavon), M. James (4) (Cardiff), C. Davies 7 (Cardiff), J.A. Gwilliam 1 (Cambridge U.), J.R.G. Stephens 5 (Neath), O. Williams (6) (Llanelli), G.W. Evans 8 (Cardiff), L. Manfield (6) (Cardiff).

Referee M.A. Allan (Scotland)

SCOTLAND v ENGLAND 51/385

20 March 1948
Murrayfield
Scotland 6 (2T) England 3 (1PG)

Scotland T: Drummond, Young.
England PG: Uren.

Having won their previous two matches at Murrayfield, England were seeking a first-ever hat-trick at the headquarters of the SRU. A series of injuries ruined the attempt, the most crucial of which was the loss through torn ligaments of Madge, their scrum-half, after ten minutes. Madge's place was taken by Mickey Steele-Bodger, switching from flank. Steele-Bodger took to his new position as to the manner born: few remembered at the time that Steele-Bodger – 'all blond curly hair and bow legs' – had played scrum-half for most of his years of pupillage at Rugby School. However, Steele-Bodger was concussed in the second half and that added to a fractured jaw suffered by the captain, E.K. Scott, weakened the resolve of the England team. It was a match to remember also for W.B. Young, scorer of one of Scotland's tries, who was recalled for his tenth and last cap after a nine-year absence.

SCOTLAND W.C.W. Murdoch (8) (Hillhead HSFP); T.G.H. Jackson 7 (London Scottish), *J.R.S. Innes (7) (Aberdeen GSFP), L. Bruce-Lockhart 1 (London Scottish), C.W. Drummond 7 (Melrose); D.P. Hepburn 4 (Woodford), A.W. Black 3 (Edinburgh U.); I.C. Henderson (7) (Edinburgh Acads), G.G. Lyall (4) (Gala), H.H. Campbell (4) (London Scottish), W.P. Black 4 (Glasgow HSFP), R. Finlay (1) (Watsonians), W.I.D. Elliot 7 (Edinburgh Acads), W.B. Young (10) (London Scottish), J.B. Lees (4) (Gala).

ENGLAND R. Uren 2 (Waterloo); R.H. Guest 10 (Waterloo), N.O. Bennett (6) (US Portsmouth), *E.K. Scott (4) (Redruth), M.F. Turner 1 (Blackheath); I. Preece 2 (Coventry), R.J.P. Madge (3) (Exeter); H.W. Walker 7 (Coventry), A.P. Henderson 6 (Edinburgh Wands), T.W. Price 1 (Gloucester), S.V. Perry 5 (Cambridge U.), H.F. Luya 3 (Headingley), M.R. Steele-Bodger 7 (Edinburgh U.), D.B. Vaughan 3 (Devonport Services), R.H.G. Weighill 3 (Harlequins).

Referee N.H. Lambert (Ireland)

FRANCE v ENGLAND 19/386

29 March 1948
Stade Colombes, Paris
France 15 (1G, 2T, 1DG) England 0

France T: Pomathios, Prat, Soro. C: Alvarez. DG: Bergougnan.

This was France's biggest score and widest winning margin against England in the 19 Championship matches played since 1910. It was only the second time that England had failed to score against France. The result elevated France to second place behind Grand Slamming Ireland and left England with the Wooden Spoon. The nearest England came to a try was when Mickey Steele-Bodger tried to dive over André Alvarez. As he fell the English flanker broke his wrist. As this was Easter Monday few public services were operating: when a French official took Steele-Bodger to hospital after the game they found themselves at the end of a very long queue. With the prospect of a long wait for treatment, the Frenchman suggested a couple of bottles of champagne as an alternative. Steele-Bodger agreed with alacrity.

FRANCE A. Alvarez 8 (A. Bayonne); M. Siman 1 (AS Montferrand), P. Dizabo 2 (US Tyrosse), M. Terreau 7 (US Bressane), M. Pomathios 4 (SU Agen); L. Bordenave 3 (RC Toulon) Y. Bergougnan 7 (S. Toulouse); L. Caron 4 (Castres Ol), L. Martin 4 (S. Pau), E. Buzy 8 (FC Lourdes), R. Soro 8 (US Romans), A. Moga 8 (CA Bègles), J. Prat 8 (FC Lourdes), J. Matheu 8 (Castres Ol), *G. Basquet 8 (SU Agen).

ENGLAND R. Uren 3 (Waterloo); M.F. Turner (2) (Blackheath), L.B. Cannell 1 (Northampton), A.C. Towell 1 (Leicester), C.B. Holmes (3) (Manchester); I. Preece 3 (Coventry), P.W. Sykes 1 (Wasps); H.W. Walker (8) (Coventry), A.P. Henderson 7 (Edinburgh Wands), T.W. Price 2 (Gloucester), S.V. Perry (6) (Cambridge U.), H.F. Luya 4 (Headingley), M.R. Steele-Bodger (8) (Edinburgh U.), D.F. White 5 (Northampton), *R.H.G. Weighill (4) (Harlequins).

Referee T. Jones (Wales)

1949

PARIS Scotland beat France 8-0 · CARDIFF Wales beat England 9-3
DUBLIN France beat Ireland 16-9 · MURRAYFIELD Scotland beat Wales 6-5
DUBLIN Ireland beat England 14-5 · TWICKENHAM England beat France 8-3
MURRAYFIELD Ireland beat Scotland 13-3 · SWANSEA Ireland beat Wales 5-0
TWICKENHAM England beat Scotland 19-3 · PARIS France beat Wales 5-3

CHAMPIONSHIP TABLE
Ireland – Championship, Triple Crown

Pos	Country	P	W	D	L	F	A	Pts	Tries F	A
1	Ireland (1)	4	3	0	1	41	24	6	5	3
2	England (5)	4	2	0	2	35	29	4	7	5
3	France (2)	4	2	0	2	24	28	4	3	4
4	Scotland (3)	4	2	0	2	20	37	4	4	8
5	Wales (4)	4	1	0	3	17	19	2	5	4

The 1949 Championship was notable for its anomalies, apart from the fact that Ireland triumphed again, the only time they have won two titles in succession. The Champions started their campaign by losing to France and winning the next three, which was curious in itself. Wales's fate was unusual; they scored five tries, the same number as Ireland, and conceded only 19 points, the lowest of any country yet they still finished bottom. England on the other hand scored most tries, seven, but they were only runners-up. Scotland had more right to be frustrated than anyone. They won their first two matches but finished with only Wales below them in the table. Third-placed France completed the quirkiness by losing to Scotland and ending up above them in the table, and beating Ireland, who won the title.

The English XV which lost for a fourth time in a row against Ireland when they were beaten 14-5 on 12 February 1949

FRANCE v SCOTLAND   19/387

15 January 1949
Stade Colombes, Paris
Scotland 8 (1G, 1T) France 0

Scotland   T: Elliot, Kininmonth. C: Allardice.

France, who had often been accused of all manner of malpractice regarding the transfer of players within their club system, must have been amazed to find the Scottish team captained by Des Keller, whom they had last met playing for Australia on 11 January 1948. Keller had also played against Scotland at the beginning of the Australian tour. Despite his Scottish ancestry, the selection of Keller caused quite a stir, because he had already played internationally for another country. Scotland, however, had not created a precedent. In 1923 they had capped A.C. Wallace, the New South Wales wing, who was studying at Oxford and had played for New South Wales before coming to Britain. Wallace, however, had not represented Australia, though in those days playing for New South Wales virtually amounted to being capped.

FRANCE   N. Baudry 1 (AS Montferrand); M. Pomathios 5 (Lyon OU), M. Terreau 8 (US Bressane), P. Dizabo 3 (US Tyrosse), M. Siman 2 (AS Montferrand); L. Bordenave (4) (RC Toulon), Y. Bergougnan 8 (S. Toulouse); E. Buzy 9 (FC Lourdes), M. Jol 5 (Biarritz Ol), L. Caron 5 (Lyon OU), R. Soro 9 (US Romans), A. Moga 9 (CA Bégles), J. Prat 9 (FC Lourdes), J. Matheu 9 (Castres Ol), *G. Basquet 9 (SU Agen).

SCOTLAND   I.J.M. Lumsden 3 (Bath); T.G.H. Jackson 8 (London Scottish), L.G. Gloag 1 (Cambridge U.), D.P. Hepburn 5 (Woodford), D.W.C. Smith 1 (London Scottish); C.R. Bruce 5 (Glasgow Acads), W.D. Allardice 4 (Aberdeen GSFP); J.C. Dawson 3 (Glasgow Acads), J.G. Abercrombie 1 (Edinburgh U.), S. Coltman 2 (Hawick), L.R. Currie 4 (Dunfermline), G.A. Wilson 1 (Oxford U.), *D.H. Keller 1 (London Scottish), W.I.D. Elliot 8 (Edinburgh Acads), P.W. Kininmonth 1 (Oxford U.).

Referee T.N. Pearce (England)

WALES v ENGLAND   53/388

15 January 1949
Cardiff Arms Park
Wales 9 (3T) England 3 (1DG)

Wales   T: Les Williams (2), Meredith.
England   DG: Hall.

England, who had finished with the Wooden Spoon in 1948, demonstrated their eagerness to try out new talent by playing nine new caps against Wales. The experiment must be considered a failure, not only because they lost but because four of the newcomers were at once discarded. Wales too had four new players, all in the pack, but their selectors clearly believed that if they were good enough to be picked in the first place, they were good enough to be retained. There were not all new faces at Cardiff: Bunny Travers, the Newport hooker, returned to the Welsh side ten years after his last appearance. Haydn Tanner, too, was in the veteran class. He had made his first Championship appearance in 1936 but had been capped a year earlier, against New Zealand. The dropped goal was now worth three points and Nim Hall became the first player to score one at the new value.

WALES   R.F. Trott 5 (Cardiff); K.J. Jones 9 (Newport), J. Matthews 5 (Cardiff), B.L. Williams 9 (Cardiff), L. Williams (6) (Cardiff); G. Davies 6 (Cambridge U.), *H. Tanner 21 (Cardiff); E. Coleman 1 (Newport), W.H. Travers 9 (Newport), D. Jones 4 (Swansea), D. Hayward 1 (Newbridge), A. Meredith 1 (Devonport Services), W.R. Cale 1 (Newbridge), G.W. Evans 9 (Cardiff), J.A. Gwilliam 2 (Cambridge U.).

ENGLAND   W.B. Holmes 1 (Cambridge U.); J.A. Gregory (1) (Blackheath), L.B. Cannell 2 (Oxford U.), C.B. van Ryneveld 1 (Oxford U.), T. Danby (1) (Harlequins); *N.M. Hall 5 (Huddersfield), G. Rimmer 1 (Waterloo); T.W. Price 3 (Cheltenham), A.P. Henderson 8 (Edinburgh Wands), M.J. Berridge 1 (Northampton), H.F. Luya (5) (Headingley), G.R.d'A. Hosking 1 (Devonport Services), E.L. Horsfall (1) (Harlequins), V.G. Roberts 2 (Penryn), B. Braithwaite-Exley (1) (Headingley).

Referee N.H. Lambert (Ireland)

IRELAND v FRANCE 20/389

29 January 1949
Lansdowne Road, Dublin
France 16 (2G, 2PG) Ireland 9 (3PG)

Ireland PG: Norton (3).
France T: Basquet, Lassegue. C: Prat (2). PG:
Prat (2).

A footnote beneath the match report in one Irish
newspaper read: 'The Irish Rugby Football
Union premises at Lansdowne Road were dis-
infected with Jeyes' fluid'. No explanation was
given, nor was there any information as to
whether the action was taken before, during or
after the match. France performed their own
clean-up: while not matching the four-try blitz
of 1947, they registered their biggest score in
Ireland to run up a third victory in a row on
Irish soil. They have never bettered that
sequence.

IRELAND G.W. Norton 1 (Bective Rangers);
M.F. Lane 2 (UC Cork), W.D. McKee 5 (NIFC),
T.J. Gavin 1 (London Irish), B. O'Hanlon 8
(Dolphin); J.W. Kyle 9 (Queen's U. Belfast), T.J.
Cullen (1) (UC Dublin); A.A. McConnell 5
(Belfast Collegians), *K.D. Mullen 9 (Old Belve-
dere), T. Clifford 1 (Young Munster), J.E. Nelson
4 (Malone), C.P. Callan 9 (Lansdowne), J.W.
McKay 9 (Queen's U. Belfast), J.S. McCarthy 5
(Dolphin), D.J. O'Brien 4 (London Irish).

FRANCE N. Baudry 2 (AS Montferrand); J.
Lassegue 5 (S. Toulouse), H. Dutrain 2 (S.
Toulouse), P. Dizabo 4 (US Tyrosse), M. Poma-
thios 6 (Lyon OU); A. Alvarez 9 (US Tyrosse), G.
Dufau 2 (RCF); E. Buzy 10 (FC Lourdes), M. Jol 6
(Biarritz Ol), L. Caron 6 (Lyon OU), R. Soro 10
(US Romans), A. Moga 10 (CA Bègles), J. Prat 10
(FC Lourdes), J. Matheu 10 (Castres Ol), *G.
Basquet 10 (SU Agen).

Referee T.N. Pearce (England)

SCOTLAND v WALES 53/390

5 February 1949
Murrayfield
Scotland 6 (2T) Wales 5 (1G)

Scotland T: Gloag, Smith.
Wales T: Williams. C: Trott.

Thick fog threatened to postpone the match but
it lifted in time for it to start five minutes late.
Some accounts castigated Wales for inflexibility
in their tactics. Others gave warm praise to
Scotland for their smother-and-poach play, of
which the tackling of the flankers Doug Elliot
and Doug Keller, was the significant element.

SCOTLAND I.J.M. Lumsden 4 (Bath); T.G.H.
Jackson 9 (London Scottish), L.G. Gloag 2 (Cam-
bridge U.), D.P. Hepburn 6 (Woodford), D.W.C.
Smith 2 (London Scottish); C.R. Bruce 6 (Glas-
gow Acads), W.D. Allardice 5 (Aberdeen GSFP);
J.C. Dawson 4 (Glasgow Acads), J.G. Aber-
crombie 2 (Edinburgh U.), S. Coltman 3
(Hawick), L.R. Currie 5 (Dunfermline), G.A.
Wilson 2 (Oxford U.), *D.H. Keller 2 (London
Scottish), W.I.D. Elliot 9 (Edinburgh Acads),
P.W. Kininmonth 2 (Oxford U.).

WALES R.F. Trott 6 (Cardiff); K.J. Jones 10
(Newport), J. Matthews 6 (Cardiff), B.L. Williams 10 (Cardiff), T. Cook 1 (Cardiff); G. Davies
7 (Cambridge U.), *H. Tanner 22 (Cardiff); E.
Coleman 2 (Newport), W.H. Travers 10 (Newport), D. Jones 5 (Swansea), J.A. Gwilliam 3
(Cambridge U.), A. Meredith 2 (Devonport Services), W.R. Cale 2 (Newbridge), G.W. Evans 10
(Cardiff), J.R.G. Stephens 6 (Cardiff).

Referee N.H. Lambert (Ireland)

IRELAND v ENGLAND   53/391

12 February 1949
Lansdowne Road, Dublin
Ireland 14 (1G, 1T, 2PG) England 5 (1G)

Ireland   T: O'Hanlon, McKee. C: Norton. PG: Norton (2).
England   T: van Ryneveld. C: Holmes.

England lost to Ireland for a fourth time in succession, which had last happened in 1896–99. England in fact had not won a match since beating France in April 1947, a run of six matches without victory. Ireland, Grand Slam winners in 1948, reaped the benefits of efficient team-work, in which individuals like Kyle and Strathdee blossomed and a back-row of McKay, McCarthy and O'Brien had no peers at the time.

IRELAND   G.W. Norton 2 (Bective Rangers); M.F. Lane 3 (UC Cork), T.J. Gavin (2) (London Irish), W.D. McKee 6 (NIFC), B. O'Hanlon 9 (Dolphin); J.W. Kyle 10 (Queen's U. Belfast), E. Strathdee 6 (Queen's U. Belfast); A.A. McConnell (6) (Belfast Collegians), *K.D. Mullen 10 (Old Belvedere), T. Clifford 2 (Young Munster), J.E. Nelson 5 (Malone), C.P. Callan (10) (Lansdowne), J.M. McKay 10 (Queen's U. Belfast), J.S. McCarthy 6 (Dolphin), D.J. O'Brien 5 (London Irish).

ENGLAND   W.B. Holmes 2 (Cambridge U.); D.W. Swarbrick (5) (Oxford U.), L.B. Cannell 3 (Oxford U.), C.B. van Ryneveld 2 (Oxford U.), R.D. Kennedy 1 (Camborne School of Mines); *N.M. Hall 6 (Huddersfield), G. Rimmer 2 (Waterloo); T.W. Price 4 (Cheltenham), A.P. Henderson (9) (Edinburgh Wands), M.J. Berridge (2) (Northampton), G.R.d'A. Hosking 2 (Devonport Services), J.T. George (3) (Falmouth), D.B. Vaughan 4 (Headingley), V.G. Roberts 3 (Penryn), J.M.K. Kendall-Carpenter 1 (Oxford U.).

Referee R.A. Beattie (Scotland)

ENGLAND v FRANCE   20/392

26 February 1949
Twickenham
England 8 (1G, 1DG) France 3 (1DG)

England   T: Cannell. C: Holmes. DG: Preece.
France   DG: Alvarez.

England scored their first victory in seven Championship matches, thanks to a splendid forward display. The French were no longer the lambs of pre-war years and far more was expected of their forwards, who were more experienced in Championship rugby than the English pack. The French problem seemed to be a psychological barrier when playing at Twickenham, 'La Cathedrale'; they had never won there. The dropped goal was now worth three points and as if to mark the devaluation, each side scored one. England's was their first against the French in England.

ENGLAND   W.B. Holmes 3 (Cambridge U.); R.H. Guest 11 (Waterloo), L.B. Cannell 4 (Oxford U.), C.B. van Ryneveld 3 (Oxford U.), R.D. Kennedy 2 (Camborne School of Mines); *I. Preece 4 (Coventry), W.K.T. Moore 3 (Leicester); T.W. Price 5 (Cheltenham), J.H. Steeds 1 (Middlesex H.), J.M.K. Kendall-Carpenter 2 (Oxford U.), J.R.C. Matthews 1 (Harlequins), G.R.d'A. Hosking 3 (Devonport Services), B.H. Travers 4 (Harlequins), V.G. Roberts 4 (Penryn), D.B. Vaughan 5 (Headingley).

FRANCE   A.J. Alvarez 10 (US Tyrosse); M. Pomathios 7 (Lyon OU), P. Dizabo 5 (US Tyrosse), H. Dutrain 3 (S. Toulouse), J. Lassegue 6 (S. Toulouse); J. Pilon 1 (CA Périgueux), Y. Bergougnan (9) (S. Toulouse); L. Caron 7 (Lyon OU), M. Jol 7 (Biarritz Ol), E. Buzy 11 (FC Lourdes), A. Moga 11 (CA Bègles), R. Soro 11 (US Romans), J. Prat 11 (FC Lourdes), J. Matheu 11 (Castres Ol), *G. Basquet 11 (SU Agen).

Referee T. Jones (Wales)

SCOTLAND v IRELAND   55/393

26 February 1949
Murrayfield
Ireland 13 (2G, 1PG) Scotland 3 (1PG)

Scotland   PG: Allardice.
Ireland   T: McCarthy (2). C: Norton (2). PG: Norton.

Scottish rugby was so unproductive during this period that they were finding it a problem to produce a winning combination even with the home advantage. This was Ireland's seventh win at Murrayfield since 1926, in which time Scotland had won but twice. The match was a personal triumph for Jim McCarthy, who scored both Irish tries. The flame-haired Dolphin breakaway was a master of aggressive harassment; he was also adept at supporting and linking with Jackie Kyle. Between them they plotted the downfall of many a defence, a strike-force which often led to scores for others but on this occasion was more suitably accredited.

SCOTLAND   I.J.M. Lumsden 5 (Bath); T.G.H. Jackson 10 (London Scottish), L.G. Gloag 3 (Cambridge U.), D.P. Hepburn 7 (Woodford), D.W.C. Smith 3 (London Scottish); C.R. Bruce 7 (Glasgow Acads), W.D. Allardice 6 (Aberdeen GSFP); J.C. Dawson 5 (Glasgow Acads), J.G. Abercrombie 3 (Edinburgh U.), S. Coltman 4 (Hawick), L.R. Currie 6 (Dunfermline), A.M. Thomson (1) (St Andrew's U.), *D.H. Keller 3 (London Scottish), W.I.D. Elliot 10 (Edinburgh Acads), P.W. Kininmonth 3 (Oxford U.).

IRELAND   G.W. Norton 3 (Bective Rangers); B. O'Hanlon 10 (Dolphin), N.J. Henderson 1 (Queen's U. Belfast), W.D. McKee 7 (NIFC), M.F. Lane 4 (UC Cork); J.W. Kyle 11 (Queen's U. Belfast) E. Strathdee 7 (Queen's U. Belfast); T. Clifford 3 (Young Munster), *K.D. Mullen 11 (Old Belvedere), J.L. Griffin 1 (Wanderers), J.E. Nelson 6 (Malone), R.D. Agar 6 (Malone), J.W. McKay 11 (Queen's U. Belfast), J.S. McCarthy 7 (Dolphin), D.J. O'Brien 6 (London Irish).

Referee A.S. Bean (England)

WALES v IRELAND   51/394

12 March 1949
St Helen's, Swansea
Ireland 5 (1G) Wales 0

Ireland   T: McCarthy. C: Norton.

Ireland carried off the Triple Crown for the second season in a row, largely due to a try by Jim McCarthy, converted by George Norton. Norton was one of those players who achieved only momentary greatness, his promising career cut short when he so badly injured a shoulder against Scotland in 1951 that he did not play again. Norton's reputation was based on resolute head-on tackling. His other qualities were safe hands, an uncanny positional sense and accurate line-kicking. He was also a superb place-kicker as proved in this, his first season, when almost unnoticed he contributed a record 26 points out of Ireland's total of 41 in winning the Championship. While Ireland were so successful, Wales's lack of wins was an enigma. They had plenty of good-quality players, but some essential ingredient was missing as they scraped together two victories only during the two seasons Ireland dominated.

WALES   R.F. Trott 7 (Cardiff); K.J. Jones 11 (Newport), J. Matthews 7 (Cardiff), B.L. Williams 11 (Cardiff), T. Cook (2) (Cardiff); W.B. Cleaver 9 (Cardiff), *H. Tanner 23 (Cardiff); E. Coleman (3) (Newport), W.H. Travers 11 (Newport), D. Jones 6 (Swansea), J.A. Gwilliam 4 (Cambridge U.), A. Meredith (3) (Devonport Services), W.R. Cale 3 (Newbridge), G.W. Evans (11) (Cardiff), J.R.G. Stephens 7 (Neath).

IRELAND   G.W. Norton 4 (Bective Rangers); M.F. Lane 5 (UC Cork), W.D. McKee 8 (NIFC), N.J. Henderson 2 (Queen's U. Belfast), B. O'Hanlon 11 (Dolphin); J.W. Kyle 12 (Queen's U. Belfast), E. Strathdee (8) (Queen's U. Belfast); T. Clifford 4 (Young Munster), *K.D. Mullen 12 (Old Belvedere), J.L. Griffin (2) (Wanderers), R.D. Agar 7 (Malone), J.E. Nelson 7 (Malone), J.W. McKay 12 (Queen's U. Belfast), J.S. McCarthy 8 (Dolphin), D.J. O'Brien 7 (London Irish).

Referee T.N. Pearce (England)

ENGLAND v SCOTLAND 52/395

19 March 1949
Twickenham
England 19 (2G, 3T) Scotland 3 (1PG)

England T: van Ryneveld (2), Guest, Hosking, Kennedy. C: Travers (2).
Scotland PG: Wilson.

Six of the England side made their final Championship appearances in this match, including the highly-talented Waterloo wing, Dicky Guest, and W.B. Holmes, the polished Cambridge full-back. Guest first played for England in 1939 and although advancing years blunted his blistering speed, he still retained his ability to bewilder defences with jink and side-step. In contrast Holmes played in this season only – a promising career cut short when he died later in the year on a visit to his homeland, Argentina. Coincidentally, two others who played their last match were also expatriates employed by England. Clive van Ryneveld, a South African, and B.H. Travers, of Australia. In contrast to England's modest clear-out, Scotland's was genocidal: eleven players were axed.

ENGLAND W.B. Holmes (4) (Cambridge U.); R.H. Guest (12) (Waterloo), L.B. Cannell 5 (Oxford U.), C.B. van Ryneveld (4) (Oxford U.), R.D. Kennedy (3) (Camborne School of Mines); *I. Preece 5 (Coventry), W.K.T. Moore 4 (Leicester); T.W. Price (6) (Cheltenham), J.H. Steeds 2 (Middlesex H.), J.M.K. Kendall-Carpenter 3 (Oxford U.), J.R.C. Matthews 2 (Harlequins), G.R.d'A. Hosking 4 (Devonport Services), B.H. Travers (5) (Harlequins), V.G. Roberts 5 (Penryn), D.B. Vaughan 6 (Headingley).

SCOTLAND I.J.M. Lumsden (6) (Bath); T.G.H. Jackson (11) (London Scottish), L.G. Gloag (4) (Cambridge U.), D.P. Hepburn (8) (Woodford), D.W.C. Smith 4 (The Army); C.R. Bruce (8) (Glasgow Acads), W.D. Allardice (7) (Aberdeen GSFP); S.T.H. Wright (1) (Stewart's FP), J.A.R. Macphail (1) (Edinburgh Acads), S. Coltman (5) (Hawick), L.R. Currie (7) (Dunfermline), G.A. Wilson (3) (Oxford U.), *D.H. Keller 4 (London Scottish), W.I.D. Elliot 11 (Edinburgh Acads), P.W. Kininmonth 4 (Oxford U.).

Referee N.H. Lambert (Ireland)

FRANCE v WALES 20/396

26 March 1949
Stade Colombes, Paris
France 5 (1G) Wales 3 (1T)

France T: Lassegue. C: Alvarez.
Wales T: Ken Jones.

The last link with the pre-War Championship was severed in this match when Haydn Tanner, the great Cardiff scrum-half, played his final match for Wales. Tanner was 18 when his international career had begun, against New Zealand, in 1935 and he played the first of 24 Championship matches the following year. It speaks volumes for his fitness and skill that he bridged the war-years gap to come back and captain Wales. The speed, length and accuracy of Tanner's pass was arguably his greatest asset. But he was far more than just a feeder of the fly-half: he possessed an incisive break from the scrum, could accelerate and swerve in the open and was a better defender than often given credit for. Some believe that he is the greatest scrum-half ever. As one chapter of Welsh history closed, two others opened: Malcolm Thomas and Clem Thomas made their début appearances.

FRANCE N. Baudry (3) (AS Montferrand); M. Pomathios 8 (Lyon OU), P. Dizabo 6 (US Tyrosse), H. Dutrain (4) (S. Toulouse), J. Lassegue (7) (S. Toulouse); A. Alvarez 11 (US Tyrosse), G. Dufau 3 (RCF): E. Buzy (12) (FC Lourdes), M. Jol (8) (Biarritz Ol), L. Caron (8) (Lyon OU), A. Moga (12) (CA Bègles), R. Soro (12) (US Romans), J. Matheu 12 (Castres Ol), J. Prat 12 (FC Lourdes), *G. Basquet 12 (SU Agen).

WALES R.F. Trott (8) (Cardiff); K.J. Jones 12 (Newport), M.C. Thomas 1 (Newport), J. Matthews 8 (Cardiff), W. Major 1 (Maesteg); G. Davies 8 (Pontypridd), *H. Tanner (24) (Cardiff); C. Davies 8 (Cardiff), W.H. Travers (12) (Newport), D. Jones (7) (Swansea), D. Hayward 2 (Newport), J.A. Gwilliam 5 (Cambridge U.), P. Stone (1) (Llanelli), R.C.C. Thomas 1 (Swansea), J.R.G. Stephens 8 (Neath).

Referee N.H. Lambert (Ireland)

1950

MURRAYFIELD Scotland beat France 8-5 · TWICKENHAM Wales beat England 11-5
PARIS France drew Ireland 3-3 · SWANSEA Wales beat Scotland 12-0
TWICKENHAM England beat Ireland 3-0 · PARIS France beat England 6-3
DUBLIN Ireland beat Scotland 21-0 · BELFAST Wales beat Ireland 6-3
MURRAYFIELD Scotland beat England 13-11 · CARDIFF Wales beat France 21-0

CHAMPIONSHIP TABLE
Wales – Championship, Triple Crown, Grand Slam

Pos	Country	P	W	D	L	F	A	Pts	Tries F	A
1	Wales (5)	4	4	0	0	50	8	8	10	1
2	Scotland (4)	4	2	0	2	21	49	4	5	8
3	Ireland (1)	4	1	1	2	27	12	3	3	3
4	France (3)	4	1	1	2	14	35	3	3	7
5	England (2)	4	1	0	3	22	30	2	5	7

Wales defied all expectations for having been Wooden Spoon holders in 1949, they won the Grand Slam for the first time since 1911. Their four-match aggregate of 50 points, even though it contained ten tries, was not particularly impressive. Their defence, however, was dramatic for they conceded only eight points. Only England, who yielded four points in 1913, had won a Grand Slam with fewer points against them. The other major surprise of the 1950 Championship was Scotland's improvement; they had finished only one place above Wales the previous season, but managed two victories and second place. England had the misfortune to finish bottom for a second time in three seasons, even though only Wales and Ireland outscored them overall.

SCOTLAND v FRANCE   20/397

14 January 1950
Murrayfield
Scotland 8 (1G, 1T) France 5 (1G)

Scotland T: Macdonald, Budge. C: Bruce-Lockhart.
France T: Merquey. C: Prat.

Tries by newcomers, R. Macdonald and G.M. Budge enabled Scotland to register their seventh consecutive home victory over France, their best sequence ever against them.

SCOTLAND   G. Burrell 1 (Gala); D.W.C. Smith 5 (London Scottish), R. Macdonald 1 (Edinburgh U.), D.A. Sloan 1 (Edinburgh Acads), C.W. Drummond 8 (Melrose); L. Bruce-Lockhart 2 (London Scottish), A.F. Dorward 1 (Cambridge U.); J.C. Dawson 6 (Glasgow Acads), J.G. Abercrombie 4 (Edinburgh U.), G.M. Budge 1 (Edinburgh Wands), D.E. Muir 1 (Heriot's FP), R. Gemmill 1 (Glasgow HSFP), *W.I.D. Elliot 12 (Edinburgh Acads), D.H. Keller 5 (Sheffield), P.W. Kininmonth 5 (Richmond).

FRANCE   R. Arcalis 1 (CA Brive); M. Pomathios 9 (Lyon OU), J. Merquey 1 (RC Toulon), P. Dizabo 7 (RCF), M. Siman 3 (Castres Ol); P. Lauga 1 (RC Vichy), G. Dufau 4 (RCF); P. Lavergne (1), (US Limoges), L. Martin (5) (S. Pau), P. Aristouy 2 (S. Pau), R. Ferrien 1 (S. Tarbes); F. Bonnus 1 (RC Toulon), J. Prat 13 (FC Lourdes), R. Biénès 1 (US Cognac), *G. Basquet 13 (SU Agen).

Referee T. Jones (Wales)

ENGLAND v WALES   54/398

21 January 1950
Twickenham
Wales 11 (1G, 1T, 1PG) England 5 (1G)

England   T: Smith. C: Hofmeyr.
Wales   T: Cale, Cliff Davies. C: Lewis Jones.
PG: Lewis Jones.

An attendance of 75,532, Twickenham's largest ever crowd, persuaded the RFU to make future home internationals all-ticket affairs. It was Wales's second victory only in 15 visits to Twickenham since 1910. As in 1949, England introduced nine new players – but only one of them, Eric Evans, the Sale hooker resisted selectorial whims eventually to become a regular first-choice. Wales, bottom of the table in 1949, had five newcomers on show. One of them, Lewis Jones, became a Welsh folk hero, and it was said that half the Principality went into mourning when, after only nine caps, the multi-talented utility back became a professional rugby league player. However, on this occasion Jones made his presence felt; a brilliant, diagonal run produced a try for Cliff Davies and his accurate place kicking brought a conversion and a penalty.

ENGLAND   M.B. Hofmeyr 1 (Oxford U.); J.V. Smith 1 (Cambridge U.), B. Boobyer 1 (Oxford U.), L.B. Cannell 6 (Oxford U.), I.J. Botting 1 (Oxford U.); *I. Preece 6 (Coventry), G. Rimmer 3 (Waterloo); J.M.K. Kendall-Carpenter 4 (Oxford U.), E. Evans 1 (Sale), W.A. Holmes 1 (Nuneaton), G.R.d'A. Hosking (5) (Devonport Services), H.A. Jones 1 (Barnstaple), H.D. Small 1 (Oxford U.), J.J. Cain (1) (Waterloo), D.B. Vaughan (7) (Headingley).

WALES   B. Lewis Jones 1 (Devonport Services); K.J. Jones 13 (Newport), M.C. Thomas 2 (Newport), J. Matthews 9 (Cardiff), T.J. Brewer 1 (Newport); W.B. Cleaver 10 (Cardiff), W.R. Willis 1 (Cardiff); J.D. Robins 1 (Birkenhead Park), D.M. Davies 1 (Somerset Police), C. Davies 9 (Cardiff), D. Hayward 3 (Newbridge), E.R. John 1 (Neath), W.R. Cale 4 (Pontypool), R.T. Evans 3 (Newport), *J.A. Gwilliam 6 (Edinburgh Wands).

Referee M.H. Lambert (Ireland)

FRANCE v IRELAND   21/399

28 January 1950
Stade Colombes, Paris
France 3 (1DG) Ireland 3 (1PG)

France   DG: Lauga.
Ireland   PG: Burges.

The first Championship match between Ireland and France to end in a draw. Burges was the fourth player Ireland tried as a place kicker – and he succeeded with his first kick.

FRANCE   R. Arcalis 2 (CA Brive); M. Siman 4 (Castres Ol), J. Merquey 2 (RC Toulon), P. Dizabo (8) (RCF), M. Pomathios 10 (Lyon OU); P. Lauga 2 (RC Vichy), P. Lasâosa 1 (US Dax); R. Biénès 2 (US Cognac), P. Pascalin 1 (S. Mont-de-Marsan), R. Ferrien 2 (S. Tarbes), F. Bonnus 2 (RC Toulon), P. Aristouy 3 (S. Pau), D. Herice (1) (CA Bègles), J. Prat 14 (FC Lourdes), *G. Basquet 14 (SU Agen).

IRELAND   G.W. Norton 5 (Bective Rangers); M.F. Lane 6 (UC Cork), N.J. Henderson 3 (Queen's U. Belfast), W.D. McKee 9 (NIFC), B. O'Hanlon (12) (Dolphin); J.W. Kyle 13 (Queen's U. Belfast), J.H. Burges 1 (Rosslyn Park); T. Clifford 5 (Young Munster), *K.D. Mullen 13 (Old Belvedere), D. McKibbin 1 (Instonians), J.E. Nelson 8 (Malone), R.D. Agar 8 (Malone), A.B. Curtis 1 (Oxford U.), J.W. McKay 13 (Queen's U. Belfast), D.J. O'Brien 8 (London Irish).

Referee T.N. Pearce (England)

WALES v SCOTLAND   54/400

4 February 1950
St Helen's, Swansea
Wales 12 (2T, 1DG, 1PG) Scotland 0

Wales   T: Thomas, Ken Jones. DG: Cleaver. PG: Lewis Jones.

Remarkably, three members of the Welsh pack played most of their rugby outside Wales: John Robins (Birkenhead Park), Dai Davies (Somerset Police) and John Gwilliam (Edinburgh Wanderers). Each was an important cog in what had become a smoothly efficient machine. The aim was to subdue the opposition in the opening half-an-hour and then release the backs to reap the benefit against psychologically beaten opponents. This was classic strategy, and it was employed even more tellingly 20 years later.

WALES   B. Lewis Jones 2 (Devonport Services); K.J. Jones 14 (Newport), M.C. Thomas 3 (Newport), J. Matthews 10 (Cardiff), W. Major (2) (Maesteg); W.B. Cleaver 11 (Cardiff), W.R. Willis 2 (Cardiff); J.D. Robins 2 (Birkenhead Park), D.M. Davies 2 (Somerset Police), C. Davies 10 (Cardiff), D. Hayward 4 (Newbridge), E.R. John 2 (Neath), W.R. Cale 5 (Pontypool), R.T. Evans 4 (Newport), *J.A. Gwilliam 7 (Edinburgh Wands).

SCOTLAND   G. Burrell 2 (Gala); D.W.C. Smith 6 (London Scottish), R. Macdonald 2 (Edinburgh U.), D.A. Sloan 2 (Edinburgh Acads), C.W. Drummond 9 (Melrose); L. Bruce-Lockhart 3 (London Scottish), A.W. Black 4 (Edinburgh U.); J.C. Dawson 7 (Glasgow Acads), J.G. Abercrombie 5 (Edinburgh U.), G.M. Budge 2 (Edinburgh Wands), D.E. Muir 2 (Heriot's FP), R. Gemmill 2 (Glasgow HSFP), *W.I.D. Elliot 13 (Edinburgh Acads), D.H. Keller 6 (Sheffield), P.W. Kininmonth 6 (Richmond).

Referee Captain M.J. Dowling (Ireland)

ENGLAND v IRELAND   54/401

11 February 1950
Twickenham
England 3 (1T) Ireland 0

England   T: Roberts.

Ireland were denied what would have been a record five successive victories over England because of a first-half injury to Des McKee. The powerful, extremely quick NIFC centre, was as vital to Irish midfield strategy as the brilliant Jackie Kyle was in orchestrating it. When McKee went off at half-time – to end, incidentally, his international career – the consequent reshuffling restricted the range of Irish attacking, even though their seven forwards often had the better of the opposition. England's one victory of the season came from a well-worked move which ended with Roberts storming over.

ENGLAND   R. Uren (4) (Waterloo); J.V. Smith 2 (Cambridge U.), B. Boobyer 2 (Oxford U.), L.B. Cannell 7 (Oxford U.), I.J. Botting (2) (Oxford U.); *I. Preece 7 (Coventry), W.K.T. Moore 5 (Leicester); J.M.K. Kendall-Carpenter 5 (Oxford U.), J.H. Steeds 3 (Saracens), W.A. Holmes 2 (Nuneaton), J.R.C. Matthews 3 (Harlequins), H.A. Jones 2 (Barnstaple), H.D. Small 2 (Oxford U), V.G. Roberts 6 (Penryn), S.J. Adkins 1 (Coventry).

IRELAND   G.W. Norton 6 (Bective Rangers); M.F. Lane 7 (UC Cork), G.C. Phipps 1 (Rosslyn Park), W.D. McKee (10) (NIFC), L. Crowe 1 (Old Belvedere); J.W. Kyle 14 (Queen's U. Belfast), J.H. Burges (2) (Rosslyn Park); T. Clifford 6 (Young Munster), *K.D. Mullen 14 (Old Belvedere), D. McKibbin 2 (Instonians), J.E. Nelson 9 (Malone), R.D. Agar 9 (Malone), A.B. Curtis 2 (Oxford U.), J.W. McKay 14 (Queen's U. Belfast), D.J. O'Brien 9 (London Irish).

Referee R.A. Beattie (Scotland)

FRANCE v ENGLAND   21/402

25 February 1950
Stade Colombes, Paris
France 6 (2T) England 3 (1T)

France   T: Cazenave, Pilon.
England   T: Smith.

Stade Colombes, close to the Seine and with poor drainage, usually ended as a quagmire whenever Paris suffered heavy rain. This match was no exception, and both sides had to adjust tactically. The tries came from defensive mistakes while shaky handling by both sets of backs might have brought others. The French victory was important for them: it was their third home win in a row, and their first hat-trick against England in the Championship.

FRANCE   G. Brun 1 (CS Vienne); M. Siman 5 (Castres Ol), P. Lauga 3 (RC Vichy), J. Merquey 3 (RC Toulon), F. Cazenave 1 (RCF); J. Pilon (2) (CA Périgueux), G. Dufau 5 (RCF); R. Biénès 3 (US Cognac), P. Pascalin 2 (S. Mont-de-Marsan), R. Ferrien 3 (S. Tarbes), P. Aristouy 4 (S. Pau) F. Bonnus 3 (RC Toulon), J. Prat 15 (FC Lourdes), J. Matheu 13 (Castres Ol), *G. Basquet 15 (SU Agen).

ENGLAND   M.B. Hofmeyr 2 (Oxford U.); J.V. Smith 3 (Cambridge U.), B. Boobyer 3 (Oxford U.), L.B. Cannell 8 (Oxford U.), J.P. Hyde 1 (Northampton); *I. Preece 8 (Coventry), W.K.T. Moore 6 (Leicester); J.M.K. Kendall-Carpenter 6 (Oxford U.), J.H. Steeds 4 (Saracens), W.A. Holmes 3 (Nuneaton), J.R.C. Matthews 4 (Harlequins), H.A. Jones (3) (Barnstaple), H.D. Small 3 (Oxford U.), V.G. Roberts 7 (Penryn), S.J. Adkins 2 (Coventry).

Referee N.H. Lambert (Ireland)

IRELAND v SCOTLAND   56/403

25 February 1950
Lansdowne Road, Dublin
Ireland 21 (3G, 2PG) Scotland 0

Ireland   T: Blayney, Curtis, Crowe. C: Norton (3). PG: Norton (2).

George Norton's 12 points from two penalty goals and three conversions represented most points from kicks for Ireland at the time. It was also the biggest margin of victory in any Scotland-Ireland match. Making his last appearance for Scotland was George Burrell, the Gala full-back. Burrell became a referee of some note, even though his international experience was limited to two matches. He became better known as the manager of the 1977 British tour of New Zealand. Other players in the match had links with British tours to New Zealand: Karl Mullen captained the 1950 side, Des O'Brien managed the 1966 tourists and Doug Smith managed the 1971 team.

IRELAND   G.W. Norton 7 (Bective Rangers); L. Crowe 2 (Old Belvedere), J. Blayney (1) (Wanderers), R.J.H. Uprichard 1 (Harlequins), M.F. Lane 8 (UC Cork); J.W. Kyle 15 (Queen's U. Belfast), R. Carroll 2 (Lansdowne); T. Clifford 7 (Young Munster), *K.D. Mullen 15 (Old Belvedere), D. McKibbin 3 (Instonians), J.E. Nelson 10 (Malone), J. Maloney (1) (UC Dublin), A.B. Curtis (3) (Oxford U.), J.W. McKay 15 (Queen's U. Belfast), D.J. O'Brien 10 (London Irish).

SCOTLAND   G. Burrell (3) (Gala); D.W.C. Smith 7 (London Scottish), R. Macdonald 3 (Edinburgh U.), C.W. Drummond 10 (Melrose), D.M. Scott 1 (Langholm); A. Cameron 2 (Glasgow HSFP), A.W. Black 5 (Edinburgh U.); J.C. Dawson 8 (Glasgow Acads), J.G. Abercrombie 6 (Edinburgh U.), G.M. Budge 3 (Edinburgh Wands), D.E. Muir 3 (Heriot's FP), R. Gemmill 3 (Glasgow HSFP), *W.I.D. Elliot 14 (Edinburgh Acads), D.H. Keller (7) (Sheffield), P.W. Kininmonth 7 (Richmond).

Referee T.N. Pearce (England)

IRELAND v WALES   52/404

11 March 1950
Ravenhill, Belfast
Wales 6 (2T) Ireland 3 (1PG)

Ireland   PG: Norton.
Wales   T: Ken Jones, Thomas.

Wales won their eighth Triple Crown, their first since 1911, when Malcolm Thomas, with tacklers clinging to him like leeches, dived in at the corner after a fine countering attack which followed an uncustomary lapse by the Irish defence. Celebrations, though, were silenced by an appalling tragedy the next day when a plane carrying home Welsh supporters crashed at Llandow, near Cardiff, killing 80.

IRELAND   G.W. Norton 8 (Bective Rangers); M.F. Lane 9 (UC Cork), R.J.H. Uprichard (2) (Harlequins), G.C. Phipps 2 (Rosslyn Park), L. Crowe (3) (Old Belvedere); J.W. Kyle 16 (Queen's U. Belfast), R. Carroll (3) (Lansdowne); T. Clifford 8 (Young Munster), *K.D. Mullen 16 (Old Belvedere), D. McKibbin 4 (Instonians), J.E. Nelson 11 (Malone), R.D. Agar (10) (Malone), J.W. McKay 16 (Queen's U. Belfast), J.S. McCarthy 9 (Dolphin), D.J. O'Brien 11 (London Irish).

WALES   G. Williams 1 (London Welsh); K.J. Jones 15 (Newport), B. Lewis Jones 3 (Devonport Services), J. Matthews 11 (Cardiff), M.C. Thomas 4 (Devonport Services); W.B. Cleaver 12 (Cardiff), W.R. Willis 3 (Cardiff); J.D. Robins 3 (Birkenhead Park), D.M. Davies 3 (Somerset Police), C. Davies 11 (Cardiff), E.R. John 3 (Neath), D. Hayward 5 (Newbridge), W.R. Cale 6 (Pontypool), R.T. Evans 5 (Newport), *J.A. Gwilliam 8 (Edinburgh Wanderers).

Referee R.A. Beattie (Scotland)

SCOTLAND v ENGLAND 53/405

18 March 1950
Murrayfield
Scotland 13 (2G, 1T) England 11 (1G, 1T, 1PG)

Scotland T: Sloan (2), Abercrombie. C: Gray (2).
England T: Smith (2). C: Hofmeyr. PG: Hofmeyr.

This was Scotland's last victory over England for 14 depressing years, so T. Gray's match-winning conversion, the final act of a rain-sodden encounter, was quite rightly of reverential distinction. England came close to winning – indeed some observers thought they deserved to win – but for the second time in three years they became Wooden Spoonists.

SCOTLAND T. Gray 1 (Northampton); C.W. Drummond (11) (Melrose), R. Macdonald (4) (Edinburgh U.), D.A. Sloan 3 (Edinburgh Acads), D.M. Scott 2 (Langholm); A. Cameron 3 (Glasgow HSFP), A.W. Black (6) (Edinburgh U.); J.C. Dawson 9 (Glasgow Acads), J.G. Abercrombie (7) (Edinburgh U.), G.M. Budge (4) (Edinburgh Wands), D.E. Muir 4 (Heriot's FP), R. Gemmill 4 (Glasgow HSFP), W.I.D. Elliot 15 (Edinburgh Acads), J.S. Scott (1) (St Andrew's U.), *P.W. Kininmonth 8 (Richmond).

ENGLAND M.B. Hofmeyr (3) (Oxford U.); J.V. Smith (4) (Cambridge U.), B. Boobyer 4 (Oxford U.), L.B. Cannell 9 (Oxford U.), J.P. Hyde (2) (Northampton); *I. Preece 9 (Coventry), W.K.T. Moore (7) (Leicester); J.L. Baume (1) (Northern), J.H. Steeds (5) (Saracens), W.A. Holmes 4 (Nuneaton), J.R.C. Matthews 5 (Harlequins), S.J. Adkins 3 (Coventry), H.D. Small (4) (Oxford U.), V.G. Roberts 8 (Penryn), J.M.K. Kendall-Carpenter 7 (Oxford U.).

Referee Captain M.J. Dowling (Ireland)

WALES v FRANCE 21/406

25 March 1950
Cardiff Arms Park
Wales 21 (3G, 1T, 1PG) France 0

Wales T: Ken Jones (2), John, Matthews. C: Lewis Jones (3). PG: Lewis Jones.

Wales won the Grand Slam for the first time since 1911 with this convincing display against a rebuilt French team that was about to be reshuffled again. Seven players made their last appearance in the Championship, but the four musketeers, Michel Pomathios, Jean Prat, Jean Matheu and Guy Basquet survived one of the biggest French purges since before the War. Before kick-off the crowd stood in silence as five buglers sounded a Last Post tribute to the memory of the Welsh rugby supporters who had died in the Dublin-Cardiff aeroplane disaster a fortnight earlier.

WALES G. Williams 2 (London Welsh); K.J. Jones 16 (Newport), J. Matthews 12 (Cardiff), B. Lewis Jones 4 (Devonport Services), M.C. Thomas 5 (Devonport Services); W.B. Cleaver (13) (Cardiff), W.R. Willis 4 (Cardiff); J.D. Robins 4 (Birkenhead Park), D.M. Davies 4 (Somerset Police), C. Davies 12 (Cardiff), D. Hayward 6 (Newbridge), E.R. John 4 (Neath), W.R. Cale (7) (Pontypool), R.T. Evans 6 (Newport), *J.A. Gwilliam 9 (Edinburgh Wands).

FRANCE G. Brun 2 (CS Vienne); M. Siman (6) (Castres Ol), P. Lauga (4) (RC Vichy), J. Merquey (4) (RC Toulon), M. Pomathios 11 (Lyon OU); F. Fournet (1) (AS Montferrand), G. Dufau 6 (RCF), P. Pascalin 3 (S. Mont-de-Marsan), R. Biénès 4 (US Cognac), R. Ferrien (4) (S. Tarbes), P. Aristouy (5) (S. Pau), F. Bonnus (4) (RC Toulon), J. Prat 16 (FC Lourdes), J. Matheu 14 (Castres Ol), *G. Basquet 16 (SU Agen).

Referee Captain M.J. Dowling (Ireland)

1951

PARIS France beat Scotland 14-12 · SWANSEA Wales beat England 23-5
DUBLIN Ireland beat France 9-8 · MURRAYFIELD Scotland beat Wales 19-0
DUBLIN Ireland beat England 3-0 · TWICKENHAM France beat England 11-3
MURRAYFIELD Ireland beat Scotland 6-5 · CARDIFF Wales drew Ireland 3-3
TWICKENHAM England beat Scotland 5-3 · PARIS France beat Wales 8-3

CHAMPIONSHIP TABLE
Ireland – Championship

									Tries	
Pos	Country	P	W	D	L	F	A	Pts	F	A
1	Ireland (3)	4	3	1	0	21	16	7	4	3
2	France (4)	4	3	0	1	41	27	6	7	6
3	Wales (1)	4	1	1	2	29	35	3	6	6
4	Scotland (2)	4	1	0	3	39	25	2	7	4
5	England (5)	4	1	0	3	13	40	2	3	8

France had been accepted back into the Championship in 1947 but the International Board still felt some unease as to the state of the game there. Professionalism, they believed, was still rife. Accordingly they sent a formal warning to the French, reiterating the conditions of acceptance of 1939. The French diplomatically promised action. They promised again in 1952, again in 1953 and by 1958 the Four Home Unions were left with but two decisions: ban France again, because in effect nothing had changed, or forget the matter. The latter was decided upon. By 1978 France had become full members of the International Board, which effectively ruled out any further possibility of their being excluded.

In 1951 other events were of more importance to France. For the first time they won three matches in the Championship, and only a narrow 8-9 defeat by Ireland in Dublin, had stopped them winning the most cherished prize of all, the Grand Slam and the Championship. The threat was obvious, for no one scored more points or tries. The years of easy matches and try-scoring sprees against the French were over.

FRANCE v SCOTLAND   21/407

13 January 1951
Stade Colombes, Paris
France 14 (1G, 1T, 2PG) Scotland 12 (2T, 2PG)

France   T: Miâs, Porthault. C: Prat. PG: Prat (2).
Scotland   T: Rose (2). PG: Gray (2).

Scotland usually fared well when playing in France. This defeat proved the turning-point, with the French citadel all but unassailable to the Scots, who were to win only four more matches there. This match had one other significance. It was the first appearance in the Championship of Lucien Miâs, arguably the man responsible for elevating France to world-class status. Miâs took over where Guy Basquet left off, transforming not only a collection of individuals into a team but giving French rugby as a whole an example to follow.

Miâs recognised the French problems instantly: indiscipline, poor organization, lack of strong leadership and team spirit. Out went any unable to accept the physical challenge of the game. In came towering giants, hard, robust and instilled with disciplined technique. Suddenly the French backs, brilliant, fast, unorthodox, became part of a unified team effort. The result was staggering. In 1958 Miâs's 15-man game was demonstrated tellingly against Australia, South Africa in South Africa, and Wales in Cardiff. Miâs's – and French rugby's – supreme moment came the following year when they won the Championship for the first time.

FRANCE   A.O. Alvarez 12 (US Tyrosse); A. Porthault 1 (RCF), M. Terreau (9) (US Bressane), G. Brun 3 (CS Vienne), M. Pomathios 12 (Lyon OU);

J. Carabignac 1 (SU Agen), G. Dufau 7 (RCF); R. Bernard 1 (US Bergerac), P. Pascalin 4 (S. Mont-de-Marsan), R. Biénès 5 (US Cognac), L. Miâs 1 (SC Mazamet), H. Fourès 1 (S. Toulouse), J. Prat 17 (FC Lourdes), J. Matheu 15 (Castres Ol), *G. Basquet 17 (SU Agen).

SCOTLAND   T. Gray 2 (Northampton); A.D. Cameron 1 (Hillhead HSFP), I.D.F. Coutts 1 (Old Alleynians), F.O. Turnbull (1) (Kelso), D.M. Rose 1 (Jedforest); A. Cameron 4 (Glasgow HSFP), I.A. Ross 1 (Hillhead HSFP); J.C. Dawson 10 (Glasgow Acads), N.G.R. Mair 1 (Edinburgh U.), R.L. Wilson 1 (Gala), H.M. Inglis 1 (Edinburgh Acads), R. Gemmill 5 (Glasgow HSFP), W.I.D. Elliot 16 (Edinburgh Acads), J.J. Hegarty 1 (Hawick), *P.W. Kininmonth 9 (Richmond).

Referee T.N. Pearce (England)

WALES v ENGLAND   55/408

20 January 1951
St Helen's, Swansea
Wales 23 (4G, 1T) England 5 (1G)

Wales   T: Matthews (2). Thomas (2), Ken Jones. C: Lewis Jones (4).
England   T: Rittson-Thomas. C: Hewitt.

With ten players new to international rugby, England were no match for a Wales side that contained eleven players who had toured with the British Isles to New Zealand in 1950, and was essentially the same side that had carried off the Grand Slam the previous season. Not since 1922, when they scored eight tries, had Wales run up so many tries against England in Wales. The weakness of the England side was overlooked in the euphoria of the Welsh victory: 'scintillating', 'magnificent', 'unbeatable', read the headlines. Unbeatable they most certainly were not.

WALES   G. Williams 3 (London Welsh); K.J. Jones 17 (Newport), J. Matthews 13 (Cardiff), B. Lewis Jones 5 (Devonport Services), M.C. Thomas 6 (Devonport Services); G. Davies 9 (Cambridge U.), W.R. Willis 5 (Cardiff); J.D. Robins 5 (Birkenhead Park), D.M. Davies 5 (Somerset Police), C. Davies 13 (Cardiff), E.R. John 5 (Neath), D. Hayward 7 (Newbridge), P. Evans 1 (Llanelli), R.T. Evans 7 (Newport), *J.A. Gwilliam 10 (Edinburgh Wands).

ENGLAND   E.N. Hewitt 1 (Coventry); C.G. Woodruff 1 (Harlequins), L.F.L. Oakley (1) (Bedford), B. Boobyer 5 (Oxford U.), V.R. Tindall 1 (Liverpool U.); I. Preece 10 (Coventry), G. Rimmer 4 (Waterloo); R.V. Stirling 1 (Leicester), T. Smith (1) (Northampton), W.A. Holmes 5 (Nuneaton), D.T. Wilkins 1 (Roundhay), J.T. Bartlett (1) (Waterloo), *V.G. Roberts 9 (Penryn), G.C. Rittson-Thomas 1 (Oxford U.), P.B.C. Moore (1) (Blackheath).

Referee Captain M.J. Dowling (Ireland)

IRELAND v FRANCE   22/409

27 January 1951
Lansdowne Road, Dublin
Ireland 9 (2T, 1PG) France 8 (1G, 1T)

Ireland   T: Nelson, Clifford. PG: Henderson.
France   T: Olive, Matheu. C: Bertrand.

Ireland's penalty goal was taken by Noel Henderson with his first place kick in international rugby. France's chances were diminished by the withdrawal on the morning of the match of their ace goal-kicker, Jean Prat, who had gone down with influenza. After scoring only one try in the previous three matches against France at Lansdowne Road, their two tries were welcome.

IRELAND   G.W. Norton 9 (Bective Rangers); C.S. Griffin 1 (London Irish), N.J. Henderson 4 (Queen's U. Belfast), R.R. Chambers 1 (Instonians), M.F. Lane 10 (UC Cork); J.W. Kyle 17 (Queen's U. Belfast), J.A. O'Meara 1 (UC Cork); T. Clifford 9 (Young Munster), *K.D. Mullen 17 (Old Belvedere), J.H. Smith 1 (London Irish), J.E. Nelson 12 (Malone), D. McKibbin 5 (Instonians), J.S. McCarthy 10 (Dolphin), J.W. McKay 17 (Queen's U. Belfast), D.J. O'Brien 12 (London Irish).

FRANCE   R. Arcalis 3 (CA Brive); D. Olive 1 (AS Montferrand), G. Belletante 1 (S. Nantes), M. Prat 1 (FC Lourdes), M. Pomathios 13 (Lyon OU); J. Carabignac 2 (SU Agen), G. Dufau 8 (RCF); R. Bernard 2 (US Bergerac), P. Pascalin 5 (S. Mont-de-Marsan), P. Bertrand 1 (US Bressane), H. Fourès 2 (S. Toulouse), L. Miâs 2 (SC Mazamet), J. Matheu (16) (Castres Ol), R. Biénès 6 (US Cognac), *G. Basquet 18 (SU Agen).

Referee: T.N. Pearce (England)

SCOTLAND v WALES　　55/410

3 February 1951
Murrayfield
Scotland 19 (2G, 1T, 1DG, 1PG) Wales 0

Scotland　T: Gordon (2), Dawson. C: Inglis, Thomson. DG: Kininmonth. PG: Thomson.

Few would argue that this was the most unexpected result of any match in the history of the Championship. Scotland, supposedly the no-hopers, fielded a side best described as anonymous, even in Scotland. Yet they decisively toppled what was regarded as one of Wales's finest sides. Those that considered it a fluke had much to justify their view: Scotland had to wait until 1955 for their next victory; and their sequence of 17 defeats, 15 in the Championship, was the worst suffered by any country. However, Scotland played magnificently in this match; Wales were totally outclassed. The post-mortems in the Valleys were to state the obvious, acrimonious. The selectors, however, baffled everyone yet again. Instead of the expected clear-out, they made only a few minor reshuffles for the Irish match. Only one player, Glyn Davies, never played again.

SCOTLAND　I.H.M. Thomson 1 (Heriot's FP); R. Gordon 1 (Edinburgh Wands), D.A. Sloan 4 (Edinburgh Acads), D.M. Scott 3 (Langholm), D.M. Rose 2 (Jedforest); A. Cameron 5 (Glasgow HSFP), I.A. Ross 2 (Hillhead HSFP); J.C. Dawson 11 (Glasgow Acads), N.G.R. Mair 2 (Edinburgh U.), R.L. Wilson 2 (Gala), R. Gemmill 6 (Glasgow HSFP), H.M. Inglis 2 (Edinburgh Acads), W.I.D. Elliot 17 (Edinburgh Acads), R.C. Taylor 1 (Kelvinside-West), *P.W. Kininmonth 10 (Richmond).

WALES　G. Williams 4 (Llanelli); K.J. Jones 18 (Newport), J. Matthews 14 (Cardiff), B. Lewis Jones 6 (Devonport Services), M.C. Thomas 7 (Devonport Services); G. Davies (10) (Cambridge U.), W.R. Willis 6 (Cardiff); J.D. Robins 6 (Birkenhead Park), D.M. Davies 6 (Somerset Police), C. Davies 14 (Cardiff), E.R. John 6 (Neath), D. Hayward 8 (Newbridge), A. Forward 1 (Pontypool), R.T. Evans 8 (Newport), *J.A. Gwilliam 11 (Edinburgh Wands).

Referee Captain M.J. Dowling (Ireland)

IRELAND v ENGLAND　　55/411

10 February 1951
Lansdowne Road, Dublin
Ireland 3 (1PG) England 0

Ireland　PG: McKibbin.

This was Ireland's fifth success in the last six encounters with England. It was not without significance, however, that it was the first time since 1921 that the Irish had failed to score a try against them.

IRELAND　G.W. Norton 10 (Bective Rangers); C.S. Griffin (2) (London Irish), N.J. Henderson 5 (Queen's U. Belfast), R.R. Chambers 2 (Instonians), W.H.J. Millar 1 (Queen's U. Belfast); J.W. Kyle 18 (Queen's U. Belfast), J.A. O'Meara 2 (UC Cork); T. Clifford 10 (Young Munster), *K.D. Mullen 18 (Old Belvedere), J.H. Smith 2 (Queen's U. Belfast), J.E. Nelson 13 (Malone), D. McKibbin 6 (Instonians), J.W. McKay 18 (Queen's U. Belfast), J.S. McCarthy 11 (Dolphin), D.J. O'Brien 13 (London Irish).

ENGLAND　E.N. Hewitt 2 (Coventry); C.G. Woodruff 2 (Harlequins), I. Preece 11 (Coventry), J.M. Williams 1 (Penzance & Newlyn), V.R. Tindall 2 (Liverpool U.); E.M.P. Hardy 1 (Blackheath), G. Rimmer 5 (Waterloo); R.V. Stirling 2 (Leicester), E. Evans 2 (Sale), W.A. Holmes 6 (Nuneaton), D.T. Wilkins 2 (Roundhay), B.A. Neale 1 (Rosslyn Park), V.G. Roberts 10 (Penryn), G.C. Rittson-Thomas 2 (Oxford U.), *J.M.K. Kendall-Carpenter 8 (Oxford U.).

Referee T. Jones (Wales)

ENGLAND v FRANCE　　22/412

24 February 1951
Twickenham
France 11 (1G, 1T, 1DG) England 3 (1T)

England　T: Boobyer.
France　T: Basquet, Prat. C: Prat. DG: Prat.

France's first win over England at Twickenham. England had won nine and drawn one of the previous ten home matches against the French. It was a singular triumph for their back-row.

ENGLAND   E.N. Hewitt (3) (Coventry); C.G. Woodruff 3 (Harlequins), I. Preece (12) (Coventry), B. Boobyer 6 (Oxford U.), V.R. Tindall 3 (Liverpool U.); E.M.P. Hardy 2 (Blackheath), G. Rimmer 6 (Waterloo); R.V. Stirling 3 (Leicester), E. Evans 3 (Sale), W.A. Holmes 7 (Nuneaton), D.T. Wilkins 3 (Roundhay), B.A. Neale 2 (The Army), V.G. Roberts 11 (Penryn), G.C. Rittson-Thomas (3) (Oxford U.), *J.M.K. Kendall-Carpenter 9 (Penzance & Newlyn).

FRANCE   R. Arcalis 4 (CA Brive); A. Porthault 2 (RCF), G. Brun 4 (CS Vienne), G. Belletante 2 (S. Nantes), M. Pomathios 14 (Lyon OU); A.J. Alvarez 13 (US Tyrosse), G. Dufau 9 (RCF); R. Bernard 3 (US Bergerac), P. Pascalin 6 (S. Mont-de-Marsan), P. Bertrand 2 (US Bressane), L. Miâs 3 (SC Mazamet), H. Fourès 3 (S. Toulouse), J. Prat 18 (FC Lourdes), R. Biénès 7 (US Cognac), *G. Basquet 19 (SU Agen).

Referee V.S. Llewellyn (Wales)

SCOTLAND v IRELAND   57/413

24 February 1951
Murrayfield
Ireland 6 (1T, 1DG) Scotland 5 (1G)

Scotland   T: Sloan. C: Thomson.
Ireland   T: O'Brien. DG: Henderson.

George Norton suffered such a severe shoulder injury that not only did he have to leave the field after only quarter of an hour, but it ended his international career.

SCOTLAND   I.H.M. Thomson 2 (Heriot's FP); K.J. Dalgleish 1 (Edinburgh Wands), D.A. Sloan 5 (Edinburgh Acads), D.M. Scott 4 (Langholm), D.M. Rose 3 (Jedforest); A. Cameron 6 (Glasgow HSFP), I.A. Ross 3 (Hillhead HSFP); J.C. Dawson 12 (Glasgow Acads), N.G.R. Mair 3 (Edinburgh U.), R.L. Wilson 3 (Gala), H.M. Inglis 3 (Edinburgh Acads), R. Gemmill (7) (Glasgow HSFP), W.I.D. Elliot 18 (Edinburgh Acads), R.C. Taylor 2 (Kelvinside-West), *P.W. Kininmonth 11 (Richmond).

IRELAND   G.W. Norton (11) (Bective Rangers); M.F. Lane 11 (UC Cork), R.R. Chambers 3 (Instonians), N.J. Henderson 6 (Queen's U. Belfast), W.H.J. Millar 2 (Queen's U. Belfast); J.W. Kyle 19 (Queen's U. Belfast), J.A. O'Meara 3 (UC Cork); J.H. Smith 3 (Queen's U. Belfast), *K.D. Mullen 19 (Old Belvedere), D. McKibbin 7 (Instonians), P.J. Lawler 1 (Clontarf), J.R. Brady 1 (CIYMS), J.S. McCarthy 12 (Dolphin), J.W. McKay 19 (Queen's U. Belfast), D.J. O'Brien 14 (London Irish).

Referee T.N. Pearce (England)

WALES v IRELAND   53/414

10 March 1951
Cardiff Arms Park
Wales 3 (1PG) Ireland 3 (1T)

Wales   PG: Edwards.
Ireland   T: Kyle.

Ireland were frustrated in their hopes of what would have been a second Grand Slam by a penalty goal from a man who made only this one appearance for Wales, Ben Edwards. The Newport lock-forward's presence meant that Roy John had to play at flank-forward, a curious selection for whatever qualities John possessed certainly they were not of a flanker. But what is international selection if not a mixture of compromise, blind faith and prejudice? The process of selection, inadvertently perhaps, continues the combination of old and new that characterizes one of the more emotive and compelling ingredients of the Championship. This match, for instance, brought to an end the career of the veteran prop, Cliff Davies, while introducing Cliff Morgan, just out of school.

WALES   G. Williams 5 (Llanelli); K.J. Jones 19 (Newport), J. Matthews 15 (Cardiff), B.L. Williams 12 (Cardiff), M.C. Thomas 8 (Devonport Services); C.I. Morgan 1 (Cardiff), W.R. Willis 7 (Cardiff); J.D. Robins 7 (Birkenhead Park), D.M. Davies 7 (Somerset Police), C. Davies (15) (Cardiff), D. Hayward 9 (Newbridge), B. Edwards (1) (Newport), R.T. Evans 9 (Newport), E.R. John 7 (Neath), *J.A. Gwilliam 12 (Edinburgh Wands)

IRELAND   A. McMorrow (1) (Garryowen), W.H.J. Millar 3 (Queen's U. Belfast), N.J. Henderson 7 (Queen's U. Belfast), R.R. Chambers 4 (Instonians), M.F. Lane 12 (UC Cork); J.W. Kyle

20 (Queen's U. Belfast), J.A. O'Meara 4 (UC Cork); D. McKibbin (8) (Instonians), *K.D. Mullen 20 (Old Belvedere), J.H. Smith 4 (Queen's U. Belfast), J.R. Brady 2 (CIYMS), J.E. Nelson 14 (Malone), J.W. McKay 20 (Queen's U. Belfast), J.C. McCarthy 13 (Dolphin), D.J. O'Brien 15 (Cardiff).

Referee W.C.W. Murdoch (Scotland)

ENGLAND v SCOTLAND 54/415

17 March 1951
Twickenham
England 5 (1G) Scotland 3 (1T)

England T: White. C: Hook.
Scotland T: Cameron.

This was one of the lowest-scoring England sides of all time and, despite this victory, it was this deficiency which condemned them to the Wooden Spoon for a second season running. The whole of the threequarter line was abandoned afterwards. Scotland were more selective, pruning five players throughout the line-up.

ENGLAND W.G. Hook 1 (Gloucester); C.G. Woodruff (4) (Harlequins), A.C. Towell (2) (Bedford), J.M. Williams (2) (Penzance & Newlyn), V.R. Tindall (4) (Liverpool U.); E.M.P. Hardy (3) (Blackheath), D.W. Shuttleworth 1 (Headingley); R.V. Stirling 4 (Leicester), E. Evans 4 (Sale), W.A. Holmes 8 (Nuneaton), D.T. Wilkins 4 (Roundhay), B.A. Neale (3) (Rosslyn Park), D.F. White 6 (Northampton), V.G. Roberts 12 (Penryn), *J.M.K. Kendall-Carpenter 10 (Penzance & Newlyn).

SCOTLAND T. Gray (3) (Northampton); K.J. Dalgleish 2 (Edinburgh Wands), D.A. Sloan 6 (Edinburgh Acads), D.M. Scott 5 (Langholm), D.M. Rose 4 (Jedforest); A. Cameron 7 (Glasgow HSFP), I.A. Ross (4) (Hillhead HSFP); J.C. Dawson 13 (Glasgow Acads), N.G.R. Mair (4) (Edinburgh U.), R.L. Wilson 4 (Gala), W.P. Black (5) (Glasgow HSFP), H.M. Inglis 4 (Edinburgh Acads), W.I.D. Elliot 19 (Edinburgh Acads), R.C. Taylor (3) (Kelvinside-West), *P.W. Kininmonth 12 (Richmond).

Referee Captain M.J. Dowling (Ireland)

FRANCE v WALES 22/416

7 April 1951
Stade Colombes, Paris
France 8 (1G, 1PG) Wales 3 (1T)

France T: Alvarez. C: Prat. PG: Alvarez.
Wales T: Ken Jones.

Ineffective performances by Wales against Scotland and Ireland led to John Gwilliam losing the captaincy and his place. His successor, Jack Matthews, lasted this match only, as did Bob Evans and Peter Evans. Matthews was a cross between a bulldozer and a brick wall, and he won fame far and wide for his strength and tackling. Yet he was a fine centre in his own right, although occasionally Wales did not employ his midfield talents to the full by 'relegating' him to the wing. An interesting newcomer to the Welsh pack was Billy Williams, claimed by Swansea to have developed the finest scrummaging technique they had ever seen. Williams fully justified his inclusion and went on to contribute mightily to the Welsh scrum in 19 Championship matches. France had won three of the last four matches against Wales but their fortunes were about to change. They lost the next six.

FRANCE R. Arcalis (5) (CA Brive): A. Porthault 3 (RCF), G. Brun 5 (CS Vienne), G. Belletante (3) (S. Nantes), M. Pomathios 15 (Lyon OU); A. Alvarez (14) (US Tyrosse), G. Dufau 10 (RCF); R. Bernard (4) (US Bergerac), P. Pascalin (7) (S. Mont-de-Marsan), P. Bertrand 3 (US Bressane), L. Miâs 4 (SC Mazamet), H. Fourès (4) (S. Toulouse), R. Biénès 8 (US Cognac), J. Prat 19 (FC Lourdes), *G. Basquet 20 (SU Agen).

WALES G. Williams 6 (Llanelli); K.J. Jones 20 (Newport), M.C. Thomas 9 (Newport), *J. Matthews (16) (Cardiff), H.T. Morris 1 (Cardiff); C.I. Morgan 2 (Cardiff), W.R. Willis 8 (Cardiff); W.O.G. Williams 1 (Swansea), D.M. Davies 8 (Somerset Police), J.D. Robins 8 (Birkenhead Park), D. Hayward 10 (Newbridge), E.R. John 8 (Neath), R.T. Evans (10) (Newport), P. Evans (2) (Llanelli), J.R.G. Stephens 9 (Neath).

Referee Captain M.J. Dowling (Ireland)

1952

MURRAYFIELD France beat Scotland 13-11 · TWICKENHAM Wales beat England 8-6
PARIS Ireland beat France 11-8 · CARDIFF Wales beat Scotland 11-0
DUBLIN Ireland beat Scotland 12-8 · DUBLIN Wales beat Ireland 14-3
MURRAYFIELD England beat Scotland 19-3 · SWANSEA Wales beat France 9-5
TWICKENHAM England beat Ireland 3-0 · PARIS England beat France 6-3

CHAMPIONSHIP TABLE
Wales – Championship, Triple Crown, Grand Slam

| | | | | | | | | | Tries | |
Pos	Country	P	W	D	L	F	A	Pts	F	A
1	Wales (3)	4	4	0	0	42	14	8	6	3
2	England (5)	4	3	0	1	34	14	6	7	4
3	Ireland (1)	4	2	0	2	26	33	4	5	6
4	France (2)	4	1	0	3	29	37	2	5	3
5	Scotland (4)	4	0	0	4	22	55	0	3	10

Ireland extended their sequence of matches without defeat to six, their longest in the Championship until equalled in 1968–69. It awarded them only third place, however, in a Championship dominated by two sides, Wales and England. For Wales their third Championship Grand Slam was the reward for consistency, if not brilliant attacking play. The crucial match turned out to be between England and Wales at Twickenham, where the Welsh recovered from a six-point deficit to stage a dramatic revival in front of a packed house of 73,000. After finishing in bottom place in 1951 England had every reason to feel happy with three victories and second position. The French threat did not materialize, and they won only one match, against Scotland. For the Scots, beaten in all four matches, it was a distressing period and ominous of even worse to come.

The Wales XV which defeated Ireland 14-3 on 8 March 1952 to win the Triple Crown for the ninth time
Back row: Dr P.F. Cooper, A. Forward, R.C.C. Thomas, W.O. Williams, D. Hayward, D.M. Davies, A. Thomas, I. Jones.
Middle row: W.O.G. Williams, M.C. Thomas, R.G. Stephens, J.A. Gwilliam, E.R. John, K.J. Jones, B.L. Jones. Seated: W.A. Williams, C.I. Morgan

SCOTLAND v FRANCE 22/417

12 January 1952
Murrayfield
France 13 (2G, 1PG) Scotland 11 (1G, 2PG)

Scotland T: Cordial. C: Thomson. PG: Thomson (2).
France T: Jean Prat, Basquet. C: Jean Prat (2). PG: Jean Prat.

After six consecutive defeats at Murrayfield, France won there for a first time. Jean Prat, the French flanker, had a magnificent game, not the least for his contribution of 10 of France's 13 points. On only two other occasions, 1978 and 1980, have France scored more points at the headquarters of Scottish rugby. The match took place six weeks after Scotland had suffered the most humiliating defeat in their history, 44-0 at the hands of South Africa. Scotland introduced eight new caps – coincidentally the same number as France – in an effort to rebuild not only their side but their shattered pride. Victory over France, which was nearly achieved, might have helped. In the event matters steadily worsened and they endured 13 successive defeats. Scotland's Dark Age had arrived.

SCOTLAND I.H.M. Thomson 3 (Heriot's FP); R. Gordon 2 (Edinburgh Wands), I.F. Cordial 1 (Edinburgh Wands), J.L. Allan 1 (Melrose), D.M. Scott 6 (London Scottish); J.N.G. Davidson 1 (Edinburgh U.), A.K. Fulton 1 (Edinburgh U.); J.C. Dawson 14 (Glasgow Acads), N.M. Munnoch 1 (Watsonians), J. Fox 1 (Gala), M. Walker 1 (Oxford U.), J. Johnston 1 (Melrose), W.I.D. Elliot 20 (Edinburgh Acads), J.T. Greenwood 1 (Dunfermline), *P.W. Kininmonth 13 (Richmond).

FRANCE R. Labarthete (1) (S. Pau); G. Brun 6 (CS Vienne), M. Prat (2) (FC Lourdes), R. Martine 1 (FC Lourdes), F. Cazenave 2 (S. Mont-de--Marsan); R. Furcade (1) (US Perpignan), P. Lasâosa 2 (US Dax); R. Bréjassou 1 (S. Tarbes), P. Labadie 1 (A. Bayonne), R. Biénès 9 (US Cognac), B. Chevallier 1 (AS Montferrand), F. Varenne (1) (RCF), J. Prat 20 (FC Lourdes), J-R. Bourdeu 1 (FC Lourdes), *G. Basquet 21 (SU Agen).

Referee I. David (Wales)

ENGLAND v WALES 56/418

19 January 1952
Twickenham
Wales 8 (1G, 1T) England 6 (2T)

England T: Agar, Woodward.
Wales T: Ken Jones (2). C: Malcolm Thomas.

This was Wales's fourth successive victory over England, who now had not beaten their rivals at Twickenham since before the War. The win was even more creditable because while Lewis Jones was off the field receiving treatment for a thigh injury, England scored two tries through their new right-wing combination of Albert Agar and Ted Woodward. The Welsh forwards, with Roy John totally dominating the line-out, responded to the challenge by gradually overtaking England in a pulsating second half.

ENGLAND W.G. Hook (2) (Gloucester); J.E. Woodward 1 (Wasps), A.E. Agar 1 (Harlequins), L.B. Cannell 10 (St Mary's H.), C.E. Winn 1 (Rosslyn Park); *N.M. Hall 7 (Richmond), G. Rimmer 7 (Waterloo); E.E. Woodgate (1) (Paignton), E. Evans 5 (Sale), R.V. Stirling 5 (Leicester), J.R.C. Matthews 6 (Harlequins), D.T. Wilkins 5 (US Portsmouth), D.F. White 7 (Northampton), A.O. Lewis 1 (Bath), J.M.K. Kendall-Carpenter 11 (Penzance & Newlyn).

WALES G. Williams 7 (Llanelli); K.J. Jones 21 (Newport), M.C. Thomas 10 (Newport), A.G. Thomas 1 (Cardiff), B. Lewis Jones 7 (Llanelli); C.I. Morgan 3 (Cardiff), W.R. Willis 9 (Cardiff); W.O.G. Williams 2 (Swansea), D.M. Davies 9 (Somerset Police), D. Hayward 11 (Newbridge), E.R. John 9 (Neath), J.R.G. Stephens 10 (Neath), L. Blyth 1 (Swansea), A. Forward 2 (Pontypool), *J.A. Gwilliam 13 (Edinburgh Wands).

Referee N.H. Lambert (England)

FRANCE v IRELAND   23/419

26 January 1952
Stade Colombes, Paris
Ireland 11 (1G, 1T, 1PG) France 8 (1G, 1PG)

France   T: Jean Prat. C: Jean Prat. PG: Jean Prat.
Ireland   T: McCarthy (2). C: Notley. PG: Henderson.

This victory marked the end of Ireland's period of success in France. Since 1910, they had won 8 of the 12 matches there, and France had won only 3.

FRANCE   G. Brun 7 (CS Vienne); A. Porthault 4 (RCF), M. Prat 3 (FC Lourdes), R. Martine 2 (FC Lourdes), D. Olive (2) (AS Montferrand); A. Labazuy 1 (FC Lourdes), P. Lasâosa 3 (US Dax); R. Bréjassou 2 (S. Tarbes), P. Labadie 2 (A. Bayonne), R. Biénès 10 (US Cognac), L. Miâs 5 (SC Mazamet), B. Chevallier 2 (AS Montferrand), J-R. Bourdeu 2 (FC Lourdes), J. Prat 21 (FC Lourdes), *G. Basquet 22 (SU Agen).

IRELAND   J.R. Notley 1 (Wanderers); M.F. Lane 13 (UC Cork), N.J. Henderson 8 (Queen's U. Belfast), R.R. Chambers 5 (Instonians), G.C. Phipps 3 (Rosslyn Park); J.W. Kyle 21 (NIFC), J.A. O'Meara 5 (UC Cork); T. Clifford 11 (Young Munster), K.D. Mullen 21 (Old Belvedere), J.H. Smith 5 (London Irish), R.H. Thompson 1 (Instonians), P.J. Lawler 2 (Clontarf), J.W. McKay (21) (Queen's U. Belfast), J.S. McCarthy 14 (Dolphin), *D.J. O'Brien 16 (Cardiff).

Referee T.N. Pearce (England)

WALES v SCOTLAND   56/420

2 February 1952
Cardiff Arms Park
Wales 11 (1G, 2PG) Scotland 0

Wales   T: Ken Jones. C: Malcolm Thomas. PG: Malcolm Thomas (2)

A crowd of 56,000 produced then record Arms Park receipts of £14,506. Newspapers forecast a Welsh fifteen eager to exact revenge for the humiliation of Murrayfield the year before. This prescient 'insight' into the collective thinking of 15 individuals was no less absurd then than it is today: each match is taken as it comes, and for each player it is a private and different experience, regardless of the fact they are participating in a team effort. In 1952 the response from 'eager' Wales was a dour one, lacking the urgency of a side hellbent on revenge, which of course they were not. On this occasion Wales did what was required to achieve victory, no more.

WALES   G. Williams 8 (Llanelli); K.J. Jones 22 (Newport), M.C. Thomas 11 (Newport), A.G. Thomas 2 (Cardiff), B.L. Williams 13 (Cardiff); C.I. Morgan 4 (Cardiff), W.R. Willis 10 (Cardiff); W.O.G. Williams 3 (Swansea), D.M. Davies 10 (Somerset Police), D. Hayward 12 (Newbridge), E.R. John 10 (Neath), J.R.G. Stephens 11 (Neath), L. Blyth (2) (Swansea), A. Forward 3 (Pontypool), *J.A. Gwilliam 14 (Edinburgh Wands).

SCOTLAND   I.H.M. Thomson 4 (Heriot's FP); R. Gordon 3 (Edinburgh Wands), I.F. Cordial 2 (Edinburgh Wands), J.L. Allan 2 (Melrose), D.M. Scott 7 (London Scottish); J.N.G. Davidson 2 (Edinburgh U.), A.F. Dorward 2 (Gala); J.C. Dawson 15 (Glasgow Acads), N.M. Munnoch 2 (Watsonians), J. Fox 2 (Gala), J. Johnston 2 (Melrose), D.E. Muir 5 (Heriot's FP), W.I.D. Elliot 21 (Edinburgh Acads), *P.W. Kininmonth 14 (Richmond), H.M. Inglis 5 (Edinburgh Acads).

Referee Captain M.J. Dowling (Ireland)

IRELAND v SCOTLAND   58/421

23 February 1952
Lansdowne Road, Dublin
Ireland 12 (3T, 1PG) Scotland 8 (1G, 1PG)

Ireland   T: Lane, Kyle, Henderson. PG: Henderson.
Scotland   T: Davidson. C: Thomson. PG: Thomson.

Scotland were beaten by Ireland for the seventh time in a row, and according to one account they were outscored in every way except courage. As in the previous year, Ireland lost a player in the first half because of injury. The unfortunate was Mick Lane, who having scored Ireland's first try, broke his wrist in a tackle.

IRELAND   J.G.M.W. Murphy 1 (Dublin U.); W.H.J. Millar 4 (Queen's U. Belfast), N.J. Henderson 9 (Queen's U. Belfast), J.R. Notley (2) (Wanderers), M.F. Lane 14 (UC Cork); J.W. Kyle 22 (NIFC), J.A. O'Meara 6 (UC Cork); T. Clifford 12 (Young Munster), K.D. Mullen 22 (Old Belvedere), J.H. Smith 6 (Belfast Collegians), P.J. Lawler 3 (Clontarf), A. O'Leary 1 (Cork Constitution), M. Dargan 1 (Old Belvedere), J.S. McCarthy 15 (Dolphin), *D.J. O'Brien 17 (Cardiff).

SCOTLAND   I.H.M. Thomson 5 (Heriot's FP); R. Gordon 4 (Edinburgh Wands), I.F. Cordial 3 (Edinburgh Wands), J.L. Allan 3 (Melrose), D.M. Scott 8 (London Scottish); J.N.G. Davidson 3 (Edinburgh U.), A.F. Dorward 3 (Gala); J.C. Dawson 16 (Glasgow Acads), N.M. Munnoch (3) (Watsonians), J. Fox 3 (Gala), J. Johnston 3 (Melrose), D.E. Muir 6 (Heriot's FP), W.I.D. Elliot 22 (Edinburgh Acads), *P.W. Kininmonth 15 (Richmond), H.M. Inglis (6) (Edinburgh Acads).

Referee I. David (Wales)

IRELAND v WALES   54/422

8 March 1952
Lansdowne Road, Dublin
Wales 14 (1G, 2T, 1PG) Ireland 3 (1PG)

Ireland   PG: Murphy.
Wales   T: Clem Thomas, Ken Jones, Stephens. C: Lewis Jones. PG: Lewis Jones.

It was appropriate that Karl Mullen's illustrious career for Ireland should come to an end against a Wales side seeking the Triple Crown. The two countries had dominated the Championship since 1948, and Mullen had played more than a significant part in the battles for honour and supremacy that were the climax of each season. That so much was at stake in Ireland-Wales matches was, of course, entirely accidental and in no way ordained. Ireland v Wales usually was the last fixture of the season, and with both countries doing well in their early matches, a

Championship, a Triple Crown or a Grand Slam was the inevitable prize for one or the other, and sometimes both. For the record, this victory gave Wales their third Championship Grand Slam, their ninth Triple Crown and their fourteenth Championship. Some are of the view that this 1952 Wales side was among the best ever.

IRELAND   J.G.M.W. Murphy 2 (Dublin U.); W.H.J. Millar (5) (Queen's U. Belfast), N.J. Henderson 10 (Queen's U. Belfast), R.R. Chambers (6) (Instonians), G.C. Phipps 4 (Rosslyn Park); J.W. Kyle 23 (NIFC), J.A. O'Meara 7 (UC Cork), T. Clifford (13) (Young Munster), K.D. Mullen (23) (Old Belvedere), J.H. Smith 7 (Belfast Collegians), P.J. Lawler 4 (Clontarf), A. O'Leary 2 (Cork Constitution), M. Dargan (2) (Old Belvedere), J.S. McCarthy 16 (Dolphin), *D.J. O'Brien 18 (Cardiff).

WALES   G. Williams 9 (Llanelli); K.J. Jones 23 (Newport), M.C. Thomas 12 (Newport), A.G. Thomas 3 (Cardiff), B. Lewis Jones 8 (Llanelli); C.I. Morgan 5 (Cardiff), W.A. Williams 1 (Newport); W.O.G. Williams 4 (Swansea), D.M. Davies 11 (Somerset Police), D. Hayward 13 (Newbridge), E.R. John 11 (Neath), J.R.G. Stephens 12 (Neath), R.C.C. Thomas 2 (Swansea), A. Forward 4 (Pontypool), *J.A. Gwilliam 15 (Edinburgh Wands).

Referee Dr P.F. Cooper (England)

SCOTLAND v ENGLAND   55/423

15 March 1952
Murrayfield
England 19 (2G, 2T, 1DG) Scotland 3 (1T)

Scotland   T: Johnston.
England   T: Evans, Kendall-Carpenter, Winn, Woodward. C: Hall (2). DG: Agar.

This equalled England's highest score in Scotland, achieved in 1931, and meant that Scotland had lost all four matches in the season for the first time since 1947. It also confirmed that England, after two bleak seasons, had recovered; there was much praise for a side which produced four tries, two of them by their wings.

SCOTLAND   N.W. Cameron 1 (Glasgow U.); R. Gordon 5 (Edinburgh Wands), I.F. Cordial (4) (Edinburgh Wands), I.D.F. Coutts (2) (Old Alleynians), T.G. Weatherstone 1 (Stewart's FP); J.N.G. Davidson 4 (Edinburgh U.), *A.F. Dorward 4 (Gala); J.C. Dawson 17 (Glasgow Acads), J. Fox (4) (Gala), J.M. Inglis (1) (Selkirk), J. Johnston (4) (Melrose), D.E. Muir (7) (Heriot's FP), W.I.D. Elliot 23 (Edinburgh Acads), D.S. Gilbert-Smith (1) (London Scottish), J.P. Friebe (1) (Glasgow HSFP).

ENGLAND   P.J. Collins 1 (Camborne School of Mines); J.E. Woodward 2 (Wasps), A.E. Agar 2 (Harlequins), B. Boobyer 7 (Rosslyn Park), C.E. Winn 2 (Rosslyn Park); *N.M. Hall 8 (Richmond), P.W. Sykes 2 (Wasps); W.A. Holmes 9 (Nuneaton), E. Evans 6 (Sale), R.V. Stirling 6 (Leicester), J.R.C. Matthews 7 (Harlequins), D.T. Wilkins 6 (US Portsmouth), D.F. White 8 (Northampton), A.O. Lewis 2 (Bath), J.M.K. Kendall-Carpenter 12 (Penzance & Newlyn).

Referee Captain M.J. Dowling (Ireland)

WALES v FRANCE   23/424

---

22 March 1952
St Helen's, Swansea
Wales 9 (1DG, 2PG) France 5 (1G)

Wales   DG: Alun Thomas. PG: Lewis Jones (2).
France   T: Pomathios. C: Jean Prat.

Wales won their second Grand Slam in three years, but clearly missed the flair of Cliff Morgan, absent through injury. Lewis Jones's place kicking, normally so reliable, was also a disappointment. He missed six kicks at goal. No one knew at the time but it was to be his last game. In October he signed professional rugby league forms for Leeds and one of Wales's most outstanding players departed after only nine Championship matches. Wales won eight of those matches and two Grand Slams. Lewis Jones's contribution to the number of points was 36; in terms of midfield, wing and full-back artistry it was incalculable.

WALES   G. Williams 10 (Llanelli); K. J. Jones 24 (Newport), M.C. Thomas 13 (Newport), B. Lewis Jones (9) (Llanelli), H. Phillips (1) (Swansea); A.G. Thomas 4 (Cardiff), W.A. Williams 2 (Newport); W.O.G. Williams 5 (Swansea), D.M. Davies 12 (Somerset Police), D. Hayward (14) (Newbridge), E.R. John 12 (Neath), J.R.G. Stephens 13 (Neath), R.C.C. Thomas 3 (Swansea), A. Forward (5) (Pontypool), *J.A. Gwilliam 16 (Edinburgh Wands).

FRANCE   G. Brun 8 (CS Vienne); M. Pomathios 16 (Lyon OU), J. Mauran 1 (Castres Ol), M. Prat 4 (FC Lourdes), J. Colombier 1 (AS St Junien); J. Carabignac 3 (SU Agen), G. Dufau 11 (RCF); R. Biénès 11 (US Cognac), R. Bréjassou 3 (S. Tarbes), P. Labadie 3 (A. Bayonne), B. Chevallier 3 (AS Montferrand), L. Miâs 6 (SC Mazamet), J-R. Bourdeu 3 (FC Lourdes), J. Prat 22 (FC Lourdes), *G. Basquet 23 (SU Agen).

Referee A.W.C. Austin (Scotland)

The English XV which defeated France 6-3 on 5 April 1952

ENGLAND v IRELAND 56/425

29 March 1952
Twickenham
England 3 (1T) Ireland 0

England T: Boobyer.

A blizzard made playing conditions almost impossible for a match scheduled to be played on 9 February but postponed because of the death of King George VI. Ireland, Champions in three out of the four previous years, were not the force they had been, while England, Wooden Spoonists in 1951, continued the improvement displayed in the Scottish match a fortnight earlier. Ireland had introduced five new players. Two new wings, Hillary and Bailey, were discarded after this one appearance. It was also the nineteenth and last Championship appearance of Des O'Brien, who added a new dimension to Irish back-row play with his ball skill, distribution and speed in the loose. His leadership through example was badly missed by Ireland, who went downhill rapidly from 1952, never winning more than two games a season until 1969 when they won three and finished runners-up to Wales.

ENGLAND P.J. Collins 2 (Camborne School of Mines); C.E. Winn 3 (Rosslyn Park), A.E. Agar 3 (Harlequins), B. Boobyer 8 (Rosslyn Park), R.C. Bazley 1 (Waterloo); *N.M. Hall 9 (Richmond), P.W. Sykes 3 (Wasps); W.A. Holmes 10 (Nuneaton), E. Evans 7 (Sale), R.V. Stirling 7 (Leicester), J.R.C. Matthews 8 (Harlequins), D.T. Wilkins 7 (US Portsmouth), D.F. White 9 (Northampton), A.O. Lewis 3 (Bath), J.M.K. Kendall-Carpenter 13 (Penzance & Newlyn).

IRELAND J.G.M.W. Murphy 3 (Dublin U.); M. Hillary (1) (UC Dublin), N.J. Henderson 11 (Queen's U. Belfast), G.C. Phipps (5) (Rosslyn Park), N. Bailey (1) (Northampton); J.W. Kyle 24 (NIFC), J.A. O'Meara 8 (UC Cork); W.A. O'Neill 1 (UC Dublin), R. Roe 1 (Dublin U.), J.H. Smith 8 (Belfast Collegians), P.J. Lawler 5 (Clontarf), A. O'Leary (3) (Cork Constitution), P. Kavanagh 1 (UC Dublin), J.S. McCarthy 17 (Dolphin), *D.J. O'Brien (19) (Cardiff).

Referee I. David (Wales)

FRANCE v ENGLAND 23/426

5 April 1952
Stade Colombes, Paris
England 6 (2PG) France 3 (1T)

France T: Pomathios.
England PG: Hall (2).

Guy Basquet, veteran captain of France, ended his distinguished Championship career in this match. Basquet, winner of 24 caps since 1947, was one of the proponents of modern French rugby. Not only a talented, productive No. 8, Basquet drilled into his contemporaries the need for organization and discipline in the pack. While he was captain, no French side suffered the kind of humiliating defeat undergone by pre-war sides: in other words, they had learned the facts of Championship life, and, after Basquet, France were primed to take on any opposition. Nim Hall, England's fly-half, kicked both penalty goals. With one he turned back the pages of history, to drop kick the penalty, a marvellous effort from over 50 yards.

FRANCE G. Brun 9 (CS Vienne); M. Pomathios 17 (Lyon OU), J. Mauran 2 (Castres Ol), M. Prat 5 (FC Lourdes), J. Colombier (2) (AS St Junien); J. Carabignac 4 (SU Agen), P. Lasâosa (4) (US Dax); R. Biénès 12 (US Cognac), P. Labadie 4 (A. Bayonne), R. Bréjassou 4 (S. Tarbes), L. Miâs 7 (SC Mazamet), B. Chevallier 4 (AS Montferrand), J. Prat 23 (FC Lourdes), J-R. Bourdeu 4 (FC Lourdes), *G. Basquet (24) (SU Agen).

ENGLAND P.J. Collins (3) (Camborne School of Mines); C.E. Winn 4 (Rosslyn Park), B. Boobyer (9) (Rosslyn Park), A.E. Agar 4 (Harlequins), R.C. Bazley 2 (Waterloo); *N.M. Hall 10 (Richmond), P.W. Sykes 4 (Wasps); W.A. Holmes 11 (Nuneaton), E. Evans 8 (Sale), R.V. Stirling 8 (Leicester), J.R.C. Matthews (9) (Harlequins), D.T. Wilkins 8 (US Portsmouth), D.F. White 10 (Northampton), A.O. Lewis 4 (Bath), J.M.K. Kendall-Carpenter 14 (Penzance & Newlyn).

Referee W.C.W. Murdoch (Scotland)

1953

PARIS France beat Scotland 11-5 · CARDIFF England beat Wales 8-3
BELFAST Ireland beat France 16-3 · MURRAYFIELD Wales beat Scotland 12-0
DUBLIN Ireland drew England 9-9 · TWICKENHAM England beat France 11-0
MURRAYFIELD Ireland beat Scotland 26-8 · SWANSEA Wales beat Ireland 5-3
TWICKENHAM England beat Scotland 26-8 · PARIS Wales beat France 6-3

CHAMPIONSHIP TABLE
England – Championship

Pos	Country	P	W	D	L	F	A	Pts	Tries F	A
1	England (2)	4	3	1	0	54	20	7	11	3
2	Wales (1)	4	3	0	1	26	14	6	6	2
3	Ireland (3)	4	2	1	1	54	25	5	12	3
4	France (4)	4	1	0	3	17	38	2	1	10
5	Scotland (5)	4	0	0	4	21	75	0	4	16

A victory in Cardiff and a draw in Dublin, followed by impressive home victories over France and Scotland earned England their first Championship title since 1947. Their points aggregate of 54 was the highest since the resumption of the Championship after the War and was largely due to their scoring spree against Scotland in their last match. England scored six tries, a record number against Scotland, and with Nim Hall converting four of them they romped home 26-8. Strangely, it was an identical score to the one when Scotland had lost to Ireland at Murrayfield in their previous match. It was Ireland's biggest score ever in the Championship and stood until their 1974 team equalled it against England. Ireland mustered 12 tries from their 4 matches, to equal their best ever aggregate established in 1928.

In contrast, France managed one try only, which represented their poorest performance ever in the Championship. Wales, Champions in 1952, never truly recovered from their initial defeat by England, and though they went on to win their next three matches, they achieved complete mastery only over Scotland. So not only did Scotland find themselves at the foot of the table for the third time in four seasons, but in the process they conceded a massive 75 points.

FRANCE v SCOTLAND   23/427

10 January 1953
Stade Colombes, Paris
France 11 (1G, 1DG, 1PG) Scotland 5 (1G)

France T: Bourdeu. C: Bertrand. DG: Carabignac. PG: Bertrand.
Scotland T: Rose. C: Cameron.

Scotland went down to a third successive defeat against France on a Colombes pitch that was barely playable after a week of frost and snow. The Scottish pack, which included six newcomers, gave away height and weight all round but it was not until late in the second half that the French were able to establish complete mastery.

FRANCE J-C. Rouan 1 (RC Narbonne); M. Pomathios 18 (US Bressane), J. Dauger (1) (A. Bayonne), M. Prat 6 (FC Lourdes) A. Porthault 5 (RCF); J. Carabignac 6 (SU Agen), G. Dufau 12 (RCF); A. Sanac 1 (US Perpignan), P. Labadie 5 (A. Bayonne), P. Bertrand 4 (US Bressane), P. Tignol 1 (S. Toulouse), L. Miàs 8 (SC Mazamet), *J. Prat 24 (FC Lourdes), J-R. Bourdeu 5 (FC Lourdes), R. Biénès 13 (US Cognac).

SCOTLAND   N.W. Cameron 2 (Glasgow U.); K.J. Dalgleish 3 (Cambridge U.), D.A. Sloan (7) (London Scottish), D.M. Scott (9) (Watsonians), D.M. Rose 5 (Jedforest); J.N.G. Davidson 5 (Edinburgh U.), *A.F. Dorward 5 (Gala); B.E. Thomson 1 (Oxford U.), J.H.F. King 1 (Selkirk), R.L. Wilson 5 (Gala), J.H. Henderson 1 (Oxford U.), J.J. Hegarty 2 (Hawick), A.R. Valentine 1 (RNAS Anthorn), K.H.D. McMillan 1 (Sale), D.C. Macdonald 1 (Edinburgh U.).

Referee O.B. Glasgow (Ireland)

WALES v ENGLAND   57/428

17 January 1953
Cardiff Arms Park
England 8 (1G, 1PG) Wales 3 (1PG)

Wales   PG: Davies.
England   T: Cannell. C: Hall. PG: Woodward.

Selectors could often be accused of making odd decisions. None perhaps was as eccentric as the omission of Cliff Morgan for this match, simply because they felt he would not be as effective without Rex Willis, who was unable to play because of injury. Instead they plumped for the Newport halves, the highly-talented Roy Burnett and Billy Williams. England won, and neither played again for Wales. Wales were criticized for the deafeat; but in fact this was a very good English side, which with few changes in personnel, went unbeaten for another six consecutive Championship matches.

WALES   T.J. Davies 1 (Swansea); K.J. Jones 25 (Newport), M.C. Thomas 14 (Newport), B.L. Williams 14 (Cardiff), G.M. Griffiths 1 (Cardiff); R. Burnett (1) (Newport), W.A. Williams (3) (Newport); J.D. Robins 9 (Bradford), G. Beckingham 1 (Cardiff), W.O.G. Williams 6 (Swansea), E.R. John 13 (Neath), J.R.G. Stephens 14 (Neath), S. Judd 1 (Cardiff), W.D. Johnson (1) (Swansea), *J.A. Gwilliam 17 (Gloucester).

ENGLAND   *N.M. Hall 11 (Richmond); J.E. Woodward 3 (Wasps), A.E. Agar 5 (Harlequins), L.B. Cannell 11 (St Mary's H.), R.C. Bazley 3 (Waterloo); M. Regan 1 (Liverpool), P.W. Sykes 5 (Wasps); W.A. Holmes 12 (Nuneaton), N.A. Labuschagne 1 (Harlequins), R.V. Stirling 9 (Leicester), S.J. Adkins 4 (Coventry), D.T. Wilkins 9 (US Portsmouth), D.F. White 11 (Northampton), A.O. Lewis 5 (Bath), J.M.K. Kendall-Carpenter 15 (Bath).

Referee Captain M.J. Dowling (Ireland)

IRELAND v FRANCE   24/429

24 January 1953
Ravenhill, Belfast
Ireland 16 (2G, 2T) France 3 (1DG)

Ireland   T: Lawler, McCarthy, Kyle, Mortell. C: Gregg (2).
France   DG: Carabignac.

This was Ireland's biggest score against France since they beat them 24-0 in 1913. The French reacted by ending the Championship careers of four of their team.

The Irish team, captained by Jackie Kyle, which defeated France 16-3 at Ravenhill, Belfast

IRELAND R.J. Gregg 1 (Queen's U. Belfast); M.F. Lane 15 (UC Cork), N.J. Henderson 12 (NIFC), K. Quinn 2 (Old Belvedere), M. Mortell 1 (Dolphin); *J.W. Kyle 25 (NIFC), J.A. O'Meara 9 (Dolphin); W.A. O'Neill 2 (UC Dublin), R. Roe 2 (Dublin U.), F.E. Anderson 1 (NIFC), J.R. Brady 3 (CIYMS), P.J. Lawler 6 (Clontarf), J.S. McCarthy 18 (Dolphin), W.E. Bell 1 (Belfast Collegians), J.R. Kavanagh 1 (UC Dublin).

FRANCE J-C. Rouan (2) (RC Narbonne); A. Porthault (6) (RCF), J. Mauran 3 (Castres Ol), M. Prat 7 (FC Lourdes), M. Pomathios 19 (US Bressane); J. Carabignac (6) (SU Agen), G. Dufau 13 (RCF); R. Biénès 14 (US Cognac), P. Labadie 6 (A. Bayonne) P. Bertrand 5 (US Bressane), L. Miâs 9 (SC Mazamet), A. Sanac 2 (US Perpignan), J-R. Bourdeu 6 (FC Lourdes), *J. Prat 25 (FC Lourdes), P. Tignol (2) (S. Toulouse).

Referee T.E. Priest (England)

SCOTLAND v WALES 57/430

7 February 1953
Murrayfield
Wales 12 (3T) Scotland 0

Wales T: Bleddyn Williams (2), Jones. PG: Davies.

After this match Scotland dropped all their backs. Only the half-backs were invited to play again. Bleddyn Williams, appointed captain of Wales, gilded the honour by scoring two tries. Cliff Morgan played his first game for Wales at scrum-half, having being moved there after Rex Willis had left the field because of injury. Coincidentally Morgan took over from Willis in similar circumstances when Wales played England on 16 January 1954.

SCOTLAND N.W. Cameron (3) (Glasgow U.); R. Gordon (6) (Edinburgh Wands), K.J. Dalgleish (4) (Cambridge U.), J.L. Allan (4) (Melrose), D.M. Rose (6) (Jedforest); J.N.G. Davidson 6 (Edinburgh U), *A.F. Dorward 6 (Gala); B.E. Thomson 2 (Oxford U.), J.H.F. King 2 (Selkirk), R.L. Wilson 6 (Gala), J.H. Henderson 2 (Oxford U.), J.J. Hegarty 3 (Hawick), A.R. Valentine 2 (RNAS Anthorn), K.H.D. McMillan 2 (Sale), D.C. Macdonald 2 (Edinburgh U.).

WALES T.J. Davies 2 (Swansea); K.J. Jones 26 (Newport), A.G. Thomas 5 (Cardiff), *B.L. Williams 15 (Cardiff), G.M. Griffiths 2 (Cardiff); C.I. Morgan 6 (Cardiff), W.R. Willis 11 (Cardiff); W.O.G. Williams 7 (Swansea), G. Beckingham 2 (Cardiff), C.C. Meredith 1 (Neath), E.R. John 14 (Neath), J.R.G. Stephens 15 (Neath), S. Judd 2 (Cardiff), R.C.C. Thomas 4 (Swansea), R.J. Robins 1 (Pontypridd).

Referee Dr P.F. Cooper (England)

IRELAND v ENGLAND 57/431

14 February 1953
Lansdowne Road, Dublin
Ireland 9 (1T, 2PG) England 9 (1T, 2PG)

Ireland T: Mortell. PG: Henderson (2).
England T: Evans. PG: Hall (2).

England had not won at Lansdowne Road since their record 36-14 triumph of 1938, but they did well to hold Ireland to the first drawn match between the sides in Dublin. It was the last Championship match for Mick Lane, one of a host of fast, opportunist wings Ireland habitually produced.

IRELAND R.J. Gregg 2 (Queen's U. Belfast); M.F. Lane (16) (UC Cork), N.J. Henderson 13 (NIFC), K. Quinn 3 (Old Belvedere), M. Mortell 2 (Bective Rangers); *J.W. Kyle 26 (NIFC), J.A. O'Meara 10 (UC Cork); W.A. O'Neill 3 (UC Dublin), R. Roe 3 (Dublin U.), F.E. Anderson 2 (Queen's U. Belfast), J.R. Brady 4 (CIYMS), T.E. Reid 1 (Garryowen), J.S. McCarthy 19 (Dolphin), W.E. Bell 2 (Belfast Collegians), J.R. Kavanagh 2 (UC Dublin).

ENGLAND *N.M. Hall 12 (Richmond); J.E. Woodward 4 (Wasps), A.E. Agar (6) (Harlequins), L.B. Cannell 12 (St Mary's H.), R.C. Bazley 4 (Waterloo); M. Regan 2 (Liverpool), P.W. Sykes 6 (Wasps); W.A. Holmes 13 (Nuneaton), E. Evans 9 (Sale), R.V. Stirling 10 (Leicester), D.T. Wilkins 10 (US Portsmouth), S.J. Adkins 5 (Coventry), D.F. White 12 (Northampton), A.O. Lewis 6 (Bath), J.M.K. Kendall-Carpenter 16 (Bath).

Referee A.W.C. Austin (Scotland)

ENGLAND v FRANCE   24/432

28 February 1953
Twickenham
England 11 (1G, 2T) France 0

England   T: Butterfield, Evans, Woodward. C: Hall.

Jeff Butterfield made a notable début by scoring one try and making another in England's most convincing victory over France at Twickenham since their win of 18-8 in 1928.

ENGLAND   *N.M. Hall 13 (Richmond); J.E. Woodward 5 (Wasps), J. Butterfield 1 (Northampton), L.B. Cannell 13 (St Mary's H.), R.C. Bazley 5 (Waterloo); M. Regan 3 (Liverpool), P.W. Sykes (7) (Wasps); W.A. Holmes 14 (Nuneaton), E. Evans 10 (Sale), R.V. Stirling 11 (Leicester), D.T. Wilkins 11 (US Portsmouth), S.J. Adkins 6 (Coventry), A.O. Lewis 7 (Bath), D.S. Wilson 1 (Harlequins), J.M.K. Kendall-Carpenter 17 (Bath).

FRANCE   G. Brun 10 (CS Vienne); J-R. Bourdeu (7) (FC Lourdes), M. Prat 8 (FC Lourdes), J. Mauran (4) (Castres Ol), L. Rogé 1 (AS Béziers); A. Haget 1 (PUC), G. Dufau 14 (RCF); P. Bertrand 6 (US Bourg), J. Arrieta 1 (S. Français), R. Carrère (1) (S. Mont-de-Marsan), R. Bréjassou 5 (S. Tarbes), B. Chevallier 5 (AS Montferrand), *J. Prat 26 (FC Lourdes), R. Biénès 15 (US Cognac), M. Celaya 1 (Biarritz Ol).

Referee V.J. Parfitt (Wales)

SCOTLAND v IRELAND   59/433

28 February 1953
Murrayfield
Ireland 26 (4G, 2T) Scotland 8 (1G, 1PG)

Scotland   T: Henderson. C: Ian Thomson. PG: Ian Thomson.
Ireland   T: McCarthy, Byrne (3), Mortell, Kavanagh. C: Gregg (4).

Sean Byrne became the first Irish player to score a hat-trick of tries since Eugene Davy, also against Scotland, in 1930. He helped Ireland register their biggest Championship score, their six tries were the most ever against Scotland, and it was their fourth successive win at Murrayfield, which equalled their best winning sequence there. Seven of the outclassed Scottish side did not play again in the Championship.

SCOTLAND   I.H.M. Thomson 6 (Heriot's FP); T.G. Weatherstone 2 (Stewart's FP), *A. Cameron 8 (Glasgow HSFP), D. Cameron 1 (Glasgow HSFP), D.W.C. Smith (8) (London Scottish); L. Bruce-Lockhart 4 (London Scottish), K.M. Spence (1) (London Scottish); B.E. Thomson (3) (Oxford U.), G.C. Hoyer-Miller (1) (Oxford U.), J.H. Wilson (1) (Watsonians), J.H. Henderson 3 (Oxford U.), J.J. Hegarty 4 (Hawick), A.R. Valentine (3) (RNAS Anthorn), K.H.D. McMillan 3 (Sale), E.H. Henriksen (1) (Royal HSFP).

IRELAND   R.J. Gregg 3 (Queen's U. Belfast); S.J. Byrne 1 (Lansdowne), N.J. Henderson 14 (Queen's U. Belfast), K. Quinn (4) (Old Belvedere), M. Mortell 3 (Bective Rangers); * J.W. Kyle 27 (NIFC), J.A. O'Meara 11 (UC Cork); F.E. Anderson 3 (Queen's U. Belfast), R. Roe 4 (Dublin U.), W.A. O'Neill 4 (UC Dublin), J.R. Brady 5 (CIYMS), T.E. Reid 2 (Garryowen), W.E. Bell 3 (Belfast Collegians), J.S. McCarthy 20 (Dolphin), J.R. Kavanagh 3 (UC Dublin).

Referee I. David (Wales)

WALES v IRELAND   55/434

14 March 1953
St Helen's, Swansea
Wales 5 (1G) Ireland 3 (1T)

Wales   T: Griffiths. C: Terry Davies.
Ireland   T: Pedlow.

Ireland, who had won only one game in Wales since 1932, matched the Welsh in terms of tries but were beaten by Terry Davies's conversion. Cecil Pedlow, making his début in the centre, had the distinction of scoring Ireland's try.

WALES   T.J. Davies 3 (Swansea); K.J. Jones 27 (Newport), A.G. Thomas 6 (Cardiff), *B.L. Williams 16 (Cardiff), G.M. Griffiths 3 (Cardiff); C.I. Morgan 7 (Cardiff), T. Lloyd 1 (Maesteg); J.D. Robins 10 (Bradford), D.M. Davies 13 (Somerset Police), W.O.G. Williams 8 (Swansea), E.R. John

15 (Neath), J.R.G. Stephens 16 (Neath), S. Judd 3 (Cardiff), R.C.C. Thomas 5 (Swansea), J.A. Gwilliam 18 (Gloucester).

IRELAND   R.J. Gregg 4 (Queen's U. Belfast); S.J. Byrne 2 (Lansdowne), N.J. Henderson 15 (NIFC), A.C. Pedlow 1 (Queen's U. Belfast), M. Mortell 4 (Bective Rangers); *J.W. Kyle 28 (NIFC), J.A. O'Meara 12 (UC Cork); W.A. O'Neill (5) (UC Dublin), R. Roe 5 (Dublin U.), F.E. Anderson 4 (Queen's U. Belfast), J.R. Brady 6 (CIYMS), T.E. Reid 3 (Garryowen), G.F. Reidy 1 (Dolphin), W.E. Bell 4 (Belfast Collegians), J.R. Kavanagh (4) (UC Dublin).

Referee Dr P.F. Cooper (England)

ENGLAND v SCOTLAND   56/435

21 March 1953
Twickenham
England 26 (4G, 2T) Scotland 8 (1G, 1T)

England T: Bazley (2), Adkins, Butterfield, Stirling, Woodward. C: Hall (4).
Scotland T: Henderson, Weatherstone. C: Thomson.

Stan Adkins, the Coventry lock-forward, celebrated his seventh and last appearance for England by scoring a try, the hundredth by England against Scotland in the Championship. More important, England's six tries were their best plunder against Scotland in any match, and Nim Hall's four conversions equalled the 1947 highest total. On only one other occasion, 1967, have the English scored more points against the Scots at Twickenham. All this meant that England had won the Championship for the first time since 1947. None of this was remembered, however, when selection was made the next season. As well as Adkins, four other players did not attain England status again, including that scourge of fly-halves, Don White.

ENGLAND   *N.M. Hall 14 (Richmond); J.E. Woodward 6 (Wasps), J. Butterfield 2 (Northampton), W.P.C. Davies 1 (Harlequins), R.C. Bazley 6 (Waterloo); M. Regan 4 (Liverpool), D.W. Shuttleworth (2) (Headingley); R.V. Stirling 12 (Leicester), E. Evans 11 (Sale), W.A. Holmes (15) (Nuneaton), D.T. Wilkins (12) (US

Portsmouth), S.J. Adkins (7) (Coventry), A.O. Lewis 8 (Bath), D.F. White (13) (Northampton), J.M.K. Kendall-Carpenter 18 (Bath).

SCOTLAND   I.H.M. Thomson (7) (Heriot's FP); T.G. Weatherstone 3 (Stewart's FP), *A. Cameron 9 (Glasgow HSFP), D. Cameron 2 (Glasgow HSFP), J.S. Swan 1 (St Andrew's U.); L. Bruce-Lockhart (5) (London Scottish), A.F. Dorward 7 (Gala); J.C. Dawson (18) (Glasgow Acads), J.H.F. King 3 (Selkirk), R.L. Wilson (7) (Gala), J.H. Henderson 4 (Oxford U.), J.J. Hegarty 5 (Hawick), W. Kerr (1) (London Scottish), K.H.D. McMillan (4) (Sale), W.L.K. Cowie (1) (Edinburgh Wands).

Referee Captain M.J. Dowling (Ireland)

FRANCE v WALES   24/436

28 March 1953
Stade Colombes, Paris
Wales 6 (2T) France 3 (1PG)

Wales T: Griffiths (2).
France PG: Bertrand.

After successive defeats in France, Wales returned to winning form against a French side with talent but few productive attacking ideas. It proved an uncomfortable début for Michel Vannier at full-back as he tried to cover the gaps left by a loose defence.

FRANCE   M. Vannier 1 (RCF); M. Pomathios 20 (US Bressane), J. Galy (1) (US Perpignan), G. Brun (11) (CS Vienne), L. Rogé 2 (AS Béziers); L. Bidart (1) (S. La Rochelle), G. Dufau 15 (RCF); P. Bertrand (7) (US Bourg), J. Arrieta (2) (S. Français), R. Bréjassou 6 (S. Tarbes), L. Miàs 10 (SC Mazamet), B. Chevallier 6 (AS Montferrand), *J. Prat 27 (FC Lourdes), M. Celaya 2 (Biarritz Ol), H. Domec 1 (FC Lourdes).

WALES   T.J. Davies 4 (Swansea); K.J. Jones 28 (Newport), A.G. Thomas 7 (Cardiff), *B.L. Williams 17 (Cardiff), G.M. Griffiths 4 (Cardiff); C.I. Morgan 8 (Cardiff), T. Lloyd (2) (Maesteg); W.O.G. Williams 9 (Swansea), D.M. Davies 14 (Somerset Police), J.D. Robins (11) (Bradford), E.R. John 16 (Neath), J.R.G. Stephens 17 (Neath), S. Judd 4 (Cardiff), R.C.C. Thomas 6 (Swansea), J.A. Gwilliam 19 (Gloucester).

Referee O.B. Glasgow (Ireland)

1954

MURRAYFIELD France beat Scotland 3-0 · TWICKENHAM England beat Wales 9-6
PARIS France beat Ireland 8-0 · TWICKENHAM England beat Ireland 14-3
BELFAST Ireland beat Scotland 6-0 · DUBLIN Wales beat Ireland 12-9
MURRAYFIELD England beat Scotland 13-3 · CARDIFF Wales beat France 19-13
PARIS France beat England 11-3 · SWANSEA Wales beat Scotland 15-3

CHAMPIONSHIP TABLE
Wales – Championship, England, Triple Crown

								Tries	
Pos Country	P	W	D	L	F	A	Pts	F	A
1 Wales (2)	4	3	0	1	52	34	6	7	7
2 England (1)	4	3	0	1	39	23	6	10	4
3 France (4)	4	3	0	1	35	22	6	7	3
4 Ireland (3)	4	1	0	3	18	34	2	3	5
5 Scotland (5)	4	0	0	4	6	37	0	2	10

The Championship was only half complete when it became obvious that it would be a three horse-race between England, France and Wales, with England favourites because they had beaten Wales in their opening match. France had won both their opening matches, so the crunch came when they met Wales in Cardiff. By this time England had already beaten Scotland to win the Triple Crown but when Wales accounted for France, the issue once more became wide open.

The Day of Judgement was on 10 April when all three contenders were in action. England allowed their Grand Slam opportunity to pass away by losing in Paris which meant that Wales had only to beat Scotland at Swansea to nip past both to take the title. The Welsh achieved their objective by a wide margin which was hardly surprising against such a dispirited Scottish team. Thus Scotland lost all four matches for a third season in a row, a fate which had befallen no other country. To add to the misery north of the border, the Scots totalled only six points, their worst return since they scraped three points from three matches in 1900.

SCOTLAND v FRANCE 24/437

9 January 1954
Murrayfield
France 3 (1T) Scotland 0

France T: Bréjassou.

Hugh McLeod was one of six new caps in a Scotland side that failed to score against France at home for the first time since 1921. T.P.L. McGlashan returned to the side after a seven-year absence. Michel Pomathios, who had been a regular member of the French team since 1948, made his twenty-first and final appearance.

SCOTLAND J.C. Marshall 1 (London Scottish); J.S. Swan 2 (London Scottish), A.D. Cameron 2 (Hillhead HSFP), D. Cameron 3 (Glasgow HSFP), T.G. Weatherstone 4 (Stewart's FP); *J.N.G. Davidson (7) (Edinburgh U.), A.K. Fulton (2) (Dollar Academy); T.P.L. McGlashan 4 (Royal HSFP), R.K.G. MacEwan 1 (Cambridge U.), H.F. McLeod 1 (Hawick), E.A.J. Fergusson 1 (Oxford U.), E.J.S. Michie 1 (Aberdeen U.), A. Robson 1 (Hawick), J.H. Henderson 5 (Richmond), P.W. Kininmonth 16 (Richmond).

FRANCE M. Vannier 2 (RCF); L. Rogé 3 (AS Béziers), R. Martine 3 (FC Lourdes), J. Bouquet 1 (CS Bourg), M. Pomathios (21) (US Bressane); A. Labazuy 2 (FC Lourdes), G. Dufau 16 (RCF); R. Biénès 16 (US Cognac), P. Labadie 7 (A. Bayonne), R. Bréjassou 7 (S. Tarbes), B. Chevallier 7 (AS Montferrand), L. Miàs 11 (SC Mazamet), H. Domec 2 (FC Lourdes), *J. Prat 28 (FC Lourdes), R. Baulon 1 (CS Vienne).

Referee I. David (Wales)

ENGLAND v WALES 58/438

16 January 1954
Twickenham
England 9 (3T) Wales 6 (1T, 1PG)

England   T: Woodward (2), Winn.
Wales   T: Rowlands. PG: Rowlands.

The first all-ticket international to be staged at Twickenham was won by England with a last-minute try by Chris Winn; England's previous home win over Wales had been in 1939. Wales were hit by several injuries on this occasion with Billy Williams, Rex Willis and Gerwyn Williams all needing treatment. Some critics considered Wales unlucky to lose; but England deserved great credit for a sustained performance.

ENGLAND   I. King 1 (Harrogate); J.E. Woodward 7 (Wasps), J.P. Quinn 1 (New Brighton), J. Butterfield 3 (Northampton), C.E. Winn 5 (Rosslyn Park); M. Regan 5 (Liverpool), G. Rimmer 8 (Waterloo); *R.V. Stirling 13 (Wasps), E. Evans 12 (Sale), D.L. Sanders 1 (Harlequins), P.D. Young 1 (Dublin Wands), P.G. Yarranton 1 (Wasps), D.S. Wilson 2 (Metropolitan Police), R. Higgins 1 (Liverpool), J.M.K. Kendall-Carpenter 19 (Bath).

WALES   G. Williams (11) (London Welsh); K.J. Jones 29 (Newport), A.G. Thomas 8 (Cardiff), G. John 1 (St Luke's College), G. Rowlands 1 (Cardiff); C.I. Morgan 9 (Cardiff), W.R. Willis 12 (Cardiff); W.O.G. Williams 10 (Swansea), D.M. Davies (15) (Somerset Police), C.C. Meredith 2 (Neath), E.R. John (17) (Neath), J.A. Gwilliam (20) (Gloucester), S. Judd 5 (Cardiff), R.C.C. Thomas 7 (Swansea), *J.R.G. Stephens 18 (Neath).

Referee Captain M.J. Dowling (Ireland)

FRANCE v IRELAND 25/439

23 January 1954
Stade Colombes, Paris
France 8 (1G, 1T) Ireland 0

France   T: Maurice Prat (2). C: Jean Prat.

Ireland had lost on only three occasions in twelve previous visits to France but this defeat was to prove the turning-point. France went on to beat Ireland in 14 out of the next 15 matches on French soil, which included a run of nine consecutive victories until 1972 when Ireland achieved their one success, by 14-9.

FRANCE   M. Vannier 3 (RCF); F. Cazenave 3 (S. Mont-de-Marsan), R. Martine 4 (FC Lourdes), M. Prat 9 (FC Lourdes), A. Boniface 1 (S. Mont-de-Marsan); A. Haget 2 (PUC), G. Dufau 17 (RCF); R. Biénès 17 (US Cognac), P. Labadie 8 (A. Bayonne), R. Bréjassou 8 (S. Tarbes), L. Miâs 12 (SC Mazamet), B. Chevallier 8 (AS Montferrand), H. Domec 3 (FC Lourdes), *J. Prat 29 (FC Lourdes), M. Celaya 3 (Biarritz Ol).

IRELAND   R.J. Gregg 5 (Queen's U. Belfast); M. Mortell 5 (Dolphin), N.J. Henderson 16 (NIFC), A.C. Pedlow 2 (Queen's U. Belfast), J.T. Gaston 1 (Dublin U.); J.W. Kyle 29 (NIFC), J.A. O'Meara 13 (Dolphin); F.E. Anderson 5 (Queen's U. Belfast), R. Roe 6 (Lansdowne), J.H. Smith 9 (London Irish), R.H. Thompson 2 (Instonians), J.E. Nelson (15) (Malone), G.F. Reidy 2 (Lansdowne), *J.S. McCarthy 21 (Dolphin), T.E. Reid 4 (Garryowen).

Referee A.I. Dickie (Scotland)

ENGLAND v IRELAND 58/440

13 February 1954
Twickenham
England 14 (1G, 2T, 1PG) Ireland 3 (1PG)

England   T: Butterfield, Regan, Wilson. C: King. PG: King.
Ireland   PG: Murphy-O'Connor.

England scored a third successive win over Ireland at Twickenham and their try return was their best against the Irish since they scored five in 1933. In contrast Ireland found scoring at Twickenham difficult: Murphy-O'Connor's penalty goal was in fact their only score in five visits between 1950–58.

ENGLAND   I. King (2) (Harrogate); J.E. Woodward 8 (Wasps), J. Butterfield 4 (Northampton), J.P. Quinn 2 (New Brighton), W.P.C. Davies 2 (Harlequins); M. Regan 6 (Liverpool), G. Rimmer

9 (Waterloo); *R.V. Stirling 14 (Wasps), E. Evans 13 (Sale), D.L. Sanders 2 (Harlequins), P.D. Young 2 (Dublin Wands), P.G. Yarranton 2 (Wasps), D.S. Wilson 3 (Metropolitan Police), R. Higgins 2 (Liverpool), J.M.K. Kendall-Carpenter 20 (Bath).

IRELAND   R.J. Gregg 6 (Queen's U. Belfast); M. Mortell 6 (Bective Rangers), N.J. Henderson 17 (NIFC), A.C. Pedlow 3 (Queen's U. Belfast), J.T. Gaston 2 (Dublin U.); W.J. Hewitt 1 (Instonians), J.A. O'Meara 14 (Dolphin); F.E. Anderson 6 (Queen's U. Belfast), R. Roe 7 (Lansdowne), B.G.M. Wood 1 (Garryowen), R.H. Thompson 3 (Instonians), P.J. Lawler 7 (Clontarf), G.F. Reidy 3 (Lansdowne), *J.S. McCarthy 22 (Dolphin), J. Murphy-O'Connor (1) (Bective Rangers).

Referee A.I. Dickie (Scotland)

IRELAND v SCOTLAND   60/441

27 February 1954
Ravenhill, Belfast
Ireland 6 (2T) Scotland 0

Ireland   T: Mortell (2).

This was Ireland's ninth win in a row over Scotland, which was also their best winning sequence against any opposition. One of the two Irish tries was remarkable in that it began speculatively on their own line with a pass by Kavanagh to the fleet-footed and unmarked Gaston. The wing ran clear, kicked on when challenged well inside the Scottish half and the try was completed when Godfrey scooped up the ball for Henderson to put Mortell over for a sensational score.

IRELAND   R.J. Gregg (7) (Queen's U. Belfast); M. Mortell 7 (Bective Rangers), N.J. Henderson 18 (NIFC), R.P. Godfrey 1 (UC Dublin), J.T. Gaston 3 (Dublin U.); S. Kelly 1 (Lansdowne), J.A. O'Meara 15 (Dolphin); F.E. Anderson 7 (Queen's U. Belfast), R. Roe 8 (Lansdowne), B.G.M. Wood 2 (Garryowen), R.H. Thompson 4 (Instonians), P.J. Lawler 8 (Clontarf), G.F. Reidy 4 (Lansdowne), *J.S. McCarthy 23 (Dolphin), J.R. Kavanagh 5 (Wanderers).

SCOTLAND   J.C. Marshall 2 (London Scottish); J.S. Swan 3 (London Scottish), M.K. Elgie 1 (London Scottish), D. Cameron 4 (Glasgow HSFP), T.G. Weatherstone 5 (Stewart's FP); G.T. Ross 1 (Watsonians), L.P. MacLachlan 1 (London Scottish); T.P.L. McGlashan 5 (Royal HSFP), R.K.G. MacEwan 2 (Cambridge U.), H.F. McLeod 2 (Hawick), E.A.J. Fergusson 2 (Oxford U.), E.J.S. Michie 2 (Aberdeen U.), *W.I.D. Elliot 24 (Edinburgh Acads), J.H. Henderson 6 (Richmond), P.W. Kininmonth 17 (Richmond).

Referee V.J. Parfitt (Wales)

IRELAND v WALES   56/442

13 March 1954
Lansdowne Road, Dublin
Wales 12 (1DG, 3PG) Ireland 9 (1T, 2PG)

Ireland   T: Gaston. PG: Henderson, Kelly.
Wales   DG: Denzil Thomas. PG: Evans (3).

Harry McCracken, the NIFC scrum-half, won his only cap for Ireland due to the most unusual circumstances; he came into the side because first choice John O'Meara had withdrawn after ricking a back muscle in bed in the team hotel on the morning of the match. Two other newcomers won the match: Viv Evans, with three penalty goals, and Denzil Thomas, with a last-minute dropped goal. Thomas never played again for Wales.

IRELAND   P.J. Berkery 1 (Lansdowne); M. Mortell (8) (Bective Rangers), N.J. Henderson 19 (NIFC), R.P. Godfrey (2) (UC Dublin), J.T. Gaston 4 (Dublin U.); S. Kelly 2 (Lansdowne), H. McCracken (1) (NIFC); J.H. Smith (10) (London Irish), R. Roe 9 (Lansdowne), F.E. Anderson 8 (Queen's U. Belfast), J.R. Brady 7 (CIYMS), R.H. Thompson 5 (Instonians), G.F. Reidy (5) (Lansdowne), *J.S. McCarthy 24 (Dolphin), J.R. Kavanagh 6 (Wanderers).

WALES   V. Evans 1 (Neath); K.J. Jones 30 (Newport), D. Thomas (1) (Llanelli), A.G. Thomas 9 (Cardiff), G.M. Griffiths 5 (Cardiff); C.I. Morgan 10 (Cardiff), W.R. Willis 13 (Cardiff); W.O.G. Williams 11 (Swansea), B.V. Meredith 1 (Newport), C.C. Meredith 3 (Neath), *J.R.G. Stephens 19 (Neath), R.H. Williams 1 (Llanelli), R.C.C. Thomas 8 (Swansea), B. Sparks 1 (Neath), L.H. Jenkins 1 (Newport).

Referee A.W.C. Austin (Scotland)

Jean Prat's 1958 French XV which defeated Ireland 8-0 at Stade Colombes to start a sequence of 14 victories in 15 matches against the Irish in France

SCOTLAND v ENGLAND   57/443

20 March 1954
Murrayfield
England 13 (2G, 1T) Scotland 3 (1T)

Scotland   T: Elgie.
England   T: Wilson (2), Young. C: Gibbs (2).

England's three tries meant that they had totalled nine in their last three visits to Murrayfield, which was as much a measure of the desperate state of Scottish rugby as English flair. Victory meant a Triple Crown for England, while all the luckless Scots had to look forward to was a visit to Swansea where they were to play their postponed match against Wales in April.

SCOTLAND   J.C. Marshall 3 (London Scottish); J.S. Swan 4 (London Scottish), M.K. Elgie 2 (London Scottish), D. Cameron (5) (Glasgow HSFP), T.G. Weatherstone 6 (Stewart's FP); G.T. Ross 2 (Watsonians), L.P. MacLachlan 2 (Oxford U.); T.P.L. McGlashan 6 (Royal HSFP), J.H.F. King (4) (Selkirk), H.F. McLeod 3 (Hawick), E.A.J. Fergusson 3 (Oxford U.), E.J.S. Michie 3 (Aberdeen U.), *W.I.D. Elliot 25 (Edinburgh Acads), J.H. Henderson 7 (Richmond), P.W. Kininmonth 18 (Richmond).

ENGLAND   N. Gibbs 1 (Harlequins); J.E. Woodward 9 (Wasps), J. Butterfield 5 (Northampton), J.P. Quinn 3 (New Brighton), C.E. Winn 6 (Rosslyn Park); M. Regan 7 (Liverpool), G. Rimmer (10) (Waterloo); *R.V. Stirling 15

(Wasps), E.F. Robinson 1 (Coventry), D.L. Sanders 3 (Harlequins), P.D. Young 3 (Dublin Wands), J.F. Bance (1) (Bedford), D.S. Wilson 4 (Metropolitan Police), R. Higgins 3 (Liverpool), V.H. Leadbetter 1 (Edinburgh Wands).

Referee O.B. Glasgow (Ireland)

WALES v FRANCE   25/444

27 March 1954
Cardiff Arms Park
Wales 19 (2G, 3PG) France 13 (2G, 1PG)

Wales   T: Griffiths, Billy Williams. C: Evans (2). PG: Evans (3).
France   T: Martine, Baulon. C: Jean Prat (2). PG: Jean Prat.

Viv Evans, the Neath full-back, played only three Championship matches for Wales but scored 25 points, 13 of them in this match. Another Welsh player who had something to celebrate was Gareth Griffiths – his try was the fiftieth Wales had scored against France in Wales.

WALES   V. Evans 2 (Neath); K.J. Jones 31 (Newport), A.G. Thomas 10 (Cardiff), G.M. Griffiths 6 (Cardiff), G. Rowlands 2 (Cardiff); G. John (2) (St Luke's College), *W.R. Willis 14 (Cardiff);

W.O.G. Williams 12 (Swansea), B.V. Meredith 2 (Newport), C.C. Meredith 4 (Neath), R.J. Robins 2 (Pontypridd), R.H. Williams 2 (Llanelli), L. Davies 1 (Llanelli), R.C.C. Thomas 9 (Swansea), S. Judd 6 (Cardiff).

FRANCE   H. Claverie (1) (FC Lourdes); A. Boniface 2 (S. Mont-de-Marsan), M. Prat 10 (FC Lourdes), R. Martine 5 (FC Lourdes), F. Cazenave 4 (S. Mont-de-Marsan); A. Labazuy 3 (FC Lourdes), G. Dufau 18 (RCF); A. Domenech 1 (RC Vichy), P. Labadie 9 (A. Bayonne), R. Biénès 18 (US Cognac), L. Miâs 13 (SC Mazamet), B. Chevallier 9 (AS Montferrand), *J. Prat 30 (FC Lourdes), H. Domec 4 (FC Lourdes), R. Baulon 2 (CS Vienne).

Referee A.I. Dickie (Scotland)

FRANCE v ENGLAND   25/445

10 April 1954
Stade Colombes, Paris
France 11 (1G, 1T, 1DG) England 3 (1T)

France   T: Boniface, Maurice Prat. C: Jean Prat. DG: Jean Prat.
England   T: Wilson.

France won a third Championship victory in a season for a first time but had to be content with third place behind Wales and England, both of whom aggregated more points. England, bidding for a Grand Slam, failed to exert their expected forward superiority with the odd sequel that seven players of a Triple Crown winning side never again played in the Championship. Two of those dropped were considered by some to be among England's best forwards of the post-war period, Bob Stirling and John Kendall-Carpenter.

FRANCE   P. Albaladejo 1 (US Dax); A. Boniface 3 (S. Mont-de-Marsan), R. Martine 6 (FC Lourdes), M. Prat 11 (FC Lourdes), F. Cazenave (5) (S. Mont-de-Marsan); A. Haget 3 (PUC), G. Dufau 19 (RCF); R. Biénès 19 (US Cognac), P. Labadie 10 (A. Bayonne), A. Domenech 2 (RC Vichy), A. Sanac 3 (US Perpignan), M. Celaya 4 (Biarritz Ol), *J. Prat 31 (FC Lourdes), H. Domec 5 (FC Lourdes), R. Baulon 3 (CS Vienne).

ENGLAND N. Gibbs (2) (Harlequins); J.E. Woodward 10 (Wasps), J. Butterfield 6 (North-

ampton), J.P. Quinn (4) (New Brighton), C.E. Winn (7) (Rosslyn Park); M. Regan 8 (Liverpool), J.E. Williams 1 (Old Millhillians); *R.V. Stirling (16) (Leicester), E. Evans 14 (Sale), D.L. Sanders 4 (Harlequins), P.D. Young 4 (Dublin Wands), V.H. Leadbetter (2) (Edinburgh Wands), D.S. Wilson 5 (Metropolitan Police), A.O. Lewis (9) (Bath), J.M.K. Kendall-Carpenter (21) (Bath).

Referee I. David (Wales)

WALES v SCOTLAND   58/446

10 April 1954
St Helen's, Swansea
Wales 15 (4T, 1PG) Scotland 3 (1T)

Wales   T: Rhys Williams, Meredith, Ray Williams, Morgan. PG: Evans.
Scotland   T: Henderson.

The last international to be played at St Helen's, Swansea, had been postponed from 30 January because of frost. Ken Jones was honoured with the Wales captaincy for the only time, to mark his equalling of Dicky Owen's 35-cap record in all matches. It was also the last appearance for two of Scotland's longest serving forwards, Doug Elliot and Peter Kininmonth, who had earned 45 caps between them.

WALES   V. Evans (3) (Neath); *K.J. Jones 32 (Newport), G.M. Griffiths 7 (Cardiff), B.L. Williams 18 (Cardiff), R. Williams 1 (Llanelli); C.I. Morgan 11 (Cardiff), W.R. Willis 15 (Cardiff); W.O.G. Williams 13 (Swansea), B.V. Meredith 3 (Newport), C.C. Meredith 5 (Neath), R.J. Robins 3 (Pontypridd), R.H. Williams 3 (Llanelli), L. Davies 2 (Llanelli), R.C.C. Thomas 10 (Swansea), S. Judd 7 (Cardiff).

SCOTLAND   J.C. Marshall (4) (London Scottish); J.S. Swan 5 (London Scottish), M.K. Elgie 3 (London Scottish), A.D. Cameron (3) (Hillhead HSFP), T.G. Weatherstone 7 (Stewart's FP); G.T. Ross (3) (Watsonians), L.P. MacLachan (3) (Oxford U.); T.P.L. McGlashan (7) (Royal HSFP), R.K.G. MacEwan 3 (Cambridge U.), H.F. McLeod 4 (Hawick), E.A.J. Fergusson (4) (Oxford U.), J.W.Y. Kemp 1 (Glasgow HSFP), *W.I.D. Elliot (26) (Edinburgh Acads), J.H. Henderson (8) (Richmond), P.W. Kininmonth (19) (Richmond).

Referee Dr P.F. Cooper (England)

1955

PARIS France beat Scotland 15-0 · DUBLIN France beat Ireland 5-3
CARDIFF Wales beat England 3-0 · MURRAYFIELD Scotland beat Wales 14-8
DUBLIN Ireland drew England 6-6 · TWICKENHAM France beat England 16-9
MURRAYFIELD Scotland beat Ireland 12-3 · CARDIFF Wales beat Ireland 21-3
TWICKENHAM England beat Scotland 9-6 · PARIS Wales beat France 16-11

CHAMPIONSHIP TABLE
Wales – Championship

| | | | | | | | | | Tries | |
Pos	Country	P	W	D	L	F	A	Pts	F	A
1	Wales (1)	4	3	0	1	48	28	6	8	3
2	France (3)	4	3	0	1	47	28	6	8	3
3	Scotland (5)	4	2	0	2	32	35	4	4	8
4	England (2)	4	1	1	2	24	31	3	5	4
5	Ireland (4)	4	0	1	3	15	44	1	1	8

The 1955 season was notable for the departure from the international scene of many of the Championship's best-known players, some approaching veteran status but others victims of selectorial inconsistency. Wales lost the services of Bleddyn Williams, Rex Willis and Alun Thomas while on their way to winning the Championship for the second successive year while France, narrowly outpointed into second place, bade farewell to Jean Prat, arguably one of their greatest forwards of all time. There was no further use in Ireland for that tearaway flanker, Jim McCarthy, in a season in which the Irish tried all sorts of combinations from 25 players – and finished without one victory and the Wooden Spoon. Scotland, too, made many changes and experimented with 23 players in an effort to end their miserable run of failures, which had extended to 15 matches after they lost to France. They made six changes for the next match and, incredibly, became the only side to beat Wales in the season. At last, the Scots avoided the Wooden Spoon. England employed 21 players in all and of these 14 were discarded before the season was out, including Nim Hall, slower certainly, but still one of the game's craftsmen. England tried two replacements for Hall, both became one-cap wonders.

The Championship was the proving ground, of course, for selection for the British Isles forthcoming tour of South Africa and it is intriguing that of the 30 selected, 7 never played for their countries again in the Championship. Wales and Scotland provided the bulk of the tourists' forwards and England supplied the majority of the backs, plus three of the half-backs. Players of the ilk of Jackie Kyle, Noel Henderson, John O'Meara, Jim McCarthy, Ronnie Kavanagh (all Ireland), Ken Jones, Bleddyn Williams, Gordon Wells, Rex Willis (Wales), Alan Dorward (Scotland), Nim Hall, Ted Woodward, George Hastings and Phil Taylor (England) were ignored. The British drew the series 2-2, playing brilliant rugby at times, and understandably the selectors were applauded in their choices.

FRANCE v SCOTLAND 25/447

8 January 1955
Stade Colombes, Paris
France 15 (4T, 1PG) Scotland 0

France T: Boniface, Jean Prat, Domenech, Dufau. PG: Vannier.

After 14 successive Championship defeats, Scotland attempted to change their fortunes by playing a reconstructed side in this, their first match of the 1955 campaign. Only five players had survived from the side beaten by Wales at the end of the previous season, and there were five new caps. Lack of teamwork was soon cruelly exposed by the French, who cruised to a fifth successive victory over the Scots. It also proved to be France's biggest winning margin over them until 1977 when they won 23-3.

FRANCE   M. Vannier 4 (RCF); J. Lepatey 1 (SC Mazamet), L. Rogé 4 (AS Béziers), M. Prat 12 (FC Lourdes), A. Boniface 4 (S. Mont-de-Marsan); R. Martine 7 (FC Lourdes), G. Dufau 20 (RCF); A. Domenech 3 (RC Vichy), P. Labadie 11 (A. Bayonne), R. Bréjassou 9 (S. Tarbes), B. Chevallier 10 (AS Montferrand), J. Barthe 1 (FC Lourdes), *J. Prat 32 (FC Lourdes), H. Domec 6 (FC Lourdes), M. Celaya 5 (Biarritz Ol).

SCOTLAND   A. Cameron 10 (Glasgow HSFP); J.S. Swan 6 (London Scottish), M.K. Elgie 4 (London Scottish), M.L. Grant 1 (Harlequins), T.G. Weatherstone 8 (Stewart's FP); J.T. Docherty 1 (Glasgow HSFP), A.F. Dorward 8 (Gala); H.F. McLeod 5 (Hawick), W.K.L. Relph 1 (Stewart's FP), I.R. Hastie 1 (Kelso), J.J. Hegarty (6) (Hawick), J.W.Y. Kemp 2 (Glasgow HSFP), H. Duffy (1) (Jedforest), A. Robson 2 (Hawick), *J.T. Greenwood 2 (Dunfermline).

Referee H.B. Elliot (England)

IRELAND v FRANCE   26/448

22 January 1955
Lansdowne Road, Dublin
France 5 (1G) Ireland 3 (1PG)

Ireland   PG: Henderson.
France   T: Domenech. C: Vannier.

This was France's fourth victory in their last six visits to Ireland, and was a disheartening start for the reconstructed Irish side. One of their five newcomers was Tony O'Reilly, just 18 and fresh out of school. O'Reilly was undoubtedly one of the personalities of Irish rugby and was ultimately regarded as one their finest backs – he played with dash and power at centre and wing. O'Reilly was a major try scorer for the British Isles on tour, but strangely rarely produced great try-scoring feats in the Championship in a 27-match career which spanned 15 years. Nor did he play in an Irish side which won the Championship. His career seemed effectively finished when he was dropped in 1963, but he made a much-publicized one-match return to

international rugby, against England, in 1970. As an after-dinner speaker and raconteur, O'Reilly was without equal and if all the stories attributed to him were truly of his authorship, he would have left Aesop, the brothers Grimm and Confucius trailing.

IRELAND   W.R. Tector 1 (Wanderers); S.J.Byrne (3) (Lansdowne), N.J. Henderson 20 (NIFC), A.J.F. O'Reilly 1 (Old Belvedere), A.C. Pedlow 4 (Queen's U. Belfast); J.W. Kyle 30 (NIFC), J.A. O'Meara 16 (Dolphin); F.E. Anderson 9 (NIFC), R. Roe 10 (Lansdowne), P.J. O'Donoghue 1 (Bective Rangers), R.H. Thompson 6 (Instonians), W.J. O'Connell (1) (Lansdowne), M.J. Cunningham 1 (UC Cork), *J.S. McCarthy 25 (Dolphin), J.R. Kavanagh 7 (UC Dublin).

FRANCE   M. Vannier 5 (RCF); J. Lepatey 2 (SC Mazamet), L. Rogé 5 (AS Béziers), M. Prat 13 (FC Lourdes), A. Boniface 5 (S. Mont-de-Marsan); R. Martine 8 (FC Lourdes), G. Dufau 21 (RCF); A. Domenech 4 (RC Vichy), P. Labadie 12 (A. Bayonne), R. Bréjassou 10 (S. Tarbes), M. Celaya 6 (Biarritz Ol), B. Chevallier 11 (AS Montferrand), H. Domec 7 (FC Lourdes), *J. Prat 33 (FC Lourdes), R. Baulon 4 (CS Vienne).

Referee I. David (Wales)

WALES v ENGLAND   59/449

22 January 1955
Cardiff Arms Park
Wales 3 (1PG) England 0

Wales   PG: Edwards.

Ken Jones became Wales's most capped player on his thirty-sixth (thirty-third Championship) appearance, Bleddyn Williams played his nineteenth and final Championship match, and late replacement Arthur Edwards, who had come in for Garfield Owen who had been injured at match practice, won the match with a penalty goal on his Championship début. The match had been postponed a week because of heavy snow.

WALES   A.B. Edwards 1 (London Welsh); K.J. Jones 33 (Newport), G.T. Wells 1 (Cardiff), *B.L. Williams (19) (Cardiff), T.J. Brewer 2 (London Welsh); C.I. Morgan 12 (Bective Rangers), W.R.

Willis 16 (Cardiff); W.O.G. Williams 14 (Swansea), B.V. Meredith 4 (Newport), C.C. Meredith 6 (Neath), J.R.G. Stephens 20 (Neath), R.J. Robins 4 (Pontypridd), B. Sparks 2 (Neath), N.G. Davies (1) (London Welsh), S. Judd 8 (Cardiff).

ENGLAND *N.M. Hall 15 (Richmond); J.E. Woodward 11 (Wasps), J. Butterfield 7 (Northampton), W.P.C. Davies 3 (Harlequins), R.C. Bazley 7 (Waterloo); D.G.S. Baker 1 (OMT), J.E. Williams 2 (Old Millhillians); G.W.D. Hastings 1 (Gloucester), N.A. Labuschagne 2 (Guy's H.), D. St G. Hazell 1 (Leicester), P.D. Young 5 (Dublin Wanderers), J.H. Hancock 1 (Newport), P.H. Ryan 1 (Richmond), R. Higgins 4 (Liverpool), P.J. Taylor 1 (Northampton).

Referee O.B. Glasgow (Ireland)

SCOTLAND v WALES   59/450

5 February 1955
Murrayfield
Scotland 14 (1G, 1T, 1DG, 1PG) Wales 8 (1G, 1T)

Scotland   T: Smith, Nichol. C: Elgie. DG: Docherty. PG: Elgie.
Wales   T: Brewer (2). C: Stephens.

Scotland ended their dismal run of 15 consecutive Championship defeats over 4 seasons. One of their tries was scored by Arthur Smith, who was making the first of a record 30 Championship appearances on the wing for Scotland. The Welsh team included five players who had played against Scotland in their previous Championship win in 1951 – Ken Jones, Cliff Morgan, Rex Willis, Billy Williams and Rhys Stephens – when the Scots won 19-0. Trevor Brewer, scorer of both Welsh tries, did not play in the Championship again.

SCOTLAND *A. Cameron 11 (Glasgow HSFP); A.R. Smith 1 (Cambridge U.), M.K. Elgie 5 (London Scottish), R.G. Charters 1 (Hawick), J.S. Swan 7 (London Scottish); J.T. Docherty 2 (Glasgow HSFP), J.A. Nichol 1 (Royal HSFP), H.F. McLeod 6 (Hawick), W.K.L. Relph 2 (Stewart's FP), T. Elliot 1 (Gala), E.J.S. Michie 4 (Aberdeen U.), J.W.Y. Kemp 3 (Glasgow HSFP), W.S. Glen (1) (Edinburgh Wands), A. Robson 3 (Hawick), J.T. Greenwood 3 (Dunfermline).

WALES   A.B. Edwards (2) (London Welsh); K.J.

Jones 34 (Newport), G.T. Wells 2 (Cardiff), A.G. Thomas 11 (Llanelli), T.J. Brewer (3) (London Welsh); C.I. Morgan 13 (Bective Rangers), *W.R. Willis 17 (Cardiff); W.O.G. Williams 15 (Swansea), B.V. Meredith 5 (Newport), C.C. Meredith 7 (Neath), R.J. Robins 5 (Pontypridd), R.H. Williams 4 (Llanelli), S. Judd (9) (Cardiff), R.C.C. Thomas 11 (Swansea), J.R.G. Stephens 21 (Neath).

Referee Captain M.J. Dowling (Ireland)

IRELAND v ENGLAND   59/451

12 February 1955
Lansdowne Road, Dublin
Ireland 6 (1T, 1PG) England 6 (2T)

Ireland   T: O'Reilly. PG: Henderson.
England   T: Butterfield, Hastings.

England scored two tries in the first nine minutes and seemed assured of their first win on Irish soil since 1938, until a late penalty goal by Noel Henderson produced a drawn match for the second year running in Dublin. It resulted in the end of the Championship careers of the captains of each side, the veterans Jim McCarthy and Nim Hall.

IRELAND   W.R. Tector 2 (Wanderers); R.E. Roche 1 (UC Galway), N.J. Henderson 21 (NIFC), A.J.F. O'Reilly 2 (Old Belvedere), A.C. Pedlow 5 (Queen's U. Belfast); J.W. Kyle 31 (NIFC), J.A. O'Meara 17 (Dolphin); F.E. Anderson 10 (NIFC), R. Roe 11 (Lansdowne), P.J. O'Donoghue 2 (Bective Rangers), M.N. Madden 1 (Sunday's Well), T.E. Reid 5 (London Irish), M.J. Cunningham 2 (UC Cork), *J.S. McCarthy (26) (Dolphin), J.R. Kavanagh 8 (Wanderers).

ENGLAND   *N.M. Hall (16) (Richmond); J.E. Woodward 12 (Wasps), J. Butterfield 8 (Northampton), W.P.C. Davies 4 (Harlequins), R.C. Bazley 8 (Waterloo); D.G.S. Baker 2 (OMT), J.E. Williams 3 (Old Millhillians); G.W.D. Hastings 2 (Gloucester), N.A. Labuschagne 3 (Guy's H.), D. St G. Hazell 2 (Leicester), P.D. Young 6 (Dublin Wanderers), J.H. Hancock (2) (Newport), P.H. Ryan (2) (Richmond), R. Higgins 5 (Liverpool), P.J. Taylor 2 (Northampton).

Referee A.I. Dickie (Scotland)

ENGLAND v FRANCE   26/452

26 February 1955
Twickenham
France 16 (2G, 2DG) England 9 (1T, 2PG)

England   T: Higgins. PG: Hazell (2).
France   T: Baulon, Celaya. C: Vannier (2). DG:
Jean Prat (2).

France registered their biggest score at Twickenham to date mainly due to the accuracy of
Michel Vannier's place kicking and two dropped goals from the French scoring machine
Jean Prat.

ENGLAND   H. Scott (1) (Manchester); F.D. Sykes
1 (Northampton), J. Butterfield 9 (Northampton), W.P.C. Davies 5 (Harlequins), R.C. Bazley 9
(Waterloo); D.G.S. Baker 3 (OMT), J.E. Williams
4 (Old Millhillians); G.W.D. Hastings 3 (Gloucester), N.A. Labuschagne 4 (Guy's H.), D. St G.
Hazell 3 (Leicester), *P.D. Young 7 (Dublin
Wands), P.G. Yarranton 3 (Wasps), D.S. Wilson
6 (Metropolitan Police), R. Higgins 6 (Liverpool), I.D.S. Beer 1 (Harlequins).

FRANCE   M. Vannier 6 (RCF); H. Rancoule 1 (FC
Lourdes), M. Prat 14 (FC Lourdes), J. Bouquet 2
(CS Bourg), J. Lepatey 3 (SC Mazamet); A. Haget
4 (PUC), G. Dufau 22 (RCF); A. Domenech 5 (RC
Vichy), P. Labadie 13 (A. Bayonne) R. Bréjassou
11 (S. Tarbes), B. Chevallier 12 (AS Montferrand), M. Celaya 7 (Biarritz Ol), *J. Prat 34 (FC
Lourdes), H. Domec 8 (FC Lourdes), R. Baulon 5
(CS Vienne).

Referee R. Mitchell (Ireland)

SCOTLAND v IRELAND   61/453

26 February 1955
Murrayfield
Scotland 12 (1T, 1DG, 2PG) Ireland 3 (1PG)

Scotland   T: Swan. DG: Cameron. PG: Elgie (2).
Ireland   PG: Kelly.

After nine successive defeats Scotland at last
managed a victory over Ireland. Even so it was
only the Scots' second win against the Irish in 20
matches between 1935–59.

SCOTLAND   R.W.T. Chisholm 1 (Melrose); A.R.
Smith 2 (Cambridge U.), M.K. Elgie 6 (London
Scottish), R.G. Charters 2 (Hawick), J.S. Swan 8
(Coventry); *A. Cameron 12 (Glasgow HSFP),
J.A. Nichol 2 (Royal HSFP); H.F. McLeod 7
(Hawick), W.K.L. Relph 3 (Stewart's FP), T.
Elliot 2 (Gala), E.J.S. Michie 5 (Aberdeen U.),
J.W.Y. Kemp 4 (Glasgow HSFP), I.A.A.
MacGregor 1 (Hillhead HSFP), A. Robson 4
(Hawick), J.T. Greenwood 4 (Dunfermline).

IRELAND   W.R. Tector (3) (Wanderers); A.C.
Pedlow 6 (Queen's U. Belfast), A.J.F. O'Reilly 3
(Old Belvedere), N.J. Henderson 22 (NIFC), R.E.
Roche 2 (UC Galway); S. Kelly 3 (Lansdowne),
S.J. McDermott 1 (London Irish); P.J.
O'Donoghue 3 (Bective Rangers), R. Roe 12
(Lansdowne), F.E. Anderson 11 (NIFC), T.E.
Reid 6 (London Irish), M.N. Madden 2
(Sunday's Well), D.A. McSweeney (1) (Blackrock College), M.J. Cunningham 3 (UC Cork),
*R.H. Thompson 7 (Instonians).

Referee L.M. Boundy (England)

WALES v IRELAND   57/454

12 March 1955
Cardiff Arms Park
Wales 21 (3G, 1T, 1PG) Ireland 3 (1PG)

Wales   T: Courtney Meredith, Griffiths, Morgan, Morris. C: Owen (3). PG: Owen.
Ireland   PG: Henderson.

Wales scored a fourth win in a row over Ireland
owing to a four-try blitz in the final quarter of
an hour. Five of the Irishmen did not play again
in the Championship, including four of a pack
which had done well up to half-time but then
wilted noticeably.

WALES   G. Owen 1 (Newport); K.J. Jones 35
(Newport), A.G. Thomas 12 (Cardiff), G.M.
Griffiths 8 (Cardiff), H.T. Morris 2 (Cardiff); C.I.
Morgan 14 (Bective Rangers), W.R. Willis 18
(Cardiff); W.O.G. Williams 16 (Swansea), B.V.
Meredith 6 (Newport), C.C. Meredith 8 (Neath),
R.J. Robins 6 (Pontypridd), R.H. Williams 5
(Llanelli), I. Davies (3) (Llanelli), R.C.C. Thomas
12 (Swansea), *J.R.G. Stephens 22 (Neath).

IRELAND P.J. Berkery 2 (Lansdowne); A.C. Pedlow 7 (Queen's U. Belfast), N.J. Henderson 23 (NIFC), A.J.F. O'Reilly 4 (Old Belvedere), J.T. Gaston 5 (Dublin U.); J.W. Kyle 32 (NIFC), S.J. McDermott (2) (London Irish); P.J. O'Donoghue 4 (Bective Rangers), R. Roe 13 (Lansdowne), F.E. Anderson (12) (NIFC), M.N. Madden (3) (Sunday's Well), *R.H. Thompson 8 (Instonians), M.J. Cunningham 4 (UC Cork), P. Kavanagh (2) (Wanderers), G.R.P. Ross (1) (CIYMS).

Referee A.I. Dickie (Scotland)

ENGLAND v SCOTLAND 58/455

19 March 1955
Twickenham
England 9 (2T, 1PG) Scotland 6 (1T, 1PG)

England T: Beer, Sykes. PG: Hazell.
Scotland T: Cameron. PG: Cameron.

England gained their only victory of the season and in so doing deprived Scotland of the Triple Crown. Fourteen of the players involved, ten of them English, never played in another Championship match.

ENGLAND N.S.D. Estcourt (1) (Blackheath); F.D. Sykes (2) (Northampton), J. Butterfield 10 (Northampton), W.P.C. Davies 6 (Harlequins), R.C. Bazley (10) (Waterloo); D.G.S. Baker (4) (OMT), J.E. Williams 5 (Old Millhillians); G.W.D. Hastings 4 (Gloucester), N.A. Labuschagne (5) (Guy's H.), D. St G. Hazell (4) (Leicester), *P.D. Young (8) (Dublin Wands), P.G. Yarranton (4) (Wasps), D.S. Wilson (7) (Metropolitan Police), R. Higgins 7 (Liverpool), I.D.S. Beer (2) (Harlequins).

SCOTLAND R.W.T. Chisholm 2 (Melrose); A.R. Smith 3 (Cambridge U.), M.K. Elgie (7) (London Scottish), R.G. Charters (3) (Hawick), J.S. Swan 9 (Coventry); *A. Cameron 13 (Glasgow HSFP), J.A. Nichol (3) (Royal HSFP); H.F. McLeod 8 (Hawick), W.K.L. Relph (4) (Stewart's FP), T. Elliot 3 (Gala), E.J.S. Michie 6 (Aberdeen U.), J.W.Y. Kemp 5 (Glasgow HSFP), I.A.A. Mac-Gregor 2 (Hillhead HSFP), A. Robson 5 (Hawick), J.T. Greenwood 5 (Dunfermline).

Referee D.C. Joynson (Wales)

FRANCE v WALES 26/456

26 March 1955
Stade Colombes, Paris
Wales 16 (2G, 2PG) France 11 (1G, 1DG, 1PG)

Wales T: Thomas, Morris. C: Owen (2). PG: Owen (2).
France T: Baulon. C: Vannier. DG: Maurice Prat. PG: Vannier.

Wales travelled to Paris to face a French side which had already beaten Scotland, Ireland and England and their victory proved just enough to edge the Grand Slam seeking French into second place in the Championship. It was also Wales's biggest score in France to date, although they were to surpass it on their next visit in 1957 and in 1975. It was the great Jean Prat's final match.

FRANCE M. Vannier 7 (RCF); H. Rancoule 2 (FC Lourdes), M. Prat 15 (FC Lourdes), R. Martine 9 (FC Lourdes), J. Lepatey (4) (SC Mazamet); A. Haget 5 (PUC), G. Dufau 23 (RCF); R. Bréjassou (12) (S. Tarbes), P. Labadie 14 (A. Bayonne), A. Domenech 6 (RC Vichy), R. Baulon 6 (CS Vienne), B. Chevallier 13 (AS Montferrand), M. Celaya 8 (Biarritz Ol), H. Domec 9 (FC Lourdes), *J. Prat (35) (FC Lourdes).

WALES G. Owen 2 (Newport); K.J. Jones 36 (Newport), A.G. Thomas (13) (Llanelli), G.M. Griffiths 9 (Cardiff), H.T. Morris (3) (Cardiff); C.I. Morgan 15 (Bective Rangers), W.R. Willis (19) (Cardiff); W.O.G. Williams 17 (Swansea), B.V. Meredith 7 (Newport), C.C. Meredith 9 (Neath), R.J. Robins 7 (Pontypridd), R.H. Williams 6 (Llanelli), B. Sparks 3 (Neath), C.D. Williams 1 (Cardiff), *J.R.G. Stephens 23 (Neath).

Referee O.B. Glasgow (Ireland)

1956

MURRAYFIELD Scotland beat France 12-0 · TWICKENHAM Wales beat England 8-3
PARIS France beat Ireland 14-8 · CARDIFF Wales beat Scotland 9-3
TWICKENHAM England beat Ireland 20-0 · DUBLIN Ireland beat Scotland 14-10
DUBLIN Ireland beat Wales 11-3 · MURRAYFIELD England beat Scotland 11-6
CARDIFF Wales beat France 5-3 · PARIS France beat England 14-9

CHAMPIONSHIP TABLE
Wales – Championship

Pos	Country	P	W	D	L	F	A	Pts	Tries F	A
1	Wales (1)	4	3	0	1	25	20	6	6	2
2	England (4)	4	2	0	2	43	28	4	5	5
3	Ireland (5)	4	2	0	2	33	47	4	6	7
4	France (2)	4	2	0	2	31	34	4	5	5
5	Scotland (3)	4	1	0	3	31	34	2	5	8

After the great attacking flair displayed by the British team in South Africa the previous summer, expectations were high that the 1956 Championship would confirm a new golden era for British rugby. It did not happen. The most emphatic victory was England's three-try 20-0 rout of Ireland, but that was very much the exception in a series of tight, closely-fought encounters. Wales, Champions for a third year in a row – which meant they had won five times in seven seasons – were unquestionably the best side, despite an inexplicable defeat in their bid to win the Triple Crown in Dublin. Yet the Welsh aggregate was a mere 25 points, the lowest by a title-winning side when five countries competed, with the exception of Ireland's 21 points in 1951 and England's 25 points in 1930. Because of their heavy defeat of Ireland, England were the highest points plunderers, only to surrender their title chance by submitting to France in their last match.

The Irish experience was curious. They tried 28 players in various permutations, which hardly suggested that their selectors had embarked on a reasoned team policy. Even after they had got it right, seemingly, by defeating Scotland with seven changes, they made four more for the next match. Their audacity was rewarded: they beat Wales. France certainly struggled for a cohesive team after losing their first match, against Scotland. By the time they had finished, however, they had used 23 players and gained 2 victories. Scotland, like England, tried to engender team spirit and team building. Admirable though this was, it brought few rewards for they won only one match, their first, and once again found themselves propping up the rest at the foot of the table.

SCOTLAND v FRANCE   26/457

14 January 1956
Murrayfield
Scotland 12 (2T, 2PG) France 0

Scotland   T: Kemp (2). PG: Smith, Cameron.

After losing the two previous matches against France at Murrayfield, Scotland produced an emphatic victory, though it proved to be their only one of the season.

SCOTLAND   R.W.T. Chisholm 3 (Melrose); A.R. Smith 4 (Cambridge U.), *A. Cameron 14 (Glasgow HSFP), K.R. Macdonald 1 (Stewart's FP), J.S. Swan 10 (Coventry); M.L. Grant 2 (Harlequins), N.M. Campbell 1 (London Scottish); H.F. McLeod 9 (Hawick), R.K.G. MacEwan 4 (London Scottish), T. Elliot 4 (Gala), E.J.S. Michie 7 (Aberdeen GSFP), J.W.Y. Kemp 6 (Glasgow HSFP), I.A.A. MacGregor 3 (Llanelli), A. Robson 6 (Hawick), J.T. Greenwood 6 (Dunfermline).

FRANCE   M. Vannier 8 (RCF); J. Dupuy 1 (S.

Tarbes), A. Boniface 6 (S. Mont-de-Marsan), G. Stener 1 (PUC), S. Torreilles (1) (US Perpignan); J. Bouquet 3 (CS Vienne), *G. Dufau 24 (RCF); A. Domenech 7 (CA Brive), R. Vigier 1 (AS Montferrand), R. Biénès 20 (US Cognac), B. Chevallier 14 (AS Montferrand), G. Roucaries (1) (US Perpignan), J. Carrère 1 (RC Vichy), R. Baulon 7 (A. Bayonne), M. Celaya 9 (Biarritz Ol).

Referee Captain M.J. Dowling (Ireland)

ENGLAND v WALES 60/458

21 January 1956
Twickenham
Wales 8 (1G, 1T) England 3 (1PG)

England PG: Allison.
Wales T: Davies, Robins. C: Owen.

A huge crowd of 75,000 watched Wales win for a third time in four visits to Twickenham. England played ten new caps and one player, Vic Roberts, made his reappearance in the side after a five-year absence. Most of the débutants, however, were to play significant roles in the future: Jackson, Thompson, Jeeps, Jacobs, Marques, Currie, Robbins and Ashcroft. One of the other newcomers, Mike Smith, played in this match only – coincidentally against Onllwyn Brace, the Welsh scrum-half, with whom he had struck up a superb half-back partnership at Oxford University.

ENGLAND D.F. Allison 1 (Coventry); P.B. Jackson 1 (Coventry), J. Butterfield 11 (Northampton), W.P.C. Davies 7 (Harlequins), P.H. Thompson 1 (Headingley); M.J.K. Smith (1) (Oxford U.), R.E.G. Jeeps 1 (Northampton); D.L. Sanders 5 (Harlequins), *E. Evans 15 (Sale), C.R. Jacobs 1 (Northampton), R.W.D. Marques 1 (Cambridge U.), J.D. Currie 1 (Oxford U.), P.G.D. Robbins 1 (Oxford U.), V.G. Roberts 13 (Harlequins), A. Ashcroft 1 (Waterloo).

WALES G. Owen 3 (Newport); K.J. Jones 37 (Newport), H.P. Morgan 1 (Newport), M.C. Thomas 15 (Newport), C.L. Davies 1 (Cardiff); *C.I. Morgan 16 (Cardiff), D.O. Brace 1 (Newport); W.O.G. Williams 18 (Swansea), B.V. Meredith 8 (Newport), C.C. Meredith 10 (Neath),

R.H. Williams 7 (Llanelli), R. J. Robins 8 (Pontypridd), B. Sparks 4 (Neath), R.C.C. Thomas 13 (Swansea), L.H. Jenkins 2 (Newport).

Referee R. Mitchell (Ireland)

FRANCE v IRELAND 27/459

28 January 1956
Stade Colombes, Paris
France 14 (1G, 1T, 2DG) Ireland 8 (1G, 1PG)

France T: Boniface, Baulon. C: Vannier. DG: Vannier, Bouquet.
Ireland T: O'Reilly. C: Pedlow. PG: Pedlow.

Ireland, who had won only one of their previous eight Championship matches, blooded six players new to the Championship, including a slim, willowy scrum-half, Andy Mulligan. Mulligan matured into a fine attacking player, whose elegant running and passing made him one of the outstanding scrum-halves of the late 1950s. Mulligan was at the centre of a great controversy at the height of his playing career for, seemingly in contravention of the Law as it stood, he became a professional rugby writer. Diehards reckoned Mulligan should be banned from playing and there was much speculation that this would happen. Ultimately the Irish Rugby Union decided that as journalism was Mulligan's full-time occupation he would be able to continue playing – a decision which led to the Law being amended so that all those who made their living from writing, television and radio could still play if they so wished.

FRANCE M. Vannier 9 (RCF); A. Boniface 7 (S. Mont-de-Marsan) M. Prat 16 (FC Lourdes), G. Stener 2 (PUC), J. Dupuy 2 (S. Tarbes); J. Bouquet 4 (CS Vienne), *G. Dufau 25 (RCF); A. Domenech 8 (CA Brive), P. Labadie 15 (A. Bayonne), R. Biénès 21 (US Cognac), M. Celaya 10 (Biarritz Ol), B. Chevallier 15 (AS Montferrand), H. Domec 10 (FC Lourdes), R. Baulon 8 (A. Bayonne), J. Barthe 2 (FC Lourdes).

IRELAND J.M. McKelvey 1 (Queen's U. Belfast); S.V.J. Quinlan 1 (Highfield), A.J.F. O'Reilly 5 (Old Belvedere), A.C. Pedlow 8 (Queen's U. Belfast), J.T. Gaston 6 (Monkstown); J.W. Kyle 33 (NIFC), A.A. Mulligan 1 (Wanderers); C. Fagan 1 (Wanderers), R. Roe 14 (Lansdowne),

B.G.M. Wood 3 (Garryowen), P.J. Lawler 9 (Clontarf), T.E. Reid 7 (London Irish), M.J. Cunningham 5 (UC Cork), *J.S. Ritchie 1 (London Irish), A.G. Kennedy (1) (Belfast Collegians).

Referee Dr P.F. Cooper (England)

WALES v SCOTLAND 60/460

4 February 1956
Cardiff Arms Park
Wales 9 (3T) Scotland 3 (1PG)

Wales T: Harry Morgan, Cliff Morgan, Davies.
Scotland PG: Cameron.

The new South Stand at the Arms Park was officially opened at this match though it had been uncertain whether it would take place because of severe frost. Volunteers had manned braziers dotted around the pitch throughout the night, activity reminiscent of the battle which saved the match against England in 1893. There were misgivings on both sides about playing because several parts of the ground remained frozen over at kick-off and in places it was like an ice-skating rink. To score at all was miraculous, but Wales somehow contrived three tries to register their sixth victory in a row over Scotland in Wales.

WALES   G. Owen 4 (Newport); K.J. Jones 38 (Newport), H.P. Morgan 2 (Newport), M.C. Thomas 16 (Newport), C.L. Davies 2 (Cardiff); *C.I. Morgan 17 (Cardiff), D.O. Brace 2 (Newport); W.O.G. Williams 19 (Swansea), B.V. Meredith 9 (Newport), R. Prosser 1 (Pontypool), R.H. Williams 8 (Llanelli), J.R.G. Stephens 24 (Neath), B. Sparks 5 (Neath), R.C.C. Thomas 14 (Swansea), L.H. Jenkins 3 (Newport).

SCOTLAND   R.W.T. Chisholm 4 (Melrose); A.R. Smith 5 (Cambridge U.), *A. Cameron 15 (Glasgow HSFP), K.R. Macdonald 2 (Stewart's FP), J.S. Swan 11 (Coventry); M.L. Grant 3 (Harlequins), N.M. Campbell (2) (London Scottish); H.F. McLeod 10 (Hawick), R.K.G. MacEwan 5 (London Scottish), T. Elliot 5 (Gala), E.J.S. Michie 8 (Aberdeen GSFP), J.W.Y. Kemp 7 (Glasgow HSFP), I.A.A. MacGregor 4 (Llanelli), A. Robson 7 (Hawick), J.T. Greenwood 7 (Dunfermline).

Referee L.M. Boundy (England)

ENGLAND v IRELAND 60/461

11 February 1956
Twickenham
England 20 (1G, 2T, 3PG) Ireland 0

England T: Butterfield, Evans, Jackson. C: Currie. PG: Currie (2), Allison.

England achieved their biggest margin of victory over Ireland at Twickenham, and it was only two points fewer than their record 36-14 triumph at Lansdowne Road in 1938. England had now scored eight tries without reply in the last four home matches against Ireland who reacted predictably by ending the Championship careers of five of their side.

ENGLAND   D.F. Allison 2 (Coventry); P.B. Jackson 2 (Coventry), J. Butterfield 12 (Northampton), L.B. Cannell 14 (St Mary's H.), P.H. Thompson 2 (Headingley); M. Regan 9 (Liverpool), J.E. Williams 6 (Old Millhillians); D.L. Sanders 6 (Harlequins), *E. Evans 16 (Sale), C.R. Jacobs 2 (Northampton), R.W.D. Marques 2 (Cambridge U.), J.D. Currie 2 (Oxford U.), P.G.D. Robbins 2 (Oxford U.), V.G. Roberts 14 (Harlequins), A. Ashcroft 2 (Waterloo).

IRELAND   J.M. McKelvey (2) (Queen's U. Belfast); S.V.J. Quinlan 2 (Highfield), A.J.F. O'Reilly 6 (Old Belvedere), A.C. Pedlow 9 (Queen's U. Belfast), J.T. Gaston (7) (Monkstown); J.W. Kyle 34 (NIFC), A.A. Mulligan 2 (Cambridge U.); C. Fagan 2 (Morley), R. Roe 15 (Lansdowne), B.G.M. Wood 4 (Garryowen), P.J. Lawler (10) (Clontarf), T.E. Reid 8 (London Irish), *J.S. Ritchie (2) (London Irish), N. Feddis (1) (Lansdowne), J.R. Kavanagh 9 (Wanderers).

Referee A.I. Dickie (Scotland)

IRELAND v SCOTLAND   62/462

25 February 1956
Lansdowne Road, Dublin
Ireland 14 (1G, 3T) Scotland 10 (2G)

Ireland   T: Henderson, O'Reilly, Kyle, O'Meara.
C: Pedlow.
Scotland   T: Michie, Smith. C: McClung (2).

Alex Cameron, the Glasgow HSFP fly-half, was badly concussed early in the match and had to go off never to play again for Scotland. He had appeared in 16 Championship matches over eight seasons.

IRELAND   P.J. Berkery 3 (Lansdowne); A.C. Pedlow 10 (Queen's U. Belfast), A.J.F. O'Reilly 7 (Old Belvedere), *N.J. Henderson 24 (NIFC), W.J. Hewitt 2 (Instonians); J.W. Kyle 35 (NIFC), J.A. O' Meara 18 (Dolphin); C. Fagan (3) (Morley), R. Roe 16 (London Irish), B.G.M. Wood 5 (Garryowen), B.N. Guerin (1) (Galwegians), L.M. Lynch (1) (Lansdowne), C.T.J. Lydon (1) (Galwegians), M.J. Cunningham 6 (Cork Constitution), J.R. Kavanagh 10 (Wanderers).

SCOTLAND   R.W.T. Chisholm 5 (Melrose); A.R. Smith 6 (Cambridge U.), T. McClung 1 (Edinburgh Acads), K.R. Macdonald 3 (Stewart's FP), J.S. Swan 12 (Coventry); *A. Cameron (16) (Glasgow HSFP), A.F. Dorward 9 (Gala); H.F. McLeod 11 (Hawick), R.K.G. MacEwan 6 (London Scottish), T. Elliot 6 (Gala), E.J.S. Michie 9 (Aberdeen GSFP), J.W.Y. Kemp 8 (Glasgow HSFP), I.A.A. McGregor 5 (Llanelli), A. Robson 8 (Hawick), J.T. Greenwood 8 (Dunfermline).

Referee H.B. Elliott (England)

IRELAND v WALES   58/463

10 March 1956
Lansdowne Road, Dublin
Ireland 11 (1G, 1DG, 1PG) Wales 3 (1PG)

Ireland   T: Cunningham. C: Pedlow. DG: Kyle.
PG: Pedlow.
Wales   PG: Owen.

Ireland gained their first victory against Wales since 1949 and in so doing wrecked their Triple Crown bid. A record crowd of over 50,000 saw the Irish pack in total control and the Welsh backs engulfed by swarm after swarm of tacklers.

IRELAND   P.J. Berkery 4 (Lansdowne); S.V.J. Quinlan 3 (Highfield), *N.J. Henderson 25 (NIFC), A.J.F. O'Reilly 8 (Old Belvedere), A.C. Pedlow 11 (Queen's U. Belfast); J.W. Kyle 36 (NIFC), J.A. O'Meara 19 (Dolphin); P.J. O'Donoghue 5 (Bective Rangers), R. Roe 17 (London Irish), B.G.M. Wood 6 (Garryowen), R.H. Thompson (9) (Instonians), J.R. Brady 8 (CIYMS), M.J. Cunningham (7) (Cork Constitution), J.R. Kavanagh 11 (Wanderers), T. McGrath 1 (Garryowen).

WALES   G. Owen 5 (Newport); K.J. Jones 39 (Newport), H.P. Morgan 3 (Newport), M.C. Thomas 17 (Newport), C.L. Davies (3) (Cardiff); *C.I. Morgan 18 (Cardiff), D.O. Brace 3 (Newport); W.O.G. Williams (20) (Swansea), B.V. Meredith 10 (Newport), C.C. Meredith 11 (Neath), J.R.G. Stephens 25 (Neath), R.H. Williams 9 (Llanelli), B. Sparks 6 (Neath), R.C.C. Thomas 15 (Swansea), L.H. Jenkins 4 (Newport).

Referee A.I. Dickie (Scotland)

SCOTLAND v ENGLAND   59/464

17 March 1956
Murrayfield
England 11 (1G, 2PG) Scotland 6 (1T, 1PG)

Scotland   T: Stevenson. PG: Smith.
England   T: Williams. C: Currie. PG: Currie (2).

England won in Scotland for a third year running, a feat only once previously achieved, in 1914–23. John Currie, fast developing his technique in the line-out and mauls, confirmed another quality – that of goal-kicking. He landed two penalty goals, one an extremely difficult one, and a conversion. In contrast, Scotland missed five penalty goal attempts.

SCOTLAND   R.W.T. Chisholm 6 (Melrose); A.R. Smith 7 (Cambridge U.), J.T. Docherty 3 (Glasgow HSFP), G.D. Stevenson 1 (Hawick), J.S. Swan 13 (Coventry); T. McClung 2 (Edinburgh Acads), A.F. Dorward 10 (Gala); H.F. McLeod 12 (Hawick), R.K.G. MacEwan 7 (London Scottish), T. Elliot 7 (Gala), E.J.S. Michie 10 (Aberdeen GSFP), J.W.Y. Kemp 9 (Glasgow HSFP), I.A.A. MacGregor 6 (Llanelli), A. Robson 9 (Hawick), *J.T. Greenwood 9 (Dunfermline).

ENGLAND D.F. Allison 3 (Coventry); J.E. Woodward (13) (Wasps), J. Butterfield 13 (Northampton), L.B. Cannell 15 (St Mary's H.), P.H. Thompson 3 (Headingley); M. Regan 10 (Liverpool), J.E. Williams 7 (Old Millhillians); D.L. Sanders 7 (Harlequins), *E. Evans 17 (Sale), C.R. Jacobs 3 (Northampton), R.W.D. Marques 3 (Cambridge U.), J.D. Currie 3 (Oxford U.), P.G.D. Robbins 3 (Oxford U.), V.G. Roberts 15 (Harlequins), A. Ashcroft 3 (Waterloo).

Referee Captain M.J. Dowling (Ireland)

WALES v FRANCE 27/465

24 March 1956
Cardiff Arms Park
Wales 5 (1G) France 3 (1T)

Wales T: Williams. C: Owen.
France T: Bouquet.

This was Wales's fourth successive home win over France, and some French observers were convinced that Derek Williams had grounded the ball over the dead-ball line and therefore should not have been allowed what turned out to be a match-winning try. Victory meant Wales had won the Championship for the third season in a row. It was also a match to remember for the Newport wing, Ken Jones: it was his fortieth Championship appearance for Wales.

WALES G. Owen (6) (Newport); K.J. Jones 40 (Newport), H.P. Morgan (4) (Newport), M.C. Thomas 18 (Newport), G. Rowlands (3) (Cardiff); *C.I. Morgan 19 (Cardiff), D.O. Brace 4 (Newport); R. Richards (1) (Cross Keys), B.V. Meredith 11 (Newport), R. Prosser 2 (Pontypool), L.H. Jenkins (5) (Newport), J.R.G. Stephens 26 (Neath), C.D. Williams (2) (Neath), G. Whitson 1 (Newport), R.J. Robins 9 (Pontypridd).

FRANCE M. Vannier 10 (RCF); J. Dupuy 3 (S. Tarbes), M. Prat 17 (FC Lourdes), A. Boniface 8

(S. Mont-de-Marsan), L. Rogé 6 (AS Béziers); J. Bouquet 5 (CS Vienne), *G. Dufau 26 (RCF); A. Domenech 9 (CA Brive), R. Vigier 2 (AS Montferrand), R. Biénès 22 (US Cognac), B. Chevallier 16 (AS Montferrand), M. Celaya 11 (Biarritz Ol), R. Baulon 9 (A. Bayonne), H. Domec 11 (FC Lourdes), J. Barthe 3 (FC Lourdes).

Referee Dr P.F. Cooper (England)

FRANCE v ENGLAND 27/466

14 April 1956
Stade Colombes, Paris
France 14 (1G, 1T, 2PG) England 9 (1T, 2PG)

France T: Dupuy, Pauthe. C: Labazuy. PG: Labazuy (2).
England T: Thompson. PG: Allison (2).

England would have pipped Wales to the Championship had they been able to win this match, which had been postponed from February because of frost. But France, stout in defence and quick to find scoring opportunities in attack, won handsomely to record three successive wins over England for a first time. The wheel certainly had turned full circle for England in France – they had won their first six matches there, but since 1927 they had won only twice, in 1929 and 1952.

FRANCE M. Vannier 11 (RCF); J. Dupuy 4 (S. Tarbes), J. Bouquet 6 (CS Vienne), G. Stener (3) (PUC), L. Rogé 7 (AS Béziers); A. Labazuy 4 (FC Lourdes), G. Pauthe (1) (SC Graulhet); A. Domenech 10 (CA Brive), R. Vigier 3 (AS Montferrand), R. Biénès (23) (US Cognac), B. Chevallier 17 (AS Montferrand), *M. Celaya 12 (Biarritz Ol) H. Lazies 1 (S. Toulouse), R. Baulon 10 (A. Bayonne), J. Barthe 4 (FC Lourdes).

ENGLAND D.F. Allison 4 (Coventry); P.B. Jackson 3 (Coventry), J. Butterfield 14 (Northampton), L.B. Cannell 16 (St Mary's H.), P.H. Thompson 4 (Headingley); M. Regan (11) (Liverpool), J.E. Williams 8 (Old Millhillians); D.L. Sanders (8) (Harlequins), *E. Evans 18 (Sale), C.R. Jacobs 4 (Northampton), R.W.D. Marques 4 (Cambridge U.), J.D. Currie 4 (Oxford U.), P.G.D. Robbins 4 (Oxford U.), V.G. Roberts (16) (Harlequins), A. Ashcroft 4 (Waterloo).

Referee I. David (Wales)

1957

PARIS Scotland beat France 6-0 · CARDIFF England beat Wales 3-0
DUBLIN Ireland beat France 11-6 · MURRAYFIELD Scotland beat Wales 9-6
DUBLIN England beat Ireland 6-0 · TWICKENHAM England beat France 9-5
MURRAYFIELD Ireland beat Scotland 5-3 · CARDIFF Wales beat Ireland 6-5
TWICKENHAM England beat Scotland 16-3 · PARIS Wales beat France 19-13

CHAMPIONSHIP TABLE
England – Championship, Triple Crown, Grand Slam

Pos	Country	P	W	D	L	F	A	Pts	Tries F	A
1	England (2)	4	4	0	0	34	8	8	7	1
2	Wales (1)	4	2	0	2	31	30	4	5	5
3	Ireland (3)	4	2	0	2	21	21	4	4	1
4	Scotland (5)	4	2	0	2	21	27	4	1	5
5	France (4)	4	0	0	4	24	45	0	4	9

England carried all before them, having begun the season with a 3-0 win at Cardiff, and completing it with resounding success over Scotland to take the Triple Crown and Grand Slam. They made two changes only during the season, and an indication of their playing tactics was that four of their six tries were scored by their wings. Peter Jackson scored three of them bringing his total to four out of seven appearances, just reward for the Houdini of the wing position. Scotland, under a new captain Jim Greenwood, and with a highly promising full-back in Ken Scotland, must have felt their fortunes were ready for a significant upturn when they won both opening matches. An injury to Greenwood, and other enforced reshuffles of their back division, left them vulnerable to their Murrayfield bogey side, Ireland. It was then only misfortune that their last match was against an England side intent on Grand Slamming, hardly the occasion for the introduction of a newcomer, Gordon Wadell, on whom many in Scotland fixed high hopes.

France, in contrast, achieved little. They lost all four matches for the first time since 1929. In the consequent axing of players, nine in total, out went Gérard Dufau, their ebullient little scrum-half, who since 1948 had appeared in 30 matches and had won admirers with friend and foe alike. The big, burly Bernard Chevallier was another of the casualties of a disastrous season for the French. Ken Jones, Gareth Griffiths, Rhys Stephens, Russell Robins and Courtney Meredith also left Championship rugby as Wales suffered the unusual experience of losing their first two matches and winning the next two. Ireland changed their policy decisively. In contrast to the previous season, they played with nearly the same side in all four matches, and were perhaps unlucky to win but two of them.

The year had its moment of sadness and reflection with the death, aged 93, of Frank Pease, one of the few surviving links with the nineteenth-century Championship. Pease, a forward from Hartlepool Rovers, played for England against Ireland in Dublin in 1887.

FRANCE v SCOTLAND 27/467

12 January 1957
Stade Colombes, Paris
Scotland 6 (1DG, 1PG) France 0

Scotland DG: Scotland. PG: Scotland.

Scotland's first victory in France since 1949 was also their only win of the season. It was a tough match in which the Scottish defence performed soundly, preventing the French from scoring for only the third time in Paris. The French reaction was to drop two players, Henri Lazies, the Auch prop, and Bernard Chevallier, of Montferrand, who had been a regular at lock-forward since 1952.

FRANCE   M. Vannier 12 (RCF); J. Dupuy 5 (S. Tarbes), L. Rogé 8 (AS Béziers), M. Prat 18 (FC Lourdes), A. Boniface 9 (S. Mont-de-Marsan); J. Bouquet 7 (CS Vienne), G. Dufau 27 (RCF); A. Domenech 11 (CA Brive), R. Vigier 4 (AS Montferrand), H. Lazies (2) (S. Toulouse), B. Chevallier (18) (AS Montferrand), A. Sanac 4 (US Perpignan), R. Baulon 11 (A. Bayonne), J. Barthe 5 (FC Lourdes), *M. Celaya 13 (Biarritz Ol).

SCOTLAND   K.J.F. Scotland 1 (Royal Signals); A.R. Smith 8 (Cambridge U.), E. McKeating 1 (Heriot's FP), G.D. Stevenson 2 (Hawick), J.S. Swan 14 (Coventry); M.L. Grant (4) (Harlequins), A.F. Dorward 11 (Gala); H.F. McLeod 13 (Hawick), R.K.G. MacEwan 8 (London Scottish), T. Elliot 8 (Gala), E.J.S. Michie 11 (London Scottish), J.W.Y. Kemp 10 (Glasgow HSFP), I.A.A. MacGregor 7 (Llanelli), A. Robson 10 (Hawick), *J.T. Greenwood 10 (Perthshire Acads).

Referee L.M. Boundy (England)

WALES v ENGLAND   61/468

19 January 1957
Cardiff Arms Park
England 3 (1PG) Wales 0

England   PG: Allison.

England won with a penalty goal given away by Keith Maddocks, the Neath wing, because he encroached offside as a line-out was taken. The unfortunate Maddocks never played again for Wales.

WALES   T.J. Davies 5 (Llanelli); G. Howells 1 (Llanelli), G.M. Griffiths 10 (Cardiff), *M.C. Thomas 19 (Newport), K. Maddocks (1) (Neath); C.I. Morgan 20 (Cardiff), D.O. Brace 5 (Newport); R. Prosser 3 (Pontypool), B.V. Meredith 12 (London Welsh), C.C. Meredith 12 (Neath), J.R.G. Stephens 27 (Neath), R.H. Williams 10 (Llanelli), R. O'Connor (1) (Aberavon), R.C.C. Thomas 16 (Swansea), R.J. Robins 10 (Pontypridd).

ENGLAND   D.F. Allison 5 (Coventry); P.B. Jackson 4 (Coventry), J. Butterfield 15 (Northampton), L.B. Cannell 17 (St Mary's H.), P.H. Thompson 5 (Headingley); R.M. Bartlett 1 (Harlequins), R.E.G. Jeeps 2 (Northampton); C.R. Jacobs 5 (Northampton), *E. Evans 19 (Sale),

Wales's fly-half maestro, Cliff Morgan, scythes through England's defence and sets up Terry Davies on 19 January 1957

G.W.D. Hastings 5 (Gloucester), J.D. Currie 5 (Oxford U.), R.W.D. Marques 5 (Cambridge U.), P.G.D. Robbins 5 (Oxford U.), R. Higgins 8 (Liverpool), A. Ashcroft 5 (Waterloo).

Referee A.I. Dickie (Scotland)

IRELAND v FRANCE   28/469

26 January 1957
Lansdowne Road, Dublin
Ireland 11 (1G, 1T, 1PG) France 6 (2PG)

Ireland   T: Brophy, Kyle. C: Pedlow. PG: Pedlow.
France   PG: Vannier (2).

Christian Darrouy and François Moncla, arguably two of France's finest post-war players, made their Championship débuts but appeared in a side which was completely outplayed. Ireland failed to keep the momentum, however, while the French went from bad to worse, eventually losing all four matches for the first time since 1929.

IRELAND   P.J. Berkery 5 (Lansdowne); A.C. Pedlow 12 (CIYMS), *N.J. Henderson 26 (NIFC), A.J.F. O'Reilly 9 (Old Belvedere), N.H. Brophy 1 (UC Dublin); J.W. Kyle 37 (NIFC), A.A. Mulligan

3 (Cambridge U.); P.J. O'Donoghue 6 (Bective Rangers), R. Roe 18 (Lansdowne), B.G.M. Wood 7 (Garryowen), T.E. Reid 9 (London Irish), J.R. Brady 9 (CIYMS), J.R. Kavanagh 12 (Wanderers), H.S. O'Connor 1 (Dublin U.), P.J.A. O'Sullivan 1 (Galwegians).

FRANCE   M. Vannier 13 (RCF); J. Dupuy 6 (S. Tarbes), M. Prat 19 (FC Lourdes), A. Boniface 10 (S. Mont-de-Marsan), C. Darrouy 1 (S. Mont-de-Marsan); A. Haget 6 (PUC), G. Dufau 28 (RCF); A. Sanac 5 (US Perpignan), P. Labadie (16) (A. Bayonne), A. Domenech 12 (CA Brive), *M. Celaya 14 (Biarritz Ol), M. Hoche 1 (PUC), R. Baulon (12) (A. Bayonne), F. Moncla 1 (RCF), J. Barthe 6 (FC Lourdes).

Referee L.M. Boundy (England)

(London Scottish), T. Elliot 9 (Gala), E.J.S. Michie 12 (London Scottish), J.W.Y. Kemp 11 (Glasgow HSFP), I.A.A. MacGregor 8 (Hillhead HSFP), A. Robson 11 (Hawick), *J.T. Greenwood 11 (Perthshire Acads).

WALES   T.J. Davies 6 (Llanelli); K.J. Jones (41) (Newport), G.M. Griffiths (11) (Cardiff), *M.C. Thomas 20 (Newport), G. Howells 2 (Llanelli); C.I. Morgan 21 (Cardiff), L.H. Williams 1 (Cardiff); C.C. Meredith (13) (Neath), B.V. Meredith 13 (London Welsh), R. Prosser 4 (Pontypool), R.H. Williams 11 (Llanelli), J.R.G. Stephens 28 (Neath), R.H. Davies 1 (Oxford U.), B. Sparks (7) (Neath), R.J. Robins 11 (Pontypridd).

Referee R.C. Williams (Ireland)

SCOTLAND v WALES   61/470

2 February 1957
Murrayfield
Scotland 9 (1T, 1DG, 1PG)   Wales 6 (1T, 1PG)

Scotland T: Smith. DG: Dorward. PG: Scotland.
Wales T: Robin Davies. PG: Terry Davies.

Ken Jones, probably Wales's greatest wing, made his forty-first and final Championship appearance. In a career which had started in the first international to be played after the War, against England in 1947, Jones scored 16 tries. Although his speed was his greatest asset – as befitting someone who represented Great Britain in the 1948 Olympic Games – Jones was also a shrewd coverer and rarely missed his tackles. No doubt had he been playing in a different era, when right wings were given many more scoring opportunities, this tall, raw-boned athlete from Blaenavon would have shattered all try-scoring records. 'People ask me often which match I enjoyed most,' said Jones once, 'the truth is I enjoyed them all. It was a marvellous experience playing for Wales.'

SCOTLAND   K.J.F. Scotland 2 (Royal Signals); A.R. Smith 9 (Cambridge U.), E. McKeating 2 (Heriot's FP), K.R. Macdonald 4 (Stewart's FP, J.S. Swan 15 (Coventry); T. McClung 3 (Edinburgh Acads), A.F. Dorward 12 (Gala); H.F. McLeod 14 (Hawick), R.K.G. MacEwan 9

IRELAND v ENGLAND   61/471

9 February 1957
Lansdowne Road, Dublin
England 6 (1T, 1PG)   Ireland 0

England T: Jackson. PG: Challis.

England ended a 19-year wait to win in Ireland and it was entirely due to a heroic performance by their forwards, who were down to 7 after 20 minutes when Ashcroft replaced the injured wing, Thompson. It was the final Championship match for Lewis Cannell, who had made 18 appearances since 1948. Cannell was exceptionally quick, a shrewd tactical kicker and a master timer of his passes. Without doubt, he was one of the finest creators of scores for others that England have ever possessed.

IRELAND   P.J. Berkery 6 (Lansdowne); A.J.F. O'Reilly 10 (Old Belvedere), *N.J. Henderson 27 (NIFC), A.C. Pedlow 13 (CIYMS), N.H. Brophy 2 (UC Dublin); J.W. Kyle 38 (NIFC), A.A. Mulligan 4 (Cambridge U.); P.J. O'Donoghue 7 (Bective Rangers), R. Roe 19 (London Irish), B.G.M. Wood 8 (Garryowen), T.E. Reid 10 (London Irish), J.R. Brady 10 (CIYMS), H.S. O'Connor 2 (Dublin U.), J.R. Kavanagh 13 (Wanderers), P.J.A. O'Sullivan 2 (Galwegians).

ENGLAND   R. Challis 1 (Bristol); P.B. Jackson 5 (Coventry), L.B. Cannell (18) (St Mary's H.), J. Butterfield 16 (Northampton), P.H. Thompson 6

(Headingley); R.M. Bartlett 2 (Harlequins), R.E.G. Jeeps 3 (Northampton); C.R. Jacobs 6 (Northampton), *E. Evans 20 (Sale), G.W.D. Hastings 6 (Gloucester), J.D. Currie 6 (Oxford U.), R.W.D. Marques 6 (Cambridge U.), P.G.D. Robbins 6 (Oxford U.), R. Higgins 9 (Liverpool), A. Ashcroft 6 (Waterloo).

Referee A.I. Dickie (Scotland)

ENGLAND v FRANCE   28/472

23 February 1957
Twickenham
England 9 (3T) France 5 (1G)

England T: Jackson (2), Evans.
France T: Darrouy. C: Vannier.

England's victory ensured that they would win the Championship and that France, beaten for the third time in the season, would end up with the Wooden Spoon, a fate they had not suffered since 1929. Peter Jackson's two tries, one a gem, meant that he had now scored four in six Championship appearances.

ENGLAND R. Challis 2 (Bristol); P.B. Jackson 6 (Coventry), J. Butterfield 17 (Northampton), W.P.C. Davies 8 (Harlequins), P.H. Thompson 7 (Headingley); R.M. Bartlett 3 (Harlequins), R.E.G. Jeeps 4 (Northampton); C.R. Jacobs 7 (Northampton), *E. Evans 21 (Sale), G.W.D. Hastings 7 (Gloucester), J.D. Currie 7 (Oxford U.), R.W.D. Marques 7 (Cambridge U.), P.G.D. Robbins 7 (Oxford U.), R. Higgins 10 (Liverpool), A. Ashcroft 7 (Waterloo).

FRANCE M. Vannier 14 (RCF); C. Darrouy 2 (S. Mont-de-Marsan), J. Bouquet 8 (CS Vienne), R. Monie (1) (US Perpignan), J. Dupuy 7 (S. Tarbes); A. Haget (7) (PUC), G. Dufau 29 (RCF); A. Domenech 13 (CA Brive), R. Vigier 5 (AS Montferrand), A. Sanac 6 (US Perpignan), *M. Celaya 15 (Biarritz Ol), M. Hoche 2 (PUC), J. Carrère 2 (RC Vichy), F. Moncla 2 (RCF), J. Barthe 7 (FC Lourdes).

Referee R.C. Williams (Ireland)

SCOTLAND v IRELAND   63/473

23 February 1957
Murrayfield
Ireland 5 (1G) Scotland 3 (IPG)

Scotland PG: Scotland.
Ireland T: O'Sullivan. C: Berkery.

Ireland won for the fifth time in six visits to Murrayfield, where a pre-match snowfall and flurries during the game caused the players more than a few problems.

SCOTLAND K.J.F. Scotland 3 (Royal Signals); *A.R. Smith 10 (Cambridge U.), T. McClung 4 (Edinburgh Acads), K.R. Macdonald 5 (Stewart's FP), J.L.F. Allan 1 (Cambridge U.); J.M. Maxwell (1) (Langholm), A.F. Dorward 13 (Gala); H.F. McLeod 15 (Hawick), R.K.G. MacEwan 10 (London Scottish), T. Elliot 10 (Gala), E.J.S. Michie 13 (London Scottish), J.W.Y. Kemp 12 (Glasgow HSFP), I.A.A. MacGregor (9) (Hillhead HSFP), A. Robson 12 (Hawick), G.K. Smith 1 (Kelso).

IRELAND P.J. Berkery 7 (Lansdowne); A.C. Pedlow 14 (CIYMS), *N.J. Henderson 28 (NIFC), A.J.F. O'Reilly 11 (Old Belvedere), R.E. Roche 3 (Galwegians); J.W. Kyle 39 (NIFC), A.A. Mulligan 5 (Cambridge U.); B.G.M. Wood 9 (Garryowen), R. Roe 20 (London Irish), J.I. Brennan 1 (CIYMS), T.E. Reid 11 (London Irish), J.R. Brady 11 (CIYMS), J.R. Kavanagh 14 (Wanderers), H.S. O'Connor 3 (Dublin U.), P.J.A. O'Sullivan 3 (Galwegians).

Referee L.M. Boundy (England)

WALES v IRELAND   59/474

9 March 1957
Cardiff Arms Park
Wales 6 (2PG) Ireland 5 (1G)

Wales PG: Terry Davies (2).
Ireland T: Kavanagh. C: Pedlow.

Ireland had a much more experienced back division but on a heavy, muddy pitch it was the Welsh pack which dominated a gruelling struggle. During the second half the players had become so mud-spattered that the referee could not differentiate between jersey colours. His solution was to send the Welsh players to the changing-rooms to change into clean jerseys.

WALES   T.J. Davies 7 (Llanelli); G. Howells 3 (Llanelli), C.H.A. Davies 1 (Llanelli), G. Powell 1 (Ebbw Vale), G.T. Wells 3 (Cardiff); C.I. Morgan 22 (Cardiff), L.H. Williams 2 (Cardiff); R. Prosser 5 (Pontypool), B.V. Meredith 14 (London Welsh), C.H. Morgan 1 (Llanelli), R.H. Williams 12 (Llanelli), *J.R.G. Stephens 29 (Neath), R.J. Robins 12 (Pontypridd), R.H. Davies 2 (London Welsh), J. Faull 1 (Swansea).

IRELAND   P.J. Berkery 8 (Lansdowne); R.E. Roche (4) (Galwegians), A.J.F. O'Reilly 12 (Old Belvedere), *N.J. Henderson 29 (NIFC), A.C. Pedlow 15 (CIYMS); J.W. Kyle 40 (NIFC), A.A. Mulligan 6 (London Irish); J.I. Brennan (2) (CIYMS), R. Roe (21) (London Irish), B.G.M. Wood 10 (Garryowen), T.E. Reid (12) (London Irish), J.R. Brady (12) (CIYMS), J.R. Kavanagh 15 (Wanderers), H.S. O'Connor (4) (Dublin U.), P.J.A. O'Sullivan 4 (Galwegians).

Referee J.A.S. Taylor (Scotland)

ENGLAND v SCOTLAND   60/475

16 March 1957
Twickenham
England 16 (2G, 1T, 1PG) Scotland 3 (1PG)

England   T: Davies, Higgins, Thompson. C: Challis (2). PG: Challis.
Scotland   PG: Scotland.

England won their seventh Grand Slam, their thirteenth Triple Crown and their seventh Calcutta Cup triumph in a row. It was also roughly the half-way point in a notable period of ascendancy over Scotland: England winning 13 and drawing 4 of 19 matches. John Griffiths, in *The Book of English International Rugby*, noted that in their report of the match *The Times* employed the term 'Grand Slam', thus giving authorship to a now generally-accepted expression in rugby. The term, Grand Slam, is derived from the game of Bridge and means the winning of all tricks,

Jim Greenwood's Scotland XV which defeated France at Stade Colombes on 12 January 1957

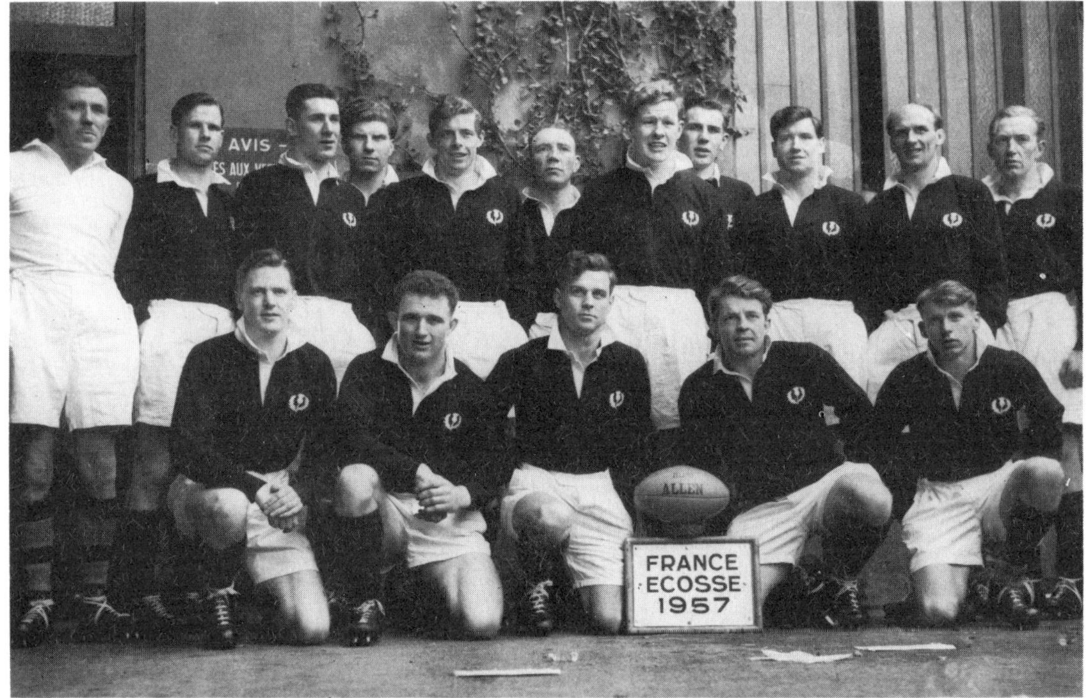

entirely appropriate in a rugby context. No one yet, as far as can be traced, has adopted another Bridge term, a Small Slam, meaning winning all but one trick – which could be an apposite term to differentiate between the Triple Crown and the winning of any three other Championship matches.

ENGLAND   R. Challis (3) (Bristol); P.B. Jackson 7 (Coventry), J. Butterfield 18 (Northampton), W.P.C. Davies 9 (Harlequins), P.H. Thompson 8 (Headingley); R.M. Bartlett 4 (Harlequins), R.E.G. Jeeps 5 (Northampton); C.R. Jacobs 8 (Northampton), *E. Evans 22 (Sale), G.W.D. Hastings 8 (Gloucester), J.D. Currie 8 (Oxford U.), R.W.D. Marques 8 (Cambridge U.), P.G.D. Robbins 8 (Oxford U.), R. Higgins 11 (Liverpool), A. Ashcroft 8 (Waterloo).

SCOTLAND   K.J.F. Scotland 4 (Heriot's FP); A.R. Smith 11 (Cambridge U.), T. McClung 5 (Edinburgh Acads), K.R. Macdonald (6) (Stewart's FP), J.L.F. Allan (2) (Cambridge U.); G.H. Waddell 1 (London Scottish), A.F. Dorward (14) (Gala); H.F. McLeod 16 (Hawick), R.K.G. MacEwan 11 (London Scottish), T. Elliot 11 (Gala), E.J.S. Michie (14) (London Scottish), J.W.Y. Kemp 13 (Glasgow HSFP), G.K. Smith 2 (Kelso), A. Robson 13 (Hawick), *J.T. Greenwood 12 (Perthshire Acads).

Referee R. Mitchell (Ireland)

FRANCE   M. Vannier 15 (RCF); J. Dupuy 8 (S. Tarbes), M. Prat 20 (FC Lourdes), A. Boniface 11 (S. Mont-de-Marsan) C. Darrouy 3 (S. Mont-de-Marsan); J. Bouquet 9 (CS Vienne), G. Dufau (30) (RCF); A. Domenech 14 (CA Brive), R. Vigier 6 (AS Montferrand), A. Sanac (7) (US Perpignan), *M. Celaya 16 (Biarritz Ol), M. Hoche (3) (PUC), F. Moncla 3 (RCF), J. Carrère 3 (RC Vichy), J. Barthe 8 (FC Lourdes).

WALES   T.J. Davies 8 (Llanelli); R. Williams (2) (Llanelli), G. Powell (2) (Ebbw Vale), G.T. Wells 4 (Cardiff), G. Howells (4) (Llanelli); C.I. Morgan 23 (Cardiff), L.H. Williams 3 (Cardiff); R. Prosser 6 (Pontypool), B.V. Meredith 15 (London Welsh), C.H. Morgan (2) (Llanelli), R.H. Williams 13 (Llanelli), *J.R.G. Stephens (30) (Neath), R.J. Robins (13) (Pontypridd), R.H. Davies 3 (London Welsh), J. Faull 2 (Swansea).

Referee Dr P.F. Cooper (England)

FRANCE v WALES   28/476

23 March 1957
Stade Colombes, Paris
Wales 19 (2G, 2T, 1PG) France 13 (2G, 1T)

France   T: Dupuy, Prat, Sanac. C: Bouquet (2).
Wales   T: Prosser, Howells, Faull, Meredith. C: Terry Davies (2). PG: Terry Davies.

This was Wales's third victory in a row in France, and their sixth overall. The four-try haul too was their biggest in France to date and has been bettered on only one other occasion – when the 1975 side scored five. The match, however, signified the end of Wales's dominance in France. They were not to win there again until 1971 and the 1975 triumph is their only other victory in 24 years.

MURRAYFIELD Scotland beat France 11-9 · TWICKENHAM England drew Wales 3-3
CARDIFF Wales beat Scotland 8-3 · TWICKENHAM England beat Ireland 6-0
PARIS England beat France 14-0 · DUBLIN Ireland beat Scotland 12-6
DUBLIN Wales beat Ireland 9-6 · MURRAYFIELD Scotland drew England 3-3
CARDIFF France beat Wales 16-6 · PARIS France beat Ireland 11-6

CHAMPIONSHIP TABLE
England – Championship

									Tries	
Pos	Country	P	W	D	L	F	A	Pts	F	A
1	England (1)	4	2	2	0	26	6	6	5	0
2	Wales (2)	4	2	1	1	26	28	5	6	4
3	France (5)	4	2	0	2	36	37	4	4	6
4	Scotland (4)	4	1	1	2	23	32	3	4	5
5	Ireland (3)	4	1	0	3	24	32	2	3	7

There were many changes to the Laws during this season, which included allowing near-foot heeling by the hooker and decreeing that it was no longer necessary for the ball to be played with the foot after a tackle. Both had the object of speeding up the game and making it more fluid. But, as ever, changes do not always have the desired effect and it was one of the game's basic skills, so often overlooked by reformers, the art of tackling and defending, which was the feature of the Championship. England provided indisputable evidence of this in winning the title with two wins and two draws, in the process of which their defence was impeccable for it conceded but two penalty goals.

The Championship also lost one of its great characters in Jackie Kyle, the evergreen Irish fly-half. He played his forty-second and final match in a 12-6 victory over Scotland – Ireland's only win of the season – which left Noel Henderson alone to carry his country's veteran status. Arthur Smith, uniquely endowed with the ability to change pace at speed, became Scotland's new captain, but even with the potentially high-class half-back partnership of Tremayne Rodd and Gordon Waddell, the Scots still found winning difficult.

The most significant event of the season, however, was France's remarkable improvement. Outclassed by England, they made six changes and went to Cardiff to score their first ever win in Wales. An indication of their transformation was that it remains their highest winning margin against the Welsh. Maurice Prat, their veteran centre, retired after the next match, and with Lucien Miàs back in the side after an enforced absence, the end of the 1958 season signalled the beginning the great French assault on the Championship.

SCOTLAND v FRANCE 28/477

11 January 1958
Murrayfield
Scotland 11 (1G, 1T, 1PG) France 9 (1T, 2PG)

Scotland T: Stevenson, Hastie. C: Chisholm. PG: Chisholm.
France T: Dupuy. PG: Vannier (2).

This defeat meant that France had lost five Championship games in a row and had not won a match since beating England 14-9 on 14 April 1956. It was Scotland's third successive win over France, though it was to be their only victory of the season.

SCOTLAND R.W.T. Chisholm 7 (Melrose); *A.R. Smith 12 (Cambridge U.), G.D. Stevenson 3 (Hawick), J.T. Docherty 4 (Glasgow HSFP), J.S. Swan (16) (Leicester); G.H. Waddell 2 (Devonport Services), J.A.T. Rodd 1 (US Portsmouth); H.F. McLeod 17 (Hawick), N.S. Bruce 1 (Blackheath), I.R. Hastie 2 (Kelso), M.W. Swan 1 (Oxford U.), J.W.Y. Kemp 14 (Glasgow HSFP),

G.K. Smith 3 (Kelso), M.A. Robertson (1) (Gala), J.T. Greenwood 13 (Perthshire Acads).

FRANCE   M. Vannier 16 (RCF); G. Mauduy 1 (CA Périgueux), A. Boniface 12 (S. Mont-de-Marsan), J. Bouquet 10 (CS Vienne), J. Dupuy 9 (S. Tarbes); C. Vignes 1 (RCF), P. Danos 1 (AS Béziers); A. Domenech 15 (CA Brive), R. Vigier 7 (AS Montferrand), A. Quaglio 1 (SC Mazamet), L. Miâs 14 (SC Mazamet), *M. Celaya 17 (Biarritz Ol), M. Crauste 1 (RCF), J. Carrère 4 (RC Toulon), J. Barthe 9 (FC Lourdes).

Referee L.M. Boundy (England)

ENGLAND v WALES   62/478

18 January 1958
Twickenham
England 3 (1T) Wales 3 (1PG)

England   T: Thompson.
Wales   PG: Terry Davies.

The famed and talented centre partnership of Jeff Butterfield and Phil Davies ended in this match when Davies played his last game. They had played together in mid-field in nine Championship matches since 1953, and the partnership could have continued but for the 'intervention' of Pat Quinn and Lewis Cannell. Davies's last game coincided with the first appearance for England of Phil Horrocks-Taylor, who had to wait until 1961 for his second cap, and then only because of an injury to Richard Sharp.

Wales played in plain red jerseys; their emblem had been 'overlooked' by the manufacturers. Bill Clement, secretary of the WRU, spotted the omission as he handed out the jerseys in the changing-room. 'It was amazing,' said Clement, 'I don't think anyone realized they were plain jerseys before, during or after the match.' However, the Welsh badge was not the only thing missing at Twickenham that day. During the night after the match Welsh souvenir hunters returned to the ground in search of a trophy. They left with a sizeable chunk of the cross-bar over which Terry Davies's match-saving penalty had crossed.

ENGLAND   D.F. Allison 6 (Coventry); P.B. Jackson 8 (Coventry), J. Butterfield 19 (Northampton), W.P.C. Davies (10) (Harlequins), P.H. Thompson 9 (Headingley); J.P. Horrocks-Taylor 1 (Cambridge U.), R.E.G. Jeeps 6 (Northampton); C.R. Jacobs 9 (Northampton), *E. Evans 23 (Sale), G.W.D. Hastings 9 (Gloucester), R.W.D. Marques 9 (Cambridge U.), J.D. Currie 9 (Oxford U.), P.G.D. Robbins 9 (Oxford U.), R.E. Syrett 1 (Wasps), A. Ashcroft 9 (Waterloo).

WALES   T.J. Davies 9 (Llanelli); J.R. Collins 1 (Aberavon), M.C. Thomas 21 (Newport), C.H.A. Davies 2 (Llanelli), G.T. Wells 5 (Cardiff); C.I. Morgan 24 (Cardiff), L.H. Willliams 4 (Cardiff); R. Prosser 7 (Pontypool), B.V. Meredith 16 (Newport), D. Devereux 1 (Neath), R.H. Williams 14 (Llanelli), W.R. Evans 1 (Cardiff), *R.C.C. Thomas 17 (Swansea), H.J. Morgan 1 (Abertillery), J. Faull 3 (Swansea).

Referee R.C. Williams (Ireland)

WALES v SCOTLAND   62/479

1 February 1958
Cardiff Arms Park
Wales 8 (1G, 1T) Scotland 3 (1PG)

Wales   T: Wells, Collins. C: Terry Davies.
Scotland   PG: Arthur Smith.

Scotland were not only finding winning at Cardiff difficult, but scoring as well. Arthur Smith's penalty goal brought their total to a miserly 12 points from the 7 games played in Wales since they last achieved a respectable score, 13-6 in 1937.

WALES   T.J. Davies 10 (Llanelli); J.R. Collins 2 (Aberavon), M.C. Thomas 22 (Newport), C.H.A. Davies 3 (Llanelli), G.T. Wells (6) (Cardiff); C.I. Morgan 25 (Cardiff), L.H. Williams 5 (Cardiff); R. Prosser 8 (Pontypool), B.V. Meredith 17 (Newport), D. Devereux (2) (Neath), R.H. Williams 15 (Llanelli), W.R. Evans 2 (Cardiff), *R.C.C. Thomas 18 (Swansea), H.J. Morgan 2 (Abertillery), J. Faull 4 (Swansea).

SCOTLAND   R.W.T. Chisholm 8 (Melrose); *A.R. Smith 13 (Cambridge U.), G.D. Stevenson 4 (Hawick), J.T. Docherty 5 (Glasgow HSFP), T.G. Weatherstone 9 (Stewart's FP); G.H. Waddell 3 (Devonport Services), J.A.T. Rodd 2 (US Portsmouth); H.F. McLeod 18 (Hawick), R.K.G. MacEwan (12) (Lansdowne), T. Elliot 12 (Gala),

M.W. Swan 2 (Oxford U.), J.W.Y. Kemp 15 (Glasgow HSFP), G.K. Smith 4 (Kelso), A. Robson 14 (Hawick), J.T. Greenwood 14 (Perthshire Acads).

Referee Dr N.M. Parkes (England)

ENGLAND v IRELAND 62/480

8 February 1958
Twickenham
England 6 (1T, 1PG) Ireland 0

England   T: Ashcroft. PG: Hetherington.

Ireland, who had just toppled the Australian touring side, played the same team at Twickenham. However, with six members, including five of the pack, new to Championship rugby the issue though close was never in doubt. Several very famous Irish players made their début appearances, including Ronnie Dawson, Bill Mulcahy and Noel Murphy, while England introduced two highly-promising new backs, Malcolm Phillips and John Young, and a full-back in Jim Hetherington who many considered would prove the most accomplished in the position since the War.

ENGLAND   J.G.G. Hetherington 1 (North-ampton); J.R.C. Young 1 (Oxford U.), J. Butterfield 20 (Northampton), M.S. Phillips 1 (Oxford U.), P.H. Thompson 10 (Headingley); R.M. Bartlett 5 (Harlequins), R.E.G. Jeeps 7 (Northampton); C.R. Jacobs 10 (Northampton), *E. Evans 24 (Sale), G.W.D. Hastings 10 (Glouce-ster), R.W.D. Marques 10 (Cambridge U.), J.D. Currie 10 (Oxford U.), P.G.D. Robbins 10 (Oxford U.), R.E. Syrett 2 (Wasps), A. Ashcroft 10 (Waterloo).

IRELAND   P.J. Berkery 9 (London Irish); A.J.F. O'Reilly 13 (Old Belvedere), *N.J. Henderson 30 (NIFC), D. Hewitt 1 (Queen's U. Belfast), A.C. Pedlow 16 (CIYMS); J.W. Kyle 41 (NIFC), A.A. Mulligan 7 (London Irish); P.J. O'Donoghue 8 (Bective Rangers), A.R. Dawson 1 (Wanderers), B.G.M. Wood 11 (Garryowen), J.B. Stevenson 1 (Instonians), W.A. Mulcahy 1 (UC Dublin), J.A. Donaldson 1 (Belfast Collegians), N.A.A. Murphy 1 (Cork Constitution), J.R. Kavanagh 16 (Wanderers).

Referee G. Burrell (Scotland)

FRANCE v ENGLAND 29/481

1 March 1958
Stade Colombes, Paris
England 14 (1G, 2T, 1PG) France 0

England   T: Thompson (2), Jackson. C: Hastings. PG: Hastings.

Not since their early Championship encounters had England handed France such a drubbing in Paris and that added to the fact that the French had now lost six Championship matches in a row had the crowd calling for the selectors' blood.

FRANCE   M. Vannier 17 (RCF); G. Mauduy 2 (CA Périgueux), A. Boniface 13 (S. Mont-de-Marsan), C. Vignes (2) (RCF), J. Dupuy 10 (S. Tarbes); J. Bouquet 11 (CS Vienne), P. Danos 2 (AS Béziers); A. Domenech 16 (CA Brive), R. Vigier 8 (AS Montferrand), A. Quaglio 2 (SC Mazamet), L. Miâs 15 (SC Mazamet), *M. Celaya 18 (Biarritz Ol), M. Crauste 2 (RCF), H. Domec 12 (FC Lourdes), J. Barthe 10 (FC Lourdes).

ENGLAND   J.S.M. Scott (1) (Oxford U.); P.B. Jackson 9 (Coventry), J. Butterfield 21 (North-ampton), M.S. Phillips 2 (Oxford U.), P.H. Thompson 11 (Headingley); R.M. Bartlett 6 (Harlequins), R.E.G. Jeeps 8 (Northampton); C.R. Jacobs 11 (Northampton), *E. Evans 25 (Sale), G.W.D. Hastings 11 (Gloucester), R.W.D. Marques 11 (Cambridge U.), J.D. Currie 11 (Oxford U.), A.J. Herbert 1 (Wasps), R.E. Syrett 3 (Wasps), A. Ashcroft 11 (Waterloo).

Referee W.J. Evans (Wales)

IRELAND v SCOTLAND 64/482

1 March 1958
Lansdowne Road, Dublin
Ireland 12 (2T, 2PG) Scotland 6 (2T)

Ireland   T: Pedlow (2). PG: Henderson, Berkery.
Scotland   T: Smith, Weatherstone.

This was Ireland's ninth successive home victory over Scotland, their best ever sequence against the Scots – which was something for

Jackie Kyle, playing his forty-second and final Championship match, to savour. The irrepressible Kyle, often brilliant, occasionally erratic, had been an Irish regular since the resumption of the Championship in 1947. He played in 11 matches against Scotland and was on the winning side each time. On one of the two occasions Kyle did not play against the Scots, 1955, Ireland were beaten.

IRELAND   P.J. Berkery (10) (London Irish); A.C. Pedlow 17 (CIYMS), D. Hewitt 2 (Queen's U. Belfast), *N.J. Henderson 31 (NIFC), A.J.F. O'Reilly 14 (Old Belvedere); J.W. Kyle (42) (NIFC), A.A. Mulligan 8 (Wanderers); P.J. O'Donoghue 9 (Bective Rangers), A.R. Dawson 2 (Wanderers), B.G.M. Wood 12 (Garryowen), J.B. Stevenson 2 (Instonians), W.A. Mulcahy 2 (UC Dublin), J.A. Donaldson 2 (Belfast Collegians), N.A.A. Murphy 2 (Cork Constitution), J.R. Kavanagh 17 (Wanderers).

SCOTLAND   R.W.T. Chisholm (9) (Melrose); *A.R. Smith 14 (Gosforth), G.D. Stevenson 5 (Hawick), J.T. Docherty 6 (Glasgow HSFP), T.G. Weatherstone 10 (Stewart's FP); G.H. Waddell 4 (Devonport Services), J.A.T. Rodd 3 (US Portsmouth); H.F. McLeod 19 (Hawick), N.S. Bruce 2 (Blackheath), T. Elliot (13) (Gala), M.W. Swan 3 (Oxford U.), J.W.Y. Kemp 16 (Glasgow HSFP), D.C. Macdonald 3 (Edinburgh U.), A. Robson 15 (Hawick), J.T. Greenwood 15 (Perthshire Acads).

Referee W.N. Gillmore (England)

IRELAND v WALES   60/483

15 March 1958
Lansdowne Road, Dublin
Wales 9 (3T) Ireland 6 (1T, 1PG)

Ireland   T: O'Meara. PG: Henderson.
Wales   T: Haydn Morgan, Meredith, Roberts.

Wales pulled off their fourth win in the last five visits to Ireland with three late tries. Ireland, however, were decidedly unlucky to lose their vastly experienced scrum-half, John O'Meara, who was injured 20 minutes from time. O'Meara, along with four others, never played for Ireland again. O'Meara possessed a long, quick pass and its value to fly-halves, particu-

larly Jackie Kyle, in giving that extra yard of room against the tight, close-up defences of the day, was immeasurable.

IRELAND   J.G.M.W. Murphy (4) (London Irish); S.V.J. Quinlan (4) (Blackrock College), *N.J. Henderson 32 (NIFC), A.J.F. O'Reilly 15 (Old Belvedere), A.C. Pedlow 18 (CIYMS); M.A.F. English 1 (Bohemians), J.A. O'Meara (20) (Dolphin); P.J. O'Donoghue (10) (Bective Rangers), A.R. Dawson 3 (Wanderers), B.G.M. Wood 13 (Garryowen), J.B. Stevenson 3 (Instonians), W.A. Mulcahy 3 (UC Dublin), J.A. Donaldson (3) (Belfast Collegians), N.A.A. Murphy 3 (Cork Constitution), J.R. Kavanagh 18 (Wanderers).

WALES   A.J. Priday 1 (Cardiff); C. Roberts 1 (Neath), M.C. Thomas 23 (Newport), C.H.A. Davies 4 (Llanelli), H. Nicholls (1) (Cardiff); C.I. Morgan 26 (Cardiff), L.H. Williams 6 (Cardiff); R. Prosser 9 (Pontypool), B.V. Meredith 18 (Newport), J.D. Evans 1 (Cardiff), W.R. Evans 3 (Cardiff), R.H. Williams 16 (Llanelli), *R.C.C. Thomas 19 (Swansea), H.J. Morgan 3 (Abertillery), J. Faull 5 (Swansea).

Referee Dr N.M. Parkes (England)

SCOTLAND v ENGLAND   61/484

15 March 1958
Murrayfield
Scotland 3 (1PG) England 3 (1PG)

Scotland   PG: Elliot.
England   PG: Hastings.

George Hastings, the Gloucester prop who saved England from defeat with a late penalty goal, did not play for his country again. Neither did Eric Evans, the captain, Allison, the competent Coventry full-back, or Ricky Bartlett, the tricky little Harlequins fly-half. The emergence of Bev Risman, brilliant Manchester University youngster, was the prime factor in the discarding of Bartlett. Many considered the Harlequin badly treated particularly as he had played a major part in six victories England achieved while he was in the side. The only blemish in Bartlett's career was this draw in his seventh and final match.

SCOTLAND   K.J.F. Scotland 5 (Heriot's FP); C. Elliot 1 (Langholm), G.D. Stevenson 6 (Hawick),

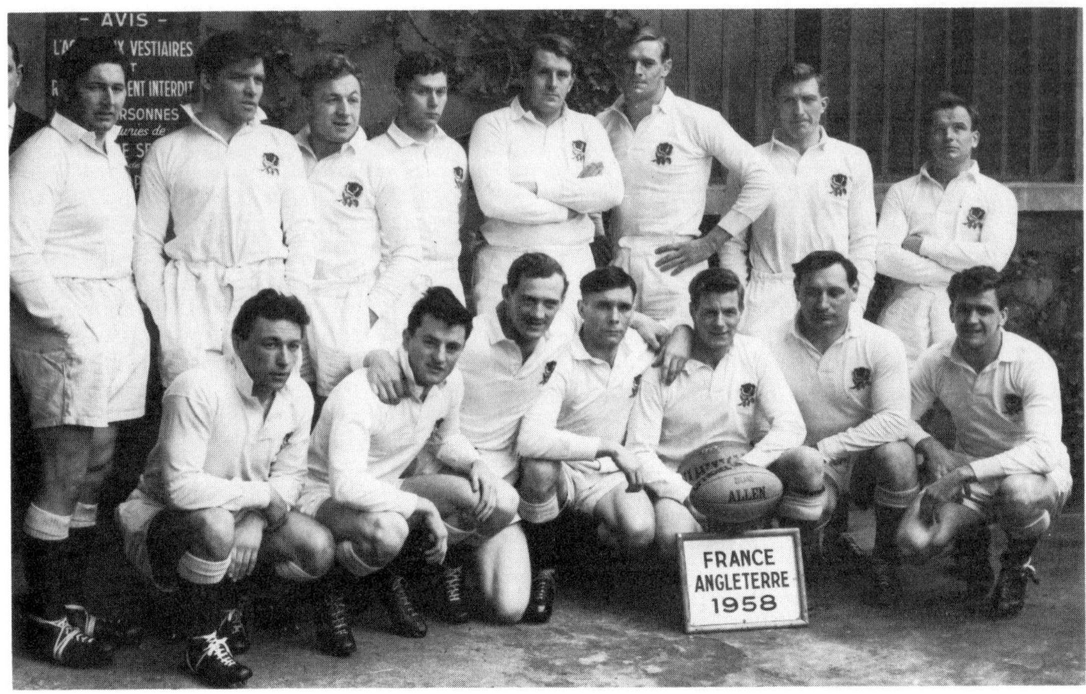

France were clearly outclassed by this England XV at Stade Colombes on 1 March 1958

J.T. Docherty (7) (Glasgow HSFP), T.G. Weatherstone 11 (Stewart's FP); G.H. Waddell 5 (Devonport Services), J.A.T. Rodd 4 (US Portsmouth); H.F. McLeod 20 (Hawick), N.S. Bruce 3 (Blackheath), I.R. Hastie 3 (Kelso), M.W. Swan 4 (London Scottish), J.W.Y. Kemp 17 (Glasgow HSFP), D.C. Macdonald (4) (Edinburgh U.), A. Robson 16 (Hawick), *J.T. Greenwood 16 (Perthshire Acads).

ENGLAND D.F. Allison (7) (Coventry); P.B. Jackson 10 (Coventry), J. Butterfield 22 (Northampton), M.S. Phillips 3 (Oxford U.), P.H. Thompson 12 (Headingley); R.M. Bartlett (7) (Harlequins), R.E.G. Jeeps 9 (Northampton); C.R. Jacobs 12 (Northampton), *E. Evans (26) (Sale), G.W.D. Hastings (12) (Gloucester), R.W.D. Marques 12 (Cambridge U.), J.D. Currie 12 (Oxford U.), P.G.D. Robbins 11 (Oxford U.), A. J. Herbert 2 (Wasps), A. Ashcroft 12 (Waterloo).

Referee R.C. Williams (Ireland)

WALES v FRANCE 29/485

29 March 1958
Cardiff Arms Park
France 16 (2G, 2DG) Wales 6 (1T, 1PG)

Wales T: Collins. PG: Davies.
France T: Danos, Tarricq. C: Labazuy (2). DG: Vannier (2).

France's first win at Cardiff was also their highest winning margin against Wales. It was all the more remarkable for the fact that in their previous Championship match France had been humbled 0-14 by England. Having dispelled the Arms Park bogey France experienced a spectacular run, beating Italy, Ireland, drawing with and beating South Africa in South Africa before going through 1959 unbeaten until losing to Ireland in Dublin. Wales were understandably shell-shocked by the role reversal. They had won 24 of the previous 28 matches against the French and the only matches they had lost were by narrow margins. Now, even with flitting geniuses like Cliff Morgan and Carywn James in their side, they did not have the flair to match the dazzling French players. 'We were outplayed,' James admitted later, 'and we all knew, I think that there was much, much more to come. It was a bad day for Wales but a great day for rugby football.'

WALES   T.J. Davies 11 (Llanelli); C. Roberts (2) (Neath), M.C. Thomas 24 (Newport), C.R. James (1) (Llanelli), J.R. Collins 3 (Aberavon); C.I. Morgan (27) (Cardiff), L.H. Williams 7 (Cardiff); R. Prosser 10 (Pontypool), G. Beckingham (3) (Cardiff), J.D. Evans (2) (Cardiff), W.R. Evans 4 (Cardiff), R.H. Williams 17 (Llanelli), *R.C.C. Thomas 20 (Swansea), H.J. Morgan 4 (Abertillery), J. Faull 6 (Swansea).

FRANCE   M. Vannier 18 (RCF); H. Rancoule 3 (FC Lourdes), M. Prat 21 (FC Lourdes), R. Martine 10 (FC Lourdes), P. Tarricq 1 (FC Lourdes); A. Labazuy 5 (FC Lourdes), P. Danos 3 (AS Béziers); A. Roques 1 (S. Cahors), R. Vigier 9 (AS Montferrand), A. Quaglio 3 (SC Mazamet), L. Miâs 16 (SC Mazamet), *M. Celaya 19 (Biarritz Ol), M. Crauste 3 (RCF), H. Domec 13 (FC Lourdes), J. Barthe 11 (FC Lourdes).

Referee A.I. Dickie (Scotland)

A. Quaglio 4 (SC Mazamet), R. Vigier 10 (AS Montferrand), A. Roques 2 (S. Cahors), *L. Miâs 17 (SC Mazamet), B. Mommejat 1 (S. Cahors), H. Domec (14) (FC Lourdes), M. Crauste 4 (RCF), J. Barthe 12 (FC Lourdes).

IRELAND   D.C. Glass 1 (Belfast Collegians); A.C. Pedlow 19 (CIYMS), *N.J. Henderson 33 (NIFC), D. Hewitt 3 (Queen's U. Belfast), A.J.F. O'Reilly 16 (Old Belvedere); M.A.F. English 2 (Limerick Bohemians), A.A. Mulligan 9 (Wanderers); S. Millar 1 (Ballymena), A.R. Dawson 4 (Wanderers), B.G.M. Wood 14 (Garryowen), W.A. Mulcahy 4 (Bective Rangers), J.B. Stevenson (4) (Instonians), E.L. Brown (1) (Instonians), N.A.A. Murphy 4 (Cork Constitution), T. McGrath 2 (Garryowen).

Referee Dr N.M. Parkes (England)

FRANCE v IRELAND   29/486

19 April 1958
Stade Colombes, Paris
France 11 (1G, 1DG, 1PG) Ireland 6 (2PG)

France   T: Danos. C: Labazuy. DG: Vannier. PG: Labazuy.
Ireland   PG: Henderson (2).

Maurice Prat made his twenty-second and final Championship appearance in the same match that Syd Millar made his first for Ireland. Prat was a fine, resourceful player but tended to be overshadowed by his more famous brother, Jean, who had retired in 1955. Millar went on to make 33 Championship appearances and earned a reputation as one of the finest loose-head props produced by Ireland, whom he also coached when he retired.

FRANCE   M. Vannier 19 (RCF); H. Rancoule 4 (FC Lourdes), M. Prat (22) (FC Lourdes), R. Martine 11 (FC Lourdes), P. Tarricq (2) (FC Lourdes); A. Labazuy 6 (FC Lourdes), P. Danos 4 (AS Béziers);

1959

PARIS France beat Scotland 9-0 · CARDIFF Wales beat England 5-0
MURRAYFIELD Scotland beat Wales 6-5 · DUBLIN England beat Ireland 3-0
TWICKENHAM England drew France 3-3 · MURRAYFIELD Ireland beat Scotland 8-3
CARDIFF Wales beat Ireland 8-6 · TWICKENHAM England drew Scotland 3-3
PARIS France beat Wales 11-3 · DUBLIN Ireland beat France 9-5

CHAMPIONSHIP TABLE
France – Championship

Pos	Country	P	W	D	L	F	A	Pts	Tries F	A
1	France (3)	4	2	1	1	28	15	5	4	1
2	Ireland (5)	4	2	0	2	23	19	4	3	3
3	Wales (2)	4	2	0	2	21	23	4	4	4
4	England (1)	4	1	2	1	9	11	4	0	1
5	Scotland (4)	4	1	1	2	12	25	3	1	3

France won the title for the first time, and although it was achieved without the full extent of attacking brilliance that was to be the hallmark of their future play, the signs were there for all to see. Powerful, disciplined forwards who could run and handle and who could support and vary their ploys were impossible to counter by the more orthodox approach of the other countries. It was quite some achievement that England held the French to 3-3 and that Ireland outwitted them in their last match.

Lucien Miàs, the founder figure of modern French rugby

By this time France were already assured of the title, and possibly Lucien Miâs, the architect of their emergence, found motivation difficult to instil in this his final Championship appearance.

England's fate made an interesting contrast. It was the only time that they failed to score a try in a Championship season, and their 9 points' aggregate was their lowest for 58 years and only 6 points more than their worst ever total of 1899. England's new captain was Jeff Butterfield, and it was one of the ironies of the Championship that one of the great proponents of a fluent, expansive game, should have been leader of an English side with brilliant attacking potential, which floundered and were frustrated. By the end of the season nine Englishmen had played their last Championship match, including Butterfield himself, the high-scoring Phil Thompson, Alan Ashcroft and Gordon Bendon.

The expulsion of Bendon, who had played four matches only, puzzled contemporaries. In retrospect it was amazing because the Wasps tight-prop was one of the strongest, technically soundest of his time. Even today, props who played against Bendon talk of him with awe and respect. Noel Henderson played his last season for Ireland as a makeshift full-back, and he contributed as much as anyone in their two victories, over Scotland and France. Another veteran whose last season it was, was Wales's Malcolm Thomas. In Scotland it was also farewell to Greenwood and Weatherstone as the Scots finished with the Wooden Spoon yet again. In the final analysis, however, the 1959 season was significant not for the departure of so many top players or the long-awaited French victory, it was the Championship's nadir in terms of points and tries – the 93 points and 12 tries were the lowest ever aggregates when five countries competed.

FRANCE v SCOTLAND 29/487

10 January 1959
Stade Colombes, Paris
France 9 (1T, 2DG) Scotland 0

France T: Moncla. DG: Lacaze (2).

This was the first international to be refereed by Gwynne Walters. The diminuitive, dapper Welshman went on to officiate at a record 19 Championship matches in which he won the respect of both players and spectators because he tried to promote fast and flowing matches. Gentle rebukes accompanied by a smile were regarded as flaws by some of his critics; but Walters abhorred dirty play and he was a strict disciplinarian whenever villainy reared its ugly head.

FRANCE   P. Lacaze 1 (FC Lourdes); J. Dupuy 11 (S. Tarbes), A. Marquesuzaa 1 (RCF), J. Bouquet 12 (CS Vienne), H. Rancoule 5 (FC Lourdes); A. Labazuy 7 (FC Lourdes), P. Danos 5 (AS Béziers); A. Quaglio 5 (SC Mazamet), R. Vigier 11 (AS Montferrand), A. Roques 3 (S. Cahors), *L. Miâs 18 (SC Mazamet), B. Mommejat 2 (S. Cahors), F. Moncla 4 (RCF), M. Celaya 20 (Biarritz Ol), J. Barthe 13 (FC Lourdes).

SCOTLAND   K.J.F. Scotland 6 (Cambridge U.); A.R. Smith 15 (Gosforth), T. McClung 6 (Edinburgh Acads), I.H.P. Laughland 1 (London Scottish), C. Elliot 2 (Langholm); G.H. Waddell 6 (Cambridge U.), S. Coughtrie 1 (Edinburgh Acads); H.F. McLeod 21 (Hawick), N.S. Bruce 4 (Blackheath), I.R. Hastie 4 (Kelso), M.W. Swan 5 (London Scottish), J.W.Y. Kemp 18 (Glasgow HSFP), G.K. Smith 5 (Kelso), A. Robson 17 (Hawick), *J.T. Greenwood 17 (Perthshire Acads).

Referee D.G. Walters (Wales)

WALES v ENGLAND 63/488

17 January 1959
Cardiff Arms Park
Wales 5 (1G) England 0

Wales T: Bebb. C: Terry Davies.

There were 13 players new to international rugby and one of them, Dewi Bebb, joined the select band of players to score a try on his début. It was also Wales's first try scored against England at Cardiff for ten years. Conditions were appalling: heavy rain lay in pools and many parts of the ground were inches deep in mud.

WALES   T.J. Davies 12 (Llanelli); J.R. Collins 4 (Aberavon), H.J. Davies 1 (Cambridge U.), M.J.

Price 1 (Pontypool), D.I.E. Bebb 1 (Carmarthen Training College); C. Ashton 1 (Aberavon), L.H. Williams 8 (Cardiff); R. Prosser 11 (Pontypool), B.V. Meredith 19 (Newport), D.R. Main 1 (London Welsh), I. Ford 1 (Newport), R.H. Williams 18 (Llanelli), *R.C.C. Thomas 21 (Swansea), J. Leleu 1 (London Welsh), J. Faull 7 (Swansea).

ENGLAND   J.G.G. Hetherington 2 (Northampton); P.B. Jackson 11 (Coventry), M.S. Phillips 4 (Oxford U.), *J. Butterfield 23 (Northampton), P.H. Thompson 13 (Waterloo); A.B.W. Risman 1 (Manchester U.), S.R. Smith 1 (Cambridge U.); St L.H. Webb 1 (Bedford), J.A.S. Wackett 1 (Rosslyn Park), G.J. Bendon 1 (Wasps), J.D. Currie 13 (Harlequins), R.W.D. Marques 13 (Harlequins), A.J. Herbert 3 (Wasps), R. Higgins (12) (Liverpool), B.J. Wightman 1 (Moseley).

Referee R.C. Williams (Ireland)

SCOTLAND v WALES   63/489

7 February 1959
Murrayfield
Scotland 6 (1T, 1PG) Wales 5 (1G)

Scotland   T: Bruce. PG: Scotland.
Wales   T: Price. C: Terry Davies.

'Feet, feet, Scotland' had long been the Murrayfield battle cry, but never was the response from the forwards more devastating than in this match. From close to their own line the Scots tore away in a headlong, unstoppable and controlled dribble which ended after about 70 yards with a pick-up by Gordon Waddell, who quickly passed to Norman Bruce to climax Scotland's demonstrably best tactic with a corner flag try.

SCOTLAND   K.J.F. Scotland 7 (Cambridge U.); A.R. Smith 16 (Gosforth), T. McClung 7 (Edinburgh Acads), G.D. Stevenson 7 (Hawick), T.G. Weatherstone 12 (Stewart's FP); G.H. Waddell 7 (Cambridge U.), S. Coughtrie 2 (Edinburgh Acads); H.F. McLeod 22 (Hawick), N.S. Bruce 5 (Blackheath), I.R. Hastie 5 (Kelso), M.W. Swan 6 (London Scottish), J.W.Y. Kemp 19 (Glasgow HSFP), G.K. Smith 6 (Kelso), A. Robson 18 (Hawick), *J.T. Greenwood 18 (Perthshire Acads).

WALES   T.J. Davies 13 (Llanelli); J.R. Collins 5 (Aberavon), H.J. Davies (2) (Cambridge U.), M.J. Price 2 (Pontypool), D.I.E. Bebb 2 (Carmarthen Training College); C. Ashton 2 (Aberavon), L.H. Williams 9 (Cardiff); R. Prosser 12 (Pontypool), B.V. Meredith 20 (Newport), D.R. Main 2 (London Welsh), R.H. Williams 19 (Llanelli), I. Ford (2) (Newport), *R.C.C. Thomas 22 (Swansea), J. Leleu 2 (London Welsh), J. Faull 8 (Swansea).

Referee R.C. Williams (Ireland)

IRELAND v ENGLAND   63/490

14 February 1959
Lansdowne Road, Dublin
England 3 (1PG) Ireland 0

England   PG: Risman.

The fourth match in a row that Ireland failed to score against England, which was a sour reward for the efforts of their rampaging pack of forwards. There was much newspaper criticism of the failure of the Irish backs; many overlooked the fact that Butterfield and Phillips hardly missed a tackle, and that Jeeps played a resourceful tactical game behind a beaten pack.

IRELAND   N.J. Henderson 34 (NIFC); N.H. Brophy 3 (UC Dublin), A.J.F. O'Reilly 17 (Old Belvedere), J.F. Dooley 1 (Galwegians), A.C. Pedlow 20 (CIYMS), M.A.F. English 3 (Bohemians), A.A. Mulligan 10 (London Irish); B.G.M. Wood 15 (Garryowen), *A.R. Dawson 5 (Wanderers), S. Millar 2 (Ballymena), W.A. Mulcahy 5 (UC Dublin), M.G. Culliton 1 (Wanderers), N.A.A. Murphy 5 (Cork Constitution), J.R. Kavanagh 19 (Wanderers), P.J.A. O'Sullivan 5 (Galwegians).

ENGLAND   J.G.G. Hetherington 3 (Northampton); P.B. Jackson 12 (Coventry), M.S. Phillips 5 (Oxford U.), *J. Butterfield 24 (Northampton), P.H. Thompson 14 (Waterloo); A.B.W. Risman 2 (Manchester U.), R.E.G. Jeeps 10 (Northampton); St L.H. Webb 2 (Bedford), J.A.S. Wackett (2) (Rosslyn Park), G.J. Bendon 2 (Wasps), J.D. Currie 14 (Harlequins), R.W.D. Marques 14 (Harlequins), A.J. Herbert 4 (Wasps), J.W. Clements 1 (Old Cranleighans), A. Ashcroft 13 (Waterloo).

Referee D.G. Walters (Wales)

ENGLAND v FRANCE   30/491

28 February 1959
Twickenham
England 3 (1PG) France 3 (1PG)

England   PG: Hetherington.
France   PG: Labazuy.

Although much was made of the dominance of the English pack and the superiority of their backs, this was the first time in 15 matches against France at Twickenham that England failed to score a try.

ENGLAND   J.G.G. Hetherington 4 (Northampton); P.B. Jackson 13 (Coventry), M.S. Phillips 6 (Oxford U.), *J. Butterfield 25 (Northampton), P.H. Thompson 15 (Waterloo); A.B.W. Risman 3 (Manchester U.), S.R. Smith 2 (Cambridge U.); St L.H. Webb 3 (Bedford), H.O. Godwin 1 (Coventry), G.J. Bendon 3 (Wasps), R.W.D. Marques 15 (Harlequins), J.D. Currie 15 (Harlequins), A.J. Herbert 5 (Wasps), J.W. Clements 2 (Old Cranleighans), A. Ashcroft 14 (Waterloo).

FRANCE   P. Lacaze 2 (FC Lourdes); C. Darrouy 4 (S. Mont-de-Marsan), A. Boniface 14 (S. Mont-de-Marsan), A. Marquesuzaa 2 (RCF), J. Dupuy 12 (S. Tarbes); A. Labazuy 8 (FC Lourdes), P. Danos 6 (AS Béziers); A. Quaglio 6 (SC Mazamet), R. Vigier 12 (AS Montferrand), A. Roques 4 (S. Cahors), M. Celaya 21 (Biarritz Ol), B. Mommejat 3 (S. Cahors), M. Crauste 5 (RCF), F. Moncla 5 (RCF), *J. Barthe 14 (FC Lourdes).

Referee R.C. Williams (Ireland)

SCOTLAND v IRELAND   65/492

28 February 1959
Murrayfield
Ireland 8 (1G, 1PG) Scotland 3 (1PG)

Scotland   PG: Scotland.
Ireland   T: Dooley. C: Hewitt. PG: Hewitt.

For a second match in a row at Murrayfield, Scotland had to be satisfied with the paltry return of just one penalty goal against Ireland.

The Scots were handicapped by an injury to Jim Greenwood, who played on after treatment with a dislocated shoulder. It was to be his nineteenth and final Championship match. After his distinguished playing days were over, Greenwood took up coaching, and he helped to produce some outstanding sides at Loughborough College where 15-man rugby became a byword.

SCOTLAND   K.J.F. Scotland 8 (Cambridge U.); A.R. Smith 17 (Ebbw Vale), T. McClung 8 (Edinburgh Wands), G.D. Stevenson 8 (Hawick), T.G. Weatherstone 13 (Stewart's FP); G.H. Waddell 8 (Cambridge U.), S. Coughtrie 3 (Edinburgh Acads); H.F. McLeod 23 (Hawick), N.S. Bruce 6 (Blackheath), I.R. Hastie (6) (Kelso), M.W. Swan (7) (London Scottish), J.W.Y. Kemp 20 (Glasgow HSFP), G.K. Smith 7 (Kelso), A. Robson 19 (Hawick), *J.T. Greenwood (19) (Perthshire Acads).

IRELAND   N.J. Henderson 35 (NIFC); N.H. Brophy 4 (UC Dublin), D. Hewitt 4 (Queen's U. Belfast), J.F. Dooley 2 (Galwegians), A.J.F. O'Reilly 18 (Old Belvedere); M.A.F. English 4 (Bohemians), A.A. Mulligan 11 (London Irish); B.G.M. Wood 16 (Garryowen), *A.R. Dawson 6 (Wanderers), S. Millar 3 (Ballymena), W.A. Mulcahy 6 (UC Dublin), M.G. Culliton 2 (Wanderers), N.A.A. Murphy 6 (Cork Constitution), J.R. Kavanagh 20 (Wanderers), P.J.A. O'Sullivan 6 (Galwegians).

Referee L.M. Boundy (England)

WALES v IRELAND   61/493

14 March 1959
Cardiff Arms Park
Wales 8 (1G, 1T) Ireland 6 (1T, 1PG)

Wales   T: Ashton, Price. C: Davies.
Ireland   T: O'Reilly. PG: David Hewitt.

Wales-Ireland matches had traditionally been keenly contested affairs, the issue usually being decided by one score. But few expected that the Welsh, 0-6 at half-time, could establish a lead over the Irish once again, particularly as the Irish forwards seemed to have gained full control. But a try by the chirpy Cliff Ashton gave the Welsh hope and five minutes from time another, by Malcolm Thomas, converted by

Terry Davies, frustrated the Irish yet again, to wreck effectively their chance of winning the Championship.

WALES   T.J. Davies 14 (Llanelli); J.R. Collins 6 (Aberavon), M.C. Thomas 25 (Newport), M.J. Price 3 (Pontypool), D.I.E. Bebb 3 (Swansea); C. Ashton 3 (Aberavon), L.H. Williams 10 (Cardiff); R. Prosser 13 (Pontypool), B.V. Meredith 21 (Newport), D.R. Main 3 (London Welsh), R.H. Williams 20 (Llanelli), D.J.E. Harris 1 (Pontypridd), *R.C.C. Thomas 23 (Swansea), H.J. Morgan 5 (Abertillery), J. Faull 9 (Swansea).

IRELAND   N.J. Henderson 36 (NIFC); A.J.F. O'Reilly 19 (Old Belvedere), J.F. Dooley (3) (Galwegians), D. Hewitt 5 (Queen's U. Belfast), N.H. Brophy 5 (UC Dublin); W.J. Hewitt (3) (Instonians), A.A. Mulligan 12 (London Irish); B.G.M. Wood 17 (Garryowen), *A.R. Dawson 7 (Wanderers), S. Millar 4 (Ballymena), W.A. Mulcahy 7 (UC Dublin), M.G. Culliton 3 (Wanderers), N.A.A. Murphy 7 (Cork Constitution), J.R. Kavanagh 21 (Wanderers), P.J.A. O'Sullivan 7 (Galwegians).

Referee G. Burrell (Scotland)

ENGLAND v SCOTLAND   62/494

21 March 1959
Twickenham
England 3 (1PG) Scotland 3 (1PG)

England   PG: Risman.
Scotland   PG: Scotland.

After six consecutive Twickenham victories over Scotland, England were held to a draw by a side which included four new caps, two of them menacingly large and raw-boned, David Rollo and Franz ten Bos. Jeff Butterfield, the Prince of English centres since the War, was one of the eight English players whose last match it was to be. Neither side could have been particularly happy about the absence of tries – England had not scored one since 1 March 1958, when they managed three against France, and for Scotland it was their third successive match at Twickenham without one.

ENGLAND   J.G.G. Hetherington (5) (Northampton); P.B. Jackson 14 (Coventry), M.S. Phillips 7 (Oxford U.), *J. Butterfield (26) (Northampton), P.H. Thompson (16) (Waterloo); A.B.W. Risman 4 (Manchester U.), S.R. Smith 3 (Cambridge U.); St L.H. Webb (4) (Bedford), H.O. Godwin 2 (Coventry), G.J. Bendon (4) (Wasps), R.W.D. Marques 16 (Harlequins), J.D. Currie 16 (Harlequins), A.J. Herbert (6) (Wasps), J.W. Clements (3) (Old Cranleighans), A. Ashcroft (15) (Waterloo).

SCOTLAND   K.J.F. Scotland 9 (Cambridge U.); A.R. Smith 18 (Ebbw Vale), J.A.P. Shackleton 1 (London Scottish), G.D. Stevenson 9 (Hawick), T.G. Weatherstone (14) (Stewart's FP); *G.H. Waddell 9 (Cambridge U.), S. Coughtrie 4 (Edinburgh Acads); D.M.D. Rollo 1 (Howe of Fife), N.S. Bruce 7 (Blackheath), H.F. McLeod 24 (Hawick), F.H. ten Bos 1 (Oxford U.), J.W.Y. Kemp 21 (Glasgow HSFP), G.K. Smith 8 (Kelso), A. Robson 20 (Hawick), J.A. Davidson 1 (London Scottish).

Referee D.G. Walters (Wales)

FRANCE v WALES   30/495

4 April 1959
Stade Colombes, Paris
France 11 (1G, 1T, 1PG) Wales 3 (1PG)

France   T: Moncla (2). C: Labazuy. PG: Labazuy.
Wales   PG: Davies.

Even though they had one match still to play – against Ireland in Dublin – for the first time France won the Championship by out-thinking, outrunning and outscoring Wales. Paris started to celebrate from the moment Lucien Miâs was carried from the field by jubilant spectators convinced they had a brilliant captain and a superb side in the making. How right they were! Despite losing that last match in Ireland, the French went on to win four successive Championships, losing one match only, against Wales in 1962, in the process. It was described as champagne rugby and it certainly was sparkling.

FRANCE   P. Lacaze 3 (FC Lourdes); H. Rancoule 6 (FC Lourdes) J. Bouquet 13 (CS Vienne), A. Marquesuzaa 3 (RCF), J. Dupuy 13 (S. Tarbes); A. Labazuy (9) (FC Lourdes), P. Danos 7 (AS

Béziers); A. Quaglio 7 (SC Mazamet), R. Vigier 13 (AS Montferrand), A. Roques 5 (S. Cahors), B. Mommejat 4 (S. Cahors), *L. Miâs 19 (SC Mazamet), M. Crauste 6 (RCF), F. Moncla 6 (RCF), J. Barthe (15) (FC Lourdes).

WALES   T.J. Davies 15 (Llanelli); J.R. Collins 7 (Aberavon), J.E. Hurrell (1) (Newport), M.J. Price 4 (Pontypool), D.I.E. Bebb 4 (Swansea); M.C. Thomas (26) (Newport), W. Watkins (1) (Newport); R. Prosser 14 (Pontypool), B.V. Meredith 22 (Newport), D.R. Main (4) (London Welsh), R.H. Williams 21 (Llanelli), D.J.E. Harris 2 (Pontypridd), *R.C.C. Thomas (24) (Swansea), H.J. Morgan 6 (Abertillery), G.D. Davidge 1 (Newport).

Referee Dr N.M. Parkes (England)

ick Bohemians), A.A. Mulligan 13 (London Irish); S. Millar 5 (Ballymena), *A.R. Dawson 8 (Wanderers), B.G.M. Wood 18 (Garryowen), W.A. Mulcahy 8 (Bective Rangers), M.G. Culliton 4 (Wanderers), N.A.A. Murphy 8 (Cork Constitution), J.R. Kavanagh 22 (Wanderers), P.J.A. O'Sullivan 8 (Galwegians).

FRANCE   P. Lacaze (4) (FC Lourdes), J. Dupuy 14 (S. Tarbes), J. Bouquet 14 (CS Vienne), L. Casaux 1 (S. Tarbes), S. Mericq 1 (SU Agen); C. Mantoulan (1) (S. Pau), P. Danos 8 (AS Béziers); A. Quaglio (8) (SC Mazamet), R. Vigier (14) (AS Montferrand), A. Roques 6 (S. Cahors), B. Mommejat 5 (S. Cahors), *L. Miâs (20) (SC Mazamet), J. Carrère (5) (RC Vichy), F. Moncla 7 (RCF), M. Crauste 7 (RCF).

Referee D.G. Walters (Wales)

IRELAND v FRANCE   30/496

18 April 1959
Lansdowne Road, Dublin
Ireland 9 (1T, 1DG, 1PG) France 5 (1G)

Ireland   T: Brophy. DG: English. PG: Hewitt.
France   T: Dupuy. C: Lacaze.

France came to Lansdowne Road already assured of their first ever Championship title, but the match was notable for other reasons in that it proved to be Ireland's last victory over the French for ten years, and was the final international for several notable players on both sides. Noel Henderson, who was first capped in 1949, had made 37 appearances for Ireland and was a centre of some stature and poise, even though in this and the other three matches of the season he played at full-back. Of the six French players who bade farewell to international rugby Lucien Miâs was the most renowned, for he had set out with single-minded determination to raise the standard of French rugby. The measure of Miâs's success was the winning of the Championship, in which he had played 20 times, and having achieved his ambition he was quite happy to stand aside and allow others to follow and sustain the improvement.

IRELAND   N.J. Henderson (37) (NIFC); N.H. Brophy 6 (Blackrock College), D. Hewitt 6 (Instonians), M.K. Flynn 1 (Wanderers), A.J.F. O'Reilly 20 (Leicester); M.A.F. English 5 (Limer-

1960

MURRAYFIELD France beat Scotland 13-11 · TWICKENHAM England beat Wales 14-6
CARDIFF Wales beat Scotland 8-0 · TWICKENHAM England beat Ireland 8-5
PARIS France drew England 3-3 · DUBLIN Scotland beat Ireland 6-5
DUBLIN Wales beat Ireland 10-9 · MURRAYFIELD England beat Scotland 21-12
CARDIFF France beat Wales 16-8 · PARIS France beat Ireland 23-6

CHAMPIONSHIP TABLE
France – Championship, England – Triple Crown

Pos	Country	P	W	D	L	F	A	Pts	Tries F	A
1	France (1)	4	3	1	0	55	28	7	11	6
2	England (4)	4	3	1	0	46	26	7	7	2
3	Wales (3)	4	2	0	2	32	39	4	4	7
4	Scotland (5)	4	1	0	3	29	47	2	4	8
5	Ireland (2)	4	0	0	4	25	47	0	5	8

After the dearth of tries the previous season, the 31 tries of this season gave rise to some high-scoring matches with a total of 187 points, the highest since 1931. France, Champions again, played an important part in the try-spree. They scored 11, a total they have bettered only once, in 1976, when they ran in 13. Only England, who restricted them to a Michel Vannier penalty goal, had any defence against the brilliant French attacking machine, which moved into top gear on the return, six years after his first cap, of Pierre Albaladejo, against Wales and Ireland. Tom Kiernan played his first Championship season for Ireland – and it was one he would probably like to forget since they lost all four matches for the first time since 1920. The first three matches were narrow defeats before their final capitulation to the dominant French in Paris, a match in which all sorts of records were broken.

Neither Wales or Scotland achieved anything memorable, except between them they tried out 49 players in their search for winning combinations. England, on the other hand, played extremely well at times and deserved their Triple Crown success, in which only the Irish

provided serious opposition. After failing to score a try the previous year, the English produced seven, Jim Roberts scoring three, two of them on his début, against Wales.

SCOTLAND v FRANCE 30/497

9 January 1960
Murrayfield
France 13 (2G, 1T) Scotland 11 (1G, 1T, 1PG)

Scotland T: Arthur Smith (2). C: Elliot. PG: Elliot.
France T: Meyer, Mericq, Moncla. C: Vannier (2).

France's three tries were the most they have scored in Scotland, which was even more commendable considering that for most of the match Lucien Rogé, the Béziers wing, was a passenger with a broken hand.

SCOTLAND K.J.F. Scotland 10 (Cambridge U.); *A.R. Smith 19 (Ebbw Vale), J.J. McPartlin 1 (Harlequins), I.H.P. Laughland 2 (London Scottish), C. Elliot 3 (Langholm); G. Sharp 1 (Stewart's FP), J.A.T. Rodd 5 (US Portsmouth); H.F. McLeod 25 (Hawick), N.S. Bruce 8 (London Scottish), D.M.D. Rollo 2 (Howe of Fife), F.H. ten Bos 2 (Oxford U.), J.W.Y. Kemp 22 (Glasgow HSFP), G.K. Smith 9 (Kelso), A. Robson (21) (Hawick), K.R.F. Bearne 1 (Cambridge U.).

FRANCE M. Vannier 20 (RCF); L. Rogé 9 (AS Béziers), J. Bouquet 15 (CS Vienne), A. Marquesuzaa 4 (FC Lourdes), S. Mericq 2 (SU Agen); R. Martine 12 (FC Lourdes), P. Danos 9 (AS Béziers); A. Domenech 17 (CA Brive), J. de

Gregorio 1 (FC Grenoble), A. Roques 7 (S. Cahors), B. Mommejat 6 (S. Cahors), M. Celaya 22 (SBUC), *F. Moncla 8 (S. Pau), S. Meyer 1 (CA Périgueux), M. Crauste 8 (FC Lourdes).

Referee D.G. Walters (Wales)

ENGLAND v WALES   64/498

16 January 1960
Twickenham
England 14 (1G, 1T, 2PG) Wales 6 (2PG)

England   T: Roberts (2). C: Rutherford. PG: Rutherford (2).
Wales   PG: Davies (2).

Haydn Morgan, who had given Phil Horrocks-Taylor such a harrowing time on Wales's previous visit to Twickenham, found another England fly-half newcomer, Richard Sharp, an altogether different proposition. Although in effect Morgan missed but one vital tackle on the slight, elusive Sharp, the myth has grown up that he was completely mesmerized by probably the most elegant player England has ever had in the position. Altogether England fielded seven new caps. One of them, Jim Roberts, had the distinction of scoring both tries, and another, Don Rutherford, supplied the remainder of the points with a conversion and two penalties. It was England's biggest score against Wales since 1921, and was a sad way for Rhys Williams, the Welsh captain, to end his illustrious 22-cap Championship career.

ENGLAND   D. Rutherford 1 (Percy Park); J.R.C. Young 2 (Harlequins), M.S. Phillips 8 (Oxford U.), M.P. Weston 1 (Richmond), J. Roberts 1 (Old Millhillians); R.A.W. Sharp 1 (Oxford U.), *R.E.G. Jeeps 11 (Northampton); C.R. Jacobs 13 (Northampton), S.A.M. Hodgson 1 (Durham City), T.P. Wright 1 (Blackheath), R.W.D. Marques 17 (Harlequins), J.D. Currie 17 (Harlequins), P.G.D. Robbins 12 (Moseley), R.E. Syrett 4 (Wasps), W.G.D. Morgan 1 (Medicals).

WALES   T.J. Davies 16 (Llanelli); J.R. Collins 8 (Aberavon), M.J. Price 5 (Pontypool), G.W. Lewis 1 (Richmond), D.I.E. Bebb 5 (Swansea); C. Ashton 4 (Aberavon), C. Evans (1) (Pontypool); R. Prosser 15 (Pontypool), B.V. Meredith 23 (Newport), L.J. Cunningham 1 (Aberavon),

G.W. Payne 1 (Pontypridd), *R.H. Williams (22) (Llanelli), B. Cresswell 1 (Newport), H.J. Morgan 7 (Abertillery), J. Faull 10 (Swansea).

Referee J.A.S. Taylor (Scotland)

WALES v SCOTLAND   64/499

6 February 1960
Cardiff Arms Park
Wales 8 (1G, 1PG) Scotland 0

Wales   T: Bebb. C: Morgan. PG: Morgan.

This was the first international to be handled by Kevin Kelleher, of Ireland. Kelleher became one of the most respected referees in the game and altogether officiated at 17 Championship matches, a total bettered only by Gwynne Walters, of Wales. Wales completed a run of eight successive home wins over Scotland.

WALES   N. Morgan 1 (Newport); F.C. Coles 1 (Pontypool), M.J. Price 6 (Pontypool), G.W. Lewis (2) (Richmond), D.I.E. Bebb 6 (Swansea); C. Ashton 5 (Aberavon), D.O. Brace 6 (Llanelli); R. Prosser 16 (Pontypool), *B.V. Meredith 24 (Newport), L.J. Cunningham 2 (Aberavon), G.W. Payne 2 (Pontypridd), D.J.E. Harris 3 (Cardiff), B. Cresswell 2 (Newport), G. Whitson 2 (Newport), G.D. Davidge 2 (Newport).

SCOTLAND   K.J.F. Scotland 11 (Cambridge U.); *A.R. Smith 20 (Ebbw Vale), J.J. McPartlin 2 (Harlequins), I.H.P. Laughland 3 (London Scottish), G.D. Stevenson 10 (Hawick); T. McClung (9) (Edinburgh Acads), J.A.T. Rodd 6 (US Portsmouth); H.F. McLeod 26 (Hawick), N.S. Bruce 9 (London Scottish), D.M.D. Rollo 3 (Howe of Fife), F.H. ten Bos 3 (Oxford U.), J.W.Y. Kemp 23 (Glasgow HSFP), G.K. Smith 10 (Kelso), C.E.B. Stewart 1 (Kelso), K.R.F. Bearne (2) (Cambridge U.).

Referee K.D. Kelleher (Ireland)

ENGLAND v IRELAND   64/500

13 February 1960
Twickenham
England 8 (1G, 1DG) Ireland 5 (1G)

England   T: Marques. C: Rutherford. DG: Sharp.
Ireland   T: Culliton. C: Kiernan.

Michael Culliton, the rugged, uncompromising Wanderers lock-forward, scored Ireland's first try at Twickenham in six visits since 1948. It was still not enough to prevent England chalking up their sixth home win in a row over Ireland, whose chances were diminished when Tony O'Reilly was injured in the second half. David Marques scored his first try in 18 Championship matches, and with Don Rutherford converting, it proved to be the match-winner.

ENGLAND   D. Rutherford 2 (Percy Park); J.R.C. Young 3 (Harlequins), M.S. Phillips 9 (Oxford U.), M.P. Weston 2 (Richmond), J. Roberts 2 (Old Millhillians); R.A.W. Sharp 2 (Oxford U.), *R.E.G. Jeeps 12 (Northampton); C.R. Jacobs 14 (Northampton), S.A.M. Hodgson 2 (Durham City), T.P. Wright 2 (Blackheath), R.W.D. Marques 18 (Harlequins), J.D. Currie 18 (Harlequins), P.G.D. Robbins 13 (Moseley), R.E. Syrett 5 (Wasps), W.G.D. Morgan 2 (Medicals).

IRELAND   T.J. Kiernan 1 (UC Cork); W.W. Bornemann 1 (Wanderers), A.C. Pedlow 21 (CIYMS), D. Hewitt 7 (Queen's U. Belfast), A.J.F. O'Reilly 21 (Leicester); M.A.F. English 6 (Bohemians), *A.A. Mulligan 14 (London Irish); B.G.M. Wood 19 (Lansdowne), B. McCallan 1 (Ballymena), S. Millar 6 (Ballymena), W.A. Mulcahy 9 (UC Dublin), M.G. Culliton 5 (Wanderers), N.A.A. Murphy 9 (Cork Constitution), J.R. Kavanagh 23 (Wanderers), T. McGrath 3 (Garryowen).

Referee D.G. Walters (Wales)

FRANCE v ENGLAND   31/501

27 February 1960
Stade Colombes, Paris
France 3 (1PG) England 3 (1T)

France   PG: Vannier.
England   T: Weston.

The Championship careers of four French players were ended after this draw, which ultimately prevented France from winning the Grand Slam for the first time and England from winning it for the eighth time. Considering the high quality of play of both sides before and after, this encounter was a bitter disappointment. Some observers, however, noted the effectiveness of the England back-row in containing their French counterparts – which was an achievement in itself – and the coolness under long bombardment from Don Rutherford, a stribling at full-back.

FRANCE   M. Vannier 21 (RCF); L. Rogé (10) (AS Béziers), J. Bouquet 16 (CS Vienne), A. Marquesuzaa (5) (FC Lourdes), S. Mericq 3 (SU Agen); R. Martine 13 (FC Lourdes), P. Danos (10) (AS Béziers); A. Domenech 18 (CA Brive), J. de Gregorio 2 (FC Grenoble), A. Roques 8 (S. Cahors), B. Mommejat 7 (S. Cahors), M. Celaya 23 (SBUC), *F. Moncla 9 (S. Pau), S. Meyer (2) (CA Périgueux), M. Crauste 9 (FC Lourdes).

ENGLAND   D. Rutherford 3 (Percy Park); J.R.C. Young 4 (Harlequins), M.S. Phillips 10 (Oxford U.), M.P. Weston 3 (Richmond), J. Roberts 3 (Old Millhillians); R.A.W. Sharp 3 (Oxford U.), *R.E.G. Jeeps 13 (Northampton); C.R. Jacobs 15 (Northampton), S.A.M. Hodgson 3 (Durham City), T.P. Wright 3 (Blackheath), R.W.D. Marques 19 (Harlequins), J.D. Currie 19 (Harlequins), P.G.D. Robbins 14 (Moseley), R.E. Syrett 6 (Wasps), W.G.D. Morgan 3 (Medicals).

Referee J.A.S. Taylor (Scotland)

IRELAND v SCOTLAND 66/502

27 February 1960
Lansdowne Road, Dublin
Scotland 6 (1T, 1DG) Ireland 5 (1G)

Ireland T: Wood. C: Hewitt.
Scotland T: Thomson. DG: Scotland.

After nine defeats in a row in Ireland, Scotland finally found the formula for victory. It was the reward for speculation for the Scots reshuffled their forces and brought in four new caps, one of them, Ronnie Thomson, scoring their try.

IRELAND   T.J. Kiernan 2 (UC Cork); A.C. Pedlow 22 (CIYMS), D. Hewitt 8 (Queen's U. Belfast), J.C. Walsh 1 (UC Cork), W.W. Bornemann 2 (Wanderers); M.A.F. English 7 (Bohemians), *A.A. Mulligan 15 (London Irish); B.G.M. Wood 20 (Lansdowne), B. McCallan (2) (Ballymena), S. Millar 7 (Ballymena), W.A. Mulcahy 10 (UC Dublin), M.G. Culliton 6 (Wanderers), N.A.A. Murphy 10 (Cork Constitution), J.R. Kavanagh 24 (Wanderers), T. McGrath 4 (Garryowen).

SCOTLAND   K.J.F. Scotland 12 (UC Cork); A.R. Smith 21 (Ebbw Vale), G.D. Stevenson 11 (Hawick), I.H.P. Laughland 4 (London Scottish), R.H. Thomson 1 (London Scottish); *G.H. Waddell 10 (Cambridge U.), R.B. Shillinglaw 1 (KOSB); D.M.D. Rollo 4 (Howe of Fife), N.S. Bruce 10 (London Scottish), H.F. McLeod 27 (Hawick), T.O. Grant 1 (Hawick), J.W.Y. Kemp 24 (Glasgow HSFP), G.K. Smith 11 (Kelso), D.B. Edwards 1 (Heriot's FP), J.A. Davidson 2 (Edinburgh Wands).

Referee D.G. Walters (Wales)

IRELAND v WALES 62/503

12 March 1960
Lansdowne Road, Dublin
Wales 10 (2G) Ireland 9 (1T, 2PG)

Ireland T: Murphy. PG: Kelly (2).
Wales T: Cresswell, Brace. C: Morgan (2).

This defeat meant that Ireland had won only one of their last six home matches against Wales,

easily the bleakest period at Lansdowne Road against any country. As on so many occasions, victory came late in the contest when Norman Morgan converted a try by Onllwyn Brace.

IRELAND   T.J. Kiernan 3 (UC Cork); W.W. Bornemann (3) (Wanderers), D. Hewitt 9 (Queen's U. Belfast), A.C. Pedlow 23 (CIYMS), D.C. Glass 2 (Belfast Collegians); S. Kelly 4 (Lansdowne), *A.A. Mulligan 16 (London Irish); S. Millar 8 (Ballymena), L. Butler (1) (Blackrock College), B.G.M. Wood 21 (Lansdowne), W.A. Mulcahy 11 (UC Dublin), M.G. Culliton 7 (Wanderers), J.R. Kavanagh 25 (Wanderers), N.A.A. Murphy 11 (Cork Constitution), T. McGrath 5 (Garryowen).

WALES   N. Morgan 2 (Newport); F.C. Coles 2 (Pontypool), M.J. Price 7 (Pontypool), B.J. Jones 1 (Newport), D.I.E. Bebb 7 (Swansea); C. Ashton 6 (Aberavon), *D.O. Brace 7 (Llanelli); R. Prosser 17 (Pontypool), N.R. Gale 1 (Swansea), L.J. Cunningham 3 (Aberavon), D.J.E. Harris 4 (Cardiff), G.W. Payne (3) (Pontypridd), B. Cresswell 3 (Newport), G. Whitson (3) (Newport), G.D. Davidge 3 (Newport).

Referee D.A. Brown (England)

SCOTLAND v ENGLAND 63/504

19 March 1960
Murrayfield
England 21 (3G, 1DG, 1PG) Scotland 12 (1T, 3PG)

Scotland T: Arthur Smith. PG: Scotland (3).
England T: Roberts, Syrett, Young. C: Rutherford (3). DG: Sharp. PG: Rutherford.

England played the same XV which had beaten Wales and Ireland and had drawn in Paris, and were rewarded with their biggest victory in Scotland, a score surpassed only by the 1980 side. It meant also their fourteenth Triple Crown.

SCOTLAND   K.J.F. Scotland 13 (Cambridge U.); A.R. Smith 22 (Ebbw Vale), G.D. Stevenson 12 (Hawick), I.H.P. Laughland 5 (London Scottish), R.H. Thomson 2 (London Scottish); *G.H. Waddell 11 (Cambridge U.), R.B. Shillinglaw 2 (KOSB); D.M.D. Rollo 5 (Howe of Fife), N.S.

Bruce 11 (London Scottish), H.F. McLeod 28 (Hawick), T.O. Grant 2 (Hawick), J.W.Y. Kemp (25) (Glasgow HSFP), G.K. Smith 12 (Kelso), D.B. Edwards (2) (Heriot's FP), J.A. Davidson (3) (Edinburgh Wands).

ENGLAND D. Rutherford 4 (Percy Park); J.R.C. Young 5 (Harlequins), M.S. Phillips 11 (Oxford U.), M.P. Weston 4 (Richmond), J. Roberts 4 (Old Millhillians); R.A.W. Sharp 4 (Oxford U.), *R.E.G. Jeeps 14 (Northampton); C.R. Jacobs 16 (Northampton), S.A.M. Hodgson 4 (Durham City), T.P. Wright 4 (Blackheath), R.W.D. Marques 20 (Harlequins), J.D. Currie 20 (Harlequins), P.G.D. Robbins 15 (Moseley), R.E. Syrett 7 (Wasps), W.G.D. Morgan 4 (Medicals).

Referee R.C. Williams (Ireland)

WALES v FRANCE 31/505

26 March 1960
Cardiff Arms Park
France 16 (2G, 2T) Wales 8 (1G, 1PG)

Wales T: Cresswell. C: Morgan. PG: Morgan.
France T: Celaya, Lacroix, Mericq, Dupuy. C: Vannier, Albaladejo.

France's four tries were the highest number they had registered against Wales in Wales. It was also the only time that France had scored two successive wins in Wales. These records should not be surprising for, in the view of many, this was one of France's finest sides with unmatched technique in the tight, fluency and power in the loose and capable of scoring spectacular tries by either forwards or backs or a thrilling combination of both.

WALES N. Morgan (3) (Newport); F.C. Coles (3) (Pontypool), M.J. Price 8 (Pontypool), B.J. Jones (2) (Newport), D.I.E. Bebb 8 (Swansea); B. Richards (1) (Swansea), D.O. Brace 8 (Llanelli); R. Prosser 18 (Pontypool), *B.V. Meredith 25 (Newport), L.J. Cunningham 4 (Aberavon), J. Faull (11) (Swansea), D.J.E. Harris 5 (Cardiff), B. Cresswell (4) (Newport), J. Leleu (3) (Swansea), G.D. Davidge 4 (Newport).

FRANCE M. Vannier 22 (RCF); S. Mericq 4 (SU Agen), G. Boniface 1 (S. Mont-de-Marsan), J. Bouquet 17 (CS Vienne), J. Dupuy 15 (S. Tarbes);

P. Albaladejo 2 (US Dax), P. Lacroix 1 (S. Mont-de-Marsan); A. Domenech 19 (CA Brive), J. de Gregorio 3 (FC Grenoble), A. Roques 9 (S. Cahors), J-P. Saux 1 (S. Pau), H. Larrue 1 (US Carmaux), *F. Moncla 10 (S. Pau), M. Crauste 10 (FC Lourdes), M. Celaya 24 (SBUC).

Referee Dr N.M. Parkes (England)

FRANCE v IRELAND 31/506

9 April 1960
Stade Colombes, Paris
France 23 (1G, 3T, 3DG) Ireland 6 (2T)

France T: Celaya, Domenech, Moncla, Rancoule. C: Bouquet. DG: Albaladejo (3).
Ireland T: Brophy (2)

Pierre Albaladejo's three dropped goals were a record score for both an individual player and a team in a Championship match, helping France to initiate their longest sequence of matches without defeat against any side in the Championship: eight wins and one draw, before they lost 9-17 in Dublin in 1969. Victory also brought France the title for the second successive season and their 55 points' aggregate was the highest since Wales had totalled 74 in 1931.

FRANCE M. Vannier 23 (RCF); J. Dupuy 16 (S. Tarbes), J. Bouquet 18 (CS Vienne), G. Boniface 2 (S. Mont-de-Marsan), H. Rancoule 7 (RC Toulon); P. Albaladejo 3 (US Dax), P. Lacroix 2 (S. Mont-de-Marsan); A. Domenech 20 (CA Brive), J. de Gregorio 4 (FC Grenoble), A. Roques 10 (S. Cahors), H. Larrue (2) (US Carmaux), B. Mommejat 8 (S. Cahors), M. Crauste 11 (FC Lourdes), *F. Moncla 11 (S. Pau), M. Celaya 25 (SBUC).

IRELAND T.J. Kiernan 4 (UC Cork); N.H. Brophy 7 (Blackrock College), D. Hewitt 10 (Instonians), M.K. Flynn 2 (Wanderers), A.C. Pedlow 24 (CIYMS); S. Kelly (5) (Lansdowne), *A.A. Mulligan 17 (London Irish); S. Millar 9 (Ballymena), A.R. Dawson 9 (Wanderers), B.G.M. Wood 22 (Garryowen), P. Costello (1) (Bective Rangers), M.G. Culliton 8 (Wanderers), N.A.A. Murphy 12 (Cork Constitution), J.R. Kavanagh 26 (Wanderers), T. McGrath (6) (Garryowen).

Referee D.G. Walters (Wales)

1961

PARIS France beat Scotland 11-0 · CARDIFF Wales beat England 6-3
DUBLIN Ireland beat England 11-8 · MURRAYFIELD Scotland beat Wales 3-0
TWICKENHAM England drew France 5-5 · MURRAYFIELD Scotland beat Ireland 16-8
CARDIFF Wales beat Ireland 9-0 · TWICKENHAM England beat Scotland 6-0
PARIS France beat Wales 8-6 · DUBLIN France beat Ireland 15-3

CHAMPIONSHIP TABLE
France – Championship

									Tries	
Pos	Country	P	W	D	L	F	A	Pts	F	A
1	France (1)	4	3	1	0	39	14	7	5	3
2	Wales (3)	4	2	0	2	21	14	4	5	4
3	Scotland (4)	4	2	0	2	19	25	4	4	4
4	England (2)	4	1	1	2	22	22	3	5	4
5	Ireland (5)	4	1	0	3	22	48	2	3	7

The scintillating rugby being produced by France forced all the other countries to scurry around looking for ways to emulate it and to find players with similar flair. Consequently the 1961 Championship was one of new faces, with only one country, Scotland, keeping the same XV for two matches in a row. Scotland were at the foot of the new player league – they tried out only 20 players. Even France, anxious to maintain their momentum, capped 21 newcomers. Top of the league, however, were Wales (26 players), followed by England (25) and Ireland (23). Not since the beginning of the Championship had so many played so few matches. None of this reshuffling made the slightest difference to the balance of power: France won the title again without any serious argument or challenge, while the others battled to avoid bottom place.

FRANCE v SCOTLAND   31/507

7 January 1961
Stade Colombes, Paris
France 11 (1G, 1DG, 1PG) Scotland 0

France   T: Boniface. C: Albaladejo. DG: Albaladejo. PG: Albaladejo.

For Scotland, this match was sandwiched between two defeats by South Africa, and was more clear-cut than either of them. Much of Scotland's trouble stemmed from an early injury to Stewart.

FRANCE   R. Martine (14) (FC Lourdes); J. Dupuy 17 (S. Tarbes), J. Bouquet 19 (CS Vienne), G. Boniface 3 (S. Mont-de-Marsan), J. Gachassin 1 (FC Lourdes); P. Albaladejo 4 (US Dax), P. Lacroix 3 (SU Agen); A. Domenech 21 (CA Brive), J. de Gregorio 5 (FC Grenoble), A. Roques 11 (S. Cahors), L. Echave (1) (SU Agen), M. Celaya 26 (Biarritz Ol), *F. Moncla 12 (S. Pau), M. Crauste 12 (FC Lourdes), R. Crancee (1) (FC Lourdes).

SCOTLAND   K.J.F. Scotland 14 (London Scottish); A.R. Smith 23 (Edinburgh Wands), R.C. Cowan 1 (Selkirk), G.D. Stevenson 13 (Hawick), R.H. Thomson 3 (London Scottish); *G.H. Waddell 12 (Cambridge U.), R.B. Shillinglaw (3) (KOSB); H.F. McLeod 29 (Hawick), N.S. Bruce 12 (London Scottish), D.M.D. Rollo 6 (Howe of Fife), F.H. ten Bos 4 (Oxford U.), M.J. Campbell-Lamerton 1 (Blackheath), G.K. Smith 13 (Kelso), J. Douglas 1 (Stewart's FP), C.E.B. Stewart (2) (Kelso).

Referee R.C. Williams (Ireland)

WALES v ENGLAND   65/508

21 January 1961
Cardiff Arms Park
Wales 6 (2T) England 3 (1T)

Wales   T: Bebb (2).
England   T: Young.

A knee injury to Cyril Davies, the Cardiff centre, not only ended his international career but meant Wales had to play most of the second half with only 14 players. Haydn Morgan was moved from flank to replace Davies and performed with merit in the position in which he had started his club career with Abertillery.

WALES   *T.J. Davies 17 (Llanelli); P.M. Rees 1 (Newport), C.H.A. Davies (5) (Cardiff), H.M. Roberts 1 (Cardiff), D.I.E. Bebb 9 (Swansea); K.H.L. Richards 1 (Bridgend), A. O'Connor 1 (Aberavon); P.E.J. Morgan 1 (Aberavon), B.V. Meredith 26 (Newport), K.D. Jones 1 (Cardiff), D.J.E. Harris 6 (Cardiff), W.R. Evans 5 (Bridgend), G.D. Davidge 5 (Newport), H.J. Morgan 8 (Abertillery), D. Nash 1 (Ebbw Vale).

ENGLAND   M.N. Gavins (1) (Leicester); J.R.C. Young 6 (Harlequins), M.S. Phillips 12 (Fylde), M.P. Weston 5 (Richmond), J. Roberts 5 (Old Millhillians); A.B.W. Risman 5 (Loughborough College), *R.E.G. Jeeps 15 (Northampton); C.R. Jacobs 17 (Northampton), S.A.M. Hodgson 5 (Durham City), T.P. Wright 5 (Blackheath), R.W.D. Marques (21) (Harlequins), R.J. French 1 (St Helens), L.I. Rimmer 1 (Bath), P.G.D. Robbins 16 (Moseley), W.G.D. Morgan 5 (Medicals).

Referee K.D. Kelleher (Ireland)

IRELAND v ENGLAND   65/509

11 February 1961
Lansdowne Road, Dublin
Ireland 11 (1G, 2PG) England 8 (1G, 1T)

Ireland   T: Kavanagh. C: Moffett. PG: Moffett (2).
England   T: Roberts, Rogers. C: Risman.

After winning on their two previous visits to Lansdowne Road, England came unstuck against an Irish side that gambled on a new wing in Ronnie McCarten and new half-back pairing of Armstrong and Moffett. The little Ballymena scrum-half proved the match-winner with eight points. England's only satisfaction was that they outscored Ireland in tries, 2-1, that Jeeps enjoyed one of his best games, and that Ernie Robinson, recalled to hook after a seven-year absence, gave an excellent account of himself against Ronnie Dawson.

IRELAND   T.J. Kiernan 5 (UC Cork); R.J. McCarten 1 (London Irish), D. Hewitt 11 (Queen's U. Belfast), J.C. Walsh 2 (UC Cork), A.J.F. O'Reilly 22 (Dolphin); W.K. Armstrong (1) (NIFC), J.W. Moffett 1 (Ballymena); B.G.M. Wood 23 (Lansdowne), *A.R. Dawson 10 (Wanderers), S. Millar 10 (Ballymena), W.A. Mulcahy 12 (UC Dublin), M.G. Culliton 9 (Wanderers), J.R. Kavanagh 27 (Wanderers), N.A.A. Murphy 13 (Garryowen), P.J.A. O'Sullivan 9 (Galwegians).

ENGLAND   J.G. Willcox 1 (Oxford U.); J.R.C. Young 7 (Harlequins), A.B.W. Risman 6 (Loughborough College), M.P. Weston 6 (Richmond), J. Roberts 6 (Sale); R.A.W. Sharp 5 (Oxford U.), *R.E.G. Jeeps 16 (Northampton); C.R. Jacobs 18 (Northampton), E.F. Robinson 2 (Coventry), T.P. Wright 6 (Blackheath), R.J. French 2 (St Helens), J. Price (1) (Coventry), L.I. Rimmer 2 (Bath), D.P. Rogers 1 (Bedford), W.G.D. Morgan 6 (Medicals).

Referee G.J. Treharne (Wales)

SCOTLAND v WALES   65/510

11 February 1961
Murrayfield
Scotland 3 (1T) Wales 0

Scotland   T: Arthur Smith.

This was Scotland's fourth consecutive win over Wales at Murrayfield, equalling their best winning sequence at home against Wales established in 1895–1903.

SCOTLAND   K.J.F. Scotland 15 (London Scottish); *A.R. Smith 24 (Edinburgh Wands), E.

McKeating 3 (Heriot's FP), G.D. Stevenson 14 (Hawick), R.H. Thomson 4 (London Scottish); I.H.P. Laughland 6 (London Scottish), A.J. Hastie 1 (Melrose); H.F. McLeod 30 (Hawick), N.S. Bruce 13 (London Scottish), D.M.D. Rollo 7 (Howe of Fife), F.H. ten Bos 5 (London Scottish), M.J. Campbell-Lamerton 2 (Halifax), K.I. Ross 1 (Boroughmuir FP), G.K. Smith 14 (Kelso), J. Douglas 2 (Stewart's FP).

WALES *T.J. Davies 18 (Llanelli); P.M. Rees 2 (Newport), G.R. Britton (1) (Newport), H.M. Roberts 2 (Cardiff), D.I.E. Bebb 10 (Swansea); K.H.L. Richards 2 (Bridgend), A. O'Connor 2 (Aberavon); P.E.J. Morgan 2 (Aberavon), B.V. Meredith 27 (Newport), K.D. Jones 2 (Cardiff), D.J.E. Harris (7) (Cardiff), W.R. Evans 6 (Bridgend), G.D. Davidge 6 (Newport), H.J. Morgan 9 (Abertillery), D. Nash 2 (Ebbw Vale).

Referee R.C. Williams (Ireland)

ENGLAND v FRANCE 32/511

25 February 1961
Twickenham
England 5 (1G) France 5 (1G)

England T: Harding. C: Willcox.
France T: Crauste. C: Vannier.

For the second season running, a draw with England meant that France lost the opportunity of winning the Grand Slam for a first time.

ENGLAND J.G. Willcox 2 (Oxford U.); J.R.C. Young (8) (Harlequins), A.B.W. Risman (7) (Loughborough College), M.P. Weston 7 (Richmond), J. Roberts 7 (Sale); R.A.W. Sharp 6 (Oxford U.), *R.E.G. Jeeps 17 (Northampton); C.R. Jacobs 19 (Northampton), E.F. Robinson 3 (Coventry), T.P. Wright 7 (Blackheath), R.J. French 3 (St Helens), V.S.J. Harding 1 (Cambridge U.), L.I. Rimmer 3 (Bath), D.P. Rogers 2 (Bedford), W.G.D. Morgan 7 (Medicals).

FRANCE M. Vannier 24 (RC Chalon); H. Rancoule 8 (RC Toulon), G. Boniface 4 (S. Mont-de-Marsan), J. Bouquet 20 (CS Vienne), J. Dupuy 18 (S. Tarbes); P. Albaladejo 5 (US Dax), P. Lacroix 4 (SU Agen); A. Domenech 22 (CA Brive), J. de Gregorio 6 (FC Grenoble), A. Roques 12 (S. Cahors), G. Bouguyon 1 (FC Grenoble), J-P. Saux

2 (S. Pau), *F. Moncla 13 (S. Pau), M. Crauste 13 (FC Lourdes), M. Celaya 27 (SBUC).

Referee D.G. Walters (Wales)

SCOTLAND v IRELAND 67/512

25 February 1961
Murrayfield
Scotland 16 (2G, 1T, 1PG) Ireland 8 (1G, 1T)

Scotland T: Douglas, Ross (2). C: Scotland (2). PG: Scotland.
Ireland T: Kavanagh, Hewitt. C: Moffett.

After failing to score a try in their two previous encounters with Ireland at Murrayfield, Scotland unleashed a shattering three-try burst. Ireland responded with two themselves, and the crowd enjoyed a spectacularly open match. A conversion brought Moffett's total to ten points in two matches for Ireland, but the Ballymena scrum-half was not selected again.

SCOTLAND K.J.F. Scotland 16 (London Scottish); *A.R. Smith 25 (Edinburgh Wands), E. McKeating 4 (Heriot's FP), G.D. Stevenson 15 (Hawick), R.H. Thomson 5 (London Scottish); I.H.P. Laughland 7 (London Scottish), A.J. Hastie 2 (Melrose); H.F. McLeod 31 (Hawick), N.S. Bruce 14 (London Scottish), D.M.D. Rollo 8 (Howe of Fife), F.H. ten Bos 6 (London Scottish), M.J. Campbell-Lamerton 3 (Halifax), K.I. Ross 2 (Boroughmuir FP), G.K. Smith 15 (Kelso), J. Douglas 3 (Stewart's FP).

IRELAND T.J. Kiernan 6 (UC Cork); A.C. Pedlow 25 (CIYMS), D. Hewitt 12 (Queen's U. Belfast), J.C. Walsh 3 (UC Cork), N.H. Brophy 8 (Blackrock College); M.A.F. English 8 (Bohemians), J.W. Moffett (2) (Ballymena); B.G.M. Wood 24 (Lansdowne), *A.R. Dawson 11 (Wanderers), S. Millar 11 (Ballymena), W.A. Mulcahy 13 (UC Dublin), M.G. Culliton 10 (Wanderers), J.R. Kavanagh 28 (Wanderers), N.A.A. Murphy 14 (Garryowen), P.J.A. O'Sullivan 10 (Galwegians).

Referee M.H.R. King (England)

WALES v IRELAND　　63/513

11 March 1961
Cardiff Arms Park
Wales 9 (1T, 2PG) Ireland 0

Wales　T: Richards. PG: Richards (2).

This was Onllwyn Brace's last appearance for Wales, whose flair, unorthodoxy and trickery made him the epitomy of what everyone thought a Welsh scrum-half should be. Yet Wales did not want him. The exceptionally talented Brace hiccupped his way through a five-year international career winning just nine caps.

WALES　A.J. Priday (2) (Cardiff); P.M. Rees 3 (Newport), D. Thomas (1) (Aberavon), H.M. Roberts 3 (Cardiff), D.I.E. Bebb 11 (Swansea); K.H.L. Richards 3 (Bridgend), *D.O. Brace (9) (Llanelli); R. Prosser 19 (Pontypool), B.V. Meredith 28 (Newport), K.D. Jones 3 (Cardiff), W.R. Evans 7 (Bridgend), B. Price 1 (Newport), G.D. Davidge 7 (Newport), H.J. Morgan 10 (Abertillery), D. Nash 3 (Ebbw Vale).

IRELAND　T.J. Kiernan 7 (UC Cork); N.H. Brophy 9 (Blackrock College), D. Hewitt 13 (Queen's U. Belfast), D.C. Glass (3) (Belfast Collegians), R.J. McCarten 2 (London Irish);

M.A.F. English 9 (Bohemians), A.A. Mulligan 18 (London Irish); B.G.M. Wood 25 (Lansdowne), *A.R. Dawson 12 (Wanderers), S. Millar 12 (Ballymena), C.J. Dick 1 (Ballymena), W.A. Mulcahy 14 (UC Dublin), M.G. Culliton 11 (Wanderers), N.A.A. Murphy 15 (Garryowen), J.R. Kavanagh 29 (Wanderers).

Referee D.C.J. McMahon (Scotland)

ENGLAND v SCOTLAND　　64/514

18 March 1961
Twickenham
England 6 (1T, 1PG) Scotland 0

England　T: Roberts. PG: Horrocks-Taylor.

Having beaten Wales and Ireland at Murray-field, Scotland came to Twickenham in search of their first victory there since 1938 and the Triple Crown. They were denied both, as much by their own inefficiency as by a try by Jim Roberts and a penalty from Phil Horrocks-Taylor.

ENGLAND　J.G. Willcox 3 (Oxford U.); P.B. Jackson 15 (Coventry), W.M. Patterson (1) (Sale), M.P. Weston 8 (Richmond), J. Roberts 8 (Sale); J.P. Horrocks-Taylor 2 (Leicester), *R.E.G. Jeeps 18 (Northampton); C.R. Jacobs 20

The Scottish XV defeated by France on 7 January 1961. Back row: H.F. McLeod, N.S. Bruce, C.E.B. Stewart, J. Douglas, F.H. ten Bos, M.J. Campbell-Lamerton, G.K. Smith, D.M.D. Rollo. Front row: A.R. Smith, G.D. Stevenson, R.C. Cowan, G.H. Waddell, R.B. Shillinglaw, R.H. Thomson, K.J.F. Scotland

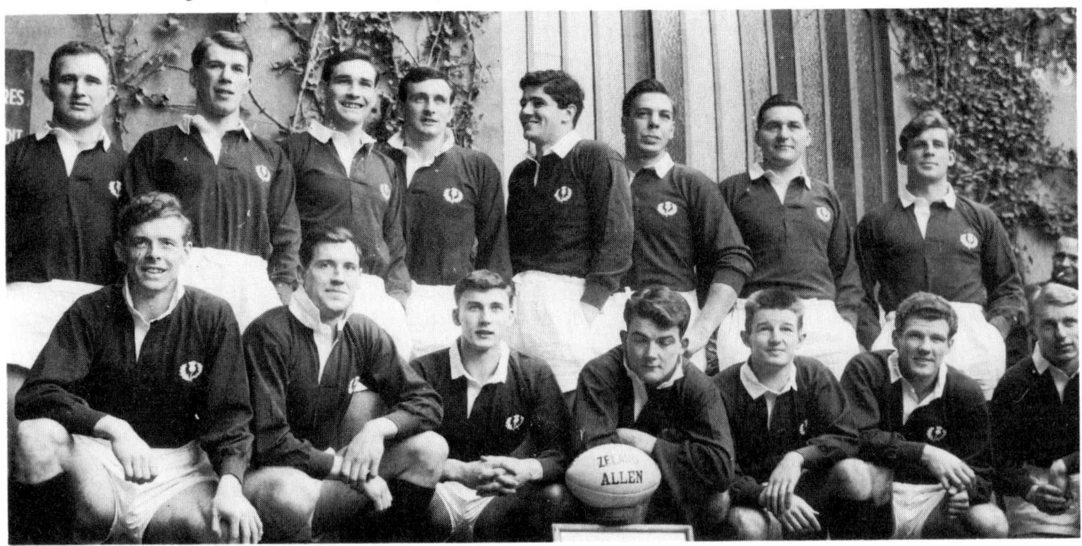

(Northampton), E.F. Robinson (4) (Coventry), T.P. Wright 8 (Blackheath), R.J. French (4) (St Helens), V.S.J. Harding 2 (Cambridge U.), L.I. Rimmer (4) (Bath), D.P. Rogers 3 (Bedford), W.G.D. Morgan (8) (Medicals).

SCOTLAND K.J.F. Scotland 17 (Heriot's FP); *A.R. Smith 26 (Edinburgh Wands), E. McKeating (5) (Heriot's FP), G.D. Stevenson 16 (Hawick), R.H. Thomson 6 (London Scottish); I.H.P. Laughland 8 (London Scottish), A.J. Hastie 3 (Melrose); H.F. McLeod 32 (Hawick), N.S. Bruce 15 (London Scottish), D.M.D. Rollo 9 (Howe of Fife), F.H. ten Bos 7 (London Scottish), J. Douglas 4 (Stewart's FP), K.I. Ross 3 (Boroughmuir FP), J.C. Brash (1) (Cambridge U.), G.K. Smith (16) (Kelso).

Referee K.D. Kelleher (Ireland)

FRANCE v WALES 32/515

25 March 1961
Stade Colombes, Paris
France 8 (1G, 1T) Wales 6 (2T)

France T: Boniface, Saux. C: Vannier.
Wales T: Pask, Bebb.

France established their best ever winning sequence of four victories in a row against Wales, which was beaten only by five successive home wins 1959–67. It also meant that they had won the Championship for a third season in a row, regardless of the outcome of their final match, against Ireland.

FRANCE M. Vannier 25 (RC Chalon); G. Mauduy (3) (CA Périgueux), J. Bouquet 21 (CS Vienne), G. Boniface 5 (S. Mont-de-Marsan), H. Rancoule 9 (RC Toulon); P. Albaladejo 6 (US Dax), P. Lacroix 5 (SU Agen); A. Domenech 23 (CA Brive), J. de Gregorio 7 (FC Grenoble), A. Roques 13 (S. Cahors), G. Bouguyon 2 (FC Grenoble), J-P. Saux 3 (S. Pau), *F. Moncla 14 (S. Pau), M. Crauste 14 (FC Lourdes), M. Celaya 28 (SBUC).

WALES T.J. Davies (19) (Llanelli); J.R. Collins (9) (Aberavon), H.M. Roberts 4 (Cardiff), H.J. Mainwaring (1) (Swansea), D.I.E. Bebb 12 (Swansea); K.H.L. Richards (4) (Bridgend), *L.H. Williams 11 (Cardiff); R. Prosser (20) (Pontypool), W.J. Thomas 1 (Cardiff), P.E.J. Morgan (3)

(Aberavon), W.R. Evans 8 (Bridgend), B. Price 2 (Newport), A.E.I. Pask 1 (Abertillery), H.J. Morgan 11 (Abertillery), D. Nash 4 (Ebbw Vale).

Referee Dr N.M. Parkes (England)

IRELAND v FRANCE 32/516

15 April 1961
Lansdowne Road, Dublin
France 15 (1T, 2DG, 2PG) Ireland 3 (1PG)

Ireland PG: Kiernan.
France T: Gachassin. DG: Bouquet, Albaladejo. PG: Vannier, Albaladejo.

With their third successive Championship already assured, France confirmed their superiority with this emphatic victory in Dublin, which left Ireland with the Wooden Spoon for a second year running. Of the seven Frenchmen who played in all three Championship successes, Michel Celaya, Michel Vannier and François Moncla would not play again: but each in his way left a lasting impression on French rugby history. Celaya and Moncla were giants in every sense in successive French packs, but their speed and handling skills in the loose made them exceptional. Vannier was a superb full-back, calm, assured and pacy.

IRELAND T.J. Kiernan 8 (UC Cork); R.J. McCarten (3) (London Irish), D. Hewitt 14 (Instonians), J.C. Walsh 4 (UC Cork), A.J.F. O'Reilly 23 (Leicester); M.A.F. English 10 (Lansdowne), A.A. Mulligan (19) (London Irish); B.G.M. Wood (26) (Lansdowne), *A.R. Dawson 13 (Wanderers), S. Millar 13 (Ballymena), C.J. Dick 2 (Ballymena), M.G. Culliton 12 (Wanderers), T.J. Nesdale (1) (Garryowen), J.R. Kavanagh 30 (Wanderers), D. Scott 1 (Malone).

FRANCE M. Vannier (26) (RC Chalon); S. Mericq (5) (SU Agen), G. Boniface 6 (S. Mont-de-Marsan), J. Bouquet 22 (CS Vienne), J. Gachassin 2 (FC Lourdes); P. Albaladejo 7 (US Dax), P. Lacroix 6 (SU Agen); A. Roques 14 (S. Cahors), J. de Gregorio 8 (FC Grenoble), A. Domenech 24 (CA Brive), J-P. Saux 4 (S. Pau), G. Bouguyon (3) (FC Grenoble), *F. Moncla (15) (S. Pau), M. Crauste 15 (FC Lourdes), M. Celaya (29) (SBUC).

Referee G.J. Treharne (Wales)

1962

MURRAYFIELD France beat Scotland 11-3 · TWICKENHAM England drew Wales 0-0
CARDIFF Scotland beat Wales 8-3 · TWICKENHAM England beat Ireland 16-0
PARIS France beat England 13-0 · DUBLIN Scotland beat Ireland 20-6
MURRAYFIELD Scotland drew England 3-3 · CARDIFF Wales beat France 3-0
PARIS France beat Ireland 11-0 · DUBLIN Ireland drew Wales 3-3

CHAMPIONSHIP TABLE
France – Championship

Pos	Country	P	W	D	L	F	A	Pts	Tries F	A
1	France (1)	4	3	0	1	35	6	6	7	0
2	Scotland (3)	4	2	1	1	34	23	5	5	2
3	England (4)	4	1	2	1	19	16	4	3	3
4	Wales (2)	4	1	2	1	9	11	4	0	2
5	Ireland (5)	4	0	1	3	9	50	1	1	9

Despite losing to Wales, France won the title for the fourth consecutive season, the best sequence of title wins by any country. The run included a sequence of ten successive matches without defeat, an achievement bettered only by England, who went unbeaten in 13 matches (1922–25) and 12 matches (1883–87). Furthermore, the French conceded only six points, penalty goals by Scotland and Wales.

Wales, in scoring terms, had a miserable season; they extracted a mere nine points, their worst total since 1892 when they had managed two. They also failed to score a try, which had happened only once before, in 1889. Not that they did not endeavour to find a try-scoring side. They experimented with 26 players in the quest for a winning formula. Even that number of try-outs was dwarfed by Ireland who fielded two sides plus one – 31 players, permutations rewarded only by three defeats and a 3-3 draw, in their last match, against equally frustrated Wales. England, on the other hand, kept the same XV for their first three matches, but then caught the Irish-Welsh disease and made six changes for their last match. It resulted in a 3-3 draw against Scotland, and ultimately no more Championship call-ups for 11 of their players.

The Wales-Ireland match actually took place at the beginning of the 1962–63 season, on 17 November. It had been postponed because of an outbreak of smallpox in the Rhondda in March. Three of the five tries which Scotland scored to help them into second place came from Arthur Smith in his last Championship season.

SCOTLAND v FRANCE 32/517

13 January 1962
Murrayfield
France 11 (1G, 2PG) Scotland 3 (1PG)

Scotland PG: Smith.
France T: Rancoule. C: Albaladejo. PG: Albaladejo (2).

This defeat, their second in a row at home against France, was Scotland's only setback of the season and without doubt cost them the Championship. France, who went on to win the title for a fourth successive season, had their defence abilities to thank for it.

SCOTLAND K.J.F. Scotland 18 (Leicester); *A.R. Smith 27 (Edinburgh Wands), J.J. McPartlin 3 (Oxford U.), I.H.P. Laughland 9 (London Scottish), R.C. Cowan 2 (Selkirk); G.H. Waddell 13 (London Scottish), J.A.T. Rodd 7 (London Scottish); H.F. McLeod 33 (Hawick), N.S. Bruce 16 (London Scottish), D.M.D. Rollo 10 (Howe of Fife), F.H. ten Bos 8 (London Scottish), M.J. Campbell-Lamerton 4 (Halifax), R.J.C. Glasgow 1 (Dunfermline), K.I. Ross 4 (Boroughmuir FP), J. Douglas 5 (Stewart's FP).

FRANCE   L. Casaux (2) (S. Tarbes); J. Dupuy 19 (S. Tarbes), J. Piqué 1 (S. Pau), J. Bouquet 23 (CS Vienne), H. Rancoule 10 (S. Tarbes); P. Albaladejo 8 (US Dax), *P. Lacroix 7 (SU Agen); A. Domenech 25 (CA Brive), J. de Gregorio 9 (FC Grenoble), A. Roques 15 (S. Cahors), B. Mommejat 9 (SC Albi), J-P. Saux 5 (S. Pau), M. Crauste 16 (FC Lourdes), R. Gensanne 1 (AS Béziers), H. Romero 1 (US Montauban).

Referee R.C. Williams (Ireland)

ENGLAND v WALES   66/518

20 January 1962
Twickenham
England 0 Wales 0

Considering the attacking qualities of both sets of backs, this was an extraordinary result, which was confirmed by the fact that it was the only occasion when England failed to score in a home match against Wales. England had ended the Championship careers of two of their back-row players, Derek Morgan and Laurie Rimmer, in the previous match – against Scotland – but it was hardly to make way for new blood. Ron Syrett was recalled after a year's absence and Phil Taylor, the big, burly Northampton No. 8, returned after seven years. Wales also brought in a different No. 8, Alun Pask playing in place of David Nash, who withdrew on the morning of the match with a heavy cold. They also experimented with four new caps. One of them, Kelvin Coslett, the Aberavon full-back, found it impossible to fathom the notorious Twickenham wind eddies; he missed five penalty kicks.

ENGLAND   J.G. Willcox 4 (Oxford U.); A.M. Underwood 1 (Northampton), M.R. Wade 1 (Cambridge U.), M.P. Weston 9 (Richmond), J. Roberts 9 (Sale); R.A.W. Sharp 7 (Oxford U.), *R.E.G. Jeeps 19 (Northampton); P.E. Judd 1 (Coventry), S.A.M. Hodgson 6 (Durham City), T.P. Wright 9 (Blackheath), V.S.J. Harding 3 (Sale), J.D. Currie 21 (Bristol), R.E. Syrett 8 (Wasps), D.P. Rogers 4 (Bedford), P.J. Taylor 3 (Northampton).

WALES   K. Coslett 1 (Aberavon); D.R.R. Morgan 1 (Llanelli), D.K. Jones 1 (Llanelli), M.J. Price (9) (Pontypool), D.I.E. Bebb 13 (Swansea); A. Rees 1 (Maesteg), *L.H. Williams 12 (Cardiff); K.D.

Jones 4 (Cardiff), B.V. Meredith 29 (Newport), L.J. Cunningham 5 (Aberavon), W.R. Evans 9 (Bridgend), B. Price 3 (Newport), R.H. Davies 4 (London Welsh), H.J. Morgan 12 (Abertillery), A.E.I. Pask 2 (Abertillery).

Referee J.A.S. Taylor (Scotland)

WALES v SCOTLAND   66/519

3 February 1962
Cardiff Arms Park
Scotland 8 (1G, 1T) Wales 3 (1DG)

Wales   DG: Rees.
Scotland   T: Glasgow, ten Bos. C: Scotland.

After eight successive defeats in Wales, Scotland won at last, but as it turned out it was to be their only victory in 18 visits between 1939–80, 17 of which Wales won. Wet and windy conditions determined tactics, and Coughtrie at scrum-half produced one of his best ever displays for Scotland.

WALES   K. Coslett 2 (Aberavon); D.R.R. Morgan 2 (Llanelli), D.K. Jones 2 (Llanelli), H.M. Roberts 5 (Cardiff), D.I.E. Bebb 14 (Swansea); A. Rees 2 (Maesteg), *L.H. Williams (13) (Cardiff); L.J. Cunningham 6 (Aberavon), B.V. Meredith 30 (Newport), D. Greenslade (1) (Newport), B. Price 4 (Newport), W.R. Evans 10 (Bridgend), R.H. Davies (5) (London Welsh), H.J. Morgan 13 (Abertillery), A.I.E. Pask 3 (Abertillery).

SCOTLAND   K.J.F. Scotland 19 (Leicester); *A.R. Smith 28 (Edinburgh Wands), J.J. McPartlin 4 (Oxford U.), I.H.P. Laughland 10 (London Scottish), R.C. Cowan 3 (Selkirk); G.H. Waddell 14 (London Scottish), S. Coughtrie 5 (Edinburgh Acads); H.F. McLeod 34 (Hawick), N.S. Bruce 17 (London Scottish), D.M.D. Rollo 11 (Howe of Fife), F.H. ten Bos 9 (London Scottish), M.J. Campbell-Lamerton 5 (Halifax), R.J.C. Glasgow 2 (Dunfermline), K.I. Ross 5 (Boroughmuir FP), J. Douglas 6 (Stewart's FP).

Referee Dr N.M. Parkes (England)

ENGLAND v IRELAND   66/520

10 February 1962
Twickenham
England 16 (2G, 1T, 1PG) Ireland 0

England   T: Roberts, Sharp, Wade. C: Sharp (2). PG: Sharp.

Inspired by Dickie Jeeps and Richard Sharp, who had ample possession, England ran riot to score their seventh successive victory, their longest winning sequence against Ireland at Twickenham. The Irish played nine new caps, including a craggy, raw-boned young man from Ballymena called Willie John McBride, a square-shouldered prop with no neck named Ray McLoughlin, and a terrier at No. 8 in Mick Hipwell. Another newcomer, Johnny Quirke, at scrum-half was just 17, Ireland's youngest ever player. Quirke's service matched his humour — quick and to the point. It was he who sent an immortal telegram to canned food executive Tony O'Reilly on the occasion of his shock one-off recall to the Irish side in 1970, seven years after the proclaimed end of the veteran Irish centre's career. Quirke's telegram read: 'Heinz beanz are haz beanz.'

ENGLAND   J.G. Willcox 5 (Oxford U.); A.M. Underwood 2 (Northampton), M.R. Wade 2 (Cambridge U.), M.P. Weston 10 (Richmond), J. Roberts 10 (Sale); R.A.W. Sharp 8 (Oxford U.), *R.E.G. Jeeps 20 (Northampton); P.E. Judd 2 (Coventry), S.A.M. Hodgson 7 (Durham City), T.P. Wright 10 (Blackheath), V.S.J. Harding 4 (Sale), J.D. Currie 22 (Bristol), R.E. Syrett 9 (Wasps), D.P. Rogers 5 (Bedford), P.J. Taylor 4 (Northampton).

IRELAND   T.J. Kiernan 9 (UC Cork); L.P.F. L'Estrange (1) (Dublin U.), M.K. Flynn 3 (Wanderers), W.R. Hunter 1 (CIYMS), N.H. Brophy 10 (Blackrock College); F.G. Gilpin 1 (Queen's U. Belfast), J.T.M. Quirke 1 (Blackrock College); S. Millar 14 (Ballymena), J.S. Dick (1) (Queen's U. Belfast), R.J. McLoughlin 1 (UC Dublin), *W.A. Mulcahy 15 (Bohemians), W.J. McBride 1 (Ballymena), N. Turley (1) (Blackrock College), N.A.A. Murphy 16 (Cork Constitution), M.L. Hipwell 1 (Terenure).

Referee D.G. Walters (Wales)

FRANCE v ENGLAND   33/521

24 February 1962
Stade Colombes, Paris
France 13 (2G, 1T) England 0

France   T: Crauste (3). C: Albaladejo (2).

The three previous England-France matches had been drawn but this time France won decisively, by their biggest winning margin against England to date. The match was a singular triumph for Michel Crauste, who became the only forward in the history of the Championship to score three tries. (Jehoida Hodges, of Wales, scored a hat-trick of tries against England at Swansea in 1903, but only after he had been brought out of the pack to play on the wing, following an injury to another player.) Consequently three England players were dropped, including the redoubtable John Currie, who had started his Championship career in harness with David Marques in 1956.

FRANCE   C. Lacaze 1 (FC Lourdes); H. Rancoule 11 (S. Tarbes), A. Boniface 15 (S. Mont-de-Marsan), J. Bouquet 24 (CS Vienne), J. Dupuy 20 (S. Tarbes); P. Albaladejo 9 (US Dax), *P. Lacroix 8 (SU Agen); A. Domenech 26 (CA Brive), J. de Gregorio 10 (FC Grenoble), A. Roques 16 (S. Cahors), J-P. Saux 6 (S. Pau), B. Mommejat 10 (SC Albi), R. Gensanne 2 (AS Béziers), M. Crauste 17 (FC Lourdes), H. Romero 2 (US Montauban).

ENGLAND   J.G. Willcox 6 (Oxford U.); A.M. Underwood 3 (Northampton), M.R. Wade (3) (Cambridge U.), M.P. Weston 11 (Richmond), J. Roberts 11 (Sale); R.A.W. Sharp 9 (Oxford U.), *R.E.G. Jeeps 21 (Northampton); P.E. Judd 3 (Coventry), S.A.M. Hodgson 8 (Durham City), T.P. Wright 11 (Blackheath), V.S.J. Harding 5 (Sale), J.D. Currie (23) (Bristol), R.E. Syrett (10) (Wasps), D.P. Rogers 6 (Bedford), P.J. Taylor 5 (Northampton).

Referee D.G. Walters (Wales)

Pierre Lacroix, astute French captain and scrum-half tactician, puts pressure on Ireland on 14 April 1962

IRELAND v SCOTLAND 68/522

24 February 1962
Lansdowne Road, Dublin
Scotland 20 (1G, 2T, 1DG, 2PG) Ireland 6 (1T, 1PG)

Ireland T: Hunter. PG. Hunter.
Scotland T: Smith (2), Cowan. C: Scotland. DG: Coughtrie. PG: Scotland (2).

Scotland's biggest score in Ireland was curious insofar that the Irish pack dominated for much of the contest. Arthur Smith, who was to play one more Championship match only, was the Scottish hero with two tries, the veteran wing finishing off some excellent creative work initiated by Waddell and Coughtrie.

IRELAND F.G. Gilpin 2 (Queen's U. Belfast); W.R. Hunter 2 (CIYMS), M.K. Flynn 4 (Wanderers), D. Hewitt 15 (Instonians), N.H. Brophy 11 (Blackrock College); G.G. Hardy (1) (Bective Rangers), J.T.M. Quirke 2 (Blackrock College); S. Millar 15 (Ballymena), A.R. Dawson 14 (Wanderers), R.J. McLoughlin 2 (UC Dublin), *W.A. Mulcahy 16 (Bohemians), W.J. McBride 2 (Ballymena), D. Scott (2) (Malone), M.L. Hipwell 2 (Terenure), M.G. Culliton 13 (Wanderers).

SCOTLAND K.J.F. Scotland 20 (Leicester); *A.R. Smith 29 (Edinburgh Wands), J.J. McPartlin 5 (Oxford U.), I.H.P. Laughland 11 (London Scottish), R.C. Cowan 4 (Selkirk); G.H. Waddell 15 (London Scottish), S. Coughtrie 6 (Edinburgh Acads); H.F. McLeod 35 (Hawick), N.S. Bruce 18 (London Scottish), R. Steven (1) (Edinburgh Wands), F.H. ten Bos 10 (London Scottish), M.J. Campbell-Lamerton 6 (Halifax), R.J.C. Glasgow 3 (Dunfermline), K.I. Ross 6 (Boroughmuir FP), J. Douglas 7 (Stewart's FP).

Referee Dr N.M. Parkes (England)

SCOTLAND v ENGLAND   65/523

17 March 1962
Murrayfield
Scotland 3 (1PG)   England 3 (1PG)

Scotland   PG: Scotland.
England   PG: Willcox.

The third time in five years Scotland and England produced a draw with a penalty apiece. It was most disappointing for Scotland, who had earlier beaten Wales after eight successive defeats in Wales, and had run up a record 20 points against Ireland. They fell at the Triple Crown hurdle yet again because of their failure to breach the resolute English defence. For Arthur Smith, Gordon Waddell and Hugh McLeod it proved the finale of their great careers. It was puzzling to many keen observers that Scotland did not fare better considering that it had players of such quality; at least all three went out on a high note, having contributed to a side which finished second, Scotland's highest Championship placing since 1950.

SCOTLAND   K.J.F. Scotland 21 (Leicester); *A.R. Smith (30) (Edinburgh Wands), J.J. McPartlin (6) (Oxford U.), I.H.P. Laughland 12 (London Scottish), R.C. Cowan (5) (Selkirk); G.H. Waddell (16) (London Scottish), S. Coughtrie 7 (Edinburgh Acads); H.F. McLeod (36) (Hawick), N.S. Bruce 19 (London Scottish), D.M.D. Rollo 12 (Howe of Fife), F.H. ten Bos 11 (London Scottish), M.J. Campbell-Lamerton 7 (Halifax), R.J.C. Glasgow 4 (Dunfermline), K.I. Ross 7 (Boroughmuir FP), J. Douglas 8 (Stewart's FP).

ENGLAND   J.G. Willcox 7 (Oxford U.); A.C.B. Hurst (1) (Wasps), A.M. Underwood 4 (Northampton), J.M. Dee (1) (Hartlepool Rovers), J. Roberts 12 (Sale); J.P. Horrocks-Taylor 3 (Leicester), *R.E.G. Jeeps (22) (Northampton); P.E. Judd 4 (Coventry), S.A.M. Hodgson 9 (Durham City), T.P. Wright (12) (Blackheath), T.A. Pargetter 1 (Coventry), V.S.J. Harding (6) (Sale), S.J. Purdy (1) (Rugby), P.G.D. Robbins (17) (Coventry), P.J. Taylor (6) (Northampton).

Referee K.D. Kelleher (Ireland)

WALES v FRANCE   33/524

24 March 1962
Cardiff Arms Park
Wales 3 (1PG)   France 0

Wales   PG: Coslett.

This was only the third occasion Wales had failed to register a try against France in matches in Wales, the previous two occasions being in 1948, when France won in Wales for a first time, and in 1952. In contrast, it was the last time that France failed to score against Wales and it was their first defeat against them since 1957.

WALES   K. Coslett (3) (Aberavon); D.R.R. Morgan 3 (Llanelli), D.K. Jones 3 (Llanelli), H.M. Roberts 6 (Cardiff), D.I.E. Bebb 15 (Swansea); A. Rees (3) (Maesteg), A. O'Connor 3 (Aberavon); L.J. Cunningham 7 (Aberavon), *B.V. Meredith 31 (Newport), K.D. Jones 5 (Cardiff), K.A. Rowlands 1 (Cardiff), D. Nash (5) (Ebbw Vale), G.D. Davidge (8) (Newport), H.J. Morgan 14 (Abertillery), A.E.I. Pask 4 (Abertillery).

FRANCE   C. Lacaze 2 (FC Lourdes); H. Rancoule 12 (S. Tarbes), A. Boniface 16 (S. Mont-de-Marsan), J. Bouquet 25 (CS Vienne), J. Dupuy 21 (S. Tarbes); P. Albaladejo 10 (US Dax), *P. Lacroix 9 (SU Agen); A. Domenech 27 (CA Brive), J. de Gregorio 11 (FC Grenoble), A. Roques 17 (S. Cahors), B. Mommejat 11 (SC Albi), J-P. Saux 7 (S. Pau), R. Gensanne 3 (AS Béziers), M. Crauste 18 (FC Lourdes), H. Romero 3 (US Montauban).

Referee K.D. Kelleher (Ireland)

FRANCE v IRELAND   33/525

14 April 1962
Stade Colombes, Paris
France 11 (1G, 2T)   Ireland 0

France   T: Mommejat, Lacaze, Crauste. C: Albaladejo.

France extended their run of matches without defeat to ten, their longest sequence. It left them clearly in the lead at the top of the table for a fourth season in a row, with Ireland condemned to bottom place for a third year running. The Irish had suffered a miserable period with one victory only in 12 Championship matches.

FRANCE   C. Lacaze 3 (FC Lourdes); H. Rancoule (13) (S. Tarbes), A. Boniface 17 (S. Mont-de-Marsan), J. Bouquet (26) (CS Vienne), J. Dupuy 22 (S. Tarbes); P. Albaladejo 11 (US Dax), *P. Lacroix 10 (SU Agen); A. Domenech 28 (CA Brive), J. Laudouar (1) (AS Soustons), A. Roques 18 (S. Cahors), J-P. Saux 8 (S. Pau), B. Mommejat 12 (SC Albi), H. Romero 4 (SU Montauban), R. Gensanne 4 (AS Béziers), M. Crauste 19 (FC Lourdes).

IRELAND   F.G. Gilpin (3) (Queen's U. Belfast); W.R. Hunter 3 (CIYMS), M.K. Flynn 5 (Wanderers), D. Hewitt 16 (Instonians), F. Byrne (1) (UC Dublin); M.A.F. English 11 (Lansdowne), J.C. Kelly 1 (UC Dublin); R.J. McLoughlin 3 (Blackrock College), A.R. Dawson 15 (Wanderers), S. Millar 16 (Ballymena), W.J. McBride 3 (Ballymena), *W.A. Mulcahy 17 (Bective Rangers), M.G. Culliton 14 (Wanderers), J.R. Kavanagh (31) (Wanderers), P.J.A. O'Sullivan 11 (Galwegians).

Referee J.A.S. Taylor (Scotland)

IRELAND   T.J. Kiernan 10 (UC Cork); W.R. Hunter 4 (CIYMS), A.C. Pedlow 26 (CIYMS), M.K. Flynn 6 (Wanderers), N.H. Brophy 12 (London Irish); M.A.F. English 12 (Lansdowne), J.C. Kelly 2 (UC Dublin); M.P. O'Callaghan 1 (Sunday's Well), A.R. Dawson 16 (Wanderers), P.J. Dwyer 1 (UC Dublin), W.J. McBride 4 (Ballymena), *W.A. Mulcahy 18 (Bective Rangers), P.J.A. O'Sullivan 12 (Galwegians), M.D. Kiely 1 (Lansdowne), C.J. Dick 3 (Ballymena).

WALES   G.T.R. Hodgson 1 (Neath); D.R.R. Morgan 4 (Llanelli), D.K. Jones 4 (Llanelli), D.B. Davies 1 (Llanelli), D.I.E. Bebb 16 (Swansea); C. Ashton (7) (Aberavon), A. O'Connor (4) (Aberavon); J. Warlow (1) (Llanelli), *B.V. Meredith (32) (Newport), L.J. Cunningham 8 (Aberavon), W.R. Evans (11) (Bridgend), K.A. Rowlands 2 (Cardiff), D.J. Davies (1) (Neath), H.J. Morgan 15 (Abertillery), A.E.I. Pask 5 (Abertillery).

Referee J.A.S. Taylor (Scotland)

IRELAND v WALES   64/526

17 November 1962
Lansdowne Road, Dublin
Ireland 3 (1DG) Wales (1PG)

Ireland   DG: English.
Wales   PG: Hodgson.

This match was postponed from March because of an outbreak of smallpox in the Rhondda. While Ireland were satisfied with keeping their reconstructed side intact, Wales decided that six of their players would not play in the Championship again, including their captain, Bryn Meredith, whose record of 32 caps as hooker still stands. Meredith faced few men who could outstrike him, he had the strength and technique for all-out scrummaging and he was also a fast ball-handler in the loose. Other Welsh hookers may have been better than Meredith in specific skills; but none compared in all-round ability.

1963

PARIS Scotland beat France 11-6 · CARDIFF England beat Wales 13-6
DUBLIN France beat Ireland 24-5 · MURRAYFIELD Wales beat Scotland 6-0
DUBLIN Ireland drew England 0-0 · TWICKENHAM England beat France 6-5
MURRAYFIELD Scotland beat Ireland 3-0 · CARDIFF Ireland beat Wales 14-6
TWICKENHAM England beat Scotland 10-8 · PARIS France beat Wales 5-3

CHAMPIONSHIP TABLE
England – Championship

| | | | | | | | | | Tries | |
Pos	Country	P	W	D	L	F	A	Pts	F	A
1	England (3)	4	3	1	0	29	19	7	4	3
2	France (1)	4	2	0	2	40	25	4	6	2
3	Scotland (2)	4	2	0	2	22	22	4	2	2
4	Ireland (5)	4	1	1	2	19	33	3	2	5
5	Wales (4)	4	1	0	3	21	32	2	2	4

England ended France's four-year domination of the Championship, by winning the title with three narrow wins. They were prevented from taking the Grand Slam by a 0-0 draw against Ireland, but it was nevertheless a fitting finale to the Championship careers of Jim Roberts, Peter Jackson and Richard Sharp. France may have been denied another title, but they still achieved the distinction of keeping their try-line intact for the only time in their Championship history.

Ireland's 14-6 victory over Wales in Cardiff ended for them a run of ten Championship matches without a victory, which had been their longest sequence. The defeat condemned Wales to the Wooden Spoon for the first time since 1949, although they could still have avoided that indignity had they wrung out even a draw in their last match, against France. Scotland started their campaign by beating France but they could not maintain momentum. Even so, for the Scots to win two matches for a second season in a row suggested their worst days were over, and that the future boded well.

FRANCE v SCOTLAND   33/527

12 January 1963
Stade Colombes, Paris
Scotland 11 (1G, 1DG, 1PG) France 6 (1DG, 1PG)

France DG: André Boniface. PG: Albaladejo.
Scotland T: Thomson. C: Scotland. DG: Scotland. PG: Scotland.

This match, best remembered for a remarkable late try by Ronnie Thomson after a dropped goal attempt had gone wide, was also the first appearance together of the Boniface brothers, André and Guy, for France. Each was an outstanding attacking player, with a panache for dropped goals, but on this occasion the light French forwards were so convincingly outplayed that scoring opportunities were rare. It was the last Championship appearance of Alfred 'The Rock' Roques, the Cahors prop, who earned an awesome reputation for his scrummage technique and strength.

FRANCE   J-P. Razat 1 (SU Agen); P. Besson 1 (CA Brive), A. Boniface 18 (S. Mont-de-Marsan), G. Boniface 7 (S. Mont-de-Marsan), C. Darrouy 5 (S. Mont-de-Marsan); P. Albaladejo 12 (US Dax), *P. Lacroix 11 (SU Agen); F. Mas 1 (AS Béziers), J. de Gregorio 12 (FC Grenoble), A. Roques (19) (S. Cahors), B. Mommejat 13 (SC Albi), J-P. Saux 9 (S. Pau), R. Gensanne (5) (AS Béziers), M. Crauste 20 (FC Lourdes), J. Fabre 1 (S. Toulouse).

SCOTLAND   *K.J.F. Scotland 22 (Leicester); R.H. Thomson 7 (London Scottish), J.A.P. Shackleton 2 (London Scottish), D.M. White 1 (Kelvinside Acads), G.D. Stevenson 17 (Hawick); I.H.P.

Laughland 13 (London Scottish), S. Coughtrie 8 (Edinburgh Acads); A.C.W. Boyle 1 (London Scottish), N.S. Bruce 20 (London Scottish), D.M.D. Rollo 13 (Howe of Fife), F.H. ten Bos 12 (London Scottish), M.J. Campbell-Lamerton 8 (Halifax), K.I. Ross 8 (Boroughmuir FP), W.R.A. Watherston 1 (London Scottish), J. Douglas 9 (Stewart's FP).

Referee R.C. Williams (Ireland)

WALES v ENGLAND 67/528

19 January 1963
Cardiff Arms Park
England 13 (2G, 1DG) Wales 6 (1T, 1PG)

Wales T: Hayward. PG: Hodgson.
England T: Owen, Phillips. C: Sharp (2). DG: Sharp.

This was a victory for England to savour for it was their only one in 13 matches in Cardiff between 1959–83. Six of the English pack had not played in an international before and Simon Clarke, cherubic-looking Cambridge University scrum-half, had the unenviable task as successor to the great Dickie Jeeps. Wales also fielded new faces, six in all, including David Watkins and Clive Rowlands at half-back, and two formidable-looking giants in the pack, Denzil Williams and Brian Thomas. Another newcomer, Dai Hayward, scored the Welsh try heralding his comparatively short but explosive entry into the international game.

WALES G.T.R. Hodgson 2 (Neath); D.R.R. Morgan 5 (Llanelli), D.K. Jones 5 (Llanelli), D.B. Davies 2 (Llanelli), D.I.E. Bebb 17 (Swansea); D. Watkins 1 (Newport), *D.C.T. Rowlands 1 (Pontypool); K.D. Jones 6 (Cardiff), N.R. Gale 2 (Llanelli), D. Williams 1 (Ebbw Vale), B.E. Thomas 1 (Neath), B. Price 5 (Newport), A.E.I. Pask 6 (Abertillery), D.J. Hayward 1 (Cardiff), R.C.B. Michaelson (1) (Cambridge U.).

ENGLAND J.G. Willcox 8 (Oxford U.); P.B. Jackson 16 (Coventry), M.S. Phillips 13 (Fylde), M.P. Weston 12 (Durham City), J. Roberts 13 (Sale); *R.A.W. Sharp 10 (Wasps), S.J.S. Clarke 1 (Cambridge U.); N.J. Drake-Lee 1 (Cambridge U.), J.D. Thorne 1 (Bristol), B.A. Dovey 1 (Rosslyn Park), A.M. Davis 1 (Torquay Athletic), J.E. Owen 1 (Coventry), D.C. Manley 1 (Exeter), D.P. Rogers 7 (Bedford), B.J. Wightman 2 (Coventry).

Referee K.D. Kelleher (Ireland)

IRELAND v FRANCE 34/529

26 January 1963
Lansdowne Road, Dublin
France 24 (3G, 1T, 2DG) Ireland 5 (1G)

Ireland T: O'Reilly. C: Kiernan.
France T: Guy Boniface, Darrouy (3). C: Albaladejo (3). DG: Albaladejo, André Boniface.

This was France's highest score and biggest winning points margin in matches with Ireland in Ireland, and they achieved success with what was substantially a new side. Ireland, at the time, were not endowed with a surplus of top-class players, which was probably why three players only were axed. Two of them, however, were stalwarts of the side, Cecil Pedlow and Tony O'Sullivan. With a yard or so more pace, the gifted Pedlow would have been one of the outstanding backs of the late 1950s; as it was he played with skill and determination whether he was selected as a wing or a centre. O'Sullivan, a rugged, lusty back-row forward was considerably underrated and possibly would have won many more than his 13 Championship caps had not Ireland been a struggling side during his playing career.

IRELAND T.J. Kiernan 11 (Cork Constitution); W.R. Hunter 5 (CIYMS), J.B. Murray (1) (UC Dublin), A.C. Pedlow (27) (CIYMS), A.J.F. O'Reilly 24 (Old Belvedere); P.J. Casey 1 (Lansdowne), J.C. Kelly 3 (UC Dublin); P.J. Dwyer 2 (UC Dublin), A.R. Dawson 17 (Wanderers), S. Millar 17 (Ballymena), W.J. McBride 5 (Ballymena), *W.A. Mulcahy 19 (Bective Rangers), P.J.A. O'Sullivan (13) (Galwegians), M.D. Kiely 2 (Lansdowne), C.J. Dick 4 (Ballymena).

FRANCE J-P. Razat (2) (SU Agen); P. Besson 2 (CA Brive), A. Boniface 19 (S. Mont-de-Marsan), G. Boniface 8 (S. Mont-de-Marsan), C. Darrouy 6 (S. Mont-de-Marsan); P. Albaladejo 13 (US Dax), *P. Lacroix 12 (SU Agen); F. Mas 2 (AS Béziers), J. Rollet (1) (A. Bayonne), F. Zago 1 (US Montauban), J-P. Saux 10 (S. Pau), B. Mommejat 14

(SC Albi), J. Fabre 2 (S. Toulouse), M. Crauste 21 (FC Lourdes), M. Lira 1 (La Voulte S.).

Referee F.G. Price (Wales)

SCOTLAND v WALES   67/530

2 February 1963
Murrayfield
Wales 6 (1DG, 1PG) Scotland 0

Wales   DG: Rowlands. PG: Hodgson.

This was Wales's only victory of the season and was the result of unadulterated nine-man rugby. Clive Rowlands, the Wales captain and scrum-half, kicked, kicked and kicked again, tactics which not only effectively pinned down Scotland in their own half, but produced a flush of lines-out. One statistician counted over 100, though that figure is unlikely since there would have been little or no time for scrums, mauls or even the few passes that did break the monotony.

SCOTLAND   *K.J.F. Scotland 23 (Heriot's FP); R.H. Thomson 8 (London Scottish), J.A.P. Shackleton 3 (London Scottish), D.W. White 2 (Kelvinside Acads), G.D. Stevenson 18 (Hawick); I.H.P. Laughland 14 (London Scottish), S. Coughtrie 9 (Edinburgh Acads); A.C.W. Boyle 2 (London Scottish), N.S. Bruce 21 (London Scottish), D.M.D. Rollo 14 (Howe of Fife), F.H. ten Bos 13 (London Scottish), M.J. Campbell-Lamerton 9 (Halifax), K.I. Ross 9 (Boroughmuir FP), W.R.A. Watherston 2 (London Scottish), J. Douglas 10 (Stewart's FP).

WALES   G.T.R. Hodgson 3 (Neath); D.R.R. Morgan 6 (Llanelli), D.B. Davies (3) (Llanelli), R. Evans 1 (Bridgend), W.J. Morris 1 (Pontypool); D. Watkins 2 (Newport), * D.C.T. Rowlands 2 (Pontypool); D. Williams 2 (Ebbw Vale), N.R. Gale 3 (Llanelli), K.D. Jones 7 (Cardiff), B. Price 6 (Newport), B.E. Thomas 2 (Cambridge U.), G. Jones 1 (Ebbw Vale), H.J. Morgan 16 (Abertillery), A.E.I. Pask 7 (Abertillery).

Referee R.C. Williams (Ireland)

IRELAND v ENGLAND   67/531

9 February 1963
Lansdowne Road, Dublin
Ireland 0 England 0

England had won two matches only at Lansdowne Road since 1938 and luck was against them on this occasion, marred by continual rain and a slippery surface. The relatively inexperienced English pack, which had surprised Wales at Cardiff the previous month, could not match the Irish in either beef or brain, but their threequarters always had the edge in ideas and speed over the surprisingly ineffective Irish backs.

IRELAND   B.D.E. Marshall (1) (Queen's U. Belfast); W.R. Hunter 6 (CIYMS), J.C. Walsh 5 (UC Cork), P.J. Casey 2 (UC Dublin), N.H. Brophy 13 (Blackrock College); M.A.F. English 13 (Lansdowne), J.C. Kelly 4 (UC Dublin); R.J. McLoughlin 4 (Blackrock College), A.R. Dawson 18 (Wanderers), S. Millar 18 (Ballymena), *W.A. Mulcahy 20 (Bective Rangers), W.J. McBride 6 (Ballymena), E.P. McGuire 1 (UC Galway), M.D. Kiely 3 (Lansdowne), C.J. Dick 5 (Ballymena).

ENGLAND   J.G. Willcox 9 (Oxford U.); P.B. Jackson 17 (Coventry), M.S. Phillips 14 (Fylde), M.P. Weston 13 (Durham City), J. Roberts 14 (Sale); *R.A.W. Sharp 11 (Wasps), S.J.S. Clarke 2 (Cambridge U.); N.J. Drake-Lee 2 (Cambridge U.), J.D. Thorne 2 (Bristol), B.A. Dovey (2) (Rosslyn Park), A.M. Davis 2 (Torquay Athletic), J.E. Owen 2 (Coventry), D.C. Manley 2 (Exeter), D.P. Rogers 8 (Bedford), B.J. Wightman (3) (Coventry).

Referee H.B. Laidlaw (Scotland)

ENGLAND v FRANCE 34/532

23 February 1963
Twickenham
England 6 (2PG) France 5 (1G)

England PG: Willcox (2).
France T: Guy Boniface. C: Albaladejo.

After draws in the previous two matches at Twickenham, this was a close encounter of a third kind, a single-point victory going to England thanks to two penalties by John Willcox. Neither side played particularly well and consequently eight players, five of them French, were not invited again for Championship duty.

ENGLAND J.G. Willcox 10 (Oxford U.); P.B. Jackson 18 (Coventry), M.S. Phillips 15 (Fylde), M.P. Weston 14 (Durham City), J. Roberts 15 (Sale); *R.A.W. Sharp 12 (Wasps), S.J.S. Clarke 3 (Cambridge U.); K.J. Wilson (1) (Gloucester), J.D. Thorne (3) (Bristol), N.J. Drake-Lee 3 (Cambridge U.), T.A. Pargetter (2) (Coventry), J.E. Owen 3 (Coventry), D.C. Manley 3 (Exeter), D.P. Rogers 9 (Bedford), D.G. Perry 1 (Bedford).

FRANCE P. Dedieu 1 (AS Béziers); P. Besson (3) (CA Brive), G. Boniface 9 (S. Mont-de-Marsan), A. Boniface 20 (S. Mont-de-Marsan), C. Darrouy 7 (S. Mont-de-Marsan); P. Albaladejo 14 (US Dax), *P. Lacroix 13 (SU Agen); F. Mas 3 (AS Béziers), R. Rebujent (1) (RCF), F. Zago (2) (US Montauban), M. Lira 2 (La Voulte S.), J-P. Saux (11) (S. Pau), J. Fabre 3 (S. Toulouse), M. Crauste 22 (FC Lourdes), H. Romero (5) (US Montauban).

Referee D.C.J. McMahon (Scotland)

SCOTLAND v IRELAND 69/533

23 February 1963
Murrayfield
Scotland 3 (1PG) Ireland 0

Scotland PG: Coughtrie.

Irish rugby plunged to the point of despair with this defeat for it was their tenth consecutive match without a victory, their longest ever sequence. An indication of the differing attitudes of the selectors was that the Irish kept faith in their side – which probably was unlucky to lose anyway – while the Scottish dropped three of their pack, including Cameron Boyle who because of injury had to swap positions with Franz ten Bos.

SCOTLAND C.F. Blaikie 1 (Heriot's FP); R.H. Thomson 9 (London Scottish), I.H.P. Laughland 15 (London Scottish), D.M. White 3 (Kelvinside Acads), G.D. Stevenson 19 (Hawick); *K.J.F. Scotland 24 (Heriot's FP), S. Coughtrie 10 (Edinburgh Acads); A.C.W. Boyle (3) (London Scottish), N.S. Bruce 22 (London Scottish), D.M.D. Rollo 15 (Howe of Fife), F.H. ten Bos 14 (London Scottish), M.J. Campbell-Lamerton 10 (Halifax), R.J.C. Glasgow 5 (Dunfermline), W.R.A. Watherston (3) (London Scottish), J. Douglas (11) (Stewart's FP).

IRELAND T.J. Kiernan 12 (UC Cork); W.R. Hunter 7 (CIYMS), J.C. Walsh 6 (UC Cork), P.J. Casey 3 (UC Dublin), A.J.F. O'Reilly 25 (Old Belvedere); M.A.F. English 14 (Lansdowne), J.C. Kelly 5 (UC Dublin); S. Millar 19 (Ballymena), A.R. Dawson 19 (Wanderers), R.J. McLoughlin 5 (Gosforth), *W.A. Mulcahy 21 (Bective Rangers), W.J. McBride 7 (Ballymena), E.P. McGuire 2 (UC Galway), M.D. Kiely 4 (Lansdowne), C.J. Dick 6 (Ballymena).

Referee G.J. Treharne (Wales)

The irrepressible Michel Crauste, one of the all-time great French forwards

WALES v IRELAND   65/534

9 March 1963
Cardiff Arms Park
Ireland 14 (1G, 1DG, 2PG) Wales 6 (1T, 1DG)

Wales   T: Graham Jones. DG: Watkins.
Ireland   T: Casey. C: Kiernan. DG: English. PG: Kiernan (2).

Ireland won their only game of the season at Cardiff, their first triumph on Welsh soil since 1949, with their biggest score in Wales to date. The Irish forwards were irresistible and the covering and tackling was so good that Wales rarely threatened.

WALES   G.T.R. Hodgson 4 (Neath); D.R.R. Morgan 7 (Llanelli), R. Evans 2 (Bridgend), H.M. Roberts (7) (Cardiff), W.J. Morris (2) (Pontypool); D. Watkins 3 (Newport), *D.C.T. Rowlands 3 (Pontypool); D. Williams 3 (Ebbw Vale), N.R. Gale 4 (Llanelli), K.D. Jones (8) (Cardiff), K.A. Rowlands 3 (Cardiff), B.E. Thomas 3 (Neath), G. Jones 2 (Ebbw Vale), H.J. Morgan 17 (Abertillery), A.E.I. Pask 8 (Abertillery).

IRELAND   T.J. Kiernan 13 (Cork Constitution); A.J.F. O'Reilly 26 (Old Belvedere), J.C. Walsh 7 (UC Cork), P.J. Casey 4 (UC Dublin), N.H. Brophy 14 (Blackrock College); M.A.F. English (15) (Lansdowne), J.C. Kelly 6 (UC Dublin); R.J. McLoughlin 6 (Gosforth), A.R. Dawson 20 (Wanderers), S. Millar 20 (Ballymena), W.J. McBride 8 (Ballymena), *W.A. Mulcahy 22 (Bective Rangers), M.D. Kiely (5) (Lansdowne), E.P. McGuire 3 (UC Galway), C.J. Dick (7) (Ballymena).

Referee A.C. Luff (England)

ENGLAND v SCOTLAND   66/535

16 March 1963
Twickenham
England 10 (2G) Scotland 8 (1G, 1DG)

England   T: Drake-Lee, Sharp. C: Willcox (2).
Scotland   T: Glasgow. C: Coughtrie. DG: Scotland.

This was the thirteenth successive match in which Scotland failed to beat England, who thus won the Championship and left the Scots, also seeking the title, in third place. The repercussions were that White, Coughtrie, ten Bos and Ross joined the ranks of Scottish ex-internationals; and three great English backs, Peter Jackson, Jim Roberts and Richard Sharp, did not play again in the Championship. Some historians have suggested that the loss of these three players was a major cause of the decline of England as international force, an hypothesis supported by results: England won only 2 of their next 17 internationals, both against France.

ENGLAND   J.G. Willcox 11 (Harlequins); P.B. Jackson (19) (Coventry), M.S. Phillips 16 (Fylde), M.P. Weston 15 (Durham City), J. Roberts (16) (Sale); *R.A.W. Sharp (13) (Wasps), S.J.S. Clarke 4 (Cambridge U.); P.E. Judd 5 (Coventry), H.O. Godwin 3 (Coventry), N.J. Drake-Lee 4 (Cambridge U.), A.M. Davis 3 (Torquay Athletic), J.E. Owen 4 (Coventry), D.C. Manley (4) (Exeter), D.P. Rogers 10 (Bedford), D.G. Perry 2 (Bedford).

SCOTLAND   C.F. Blaikie 2 (Heriot's FP); C. Elliot 4 (Langholm), B.C. Henderson 1 (Edinburgh Wands), D.M. White (4) (Kelvinside Acads), R.H. Thomson 10 (London Scottish); *K.J.F. Scotland 25 (Heriot's FP), S. Coughtrie (11) (Edinburgh Acads); J.B. Neill 1 (Edinburgh Acads), N.S. Bruce 23 (London Scottish), D.M.D. Rollo 16 (Howe of Fife), F.H. ten Bos (15) (London Scottish), M.J. Campbell-Lamerton 11 (Halifax), R.J.C. Glasgow 6 (Dunfermline), K.I. Ross (10) (Boroughmuir), J.P. Fisher 1 (Royal HSFP).

Referee D.G. Walters (Wales)

FRANCE v WALES   34/536

23 March 1963
Stade Colombes, Paris
France 5 (1G) Wales 3 (1PG)

France   T: Guy Boniface. C: Albaladejo.
Wales   PG: Hodgson.

Defeat, their third of the season, firmly placed Wales at the bottom of the Championship for a first time since 1949. The French, who had suffered many such indignities at Welsh hands, thus had won five out of their last six meetings, an unprecedented run of success for them. It was a fitting climax to the Championship careers of three of France's outstanding players: Amédée Domenech, Bernard Mommejat and Pierre Lacroix.

FRANCE   C. Lacaze 4 (SC Angoulême); C. Darrouy 8 (S. Mont-de-Marsan), A. Boniface 21 (S. Mont-de-Marsan), G. Boniface 10 (S. Mont-de-Marsan), J. Dupuy 23 (S. Tarbes); P. Albaladejo 15 (US Dax), *P. Lacroix (14) (SU Agen); F. Mas (4) (AS Béziers), J. de Gregorio 13 (FC Grenoble), A. Domenech (29) (CA Brive), R. Fite (1) (CA Brive), B. Mommejat (15) (SC Albi), M. Lira 3 (La Voulte S.), M. Crauste 23 (FC Lourdes), J. Fabre 4 (S. Toulouse).

WALES   G.T.R. Hodgson 5 (Neath); D.R.R. Morgan 8 (Llanelli), D.K. Jones 6 (Llanelli), R. Evans (3) (Bridgend), D.I.E. Bebb 18 (Swansea); D. Watkins 4 (Newport), *D.C.T. Rowlands 4 (Pontypool); D. Williams 4 (Ebbw Vale), W.J. Thomas (2) (Cardiff), C.H. Norris 1 (Cardiff), B. Price 7 (Newport), B.E. Thomas 4 (Neath), G. Jones (3) (Ebbw Vale), H.J. Morgan 18 (Abertillery), A.E.I. Pask 9 (Abertillery).

Referee P.G. Brook (England)

1964

MURRAYFIELD Scotland beat France 10-0 · TWICKENHAM England drew Wales 6-6
CARDIFF Wales beat Scotland 11-3 · TWICKENHAM Ireland beat England 18-5
PARIS England beat France 6-3 · DUBLIN Scotland beat Ireland 6-3
DUBLIN Wales beat Ireland 15-6 · MURRAYFIELD Scotland beat England 15-6
CARDIFF Wales drew France 11-11 · PARIS France beat Ireland 27-6

CHAMPIONSHIP TABLE
Wales – Championship

Pos	Country	P	W	D	L	F	A	Pts	Tries F	Tries A
1	Wales (5)	4	2	2	0	43	26	6	8	4
2	Scotland (3)	4	3	0	1	34	20	6	6	3
3	France (2)	4	1	1	2	41	33	3	8	5
4	England (1)	4	1	1	2	23	42	3	5	10
5	Ireland (4)	4	1	0	3	33	53	2	5	10

After seven lean years, Wales at last won the Championship again, ending their longest period without a title success since an eight-year break up to 1931 and the ten-year wait from 1883 before they won for the first time. Scotland won three matches, one more than Wales, to finish second and they took greatest pleasure of all from the last of these, a 15-6 defeat over England. It was their first victory over the traditional enemy in 14 matches and was interesting in that all three of their tries came from a forward.

It was a curious season for Ireland. They started in brilliant form, storming to an 18-3 win at Twickenham, where Mike Gibson enjoyed a scintillating début. The new Irish fly-half could not inspire his countrymen to similar heights in the remaining matches, all of which were lost and culminated in a terrible beating by France in Paris. In that match Christian Darrouy scored two tries to follow on his hat-trick against Ireland the previous season. Michel Crauste also scored a try to bring his total for France to 7 in 27 appearances.

SCOTLAND v FRANCE 34/537

4 January 1964
Murrayfield
Scotland 10 (2G) France 0

Scotland T: Laughland, Thomson. C: Wilson (2).

Stewart Wilson, Jim Telfer and Peter Brown, each of whom was to captain Scotland in the future, made their Championship début appearances on a wet greasy pitch which favoured the more orthodox Scottish approach. The French – playing six new men in their pack – frittered many a scoring chance with over-complicated passing movements, with the result that they failed to score for only a third time in 17 visits.

SCOTLAND   S. Wilson 1 (Oxford U.); C. Elliot 5 (Langholm), B.C. Henderson 2 (Edinburgh Wands), I.H.P. Laughland 16 (London Scottish), R.H. Thomson 11 (London Scottish); G. Sharp 2 (Stewart's FP), J.A.T. Rodd 8 (London Scottish); *J.B. Neill 2 (Edinburgh Acads), N.S. Bruce 24 (London Scottish), D.M.D. Rollo 17 (Howe of Fife), W.J. Hunter 1 (Hawick), P.C. Brown 1 (W. of Scotland), J.W. Telfer 1 (Melrose), J.P. Fisher 2 (Royal HSFP), T.O. Grant 3 (Hawick).

FRANCE   C. Lacaze 5 (SC Angoulême); J. Gachassin 3 (FC Lourdes), G. Boniface 11 (S. Mont-de-Marsan), A. Boniface 22 (S. Mont-de-Marsan), J. Dupuy (24) (S. Tarbes); P. Albaladejo 16 (US Dax), J-C. Lasserre 1 (US Dax); J-C. Berejnoi 1 (SC Tulle), J-M. Cabanier 1 (US Montauban), J. Bayardon 1 (RC Chalon), B. Dauga 1 (S. Mont-de-

Marsan), J. le Droff 1 (FC Auch), J-J. Rupert 1 (US Tyrosse), M. Crauste 24 (FC Lourdes), *J. Fabre 5 (S. Toulouse).

Referee R.C. Williams (Ireland)

ENGLAND v WALES 68/538

18 January 1964
Twickenham
England 6 (2T) Wales 6 (2T)

England T: Perry, Ranson.
Wales T: Bebb (2).

This was Phil Horrocks-Taylor's fourth and final Championship match, though he had played on five other occasions for England. The Welsh hero of the day was unquestionably that master try poacher, Dewi Bebb. His brace of tries at Twickenham had been achieved by a Welsh player only once previously, by Ken Jones in 1952, though Bebb had scored two tries against England at Cardiff in 1961.

ENGLAND *J.G. Willcox 12 (Harlequins); M.S. Phillips 17 (Fylde), M.P. Weston 16 (Durham City), R.D. Sangwin (1) (Hull & ER), J.M. Ranson 1 (Rosslyn Park); J.P. Horrocks-Taylor (4) (Middlesbrough), S.J.S. Clarke 5 (Cambridge U.); C.R. Jacobs 21 (Northampton), S.A.M. Hodgson (10) (Durham City), N.J. Drake-Lee 5 (Cambridge U.), A.M. Davis 4 (Torquay Athletic), R.E. Rowell 1 (Leicester), P.J. Ford 1 (Gloucester), D.P. Rogers 11 (Bedford), D.G. Perry 3 (Bedford).

WALES G.T.R. Hodgson 6 (Neath); D. Weaver (1) (Swansea), D.K. Jones 7 (Llanelli), K. Bradshaw 1 (Bridgend), D.I.E. Bebb 19 (Swansea); D. Watkins 5 (Newport), *D.C.T. Rowlands 5 (Pontypool); D. Williams 5 (Ebbw Vale), N.R. Gale 5 (Llanelli), L.J. Cunningham 9 (Aberavon), B.E. Thomas 5 (Neath), B. Price 8 (Newport), J.T. Mantle (1) (Loughborough College), A. Thomas (1) (Newport), A.E.I. Pask 10 (Abertillery).

Referee K.D. Kelleher (Ireland)

WALES v SCOTLAND 68/539

1 February 1964
Cardiff Arms Park
Wales 11 (1G, 1T, 1PG) Scotland 3 (1T)

Wales T: Bradshaw, Thomas. C: Bradshaw. PG: Bradshaw.
Scotland T: Laughland.

This was the only defeat of the season for Scotland, who a fortnight earlier had been the only Championship side to avoid defeat against the touring New Zealanders.

WALES G.T.R. Hodgson 7 (Neath); S.J. Watkins 1 (Newport), D.K. Jones 8 (Llanelli), K. Bradshaw 2 (Bridgend), D.I.E. Bebb 20 (Swansea); D. Watkins 6 (Newport), *D.C.T. Rowlands 6 (Pontypool); D. Williams 6 (Ebbw Vale), N.R. Gale 6 (Llanelli), L.J. Cunningham 10 (Aberavon), B. Price 9 (Newport), B.E. Thomas 6 (Neath), G.J. Prothero 1 (Bridgend), D.J. Hayward 2 (Cardiff), A.E.I. Pask 11 (Abertillery).

SCOTLAND S. Wilson 2 (Oxford U.); C. Elliot 6 (Langholm), J.A.P. Shackleton 4 (London Scottish), I.H.P. Laughland 17 (London Scottish), R.H. Thomson (12) (London Scottish); G. Sharp (3) (Stewart's FP), J.A.T. Rodd 9 (London Scottish); *J.B. Neill 3 (Edinburgh Acads), N.S. Bruce 25 (London Scottish), D.M.D. Rollo 18 (Howe of Fife), W.J. Hunter 2 (Hawick), P.C. Brown 2 (W. of Scotland), J.W. Telfer 2 (Melrose), J.P. Fisher 3 (Royal HSFP), T.O. Grant (4) (Hawick).

Referee P.G. Brook (England)

ENGLAND v IRELAND 68/540

8 February 1964
Twickenham
Ireland 18 (3G, 1T) England 5 (1G)

England T: Rogers. C: Willcox.
Ireland T: Flynn (2), Casey, Murphy. C: Kiernan (3).

A pale, deceptively frail-looking figure called Mike Gibson made his début, at fly-half, for Ireland, and was responsible for transforming them into a volatile, occasionally brilliant attacking side. The victory which he inspired ended a run of seven Irish defeats at Twickenham since 1948 and was their biggest score there until the 1974 side, again orchestrated by Gibson, scored a record 26 points. Coincidentally, England also had a brilliant newcomer at fly-half in Tom Brophy, and had his forwards won a little more ball he rather than Gibson might have made the headlines. In the event, for those present, it was one of the best, most fluid internationals at Twickenham for many years.

ENGLAND *J.G. Willcox 13 (Harlequins); A.M. Underwood (5) (Exeter), M.S. Phillips 18 (Fylde), M.P. Weston 17 (Durham City), J.M. Ranson 2 (Rosslyn Park); T.J. Brophy 1 (Liverpool), S.J.S. Clarke 6 (Blackheath); C.R. Jacobs 22 (Northampton), H.O. Godwin 4 (Coventry), N.J. Drake-Lee 6 (Cambridge U.), C.M. Payne 1 (Harlequins), A.M. Davis 5 (Torquay Athletic), P.J. Ford 2 (Gloucester), D.P. Rogers 12 (Bedford), D.G. Perry 4 (Bedford).

IRELAND T.J. Kiernan 14 (Cork Constitution); P.J. Casey 5 (UC Dublin), J.C. Walsh 8 (UC Cork), M.K. Flynn 7 (Wanderers), J.J. Fortune (1) (Clontarf); C.M.H. Gibson 1 (Cambridge U.), J.C. Kelly 7 (UC Dublin); M.P. O'Callaghan 2 (London Irish), A.R. Dawson 21 (Wanderers), R.J. McLoughlin 7 (Gosforth), W.J. McBride 9 (Ballymena), *W.A. Mulcahy 23 (Bective Rangers), E.P. McGuire 4 (UC Galway), N.A.A. Murphy 17 (Cork Constitution), M.G. Culliton 15 (Wanderers).

Referee D.G. Walters (Wales)

FRANCE v ENGLAND 35/541

22 February 1964
Stade Colombes, Paris
England 6 (1T, 1PG) France 3 (1T)

France T: Darrouy.
England T: Phillips. PG: Hosen.

French supporters were so disappointed with their team's performance that at the end of the match they gathered in front of the committee box, to demand vociferously the resignation of their selectors. The selectors stayed but six players went, including the whole front-row,

which had been comprehensively outscrummaged by Les Formidables, Jacobs, Godwin and Wrench. England, though they won, had no cause for complacency – a suspicion confirmed a month later when the same side were thrashed by Scotland.

FRANCE C. Lacaze 6 (SC Angoulême); J. Gachassin 4 (FC Lourdes), A. Boniface 23 (S. Mont-de-Marsan), J. Piqué 2 (S. Pau), C. Darrouy 9 (S. Mont-de-Marsan); J-C. Hiquet (1) (SU Agen), J-C. Lasserre 2 (US Dax); J.B. Amestoy (1) (S. Mont-de-Marsan), J. de Gregorio (14) (FC Grenoble), J. Bayardon (2) (RC Chalon), J. le Droff 2 (FC Auch), B. Dauga 2 (S. Mont-de-Marsan), M. Crauste 25 (FC Lourdes), A. Herrero 1 (RC Toulon), *J. Fabre (6) (S. Toulouse).

ENGLAND J.G. Willcox 14 (Harlequins); R.W. Hosen 1 (Northampton), M.S. Phillips 19 (Fylde), M.P. Weston 18 (Durham City), J.M. Ranson 3 (Rosslyn Park); T.J. Brophy 2 (Liverpool), S.R. Smith 4 (Richmond); *C.R. Jacobs 23 (Northampton), H.O. Godwin 5 (Coventry), D.F.B. Wrench 1 (Harlequins), C.M. Payne 2 (Harlequins), A.M. Davis 6 (Torquay Athletic), P.J. Ford 3 (Gloucester), D.P. Rogers 13 (Bedford), T.G.A.H. Peart 1 (Hartlepool Rovers).

Referee D.G. Walters (Wales)

IRELAND v SCOTLAND 70/542

22 February 1964
Lansdowne Road, Dublin
Scotland 6 (2PG) Ireland 3 (1PG)

Ireland PG: Kiernan.
Scotland PG: Wilson (2).

This was Scotland's fifth win in a row over Ireland, their best sequence against them since winning ten matches between 1883–92. The sequence had started in 1960 after Ireland had won 16 of the previous 18 matches between the countries.

IRELAND T.J. Kiernan 15 (Cork Constitution); P.J. Casey 6 (UC Dublin), M.K. Flynn 8 (Wanderers), J.C. Walsh 9 (UC Cork), K.J. Houston 1 (Queen's U. Belfast); C.M.H. Gibson 2 (Cambridge U.), J.C. Kelly 8 (UC Dublin); P.J. Dwyer 3 (UC Dublin), A.R. Dawson 22 (Wanderers),

R.J. McLoughlin 8 (Gosforth), *W.A. Mulcahy 24 (Bective Rangers), W.J. McBride 10 (Ballymena), E.P. McGuire 5 (UC Galway), N.A.A. Murphy 18 (Cork Constitution), M.G. Culliton 16 (Wanderers).

SCOTLAND   S. Wilson 3 (Oxford U.); C. Elliot 7 (Langholm), B.C. Henderson 3 (Edinburgh Wands), I.H.P. Laughland 18 (London Scottish), W.D. Jackson 1 (Hawick); D.H. Chisholm 1 (Melrose), A.J. Hastie 4 (Melrose); *J.B. Neill 4 (Edinburgh Acads), N.S. Bruce 26 (London Scottish), D.M.D. Rollo 19 (Howe of Fife), P.C. Brown 3 (W. of Scotland), M.J. Campbell-Lamerton 12 (London Scottish), J.W. Telfer 3 (Melrose), R.J.C. Glasgow 7 (Dunfermline), J.P. Fisher 4 (Royal HSFP).

Referee A.C. Luff (England)

IRELAND v WALES   66/543

7 March 1964
Lansdowne Road, Dublin
Wales 15 (3G) Ireland 6 (2PG)

Ireland   PG: Keogh (2).
Wales   T: Stuart Watkins, Dawes, David Watkins. C: Bradshaw (3).

Wales scored their sixth victory at Lansdowne Road since 1950, in a match which was notable for the number of students Ireland played and that it was the first appearance for Wales of John Dawes, who joined that elite band of players to score a try on his début.

IRELAND   F.S. Keogh 1 (Bective Rangers); P.J. Casey 7 (UC Dublin), M.K. Flynn 9 (Wanderers), J.C. Walsh 10 (UC Cork), K.J. Houston 2 (Queen's U. Belfast); C.M.H. Gibson 3 (NIFC), J.C. Kelly 9 (UC Dublin); P.J. Dwyer (4) (UC Dublin), P. Lane (1) (Old Crescent), T.A. Moroney 1 (UC Dublin), M.W. Leahy (1) (UC Cork), *W.A. Mulcahy 25 (Bective Rangers), E.P. McGuire 6 (UC Galway), N.A.A. Murphy 19 (Cork Constitution), M.G. Culliton 17 (Wanderers).

WALES   G.T.R. Hodgson 8 (Neath); S.J. Watkins 2 (Newport), S.J. Dawes 1 (London Welsh), K. Bradshaw 3 (Bridgend), P.M. Rees (4) (Newport); D. Watkins 7 (Newport), *D.C.T. Rowlands 7 (Pontypool); D. Williams 7 (Ebbw Vale), N.R.

Gale 7 (Llanelli), L.J. Cunningham 11 (Aberavon), B. Price 10 (Newport), B.E. Thomas 7 (Neath), G.J. Prothero 2 (Bridgend), D.J. Hayward 3 (Cardiff), A.E.I. Pask 12 (Abertillery).

Referee A.C. Luff (England)

SCOTLAND v ENGLAND   67/544

21 March 1964
Murrayfield
Scotland 15 (3G) England 6 (1T, 1PG)

Scotland   T: Glasgow, Bruce, Telfer. C: Wilson (3).
England   T: Rogers. PG: Hosen.

After 13 successive matches in which they had failed to register one victory over England, Scotland at last ended their worst sequence against any country. Confirming that the bad run was over, Scotland won five of their next six home matches against England. The English reaction to their fall from Championship-holders to fourth place was to end the international careers of nine of the team, including the mighty Ron Jacobs (24 caps), the underrated centre Malcolm Phillips (20) and that most immaculate of full-backs, John Willcox (15).

SCOTLAND   S. Wilson 4 (Oxford U.); C. Elliot 8 (Langholm), B.C. Henderson 4 (Edinburgh Wands), I.H.P. Laughland 19 (London Scottish), G.D. Stevenson 20 (Hawick); D.H. Chisholm 2 (Melrose), A.J. Hastie 5 (Melrose); *J.B. Neill 5 (Edinburgh Acads), N.S. Bruce (27) (London Scottish), D.M.D. Rollo 20 (Howe of Fife), P.C. Brown 4 (W. of Scotland), M.J. Campbell-Lamerton 13 (London Scottish), J.P. Fisher 5 (Royal HSFP), R.J.C. Glasgow 8 (Dunfermline), J.W. Telfer 4 (Melrose).

ENGLAND   J.G. Willcox (15) (Harlequins); R.W. Hosen 2 (Northampton), M.S. Phillips (20) (Fylde), M.P. Weston 19 (Durham City), J.M. Ranson (4) (Rosslyn Park); T.J. Brophy 3 (Liverpool), S.R. Smith (5) (Blackheath); *C.R. Jacobs (24) (Northampton), H.O. Godwin (6) (Coventry), D.F.B. Wrench (2) (Harlequins), C.M. Payne 3 (Harlequins), A.M. Davis 7 (Torquay Athletic), P.J. Ford (4) (Gloucester), D.P. Rogers 14 (Bedford), T.G.A.H. Peart (2) (Hartlepool Rovers).

Referee R.C. Williams (Ireland)

WALES v FRANCE   35/545

21 March 1964
Cardiff Arms Park
Wales 11 (1G, 2PG) France 11 (1G, 2PG)

Wales T: Stuart Watkins. C: Bradshaw. PG: Bradshaw (2).
France T: Crauste. C: Albaladejo. PG: Albaladejo (2).

This draw, the first between the countries, enabled Wales to win the Championship ahead of Scotland on superior points-scoring. Wales, who had won only one of the previous three home matches against France, were fortunate to escape another defeat and managed to do so only because of a late try by Stuart Watkins which Bradshaw converted from wide out. Thus two of the great characters of Welsh rugby at the time, Len Cunningham and Dai Hayward, were able to end their Championship careers on a high note.

WALES G.T.R. Hodgson 9 (Neath); S.J. Watkins 3 (Newport), S.J. Dawes 2 (London Welsh), K. Bradshaw 4 (Bridgend), D.I.E. Bebb 21 (Swansea); D. Watkins 8 (Newport), *D.C.T. Rowlands 8 (Pontypool); D. Williams 8 (Ebbw Vale), N.R. Gale 8 (Llanelli), L.J. Cunningham (12) (Aberavon), B. Price 11 (Newport), B.E. Thomas 8 (Neath), G.J. Prothero 3 (Bridgend), D.J. Hayward (4) (Cardiff), A.E.I. Pask 13 (Abertillery).

FRANCE P. Dedieu 2 (AS Béziers); J. Gachassin 5 (FC Lourdes), J. Piqué 3 (S. Pau), A. Boniface 24 (S. Mont-de-Marsan), C. Darrouy 10 (S. Mont-de-Marsan); P. Albaladejo 17 (US Dax), J-C. Lasserre 3 (US Dax); J-C. Berejnoi 2 (SC Tulle), Y. Menthiller 1 (US Romans), A. Gruarin 1 (RC Toulon), A. Herrero 2 (RC Toulon), B. Dauga 3 (S. Mont-de-Marsan), M. Sitjar 1 (SU Agen), *M. Crauste 26 (FC Lourdes), M. Lira 4 (La Voulte S.).

Referee H.B. Laidlaw (Scotland)

FRANCE v IRELAND   35/546

11 April 1964
Stade Colombes, Paris
France 27 (3G, 3T, 1DG) Ireland 6 (1T, 1DG)

France T: Crauste, Lira, Darrouy (2), Arnaudet, Herrero. C: Albaladejo (3). DG: Dedieu.
Ireland T: Casey. DG: Gibson.

This was France's highest score and most number of tries against Ireland. It was also France's fifth successive victory over the Irish – their longest winning sequence against them to date. Curiously, it was France's only victory of the season, and the last match for their outstanding tactical kicker, Pierre Albaladejo, who played a record 17 matches at fly-half, and one, his first against England in 1954, at full-back. There was some consolation for Ireland in that it was the last year until 1977 that they ended up with the Wooden Spoon.

FRANCE P. Dedieu 3 (AS Béziers); J. Gachassin 6 (FC Lourdes), M. Arnaudet 1 (FC Lourdes), J. Piqué 4 (S. Pau), C. Darrouy 11 (S. Mont-de-Marsan); P. Albaladejo (18) (US Dax), J-C. Lasserre 4 (US Dax); A. Gruarin 2 (RC Toulon), A. Abadie (1) (S. Pau), J-C. Berejnoi 3 (SC Tulle), A. Herrero 3 (RC Toulon), B. Dauga 4 (S. Mont-de-Marsan), *M. Crauste 27 (FC Lourdes), M. Sitjar 2 (SU Agen), M. Lira 5 (La Voulte S.).

IRELAND F.S. Keogh (2) (Bective Rangers); P.J. Casey 8 (Lansdowne), M.K. Flynn 10 (Wanderers), J.C. Walsh 11 (UC Cork), A.T.A. Duggan 1 (Lansdowne); C.M.H. Gibson 4 (Cambridge U.), J.C. Kelly (10) (UC Dublin); S. Millar 21 (Ballymena), A.R. Dawson (23) (Wanderers), M.P. O'Callaghan (3) (Sunday's Well), W.J. McBride 11 (Ballymena), *W.A. Mulcahy 26 (Bective Rangers), E.P. McGuire (7) (UC Galway), N.A.A. Murphy 20 (Cork Constitution), M.G. Culliton (18) (Wanderers).

Referee D.G. Walters (Wales)

1965

PARIS France beat Scotland 16-8 · CARDIFF Wales beat England 14-3
DUBLIN Ireland drew France 3-3 · MURRAYFIELD Wales beat Scotland 14-12
DUBLIN Ireland beat England 5-0 · MURRAYFIELD Ireland beat Scotland 16-6
TWICKENHAM England beat France 9-6 · CARDIFF Wales beat Ireland 14-8
TWICKENHAM England drew Scotland 3-3 · PARIS France beat Wales 22-13

CHAMPIONSHIP TABLE
Wales – Championship, Triple Crown

Pos	Country	P	W	D	L	F	A	Pts	Tries F	A
1	Wales (1)	4	3	0	1	55	45	6	10	5
2	France (3)	4	2	1	1	47	33	5	10	7
3	Ireland (5)	4	2	1	1	32	23	5	6	3
4	England (4)	4	1	1	2	15	28	3	2	5
5	Scotland (2)	4	0	1	3	29	49	1	2	10

Wales won the title again, by producing effective, attractive rugby which brought ten tries and the Triple Crown. Even defeat, by 22-13, against France in their last match did not curb their scoring ability for they still managed to score three tries. Stuart Watkins was the principal beneficiary of the great try-maker, John Dawes, in the centre: Watkins scored four in the season, making his total six in his first seven appearances on Wales's right wing.

Christian Darrouy whose 13 tries in the Championship are a record for a French player

Ireland, inspiringly led for the first time by Ray McLoughlin, also fared comparatively well, losing only their last match against Wales in Cardiff. The anomaly of 1965 was Scotland, who after their encouraging play and series of good results the year before, unaccountably fell from favour. Their only positive achievement was a draw with England. Christian Darrouy, the French try-scoring phenomenon, managed a try in each of the first three matches – but missed the last game because of injury and watched in the stands as France thrashed Wales.

FRANCE v SCOTLAND 35/547

9 January 1965
Stade Colombes, Paris
France 16 (2G, 2T) Scotland 8 (1G, 1T)

France T: Gachassin, Piqué, Darrouy (2). C: Dedieu (2).
Scotland T: Henderson (2). C: Scotland.

After a comparatively successful season in 1964, Scotland disappointed their supporters in the first match of the new campaign. It was only the fourth time that the French had registered four tries against the Scots in Paris. The axe was bound to fall, but the heads which rolled were somewhat surprising: the captain, Neill, and the two most experienced players in the side, Ken Scotland, and Stevenson.

FRANCE   P. Dedieu 4 (AS Béziers); J. Gachassin 7 (FC Lourdes), G. Boniface 12 (S. Mont-de-Marsan), J. Piqué 5 (S. Pau), C. Darrouy 12 (S. Mont-de-Marsan); J. Capdouze 1 (S. Pau), L. Camberabero 1 (La Voulte S.); A. Gruarin 3 (RC

Toulon), J-M. Cabanier 2 (US Montauban), J-C. Berejnoi 4 (SC Tulle), W. Spanghero 1 (RC Narbonne), B. Dauga 5 (S. Mont-de-Marsan), M. Lira 6 (La Voulte S.), *M. Crauste 28 (FC Lourdes), A. Herrero 4 (RC Toulon).

SCOTLAND K.J.F. Scotland (26) (Aberdeenshire); C. Elliot 9 (Langholm), B.C. Henderson 5 (Edinburgh Wands), I.H.P. Laughland 20 (London Scottish), G.D. Stevenson (21) (Hawick); B.M. Simmers 1 (Glasgow Acads), J.A.T. Rodd 10 (London Scottish); *J.B. Neill (6) (Edinburgh Acads), F.A.L. Laidlaw 1 (Melrose), D.M.D. Rollo 21 (Howe of Fife), P.K. Stagg 1 (Sale), M.J. Campbell-Lamerton 14 (London Scottish), D. Grant 1 (Hawick), J.P. Fisher 6 (London Scottish), J.W. Telfer 5 (Melrose).

Referee K.D. Kelleher (Ireland)

WALES v ENGLAND 69/548

16 January 1965
Cardiff Arms Park
Wales 14 (1G, 2T, 1DG) England 3 (1PG)

Wales T: Stuart Watkins (2), Morgan. C: Terry Price. DG: David Watkins.
England PG: Rutherford.

The début appearance of Terry Price, the Llanelli Grammar schoolboy prodigy, whose burgeoning talent was seen at club and trial matches earlier in the season, was eagerly anticipated. Price, who could play wing, fly-half or centre, came in as a full-back and performed well. There were those who believed he would have been better employed elsewhere, for few contemporary players possessed his speed, swaggering, aggressive power or innate timing of a break. His loss to rugby league, after a mere seven Championship matches, was immeasurable, but it can be presumed that had circumstances allowed maturity and development of his skill he would have become one of the all-time great players.

WALES T.G. Price 1 (Llanelli); S.J. Watkins 4 (Newport), J.R. Uzzell 1 (Newport), S.J. Dawes 3 (London Welsh), D.I.E. Bebb 22 (Swansea); D. Watkins 9 (Newport), *D.C.T. Rowlands 9 (Pontypool); D. Williams 9 (Ebbw Vale), N.R. Gale 9 (Llanelli), R. Waldron 1 (Neath), B.E. Thomas 9

(Neath), B. Price 12 (Newport), G.J. Prothero 4 (Bridgend), H.J. Morgan 19 (Abertillery), A.E.I. Pask 14 (Abertillery).

ENGLAND D. Rutherford 5 (Gloucester); E.L. Rudd 1 (Oxford U.), D.W.A. Rosser 1 (Cambridge U.), G.P. Frankcom 1 (Cambridge U.), C.P. Simpson (1) (Harlequins); T.J. Brophy 4 (Liverpool), J.E. Williams (9) (Sale); A.L. Horton 1 (Blackheath), S.B. Richards 1 (Richmond), N.J. Drake-Lee (7) (Leicester), J.E. Owen 5 (Coventry), R.E. Rowell (2) (Leicester), N. Silk 1 (Harlequins), D.P. Rogers 15 (Bedford), *D.G. Perry 5 (Bedford).

Referee K.D. Kelleher (Ireland)

IRELAND v FRANCE 36/549

23 January 1965
Lansdowne Road, Dublin
Ireland 3 (1T) France 3 (1T)

Ireland T: Doyle.
France T: Darrouy.

This was only the second draw in the 36 Championship matches played to date between Ireland and France — but for Ireland it was important in that it ended a run of five French victories. While France were content to rely largely on seasoned players, Ireland continued their rebuilding, bringing in five new players, each of whom were to play a significant part in lifting their country if not to the Championship title, at least out of the rut in which usually they had found themselves in the previous seven seasons.

IRELAND T.J. Kiernan 16 (Cork Constitution); P.J. Casey 9 (Lansdowne), M.K. Flynn 11 (Wanderers), K.J. Houston 3 (Oxford U.), J.C. Walsh 12 (Sunday's Well); C.M.H. Gibson 5 (Cambridge U.), R.M. Young 1 (Belfast Collegians); S. MacHale 1 (Lansdowne), K.W. Kennedy 1 (Queen's U. Belfast), *R.J. McLoughlin 9 (Gosforth), W.J. McBride 12 (Ballymena), W.A. Mulcahy 27 (Bective Rangers), M.G. Doyle 1 (UC Dublin), N.A.A. Murphy 21 (Cork Constitution), R.A. Lamont 1 (Instonians).

FRANCE P. Dedieu 5 (AS Beziers); C. Darrouy 13 (S. Mont-de-Marsan), J. Piqué 6 (S. Pau), G. Boniface 13 (S. Mont-de-Marsan), J. Gachassin 8

(FC Lourdes); J. Capdouze 2 (S. Pau), L. Cambera-bero 2 (La Voulte S.); J-C. Berejnoi 5 (SC Tulle), J-M. Cabanier 3 (US Montauban), A. Gruarin 4 (RC Toulon), B. Dauga 6 (S. Mont-de-Marsan), W. Spanghero 2 (RC Narbonne), *M. Crauste 29 (FC Lourdes), M. Lira (7) (La Voulte S.), A. Herrero 5 (RC Toulon).

Referee D.G. Walters (Wales)

SCOTLAND v WALES   69/550

6 February 1965
Murrayfield
Wales 14 (1G, 1T, 2PG) Scotland 12 (2DG, 2PG)

Scotland   DG: Simmers (2). PG: Wilson (2).
Wales   T: Stuart Watkins, Gale. C: Terry Price. PG: Terry Price (2).

Wales gained their second consecutive victory at Murrayfield, which was something they had not achieved since the early 1930s. It was attained against what many considered a very good, balanced Scottish side, which had power and pace in the back-row, giants in the second row, solid scrummagers in the front-row and backs of flair and pace. Yet the team failed to win this or any other match in the season for the basic reason they gave away more points than they were able to score: an indictment of many Scotland sides of other eras.

SCOTLAND   S. Wilson 5 (London Scottish); C. Elliot 10 (Langholm), B.C. Henderson 6 (Edinburgh Wands), I.H.P. Laughland 21 (London Scottish), D.J. Whyte 1 (Edinburgh Wands); B.M. Simmers 2 (Glasgow Acads), J.A.T. Rodd 11 (London Scottish); N. Suddon 1 (Hawick), F.A.L. Laidlaw 2 (Melrose), D.M.D. Rollo 22 (Howe of Fife), P.K. Stagg 2 (Sale), *M.J. Campbell-Lamerton 15 (London Scottish), J.P. Fisher 7 (London Scottish), R.J.C. Glasgow 9 (Dunfermline), J.W. Telfer 6 (Melrose).

WALES   T.G. Price 2 (Llanelli); S.J. Watkins 5 (Newport), J.R. Uzzell 2 (Newport), S.J. Dawes 4 (London Welsh), D.I.E. Bebb 23 (Swansea); D. Watkins 10 (Newport), *D.C.T. Rowlands 10 (Pontypool); D. Williams 10 (Ebbw Vale), N.R. Gale 10 (Llanelli), R. Waldron 2 (Neath), B. Price 13 (Newport), W.J. Morris 1 (Newport), G.J. Prothero 5 (Bridgend), H.J. Morgan 20 (Abertillery), A.E.I. Pask 15 (Abertillery).

Referee R.W. Gilliland (Ireland)

IRELAND v ENGLAND   69/551

13 February 1965
Lansdowne Road, Dublin
Ireland 5 (1G) England 0

Ireland   T: Lamont. C: Kiernan.

For the second match in a row England were unable to score at Lansdowne Road, their failure attributable to excellent Irish defence and covering which was exemplified by Tom Kiernan. The Irish full-back was not the fastest player of his day; but his tactical know-how and positional sense were often underrated. Another Irish player to perform well was Roger Young, winning his second cap. It was the scrum-half's lunge from a scrum which led to the only try, scored by another highly promising newcomer Ronnie Lamont.

IRELAND   T.J. Kiernan 17 (Cork Constitution); P.J. Casey 10 (Lansdowne), M.K. Flynn 12 (Wanderers), K.J. Houston (4) (Oxford U.), P.J. McGrath 1 (UC Cork); C.M.H. Gibson 6 (Cambridge U.), R.M. Young 2 (Queen's U. Belfast); S. MacHale 2 (Lansdowne), K.W. Kennedy 2 (Queen's U. Belfast), *R.J. McLoughlin 10 (Gosforth), W.J. McBride 13 (Ballymena), W.A. Mulcahy 28 (Bective Rangers), M.G. Doyle 2 (UC Dublin), N.A.A. Murphy 22 (Cork Constitution), R.A. Lamont 2 (Instonians).

ENGLAND   D. Rutherford 6 (Gloucester); E.L. Rudd 2 (Oxford U.), D.W.A. Rosser 2 (Cambridge U.), G.P. Frankcom 2 (Cambridge U.), P.W. Cook 1 (Richmond); T.J. Brophy 5 (Liverpool), S.J.S. Clarke 7 (Blackheath); A.L. Horton 2 (Blackheath), S.B. Richards 2 (Richmond), P.E. Judd 6 (Coventry), J.E. Owen 6 (Coventry), C.M. Payne 4 (Harlequins), N. Silk 2 (Harlequins), D.P. Rogers 16 (Bedford), *D.G. Perry 6 (Bedford).

Referee H.B. Laidlaw (Scotland)

ENGLAND v FRANCE   36/552

27 February 1965
Twickenham
England 9 (1T, 2PG) France 6 (1T, 1PG)

England   T: Payne. PG: Rutherford (2).
France   T: Darrouy. PG: Dedieu.

France had always found winning at Twickenham difficult – they had won there only twice in 17 visits – and some critics were of the opinion that it was mostly due to an hereditary French disease, an inferiority complex. Certainly, in this match France had more than enough opportunities to prevail, but the discipline of England once again proved too much. The French selectors had to have their scapegoats. Out went the half-backs, Laborde and Capdouze, who had not played badly by any means, and the hooker Yves Menthiller, hapless victim of the fastest striker in the game, Steve Richards.

ENGLAND   D. Rutherford 7 (Gloucester); A.W. Hancock 1 (Northampton), D.W.A. Rosser 3 (Cambridge U.), G.P. Frankcom 3 (Cambridge U.), P.W. Cook (2) (Richmond); M.P. Weston 20 (Durham City), S.J.S. Clarke 8 (Blackheath); A.L. Horton 3 (Blackheath), S.B. Richards 3 (Richmond), P.E. Judd 7 (Coventry), J.E. Owen 7 (Coventry), C.M. Payne 5 (Harlequins), N. Silk 3 (Harlequins), D.P. Rogers 17 (Bedford), *D.G. Perry 7 (Bedford).

FRANCE   P. Dedieu 6 (AS Béziers); J. Gachassin 9 (FC Lourdes), G. Boniface 14 (S. Mont-de-Marsan), J. Piqué 7 (S. Pau), C. Darrouy 14 (S. Mont-de-Marsan); J-R. Capdouze (3) (S. Pau), C. Laborde (1) (RCF); A. Gruarin 5 (RC Toulon), Y. Menthiller (2) (US Romans), J-C. Berejnoi 6 (SC Tulle), W. Spanghero 3 (RC Narbonne), B. Dauga 7 (S. Mont-de-Marsan), J-J. Rupert 2 (US Tyrosse), *M. Crauste 30 (FC Lourdes), A. Herrero 6 (RC Toulon).

Referee R.W. Gilliland (Ireland)

SCOTLAND v IRELAND   71/553

27 February 1965
Murrayfield
Ireland 16 (2G, 1T, 1DG) Scotland 6 (1DG, 1PG)

Scotland   DG: Laughland. PG: Wilson.
Ireland   T. McGrath, Young, Murphy. C: Kiernan (2). DG: Gibson.

Ireland enjoyed unprecedented success since first playing at Murrayfield in 1926 and this was the latest example of their ability to score freely on a large, expansive ground. Mike Gibson was credited with master-minding the triumph but the Irish were clearly helped by sluggish performances from several of the more experienced Scottish players. The selectors made no bones about culpability: the careers of Elliot, Shackleton, Rodd and Glasgow were ended, a cruel finale for players of their calibre and skill.

SCOTLAND   S. Wilson 6 (London Scottish); C. Elliot (11) (Langholm), B.C. Henderson 7 (Edinburgh Wands), J.A.P. Shackleton (5) (London Scottish), D.J. Whyte 2 (Edinburgh Wands); I.H.P. Laughland 22 (London Scottish), J.A.T. Rodd (12) (London Scottish); N. Suddon 2 (Hawick), F.A.L. Laidlaw 3 (Melrose), D.M.D. Rollo 23 (Howe of Fife), P.C. Brown 5 (W. of Scotland), *M.J. Campbell-Lamerton 16 (London Scottish), J.P. Fisher 8 (London Scottish), R.J.C. Glasgow (10) (Dunfermline), J.W. Telfer 7 (Melrose).

IRELAND   T.J. Kiernan 18 (Cork Constitution); P.J. Casey (11) (Lansdowne), J.C. Walsh 13 (Sunday's Well), M.K. Flynn 13 (Wanderers), P.J. McGrath 2 (UC Cork); C.M.H. Gibson 7 (Cambridge U.), R.M. Young 3 (Queen's U. Belfast); S. MacHale 3 (Lansdowne), K.W. Kennedy 3 (Queen's U. Belfast), *R.J. McLoughlin 11 (Gosforth), W.J. McBride 14 (Ballymena), W.A. Mulcahy 29 (Bective Rangers), M.G. Doyle 3 (US Dublin), N.A.A. Murphy 23 (Cork Constitution), H. Wall 1 (Dolphin).

Referee D.G. Walters (Wales)

WALES v IRELAND 67/554

13 March 1965
Cardiff Arms Park
Wales 14 (1G, 1T, 1DG, 1PG) Ireland 8 (1G, 1PG)

Wales T: David Watkins, Bebb. C: Terry Price.
DG: Terry Price. PG: Terry Price.
Ireland T: Flynn. C: Kiernan. PG: Kiernan.

Wales won the Triple Crown for a tenth time in a match in which the fiery, aggressive Irish matched them at almost every phase. But this Welsh side was endowed with courage and character, which was underlined when they had to reshuffle their forces after losing John Dawes early on. Terry Price was moved to centre to replace Dawes and Alun Pask went to full-back. Ireland, also bidding to win the Triple Crown, tried everything against Wales – and Pask – but they hung on grimly until Dawes returned to tip the balance. Price's 8 points brought his total in his first season to 12.

It was to be the last Championship match for two famous Irish players: Bill Mulcahy and Dave Hewitt. Mulcahy was a marvellous forward in the Irish tradition, hard and committed, though rather lightweight for a lock. Hewitt was a member of a family which produced six Irish internationals, but like Tony O'Reilly, he was appreciated more for his contribution to British Isles rugby than for his country.

WALES T.G. Price 3 (Llanelli); S.J. Watkins 6 (Newport), J.R. Uzzell 3 (Newport), S.J. Dawes 5 (London Welsh), D.I.E. Bebb 24 (Swansea); D. Watkins 11 (Newport), *D.C.T. Rowlands 11 (Pontypool); D. Williams 11 (Ebbw Vale), N.R. Gale 11 (Llanelli), R. Waldron 3 (Neath), B. Price 14 (Newport), K.A. Rowlands 4 (Cardiff), G.J. Prothero 6 (Bridgend), H.J. Morgan 21 (Abertillery), A.E.I. Pask 16 (Abertillery).

IRELAND T.J. Kiernan 19 (Cork Constitution); D. Hewitt (17) (Instonians), M.K. Flynn 14 (Wanderers), J.C. Walsh 14 (Sunday's Well), P.J. McGrath 3 (UC Cork); C.M.H. Gibson 8 (Cambridge U.), R.M. Young 4 (Queen's U. Belfast); S. MacHale 4 (Lansdowne), K.W. Kennedy 4 (Queen's U. Belfast), *R.J. McLoughlin 12 (Gosforth), W.J. McBride 15 (Ballymena), W.A. Mulcahy (30) (Bective Rangers), M.G. Doyle 4

(UC Dublin), N.A.A. Murphy 24 (Cork Constitution), H. Wall (2) (Dolphin).

Referee P.G. Brook (England)

ENGLAND v SCOTLAND 68/555

20 March 1965
Twickenham
England 3 (1T) Scotland 3 (1DG)

England T: Hancock.
Scotland DG: Chisholm.

This match will always be famous for one of the greatest tries in the history of the Championship; scored by Andy Hancock, the chunky little Northampton wing. With only seconds remaining, and Scotland ahead by a dropped goal from Chisholm, a sensational finish was the last anyone expected. But sensational it was. A Scottish attack broke down on the England 25 and when England won the ball, Weston had the option of kicking for safety or gambling on a miracle. His pass to Hancock was innocuity itself; and even when the wing loped outside a few Scottish skirmishers, no danger seemed imminent. Hancock, who was not a particularly fast wing, suddenly gathered speed: 'I just ran and ran,' he said later. But what a run it was, for in a moment he was over halfway making for the corner-flag inches away from touch. Scotland were completely taken by surprise and only Laughland gave serious chase, actually managing a despairing last-ditch tackle as the exhausted Hancock hurled himself in at the corner.

ENGLAND D. Rutherford 8 (Gloucester); E.L. Rudd 3 (Oxford U.), D.W.A. Rosser 4 (Cambridge U.), G.P. Frankcom (4) (Cambridge U.), A.W. Hancock 2 (Northampton); M.P. Weston 21 (Durham City), S.J.S. Clarke (9) (Blackheath); A.L. Horton 4 (Blackheath), S.B. Richards 4 (Richmond), P.E. Judd 8 (Coventry), J.E. Owen 8 (Coventry), C.M. Payne 6 (Harlequins), N. Silk (4) (Harlequins), D.P. Rogers 18 (Bedford), *D.G. Perry 8 (Bedford).

SCOTLAND *S. Wilson 7 (London Scottish); D.J. Whyte 3 (Edinburgh Wands), B.C. Henderson 8 (Edinburgh Wands), I.H.P. Laughland 23 (London Scottish), W.D. Jackson 2 (Hawick); D.H. Chisholm 3 (Melrose), A.J. Hastie 6 (Melrose); N. Suddon 3 (Hawick), F.A.L. Laidlaw 4 (Melrose), D.M.D. Rollo 24 (Howe of Fife), P.K. Stagg 3 (Sale), M.J. Campbell-Lamerton 17 (London Scottish), J.P. Fisher 9 (London Scottish), D. Grant 2 (Hawick), P.C. Brown 6 (W. of Scotland).

Referee D.G. Walters (Wales)

Watkins 12 (Newport), *D.C.T. Rowlands (12) (Pontypool); D. Williams 12 (Ebbw Vale), N.R. Gale 12 (Llanelli), R. Waldron (4) (Neath), B. Price 15 (Newport), K.A. Rowlands (5) (Cardiff), G.J. Prothero 7 (Bridgend), H.J. Morgan 22 (Abertillery), A.E.I. Pask 17 (Abertillery).

Referee R.W. Gilliland (Ireland), replaced by B. Marie (France) after 32 minutes

FRANCE v WALES   36/556

27 March 1965
Stade Colombes, Paris
France 22 (2G, 2T, 1DG, 1PG) Wales 13 (2G, 1T)

France T: Guy Boniface (2), Herrero (2). C: Dedieu (2). DG: Lasserre. PG: Dedieu.
Wales T: Dawes, Stuart Watkins, Bebb. C: Terry Price (2).

This was France's highest score in any match against Wales, and they have scored as many tries against them on only one other occasion, 1960. It was all the more remarkable because Wales had already won the Triple Crown and the Championship and were aiming to round off the season with the Grand Slam. By the time France had completed their scoring the referee, R.W. Gilliland, had gone off with an injured leg and had been replaced by the French touch-judge, Bernard Marie. Wales made a determined effort to catch up but though they produced three tries the leeway proved far too great. For four of the Welsh team, it meant a final inter-national appearance, including Clive Rowlands, who had been captain in all his 11 Champion-ship matches.

FRANCE   P. Dedieu (7) (AS Béziers); J. Piqué (8) (S. Pau), G. Boniface 15 (S. Mont-de-Marsan), A. Boniface 25 (S. Mont-de-Marsan), A. Campaes 1 (FC Lourdes); J. Gachassin 10 (FC Lourdes), J-C. Lasserre 5 (US Dax); A. Gruarin 6 (RC Toulon), J-M. Cabanier 4 (US Montauban), J-C. Berejnoi 7 (SC Tulle), B. Dauga 8 (S. Mont-de-Marsan), W. Spanghero 4 (RC Narbonne), J-J. Rupert 3 (US Tyrosse), *M Crauste 31 (FC Lourdes), A. Her-rero 7 (RC Toulon).

WALES   T.G. Price 4 (Llanelli); S.J. Watkins 7 (Newport), J.R. Uzzell (4) (Newport), S.J. Dawes 6 (London Welsh), D.I.E. Bebb 25 (Swansea); D.

1966

TWICKENHAM Wales beat England 11-6 · MURRAYFIELD Scotland drew France 3-3
PARIS France beat Ireland 11-6 · CARDIFF Wales beat Scotland 8-3
TWICKENHAM England drew Ireland 6-6 · PARIS France beat England 13-0
DUBLIN Scotland beat Ireland 11-3 · DUBLIN Ireland beat Wales 9-6
MURRAYFIELD Scotland beat England 6-3 · CARDIFF Wales beat France 9-8

CHAMPIONSHIP TABLE
Wales – Championship

| | | | | | | | | Tries | |
Pos Country	P	W	D	L	F	A	Pts	F	A
Wales (1)	4	3	0	1	34	26	6	5	4
France (2)	4	2	1	1	35	18	5	7	2
Scotland (5)	4	2	1	1	23	17	5	5	2
Ireland (3)	4	1	1	2	24	34	3	2	7
England (4)	4	0	1	3	15	36	1	2	6

Wales won the Championship for the third year in succession, equalling their most title wins in sequence of 1954–56. The title was not easily gained, however, and after being surprised by Ireland in Dublin, the Welsh had to struggle to ensure top place against France at Cardiff in their last match. But what a match it was; France led 8-0 and had success snatched from their grasp by an incredible 75-yard try by Stuart Watkins ten minutes from time. The Irish defeat was all the more remarkable for it came after the Irish had been beaten by Scotland and France and drawn with England.

Lilian Camberabero receives much needed protection from his line-out forwards, against Wales on 26 March 1966

Scotland, bottom of the table the year before, showed the most improvement and came within a whisker of winning the title. Their chief regret was that they had let their opportunity pass by because of their 3-3 draw against France at Murrayfield in their opening match. Little had gone right for England since they last won the title in 1963, and they reached a nadir in terms of results in 1966 when they failed to win a match and ended up bottom for the first time since 1951.

ENGLAND v WALES   70/557

15 January 1966
Twickenham
Wales 11 (1G, 2PG) England 6 (1T, 1PG)

England T: Perry. PG: Rutherford.
Wales T: Pask. C: Terry Price. PG: Terry Price (2).

England, who had conquered Wales at Twickenham only once since 1954, were beaten yet again, on this occasion by the exceptional kicking ability of Terry Price. The Llanelli full-back scored 8 of Wales's points, and had now totalled 30 points having scored on each of his 5 international appearances. An injury kept Price out of the firing line for the rest of Wales's matches in the season.

ENGLAND D. Rutherford 9 (Gloucester); E.L. Rudd 4 (Liverpool), T.G. Arthur 1 (Wasps), D.W.A. Rosser (5) (Wasps), K.F. Savage 1 (Northampton); T.J. Brophy 6 (Liverpool), J. Spencer (1) (Harlequins); P.E. Judd 9 (Coventry), J.V. Pullin 1 (Bristol), D.L. Powell 1 (Northampton), C.M. Payne 7 (Harlequins), A.M. Davis 8 (Devonport Services), R.B. Taylor 1 (Northampton), *D.P. Rogers 19 (Bedford), D.G. Perry 9 (Bedford).

WALES T.G. Price 5 (Llanelli); S.J. Watkins 8 (Newport), D.K. Jones 9 (Cardiff), K. Bradshaw 5 (Bridgend), L. Davies 1 (Bridgend); D. Watkins 13 (Newport), A.R. Lewis 1 (Abertillery); D. Williams 13 (Ebbw Vale), N.R. Gale 13 (Llanelli), D.J. Lloyd 1 (Bridgend), B. Price 16 (Newport), B.E. Thomas 10 (Neath), G.J. Prothero 8 (Bridgend), H.J. Morgan 23 (Abertillery), *A.E.I. Pask 18 (Abertillery).

Referee R.W. Gilliland (Ireland)

SCOTLAND v FRANCE   36/558

15 January 1966
Murrayfield
Scotland 3 (1T) France 3 (1PG)

Scotland T: Whyte.
France PG: Lacaze.

France had treated Murrayfield aficionados to some spectacular tries over the years but on this occasion the only French points came from a penalty goal by Lacaze. Much of France's difficulty in creating chances to score lay in their new half-backs, Puget and Roques. Each was a tricky, quick operator but they did not combine well and Hastie, along with the Scottish back-row, regularly harassed and dispossessed them. Scotland deserved to win; they scored a fine try after a sustained handling move, but Stewart Wilson failed to convert. Normally the most reliable of place kickers, Wilson also missed several penalty goal attempts, any of which would have settled the matter. Consequently it ended in a draw, only the second between the countries.

SCOTLAND *S. Wilson 8 (London Scottish); A.J.W. Hinshelwood 1 (London Scottish), B.C. Henderson 9 (Edinburgh Wands), I.H.P. Laughland 24 (London Scottish), D.J. Whyte 4 (Edinburgh Wands); D.H. Chisholm 4 (Melrose), A.J. Hastie 7 (Melrose); J.D. Macdonald 1 (London Scottish), F.A.L. Laidlaw 5 (Melrose), D.M.D. Rollo 25 (Howe of Fife), P.K. Stagg 4 (Sale), M.J. Campbell-Lamerton 18 (London Scottish), J.P. Fisher 10 (London Scottish), D. Grant 3 (Hawick), J.W. Telfer 8 (Melrose).

FRANCE C. Lacaze 7 (SC Angoulême); J. Gachassin 11 (FC Lourdes), G. Boniface 16 (S. Mont-de-Marsan), A. Boniface 26 (S. Mont-de-Marsan), C. Darrouy 15 (S. Mont-de-Marsan); J-C. Roques 1 (CA Brive), M. Puget 1 (CA Brive); A. Gruarin 7 (RC Toulon), J-M. Cabanier 5 (US Montauban), J-C. Berejnoi 8 (SC Tulle), W. Spanghero 5 (RC Narbonne), E. Cester 1 (TOEC), J-J. Rupert 4 (US Tyrosse), *M. Crauste 32 (FC Lourdes), B. Dauga 9 (S. Mont-de-Marsan).

Referee D.M. Hughes (Wales)

FRANCE v IRELAND — 37/559

29 January 1966
Stade Colombes, Paris
France 11 (1G, 1T, 1PG) Ireland 6 (1DG, 1PG)

France T: Darrouy (2). C: Lacaze. PG: Lacaze.
Ireland DG: Kiernan. PG: Gibson.

This was Ireland's seventh consecutive defeat in Paris since they last won there in 1952 but at least they had the satisfaction of denying France their normal runaway victory. But they must have trembled at the presence of Christian Darrouy, whose two tries meant that he had scored eight against them in four matches since 1963.

FRANCE C. Lacaze 8 (SC Angoulême); J. Gachassin 12 (FC Lourdes), G. Boniface 17 (S. Mont-de-Marsan), A. Boniface 27 (S. Mont-de-Marsan), C. Darrouy 16 (S. Mont-de-Marsan); J-C. Roques (2) (CA Brive), M. Puget 2 (CA Brive); A. Gruarin 8 (RC Toulon), J-M. Cabanier 6 (US Montauban), J-C. Berejnoi 9 (SC Tulle), E. Cester 2 (TOEC), W. Spanghero 6 (RC Narbonne), *M. Crauste 33 (FC Lourdes), J-J. Rupert 5 (US Tyrosse), B. Dauga 10 (S. Mont-de-Marsan).

IRELAND T.J. Kiernan 20 (Cork Constitution); W.R. Hunter 8 (CIYMS), M.K. Flynn 15 (Wanderers), J.C. Walsh 15 (Sunday's Well), P.J. McGrath 4 (UC Cork); C.M.H. Gibson 9 (NIFC), R.M. Young 5 (Belfast Collegians); S. MacHale 5 (Lansdowne), K.W. Kennedy 5 (CIYMS), *R.J. McLoughlin 13 (Blackrock College), W.J. McBride 16 (Ballymena), M.G. Molloy 1 (UC Galway), N.A.A. Murphy 25 (Cork Constitution), M.G. Doyle 5 (Cambridge U.), R.A. Lamont 3 (Instonians).

Referee P.G. Brook (England)

WALES v SCOTLAND — 70/560

5 February 1966
Cardiff Arms Park
Wales 8 (1G, 1T) Scotland 3 (1PG)

Wales T: Ken Jones (2). C: Bradshaw.
Scotland PG: Wilson.

Scotland's gamble in playing against the wind during the first half did not come off. Wales led only 3-0 but with David Watkins in masterful form and the forwards responding well to the challenge it was the Scots who faded rather than taking control as expected. It was Wales's fourth win in a row against the Scots.

WALES T.G.R. Hodgson 10 (Neath); S.J. Watkins 9 (Newport), D.K. Jones 10 (Cardiff), K. Bradshaw 6 (Bridgend), L. Davies 2 (Bridgend); D. Watkins 14 (Newport), A.R. Lewis 2 (Abertillery); D. Williams 14 (Ebbw Vale), N.R. Gale 14 (Llanelli), D.J. Lloyd 2 (Bridgend), B. Price 17 (Newport), B.E. Thomas 11 (Neath), G.J. Prothero 9 (Bridgend), H.J. Morgan 24 (Abertillery), *A.I.E. Pask 19 (Abertillery).

SCOTLAND *S. Wilson 9 (London Scottish); A.J.W. Hinshelwood 2 (London Scottish), B.C. Henderson 10 (Edinburgh Wands), I.H.P. Laughland 25 (London Scottish), D.J. Whyte 5 (Edinburgh Wands); J.W.C. Turner 1 (Gala), A.J. Hastie 8 (Melrose); J.D. Macdonald 2 (London Scottish), F.A.L. Laidlaw 6 (Melrose), D.M.D. Rollo 26 (Howe of Fife), P.K. Stagg 5 (Sale), M.J. Campbell-Lamerton 19 (London Scottish), J.P. Fisher 11 (London Scottish), D. Grant 4 (Hawick), J.W. Telfer 9 (Melrose).

Referee M.H. Titcomb (England)

ENGLAND v IRELAND   70/561

12 February 1966
Twickenham
England 6 (1T, 1PG) Ireland 6 (1T, 1PG)

England   T: Greenwood. PG: Rutherford.
Ireland   T: McGrath. PG: Kiernan.

England had not beaten Ireland since 1962 and failed to win again because they created hardly any chances. The prospect of a dazzling clash between Tom Brophy and Mike Gibson did not materialize either, and the match petered out to an uninspiring draw between the two sides who were to end the season at the foot of the table. It was the first Championship match in which a French referee was appointed. Bernard Marie had proved his worth when he left his role as touch-judge in the France-Wales match of 1965 in Paris to take over from the Scottish referee, R.W. Gilliland, who had to retire because of injury.

ENGLAND   D. Rutherford 10 (Gloucester); E.L. Rudd 5 (Liverpool), T.G. Arthur (2) (Wasps), C.W. McFadyean 1 (Moseley), K.F. Savage 2 (Northampton); T.J. Brophy 7 (Liverpool), R.C. Ashby 1 (Wasps); P.E. Judd 10 (Coventry), W.T. Treadwell 1 (Wasps), D.L. Powell 2 (Northampton), C.M. Payne 8 (Harlequins), J.E. Owen 9 (Coventry), J.R.H. Greenwood 1 (Waterloo), *D.P. Rogers 20 (Bedford), D.G. Perry 10 (Bedford).

IRELAND   T.J. Kiernan 21 (Cork Constitution); W.R. Hunter 9 (CIYMS), M.K. Flynn 16 (Wanderers), F.P.K. Bresnihan 1 (UC Dublin), P.J. McGrath 5 (UC Cork); C.M.H. Gibson 10 (NIFC), R.M. Young 6 (Queen's U. Belfast); S. MacHale 6 (Lansdowne), K.W. Kennedy 6 (CIYMS), *R.J. McLoughlin 14 (Gosforth), W.J. McBride 17 (Ballymena), M.G. Molloy 2 (UC Galway), N.A.A. Murphy 26 (Cork Constitution), M.G. Doyle 6 (Cambridge U.), R.A. Lamont 4 (Instonians).

Referee B. Marie (France)

FRANCE v ENGLAND   37/562

26 February 1966
Stade Colombes, Paris
France 13 (2G, 1T) England 0

France   T: André Boniface, Gachassin, Gruarin. C: Lacaze (2).

This was Gwynne Walter's nineteenth and last Championship match as a referee, a record challenged only remotely by one other man, Ireland's Kevin Kelleher, who officiated at 17. As a devotee of an open, running game Walters could not have wished for a better finale, for France were superb, often launching unstoppable attacks from inside their own 25, with forwards and backs linking with bewildering flair and pace. It was a miracle that England's defence stood up to them so well, particularly as several English players were handicapped by injury. Four of the team did not play again in the Championship, including the saviour in the 1965 Scotland match, Andy Hancock: a hero one day, a has-been the next.

FRANCE   C. Lacaze 9 (SC Angoulême); B. Duprat 1 (A. Bayonne), G. Boniface 18 (S. Mont-de-Marsan), A. Boniface 28 (S. Mont-de-Marsan), C. Darrouy 17 (S. Mont-de-Marsan); J. Gachassin 13 (FC Lourdes), L. Camberabero 3 (La Voulte S.); A. Gruarin 9 (RC Toulon), J-M. Cabanier 7 (US Montauban), J-C. Berejnoi 10 (SC Tulle), W. Spanghero 7 (RC Narbonne), E. Cester 3 (TOEC), J-J. Rupert 6 (US Tyrosse), *M. Crauste 34 (FC Lourdes), B. Dauga 11 (S. Mont-de-Marsan).

ENGLAND   D. Rutherford 11 (Gloucester); A.W. Hancock (3) (Northampton), R.D. Hearn 1 (Bedford), C.W. McFadyean 2 (Moseley), K.F. Savage 3 (Northampton); T.J. Brophy (8) (Liverpool), R.C. Ashby (2) (Wasps); P.E. Judd 11 (Coventry), W.T. Treadwell 2 (Wasps), A.L. Horton 5 (Blackheath), C.M. Payne 9 (Harlequins), J.E. Owen 10 (Coventry), J.R.H. Greenwood 2 (Waterloo), *D.P. Rogers 21 (Bedford), D.G. Perry (11) (Bedford).

Referee D.G. Walters (Wales)

IRELAND v SCOTLAND   72/563

26 February 1966
Lansdowne Road, Dublin
Scotland 11 (1G, 2T) Ireland 3 (1PG)

Ireland   PG: Kiernan.
Scotland   T: Hinshelwood (2), Grant. C: Wilson.

Scotland would not claim to have been the innovators of the shortened line-out, but they employed the technique effectively in this match, utilizing Pringle Fisher's one-handed flips. The Scottish scrummage too was immovably solid. With Sandy Hinshelwood running in two fine tries it added up to Scotland's fourth consecutive win at Lansdowne Road and their sixth in the last seven meetings with Ireland. The Irish performance was so abject and lacking in spirit that at the end their supporters made their feelings perfectly clear.

IRELAND   T.J. Kiernan 22 (Cork Constitution); W.R. Hunter (10) (CIYMS), M.K. Flynn 17 (Wanderers), J.C. Walsh 16 (Sunday's Well), P.J. McGrath 6 (UC Cork); C.M.H. Gibson 11 (Cambridge U.), R.M. Young 7 (Queen's U. Belfast); S. MacHale 7 (Lansdowne), A.M. Brady 1 (Dublin U.), *R.J. McLoughlin 15 (Gosforth), W.J. McBride 18 (Ballymena), O.C. Waldron 1 (Oxford U.), N.A.A. Murphy 27 (Cork Constitution), M.G. Doyle 7 (Cambridge U.), R.A. Lamont 5 (Instonians).

SCOTLAND   S. Wilson 10 (London Scottish); A.J.W. Hinshelwood 3 (London Scottish), B.C. Henderson 11 (Edinburgh Wands), *I.H.P. Laughland 26 (London Scottish), D.J. Whyte 6 (Edinburgh Wands); D.H. Chisholm 5 (Melrose), A.J. Hastie 9 (Melrose); J.D. Macdonald 3 (London Scottish), F.A.L. Laidlaw 7 (Melrose), D.M.D. Rollo 27 (Howe of Fife), P.K. Stagg 6 (Sale), M.J. Campbell-Lamerton 20 (London Scottish), J.P. Fisher 12 (London Scottish), D. Grant 5 (Hawick), J.W. Telfer 10 (Melrose).

Referee D.M. Hughes (Wales)

IRELAND v WALES   68/564

12 March 1966
Lansdowne Road, Dublin
Ireland 9 (1T, 1DG, 1PG) Wales 6 (1T, 1PG)

Ireland   T: Bresnihan. DG: Gibson. PG: Gibson.
Wales   T: Prothero. PG: Bradshaw.

Wales went to Lansdowne Road in search of an eleventh Triple Crown, confident not only of their own ability, but in the knowledge that Ireland had beaten them on their own turf only once since 1948. There was also the indisputable fact that Ireland had just played extremely badly against Scotland, and it would take enormous effort to improve their game. In the event the Irish were marvellous, completely dominating the match, covering, tackling and smothering every Welsh ploy. The villains of the Scottish match suddenly became heroes who were carried, shoulder-high, from the field by delighted fans after the final whistle.

IRELAND   *T.J. Kiernan 23 (Cork Constitution); A.T.A. Duggan 2 (Lansdowne), F.P.K. Bresnihan 2 (UC Dublin), J.C. Walsh 17 (Sunday's Well), P.J. McGrath (7) (UC Cork); C.M.H. Gibson 12 (NIFC), R.M. Young 8 (Queen's U. Belfast); S. MacHale 8 (Lansdowne), K.W. Kennedy 7 (CIYMS), R.J. McLoughlin 16 (Gosforth), O.C. Waldron (2) (Oxford U.), W.J. McBride 19 (Ballymena), N.A.A. Murphy 28 (Cork Constitution), M.G. Doyle 8 (Cambridge U.), R.A. Lamont 6 (Instonians).

WALES   G.T.R. Hodgson 11 (Neath); S.J. Watkins 10 (Newport), D.K. Jones 11 (Cardiff), K. Bradshaw 7 (Bridgend), L. Davies (3) (Bridgend); D. Watkins 15 (Newport), A.R. Lewis 3 (Abertillery); D. Williams 15 (Ebbw Vale), N.R. Gale 15 (Llanelli), D.J. Lloyd 3 (Bridgend), B. Price 18 (Newport), B.E. Thomas 12 (Neath), G.J. Prothero 10 (Bridgend), H.J. Morgan 25 (Abertillery), *A.E.I. Pask 20 (Abertillery).

Referee R.P. Burrell (Scotland)

SCOTLAND v ENGLAND 69/565

19 March 1966
Murrayfield
Scotland 6 (1T, 1PG) England 3 (1DG)

Scotland T: Whyte. PG: Blaikie.
England DG: McFadyean.

This victory elevated Scotland to a respectable third place in the Championship, which was a vast improvement in their fortunes from 1965. Defeat for England in fact brought them the Wooden Spoon for the first time since 1951, a failure which resulted in last caps for seven of the team, including five of the pack.

SCOTLAND C.F. Blaikie 3 (Heriot's FP); A.J.W. Hinshelwood 4 (London Scottish), B.C. Henderson (12) (Edinburgh Wands), *I.H.P. Laughland 27 (London Scottish), D.J. Whyte 7 (Edinburgh Wands); D.H. Chisholm 6 (Melrose), A.J. Hastie 10 (Melrose); J.D. Macdonald 4 (London Scottish), F.A.L. Laidlaw 8 (Melrose), D.M.D. Rollo 28 (Howe of Fife), P.K. Stagg 7 (Sale), M.J. Campbell-Lamerton (21) (London Scottish), J.P. Fisher 13 (London Scottish), D. Grant 6 (Hawick), J.W. Telfer 11 (Melrose).

ENGLAND D. Rutherford (12) (Gloucester); E.L. Rudd (6) (Liverpool), R.D. Hearn 2 (Bedford), C.W. McFadyean 3 (Moseley), K.F. Savage 4 (Northampton); M.P. Weston 22 (Durham City), T.C. Wintle 1 (Northampton); A.L. Horton (6) (Blackheath), W.T. Treadwell (3) (Wasps), P.E. Judd 12 (Coventry), J.E. Owen (11) (Coventry), C.M. Payne (10) (Harlequins), J.R.H. Greenwood 3 (Waterloo), *D.P. Rogers 22 (Bedford), G.A. Sherriff (1) (Saracens).

Referee K.D. Kelleher (Ireland)

WALES v FRANCE 37/566

26 March 1966
Cardiff Arms Park
Wales 9 (1T, 2PG) France 8 (1G, 1T)

Wales T: Stuart Watkins. PG: Bradshaw (2).
France T: Duprat, Rupert. C: Lacaze.

Wales, who had won only one of their previous eight encounters with France, pulled off a remarkable victory after trailing by eight points. The man who won the match – and the Championship as it happened – was Stuart Watkins, who raced 75 yards for a memorable try after Keith Bradshaw had resurrected fading Welsh hopes with two penalty goals. France, themselves bidding for the title, had a last-minute chance to triumph when Bill Morris, desperately and deliberately threw in the ball to touch near the Welsh goal-line. The penalty kick, taken by Claude Lacaze from near the touchline, was a brilliant attempt but a strong wind sent the ball veering slightly off target. Thus ended the match and the Championship careers of three great French players, their marvellous captain, Michel Crauste, and the Boniface brothers, André and Guy. It was the only time Lilian Camberabero played on a losing French side.

WALES G.T.R. Hodgson 12 (Neath); S.J. Watkins 11 (Newport), D.K. Jones (12) (Cardiff), K. Bradshaw (8) (Bridgend), D.I.E. Bebb 26 (Swansea); D. Watkins 16 (Newport), A.R. Lewis 4 (Abertillery); C.H. Norris (2) (Cardiff), N.R. Gale 16 (Llanelli), D.J. Lloyd 4 (Bridgend), B. Price 19 (Newport), W.J. Morris (2) (Newport), G.J. Prothero (11) (Bridgend), H.J. Morgan (26) (Abertillery), *A.E.I. Pask 21 (Abertillery).

FRANCE C. Lacaze 10 (SC Angoulême); B. Duprat 2 (A. Bayonne), G. Boniface (19) (S. Mont-de-Marsan), A. Boniface (29) (S. Mont-de-Marsan), C. Darrouy 18 (S. Mont-de-Marsan); J. Gachassin 14 (FC Lourdes), L. Camberabero 4 (La Voulte S.); A. Gruarin 10 (RC Toulon), J-M. Cabanier 8 (US Montauban), J-C. Berejnoi 11 (SC Tulle), W. Spanghero 8 (RC Narbonne), B. Dauga 12 (S. Mont-de-Marsan), J-J. Rupert 7 (US Tyrosse), *M. Crauste (35) (FC Lourdes), A. Herrero 8 (RC Toulon).

Referee K.D. Kelleher (Ireland)

1967

PARIS Scotland beat France 9-8 · MURRAYFIELD Scotland beat Wales 11-5
DUBLIN England beat Ireland 8-3 · TWICKENHAM France beat England 16-12
MURRAYFIELD Ireland beat Scotland 5-3 · CARDIFF Ireland beat Wales 3-0
TWICKENHAM England beat Scotland 27-14 · PARIS France beat Wales 11-6
DUBLIN France beat Ireland 11-6 · CARDIFF Wales beat England 34-21

CHAMPIONSHIP TABLE
France – Championship

Pos	Country	P	W	D	L	F	A	Pts	Tries F	A
1	France (2)	4	3	0	1	55	41	6	8	2
2	England (5)	4	2	0	2	68	67	4	8	9
3	Scotland (3)	4	2	0	2	37	45	4	4	8
4	Ireland (4)	4	2	0	2	17	22	4	3	2
5	Wales (1)	4	1	0	3	53	55	2	7	9

The 1967 Championship was notable for the large increase in scoring, for the 10 matches produced a massive 230 points, the first time since 1931 that the 200-barrier had been breached. Only Ireland failed to respond with big scores, although in accumulating just 17 points, they still managed 2 victories. The Irish total, remarkably, was 36 fewer than Wales scored and yet the Welsh finished bottom of the table.

Wales, Champions in 1966, lost their first three matches and then, in the most extraordinary reversal for many years, gave a superb performance to overwhelm England in their last match, 34-21 at Cardiff. It was Wales's highest ever score against England, who readily responded to the free scoring, so much so that they came extremely close to their own record score against Wales, 25-0 of 1896. It was a fitting finale for Wales, who had cause to celebrate for the WRU had just completed the purchase of Cardiff Arms Park where they planned a vast, expensive redevelopment. Scotland started their campaign handsomely, beating France (in Paris) and Wales, only to lose to Ireland at Murrayfield and then be blasted 27-14 by England at Twickenham. The year, however,

belonged to France who captured the title with three impressive victories which brought them their highest points return to date, 55, a total swollen by a record 32 points from Guy Camberabero, a master place and drop kicker.

FRANCE v SCOTLAND 37/567

14 January 1967
Stade Colombes, Paris
Scotland 9 (1DG, 2PG) France 8 (1G, 1T)

France T: Duprat, Carrère. C: Gachassin.
Scotland DG: Simmers. PG: Wilson (2).

France, always difficult to beat at home now, were unfortunate to succumb on this occasion. They lost Jean Maso, their talented newcomer in the centre, with a leg injury in the first half and the consequent reshuffling of the side restricted their scoring potential, particularly in the crucial area of back-row play. But this was a better Scottish side than usually accredited, and their pack and half-backs diligently kept up the pressure on the depleted French. Pringle Fisher had a particularly good game, and he was not only in the thick of the defensive set-up but occasionally inspired some dangerous Scottish counter-thrusts. It was from one of these that Scotland won, Brian Simmers dropping a fine goal.

FRANCE C. Lacaze 11 (SC Angoulême); B. Duprat 3 (A. Bayonne), C. Dourthe 1 (US Dax), J. Maso 1 (US Perpignan), *C. Darrouy 19 (S. Mont-de-Marsan); J. Gachassin 15 (FC Lourdes), J-C. Lasserre (6) (US Dax); A. Gruarin 11 (RC Toulon), J-M. Cabanier 9 (US Montauban), J-C. Berejnoi

12 (SC Tulle), W. Spanghero 9 (RC Narbonne), B. Dauga 13 (S. Mont-de-Marsan), J-P. Salut 1 (S. Toulouse), C. Carrère 1 (RC Toulon), A. Herrero 9 (RC Toulon).

SCOTLAND   S. Wilson 11 (London Scottish); A.J.W. Hinshelwood 5 (London Scottish), J.W.C. Turner 2 (Gala), B.M. Simmers 3 (Glasgow Acads), D.J. Whyte 8 (Edinburgh Wands); D.H. Chisholm 7 (Melrose), A.J. Hastie 11 (Melrose); J.D. MacDonald 5 (London Scottish), F.A.L. Laidlaw 9 (Melrose), D.M.D. Rollo 29 (Howe of Fife), P.K. Stagg 8 (Sale), W.J. Hunter 3 (Hawick), *J.P. Fisher 14 (London Scottish), D. Grant 7 (Hawick), A.H.W. Boyle 1 (St Thomas's H.).

Referee K.D. Kelleher (Ireland)

SCOTLAND v WALES   71/568

4 February 1967
Murrayfield
Scotland 11 (1G, 1T, 1DG) Wales 5 (1G)

Scotland   T: Hinshelwood, Telfer. C: Wilson. DG: Chisholm.
Wales   T: Watkins. C: Terry Price.

This was the only victory against Wales to console Scotland in the ten-year period, 1963–72, and as it was after Wales had beaten France it gave back the Scots some self-respect, not to mention prestige. Their pack played extremely well at times, controlling most of the game against a Welsh side containing nine players new to Championship rugby. Considering the quality and flair of some of these newcomers – Billy Raybould, Gerald Davies, Barry John and John Taylor – the general play was unimaginative, often negative.

SCOTLAND   S. Wilson 12 (London Scottish); A.J.W. Hinshelwood 6 (London Scottish), J.W.C. Turner 3 (Gala), B.M. Simmers 4 (Glasgow Acads), D.J. Whyte 9 (Edinburgh Wands); D.H. Chisholm 8 (Melrose), A.J. Hastie 12 (Melrose); J.D. Macdonald 6 (London Scottish), F.A.L. Laidlaw 10 (Melrose), D.M.D. Rollo 30 (Howe of Fife), P.K. Stagg 9 (Sale), W.J. Hunter 4 (Hawick), *J.P. Fisher 15 (London Scottish), D. Grant 8 (Hawick), J.W. Telfer 12 (Melrose).

WALES   T.G. Price 6 (Leicester U.); D.I.E. Bebb 27 (Swansea), T.G.R. Davies 1 (Cardiff), W.H. Raybould 1 (Cambridge U.), S.J. Watkins 12 (Newport); B. John 1 (Llanelli), W.G. Hullin (1) (Cardiff); J. P. O'Shea 1 (Cardiff), B.I. Rees 1 (London Welsh), D.J. Lloyd 5 (Bridgend), B. Price 20 (Newport), W.T. Mainwaring 1 (Aberavon), K.J. Braddock 1 (Newbridge), J. Taylor 1 (London Welsh), *A.E.I. Pask 22 (Abertillery).

Referee K.D. Kelleher (Ireland)

IRELAND v ENGLAND   71/569

11 February 1967
Lansdowne Road, Dublin
England 8 (1G, 1PG) Ireland 3 (1PG)

Ireland   PG: Kiernan.
England   T: McFadyean. C: Hosen. PG: Hosen.

England won at Lansdowne Road for the first time since 1959 with a team which included eight new caps, five in the pack and a fresh half-back pairing. It was somewhat of a risk against a seasoned Irish side in which the first appearance of a lanky, lithe No. 8 Ken Goodall was eagerly awaited in Dublin. Goodall and the other Irish forwards did well enough, but the old weakness of failing to take advantage of scoring opportunities left the sides in impasse until near the end. Then Ireland's luck deserted them; a misplaced Irish pass was catapulted forwards from Colin McFadyean's thigh and the wing followed up to take a perfect bounce and cross unchallenged for a try.

IRELAND   T.J. Kiernan 24 (Cork Constitution); R.D. Scott 1 (Queen's U. Belfast), F.P.K. Bresnihan 3 (UC Dublin), J.C. Walsh 18 (Sunday's Well), N.H. Brophy 15 (Blackrock College); C.M.H. Gibson 13 (NIFC), B.F. Sherry 1 (Terenure College); T.A. Moroney (2) (UC Dublin), K.W. Kennedy 8 (CIYMS), P. O'Callaghan 1 (Dolphin), W.J. McBride 20 (Ballymena), M.G. Molloy 3 (UC Galway), *N.A.A. Murphy 29 (Cork Constitution), M.G. Doyle 9 (Edinburgh Wands), K.G. Goodall 1 (Newcastle U.).

ENGLAND   R.W. Hosen 3 (Bristol); K.F. Savage 5 (Northampton), R.D. Hearn 3 (Bedford), C.R. Jennins 1 (Waterloo), C.W. McFadyean 4 (Moseley); J.F. Finlan 1 (Moseley), R.D.A. Pickering 1 (Bradford); *P.E. Judd 13 (Coventry), S.B. Richards 5 (Richmond), M.J. Coulman 1 (Moseley), J. Barton 1 (Coventry), D.E.J. Watt 1 (Bristol), D.M. Rollitt 1 (Bristol), R.B. Taylor 2 (Northampton), J.N. Pallant 1 (Notts).

Referee D.M. Hughes (Wales)

ENGLAND v FRANCE   38/570

25 February 1967
Twickenham
France 16 (2G, 1DG, 1PG) England 12 (1DG, 3PG)

England   DG: Finlan. PG: Hosen (3).
France   T: Dourthe, Duprat. C: Guy Camberabero (2). DG: Guy Camberabero. PG: Guy Camberabero.

France gained their first victory at Twickenham since 1955, and it proved a fascinating contrast of styles. The French zipped all around the pitch, maintaining momentum with short, crisp passes, while the more orthodox English approach swung the ball about in long, wide movements. Roger Hosen, unquestionably one of the finest straight-on place kickers ever seen in the Championship, landed three penalty goals, two from long range. In contrast France's newcomer, Guy Camberabero, made a sensational début contributing ten of their points. It seemed Camberabero could drop kick from any angle and he was a deadly, quick, unfussed place kicker, an asset which was to win France many matches they might otherwise have lost. Camberabero's son, Didier, coincidentally played his first Championship match at Twickenham in 1983. His kicking was, however, indifferent and his only success was a penalty goal which he drop kicked.

ENGLAND   R.W. Hosen 4 (Bristol); K.F. Savage 6 (Northampton), R.D. Hearn 4 (Bedford), C.R. Jennins (2) (Waterloo), C.W. McFadyean 5 (Moseley); J.F. Finlan 2 (Moseley), R.D.A. Pickering 2 (Bradford); *P.E. Judd 14 (Coventry), S.B. Richards 6 (Richmond), M.J. Coulman 2 (Moseley), J. Barton 2 (Coventry), D.E.J. Watt 2 (Bristol), D.M. Rollitt 2 (Bristol), R.B. Taylor 3 (Northampton), J.N. Pallant 2 (Notts).

FRANCE   C. Lacaze 12 (SC Angoulême); B. Duprat 4 (A. Bayonne), C. Dourthe 2 (US Dax), J-P. Lux 1 (US Tyrosse), *C. Darrouy 20 (S. Mont-de-Marsan); G. Camberabero 1 (La Voulte S.), L. Camberabero 5 (La Voulte S.); A. Gruarin 12 (RC Toulon), J-M. Cabanier 10 (US Montauban), J-C. Berejnoi 13 (SC Tulle), W. Spanghero 10 (RC Narbonne), B. Dauga 14 (S. Mont-de-Marsan), M. Sitjar 3 (SU Agen), C. Carrère 2 (RC Toulon), A. Herrero 10 (RC Toulon).

Referee D.P. d'Arcy (Ireland)

SCOTLAND v IRELAND   73/571

25 February 1967
Murrayfield
Ireland 5 (1G) Scotland 3 (1PG)

Scotland   PG: Wilson.
Ireland   T: Murphy. C: Kiernan.

Ireland gained one of their rare victories of the era over Scotland, thanks to a well-taken try by their veteran flank-forward Noel Murphy, which Tom Kiernan converted. It was a disappointing outcome for Scotland who in their match earlier in the month had won convincingly against Wales, while Ireland in their opening match had been beaten by England. Mike Gibson was credited as man of the match by many critics; but there were also notable contributions from Bresnihan, Goodall and Doyle.

SCOTLAND   S. Wilson 13 (London Scottish); A.J.W. Hinshelwood 7 (London Scottish), J.W.C. Turner 4 (Gala), R.B. Welsh 1 (Hawick), D.J. Whyte 10 (Edinburgh Wands); B.M. Simmers 5 (Glasgow Acads), A.J. Hastie 13 (Melrose); J.D. Macdonald 7 (London Scottish), F.A.L. Laidlaw 11 (Melrose), A.B. Carmichael 1 (W. of Scotland), P.K. Stagg 10 (Sale), W.J. Hunter 5 (Hawick), *J.P. Fisher 16 (London Scottish). D. Grant 9 (Hawick), J.W. Telfer 13 (Melrose).

IRELAND   T.J. Kiernan 25 (Cork Constitution); N.H. Brophy 16 (Blackrock College), J.C. Walsh 19 (Sunday's Well), F.P.K. Bresnihan 4 (UC Dublin), A.T.A. Duggan 3 (Lansdowne); C.M.H. Gibson 14 (NIFC), B.F. Sherry 2 (Terenure College); S. MacHale 9 (Lansdowne), K.W. Kennedy 9 (CIYMS), S.A. Hutton 1 (Malone), W.J.

McBride 21 (Ballymena), M.G. Molloy 4 (UC Galway), *N.A.A. Murphy 30 (Cork Constitution), M.G. Doyle 10 (Edinburgh Wands), K.G. Goodall 2 (Newcastle U.).

Referee D.M. Hughes (Wales)

WALES v IRELAND 69/572

11 March 1967
Cardiff Arms Park
Ireland 3 (1T) Wales 0

Ireland T: Duggan.

This was Ireland's hundredth Championship victory, achieved by a try after only four minutes when Alan Duggan pounced on an angled kick to the corner. The Irish deserved their success, for their pack played with gusto, particularly in the mauls and loose. For Wales it was the third time only that they had failed to score against Ireland at home, and after the inevitable post-mortem the heads that rolled were those of Grahame Hodgson, Allan Lewis, Ken Braddock and Alun Pask.

WALES   G.T.R. Hodgson (13) (Neath); S.J. Watkins 13 (Newport), W.H. Raybould 2 (London Welsh), T.G.R. Davies 2 (Cardiff), D.I.E. Bebb 28 (Swansea); *D. Watkins 17 (Newport), A.R. Lewis (5) (Abertillery); J.P. O'Shea 2 (Cardiff), B.I. Rees 2 (London Welsh), D.J. Lloyd 6 (Bridgend), W.T. Mainwaring 2 (Aberavon), B. Price 21 (Newport), K.J. Braddock (2) (Newbridge), J. Taylor 2 (London Welsh), A.E.I. Pask (23) (Abertillery).

IRELAND   T.J. Kiernan 26 (Cork Constitution); A.T.A. Duggan 4 (Lansdowne), F.P.K. Bresnihan 5 (UC Dublin), J.C. Walsh 20 (Sunday's Well), N.H. Brophy 17 (Blackrock College); C.M.H. Gibson 15 (NIFC), R.M. Young 9 (Queen's U. Belfast); S. MacHale 10 (Lansdowne), K.W. Kennedy 10 (CIYMS), S.A. Hutton 2 (Malone), W.J. McBride 22 (Ballymena), M.G. Molloy 5 (UC Galway), *N.A.A. Murphy 31 (Cork Constitution), M.G. Doyle 11 (Edinburgh Wands), K.G. Goodall 3 (Newcastle U.).

Referee M.H. Titcomb (England)

ENGLAND v SCOTLAND 70/573

18 March 1967
Twickenham
England 27 (3G, 1T, 1DG, 2PG) Scotland 14 (1G, 1T, 2PG)

England T: McFadyean (2), Taylor, Webb. C: Hosen (3). DG: Finlan. PG: Hosen (2).
Scotland T: Hinshelwood, Turner. C: Wilson. PG: Wilson (2).

This was England's biggest score at home against Scotland, and confirmed that while they had some skilled, fast attacking players, their defence was not as strong as it could have been. England in fact ended the season by scoring 68 points, more than anyone else, but they also conceded 67, by far the highest of any team which finished in the top two of the table. The frantic pace of the match was obviously too much for Scotland, for while they competed valiantly for most of the game, their defence fell apart in the later stages, England adding 13 points in 6 minutes. Four of their team never played another Championship match, including Ian Laughland, arguably the best all-round Scottish back since the War; he had made 28 appearances.

ENGLAND   R.W. Hosen 5 (Bristol); K.F. Savage 7 (Northampton), R.D. Hearn 5 (Bedford), C.W. McFadyean 6 (Moseley), R.E. Webb 1 (Coventry); J.F. Finlan 3 (Moseley), R.D.A. Pickering 3 (Bradford); *P.E. Judd 15 (Coventry), S.B. Richards 7 (Richmond), M.J. Coulman 3 (Moseley), J.N. Pallant (3) (Notts), D.E.J. Watt 3 (Bristol), D.P. Rogers 23 (Bedford), R.B. Taylor 4 (Northampton), D.M. Rollitt 3 (Bristol).

SCOTLAND   S. Wilson 14 (London Scottish); A.J.W. Hinshelwood 8 (London Scottish), J.W.C. Turner 5 (Gala), R.B. Welsh (2) (Hawick), D.J. Whyte (11) (Edinburgh Wands); I.H.P. Laughland (28) (London Scottish), I.G. McCrae 1 (Gordonians); J.D. MacDonald (8) (London Scottish), F.A.L. Laidlaw 12 (Melrose), D.M.D. Rollo 31 (Howe of Fife), P.K. Stagg 11 (Sale), W.J. Hunter (6) (Hawick), *J.P. Fisher 17 (London Scottish), D. Grant 10 (Hawick), J.W. Telfer 14 (Melrose).

Referee D.P. d'Arcy (Ireland)

FRANCE v WALES   38/574

1 April 1967
Stade Colombes, Paris
France 20 (1G, 2T, 2DG, 1PG) Wales 14 (1G, 1DG, 1PG)

Keith Jarrett who scored 19 points on his début for Wales against England on 15 April 1967

France   T: Guy Camberabero, Dauga, Dourthe. C: Guy Camberabero. DG: Guy Camberabero (2). PG: Guy Camberabero.
Wales   T: Bebb. C: Terry Price. DG: David Watkins. PG: Terry Price (2).

Gareth Edwards's first appearance coincided with France's fifth win in a row against Wales in Paris, their longest winning sequence against them. It was a benefit day for Guy Camberabero, who in scoring 14 of the French points completely overshadowed the Welsh scoring machine, Terry Price. It was in fact Price's last appearance; he was lured by a signing-on fee, purported to be £10,000, to play rugby league for Bradford. In 7 Championship matches Price scored 40 points, and though there were some who felt little regret that this swaggering, seemingly arrogant player left the game, there were many who realized Wales had lost a magnificent competitor whose full potential had not been realized. The game is always bigger than its players, but. . . .

FRANCE   J. Gachassin 16 (FC Lourdes); M. Arnaudet (2) (FC Lourdes), C. Dourthe 3 (US Dax), J-P. Lux 2 (US Tyrosse), *C. Darrouy 21 (S. Mont-de-Marsan); G. Camberabero 2 (La Voulte S.), L. Camberabero 6 (La Voulte S.); A. Gruarin 13 (RC Toulon), J-M. Cabanier 11 (US Montauban), J-C. Berejnoi 14 (SC Tulle), E. Cester 4 (S. Toulouse), J. Fort 1 (SU Agen), M. Sitjar 4 (SU Agen), C. Carrère 3 (RC Toulon), B. Dauga 15 (S. Mont-de-Marsan).

WALES   T.G. Price (7) (London Welsh); S.J. Watkins 14 (Newport), W.H. Raybould 3 (London Welsh), T.G.R. Davies 3 (Cardiff), D.I.E. Bebb 29 (Swansea); *D. Watkins 18 (Newport), G.O. Edwards 1 (Cardiff Training College); D. Williams 16 (Ebbw Vale), B.I. Rees (3) (London Welsh), D.J. Lloyd 7 (Bridgend), B. Price 22 (Newport), W.T. Mainwaring 3 (Aberavon), R.E. Jones 1 (Coventry), J. Taylor 3 (London Welsh), W.D. Morris 1 (Neath).

Referee D.P. d'Arcy (Ireland)

IRELAND v FRANCE   38/575

15 April 1967
Lansdowne Road, Dublin
France 11 (1G, 2DG) Ireland 6 (1T, 1PG)

Ireland   T: Molloy. PG: Kiernan.
France   T: Cabanier. C: Guy Camberabero. DG: Guy Camberabero (2).

Guy Camberabero's 8 points brought this season's Championship total to 32, a record for a Frenchman. It was the twenty-second and last appearance of Christian Darrouy, the French captain, which must have been of some relief to the Irish for the flying wing had scored 8 tries against them on his way to a French try record of 14. Darrouy shared with Michel Crauste the distinction of scoring most tries in a match, three, for France and that was also against Ireland in 1963. He and Crauste also shared the French record for most tries in a season, four, until Patrick Estève went one better in 1983.

IRELAND   T.J. Kiernan 27 (Cork Constitution); R.D. Scott 2 (Queen's U. Belfast), F.P.K. Bresnihan 6 (UC Dublin), J.C. Walsh (21) (Sunday's Well), N.H. Brophy (18) (Blackrock College); C.M.H. Gibson 16 (NIFC), R.M. Young 10 (Belfast Collegians); S. MacHale (11) (Lansdowne), K.W. Kennedy 11 (CIYMS), S.A. Hutton (3) (Malone), W.J. McBride 23 (Ballymena), M.G. Molloy 6 (London Irish), *N.A.A. Murphy 32 (Cork Constitution), M.G. Doyle 12 (Blackrock College), K.G. Goodall 4 (City of Derry).

FRANCE   P. Villepreux 1 (S Toulouse); J. Gachassin 17 (FC Lourdes), C. Dourthe 4 (US Dax), J-P. Lux 3 (US Tyrosse), *C. Darrouy (22) (S. Mont-de-Marsan); G. Camberabero 3 (La Voulte S.), L. Camberabero 7 (La Voulte S.); J-C. Berejnoi (15) (SC Tulle), J-M. Cabanier 12 (US Montauban), A. Gruarin 14 (RC Toulon), J. Fort (2) (SU Agen), A. Herrero (11) (RC Toulon), C. Carrère 4 (RC Toulon), M. Sitjar (5) (SU Agen), B. Dauga 16 (S. Mont-de-Marsan).

Referee R.P. Burrell (Scotland)

WALES v ENGLAND   71/576

15 April 1967
Cardiff Arms Park
Wales 34 (5G, 1DG, 2PG) England 21 (3T, 4PG)

Wales   T: Davies (2), Jarrett, Morris, Bebb. C: Jarrett (5). DG: Raybould. PG: Jarrett (2).
England   T: Barton (2), Savage. PG: Hosen (4).

Wales's highest score against England and their biggest victory since beating France 49-14 in 1910 was made possible by the remarkable début of Keith Jarrett, who scored 19 points to equal Jack Bancroft's record, also against France in 1910. Jarrett's total included a try, curiously only the second time in rugby history for a Wales full-back to achieve the feat, the first being by Vivian Jenkins against Ireland in 1934. England, deprived of the Triple Crown by the defeat, had little to console them: one cheering note was Roger Hosen's 4 penalties which gave him 38 points, the most to date in a Championship season by an England player. It was also England's biggest points' haul in Wales and the match aggregate of 55 points was the highest of all England-Wales matches.

WALES   K.S. Jarrett 1 (Newport); S.J. Watkins 15 (Newport), W.H. Raybould 4 (London Welsh), T.G.R. Davies 4 (Cardiff), D.I.E. Bebb (30) (Swansea); *D. Watkins (19) (Newport), G.O. Edwards 2 (Cardiff Training College); D. Williams 17 (Ebbw Vale), N.R. Gale 17 (Llanelli), D.J. Lloyd 8 (Bridgend), B. Price 23 (Newport), W.T. Mainwaring 4 (Aberavon), R.E. Jones 2 (Coventry), J. Taylor 4 (London Welsh), W.D. Morris 2 (Neath).

ENGLAND   R.W. Hosen (6) (Bristol); K.F. Savage 8 (Northampton), R.D. Hearn (6) (Bedford), C.W. McFadyean 7 (Moseley), R.E. Webb 2 (Coventry); J.F. Finlan 4 (Moseley), R.D.A. Pickering 4 (Bradford); *P.E. Judd (16) (Coventry), S.B. Richards (8) (Richmond), M.J. Coulman 4 (Moseley), J. Barton 3 (Coventry), D.E.J. Watt (4) (Bristol), D.P. Rogers 24 (Bedford), R.B. Taylor 5 (Northampton), D.M. Rollitt 4 (Bristol).

Referee D.C.J. McMahon (Scotland)

1968

MURRAYFIELD France beat Scotland 8-6 · TWICKENHAM England drew Wales 11-11
PARIS France beat Ireland 16-6 · CARDIFF Wales beat Scotland 5-0
TWICKENHAM England drew Ireland 9-9 · DUBLIN Ireland beat Wales 9-6
PARIS France beat England 14-9 · DUBLIN Ireland beat Scotland 14-6
MURRAYFIELD England beat Scotland 8-6 · CARDIFF France beat Wales 14-9

CHAMPIONSHIP TABLE
France – Championship, Triple Crown

Pos	Country	P	W	D	L	F	A	Pts	Tries F	A
1	France (1)	4	4	0	0	52	30	8	7	2
2	Ireland (4)	4	2	1	1	38	37	5	4	2
3	England (2)	4	1	2	1	37	40	4	3	3
4	Wales (5)	4	1	1	2	31	34	3	4	5
5	Scotland (3)	4	0	0	4	18	35	0	1	7

After 39 years of competing, France finally achieved their ambition and won the Grand Slam. Guy Camberabero, their record points-scorer of the previous season, set them on course with a vital five points in a close, tough opening match at Murrayfield. From that moment the French won in style, with a 14-9 triumph over Wales in Cardiff to set the seal on their most momentous season since joining the Championship in 1910. The Scots, who had given the all-conquering French their biggest fright, did not repeat that spirit or performance and slumped to four defeats for the first time since 1954. If the remaining contests were of less importance at least the Irish had something to celebrate in that they came second in the table, their highest position since they were runners-up to France in 1959.

SCOTLAND v FRANCE 38/577

13 January 1968
Murrayfield
France 8 (1G, 1T) Scotland 6 (1T, 1PG)

Scotland T: Keith. PG: Wilson.
France T: Duprat, Campaes. C. Guy Camberabero.

Having failed to score a try on either of their two previous visits to Murrayfield, France regained their touch with two splendidly opportunist scores. The match was evenly balanced and it seems incongruous that Scotland slumped to four defeats.

SCOTLAND S. Wilson 15 (London Scottish); A.J.W. Hinshelwood 9 (London Scottish), J.W.C. Turner 6 (Gala), J.N.M. Frame 1 (Edinburgh U.), G.J. Keith 1 (Wasps); D.H. Chisholm 9 (Melrose), A.J. Hastie 14 (Melrose); A.B. Carmichael 2 (W. of Scotland), F.A.L. Laidlaw 13 (Melrose), D.M.D. Rollo 32 (Howe of Fife), P.K. Stagg 12 (Sale), G.W.E. Mitchell 1 (Edinburgh Wands), *J.P. Fisher 18 (London Scottish), D. Grant (11) (Hawick), A.H.W. Boyle 2 (London Scottish).

FRANCE C. Lacaze 13 (SC Angoulême); A. Campaes 2 (FC Lourdes), J. Trillo 1 (CA Bègles), J. Maso 2 (US Perpignan), B. Duprat 5 (A. Bayonne); G. Camberabero 4 (La Voulte S.), L. Camberabero 8 (La Voulte S.); A. Abadie 1 (SC Graulhet), J-M. Cabanier 13 (US Montauban), A. Gruarin 15 (RC Toulon), B. Dauga 17 (S Mont-de-Marsan), E. Cester 5 (TOEC), J-J. Rupert (8) (US Tyrosse), *C. Carrère 5 (RC Toulon), W. Spanghero 11 (RC Narbonne).

Referee K.D. Kelleher (Ireland)

ENGLAND v WALES 72/578

20 January 1968
Twickenham
England 11 (1G, 1T, 1PG) Wales 11 (1G, 1T, 1DG)

England T: McFadyean, Redwood. C: Hiller. PG: Hiller.
Wales T: Edwards, Wanbon. C: Jarrett. DG: John.

David Nash had the distinction of becoming Wales's first coach, but even he would have agreed that his maiden team was somewhat fortunate to escape with a draw. England led 11-3 but were thwarted when Welsh tries emanated from failed penalty goals by Keith Jarrett. Both kicks were knocked on by a defender and from the resultant scrummages first Gareth Edwards scored, then Bobby Wanbon. Jarrett converted the second and a dropped goal by Barry John completed the misery of an England side which, with ten new caps, had exceeded all expectations.

ENGLAND R. Hiller 1 (Harlequins); D.H. Prout 1 (Northampton), *C.W. McFadyean 8 (Moseley), R.H. Lloyd 1 (Harlequins), K.F. Savage 9 (Northampton); J.F. Finlan 5 (Moseley), B.W. Redwood 1 (Bristol); B.W. Keen 1 (Newcastle U.), J.V. Pullin 2 (Bristol), M.J. Coulman 5 (Moseley), M.J. Parsons 1 (Northampton), P.J. Larter 1 (Northampton), P.J. Bell 1 (Blackheath), B.R. West 1 (Loughborough College), D.J. Gay 1 (Bath).

WALES P.J. Wheeler (1) (Aberavon); S.J. Watkins 16 (Newport), K.S. Jarrett 2 (Newport), T.G.R. Davies 5 (Cardiff), W.K. Jones 1 (Cardiff); B. John 2 (Cardiff), G.O. Edwards 3 (Cardiff); D. Williams 18 (Ebbw Vale), *N.R. Gale (18) (Llanelli), B. James (1) (Bridgend), M. Wiltshire 1 (Aberavon), W.T. Mainwaring (5) (Aberavon), W.D. Morris 3 (Neath), A.J. Gray 1 (London Welsh), R. Wanbon (1) (Aberavon).

Referee D.P. d'Arcy (Ireland)

FRANCE v IRELAND 39/579

27 January 1968
Stade Colombes, Paris
France 16 (2G, 1DG, 1PG) Ireland 6 (2PG)

France T: Campaes, Dauga. C: Villepreux (2). DG: Gachassin. PG: Villepreux.
Ireland PG: McCombe (2).

France extended their sequence of matches without defeat against Ireland to nine, their longest unbeaten run against them. After a comparatively difficult match at Murrayfield, the French completed refining their scoring machine on their way to their first Grand Slam. Ireland did well to limit them to two tries for the French continually attacked and probed. It was a tough baptism for Billy McCombe, who contributed all the Irish points with two penalty goals.

FRANCE P. Villepreux 2 (S. Toulouse); B. Duprat 6 (A. Bayonne), J-P. Lux 4 (US Tyrosse), J. Trillo 2 (CA Bègles), A. Campaes 3 (FC Lourdes); J. Gachassin 18 (FC Lourdes), J-H. Mir (1) (FC Lourdes); A. Abadie (2) (SC Graulhet), J-M. Cabanier (14) (US Montauban), A. Gruarin (16) (RC Toulon), B. Dauga 18 (S. Mont-de-Marsan), E. Cester 6 (TOEC), *C. Carrère 6 (RC Toulon) J-P. Salut 2 (TOEC), W. Spanghero 12 (RC Narbonne).

IRELAND *T.J. Kiernan 28 (Cork Constitution); A.T.A. Duggan 5 (Lansdowne), B.A.P. O'Brien 1 (Shannon), F.P.K. Bresnihan 7 (Lansdowne), R.D. Scott 3 (Queen's U. Belfast); W.McM. McCombe 1 (Dublin U.), B.F. Sherry 3 (Terenure College); S. Millar 22 (Ballymena), K.W. Kennedy 12 (London Irish), P. O'Callaghan 2 (Dolphin), W.J. McBride 24 (Ballymena), M.G. Molloy 7 (UC Galway), M.G. Doyle 13 (Blackrock College), M.L. Hipwell 3 (Terenure College), K.G. Goodall 5 (City of Derry).

Referee G.C. Lamb (England)

WALES v SCOTLAND 72/580

3 February 1968
Cardiff Arms Park
Wales 5 (1G) Scotland 0

Wales T: Keri Jones. C: Jarrett.

This was Wales's only victory of the season and the fifth time in 12 visits that the Scots failed to register a score on Welsh soil. Like Wales, they had had plenty of opportunities, but the finishing was poor, and the only score was a try for Keri Jones after Keith Jarrett had skilfully bisected Turner and Frame. Three of the Scottish team were immediately dropped, including Alex Hastie, the tough, resourceful Melrose scrum-half.

WALES D. Rees 1 (Swansea); S.J. Watkins 17 (Newport), K.S. Jarrett 3 (Newport), T.G.R. Davies 6 (Cardiff), W.K. Jones 2 (Cardiff); B. John 3 (Cardiff), *G.O. Edwards 4 (Cardiff); D.J. Lloyd 9 (Bridgend), J. Young 1 (Bridgend), J.P. O'Shea 3 (Cardiff), M. Wiltshire 2 (Aberavon), W.D. Thomas 1 (Llanelli), W.D. Morris 4 (Neath), A.J. Gray (2) (London Welsh), R.E. Jones 3 (Coventry).

SCOTLAND S. Wilson 16 (London Scottish); A.J.W. Hinshelwood 10 (London Scottish), J.W.C. Turner 7 (Gala), J.N.M. Frame 2 (Edinburgh U.), G.J. Keith (2) (Wasps); D.H. Chisholm 10 (Melrose), A.J. Hastie (15) (Melrose); A.B. Carmichael 3 (W. of Scotland), F.A.L. Laidlaw 14 (Melrose), D.M.D. Rollo 33 (Howe of Fife), P.K. Stagg 13 (Sale), G.W.E. Mitchell (2) (Edinburgh Wands), *J.P. Fisher 19 (London Scottish), T.G. Elliot 1 (Langholm), A.H.W. Boyle 3 (London Scottish).

Referee G.C. Lamb (England)

ENGLAND v IRELAND 72/581

10 February 1968
Twickenham
England 9 (1DG, 2PG) Ireland 9 (3PG)

England DG: Finlan. PG. Hiller (2).
Ireland PG: Kiernan (3).

The new English pack, which had performed so effectively against Wales the previous month, were severely handicapped when after half-an-hour Peter Bell had to switch from flank to scrum-half because of an injury to Bill Redwood. It was reminiscent of Mickey Steele-Bodger's scrum-half takeover against Scotland in 1948, but Bell was far less effective in either feeding the scrum or providing Finlan with adequate support. Surprisingly the Irish failed to take control of the proceedings, though they were 9-6 ahead with a minute to go. The match was then quite literally thrown away. Brendan Sherry, the Terenure scrum-half, was adjudged by Welsh referee Meirion Joseph to have deliberately thrown in the ball to touch, as the Irishman was trying to tidy up on his own 25. Bob Hiller was presented with a difficult, angled kick but he succeeded brilliantly to save England. Ireland never picked the unfortunate Sherry again.

ENGLAND R. Hiller 2 (Harlequins); D.H. Prout (2) (Northampton), *C.W. McFadyean (9) (Moseley), R.H. Lloyd 2 (Harlequins), R.E. Webb 3 (Coventry); J.F. Finlan 6 (Moseley), B.W. Redwood (2) (Bristol); B.W. Keen 2 (Newcastle U.), J.V. Pullin 3 (Bristol), M.J. Coulman 6 (Moseley), M.J. Parsons 2 (Northampton), P.J. Larter 2 (Northampton), P.J. Bell 2 (Blackheath), B.R. West 2 (Loughborough College), D.J. Gay 2 (Bath).

IRELAND *T.J. Kiernan 29 (Cork Constitution); A.T.A. Duggan 6 (Lansdowne), B.A.P. O'Brien 2 (Shannon), F.P.K. Bresnihan 8 (UC Dublin), R.D. Scott 4 (Queen's U. Belfast); C.M.H. Gibson 17 (NIFC), B.F. Sherry (4) (Terenure College); S. Millar 23 (Ballymena), A.M. Brady 2 (Malone), P. O'Callaghan 3 (Dolphin), M.G. Molloy 8 (UC Galway), W.J. McBride 25 (Ballymena), M.G. Doyle 14 (Blackrock College), T.J. Doyle 1 (Wanderers), K.G. Goodall 6 (Newcastle U.).

Referee M. Joseph (Wales)

FRANCE v ENGLAND 39/582

24 February 1968
Stade Colombes, Paris
France 14 (1G, 2DG, 1PG) England 9 (1DG, 2PG)

France T: Gachassin. C: Guy Camberabero. DG: Guy Camberabero, Lacaze. PG: Guy Camberabero.
England DG: Weston. PG: Hiller (2).

Although France had beaten both Scotland and Ireland, they introduced five new players, including the whole front-row. They also played Jean Gachassin at centre to allow the return of Guy Camberabero to fly-half, a bold decision for although Gachassin had midfield experience he was essentially a wing. In the event the sheer footballing ability of both players paid off: Gachassin scored a try and Camberabero supplied eight other points. England, however, were unfortunate not to have won for they led 9-3 until late in the game, and had other opportunities to add to their score, with Mike Weston dictating affairs. Earlier French teams might have submitted but this one suddenly came to life with some brilliant switches and support play, and they swung the match in the second half.

FRANCE   C. Lacaze 14 (SC Angoulême); J-M. Bonal 1 (S. Toulouse), J. Gachassin 19 (FC Lourdes), J-P. Lux 5 (US Tyrosse), A. Campaes 4 (FC Lourdes); G. Camberabero 5 (La Voulte S.), L. Camberabero 9 (La Voulte S.); M. Lasserre 1 (SU Agen), M. Yachvili 1 (SC Tulle), J-C. Noble 1 (La Voulte S.), E. Cester 7 (TOEC), A. Plantefol 1 (SU Agen), J-P. Salut 3 (TOEC), *C. Carrère 7 (RC Toulon), W. Spanghero 13 (RC Narbonne).

ENGLAND   R. Hiller 3 (Harlequins); K.F. Savage 10 (Northampton), T.J. Brooke 1 (Richmond), R.H. Lloyd 3 (Harlequins), R.E. Webb 4 (Coventry); *M.P. Weston 23 (Durham City), R.D.A. Pickering 5 (Bradford); B.W. Keen 3 (Newcastle U.), J.V. Pullin 4 (Bristol), M.J. Coulman 7 (Moseley), M.J. Parsons 3 (Northampton), P.J. Larter 3 (Northampton), P.J. Bell 3 (Blackheath), B.R. West 3 (Loughborough College), D.J. Gay 3 (Bath).

Referee H.B. Laidlaw (Scotland)

IRELAND v SCOTLAND 74/583

24 February 1968
Lansdowne Road, Dublin
Ireland 14 (1G, 2T, 1PG) Scotland 6 (2PG)

Ireland T: Duggan (2), Bresnihan. C: Kiernan. PG: Kiernan.
Scotland PG: Wilson (2).

Johnny Quirke, who became Ireland's youngest player when he was first capped at the age of 17, was recalled six years later to make his third and final appearance. It was also the final Championship match for David Rollo, the Howe of Fife tight-head prop. Rollo played 34 times since 1959 and was the cornerstone of a series of Scottish packs who often did not do themselves justice. Rollo was an out-and-out scrummager, sturdily built with strong legs. He was also a committed competitor in the mauls.

IRELAND   *T.J. Kiernan 30 (Cork Constitution); A.T.A. Duggan 7 (Lansdowne), B.A.P. O'Brien (3) (Shannon), F.P.K. Bresnihan 9 (UC Dublin), R.D. Scott (5) (Queen's U. Belfast); C.M.H. Gibson 18 (NIFC), J.T.M. Quirke (3) (Blackrock College); S. Millar 24 (Ballymena), A.M. Brady 3 (Malone), P. O'Callaghan 4 (Dolphin), M.G. Molloy 9 (UC Galway), W.J. McBride 26 (Ballymena), M.G. Doyle 15 (Blackrock College), T.J. Doyle 2 (Wanderers), K.G. Goodall 7 (Newcastle U.).

SCOTLAND   S. Wilson 17 (London Scottish); A.J.W. Hinshelwood 11 (London Scottish), J.W.C. Turner 8 (Gala), J.N.M. Frame 3 (Edinburgh U.), C.G. Hodgson 1 (London Scottish); D.H. Chisholm (11) (Melrose), I.G. McCrae 2 (Gordonians); A.B. Carmichael 4 (W. of Scotland), F.A.L. Laidlaw 15 (Melrose), D.M.D. Rollo (34) (Howe of Fife), P.K. Stagg 14 (Sale), A.F. McHarg 1 (W. of Scotland), *J.P. Fisher 20 (London Scottish), R.J. Arneil 1 (Edinburgh Acads), A.H.W. Boyle (4) (London Scottish).

Referee M. Joseph (Wales)

Tom Kiernan, Ireland's record holder for the most number of Championship points, 115, until Ollie Campbell swept him into second place

IRELAND v WALES 70/584

9 March 1968
Lansdowne Road, Dublin
Ireland 9 (1T, 1DG, 1PG) Wales 6 (1DG, 1PG)

Ireland T: Mick Doyle. DG: Gibson. PG: Kiernan.
Wales DG: Edwards. PG: Rees.

Spectators invaded the playing area and held up play for five minutes after Mike Titcomb, the indefatigable English referee, had ruled that a Gareth Edwards dropped goal had gone over, when it had clearly passed outside a post. Titcomb, not one of those referees afraid to admit to being mistaken, did so afterwards, though he was clearly shaken at the time by the fury of the demonstration. The Irish team in fact did him a favour by restoring their spectators' good humour by winning and winning well, and the police escort for the smiling Englishman at the end proved quite unnecessary. He was to officiate at three other internationals, but none involving Ireland.

IRELAND   *T.J. Kiernan 31 (Cork Constitution); A.T.A. Duggan 8 (Lansdowne), L. Hunter (1) (Ulster Civil Service), F.P.K. Bresnihan 10 (UC Dublin, J.C.M. Moroney 1 (London Irish); C.M.H. Gibson 19 (NIFC), R.M. Young 11 (Queen's U. Belfast); P. O'Callaghan 5 (Dolphin), A.M. Brady (4) (Malone), S. Millar 25 (Ballymena), W.J. McBride 27 (Ballymena), M.G. Molloy 10 (UC Galway), M.G. Doyle (16) (Blackrock College), T.J. Doyle (3) (Wanderers), K.G. Goodall 8 (Newcastle U.).

WALES   D. Rees 2 (Swansea); W.K. Jones 3 (Cardiff), *S.J. Dawes 7 (London Welsh), W.H. Raybould 5 (London Welsh), M.C.R. Richards 1 (Cardiff); B. John 4 (Cardiff), G.O. Edwards 5 (Cardiff); J.P. O'Shea 4 (Cardiff), J. Young 2 (Bridgend), D.J. Lloyd 10 (Bridgend), I.C. Jones (1) (London Welsh), W.D. Thomas 2 (Llanelli), W.D. Morris 5 (Neath), J. Taylor 5 (London Welsh), R.E. Jones 4 (Coventry).

Referee M.H. Titcomb (England)

SCOTLAND v ENGLAND 71/585

16 March 1968
Murrayfield
England 8 (1G, 1PG) Scotland 6 (1DG, 1PG)

Scotland DG: Connell. PG: Wilson.
England T: Coulman. C: Hiller. PG: Hiller.

This was England's first victory at Murrayfield since 1960, but even worse it was Scotland's fourth defeat of the season, a misfortune they had not suffered since 1954. Four of the Scottish team were never capped again, including Stewart Wilson and Pringle Fisher. England's clear-out was even more dramatic. Ten of their players played their final international, including Mike Weston, their long-serving utility player who had appeared in 24 Championship matches.

SCOTLAND   S. Wilson (18) (London Scottish); A.J.W. Hinshelwood 12 (London Scottish), J.W.C. Turner 9 (Gala), J.N.M. Frame 4 (Edinburgh U.), C.G. Hodgson (2) (London Scottish); I. Robertson 1 (London Scottish), G.C. Connell 1 (Trinity Acads); N. Suddon 4 (Hawick), D.T. Deans (1) (Hawick), A.B. Carmichael 5 (W. of Scotland), P.K. Stagg 15 (Sale), A.F. McHarg 2

(W. of Scotland), J.P. Fisher (21) (London Scottish), R.J. Arneil 2 (Edinburgh Acads), *J.W. Telfer 15 (Melrose).

ENGLAND   R. Hiller 4 (Harlequins); K.F. Savage (11) (Northampton), T.J. Brooke (2) (Richmond), R.H. Lloyd (4) (Harlequins), R.E. Webb 5 (Coventry); *M.P. Weston (24) (Durham City), R.D.A. Pickering (6) (Bradford); B.W. Keen (4) (Newcastle U.), J.V. Pullin 5 (Bristol), M.J. Coulman (8) (Moseley), P.J. Larter 4 (Northampton), M.J. Parsons (4) (Northampton), P.J. Bell (4) (Blackheath), B.R. West 4 (Loughborough College), D. Gay (4) (Bath).

Referee D.P. d'Arcy

FRANCE   C. Lacaze 15 (SC Angoulême); J-M. Bonal 2 (S. Toulouse), J. Maso 3 (US Perpignan), C. Dourthe 5 (US Dax), A. Campaes 5 (FC Lourdes); G. Camberabero (6) (La Voulte S.), L. Camberabero (10) (La Voulte S.); J-C. Noble (2) (La Voulte S.), M. Yachvili 2 (SC Tulle), M. Lasserre 2 (SU Agen), A. Plantefol 2 (SU Agen), E. Cester 8 (S. Toulouse), W. Spanghero 14 (RC Narbonne), *C. Carrère 8 (RC Toulon), M. Greffe (1) (FC Grenoble).

Referee H.B. Laidlaw (Scotland)

WALES v FRANCE   39/586

23 March 1968
Cardiff Arms Park
France 14 (1G, 1T, 1DG, 1PG) Wales 9 (1T, 2PG)

Wales   T: Keri Jones. PG: Rees (2).
France   T: Lilian Camberabero, Carrère. C: Guy Camberabero. DG: Guy Camberabero. PG: Guy Camberabero.

This was France's seventh Championship victory in a row, and it brought them the Grand Slam for the first time. It was a rough match and France had to fight back from a 3-9 deficit. Their match-winners were the Camberabero brothers, who scored 11 points between them. It was to be their swan-song as neither played for France again. In many people's opinion Wales had been a better side than their results indicated. The axe still had to fall and in the process of ending the careers of five of this team, the selectors paved the way for the creation of the splendid side of 1969 which took over from France as Champions.

WALES   D. Rees (3) (Swansea); W.K. Jones (4) (Cardiff), S.J. Dawes 8 (London Welsh), W.H. Raybould 6 (London Welsh), M.C.R. Richards 2 (Cardiff); B. John 5 (Cardiff), *G.O. Edwards 6 (Cardiff); D.J. Lloyd 11 (Bridgend), J. Young 3 (Bridgend), J.P. O'Shea (5) (Cardiff), W.D. Thomas 3 (Llanelli), M. Wiltshire (3) (Aberavon), W.D. Morris 6 (Neath), J. Taylor 6 (London Welsh), R.E. Jones (5) (Coventry).

1969

PARIS Scotland beat France 6-3 · MURRAYFIELD Wales beat Scotland 17-3
DUBLIN Ireland beat England 17-15 · DUBLIN Ireland beat France 17-9
TWICKENHAM England beat France 22-8 · MURRAYFIELD Ireland beat Scotland 16-0
CARDIFF Wales beat Ireland 24-11 · TWICKENHAM England beat Scotland 8-3
PARIS France drew Wales 8-8 · CARDIFF Wales beat England 30-9

CHAMPIONSHIP TABLE
Wales – Championship, Triple Crown

Pos	Country	P	W	D	L	F	A	Pts	Tries F	A
1	Wales (4)	4	3	1	0	79	31	7	14	2
2	Ireland (2)	4	3	0	1	61	48	6	8	6
3	England (3)	4	2	0	2	54	58	4	6	8
4	Scotland (5)	4	1	0	3	12	44	2	1	9
5	France (1)	4	0	1	3	28	53	1	3	7

J.P.R. Williams, the Wales full-back, who has played on more winning sides in the Championship, 34, than any other player

International rugby took a major step forward this season with the introduction of two Laws: replacements for players injured in a match were now allowed and what had become known as the Australian dispensation rule was adopted. Permitting players to be replaced had been long overdue, while for many years the Australians had produced a far better game with kicking directly to touch allowed only from inside the kicker's 25. The first replacement in the Championship came in the very first match of the 1969 campaign when Ian McCrae came on for Gordon Connell in the France v Scotland match at Stade Colombes on 11 January. McCrae gained his historical distinction only narrowly: as the French team ran on to the field for the kick-off, Jean Salut twisted an ankle and his place went to Jean Iraçabal, one of the official French replacements.

Whether the kicking to touch limitation substantially affected this or any other match, it was impossible to tell. One indisputable fact was that 1969, in contrast with 1968, produced a glut of tries in the Championship, 32 in all, and the biggest number of points, 234, since 247 were amassed in 1911. Wales manufactured 14 of the try total with some marvellously open, attacking rugby. Only the French, who held them to 8-8 in Paris, contained the dominant Welsh. Ireland, too, played well and had won their three opening matches when they went to Cardiff in search of a record sixth Championship win in a row, the Triple Crown and the Grand Slam. Ireland were beaten convincingly, though the match unfortunately was remembered most for the punch by Brian Price which dropped Noel Murphy. France had an unusually poor season, finishing with the Wooden Spoon for a first time since 1957, and it was odd that after losing to every country, their only match point came from the Welsh clash.

FRANCE v SCOTLAND 39/587

11 January 1969
Stade Colombes, Paris
Scotland 6 (1T, 1PG) France 3 (1PG)

France PG: Villepreux.
Scotland T: Jim Telfer. PG: Blaikie.

Ian McCrae, the Gordonians scrum-half, became the Championship's first replacement for an injured player, when he came on for Gordon Connell in the first half. A tremendous try by Jim Telfer near the end won the game for Scotland, their third in four visits to Paris. Strangely it was to be the Scots' only victory of the season and was the last occasion when France failed to produce a try against Scotland in Paris.

FRANCE P. Villepreux 3 (S. Toulouse); J-M. Bonal 3 (S. Toulouse), J-P. Lux 6 (US Tyrosse), J. Maso 4 (RC Narbonne), A. Campaes 6 (FC Lourdes); J. Gachassin 20 (FC Lourdes), J-L. Berot 1 (S. Toulouse); M. Lasserre 3 (SU Agen), M. Yachvili 3 (SC Tulle), J-M. Esponda 1 (US Perpignan), E. Cester 9 (TOEC), B. Dauga 19 (S. Mont-de-Marsan), J. Iraçabal 1 (A. Bayonne), *C. Carrère 9 (RC Toulon), W. Spanghero 15 (RC Narbonne).

SCOTLAND C.F. Blaikie 4 (Heriot's FP); A.J.W. Hinshelwood 13 (London Scottish), J.W.C. Turner 10 (Gala), C.W.W. Rea 1 (W. of Scotland), W.D. Jackson 3 (Hawick); C.M. Telfer 1 (Hawick), G.C. Connell 2 (London Scottish); N. Suddon 5 (Hawick), F.A.L. Laidlaw 16 (Melrose), A.B. Carmichael 6 (W. of Scotland), P.K. Stagg 16 (Sale), A.F. McHarg 3 (London Scottish), T.G. Elliot 2 (Langholm), R.J. Arneil 3 (Edinburgh Acads), *J.W. Telfer 16 (Melrose).
Replacement I.G. McCrae 3 (Gordonians) for Connell

Referee G.C. Lamb (England)

IRELAND v FRANCE 40/588

25 January 1969
Lansdowne Road, Dublin
Ireland 17 (1G, 1DG, 3PG) France 9 (1T, 2PG)

Ireland T: Moroney. C: Moroney. DG: McGann. PG: Moroney (3).
France T: Trillo. PG: Villepreux (2).

Ireland ended their worst-ever sequence of non-wins against France in the Championship: eight defeats, one draw since 1960. It was a personal triumph for John Moroney, who on his second appearance for Ireland, contributed 14 points, which was then the Irish record individual score. Moroney's blitz helped the Irish to their biggest score against the French at Lansdowne Road since they won 24-0 in 1913.

IRELAND *T.J. Kiernan 32 (Cork Constitution); A.T.A. Duggan 9 (Lansdowne), F.P.K. Bresnihan 11 (Lansdowne), H.H. Rea (1) (Edinburgh U.), J.C.M. Moroney 2 (Garryowen); B.J. McGann 1 (Lansdowne), R.M. Young 12 (Belfast Collegians); S. Millar 26 (Ballymena), K.W. Kennedy 13 (London Irish), P. O'Callaghan 6 (Dolphin), W.J. McBride 28 (Ballymena), M.G. Molloy 11 (London Irish), J.C. Davidson 1 (Dungannon), N.A.A. Murphy 33 (Cork Constitution), K.G. Goodall 9 (City of Derry).
Replacement M.L. Hipwell 4 (Terenure) for Murphy

FRANCE P. Villepreux 4 (S. Toulouse); J-M. Bonal 4 (S. Toulouse), J. Maso 5 (RC Narbonne), J. Trillo 3 (CA Bègles), J-P. Lux 7 (US Tyrosse); J. Gachassin (21) (FC Lourdes), J-L. Berot 2 (S. Toulouse); J. Iraçabal 2 (A. Bayonne), M. Yachvili 4 (SC Tulle), M. Lasserre 4 (SU Agen), B. Dauga 20 (S. Mont-de-Marsan), E. Cester 10 (TOEC), *C. Carrère 10 (RC Toulon), J-P. Salut (4) (TOEC), W. Spanghero 16 (RC Narbonne).
Replacement J-M. Esponda 2 (US Perpignan) for Lasserre

Referee G.C. Lamb (England)

SCOTLAND v WALES   73/589

1 February 1969
Murrayfield
Wales 17 (1G, 2T, 2PG) Scotland 3 (1PG)

Scotland PG: Blaikie.
Wales T: John, Edwards, Richards. C: Jarrett.
PG: Jarrett (2).

The Scottish team was widely criticized for not taking their chances and for a number of mistakes which led to Welsh scores. A few of the players, however, recognized that Scotland were put under enormous pressure immediately after kick-off by an aggressive, highly-motivated Wales team. Mature performances from two débutants, J.P.R. Williams and Mervyn Davies, did not go unnoticed either.

SCOTLAND   C.F. Blaikie 5 (Heriot's FP); A.J.W. Hinshelwood 14 (London Scottish), J.N.M. Frame 5 (Gala), C.W.W. Rea 2 (W. of Scotland), W.D. Jackson 4 (Hawick); C.M. Telfer 2 (Hawick), I.G. McCrae 4 (Gordonians); N. Suddon 6 (Hawick), F.A.L. Laidlaw 17 (Melrose), A.B. Carmichael 7 (W. of Scotland), P.K. Stagg 17 (Sale), A.F. McHarg 4 (London Scottish), T.G. Elliot 3 (Langholm), R.J. Arneil 4 (Edinburgh Acads), *J.W. Telfer 17 (Melrose).

WALES   J.P.R. Williams 1 (London Welsh); M.C.R. Richards 3 (Cardiff), T.G.R. Davies 7 (Cardiff), K.S. Jarrett 4 (Newport), S.J. Watkins 18 (Newport); B. John 6 (Cardiff), G.O. Edwards 7 (Cardiff); D. Williams 19 (Ebbw Vale), J. Young 4 (Harrogate), D.J. Lloyd 12 (Bridgend), *B. Price 24 (Newport), B.E. Thomas 13 (Neath), W.D. Morris 7 (Neath), J. Taylor 7 (London Welsh), T.M. Davies 1 (London Welsh).

Referee K.D. Kelleher (Ireland)

IRELAND v ENGLAND   73/590

8 February 1969
Lansdowne Road, Dublin
Ireland 17 (1G, 1T, 1DG, 2PG) England 15 (1T, 4PG)

Ireland T: Bresnihan, Murphy. C: Kiernan. DG: McGann. PG: Kiernan (2).
England T: Duckham. PG: Hiller (4).

Colin Grimshaw became Ireland's first replacement, as permissible under the new Law, when he came on for the injured Roger Young after 24 minutes. It was Grimshaw's only international appearance and he made many telling contributions in a close and exciting match. England played five newcomers: Keith 'I hate Welshmen' Fairbrother at tight-head prop, the competitive Nigel Horton at lock, the Loughborough flier, Keith Fielding, on the right wing, and David Duckham and John Spencer at centre. Duckham and Spencer in harness were to provide England with their most explosive and creative centre partnership since Butterfield and Davies.

IRELAND   *T.J. Kiernan 33 (Cork Constitution); A.T.A. Duggan 10 (Lansdowne), C.M.H. Gibson 20 (NIFC), F.P.K. Bresnihan 12 (UC Dublin), J.C.M. Moroney 3 (London Irish); B.J. McGann 2 (Lansdowne), R.M. Young 13 (Queen's U. Belfast); S. Millar 27 (Ballymena), K.W. Kennedy 14 (London Irish), P. O'Callaghan 7 (Dolphin), W.J. McBride 29 (Ballymena), M.G. Molloy 12 (London Irish), N.A.A. Murphy 34 (Cork Constitution), J.C. Davidson 2 (Dungannon), K.G. Goodall 10 (City of Derry).
Replacement C. Grimshaw (1) (Queen's U. Belfast) for Young

ENGLAND   R. Hiller 5 (Harlequins); K.J. Fielding 1 (Loughborough College), D.J. Duckham 1 (Coventry), J.S. Spencer 1 (Cambridge U.); R.E. Webb 6 (Coventry); J.F. Finlan 7 (Moseley), T.C. Wintle 2 (Northampton); D.L. Powell 3 (Northampton), J.V. Pullin 6 (Bristol), K.E. Fairbrother 1 (Coventry), P.J. Larter 5 (Northampton), N.E. Horton 1 (Moseley), *J.R.H. Greenwood (4) (Waterloo), D.P. Rogers 25 (Bedford), D.M. Rollitt 5 (Bristol).

Referee R.P. Burrell (Scotland)

ENGLAND v FRANCE   40/591

22 February 1969
Twickenham
England 22 (2G, 1T, 3PG) France 8 (1G, 1DG)

England   T: Fielding, Rollitt, Webb. C: Hiller (2). PG: Hiller (3).
France   T: Bonal. C: Lacaze. DG: Lacaze.

Bob Hiller kicked 13 points in this, the third defeat of the season for the Champions of 1968. France had also won the previous three games against England, so their total eclipse was even more surprising. England's satisfaction did not end there; they scored three tries against their visitors which equalled their total in the previous eight matches. There could easily have been more tries for Duckham and Spencer gave the French defence many problems, except for the brave Pierre Villepreux, whose tackling and covering became one of the memorable features of the match.

ENGLAND   R. Hiller 6 (Harlequins); K.J. Fielding 2 (Loughborough College), J.S. Spencer 2 (Cambridge U.), D.J. Duckham 2 (Coventry), R.E. Webb 7 (Coventry); J.F. Finlan 8 (Moseley), T.C. Wintle 3 (Northampton); D.L. Powell 4 (Northampton), J.V. Pullin 7 (Bristol), K.E. Fairbrother 2 (Coventry), N.E. Horton 2 (Moseley), P.J. Larter 6 (Northampton), R.B. Taylor 6 (Northampton), *D.P. Rogers 26 (Bedford), D.M. Rollitt 6 (Bristol).

FRANCE   P. Villepreux 5 (S. Toulouse); B. Moraitis 1 (RC Toulon), J-P. Lux 8 (US Tyrosse), J. Trillo 4 (CA Bègles), J-M. Bonal 5 (S. Toulouse); C. Lacaze (16) (SC Angoulême), *M. Puget 3 (CA Brive); M. Lasserre 5 (SU Agen), C. Swierczinski (1) (CA Bégles), J-M. Esponda (3) (US Perpignan), E. Cester 11 (TOEC), A. Plantefol 3 (SU Agen), J-P. Biemouret 1 (SU Agen), M. Hauser (1) (FC Lourdes), B. Dauga 21 (S. Mont-de-Marsan).

Referee D.P. d'Arcy (Ireland)

SCOTLAND v IRELAND   75/592

22 February 1969
Murrayfield
Ireland 16 (2G, 2T) Scotland 0

Ireland   T: Duggan, McGann, Gibson, Bresnihan. C: Moroney (2).

Ireland had beaten Scotland in Scotland by a larger margin only once before – 26-8 in 1953 – but more significant was that it was their fifth successive Championship victory, their best ever winning sequence, and their sixth match without defeat, to equal their run in 1951–52. The match was significant in other respects for it was the first time in the Championship that three replacements were necessary, and it was the sixth time in the last seven matches against Ireland at Murrayfield that Scotland failed to score a try.

SCOTLAND   C.F. Blaikie 6 (Heriot's FP); A.J.W. Hinshelwood 15 (London Scottish), J.N.M. Frame 6 (Gala), C.W.W. Rea 3 (W. of Scotland), W.D. Jackson 5 (Hawick); C.M. Telfer 3 (Hawick), R.C. Allan (1) (Hutchesons' GSFP); N. Suddon 7 (Hawick), F.A.L. Laidlaw 18 (Melrose), A.B. Carmichael 8 (W. of Scotland), P.C. Brown 7 (Gala), A.F. McHarg 5 (London Scottish), W. Lauder 1 (Neath), R.J. Arneil 5 (Edinburgh Acads), *J.W. Telfer 18 (Melrose). *Replacements* P.K. Stagg 18 (Sale) for Telfer, W.G. Macdonald (1) (London Scottish) for Rea

IRELAND   *T.J. Kiernan 34 (Cork Constitution); A.T.A. Duggan 11 (Lansdowne), F.P.K. Bresnihan 13 (UC Dublin), C.M.H. Gibson 21 (NIFC), J.C.M. Moroney 4 (London Irish); B.J. McGann 3 (Lansdowne), R.M. Young 14 (Queen's U. Belfast); S. Millar 28 (Ballymena), K.W. Kennedy 15 (London Irish), P. O'Callaghan 8 (Dolphin), W.J. McBride 30 (Ballymena), M.G. Molloy 13 (London Irish), J.C. Davidson 3 (Dungannon), N.A.A. Murphy 35 (Cork Constitution), K.G. Goodall 11 (City of Derry). *Replacement* M.L. Hipwell 5 (Terenure) for Goodall

Referee M. Joseph (Wales)

WALES v IRELAND   71/593

8 March 1969
Cardiff Arms Park
Wales 24 (3G, 1T, 1DG, 1PG) Ireland 11 (1G, 2PG)

Wales T: Watkins, Denzil Williams, Morris, Taylor. C: Jarrett (3). DG: John. PG: Jarrett.
Ireland T: Gibson. C: Kiernan. PG: Kiernan (2).

Ireland had enjoyed a run of six Championship matches without defeat, equalling their best ever, until Wales handed out this hiding. The Irish were also bidding for the Grand Slam, having accounted with style for England, France and Scotland. The surprise was the ease with which the Welsh pack dominated. None played better than Dai Morris. Barry John, too, had one of his best games at fly-half, keeping pressure on the Irish with long touch kicks and only opening up when Wales were in a strong position.

WALES J.P.R. Williams 2 (London Welsh); S.J. Watkins 19 (Newport), K.S. Jarrett 5 (Newport), T.G.R. Davies 8 (Cardiff), M.C.R. Richards 4 (Cardiff); B. John 7 (Cardiff), G.O. Edwards 8 (Cardiff); D. Williams 20 (Ebbw Vale), J. Young 5 (Harrogate), D.J. Lloyd 13 (Bridgend), *B. Price 25 (Newport), B.E. Thomas 14 (Neath), W.D. Morris 8 (Neath), J. Taylor 8 (London Welsh), T.M. Davies 2 (London Welsh).

IRELAND *T.J. Kiernan 35 (Cork Constitution); A.T.A. Duggan 12 (Lansdowne), F.P.K. Bresnihan 14 (UC Dublin), C.M.H. Gibson 22 (NIFC), J.C.M. Moroney (5) (London Irish); B.J. McGann 4 (Lansdowne), R.M. Young 15 (Queen's U. Belfast); P. O'Callaghan 9 (Dolphin), K.W. Kennedy 16 (London Irish), S. Millar 29 (Ballymena), W.J. McBride 31 (Ballymena), M.G. Molloy 14 (London Irish), J.C. Davidson (4) (Dungannon), N.A.A. Murphy (36) (Cork Constitution), M.L. Hipwell 6 (Terenure).

Referee D.C.J. McMahon (Scotland)

ENGLAND v SCOTLAND   72/594

15 March 1969
Twickenham
England 8 (1G, 1T) Scotland 3 (1PG)

England T: Duckham (2). C: Hiller.
Scotland PG: Brown.

Tim Dalton became England's first replacement when he came on for Keith Fielding after half-an-hour. It was Dalton's only cap. England had beaten France by a comfortable margin a month earlier but apart from some nice touches by John Finlan and two well-taken tries by David Duckham the team never really worked. Scotland had also beaten France, in Paris, but heavy defeats by Wales and Ireland were not encouraging omens for a visit to Twickenham. As it turned out they played well, without taking their chances, particularly in the first half. In the end there was one more defeat for them at Twickenham, a bogey ground in every sense. The Scots had won there but once, in 1938, in 18 visits since 1928.

ENGLAND R. Hiller 7 (Harlequins); K.J. Fielding 3 (Moseley), J.S. Spencer 3 (Headingley), D.J. Duckham 3 (Coventry), R.E. Webb 8 (Coventry); J.F. Finlan 9 (Moseley), T.C. Wintle 4 (Northampton); D.L. Powell 5 (Northampton), J.V. Pullin 8 (Bristol), K.E. Fairbrother 3 (Coventry), N.E. Horton 3 (Moseley), P.J. Larter 7 (Northampton), R.B. Taylor 7 (Northampton), *D.P. Rogers 27 (Bedford), D.M. Rollitt 7 (Bristol).
Replacement T.J. Dalton (1) (Coventry) for Fielding

SCOTLAND C.F. Blaikie (7) (Heriot's FP); W.C.C. Steele 1 (Langholm), J.N.M. Frame 7 (Gala), I. Robertson 2 (Watsonians), W.D. Jackson (6) (Hawick); C.M. Telfer 4 (Hawick), G.C. Connell 3 (London Scottish); J. McLauchlan 1 (Jordanhill), F.A.L. Laidlaw 19 (Melrose), A.B. Carmichael 9 (W. of Scotland), P.C. Brown 8 (Gala), A.F. McHarg 6 (London Scottish), W. Lauder 2 (Neath), R.J. Arneil 6 (Edinburgh Acads), *J.W. Telfer 19 (Melrose).

Referee C. Durand (France)

FRANCE v WALES 40/595

22 March 1969
Stade Colombes, Paris
France 8 (1G, 1PG) Wales 8 (1G, 1T)

France T: Campaes. C: Villepreux. PG: Villepreux.
Wales T: Edwards, Richards. C: Jarrett.

The first time in 12 matches since 1957 that Wales outscored France in the matter of tries, but they still were unable to force victory. Their last win in Paris was also in 1957. Even more galling was that this draw prevented Wales from gaining the Grand Slam, for they went on to win their final match, against England. The occasion will be well remembered by Phil Bennett and Brian Price. Bennett gained his first cap, coming on as a wing replacement at the end for Gerald Davies, who injured his arm. Price ended his fine career after 26 appearances, and some critics considered the Newport lock to be among the best all-round forwards who played for Wales. Price was without peer as a No. 5 jumper, he was a good scrummager and also contributed much in maul and loose.

FRANCE P. Villepreux 6 (S. Toulouse); B. Moraitis (2) (RC Toulon), C. Dourthe 6 (US Dax), J. Trillo 5 (A. Bégles), A. Campaes (7) (FC Lourdes); J. Maso 6 (RC Narbonne), G. Sutra 1 (RC Narbonne); J. Iraçabal 3 (A. Bayonne), R. Bénésis 1 (RC Narbonne), J-L. Azarete 1 (US Dax), A. Plantefol (4) (SU Agen), E. Cester 12 (TOEC), J-P. Biemouret 2 (SU Agen), G. Viard 1 (RC Narbonne), *W. Spanghero 17 (RC Narbonne).

WALES J.P.R. Williams 3 (London Welsh); S.J. Watkins 20 (Newport), K.S. Jarrett 6 (Newport), T.G.R. Davies 9 (Cardiff), M.C.R. Richards 5 (Cardiff); B. John 8 (Cardiff), G.O. Edwards 9 (Cardiff); D. Williams 21 (Ebbw Vale), J. Young 6 (Harrogate), D.J. Lloyd 14 (Bridgend), *B. Price (26) (Newport), B.E. Thomas 15 (Neath), W.D. Morris 9 (Neath), J. Taylor 9 (London Welsh), T.M. Davies 3 (London Welsh).
Replacement P. Bennett 1 (Llanelli) for T.G.R. Davies

Referee R.P. Burrell (Scotland)

WALES v ENGLAND 73/596

12 April 1969
Cardiff Arms Park
Wales 30 (3G, 2T, 1DG, 2PG) England 9 (3PG)

Wales T: Richards (4), John. C: Jarrett (3). DG: John. PG: Jarrett (2).
England PG: Hiller (3).

Maurice Richards, the long-striding Cardiff wing, earned himself a special place in Welsh rugby history by scoring four tries in a victory which acquired the Triple Crown and the Championship for Wales. Richards equalled the Welsh individual try record of Willie Llewellyn (against England in 1899) and Reggie Gibbs (against France in 1908), and his six-try total for the season equalled Gibbs's performance of 1908. In contrast, Bob Hiller's three penalty goals for England brought his season's total to 36 points, all from kicks.

WALES J.P.R. Williams 4 (London Welsh); S.J. Watkins 21 (Newport), K.S. Jarrett (7) (Newport), S.J. Dawes 9 (London Welsh), M.C.R. Richards (6) (Cardiff); B. John 9 (Cardiff), *G.O. Edwards 10 (Cardiff); D. Williams 22 (Ebbw Vale), J. Young 7 (Harrogate), D.J. Lloyd 15 (Bridgend), W.D. Thomas 4 (Llanelli), B.E. Thomas (16) (Neath), W.D. Morris 10 (Neath), J. Taylor 10 (London Welsh), T.M. Davies 4 (London Welsh).

ENGLAND R. Hiller 8 (Harlequins); K.C. Plummer 1 (Bristol), J.S. Spencer 4 (Headingley), D.J. Duckham 4 (Coventry), R.E. Webb 9 (Coventry); J.F. Finlan 10 (Moseley), T.C. Wintle (5) (Northampton); D.L. Powell 6 (Northampton), J.V. Pullin 9 (Bristol), K.E. Fairbrother 4 (Coventry), N.E. Horton 4 (Moseley), P.J. Larter 8 (Northampton), R.B. Taylor 8 (Northampton), *D.P. Rogers (28) (Bedford), D.M. Rollitt 8 (Bristol).

Referee P. D'Arcy (Ireland)

1970

MURRAYFIELD France beat Scotland 11-9 · PARIS France beat Ireland 8-0
CARDIFF Wales beat Scotland 18-9 · TWICKENHAM England beat Ireland 9-3
TWICKENHAM Wales beat England 17-13 · DUBLIN Ireland beat Scotland 16-11
DUBLIN Ireland beat Wales 14-0 · MURRAYFIELD Scotland beat England 14-5
CARDIFF Wales beat France 11-6 · PARIS France beat England 35-13

CHAMPIONSHIP TABLE
France – Championship

Pos	Country	P	W	D	L	F	A	Pts	Tries F	A
1	France (5)	4	3	0	1	60	33	6	11	4
2	Wales (1)	4	3	0	1	46	42	6	9	7
3	Ireland (2)	4	2	0	2	33	28	4	6	4
4	Scotland (4)	4	1	0	3	43	50	2	5	12
5	England (3)	4	1	0	3	40	69	2	7	11

Although the number of points scored in the Championship was slightly down on 1969, the try return of 38 was the best since 1931. France, the Champions, and runners-up Wales were mainly responsible for this significant upsurge for they scored 20 tries between them. Even England, who finished bottom of the Championship, managed seven.

At first sight, such a glut of tries may suggest a marvellous Championship, memorable for high-quality rugby and exciting matches. The reality was rather different. Certainly there were contests which had the stamp of special: Wales's dramatic victory at Twickenham stage-managed by Chico Hopkins, for instance; Ireland's emphatic crushing of Welsh Triple Crown ambitions; France's record-breaking points-spree against England; and Scotland's brave but fruitless recovery against Ireland. There were also some thrilling tries. But in the final analysis, most of the rugby produced was dull and uninspired, with the set ploy beginning to predominate. Most countries began to put all their efforts into learning how to win and how not to make mistakes. Winning had become very, very important; the coaches had become kings.

SCOTLAND v FRANCE   40/597

10 January 1970
Murrayfield
France 11 (1G, 1T, 1DG) Scotland 9 (1T, 2PG)

Scotland   T: Smith. PG: Lauder (2).
France   T: Dauga, Lux. C: Paries. DG: Paries.

Although Scotland had a comparatively good track record against France in Paris, their performance against the French at Murrayfield was poor. This defeat meant they had won only once, in 1964, in six French visits since 1960. Three Scots made their Championship début appearances, including Gordon Brown, who was to become one of Scotland's finest lock-forwards since the War. France introduced five new caps including Jean-Pierre Bastiat, who was also to prove an outstanding forward during his eight-year career with France.

SCOTLAND   I.S.G. Smith 1 (London Scottish); A.G. Biggar 1 (London Scottish), J.N.M. Frame 8 (Gala), C.W.W. Rea 4 (W. of Scotland), A.J.W. Hinshelwood 16 (London Scottish); I. Robertson 3 (Watsonians), G.C. Connell (4) (London Scottish); J. McLauchlin 2 (Jordanhill), F.A.L. Laidlaw 20 (Melrose), A.B. Carmichael 10 (W. of Scotland), P.K. Stagg 19 (Sale), G.L. Brown 1 (W. of Scotland), W. Lauder 3 (Neath), R.J. Arneil 7 (Leicester), *J.W. Telfer 20 (Melrose).

FRANCE   P. Villepreux 7 (S. Toulouse); J. Sillières 1 (S. Tarbes), J-P. Lux 9 (US Tyrosse), A. Marot 1 (CA Brive), R. Bourgarel 1 (S. Toulouse); L. Paries 1 (Biarritz Ol), G. Sutra 2 (RC Narbonne); J. Iraçabal 4 (A. Bayonne), R. Bénésis 2 (RC Narbonne), J-L. Azarete 2 (US Dax), J-P.

Bastiat 1 (US Dax), E. Cester 13 (TOEC), *C. Carrère 11 (RC Toulon), B. Dauga 22 (S. Mont-de-Marsan), G. Viard 2 (RC Narbonne).

Referee G.C. Lamb (England)

FRANCE v IRELAND 41/598

24 January 1970
Stade Colombes, Paris
France 8 (1G, 1DG) Ireland 0

France T: Sillières. C: Paries. DG: Paries.

France's ninth successive home victory over Ireland, their longest winning sequence against them. The Irish certainly had no resistance to French domination; their only victory in 11 years had been at Lansdowne Road in 1969. Their one crumb of comfort was contained in a début of high promise by a tearaway young flanker, Fergus Slattery.

FRANCE P. Villepreux 8 (S. Toulouse); R. Bourgarel 2 (S. Toulouse), A. Marot 2 (CA Brive), J-P. Lux 10 (US Tyrosse), J. Sillières 2 (S. Tarbes); L. Paries 2 (Biarritz Ol), G. Sutra (3) (RC Narbonne); J. Iraçabal 5 (A. Bayonne), R. Bénésis 3 (RC Narbonne), J-L. Azarete 3 (US Dax), E. Cester 14 (TOEC), J-P. Bastiat 2 (US Dax), *C. Carrère 12 (RC Toulon), J-P. Biemouret 3 (SU Agen), B. Dauga 23 (S. Mont-de-Marsan).

IRELAND *T.J. Kiernan 36 (Cork Constitution); A.T.A. Duggan 13 (Lansdowne), F.P.K. Bresnihan 15 (London Irish), C.M.H. Gibson 23 (NIFC), W.J. Brown 1 (Malone); B.J. McGann 5 (Lansdowne), R.M. Young 16 (Belfast Collegians); S. Millar 30 (Ballymena), K.W. Kennedy 17 (London Irish), P. O'Callaghan 10 (Dolphin), W.J. McBride 32 (Ballymena), M.G. Molloy 15 (London Irish), R.A. Lamont 7 (Instonians), J.F. Slattery 1 (UC Dublin), K.G. Goodall 12 (City of Derry).

Referee R.F. Johnson (England)

WALES v SCOTLAND 74/599

7 February 1970
Cardiff Arms Park
Wales 18 (3G, 1T) Scotland 9 (1T, 1DG, 1PG)

Wales T: Daniel, Llewelyn, Dawes, Morris. C: Edwards (2), Daniel.
Scotland T: Robertson. DG: Robertson. PG: Lauder.

Scotland, beaten in 11 of their previous 12 visits to Wales, had every reason to believe their fortunes were going to change when they stormed 9-0 ahead. This early injury to Welsh morale was inflicted largely by Ian Robertson, who dropped a goal and then scored a try with a final imperious dummy to a confused defence. Gradually the Welsh pack took the initiative and with John Dawes at the heart of some sustained attacks, the Scottish advantage was whittled away. Wales scored four tries, one after heaving the Scots over their own line. Gordon Brown, who won his first cap against France the previous month, was omitted in favour of his older brother, Peter; Gordon played, however, coming on when Peter retired injured near half-time.

WALES J.P.R. Williams 5 (London Welsh); L.T.D. Daniel (1) (Newport), S.J. Dawes 10 (London Welsh), P. Bennett 2 (Llanelli), I. Hall 1 (Aberavon); B. John 10 (Cardiff), *G.O. Edwards 11 (Cardiff); D.B. Llewelyn 1 (Newport), V.C. Perrins (1) (Newport), D. Williams 23 (Ebbw Vale), W.D. Thomas 5 (Llanelli), T.G. Evans 1 (London Welsh), W.D. Morris 11 (Neath), D. Hughes 1 (Newbridge), T.M. Davies 5 (London Welsh).

SCOTLAND I.S.G. Smith 2 (London Scottish); M.A. Smith 1 (London Scottish), J.N.M. Frame 9 (Gala), C.W.W. Rea 5 (W. of Scotland), A.J.W. Hinshelwood (17) (London Scottish); I. Robertson 4 (Watsonians), R.G. Young (1) (Watsonians); J. McLauchlan 3 (Jordanhill), F.A.L. Laidlaw 21 (Melrose), A.B. Carmichael 11 (W. of Scotland), P.K. Stagg 20 (Sale), P.C. Brown 9 (Gala), W. Lauder 4 (Neath), R.J. Arneil 8 (Leicester), *J.W. Telfer 21 (Melrose).
Replacement G.L. Brown 2 (W. of Scotland) for P.C. Brown

Referee D.P. d'Arcy (Ireland)

ENGLAND v IRELAND   74/600

14 February 1970
Twickenham
England 9 (1T, 2DG) Ireland 3 (1PG)

England   T: Shackleton. DG: Hiller (2).
Ireland   PG: Kiernan.

The recall of Tony O'Reilly after a seven-year absence from international rugby to make his twenty-seventh Championship appearance 15 years after his first, proved if nothing else that the Irish are masters of the unexpected. Arguably O'Reilly should not have been overlooked for so long for despite the other claims on his time – his developing world-wide business interests for instance – he had never announced that he was unavailable to play nor was there any evidence that others were better. In the event Bill Brown, who was scheduled to play on the wing against England, broke down at a training session and O'Reilly was called up to play in a match for which he had written an article in the programme. Alas, there was no great final flourish from the Irish folk hero or dramatic ending. O'Reilly barely got a pass, and mostly he was silent witness as Ireland were beaten by an England side that didn't believe in fairy stories.

ENGLAND   *R. Hiller 9 (Harlequins); K.J. Fielding 4 (Moseley), J.S. Spencer 5 (Headingley), D.J. Duckham 5 (Coventry), P.M. Hale 1 (Moseley); I.R. Shackleton 1 (Harrogate), N.C. Starmer-Smith 1 (Harlequins); C.B. Stevens 1 (Penzance & Newlyn), J.V. Pullin 10 (Bristol), K.E. Fairbrother 5 (Coventry), A.M. Davis 9 (Harlequins), P.J. Larter 9 (Northampton), A.L. Bucknall 1 (Richmond), B.R. West 5 (Northampton), R.B. Taylor 9 (Northampton).

IRELAND   *T.J. Kiernan 37 (Cork Constitution); A.T.A. Duggan 14 (Lansdowne), F.P.K. Bresnihan 16 (London Irish), C.M.H. Gibson 24 (NIFC), A.J.F. O'Reilly (27) (London Irish); B.J. McGann 6 (Lansdowne), R.M. Young 17 (Belfast Collegians); S. Millar 31 (Ballymena), K.W. Kennedy 18 (London Irish), P. O'Callaghan 11 (Dolphin), W.J. McBride 33 (Ballymena), M.G. Molloy 16 (London Irish), R.A. Lamont 8 (Instonians), J.F. Slattery 2 (UC Dublin), K.G. Goodall 13 (City of Derry).

Referee A.R. Lewis (Wales)

ENGLAND v WALES   74/601

28 February 1970
Twickenham
Wales 17 (1G, 3T, 1DG) England 13 (2G, 1PG)

England   T: Duckham, Novak. C: Hiller (2). PG: Hiller.
Wales   T: Davies, John, J.P.R. Williams, Hopkins. C: J.P.R. Williams. DG: John.

This was Wales's biggest haul of tries in England since Boxer Harding's side scored five at Bristol City Football Club Ground in 1908. At one stage England led 13-3, with Duckham and Spencer threatening every time they were in possession. A try by Barry John lifted Welsh hopes, but these were soon dashed when Gareth Edwards went off injured after an hour. It was Chico Hopkins, the replacement, who performed the miracle. He took charge at once, setting up J.P.R. for a try and then scoring one himself. By this time Johnny Johnson, the English touch-judge, had taken over as referee because Robert Calmet had left the field with a broken leg, sustained in a collision with a player. J.P.R. converted Hopkins' try and Barry John wrote the final chapter with a drop goal.

ENGLAND   *R. Hiller 10 (Harlequins); M.J. Novak 1 (Harlequins), J.S. Spencer 6 (Headingley), D.J. Duckham 6 (Coventry), P.M. Hale (2) (Moseley); I.R. Shackleton 2 (Harrogate), N.C. Starmer-Smith 2 (Harlequins); C.B. Stevens 2 (Penzance & Newlyn), J.V. Pullin 11 (Bristol), K.E. Fairbrother 6 (Coventry), A.M. Davis 10 (Harlequins), P.J. Larter 10 (Northampton), A.L. Bucknall 2 (Richmond), B.R. West 6 (Northampton), R.B. Taylor 10 (Northampton).

WALES   J.P.R. Williams 6 (London Welsh); S.J. Watkins 22 (Cardiff), W.H. Raybould 7 (Newport), S.J. Dawes 11 (London Welsh), I. Hall 2 (Aberavon); B. John 11 (Cardiff), *G.O. Edwards 12 (Cardiff); D. Williams 24 (Ebbw Vale), J. Young 8 (Harrogate), D.B. Llewelyn 2 (Newport), W.D. Thomas 6 (Llanelli), T.G. Evans 2 (London Welsh), W.D. Morris 12 (Neath), D. Hughes 2 (Newbridge), T.M. Davies 6 (London Welsh).

Replacement R. Hopkins (1) (Maesteg) for Edwards

Referee R. Calmet (France), replaced at half-time by R.F. Johnson (England)

IRELAND v SCOTLAND 76/602

28 February 1970
Lansdowne Road, Dublin
Ireland 16 (2G, 2T) Scotland 11 (1G, 1T, 1DG)

Ireland T: Molloy, Goodall, Gibson, Brown. C: Kiernan (2).
Scotland T: Lauder, M.A. Smith. C: Ian Smith. DG: Robertson.

Scotland went down to a fourth successive defeat by Ireland, who at one time seemed certain to run up a massive score. But the Scots rallied courageously and gave respectability to the scoreline with two late tries. It was Jim Telfer's twenty-second and final Championship appearance.

IRELAND *T.J. Kiernan 38 (Cork Constitution); A.T.A. Duggan 15 (Lansdowne), F.P.K. Bresnihan 17 (London Irish), C.M.H. Gibson 25 (NIFC), W.J. Brown 2 (Malone); B.J. McGann 7 (Cork Constitution), R.M. Young 18 (Belfast Collegians); S. Millar 32 (Ballymena), K.W. Kennedy 19 (London Irish), P. O'Callaghan 12 (Dolphin), W.J. McBride 34 (Ballymena), M.G. Molloy 17 (London Irish), R.A. Lamont 9 (Instonians), J.F. Slattery 3 (UC Dublin), K.G. Goodall 14 (City of Derry).

SCOTLAND I.S.G. Smith 3 (London Scottish); M.A. Smith 2 (London Scottish), J.N.M. Frame 10 (Gala), C.W.W. Rea 6 (W. of Scotland), A.G. Biggar 2 (London Scottish); I. Robertson 5 (Watsonians), D.S. Paterson 1 (Gala); N. Suddon 8 (Hawick), F.A.L. Laidlaw 22 (Melrose), A.B. Carmichael 12 (W. of Scotland), P.K. Stagg 21 (Sale), G.L. Brown 3 (W. of Scotland), W. Lauder 5 (Neath), R.J. Arneil 9 (Leicester), J.W. Telfer (22) (Melrose).

Referee C. Durand (France)

Fergus Slattery, the tearaway Irish flank-forward, closes on Barry John during the Wales-Ireland match on 14 March 1970

IRELAND v WALES 72/603

14 March 1970
Lansdowne Road, Dublin
Ireland 14 (1G, 1T, 1DG, 1PG) Wales 0

Ireland T: Duggan, Goodall. C: Kiernan. DG: McGann. PG: Kiernan.

With convincing wins over Scotland and England to their credit, Wales went to Lansdowne Road understandably confident that they would win the Triple Crown for a twelfth time, particularly as Ireland had been beaten in two of their first three matches. The Irish, not for the first time, responded to such impudence with their best rugby of the season, and inspired by Barry McGann, bombarded Wales from all sides. Even

Gareth Edwards and Barry John were made to look ordinary. It was a splendid way for Irish stalwarts, Sid Millar, Ronnie Lamont and Ken Goodall to end their Championship careers. Wales's response was to drop Stewart Watkins and Dennis Hughes and to relieve Edwards of the captaincy in favour of John Dawes.

IRELAND *T.J. Kiernan 39 (Cork Constitution); A.T.A. Duggan 16 (Lansdowne), F.P.K. Bresnihan 18 (London Irish), C.M.H. Gibson 26 (NIFC), W.J. Brown (3) (Malone); B.J. McGann 8 (Cork Constitution), R.M. Young 19 (Belfast Collegians); P. O'Callaghan 13 (Dolphin), K.W. Kennedy 20 (London Irish), S. Millar (33) (Ballymena), W.J. McBride 35 (Ballymena), M.G. Molloy 18 (London Irish), R.A. Lamont (10) (Instonians), J.F. Slattery 4 (UC Dublin), K.G. Goodall (15) (City of Derry).

WALES J.P.R. Williams 7 (London Welsh); S.J. Watkins (23) (Newport), S.J. Dawes 12 (London Welsh), W.H. Raybould 8 (Newport), K. Hughes 1 (Cambridge U.); B. John 12 (Cardiff), *G.O. Edwards 13 (Cardiff); D. Williams 25 (Ebbw Vale), J. Young 9 (Harrogate), D.B. Llewelyn 3 (Newport), W.D. Thomas 7 (Llanelli), T.G. Evans 3 (London Welsh), W.D. Morris 13 (Neath), D. Hughes (3) (Newbridge), T.M. Davies 7 (London Welsh).

Referee G.C. Lamb (England)

SCOTLAND v ENGLAND 73/604

21 March 1970
Murrayfield
Scotland 14 (1G, 1T, 2PG) England 5 (1G)

Scotland T: Biggar, Turner. C: Peter Brown. PG: Peter Brown (2).
England T: Spencer. C: Hiller.

Alastair Biggar scored Scotland's one-hundredth Championship try against England, and it could not have been more timely for it helped them to their only victory of the season. The try that will be better remembered was that of John Spencer, who covered nearly 70 yards from the receipt of a pass from a short penalty by Roger Shackleton to plunge over at the corner.

SCOTLAND I.S.G. Smith 4 (London Scottish); M.A. Smith (3) (London Scottish), J.N.M. Frame 11 (Gala), J.W.C. Turner 11 (Gala), A.G. Biggar 3 (London Scottish); I. Robertson (6) (Watsonians), D.S. Paterson 2 (Gala); N. Suddon (9) (Hawick), *F.A.L. Laidlaw 23 (Melrose), A.B. Carmichael 13 (W. of Scotland), P.K. Stagg (22) (Sale), G.L. Brown 4 (W. of Scotland), T.G. Elliot (4) (Langholm), R.J. Arneil 10 (Leicester), P.C. Brown 10 (Gala).

ENGLAND *R. Hiller 11 (Harlequins); M.J. Novak 2 (Harlequins), J.S. Spencer 7 (Headingley), D.J. Duckham 7 (Coventry), M.P. Bulpitt (1) (Blackheath); I.R. Shackleton (3) (Harrogate), N.C. Starmer-Smith 3 (Harlequins); C.B. Stevens 3 (Penzance & Newlyn), J.V. Pullin 12 (Bristol), K.E. Fairbrother 7 (Coventry), A.M. Davis (11) (Harlequins), P.J. Larter 11 (Northampton), A.L. Bucknall 3 (Richmond), B.R. West (7) (Northampton), R.B. Taylor 11 (Northampton).
Replacement B.S. Jackson 1 (Broughton Park) for West

Referee M. Joseph (Wales)

WALES v FRANCE 41/605

4 April 1970
Cardiff Arms Park
Wales 11 (1G, 2PG) France 6 (2T)

Wales T: Morris. C: Williams. PG: Williams (2).
France T: Cantoni, Bonal.

Wales fielded a side with seven changes from the one trounced in Ireland the previous month, and inflicted the only defeat of the season on France. Industry and assiduity rather than flair or inspiration were the ingredients of a hard-won but deserved success. When Billy Raybould came on for the injured Jim Shanklin, it was to be his ninth and final Championship match. Bonal and Cantoni, two of three French changes from the Irish match, justified their promotion with a try apiece.

WALES J.P.R. Williams 8 (London Welsh); J.L. Shanklin 1 (London Welsh), *S.J. Dawes 13 (London Welsh), A.J. Lewis 1 (Ebbw Vale), R. Mathias (1) (Llanelli); P. Bennett 3 (Llanelli), G.O. Edwards 14 (Cardiff); D.J. Lloyd 16

(Bridgend), J. Young 10 (Harrogate), D.B. Llewelyn 4 (Newport), W.D. Thomas 8 (Llanelli), I.S. Gallacher (1) (Llanelli), W.D. Morris 14 (Neath), J. Taylor 11 (London Welsh), T.M. Davies 8 (London Welsh).
Replacement W.H. Raybould (9) (Newport) for Shanklin

FRANCE   P. Villepreux 9 (S. Toulouse); J. Cantoni 1 (AS Béziers), A. Marot (3) (CA Brive), J-P. Lux 11 (US Tyrosse), J-M. Bonal 6 (S. Toulouse); L. Paries 3 (Biarritz Ol), M. Puget (4) (CA Brive); J. Iraçabal 6 (A. Bayonne), R. Bénésis 4 (RC Narbonne), J-L. Azarete 4 (US Dax), J-P. Bastiat 3 (US Dax), E. Cester 15 (TOEC), J-P. Biemouret 4 (SU Agen), *C. Carrère 13 (RC Toulon), B. Dauga 24 (S. Mont-de-Marsan).

Referee K.D. Kelleher (Ireland)

ENGLAND   A.M. Jorden 1 (Cambridge U.); K.J. Fielding 5 (Moseley), J.S. Spencer 8 (Headingley), D.J. Duckham 8 (Coventry), M.J. Novak (3) (Harlequins); J.F. Finlan (11) (Moseley), N.C. Starmer-Smith (4) (Harlequins); B.S. Jackson (2) (Broughton Park), J.V. Pullin 13 (Bristol), K.E. Fairbrother 8 (Coventry), M.M. Leadbetter (1) (Broughton Park), P.J. Larter 12 (Northampton), A.L. Bucknall 4 (Richmond), *R.B. Taylor 12 (Northampton), G.F. Redmond (1) (Cambridge U.).

Referee W.K.M. Jones (Wales)

FRANCE v ENGLAND   41/606

18 April 1970
Stade Colombes, Paris
France 35 (4G, 2T, 2DG, 1PG) England 13 (2G, 1PG)

France   T: Berot, Bonal, Bourgarel, Dauga, Lux, Trillo. C: Villepreux (4). DG: Berot, Villepreux. PG: Villepreux.
England   T: Spencer, Taylor. C: Jorden (2). PG: Jorden.

This annihilation, then a record score for France and England's worst defeat, relegated England to the bottom of the Championship and spelled the end of the international careers of six of the team. For France, it meant a third title in four seasons, and amply compensated for their extraordinary changes in fortunes the previous year when they finished with the Wooden Spoon.

FRANCE   P. Villepreux 10 (S. Toulouse); R. Bourgarel 3 (S. Toulouse), J. Trillo 6 (CA Bègles), J-P. Lux 12 (US Tyrosse), J-M. Bonal (7) (S. Toulouse); J-L. Bergot 3 (S. Toulouse), M. Pebeyre 1 (RC Vichy); M. Lasserre 6 (SU Agen), R. Bénésis 5 (RC Narbonne), J. Iraçabal 7 (A. Bayonne), J. le Droff 3 (FC Auch), E. Cester 16 (TOEC), J-P. Biémouret 5 (SU Agen), *C. Carrère 14 (RC Toulon), B. Dauga 25 (S. Mont-de-Marsan).

PARIS France beat Scotland 13-8 · CARDIFF Wales beat England 22-6
DUBLIN Ireland drew France 9-9 · MURRAYFIELD Wales beat Scotland 19-18
DUBLIN England beat Ireland 9-6 · TWICKENHAM England drew France 14-14
MURRAYFIELD Ireland beat Scotland 17-5 · CARDIFF Wales beat Ireland 23-9
TWICKENHAM Scotland beat England 16-15 · PARIS Wales beat France 9-5

CHAMPIONSHIP TABLE
Wales – Championship, Triple Crown, Grand Slam

Pos	Country	P	W	D	L	F	A	Pts	Tries F	A
1	Wales (2)	4	4	0	0	73	38	8	13	4
2	France (1)	4	1	2	1	41	40	4	5	5
3	England (5)	4	1	1	2	44	58	3	5	9
4	Ireland (3)	4	1	1	2	41	46	3	6	5
5	Scotland (4)	4	1	0	3	47	64	2	6	12

A new era in Welsh rugby began in more respects than one in 1971, when they played their first Championship match at their new stadium at Cardiff Arms Park, against England in January, and finished the season by winning the Grand Slam for the first time since 1952. The new ground – erroneously described by some as the National Stadium – was officially opened in October 1970, when Wales played an RFU President's XV, but the first authentic occasion that the up-dated stadium was put to use was against England, who were themselves seeking an auspicious start in the RFU's centenary season. Wales, quite rightly, had built their side around the exciting talent of London Welsh players such as J.P.R. Williams, Gerald Davies, John Dawes, Mike Roberts, Mervyn Davies and John Taylor and it was of little surprise that all of these, plus another, Geoff Evans, became part of the highly successful British Lions tour to New Zealand after the Grand Slam had been won.

The fluency of the Wales side was seriously challenged only once, at Murrayfield, where a match of high drama was won by a remarkable touchline kick by Taylor. Altogether Wales scored 13 tries and 73 points, which was a good chunk of the Championship total of 243 points, the highest, incidentally for a five-nation competition up to the advent of the four-point try, but which was part of a trend of higher scoring which had effectively started in 1967.

If Wales were unquestionably the team of 1971, there was little to choose between the remainder, and it is significant that the two countries who finished in the bottom positions scored more tries than France and England, who finished second and third. In fact Wales alone scored more points than the Wooden Spoonists, Scotland, who disgraced themselves only in respect of allowing the opposition to score 12 tries. There were those that regretted the passing from the scene of England's exciting midfield pair, David Duckham and John Spencer, for Spencer was never picked again for his country. However, England received more than enough compensation in Bob Hiller: a great team man, popular, jovial. Hiller's place kicking was also England's most priceless asset. Although he did not play against Wales he scored all England's points against Ireland and France and 12 out of 15 against Scotland, so that by the end of the season he had totalled 35.

FRANCE v SCOTLAND   41/607

16 January 1971
Stade Colombes, Paris
France 13 (2G, 1PG) Scotland 8 (1G, 1PG)

France   T: Sillières, Villepreux. C: Villepreux (2). PG: Villepreux.
Scotland   T: Steele. C: Peter Brown. PG: Smith.

Scotland, who had won on three of their previous visits to Paris, were somewhat unfortunate not to have extended the sequence. At one stage they led 8-3, and were full value for that advantage. But an injury to Ian Smith and the consequent reshuffling on their personnel disjointed their defence, which allowed France to rally and snatch victory with two late tries.

FRANCE   P. Villepreux 11 (S. Toulouse); J. Sillières 3 (S. Tarbes), J. Trillo 7 (CA Bègles), J-P. Lux 13 (US Tyrosse), J. Cantoni 2 (AS Béziers); J-L. Berot 4 (S. Toulouse), M. Barrau 1 (RC Beaumont); M. Etcheverry 1 (S. Pau), R. Bénésis 6 (RC Narbonne), J-L. Azarete 5 (St-Jean-de-Luz Ol), J-P. Bastiat 4 (US Dax), J. le Droff 4 (FC Auch), G. Viard 3 (RC Narbonne), J. Dubois (1) (CA Bègles), *B. Dauga 26 (S. Mont-de-Marsan).

SCOTLAND   I.S.G. Smith 5 (London Scottish); A.G. Biggar 4 (London Scottish), J.N.M. Frame 12 (Gala), C.W.W. Rea 7 (Headingley), W.C.C. Steele 2 (Bedford); J.W.C. Turner 12 (Gala), D.S. Paterson 3 (Gala); J. McLauchlan 4 (Jordanhill), F.A.L. Laidlaw 24 (Melrose), A.B. Carmichael 14 (W. of Scotland), A.F. McHarg 7 (London Scottish), G.L. Brown 5 (W. of Scotland), N.A. MacEwan 1 (Gala), R.J. Arneil 11 (Leicester), *P.C. Brown 11 (Gala).
Replacement B.M. Simmers (6) (Glasgow Acads) for Smith

Referee K.D. Kelleher (Ireland)

WALES v ENGLAND   75/608

16 January 1971
Cardiff Arms Park
Wales 22 (2G, 1T, 2DG, 1PG) England 6 (1T, 1PG)

Wales T: Gerald Davies (2), Bevan. C: Taylor (2). DG: John (2). PG: J.P.R. Williams.
England   T: Hannaford. PG: Rossborough.

An England team with eight new caps was easy prey for a Wales team without perceivable weakness. In fact in all-round strength, power, pace and flair this XV earned the title of the greatest ever to be fielded by Wales.

WALES   J.P.R. Williams 9 (London Welsh); T.G.R. Davies 10 (London Welsh), *S.J. Dawes 14 (London Welsh), A.J. Lewis 2 (Ebbw Vale), J.C. Bevan 1 (Cardiff); B. John 13 (Cardiff), G.O. Edwards 15 (Cardiff); D.B. Llewelyn 5 (Llanelli), J. Young 11 (Harrogate), D. Williams 26 (Ebbw Vale), W.D. Thomas 9 (Llanelli), M.G. Roberts 1 (London Welsh), W.D. Morris 15 (Neath), J. Taylor 12 (London Welsh), T.M. Davies 9 (London Welsh).

ENGLAND   P.A. Rossborough 1 (Coventry); J.P.A.G. Janion 1 (Bedford), C.S. Wardlow 1 (Northampton), J.S. Spencer 9 (Headingley), D.J. Duckham 9 (Coventry); I.D. Wright 1 (Northampton), J.J. Page 1 (Bedford); D.L. Powell 7 (Northampton), J.V. Pullin 14 (Bristol), K.E. Fairbrother 9 (Coventry), P.J. Larter 13 (Northampton), B.F. Ninnes (1) (Coventry), *A.L. Bucknall 5 (Richmond), A. Neary 1 (Broughton Park), R.C. Hannaford 1 (Bristol).

Referee D.P. d'Arcy (Ireland)

IRELAND v FRANCE   42/609

30 January 1971
Lansdowne Road, Dublin
Ireland 9 (1T, 2PG) France 9 (1DG, 2PG)

Ireland   T: Grant. PG: O'Driscoll (2).
France   DG: Berot. PG: Villepreux (2).

In recent seasons Ireland had been treated

rather uncharitably by a succession of highly-motivated French sides, and they had achieved one victory only, in 1969, in ten years. So this draw came as something of a welcome change, though the Irish had several chances to have won clearly.

IRELAND   *T.J. Kiernan 40 (Cork Constitution); A.T.A. Duggan 17 (Lansdowne), F.P.K. Bresnihan 19 (London Irish), C.M.H. Gibson 27 (NIFC), E.L. Grant 1 (CIYMS); B.J. McGann 9 (Lansdowne), R.M. Young 20 (Belfast Collegians); R.J. McLoughlin 17 (Blackrock College), K.W. Kennedy 21 (London Irish), J.F. Lynch 1 (St Mary's College), W.J. McBride 36 (Ballymena), M.G. Molloy 19 (London Irish), M.L. Hipwell 7 (Terenure College), J.F. Slattery 5 (UC Dublin), D.J. Hickie 1 (St Mary's College). *Replacement* B.J. O'Driscoll 1 (Manchester) for Kiernan

FRANCE   P. Villepreux 12 (S. Toulouse); J. Sillières 4 (S. Tarbes), J. Trillo 8 (CA Bègles), J-P. Lux 14 (US Tyrosse), J. Cantoni 3 (AS Béziers); J-L. Berot 5 (S. Toulouse), M. Pebeyre 2 (AS Montferrand); M. Etcheverry (2) (S. Pau), R. Bénésis 7 (RC Narbonne), J-L. Azarete 6 (St Jean-de-Luz Ol). J-P. Bastiat 5 (US Dax), J. le Droff (5) (FC Auch), G. Viard (4) (RC Narbonne), *B. Bauga 27 (S. Mont-de-Marsan), A. Quilis (1) (RC Narbonne).

Referee G.C. Lamb (England)

SCOTLAND v WALES   75/610

6 February 1971
Murrayfield
Wales 19 (2G, 2T, 1PG) Scotland 18 (2T, 4PG)

Scotland   T: Carmichael, Rea. PG: Peter Brown (4).
Wales   T: Taylor, Edwards, John, Gerald Davies. C: John, Taylor. PG: John.

Scotland's four penalty goals were the most they have registered against Wales in any match, but the most memorable and crucial kick was that which won the match. Perpetrator of Scotland's downfall and Welsh success was John Taylor. The London Welsh flanker, one of the new breed of round-the-corner kickers, was a left-footed kicker, which was the reason why he was appointed to take the kick close to the right-hand touchline after Gerald Davies had scored a try which brought the score to 18-17. With only minutes remaining it was obvious that this exciting, see-saw struggle would be settled by this conversion. Many of the Welsh players could not bear to watch as Taylor, cool, unfussed and unhurried, lined up the kick. It was a fine kick in any circumstances; as a match-winner on which so much depended it was brilliant. Only Taylor seemed completely unaffected by the unbearable tension but he made no mistake.

SCOTLAND   I.S.G. Smith 6 (London Scottish); W.C.C. Steele 3 (Bedford), J.N.M. Frame 13 (Gala), C.W.W. Rea 8 (Headingley), A.G. Biggar 5 (London Scottish); J.W.C. Turner 13 (Gala), D.S. Paterson 4 (Gala); J. McLauchlan 5 (Jordanhill), F.A.L. Laidlaw 25 (Melrose), A.B. Carmichael 15 (W. of Scotland), A.F. McHarg 8 (London Scottish), G.L. Brown 6 (W. of Scotland), N.A. MacEwan 2 (Gala), R.J. Arneil 12 (Leicester), *P.C. Brown 12 (Gala).

WALES   J.P.R. Williams 10 (London Welsh); T.G.R. Davies 11 (London Welsh), *S.J. Dawes 15 (London Welsh), I. Hall 3 (Aberavon), J.C. Bevan 2 (Cardiff); B. John 14 (Cardiff), G.O. Edwards 16 (Cardiff); D.B. Llewelyn 6 (Llanelli), J. Young 12 (Harrogate), D. Williams 27 (Ebbw Vale), W.D. Thomas 10 (Llanelli), M.G. Roberts 2 (London Welsh), W.D. Morris 16 (Neath), J. Taylor 13 (London Welsh), T.M. Davies 10 (London Welsh).

Referee M.H. Titcomb (England)

IRELAND v ENGLAND   75/611

13 February 1971
Lansdowne Road, Dublin
England 9 (3PG) Ireland 6 (2T)

Ireland   T: Duggan, Grant.
England   PG: Hiller (3).

The Irish must have positively hated the sight of Bob Hiller. His three penalty goals won not only the match, but brought his total points against them to 33 from 4 matches since 1968. Ireland, however, had the distinction of scoring the only tries, one a marvellous effort by Grant, who ran like a stag for 70 yards after an interception.

IRELAND   B.J.   O'Driscoll   2   (Manchester); A.T.A. Duggan 18 (Lansdowne), F.P.K. Bresnihan 20 (London Irish), *C.M.H. Gibson 28 (NIFC), E.L. Grant 2 (CIYMS); B.J. McGann 10 (Cork Constitution), R.M. Young 21 (Collegians); R.J. McLoughlin 18 (Blackrock College), K.W. Kennedy 22 (London Irish), J.F. Lynch 2 (St Mary's College), W.J. McBride 37 (Ballymena), M.G. Molloy 20 (London Irish), M.L. Hipwell 8 (Terenure College), J.F. Slattery 6 (UC Dublin), D.J. Hickie 2 (St Mary's College).

ENGLAND   R. Hiller 12 (Harlequins); J.P.A.G. Janion 2 (Bedford), *J.S. Spencer 10 (Headingley), C.S. Wardlow 2 (Northampton), D.J. Duckham 10 (Coventry); I.D. Wright 2 (Northampton), J.J. Page 2 (Bedford); D.L. Powell 8 (Northampton), J.V. Pullin 15 (Bristol), K.E. Fairbrother 10 (Coventry), N.E. Horton 5(Moseley), P.J. Larter 14 (Northampton), A.L. Bucknall 6 (Richmond), A. Neary 2 (Broughton Park), R.C. Hannaford 2 (Bristol).

Referee M. Joseph (Wales)

ENGLAND v FRANCE   42/612

27 February 1971
Twickenham
England 14 (1G, 3PG) France 14 (1G, 1T, 1DG, 1PG)

England   T: Hiller. C: Hiller. PG: Hiller (3).
France   T: Bertranne, Cantoni. C: Villepreux. DG: Berot. PG: Villepreux

England were lucky to have drawn this match, for France were often much the superior side and whenever their backs were in possession they looked capable of a hatful of tries. In the event Bob Hiller played a true captain's role by supplying all of England's points, while his opposite number, Pierre Villepreux, missed four kicks that on another day he would have landed with ease.

ENGLAND   *R. Hiller 13 (Harlequins); J.P.A.G. Janion 3 (Bedford), C.S. Wardlow 3 (Northampton), D.J. Duckham 11 (Coventry), P.B. Glover (1) (Bath); I.D. Wright 3 (Northampton), J.J. Page 3 (Bedford); D.L. Powell 9 (Northampton), J.V. Pullin 16 (Bristol), K.E. Fairbrother (11) (Coventry), P.J. Larter 15 (Northampton),

N.E. Horton 6 (Moseley), A.L. Bucknall 7 (Richmond), A. Neary 3 (Broughton Park), R.C. Hannaford (3) (Bristol).

FRANCE   P. Villepreux 13 (S. Toulouse); J. Sillières 5 (S. Tarbes), R. Bertranne 1 (S. Bagnères), J-P. Lux 15 (US Tyrosse), J. Cantoni 4 (AS Béziers); J-L. Berot 6 (S. Toulouse), M. Barrau 2 (S. Beaumont); M. Lasserre 7 (SU Agen), R. Bénésis 8 (RC Narbonne), J-L. Azarete 7 (St-Jean-de-Luz Ol), W. Spanghero 18 (RC Narbonne), C. Spanghero 1 (RC Narbonne), M. Yachvili (5) (CA Brive), *C. Carrère 15 (RC Toulon), B. Dauga 28 (S. Mont-de-Marsan).

Referee A.R. Lewis (Wales)

SCOTLAND v IRELAND   77/613

27 February 1971
Murrayfield
Ireland 17 (1G, 2T, 2PG) Scotland 5 (1G)

Scotland   T: Frame. C: Peter Brown.
Ireland   T: Duggan (2), Grant. C: Gibson. PG: Gibson (2).

At times, particularly during the first half, the Irish pack were totally dominant and their vigour and urgency undoubtedly provided the platform for Ireland's fifth consecutive defeat of Scotland. It was also Ireland's biggest score against Scotland since 1953. Frank Laidlaw, a prince among hookers, did not play in another Championship match. He had served Scotland well, often brilliantly, in 26 Championship matches since 1965.

SCOTLAND   I.S.G. Smith (7) (London Scottish); W.C.C. Steele 4 (Bedford), J.N.M. Frame 14 (Gala), A.G. Biggar 6 (London Scottish), R.S.M. Hannah (1) (W. of Scotland); J.W.C. Turner 14 (Gala), D.S. Paterson 5 (Gala); J. McLauchlan 6 (Jordanhill), F.A.L. Laidlaw (26) (Melrose), A.B. Carmichael 16 (W. of Scotland), A.F. McHarg 9 (London Scottish), G.L. Brown 7 (W. of Scotland), N.A. MacEwan 3 (Gala), R.J. Arneil 13 (Leicester), P.C. Brown 13 (Gala).

IRELAND   B.J.   O'Driscoll   3   (Manchester); A.T.A. Duggan 19 (Lansdowne), F.P.K. Bresnihan 21 (London Irish), *C.M.H. Gibson 29 (NIFC), E.L. Grant 3 (CIYMS); B.J. McGann 11 (Cork Constitution), R.M. Young 22 (Belfast

Action during the Wales-Ireland match; McBride's 53 Championship appearances have been bettered only by Mike Gibson

Collegians); R.J. McLoughlin 19 (Blackrock College), K.W. Kennedy 23 (London Irish), J.F. Lynch 3 (St Mary's College), W.J. McBride 38 (Ballymena), M.G. Molloy 21 (London Irish), M.L. Hipwell 9 (Terenure College), J.F. Slattery 7 (UC Dublin), D.J. Hickie 3 (St Mary's College).

Referee W.K.M. Jones (Wales)

WALES v IRELAND   73/614

13 March 1971
Cardiff Arms Park
Wales 23 (1G, 3T, 1DG, 2PG) Ireland 9 (3PG)

Wales   T: Gerald Davies (2), Edwards (2). C: John. DG: John. PG: John (2).
Ireland   PG: Gibson (3).

A burst of 14 points in a little over a quarter-of-an-hour during the second half destroyed Irish hopes of winning for a second time in three visits to the Arms Park. It was Wales's third win of the season, and in some ways their best performance, for not only did their forwards have to subdue a fiery, hard-working Irish pack but their backs were subjected to claustrophobic attention by the Irish midfield players. The telling blows were inflicted by Gareth Edwards, producing a try for himself and for Gerald Davies. Roger Young, Edwards's opposite number, suffered not at all in comparison but the match proved to be his last in the Championship, a fate which also befell Bresnihan and Grant.

WALES   J.P.R. Williams 11 (London Welsh); T.G.R. Davies 12 (London Welsh), *S.J. Dawes 16 (London Welsh), A.J. Lewis 3 (Ebbw Vale), J.C. Bevan 3 (Cardiff); B. John 15 (Cardiff), G.O. Edwards 17 (Cardiff); D.B. Llewelyn 7 (Llanelli), J. Young 13 (Harrogate), D. Williams 28 (Ebbw Vale), W.D. Thomas 11 (Llanelli), M.G. Roberts 3 (London Welsh), W.D. Morris 17 (Neath), J. Taylor 14 (London Welsh), T.M. Davies 11 (London Welsh).

IRELAND   B.J. O'Driscoll (4) (Manchester); A.T.A. Duggan (20) (Lansdowne), F.P.K. Bresnihan (22) (London Irish), *C.M.H. Gibson 30 (NIFC), E.L. Grant (4) (CIYMS); B.J. McGann 12 (Cork Constitution), R.M. Young (23) (Belfast Collegians); J.F. Lynch 4 (St Mary's College), K.W. Kennedy 24 (London Irish), R.J. McLoughlin 20 (Blackrock College), W.J. McBride 39 (Ballymena), M.G. Molloy 22 (London Irish), M.L. Hipwell (10) (Terenure College), J.F. Slattery 8 (UC Dublin), D.J. Hickie 4 (St Mary's College).

Referee R.F. Johnson (England)

ENGLAND v SCOTLAND   74/615

20 March 1971
Twickenham
Scotland 16 (2G, 1T, 1DG) England 15 (2T, 3PG)

England   T: Hiller, Neary. PG: Hiller (3).
Scotland   T: Peter Brown, Paterson, Rea. C: Peter Brown (2). DG: Paterson.

Scotland were responsible for a disappointing finale to the RFU's centenary season by beating England for the first time at Twickenham since 1938. Victory came with the last kick of the game, Peter Brown converting a cleverly-taken try by Chris Rea. It was to be the last occasion when David Duckham and John Spencer played together in the England threequarter line, for Spencer along with five others – four of them from the Northampton club – never played in another Championship match. Rea, despite his match-winning try, suffered the same fate as did three other Scots.

ENGLAND   R. Hiller 14 (Harlequins); J.P.A.G. Janion 4 (Bedford), C.S. Wardlow (4) (Northampton), *J.S. Spencer (11) (Headingley), D.J. Duckham 12 (Coventry); A.R. Cowman 1 (Loughborough College), J.J. Page 4 (Bedford); D.L. Powell (10) (Northampton), J.V. Pullin 17 (Bristol), F.E. Cotton 1 (Loughborough College), P.J. Larter 16 (Northampton), N.E. Horton 7 (Moseley), A.L. Bucknall (8) (Richmond), A. Neary 4 (Broughton Park), R.B. Taylor (13) (Northampton).
Replacement   I.D. Wright (4) (Northampton) for Wardlow

SCOTLAND   A.R. Brown 1 (Gala); W.C.C. Steele 5 (Bedford), J.N.M. Frame 15 (Gala), C.W.W. Rea (9) (Headingley), A.G. Biggar 7 (London Scottish); J.W.C. Turner (15) (Gala), D.S. Paterson 6 (Gala); J. McLauchlan 7 (Jordanhill), Q. Dunlop (1) (W. of Scotland), A.B. Carmichael 17 (W. of Scotland), A.F. McHarg 10 (London Scottish), G.L. Brown 8 (W. of Scotland), N.A. MacEwan 4 (Gala), R.J. Arneil 14 (Leicester), *P.C. Brown 14 (Gala).
Replacement   A.S. Turk (1) (Langholm) for Frame

Referee C. Durand (France)

FRANCE v WALES   42/616

27 March 1971
Stade Colombes, Paris
Wales 9 (2T, 1PG) France 5 (1G)

France   T: Dauga. C: Villepreux.
Wales   T: Edwards, John. PG: John.

Despite the paucity in scoring, this was a match of the highest quality, and brought Wales their first Grand Slam since 1952. France's contribution was one of skill, endeavour and relentless pressure. Resilient Wales responded with two fine tries. It proved to be the twenty-ninth and final appearance of the Ebbw Vale veteran, Denzil Williams.

FRANCE   P. Villepreux 14 (S. Toulouse); R. Bourgarel 4 (S. Toulouse), R. Bertranne 2 (S. Bagnères), J-P. Lux 16 (US Tyrosse), J. Cantoni 5 (AS Béziers); J-L. Berot 7 (S. Toulouse), M. Barrau 3 (S. Beaumont); J. Iraçabal 8 (A. Bayonne), R. Bénésis 9 (RC Narbonne), M. Lasserre (8) (SU Agen), C. Spanghero 2 (RC Narbonne), W. Spanghero 19 (RC Narbonne), B. Dauga 29 (S. Mont-de-Marsan), J-P. Biemouret 6 (SU Agen), *C. Carrère (16) (RC Toulon).

WALES   J.P.R. Williams 12 (London Welsh); T.G.R. Davies 13 (London Welsh), *S.J. Dawes (17) (London Welsh), A.J. Lewis 4 (Ebbw Vale), J.C. Bevan 4 (Cardiff); B. John 16 (Cardiff), G.O. Edwards 18 (Cardiff); D.B. Llewelyn 8 (Llanelli), J. Young 14 (Harrogate), D. Williams (29) (Ebbw Vale), W.D. Thomas 12 (Llanelli), M.G. Roberts 4 (London Welsh), W.D. Morris 18 (Neath), J. Taylor 15 (London Welsh), T.M. Davies 12 (London Welsh).

Referee J. Young (Scotland)

1972

TWICKENHAM Wales beat England 12-3 · MURRAYFIELD Scotland beat France 20-9
PARIS Ireland beat France 14-9 · CARDIFF Wales beat Scotland 35-12
TWICKENHAM Ireland beat England 16-12 · PARIS France beat England 37-12
MURRAYFIELD Scotland beat England 23-9 · CARDIFF Wales beat France 20-6
NB Ireland v Wales and Ireland v Scotland not played

CHAMPIONSHIP TABLE
Wales – Championship

Pos	Country	P	W	D	L	F	A	Pts	Tries F	A
1	Wales (1)	3	3	0	0	67	21	6	8	1
2	Scotland (5)	3	2	0	1	55	53	4	6	6
3	Ireland (4)	2	2	0	0	30	21	4	4	2
4	France (2)	4	1	0	3	61	66	2	8	8
5	England (3)	4	0	0	4	36	88	0	2	11

The 1972 Championship was marred by the decision of Scotland and Wales not to play Ireland in Dublin because of the increased violence in Ulster and the possible repercussions in the Republic. Some ambivalence was obvious at both Murrayfield and Cardiff over their failure to honour their matches with Ireland, and even their suggestion that the matches be played at an alternative neutral venue failed to mollify Ireland. It meant, of course, that the Irish Rugby Union was deprived of essential gate-money from the cancellations and their disappointment was understandable. Consequently Ireland played only two matches, both away, and as they won both they had yet another reason to regret the pull-outs for clearly they possessed a side with the potential to win the Championship. From a purely rugby viewpoint, Wales had some cause for regret too. They had won their three opening matches before they decided against playing in Dublin. Thus they deprived themselves of the opportunity of winning the Championship's most coveted prize, the Grand Slam.

This season also saw the introduction of the four-point try as an incentive to increase try-scoring. The incomplete Championship was hardly the test-bed to prove the idea would work – but there were certainly some very high-scoring matches. Wales for instance, beat Scotland 35-12, which was their highest score ever against them. Scotland partly compensated for this hammering by beating England for a fourth successive year, a feat they had previously achieved only once in 1893–96. England had reason to lament 1972; it was the first time they lost all four Championship matches and they

The classical place-kicking technique of Bob Hiller, here landing one of his 29 Championship penalty goals for England against Wales on 15 January 1972

conceded a record 88 points. This total was swelled by their 12-37 defeat in Paris, which was France's highest score against any opposition and their biggest winning margin against England.

ENGLAND v WALES 76/617

15 January 1972
Twickenham
Wales 12 (1G, 2PG) England 3 (1PG)

England PG: Hiller.
Wales T: Williams. C: John. PG: John (2).

This victory meant that England had not beaten Wales at Twickenham since 1960, which in effect was their worst sequence at home against any opposition. However, it was by no means an easy triumph for Wales. For long periods Wales were under much pressure from an inspired English team which included eight new caps. England, however, could not improve on a Bob Hiller penalty goal and Wales won the game in the second half through a well-worked short-side movement which ended with J.P.R. Williams scoring a try, his second at Twickenham.

ENGLAND *R. Hiller 15 (Harlequins); J.P.A.G. Janion 5 (Bedford), M.C. Beese 1 (Liverpool), D.J. Duckham 13 (Coventry), K.J. Fielding 6 (Moseley); A.G.B. Old 1 (Middlesbrough), J.G. Webster 1 (Moseley); C.B. Stevens 4 (Harlequins), J.V. Pullin 18 (Bristol), M.A. Burton 1 (Gloucester), A. Brinn 1 (Gloucester), C.W. Ralston 1 (Richmond), P.J. Dixon 1 (Harlequins), A. Neary 5 (Broughton Park), A.G. Ripley 1 (Rosslyn Park).

WALES J.P.R. Williams 13 (London Welsh); T.G.R. Davies 14 (London Welsh), R.T.E. Bergiers 1 (Cardiff College of Educ.), A.J. Lewis 5 (Ebbw Vale), J.C. Bevan 5 (Cardiff); B. John 17 (Cardiff), G.O. Edwards 19 (Cardiff); *D.J. Lloyd 17 (Bridgend), J. Young 15 (Harrogate), D.B. Llewelyn 9 (Llanelli), W.D. Thomas 13 (Llanelli), T.G. Evans 4 (London Welsh), W.D. Morris 19 (Neath), J. Taylor 16 (London Welsh), T.M. Davies 13 (London Welsh).

Referee J. Young (Scotland)

SCOTLAND v FRANCE 42/618

15 January 1972
Murrayfield
Scotland 20 (1G, 2T, 1DG, 1PG) France 9 (1G, 1PG)

Scotland T: Telfer, Renwick, Frame. C: Arthur Brown. DG: Telfer. PG: Peter Brown.
France T: Dauga. C: Villepreux. PG: Villepreux.

This was regarded as one of Scotland's outstanding victories of the 1970s, for there were times when they completely outplayed France who admittedly were not a difficult opposition, and were in the process of rebuilding the side which finished second in the 1971 Championship.

SCOTLAND A.R. Brown 2 (Gala); W.C.C. Steele 6 (Bedford), J.N.M. Frame 16 (Gala), J.M. Renwick 1 (Hawick), A.G. Biggar 8 (London Scottish); C.M. Telfer 5 (Hawick), I.G. McCrae (5) (Gordonians); J. McLauchlan 8 (Jordanhill), R.L. Clark 1 (Edinburgh Wands), A.B. Carmichael 18 (W. of Scotland), A.F. McHarg 11 (London Scottish), G.L. Brown 9 (W. of Scotland), N.A. MacEwan 5 (Gala), R.J. Arneil 15 (Northampton), *P.C. Brown 15 (Gala).
Replacement A.J.M. Lawson 1 (Edinburgh Wands) for McCrae

FRANCE P. Villepreux 15 (S. Toulouse); R. Bertranne 3 (S. Bagnères), J. Trillo 9 (CA Bègles), J-P. Lux 17 (US Dax), J. Cantoni 6 (AS Béziers); J-L. Berot 8 (S. Toulouse), J-M. Aguirre 1 (S. Bagnères); A. Vaquerin 1 (AS Béziers), S.R. Bénésis 10 (SU Agen), J-L. Martin 1 (AS Béziers), J-P. Bastiat 6 (US Dax), *B. Dauga 30 (S. Mont-de-Marsan), O. Saisset 1 (AS Béziers), V. Boffelli 1 (S. Aurillac), C. Spanghero 3 (RC Narbonne).

Referee M. Joseph (Wales)

FRANCE v IRELAND   43/619

29 January 1972
Stade Colombes, Paris
Ireland 14 (2T, 2PG) France 9 (1G, 1PG)

France   T: Lux. C: Villepreux. PG: Villepreux.
Ireland   T: Moloney, McLoughlin. PG: Kiernan
(2).

Because of the refusal by Scotland and Wales to
play in Dublin, Ireland's Championship activity
was confined to two away matches, the other
being against England at Twickenham in February. The victory at Stade Colombes therefore
was of psychological importance in a very
trying time for the Irish Rugby Union. It was
also significant historically, in that it was
Ireland's first success in Paris after a string of
nine defeats since 1952. France fielded a very
experimental side while Ireland, also in the
process of reconstructing their team, had three
newcomers including Tom Grace, a wing of
exceptional promise, and a lively young scrum-
half, John Moloney, who distinguished himself
by scoring a try on his début.

FRANCE   P. Villepreux 16 (S. Toulouse); R.
Bertranne 4 (S. Bagnères), C. Dourthe 7 (US Dax),
J-P. Lux 18 (US Tyrosse), J. Cantoni 7 (AS
Béziers); J-L. Berot 9 (S. Toulouse), R. Astre 1
(AS Béziers); J-L. Martin (2) (AS Béziers), R.
Bénésis 11 (SU Agen), A. Vaquerin 2 (AS
Béziers), A. Estève 1 (AS Béziers), *B. Dauga 31
(S. Mont-de-Marsan), V. Boffelli 2 (S. Aurillac),
O. Saisset 2 (AS Béziers), Y. Buonomo (1) (AS
Béziers).
Replacement J-C. Skréla 1 (S. Toulouse) for
Boffelli

IRELAND   *T.J. Kiernan 41 (Cork Constitution);
A.W. McMaster 1 (Ballymena), C.M.H. Gibson
31 (NIFC), M.K. Flynn 18 (Wanderers), T.O.
Grace 1 (UC Dublin); B.J. McGann 13 (Lans-
downe), J.J. Moloney 1 (St Mary's College); J.F.
Lynch 5 (St Mary's College), K.W. Kennedy 25
(London Irish), R.J. McLoughlin 21 (Blackrock
College), W.J. McBride 40 (Ballymena), C.F.P.
Feighery 1 (Lansdowne), J.F. Slattery 9 (UC
Dublin), S.A. McKinney 2 (Dungannon), D.J.
Hickie 5 (St Mary's College).

Referee A.R. Lewis (Wales)

WALES v SCOTLAND   76/620

5 February 1972
Cardiff Arms Park
Wales 35 (3G, 2T, 3PG) Scotland 12 (1G, 2PG)

Wales   T: Edwards (2), Bergiers, Gerald Davies,
Taylor. C: John (3). PG: John (3).
Scotland   T: Clark. C: Peter Brown. PG: Ren-
wick, Peter Brown.

In Championship terms, this was the highest
score against Scotland and also their biggest
losing points margin. Moreover, Wales's five
tries were the most they have scored against
Scotland in Wales which helped them to a fifth
consecutive victory against the Scots, their best
sequence since 1909–13. It was a match in which
J.P.R. Williams was proved human after all. He
was taken off with a broken jaw, and was
replaced by Llanelli's Phil Bennett. Thus Bennett had the unusual distinction of playing in
four different positions in his first four Championship matches: wing, fly-half, centre and
full-back.

WALES   J.P.R. Williams 14 (London Welsh);
T.G.R. Davies 15 (London Welsh), A.J. Lewis 6
(Ebbw Vale), R.T.E. Bergiers 2 (Cardiff College of
Educ.), J.C. Bevan 6 (Cardiff); B. John 18 (Car-
diff), G.O. Edwards 20 (Cardiff); D.B. Llewelyn
10 (Llanelli), J. Young 16 (Harrogate), *D.J.
Lloyd 18 (Bridgend), W.D. Thomas 14 (Llanelli),
T.G. Evans 5 (London Welsh), W.D. Morris 20
(Neath), J. Taylor 17 (London Welsh), T.M.
Davies 14 (London Welsh).
Replacement P. Bennett 4 (Llanelli) for Williams

SCOTLAND   A.R. Brown 3 (Gala); W.C.C. Steele 7
(Bedford), J.N.M. Frame 17 (Gala), J.M. Ren-
wick 2 (Hawick), A.G. Biggar (9) (London
Scottish); C.M. Telfer 6 (Hawick), D.S. Paterson
(7) (Gala); J. McLauchlan 9 (Jordanhill), R.L.
Clark 2 (Edinburgh Wands), A.B. Carmichael 19
(W. of Scotland), I.A. Barnes 1 (Hawick), G.L.
Brown 10 (W. of Scotland), N.A. MacEwan 6
(Gala), R.J. Arneil 16 (Northampton), *P.C.
Brown 16 (Gala).
Replacement L.G. Dick 1 (Loughborough Col-
lege) for Biggar

Referee G.A. Jamieson (Ireland)

ENGLAND v IRELAND 76/621

12 February 1972
Twickenham
Ireland 16 (1G, 1T, 1DG, 1PG) England 12 (1G, 2PG)

England T: Ralston. C: Hiller. PG: Hiller (2).
Ireland T: Flynn, Grace. C: Kiernan. DG: McGann. PG: Kiernan.

This was Ireland's third victory only at Twickenham since the War, and was significant in that it was Tom Kiernan's fiftieth international appearance (his forty-second Championship match) and that his opposite number, Bob Hiller, played his sixteenth and final match for England. Both marked the occasion with a scoring flourish, Hiller providing eight points and Kiernan five.

ENGLAND *R. Hiller (16) (Harlequins); K.J. Fielding 7 (Moseley), M.C. Beese 2 (Liverpool), D.J. Duckham 14 (Coventry), R.E. Webb 10 (Coventry); A.G.B. Old 2 (Middlesbrough), J.G. Webster 2 (Moseley); C.B. Stevens 5 (Harlequins), J.V. Pullin 19 (Bristol), M.A. Burton 2 (Gloucester), A. Brinn 2 (Gloucester), C.W. Ralston 2 (Richmond), P.J. Dixon 2 (Harlequins), A. Neary 6 (Broughton Park), A.G. Ripley 2 (Rosslyn Park).

IRELAND *T.J. Kiernan 42 (Cork Constitution); T.O. Grace 2 (UC Dublin), C.M.H. Gibson 32 (NIFC), M.K. Flynn (19) (Wanderers), A.W. McMaster 2 (Ballymena); B.J. McGann 14 (Cork Constitution), J.J. Moloney 2 (St Mary's College); J.F. Lynch 6 (St Mary's College), K.W. Kennedy 26 (London Irish), R.J. McLoughlin 22 (Blackrock College), W.J. McBride 41 (Ballymena), C.F.P. Feighery (2) (Lansdowne), J.F. Slattery 10 (Blackrock College), S.A. McKinney 2 (Dungannon), D.J. Hickie (6) (St Mary's College).

Referee R. Austry (France)

FRANCE v ENGLAND 43/622

26 February 1972
Stade Colombes, Paris
France 37 (5G, 1T, 1PG) England 12 (1G, 2PG)

France T: Duprat (2), Biemouret, Lux, Sillières, Walter Spanghero. C: Villepreux (5). PG: Villepreux.
England T: Beese. C: Old. PG: Old (2).

France marked the last international to be played at Stade Colombes by running up their biggest score in a Championship match, which was also the highest score ever by any country against England. It also equalled England's biggest losing points margin (0-25 against Wales in 1905) and was their fourth consecutive defeat in France, their longest losing sequence there. To make matters worse, it was the second match in a row in France in which England conceded six tries, four of them coming in a blaze of brilliant attacking rugby towards the end.

FRANCE P. Villepreux 17 (S. Toulouse); B. Duprat 7 (A. Bayonne), J. Maso 7 (RC Narbonne), J-P. Lux 19 (US Dax), J. Sillières 6 (S. Tarbes); J-L. Berot 10 (S. Toulouse), M. Barrau 4 (S. Beaumont); J. Iraçabal 9 (A. Bayonne), R. Bénésis 12 (SU Agen), J-L. Azarete 8 (St-Jean-de-Luz Ol), A. Estève 2 (AS Béziers), C. Spanghero 4 (RC Narbonne), J-C. Skréla 2 (S. Toulouse), J-P. Biemouret 7 (SU Agen), *W. Spanghero 20 (RC Narbonne).

ENGLAND P.M. Knight 1 (Bristol); K.J. Fielding 8 (Moseley), M.C. Beese (3) (Liverpool), D.J. Duckham 15 (Coventry), R.E. Webb (11) (Coventry); A.G.B. Old 3 (Middlesbrough), L.E. Weston 1 (W. of Scotland); C.B. Stevens 6 (Harlequins), J.V. Pullin 20 (Bristol), M.A. Burton 3 (Gloucester), J. Barton (4) (Coventry), C.W. Ralston 3 (Richmond), *P.J. Dixon 3 (Harlequins), A. Neary 7 (Broughton Park), A.G. Ripley 3 (Rosslyn Park).
Replacement N.O. Martin (1) (Harlequins) for Neary

Referee T.F.E. Grierson (Scotland)

SCOTLAND v ENGLAND 75/623

18 March 1972
Murrayfield
Scotland 23 (2T, 1DG, 4PG) England 9 (3PG)

Scotland T: Peter Brown, MacEwan. DG: Telfer. PG: Peter Brown (3), Arthur Brown.
England PG: Old (3).

Although not the biggest score by Scotland against England (28-19 in 1931), this was Scotland's widest winning margin when at home. It was the fourth defeat of the season for England, which was the first time they suffered that particular misfortune. The sombre statistics did not end there: Scotland's four penalty goals were the most either side had scored in their series of matches and the match total of seven penalties was also a record for the fixture.

SCOTLAND A.R. Brown (4) (Gala); W.C.C. Steele 8 (Bedford), J.N.M. Frame (18) (Gala), J.M. Renwick 3 (Hawick), L.G. Dick 2 (Loughborough College); C.M. Telfer 7 (Hawick), A.J.M. Lawson 2 (Edinburgh Wands); J. McLauchlan 10 (Jordanhill), R.L. Clark 3 (Edinburgh Wands), A.B. Carmichael 20 (W. of Scotland), A.F. McHarg 12 (London Scottish), G.L. Brown 11 (W. of Scotland), N.A. MacEwan 7 (Gala), R.J. Arneil (17) (Northampton), *P.C. Brown 17 (Gala).

ENGLAND P.M. Knight (2) (Bristol); K.J. Fielding (9) (Moseley), J.P.A.G. Janion (6) (Bedford), G.W. Evans 1 (Coventry), D.J. Duckham 16 (Coventry); A.G.B. Old 4 (Middlesbrough), L.E. Weston (2) (W. of Scotland); C.B. Stevens 7 (Harlequins), J.V. Pullin 21 (Bristol), M.A. Burton 4 (Gloucester), A. Brinn (3) (Gloucester), C.W. Ralston 4 (Richmond), *P.J. Dixon 4 (Harlequins), A. Neary 8 (Broughton Park), A.G. Ripley 4 (Rosslyn Park).

Referee M. Joseph (Wales)

WALES v FRANCE 43/624

25 March 1972
Cardiff Arms Park
Wales 20 (2T, 4PG) France 6 (2PG)

Wales T: Gerald Davies, Bevan. PG: John (4).
France PG: Villepreux (2).

This was Wales's eighth consecutive Championship victory and secured them the Championship. The ease with which the Welsh commanded the scrums, lines-out and mauls was surprising. Towards the end of an unusually one-sided match between these particular contestants, Wales's captain Mervyn Davies, had to go off injured leaving just enough time for Derek Quinnell to rid himself quickly of his tracksuit and rush out to win his first cap before Mike Titcomb blew for no side.

WALES J.P.R. Williams 15 (London Welsh); T.G.R. Davies 16 (London Welsh), A.J. Lewis 7 (Ebbw Vale), R.T.E. Bergiers 3 (Cardiff College of Educ.), J.C. Bevan 7 (Cardiff); B. John (19) (Cardiff), G.O. Edwards 21 (Cardiff); D.B. Llewelyn (11) (Llanelli), J. Young 17 (Harrogate), *D.J. Lloyd 19 (Bridgend), W.D. Thomas 15 (Llanelli), T.G. Evans (6) (London Welsh), W.D. Morris 21 (Neath), J. Taylor 18 (London Welsh), T.M. Davies 15 (London Welsh).
Replacement D.L. Quinnell 1 (Llanelli) for T.M. Davies

FRANCE *P. Villepreux (18) (S. Toulouse); B. Duprat (8) (A. Bayonne), J. Maso 8 (RC Narbonne), J-P. Lux 20 (US Dax), J. Sillières (7) (S. Tarbes); J-L. Berot 11 (S. Toulouse), M. Barrau 5 (S. Beaumont); J. Iraçabal 10 (A. Bayonne), R. Bénésis 13 (SU Agen), J-L. Azarete 29 (St-Jean-de-Luz-Ol), A. Estève 3 (AS Béziers), C. Spanghero 5 (RC Narbonne), J-C. Skréla 3 (S. Toulouse), B. Dauga (32) (S. Mont-de-Marsan), J-P. Biemouret 8 (SU Agen).

Referee M.H. Titcomb (England)

1973

PARIS France beat Scotland 16-13 · CARDIFF Wales beat England 25-9
MURRAYFIELD Scotland beat Wales 10-9 · DUBLIN Ireland beat England 18-9
TWICKENHAM England beat France 14-6 · MURRAYFIELD Scotland beat Ireland 19-15
CARDIFF Wales beat Ireland 16-12 · TWICKENHAM England beat Scotland 20-13
PARIS France beat Wales 12-3 · DUBLIN Ireland beat France 6-4

CHAMPIONSHIP TABLE
Scotland – Championship

Pos	Country	P	W	D	L	F	A	Pts	Tries F	A
1	Scotland (2)	4	2	0	2	55	59	4	4	7
2	Wales (1)	4	2	0	2	53	43	4	7	3
3	England (5)	4	2	0	2	52	62	4	7	8
4	Ireland (3)	4	2	0	2	50	48	4	5	5
5	France (4)	4	2	0	2	38	36	4	3	3

The 1973 Championship was unique in that each country won their home matches and lost their away ones. This meant, of course, that they all finished level on points, which led some editors and compilers to conjure up that most eccentric of phrases, a quintuple tie. However, there was no tie in aggregate points, not even in the minor places, and Scotland won the Championship simply because they scored more match points than any other country. A Scottish title win was very much overdue; they had not won the Championship for 27 years which was the longest period any country had to endure without winning it save for France, who had to wait 29 years before their first success, in 1959. In contrast, England lost their seventh Championship match in a row during the season, their longest losing sequence ever.

The Championship had kicked off appropriately with the first international to be staged at France's superb new stadium at Parc des Princes, where Scotland provided the opposition. The biggest score of the season was Wales's 25-9 demolition of England at Cardiff. This was Wales's ninth successive Championship victory and their fifth in a row against England. The end of the international careers in 1972 of such players as Barry John and John Dawes clearly had not affected the Welsh supply line. Two other great players of the Championship were also to bow out before the end of the season, Ireland's Tom Kiernan and France's Walter Spanghero.

FRANCE v SCOTLAND 43/625

13 January 1973
Parc des Princes, Paris
France 16 (1T, 1DG, 3PG) Scotland 13 (1T, 1DG, 2PG)

France T: Dourthe. DG: Romeu. PG: Romeu (3).
Scotland T: Lawson. DG: McGeechan. PG: Brown (2).

Andy Irvine, Ian McGeechan and Jean-Pierre Romeu made their Championship débuts in the first international to be staged at the new multi-purpose Parc des Princes, a showpiece stadium built at a cost of £8 million. Almost as if inhibited by their new surroundings, the French played with uncharacteristic caution, Romeu employing widely-angled kicks in preference to releasing his centres. Ken Pattinson, the English referee, suffered a leg injury soon after the start and was replaced by the touch-judge, François Palmade, who thus officiated at his first Championship match. His second, and first formal appointment, was Scotland's next match, against Wales at Murrayfield.

FRANCE   J. Cantoni 8 (AS Béziers); J-P. Lux 21 (US Dax), C. Dourthe 8 (US Dax), J. Trillo 10 (CA

Bègles), R. Bourgarel (5) (S. Toulouse); J-P. Romeu 1 (AS Montferrand), M. Barrau 6 (S. Toulouse); A. Vaquerin 3 (AS Béziers), A. Lubrano (1) (AS Béziers), J. Iraçabal 11 (A. Bayonne), E. Cester 17 (Valence Sp), A. Estève 4 (AS Béziers), O. Saisset 3 (AS Béziers), J-P. Biemouret 9 (SU Agen), *W. Spanghero 21 (RC Narbonne).

SCOTLAND   A.R. Irvine 1 (Heriot's FP); W.C.C. Steele 9 (Bedford), I.W. Forsyth 1 (Stewart's FP), J.M. Renwick 4 (Hawick), D. Shedden 1 (W. of Scotland); I.R. McGeechan 1 (Headingley), A.J.M. Lawson 3 (Edinburgh Wands); J. McLauchlan 11 (Jordanhill), R.L. Clark 4 (Edinburgh Wands), A.B. Carmichael 21 (W. of Scotland), A.F. McHarg 13 (London Scottish), R.W.J. Wright (1) (Edinburgh Wands), N.A. MacEwan 8 (Gala), W. Lauder 6 (Neath), *P.C. Brown 18 (Gala).

Referee K.A. Pattinson (England), replaced after 14 minutes by F. Palmade (France)

WALES v ENGLAND   77/626

20 January 1973
Cardiff Arms Park
Wales 25 (1G, 4T, 1PG) England 9 (1DG, 2PG)

Wales   T: Bevan (2), Gerald Davies, Edwards, Lewis. C: Bennett. PG: Taylor.
England   DG: Cowman. PG: Doble (2).

This was Wales's ninth successive Championship victory. Only England, with ten wins in 1883–86 and 1922–25, have bettered the sequence. It was also their fifth win in a row against England, who had now gone nine matches without a victory against Wales. The well-established technique of subduing the opposition pack, wearing down their will and stamina, and then piling on the scores worked once again for Wales.

WALES   J.P.R. Williams 16 (London Welsh); T.G.R. Davies 17 (London Welsh), R.T.E. Bergiers 4 (Llanelli), *A.J. Lewis 8 (Ebbw Vale), J.C. Bevan 8 (Cardiff); P. Bennett 5 (Llanelli), G.O. Edwards 22 (Cardiff); G. Shaw 1 (Neath), J. Young 18 (London Welsh), D.J. Lloyd 20 (Bridgend), W.D. Thomas 16 (Llanelli), D.L. Quinnell 2 (Llanelli), J. Taylor 19 (London Welsh), W.D. Morris 22 (Neath), T.M. Davies 16 (Swansea).

ENGLAND   S.A. Doble (1) (Moseley); A.J. Morley 1 (Bristol), P.J. Warfield 1 (Rosslyn Park), P.S. Preece 1 (Coventry), D.J. Duckham 17 (Coventry); A.R. Cowman 2 (Coventry), J.G. Webster 3 (Moseley); C.B. Stevens 8 (Penzance & Newlyn), *J.V. Pullin 22 (Bristol), F.E. Cotton 2 (Loughborough College), P.J. Larter (17) (Northampton), C.W. Ralston 5 (Richmond), A. Neary 9 (Broughton Park), J.A. Watkins 1 (Gloucester), A.G. Ripley 5 (Rosslyn Park).
Replacement G.W. Evans 2 (Coventry) for Warfield

Referee G. Domercq (France)

SCOTLAND v WALES   77/627

3 February 1973
Murrayfield
Scotland 10 (1G, 1T) Wales 9 (3PG)

Scotland   T: Telfer, Steele. C: Morgan.
Wales   PG: Bennett (2), Taylor.

John Lloyd and John Bevan, both outstanding players in their respective positions, made their farewell appearances as Scotland scored their first win over the Welsh at Murrayfield since 1967. After 20 minutes Scotland led 10-0 and held on purposefully. It was a perfect start for the Scots' new captain, Ian McLauchlan, who had succeeded Peter Brown after their defeat in Paris the previous month.

SCOTLAND   A.R. Irvine 2 (Heriot's FP); W.C.C. Steele 10 (Bedford), I.R. McGeechan 2 (Headingley), I.W. Forsyth 2 (Stewart's FP), D. Shedden 2 (W. of Scotland); C.M. Telfer 8 (Hawick), D.W. Morgan 1 (Melville College FP); *J. McLauchlan 12 (Jordanhill), R.L. Clark 5 (Edinburgh Wands), A.B. Carmichael 22 (W. of Scotland), A.F. McHarg 14 (London Scottish), P.C. Brown 19 (Gala), N.A. MacEwan 9 (Gala), J.G. Millican 1 (Edinburgh U.), G.M. Strachan 1 (Jordanhill).

WALES   J.P.R. Williams 17 (London Welsh); T.G.R. Davies 18 (London Welsh), R.T.E. Bergiers 5 (Llanelli), *A.J. Lewis 9 (Ebbw Vale), J.C. Bevan (9) (Cardiff); P. Bennett 6 (Llanelli), G.O. Edwards 23 (Cardiff); G. Shaw 2 (Neath), J. Young 19 (London Welsh), D.J. Lloyd (21) (Bridgend), W.D. Thomas 17 (Llanelli), D.L. Quinnell 3 (Llanelli), W.D. Morris 23 (Neath), J.

Taylor 20 (London Welsh), T.M. Davies 17 (Swansea).

Referee F. Palmade (France)

IRELAND v ENGLAND 77/628

10 February 1973
Lansdowne Road, Dublin
Ireland 18 (2G, 1DG, 1PG) England 9 (1G, 1PG)

Ireland T: Grace, Milliken. C: McGann (2). DG: McGann. PG: McGann.
England T: Neary. C: Jorden. PG: Jorden.

This defeat stretched England's losing sequence to seven, their worst in the Championship. It was also their eighth match without a victory, another record sequence. This was Ireland's first match at Lansdowne Road since 13 February 1971, because Scotland and Wales had refused to play there in 1972. When John Pullin led out the England team, the spontaneity and warmth of the reception they received was an eloquent demonstration of the Irish supporters placing sport, and particularly rugby, high on their list of priorities.

IRELAND *T.J. Kiernan 43 (Cork Constitution); T.O. Grace 3 (St Mary's College), R.A. Milliken 1 (Bangor), C.M.H. Gibson 33 (NIFC), A.W. McMaster 3 (Ballymena); B.J. McGann 15 (Cork Constitution), J.J. Moloney 3 (St Mary's College); R.J. McLoughlin 23 (Blackrock College), K.W. Kennedy 27 (London Irish), J.F. Lynch 7 (St Mary's College), K.M.A. Mays 1 (UC Dublin), W.J. McBride 42 (Ballymena), J.F. Slattery 11 (Blackrock College), J.H. Buckley 1 (Sunday's Well), T.A.P. Moore 1 (Highfield).

ENGLAND A.M. Jorden 2 (Blackheath); A.J. Morley 2 (Bristol), P.J. Warfield 2 (Rosslyn Park), P.S. Preece 2 (Coventry), D.J. Duckham 18 (Coventry); A.R. Cowman (3) (Coventry), S.J. Smith 1 (Sale); C.B. Stevens 9 (Penzance & Newlyn), *J.V. Pullin 23 (Bristol), F.E. Cotton 3 (Loughborough College), R.M. Uttley 1 (Gosforth), C.W. Ralston 6 (Richmond), P.J. Dixon 5 (Gosforth), A. Neary 10 (Broughton Park), A.G. Ripley 6 (Rosslyn Park).

Referee A.M. Hosie (Scotland)

ENGLAND v FRANCE 44/629

24 February 1973
Twickenham
England 14 (2T, 2PG) France 6 (1G)

England T: Duckham (2). PG: Jorden (2).
France T: Bertranne. C: Romeu.

This was an historical win for England because it halted a run of eight Championship matches without victory, their longest ever sequence.

ENGLAND A.M. Jorden 3 (Blackheath); P.J. Squires 1 (Harrogate), G.W. Evans 3 (Coventry), P.S. Preece 3 (Coventry), D.J. Duckham 19 (Coventry); M.J. Cooper 1 (Moseley), S.J. Smith 2 (Sale); C.B. Stevens 10 (Penzance & Newlyn), *J.V. Pullin 24 (Bristol), F.E. Cotton 4 (Loughborough College), R.M. Uttley 2 (Gosforth), C.W. Ralston 7 (Richmond), P.J. Dixon 6 (Gosforth), A. Neary 11 (Broughton Park), A.G. Ripley 7 (Rosslyn Park).

FRANCE M. Droitecourt 1 (AS Montferrand); R. Bertranne 5 (RC Toulon), C. Dourthe 9 (US Dax), J. Trillo (11) (CA Bègles), J-P. Lux 22 (US Dax); J-P. Romeu 2 (AS Montferrand), M. Barrau 7 (S. Toulouse); A. Darrieussecq (1) (Biarritz Ol), R. Bénésis 14 (SU Agen), J. Iraçabal 12 (A. Bayonne), A. Estève 5 (AS Béziers), J-P. Bastiat 7 (US Dax), O. Saisset 4 (AS Béziers), J-P. Biemouret 10 (SU Agen), *W. Spanghero 22 (RC Narbonne).
Replacement R. Astre 2 (AS Béziers) for Barrau

Referee K.H. Clark (Ireland)

SCOTLAND v IRELAND 78/630

24 February 1973
Murrayfield
Scotland 19 (1T, 3DG, 2PG) Ireland 14 (2T, 2PG)

Scotland T: Forsyth. DG: Morgan (2), McGeechan. PG: Morgan (2).
Ireland T: McMaster, Kiernan. PG: McGann (2).

This was Tom Kiernan's final Championship appearance. The veteran Cork Constitution full-back finished with a record number of points in international rugby, 158 from 54 appearances (44 in the Championship) over 14 seasons (1960–73). Kiernan celebrated the occasion by scoring a try, but the issue was settled by a hat-trick of dropped goals by Scotland.

SCOTLAND   A.R. Irvine 3 (Heriot's FP); W.C.C. Steele 11 (Bedford), I.R. McGeechan 3 (Headingley), I.W. Forsyth 3 (Stewart's FP), D. Shedden 3 (W. of Scotland); C.M. Telfer 9 (Hawick), D.W. Morgan 2 (Melville College FP); *J. McLauchlan 13 (Jordanhill), R.L. Clark 6 (Edinburgh Wands), A.B. Carmichael 23 (W. of Scotland), A.F. McHarg 15 (London Scottish), P.C. Brown 20 (Gala), N.A. MacEwan 10 (Gala), J.G. Millican 2 (Edinburgh U.), G.M. Strachan 2 (Jordanhill). *Replacement* R.D.H. Bryce (1) (W. of Scotland) for McLauchlan

IRELAND   *T.J. Kiernan (44) (Cork Constitution); T.O. Grace 4 (St Mary's College), R.A. Milliken 2 (Bangor), C.M.H. Gibson 34 (NIFC), A.W. McMaster 4 (Ballymena); B.J. McGann 16 (Cork Constitution), J.J. Moloney 4 (St Mary's College); R.J. McLoughlin 24 (Blackrock College), K.W. Kennedy 28 (London Irish), J.F. Lynch 8 (St Mary's College), K.M.A. Mays 2 (UC Dublin), W.J. McBride 43 (Ballymena), J.F. Slattery 12 (Blackrock College), J.H. Buckley (2) (Sunday's Well), T.A.P. Moore 2 (Highfield).

Referee A.R. Lewis (Wales)

WALES v IRELAND   74/631

10 March 1973
Cardiff Arms Park
Wales 16 (1G, 1T, 2PG) Ireland 12 (1G, 2PG)

Wales   T: Shanklin, Edwards. C: Bennett. PG: Bennett (2).
Ireland   T: Gibson. C: McGann. PG: McGann (2).

By beating Ireland, Wales established a run of nine matches without defeat, their longest sequence in the Championship. Their match-winner, as in 1971, was Gareth Edwards, who produced two supreme pieces of football to turn the match decisively.

WALES   J.P.R. Williams 18 (London Welsh); T.G.R. Davies 19 (London Welsh), R.T.E. Ber-

giers 6 (Llanelli), *A.J. Lewis 10 (Ebbw Vale), J.L. Shanklin 2 (London Welsh); P. Bennett 7 (Llanelli), G.O. Edwards 24 (Cardiff); P.D. Llewellyn 1 (Swansea), J. Young 20 (London Welsh), G. Shaw 3 (Neath), W.D. Thomas 18 (Llanelli), M.G. Roberts 5 (London Welsh), J. Taylor 21 (London Welsh), W.D. Morris 24 (Neath), T.M. Davies 18 (Swansea).

IRELAND   A.H. Ensor 1 (Wanderers); T.O. Grace 5 (St Mary's College), R.A. Milliken 3 (Bangor), C.M.H. Gibson 35 (NIFC), A.W. McMaster 5 (Ballymena); B.J. McGann 17 (Cork Constitution), J.J. Moloney 5 (St Mary's College); J.F. Lynch 9 (St Mary's College), K.W. Kennedy 29 (London Irish), R.J. McLoughlin 25 (Blackrock College), *W.J. McBride 44 (Ballymena), K.M.A. Mays (3) (UC Dublin), S.A. McKinney 3 (Dungannon), J.F. Slattery 13 (Blackrock College), T.A.P. Moore 3 (Highfield).

Referee T.F.E. Grierson (Scotland)

ENGLAND v SCOTLAND   76/632

17 March 1973
Twickenham
England 20 (2G, 2T) Scotland 13 (1G, 1T, 1PG)

England   T: Dixon (2), Evans, Squires. C: Jorden (2).
Scotland   T: Steele (2). C: Irvine. PG: Morgan.

A powerful performance from their pack and a disciplined, controlled game at fly-half by young Martin Cooper were the chief ingredients for England's victory over Triple Crown-seeking Scotland. The Scots came perilously close to achieving their ambition when Peter Brown made a try for Billy Steele with a speculative long pass. Andy Irvine's conversion brought the score to 14-13. One more score now would settle it – but much to the chagrin of Scottish supporters, it was England who obtained the match-winner when a diagonal kick bounced badly for the Scots' defence but perfectly for Geoff Evans. Jorden's conversion was a formality.

ENGLAND   A.M. Jorden 4 (Blackheath); P.J. Squires 2 (Harrogate), G.W. Evans 4 (Coventry), P.S. Preece 4 (Coventry), D.J. Duckham 20 (Coventry); M.J. Cooper 2 (Moseley), S.J. Smith

Billy Steele at full stretch in his attempt to cut off David Duckham during England's 20-13 victory over Scotland at Twickenham on 17 March 1973

3 (Sale); C.B. Stevens 11 (Penzance & Newlyn), *J.V. Pullin 25 (Bristol), F.E. Cotton 5 (Loughborough College), R.M. Uttley 3 (Gosforth), C.W. Ralston 8 (Richmond), P.J. Dixon 7 (Gosforth), A. Neary 12 (Broughton Park), A.G. Ripley 8 (Rosslyn Park).

SCOTLAND   A.R. Irvine 4 (Heriot's FP); W.C.C. Steele 12 (Bedford), I.R. McGeechan 4 (Headingley), I.W. Forsyth (4) (Stewart's FP), D. Shedden 4 (W. of Scotland); C.M. Telfer 10 (Hawick), D.W. Morgan 3 (Melville College FP); *J.

McLauchlan 14 (Jordanhill), R.L. Clark (7) (Edinburgh Wands), A.B. Carmichael 24 (W. of Scotland), A.F. McHarg 16 (London Scottish), P.C. Brown (21) (Gala), N.A. MacEwan 11 (Gala), J.G. Millican (3) (Edinburgh U.), G.M. Strachan (3) (Jordanhill).
Replacement G.L. Brown 12 (W. of Scotland) for Millican

Referee J.C. Kelleher (Wales)

FRANCE v WALES   44/633

24 March 1973
Parc des Princes, Paris
France 12 (1DG, 3PG) Wales 3 (1DG)

France   DG: Romeu. PG: Romeu (3).
Wales   DG: Bennett.

Four of the Welsh team played their last Championship match in this, Wales's first appearance at the new Parc des Princes. One of them, Arthur Lewis was forced into an early departure because of injury, an event which allowed J.J. Williams to come on and win his first cap.

FRANCE   J-M. Aguirre 2 (A. Bagnères); J-F. Phliponeau 1 (AS Montferrand), C-F. Badin 1 (RC Chalon), J. Maso 9 (RC Narbonne), J. Cantoni 9 (AS Béziers); J-P. Romeu 3 (AS Montferrand), M. Pebeyre (3) (AS Montferrand); J. Iraçabal 13 (A. Bayonne), R. Bénésis 15 (SU Agen), J-L. Azarete 10 (St-Jean-de-Luz Ol), E. Cester 18 (Valence Sp), *W. Spanghero 23 (RC Narbonne), J-C. Skréla 4 (S. Toulouse), J-P. Biemouret 12 (SU Agen), O. Saisset 5 (AS Béziers).

WALES   J.P.R. Williams 19 (London Welsh); T.G.R. Davies 20 (London Welsh), A.J. Lewis (11) (Ebbw Vale), R.T.E. Bergiers 7 (Llanelli), J.L. Shanklin (3) (London Welsh); P. Bennett 8 (Llanelli), *G.O. Edwards 25 (Cardiff); P.D. Llewellyn 2 (Swansea), J. Young (21) (London Welsh), G. Shaw 4 (Neath), W.D. Thomas 19 (Llanelli), M.G. Roberts 6 (London Welsh), T.P. David 1 (Llanelli), J. Taylor (22) (London Welsh), T.M. Davies 19 (Swansea).
Replacement J.J. Williams 1 (Llanelli) for Lewis

Referee D.P. d'Arcy (Ireland)

IRELAND v FRANCE   44/634

14 April 1973
Lansdowne Road, Dublin
Ireland 6 (2PG) France 4 (1T)

Ireland   PG: Gibson (2).
France   T: Phliponeau.

This was Walter Spanghero's last Championship appearance, arguably one of France's greatest forwards.

IRELAND   A.H. Ensor 2 (Wanderers); J.P. Dennison 1 (Garryowen), C.M.H. Gibson 36 (NIFC), R.A. Milliken 4 (Bangor), A.W. McMaster 6 (Ballymena); M.A.M. Quinn 1 (Lansdowne), J.J. Moloney 6 (St Mary's College); R.J. McLoughlin 26 (Blackrock College), K.W. Kennedy 30 (London Irish), R.J. Clegg 1 (Bangor), *W.J. McBride 45 (Ballymena), M.G. Molloy (23) (London Irish), J.F. Slattery 14 (Blackrock College), S.A. McKinney 4 (Dungannon), T.A.P. Moore 4 (Highfield).

FRANCE   J-M. Aguirre 3 (S. Bagnères); J-F. Phliponeau (2) (AS Montferrand), J. Maso (10) (RC Narbonne), C-F. Badin (2) (RC Chalon), J. Cantoni 10 (AS Béziers); J-P. Romeu 4 (AS Montferrand), M. Barrau 8 (S. Toulouse), J-L. Azarete 11 (St-Jean-de-Luz Ol), R. Bénésis 16 (SU Agen), J. Iraçabal 14 (A. Bayonne), A. Estève 6 (AS Béziers), E. Cester 19 (Valence Sp), J-P. Biemouret (12) (SU Agen), O. Saisset 6 (AS Béziers), *W. Spanghero (24) (RC Narbonne).

Referee R.F. Johnson (England)

1974

PARIS France beat Ireland 9-6 · CARDIFF Wales beat Scotland 6-0
DUBLIN Ireland drew Wales 9-9 · MURRAYFIELD Scotland beat England 16-14
TWICKENHAM Ireland beat England 26-21 · CARDIFF Wales drew France 16-16
PARIS France drew England 12-12 · DUBLIN Ireland beat Scotland 9-6
TWICKENHAM England beat Wales 16-12 · MURRAYFIELD Scotland beat France 19-6

CHAMPIONSHIP TABLE
Ireland – Championship

Pos	Country	P	W	D	L	F	A	Pts	Tries F	A
1	Ireland (4)	4	2	1	1	50	45	5	5	3
2	Wales (2)	4	1	2	1	43	41	4	4	3
3	France (5)	4	1	2	1	43	53	4	3	4
4	Scotland (1)	4	2	0	2	41	35	4	4	4
5	England (3)	4	1	1	2	63	66	3	6	8

Ireland, probably the team least expected to win, took the Championship. As in the case of Scotland the previous season, their success was long overdue for their last title win had been in 1951; it was their longest period without a title win, 22 years. The figure 22 was significant too in that it was the number of tries produced in the Championship, which was the lowest total since 19 tries were scored in 1968. Two points separated Ireland from bottom-placed England only and they clinched the title by a narrow 6–4 win over France. The result which gave the Irish the greatest satisfaction was their 26-21 victory over England at Twickenham – their biggest score against the English and which equalled their highest score against any country, which was their 26-8 win over Scotland in 1953. Of the three draws which were the feature of the Championship, the 16-16 tie between Wales and France at Cardiff was the most significant as it was the highest scoring draw in the history of the Championship. The most tragic event of the season occurred on the day after England had played France in Paris when the Turkish airliner bringing the rugby supporters home crashed soon after take-off from Orly Airport killing many.

This was also the season when the organization of the Championship took a step forward, though it was not universally agreed as being for the good of the game. The Five Nations Committee decided to play all Championship matches in rotation with two matches being played on one day, with a gap of a fortnight between each double international. This meant that the Championship was effectively reduced to five Saturdays in the season and those Saturdays would always be the same ones, though with different fixtures, each successive year, for five years. Then the rotation would start all over again. Thus, for instance, on the first allocated Saturday of 1974 France played Ireland and Wales played Scotland, but those fixtures would not be repeated until 1979.

FRANCE v IRELAND 45/635

19 January 1974
Parc des Princes, Paris
France 9 (1G, 1PG)   Ireland 6 (2PG)

France T: Boffelli. C: Aguirre. PG: Berot.
Ireland PG: Ensor (2).

Ireland, who had not been beaten by France since 1970, failed at the first hurdle of their 1974 campaign, but it was to be their only defeat of the season. It was Moss Keane's first taste of Championship rugby – he went on to win 40 successive caps.

FRANCE J-M. Aguirre 4 (S. Bagnères); R. Bertranne 6 (S. Bagnères), C. Dourthe 10 (US Dax), J-P. Lux 23 (US Tyrosse), A. Dubertrand 1 (AS Montferrand); J-L. Berot (12) (S. Toulouse), M. Barrau 9 (S. Toulouse); J. Iraçabal 15 (A. Bayonne), R. Bénésis 17 (SU Agen), J-L. Azarete

12 (St-Jean-de-Luz Ol), *E. Cester 20 (Valence Sp), A. Estève 7 (AS Béziers), V. Boffelli 3 (S. Aurillac), O. Saisset 7 (AS Béziers), C. Spanghero 6 (RC Narbonne).
Replacement D. Kaczorowski (1) (Le Creusot) for Saisset

IRELAND   A.H. Ensor 3 (Wanderers); V. Becker 1 (Lansdowne), R.A. Milliken 5 (Bangor), C.M.H. Gibson 37 (NIFC), A.W. McMaster 7 (Ballymena); M.A.M. Quinn 2 (Lansdowne), J.J. Moloney 7 (St Mary's College); J.F. Lynch 10 (St Mary's College), K.W. Kennedy 31 (London Irish), R.J. McLoughlin 27 (Blackrock College), *W.J. McBride 46 (Ballymena), M.I. Keane 1 (Lansdowne), J.F. Slattery 15 (Blackrock College), S.A. McKinney 5 (Dungannon), T.A.P. Moore 5 (Highfield).
Replacement P.J. Agnew (1) (CIYMS) for McLoughlin

Referee A.M. Hosie (Scotland)

WALES v SCOTLAND   78/636

19 January 1974
Cardiff Arms Park
Wales 6 (1G) Scotland 0

Wales   T: Cobner. C: Bennett.

This was the ninth occasion that Scotland failed to register any points in Wales and the fifteenth time in all its Championship matches with Wales. Much of this was due to some fine covering and tackling, notably by J.P.R. Williams. This was a very useful Scottish pack, with some formidable and experienced scrummagers and the new boys in a reshaped Welsh pack must have learned some valuable lessons. One of these newcomers was Terry Cobner who had the distinction of scoring the only try, set up by the inimitable Gerald Davies.

WALES   J.P.R. Williams 20 (London Welsh); T.G.R. Davies 21 (London Welsh), K. Hughes (2) (London Welsh), I. Hall 4 (Aberavon), J.J. Williams 2 (Llanelli); P. Bennett 9 (Llanelli), *G.O. Edwards 26 (Cardiff); P.D. Llewellyn 3 (Swansea), R.W. Windsor 1 (Pontypool), G. Shaw 5 (Neath), A.J. Martin 1 (Aberavon), D.L. Quinnell 4 (Llanelli), T.J. Cobner 1 (Pontypool), W.D. Morris 25 (Neath), T.M. Davies 20 (Swansea).

SCOTLAND   A.R. Irvine 5 (Heriot's FP); A.D. Gill 1 (Gala), J.M. Renwick 5 (Hawick), I.R. McGeechan 5 (Headingley), L.G. Dick 3 (Jordanhill); C.M. Telfer 11 (Hawick), A.J.M. Lawson 4 (Edinburgh Wands); *J. McLauchlan 15 (Jordanhill), D.F. Madsen 1 (Gosforth), A.B. Carmichael 25 (W. of Scotland), A.F. McHarg 17 (London Scottish), G.L. Brown 13 (W. of Scotland), N.A. MacEwan 12 (Highland), W. Lauder 7 (Neath), W.S. Watson 1 (Boroughmuir).

Referee R.F. Johnston (England)

IRELAND v WALES   75/637

2 February 1974
Lansdowne Road, Dublin
Ireland 9 (3PG) Wales 9 (1G, 1DG)

Ireland   PG: Ensor (3).
Wales   T: J.J. Williams. C: Bennett. PG: Bennett.

Ireland's forwards played with heroic defiance against the wind in the second half to prevent Wales achieving what would have been a record fourth victory in a row in Ireland.

IRELAND   A.H. Ensor 4 (Wanderers); V. Becker (2) (Lansdowne), C.M.H. Gibson 38 (NIFC), R.A. Milliken 6 (Bangor), P.J. Lavery 1 (London Irish); M.A.M. Quinn 3 (Lansdowne), J.J. Moloney 8 (St Mary's College); J.F. Lynch 11 (St Mary's College), K.W. Kennedy 32 (London Irish), R.J. McLoughlin 28 (Blackrock College), M.I. Keane 2 (Lansdowne), *W.J. McBride 47 (Ballymena), J.F. Slattery 16 (Blackrock College), S.M. Deering 1 (Garryowen), T.A.P. Moore 6 (Highfield).

WALES   J.P.R. Williams 21 (London Welsh); C.F.W. Rees 1 (London Welsh), I. Hall 5 (Aberavon), A.A.J. Finlayson 1 (Cardiff), J.J. Williams 3 (Llanelli); P. Bennett 10 (Llanelli), *G.O. Edwards 27 (Cardiff); G. Shaw 6 (Neath), R.W. Windsor 2 (Pontypool), W.P.J. Williams 1 (Neath), G.A.D. Wheel 1 (Swansea), A.J. Martin 2 (Aberavon), W.D. Morris 26 (Neath), T.J. Cobner 2 (Pontypool), T.M. Davies 21 (Swansea).

Referee K.A. Pattinson (England)

Two of the Championship's outstanding backs in contention, Mike Gibson being caught by Peter Squires in the England-Ireland match

SCOTLAND v ENGLAND 77/638

2 February 1974
Murrayfield
Scotland 16 (1G, 1T, 2PG) England 14 (2T, 1DG, 1PG)

Scotland T: Irvine, Lauder. C: Irvine. PG: Irvine (2).
England T: Cotton, Neary. DG: Rossborough. PG: Old.

A touchline 45-yard penalty goal by Andy Irvine in injury time condemned England to their third consecutive defeat at Murrayfield. It was the final act of an extraordinary last 20 minutes during which the lead changed four times.

SCOTLAND   A.R. Irvine 6 (Heriot's FP); A.D. Gill 2 (Gala), J.M. Renwick 6 (Hawick), I.R. McGeechan 6 (Headingley), L.G. Dick 4 (Jordanhill); C.M. Telfer 12 (Hawick), A.J.M. Lawson 5 (Edinburgh Wands); *J. McLauchlan 16 (Jordanhill), D.F. Madsen 2 (Gosforth), A.B. Carmichael 26 (W. of Scotland), A.F. McHarg 18 (London Scottish), G.L. Brown 14 (W. of Scotland), N.A. MacEwan 13 (Highland), W. Lauder 8 (Neath), W.S. Watson 2 (Boroughmuir).

ENGLAND   P.A. Rossborough 2 (Coventry); P.J. Squires 3 (Harrogate), D.F.K. Roughley 1 (Liverpool), G.W. Evans 5 (Coventry), D.J. Duckham 21 (Coventry); A.G.B. Old 5 (Leicester), J.G. Webster 4 (Moseley); C.B. Stevens 12 (Penzance & Newlyn), *J.V. Pullin 26 (Bristol), F.E. Cotton 6 (Coventry), N.E. Horton 8 (Moseley), C.W. Ralston 9 (Richmond), P.J. Dixon 8 (Gosforth), A. Neary 13 (Broughton Park), A.G. Ripley 9 (Rosslyn Park).

Referee J. St Guilhem (France)

ENGLAND v IRELAND   78/639

16 February 1974
Twickenham
Ireland 26 (2G, 2T, 1DG, 1PG) England 21 (1G, 5PG)

England   T: Squires. C: Old. PG: Old (5).
Ireland   T: Gibson (2), Moloney, Moore. C: Gibson (2). DG: Quinn. PG: Ensor.

Ireland recorded their highest score against England and thus equalled their biggest score against any country, which was their 26 points against Scotland in 1953. England were not without their share of record-making. Alan Old's five penalty goals were the most in a Championship match by an Englishman, a record which he held until it was equalled by Dusty Hare three times, in 1981, 1982 and 1983.

ENGLAND   P.A. Rossborough 3 (Coventry); P.J. Squires 4 (Harrogate), G.W. Evans 6 (Coventry), D.F.K. Roughley (2) (Liverpool), D.J. Duckham 22 (Coventry); A.G.B. Old 6 (Leicester), S.J. Smith 4 (Sale); C.B. Stevens 13 (Penzance & Newlyn), *J.V. Pullin 27 (Bristol), F.E. Cotton 7 (Coventry), R.M. Uttley 4 (Gosforth), C.W. Ralston 10 (Richmond), P.J. Dixon 9 (Gosforth), A. Neary 14 (Broughton Park), A.G. Ripley 10 (Rosslyn Park).

IRELAND   A.H. Ensor 5 (Lansdowne); T.O. Grace 6 (UC Dublin), R.A. Millken 7 (Bangor), C.M.H. Gibson 39 (NIFC), A.W. McMaster 8 (Ballymena); M.A.M. Quinn 4 (Lansdowne), J.J. Moloney 9 (St Mary's College); R.J. McLoughlin 29 (Blackrock College), K.W. Kennedy 33 (London Irish), J.F. Lynch 12 (St Mary's College), *W.J. McBride 48 (Ballymena), M.I. Keane 3 (Lansdowne), J.F. Slattery 17 (Blackrock College), S.A. McKinney 6 (Dungannon), T.A.P. Moore 7 (Highfield).

Referee M. Joseph (Wales)

WALES v FRANCE   45/640

16 February 1974
Cardiff Arms Park
Wales 16 (1T, 1DG, 3PG) France 16 (1T, 1DG, 3PG)

Wales   T: J.J. Williams. DG: Edwards. PG: Bennett (3).
France   T: Lux. DG: Romeu. PG: Romeu (3).

France's 16 points equalled their highest score in Wales, previously recorded in 1958 and 1960 and with Wales replying in kind, the result was the highest-scoring draw in the history of the Championship.

WALES   J.P.R. Williams 22 (London Welsh); T.G.R. Davies 22 (London Welsh), I. Hall (6) (Aberavon), A.A.J. Finlayson 2 (Cardiff), J.J. Williams 4 (Llanelli); P. Bennett 11 (Llanelli), *G.O. Edwards 28 (Cardiff); W.P.J. Williams (2) (Neath), R.W. Windsor 3 (Pontypool), G. Shaw 7 (Neath), D.L. Quinnell 5 (Llanelli), I.R. Robinson 1 (Cardiff), W.D. Morris 27 (Neath), T.J. Cobner 3 (Pontypool), T.M. Davies 22 (Swansea).

FRANCE   J-M. Aguirre 5 (A. Bagnères); R. Bertranne 7 (A. Bagnères), J. Pecune 1 (S. Tarbes), J-P. Lux 24 (US Dax), A. Dubertrand 2 (AS Montferrand); J-P. Romeu 5 (AS Montferrand), J. Fouroux 1 (La Voulte S.); A. Vaquerin 4 (AS (Béziers), R. Bénésis 18 (SU Agen), J. Iraçabal 16 (A. Bayonne), A. Estève 8 (AS Béziers), *E. Cester 21 (Valence Sp), J-C. Skréla 5 (S. Toulouse), V. Boffelli 4 (S. Aurillac), C. Spanghero 7 (RC Narbonne).

Referee N.R. Sanson (Scotland)

FRANCE v ENGLAND 45/641

2 March 1974
Parc des Princes, Paris
France 12 (1G, 1DG, 1PG) England 12 (1G, 1DG, 1PG)

France T: Romeu. C: Romeu. DG: Romeu. PG: Romeu.
England T: Duckham. C: Old. DG: Evans. PG: Old.

Jean-Pierre Romeu had scored 12 points to earn a draw for France in Cardiff the previous month and he repeated the coup to help his country to another draw, this time against England. The following day many England supporters were killed when a Turkish airliner taking them home crashed near Paris soon after take-off. Among those who died were Larry Webb, the Bedford prop-forward, who won four caps for England in 1959, and rugby writer Lloyd Lewis. The Man of the Match Award in the final of the Welsh Cup was inaugurated in 1975 in memory of Lewis.

FRANCE M. Droitecourt 2 (AS Montferrand); R. Bertranne 8 (S. Bagnères), J. Pecune 2 (S. Tarbes), J-P. Lux 25 (US Dax), A. Dubertrand 3 (AS Montferrand); J-P. Romeu 6 (AS Montferrand), J. Fouroux 2 (La Voulte S.); J. Iraçabal 17 (A. Bayonne), R. Bénésis 19 (SU Agen), A. Vaquerin 5 (AS Béziers), *E. Cester 22 (Valence Sp), A. Estève 9 (AS Béziers), J-C. Skréla 6 (S. Toulouse), V. Boffelli 5 (S. Aurillac), C. Spanghero 8 (RC Narbonne).

ENGLAND A.M. Jorden 5 (Blackheath); P.J. Squires 5 (Harrogate), G.W. Evans 7 (Coventry), K. Smith 1 (Roundhay), D.J. Duckham 23 (Coventry); A.G.B. Old 7 (Leicester), S.J. Smith 5 (Sale); C.B. Stevens 14 (Penzance & Newlyn), *J.V. Pullin 28 (Bristol), M.A. Burton 5 (Gloucester), R.M. Uttley 5 (Gosforth), C.W. Ralston 11 (Richmond), P.J. Dixon 10 (Gosforth), A. Neary 15 (Broughton Park), A.G. Ripley 11 (Rosslyn Park).

Referee J.C. Kelleher (Wales)

IRELAND v SCOTLAND 79/642

2 March 1974
Lansdowne Road, Dublin
Ireland 9 (1G, 1PG) Scotland 6 (2PG)

Ireland T: Milliken. C: Gibson. PG: McKinney.
Scotland PG: Irvine (2).

This victory gained Ireland the Championship for a first time since 1951, though they had to wait until Scotland beat France on the final day of the season before they were certain of celebration. Four senior members of the Irish side, Willie John McBride, Mike Gibson, Ken Kennedy and Ray McLoughlin, had waited a long time for the triumph and must have doubted at one time whether they would ever play in a Championship winning side.

IRELAND A.H. Ensor 6 (Lansdowne); T.O. Grace 7 (UC Dublin), R.A. Milliken 8 (Bangor), C.M.H. Gibson 40 (NIFC), A.W. McMaster 9 (Ballymena); M.A.M. Quinn 5 (Lansdowne), J.J. Moloney 10 (St Mary's College); R.J. McLoughlin 30 (Blackrock College), K.W. Kennedy 34 (London Irish), J.F. Lynch (13) (St Mary's College), M.I. Keane 4 (Lansdowne), *W.J. McBride 49 (Ballymena), S.A. McKinney 7 (Dungannon), J.F. Slattery 18 (Blackrock College), T.A.P. Moore (8) (Highfield).

SCOTLAND A.R. Irvine 7 (Heriot's FP); A.D. Gill 3 (Gala), J.M. Renwick 7 (Hawick), I.R. McGeechan 7 (Headingley), L.G. Dick 5 (Jordanhill); C.M. Telfer 13 (Hawick), D.W. Morgan 4 (Stewart's FP); *J. McLauchlan 17 (Jordanhill), D.F. Madsen 3 (Gosforth), A.B. Carmichael 27 (W. of Scotland), A.F. McHarg 19 (London Scottish), G.L. Brown 15 (W. of Scotland), N.A. MacEwan 14 (Highland), W. Lauder 9 (Neath), W.S. Watson 3 (Boroughmuir).

Referee F. Palmade (France)

ENGLAND v WALES 78/643

16 March 1974
Twickenham
England 16 (1G, 1T, 2PG) Wales 12 (1G, 2PG)

England T: Duckham, Ripley. C: Old. PG: Old (2).
Wales T: Mervyn Davies. C: Bennett. PG: Bennett (2).

This was England's only victory over Wales in 16 matches played between 1964–79. Defeat cost Wales the Championship, but they could have no excuses for England, with Ralston and Ripley outstanding in the pack, and Alan Old, a supreme dictator at fly-half, were the better side on the day. It was the last Championship match for two of Wales's greatest forwards, Delme Thomas and Dai Morris. The athletic, always supremely fit Thomas was a two-handed line-out jumper, which says it all. No braver man ever wore a Welsh jersey than Morris, the 'dog' who divided into the thick of the mauls, to strong-arm back the ball, impervious to the kicks and knocks that the role entailed, and still had had the pace and stamina to run all afternoon.

ENGLAND W.H. Hare 1 (Nottingham); P.J. Squires 6 (Harrogate), G.W. Evans (8) (Coventry), K. Smith 2 (Roundhay), D.J. Duckham 24 (Coventry); A.G.B. Old 8 (Leicester), J.G. Webster 5 (Moseley); C.B. Stevens 15 (Penzance & Newlyn), *J.V. Pullin 29 (Bristol), M.A. Burton 6 (Gloucester), R.M. Uttley 6 (Gosforth), C.W. Ralston 12 (Richmond), P.J. Dixon 11 (Gosforth), A. Neary 16 (Broughton Park), A.G. Ripley 12 (Rosslyn Park).

WALES W.R. Blyth 1 (Swansea); T.G.R. Davies 23 (London Welsh), R.T.E. Bergiers 8 (Llanelli), A.A.J. Finlayson (3) (Cardiff), J.J. Williams 5 (Llanelli); P. Bennett 12 (Llanelli), *G.O. Edwards 29 (Cardiff); P.D. Llewellyn (4) (Swansea), R.W. Windsor 4 (Pontypool), G. Shaw 8 (Neath), I.R. Robinson (2) (Cardiff), W.D. Thomas (20) (Llanelli), W.D. Morris (28) (Neath), T.J. Cobner 4 (Pontypool), T.M. Davies 23 (Swansea).
Replacement G.A.D. Wheel 2 (Swansea) for Robinson

Referee J.R. West (Ireland)

SCOTLAND v FRANCE 44/644

16 March 1974
Murrayfield
Scotland 19 (1G, 1T, 3PG) France 6 (1DG, 1PG)

Scotland T: McHarg, Dick. C: Irvine. PG: Morgan, Irvine (2).
France DG: Romeu. PG: Romeu.

France were contenders for the Championship but were thoroughly beaten by a Scotland side which produced two wonderful tries, one via a dozen pairs of hands and the other the result of great inter-passing and support.

SCOTLAND A.R. Irvine 8 (Heriot's FP); A.D. Gill (4) (Gala), J.M. Renwick 8 (Hawick), M.D. Hunter (1) (Glasgow HSFP), L.G. Dick 6 (Jordanhill); I.R. McGeechan 8 (Headingley), D.W. Morgan 5 (Stewart's FP); *J. McLauchlan 18 (Jordanhill), D.F. Madsen 4 (Gosforth), A.B. Carmichael 28 (W. of Scotland), A.F. McHarg 20 (London Scottish), G.L. Brown 16 (W. of Scotland), N.A. MacEwan 15 (Highland), W. Lauder 10 (Neath), W.S. Watson 4 (Boroughmuir).
Replacement I.A. Barnes 2 (Hawick) for MacEwan

FRANCE M. Droitecourt 3 (AS Montferrand); J-F. Gourdon 1 (RCF), J-P. Lux 26 (US Dax), J. Pecune 3 (S. Tarbes), R. Bertranne 9 (S. Bagnères); J-P. Romeu 7 (AS Montferrand), M. Barrau (10) (SU Agen); J. Iraçabal (18) (A. Bayonne), R. Bénésis (20) (SU Agen), A. Vaquerin 6 (AS Béziers), *E. Cester (23) (Valence Sp), A. Estève 10 (AS Béziers), J-C. Skréla 7 (S. Toulouse), V. Boffelli 6 (S. Aurillac), C. Spanghero 9 (RC Narbonne).

Referee K.H. Clark (Ireland)

PARIS Wales beat France 25-10 · DUBLIN Ireland beat England 12-9
TWICKENHAM France beat England 27-20 · MURRAYFIELD Scotland beat Ireland 20-15
PARIS France beat Scotland 10-9 · CARDIFF Wales beat England 20-4
DUBLIN Ireland beat France 25-6 · MURRAYFIELD Scotland beat Wales 12-10
TWICKENHAM England beat Scotland 7-6 · CARDIFF Wales beat Ireland 32-4

CHAMPIONSHIP TABLE
Wales – Championship

Pos	Country	P	W	D	L	F	A	Pts	Tries F	A
1	Wales (2)	4	3	0	1	87	30	6	14	3
2	Ireland (1)	4	2	0	2	54	67	4	8	8
3	France (3)	4	2	0	2	53	79	4	6	10
4	Scotland (4)	4	2	0	2	47	40	4	2	5
5	England (5)	4	1	0	3	40	65	2	5	9

This was the Irish Rugby Union's centenary season, but they were not to follow up their 1974 success by winning the title. The deciding match was the final one, when Ireland played Wales at Cardiff, with both countries bidding for the prize. Wales won handsomely, 32-4, which was their biggest score against Ireland in Wales. It was the last Championship match for three of Ireland's greatest forwards, Willie John McBride, Ray McLoughlin and Ken Kennedy, and was a galling note on which to end their international careers.

Wales were led inspiringly by a new captain, Mervyn Davies, and under this long, lithe No. 8 they were to lose but one match while winning two titles. The scoring power of the Welsh team was confirmed in that final spree against Ireland, which helped them to an aggregate 87 points, a total bettered only twice, also by Welsh sides, in 1910 (88 points), and 1976 (102).

If Ireland came unstuck in Cardiff, they were able to look back with some satisfaction that their 25-6 conquest of France was the highest score against them, equalling their win in Cork in 1911. The game, and the Championship, had never been more popular and every inter-national match was a sell-out, with tickets now valuable commodities. This popularity reached its peak at the Scotland v Wales match at Murrayfield on St David's Day when a world record crowd of 104,000 paid to watch Scotland inflict the only defeat of the season on the 'unbeatable' Welsh.

There was little cause for France, who conceded 79 points, Scotland or England to celebrate – except in England's case a player emerged who was to help change their fortunes in years to come. On the day that Willie John McBride won his fiftieth Championship cap, Billy Beaumont, playing against him, won his first.

FRANCE v WALES 46/645

18 January 1975
Parc des Princes, Paris
Wales 25 (1G, 4T, 1PG) France 10 (1T, 2PG)

France T: Gourdon. PG: Taffary (2).
Wales T: Fenwick, Cobner, Gerald Davies, Edwards, Price. C: Fenwick. PG: Fenwick.

Wales's five tries was their best haul against France away, beating the four they scored in 1957. The match marked the first appearance for Wales of the Pontypool Front-Row, Graham Price and Charlie Faulkner propping the five-times capped Bobby Windsor. The three became legends during their playing careers, for they were to prove a formidable unit against all opposition. The folk singer Max Boyce even wrote a song about them. For Price it was a match to remember for another reason: he ran nearly 70 yards to snatch up a loose ball and score Wales's final try.

FRANCE   M. Taffary 1 (RCF); J-F. Gourdon 2 (RCF), C. Dourthe 11 (US Dax), R. Bertranne 10 (S. Bagnères), J-P. Lux (27) (US Dax); J-P. Romeu 8 (AS Montferrand), *J. Fouroux 3 (La Voulte S.); J-L. Azarete (13) (St-Jean-de-Luz-Ol), A. Paco 1 (AS Béziers), A. Vaquerin 7 (AS Béziers), A. Estève 11 (AS Béziers), G. Senal (1) (AS Béziers), V. Boffelli 7 (S. Aurillac), O. Saisset (8) (AS Béziers), J-P. Bastiat 8 (US Dax).
Replacements J. Cantoni (11) (AS Béziers) for Gourdon, J-C. Skréla 8 (S. Toulouse) for Saisset.

WALES   J.P.R. Williams 23 (London Welsh); T.G.R. Davies 24 (Cardiff), S.P. Fenwick 1 (Bridgend), R.W.R. Gravell 1 (Llanelli), J.J. Williams 6 (Llanelli); J.D. Bevan 1 (Aberavon), G.O. Edwards 30 (Cardiff); G. Price 1 (Pontypool), R.W. Windsor 5 (Pontypool), A.G. Faulkner 1 (Pontypool), G.A.D. Wheel 3 (Swansea), A.J. Martin 3 (Aberavon), T.P. Evans 1 (Swansea), T.J. Cobner 5 (Pontypool), *T.M. Davies 24 (Swansea).

Referee K.A. Pattinson (England)

IRELAND v ENGLAND   79/646

18 January 1975
Lansdowne Road, Dublin
Ireland 12 (2G) England 9 (1G, 1DG)

Ireland   T: Gibson, McCombe. C: McCombe (2).
England   T: Stevens. C: Old DG: Old.

This was Willie John McBride's fiftieth Championship match for Ireland, while his opposite number, Billy Beaumont was making his début. It was not the only evidence of a contrast between old and new. Ireland fielded Mike Gibson, making his forty-first appearance, Ray McLoughlin making his thirty-first and Willie Duggan his first. England played David Duckham, winning his twenty-fifth cap, John Pullin his thirtieth and Tony Neary his seventeenth. The match was won by a player making his second appearance, seven years after his first cap – Billy McCombe, who scored the second Irish try and converted it.

IRELAND   A.H. Ensor 7 (Wanderers); T.O. Grace 8 (St Mary's College), R.A. Milliken 9 (Bangor),

C.M.H. Gibson 41 (NIFC), J.P. Dennison 2 (Garryowen); W.McM. McCombe 2 (Bangor), J.J. Moloney 11 (St Mary's College); R.J. McLoughlin 31 (Blackrock College), P.C. Whelan 1 (Garryowen), R.J. Clegg 2 (Bangor), *W.J. McBride 50 (Ballymena), M.I. Keane 5 (Lansdowne), J.F. Slattery 19 (Blackrock College), S.A. McKinney 8 (Dungannon), W.P. Duggan 1 (Blackrock College).

ENGLAND   P.A. Rossborough 4 (Coventry); P.J. Squires 7 (Harrogate), P.J. Warfield 3 (Cambridge U.), P.S. Preece 5 (Coventry), D.J. Duckham 25 (Coventry); A.G.B. Old 9 (Middlesbrough), J.G. Webster 6 (Moseley); C.B. Stevens 16 (Penzance & Newlyn), J.V. Pullin 30 (Bristol), *F.E. Cotton 8 (Coventry), W.B. Beaumont 1 (Fylde), C.W. Ralston 13 (Richmond), P.J. Dixon 12 (Gosforth), A. Neary 17 (Broughton Park), A.G. Ripley 13 (Rosslyn Park).

Referee F. Palmade (France)

ENGLAND v FRANCE   46/647

1 February 1975
Twickenham
France 27 (4G, 1PG) England 20 (2T, 4PG)

England   T: Duckham, Rossborough. PG: Rossborough (4).
France   T: Etchenique, Gourdon, Guilbert, Spanghero. C: Paries (4). PG: Paries.

France's biggest score in England to date, as well as their highest total of tries, was the just reward for some marvellous attacking rugby. England's only answer to the onslaught came from two of the four Coventry players in the side – a try by David Duckham and 16 points from Peter Rossborough. Only four players have scored more points in a Championship match for England, but the Rossborough spree did not save him. He never played again for his country.

ENGLAND   P.A. Rossborough (5) (Coventry); P.J. Squires 8 (Harrogate), P.J. Warfield 4 (Cambridge U.), P.S. Preece 6 (Coventry), D.J. Duckham 26 (Coventry); M.J. Cooper 3 (Moseley), J.G. Webster 7 (Moseley); C.B. Stevens 17 (Penzance & Newlyn), P.J. Wheeler 1 (Leicester), *F.E. Cotton 9 (Coventry), R.M. Uttley 7 (Gosforth), C.W. Ralston 14 (Richmond), J.A. Watkins 2 (Gloucester), A. Neary 18 (Broughton Park), A.G. Ripley 14 (Rosslyn Park).

FRANCE   M. Taffary 2 (RCF); J-F. Gourdon 3 (RCF), J-M. Etchenique (1) (Biarritz Ol), *C. Dourthe 12 (US Dax), R. Bertranne 11 (S. Bagnères); L. Paries 4 (RC Narbonne), R. Astre 3 (AS Béziers); A. Vaquerin 8 (AS Béziers), A. Paco 2 (AS Béziers), G. Cholley 1 (Castres Ol), A. Estève (12) (AS Béziers), A. Guilbert 1 (RC Toulon), J-P. Rives 1 (S. Toulouse), J-C. Skréla 9 (S. Toulouse), C. Spanghero 10 (RC Narbonne).

Referee T.F.E. Grierson (Scotland)

SCOTLAND v IRELAND   80/648

1 February 1975
Murrayfield
Scotland 20 (2T, 2DG, 2PG) Ireland 13 (1G, 1T, 1PG)

Scotland   T: Renwick, Steele. DG: Morgan, McGeechan. PG: Irvine (2).
Ireland   T: Dennison, Grace. C: McCombe. PG: McCombe.

Scotland started their campaign in a rousing manner by outwitting and outplaying the Champions of 1974. Ian McGeechan was a master tactician at fly-half, and there were encouraging contributions from the two new back-row players, Mike Biggar and David Leslie. Ireland played well at times but they were rarely able to dominate a tight, disciplined Scottish defence.

SCOTLAND   A.R. Irvine 9 (Heriot's FP); W.C.C. Steele 13 (London Scottish), J.M. Renwick 9 (Hawick), D.L. Bell 1 (Watsonians), L.G. Dick 7 (Jordanhill); I.R. McGeechan 9 (Headingley), D.W. Morgan 6 (Stewart's FP); *J. McLauchlan 19 (Jordanhill) D.F. Madsen 5 (Gosforth), A.B. Carmichael 29 (W. of Scotland), A.F. McHarg 21 (London Scottish), G.L. Brown 17 (W. of Scotland), M.A. Biggar 1 (London Scottish), W. Lauder 11 (Neath), D.G. Leslie 1 (Dundee HSFP).

IRELAND   A.H. Ensor 8 (Wanderers); T.O. Grace 9 (St Mary's College), R.A. Milliken 10 (Bangor), C.M.H. Gibson 42 (NIFC), J.P. Dennison (3) (Garryowen); W.McM. McCombe 3 (Bangor), J.J. Moloney 12 (St Mary's College); R.J. Mc-

Loughlin 32 (Blackrock College), P.C. Whelan 2 (Garryowen), R.J. Clegg 3 (Bangor), *W.J. McBride 51 (Ballymena), M.I. Keane 6 (Lansdowne), J.F. Slattery 20 (Blackrock College), S.A. McKinney 9 (Dungannon), W.P. Duggan 2 (Blackrock College).

Referee R.F. Johnson (England)

FRANCE v SCOTLAND   45/649

15 February 1975
Parc des Princes, Paris
France 10 (1T, 1DG, 1PG) Scotland 9 (3PG)

France   T: Dourthe. DG: Astre. PG: Paries.
Scotland   PG: Irvine (3).

Andy Irvine, usually the most reliable of place kickers, had a disastrous day. Any one of the six penalty kicks he missed might have given Scotland a victory which would have put them within reach of the Championship.

FRANCE   M. Taffary 3 (RCF); J-F. Gourdon 4 (RCF), *C. Dourthe (13) (US Dax), R. Bertranne 12 (S. Bagnères), J-L. Averous 1 (La Voulte S.); L. Paries 5 (RC Narbonne), R. Astre 4 (AS Béziers); A. Vaquerin 9 (AS Béziers), J-L. Ugartemendia 1 (St-Jean-de-Luz Ol), G. Cholley 2 (Castres Ol), A. Guilbert 2 (RC Toulon), C. Spanghero 11 (RC Narbonne), J-P. Rives 2 (S. Toulouse), J-C. Skréla 10 (S. Toulouse), V. Boffelli 8 (S. Aurillac).

SCOTLAND   A.R. Irvine 10 (Heriot's FP); W.C.C. Steele 14 (London Scottish), J.M. Renwick 10 (Hawick), D.L. Bell 2 (Watsonians), L.G. Dick 8 (Jordanhill); I.R. McGeechan 10 (Headingley), D.W. Morgan 7 (Stewart's FP); *J. McLauchlan 20 (Jordanhill), D.F. Madsen 6 (Gosforth), A.B. Carmichael 30 (W. of Scotland), A.F. McHarg 22 (London Scottish), G.L. Brown 18 (W. of Scotland), M.A. Biggar 2 (London Scottish), W. Lauder 12 (Neath), D.G. Leslie 2 (Dundee HSFP).

Referee M.S. Lewis (Wales)

WALES v ENGLAND 79/650

15 February 1975
Cardiff Arms Park
Wales 20 (1G, 2T, 2PG) England 4 (1T)

Wales T: Gerald Davies, Fenwick, J.J. Williams. C: Martin. PG: Martin (2).
England T: Horton.

Since 1965 Wales had been running up large scores against England at Cardiff with embarrassing regularity. This was another one, but it was no masterly exhibition, rather a remorseless, grinding down of the opposition and then, after a comfortable lead was established, a palpable easing off was evident for all to see. England must have been baffled as to what they should do to win in Wales. They had won some good line-out ball, did well in the mauls and hardly missed a tackle. But in the end, they were outpaced and outmanoeuvered by a side which only rarely required to move into top gear.

WALES J.P.R. Williams 24 (London Welsh); T.G.R. Davies 25 (London Welsh), S.P. Fenwick 2 (Bridgend), R.W.R. Gravell 2 (Llanelli), J.J. Williams 7 (Llanelli); J.D. Bevan 2 (Aberavon), G.O. Edwards 31 (Cardiff); G. Price 2 (Pontypool), R.W. Windsor 6 (Pontypool), A.G. Faulkner 2 (Pontypool), G.A.D. Wheel 4 (Swansea), A.J. Martin 4 (Aberavon), T.P. Evans 2 (Swansea), T.J. Cobner 6 (Pontypool), *T.M. Davies 25 (Swansea).
Replacement D.L. Quinnell 6 (Llanelli) for Wheel

ENGLAND A.M. Jorden 6 (Bedford); P.J. Squires 9 (Harrogate), K. Smith 3 (Roundhay), P.S. Preece 7 (Coventry), D.J. Duckham 27 (Coventry); M.J. Cooper 4 (Moseley), J.G. Webster (8) (Moseley); C.B. Stevens 18 (Penzance & Newlyn), P.J. Wheeler 2 (Leicester), *F.E. Cotton 10 (Coventry), N.E. Horton 9 (Moseley), C.W. Ralston 15 (Richmond), J.A. Watkins (3) (Gloucester), A. Neary 19 (Broughton Park), R.M. Uttley 8 (Gosforth).
Replacements S.J. Smith 6 (Sale) for Webster; J.V. Pullin 31 (Bristol) for Wheeler

Referee A.M. Hosie (Scotland)

IRELAND v FRANCE 46/651

1 March 1975
Lansdowne Road, Dublin
Ireland 25 (2G, 1T, 2DG, 1PG) France 6 (1DG, 1PG)

Ireland T: Ensor, Grace, McBride. C: McCombe (2). DG: McCombe (2). PG: McCombe.
France DG: Paries. PG: Paries.

Ireland equalled their highest score in a Championship match against France (25-5 in Cork in 1911). It was also their highest score against any opposition at Lansdowne Road. Willie John McBride had cause for personal celebration too as he scored his only try for Ireland in this his fifty-second and penultimate Championship game. Billy McCombe also won a place for himself in the history of the fixture – no other Irishman or Irish team – had scored two dropped goals against France.

IRELAND A.H. Ensor 9 (Wanderers); T.O. Grace 10 (St Mary's College), R.A. Milliken 11 (Bangor), C.M.H. Gibson 43 (NIFC), A.W. McMaster 10 (Ballymena); W.McM. McCombe 4 (Bangor), J.J. Moloney 13 (St Mary's College); R.J. McLoughlin 33 (Blackrock College), K.W. Kennedy 35 (London Irish), R.J. Clegg 4 (Bangor), *W.J. McBride 52 (Ballymena), M.I. Keane 7 (Lansdowne), J.F. Slattery 21 (Blackrock College), M.J.A. Sherry 1 (Lansdowne), W.P. Duggan 3 (Blackrock College).

FRANCE M. Taffary (4) (RCF); J-F. Gourdon 5 (RCF), R. Bertranne 13 (S. Bagnères), F. Sangali 1 (RC Narbonne), J-L. Averous 2 (La Voulte S.); L. Paries (6) (RC Narbonne), *R. Astre (5) (AS Béziers); G. Cholley 3 (Castres Ol), J-L. Ugartemendia (2) (St-Jean-de-Luz Ol), A. Vaquerin 10 (AS Béziers), C. Spanghero (12) (RC Narbonne), A. Guilbert 3 (RC Toulon), J-C. Skréla 11 (S. Toulouse), J-P. Rives 3 (S. Toulouse), V. Boffelli (9) (S. Aurillac).

Referee D.M. Lloyd (Wales)

SCOTLAND v WALES   79/652

1 March 1975
Murrayfield
Scotland 12 (1DG, 3PG) Wales 10 (1T, 2PG)

Scotland   DG: McGeechan. PG: Morgan (3).
Wales   T: Evans. PG: Fenwick (2).

A world record crowd of 104,000 paid to watch a match which was conspicuous in the lack of skill shown by both sides. Scotland won because they were the better of two poor teams, though Allan Martin had a chance to snatch victory for Wales but he failed in injury time to make a long-range conversion of a try by Trevor Evans. Steve Fenwick and John Bevan were both injured in the match and were unfit for the next match, against Ireland. The break in continuity was only temporary in Fenwick's·case, but Bevan, replaced by Phil Bennett, did not play in another Championship match.

SCOTLAND   A.R. Irvine 11 (Heriot's FP); W.C.C. Steele 15 (London Scottish), J.M. Renwick 11 (Hawick), D.L. Bell 3 (Watsonians), L.G. Dick 9 (Jordanhill); I.R. McGeechan 11 (Headingley), D.W. Morgan 8 (Stewart's FP); *J. McLauchlan 21 (Jordanhill), D.F. Madsen 7 (Gosforth), A.B. Carmichael 31 (W. of Scotland), A.F. McHarg 23 (London Scottish), G.L. Brown 19 (W. of Scotland), M.A. Biggar 3 (London Scottish), N.A. MacEwan 16 (Highland), D.G. Leslie 3 (Dundee HSFP).

WALES   J.P.R. Williams 25 (London Welsh); T.G.R. Davies 26 (Cardiff), S.P. Fenwick 3 (Bridgend), R.W.R. Gravell 3 (Llanelli), J.J. Williams 8 (Llanelli); J.D. Bevan (3) (Aberavon), G.O. Edwards 32 (Cardiff); A.G. Faulkner 3 (Pontypool), R.W. Windsor 7 (Pontypool), G. Price 3 (Pontypool), A.J. Martin 5 (Aberavon), M.G. Roberts 7 (London Welsh), T.J. Cobner 7 (Pontypool), T.P. Evans 3 (Swansea), *T.M. Davies 26 (Swansea). *Replacements* P. Bennett 13 (Llanelli) for Bevan, W.R. Blyth 2 (Swansea) for Fenwick

Referee J.R. West (Ireland)

Gerald Davies scores a brilliant try for Wales against Ireland on 15 March 1975

ENGLAND v SCOTLAND   78/653

15 March 1975
Twickenham
England 7 (1T, 1PG) Scotland 6 (2PG)

England   T: Morley. PG: Bennett.
Scotland   PG: Morgan (2).

Once again, for the fourth time since 1947, Scotland were deprived of the Triple Crown by England at Twickenham. It was England's only win of the season, and failed to lift them from their usual place at the foot of the table. Three England players' Championship careers had ended already this season and, after this match, another eight joined them. These included Jacko Page, back for this one match after a four-year absence, and Dave Rollitt, recalled after six years on the sidelines.

ENGLAND   A.M. Jorden (7) (Bedford); P.J. Squires 10 (Harrogate), P.J. Warfield (5) (Cambridge U.), K. Smith (4) (Roundhay), A.J. Morley (3) (Bristol); W.N. Bennett 1 (Bedford), J.J. Page (5) (Northampton); C.B. Stevens (19) (Penzance & Newlyn), J.V. Pullin 32 (Bristol), M.A. Burton 7 (Gloucester), R.M. Uttley 9 (Gosforth), C.W. Ralston (16) (Richmond), D.M. Rollitt (9) (Bristol), *A. Neary 20 (Broughton Park), A.G. Ripley 15 (Rosslyn Park).

SCOTLAND   A.R. Irvine 12 (Heriot's FP); W.C.C. Steele 16 (London Scottish), J.M. Renwick 12 (Hawick), D.L. Bell (4) (Watsonians), L.G. Dick 10 (Jordanhill), I.R. McGeechan 12 (Headingley), D.W. Morgan 9 (Stewart's FP); *J. McLauchlan 22 (Jordanhill), D.F. Madsen 8 (Gosforth), A.B. Carmichael 32 (W. of Scotland), A.F. McHarg 24 (London Scottish), G.L. Brown 20 (W. of Scotland), M.A. Biggar 4 (London Scottish), N.A. MacEwan (17) (Highland), D.G. Leslie 4 (Dundee HSFP).
Replacement I.A. Barnes 3 (Hawick) for MacEwan

Referee D.P. d'Arcy (Ireland)

WALES v IRELAND   76/654

15 March 1975
Cardiff Arms Park
Wales 32 (3G, 2T, 2PG) Ireland 4 (1T)

Wales   T: Edwards, Gerald Davies, Faulkner, J.J. Williams, Bergiers. C: Bennett (3). PG: Bennett (2).
Ireland   T: Duggan.

This was Wales's biggest score against Ireland in Wales and in no way flattered them. Ireland came to Cardiff also bidding for the Championship title, but they were outclassed in a match which proved to be the final internationals for three of their great forwards, Willie John McBride, Ray McLoughlin and Ken Kennedy, as well as Milliken, McCombe, Clegg and Sherry.

WALES   J.P.R. Williams 26 (London Welsh); T.G.R. Davies 27 (Cardiff), R.T.E. Bergiers (9) (Llanelli), R.W.R. Gravell 4 (Llanelli), J.J. Williams 9 (Llanelli); P. Bennett 14 (Llanelli), G.O. Edwards 33 (Cardiff); G. Price 4 (Pontypool), R.W. Windsor 8 (Pontypool), A.G. Faulkner 4 (Pontypool), A.J. Martin 6 (Aberavon), G.A.D. Wheel 5 (Swansea), T.P. Evans 4 (Swansea), T.J. Cobner 8 (Pontypool), *T.M. Davies 27 (Swansea).

IRELAND   A.H. Ensor 10 (Wanderers); T.O. Grace 11 (St Mary's College), R.A. Milliken (12) (Bangor), C.M.H. Gibson 44 (NIFC), A.W. McMaster 11 (Ballymena); W.McM. McCombe (5) (Bangor), J.J. Moloney 14 (St Mary's College); R.J. Clegg (5) (Bangor), K.W. Kennedy (36) (London Irish), R.J. McLoughlin (34) (Blackrock College), M.I. Keane 8 (Lansdowne), *W.J. McBride (53) (Ballymena), M.J.A. Sherry (2) (Lansdowne), J.F. Slattery 22 (Blackrock College), W.P. Duggan 4 (Blackrock College).

Referee J. St Guilhem (France)

MURRAYFIELD France beat Scotland 13-6 · TWICKENHAM Wales beat England 21-9
PARIS France beat Ireland 26-3 · CARDIFF Wales beat Scotland 28-6
DUBLIN Wales beat Ireland 34-9 · MURRAYFIELD Scotland beat England 22-12
TWICKENHAM Ireland beat England 13-12 · CARDIFF Wales beat France 19-13
PARIS France beat England 30-9 · DUBLIN Scotland beat Ireland 15-6

CHAMPIONSHIP TABLE
Wales – Championship, Triple Crown, Grand Slam

Pos	Country	P	W	D	L	F	A	Pts	Tries F	A
1	Wales (1)	4	4	0	0	102	37	8	11	3
2	France (3)	4	3	0	1	82	37	6	13	2
3	Scotland (4)	4	2	0	2	49	59	4	4	5
4	Ireland (2)	4	1	0	3	31	87	2	3	8
5	England (5)	4	0	0	4	42	86	0	2	15

England had endured difficult periods in the Championship before, but few compared with their current misfortune. Not only did they finish bottom of the Championship for the third year running, they lost all four matches for only the second time in their history. Their defence was vulnerable to all and they conceded a massive 86 points, which was not their worst defensive record, but the 15 tries they allowed most certainly was. From 1967–76 was a decade of disaster for England, a period in which they won the Wooden Spoon five times and had 659 points scored against them.

On the other side of the wheel of fortune, and the Championship table, was Wales, basking in the glory of another Grand Slam, made possible by the scoring of 102 points, the biggest aggregate in the history of the Championship. An indication of the power and ability of this Welsh team was that this would have been a record total even without the four-point try. Wales, architects of midfield artistry, were also demolition experts: they scored a record 34–9 win against Ireland. The leading exponent of individual artistry and scoring power was Phil Bennett. He accumulated 38 points, a Championship best by a Welsh player.

High scoring was not entirely Wales's province. France, too, scored prolifically and even recorded more tries, 13, than Wales. But France's 82 points in second place also had the effect of lifting the Championship aggregate over 300 points for a first time, 306 to be exact. Both French points and try totals were the best they had ever achieved. In face of this scoring power, Scotland did well to win two of their four matches but Ireland had a torrid time. They lost 3-26 to France which was their biggest losing margin against the French.

SCOTLAND v FRANCE   46/655

10 January 1976
Murrayfield
France 13 (1T, 3PG) Scotland 6 (1DG, 1PG)

Scotland   DG: Morgan. PG: Renwick.
France   T: Dubertrand. PG: Romeu (3).

After being beaten on their two previous visits to Murrayfield France received full benefit of repeated penalty kick misses by Andy Irvine and Doug Morgan. There were three new faces in the French pack, including Robert Paparemborde, who had 'graduated' from the three-quarter line to tight-head prop with a dabble in the back-row, reminiscent of the progress of the Wales prop, Howard Norris.

SCOTLAND B.H. Hay 1 (Boroughmuir); A.R. Irvine 13 (Heriot's FP), J.M. Renwick 13 (Hawick), I.R. McGeechan 13 (Headingley), L.G. Dick 11 (Jordanhill); C.M. Telfer (14) (Hawick), D.W. Morgan 10 (Stewart's FP); *J. McLauchlan 23 (Jordanhill), D.F. Madsen 9 (Gosforth), A.B.

Carmichael 33 (W. of Scotland), A.F. McHarg 25 (London Scottish), G.L. Brown 21 (W. of Scotland), W. Lauder 13 (Neath), D.G. Leslie 5 (W. of Scotland), G.Y. Mackie 1 (Highlahd).

FRANCE   M. Droitecourt 4 (AS Montferrand); J-F. Gourdon 6 (RCF), R. Bertranne 14 (S. Bagnères), F. Sangali 2 (RC Narbonne), A. Dubertrand (4) (AS Montferrand); J-P. Romeu 9 (AS Montferrand), *J. Fouroux 4 (La Voulte S.); G. Cholley 4 (Castres Ol), A. Paco 3 (AS Béziers), R. Paparemborde 1 (S. Pau), F. Haget 1 (SU Agen), M. Palmié 1 (AS Béziers), J-P. Rives 4 (S. Toulouse), J-C. Skréla 12 (S. Toulouse), J-P. Bastiat 9 (US Dax).

Referee K.A. Pattinson (England)

ENGLAND v WALES   80/656

17 January 1976
Twickenham
Wales 21 (3G, 1PG) England 9 (3PG)

England   PG: Hignell (3).
Wales   T: J.P.R. Williams (2), Edwards. C: Fenwick (3). PG: Martin.

This was Wales's biggest score at Twickenham, and their highest total in England apart from their demolition of England by 28 points at Bristol in 1908. Although neither needed confirmation of their greatness, Gareth Edwards and J.P.R. Williams were at their best for Wales in the match, which was necessary as England played tremendously well, particularly their pack. Edwards's variations, the surge down the blind, the kick into the box, long, fast passes to Bennett and stupendous line-kicking, kept the English caged. If J.P.R.'s only contribution had been his tackling and covering, he would have earned the highest praise; but he also scored two tries, one a classic in its enterprise and execution.

ENGLAND   A.J. Hignell 1 (Cambridge U.); P.J. Squires 11 (Harrogate), A.W. Maxwell 1 (Headingley), D.A. Cooke 1 (Harlequins), D.J. Duckham 28 (Coventry); M.J. Cooper 5 (Moseley), M.S. Lampkowski 1 (Headingley); F.E. Cotton 11 (Sale), P.J. Wheeler 3 (Leicester), M.A. Burton 8 (Gloucester), W.B. Beaumont 2 (Fylde), R.M. Wilkinson 1 (Bedford), M. Keyworth 1

(Swansea), *A. Neary 21 (Broughton Park), A.G. Ripley 16 (Rosslyn Park).
Replacement P.S. Preece (8) (Coventry) for Squires

WALES   J.P.R. Williams 27 (London Welsh); T.G.R. Davies 28 (Cardiff), R.W.R. Gravell 5 (Llanelli), S.P. Fenwick 4 (Bridgend), J.J. Williams 10 (Llanelli); P. Bennett 15 (Llanelli), G.O. Edwards 34 (Cardiff); G. Price 5 (Pontypool), R.W. Windsor 9 (Pontypool), A.G. Faulkner 5 (Pontypool), A.J. Martin 7 (Aberavon), G.A.D. Wheel 6 (Swansea), T.P. Evans 5 (Swansea), T.J. Cobner 9 (Pontypool), *T.M. Davies 28 (Swansea).

Referee G. Domercq (France)

FRANCE v IRELAND   47/657

7 February 1976
Parc des Princes, Paris
France 26 (2G, 2T, 2PG) Ireland 3 (1PG)

France   T: Pecune, Cholley, Fouroux, Rives. C: Rives, Bastiat. PG: Romeu (2).
Ireland   PG: Robbie.

This was France's highest winning points margin against Ireland in a Championship match, and proved a severe test for an Irish team which contained five new caps. France were unstoppable as they mounted wave after wave of assaults on the Irish defences, with Rives and Bastiat in particularly majestic form.

FRANCE   M. Droitecourt 5 (AS Montferrand); J-F. Gourdon 7 (RCF), R. Bertranne 15 (S. Bagnères), J. Pecune 4 (S. Tarbes), J-L. Averous 3 (La Voulte S.); J-P. Romeu 10 (AS Montferrand), *J. Fouroux 5 (La Voulte S.); R. Paparemborde 2 (S. Pau), A. Paco 4 (AS Béziers), G. Cholley 5 (Castres Ol), M. Palmié 2 (AS Béziers), J-F. Imbernon 1 (US Perpignan), J-C. Skréla 13 (S. Toulouse), J-P. Rives 5 (S. Toulouse), J-P. Bastiat 10 (US Dax).

IRELAND   A.H. Ensor 11 (Wanderers); *T.O. Grace 12 (St Mary's College), J.A. McIlrath 1 (Ballymena), C.M.H. Gibson 45 (NIFC), A.W. McMaster 12 (Ballymena); B.J. McGann 18 (Cork Constitution), J.C. Robbie 1 (Dublin U.); P.A. Orr 1 (Old Wesley), J.L. Cantrell 1 (UC Dublin),

P. O'Callaghan 14 (Dolphin), M.I. Keane 9 (Lansdowne), B.O. Foley 1 (Shannon), S.A. McKinney 10 (Dungannon), S.M. Deering 2 (Garryowen), W.P. Duggan 5 (Blackrock College).

Referee A. Welsby (England)

SCOTLAND v WALES 80/658

7 February 1976
Cardiff Arms Park
Wales 28 (2G, 1T, 1DG, 3PG) Scotland 6 (1G)

Wales T: J.J. Williams, Evans, Edwards. C: Bennett (2). DG: Fenwick. PG. Bennett (3).
Scotland T: Irvine. C: Morgan.

Scotland had become accustomed to fearful beatings at Cardiff Arms Park and although this was in that category, the match contained very little to recommend it. The lasting memory was of some marvellous football by Gareth Edwards, which included an outrageous dummy, and brought Wales's final try. At this stage the referee, Dr Cluny, of France, was hobbling about the field suffering from a strained muscle. and yet he did not retire.

WALES J.P.R. Williams 28 (London Welsh); T.G.R. Davies 29 (Cardiff), R.W.R. Gravell 6 (Llanelli), S.P. Fenwick 5 (Bridgend), J.J. Williams 11 (Llanelli); P. Bennett 16 (Llanelli), G.O. Edwards 35 (Cardiff); G. Price 6 (Pontypool), R.W. Windsor 10 (Pontypool), A.G. Faulkner 6 (Pontypool), A.J. Martin 8 (Aberavon), G.A.D. Wheel 7 (Swansea), T.P. Evans 6 (Swansea), T.J. Cobner 10 (Pontypool), *T.M. Davies 29 (Swansea).

SCOTLAND A.R. Irvine 14 (Heriot's FP); W.C.C. Steele 17 (London Scottish), A.G. Cranston 1 (Hawick), J.M. Renwick 14 (Hawick), D. Shedden 5 (W. of Scotland); I.R. McGeechan 14 (Headingley), D.W. Morgan 11 (Stewart's FP); *J. McLauchlan 24 (Jordanhill), C.D. Fisher 1 (Waterloo), A.B. Carmichael 34 (W. of Scotland), A.F. McHarg 26 (London Scottish), G.L. Brown 22 (W. of Scotland), M.A. Biggar 5 (London Scottish), D.G. Leslie 6 (W. of Scotland), G.Y. Mackie 2 (Highland).

Referee Dr A. Cluny (France)

IRELAND v WALES 77/659

21 February 1976
Lansdowne Road, Dublin
Wales 34 (3G, 1T, 4PG) Ireland 9 (3PG)

Ireland PG: McGann (3).
Wales T: Gerald Davies (2), Edwards, Bennett. C: Bennett (3). PG: Bennett (3), Martin.

Only South Africa (38 points in 1912) and England (36 in 1938) have scored more points against Ireland, but the incredible factor in Wales's huge total was that 18 of the points came in a six-minute burst when the Irish were still very much in contention, 9-16. Chief destroyer of Irish hopes was Phil Bennett, often a mysteriously cautious figure on the international field, but at Lansdowne Road finally a figure of brilliant attacking flair. Bennett featured in 3 of the Welsh tries and by the end he had registered 19 points, to equal the Welsh Championship record of Jack Bancroft (v France 1910) and Keith Jarrett (v England 1967).

IRELAND A.H. Ensor 12 (Wanderers); *T.O. Grace 13 (St Mary's College), P.J. Lavery (2) (London Irish), C.M.H. Gibson 46 (NIFC), A.W. McMaster (13) (Ballymena); B.J. McGann 19 (Cork Constitution), D.M. Canniffe 1 (Lansdowne); P. O'Callaghan 15 (Dolphin), J.L. Cantrell 2 (UC Dublin), P.A. Orr 2 (Old Wesley), R.F. Hakin 1 (CIYMS), M.I. Keane 10 (Lansdowne), S.A. McKinney 11 (Dungannon), S.M. Deering 3 (Garryowen), W.P. Duggan 6 (Blackrock College).
Replacement L.A. Moloney 1 (Garryowen) for Ensor

WALES J.P.R. Williams 29 (London Welsh); T.G.R. Davies 30 (Cardiff), R.W.R. Gravell 7 (Llanelli), S.P. Fenwick 6 (Bridgend), J.J. Williams 12 (Llanelli); P. Bennett 17 (Llanelli), G.O. Edwards 36 (Cardiff); G. Price 7 (Pontypool), R.W. Windsor 11 (Pontypool), A.G. Faulkner 7 (Pontypool), G.A.D. Wheel 8 (Swansea), A.J. Martin 9 (Aberavon), T.P. Evans 7 (Swansea), T.P. David 2 (Pontypridd), *T.M. Davies 30 (Swansea).

Referee N.R. Sanson (Scotland)

SCOTLAND v ENGLAND   79/660

21 February 1976
Murrayfield
Scotland 22 (2G, 1T, 2PG) England 12 (1G, 2PG)

Scotland   T: Lawson (2), Leslie. C: Irvine (2).
PG: Irvine (2).
England   T: Maxwell. C: Old. PG: Old (2).

This defeat meant that England had won once only at Murrayfield in eight visits since 1960. It turned out to be the final Championship match for two of England's most respected players, David Duckham and Andy Ripley, and the only appearance for Derek Wyatt, who came on as a replacement for Duckham when the Coventry wing was injured. England may have had technically better No. 8s than Ripley but none stimulated spectators as much as the Rosslyn Park flier – very fast taking huge strides, with knees sometimes up to his chin. Mervyn Davies, the great Welsh No. 8, rated Ripley as one of the best he had played against, a compliment tempered by the added comment: 'certainly he was the most awkward to play against'. Ripley had many qualities, among which was a knack for the unexpected and unusual. A seemingly carefree approach tended to disguise the fact that he was committed, competitive and above all an instinctive player.

SCOTLAND   A.R. Irvine 15 (Heriot's FP); W.C.C. Steele 18 (London Scottish), A.G. Cranston 2 (Hawick), I.R. McGeechan 15 (Headingley), D. Shedden 6 (W. of Scotland); R. Wilson 1 (London Scottish), A.J.M. Lawson 6 (London Scottish); *J. McLauchlan 25 (Jordanhill), C.D. Fisher 2 (Waterloo), A.B. Carmichael 35 (W. of Scotland), A.J. Tomes 1 (Hawick), G.L. Brown 23 (W. of Scotland), M.A. Biggar 6 (London Scottish), D.G. Leslie 7 (W. of Scotland), A.F. McHarg 27 (London Scottish).
Replacement J.M. Renwick 15 (Hawick) for Shedden

ENGLAND   A.J. Hignell 2 (Cambridge U.); K.C. Plummer 2 (Bristol), A.W. Maxwell 2 (Headingley), D.A. Cooke 2 (Harlequins), D.J. Duckham (29) (Coventry); A.G.B. Old 10 (Middlesbrough), M.S. Lampkowski 2 (Headingley); F.E. Cotton 12 (Sale), P.J. Wheeler*4 (Leicester), M.A. Burton 9 (Gloucester), W.B. Beaumont 3 (Fylde),

R.M. Wilkinson 2 (Bedford), M. Keyworth 2 (Swansea), *A. Neary 22 (Broughton Park), A.G. Ripley (17) (Rosslyn Park).
Replacements D.M. Wyatt (1) (Bedford) for Duckham, W.N. Bennett 2 (Bedford) for Maxwell

Referee D.M. Lloyd (Wales)

ENGLAND v IRELAND   80/661

6 March 1976
Twickenham
Ireland 13 (1T, 1DG, 2PG) England 12 (4PG)

England   PG: Old (4).
Ireland   T: Grace. DG: McGann. PG: McGann (2).

Ireland scored their fifth win in succession over England, and their third in a row at Twickenham. The Irish have only once before run up three victories in succession in England, 1894–98.

ENGLAND   A.J. Hignell 3 (Cambridge U.); K.C. Plummer 3 (Bristol), A.W. Maxwell 3 (Headingley), D.A. Cooke 3 (Harlequins), M.A.C. Slemen 1 (Liverpool); A.G.B. Old 11 (Middlesbrough), M.S. Lampkowski (3) (Headingley); F.E. Cotton 13 (Sale), P.J. Wheeler 5 (Leicester), M.A. Burton 10 (Gloucester), W.B. Beaumont 4 (Fylde), R.M. Wilkinson 3 (Bedford), M. Keyworth (3) (Swansea), *A. Neary 23 (Broughton Park), G.J. Adey 1 (Leicester).
Replacement B.J. Corless 1 (Coventry) for Hignell

IRELAND   A.H. Ensor 13 (Lansdowne); *T.O. Grace 14 (St Mary's College), J.A. Brady 1 (Wanderers), C.M.H. Gibson 47 (NIFC), S.E.F. Blake-Knox 1 (NIFC); B.J. McGann 20 (Cork Constitution), D.M. Canniffe (2) (Lansdowne); P.A. Orr 3 (Old Wesley), J.L. Cantrell 3 (UC Dublin), P. O'Callaghan 16 (Dolphin), M.I. Keane 11 (Lansdowne), B.O. Foley 2 (Shannon), S.M. Deering 4 (Garryowen), S.A. McKinney 12 (Dungannon), H.W. Steele 1 (Ballymena).

Referee A.M. Hosie (Scotland)

Mervyn Davies ready to snap up a loose ball in the Wales–France match on 6 March 1976

WALES v FRANCE   47/662

6 March 1976
Cardiff Arms Park
Wales 19 (1T, 5PG) France 13 (1G, 1T, 1PG)

Wales　T: J.J. Williams. PG: Bennett (2), Fenwick (2), Martin.
France　T: Gourdon, Averous. C: Romeu. PG: Romeu.

This victory not only earned Wales the Grand Slam for a fifth time, but the 19 points they scored in this match brought their season's total to a record 102 points. The only drawback to all this was that it turned out to be Mervyn Davies's last international appearance. Just over three weeks later, Wales's captain collapsed during a Welsh Cup match between Swansea and Pontypool, suffering from a brain haemorrhage. Davies made a remarkable recovery but he never played again, and Wales lost one of their greatest forwards. He had played in 31 consecutive Championship matches and met no peer as a No. 8. His line-out possession, broken play roving and support, and often his tackling and covering, made him the lynch-pin of the Welsh pack.

WALES　J.P.R. Williams 30 (London Welsh); T.G.R. Davies 31 (Cardiff), R.W.R. Gravell 8 (Llanelli), S.P. Fenwick 7 (Bridgend), J.J. Williams 13 (Llanelli); P. Bennett 18 (Llanelli), G.O. Edwards 37 (Cardiff); G. Price 8 (Pontypool), R.W. Windsor 12 (Pontypool), A.G. Faulkner 8 (Pontypool), A.J. Martin 10 (Aberavon), G.A.D. Wheel 9 (Swansea), T.P. Evans 8 (Swansea), T.P. David (3) (Pontypridd), *T.M. Davies (31) (Swansea).
Replacement F.M.D. Knill (1) (Cardiff) for Price

FRANCE   M. Droitecourt (6) (AS Montferrand); J-F. Gourdon 8 (RCF), R. Bertranne 16 (A. Bagnères), J. Pecune 5 (S. Tarbes), J-L. Averous 4 (La Voulte S.); J-P. Romeu 11 (AS Montferrand), *J. Fouroux 6 (La Voulte S.); R. Paparemborde 3 (S. Pau), A. Paco 5 (AS Béziers), G. Cholley 6 (Castres Ol), J-F. Imbernon 2 (US Perpignan), M. Palmié 3 (AS Béziers), J-C. Skréla 14 (S. Toulouse), J-P. Rives 6 (S. Toulouse), J-P. Bastiat 11 (US Dax).
Replacement J-M. Aguirre 6 (A. Bagnerès) for Droitecourt

Referee J.R. West (Ireland)

FRANCE v ENGLAND   47/663

20 March 1976
Parc des Princes, Paris
France 30 (2G, 3T) England 9 (1G, 1PG)

France   T: Paparemborde (2), Bastiat, Fouroux, Gourdon, Romeu. C: Romeu (3).
England   T: Dixon. C: Butler PG: Butler.

France enjoyed a scoring spree when England played in Paris – this was the third time in their last four visits that they scored a record six tries against them. Thus England finished the season with four defeats, a humiliation they had suffered only once previously, in 1972. Seven of the team never played in the Championship again, including the long-serving John Pullin. He first played for England in 1966, against Wales, and altogether made 42 appearances, 33 in the Championship, which made him his country's most capped hooker.

FRANCE   J-M. Aguirre 7 (S. Bagnères); J-F. Gourdon 9 (RCF), R. Bertranne 17 (S. Bagnères), J. Pecune (6) (S. Tarbes), J-L. Averous 5 (La Voulte S.); J-P. Romeu 12 (AS Montferrand), *J. Fouroux 7 (La Voulte S.); G. Cholley 7 (Castres Ol), A. Paco 6 (AS Béziers), R. Paparemborde 4 (S. Pau), J-F. Imbernon 3 (US Perpignan), M. Palmié 4 (AS Béziers), J-P. Rives 7 (S. Toulouse), J-C. Skréla 15 (S. Toulouse), J-P. Bastiat 12 (US Dax).

ENGLAND   P.E. Butler (1) (Gloucester); K.C. Plummer (4) (Bristol), A.W. Maxwell 4 (Headingley), D.A. Cooke (4) (Harlequins), M.A.C. Slemen 2 (Liverpool); C.G. Williams (1) (Glou-cester), S.J. Smith 7 (Sale); F.E. Cotton 14 (Sale), J.V. Pullin (33) (Bristol), M.A. Burton 11 (Glou-cester), W.B. Beaumont 5 (Fylde), R.M. Wilkinson (4) (Bedford), P.J. Dixon 13 (Gosforth), *A. Neary 24 (Broughton Park), G.J. Adey (2) (Leicester).

Referee K.H. Clark (Ireland)

IRELAND v SCOTLAND   81/664

20 March 1976
Lansdowne Road, Dublin
Scotland 15 (1DG, 4PG) Ireland 6 (2PG)

Ireland   PG: McGann (2).
Scotland   DG: Wilson. PG: Irvine (4).

Andy Irvine had the dubious distinction of kicking the highest number of penalty goals for Scotland in any match against Ireland. The feat, however, enabled the Scots to win at Lansdowne Road for the first time in ten years. It was to be the final Championship match for two senior players, Ireland's Barry McGann and Scotland's Gordon Brown.

IRELAND   L.A. Moloney 2 (Garryowen); *T.O. Grace 15 (St Mary's College), J.A. Brady (2) (Wanderers), C.M.H. Gibson 48 (NIFC), S.E.F. Blake-Knox 2 (NIFC); B.J. McGann (21) (Cork Constitution), J.J. Moloney 15 (St Mary's College); P.A. Orr 4 (Old Wesley), J. Cantrell 4 (UC Dublin), P. O'Callaghan (17) (Dolphin), M.I. Keane 12 (Lansdowne), R.F. Hakin 2 (CIYMS), S.M. Deering 5 (Garryowen), S.A. McKinney 13 (Dungannon), W.P. Duggan 7 (Blackrock College).
Replacement C.H. McKibbin (1) (Instonians) for Gibson

SCOTLAND   A.R. Irvine 16 (Heriot's FP); W.C.C. Steele 19 (London Scottish), A.G. Cranston 3 (Hawick), I.R. McGeechan 16 (Headingley), D. Shedden 7 (W. of Scotland); R. Wilson 2 (London Scottish), A.J.M. Lawson 7 (London Scottish); *J. McLauchlan 26 (Jordanhill), C.D. Fisher (3) (Waterloo), A.B. Carmichael 36 (W. of Scotland), A.J. Tomes 2 (Hawick), G.L. Brown (24) (W. of Scotland), M.A. Biggar 7 (London Scottish), D.G. Leslie 8 (W. of Scotland), A.F. McHarg 28 (London Scottish).
Referee M.S. Lewis (Wales)

1977

TWICKENHAM England beat Scotland 26-6 · CARDIFF Wales beat Ireland 25-9
DUBLIN England beat Ireland 4-0 · PARIS France beat Wales 16-9
TWICKENHAM France beat England 4-3 · MURRAYFIELD Scotland beat Ireland 21-18
PARIS France beat Scotland 23-3 · CARDIFF Wales beat England 14-9
DUBLIN France beat Ireland 15-6 · MURRAYFIELD Wales beat Scotland 18-9

CHAMPIONSHIP TABLE
France – Championship, Grand Slam
Wales – Triple Crown

| | | | | | | | | | Tries | |
Pos	Country	P	W	D	L	F	A	Pts	F	A
1	France (2)	4	4	0	0	58	21	8	8	0
2	Wales (1)	4	3	0	1	66	43	6	7	3
3	England (5)	4	2	0	2	42	24	4	5	3
4	Scotland (3)	4	1	0	3	39	85	2	4	11
5	Ireland (4)	4	0	0	4	33	65	0	1	8

France bludgeoned everyone aside with their massive pack to take the Championship, and it was of no matter to them that they won all four matches by scoring a paltry 58 points, 8 fewer than Wales, who were runners-up. The season was unique in that while the French won the Grand Slam, Wales also won the Triple Crown. The least coveted trophy, the Wooden Spoon, went to Ireland, who lost all four matches for a third time (the other two occasions were in 1920 and 1960) and they managed one try only.

One of England's two victories was a 26–6 triumph over Scotland, which was their biggest winning margin against their old rivals. Scotland also lost 3-23 to France, which was France's highest score and biggest winning margin against the Scots. The Scotish referee Norman Sanson, was at the centre of the season's most controversial incident, when he sent off Willie Duggan and Geoff Wheel after a fracas in the Wales v Ireland match at Cardiff.

On a less contentious note, Mike Gibson made his fiftieth Championship appearance for Ireland, against England at Lansdowne Road, a milestone not only in this great player's career, but in the Championship for only one other player, Gibson's fellow countryman, Willie John McBride, had reached and passed a half-century of Championship appearances.

ENGLAND v SCOTLAND 80/665

15 January 1977
Twickenham
England 26 (2G, 2T, 2PG) Scotland 6 (2PG)

England T: Kent, Slemen, Uttley, Young C: Hignell (2). PG: Hignell (2).
Scotland PG: Irvine (2).

The 20 points between the teams represented England's biggest margin of victory against Scotland, home or away. It could have been even larger for the Scottish pack were completely outplayed, and Alistair Hignell missed three, reasonably easy, placed kicks. The critics raved about this new England: greatly over-estimating England's chances of going on to win the title, thereby erasing the memories of three Wooden Spoons running. Alas, for writers and England alike, much more serious opposition than Scotland was to come, and some of the flaws not immediately apparent in this pot-boiler were exposed.

ENGLAND A.J. Hignell 4 (Bristol); P.J. Squires 12 (Harrogate), B.J. Corless 2 (Moseley), C.P. Kent 1 (Rosslyn Park), M.A.C. Slemen 3 (Liverpool); M.J. Cooper 6 (Moseley), M. Young 1 (Gosforth); R.J. Cowling 1 (Leicester), P.J. Wheeler 6 (Leicester), F.E. Cotton 15 (Sale), W.B. Beaumont 6 (Fylde), N.E. Horton 10 (Moseley), P.J. Dixon 14 (Gosforth), M. Rafter 1 (Bristol), *R.M. Uttley 10 (Gosforth).

SCOTLAND   A.R. Irvine 17 (Heriot's FP); W.C.C. Steele (20) (London Scottish), *I.R. McGeechan 17 (Headingley), A.G. Cranston 4 (Hawick), L.G. Dick (12) (Swansea); R. Wilson 3 (London Scottish), A.J.M. Lawson 8 (London Scottish); J. Aitken 1 (Gala), D.F. Madsen 10 (Gosforth), A.B. Carmichael 37 (W. of Scotland), A.J. Tomes 3 (Hawick), A.F. McHarg 29 (London Scottish), W. Lauder (14) (Neath), A.K. Brewster 1 (Stewart's FP), D.S.M. Macdonald 1 (Oxford U.).

Referee M. Joseph (Wales)

WALES v IRELAND   78/666

15 January 1977
Cardiff Arms Park
Wales 25 (2G, 1T, 1DG, 2PG) Ireland 9 (3PG)

Wales   T: Davies, J.P.R. Williams, Burgess. C: Bennett (2). DG: Fenwick. PG: Bennett (2).
Ireland   PG: Gibson (3).

Ireland were leading 6-0 when an exchange of punches, none of which seemed to carry much authority, led to Willie Duggan and Geoff Wheel being sent off in the thirty-eighth minute. The joint dismissal by Norman Sanson was the first ever at Cardiff, and was part of new 'get tough' policy adopted by the Four Home Unions rather than any great thuggery. Both Duggan and Wheel had committed far more reprehensible offences in their careers and this was little more than an altercation of tea-party proportions. But Sanson would not tolerate foul play in any degree and all players knew well their fate if they were spotted by the no-nonsense Scottish referee. To suggest the sendings-off affected the course of the match, as some observers did, was pure conjecture. Ireland lost their early control and Wales finished well. Neither side sorely missed their culprits.

WALES   J.P.R. Williams 31 (Bridgend); T.G.R. Davies 32 (Cardiff), S.P. Fenwick 8 (Bridgend), D.H. Burcher 1 (Newport), J.J. Williams 14 (Llanelli); *P. Bennett 19 (Llanelli), G.O. Edwards 38 (Cardiff); G. Shaw 9 (Neath), R.W. Windsor 13 (Pontypool), G. Price 9 (Pontypool), A.J. Martin 11 (Aberavon), G.A.D. Wheel 10 (Swansea), T.P. Evans (9) (Swansea), J. Squire 1 (Newport), R.C. Burgess 1 (Ebbw Vale).
Replacement D.L. Quinnell 7 (Llanelli) for Evans

Welsh team physiotherapist Gerry Lewis accompanies Geoff Wheel from the field during the Wales-Ireland match on 15 January 1977

IRELAND   F. Wilson 1 (CIYMS); *T.O. Grace 16 (St Mary's College), A.R. McKibbin 1 (Instonians), J.A. McIlrath 2 (Ballymena), D.St J. Bowen 1 (Cork Constitution); C.M.H. Gibson 49 (NIFC), R.J.M. McGrath 1 (Wanderers); P.A. Orr 5 (Old Wesley), P.C. Whelan 3 (Garryowen), T.A.O. Feighery 1 (St Mary's College), M.I. Keane 13 (Lansdowne), R.F. Hakin 3 (CIYMS), S.A. McKinney 14 (Dungannon), S.M. Deering 6 (Garryowen), W.P. Duggan 8 (Blackrock College).
Replacement B.O. Foley 3 (Shannon) for Hakin

Referee N.R. Sanson (Scotland)

FRANCE v WALES 48/667

5 February 1977
Parc des Princes, Paris
France 16 (1G, 1T, 2PG) Wales 9 (3PG)

France T: Skréla, Harize. C: Romeu. PG: Romeu (2).
Wales PG: Fenwick (3).

Wales failed in two crucial respects: their scrummaging and not obtaining a fair proportion of line-out ball. Added to this handicap, the loss of a player of Gerald Davies's match-winning capability through injury in the second half, presented them as ready prey for the French wolves. Strangely the French took a long time in devouring the meal, and this was in some measure due to some excellent tackling and defending by Steve Fenwick and J.P.R. Williams.

FRANCE J-M. Aguirre 8 (S. Bagnères); D. Harize 1 (S. Toulouse), R. Bertranne 18 (S. Bagnères), F. Sangali 3 (RC Narbonne), J-L. Averous 6 (La Voulte S.); J-P. Romeu 13 (AS Montferrand), *J. Fouroux 8 (FC Auch); R. Paparemborde 5 (S. Pau), A. Paco 7 (AS Béziers), G. Cholley 8 (Castres Ol), M. Palmié 5 (AS Béziers), J-F. Imbernon 4 (US Perpignan), J-C. Skréla 16 (S. Toulouse), J-P. Rives 8 (S. Toulouse), J-P. Bastiat 13 (US Dax).

WALES J.P.R. Williams 32 (Bridgend); T.G.R. Davies 33 (Cardiff), S.P. Fenwick 9 (Bridgend), D.H. Burcher 2 (Newport), J.J. Williams 15 (Llanelli); *P. Bennett 20 (Llanelli), G.O. Edwards 39 (Cardiff); G. Shaw (10) (Neath), R.W. Windsor 14 (Pontypool), G. Price 10 (Pontypool), A.J. Martin 12 (Aberavon), D.L. Quinnell 8 (Llanelli), T.J. Cobner 11 (Pontypool), J. Squire 2 (Pontypool), R.C. Burgess 2 (Ebbw Vale).
Replacement G.L. Evans 1 (Newport) for Davies

Referee A.M. Hosie (Scotland)

IRELAND v ENGLAND 81/668

5 February 1977
Lansdowne Road, Dublin
England 4 (1T) Ireland 0

England T: Cooper.

Mike Gibson, the 'Mr Versatile' of Irish rugby, made his fiftieth Championship appearance, to join that elite club inaugurated by another Irishman, Willie John McBride, also against England on their previous visit to Lansdowne Road, in 1975.

IRELAND F. Wilson 2 (CIYMS); *T.O. Grace 17 (St Mary's College), A.R. McKibbin 2 (Instonians), J.A. McIlrath (3) (Ballymena), D.St J. Bowen 2 (Cork Constitution); C.M.H. Gibson 50 (NIFC), R.J.M. McGrath 2 (Wanderers); P.A. Orr 6 (Old Wesley), P.C. Whelan 4 (Garryowen), T.A.O. Feighery (2) (St Mary's College), M.I. Keane 14 (Lansdowne), R.F. Hakin 4 (CIYMS), S.A. McKinney 15 (Dungannon), S.M. Deering (7) (Garryowen), W.P. Duggan 9 (Blackrock College).

ENGLAND A.J. Hignell 5 (Bristol); P.J. Squires 13 (Harrogate), B.J. Corless 3 (Moseley), C.P. Kent 2 (Rosslyn Park), M.A.C. Slemen 4 (Liverpool); M.J. Cooper 7 (Moseley), M. Young 2 (Gosforth); R.J. Cowling 2 (Leicester), P.J. Wheeler 7 (Leicester), F.E. Cotton 16 (Sale), W.B. Beaumont 7 (Fylde), N.E. Horton 11 (Moseley), P.J. Dixon 15 (Gosforth), A. Neary 25 (Broughton Park), *R.M. Uttley 11 (Gosforth).

Referee F. Palmade (France)

ENGLAND v FRANCE 48/669

19 February 1977
Twickenham
France 4 (1T) England 3 (1PG)

England PG: Hignell.
France T: Sangali.

Notwithstanding five penalty goal misses by Alistair Hignell, England should have beaten France comfortably. At least three try chances were wasted, and as France went on to win the Grand Slam, an award of the Legion d'honneur to one particular English player would not have been undeserved.

ENGLAND   A.J. Hignell 6 (Bristol); P.J. Squires 14 (Harrogate), B.J. Corless 4 (Moseley), C.P. Kent 3 (Rosslyn Park), M.A.C. Slemen 5 (Liverpool); M.J. Cooper 8 (Moseley), M. Young 3 (Gosforth); R.J. Cowling 3 (Leicester), P.J. Wheeler 8 (Leicester), F.E. Cotton 17 (Sale), W.B. Beaumont 8 (Fylde), N.E. Horton 12 (Moseley), P.J. Dixon 16 (Gosforth), M. Rafter 2 (Bristol), *R.M. Uttley 12 (Gosforth).
Replacement S.J. Smith 8 (Sale) for Young

FRANCE   J-M. Aguirre 9 (S. Bagnères); D. Harize 2 (S. Toulouse), R. Bertranne 19 (S. Bagnères), F. Sangali 4 (RC Narbonne), J-L. Averous 7 (La Voulte S.); J-P. Romeu 14 (AS Montferrand), *J. Fouroux 9 (FC Auch); G. Cholley 9 (Castres Ol), A. Paco 8 (AS Béziers), R. Paparemborde 6 (S. Pau), J-F. Imbernon 5 (US Perpignan), M. Palmié 6 (AS Béziers), J-P. Rives 9 (S. Toulouse), J-C. Skréla 17 (S. Toulouse), J-P. Bastiat 14 (US Dax).

Referee J.C. Kelleher (Wales)

SCOTLAND v IRELAND 82/670

19 February 1977
Murrayfield
Scotland 21 (3T, 1DG, 2PG) Ireland 18 (1G, 1DG, 3PG)

Scotland T: Gammell (2), Madsen. DG: Morgan. PG: Irvine (2).
Ireland T: Gibson. C: Gibson. DG: Quinn. PG: Gibson (2), Quinn.

Both sides came to this match having lost their opening matches, but they produced a fine, fluent encounter. Scotland had the edge throughout, with McGeechan and Renwick eager to demonstrate their running skill. Sandy Carmichael had been dropped in favour of Pender, but the veteran played after all when Pender had to retire with damaged ribs.

SCOTLAND   A.R. Irvine 18 (Heriot's FP); W.B.B. Gammell 1 (Edinburgh Wands), *I.R. McGeechan 18 (Headingley), J.M. Renwick 16 (Hawick), D. Shedden 8 (W. of Scotland); R. Wilson 4 (London Scottish), D.W. Morgan 12 (Stewart's FP); J. Aitken 2 (Gala), D.F. Madsen 11 (Gosforth), N.E.K. Pender 1 (Hawick), I.A. Barnes 4 (Hawick), A.F. McHarg 30 (London Scottish), M.A. Biggar 8 (London Scottish), W.S. Watson 5 (Boroughmuir), D.S.M. Macdonald 2 (London Scottish).
Replacement A.B. Carmichael 38 (W. of Scotland) for Pender

IRELAND   F. Wilson (3) (CIYMS); *T.O. Grace 18 (St Mary's College), A.R. McKibbin 3 (Instonians), C.M.H. Gibson 51 (NIFC), D.St J. Bowen (3) (Cork Constitution); M.A.M. Quinn 6 (Lansdowne), J.C. Robbie 2 (Dublin U.); P.A. Orr 7 (Old Wesley), P.C. Whelan 5 (Garryowen), E.M.J. Byrne 1 (Blackrock College), M.I. Keane 15 (Lansdowne), C.W. Murtagh (1) (Portadown), S.A. McKinney 16 (Dungannon), J.F. Slattery 23 (Blackrock College), W.P. Duggan 10 (Blackrock College).

Referee M. Joseph (Wales)

FRANCE v SCOTLAND   47/671

5 March 1977
Parc des Princes, Paris
France 23 (2G, 2T, 1PG) Scotland 3 (1PG)

France T: Paco, Harize, Bertranne, Paparemborde. C: Romeu (2). PG: Romeu.
Scotland PG: Irvine.

This was France's biggest score and widest winning margin in all matches against Scotland. It was a thoroughly disappointing performance from a side which had played well in their previous match against Ireland. The French, in contrast, played some beautiful rugby and two of their tries came from their front-row players, Paco and Paparemborde. As if not to be left out, the other member of the front row, Cholley, set about making his presence felt in other ways and among several misdemeanours was the flooring of Donald Macdonald with a punch.

FRANCE   J-M. Aguirre 10 (S. Bagnères); D. Harize 3 (S. Toulouse), R. Bertranne 20 (S. Bagnères), F. Sangali 5 (RC Narbonne), J-L. Averous 8 (La Voulte S.); J.P. Romeu 15 (AS Montferrand), *J. Fouroux 10 (FC Auch); G. Cholley 10 (Castres Ol), A. Paco 9 (AS Béziers), R. Paparemborde 7 (S. Pau), M. Palmié 7 (AS Béziers), J-F. Imbernon 6 (US Perpignan), J-P. Rives 10 (S. Toulouse), J-C. Skréla 18 (S. Toulouse), J-P. Bastiat 15 (US Dax).

SCOTLAND   A.R. Irvine 19 (Heriot's FP); W.B.B. Gammell 2 (Edinburgh Wands), *I.R. McGeechan 19 (Headingley), J.M. Renwick 17 (Hawick), D. Shedden 9 (W. of Scotland); R. Wilson 5 (London Scottish), D.W. Morgan 13 (Stewart's FP); J. Aitken 3 (Gala), D.F. Madsen 12 (Gosforth), A.B. Carmichael 39 (W. of Scotland), I.A. Barnes 5 (Hawick), A.F. McHarg 31 (London Scottish), M.A. Biggar 9 (London Scottish), W.S. Watson 6 (Boroughmuir), D.S.M. Macdonald 3 (London Scottish).

Referee M. Joseph (Wales)

WALES v ENGLAND   81/672

5 March 1977
Cardiff Arms Park
Wales 14 (2T, 2PG) England 9 (3PG)

Wales T: Edwards, J.P.R. Williams. PG: Fenwick (2).
England PG: Hignell (3).

The Triple Crown was the glittering prize for England if they won this match. As so often in the past their hopes foundered on the failure of their forwards to master their Welsh counterparts. This was a very good English pack. But the Welsh forwards had that added extra, hwyl as they call it, and it proved crucial for it allowed Gareth Edwards to control the game with masterful ease. A Welsh victory over England would not have been complete without a try by J.P.R. Williams. And he scored one, his fifth against the English.

WALES   J.P.R. Williams 33 (Bridgend); T.G.R. Davies 34 (Cardiff), S.P. Fenwick 10 (Bridgend), D.H. Burcher 3 (Newport), J.J. Williams 16 (Llanelli); *P. Bennett 21 (Llanelli), G.O. Edwards 40 (Cardiff); C. Williams 1 (Aberavon), R.W. Windsor 15 (Pontypool), G. Price 11 (Pontypool), A.J. Martin 13 (Aberavon), G.A.D. Wheel 11 (Swansea), R.C. Burgess 3 (Ebbw Vale), T.J. Cobner 12 (Pontypool), D.L. Quinnell 9 (Llanelli).

ENGLAND   A.J. Hignell 7 (Bristol); P.J. Squires 15 (Harrogate), B.J. Corless 5 (Moseley), C.P. Kent 4 (Rosslyn Park), M.A.C. Slemen 6 (Liverpool); M.J. Cooper (9) (Moseley), M. Young 4 (Gosforth); R.J. Cowling 4 (Leicester), P.J. Wheeler 9 (Leicester), F.E. Cotton 18 (Sale), W.B. Beaumont 9 (Fylde), N.E. Horton 13 (Moseley), P.J. Dixon 17 (Gosforth), M. Rafter 3 (Bristol), *R.M. Uttley 13 (Gosforth).

Referee D.I.H. Burnett (Ireland)

IRELAND v FRANCE   48/673

19 March 1977
Lansdowne Road, Dublin
France 15 (1G, 3PG) Ireland 6 (2PG)

Ireland   PG: Gibson, Quinn.
France   T: Bastiat. C: Aguirre. PG: Aguirre (2), Romeu.

This was the last Championship match for Jacques Fouroux and Jean-Pierre Romeu, arguably the best half-back pairing in the history of French rugby. Each was a brilliant individual player but they developed an almost telepathic understanding, occasionally delighting French crowds with scissors and switch moves. It was appropriate that they should have been paired in a victory which earned France the Grand Slam for a second time.

IRELAND   A.H. Ensor 14 (Wanderers); *T.O. Grace 19 (St Mary's College), R. Finn (1) (UC Dublin), C.M.H. Gibson 52 (NIFC), A.C. McLennan 1 (Wanderers); M.A.M. Quinn (7) (Lansdowne), J.C. Robbie 3 (Dublin U.); P.A. Orr 8 (Old Wesley), P.C. Whelan 6 (Garryowen), E.M.J. Byrne 2 (Blackrock College), M.I. Keane 16 (Lansdowne), R.F. Hakin (5) (CIYMS), W.P. Duggan 11 (Lansdowne), J.F. Slattery 24 (Blackrock College), H.W. Steele 2 (Ballymena).
Replacements S.E.F. Blake-Knox (3) (NIFC) for Grace, R.J.M. McGrath 3 (Wanderers) for Robbie

FRANCE   J-M. Aguirre 11 (S. Bagnères); D. Harize (4) (S. Toulouse), R. Bertranne 21 (S. Bagnères), F. Sangali (6) (RC Narbonne), J-L. Averous 9 (La Voulte S.); J-P. Romeu (16) (AS Montferrand), *J. Fouroux (11) (FC Auch); R. Paparemborde 8 (S. Pau), A. Paco 10 (AS Béziers), G. Cholley 11 (Castres Ol), J-F. Imbernon 7 (US Perpignan), M. Palmié 8 (AS Béziers), J-C. Skréla 19 (S. Toulouse), J-P. Rives 11 (S. Toulouse), J-P. Bastiat 16 (US Dax).

Referee A.M. Hosie (Scotland)

SCOTLAND v WALES   81/674

19 March 1977
Murrayfield
Wales 18 (2G, 2PG) Scotland 9 (1G, 1DG)

Scotland   T: Irvine. C: Irvine. DG: McGeechan.
Wales   T: J.J. Williams, Bennett. C: Bennett (2). PG: Bennett (2).

This was a much better Scotland side than the scoreline suggested, for they gave the Welsh a torrid time at scrummage, line-out and loose. They also produced a splendid try, by Andy Irvine. But the experience and counter-attacking ability of Wales, plus the incentive of winning the Triple Crown, tipped the balance.

SCOTLAND   A.R. Irvine 20 (Heriot's FP); W.B.B. Gammell 3 (Edinburgh Wands), J.M. Renwick 18 (Hawick), A.G. Cranston 5 (Hawick), D. Shedden 10 (W. of Scotland); *I.R. McGeechan 20 (Headingley), D.W. Morgan 14 (Stewart's FP); J. McLauchlan 27 (Jordanhill), D.F. Madsen 13 (Gosforth), A.B. Carmichael 40 (W. of Scotland), I.A. Barnes (6) (Hawick), A.F. McHarg 32 (London Scottish), M.A. Biggar 10 (London Scottish), W.S. Watson 7 (Boroughmuir), D.S.M. Macdonald 4 (London Scottish).

WALES   J.P.R. Williams 34 (Bridgend); T.G.R. Davies 35 (Cardiff), S.P. Fenwick 11 (Bridgend), D.H. Burcher (4) (Newport), J.J. Williams 17 (Llanelli); *P. Bennett 22 (Llanelli), G.O. Edwards 41 (Cardiff); C. Williams 2 (Aberavon), R.W. Windsor 16 (Pontypool), G. Price 12 (Pontypool), A.J. Martin 14 (Aberavon), G.A.D. Wheel 12 (Swansea), R.C. Burgess 4 (Ebbw Vale), T.J. Cobner 13 (Pontypool), D.L. Quinnell 10 (Llanelli).

Referee G. Domercq (France)

1978

PARIS France beat England 15-6 · DUBLIN Ireland beat Scotland 12-9
TWICKENHAM Wales beat England 9-6 · MURRAYFIELD France beat Scotland 19-16
PARIS France beat Ireland 10-9 · CARDIFF Wales beat Scotland 22-14
MURRAYFIELD England beat Scotland 15-0 · DUBLIN Wales beat Ireland 20-16
TWICKENHAM England beat Ireland 15-9 · CARDIFF Wales beat France 16-7

CHAMPIONSHIP TABLE
Wales – Championship, Triple Crown, Grand Slam

| | | | | | | | | | Tries | |
Pos	Country	P	W	D	L	F	A	Pts	F	A
1	Wales (2)	4	4	0	0	67	43	8	8	4
2	France (1)	4	3	0	1	51	47	6	6	4
3	England (3)	4	2	0	2	42	33	4	4	2
4	Ireland (5)	4	1	0	3	46	54	2	2	5
5	Scotland (4)	4	0	0	4	39	68	0	4	9

This was a very important year for France in that they were admitted into full membership of the International Board, the Lawmakers and governors of the game. As if in celebration the French, with a team much changed from that which won the Grand Slam in 1977, charged through their first three matches to establish a run of eight consecutive wins in the Championship, a sequence unique in their history. Their stumbling-block was at Cardiff where Wales, having already won the Triple Crown, were themselves bidding for the Grand Slam. Phil Bennett achieved what few Welsh fly-halves had – scoring two tries – and Wales won, a victory which proved to be not only Bennett's farewell appearance but Gareth Edwards's also. Both these talented players certainly bowed out while at the top; it was not only a Grand Slam, but Wales's Triple Crown was their third in a row, a feat which no other country had achieved.

Two famed and talented French forwards also played their last internationals: Jean-Claude Skréla and Jean-Pierre Bastiat. The Championship had rarely been without a player or a captain prepared to risk all – on this occasion it was Scotland's Doug Morgan who adhered to

tradition when he opted to go for a match-winning try at Lansdowne Road via a short penalty rather than take a simple penalty goal which would have drawn the match. One of England's two defeats was in Paris, which meant that they had endured seven matches there without victory, their longest sequence. It was a good season, however, for Ireland's Tony Ward. He equalled the Championship best for an individual with 38 points.

FRANCE v ENGLAND 49/675

21 January 1978
Parc des Princes, Paris
France 15 (2G, 1PG) England 6 (2DG)

France T: Averous, Gallion. C: Aguirre (2). PG: Aguirre.
England DG: Old (2).

The defeat meant that England had now endured seven matches without a win in France, the longest such spell of the fixture. It was also France's fourth successive victory over England, which had not occurred before. It provided further evidence of the seemingly endless production line of top-class backs which France enjoyed: Gallion and Viviès, the new half-backs, played as if they had performed at this level for years and Belascain, in the centre, made the much more experienced English centres look second-rate, which they were not. As on so many occasions, however, the master craftsman, was the inimitable Roland Bertranne, whose probes, thrusts and quick, incisive passing put him in a class of his own.

FRANCE   J-M. Aguirre 12 (S. Bagnères); J-F. Gourdon 10 (S. Bagnères), R. Bertranne 22 (S. Bagnères), C. Belascain 1 (A. Bayonne), J-L. Averous 10 (La Voulte S.); B. Viviès 1 (SU Agen), J. Gallion 1 (RC Toulon); G. Cholley 12 (Castres Ol), A. Paco 11 (AS Béziers), R. Paparemborde 9 (S. Pau), J.-F. Imbernon 8 (US Perpignan), M. Palmié 9 (AS Béziers), J-P. Rives 12 (S. Toulouse), J-C. Skréla 20 (S. Toulouse), *J-P. Bastiat 17 (US Dax).

ENGLAND   W.H. Hare 2 (Leicester); P.J. Squires 16 (Harrogate), B.J. Corless 6 (Moseley), A.W. Maxwell (5) (Headingley), M.A.C. Slemen 7 (Liverpool); A.G.B. Old (12) (Sheffield), M. Young 5 (Gosforth); R.J. Cowling 5 (Leicester), P.J. Wheeler 10 (Leicester), M.A. Burton 12 (Gloucester), *W.B. Beaumont 10 (Fylde), N.E. Horton 14 (S. Toulouse), P.J. Dixon 18 (Gosforth), M. Rafter 4 (Bristol), J.P. Scott 1 (Rosslyn Park).
Replacements C.P. Kent (5) (Rosslyn Park) for Maxwell, A. Neary 26 (Broughton Park) for Dixon

Referee N.R. Sanson (Scotland)

IRELAND v SCOTLAND   83/676

21 January 1978
Lansdowne Road, Dublin
Ireland 12 (1G, 2PG) Scotland 9 (3PG)

Ireland   T: McKinney. C: Ward. PG: Ward (2).
Scotland   PG: Morgan (3).

Scotland had a chance of drawing this match in injury-time when they were awarded a straight-forward penalty kick. Doug Morgan, in his first match as captain, controversially decided that a short penalty move which might produce a match-winning try was a gamble worth taking. In the event Ireland scrambled the ball to safety, just before the final whistle. Morgan retained the captaincy for the next three matches but he was not selected again after Scotland lost all of them.

IRELAND   A.H. Ensor 15 (Wanderers); T.O. Grace (20) (St Mary's College), A.R. McKibbin 4 (London Irish), P.P. McNaughton 1 (Greystones), A.C. McLennan 2 (Wanderers); A.J.P. Ward 1 (Garryowen), *J.J. Moloney 16 (St Mary's College); P.A. Orr 9 (Old Wesley), P.C. Whelan 7 (Garryowen), M.P. Fitzpatrick 1 (Wanderers), M.I. Keane 17 (Lansdowne), D.E. Spring 1 (Dublin U.), J.B. O'Driscoll 1 (London Irish), J.F. Slattery 25 (Blackrock College), W.P. Duggan 12 (Blackrock College).
Replacements S.A. McKinney 17 (Dungannon) for O'Driscoll, L.A. Maloney (3) (Garryowen) for Ensor

SCOTLAND   B.H. Hay 2 (Boroughmuir); A.R. Irvine 21 (Heriot's FP), J.M. Renwick 19 (Hawick), I.R. McGeechan 21 (Headingley), D. Shedden 11 (W. of Scotland); R. Wilson 6 (London Scottish), *D.W. Morgan 15 (Stewart's FP); J. McLauchlan 28 (Jordanhill), D.F. Madsen (14) (Gosforth), A.B. Carmichael (41) (W. of Scotland), A.J. Tomes 4 (Hawick), A.F. McHarg 33 (London Scottish), M.A. Biggar 11 (London Scottish), C.B. Hegarty 1 (Hawick), D.S.M. Macdonald 5 (W. of Scotland).

Referee P.E. Hughes (England)

ENGLAND v WALES   82/677

4 February 1978
Twickenham
Wales 9 (3PG) England 6 (2PG)

England   PG: Hignell (2).
Wales   PG: Bennett (3).

Celebration of Wales's fourth win in five visits to Twickenham was curbed in that it was the only time in 21 matches 1963–83 that they failed to score a try against England.

ENGLAND   A.J. Hignell 8 (Bristol); P.J. Squires 17 (Harrogate), B.J. Corless 7 (Moseley), P.W. Dodge 1 (Leicester), M.A.C. Slemen 8 (Liverpool); J.P. Horton 1 (Bath), M. Young 6 (Gosforth); B.G. Nelmes 1 (Cardiff), P.J. Wheeler 11 (Leicester), M.A. Burton (13) (Gloucester), *W.B. Beaumont 11 (Fylde), N.E. Horton 15 (S. Toulouse), R.J. Mordell (1) (Rosslyn Park), M. Rafter 5 (Bristol), J.P. Scott 2 (Rosslyn Park).

WALES   J.P.R. Williams 35 (Bridgend); T.G.R. Davies 36 (Cardiff), R.W.R. Gravell 9 (Llanelli), S.P. Fenwick 12 (Bridgend), J.J. Williams 18 (Llanelli); *P. Bennett 23 (Llanelli), G.O. Edwards 42 (Cardiff); G. Price 13 (Pontypool), R.W. Windsor 17 (Pontypool), A.G. Faulkner 9

(Pontypool), A.J. Martin 15 (Aberavon), G.A.D. Wheel 13 (Swansea), J. Squire 3 (Newport), T.J. Cobner 14 (Pontypool), D.L. Quinnell 11 (Llanelli).

Referee N.R. Sanson (Scotland)

SCOTLAND v FRANCE   48/678

4 February 1978
Murrayfield
France 19 (1G, 1T, 3PG) Scotland 16 (1G, 1T, 1DG, 1PG)

Scotland T: Shedden, Irvine. C: Morgan. DG: Morgan. PG: Morgan.
France T: Gallion, Haget. C: Aguirre. PG: Aguirre (3).

France recovered from a seemingly hopeless position, 0-13, to record their biggest ever score in Scotland. There was a measure of good fortune about the first score in their fight-back for Andy Irvine was off the field receiving treatment when Jerome Gallion scored France's first try. Irvine and Shedden both eventually had to retire through injury, by which time the French scoring momentum was in full swing.

SCOTLAND A.R. Irvine 22 (Heriot's FP); B.H. Hay 3 (Boroughmuir), J.M. Renwick 20 (Hawick), I.R. McGeechan 22 (Headingley), D. Shedden 12 (W. of Scotland); R. Wilson 7 (London Scottish), *D.W. Morgan 16 (Stewart's FP); J. McLauchlan 29 (Jordanhill), C.T. Deans 1 (Hawick), N.E.K. Pender 2 (Hawick), A.J. Tomes 5 (Hawick), A.F. McHarg 34 (London Scottish), M.A. Biggar 12 (London Scottish), C.B. Hegarty 2 (Hawick), G.Y. Mackie (3) (Highland).
Replacements A.G. Cranston 6 (Hawick) for Irvine, C.G. Hogg 1 (Boroughmuir) for Shedden.

FRANCE J-M. Aguirre 13 (S. Bagnères); J-F. Gourdon 11 (S. Bagnères), R. Bertranne 23 (S. Bagnères), C. Belascain 2 (A. Bayonne), J-L.

Jean-Pierre Bastiat, multi-talented French forward, who was one of that rare breed possessing the physique and technique to play lock and the pace and agility to be an outstanding No 8

Averous 11 (La Voulte S.); B. Viviès 2 (SU Agen), J. Gallion 2 (RC Toulon); G. Cholley 13 (Castres Ol), A. Paco 12 (AS Béziers), R. Paparemborde 10 (S. Pau), M. Palmié 10 (AS Béziers), F. Haget 2 (SU Agen), J-P. Rives 13 (S. Toulouse), J-C. Skréla 21 (S. Toulouse), *J-P. Bastiat 18 (US Dax).

Referee C.G.P. Thomas (Wales)

FRANCE v IRELAND   49/679

18 February 1978
Parc des Princes, Paris
France 10 (1T, 2PG) Ireland 9 (3PG)

France   T: Gallion. PG: Aguirre (2).
Ireland   PG: Ward (3).

This was France's eighth consecutive Championship victory, their best ever sequence. The Irish put up a very hard fight, and twice came close to obtaining a winning score through the combined efforts of Ward, McKibbin and McNaughton.

FRANCE   J-M. Aguirre 14 (S. Bagnères); L. Bilbao 1 (St-Jean-de-Luz Ol), R. Bertranne 24 (S. Bagnères), C. Belascain 3 (A. Bayonne), J-L. Averous 12 (La Voulte S.); B. Viviès 3 (SU Agen), J. Gallion 3 (RC Toulon); R. Paparemborde 11 (S. Pau), A. Paco 13 (AS Béziers), G. Cholley 14 (Castres Ol), M. Palmié 11 (AS Béziers), F. Haget 3 (Biarritz Ol), J-C. Skréla 22 (S. Toulouse), J-P. Rives 14 (S. Toulouse), *J-P. Bastiat 19 (US Dax).

IRELAND   A.H. Ensor 16 (Wanderers); C.M.H. Gibson 53 (NIFC), A.R. McKibbin 5 (London Irish), P.P. McNaughton 2 (Greystones), A.C. McLennan 3 (Wanderers); A.J.P. Ward 2 (Garryowen), *J.J. Moloney 17 (St Mary's College); P.A. Orr 10 (Old Wesley), P.C. Whelan 8 (Garryowen), E.M.J. Byrne 3 (Blackrock College), M.I. Keane 18 (Lansdowne), H.W. Steele 3 (Ballymena), S.A. McKinney 18 (Dungannon), J.F. Slattery 26 (Blackrock College), W.P. Duggan 13 (Blackrock College).

Referee C.G.P. Thomas (Wales)

WALES v SCOTLAND   82/680

18 February 1978
Cardiff Arms Park
Wales 22 (4T, 1DG, 1PG) Scotland 14 (2T, 2PG)

Wales   T: Edwards, Gravell, Fenwick, Quinnell. DG: Bennett. PG: Bennett.
Scotland   T: Renwick, Tomes. PG: Morgan (2).

Spectators who braved the bitterly cold weather conditions were rewarded with some tries of very high quality and a brave fight-back by Scotland which though never likely to affect the outcome earned them many friends. David Shedden's last Championship match lasted only three minutes before an injury forced him to go off. By curious coincidence Shedden had been injured in Scotland's match against France a fortnight earlier, and his replacement then, as on this occasion, was Hogg, who never played for Scotland in any other capacity than a replacement. Shortly after the match heavy snow isolated Cardiff from the rest of the country and many players and spectators were prevented from returning home for days.

WALES   J.P.R. Williams 36 (Bridgend); T.G.R. Davies 37 (Cardiff), R.W.R. Gravell 10 (Llanelli), S.P. Fenwick 13 (Bridgend), J.J. Williams 19 (Llanelli); *P. Bennett 24 (Llanelli), G.O. Edwards 43 (Cardiff); G. Price 14 (Pontypool), R.W. Windsor 18 (Pontypool), A.G. Faulkner 10 (Pontypool), A.J. Martin 16 (Aberavon), G.A.D. Wheel 14 (Swansea), J. Squire 4 (Newport), T.J. Cobner 15 (Pontypool), D.L. Quinnell 12 (Llanelli).

SCOTLAND   B.H. Hay 4 (Boroughmuir); W.B.B. Gammell 4 (Edinburgh Wands), J.M. Renwick 21 (Hawick), A.G. Cranston 7 (Hawick), D. Shedden (13) (W. of Scotland); I.R. McGeechan 23 (Headingley), *D.W. Morgan 17 (Stewart's FP); J. McLauchlan 30 (Jordanhill), C.T. Deans 2 (Hawick), N.E.K. Pender 3 (Hawick), A.J. Tomes 6 (Hawick), A.F. McHarg 35 (London Scottish), M.A. Biggar 13 (London Scottish), C.B. Hegarty 3 (Hawick), D.S.M. Macdonald 6 (W. of Scotland).

Replacement C.G. Hogg (2) (Boroughmuir) for Shedden

Referee J.R. West (Ireland)

IRELAND v WALES 79/681

4 March 1978
Lansdowne Road, Dublin
Wales 20 (2T, 4PG) Ireland 16 (1T, 1DG, 3PG)

Ireland T: Moloney. DG: Ward. PG: Ward (3).
Wales T: Fenwick, J.J. Williams. PG: Fenwick (4).

This was a rugged, unrestrained contest, with the Triple Crown the prize for Wales and, if Ireland won, at least they would be within grasping reach of the trophy. Traditionally, Irish-Welsh confrontations are not for the meek, and if there were a few after-match grumbles that the play had at times been a little near the knuckle, they were rather more comments than criticisms. Each side was able to hand out as much as they were given. Gerald Davies, that most accomplished of players made his last appearance.

IRELAND   A.H. Ensor 17 (Wanderers); C.M.H. Gibson 54 (NIFC), A.R. McKibbin 6 (London Irish), P.P. McNaughton 3 (Greystones), A.C. McLennan 4 (Wanderers); A.J.P. Ward 3 (Garryowen), *J.J. Moloney 18 (St Mary's College); E.M.J. Byrne 4 (Blackrock College), P.C. Whelan 9 (Garryowen), P.A. Orr 11 (Old Wesley), M.I. Keane 19 (Lansdowne), H.W. Steele 4 (Ballymena), S.A. McKinney 19 (Dungannon), J.F. Slattery 27 (Blackrock College), W.P. Duggan 14 (Blackrock College).

WALES   J.P.R. Williams 37 (Bridgend); T.G.R. Davies (38) (Cardiff), R.W.R. Gravell 11 (Llanelli), S.P. Fenwick 14 (Bridgend), J.J. Williams 20 (Llanelli); *P. Bennett 25 (Llanelli), G.O. Edwards 44 (Cardiff); G. Price 15 (Pontypool), R.W. Windsor 19 (Pontypool), A.G. Faulkner 11 (Pontypool), A.J. Martin 17 (Aberavon), G.A.D. Wheel 15 (Swansea), J. Squire 5 (Newport), T.J. Cobner 16 (Pontypool), D.L. Quinnell 13 (Llanelli).

Referee G. Domercq (France)

SCOTLAND v ENGLAND 81/682

4 March 1978
Murrayfield
England 15 (2G, 1PG) Scotland 0

England T: Nelmes, Squires. C: Young (2). PG: Dodge.

This was England's biggest margin of victory at Murrayfield since 1952, when they had won 19-3. It left the Scots with four defeats in the season, and the Wooden Spoon for the first time since 1971. The occasion was notable for the début of the giant Maurice Colclough, the 6 feet 5 inches, 19-stone lock-forward, who played most of his serious club rugby for Angoulême in France. Another 'foreigner' who played most of his rugby outside of England was Barry Nelmes, a regular in the Cardiff front-row. Nelmes scored one of England's two tries.

SCOTLAND   A.R. Irvine 23 (Heriot's FP); W.B.B. Gammell (5) (Edinburgh Wands), J.M. Renwick 22 (Hawick), A.G. Cranston (8) (Hawick), B.H. Hay 5 (Boroughmuir); R.W. Breakey (1) (Gosforth), *D.W. Morgan (18) (Stewart's FP); J. McLauchlan 31 (Jordanhill), C.T. Deans 3 (Hawick), N.E.K. Pender (4) (Hawick), A.J. Tomes 7 (Hawick), D. Gray 1 (W. of Scotland), M.A. Biggar 14 (London Scottish), C.B. Hegarty (4) (Hawick), D.S.M. Macdonald (7) (W. of Scotland).

ENGLAND   D.W.N. Caplan 1 (Headingley); P.J. Squires 18 (Harrogate), B.J. Corless 8 (Moseley), P.W. Dodge 2 (Leicester), M.A.C. Slemen 9 (Liverpool); J.P. Horton 2 (Bath), M. Young 7 (Gosforth); B.G. Nelmes 2 (Cardiff), P.J. Wheeler 12 (Leicester), F.E. Cotton 19 (Sale), *W.B. Beaumont 12 (Fylde), M.J. Colclough 1 (SC Angoulême), P.J. Dixon 19 (Gosforth), M. Rafter 6 (Bristol), J.P. Scott 3 (Rosslyn Park).

Referee J.R. West (Ireland)

ENGLAND v IRELAND   82/683

18 March 1978
Twickenham
England 15 (2G, 1PG) Ireland 9 (1DG, 2PG)

England   T: Dixon, Slemen. C: Young (2). PG: Young.
Ireland   DG: Ward. PG: Ward (2).

Tony Ward's 9 points brought his season's points total to 38, to equal the Championship best. It was the final Championship match for two long-serving flank-forwards, England's Peter Dixon and Ireland's Stewart McKinney. Both had played in 20 internationals.

ENGLAND   D.W.N. Caplan (2) (Headingley); P.J. Squires 19 (Harrogate), B.J. Corless (9) (Moseley), P.W. Dodge 3 (Leicester), M.A.C. Slemen 10 (Liverpool); J.P. Horton 3 (Bath), M. Young 8 (Gosforth); B.G. Nelmes (3) (Cardiff), P.J. Wheeler 13 (Leicester), F.E. Cotton 20 (Sale), *W.B. Beaumont 13 (Fylde), M.J. Colclough 2 (SC Angoulême), P.J. Dixon (20) (Gosforth), M. Rafter 7 (Bristol), J.P. Scott 4 (Rosslyn Park).

IRELAND   A.H. Ensor (18) (Wanderers); C.M.H. Gibson 55 (NIFC), A.R. McKibbin 7 (London Irish), P.P. McNaughton 4 (Greystones), A.C. McLennan 5 (Wanderers); A.J.P. Ward 4 (Garryowen), *J.J. Moloney 19 (St Mary's College); P.A. Orr 12 (Old Wesley), P.C. Whelan 10 (Garryowen), E.M.J. Byrne (5) (Blackrock College), M.I. Keane 20 (Lansdowne), H.W. Steele 5 (Ballymena), S.A. McKinney (20) (Dungannon), J.F. Slattery 28 (Blackrock College), W.P. Duggan 15 (Blackrock College).

Referee F. Palmade (France)

WALES v FRANCE   49/684

18 March 1978
Cardiff Arms Park
Wales 16 (1G, 1T, 2DG) France 7 (1T, 1DG)

Wales   T: Bennett (2). C: Bennett. DG: Edwards, Fenwick.
France   T: Skréla. DG: Viviès.

For a match in which the prize was the Grand Slam, Phil Bennett's two tries highlighted one of the more curious anomalies in Welsh rugby, the lack of tries scored by their fly-halves, the most emotive position of all. The last time a Welsh fly-half had scored a brace was in 1931, when Raymond Ralph contributed to the seven which Wales scored that day, also against France. The last occasion when Wales scored two dropped goals against France was even earlier, in 1930. The 1978 match, however, was notable in other ways: it was the last Championship match for Gareth Edwards and Phil Bennett, the great Welsh half-backs, the irrepressible Terry Cobner and the French back-row forwards Skréla and Bastiat.

WALES   J.P.R. Williams 38 (Bridgend); J.J. Williams 21 (Llanelli), R.W.R. Gravell 12 (Llanelli), S.P. Fenwick 15 (Bridgend), G.L. Evans (2) (Newport); *P. Bennett (26) (Llanelli), G.O. Edwards (45) (Cardiff); G. Price 16 (Pontypool), R.W. Windsor 20 (Pontypool), A.G. Faulkner 12 (Pontypool), A.J. Martin 18 (Aberavon), G.A.D. Wheel 16 (Swansea), J. Squire 6 (Newport), T.J. Cobner (17) (Pontypool), D.L. Quinnell 14 (Llanelli).

FRANCE   J-M. Aguirre 15 (S. Bagnères); D. Bustaffa 1 (US Carcassonne), R. Bertranne 25 (S. Bagnères), C. Belascain 4 (A. Bayonne), G. Noves 1 (S. Toulouse); B. Viviès 4 (SU Agen), J. Gallion 4 (S. Toulouse); R. Paparemborde 12 (S. Pau), A. Paco 14 (AS Béziers), G. Cholley 15 (Castres Ol), F. Haget 4 (Biarritz Ol), M. Palmié (12) (AS Béziers), J-C. Skréla (23) (S. Toulouse), J-P. Rives 15 (S. Toulouse), *J-P. Bastiat (20) (US Dax).

Referee A. Welsby (England)

1979

PARIS France drew Ireland 9-9 · MURRAYFIELD Wales beat Scotland 19-13
TWICKENHAM England drew Scotland 7-7 · CARDIFF Wales beat Ireland 24-21
PARIS France beat Wales 14-13 · DUBLIN Ireland beat England 12-7
TWICKENHAM England beat France 7-6 · MURRAYFIELD Scotland drew Ireland 11-11
PARIS France beat Scotland 21-17 · CARDIFF Wales beat England 27-3

CHAMPIONSHIP TABLE
Wales – Championship, Triple Crown

Pos	Country	P	W	D	L	F	A	Pts	Tries F	A
1	Wales (1)	4	3	0	1	83	51	6	10	5
2	France (2)	4	2	1	1	50	46	5	7	5
3	Ireland (4)	4	2	0	2	53	51	4	5	6
4	England (3)	4	1	1	2	24	52	3	3	8
5	Scotland (5)	4	0	2	2	48	58	2	7	8

Wales won the Championship for the second year in a row, which was the sixth time they had achieved that distinction. Their only defeat, albeit a narrow one, was against France in Paris, but they were given a fright at Cardiff where Ireland scored 21 points, their biggest total to date against Wales. Ireland played their fiftieth Championship match against France at Lansdowne Road, but it turned out to be a disappointing 9-9 draw with three penalty goals by Tony Ward salvaging Irish pride.

Another drawn match, this time at Murrayfield, was the setting for the last international of another Irishman, the great Mike Gibson. It was his fifty-sixth Championship match over 16 seasons, attributable as much to his stamina and enthusiasm as to his enduring skill. A fortnight later one of Scotland's midfield artists, Ian McGeechan, also played his last Championship match appropriately enough at Parc des Princes, the scene of his first match for his country in 1973. Two stalwart members of the Front Row Union also ended their careers in the same match, Ian McLauchlan and Gérard Cholley.

IRELAND v FRANCE　　50/685

20 January 1979
Lansdowne Road, Dublin
Ireland 9 (3PG) France 9 (1G, 1PG)

Ireland PG: Ward (3).
France T: Caussade. C: Aguirre. PG: Aguirre.

The fiftieth Championship match between Ireland and France was a somewhat disappointing event, with Ireland being saved from defeat by three penalty goals from Tony Ward. Ireland

Roland Bertranne, rated as one of the most gifted French players of all time

introduced six players to Championship rugby and France two. One of these was a highly promising newcomer, Jean-Luc Joinel, cast in the mould of the aggressive, industrious Jean-Claude Skréla.

IRELAND   R.M. Spring 1 (Lansdowne); T.J. Kennedy 1 (St Mary's College), A.R. McKibbin 8 (London Irish), P.P. McNaughton 5 (Greystones), A.C. McLennan 6 (Wanderers); A.J.P. Ward 5 (Garryowen), C.S. Patterson 1 (Instonians); P.A. Orr 13 (Old Wesley), P.C. Whelan 11 (Garryowen), G.A.J. McLoughlin 1 (Shannon), M.I. Keane 21 (Lansdowne), H.W. Steele 6 (Ballymena), *J.F. Slattery 29 (Blackrock College), C.C. Tucker 1 (Shannon), M.E. Gibson 1 (Lansdowne).

FRANCE   J-M. Aguirre 16 (S. Bagnères); L. Bilbao (2) (St-Jean-de-Luz Ol), R. Bertranne 26 (S. Bagnères), C. Belascain 5 (A. Bayonne), G. Noves 2 (S. Toulouse); A. Caussade 1 (FC Lourdes), J. Gallion 5 (RC Toulon); R. Paparemborde 13 (S. Pau), A. Paco 15 (AS Béziers), G. Cholley 16 (Castres Ol), J-F. Imbernon 9 (US Perpignan), F. Haget 5 (Biarritz Ol), J-L. Joinel 1 (CA Brive), *J-P. Rives 16 (S. Toulouse), A. Guilbert 4 (RC Toulon).

Referee R.C. Quittenton (England)

SCOTLAND v WALES   83/686

20 January 1979
Murrayfield
Wales 19 (1G, 1T, 3PG) Scotland 13 (1T, 3PG)

Scotland   T: Irvine. PG: Irvine (3).
Wales   T: Rees, Holmes. C: Fenwick. PG: Fenwick (3).

Wales's scrummaging, which had been the basis of much of their success since the late 1960s was once again the platform for a substantial victory. The Scottish scrum, even though it contained the immovable Ian McLauchlan, was in difficulty from the start and by the end was in total disarray.

It was behind this formidable Welsh scrum that Terry Holmes and Gareth Davies made their début appearances, and their subsequent high standing in the game was due largely to this aspect of the Welsh game. Interestingly, when Welsh scrummaging power waned, so too did

the effectiveness of the half-backs, Davies being made a scapegoat for the consequent general decline, and Holmes being forced to lean heavily on his strength and defensive skills.

SCOTLAND   A.R. Irvine 24 (Heriot's FP); K.W. Robertson 1 (Melrose), J.M. Renwick 23 (Hawick), *I.R. McGeechan 24 (Headingley), B.H. Hay 6 (Boroughmuir); J.Y. Rutherford 1 (Selkirk), A.J.M. Lawson 9 (London Scottish); J. McLauchlan 32 (Jordanhill), C.T. Deans 4 (Hawick), R.F. Cunningham 1 (Gala), A.J. Tomes 8 (Hawick), A.F. McHarg 36 (London Scottish), M.A. Biggar 15 (London Scottish), G. Dickson 1 (Gala), I.K. Lambie 1 (Watsonians).

WALES   *J.P.R. Williams 39 (Bridgend); H.E. Rees 1 (Neath), S.P. Fenwick 16 (Bridgend), R.W.R. Gravell 13 (Llanelli), J.J. Williams 22 (Llanelli); W.G. Davies 1 (Cardiff), T.D. Holmes 1 (Cardiff); A.G. Faulkner 13 (Pontypool), R.W. Windsor 21 (Pontypool), G. Price 17 (Pontypool), A.J. Martin 19 (Aberavon), G.A.D. Wheel 17 (Swansea), P. Ringer 1 (Llanelli), J. Squire 7 (Pontypool), D.J. Quinnell 15 (Llanelli).

Referee F. Palmade (France)

ENGLAND v SCOTLAND   82/687

3 February 1979
Twickenham
England 7 (1T, 1PG) Scotland 7 (1T, 1PG)

England   T: Sleman. PG: Bennett.
Scotland   T: Rutherford. PG: Irvine.

Followers of England's fortunes — and misfortunes — berated tactics seemingly aimed at excluding the participation of two of the finest wings in the world. Peter Squires and Mike Slemen received no more than half-a-dozen serious passes between them, and though Neil Bennett, at fly-half, came in for most criticism for kicking too much, the England midfield as a whole were not disposed to move the ball fast and wide to bring in the wings to play. The Scottish backs, with much less ball to work with, showed much more flair and imagination. But forwards win matches, and the outgunned Scottish pack deserved no more than the draw obtained.

ENGLAND   A.J. Hignell 9 (Bristol); P.J. Squires 20 (Harrogate), A.M. Bond 1 (Sale), P.W. Dodge 4 (Leicester), M.A.C. Slemen 11 (Liverpool); W.N. Bennett 3 (London Welsh), M. Young (9) (Gosforth); R.J. Cowling 6 (Leicester), P.J. Wheeler 14 (Leicester), G.S. Pearce 1 (Northampton), W.B. Beaumont 14 (Fylde), N.E. Horton 16 (S. Toulouse), A. Neary 27 (Broughton Park), M. Rafter 8 (Bristol), *R.M. Uttley 14 (Gosforth).
Replacement J.P. Scott 5 (Cardiff) for Uttley

SCOTLAND   A.R. Irvine 25 (Heriot's FP); K.W. Robertson 2 (Melrose), J.M. Renwick 24 (Hawick), *I.R. McGeechan 25 (Headingley), B.H. Hay 7 (Boroughmuir); J.Y. Rutherford 2 (Selkirk), A.J.M. Lawson 10 (London Scottish); J. McLauchlan 33 (Jordanhill), C.T. Deans 5 (Hawick), R.F. Cunningham (2) (Gala), A.J. Tomes 9 (Hawick), A.F. McHarg (37) (London Scottish), M.A. Biggar 16 (London Scottish), G. Dickson 2 (Gala), I.K. Lambie (2) (Watsonians).

Referee C. Norling (Wales)

WALES v IRELAND   80/688

3 February 1979
Cardiff Arms Park
Wales 24 (2G, 4PG) Ireland 21 (2G, 3PG)

Wales   T: Martin, Ringer. C: Fenwick (2). PG: Fenwick (4).
Ireland   T: McLennan, Patterson. C: Ward (2). PG: Ward (3).

This was Ireland's biggest score in Wales, a substantial improvement on their previous best of 14 points scored in 1963. On that occasion they won. This time their spate of scoring came too late for it was much more in the form of a reprisal than a serious challenge to the outcome.

WALES   *J.P.R. Williams 40 (Bridgend); H.E. Rees 2 (Neath), R.W.R. Gravell 14 (Llanelli), S.P. Fenwick 17 (Bridgend), J.J. Williams 23 (Llanelli); W.G. Davies 2 (Cardiff), T.D. Holmes 2 (Cardiff); A.G. Faulkner 14 (Pontypool), R.W. Windsor 22 (Pontypool), G. Price 18 (Pontypool), A.J. Martin 20 (Aberavon) G.A.D. Wheel 18 (Swansea), P. Ringer 2 (Llanelli), J. Squire 8 (Pontypool), D.L. Quinnell 16 (Llanelli).
Replacement S.M. Lane 1 (Cardiff) for Wheel

IRELAND   R.M. Spring 2 (Lansdowne); T.J. Kennedy 2 (St Mary's College), A.R. McKibbin 9 (London Irish), P.P. McNaughton 6 (Greystones), A.C. McLennan 7 (Wanderers); A.J.P. Ward 6 (Garryowen), C.S. Patterson 2 (Instonians); P.A. Orr 14 (Old Wesley), P.C. Whelan 12 (Garryowen), G.A.J. McLoughlin 2 (Shannon), M.I. Keane 22 (Lansdowne), H.W. Steele 7 (Ballymena), C.C. Tucker 2 (Shannon), *J.F. Slattery 30 (Blackrock College), M.E. Gibson 2 (Lansdowne).

Referee A.M. Hosie (Scotland)

FRANCE v WALES   50/689

17 February 1979
Parc des Princes, Paris
France 14 (2T, 2PG) Wales 13 (1T, 3PG)

France   T: Gourdon (2). PG: Aguirre (2).
Wales   T: Holmes. PG: Fenwick (3).

France narrowly succeeded in preventing Wales equalling their nine-match sequence of Championship matches without defeat. Undoubtedly the player of the match was Jean-Pierre Rives, who when not initiating back-row moves was scouring to support others. In defence, too, Rives was like a Viking on the rampage.

FRANCE   J-M. Aguirre 17 (S. Bagnères); J-F. Gourdon 12 (S. Bagnères), R. Bertranne 27 (S. Bagnères), C. Belascain 6 (A. Bayonne), G. Noves (3) (S. Toulouse); A. Caussade 2 (FC Lourdes), J. Gallion 6 (RC Toulon); A. Vaquerin 11 (AS Béziers), A. Paco 16 (AS Béziers), R. Paparemborde 14 (S. Pau), F. Haget 6 (Biarritz Ol), A. Maleig 1 (FC Oloron), J-L. Joinel 2 (CA Brive), *J-P. Rives 17 (S. Toulouse), A. Guilbert 5 (RC Toulon).

WALES   *J.P.R. Williams 41 (Bridgend); H.E. Rees 3 (Neath), D.S. Richards 1 (Swansea), S.P. Fenwick 18 (Bridgend), J.J. Williams 24 (Llanelli); W.G. Davies 3 (Cardiff), T.D. Holmes 3 (Cardiff); A.G. Faulkner (15) (Pontypool), R.W. Windsor (23) (Pontypool), G. Price 19 (Pontypool), A.J. Martin 21 (Aberavon), B.G. Clegg (1) (Swansea), P. Ringer 3 (Llanelli), J. Squire 9 (Pontypool), D.L. Quinnell 17 (Llanelli).

Referee D.I.H. Burnett (Ireland)

IRELAND v ENGLAND 83/690

17 February 1979
Lansdowne Road, Dublin
Ireland 12 (1G, 1DG, 1PG) England 7 (1T, 1PG)

Ireland T: MacLennan. C: Ward. DG: Ward. PG: Ward.
England T: Bennett. PG: Bennett.

Tony Ward, who had produced all Ireland's nine points in the previous meeting between the countries at Twickenham in 1978, reaped another harvest of points with a dropped goal, conversion and a penalty goal. It enabled Ireland to win and helped compensate for their defeat at Cardiff a fortnight earlier.

IRELAND R.M. Spring (3) (Lansdowne); M.C. Finn 1 (UC Cork), A.R. McKibbin 10 (London Irish), P.P. McNaughton 7 (Greystones), A.C. McLennan 8 (Wanderers); A.J.P. Ward 7 (Garryowen), C.S. Patterson 3 (Instonians); P.A. Orr 15 (Old Wesley), P.C. Whelan 13 (Garryowen), G.A.J. McLoughlin 3 (Shannon), M.I. Keane 23 (Lansdowne), H.W. Steele (8) (Ballymena), W.P. Duggan 16 (Blackrock College), *J.F. Slattery 31 (Blackrock College), M.E. Gibson 3 (Lansdowne).
Replacement T.J. Kennedy 3 (St Mary's College) for Finn

ENGLAND A.J. Hignell 10 (Bristol); P.J. Squires 21 (Harrogate), A.M. Bond 2 (Sale), P.W. Dodge 5 (Leicester), M.A.C. Slemen 12 (Liverpool); W.N. Bennett 4 (London Welsh), P. Kingston 1 (Gloucester); R.J. Cowling (7) (Leicester), P.J. Wheeler 15 (Leicester), G.S. Pearce 2 (Northampton), *W.B. Beaumont 15 (Fylde), N.E. Horton 17 (S. Toulouse), A. Neary 28 (Broughton Park), M. Rafter 9 (Bristol), J.P. Scott 6 (Cardiff).

Referee A.M. Hosie (Scotland)

ENGLAND v FRANCE 50/691

3 March 1979
Twickenham
England 7 (1T, 1PG) France 6 (1G)

England T: Bennett. PG: Bennett.
France T: Costes. C: Aguirre.

Neil Bennett, who had scored all England's points in the previous match against Ireland with a try and a penalty, repeated his performance exactly, and it was just enough to pip France.

ENGLAND A.J. Hignell 11 (Bristol); P.J. Squires 22 (Harrogate), R.M. Cardus 1 (Roundhay), P.W. Dodge 6 (Leicester), M.A.C. Slemen 13 (Liverpool); W.N. Bennett 5 (London Welsh), P. Kingston 2 (Gloucester); C.E. Smart 1 (Newport), P.J. Wheeler 16 (Leicester), G.S. Pearce 3 (Northampton), *W.B. Beaumont 16 (Fylde), N.E. Horton 18 (S. Toulouse), A. Neary 29 (Broughton Park), M. Rafter 10 (Bristol), J.P. Scott 7 (Cardiff).

FRANCE J-M. Aguirre 18 (S. Bagnères); J-F. Gourdon 13 (S. Bagnères), R. Bertranne 28 (S. Bagnères), C. Belascain 7 (A. Bayonne), F. Costes 1 (AS Montferrand); A. Caussade 3 (FC Lourdes), J. Gallion 7 (RC Toulon); A. Vaquerin 12 (AS Béziers), A. Paco 17 (AS Béziers), R. Paparemborde 15 (S. Pau), F. Haget 7 (Biarritz Ol), A. Maleig 2 (FC Oloron), *J-P. Rives 18 (S. Toulouse), J-L. Joinel 3 (CA Brive), A. Guilbert (6) (RC Toulon).

Referee J.R. West (Ireland)

SCOTLAND v IRELAND · 84/692

3 March 1979
Murrayfield
Scotland 11 (2T, 1PG) Ireland 11 (2T, 1PG)

Scotland T: Rutherford, Irvine. PG: Irvine.
Ireland T: Patterson (2). PG: Ward.

Mike Gibson's Championship career ended in this match. He had played 56 Championship matches in an amazing 16-year career and was unquestionably one of the most highly skilled backs in the history of the game. Like all great players, Gibson had highs and lows, but he rarely played a poor game. Whether he was feinting, dummying, turning on a sixpence or curving outside on wide arc, Gibson was a master craftsman enjoying his work. Some admired his creative ability to make tries for others; others thought he had few equals as a tactical kicker; and there were those who believed there was no one more accomplished at reading a game or fending off the opposition's attacks. Gibson was one of those rare players — an artist with complete mastery of the basic skills.

SCOTLAND   A.R. Irvine 26 (Heriot's FP); K.W. Robertson 3 (Melrose), R.M. Renwick 25 (Hawick), *I.R. McGeechan 26 (Headingley), B.H. Hay 8 (Boroughmuir); J.Y. Rutherford 3 (Selkirk), A.J.M. Lawson 11 (London Scottish); J. McLauchlan 34 (Jordanhill), C.T. Deans 6 (Hawick), I.G. Milne 1 (Heriot's FP), A.J. Tomes 10 (Hawick), D. Gray 2 (W. of Scotland), M.A. Biggar 17 (London Scottish), G. Dickson 3 (Gala). W.S. Watson 8 (Boroughmuir).

IRELAND   W.R.J. Elliott (1) (Bangor); C.M.H. Gibson (56) (NIFC), A.R. McKibbin 11 (London Irish), P.P. McNaughton 8 (Greystones), A.C. McLennan 9 (Wanderers); A.J.P. Ward 8 (Garryowen), C.S. Patterson 4 (Instonians); P.A. Orr 16 (Old Wesley), P.C. Whelan 14 (Garryowen), G.A.J. McLoughlin 4 (Shannon), M.I. Keane 24 (Lansdowne), D.E. Spring 2 (Dublin U.), W.P. Duggan 17 (Blackrock College), *J.F. Slattery 32 (Blackrock College), M.E. Gibson 4 (Lansdowne).

Referee C. Thomas (Wales)

FRANCE v SCOTLAND · 49/693

17 March 1979
Parc des Princes, Paris
France 21 (3T, 1DG, 2PG) Scotland 17 (1G, 2T, 1PG)

France T: Belascain, Malquier (2). DG: Aguerre. PG: Aguerre, Aguirre.
Scotland T: Robertson, Dickson, Irvine. C: Irvine. PG: Irvine.

This was Scotland's fifth defeat in a row at France's hands, a run they had previously suffered only once, in their bad old days 1951–55. The aggregate of points were the highest in any France-Scotland meeting, and only once before, in 1977, have the French scored more points against the Scots. It was an appropriate venue for Ian McGeechan's last game for Scotland for it was in the first match at the new Parc des Princes that this highly-talented midfield player made his Championship début in 1973. Two front-row adversaries also left the international scene after this match: Scotland's Mighty Mouse, Ian McLauchlan, and the French prop, built like a blockhouse, Gérard Cholley.

FRANCE   J-M. Aguirre 19 (S. Bagnères); J-F. Gourdon 14 (S. Bagnères), R. Bertranne 29 (S. Bagnères), C. Belascain 8 (A. Bayonne), F. Costes 2 (AS Montferrand); R. Aguerre (1) (Biarritz Ol), J. Gallion 8 (RC Toulon); G. Cholley (17) (Castres Ol), A. Paco 18 (AS Béziers), R. Paparemborde 16 (S. Pau), F. Haget 8 (Biarritz Ol), J-F. Marchal 1 (FC Lourdes), *J-P. Rives 19 (S. Toulouse), Y. Malquier (1) (RC Narbonne), J-L. Joinel 4 (CA Brive).

SCOTLAND   A.R. Irvine 27 (Heriot's FP); K.W. Robertson 4 (Melrose), J.M. Renwick 26 (Hawick), *I.R. McGeechan (27) (Headingley), B.H. Hay 9 (Boroughmuir); J.Y. Rutherford 4 (Selkirk), A.J.M. Lawson 12 (London Scottish); J. McLauchlan (35) (Jordanhill), C.T. Deans 7 (Hawick), I.G. Milne 2 (Heriot's FP), A.J. Tomes 11 (Hawick), D. Gray 3 (W. of Scotland), M.A. Biggar 18 (London Scottish), W.S. Watson (9) (Boroughmuir), G. Dickson 4 (Gala).

Referee R.C. Quittenton (England)

WALES v ENGLAND 83/694

17 March 1979
Cardiff Arms Park
Wales 27 (2G, 3T, 1DG) England 3 (1PG)

Wales T: Rees, Richards, Ringer, Roberts, J.J. Williams. C: Martin, Fenwick. DG: Davies.
England PG: Bennett.

Wales had given England some severe beatings over the years, but not since 1905 when they won 25-0, was their winning margin so large. The collapse of England was extraordinary, following their recent victory over France and with Wales having some selection problems, a close match was expected. In the event England were totally outplayed up front, scrummage, line-out and maul, and a man who had played an important part in every aspect was the veteran Mike Roberts, recalled from semi-retirement to take the injured Geoff Wheel's place. Roberts played an outstanding game, dominating Billy Beaumont at the front and making his presence felt in areas where England had anticipated control. Roberts crowned a remarkable come-back – this was his last Championship match – with a try.

Another Welshman with cause for celebration was Steve Fenwick. He missed five penalties but a conversion brought him 38 points for the season to equal Phil Bennett's Championship record. The match was unusual in that it contained the rare occurrence of ironman J.P.R. Williams' departure because of injury. It all added up to another Welsh Triple Crown, their sixteenth, and the Championship.

WALES *J.P.R. Williams 42 (Bridgend); H.E. Rees 4 (Neath), D.S. Richards 2 (Swansea), S.P. Fenwick 19 (Bridgend), J.J. Williams (25) (Llanelli); W.G. Davies 4 (Cardiff), T.D. Holmes 4 (Cardiff); S.J. Richardson (1) (Aberavon), A.J. Phillips 1 (Cardiff), G. Price 20 (Pontypool), M.G. Roberts (8) (London Welsh), A.J. Martin 22 (Aberavon), P. Ringer 4 (Llanelli), J. Squire 10 (Pontypool), D.L. Quinnell (18) (Llanelli).
Replacement C. Griffiths (1) (Llanelli) for J.P.R. Williams

ENGLAND A.J. Hignell (12) (Bristol); P.J. Squires (23) (Harrogate), R.M. Cardus (2) (Roundhay), P.W. Dodge 7 (Leicester), M.A.C. Slemen 14 (Liverpool); W.N. Bennett (6) (London Welsh), P. Kingston (3) (Gloucester); C.E. Smart 2 (Newport), P.J. Wheeler 17 (Leicester), G.S. Pearce 4 (Northampton), *W.B. Beaumont 17 (Fylde), N.E. Horton 19 (S. Toulouse), A. Neary 30 (Broughton Park), M. Rafter 11 (Bristol), J.P. Scott 8 (Cardiff).

Referee J-P. Bonnet (France)

1980

TWICKENHAM England beat Ireland 24-9 · CARDIFF Wales beat France 18-9
PARIS England beat France 17-13 · DUBLIN Ireland beat Scotland 22-15
TWICKENHAM England beat Wales 9-8 · MURRAYFIELD Scotland beat France 22-14
PARIS France beat Ireland 19-18 · CARDIFF Wales beat Scotland 17-6
MURRAYFIELD England beat Scotland 30-18 · DUBLIN Ireland beat Wales 21-7

CHAMPIONSHIP TABLE
England – Championship, Triple Crown, Grand Slam

Pos	Country	P	W	D	L	F	A	Pts	Tries F	A
1	England (4)	4	4	0	0	80	48	8	10	6
2	Ireland (3)	4	2	0	2	70	65	4	6	8
3	Wales (1)	4	2	0	2	50	45	4	10	5
4	Scotland (5)	4	1	0	3	61	83	2	8	12
5	France (2)	4	1	0	3	55	75	2	7	10

England, led by the unassuming and popular Billy Beaumont, won the Triple Crown, the Grand Slam, the Championship and the Calcutta Cup, thus ending one of their longest periods without any measure of success. It was England's first Championship title for 16 years, in fact their longest phase without a title win. If there was an outstanding moment in this long-awaited return to the top, it was definitely in their last match, a thumping great record win at Murrayfield. England's euphoria was dimmed briefly during a bitter struggle against Wales at Twickenham when Paul Ringer was sent off. The skill, courage and high drama of the match were forgotten, not just because of the sending off, but because of the other many misdemeanours which disfigured the occasion. The media made over-much of the contest, and this more than any other single factor left many, players included, perplexed and in some cases angry that the incidents had been overplayed and exaggerated.

One controversial encounter did not, however, ruin the season, at least not for Ireland who in finishing runners-up, scored a record 70 points. Another important milestone was also overshadowed. The 41 tries which were scored in the Championship was the biggest total for 50 years. Individual scoring too attained new levels. Ollie Campbell scored 46 points, a record for an Irish player, and Andy Irvine scored 35, a record for a Scot.

ENGLAND v IRELAND   84/695

19 January 1980
Twickenham
England 24 (3G, 2PG) Ireland 9 (3PG)

England   T: Scott, Slemen, Smith. C: Hare (3). PG: Hare (2).
Ireland   PG: Campbell (3).

Ollie Campbell, the Old Belvedere fly-half, made his début appearance and gave a foretaste of his extraordinary place-kicking ability by landing three penalty goals. Two England players had cause to remember the match: Nigel Horton played his twentieth and final Championship 11 years after his début and Tony Bond had the misfortune to break a leg on his third England appearance. Bond's wretched luck allowed Clive Woodward to make his English début as a replacement. It was England's biggest score against Ireland in England, beating the previous best 23-5 achieved in 1923.

ENGLAND   W.H. Hare 3 (Leicester); J. Carleton 1 (Orrell), A.M. Bond 3 (Sale), N.J. Preston 1 (Richmond), M.A.C. Slemen 15 (Liverpool); J.P. Horton 4 (Bath), S.J. Smith 9 (Sale); F.E. Cotton 21 (Sale), P.J. Wheeler 18 (Leicester), P.J. Blakeway 1 (Gloucester), *W.B. Beaumont 18 (Fylde),

N.E. Horton (20) (Moseley), R.M. Uttley 15 (Wasps), A. Neary 31 (Broughton Park), J.P. Scott 9 (Cardiff).
Replacement C.R. Woodward 1 (Leicester) for Bond

IRELAND   K.A. O'Brien (1) (Broughton Park); T.J. Kennedy 4 (St Mary's College), A.R. McKibbin 12 (London Irish), P.P. McNaughton 9 (Greystones), A.C. McLennan 10 (Wanderers); S.O. Campbell 1 (Old Belvedere), C.S. Patterson 5 (Instonians); P.A. Orr 17 (Old Wesley), C.F. Fitzgerald 1 (St Mary's College), G.A.J. McLoughlin 5 (Shannon), M.I. Keane 25 (Lansdowne), J.J. Glennon 1 (Skerries), J.B. O'Driscoll 2 (London Irish), *J.F. Slattery 33 (Blackrock College), W.P. Duggan 18 (Blackrock College).
Replacement I.J. Burns (1) (Wanderers) for McNaughton

Referee C. Thomas (Wales)

WALES v FRANCE   51/696

19 January 1980
Cardiff Arms Park
Wales 18 (1G, 3T) France 9 (1G, 1DG)

Wales   T: Rees, Holmes, Richards, Price. C: Davies.
France   T: Marchal. C: Caussade. DG: Caussade.

Wales used the French pack for scrummage practice and then gave further insult by running in four tries, their best total against the French since 1975 when they scored five in Paris. Patrick Salas suffered all manner of problems in trying to counter Graham Price's power scrummaging, but it was the hooker, Alain Paco, who found himself out of favour with the selectors. He was not chosen again for France.

WALES   W.R. Blyth 3 (Swansea); H.E. Rees 5 (Neath), D.S. Richards 3 (Swansea), S.P. Fenwick 20 (Bridgend), L. Keen 1 (Aberavon); W.G. Davies 5 (Cardiff), T.D. Holmes 5 (Cardiff); C. Williams 3 (Swansea), A.J. Phillips 2 (Cardiff), G. Price 21 (Pontypool), A.J. Martin 23 (Aberavon), G.A.D. Wheel 19 (Swansea), P. Ringer 5 (Llanelli), *J. Squire 11 (Pontypool), E.T. Butler 1 (Pontypool).

FRANCE   J-M. Aguirre 20 (S. Bagnères); D. Bustaffa 2 (US Carcassonne), R. Bertranne 30 (S. Bagnères), D. Codorniou 1 (RC Narbonne), F. Costes 3 (AS Montferrand); A. Caussade 4 (FC Lourdes), J. Gallion 9 (RC Toulon); P. Salas 1 (RC Narbonne), A. Paco (19) (AS Béziers), R. Paparemborde 17 (S. Pau), F. Haget 9 (Biarritz Ol), J-F. Marchal 2 (FC Lourdes), *J-P. Rives 20 (S. Toulouse), J-L. Joinel 5 (CA Brive), A. Maleig 3 (FC Oloron).

Referee A.M. Hosie (Scotland)

FRANCE v ENGLAND   51/697

2 February 1980
Parc des Princes, Paris
England 17 (2T, 2DG, 1PG) France 13 (1G, 1T, 1PG)

France   T: Averous, Rives. C: Caussade. PG: Caussade.
England   T: Carleton, Preston. DG: Horton (2). PG: Hare.

England had not won in Paris since 1964, so this victory was long overdue. It was attained by solid scrummaging, pressure from the back-row and the ability of the threequarters to move the ball wide and quickly. The French were so disillusioned by their forwards that they dropped three of them, including both locks, who had been outclassed in every facet of the game by Beaumont and Colclough.

FRANCE   S. Gabernet 1 (S. Toulouse); D. Bustaffa 3 (US Carcassonne), R. Bertranne 31 (S. Bagnères), D. Codorniou 2 (RC Narbonne), J-L. Averous 13 (La Voulte S.); A. Caussade 5 (FC Lourdes), J. Gallion 10 (RC Toulon); P. Salas (2) (RC Narbonne), P. Dintrans 1 (S. Tarbes), R. Paparemborde 18 (S. Pau), Y. Duhard (1) (S. Bagnères), A. Maleig (4) (FC Oloron), *J-P. Rives 21 (S. Toulouse), J-L. Joinel 6 (CA Brive), M. Carpentier 1 (FC Lourdes).

ENGLAND   W.H. Hare 4 (Leicester); J. Carleton 2 (Orrell), C.R. Woodward 2 (Leicester), N.J. Preston (2) (Richmond), M.A.C. Slemen 16 (Liverpool); J.P. Horton 5 (Bath), S.J. Smith 10 (Sale); F.E. Cotton 22 (Sale), P.J. Wheeler 19 (Leicester), P.J. Blakeway 2 (Gloucester), *W.B. Beaumont 19 (Fylde), M.J. Colclough 3 (SC Angoulême),

R.M. Uttley 16 (Wasps), A. Neary 32 (Broughton Park), J.P. Scott 10 (Cardiff).

Referee C. Norling (Wales)

IRELAND v SCOTLAND   85/698

2 February 1980
Lansdowne Road, Dublin
Ireland 22 (1G, 1T, 1DG, 3PG) Scotland 15 (2G, 1PG)

Ireland   T: Keane, Kennedy. C: Campbell. DG: Campbell. PG: Campbell (3).
Scotland   T: Johnston (2). C: Irvine (2). PG: Irvine.

Although David Johnston joined the select band of players to score two tries on their début, Ireland ran up their biggest score against Scotland since the 26-8 triumph of 1953. Five other Scots made their first Championship appearances, one of whom, Ray Laidlaw, distinguished himself with his speed of pass and ability to break from the set-pieces. Ollie Campbell, who had kicked three penalty goals on his début against England the previous month, added another 14 points, 3 of which were from a penalty in unusual circumstances. Andy Irvine, the Scottish full-back, called a mark from kick ahead, was tackled and then penalized for not releasing the ball.

IRELAND   R.C. O'Donnell 1 (St Mary's College); T.J. Kennedy 5 (St Mary's College), A.R. McKibbin (13) (London Irish), P.P. McNaughton 10 (Greystones), J.J. Moloney 20 (St Mary's College); S.O. Campbell 2 (Old Belvedere), C.S. Patterson 6 (Instonians); P.A. Orr 18 (Old Wesley), C.F. Fitzgerald 2 (St Mary's College), M.P. Fitzpatrick 2 (Wanderers), J.J. Glennon (2) (Skerries), M.I. Keane 26 (Lansdowne), J.B. O'Driscoll 3 (London Irish), *J.F. Slattery 34 (Blackrock College), D.E. Spring 3 (Dublin U.).

SCOTLAND   A.R. Irvine 28 (Heriot's FP); S. Munro 1 (Ayr), J.M. Renwick 27 (Hawick), D.I. Johnston 1 (Watsonians), B.H. Hay 10 (Boroughmuir); J.Y. Rutherford 5 (Selkirk), R.J. Laidlaw 1 (Jedforest); J.N. Burnett 1 (Heriot's FP), C.T. Deans 8 (Hawick), I.G. Milne 3 (Heriot's FP), W. Cuthbertson 1 (Kilmarnock), D. Gray 4 (W. of Scotland), *M.A. Biggar 19 (London Scottish),

A.K. Brewster 2 (Stewart's FP), J.R. Beattie 1 (Glasgow Acads).

Referee G. Chevrier (France)

ENGLAND v WALES   84/699

16 February 1980
Twickenham
England 9 (3PG) Wales 8 (2T)

England   PG: Hare (3).
Wales   T: Rees, Squire.

Wales beat England by two tries to nil but lost the match because of Dusty Hare's three penalty goals, which is another way of agreeing with New Zealand's view that you never beat Wales, you merely score more points than them. A neutral spectator might have considered Wales unlucky to have lost. Down to 14 players after the dismissal of Paul Ringer after 15 minutes, Wales, and particularly the forwards, played magnificently, a factor often overlooked in the post-mortem of a match unsurpassed in notoriety. The fierce, unrelenting competitiveness of the match, Ringer's late tackle, the recriminations, the consequences, are all well documented. The only footnote necessary is that many of the players involved, supposedly bitter enemies for life because of the match, have since established firm and sincere friendships.

ENGLAND   W.H. Hare 5 (Leicester); J. Carleton 3 (Orrell), C.R. Woodward 3 (Leicester), P.W. Dodge 8 (Leicester), M.A.C. Slemen 17 (Liverpool); J.P. Horton 6 (Bath), S.J. Smith 11 (Sale); F.E. Cotton 23 (Sale), P.J. Wheeler 20 (Leicester), P.J. Blakeway 3 (Gloucester), *W.B. Beaumont 20 (Fylde), M.J. Colclough 4 (SC Angoulême), R.M. Uttley 17 (Wasps), A. Neary 33 (Broughton Park), J.P. Scott 11 (Cardiff).
Replacement M. Rafter 12 (Bristol) for Uttley

WALES   W.R. Blyth 4 (Swansea); H.E. Rees 6 (Neath), D.S. Richards 4 (Swansea), S.P. Fenwick 21 (Bridgend), L. Keen 2 (Aberavon); W.G. Davies 6 (Cardiff), T.D. Holmes 6 (Cardiff); C. Williams 4 (Swansea), A.J. Phillips 3 (Cardiff), G. Price 22 (Pontypool), A.J. Martin 24 (Aberavon), G.A.D. Wheel 20 (Swansea), P. Ringer (6) (Llanelli), *J. Squire 12 (Pontypool), E.T. Butler 2 (Pontypool).

Referee D.I.H. Burnett (Ireland)

SCOTLAND v FRANCE   50/700

16 February 1980
Murrayfield
Scotland 22 (2G, 1T, 2PG) France 14 (2T, 1DG, 1PG)

Scotland T: Rutherford, Irvine (2). C: Irvine, Renwick. PG: Irvine (2).
France T: Gallion, Gabernet. DG: Caussade. PG: Gabernet.

Scotland celebrated their fiftieth Championship match against France with a victory which ended a run of 11 matches without a win. Scotland's previous longest sequence without victory was 15 matches from 1951–55. It was also Scotland's biggest score against their visitors since 1927 and they did it after being 4-14 in arrears at one stage.

SCOTLAND A.R. Irvine 29 (Heriot's FP); S. Munro 2 (Ayr), J.M. Renwick 28 (Hawick), D.I. Johnston 2 (Watsonians), B.H. Hay 11 (Boroughmuir); J.Y. Rutherford 6 (Selkirk), R.J. Laidlaw 2 (Jedforest); J.N. Burnett 2 (Heriot's FP), C.T. Deans 9 (Hawick), I.G. Milne 4 (Heriot's FP), A.J. Tomes 12 (Hawick), D. Gray 5 (W. of Scotland), *M.A. Biggar 20 (London Scottish), A.K. Brewster (3) (Stewart's FP), J.R. Beattie 2 (Glasgow Acads).
Replacement K.G. Lawrie 1 (Gala) for Deans

FRANCE S. Gabernet 2 (S. Toulouse); D. Bustaffa (4) (US Carcassonne), R. Bertranne 32 (S. Bagnères), D. Codorniou 3 (RC Narbonne), J-L. Averous (14) (La Voulte S.); A. Caussade 6 (FC Lourdes), F. Gallion 11 (RC Toulon); A. Vaquerin 13 (AS Béziers), P. Dintrans 2 (S. Tarbes), R. Paparemborde 19 (S. Pau), F. Haget 10 (Biarritz Ol), J-F. Marchal 3 (FC Lourdes), *J-P. Rives 22 (S. Toulouse), J-L. Joinel 7 (CA Brive), M. Clemente 1 (FC Oloron).

Referee J.R. West (Ireland)

FRANCE v IRELAND   51/701

1 March 1980
Parc des Princes, Paris
France 19 (1G, 1T, 1DG, 2PG) Ireland 18 (1G, 1DG, 3PG)

France T: Gourdon (2). C: Aguirre. DG: Pedeutour. PG: Aguirre (2).
Ireland T: McLennan. C: Campbell. DG: Campbell. PG: Campbell.

Fourteen points from Ollie Campbell's boot enabled Ireland to record their biggest ever score in France. It was a match of true cut-and-thrust, with the French recovering from a 3-9 deficit to lead 19-9 and then having to cling to their advantage as the Irish chipped away to produce a desperately close finish. Victory did not save France from winning the Wooden Spoon but at least it prevented their losing all four matches in the season.

FRANCE J-M. Aguirre (21) (S. Bagnères); J-F. Gourdon (15) (S. Bagnères), R. Bertranne 33 (S. Bagnères), D. Codornier 4 (RC Narbonne), F. Costes (4) (AS Montferrand); P. Pedeutour (1) (CA Bègles), J. Gallion (12) (RC Toulon); P. Dospital 1 (A. Bayonne), P. Dintrans 3 (S. Tarbes), A. Vaquerin (14) (AS Béziers), J-F. Marchal (4) (FC Lourdes), F. Haget (11) (Biarritz Ol), J-L. Joinel 8 (CA Brive), *J.-P. Rives 23 (S. Toulouse), M. Clemente (2) (FC Oloron).

IRELAND R.C. O'Donnell 2 (St Mary's College); T.J. Kennedy 6 (St Mary's College), D.G. Irwin 1 (Queen's U. Belfast), P.P. McNaughton 11 (Greystones), A.C. McLennan 11 (Wanderers); S.O. Campbell 3 (Old Belvedere), C.S. Patterson 7 (Instonians); M.P. Fitzpatrick 3 (Wanderers), C.F. Fitzgerald 3 (St Mary's College), P.A. Orr 19 (Old Wesley), B.O. Foley 4 (Shannon), M.I. Keane 27 (Lansdowne), J.B. O'Driscoll 4 (London Irish), *J.F. Slattery 35 (Blackrock College), D.E. Spring 4 (Dublin U.).
Replacement C.C. Tucker (3) (Shannon) for O'Driscoll

Referee A.M. Hosie (Scotland)

WALES v SCOTLAND 84/702

1 March 1980
Cardiff Arms Park
Wales 17 (1G, 2T, 1PG) Scotland 6 (1G)

Wales T: Holmes, Keen, Richards. C: Blyth.
PG: Fenwick.
Scotland T: Renwick. C: Irvine.

This was Scotland's ninth consecutive defeat in Wales, their worst sequence there since losing ten matches in a row 1894–1914. Wales took the field under implicit instructions to behave themselves, following the controversial nature of the Battle of Twickenham the previous month. With Scotland also rather subdued, the consequence was an eminently forgettable contest.

WALES W.R. Blyth 5 (Swansea); H.E. Rees 7 (Neath), D.S. Richards 5 (Swansea), S.P. Fenwick 22 (Bridgend), L. Keen 3 (Aberavon); W.G. Davies 7 (Cardiff), T.D. Holmes 7 (Cardiff); C. Williams 5 (Swansea), A.J. Phillips 4 (Cardiff), G. Price 23 (Pontypool), A.J. Martin 25 (Aberavon), G.A.D. Wheel 21 (Swansea), S.M. Lane 2 (Cardiff), *J. Squire 13 (Pontypool), E.T. Butler 3 (Pontypool).
Replacement P.J. Morgan 1 (Llanelli) for Davies.

SCOTLAND A.R. Irvine 30 (Heriot's FP); K.W. Robertson 5 (Melrose), J.M. Renwick 29 (Hawick), D.I. Johnston 3 (Watsonians), B.H. Hay 12 (Boroughmuir); B.M. Gossman 1 (W. of Scotland), R.J. Laidlaw 3 (Jedforest); J.N. Burnett 3 (Heriot's FP), K.G. Lawrie 2 (Gala), N.A. Rowan 1 (Boroughmuir), A.J. Tomes 13 (Hawick), D. Gray 6 (W. of Scotland), *M.A. Biggar 21 (London Scottish), G. Dickson 5 (Gala), J.R. Beattie 3 (Glasgow Acads).
Replacement A.J.M. Lawson (13) (Heriot's FP) for Laidlaw

Referee L.M. Prideaux (England)

IRELAND v WALES 81/703

15 March 1980
Lansdowne Road, Dublin
Ireland 21 (3G, 1PG) Wales 7 (1T, 1PG)

Ireland T: Irwin, O'Driscoll, Fitzgerald. C: Campbell (3). PG: Campbell.
Wales T: Blyth. PG: Fenwick.

Ollie Campbell established a Championship best total of 46 points for the season with 9 points in the match. Campbell also assisted in equalling Ireland's biggest score against Wales, first achieved at Cardiff in 1979. A more surprising aspect of Campbell's contribution, however, was that his three conversions were the most by an Irish player against Wales.

IRELAND R.C. O'Donnell (3) (St Mary's College); T.J. Kennedy (7) (St Mary's College), D.G. Irwin 2 (Queen's U. Belfast), P.P. McNaughton 12 (Greystones), J.J. Moloney (21) (St Mary's College); S.O. Campbell 4 (Old Belvedere), C.S. Patterson (8) (Instonians); P.A. Orr 20 (Old Wesley), C.F. Fitzgerald 4 (St Mary's College), M.P. Fitzpatrick 4 (Wanderers), M.I. Keane 28 (Lansdowne), B.O. Foley 5 (Shannon), J.B. O'Driscoll 5 (London Irish), J.F. Slattery 36 (Blackrock College), D.E. Spring 5 (Dublin U.).

WALES W.R. Blyth (6) (Swansea); H.E. Rees 8 (Neath), D.S. Richards 6 (Swansea), S.P. Fenwick 23 (Bridgend), L. Keen (4) (Aberavon); P.J. Morgan 2 (Llanelli), T.D. Holmes 8 (Cardiff); C. Williams 6 (Swansea), A.J. Phillips 5 (Cardiff), G. Price 24 (Pontypool), A.J. Martin 26 (Aberavon), G.A.D. Wheel 22 (Swansea), S.M. Lane (3) (Cardiff), *J. Squire 14 (Pontypool), E.T. Butler 4 (Pontypool).

Referee L.M. Prideaux (England)

SCOTLAND v ENGLAND   83/704

15 March 1980
Murrayfield
England 30 (2G, 3T, 2PG) Scotland 18 (2G, 2PG)

Scotland   T: Tomes, Rutherford. C: Irvine (2).
PG: Irvine (2).
England   T: Carleton (3), Slemen, Smith. C:
Hare (2). PG: Hare (2).

One of the most remarkable matches in the history of the Championship, with England assuring themselves of the Grand Slam, Triple Crown, their first Championship for 20 years and the retention of the Calcutta Cup. It was also England's biggest score against Scotland, John Carleton's hat-trick of tries was the first by an English player for 56 years, Andy Irvine established a Scottish record of 35 points in a season and the match total of 48 points was the highest in the history of the fixture. It proved a fitting climax to the Championship careers of two England forwards, Tony Neary and Roger Uttley. Neary, England's record cap holder with 43 caps, played in 34 Championship matches and Uttley played in 18.

SCOTLAND   *A.R. Irvine 31 (Heriot's FP); K.W. Robertson 6 (Melrose), J.M. Renwick 30 (Hawick), D.I. Johnston 4 (Watsonians), B.H. Hay 13 (Boroughmuir); J.Y. Rutherford 7 (Selkirk), R.J. Laidlaw 4 (Jedforest); J.N. Burnett (4) (Heriot's FP), K.G. Lawrie (3) (Gala), N.A. Rowan 2 (Boroughmuir), A.J. Tomes 14 (Hawick), D. Gray 7 (W. of Scotland), D.G. Leslie 9 (Gala), M.A. Biggar (22) (London Scottish), J.R. Beattie 4 (Glasgow Acads).
Replacement J.S. Gossman (1) (W. of Scotland) for Hay

ENGLAND   W.H. Hare 6 (Leicester); J. Carleton 4 (Orrell), C.R. Woodward 4 (Leicester), P.W. Dodge 9 (Leicester), M.A.C. Slemen 18 (Liverpool); J.P. Horton 7 (Bath), S.J. Smith 12 (Sale); F.E. Cotton 24 (Sale), P.J. Wheeler 21 (Leicester), P.J. Blakeway 4 (Gloucester), *W.B. Beaumont 21 (Fylde), M.J. Colclough 5 (SC Angoulême), R.M. Uttley (18) (Wasps), A. Neary (34) (Broughton Park), J.P. Scott 12 (Cardiff).

Referee J-P. Bonnet (France)

Paul Ringer dismissed by Irish referee David Burnett after a dangerous tackle on England's John Horton

1981

PARIS France beat Scotland 16-9 · CARDIFF Wales beat England 21-19
DUBLIN France beat Ireland 19-13 · MURRAYFIELD Scotland beat Wales 15-6
TWICKENHAM England beat Scotland 23-17 · CARDIFF Wales beat Ireland 9-8
PARIS France beat Wales 19-15 · DUBLIN England beat Ireland 10-6
TWICKENHAM France beat England 16-12 · MURRAYFIELD Scotland beat Ireland 10-9

CHAMPIONSHIP TABLE
France – Championship, Grand Slam

									Tries	
Pos	Country	P	W	D	L	F	A	Pts	F	A
1	France (5)	4	4	0	0	70	49	8	6	3
2	England (1)	4	2	0	2	64	60	4	6	6
3	Scotland (4)	4	2	0	2	51	54	4	7	6
4	Wales (3)	4	2	0	2	51	61	4	2	6
5	Ireland (2)	4	0	0	4	36	48	0	4	4

A new-look France, coached by Jacques Fouroux and captained by Jean-Pierre Rives, won the Grand Slam for a third time and it was significant that Fouroux, when captain, and Rives, when at his fastest, were both members of the previous Grand Slam French side, in 1977. Fouroux, understandably, favoured a big, heavyweight pack similar to that of four years earlier; and if this meant a certain limitation in attacking ploys, they were still extremely effective. If the best team in the Championship, France, were not scoring tries, it was no surprise that the other countries failed in this respect. The consequence was a dramatic dip in tries scored, with just 25 scored, compared with 41 during the previous season. Scotland scored most tries, seven, but finished third only, behind England who had pulled off the season's biggest victory, 23-17 against the Scots. Wales's try drought alarmed their followers, for they scored two only, the lowest return of any country in the Championship. Even Ireland, who lost all four matches, scored twice as many tries as Wales, who in their centenary season, had very little to celebrate.

During their meeting in March, held for the first time in Cardiff, the International Board introduced legislation aimed primarily at curbing the development of the pile-up, which had disfigured the game at all levels for five years. There was discussion too, about a rewrite of the Laws. Many of the top administrators admitted they were not only verbose and too complicated but were often open to misunderstanding. Sadly, that promise of a rewrite never materialized, despite the fact that several draft rewrites were undertaken. Thus rugby football still had to endure the most complex set of rules of any sport.

FRANCE v SCOTLAND 51/705

17 January 1981
Parc des Princes, Paris
France 16 (1G, 1T, 2PG) Scotland 9 (1G, 1PG)

France T: Blanco, Bertranne. C: Caussade. PG: Viviès, Gabernet.
Scotland T: Rutherford. C: Renwick. PG: Irvine.

Andy Irvine derived some personal satisfaction in this defeat of Scotland by France, their seventh in a row in Paris, in that his penalty goal pushed him ahead of Phil Bennett as the world's leading points-scorer in internationals, with 213 points.

FRANCE S. Gabernet 3 (S. Toulouse); S. Blanco 1 (Biarritz Ol), R. Bertranne 34 (S. Bagnères), D. Codorniou 5 (RC Narbonne), L. Pardo 1 (A. Bayonne); B. Viviès (5) (SU Agen), P. Berbizier 1 (FC Lourdes); P. Dospital 2 (A. Bayonne), P. Dintrans 4 (S. Tarbes), R. Paparemborde 20 (S. Pau), D. Revallier 1 (SC Graulhet), J-F. Imbernon 10 (US Perpignan), *J-P. Rives 24 (S. Toulouse),

J-L. Joinel 9 (CA Brive), M. Carpentier 2 (FC Lourdes).
Replacement A. Caussade 7 (FC Lourdes) for Viviès

SCOTLAND *A.R. Irvine 32 (Heriot's FP); S. Munro 3 (Ayr), J.M. Renwick 31 (Hawick), K.W. Robertson 7 (Melrose), B.H. Hay 14 (Boroughmuir); J.Y. Rutherford 8 (Selkirk), R.J. Laidlaw 5 (Jedforest); N.A. Rowan 3 (Boroughmuir), C.T. Deans 10 (Hawick), J. Aitken 4 (Gala), A.J. Tomes 15 (Hawick), D. Gray (8) (W. of Scotland), J.H. Calder 1 (Stewart's Melville FP), G. Dickson 6 (Gala), J.R. Beattie 5 (Glasgow Acads).

Referee K. Rowlands (Wales)

WALES v ENGLAND   85/706

17 January 1981
Cardiff Arms Park
Wales 21 (1G, 1DG, 4PG) England 19 (1T, 5PG)

Wales   T: Davies. C: Fenwick. DG: Davies. PG: Fenwick (4).
England   T: Hare. PG: Hare (5).

Wales scored a record ninth successive home victory over England due to Dusty Hare missing a penalty goal with the last kick of what had been a pulsating match. Hare was probably consoled by the fact that the five penalty goals

Action during the Wales-England match at Cardiff which produced nine penalties, the highest total for a Championship match until Ireland played England in 1983

he did kick were the most registered by England against Wales. The nine penalties in the match were, however, substantially the highest total for a Championship match, a record which held until the Ireland-England match of 1983 produced ten. Fran Cotton, who went off injured after 15 minutes, never played for England again. The Sale loose-head – who occasionally played tight-head – had appeared in 25 Championship matches.

WALES   J.P.R. Williams 43 (Bridgend); R.A. Ackerman 1 (Newport), D.S. Richards 7 (Swansea), *S.P. Fenwick 24 (Bridgend), D.L. Nicholas 1 (Llanelli); W.G. Davies 8 (Cardiff), D.B. Williams 1 (Swansea); G. Price 25 (Pontypool), A.J. Phillips 6 (Cardiff), I. Stephens 1 (Bridgend), G.A.D. Wheel 23 (Swansea), C.E. Davis 1 (Newbridge), J. Squire 15 (Pontypool), J.R. Lewis 1 (S. Glamorgan Institute), G.P. Williams 1 (Bridgend).

ENGLAND   W.H. Hare 7 (Leicester); J. Carleton 5 (Orrell), C.R. Woodward 5 (Leicester), P.W. Dodge 10 (Leicester), M.A.C. Slemen 19 (Liverpool); J.P. Horton 8 (Bath), S.J. Smith 13 (Sale); F.E. Cotton (25) (Sale), P.J. Wheeler 22 (Leicester), P.J. Blakeway 5 (Gloucester), *W.B. Beaumont 22 (Fylde), M.J. Colclough 6 (SC Angoulême), M. Rafter (13) (Bristol), D.H. Cooke 1 (Harlequins), J.P. Scott 13 (Cardiff).

Referee J.B. Anderson (Scotland)

IRELAND v FRANCE   52/707

7 February 1981
Lansdowne Road, Dublin
France 19 (1T, 2DG, 3PG) Ireland 13 (1T, 3PG)

Ireland   T: MacNeill. PG: Campbell (3).
France   T: Pardo. DG: Laporte (2). PG: Laporte (2), Gabernet.

Guy Laporte made his Championship début at 28, an age when many internationals have finished their careers, and disposed of Ireland single-handed. Laporte's killer punches were two dropped goals, both from absurdly long range, but which flew to their targets as if they had been tapped over at practice. Two swell-struck penalty goals were merely an added bonus for a French victory which had seemed most unlikely on the morning of the match when influenza vicitims Serge Blanco and Didier Codorniou had to be replaced.

IRELAND   H.P. MacNeill 1 (Dublin U.); F.P. Quinn 1 (Old Belvedere), D.G. Irwin 3 (Queen's U. Belfast), P.P. McNaughton (13) (Greystones), A.C. McLennan 12 (Wanderers); S.O. Campbell 5 (Old Belvedere), J.C. Robbie 4 (Greystones); P.A. Orr 21 (Old Wesley), P.C. Whelan 15 (Garryowen), M.P. Fitzpatrick 5 (Wanderers), M.I. Keane 29 (Lansdowne), B.O. Foley 6 (Shannon), J.B. O'Driscoll 6 (London Irish), *J.F. Slattery 37 (Blackrock College), W.P. Duggan 19 (Blackrock College).

FRANCE   S. Gabernet 4 (S. Toulouse); A. Caussade (8) (FC Lourdes), R. Bertranne 35 (S. Bagnères), P. Mesny 1 (FC Grenoble), L. Pardo 2 (A. Bayonne); G. Laporte 1 (SC Graulhet), P. Berbizier 2 (FC (Lourdes); R. Paparemborde 21 (S. Pau), P. Dintrans 5 (S. Tarbes), P. Dospital 3 (A. Bayonne), J-F. Imbernon 11 (US Perpignan), D. Revallier 2 (SC Graulhet), J-L. Joinel 10 (CA Brive), *J-P. Rives 25 (S. Toulouse), M. Carpentier 3 (FC Lourdes).
Replacement Y. Lafarge (1) (AS Montferrand) for Mesny

Referee C. Norling (Wales)

SCOTLAND v WALES   85/708

7 February 1981
Murrayfield
Scotland 15 (2G, 1PG) Wales 6 (2PG)

Scotland   T: Tomes, Irvine (penalty try). C: Renwick (2). PG: Renwick.
Wales   PG: Fenwick (2).

The only penalty try ever to be awarded in the Championship was given by Irish referee David Burnett when Gareth Davies obstructed Andy Irvine as the Scottish captain dived to score. Burnett had not endeared himself to Welsh supporters when he sent off Paul Ringer at Twickenham the previous season, but on this occasion the offence was so blatant that criticism was unjustified. Neither the Welsh fans nor the Big Five were impressed with the rest of the Welsh performance, but it was a major surprise that the match proved to be the final Championship appearances of J.P.R. Williams and Steve Fenwick. J.P.R. had become an institution in the

Welsh side – he had played a record 44 times – and Fenwick, though slower than in his prime, was still one of the most accomplished try-makers and midfield generals since John Dawes.

SCOTLAND *A.R. Irvine 33 (Heriot's FP); S. Munro 4 (Ayr), J.M. Renwick 32 (Hawick), K.W. Robertson 8 (Melrose), B.H. Hay 15 (Boroughmuir); J.Y. Rutherford 9 (Selkirk), R.J. Laidlaw 6 (Jedforest); N.A. Rowan 4 (Borough-muir), C.T. Deans 11 (Hawick), J. Aitken 5 (Gala), A.J. Tomes 16 (Hawick), W. Cuthbertson 2 (Kilmarnock), J.H. Calder 2 (Stewart's Melville FP), D.G. Leslie 10 (Gala), J.R. Beattie 6 (Heriot's FP).

WALES J.P.R. Williams (44) (Bridgend); R.A. Ackerman 2 (Newport), *S.P. Fenwick (25) (Bridgend), D.S. Richards 8 (Swansea), D.L. Nicholas 2 (Llanelli); W.G. Davies 9 (Cardiff), D.B. Williams (2) (Swansea); G. Price 26 (Ponty-pool), A.J. Phillips 7 (Cardiff), I. Stephens 2 (Bridgend), C.E. Davis (2) (Newbridge), G.A.D. Wheel 24 (Swansea), J.R. Lewis 2 (S. Glamorgan Institute), J. Squire 16 (Pontypool), G.P. Wil-liams 2 (Bridgend).
Replacement G. Evans 1 (Maesteg) for Nicholas

Referee D.I.H. Burnett (Ireland)

have been disastrous against sterner opposition. But fortune favoured the bravado of Davies, who rounded off a marvellous début by scoring what proved to be the match-winning try, after splendid creative work by Mike Slemen.

ENGLAND W.H. Hare 8 (Leicester); J. Carleton 6 (Orrell), C.R. Woodward 6 (Leicester), P.W. Dodge 11 (Leicester), M.A.C. Slemen 20 (Liver-pool); G.H. Davies 1 (Cambridge U.), S.J. Smith 14 (Sale); C.E. Smart 3 (Newport), P.J. Wheeler 23 (Leicester), P.J. Blakeway 6 (Gloucester), *W.B. Beaumont 23 (Fylde), M.J. Colclough 7 (SC Angoulême), N.C. Jeavons 1 (Moseley), D.H. Cooke 2 (Harlequins), J.P. Scott 14 (Cardiff).
Replacement R. Hesford 1 (Bristol) for Jeavons

SCOTLAND *A.R. Irvine 34 (Heriot's FP); S. Munro 5 (Ayr), J.M. Renwick 33 (Hawick), K.W. Robertson 9 (Melrose), B.H. Hay 16 (Boroughmuir); J.Y. Rutherford 10 (Selkirk), R.J. Laidlaw 7 (Jedforest); J. Aitken 6 (Gala), C.T. Deans 12 (Hawick), N.A. Rowan 5 (Boroughmuir), W. Cuthbertson 3 (Kilmarnock), A.J. Tomes 17 (Hawick), J.H. Calder 3 (Stewart's Melville FP), D.G. Leslie 11 (Gala), J.R. Beattie 7 (Heriot's FP).

Referee D.I.H. Burnett (Ireland)

ENGLAND v SCOTLAND 84/709

21 February 1981
Twickenham
England 23 (1G, 2T, 3PG) Scotland 17 (1G, 2T, 1PG)

England T: Davies, Slemen, Woodward. C: Hare. PG: Hare (3).
Scotland T: Munro (2), Calder. C: Irvine. PG: Irvine.

Each side scored three tries in a thrilling match, which at one point seemed destined to end with a Scottish victory. The Scots' forwards were shaded in the scrummages and line-out but they matched England in the loose, and there was plenty of possession for their backs to test the defences. England, however, had a match win-ner in Huw Davies, a newcomer at fly-half. Undaunted by the pressure of international rugby, Davies cut loose at will, breaking through whenever he sniffed an opportunity. It could

WALES v IRELAND 82/710

21 February 1981
Cardiff Arms Park
Wales 9 (1DG, 2PG) Ireland 8 (2T)

Wales DG: Pearce. PG: Evans (2).
Ireland T: Slattery, MacNeill.

A Welsh team unrecognizable in many respects from that which floundered at Murrayfield, were beaten 2-0 in tries by Ireland but manu-factured a victory with discipline and reso-lution. These qualities concealed the cracks and limitations of the side, which were underlined when Tony Ward exploded in two spectacular bursts that left the Welsh defence gasping and groping. It was the only occasion when Ollie Campbell failed to score for Ireland.

WALES G. Evans 2 (Maesteg); D.S. Richards 9 (Swansea), R.W.R. Gravell 15 (Llanelli), P.J. Morgan (3) (Llanelli), D.L. Nicholas 3 (Llanelli);

G.P. Pearce 1 (Bridgend), G. Williams 1 (Bridgend); G. Price 27 (Pontypool), A.J. Phillips 8 (Cardiff), I. Stephens 3 (Bridgend), A.J. Martin 27 (Aberavon), G.A.D. Wheel 25 (Swansea), R.C. Burgess 5 (Ebbw Vale), J.R. Lewis 3 (Cardiff), *J. Squire 17 (Pontypool).
Replacement A.J. Donovan 1 (Swansea) for Morgan

IRELAND   H.P. MacNeill 2 (Dublin U.); F.P. Quinn 2 (Old Belvedere), D.G. Irwin 4 (Queen's U. Belfast), S.O. Campbell 6 (Old Belvedere), A.C. McLennan 13 (Wanderers); A.J.P. Ward 9 (Garryowen), J.C. Robbie 5 (Greystones); M.P. Fitzpatrick 6 (Wanderers), P.C. Whelan 16 (Garryowen), P.A. Orr 22 (Old Wesley), M.I. Keane 30 (Lansdowne), D.E. Spring (6) (Dublin U.), *J.F. Slattery 38 (Blackrock College), J.B. O'Driscoll 7 (London Irish), W.P. Duggan 20 (Blackrock College).
Replacement M.E. Gibson (5) (Lansdowne) for Spring

Referee F. Palmade (France)

FRANCE v WALES   52/711

7 March 1981
Parc des Princes, Paris
France 19 (1T, 5PG) Wales 15 (1G, 3PG)

France   T: Gabernet. PG: Laporte (3), Gabernet (2).
Wales   T: Richards. C: Evans. PG: Evans (3).

France's five penalty goals were the biggest haul in any match against Wales, home or away, and was the least satisfactory aspect of a rugged, unyielding battle for supremacy. Clive Rees returned to the wing seven years after his first cap. ·

FRANCE   S. Gabernet 5 (S. Toulouse); S. Blanco 2 (Biarritz Ol), R. Bertranne 36 (S. Bagnères), D. Codorniou 6 (RC Narbonne), L. Pardo 3 (A. Bayonne); G. Laporte 2 (SC Graulhet), P. Berbizier 3 (FC Lourdes); R. Paparemborde 22 (S. Pau), P. Dintrans 6 (S. Tarbes), P. Dospital 4 (A. Bayonne), J-F. Imbernon 12 (US Perpignan), D. Revallier 3 (SC Graulhet), *J-P. Rives 26 (S. Toulouse), P. Lacans 1 (AS Béziers), J-L. Joinel 11 (CA Brive).
Replacement P. Mesny 2 (FC Grenoble) for Bertranne

WALES   G. Evans 3 (Maesteg); C.F.W. Rees 2 (London Welsh), R.W.R. Gravell 16 (Llanelli), D.S. Richards 10 (Swansea), D.L. Nicholas (4) (Llanelli); G.P. Pearce 2 (Bridgend), G. Williams 2 (Bridgend); G. Price 28 (Pontypool), A.J. Phillips 9 (Cardiff), I. Stephens 4 (Bridgend), A.J. Martin (28) (Aberavon), G.A.D. Wheel 26 (Swansea), J.R. Lewis 4 (Cardiff), R.C. Burgess 6 (Ebbw Vale), *J. Squire 18 (Pontypool).

Referee A. Welsby (England)

IRELAND v ENGLAND   85/712

7 March 1981
Lansdowne Road, Dublin
England 10 (1G, 1T) Ireland 6 (2DG)

Ireland   DG: Campbell, MacNeill.
England   T: Dodge, Rose. C: Rose.

Ireland played two of the most prolific scorers in the history of the Championship, Tony Ward at fly-half and Ollie Campbell at centre, but it was the kicking of a newcomer, Marcus Rose, which decided the outcome. Phil Blakeway, the Gloucester tight-head prop, suffered a serious neck injury early in the proceedings and was replaced by his club colleague, Sargent, a loosehead. Predictably the England front-row was at once in difficulty, which was only partly solved by Colin Smart switching heads occasionally to 'rescue' Sargent from the problems of technique in which he found himself. Smart's strength and knowledge of the mechanics of the front-row had been gathered on the rigorous Welsh club circuit and it is sometimes forgotten that Smart had been offered a place in the Welsh squad, in 1974.

IRELAND   H.P. MacNeill 3 (Dublin U.); F.P. Quinn (3) (Old Belvedere), D.G. Irwin 5 (Queen's U. Belfast), S.O. Campbell 7 (Old Belvedere), A.C. McLennan 14 (Wanderers); A.J.P. Ward 10 (Garryowen), J.C. Robbie 6 (Greystones); P.A. Orr 23 (Old Wesley), P.C. Whelan (17) (Garryowen), M.P. Fitzpatrick 7 (Wanderers), M.I. Keane 31 (Lansdowne), B.O. Foley 7 (Shannon), J.B. O'Driscoll 8 (London Irish), *J.F. Slattery 39 (Blackrock College), W.P. Duggan 21 (Blackrock College).

ENGLAND   W.M.H. Rose 1 (Cambridge U.); J. Carleton 7 (Orrell), C.R. Woodward 7 (Leicester), P.W. Dodge 12 (Leicester), M.A.C. Slemen 21 (Liverpool); G.H. Davies 2 (Cambridge U.), S.J. Smith 15 (Sale); C.E. Smart 4 (Newport), P.J. Wheeler 24 (Leicester), P.J. Blakeway 7 (Gloucester), *W.B. Beaumont 24 (Fylde), M.J. Colclough 8 (SC Angoulême), N.C. Jeavons 2 (Moseley), D.H. Cooke 3 (Harlequins), J.P. Scott 15 (Cardiff).
Replacement G.A.F. Sargent (1) (Gloucester) for Blakeway

Referee J-P. Bonnet (France)

ENGLAND v FRANCE   52/713

21 March 1981
Twickenham
France 16 (1G, 1T, 2DG) England 12 (4PG)

England   PG: Rose (4).
France   T: Lacans, Pardo. C: Laporte. DG: Laporte (2).

France confirmed that this was their best side for several seasons by beating England at Twickenham to take the Grand Slam. The aggression and commitment of the French forwards provided the basis for early control, and that plus the decided advantage of a strong wind helped France build an unassailable 16-0 lead by half-time. England by no means gave up the struggle, but they came close only because Marcus Rose took advantage of French mistakes with four penalty goals. It was the last appearance of Roland Bertranne, who had played in 37 Championship matches since 1971, and was undoubtedly one of the most versatile players of the decade.

ENGLAND   W.M.H. Rose 2 (Cambridge U.); J. Carleton 8 (Orrell), C.R. Woodward 8 (Leicester), P.W. Dodge 13 (Leicester), M.A.C. Slemen 22 (Liverpool); G.H. Davies 3 (Cambridge U.), S.J. Smith 16 (Sale); C.E. Smart 5 (Newport), P.J. Wheeler 25 (Leicester), P.J. Blakeway 8 (Gloucester), *W.B. Beaumont 25 (Fylde), M.J. Colclough 9 (SC Angoulême), N.C. Jeavons 3 (Moseley), D.H. Cooke (4) (Harlequins), J.P. Scott 16 (Cardiff).

FRANCE   S. Gabernet 6 (S. Toulouse); S. Blanco 3 (Biarritz Ol), R. Bertranne (37) (S. Bagnères), D. Codorniou 7 (RC Narbonne), L. Pardo 4 (A. Bayonne); G. Laporte (3) (SC Graulhet), P. Berbizier 4 (FC Lourdes); P. Dospital 5 (A. Bayonne), P. Dintrans 7 (S. Tarbes), R. Paparemborde 23 (S. Pau), D. Revallier 4 (SC Graulhet), J-F. Imbernon 13 (US Perpignan), *J-P. Rives 27 (S. Toulouse), P. Lacans 2 (AS Béziers), J-L. Joinel 12 (CA Brive).

Referee A.M. Hosie (Scotland)

SCOTLAND v IRELAND   86/714

21 March 1981
Murrayfield
Scotland 10 (1T, 1DG, 1PG) Ireland 9 (1G, 1PG)

Scotland   T: Hay. DG: Rutherford. PG: Irvine.
Ireland   T: Irwin. C: Campbell. PG: Campbell.

Ireland, most people's favourites to take the 1981 Championship, plunged to their fourth defeat in a row and although, as in the previous three losses, the margin was narrow the Irish paid the penalty for lost opportunities. Roy Laidlaw and John Rutherford were outstanding as Scotland established a 10-0 lead and then proceeded to quell the Irish revival.

SCOTLAND   *A.R. Irvine 35 (Heriot's FP); S. Munro (6) (Ayr), J.M. Renwick 34 (Hawick), K.W. Robertson 10 (Melrose), B.H. Hay (17) (Boroughmuir); J.Y. Rutherford 11 (Selkirk), R.J. Laidlaw 8 (Jedforest); N.A. Rowan (6) (Boroughmuir), C.T. Deans 13 (Hawick), J. Aitken 7 (Gala), A.J. Tomes 18 (Hawick), W. Cuthbertson 4 (Kilmarnock), J.H. Calder 4 (Stewart's Melville FP), D.G. Leslie 12 (W. of Scotland), J.R. Beattie 8 (Heriot's FP).

IRELAND   H.P. MacNeill 4 (Dublin U.); K.J. Hooks (1) (Queen's U. Belfast), D.G. Irwin 6 (Queen's U. Belfast), S.O. Campbell 8 (Old Belvedere), A.C. McLennan (15) (Wanderers); A.J.P. Ward 11 (Garryowen), J.C. Robbie (7) (Greystones); P.A. Orr 24 (Old Welsey), J.L. Cantrell (5) (Blackrock College), M.P. Fitzpatrick (8) (Wanderers), M.I. Keane 32 (Lansdowne), B.O. Foley (8) (Shannon), J.B. O'Driscoll 9 (London Irish), *J.F. Slattery 40 (Blackrock College), W.P. Duggan 22 (Blackrock College).

Referee L.M. Prideaux (England)

1982

MURRAYFIELD Scotland drew England 9-9 · DUBLIN Ireland beat Wales 20-12
TWICKENHAM Ireland beat England 16-15 · CARDIFF Wales beat France 22-12
PARIS England beat France 27-15 · DUBLIN Ireland beat Scotland 21-12
TWICKENHAM England beat Wales 17-7 · MURRAYFIELD Scotland beat France 16-7
PARIS France beat Ireland 22-9 · CARDIFF Scotland beat Wales 34-18

CHAMPIONSHIP TABLE
Ireland – Championship, Triple Crown

| | | | | | | | | | Tries | |
Pos	Country	P	W	D	L	F	A	Pts	F	A
1	Ireland (5)	4	3	0	1	66	61	6	5	5
2	Scotland (3)	4	2	1	1	71	55	5	7	2
3	England (2)	4	2	1	1	68	47	5	5	4
4	Wales (4)	4	1	0	3	59	83	2	4	11
5	France (1)	4	1	0	3	56	74	2	5	4

Ireland won the Championship and if their prize was embellished by their taking the Triple Crown as well, it was a major disappointment to lose so badly in their last match, in France. The Ireland side was a good, well-balanced one but there could be little doubt as to their star player. Ollie Campbell, who scored a record 21 points in the win over Scotland, and went on to accumulate 46, equalling the Championship best total, which he himself had established in 1980.

High scoring by all teams resulted in an aggregate of 320 points, which was a record for the Championship. Scotland, who finished second, were among the major points' plunderers; their 71 points was their highest Championship total for 57 years, and only 6 less than their record total of 1925. Wales conceded the most points, 83, in a season in which they lost three matches for the first time since 1967. Their record of being the only country never to lose all four Championship matches was maintained because they beat France 22-12 at Cardiff, a defeat which left the Grand Slammers of 1981 with the Wooden Spoon.

SCOTLAND v ENGLAND   85/715

16 January 1982
Murrayfield
Scotland 9 (1DG, 2PG) England 9 (3PG)

Scotland   DG: Rutherford. PG: Irvine (2).
England   PG: Dodge (2), Rose.

This try-less draw gave no indication that these old adversaries would become the leading points-scorers in the season, both countries even scoring more than the title winners, Ireland. Moreover Scotland headed the try list by scoring seven in their three other matches. Of the five penalty goals in the match, the most crucial was the last, which earned Scotland a draw in injury time. But what a kick it was – a howitzer from Andy Irvine from two yards inside his own half. Although no one was aware of it at the time, it was to be Billy Beaumont's last Championship match. He retired later in the season on medical advice, after being injured in the county final between North Midlands and Lancashire at Moseley on 30 January.

SCOTLAND   *A.R. Irvine 36 (Heriot's FP); K.W. Robertson 11 (Melrose), J.M. Renwick 35 (Hawick), D.I. Johnston 5 (Watsonians), G.R.T. Baird 1 (Kelso); J.Y. Rutherford 12 (Selkirk), R.J. Laidlaw 9 (Jedforest); J. Aitken 8 (Gala), C.T. Deans 14 (Hawick), I.G. Milne 5 (Heriot's FP), W. Cuthbertson 5 (Kilmarnock), A.J. Tomes 19 (Hawick), J.H. Calder 5 (Stewart's Melville FP), D.G. Leslie 13 (Gala), I.A.M. Paxton 1 (Selkirk).

ENGLAND   W.M.H. Rose 3 (Cambridge U.); J. Carleton 9 (Orrell), C.R. Woodward 9 (Leicester), P.W. Dodge 14 (Leicester), M.A.C. Slemen 23

(Liverpool); G.H. Davies 4 (Cambridge U.), S.J. Smith 17 (Sale); C.E. Smart 6 (Newport), P.J. Wheeler 26 (Leicester), G.S. Pearce 5 (Northampton), *W.B. Beaumont (26) (Fylde), M.J. Colclough 10 (SC Angoulême), N.C. Jeavons 4 (Moseley), P.J. Winterbottom 1 (Headingley), R. Hesford 2 (Bristol).

Referee K. Rowlands (Wales)

IRELAND v WALES 83/716

23 January 1982
Lansdowne Road, Dublin
Ireland 20 (1G, 2T, 2PG) Wales 12 (1G, 1DG, 1PG)

Ireland   T: Ringland, Finn (2). C: Campbell. PG: Campbell (2).
Wales   T: Holmes. C: Evans. DG: Pearce. PG: Evans.

Heavy snow had caused postponement of this match for a week, but Lansdowne Road was in excellent condition as Ireland aimed for reinstatement after their disappointing four defeats of the previous season. They achieved their victory in style, with Ollie Campbell masterminding their three tries and kicking goals whenever Wales threatened to stage a rally. It was an unlucky match for David Irwin, who broke his leg after half-an-hour. Another player to remember the match with regret was Welsh lock-forward, Geoff Wheel; it was his twenty-seventh and final match for his country.

IRELAND   H.P. MacNeill 5 (Dublin U.); T.M. Ringland 1 (Queen's U. Belfast), D.G. Irwin 7 (Queen's U. Belfast), P.M. Dean 1 (St Mary's College), M.C. Finn 2 (Cork Constitution); S.O. Campbell 9 (Old Belvedere), R.J.M. McGrath 4 (Wanderers); G.A.J. McLoughlin 6 (Shannon), *C.F. Fitzgerald 5 (St Mary's College), P.A. Orr 25 (Old Wesley), D.G. Lenihan 1 (UC Cork), M.I. Keane 33 (Lansdowne), J.B. O'Driscoll 10 (London Irish), J.F. Slattery 41 (Blackrock College), W.P. Duggan 23 (Blackrock College).
Replacements M.J. Kiernan 1 (Dolphin) for Irwin, J.J. Murphy (1) (Greystones) for Dean

WALES   G. Evans 4 (Maesteg); R.A. Ackerman 3 (Newport), D.S. Richards 11 (Swansea), P.C.T. Daniels (1) (Cardiff), C.F.W. Rees 3 (London

Welsh); *W.G. Davies 10 (Cardiff), T.D. Holmes 9 (Cardiff); G. Price 29 (Pontypool), A.J. Phillips 10 (Cardiff), I. Stephens 5 (Bridgend), G.A.D. Wheel (27) (Swansea), R.D. Moriarty 1 (Swansea), G.P. Williams 3 (Bridgend), M. Davies 1 (Swansea), J. Squire 19 (Pontypool).
Replacement G.P. Pearce 3 (Bridgend) for W.G. Davies

Referee J.A. Short (Scotland)

ENGLAND v IRELAND 86/717

6 February 1982
Twickenham
Ireland 16 (1G, 1T, 2PG) England 15 (1G, 3PG)

England   T: Slemen. C: Rose. PG: Rose (3).
Ireland   T: MacNeill, McLoughlin. C: Campbell. PG: Campbell (2).

Ollie Campbell brought his total of points scored against England to 20 in 3 matches since he made his Championship début, at Twickenham in 1980. England suffered from the absence of Billy Beaumont's inspiring leadership; he had withdrawn from the side after being injured the previous week.

ENGLAND   W.M.H. Rose (4) (Cambridge U.); J. Carleton 10 (Orrell), C.R. Woodward 10 (Leicester), A.M. Bond (4) (Sale), M.A.C. Slemen 24 (Liverpool); G.H. Davies 5 (Cambridge U.), *S.J. Smith 18 (Sale); C.E. Smart 7 (Newport), P.J. Wheeler 27 (Leicester), P.J. Blakeway 9 (Gloucester), J.P. Syddall (1) (Waterloo), M.J. Colclough 11 (SC Angoulême), N.C. Jeavons 5 (Moseley), P.J. Winterbottom 2 (Headingley), J.P. Scott 17 (Cardiff).

IRELAND   H.P. MacNeill 6 (Dublin U.); T.M. Ringland 2 (Queen's U. Belfast), M.J. Kiernan 2 (Dolphin), P.M. Dean 2 (St Mary's College), M.C. Finn 3 (Cork Constitution); S.O. Campbell 10 (Old Belvedere), R.J.M. McGrath 5 (Wanderers); G.A.J. McLoughlin 7 (Shannon), *C.F. Fitzgerald 6 (St Mary's College), P.A. Orr 26 (Old Wesley), M.I. Keane 34 (Lansdowne), D.G. Lenihan 2 (UC Cork), J.B. O'Driscoll 11 (London Irish), J.F. Slattery 42 (Blackrock College), W.P. Duggan 24 (Blackrock College).

Referee A.M. Hosie (Scotland)

WALES v FRANCE 53/718

6 February 1982
Cardiff Arms Park
Wales 22 (1T, 6PG) France 12 (1G, 2PG)

Wales T: Holmes. PG: Evans (6).
France T: Blanco. C: Sallefranque. PG: Salle-franque, Martinez.

Wales's six penalty goals were the most they had scored against France, either home or away. Their previous largest total was five in 1976. It was the second successive year that eight penalty goals were kicked in a Wales-France match altogether. All Wales's penalties were scored by Gwyn Evans, which meant he joined Don Clarke (New Zealand) and Gerald Bosch (South Africa) as world record holder for most penalty goals in a match.

WALES   G. Evans 5 (Maesteg); R.A. Ackerman 4 (Newport), D.S. Richards 12 (Swansea), R.W.R. Gravell 17 (Llanelli), C.F.W. Rees 4 (London Welsh); *W.G. Davies 11 (Cardiff), T.D. Holmes 10 (Cardiff); G. Price 30 (Pontypool), A.J. Phillips 11 (Cardiff), I. Stephens 6 (Bridgend), S. Sutton 1 (Pontypool), R.D. Moriarty 2 (Swansea), J.R. Lewis 5 (Cardiff), R.C. Burgess 7 (Ebbw Vale), J. Squire 20 (Pontypool).

FRANCE   M. Sallefranque 1 (US Dax); S. Blanco 4 (Biarritz Ol), P. Perrier 1 (A. Bayonne), C. Belascain 9 (A. Bayonne), L. Pardo 5 (A. Bayonne); J-P. Lescarboura 1 (US Dax), G. Martinez 1 (S. Toulouse); R. Paparemborde 24 (S. Pau), P. Dintrans 8 (S. Tarbes), M. Cremaschi 1 (FC Lourdes), A. Lorieux (1) (FC Grenoble), D. Revallier 5 (SC Graulhet), *J-P. Rives 28 (S. Toulouse), P. Lacans (3) (AS Béziers), L. Rodriguez 1 (S. Mont-de-Marsan).

Referee D.I.H. Burnett (Ireland)

FRANCE v ENGLAND 53/719

20 February 1982
Parc des Princes, Paris
England 27 (2G, 5PG) France 15 (1G, 1DG, 2PG)

France T: Pardo. C: Sallefranque. DG: Lescarboura. PG: Sallefranque (2).
England T: Woodward, Carleton. C: Hare (2). PG: Hare (5).

This was England's hundred-and-fiftieth Championship victory and their highest score in France since their record 39-13 victory of 1914. With Beaumont retired due to medical reasons, Steve Smith took over the captaincy, and clearly revelled in the fact that his new duties coincided with total domination by his forwards. France, who had now conceded 49 points in 2 matches, produced only spasmodic responses to the slick English back ploys, in which the new cap, Les Cusworth, made several significant contributions.

Ollie Campbell, the Championship's most remarkable points accumulator

FRANCE   M. Sallefranque 2 (US Dax); S. Blanco 5 (Biarritz Ol), P. Perrier 2 (A. Bayonne), C. Belascain 10 (A. Bayonne), L. Pardo 6 (A. Bayonne); J-P. Lescarboura 2 (US Dax), G. Martinez 2 (S. Toulouse); D. Dubroca 1 (SU Agen), P. Dintrans 9 (S. Tarbes), J-P. Wolff (1) (AS Béziers), M. Carpentier 4 (FC Lourdes), L. Rodriguez 2 (S. Mont-de-Marsan), J-P. Rives 29 (S. Toulouse), E. Buchet (1) (RRC Nice), J-L. Joinel 13 (CA Brive).

ENGLAND   W.H. Hare 9 (Leicester); J. Carleton 11 (Orrell), C.R. Woodward 11 (Leicester), P.W. Dodge 15 (Leicester), M.A.C. Slemen 25 (Liverpool); L. Cusworth 1 (Leicester), *S.J. Smith 19 (Sale); C.E. Smart 8 (Newport), P.J. Wheeler 28 (Leicester), P.J. Blakeway 10 (Gloucester), S.J. Bainbridge 1 (Gosforth), M.J. Colclough 12 (SC Angoulême), N.C. Jeavons 6 (Moseley), P.J. Winterbottom 3 (Headingley), J.P. Scott 18 (Cardiff).
Replacement R. Hesford 3 (Bristol) for Jeavons

Referee M.D.M. Rea (Ireland)

IRELAND v SCOTLAND   87/720

20 February 1982
Lansdowne Road, Dublin
Ireland 21 (1DG, 6PG) Scotland 12 (1G, 2PG)

Ireland   DG: Campbell. PG: Campbell (6).
Scotland   T: Rutherford. C: Irvine. PG: Renwick (2).

Ireland won the Triple Crown for the first time since 1949 thanks to a remarkable 21-point haul by Ollie Campbell. His six penalty goals not only equalled the world individual record for an international match, but they represented the biggest total Ireland scored in matches with Scotland.

IRELAND   H.P. MacNeill 7 (Dublin U.); M.C. Finn 4 (Cork Constitution), M.J. Kiernan 3 (Dolphin), P.M. Dean 3 (St Mary's College), K.D. Crossan (1) (Instonians); S.O. Campbell 11 (Old Belvedere), R.J.M. McGrath 6 (Wanderers); G.A.J. McLoughlin 8 (Shannon), *C.F. Fitzgerald 7 (St Mary's College), P.A. Orr 27 (Old Wesley), M.I. Keane 35 (Lansdowne), D.G. Lenihan 3 (UC Cork), J.F. Slattery 43 (Blackrock College), J.B. O'Driscoll 12 (London Irish), W.P. Duggan 25 (Blackrock College).

SCOTLAND   *A.R. Irvine 37 (Heriot's FP); K.W. Robertson 12 (Melrose), J.M. Renwick 36 (Hawick), D.I. Johnston 6 (Watsonians), G.R.T. Baird 2 (Kelso); J.Y. Rutherford 13 (Selkirk), R.J. Laidlaw 10 (Jedforest), I.G. Milne 6 (Heriot's FP), C.T. Deans 15 (Hawick), J. Aitken 9 (Gala), W. Cuthbertson 6 (Kilmarnock), A.J. Tomes 20 (Hawick), J.H. Calder 6 (Stewart's Melville FP), R.E. Paxton (1) (Kelso), I.A.M. Paxton 2 (Selkirk).

Referee C. Norling (Wales)

ENGLAND v WALES   86/721

6 March 1982
Twickenham
England 17 (2T, 3PG) Wales 7 (1T, 1DG)

England   T: Carleton, Slemen. PG: Hare (3).
Wales   T: Lewis. DG: Davies.

The English took full advantage of the ineffectiveness of this Welsh team, and there were periods when their complete ascendancy promised an abundance of points. Steve Smith, the England captain, played extremely well behind a pack that prospered not only in the line-out and loose, but in the scrummaging, once the most feared and potent element of Welsh teams. The loss in the second half of their 'extra forward', the competitive Terry Holmes, was another factor in the gradual but assured decline of the Welsh effort.

ENGLAND   W.H. Hare 10 (Leicester); J. Carleton 12 (Orrell), C.R. Woodward 12 (Leicester), P.W. Dodge 16 (Leicester), M.A.C. Slemen (26) (Liverpool); L. Cusworth 2 (Leicester), *S.J. Smith 20 (Sale); C.E. Smart 9 (Newport), P.J. Wheeler 29 (Leicester), P.J. Blakeway (11) (Gloucester), M.J. Colclough 13 (SC Angoulême), S.J. Bainbridge 2 (Gosforth), N.C. Jeavons 7 (Moseley), P.J. Winterbottom 4 (Headingley), J.P. Scott 19 (Cardiff).

WALES   G. Evans 6 (Maesteg); R.A. Ackerman 5 (Newport), R.W.R. Gravell 18 (Llanelli), A.J. Donovan 2 (Swansea), C.F.W. Rees 5 (London Welsh); *W.G. Davies (12) (Cardiff), T.D. Holmes 11 (Cardiff); G. Price 31 (Pontypool), A.J. Phillips 12 (Cardiff), I. Stephens 7 (Bridgend), S. Sutton (2) (Pontypool), R.D. Moriarty 3 (Swan-

sea), J.R. Lewis 6 (Cardiff), R.C. Burgess 8 (Ebbw Vale), J. Squire 21 (Pontypool).
Replacement: G. Williams 3 (Bridgend) for Holmes

Referee F. Palmade (France)

SCOTLAND v FRANCE 52/722

6 March 1982
Murrayfield
Scotland 16 (1T, 1DG, 3PG) France 7 (1T, 1PG)

Scotland T: Rutherford. DG: Renwick. PG: Irvine (3).
France T: Rives. PG: Sallefranque.

France slumped to their third defeat of the season, and their second in a row at Murrayfield. It was a triumph for the controlled aggression of the Scottish pack, and the opportunism of their backs, among whom Jim Renwick was outstanding.

SCOTLAND *A.R. Irvine 38 (Heriot's FP); K.W. Robertson 13 (Melrose), J.M. Renwick 37 (Hawick), D.I. Johnston 7 (Watsonians), G.R.T. Baird 3 (Kelso); J.Y. Rutherford 14 (Selkirk), R.J. Laidlaw 11 (Jedforest); I.G. Milne 7 (Heriot's FP), C.T. Deans 16 (Hawick), J. Aitken 10 (Gala), W. Cuthbertson 7 (Kilmarnock), A.J. Tomes 21 (Hawick), J.H. Calder 7 (Stewart's Melville FP), D.B. White 1 (Gala), I.A.M. Paxton 3 (Selkirk).

FRANCE M. Sallefranque (3) (US Dax); S. Blanco 6 (Biarritz Ol), P. Perrier 3 (A. Bayonne), C. Belascain 11 (A. Bayonne), L. Pardo (7) (A. Bayonne); J-P. Lescarboura 3 (US Dax), G. Martinez 3 (S. Toulouse); D. Dubroca (2) (SU Agen), P. Dintrans 10 (S. Tarbes), M. Cremaschi (2) (FC Lourdes), D. Revallier 6 (SC Graulhet), L. Rodriguez 3 (S. Mont-de-Marsan), *J-P. Rives 30 (S. Toulouse), J-L. Joinel 14 (CA Brive), M. Carpentier (5) (FC Lourdes).

Referee J.A.F. Trigg (England)

FRANCE v IRELAND 53/723

20 March 1982
Parc des Princes, Paris
France 22 (1G, 1T, 4PG) Ireland 9 (3PG)

France T: Blanco, Mesny. C: Gabernet. PG: Blanco (2), Gabernet (2).
Ireland PG: Campbell (3).

Ireland failed in their bid to win their second Grand Slam in the Championship, but Ollie Campbell equalled the Championship record total for the season, 46 points, which he had set in 1980. After the disciplined and resourceful play which had won Ireland the Triple Crown, their overall performance was somewhat disappointing, although the French did field probably their strongest, most experienced XV of the season and were committed to finish the season in style.

FRANCE S. Gabernet (7) (S. Toulouse); M. Fabre (1) (AS Béziers), P. Mesny (3) (FC Grenoble), C. Belascain 12 (A. Bayonne), S. Blanco 7 (Biarritz Ol); J-P. Lescarboura (4) (US Dax), P. Berbizier 5 (FC Lourdes); R. Paparemborde 25 (S. Pau), P. Dintrans 11 (S. Tarbes), P. Dospital 6 (A. Bayonne), J-F. Imbernon 14 (US Perpignan), D. Revallier (7) (SC Graulhet), L. Rodriguez 4 (S. Mont-de-Marsan), *J-P. Rives 31 (S. Toulouse), J-L. Joinel 15 (CA Brive).
Replacement P. Perrier (4) (A. Bayonne) for Belascain

IRELAND H.P. MacNeill 8 (Dublin U.); T.M. Ringland 3 (Queen's U. Belfast), M.J. Kiernan 4 (Dolphin), P.M. Dean (4) (St Mary's College), M.C. Finn 5 (Cork Constitution); S.O. Campbell 12 (Old Belvedere), R.J.M. McGrath 7 (Wanderers); P.A. Orr 28 (Old Wesley), *C.F. Fitzgerald 8 (St Mary's College), G.A.J. McLoughlin 9 (Shannon), M.I. Keane 36 (Lansdowne), D.G. Lenihan 4 (UC Cork), R.K. Kearney (1) (Wanderers), J.F. Slattery 44 (Blackrock College), J.B. O'Driscoll 13 (London Irish).

Referee A. Welsby (England)

WALES v SCOTLAND   86/724

20 March 1982
Cardiff Arms Park
Scotland 34 (4G, 1T, 2DG) Wales 18 (1G, 4PG)

Wales   T: Butler. C: Evans. PG: Evans (4).
Scotland   T: Calder, Renwick, Pollock, White, Johnston. C: Irvine (4). DG: Renwick, Rutherford.

Scotland's 34 points was the highest score ever recorded by any side against Wales in Wales. It was also the Scots' first win at Cardiff for 20 years, Wales's first defeat in the Championship there since 1968 (when France won) and the end of a run of 27 unbeaten Championship home matches. Scotland have scored more tries in Wales on one other occasion only: in 1925 when they registered six in their previous highest scoring match in Wales (24-14). Wales's four penalty goals were the most Wales kicked against Scotland in any match.

WALES   G. Evans 7 (Maesteg); R.A. Ackerman 6 (Newport), R.W.R. Gravell (19) (Llanelli), A.J. Donovan (3) (Swansea), C.F.W. Rees 6 (London Welsh); *W.G. Davies 13 (Cardiff), G. Williams (4) (Bridgend); G. Price 32 (Pontypool), A.J. Phillips (13) (Cardiff), I. Stephens 8 (Bridgend), R.L. Norster 1 (Cardiff), R.D. Moriarty 4 (Swansea), R.C. Burgess (9) (Ebbw Vale), J.R. Lewis (7) (Cardiff), E.T. Butler 5 (Pontypool).

SCOTLAND   *A.R. Irvine 39 (Heriot's FP); J.A. Pollock 1 (Gosforth), J.M. Renwick 38 (Hawick), D.I. Johnston 8 (Watsonians), G.R.T. Baird 4 (Kelso); J.Y. Rutherford 15 (Selkirk), R.J. Laidlaw 12 (Jedforest); I.G. Milne 8 (Heriot's FP), C.T. Deans 17 (Hawick), J. Aitken 11 (Gala), W. Cuthbertson 8 (Harlequins), A.J. Tomes 22 (Hawick), J.H. Calder 8 (Stewart's Melville FP), D.B. White (2) (Gala), I.A.M. Paxton 4 (Selkirk). *Replacement* G. Dickson (7) (Gala) for Paxton

Referee J-P. Bonnet (France)

1983

TWICKENHAM France beat England 19-15 · MURRAYFIELD Ireland beat Scotland 15-13
PARIS France beat Scotland 19-15 · CARDIFF Wales drew England 13-13
MURRAYFIELD Wales beat Scotland 19-15 · DUBLIN Ireland beat France 22-16
TWICKENHAM Scotland beat England 22-12 · CARDIFF Wales beat Ireland 23-9
DUBLIN Ireland beat England 25-15 · PARIS France beat Wales 16-9

CHAMPIONSHIP TABLE
Ireland – Championship

Pos	Country	P	W	D	L	F	A	Pts	Tries F	A
1	Ireland (1)	4	3	0	1	71	67	6	5	6
2	France (5)	4	3	0	1	70	61	6	8	4
3	Wales (4)	4	2	1	1	64	53	5	7	3
4	Scotland (2)	4	1	0	3	65	65	2	5	5
5	England (3)	4	0	1	3	55	79	1	1	8

Hardly a match in the Championship did not produce a record or statistic of note, with the consequence that a new high points-total was achieved, 325, 5 more than the previous best of 1982. For Ireland it was record-breaking all the way. Their 71 points in winning the title for the second year in a row, was their best ever return, and Ollie Campbell was largely responsible. This phenomenal scoring machine broke his own Championship record with 52 points, a total achieved largely by notching up 21 points against England – to equal his best match total – and by kicking four penalty goals against France, a record number by the Irish against any French side.

The fact that France were the top try scorers was due entirely to Patrick Estève's finishing: the wing set a French record by scoring five tries, two of them against Scotland in a match which was to prove the Scots' seventh defeat in a row in Paris, their longest losing sequence against the French. That victory also meant that France had now taken the lead, 26-25, in wins in their Championship series with Scotland. Scotland, who had opened their new stand at Murrayfield in their match against Ireland in

January, finished their season on a much happier note by beating England 22-12 at Twickenham, which was their highest ever score in England.

Wales celebrated Graham Price becoming their most capped forward when he made his thirty-ninth appearance, against England, in a match in which Dusty Hare passed Bob Hiller's 138 points' record in internationals. There were two other, more curious events in the Championship: Bob Hesford, of Bristol, became the first player to earn three caps as a replacement and in the Ireland-England match the lead switched seven times, which had not occurred in any previous Championship clash.

ENGLAND v FRANCE 54/725

15 January 1983
Twickenham
France 19 (2G, 1T, 1PG) England 15 (1DG, 4PG)

England DG: Cusworth. PG: Hare (4).
France T: Estève, Sella, Paparemborde. C: Blanco (2). PG: Camberabero.

Bob Hesford earned his third cap as a replacement, a record for the Championship, when he came on for Maurice Colclough after 50 mintues. Hesford had previously replaced Nick Jeavons (against Scotland at Twickenham in 1981 and against France in Paris in 1982). Robert Paparemborde, the Pau tight-head prop, scored his eighth try for France, a record for a prop, Paparemborde is also the most capped French prop to date. It was France's fourth win in the last five visits to Twickenham. Didier Camberabero's penalty goal taken as a dropped kick was a fairly common occurrence before the War, but the last occasion it was employed was in 1947 by Jean Prat, also for France against England at Twickenham. Two other Camberaberos had played for France: Didier's father, Guy, (1967–68) and uncle, Lilian, (1965–68).

ENGLAND W.H. Hare 11 (Leicester); J. Carleton 13 (Orrell), G.H. Davies 6 (Coventry), P.W. Dodge 17 (Leicester), A.H. Swift 1 (Swansea); L. Cusworth 3 (Leicester), *S.J. Smith 21 (Sale); C.E. Smart 10 (Newport), P.J. Wheeler 30 (Leicester), G.S. Pearce 6 (Northampton), M.J. Colclough 14 (SC Angoulême), S.J. Bainbridge 3 (Gosforth), N.C. Jeavons 8 (Moseley), P.J. Winterbottom 5 (Headingley), J.P. Scott 20 (Cardiff).
Replacement R. Hesford 4 (Bristol) for Colclough

FRANCE S. Blanco 8 (Biarritz Ol); P. Sella 1 (SU Agen), C. Belascain 13 (A. Bayonne), D. Codorniou 8 (RC Narbonne), P. Estève 1 (RC Narbonne); D. Camberabero 1 (La Voulte S.), G. Martinez 4 (S. Toulouse); P. Dospital 7 (A. Bayonne), P. Dintrans 12 (S. Tarbes), R. Paparemborde 26 (S. Pau), J. Condom 1 (Boucau S.), J-C. Orso 1 (RRC Nice), *J-P. Rives 32 (RCF), L. Rodriguez 5 (S. Mont-de-Marsan), J-L. Joinel 16 (CA Brive).

Referee D.I.H. Burnett (Ireland)

SCOTLAND v IRELAND 88/726

15 January 1983
Murrayfield
Ireland 15 (1G, 3PG) Scotland 13 (1T, 1DG, 2PG)

Scotland T: Laidlaw. DG: Renwick. PG: Dods (2).
Ireland T: Kiernan. C: Campbell. PG: Campbell (3).

Scotland's new £3 million stand was in use for the first time, and although Roy Laidlaw had the distinction of scoring his first try for Scotland in his first match as captain, Ireland nipped in for a victory. This brought them level with Scotland in Championship matches with 42 wins each.

SCOTLAND P.W. Dods 1 (Gala); K.W. Robertson 14 (Melrose), J.M. Renwick 39 (Hawick), D.I.

Johnston 9 (Watsonians), G.R.T. Baird 5 (Kelso); R. Wilson 8 (London Scottish), *R.J. Laidlaw 13 (Jedforest); G.M. McGuinness 1 (W. of Scotland), C.T. Deans 18 (Hawick), I.G. Milne 9 (Heriot's FP), W. Cuthbertson 9 (Harlequins), A.J. Tomes 23 (Hawick), J.H. Calder 9 (Stewart's Melville FP), D.G. Leslie 14 (Gala), I.A.M. Paxton 5 (Selkirk).

IRELAND H.P. MacNeill 9 (Oxford U.); T.M. Ringland 4 (Ballymena), D.G. Irwin 8 (Instonians), M.J. Kiernan 5 (Dolphin), M.C. Finn 6 (Cork Constitution), S.O. Campbell 13 (Old Belvedere), R.J.M. McGrath 8 (Wanderers); P.A. Orr 29 (Old Wesley), *C.F. Fitzgerald 9 (St Mary's College), G.A.J. McLoughlin 10 (Shannon), M.I. Keane 37 (Lansdowne), D.G. Lenihan 5 (Cork Constitution), J.F. Slattery 45 (Blackrock College), J.B. O'Driscoll 14 (Manchester), W.P. Duggan 26 (Blackrock College).

Referee J.C. Yche (France)

FRANCE v SCOTLAND 53/727

5 February 1983
Parc des Princes, Paris
France 19 (1G, 1T, 3PG) Scotland 15 (1G, 2DG, 1PG)

France T: Estève (2). C: Blanco. PG: Blanco (3).
Scotland T: Robertson. C: Dods. DG: Gossman (2). PG: Dods.

This was Scotland's seventh defeat in a row against France in Paris, their longest losing sequence against the French. Victory also put France ahead in the series between the countries, 26-25, with 2 matches drawn. Strangely, Bryan Gossman's two dropped goals were the most ever scored by Scotland against France.

FRANCE S. Blanco 9 (Biarritz Ol); P. Sella 2 (SU Agen), C. Belascain 14 (A. Bayonne), D. Codorniou 9 (RC Narbonne), P. Estève 2 (RC Narbonne); C. Delage 1 (SU Agen), P. Berbizier 6 (FC Lourdes); R. Paparemborde 27 (S. Pau), J.L. Dupont 1 (SU Agen), P. Dospital 8 (A. Bayonne), J-C. Orso 2 (RRC Nice), J. Condom 2 (Boucau S.), *J-P. Rives 33 (RCF), L. Rodriguez 6 (S. Mont-de-Marsan), J-L. Joinel 17 (CA Brive).

SCOTLAND   P.W. Dods 2 (Gala); K.W. Robertson 15 (Melrose), J.M. Renwick 40 (Hawick), D.I. Johnston 10 (Watsonians), G.R.T. Baird 6 (Kelso); B.M. Gossman 2 (W. of Scotland), *R.J. Laidlaw 14 (Jedforest); J. Aitken 12 (Gala), C.T. Deans 19 (Hawick), I.G. Milne 10 (Heriot's FP), W. Cuthbertson 10 (Harlequins), A.J. Tomes 24 (Hawick), J.H. Calder 10 (Stewart's Melville FP), D.G. Leslie 15 (Gala), J.R. Beattie 9 (Glasgow Acads).

Referee A. Richards (Wales)

WALES v ENGLAND   87/728

5 February 1983
Cardiff Arms Park
Wales 13 (1T, 1DG, 2PG) England 13 (1T, 1DG, 2PG)

Wales   T: Squire. DG: Dacey. PG: Wyatt (2).
England   T: Carleton. DG: Cusworth. PG: Hare (2).

Graham Price, the Pontypool tight-head prop, became Wales's most capped forward when he made his thirty-ninth appearance (33 Championship matches) in the first ever fully-sponsored home international (British Telecom). It was the first drawn Wales-England international in Wales since 1936, which was at Swansea. Dusty Hare's two penalties (six points) brought his total points for England to 140, beating the previous best of 138 by Bob Hiller. The match, however, was rather uninspiring, with very little productive play.

WALES   M.A. Wyatt 1 (Swansea); H.E. Rees 9 (Neath), M.G. Ring 1 (Cardiff), D.S. Richards 13 (Swansea), C.F.W. Rees 7 (London Welsh); M. Dacey 1 (Swansea), T.D. Holmes 12 (Cardiff); C. Williams 7 (Swansea), W.J. James 1 (Aberavon), G. Price 33 (Pontypool), R.L. Norster 2 (Cardiff), R.D. Moriarty 5 (Swansea), J. Squire 22 (Pontypool), D.F. Pickering 1 (Llanelli), *E.T. Butler 6 (Pontypool).

ENGLAND   W.H. Hare 12 (Leicester); J. Carleton 14 (Orrell), G.H. Davies 7 (Coventry), P.W. Dodge 18 (Leicester), A.H. Swift 2 (Swansea); L. Cusworth 4 (Leicester), *S.J. Smith 22 (Sale); C.E. Smart 11 (Newport), S.G.F. Mills 1 (Gloucester), G.S. Pearce 7 (Northampton), S.B. Boyle 1 (Gloucester), S.J. Bainbridge 4 (Gosforth), N.C. Jeavons 9 (Moseley), P.J. Winterbottom 6 (Headingley), J.P. Scott 21 (Cardiff).

Referee J.R. West (Ireland)

IRELAND v FRANCE   54/729

19 February 1983
Lansdowne Road, Dublin
Ireland 22 (1G, 1T, 4PG) France 16 (1G, 1T, 2PG)

Ireland   T: Finn (2). C: Campbell. PG: Campbell (4).
France   T: Blanco, Estève. C: Blanco. PG: Blanco (2).

Ollie Campbell's four penalty goals were the highest number scored by Ireland against France, and were to prove crucial not only in winning the match, but in swelling the Irish points' aggregate just enough for them to win the title ahead of France by the end of the campaign. France, at one stage, seemed certain to win, but a series of defensive lapses plus some Irish initiative swung the outcome in the last 10 minutes.

IRELAND   H.P. MacNeill 10 (Oxford U.); T.M. Ringland 5 (Ballymena), D.G. Irwin 9 (Instonians), M.J. Kiernan 6 (Dolphin), M.C. Finn 7 (Cork Constitution); S.O. Campbell 14 (Old Belvedere), R.J.M. McGrath 9 (Wanderers); P.A. Orr 30 (Old Wesley), *C.F. Fitzgerald 10 (St Mary's College), G.A.J. McLoughlin 11 (Shannon), M.I. Keane 38 (Lansdowne), D.G. Lenihan 6 (Cork Constitution), J.F. Slattery 46 (Blackrock College), J.B. O'Driscoll 15 (Manchester), W.P. Duggan 27 (Blackrock College).

FRANCE   S. Blanco 10 (Biarritz Ol); P. Sella 3 (SU Agen), C. Belascain 15 (A. Bayonne), D. Codorniou 10 (RC Narbonne), P. Estève 3 (RC Narbonne); C. Delage 2 (SU Agen), P. Berbizier 7 (FC Lourdes); P. Dospital 9 (A. Bayonne), B. Herrero 1 (RRC Nice), R. Paparemborde 28 (S. Pau), J. Condom 3 (Boucau S.), J-F. Imbernon 15 (US Perpignan), *J-P. Rives 34 (RCF), D. Erbani 1 (SU Agen), J-L. Joinel 18 (CA Brive).
Replacement B. Viviès 5 (SU Agen) for Delage

Referee A.M. Hosie (Scotland)

SCOTLAND v WALES 87/730

19 February 1983
Murrayfield
Wales 19 (1G, 1T, 3PG) Scotland 15 (1G, 3PG)

Scotland T: Renwick. C: Dods. PG: Dods (3).
Wales T: Jones, Elgan Rees. C: Wyatt. PG: Wyatt (3).

After the disappointing draw with England a fortnight earlier, this victory at Murrayfield was hailed as the dawn of Welsh rugby's revival which had been in the doldrums arguably since their defeat by England at Twickenham in 1980. Certainly Wales played with encouraging gusto at times and it proved a memorable first appearance for Staff Jones, the young Pontypool loose-head who scored a try and was to emerge from relative obscurity to win a British Lions test place within six months. Another débutant in the Welsh pack was Ian Eidman, the Cardiff tight-head, brought into the side after the controversial dropping of Graham Price, Wales's most capped forward.

SCOTLAND P.W. Dods 3 (Gala); K.W. Robertson 16 (Melrose), J.M. Renwick 41 (Hawick), D.I. Johnston 11 (Watsonians), G.R.T. Baird 7 (Kelso); B.M. Gossman 3 (W. of Scotland), *R.J. Laidlaw 15 (Jedforest); J. Aitken 13 (Gala), C.T. Deans 20 (Hawick), I.G. Milne 11 (Heriot's FP), W. Cuthbertson 11 (Harlequins), A.J. Tomes 25 (Hawick), J.H. Calder 11 (Stewart's Melville FP), D.G. Leslie 16 (Gala), J.R. Beattie 10 (Glasgow Acads).

WALES M.A. Wyatt 2 (Swansea); H.E. Rees 10 (Neath), D.S. Richards 14 (Swansea), R.A. Ackerman 7 (London Welsh), C.F.W. Rees 8 (London Welsh); M. Dacey 2 (Swansea), T.D. Holmes 13 (Cardiff); S.T. Jones 1 (Pontypool), W.J. James 2 (Aberavon), I. Eidman 1 (Cardiff), S.J. Perkins 1 (Pontypool), R.L. Norster 3 (Caridff), J. Squire 23 (Pontypool), D.F. Pickering 2 (Llanelli), *E.T. Butler 7 (Pontypool).

Referee R.C. Quittenton (England)

ENGLAND v SCOTLAND 86/731

5 March 1983
Twickenham
Scotland 22 (1G, 1T, 1DG, 3PG) England 12 (1DG, 3PG)

England DG: Horton. PG: Hare (3).
Scotland T: Laidlaw, Smith. C: Dods. DG: Robertson. PG: Dods (3).

This was Scotland's highest score in England, beating the 21 points they registered in their spectacular 5-try victory of 1938. The Scots had other reasons for self-congratulation. Only three other Scottish sides had won in England since 1909 but none by so decisive a margin. It was the first time since 1959 that England failed to score a try against Scotland at Twickenham and the second time only since 1905. England could derive no comfort from the fact that they were beaten by a much better side as Scotland had lost their previous three matches and needed to win to avoid the Wooden Spoon.

ENGLAND W.H. Hare 13 (Leicester); J. Carleton 15 (Orrell), G.H. Davies 8 (Coventry), P.W. Dodge 19 (Leicester), A.H. Swift 3 (Swansea); J.P. Horton 9 (Bath), S.J. Smith 23 (Sale); C.E. Smart 12 (Newport), P.J. Wheeler 31 (Leicester), G.S. Pearce 8 (Northampton), S.B. Boyle 2 (Gloucester), S.J. Bainbridge 5 (Gosforth), N.C. Jeavons 10 (Moseley), P.J. Winterbottom 7 (Headingley), *J.P. Scott 22 (Cardiff).

SCOTLAND P.W. Dods 4 (Gala); J.A. Pollock 2 (Gosforth), J.M. Renwick 42 (Hawick), K.W. Robertson 17 (Melrose), G.R.T. Baird 8 (Melrose); J.Y. Rutherford 16 (Selkirk), R.J. Laidlaw 16 (Jedforest); *J. Aitken 14 (Gala), C.T. Deans 21 (Hawick), I.G. Milne 12 (Heriot's FP), T.J. Smith 1 (Gala), I.A.M. Paxton 6 (Selkirk), J.H. Calder 12 (Stewart's Melville FP), D.G. Leslie 17 (Gala), J.R. Beattie 11 (Glasgow Acads).

Referee T. Doocey (New Zealand)

Pontypool's proudest day. Five of their forwards: Staff Jones, Jeff Squire, Eddie Butler, John Perkins and Graham Price, played together in the Wales pack for the first time, against Ireland, on 5 March 1983

WALES v IRELAND 84/732

5 March 1983
Cardiff Arms Park
Wales 23 (1G, 2T, 3PG) Ireland 9 (3PG)

Wales T: Wyatt, Holmes, Elgan Rees. C: Wyatt. PG: Wyatt (3).
Ireland PG: Campbell (2), MacNeill.

This was Wales's eighth successive win over Ireland in Wales, one victory short of their all-time best sequence established in 1901–22. Ireland were highly confident of their team's ability to shake off the Arms Park bogey, and it was somewhat of a shock for those closely involved with their selection and preparation that they were so obviously outplayed. The champagne which had been brought by the Irish for the occasion, must have tasted rather flat. Main contributors to the Welsh success were John Perkins, lustily aggressive in line-out and maul, Jeff Squire, Malcolm Dacey and Terry Holmes. There were 15 points, too, from the comparative newcomer at full-back, Mark Wyatt.

WALES M.A. Wyatt 3 (Swansea); H.E. Rees 11 (Neath), D.S. Richards 15 (Swansea), R.A. Ackerman 8 (London Welsh), C.F.W. Rees 9 (London Welsh); M. Dacey 3 (Swansea), T.D. Holmes 14 (Cardiff); S.T. Jones 2 (Pontypool), W.J. James 3 (Aberavon), G. Price 34 (Pontypool), S.J. Perkins 2 (Pontypool), R.L. Norster 4 (Cardiff), J. Squire 24 (Pontypool), D.F. Pickering 3 (Llanelli), *E.T. Butler 8 (Pontypool).

IRELAND H.P. MacNeill 11 (Oxford U.); T.M. Ringland 6 (Ballymena), D.G. Irwin 10 (Instonians), M.J. Kiernan 7 (Dolphin), M.C. Finn 8 (Cork Constitution); S.O. Campbell 15 (Old Belvedere), R.J.M. McGrath 10 (Wanderers); P.A. Orr 31 (Old Wesley), *C.F. Fitzgerald 11 (St Mary's College), G.A.J. McLoughlin 12 (Shannon), M.I. Keane 39 (Lansdowne), D.G. Lenihan 7 (Cork Constitution), J.F. Slattery 47 (Blackrock College), J.B. O'Driscoll 16 (Manchester), W.P. Duggan 28 (Blackrock College).

Referee J.A.F. Trigg (England

FRANCE v WALES 54/733

19 March 1983
Parc des Princes, Paris
France 16 (1T, 1DG, 3PG) Wales 9 (1G, 1PG)

France T: Estève. DG: Camberabero. PG: Blanco (3).
Wales T: Squire. C: Wyatt. PG: Evans.

Patrick Estève's try brought his total to five for the season, a record for a French player in the Championship, beating the four-try total held jointly by Michel Crauste (1962) and Christian Darrouy (1965). The victory also confirmed that France had established a marked superiority over Wales in France. Of 13 matches played in Paris since 1959, Wales had won twice only, in 1971 and 1975. In contrast, Wales still had the edge at home for France had won three times only in their last 13 visits. The match itself was a bloody affair and much recrimination followed.

FRANCE   S. Blanco 11 (Biarritz Ol); P. Sella 4 (SU Agen), C. Belascain 16 (A. Bayonne), D. Codorniou 11 (RC Narbonne), P. Estève 4 (RC Narbonne); D. Camberabero 2 (La Voulte S.), G. Martinez 5 (S. Toulouse); R. Paparemborde (29) (S. Pau), P. Dintrans 13 (S. Tarbes), P. Dospital 10 (A. Bayonne), J. Condom 4 (Boucau S.), J-F. Imbernon 16 (US Perpignan), *J-P. Rives 35 (RCF), D. Erbani 2 (SU Agen), J-L. Joinel 19 (CA Brive).

WALES   M.A. Wyatt 4 (Swansea); H.E. Rees 12 (Neath), G. Evans 8 (Maesteg), R.A. Ackerman 9 (London Welsh), C.F.W. Rees 10 (London Welsh); M. Dacey 4 (Swansea), T.D. Holmes 15 (Cardiff); G. Price (35) (Pontypool), W.J. James 4 (Aberavon), S.T. Jones 3 (Pontypool), S.J. Perkins 3 (Pontypool), R.L. Norster 5 (Cardiff), J. Squire (25) (Pontypool), D.F. Pickering 4 (Llanelli), *E.T. Butler 9 (Pontypool).

Referee T. Doocey (New Zealand)

IRELAND v ENGLAND   87/734

19 March 1983
Lansdowne Road, Dublin
Ireland 25 (1G, 1T, 5PG) England 15 (5PG)

Ireland   T: Slattery, Campbell. C: Campbell. PG: Campbell (5).
England   PG: Hare (5).

Ollie Campbell broke the Championship record total for a season for the second time by scoring 52 points. This was entirely due to his 21 points in this match, equalling the Irish individual record established by Campbell himself against Scotland at the same ground in 1982. Campbell's points' blitz included a try, his first for Ireland. Dusty Hare was also in record-breaking mood: his five penalties equalled the England record held by himself and Alan Old (also against

Ireland, in 1974). Hare's first penalty gave England the advantage and thereby started a sequence unique in a Championship match for the lead swung seven times before Ireland pulled away in the second half. It meant that Ireland finished the season as Champions, narrowly outpointing France, and in the process had scored 71 points, their highest Championship total.

IRELAND   H.P. MacNeill 12 (Blackrock College); T.M. Ringland 7 (Ballymena), D.G. Irwin 11 (Instonians), M.J. Kiernan 8 (Dolphin), M.C. Finn 9 (Cork Constitution); S.O. Campbell 16 (Old Belvedere), R.J.M. McGrath 11 (Wanderers); P.A. Orr 32 (Old Wesley), *C.F. Fitzgerald 12 (St Mary's College), G.A.J. McLoughlin 13 (Shannon), D.G. Lenihan 8 (Cork Constitution), M.I. Keane 40 (Lansdowne), J.F. Slattery 48 (Blackrock College), J.B. O'Driscoll 17 (Manchester), W.P. Duggan 29 (Blackrock College).
Replacement A.J.P. Ward 12 (St Mary's College) for Campbell.

ENGLAND   W.H. Hare 14 (Leicester); J. Carleton 16 (Orrell), C.R. Woodward 13 (Leicester), P.M. Dodge 20 (Leicester), D.M. Trick 1 (Bath); J.P. Horton 10 (Bath), N.G. Youngs 1 (Leicester); C.E. Smart 13 (Newport), P.J. Wheeler 32 (Leicester), G.S. Pearce 9 (Northampton), S.B. Boyle 3 (Gloucester), S.J. Bainbridge 6 (Gosforth), N.C. Jeavons 11 (Moseley), P.J. Winterbottom 8 (Headingley), *J.P. Scott 23 (Cardiff).

Referee J.B. Anderson (Scotland)

HOW POINTS HAVE INCREASED

The increase in the number of kicks, particularly penalty goals, in international rugby in general and the Championship in particular has been a matter of some concern to the rugby establishment for a number of years. The Press – supposedly the mirror of opinion within the game – have campaigned for measures to curb the plethora, their suggestions ranging from a drastic increase or decrease in the value of kicks or tries to restricting the number of penalty kicks at goal allowed for serious offences only, such as foul play. Highly-specialized players such as Ollie Campbell, Dusty Hare and Gwyn Evans, who have broken numerous records because of their kicking abilities, perhaps hold a rather sceptical view of such proposals. Certainly their accuracy has contributed significantly to modern Championship scoring which, despite the occasional hiccup, has gradually increased since the resumption after the War in 1947.

However, it is debatable that this increase in points-scoring has, as is sometimes thought, affected matches and their outcomes. There is no evidence that goal-kicking has become more crucial than, for example, tries and that there has been a consequent lowering of standards in the Championship. Statistically speaking the Championship is far from impoverished, as some critics have advocated, for while the kickers have certainly added to match aggregates, it is not through penalty goals alone. Conversions and dropped kicks have on the whole increased: there has been no outcry against this.

It is often overlooked that the number of tries is also increasing. Although not as abundant as in, say 1910–14, when France first joined the Championship (the fragile French defence was a major factor in a harvest of tries), tries nevertheless are being scored regularly by each competing nation as part of an overall increase in scoring. The try average may not yet have reached the heady 38 tries a season which was the feature of the 1920–31 era, but the number has nevertheless grown steadily since 1947. If this surge in tries is coincidental with the age of the greatest kickers the game has ever known, it surely outweighs opposition to the corresponding increase in accurate goal-kicking.

While bearing in mind that present-day kickers have many more opportunities to practise their art, it would seem that they are more skilled than ever before and are merely a factor in the evolution of the game. The critics would be among the first to comment if a contemporary international side took the field without a specialized goal-kicker.

The following tables tell their own story of scoring over the years in the Championship. The periods are self-evident: they largely embrace the 'natural' breaks caused by the intervention of two World Wars and coincide with the entries (and barring) of France. The introduction of the four-point try in 1972 was a convenient break in the period 1947–83.

Period	Seasons	Matches	Eng.	France	Ire.	Scot.	Wales	Total	Per Season	Per Match
					TRIES					
1883–90	8	38	33	—	13	46	12	104	13	2.73
1891–1909	19	111	98	—	66	87	124	375	19.73	3.37
1910–14	5	49	67	24	36	49	69	245	49	5
1920–31	12	120	116	62	76	107	106	467	38.91	3.89
1932–39	8	48	41	—	45	34	31	151	18.87	3.14
1947–59	13	130	74	66	66	45	82	333	25.61	2.56
1960–71	12	120	55	88	51	47	81	322	26.83	2.68
1972–83	12	118	56	80	51	64	92	343	28.58	2.89
	89	734	540	320	404	479	597	2340	26.29	3.18

Period	Seasons	Matches	Eng.	France	Ire.	Scot.	Wales	Total	Per Season	Per Match
				CONVERSIONS						
1883–90	8	38	8	—	4	19	6	37	4.62	0.97
1891–1909	19	111	36	—	21	35	48	140	7.36	1.26
1910–14	5	49	26	9	17	23	33	108	21.6	2.2
1920–31	12	120	53	16	28	46	40	183	15.25	1.52
1932–39	8	48	15	—	12	13	11	51	6.37	1.06
1947–59	13	130	31	35	27	18	32	143	11	1.1
1960–71	12	120	29	51	24	22	43	169	14.08	1.4
1972–83	12	118	27	41	28	31	41	168	14.00	1.42
	89	734	225	152	161	207	254	999	11.22	1.36
				DROPPED GOALS						
1883–90	8	38	0	—	1	4	2	7	0.87	0.18
1891–1909	19	111	3	—	3	11	8	25	1.31	0.22
1910–14	5	49	2	0	6	4	7	19	3.8	0.38
1920–31	12	120	7	8	5	9	16	45	3.75	0.37
1932–39	8	48	3	—	2	5	5	15	1.87	0.31
1947–59	13	130	5	17	3	5	3	33	2.53	0.25
1960–71	12	120	10	27	10	14	15	76	6.63	0.66
1972–83	12	118	11	18	15	23	13	80	6.66	0.67
	89	734	41	70	45	75	69	300	3.37	0.4
				PENALTY GOALS						
1883–90	8	38	0	—	0	0	0	0	—	—
1891–1909	19	111	7	—	8	7	9	31	1.63	0.27
1910–14	5	49	4	2	2	1	5	14	2.8	0.28
1920–31	12	120	11	4	13	14	9	51	4.25	0.42
1932–39	8	48	14	—	6	10	9	39	4.87	0.81
1947–59	13	130	29	23	37	31	36	156	12	1.2
1960–71	12	120	53	27	41	40	41	202	16.83	1.68
1972–83	12	118	99	77	95	78	101	450	37.50	3.81
	89	734	217	133	202	181	210	943	10.56	1.28
				POINTS						
1883–90	8	38	—*	—	—	—*	—	—	—	—
1891–1909	19	111	378*	—	278†	369†	519*	1544	81.26	13.9
1910–14	5	49	273	96	172	212	316	1069	213.8	21.81
1920–31	12	120	521†	265*	343	491	492*	2112	176	17.6
1932–39	8	48	207	—	188*	178	162	735	91.87	15.31
1947–59	13	130	388	389	372	279	427	1855	142.69	14.26
1960–71	12	120	412	528	354	347	497	2138	178.16	17.81
1972–83	12	118	608	687	590	621	792	3298	274.83	27.94
	89	734	2787	1965	2297	2497	3205	12,751	143.27	17.35

** includes one goal from mark*   *† includes two goals from mark*

CHAMPIONSHIP WINNERS 1883–1983

Year	Country	P	W	D	L	F	A	Pts	Tries F	A
1883	England	3	3	0	0	—	—	6	12	2
1884	England	3	3	0	0	—	—	6	5	2
1885	England	2	2	0	0	—	—	4	7	3
1886	Scotland	3	2	1	0	—	—	5	8	0
1887	Scotland	3	2	1	0	—	—	5	16	1
1888	Ireland	2	1	0	1	—	—	2	2	1
1889	Scotland	2	2	0	0	—	—	4	2	0
1890	England	3	2	0	1	—	—	4	5	1
1891	Scotland	3	3	0	0	38	3	6	14	1
1892	England	3	3	0	0	29	0	6	7	0
1893	Wales	3	3	0	0	23	11	6	8	4
1894	Ireland	3	3	0	0	15	5	6	2	1
1895	Scotland	3	3	0	0	17	7	6	4	0
1896	Ireland	3	2	1	0	18	8	5	4	0
1897	England	3	1	0	2	21	27	2	3	7
1898	England	3	1	1	1	23	19	3	6	4
1899	Ireland	3	3	0	0	18	3	6	5	0
1900	Wales	3	3	0	0	28	6	6	7	2
1901	Scotland	3	3	0	0	45	16	6	11	4
1902	Wales	3	3	0	0	38	13	6	9	3
1903	Scotland	3	3	0	0	19	6	6	4	2
1904	Scotland	3	2	0	1	28	27	4	8	6
1905	Wales	3	3	0	0	41	6	6	11	2
1906	Ireland	3	2	0	1	33	25	4	9	6
1907	Scotland	3	3	0	0	29	9	6	7	1
1908	Wales	3	3	0	0	45	28	6	10	6
1909	Wales	3	3	0	0	31	8	6	7	1
1910	England	4	3	1	0	36	14	7	9	4
1911	Wales	4	4	0	0	78	21	8	18	5
1912	England	4	3	0	1	44	16	6	12	4
1913	England	4	4	0	0	50	4	8	13	0
1914	England	4	4	0	0	82	49	8	20	9
1920	Wales	4	3	0	1	58	23	6	11	3
1921	England	4	4	0	0	61	9	8	13	1
1922	Wales	4	3	1	0	59	23	7	15	6
1923	England	4	4	0	0	50	17	8	10	4
1924	England	4	4	0	0	69	19	8	17	5
1925	Scotland	4	4	0	0	77	37	8	17	6
1926	Scotland	4	3	0	1	45	23	6	9	6
1927	Scotland	4	3	0	1	49	25	6	10	6
1928	England	4	4	0	0	41	22	8	9	6
1929	Scotland	4	3	0	1	41	30	6	9	8
1930	England	4	2	1	1	25	12	5	6	2
1931	Wales	4	3	1	0	74	25	7	15	5
1932	Ireland	3	2	0	1	40	29	4	9	5
1933	Scotland	3	3	0	0	22	9	6	3	3
1934	England	3	3	0	0	28	6	6	8	2
1935	Ireland	3	2	0	1	24	22	4	6	2
1936	Wales	3	2	1	0	16	3	5	3	1
1937	England	3	3	0	0	19	14	5	4	3
1938	Scotland	3	3	0	0	52	36	6	10	7
1939	Wales	3	2	0	1	18	6	4	3	1

Year	Country	P	W	D	L	F	A	Pts	Tries F	Tries A
1947	England	4	3	0	1	39	36	6	7	8
1948	Ireland	4	4	0	0	36	19	8	10	5
1949	Ireland	4	3	0	1	41	24	6	5	3
1950	Wales	4	4	0	0	50	8	8	10	1
1951	Ireland	4	3	1	0	21	16	7	4	3
1952	Wales	4	4	0	0	42	14	8	6	3
1953	England	4	3	1	0	54	20	7	11	3
1954	Wales	4	3	0	1	52	34	6	7	7
1955	Wales	4	3	0	1	48	28	6	8	3
1956	Wales	4	3	0	1	25	20	6	6	2
1957	England	4	4	0	0	34	8	8	7	1
1958	England	4	2	2	0	26	6	6	5	0
1959	France	4	2	1	1	28	15	5	4	1
1960	France	4	3	1	0	55	28	7	11	6
1961	France	4	3	1	0	39	14	7	5	3
1962	France	4	3	0	1	35	6	6	7	0
1963	England	4	3	1	0	29	19	7	4	3
1964	Wales	4	2	2	0	43	26	6	8	4
1965	Wales	4	3	0	1	55	45	6	10	5
1966	Wales	4	3	0	1	34	26	6	5	4
1967	France	4	3	0	1	55	41	6	8	2
1968	France	4	4	0	0	52	30	8	7	2
1969	Wales	4	3	1	0	79	31	7	14	2
1970	France	4	3	0	1	60	33	6	11	4
1971	Wales	4	4	0	0	73	38	8	13	4
1972	Wales	3	3	0	0	67	21	6	8	1
1973	Scotland	4	2	0	2	55	59	4	4	7
1974	Ireland	4	2	1	1	50	45	5	5	3
1975	Wales	4	3	0	1	87	30	6	14	3
1976	Wales	4	4	0	0	102	37	8	11	3
1977	France	4	4	0	0	58	21	8	8	0
1978	Wales	4	4	0	0	67	43	8	8	4
1979	Wales	4	3	0	1	83	51	6	10	5
1980	England	4	4	0	0	80	48	8	10	6
1981	France	4	4	0	0	70	49	8	6	3
1982	Ireland	4	3	0	1	66	61	6	5	5
1983	Ireland	4	3	0	1	71	67	6	5	6

Title wins: Wales 27   England 24   Scotland 16   Ireland 13   France 9

Highest aggregate: 102 points Wales 1976

Lowest aggregate: 15 points Ireland 1894 (4 nations)
                       25 points England 1930 (5 nations)

Fewest points against: 0 England 1892 (4 nations)
                       4 England 1913 (5 nations)

Most points against: 67 Ireland 1983

Most tries scored: 20 England 1914

Most tries against: 9 England 1914

CHAMPIONSHIP SUMMARIES

Country	Champion-ships	Titles	Runners-up	Grand Slams	Triple Crowns	Wooden Spoons
England	87	24	18	8	15	18
France	54	9	12	3	—	14
Ireland	89	13	18	1	5	26
Scotland	89	16	19	1	8	21
Wales	89	27	22	6	16	10

CHAMPIONSHIP POINTS, TRIES AND LANDMARKS

Year	M	Pts	Tries	
1883	5	—	20	
1884	6	—	15	
1885	4	—	13	
1886	5	—	11	Points-scoring introduced, but values varied until 1890 when uniform
1887	6	—	23	scoring was adopted after England joined the International Board.
1888	3	—	4	
1889	3	—	4	
1890	6	—	13	
1891	6	70	24	Points-scoring applied to Championship for the first time: points values
1892	6	49	14	in 1891 were: 1 point for a try, 2 for a conversion, 2 for a penalty goal,
1893	6	46	14	3 for a dropped goal, 3 for a goal from mark.
1894	6	60	11	In 1893 the try was upgraded to 2 points and a penalty goal to 3 points.
1895	6	61	15	In 1894 the try was upgraded to 3 points.
1896	6	68	16	
1897	4	59	12	
1898	5	64	14	
1899	6	86	18	
1900	6	53	12	
1901	6	**109**	26	100-point barrier passed for first time.
1902	6	74	19	
1903	6	75	19	
1904	6	128	32	
1905	6	91	25	
1906	6	101	27	Goal from mark now valued at 3 points.
1907	6	115	26	
1908	6	142	29	
1909	6	93	21	
1910	10	**201**	49	France enter Championship: 200-point barrier passed.
1911	10	247	**55**	Highest ever number of tries in Championship.
1912	10	195	45	
1913	10	201	46	
1914	9	225	50	Scotland did not play France: Championship suspended because of War.
1920	10	180	36	
1921	10	164	32	
1922	10	161	41	
1923	10	176	38	
1924	10	221	53	
1925	10	218	49	
1926	10	161	35	
1927	10	182	38	
1928	10	169	43	

Year	M	Pts	Tries	
1929	10	142	36	
1930	10	128	25	
1931	10	200	41	France barred from Championship.
1932	6	111	22	
1933	6	79	16	
1934	6	91	23	
1935	6	85	16	
1936	6	59	13	
1937	6	75	16	
1938	6	**176**	**35**	Highest number of tries and points in 6-match Championship.
1939	6	59	10	War prevented Championship for 8 years.
1947	10	148	30	
1948	10	130	29	
1949	10	137	24	Dropped goal now worth 3 points.
1950	10	134	26	
1951	10	143	27	
1952	10	153	26	
1953	10	172	34	
1954	10	150	29	
1955	10	166	26	
1956	10	163	27	
1957	10	131	21	
1958	10	135	22	
1959	10	**93**	12	Lowest number of tries and points for 10-match Championship.
1960	10	187	31	
1961	10	123	22	
1962	10	106	16	
1963	10	131	16	
1964	10	174	32	
1965	10	178	30	
1966	10	131	21	
1967	10	**230**	30	200-point barrier passed for the first time since 1931.
1968	10	176	19	
1969	10	234	32	
1970	10	222	38	
1971	10	246	35	
1972	8	249	28	Try now worth 4 points; Ireland did not play Scotland
1973	10	248	26	or Wales.
1974	10	240	22	
1975	10	281	35	
1976	10	**306**	33	300-point barrier passed for the first time.
1977	10	238	25	
1978	10	245	24	
1979	10	258	32	
1980	10	316	41	Highest try total for 50 years.
1981	10	272	25	
1982	10	320	26	
1983	10	**325**	26	Highest number of points in Championship.

SUMMARIES

HIGHEST NUMBER OF POINTS:	325 1983 (10 matches) 176 1938 (6 matches)	LOWEST NUMBER OF POINTS:	93 1959 (10 matches) 46 1893 (6 matches)
HIGHEST NUMBER OF TRIES:	55 1911 (10 matches) 35 1938 (6 matches)	LOWEST NUMBER OF TRIES:	12 1959 (10 matches) 10 1939 (6 matches)

CHAMPIONSHIP RECORDS 1883–1983

HIGHEST SCORE: 49 (Wales 49 France 14 1910 Swansea)

BIGGEST WINNING POINTS MARGIN: 37 (England 37 France 0 1911 Richmond)

MOST POINTS IN A SEASON: 102 Wales 1976 (4 matches)

MOST TRIES IN A SEASON: 21 Wales 1910 (4 matches)

MOST POINTS AGAINST IN A SEASON: 95 France 1910 (4 matches)

MOST TRIES IN A MATCH: 12 (Scotland v Wales 1887 Raeburn Place, Wales v France 1910 Swansea, England v France 1914 Paris)

LONGEST WINNING SEQUENCE: 10 matches (England 1883–86, 1922–25)

LONGEST LOSING SEQUENCE: 17 matches (France 1911–20)

MOST TITLE WINS IN SEQUENCE: 4 (France 1959–62)

LONGEST PERIOD WITHOUT TITLE WIN: 27 years (Scotland 1939–73)

MOST WOODEN SPOONS IN SEQUENCE: 4 France (1924–27), Ireland (1920–23)

LONGEST SEQUENCE WITHOUT DEFEAT: 13 matches (England 1922–25)

LONGEST SEQUENCE WITHOUT VICTORY: 17 matches (France 1911–20)

ENGLAND

HIGHEST SCORE: 39 (39-13 v France 1914 Paris)

BIGGEST WINNING POINTS MARGIN: 37 (37-0 v France 1911 Richmond)

BIGGEST SCORE AGAINST: 37 (12-37 v France 1972 Paris)

BIGGEST LOSING POINTS MARGIN: 25 (0-25 v Wales 1905 Cardiff, 12-37 v France 1972 Paris)

MOST POINTS IN A SEASON: 82 1914 (4 matches)

MOST TRIES IN A SEASON: 20 1914 (4 matches)

MOST POINTS AGAINST IN A SEASON: 88 1972 (4 matches)

MOST TRIES AGAINST IN A SEASON: 15 1976 (4 matches)

MOST TRIES IN A MATCH: 9 (39-13 v France 1914 Paris)

MOST TRIES AGAINST IN A MATCH: 8 (6-28 v Wales 1922 Cardiff)

FRANCE

HIGHEST SCORE: 37 (37-12 v England 1972 Paris)

BIGGEST WINNING POINTS MARGIN: 25 (37-12 v England 1972 Paris)

BIGGEST SCORE AGAINST: 49 (14-49 v Wales 1910 Swansea)

BIGGEST LOSING POINTS MARGIN: 37 (0-37 v England 1911 Twickenham)

MOST POINTS IN A SEASON: 82 1976 (4 matches)

MOST TRIES IN A SEASON: 13 1976 (4 matches)

MOST POINTS AGAINST IN A SEASON: 95 1910 (4 matches)

MOST TRIES AGAINST IN A SEASON: 22 1910 (4 matches)

MOST TRIES IN A MATCH: 6 (27-6 v Ireland 1964 Paris, 35-13 v England 1970 Paris, 37-12 v England 1972 Paris, 30-9 v England 1976 Paris)

MOST TRIES AGAINST IN A MATCH: 10 (14-49 v Wales 1910 Swansea)

IRELAND

HIGHEST SCORE: 26 (26-8 v Scotland 1953 Murrayfield, 26-21 v England, 1974 Twickenham)

BIGGEST WINNING POINTS MARGIN: 24 (24-0 v France 1913 Cork)

BIGGEST SCORE AGAINST: 36 (14-36 v England 1938 Dublin)

BIGGEST LOSING POINTS MARGIN: 29 (0-29 v Wales 1907 Cardiff)

MOST POINTS IN A SEASON: 71 1983 (4 matches)

MOST TRIES IN A SEASON: 12 (1928, 1953)

MOST POINTS AGAINST IN A SEASON: 87 1976 (4 matches)

MOST TRIES AGAINST IN A SEASON: 19 1920 (4 matches)

MOST TRIES IN A MATCH: 6 (24-0 v France 1913 Cork, 26-8 v Scotland 1953 Murrayfield)

MOST TRIES AGAINST IN A MATCH: 7 (14-36 v England 1938 Dublin, 14-29 v Scotland 1913 Inverleith)

SCOTLAND

HIGHEST SCORE: 35 (35-0 v Wales 1924 Inverleith)

BIGGEST WINNING POINTS MARGIN: 28 (31-3 v France 1912 Inverleith)

BIGGEST SCORE AGAINST: 35 (12-35 v Wales 1972 Cardiff)

BIGGEST LOSING POINTS MARGIN: 23 (12-35 v Wales, 1972 Cardiff)

MOST POINTS IN A SEASON: 77 1925 (4 matches)

MOST TRIES IN A SEASON: 17 1925 (4 matches)

MOST POINTS AGAINST IN A SEASON: 85 1977 (4 matches)

MOST TRIES AGAINST IN A SEASON: 19 1911 (4 matches)

MOST TRIES IN A MATCH: 12 (Wales 1887 Raeburn Place)

MOST TRIES AGAINST IN A MATCH: 6 (8-26 v Ireland 1953 Murrayfield)

WALES

HIGHEST SCORE: 49 (49-14 v France 1910 Swansea)

BIGGEST WINNING POINTS MARGIN: 35 (49-14 v France 1910 Swansea)

BIGGEST SCORE AGAINST: 35 (10-35 v Scotland 1924 Inverleith)

BIGGEST LOSING POINTS MARGIN: 25 (0-25 v England 1896 Blackheath, 10-35 v Scotland 1924 Inverleith)

MOST POINTS IN A SEASON: 102 1976 (4 matches)

MOST TRIES IN A SEASON: 21 1910 (4 matches)

MOST POINTS AGAINST IN A SEASON: 83 1982 (4 matches)

MOST TRIES AGAINST IN A SEASON: 18 1924 (4 matches)

MOST TRIES IN A MATCH: 10 (49-14 v France 1910 Swansea)

MOST TRIES AGAINST IN A MATCH: 12 (v Scotland 1887 Raeburn Place)

RECORD IN CHAMPIONSHIP

Year	Pos	P	W	D	L	F	A	Pts	Tries F	Tries A
ENGLAND										
*1883	1	3	3	0	0	—	—	6	12	2
*1884	1	3	3	0	0	—	—	6	5	2
1885	1	2	2	0	0	—	—	4	7	3
1886	2	3	2	1	0	—	—	5	3	1
1887	4	3	0	2	1	—	—	2	1	3
1890	1	3	2	0	1	—	—	4	5	1
1891	2	3	2	0	1	19	12	4	9	3
*1892	1	3	3	0	0	29	0	6	7	0
1893	3	3	1	0	2	15	20	2	6	3
1894	2	3	1	0	2	29	16	2	5	4
1895	2	3	2	0	1	23	15	4	6	4
1896	3	3	1	0	2	29	21	2	7	5
1897	1	3	1	0	2	21	27	2	3	7
1898	1	3	1	1	1	23	19	3	6	4
1899	4	3	0	0	3	3	37	0	1	8
1900	2	3	1	1	1	18	17	3	4	2
1901	4	3	0	0	3	9	41	0	2	9
1902	2	3	2	0	1	20	15	4	6	4
1903	4	3	0	0	3	11	37	0	3	8
1904	3	3	1	1	1	36	20	3	9	4
1905	4	3	0	0	3	3	50	0	1	14
1906	4	3	1	0	2	18	35	2	6	9
1907	4	3	0	0	3	12	47	0	3	12
1908	2	3	1	0	2	41	47	2	9	7
1909	3	3	1	0	2	19	31	2	5	7
1910	1	4	3	1	0	36	14	7	9	4
1911	3	4	2	0	2	61	26	4	13	7
1912	1	4	3	0	1	44	16	6	12	4
†*1913	1	4	4	0	0	50	4	8	13	0
†*1914	1	4	4	0	0	82	49	8	20	9
1920	2	4	3	0	1	40	37	6	9	5
†*1921	1	4	4	0	0	61	9	8	13	1
1922	2	4	2	1	1	40	47	5	10	13
†*1923	1	4	4	0	0	50	17	8	10	4
†*1924	1	4	4	0	0	69	19	8	17	5
1925	3	4	2	1	1	42	37	5	9	9
1926	4	4	1	1	2	38	39	3	10	8
1927	3	4	2	0	2	32	39	4	5	9
†*1928	1	4	4	0	0	41	22	8	9	6
1929	4	4	2	0	2	35	27	4	9	9
1930	1	4	2	1	1	25	12	5	6	2
1931	5	4	0	1	3	38	59	1	9	11
1932	2	3	2	0	1	32	23	4	6	3
1933	3	3	1	0	2	20	16	2	6	3
*1934	1	3	3	0	0	28	6	6	8	2
1935	2	3	1	1	1	24	16	3	2	4
1936	3	3	1	1	1	12	14	3	4	3
*1937	1	3	3	0	0	19	14	5	4	3
1938	3	3	1	0	2	60	49	2	10	11
1939	3	3	2	0	1	12	11	4	1	3
1947	1	4	3	0	1	39	36	6	7	8
1948	5	4	0	1	3	16	35	1	2	9
1949	2	4	2	0	2	35	29	4	7	5
1950	5	4	1	0	3	22	30	2	5	7
1951	5	4	1	0	3	13	40	2	3	8
1952	2	4	3	0	1	34	14	6	7	4
1953	1	4	3	1	0	54	20	7	11	3
*1954	2	4	3	0	1	39	23	6	10	4
1955	4	4	1	1	2	24	31	3	5	4
1956	2	4	2	0	2	43	28	4	5	5
†*1957	1	4	4	0	0	34	8	8	7	1
1958	1	4	2	2	0	26	6	6	5	0
1959	4	4	1	2	1	9	11	4	0	1
*1960	2	4	3	1	0	46	26	7	7	2
1961	4	4	1	1	2	22	22	3	5	4
1962	3	4	1	2	1	19	16	4	3	3
1963	1	4	3	1	0	29	19	7	4	3
1964	4	4	1	1	2	23	42	3	5	10
1965	4	4	1	1	2	15	28	3	2	5
1966	5	4	0	1	3	15	36	1	2	6
1967	2	4	2	0	2	68	67	4	8	9
1968	3	4	1	2	1	37	40	4	3	3
1969	3	4	2	0	2	54	58	4	6	8
1970	5	4	1	0	3	40	69	2	7	11
1971	3	4	1	1	2	44	58	3	5	9
1972	5	4	0	0	4	36	88	0	2	11
1973	3	4	2	0	2	52	62	4	7	8
1974	5	4	1	1	2	63	66	3	6	8
1975	5	4	1	0	3	40	65	2	5	9
1976	5	4	0	0	4	42	86	0	2	15
1977	3	4	2	0	2	42	24	4	5	3
1978	3	4	2	0	2	42	33	4	4	2
1979	4	4	1	1	2	24	52	3	3	8
†*1980	1	4	4	0	0	80	48	8	10	6
1981	2	4	2	0	2	64	60	4	6	6
1982	3	4	2	1	1	68	47	5	5	4
1983	5	4	0	1	3	55	79	1	1	8
Total:		314	151	36	127	2777	2631	—	542	484

Title wins: 24; Runners-up: 18; Wooden Spoons: 18

* *Triple Crown*

† *Grand Slam*

FRANCE

Year	Pos	P	W	D	L	F	A	Pts	Tries F	Tries A
1910	5	4	0	0	4	20	95	0	4	22
1911	4	4	1	0	3	21	92	2	5	18
1912	5	4	0	0	4	25	74	0	7	17
1913	5	4	0	0	4	11	76	0	3	20
1914	5	3	0	0	3	19	78	0	5	18
1920	4	4	1	0	3	23	26	2	7	5
1921	2	4	2	0	2	33	32	4	5	6
1922	4	4	0	2	2	20	33	2	6	6
1923	4	4	1	0	3	28	52	2	6	11
1924	5	4	0	0	4	23	47	0	7	10
1925	5	4	0	0	4	23	58	0	5	14
1926	5	4	0	0	4	11	49	0	2	11
1927	5	4	1	0	3	19	56	2	5	12
1928	4	4	1	0	3	30	48	2	8	14
1929	5	4	0	0	4	12	36	0	4	9
1930	4	4	2	0	2	17	25	4	3	5
1931	3	4	2	0	2	24	44	4	4	10
1947	4	4	2	0	2	23	20	4	6	3
1948	2	4	2	0	2	40	25	4	9	4
1949	3	4	2	0	2	24	28	4	3	4
1950	4	4	1	1	2	14	35	3	3	7
1951	2	4	3	0	1	41	27	6	7	6
1952	4	4	1	0	3	29	37	2	5	3
1953	4	4	1	0	3	17	38	2	1	10
1954	3	4	3	0	1	35	22	6	7	3
1955	2	4	3	0	1	47	28	6	8	3
1956	4	4	2	0	2	31	34	4	5	5
1957	5	4	0	0	4	24	45	0	4	9
1958	3	4	2	0	2	36	37	4	4	6
1959	1	4	2	1	1	28	15	5	4	1
1960	1	4	3	1	0	55	28	7	11	6
1961	1	4	3	1	0	39	14	7	5	3
1962	1	4	3	0	1	35	6	6	7	0
1963	2	4	2	0	2	40	25	4	6	2
1964	3	4	1	1	2	41	33	3	8	5
1965	2	4	2	1	1	47	33	5	10	7
1966	2	4	2	1	1	35	18	5	7	2
1967	1	4	3	0	1	55	41	6	8	2
†1968	1	4	4	0	0	52	30	8	7	2
1969	5	4	0	1	3	28	53	1	3	7
1970	1	4	3	0	1	60	33	6	11	4
1971	2	4	1	2	1	41	40	4	5	5
1972	4	4	1	0	3	61	66	2	8	8
1973	5	4	2	0	2	38	36	4	3	3
1974	3	4	1	2	1	43	53	4	3	4
1975	3	4	2	0	2	53	79	4	6	10
1976	2	4	3	0	1	82	37	6	13	2
†1977	1	4	4	0	0	58	21	8	8	0
1978	2	4	3	0	1	51	47	6	6	4
1979	2	4	2	1	1	50	46	5	7	5
1980	5	4	1	0	3	55	75	2	7	10
†1981	1	4	4	0	0	70	49	8	6	3
1982	5	4	1	0	3	56	74	2	5	4
1983	2	4	3	0	1	70	61	6	8	4
Total:		215	89	15	111	1963	2310	—	320	374

Title wins: 9; Runners-up: 12; Wooden Spoons: 14

IRELAND

Year	Pos	P	W	D	L	F	A	Pts	Tries F	Tries A
1883	3	2	0	0	2	—	—	0	1	6
1884	4	3	0	0	3	—	—	0	1	7
1885	4	2	0	0	2	—	—	0	1	5
1886	4	2	0	0	2	—	—	0	0	6
1887	3	3	1	0	2	—	—	2	5	4
1888	1	2	1	0	1	—	—	2	2	1
1889	2	2	1	0	1	—	—	2	2	0
1890	4	3	0	1	2	—	—	1	1	5
1891	4	3	0	0	3	4	29	0	1	11
1892	3	3	1	0	2	9	9	2	3	3
1893	4	3	0	1	2	0	6	1	0	4
*1894	1	3	3	0	0	15	5	6	2	1
1895	4	3	0	0	3	6	17	0	2	5
1896	1	3	2	1	0	18	8	5	4	0
1897	2	2	1	0	1	16	17	2	4	2
1898	4	3	1	0	2	12	25	2	2	5
*1899	1	3	3	0	0	18	3	6	5	0
1900	4	3	0	1	2	4	18	1	0	4
1901	3	3	1	0	2	24	25	2	6	6
1902	3	3	1	0	2	8	21	2	2	5
1903	3	3	1	0	2	6	21	2	1	7
1904	4	3	1	0	2	17	50	2	5	14
1905	2	3	2	0	1	31	18	4	9	4
1906	1	3	2	0	1	33	25	4	9	6
1907	3	3	1	0	2	20	53	2	4	11
1908	4	3	1	0	2	24	35	2	5	8
1909	4	3	0	0	3	13	38	0	2	10
1910	4	4	1	1	2	11	36	3	3	10
1911	2	4	3	0	1	44	31	6	10	6
1912	2	4	3	0	1	33	34	6	6	10
1913	4	4	1	0	3	55	60	2	10	14
1914	3	4	2	0	2	29	34	4	7	10
1920	5	4	0	0	4	22	76	0	3	19
1921	5	4	1	0	3	19	49	2	5	10
1922	5	4	1	0	3	19	32	2	4	10
1923	5	4	1	0	3	21	54	2	5	12
1924	3	4	2	0	2	30	37	4	8	9
1925	2	4	2	1	1	42	26	5	9	6
1926	2	4	3	0	1	41	26	6	8	6
1927	2	4	3	0	1	39	20	6	8	4
1928	2	4	3	0	1	44	30	6	12	6

Year	Pos	P	W	D	L	F	A	Pts	Tries F	Tries A
1929	3	4	2	1	1	24	26	5	6	6
1930	3	4	2	0	2	25	31	4	4	8
1931	4	4	2	0	2	17	28	4	4	6
1932	1	3	2	0	1	40	29	4	9	5
1933	2	3	1	0	2	22	30	2	4	6
1934	4	3	0	0	3	12	42	0	4	9
1935	1	3	2	0	1	24	22	4	6	2
1936	2	3	2	0	1	16	10	4	4	1
1937	2	3	2	0	1	24	16	4	6	2
1938	4	3	0	0	3	33	70	0	9	13
1939	2	3	2	0	1	17	10	4	3	2
1947	3	4	2	0	2	33	18	4	7	5
†*1948	1	4	4	0	0	36	19	8	10	5
*1949	1	4	3	0	1	41	24	6	5	3
1950	3	4	1	1	2	27	12	3	3	3
1951	1	4	3	1	0	21	16	7	4	3
1952	3	4	2	0	2	26	33	4	5	6
1953	3	4	2	1	1	54	25	5	12	3
1954	4	4	1	0	3	18	34	2	3	5
1955	5	4	0	1	3	15	44	1	1	8
1956	3	4	2	0	2	33	47	4	6	7
1957	3	4	2	0	2	21	21	4	4	1
1958	5	4	1	0	3	24	32	2	3	7
1959	2	4	2	0	2	23	19	4	3	3
1960	5	4	0	0	4	25	47	0	5	8
1961	5	4	1	0	3	22	48	2	3	7
1962	5	4	0	1	3	9	50	1	1	9
1963	4	4	1	1	2	19	33	3	2	5
1964	5	4	1	0	3	33	53	2	5	10
1965	3	4	2	1	1	32	23	5	6	3
1966	4	4	1	1	2	24	34	3	2	7
1967	4	4	2	0	2	17	22	4	3	2
1968	2	4	2	1	1	38	37	5	4	2
1969	2	4	3	0	1	61	48	6	8	6
1970	3	4	2	0	2	33	28	4	6	4
1971	4	4	1	1	2	41	46	3	6	5
1972	3	2	2	0	0	30	21	4	4	2
1973	4	4	2	0	2	50	48	4	5	5
1974	1	4	2	1	1	50	45	5	5	3
1975	2	4	2	0	2	54	67	4	8	8
1976	4	4	1	0	3	31	87	2	3	8
1977	5	4	0	0	4	33	65	0	1	8
1978	4	4	1	0	3	46	54	2	2	5
1979	3	4	2	0	2	53	51	4	5	6
1980	2	4	2	0	2	70	65	4	6	8
1981	5	4	0	0	4	36	48	0	4	4
*1982	1	4	3	0	1	66	61	6	5	5
1983	1	4	3	0	1	71	67	6	5	6
Total:		313	128	18	167	2297	2774	—	406	527

Title wins: 13; Runners-up: 18; Wooden Spoons: 26

SCOTLAND

Year	Pos	P	W	D	L	F	A	Pts	Tries F	Tries A
1883	2	3	2	0	1	—	—	4	6	3
1884	2	3	2	0	1	—	—	4	6	2
1885	2	2	1	1	0	—	—	3	3	0
1886	1	3	2	1	0	—	—	5	8	0
1887	1	3	2	1	0	—	—	5	16	1
1888	2	2	1	0	1	—	—	2	1	1
1889	1	2	2	0	0	—	—	4	2	0
1890	2	3	2	0	1	—	—	4	4	3
*1891	1	3	3	0	0	38	3	6	14	1
1892	2	3	2	0	1	9	7	4	3	2
1893	2	3	1	1	1	8	9	3	0	3
1894	4	3	1	0	2	6	12	2	2	2
*1895	1	3	3	0	0	17	7	6	4	0
1896	2	3	1	1	1	11	6	3	3	2
1897	4	2	1	0	1	11	15	2	2	3
1898	2	2	1	1	0	11	3	3	3	1
1899	2	3	2	0	1	29	19	4	4	5
1900	3	3	0	2	1	3	12	2	1	4
*1901	1	3	3	0	0	45	16	6	11	4
1902	4	3	0	0	3	8	25	0	2	7
*1903	1	3	3	0	0	19	6	6	4	2
1904	1	3	2	0	1	28	27	4	8	6
1905	3	3	1	0	2	16	17	2	4	5
1906	3	3	1	0	2	19	24	2	3	8
*1907	1	3	3	0	0	29	9	6	7	1
1908	3	3	1	0	2	32	32	2	5	8
1909	2	3	2	0	1	30	16	4	7	3
1910	3	4	2	0	2	46	28	4	12	8
1911	5	4	0	0	4	43	77	0	9	19
1912	3	4	2	0	2	53	37	4	12	6
1913	3	4	2	0	2	50	28	4	12	6
1914	4	3	0	0	3	20	46	0	4	9
1920	3	4	3	0	1	37	18	6	6	4
1921	4	4	1	0	3	22	38	2	5	8
1922	3	4	1	2	1	23	26	4	6	6
1923	2	4	3	0	1	46	22	6	12	4
1924	2	4	3	0	1	60	47	6	12	11
†*1925	1	4	4	0	0	77	37	8	17	6
1926	1	4	3	0	1	45	23	6	9	6
1927	1	4	3	0	1	49	25	6	10	6
1928	5	4	1	0	3	20	38	2	6	10
1929	1	4	3	0	1	41	30	6	9	8
1930	5	4	1	1	2	26	30	3	6	6
1931	2	4	2	0	2	47	44	4	9	9
1932	4	3	0	0	3	11	42	0	3	9
*1933	1	3	3	0	0	22	9	6	3	3
1934	3	3	1	0	2	25	28	2	5	8
1935	4	3	1	0	2	21	29	2	5	7
1936	4	3	0	0	3	15	32	0	2	8
1937	3	3	1	0	2	20	23	2	3	7
*1938	1	3	3	0	0	52	36	6	10	7

Year	Pos	P	W	D	L	F	A	Pts	Tries F	Tries A
1939	4	3	0	0	3	12	32	0	3	4
1947	5	4	0	0	4	16	57	0	2	12
1948	3	4	2	0	2	15	31	4	3	6
1949	4	4	2	0	2	20	37	4	4	8
1950	2	4	2	0	2	21	49	4	5	8
1951	4	4	1	0	3	39	25	2	7	4
1952	5	4	0	0	4	22	55	0	3	10
1953	5	4	0	0	4	21	75	0	4	16
1954	5	4	0	0	4	6	37	0	2	10
1955	3	4	2	0	2	32	35	4	4	8
1956	5	4	1	0	3	31	34	2	5	8
1957	4	4	2	0	2	21	27	4	1	5
1958	4	4	1	1	2	23	32	3	4	5
1959	5	4	1	1	2	12	25	3	1	3
1960	4	4	1	0	3	29	47	2	4	8
1961	3	4	2	0	2	19	25	4	4	4
1962	2	4	2	1	1	34	23	5	5	2
1963	3	4	2	0	2	22	22	4	2	2
1964	2	4	3	0	1	34	20	6	6	3
1965	5	4	0	1	3	29	49	1	2	10
1966	3	4	2	1	1	23	17	5	5	2
1967	3	4	2	0	2	37	45	4	4	8
1968	5	4	0	0	4	18	35	0	1	7
1969	4	4	1	0	3	12	44	2	1	9
1970	4	4	1	0	3	43	50	2	5	12
1971	5	4	1	0	3	47	64	2	6	12
1972	2	3	2	0	1	55	53	4	6	6
1973	1	4	2	0	2	55	59	4	4	7
1974	4	4	2	0	2	41	35	4	4	4
1975	4	4	2	0	2	47	40	4	2	5
1976	3	4	2	0	2	49	59	4	4	5
1977	4	4	1	0	3	39	85	2	4	11
1978	5	4	0	0	4	39	68	0	4	9
1979	5	4	0	2	2	48	58	2	7	8
1980	4	4	1	0	3	61	83	2	8	12
1981	3	4	2	0	2	51	54	4	7	6
1982	2	4	2	1	1	71	55	5	7	2
1983	4	4	1	0	3	65	65	2	5	5
Total:		314	136	19	159	2499	2764	—	475	524

Title wins: 16; Runners-up: 19; Wooden Spoons: 21

Year	Pos	P	W	D	L	F	A	Pts	Tries F	Tries A
1889	3	2	0	0	2	—	—	0	0	4
1890	3	3	1	1	1	—	—	3	3	4
1891	3	3	1	0	2	9	26	2	2	11
1892	4	3	0	0	3	2	33	0	1	9
*1893	1	3	3	0	0	23	11	6	8	4
1894	3	3	1	0	2	10	27	2	2	4
1895	3	3	1	0	2	15	22	2	3	6
1896	4	3	1	0	2	10	33	2	2	9
1897	3	1	1	0	0	11	0	2	3	0
1898	3	2	1	0	1	18	17	2	3	4
1899	3	3	1	0	2	36	27	2	8	5
*1900	1	3	3	0	0	28	6	6	7	2
1901	2	3	2	0	1	31	27	4	7	7
*1902	1	3	3	0	0	38	13	6	9	3
1903	2	3	2	0	1	39	11	4	11	2
1904	2	3	1	1	1	47	31	3	10	8
*1905	1	3	3	0	0	41	6	6	11	2
1906	2	3	2	0	1	31	17	4	9	4
1907	2	3	2	0	1	54	6	4	12	2
†*1908	1	3	3	0	0	45	28	6	10	6
†*1909	1	3	3	0	0	31	8	6	7	1
1910	2	4	3	0	1	88	28	6	21	5
†*1911	1	4	4	0	0	78	21	8	18	5
1912	4	4	2	0	2	40	34	4	8	8
1913	2	4	3	0	1	35	33	6	8	6
1914	2	4	3	0	1	75	18	6	14	4
1920	1	4	3	0	1	58	23	6	11	3
1921	3	4	2	0	2	29	36	4	4	7
1922	1	4	3	1	0	59	23	7	15	6
1923	3	4	1	0	3	31	31	2	5	7
1924	4	4	1	0	3	39	71	2	9	18
1925	4	4	1	0	3	34	60	2	9	14
1926	3	4	2	1	1	26	24	5	6	4
1927	4	4	1	0	3	43	42	2	10	7
1928	3	4	1	0	3	34	31	2	8	7
1929	2	4	2	1	1	30	23	5	8	4
1930	2	4	2	0	2	35	30	4	6	4
1931	1	4	3	1	0	74	25	7	15	5
1932	3	3	2	0	1	28	17	4	4	5
1933	4	3	1	0	2	15	24	2	3	4
1934	2	3	2	0	1	26	15	4	6	4
1935	3	3	1	1	1	16	18	3	3	3
1936	1	3	2	1	0	16	3	5	3	1
1937	4	3	0	0	3	12	22	0	3	4
1938	2	3	2	0	1	31	21	4	6	4
1939	1	3	2	0	1	18	6	4	3	1
1947	2	4	3	0	1	37	17	6	8	2
1948	4	4	1	1	2	23	20	3	5	5
1949	5	4	1	0	3	17	19	2	5	4
†*1950	1	4	4	0	0	50	8	8	10	1
1951	3	4	1	1	2	29	35	3	6	6
†*1952	1	4	4	0	0	42	14	8	6	3
1953	2	4	3	0	1	26	14	6	6	2

WALES

Year	Pos	P	W	D	L	F	A	Pts	Tries F	Tries A
1883	4	2	0	0	2	—	—	0	1	9
1884	3	3	1	0	2	—	—	2	3	4
1885	3	2	0	1	1	—	—	1	2	5
1886	3	2	0	0	2	—	—	0	1	5
1887	2	3	1	1	1	—	—	3	1	15
1888	3	2	1	0	1	—	—	2	1	2

Year	Pos	P	W	D	L	F	A	Pts	Tries F	A
1954	1	4	3	0	1	52	34	6	7	7
1955	1	4	3	0	1	48	28	6	8	3
1956	1	4	3	0	1	25	20	6	6	2
1957	2	4	2	0	2	31	30	4	5	5
1958	2	4	2	1	1	26	28	5	6	4
1959	3	4	2	0	2	21	23	4	4	4
1960	3	4	2	0	2	32	39	4	4	7
1961	2	4	2	0	2	21	14	4	5	4
1962	4	4	1	2	1	9	11	4	0	2
1963	5	4	1	0	3	21	32	2	2	4
1964	1	4	2	2	0	43	26	6	8	4
*1965	1	4	3	0	1	55	45	6	10	5
1966	1	4	3	0	1	34	26	6	5	4
1967	5	4	1	0	3	53	55	2	7	9
1968	4	4	1	1	2	31	34	3	4	5
*1969	1	4	3	1	0	79	31	7	14	2
1970	2	4	3	0	1	46	42	6	9	7

Year	Pos	P	W	D	L	F	A	Pts	Tries F	A
†*1971	1	4	4	0	0	73	38	8	13	4
1972	1	3	3	0	0	67	21	6	8	1
1973	2	4	2	0	2	53	43	4	7	3
1974	2	4	1	2	1	43	41	4	4	3
1975	1	4	3	0	1	87	30	6	14	3
†*1976	1	4	4	0	0	102	37	8	11	3
*1977	2	4	3	0	1	66	43	6	7	3
†*1978	1	4	4	0	0	67	43	8	8	4
*1979	1	4	3	0	1	83	51	6	10	5
1980	3	4	2	0	2	50	45	4	10	5
1981	4	4	2	0	2	51	61	4	2	6
1982	4	4	1	0	3	59	83	2	4	11
1983	3	4	2	1	1	64	53	5	7	3
Total:		312	175	22	115	3205	2262	—	598	432

Title wins: 27; Runners-up: 22; Wooden Spoons: 10

LONGEST SEQUENCES

Matches	Country	Period

WINNING

Matches	Country	Period
10	England	1883–86
10	England	1922–25
9	England	1912–14
9	Wales	1970–73

LOSING

Matches	Country	Period
17	France	1911–20
15	Scotland	1951–55
14	France	1924–27
9	Ireland	1883–86

WITHOUT DEFEAT

Matches	Country	Period
13	England	1922–25
12	England	1883–87
10	France	1960–62
9	Wales	1970–73

WITHOUT VICTORY

Matches	Country	Period
17	France	1911–20
15	Scotland	1951–55
14	France	1924–27
11	Scotland	1977–80

MOST TITLE WINS

Matches	Country	Period
4	France	1959–62
3	England	1912–14
3	England	1883–85
3	Scotland	1925–27
3	Wales	1954–56
3	Wales	1964–66

WITHOUT TITLE WIN

Matches	Country	Period
30	France	1910–59
27	Scotland	1939–73
22	Ireland	1952–74
20	Ireland	1907–32
16	England	1964–80

MOST WOODEN SPOONS

Matches	Country	Period
4	France	1924–27
4	Ireland	1920–23
3	England	1905–07
3	England	1974–76
3	Scotland	1952–54
2	Wales	1888–89

MATCHES

M	Year	Venue	R	F	A	T	C	DG	PG	GM	T	C	DG	PG	GM
ENGLAND-FRANCE															
1	1910	away	W	11	3	3	1	0	0	0	1	0	0	0	0
2	1911	home	W	37	0	7	5	0	2	0	0	0	0	0	0
3	1912	away	W	18	8	4	1	1	0	0	2	1	0	0	0
4	1913	home	W	20	0	6	1	0	0	0	0	0	0	0	0
5	1914	away	W	39	13	9	6	0	0	0	3	2	0	0	0
6	1920	home	W	8	3	1	1	0	1	0	1	0	0	0	0
7	1921	away	W	10	6	2	2	0	0	0	0	0	0	2	0
8	1922	home	D	11	11	1	1	0	2	0	3	1	0	0	0
9	1923	away	W	12	3	2	1	1	0	0	0	0	0	1	0
10	1924	home	W	19	7	5	2	0	0	0	1	0	1	0	0
11	1925	away	W	13	11	2	2	0	0	1	3	1	0	0	0
12	1926	home	W	11	0	3	1	0	0	0	0	0	0	0	0
13	1927	away	L	0	3	0	0	0	0	0	1	0	0	0	0
14	1928	home	W	18	8	4	3	0	0	0	2	1	0	0	0
15	1929	away	W	16	6	4	2	0	0	0	2	0	0	0	0
16	1930	home	W	11	5	3	1	0	0	0	1	1	0	0	0
17	1931	away	L	13	14	3	2	0	0	0	2	0	2	0	0
18	1947	home	W	6	3	2	0	0	0	0	0	0	0	1	0
19	1948	away	L	0	15	0	0	0	0	0	3	1	1	0	0
20	1949	home	W	8	3	1	1	1	0	0	0	0	1	0	0
21	1950	away	L	3	6	1	0	0	0	0	2	0	0	0	0
22	1951	home	L	3	11	1	0	0	0	0	2	1	1	0	0
23	1952	away	W	6	3	0	0	0	2	0	1	0	0	0	0
24	1953	home	W	11	0	3	1	0	0	0	0	0	0	0	0
25	1954	away	L	3	11	1	0	0	0	0	2	1	1	0	0
26	1955	home	L	9	16	1	0	0	2	0	2	2	2	0	0
27	1956	away	L	9	14	1	0	0	2	0	2	1	0	2	0
28	1957	home	W	9	5	3	0	0	0	0	1	1	0	0	0
29	1958	away	W	14	0	3	1	0	1	0	0	0	0	0	0
30	1959	home	D	3	3	0	0	0	1	0	0	0	0	1	0
31	1960	away	D	3	3	1	0	0	0	0	0	0	0	1	0
32	1961	home	D	5	5	1	1	0	0	0	1	1	0	0	0
33	1962	away	L	0	13	0	0	0	0	0	3	2	0	0	0
34	1963	home	W	6	5	0	0	0	2	0	1	1	0	0	0
35	1964	away	W	6	3	1	0	0	1	0	1	0	0	0	0
36	1965	home	W	9	6	1	0	0	2	0	1	0	0	1	0
37	1966	away	L	0	13	0	0	0	0	0	3	2	0	0	0
38	1967	home	L	12	16	0	0	1	3	0	2	2	1	1	0
39	1968	away	L	9	14	0	0	1	2	0	1	1	2	1	0
40	1969	home	W	22	8	3	2	0	3	0	1	1	1	0	0
41	1970	away	L	13	35	2	2	0	1	0	6	4	2	1	0
42	1971	home	D	14	14	1	1	0	3	0	2	1	1	1	0
43	1972	away	L	12	37	1	1	0	2	0	6	5	0	1	0
44	1973	home	W	14	6	2	0	0	2	0	1	1	0	0	0
45	1974	away	D	12	12	1	1	1	1	0	1	1	1	1	0
46	1975	home	L	20	27	2	0	0	4	0	4	4	0	1	0
47	1976	away	L	9	30	1	1	0	1	0	6	3	0	0	0
48	1977	home	L	3	4	0	0	0	1	0	1	0	0	0	0

M	Year	Venue	R	F	A	T	C	DG	PG	GM	T	C	DG	PG	GM
49	1978	away	L	6	15	0	0	2	0	0	2	2	0	1	0
50	1979	home	W	7	6	1	0	0	1	0	1	1	0	0	0
51	1980	away	W	17	13	2	0	2	1	0	2	1	0	1	0
52	1981	home	L	12	16	0	0	0	4	0	2	1	2	0	0
53	1982	away	W	27	15	2	2	0	5	0	1	1	1	2	0
54	1983	home	L	15	19	0	0	1	4	0	3	2	0	1	0
		Total:		604	526	98	46	11	56	1	89	51	20	21	0

England 28 wins; France 20; Drawn 6

ENGLAND-IRELAND

M	Year	Venue	R	F	A	T	C	DG	PG	GM	T	C	DG	PG	GM
1	1883	home	W	—	—	4	1	0	0	0	1	0	0	0	0
2	1884	away	W	—	—	1	1	0	0	0	0	0	0	0	0
3	1885	home	W	—	—	2	0	0	0	0	1	0	0	0	0
4	1886	away	W	—	—	1	0	0	0	0	0	0	0	0	0
5	1887	away	L	—	—	0	0	0	0	0	2	2	0	0	0
6	1890	home	W	—	—	3	0	0	0	0	0	0	0	0	0
7	1891	away	W	9	0	5	2	0	0	0	0	0	0	0	0
8	1892	home	W	7	0	2	1	0	0	0	0	0	0	0	0
9	1893	away	W	4	0	2	0	0	0	0	0	0	0	0	0
10	1894	home	L	5	7	1	1	0	0	0	1	0	1	0	0
11	1895	away	W	6	3	2	0	0	0	0	1	0	0	0	0
12	1896	home	L	4	10	0	0	1	0	0	2	2	0	0	0
13	1897	away	L	9	13	1	0	0	2	0	3	0	0	0	1
14	1898	home	L	6	9	1	0	0	1	0	2	0	0	1	0
15	1899	away	L	0	6	0	0	0	0	0	1	0	0	1	0
16	1900	home	W	15	4	3	1	1	0	0	0	0	1	0	0
17	1901	away	L	6	10	1	0	0	1	0	2	2	0	0	0
18	1902	home	W	6	3	2	0	0	0	0	1	0	0	0	0
19	1903	away	L	0	6	0	0	0	0	0	1	0	0	1	0
20	1904	home	W	19	0	5	2	0	0	0	0	0	0	0	0
21	1905	away	L	3	17	1	0	0	0	0	5	1	0	0	0
22	1906	home	L	6	16	2	0	0	0	0	4	2	0	0	0
23	1907	away	L	9	17	2	0	0	1	0	4	1	0	0	1
24	1908	home	W	13	3	3	2	0	0	0	0	0	0	1	0
25	1909	away	W	11	5	3	1	0	0	0	1	1	0	0	0
26	1910	home	D	0	0	0	0	0	0	0	0	0	0	0	0
27	1911	away	L	0	3	0	0	0	0	0	1	0	0	0	0
28	1912	home	W	15	0	5	0	0	0	0	0	0	0	0	0
29	1913	away	W	15	4	4	0	0	1	0	0	0	1	0	0
30	1914	home	W	17	12	5	1	0	0	0	2	1	1	0	0
31	1920	away	W	14	11	4	1	0	0	0	2	1	0	1	0
32	1921	home	W	15	0	3	1	1	0	0	0	0	0	0	0
33	1922	away	W	12	3	4	0	0	0	0	1	0	0	0	0
34	1923	home	W	23	5	5	2	1	0	0	1	1	0	0	0
35	1924	away	W	14	3	4	1	0	0	0	1	0	0	0	0
36	1925	home	D	6	6	2	0	0	0	0	2	0	0	0	0
37	1926	away	L	15	19	3	3	0	0	0	4	2	0	1	0
38	1927	home	W	8	6	2	1	0	0	0	1	0	0	1	0
39	1928	away	W	7	6	1	0	1	0	0	2	0	0	0	0
40	1929	home	L	5	6	1	1	0	0	0	2	0	0	0	0

M	Year	Venue	R	F	A	T	C	DG	PG	GM	T	C	DG	PG	GM
41	1930	away	L	3	4	1	0	0	0	0	0	0	1	0	0
42	1931	home	L	5	6	1	1	0	0	0	1	0	0	1	0
43	1932	away	W	11	8	1	1	0	2	0	1	1	0	1	0
44	1933	home	W	17	6	5	1	0	0	0	1	0	0	1	0
45	1934	away	W	13	3	3	2	0	0	0	1	0	0	0	0
46	1935	home	W	14	3	1	1	0	3	0	1	0	0	0	0
47	1936	away	L	3	6	1	0	0	0	0	2	0	0	0	0
48	1937	home	W	9	8	2	0	0	1	0	2	1	0	0	0
49	1938	away	W	36	14	7	6	0	1	0	4	1	0	0	0
50	1939	home	L	0	5	0	0	0	0	0	1	1	0	0	0
51	1947	away	L	0	22	0	0	0	0	0	5	2	0	1	0
52	1948	home	L	10	11	2	2	0	0	0	3	1	0	0	0
53	1949	away	L	5	14	1	1	0	0	0	2	1	0	2	0
54	1950	home	W	3	0	1	0	0	0	0	0	0	0	0	0
55	1951	away	L	0	3	0	0	0	0	0	0	0	0	1	0
56	1952	home	W	3	0	1	0	0	0	0	0	0	0	0	0
57	1953	away	D	9	9	1	0	0	2	0	1	0	0	2	0
58	1954	home	W	14	3	3	1	0	1	0	0	0	0	1	0
59	1955	away	D	6	6	2	0	0	0	0	1	0	0	1	0
60	1956	home	W	20	0	3	1	0	3	0	0	0	0	0	0
61	1957	away	W	6	0	1	0	0	1	0	0	0	0	0	0
62	1958	home	W	6	0	1	0	0	1	0	0	0	0	0	0
63	1959	away	W	3	0	0	0	0	1	0	0	0	0	0	0
64	1960	home	W	8	5	1	1	1	0	0	1	1	0	0	0
65	1961	away	L	8	11	2	1	0	0	0	1	1	0	2	0
66	1962	home	W	16	0	3	2	0	1	0	0	0	0	0	0
67	1963	away	D	0	0	0	0	0	0	0	0	0	0	0	0
68	1964	home	L	5	18	1	1	0	0	0	4	3	0	0	0
69	1965	away	L	0	5	0	0	0	0	0	1	1	0	0	0
70	1966	home	D	6	6	1	0	0	1	0	1	0	0	1	0
71	1967	away	W	8	3	1	1	0	1	0	0	0	0	1	0
72	1968	home	D	9	9	0	0	1	2	0	0	0	0	3	0
73	1969	away	L	15	17	1	0	0	4	0	2	1	1	2	0
74	1970	home	W	9	3	1	0	2	0	0	0	0	0	1	0
75	1971	away	W	9	6	0	0	0	3	0	2	0	0	0	0
76	1972	home	L	12	16	1	1	0	2	0	2	1	1	1	0
77	1973	away	L	9	18	1	1	0	1	0	2	2	1	1	0
78	1974	home	L	21	26	1	1	0	5	0	4	2	1	1	0
79	1975	away	L	9	12	1	1	1	0	0	2	2	0	0	0
80	1976	home	L	12	13	0	0	0	4	0	1	0	1	2	0
81	1977	away	W	4	0	1	0	0	0	0	0	0	0	0	0
82	1978	home	W	15	9	2	2	0	1	0	0	0	1	2	0
83	1979	away	L	7	12	1	0	0	1	0	1	1	1	1	0
84	1980	home	W	24	9	3	3	0	2	0	0	0	0	3	0
85	1981	away	W	10	6	2	1	0	0	0	0	0	2	0	0
86	1982	home	L	15	16	1	1	0	3	0	2	1	0	2	0
87	1983	away	L	15	25	0	0	0	5	0	2	1	0	5	0
		Total:		746	589	153	57	10	58	0	105	41	14	46	2

England 46 wins; Ireland 34; Drawn 7

M	Year	Venue	R	F	A	T	C	DG	PG	GM	T	C	DG	PG	GM

ENGLAND-SCOTLAND

M	Year	Venue	R	F	A	T	C	DG	PG	GM	T	C	DG	PG	GM
1	1883	away	W	—	—	2	0	0	0	0	1	0	0	0	0
2	1884	home	W	—	—	1	1	0	0	0	1	0	0	0	0
3	1886	away	D	—	—	0	0	0	0	0	0	0	0	0	0
4	1887	home	D	—	—	1	0	0	0	0	1	0	0	0	0
5	1890	away	W	—	—	2	1	0	0	0	0	0	0	0	0
6	1891	home	L	3	9	1	1	0	0	0	2	2	1	0	0
7	1892	away	W	5	0	1	1	0	0	0	0	0	0	0	0
8	1893	home	L	0	8	0	0	0	0	0	0	0	2	0	0
9	1894	away	L	0	6	0	0	0	0	0	2	0	0	0	0
10	1895	home	L	3	6	0	0	0	1	0	1	0	0	1	0
11	1896	away	L	0	11	0	0	0	0	0	3	1	0	0	0
12	1897	home	W	12	3	2	1	1	0	0	1	0	0	0	0
13	1898	away	D	3	3	1	0	0	0	0	1	0	0	0	0
14	1899	home	L	0	5	0	0	0	0	0	1	1	0	0	0
15	1900	away	D	0	0	0	0	0	0	0	0	0	0	0	0
16	1901	home	L	3	18	1	0	0	0	0	4	3	0	0	0
17	1902	away	W	6	3	2	0	0	0	0	1	0	0	0	0
18	1903	home	L	6	10	2	0	0	0	0	2	0	1	0	0
19	1904	away	L	3	6	1	0	0	0	0	2	0	0	0	0
20	1905	home	L	0	8	0	0	0	0	0	2	1	0	0	0
21	1906	away	W	9	3	3	0	0	0	0	1	0	0	0	0
22	1907	home	L	3	8	1	0	0	0	0	2	1	0	0	0
23	1908	away	L	10	16	2	2	0	0	0	2	1	2	0	0
24	1909	home	L	8	18	2	1	0	0	0	4	3	0	0	0
25	1910	away	W	14	5	4	1	0	0	0	1	1	0	0	0
26	1911	home	W	13	8	3	2	0	0	0	2	1	0	0	0
27	1912	away	L	3	8	1	0	0	0	0	2	1	0	0	0
28	1913	home	W	3	0	1	0	0	0	0	0	0	0	0	0
29	1914	away	W	16	15	4	2	0	0	0	3	1	1	0	0
30	1920	home	W	13	4	3	2	0	0	0	0	0	1	0	0
31	1921	away	W	18	0	4	3	0	0	0	0	0	0	0	0
32	1922	home	W	11	5	3	1	0	0	0	1	1	0	0	0
33	1923	away	W	8	6	2	1	0	0	0	2	0	0	0	0
34	1924	home	W	19	0	3	3	1	0	0	0	0	0	0	0
35	1925	away	L	11	14	2	1	0	1	0	2	2	1	0	0
36	1926	home	L	9	17	3	0	0	0	0	3	2	1	0	0
37	1927	away	L	13	21	2	2	0	1	0	5	1	1	0	0
38	1928	home	W	6	0	2	0	0	0	0	0	0	0	0	0
39	1929	away	L	6	12	2	0	0	0	0	4	0	0	0	0
40	1930	home	D	0	0	0	0	0	0	0	0	0	0	0	0
41	1931	away	L	19	28	4	2	0	1	0	6	5	0	0	0
42	1932	home	W	16	3	4	2	0	0	0	1	0	0	0	0
43	1933	away	L	0	3	0	0	0	0	0	1	0	0	0	0
44	1934	home	W	6	3	2	0	0	0	0	1	0	0	0	0
45	1935	away	L	7	10	1	0	1	0	0	2	2	0	0	0
46	1936	home	W	9	8	3	0	0	0	0	1	1	0	1	0
47	1937	away	W	6	3	2	0	0	0	0	0	0	0	1	0
48	1938	home	L	16	21	1	0	1	3	0	5	0	0	2	0
49	1939	away	W	9	6	0	0	0	3	0	2	0	0	0	0
50	1947	home	W	24	5	4	4	1	0	0	1	1	0	0	0
51	1948	away	L	3	6	0	0	0	1	0	2	0	0	0	0
52	1949	home	W	19	3	5	2	0	0	0	0	0	0	1	0
53	1950	away	L	11	13	2	1	0	1	0	3	2	0	0	0

M	Year	Venue	R	F	A	T	C	DG	PG	GM	T	C	DG	PG	GM
54	1951	home	W	5	3	1	1	0	0	0	1	0	0	0	0
55	1952	away	W	19	3	4	2	1	0	0	1	0	0	0	0
56	1953	home	W	26	8	6	4	0	0	0	2	1	0	0	0
57	1954	away	W	13	3	3	2	0	0	0	1	0	0	0	0
58	1955	home	W	9	6	2	0	0	1	0	1	0	0	1	0
59	1956	away	W	11	6	1	1	0	2	0	1	0	0	1	0
60	1957	home	W	16	3	3	2	0	1	0	0	0	0	1	0
61	1958	away	D	3	3	0	0	0	1	0	0	0	0	1	0
62	1959	home	D	3	3	0	0	0	1	0	0	0	0	1	0
63	1960	away	W	21	12	3	3	1	1	0	1	0	0	3	0
64	1961	home	W	6	0	1	0	0	1	0	0	0	0	0	0
65	1962	away	D	3	3	0	0	0	1	0	0	0	0	1	0
66	1963	home	W	10	8	2	2	0	0	0	1	1	1	0	0
67	1964	away	L	6	15	1	0	0	1	0	3	3	0	0	0
68	1965	home	D	3	3	1	0	0	0	0	0	0	1	0	0
69	1966	away	L	3	6	0	0	1	0	0	1	0	0	1	0
70	1967	home	W	27	14	4	3	1	2	0	2	1	0	2	0
71	1968	away	W	8	6	1	1	0	1	0	0	0	1	1	0
72	1969	home	W	8	3	2	1	0	0	0	0	0	0	1	0
73	1970	away	L	5	14	1	1	0	0	0	2	1	0	2	0
74	1971	home	L	15	16	2	0	0	3	0	3	2	1	0	0
75	1972	away	L	9	23	0	0	0	3	0	2	0	1	4	0
76	1973	home	W	20	13	4	2	0	0	0	2	1	0	1	0
77	1974	away	L	14	16	2	0	1	1	0	2	1	0	2	0
78	1975	home	W	7	6	1	0	0	1	0	0	0	0	2	0
79	1976	away	L	12	22	1	1	0	2	0	3	2	0	2	0
80	1977	home	W	26	6	4	2	0	2	0	0	0	0	2	0
81	1978	away	W	15	0	2	2	0	1	0	0	0	0	0	0
82	1979	home	D	7	7	1	0	0	1	0	1	0	0	1	0
83	1980	away	W	30	18	5	2	0	2	0	2	2	0	2	0
84	1981	home	W	23	17	3	1	0	3	0	3	1	0	1	0
85	1982	away	D	9	9	0	0	0	3	0	0	0	1	2	0
86	1983	home	L	12	22	0	0	1	3	0	2	1	1	3	0
		Total:		786	665	153	70	11	50	0	121	51	18	44	0

England 43 wins; Scotland 32; Drawn 11

ENGLAND-WALES

M	Year	Venue	R	F	A	T	C	DG	PG	GM	T	C	DG	PG	GM
1	1883	away	W	—	—	6	2	0	0	0	0	0	0	0	0
2	1884	home	W	—	—	3	1	0	0	0	1	1	0	0	0
3	1885	away	W	—	—	5	1	0	0	0	2	1	0	0	0
4	1886	home	W	—	—	2	0	0	0	1	1	1	0	0	0
5	1887	away	D	—	—	0	0	0	0	0	0	0	0	0	0
6	1890	home	L	—	—	0	0	0	0	0	1	0	0	0	0
7	1891	away	W	7	3	3	2	0	0	0	1	1	0	0	0
8	1892	home	W	17	0	4	3	0	0	0	0	0	0	0	0
9	1893	away	L	11	12	4	1	0	0	0	3	1	0	1	0
10	1894	home	W	24	3	4	4	0	0	1	1	0	0	0	0
11	1895	away	W	14	6	4	1	0	0	0	2	0	0	0	0
12	1896	home	W	25	0	7	2	0	0	0	0	0	0	0	0
13	1897	away	L	0	11	0	0	0	0	0	3	1	0	0	0
14	1898	home	W	14	7	4	1	0	0	0	1	0	1	0	0

M	Year	Venue	R	F	A	T	C	DG	PG	GM	T	C	DG	PG	GM
15	1899	away	L	3	26	1	0	0	0	0	6	4	0	0	0
16	1900	home	L	3	13	1	0	0	0	0	2	2	0	1	0
17	1901	away	L	0	13	0	0	0	0	0	3	2	0	0	0
18	1902	home	L	8	9	2	1	0	0	0	2	0	0	1	0
19	1903	away	L	5	21	1	1	0	0	0	5	3	0	0	0
20	1904	home	D	14	14	3	1	0	1	0	2	2	0	0	1
21	1905	away	L	0	25	0	0	0	0	0	7	2	0	0	0
22	1906	home	L	3	16	1	0	0	0	0	4	2	0	0	0
23	1907	away	L	0	22	0	0	0	0	0	6	2	0	0	0
24	1908	home	L	18	28	4	3	0	0	0	5	3	1	1	0
25	1909	away	L	0	8	0	0	0	0	0	2	1	0	0	0
26	1910	home	W	11	6	2	1	0	1	0	2	0	0	0	0
27	1911	away	L	11	15	3	1	0	0	0	4	0	0	1	0
28	1912	home	W	8	0	2	1	0	0	0	0	0	0	0	0
29	1913	away	W	12	0	2	1	1	0	0	0	0	0	0	0
30	1914	home	W	10	9	2	2	0	0	0	1	1	1	0	0
31	1920	away	L	5	19	1	1	0	0	0	2	1	2	1	0
32	1921	home	W	18	3	4	1	1	0	0	1	0	0	0	0
33	1922	away	L	6	28	2	0	0	0	0	8	2	0	0	0
34	1923	home	W	7	3	1	0	1	0	0	1	0	0	0	0
35	1924	away	W	17	9	5	1	0	0	0	3	0	0	0	0
36	1925	home	W	12	6	3	0	0	1	0	2	0	0	0	0
37	1926	away	D	3	3	1	0	0	0	0	1	0	0	0	0
38	1927	home	W	11	9	1	1	0	1	1	2	0	0	1	0
39	1928	away	W	10	8	2	2	0	0	0	2	1	0	0	0
40	1929	home	W	8	3	2	1	0	0	0	1	0	0	0	0
41	1930	away	W	11	3	2	1	0	1	0	1	0	0	0	0
42	1931	home	D	11	11	1	1	0	2	0	2	1	0	0	1
43	1932	away	L	5	12	1	1	0	0	0	1	1	1	1	0
44	1933	home	L	3	7	1	0	0	0	0	1	0	1	0	0
45	1934	away	W	9	0	3	0	0	0	0	0	0	0	0	0
46	1935	home	D	3	3	0	0	0	1	0	1	0	0	0	0
47	1936	away	D	0	0	0	0	0	0	0	0	0	0	0	0
48	1937	home	W	4	3	0	0	1	0	0	1	0	0	0	0
49	1938	away	L	8	14	2	1	0	0	0	2	1	0	2	0
50	1939	home	W	3	0	1	0	0	0	0	0	0	0	0	0
51	1947	away	W	9	6	1	1	1	0	0	2	0	0	0	0
52	1948	home	D	3	3	0	0	0	1	0	1	0	0	0	0
53	1949	away	L	3	9	0	0	1	0	0	3	0	0	0	0
54	1950	home	L	5	11	1	1	0	0	0	2	1	0	1	0
55	1951	away	L	5	23	1	1	0	0	0	5	4	0	0	0
56	1952	home	L	6	8	2	0	0	0	0	2	1	0	0	0
57	1953	away	W	8	3	1	1	0	1	0	0	0	0	1	0
58	1954	home	W	9	6	3	0	0	0	0	1	0	0	1	0
59	1955	away	L	0	3	0	0	0	0	0	0	0	0	1	0
60	1956	home	L	3	8	0	0	0	1	0	2	1	0	0	0
61	1957	away	W	3	0	0	0	0	1	0	0	0	0	0	0
62	1958	home	D	3	3	1	0	0	0	0	0	0	0	1	0
63	1959	away	L	0	5	0	0	0	0	0	1	1	0	0	0
64	1960	home	W	14	6	2	1	0	2	0	0	0	0	2	0
65	1961	away	L	3	6	1	0	0	0	0	2	0	0	0	0
66	1962	home	D	0	0	0	0	0	0	0	0	0	0	0	0
67	1963	away	W	13	6	2	2	1	0	0	1	0	0	1	0
68	1964	home	D	6	6	2	0	0	0	0	2	0	0	0	0
69	1965	away	L	3	14	0	0	0	1	0	3	1	1	0	0

M	Year	Venue	R	F	A	T	C	DG	PG	GM	T	C	DG	PG	GM
70	1966	home	L	6	11	1	0	0	1	0	1	1	0	2	0
71	1967	away	L	21	34	3	0	0	4	0	5	5	1	2	0
72	1968	home	D	11	11	2	1	0	1	0	2	1	1	0	0
73	1969	away	L	9	30	0	0	0	3	0	5	3	1	2	0
74	1970	home	L	13	17	2	2	0	1	0	4	1	1	0	0
75	1971	away	L	6	22	1	0	0	1	0	3	2	2	1	0
76	1972	home	L	3	12	0	0	0	1	0	1	1	0	2	0
77	1973	away	L	9	25	0	0	1	2	0	5	1	0	1	0
78	1974	home	W	16	12	2	1	0	2	0	1	1	0	2	0
79	1975	away	L	4	20	1	0	0	0	0	3	1	0	2	0
80	1976	home	L	9	21	0	0	0	3	0	3	3	0	1	0
81	1977	away	L	9	14	0	0	0	3	0	2	0	0	2	0
82	1978	home	L	6	9	0	0	0	2	0	0	0	0	3	0
83	1979	away	L	3	27	0	0	0	1	0	5	2	1	0	0
84	1980	home	W	9	8	0	0	0	3	0	2	0	0	0	0
85	1981	away	L	19	21	1	0	0	5	0	1	1	1	4	0
86	1982	home	W	17	7	2	0	0	3	0	1	0	1	0	0
87	1983	away	D	13	13	1	0	1	2	0	1	0	1	2	0
		Total:		651	851	136	52	9	53	3	171	69	18	44	2

England 34 wins; Wales 41; Drawn 12

IRELAND-FRANCE

M	Year	Venue	R	F	A	T	C	DG	PG	GM	T	C	DG	PG	GM
1	1910	away	W	8	3	2	1	0	0	0	1	0	0	0	0
2	1911	home	W	25	5	5	3	1	0	0	1	1	0	0	0
3	1912	away	W	11	6	3	1	0	0	0	2	0	0	0	0
4	1913	home	W	24	0	6	3	0	0	0	0	0	0	0	0
5	1914	away	W	8	6	2	1	0	0	0	2	0	0	0	0
6	1920	home	L	7	15	1	0	1	0	0	5	0	0	0	0
7	1921	away	L	10	20	2	2	0	0	0	4	4	0	0	0
8	1922	home	W	8	3	1	1	0	1	0	1	0	0	0	0
9	1923	away	L	8	14	2	1	0	0	0	4	1	0	0	0
10	1924	home	W	6	0	2	0	0	0	0	0	0	0	0	0
11	1925	away	W	9	3	2	0	0	1	0	1	0	0	0	0
12	1926	home	W	11	0	2	1	0	1	0	0	0	0	0	0
13	1927	away	W	8	3	1	1	0	1	0	1	0	0	0	0
14	1928	home	W	12	8	4	0	0	0	0	2	1	0	0	0
15	1929	away	W	6	0	2	0	0	0	0	0	0	0	0	0
16	1930	home	L	0	5	0	0	0	0	0	1	1	0	0	0
17	1931	away	L	0	3	0	0	0	0	0	1	0	0	0	0
18	1947	home	L	8	12	1	1	0	1	0	4	0	0	0	0
19	1948	away	W	13	6	3	2	0	0	0	2	0	0	0	0
20	1949	home	L	9	16	0	0	0	3	0	2	2	0	2	0
21	1950	away	D	3	3	0	0	0	1	0	0	0	1	0	0
22	1951	home	W	9	8	2	0	0	1	0	2	1	0	0	0
23	1952	away	W	11	8	2	1	0	1	0	1	1	0	1	0
24	1953	home	W	16	3	4	2	0	0	0	0	0	1	0	0
25	1954	away	L	0	8	0	0	0	0	0	2	1	0	0	0
26	1955	home	L	3	5	0	0	0	1	0	1	1	0	0	0
27	1956	away	L	8	14	1	1	0	1	0	2	1	2	0	0
28	1957	home	W	11	6	2	1	0	1	0	0	0	0	2	0

M	Year	Venue	R	F	A	T	C	DG	PG	GM	T	C	DG	PG	GM
29	1958	away	L	6	11	0	0	0	2	0	1	1	1	1	0
30	1959	home	W	9	5	1	0	1	1	0	1	1	0	0	0
31	1960	away	L	6	23	2	0	0	0	0	4	1	3	0	0
32	1961	home	L	3	15	0	0	0	1	0	1	0	2	2	0
33	1962	away	L	0	11	0	0	0	0	0	3	1	0	0	0
34	1963	home	L	5	24	1	1	0	0	0	4	3	2	0	0
35	1964	away	L	6	27	1	0	1	0	0	6	3	1	0	0
36	1965	home	D	3	3	1	0	0	0	0	1	0	0	0	0
37	1966	away	L	6	11	0	0	1	1	0	2	1	0	1	0
38	1967	home	L	6	11	1	0	0	1	0	1	1	2	0	0
39	1968	away	L	6	16	0	0	0	2	0	2	2	1	1	0
40	1969	home	W	17	9	1	1	1	3	0	1	0	0	2	0
41	1970	away	L	0	8	0	0	0	0	0	1	1	1	0	0
42	1971	home	D	9	9	1	0	0	2	0	0	0	1	2	0
43	1972	away	W	14	9	2	0	0	2	0	1	1	0	1	0
44	1973	home	W	6	4	0	0	0	2	0	1	0	0	0	0
45	1974	away	L	6	9	0	0	0	2	0	1	1	0	1	0
46	1975	home	W	25	6	3	2	2	1	0	0	0	1	1	0
47	1976	away	L	3	26	0	0	0	1	0	4	2	0	2	0
48	1977	home	L	6	15	0	0	0	2	0	1	1	0	3	0
49	1978	away	L	9	10	0	0	0	3	0	1	0	0	2	0
50	1979	home	D	9	9	0	0	0	3	0	1	1	0	1	0
51	1980	away	L	18	19	1	1	1	3	0	2	1	1	2	0
52	1981	home	L	13	19	1	0	0	3	0	1	0	2	3	0
53	1982	away	L	9	22	0	0	0	3	0	2	1	0	4	0
54	1983	home	W	22	16	2	1	0	4	0	2	1	0	2	0
		Total:		474	530	70	29	9	56	0	87	39	22	36	0

Ireland 23 wins; France 27; Drawn 4

IRELAND-WALES

M	Year	Venue	R	F	A	T	C	DG	PG	GM	T	C	DG	PG	GM
1	1884	away	L	—	—	0	0	0	0	0	2	0	1	0	0
2	1887	away	L	—	—	3	0	0	0	0	1	1	1	0	0
3	1888	home	W	—	—	2	1	1	0	0	0	0	0	0	0
4	1889	away	W	—	—	2	0	0	0	0	0	0	0	0	0
5	1890	home	D	—	—	1	1	0	0	0	1	1	0	0	0
6	1891	away	L	4	6	1	0	1	0	0	1	1	1	0	0
7	1892	home	W	9	0	3	1	0	0	0	0	0	0	0	0
8	1893	away	L	0	2	0	0	0	0	0	1	0	0	0	0
9	1894	home	W	3	0	0	0	0	1	0	0	0	0	0	0
10	1895	away	L	3	5	1	0	0	0	0	1	1	0	0	0
11	1896	home	W	8	4	2	1	0	0	0	0	0	1	0	0
12	1898	home	L	3	11	0	0	0	1	0	2	1	0	1	0
13	1899	away	W	3	0	1	0	0	0	0	0	0	0	0	0
14	1900	home	L	0	3	0	0	0	0	0	1	0	0	0	0
15	1901	away	L	9	10	3	0	0	0	0	2	2	0	0	0
16	1902	home	L	0	15	0	0	0	0	0	3	1	1	0	0
17	1903	away	L	0	18	0	0	0	0	0	6	0	0	0	0
18	1904	home	W	14	12	4	1	0	0	0	4	0	0	0	0
19	1905	away	L	3	10	1	0	0	0	0	2	2	0	0	0
20	1906	home	W	11	6	3	1	0	0	0	2	0	0	0	0
21	1907	away	L	0	29	0	0	0	0	0	6	2	1	1	0

M	Year	Venue	R	F	A	T	C	DG	PG	GM	T	C	DG	PG	GM
22	1908	home	L	5	11	1	1	0	0	0	3	1	0	0	0
23	1909	away	L	5	18	1	1	0	0	0	4	3	0	0	0
24	1910	home	L	3	19	1	0	0	0	0	5	0	1	0	0
25	1911	away	L	0	16	0	0	0	0	0	3	2	0	1	0
26	1912	home	W	12	5	2	1	1	0	0	1	1	0	0	0
27	1913	away	L	13	16	2	2	0	1	0	3	2	0	1	0
28	1914	home	L	3	11	1	0	0	0	0	3	1	0	0	0
29	1920	away	L	4	28	0	0	1	0	0	6	3	1	0	0
30	1921	home	L	0	6	0	0	0	0	0	1	0	0	1	0
31	1922	away	L	5	11	1	1	0	0	0	3	1	0	0	0
32	1923	home	W	5	4	1	1	0	0	0	0	0	1	0	0
33	1924	away	W	13	10	3	2	0	0	0	2	0	1	0	0
34	1925	home	W	19	3	4	2	0	1	0	1	0	0	0	0
35	1926	away	L	8	11	1	1	0	1	0	3	1	0	0	0
36	1927	home	W	19	9	4	2	0	1	0	1	1	1	0	0
37	1928	away	W	13	10	3	2	0	0	0	2	2	0	0	0
38	1929	home	D	5	5	1	1	0	0	0	1	1	0	0	0
39	1930	away	L	7	12	0	0	1	1	0	3	0	0	1	0
40	1931	home	L	3	15	1	0	0	0	0	3	1	1	0	0
41	1932	away	W	12	10	4	0	0	0	0	2	0	1	0	0
42	1933	home	W	10	5	1	0	1	1	0	1	1	0	0	0
43	1934	away	L	0	13	0	0	0	0	0	3	2	0	0	0
44	1935	home	W	9	3	1	0	0	2	0	0	0	0	1	0
45	1936	away	L	0	3	0	0	0	0	0	0	0	0	1	0
46	1937	home	W	5	3	1	1	0	0	0	0	0	0	1	0
47	1938	away	L	5	11	1	1	0	0	0	2	1	0	1	0
48	1939	home	L	0	7	0	0	0	0	0	1	0	1	0	0
49	1947	away	L	0	6	0	0	0	0	0	1	0	0	1	0
50	1948	home	W	6	3	2	0	0	0	0	1	0	0	0	0
51	1949	away	W	5	0	1	1	0	0	0	0	0	0	0	0
52	1950	home	L	3	6	0	0	0	1	0	2	0	0	0	0
53	1951	away	D	3	3	1	0	0	0	0	0	0	0	1	0
54	1952	home	L	3	14	0	0	0	1	0	3	1	0	1	0
55	1953	away	L	3	5	1	0	0	0	0	1	1	0	0	0
56	1954	home	L	9	12	1	0	0	2	0	0	0	1	3	0
57	1955	away	L	3	21	0	0	0	1	0	4	3	0	1	0
58	1956	home	W	11	3	1	1	1	1	0	0	0	0	1	0
59	1957	away	L	5	6	1	1	0	0	0	0	0	0	2	0
60	1958	home	L	6	9	1	0	0	1	0	3	0	0	0	0
61	1959	away	L	6	8	1	0	0	1	0	2	1	0	0	0
62	1960	home	L	9	10	1	0	0	2	0	2	2	0	0	0
63	1961	away	L	0	9	0	0	0	0	0	1	0	0	2	0
64	1962	home	D	3	3	0	0	1	0	0	0	0	0	1	0
65	1963	away	W	14	6	1	1	1	2	0	1	0	1	0	0
66	1964	home	L	6	15	0	0	0	2	0	3	3	0	0	0
67	1965	away	L	8	14	1	1	0	1	0	2	1	1	1	0
68	1966	home	W	9	6	1	0	1	1	0	1	0	0	1	0
69	1967	away	W	3	0	1	0	0	0	0	0	0	0	0	0
70	1968	home	W	9	6	1	0	1	1	0	0	0	1	1	0
71	1969	away	L	11	24	1	1	0	2	0	4	3	1	1	0
72	1970	home	W	14	0	2	1	1	1	0	0	0	0	0	0
73	1971	away	L	9	23	0	0	0	3	0	4	1	1	2	0
74	1973	away	L	12	16	1	1	0	2	0	2	1	0	2	0
75	1974	home	D	9	9	0	0	0	3	0	1	1	0	1	0
76	1975	away	L	4	32	1	0	0	0	0	5	3	0	2	0

M	Year	Venue	R	F	A	T	C	DG	PG	GM	T	C	DG	PG	GM
77	1976	home	L	9	34	0	0	0	3	0	4	3	0	4	0
78	1977	away	L	9	25	0	0	0	3	0	3	2	1	2	0
79	1978	home	L	16	20	1	0	1	3	0	2	0	0	4	0
80	1979	away	L	21	24	2	2	0	3	0	2	2	0	4	0
81	1980	home	W	21	7	3	3	0	1	0	1	0	0	1	0
82	1981	away	L	8	9	2	0	0	0	0	0	0	1	2	0
83	1982	home	W	20	12	3	1	0	2	0	1	1	1	1	0
84	1983	away	L	9	23	0	0	0	3	0	3	1	0	3	0
		Total:		549	829	94	39	13	56	0	151	66	23	55	0

Ireland 28 wins; Wales 51; Drawn 5

SCOTLAND-FRANCE

M	Year	Venue	R	F	A	T	C	DG	PG	GM	T	C	DG	PG	GM
1	1910	home	W	27	0	7	3	0	0	0	0	0	0	0	0
2	1911	away	L	15	16	3	1	1	0	0	4	2	0	0	0
3	1912	home	W	31	3	6	5	0	1	0	1	0	0	0	0
4	1913	away	W	21	3	5	3	0	0	0	1	0	0	0	0
5	1920	away	W	5	0	1	1	0	0	0	0	0	0	0	0
6	1921	home	L	0	3	0	0	0	0	0	1	0	0	0	0
7	1922	away	D	3	3	1	0	0	0	0	1	0	0	0	0
8	1923	home	W	16	3	4	2	0	0	0	0	0	0	0	1
9	1924	away	L	10	12	1	0	1	1	0	4	0	0	0	0
10	1925	home	W	25	4	7	2	0	0	0	0	0	1	0	0
11	1926	away	W	20	6	5	1	0	1	0	1	0	0	1	0
12	1927	home	W	23	6	4	4	0	1	0	2	0	0	0	0
13	1928	away	W	15	6	5	0	0	0	0	2	0	0	0	0
14	1929	home	W	6	3	1	0	0	1	0	1	0	0	0	0
15	1930	away	L	3	7	1	0	0	0	0	1	0	1	0	0
16	1931	home	W	6	4	0	0	0	2	0	0	0	1	0	0
17	1947	away	L	3	8	0	0	0	1	0	2	1	0	0	0
18	1948	home	W	9	8	1	0	0	2	0	1	1	0	1	0
19	1949	away	W	8	0	2	1	0	0	0	0	0	0	0	0
20	1950	home	W	8	5	2	1	0	0	0	1	1	0	0	0
21	1951	away	L	12	14	2	0	0	2	0	2	1	0	2	0
22	1952	home	L	11	13	1	1	0	2	0	2	2	0	1	0
23	1953	away	L	5	11	1	1	0	0	0	1	1	1	1	0
24	1954	home	L	0	3	0	0	0	0	0	1	0	0	0	0
25	1955	away	L	0	15	0	0	0	0	0	4	0	0	1	0
26	1956	home	W	12	0	2	0	0	2	0	0	0	0	0	0
27	1957	away	W	6	0	0	0	1	1	0	0	0	0	0	0
28	1958	home	W	11	9	2	1	0	1	0	1	0	0	2	0
29	1959	away	L	0	9	0	0	0	0	0	1	0	2	0	0
30	1960	home	L	11	13	2	1	0	1	0	3	2	0	0	0
31	1961	away	L	0	11	0	0	0	0	0	1	1	1	1	0
32	1962	home	L	3	11	0	0	0	1	0	1	1	0	2	0
33	1963	away	W	11	6	1	1	1	1	0	0	0	1	1	0
34	1964	home	W	10	0	2	2	0	0	0	0	0	0	0	0
35	1965	away	L	8	16	2	1	0	0	0	4	2	0	0	0
36	1966	home	D	3	3	1	0	0	0	0	0	0	0	1	0
37	1967	away	W	9	8	0	0	1	2	GM	2	1	DG	PG	GM
38	1968	home	L	6	8	1	0	0	1	0	2	1	0	0	0
39	1969	away	W	6	3	1	0	0	1	0	0	0	0	1	0
40	1970	home	L	9	11	1	0	0	2	0	2	1	1	0	0

M	Year	Venue	R	F	A	T	C	DG	PG	GM	T	C	DG	PG	GM
41	1971	away	L	8	13	1	1	0	1	0	2	2	0	1	0
42	1972	home	W	20	9	3	1	1	1	0	1	1	0	1	0
43	1973	away	L	13	16	1	0	1	2	0	1	0	1	3	0
44	1974	home	W	19	6	2	1	0	3	0	0	0	1	1	0
45	1975	away	L	9	10	0	0	0	3	0	1	0	1	1	0
46	1976	home	L	6	13	0	0	1	1	0	1	0	0	3	0
47	1977	away	L	3	23	0	0	0	1	0	4	2	0	1	0
48	1978	home	L	16	19	2	1	1	1	0	2	1	0	3	0
49	1979	away	L	17	21	3	1	0	1	0	3	0	1	2	0
50	1980	home	W	22	14	3	2	0	2	0	2	0	1	1	0
51	1981	away	L	9	16	1	1	0	1	0	2	1	0	2	0
52	1982	home	W	16	7	1	0	1	3	0	1	0	0	1	0
53	1983	away	L	15	19	1	1	2	1	0	2	1	0	3	0
		Total:		560	450	93	41	12	48	0	72	26	14	38	1

Scotland 25 wins; France 26; Drawn 2

SCOTLAND-IRELAND

M	Year	Venue	R	F	A	T	C	DG	PG	GM	T	C	DG	PG	GM
1	1883	away	W	—	—	2	1	0	0	0	0	0	0	0	0
2	1884	home	W	—	—	4	2	0	0	0	1	0	0	0	0
3	1885	home	W	—	—	3	1	0	0	0	0	0	0	0	0
4	1886	home	W	—	—	5	3	1	0	0	0	0	0	0	0
5	1887	away	W	—	—	3	1	0	0	1	0	0	0	0	0
6	1888	home	W	—	—	1	1	0	0	0	0	0	0	0	0
7	1889	away	W	—	—	0	0	1	0	0	0	0	0	0	0
8	1890	home	W	—	—	1	0	1	0	0	0	0	0	0	0
9	1891	away	W	14	0	5	3	1	0	0	0	0	0	0	0
10	1892	home	W	2	0	1	0	0	0	0	0	0	0	0	0
11	1893	away	D	0	0	0	0	0	0	0	0	0	0	0	0
12	1894	away	L	0	5	0	0	0	0	0	1	1	0	0	0
13	1895	home	W	6	0	2	0	0	0	0	0	0	0	0	0
14	1896	away	D	0	0	0	0	0	0	0	0	0	0	0	0
15	1897	home	W	8	3	1	1	0	1	0	1	0	0	0	0
16	1898	away	W	8	0	2	1	0	0	0	0	0	0	0	0
17	1899	home	L	3	9	0	0	0	1	0	3	0	0	0	0
18	1900	away	D	0	0	0	0	0	0	0	0	0	0	0	0
19	1901	home	W	9	5	3	0	0	0	0	1	1	0	0	0
20	1902	away	L	0	5	0	0	0	0	0	1	1	0	0	0
21	1903	home	W	3	0	1	0	0	0	0	0	0	0	0	0
22	1904	away	W	19	3	5	2	0	0	0	1	0	0	0	0
23	1905	home	L	5	11	1	1	0	0	0	3	1	0	0	0
24	1906	away	W	13	6	2	2	0	0	1	2	0	0	0	0
25	1907	home	W	15	3	3	3	0	0	0	0	0	0	1	0
26	1908	away	L	11	16	2	1	0	1	0	4	2	0	0	0
27	1909	home	W	9	3	3	0	0	0	0	0	0	0	1	0
28	1910	away	W	14	0	4	1	0	0	0	0	0	0	0	0
29	1911	home	L	10	16	2	0	1	0	0	4	2	0	0	0
30	1912	away	L	8	10	2	1	0	0	0	1	0	1	1	0
31	1913	home	W	29	14	7	4	0	0	0	2	2	1	0	0
32	1914	away	L	0	6	0	0	0	0	0	2	0	0	0	0
33	1920	home	W	19	0	4	2	0	1	0	0	0	0	0	0
34	1921	away	L	8	9	2	1	0	0	0	3	0	0	0	0
35	1922	home	W	6	3	2	0	0	0	0	1	0	0	0	0

M	Year	Venue	R	F	A	T	C	DG	PG	GM	T	C	DG	PG	GM
36	1923	away	W	13	3	3	2	0	0	0	1	0	0	0	0
37	1924	home	W	13	8	3	2	0	0	0	2	1	0	0	0
38	1925	away	W	14	8	2	2	1	0	0	1	1	0	1	0
39	1926	home	L	0	3	0	0	0	0	0	1	0	0	0	0
40	1927	away	L	0	6	0	0	0	0	0	2	0	0	0	0
41	1928	home	L	5	13	1	1	0	0	0	3	2	0	0	0
42	1929	away	W	16	7	4	2	0	0	0	1	0	1	0	0
43	1930	home	L	11	14	3	1	0	0	0	4	1	0	0	0
44	1931	away	L	5	8	1	1	0	0	0	2	1	0	0	0
45	1932	home	L	8	20	2	1	0	0	0	4	4	0	0	0
46	1933	away	W	8	6	0	0	2	0	0	2	0	0	0	0
47	1934	home	W	16	9	3	2	0	1	0	3	0	0	0	0
48	1935	away	L	5	12	1	1	0	0	0	4	0	0	0	0
49	1936	home	L	4	10	0	0	1	0	0	2	0	1	0	0
50	1937	away	L	4	11	0	0	1	0	0	3	1	0	0	0
51	1938	home	W	23	14	4	2	1	1	0	4	1	0	0	0
52	1939	away	L	3	12	1	0	0	0	0	2	0	0	1	1
53	1947	home	L	0	3	0	0	0	0	0	1	0	0	0	0
54	1948	away	L	0	6	0	0	0	0	0	2	0	0	0	0
55	1949	home	L	3	13	0	0	0	1	0	2	2	0	1	0
56	1950	away	L	0	21	0	0	0	0	0	3	3	0	2	0
57	1951	home	L	5	6	1	1	0	0	0	1	0	1	0	0
58	1952	away	L	8	12	1	1	0	1	0	3	0	0	1	0
59	1953	home	L	8	26	1	1	0	1	0	6	4	0	0	0
60	1954	away	L	0	6	0	0	0	0	0	2	0	0	0	0
61	1955	home	W	12	3	1	0	1	2	0	0	0	0	1	0
62	1956	away	L	10	14	2	2	0	0	0	4	1	0	0	0
63	1957	home	L	3	5	0	0	0	1	0	1	1	0	0	0
64	1958	away	L	6	12	2	0	0	0	0	2	0	0	2	0
65	1959	home	L	3	8	0	0	0	1	0	1	1	0	1	0
66	1960	away	W	6	5	1	0	1	0	0	1	1	0	0	0
67	1961	home	W	16	8	3	2	0	1	0	2	1	0	0	0
68	1962	away	W	20	6	3	1	1	2	0	1	0	0	1	0
69	1963	home	W	3	0	0	0	0	1	0	0	0	0	0	0
70	1964	away	W	6	3	0	0	0	2	0	0	0	0	1	0
71	1965	home	L	6	16	0	0	1	1	0	3	2	1	0	0
72	1966	away	W	11	3	3	1	0	0	0	0	0	0	1	0
73	1967	home	L	3	5	0	0	0	1	0	1	1	0	0	0
74	1968	away	L	6	14	0	0	0	2	0	3	1	0	1	0
75	1969	home	L	0	16	0	0	0	0	0	4	2	0	0	0
76	1970	away	L	11	16	2	1	1	0	0	4	2	0	0	0
77	1971	home	L	5	17	1	1	0	0	0	3	1	0	2	0
78	1973	home	W	19	14	1	0	3	2	0	2	0	0	2	0
79	1974	away	L	6	9	0	0	0	2	0	1	1	0	1	0
80	1975	home	W	20	13	2	0	2	2	0	2	1	0	1	0
81	1976	away	W	15	6	0	0	1	4	0	0	0	0	2	0
82	1977	home	W	21	18	3	0	1	2	0	1	1	1	3	0
83	1978	away	L	9	12	0	0	0	3	0	1	1	0	2	0
84	1979	home	D	11	11	2	0	0	1	0	2	0	0	1	0
85	1980	away	L	15	22	2	2	0	1	0	2	1	1	3	0
86	1981	home	W	10	9	1	0	1	1	0	1	1	0	1	0
87	1982	away	L	12	21	1	1	0	2	0	0	0	1	6	0
88	1983	home	L	13	15	1	0	1	2	0	1	1	0	3	0
		Total:		669	685	135	63	25	45	2	135	52	9	44	1

Scotland 42 wins; Ireland 42; Drawn 4

SCOTLAND-WALES

M	Year	Venue	R	F	A	T	C	DG	PG	GM	T	C	DG	PG	GM
1	1883	home	W	—	—	3	3	0	0	0	1	1	0	0	0
2	1884	away	W	—	—	1	0	1	0	0	0	0	0	0	0
3	1885	home	D	—	—	0	0	0	0	0	0	0	0	0	0
4	1886	away	W	—	—	3	2	0	0	0	0	0	0	0	0
5	1887	home	W	—	—	12	4	0	0	0	0	0	0	0	0
6	1888	away	L	—	—	0	0	0	0	0	1	0	0	0	0
7	1889	home	W	—	—	2	0	0	0	0	0	0	0	0	0
8	1890	away	W	—	—	3	1	0	0	0	1	0	0	0	0
9	1891	home	W	15	0	7	1	2	0	0	0	0	0	0	0
10	1892	away	W	7	2	2	1	0	0	0	1	0	0	0	0
11	1893	home	L	0	9	0	0	0	0	0	3	0	0	1	0
12	1894	away	L	0	7	0	0	0	0	0	1	0	1	0	0
13	1895	home	W	5	4	1	1	0	0	0	0	0	1	0	0
14	1896	away	L	0	6	0	0	0	0	0	2	0	0	0	0
15	1899	home	W	21	10	3	0	2	0	1	2	2	0	0	0
16	1900	away	L	3	12	1	0	0	0	0	4	0	0	0	0
17	1901	home	W	18	8	4	3	0	0	0	2	1	0	0	0
18	1902	away	L	5	14	1	1	0	0	0	4	1	0	0	0
19	1903	home	W	6	0	1	0	0	1	0	0	0	0	0	0
20	1904	away	L	3	21	1	0	0	0	0	4	3	0	1	0
21	1905	home	L	3	6	1	0	0	0	0	2	0	0	0	0
22	1906	away	L	3	9	0	0	0	1	0	3	0	0	0	0
23	1907	home	W	6	3	2	0	0	0	0	0	0	0	1	0
24	1908	away	L	5	6	1	1	0	0	0	2	0	0	0	0
25	1909	home	L	3	5	0	0	0	1	0	1	1	0	0	0
26	1910	away	L	0	14	0	0	0	0	0	4	1	0	0	0
27	1911	home	L	10	32	2	0	1	0	0	8	2	1	0	0
28	1912	away	L	6	21	2	0	0	0	0	3	2	2	0	0
29	1913	home	L	0	8	0	0	0	0	0	2	1	0	0	0
30	1914	away	L	5	24	1	1	0	0	0	3	2	2	1	0
31	1920	home	W	9	5	1	0	0	2	0	1	1	0	0	0
32	1921	away	W	14	8	3	1	0	1	0	0	0	2	0	0
33	1922	home	D	9	9	2	0	0	1	0	1	1	1	0	0
34	1923	away	W	11	8	3	1	0	0	0	1	1	0	1	0
35	1924	home	W	35	10	8	4	0	1	0	2	2	0	0	0
36	1925	away	W	24	14	6	1	1	0	0	3	1	0	1	0
37	1926	home	W	8	5	1	1	0	1	0	1	1	0	0	0
38	1927	away	W	5	0	1	1	0	0	0	0	0	0	0	0
39	1928	home	L	0	13	0	0	0	0	0	3	2	0	0	0
40	1929	away	L	7	14	0	0	1	1	0	4	1	0	0	0
41	1930	home	W	12	9	2	1	1	0	0	1	1	1	0	0
42	1931	away	L	8	13	2	1	0	0	0	3	2	0	0	0
43	1932	home	L	0	6	0	0	0	0	0	1	0	0	1	0
44	1933	away	W	11	3	2	1	0	1	0	1	0	0	0	0
45	1934	home	L	6	13	1	0	0	1	0	3	2	0	0	0
46	1935	away	L	6	10	2	0	0	0	0	2	0	1	0	0
47	1936	home	L	3	13	1	0	0	0	0	3	2	0	0	0
48	1937	away	W	13	6	3	2	0	0	0	2	0	0	0	0
49	1938	home	W	8	6	1	1	0	1	0	2	0	0	0	0
50	1939	away	L	3	11	0	0	0	1	0	2	1	0	1	0
51	1947	home	L	8	22	1	1	0	1	0	5	2	0	1	0
52	1948	away	L	0	14	0	0	0	0	0	3	1	0	1	0

M	Year	Venue	R	F	A	T	C	DG	PG	GM	T	C	DG	PG	GM
53	1949	home	W	6	5	2	0	0	0	0	1	1	0	0	0
54	1950	away	L	0	12	0	0	0	0	0	2	0	1	1	0
55	1951	home	W	19	0	3	2	1	1	0	0	0	0	0	0
56	1952	away	L	0	11	0	0	0	0	0	1	1	0	2	0
57	1953	home	L	0	12	0	0	0	0	0	3	0	0	1	0
58	1954	away	L	3	15	1	0	0	0	0	4	0	0	1	0
59	1955	home	W	14	8	2	1	1	1	0	2	1	0	0	0
60	1956	away	L	3	9	0	0	0	1	0	3	0	0	0	0
61	1957	home	W	9	6	1	0	1	1	0	1	0	0	1	0
62	1958	away	L	3	8	0	0	0	1	0	2	1	0	0	0
63	1959	home	W	6	5	1	0	0	1	0	1	1	0	0	0
64	1960	away	L	0	8	0	0	0	0	0	1	1	0	1	0
65	1961	home	W	3	0	1	0	0	0	0	0	0	0	0	0
66	1962	away	W	8	3	2	1	0	0	0	0	0	1	0	0
67	1963	home	L	0	6	0	0	0	0	0	0	0	1	1	0
68	1964	away	L	3	11	1	0	0	0	0	2	1	0	1	0
69	1965	home	L	12	14	0	0	2	2	0	2	1	0	2	0
70	1966	away	L	3	8	0	0	0	1	0	2	1	0	0	0
71	1967	home	W	11	5	2	1	1	0	0	1	1	0	0	0
72	1968	away	L	0	5	0	0	0	0	0	1	1	0	0	0
73	1969	home	L	3	17	0	0	0	1	0	3	1	0	2	0
74	1970	away	L	9	18	1	0	1	1	0	4	3	0	0	0
75	1971	home	L	18	19	2	0	0	4	0	4	2	0	1	0
76	1972	away	L	12	35	1	1	0	2	0	5	3	0	3	0
77	1973	home	W	10	9	2	1	0	0	0	0	0	0	3	0
78	1974	away	L	0	6	0	0	0	0	0	1	1	0	0	0
79	1975	home	W	12	10	0	0	1	3	0	1	0	0	2	0
80	1976	away	L	6	28	1	1	0	0	0	3	2	1	3	0
81	1977	home	L	9	18	1	1	1	0	0	2	2	0	2	0
82	1978	away	L	14	22	2	0	0	2	0	4	0	1	1	0
83	1979	home	L	13	19	1	0	0	3	0	2	1	0	3	0
84	1980	away	L	6	17	1	1	0	0	0	3	1	0	1	0
85	1981	home	W	15	6	2	2	0	1	0	0	0	0	2	0
86	1982	away	W	34	18	5	4	2	0	0	1	1	0	4	0
87	1983	home	L	15	19	1	1	0	3	0	2	1	0	3	0
	Total:			603	845	130	52	20	44	1	162	67	17	51	0

Scotland 36 wins; Wales 49; Drawn 2

WALES-FRANCE

M	Year	Venue	R	F	A	T	C	DG	PG	GM	T	C	DG	PG	GM
1	1910	home	W	49	14	10	8	0	1	0	2	1	0	2	0
2	1911	away	W	15	0	3	3	0	0	0	0	0	0	0	0
3	1912	home	W	14	8	4	1	0	0	0	2	1	0	0	0
4	1913	away	W	11	8	3	1	0	0	0	2	1	0	0	0
5	1914	home	W	31	0	7	5	0	0	0	0	0	0	0	0
6	1920	away	W	6	5	2	0	0	0	0	1	1	0	0	0
7	1921	home	W	12	4	2	0	0	2	0	0	0	1	0	0
8	1922	away	W	11	3	3	1	0	0	0	1	0	0	0	0
9	1923	home	W	16	8	3	2	DG	1	GM	2	1	DG	PG	GM
10	1924	away	W	10	6	2	0	1	0	0	2	0	0	0	0
11	1925	home	W	11	5	3	1	0	0	0	1	1	0	0	0
12	1926	away	W	7	5	1	0	1	0	0	1	1	0	0	0

M	Year	Venue	R	F	A	T	C	DG	PG	GM	T	C	DG	PG	GM
13	1927	home	W	25	7	7	2	0	0	0	1	0	1	0	0
14	1928	away	L	3	8	1	0	0	0	0	2	1	0	0	0
15	1929	home	W	8	3	2	1	0	0	0	1	0	0	0	0
16	1930	away	W	11	0	1	0	2	0	0	0	0	0	0	0
17	1931	home	W	35	3	7	5	1	0	0	1	0	0	0	0
18	1947	away	W	3	0	0	0	0	1	0	0	0	0	0	0
19	1948	home	L	3	11	0	0	0	1	0	3	1	0	0	0
20	1949	away	L	3	5	1	0	0	0	0	1	1	0	0	0
21	1950	home	W	21	0	4	3	0	1	0	0	0	0	0	0
22	1951	away	L	3	8	1	0	0	0	0	1	1	0	1	0
23	1952	home	W	9	5	0	0	1	2	0	1	1	0	0	0
24	1953	away	W	6	3	2	0	0	0	0	0	0	0	1	0
25	1954	home	W	19	13	2	2	0	3	0	2	2	0	1	0
26	1955	away	W	16	11	2	2	0	2	0	1	1	1	1	0
27	1956	home	W	5	3	1	1	0	0	0	1	0	0	0	0
28	1957	away	W	19	13	4	2	0	1	0	3	2	0	0	0
29	1958	home	L	6	16	1	0	0	1	0	2	2	2	0	0
30	1959	away	L	3	11	0	0	0	1	0	2	1	0	1	0
31	1960	home	L	8	16	1	1	0	1	0	4	2	0	0	0
32	1961	away	L	6	8	2	0	0	0	0	2	1	0	0	0
33	1962	home	W	3	0	0	0	0	1	0	0	0	0	0	0
34	1963	away	L	3	5	0	0	0	1	0	1	1	0	0	0
35	1964	home	D	11	11	1	1	0	2	0	1	1	0	2	0
36	1965	away	L	13	22	3	2	0	0	0	4	2	1	1	0
37	1966	home	W	9	8	1	0	0	2	0	2	1	0	0	0
38	1967	away	L	14	20	1	1	1	2	0	3	1	2	1	0
39	1968	home	L	9	14	1	0	0	2	0	2	1	1	1	0
40	1969	away	D	8	8	2	1	0	0	0	1	1	0	1	0
41	1970	home	W	11	6	1	1	0	2	0	2	0	0	0	0
42	1971	away	W	9	5	2	0	0	1	0	1	1	0	0	0
43	1972	home	W	20	6	2	0	0	4	0	0	0	0	2	0
44	1973	away	L	3	12	0	0	1	0	0	0	0	1	3	0
45	1974	home	D	16	16	1	0	1	3	0	1	0	1	3	0
46	1975	away	W	25	10	5	1	0	1	0	1	0	0	2	0
47	1976	home	W	19	13	1	0	0	5	0	2	1	0	1	0
48	1977	away	L	9	16	0	0	0	3	0	2	1	0	2	0
49	1978	home	W	16	7	2	1	2	0	0	1	0	1	0	0
50	1979	away	L	13	14	1	0	0	3	0	2	0	0	2	0
51	1980	home	W	18	9	4	1	0	0	0	1	1	1	0	0
52	1981	away	L	15	19	1	1	0	3	0	1	0	0	5	0
53	1982	home	W	22	12	1	0	0	6	0	1	1	0	2	0
54	1983	away	L	9	16	1	1	0	1	0	1	0	1	3	0
		Total:		680	459	113	52	11	60	0	72	36	14	38	0

Wales 34 wins; France 17; Drawn 3

LEADING SCORERS IN CHAMPIONSHIP

Player	Country	Points	Eng.	France	Ire.	Scot.	Wales
Irvine, A.R.	Scotland	194	54	61	42	—	37
Campbell, S.O.	Ireland	161	41	46	—	51	23
Bennett, P.	Wales	142	19	28	54	41	—
Fenwick, S.P.	Wales	139	32	36	38	33	—
Hare, W.H.	England	134	—	34	27	30	43
Hiller, R.	England	119	—	33	41	21	24
Kiernan, T.J.	Ireland	115	44	17	—	25	29
Romeu, J-P.	France	102	24	—	7	34	37
Gibson, C.M.H.	Ireland	96	16	15	—	31	34
Stephenson, G.V.	Ireland	93	13	25	—	18	37
John, B.	Wales	87	29	18	14	26	—
Prat, J.	France	87	25	—	23	28	11
Villepreux, P.	France	84	32	—	21	18	13
Edwards, G.O.	Wales	82	15	16	21	30	—
Old, A.G.B.	England	81	—	19	34	17	11

TRY SCORERS

Player	Country	Points	Eng.	France	Ire.	Scot.	Wales
Smith, I.S.	Scotland	24	9	6	1	—	8
Edwards, G.O.	Wales	19	4	3	5	7	—
Lowe, C.N.	England	18	—	4	6	6	2
Stephenson, G.V.	Ireland	15	1	6	—	4	4
Darrouy, C.	France	13	3	—	8	2	0

MOST CONVERSIONS

Player	Country	Points	Eng.	France	Ire.	Scot.	Wales
Bancroft, J.	Wales	32	2	16	8	6	—
Kiernan, T.J.	Ireland	18	7	1	—	6	4
Villepreux, P.	France	18	10	—	3	3	2
Irvine, A.R.	Scotland	17	7	3	1	—	6
Greenwood, J.E.	England	12	—	8	1	2	1

MOST DROPPED GOALS

Player	Country	Points	Eng.	France	Ire.	Scot.	Wales
Camberabero, G.	France	7	2	—	2	0	3
John, B.	Wales	7	5	0	2	0	—
Lloyd, R.A.	Ireland	7	2	2	—	2	1
Morgan, D.W.	Scotland	6	0	2	4	—	0
Hall, N.M.	England	3	0	0	0	1	2
Old, A.G.B.	England	3	0	2	1	0	0

MOST PENALTY GOALS

Player	Country	Points	Eng.	France	Ire.	Scot.	Wales
Campbell, S.O.	Ireland	41	10	13	—	13	5
Irvine, A.R.	Scotland	40	12	13	12	—	3
Hare, W.H.	England	38	—	10	7	8	13
Fenwick, S.P.	Wales	32	6	9	9	8	—
Romeu, J-P.	France	22	1	—	3	9	9

INDIVIDUAL SCORING SUMMARIES 1883–1983

LEADING POINTS SCORER: 194   A.R. Irvine (Scotland)
LEADING TRY SCORER: 24   I.S. Smith (Scotland)
MOST CONVERSIONS: 32   J. Bancroft (Wales)
MOST DROPPED GOALS: 7   G. Camberabero (France), R.A. Lloyd (Ireland), B. John (Wales)
MOST PENALTY GOALS: 41   S.O. Campbell (Ireland)
MOST POINTS IN A MATCH: 22   D. Lambert (England v France 1911, Twickenham)
MOST TRIES IN A MATCH: 5   G.C. Lindsay (Scotland v Wales 1887, Raeburn Place)
MOST CONVERSIONS IN A MATCH: 8   J. Bancroft (49-14 Wales v France 1910, Swansea)
MOST DROPPED GOALS IN A MATCH: 3 P. Albaladejo (France v Ireland 1960, Paris)
MOST PENALTY GOALS IN A MATCH: 6   G. Evans (Wales v France 1982, Cardiff), S.O. Campbell (Ireland v Scotland 1982, Dublin)
MOST POINTS IN A SEASON: 52   S.O. Campbell (1983)
MOST TRIES IN A SEASON: 8   C.N. Lowe (England 1914), I.S. Smith (Scotland 1925)
MOST CONVERSIONS IN A SEASON: 11   J. Bancroft (Wales 1910)
MOST DROPPED GOALS IN A SEASON: 3   P. Albaladejo (France 1960), G. Camberabero (France 1967)
MOST PENALTY GOALS IN A SEASON: 14   S.O. Campbell (1983)

MOST APPEARANCES

ALL PLAYERS

M	Player	Country	W	D	L	Career Span
56	Gibson, C.M.H.	Ireland	21	6	29	1964–79
53	McBride, W.J.	Ireland	22	7	24	1962–75
48	Slattery, J.F.	Ireland	20	4	24	1970–83
45	Edwards, G.O.	Wales	32	4	9	1967–78
44	Kiernan, T.J.	Ireland	17	5	22	1960–73
44	Williams, J.P.R.	Wales	34	3	7	1969–81
42	Kyle, J.W.	Ireland	22	4	16	1947–58
42	Renwick, J.M.	Scotland	14	3	25	1972–83
41	Carmichael, A.B.	Scotland	14	0	27	1967–78
41	Jones, K.J.	Wales	26	2	13	1947–57
40	Keane, M.I.	Ireland	15	3	22	1974–83
40	Stephenson, G.V.	Ireland	20	2	18	1920–30
39	Irvine, A.R.	Scotland	14	3	22	1973–82
38	Davies, T.G.R.	Wales	27	3	8	1967–78
37	Bertranne, R.	France	20	4	13	1971–81
37	Henderson, N.J.	Ireland	17	4	16	1949–59
37	McHarg, A.F.	Scotland	13	1	23	1968–79
36	Bannerman, J.M.	Scotland	21	2	13	1921–29
36	Kennedy, K.W.	Ireland	17	4	15	1965–75
36	McLeod, H.F.	Scotland	12	3	21	1954–62
36	Murphy, N.A.A.	Ireland	13	2	21	1958–69
35	Crauste, M.	France	19	6	10	1958–66
35	McLauchlan, J.	Scotland	11	2	22	1969–79
35	Prat, J.	France	17	1	17	1947–55
35	Price, G.	Wales	23	1	11	1975–83
35	Rives, J-P.	France	23	1	11	1975–83

ENGLAND

M	Player	W	D	L	Career Span
34	Neary, A.	11	3	20	1971–80
33	Pullin, J.V.	9	4	20	1966–76
32	Wheeler, P.J.	13	2	17	1975–83
30	Wakefield, W.W.	20	3	7	1920–27
29	Duckham, D.J.	7	2	20	1969–76
28	Rogers, D.P.	10	6	12	1961–69
27	Cove-Smith, R.	21	2	4	1921–29
26	Beaumont, W.B.	11	2	13	1975–82
26	Butterfield, J.	15	5	6	1953–59
26	Evans, E.	16	3	7	1950–58
26	Slemen, M.A.C.	13	2	11	1976–82
26	Voyce, A.T.	19	3	4	1920–26
25	Cotton, F.E.	10	0	15	1971–81
25	Tucker, J.S.	13	4	8	1922–31

FRANCE

M	Player	W	D	L	Career Span
37	Bertranne, R.	20	4	13	1971–81
35	Crauste, M.	19	6	10	1958–66
35	Prat, J.	17	1	17	1947–55
35	Rives, J-P.	23	1	11	1975–83
32	Dauga, B.	14	5	13	1964–72
30	Dufau, G.	15	0	15	1948–57
29	Boniface, A.	12	3	14	1954–66
29	Celaya, M.	15	3	11	1953–61

M	Player	W	D	L	Career Span
29	Domenech, A.	16	2	11	1954–63
29	Paparemborde, R.	20	1	8	1976–83
27	Lux, J-P.	12	4	11	1967–75
26	Bouquet, J.	15	2	9	1954–62
26	Cassayet, A.	3	2	21	1920–27
26	Vannier, M.	14	2	10	1953–61

IRELAND

M	Player	W	D	L	Career Span
56	Gibson, C.M.H.	22	6	28	1964–79
53	McBride, W.J.	23	7	23	1962–75
48	Slattery, J.F.	21	4	23	1970–83
44	Kiernan, T.J.	18	5	21	1960–73
42	Kyle, J.W.	22	4	16	1947–58
40	Keane, M.I.	15	3	22	1974–83
40	Stephenson, G.V.	20	2	18	1920–30
37	Henderson, N.J.	17	4	16	1949–59
36	Kennedy, K.W.	18	4	14	1965–75
36	Murphy, N.A.A.	13	2	21	1958–69
34	McLoughlin, R.J.	14	5	15	1962–75
33	Millar, S.	11	2	20	1958–70
32	Davy, E.O'D.	19	1	12	1925–34
32	Orr, P.A.	11	2	19	1976–83
31	Kavanagh, J.R.	11	2	18	1953–62
30	Mulcahy, W.A.	8	3	19	1958–65
29	Crawford, W.E.	12	1	16	1920–27
29	Duggan, W.P.	9	1	19	1975–83
28	Clinch, J.D.	16	2	10	1923–31
27	Farrell, J.L.	17	1	9	1926–32
27	Hamlet, G.T.	11	1	15	1902–11
27	Magee, L.M.	11	2	14	1895–1904
27	O'Reilly, A.J.F.	9	1	17	1955–70
27	O'Reilly, A.J.F.	9	1	17	1955–70
27	Pedlow, A.C.	5	2	20	1953–63
27	Sugden, M.	16	2	9	1925–31
26	McCarthy, J.S.	15	3	8	1948–55
26	Wood, B.G.M.	9	0	17	1954–61

SCOTLAND

M	Player	W	D	L	Career Span
42	Renwick, J.M.	14	3	25	1972–83
41	Carmichael, A.B.	14	0	27	1967–78
39	Irvine, A.R.	14	3	22	1973–82
37	McHarg, A.F.	13	1	23	1968–79
36	Bannerman, J.M.	21	2	13	1921–29
36	McLeod, H.F.	12	3	21	1954–62
35	McLauchlan, J.	11	2	22	1969–79
34	Rollo, D.M.D.	13	4	17	1959–68
31	Smith, I.S.	20	0	11	1924–33
30	Smith, A.R.	12	2	16	1955–62
28	Laughland, I.H.P.	12	3	13	1959–67
27	Bruce, N.S.	12	3	12	1958–64
27	McGeechan, I.R.	9	2	16	1973–79

M	Player	W	D	L	Career Span
26	Elliot, W.I.D.	7	0	19	1947–54
26	Laidlaw, F.A.L.	6	2	18	1965–71
26	Scotland, K.J.F.	10	3	13	1957–65
26	Simmers, W.M.	12	1	13	1926–32
25	Drysdale, D.	17	0	8	1923–29
25	Kemp, J.W.Y.	8	2	15	1954–60
25	Macpherson, G.P.S.	13	3	9	1922–32
25	Nelson, J.B.	15	1	9	1925–31
25	Tomes, A.J.	7	3	15	1976–83

WALES

M	Player	W	D	L	Career Span
45	Edwards, G.O.	32	4	9	1967–78
44	Williams, J.P.R.	34	3	7	1969–81
41	Jones, K.J.	26	2	13	1947–57
38	Davies, T.G.R.	27	3	18	1967–78
35	Price, G.	23	1	11	1975–83
33	Bancroft, W.J.	16	1	16	1890–1901
32	Meredith, B.V.	19	3	10	1954–62
31	Davies, T.M.	23	3	5	1969–76
30	Bebb, D.I.E.	13	4	13	1959–67
30	Owen, R.M.	23	1	6	1901–12
30	Stephens, J.R.G.	18	0	12	1947–57
29	Williams, D.	18	4	7	1963–71
28	Martin, A.J.	21	1	6	1974–81
28	Morris, W.D.	18	4	6	1967–74
27	Gould, A.J.	10	3	14	1885–97
27	Morgan, C.I.	18	2	7	1951–58
27	Wheel, G.A.D.	20	1	6	1974–82
26	Bennett, P.	18	3	5	1969–78
26	Morgan, H.J.	13	3	10	1958–66
26	Powell, W.C.	14	3	9	1926–35
26	Price, B.	13	4	9	1961–69
26	Thomas, M.C.	15	2	9	1949–59
26	Trew, W.J.	22	0	4	1900–13
25	Fenwick, S.P.	19	0	6	1975–81
25	Squire, J.	15	1	9	1977–83
25	Williams, J.J.	18	2	5	1973–79

PLAYERS WITH 100% RECORDS

P	W	D	L	Player	Country	Career Span
8	8	0	0	Wade, C.G.	England	1882–86
7	7	0	0	Wooldridge, C.S.	England	1882–85
7	7	0	0	Ritson, J.A.S.	England	1910–13
6	6	0	0	Ward, G.	England	1913–14
6	6	0	0	Bush, P.F.	Wales	1906–10
6	6	0	0	Camberabero, G.	France	1967–68

P	W	D	L	Player	Country	Career Span
6	6	0	0	Payne, J.H.	England	1882–85
6	6	0	0	Tatham, W.M.	England	1882–84
6	6	0	0	Thomson, G.T.	England	1882–85
5	5	0	0	Jacob, H.P.	England	1924–30
5	5	0	0	Henderson, R.S.F.	England	1882–85
5	5	0	0	MacIlwaine, A.H.	England	1912–20
5	5	0	0	Woods, T.	England	1920–21
4	4	0	0	Chantrill, B.S.	England	1924
4	4	0	0	Coates, V.H.M.	England	1913
4	4	0	0	Evanson, A.M.	England	1882–84
4	4	0	0	Fuller, H.G.	England	1882–84
4	4	0	0	Oakley, F.E.	England	1913–14
4	4	0	0	Price, H.L.	England	1922–23
4	4	0	0	Richardson, J.V.	England	1928
4	4	0	0	Taylor, W.J.	England	1928
4	4	0	0	Waller, P.D.	Wales	1909–10
4	4	0	0	Thomas, R.	Wales	1900–01
4	4	0	0	Williams, W.H.	Wales	1900–01
4	4	0	0	Harize, D.	France	1977
4	4	0	0	Taylor, A.S.	England	1882–86
4	4	0	0	Twynam, H.T.	England	1883–84
4	4	0	0	Dyke, L.M.	Wales	1910–11
3	3	0	0	Fry, H.A.	England	1934
3	3	0	0	Cheesman, W.I.	England	1913
3	3	0	0	Dingle, A.J.	England	1913–14
3	3	0	0	Kindersley, R.S.	England	1882–85
3	3	0	0	Brown, D.I.	Scotland	1933
3	3	0	0	Frew, A.	Scotland	1901
3	3	0	0	Knox, J.	Scotland	1903
3	3	0	0	Kennedy, N.	Scotland	1903
3	3	0	0	Forrest, J.G.S.	Scotland	1938
3	3	0	0	Hastie, J.D.H.	Scotland	1938
3	3	0	0	Henderson, J.M.	Scotland	1933
3	3	0	0	Thom, J.R.	Scotland	1933
3	3	0	0	Lamond, G.A.W.	Scotland	1899–1905
3	3	0	0	MacGregor, D.G.	Scotland	1907
3	3	0	0	Lorraine, H.B.D.	Scotland	1933
3	3	0	0	Maynard, A.F.	England	1914
3	3	0	0	Palmer, G.V.	England	1928
3	3	0	0	Prentice, F.D.	England	1928
3	3	0	0	Sanders, F.W.	England	1923
3	3	0	0	Watson, J.H.D.	England	1914
3	3	0	0	Meikle, G.W.C.	England	1934
3	3	0	0	Brunton, J.	England	1914
3	3	0	0	Briggs, A.	England	1892
3	3	0	0	Bullough, E.	England	1892
3	3	0	0	Challis, R.	England	1957
3	3	0	0	Collins, P.J.	England	1952
3	3	0	0	Hayward, G.	Wales	1908–09
3	3	0	0	Richards, R.	Wales	1913
3	3	0	0	Davies, G.	Wales	1921–25
3	3	0	0	Beatty, W.J.	Ireland	1910–12
3	3	0	0	Reid, P.J.	Ireland	1948

P	W	D	L	Player	Country	Career Span
3	3	0	0	Smyth, P.J.	Ireland	1911
3	3	0	0	Mesny, P.	France	1981–82
3	3	0	0	Laporte, G.	France	1981
3	3	0	0	Moss, F.	England	1885–86
3	3	0	0	Strong, E.L.	England	1884
3	3	0	0	Davies, I.T.	Wales	1914
3	3	0	0	Gore, W.	Wales	1947
3	3	0	0	Evans, V.	Wales	1954
3	3	0	0	Davies, L.	Wales	1954–55
3	3	0	0	Whitson, G.	Wales	1956–60

MOST APPEARANCES ON WINNING SIDE: ALL PLAYERS

W	Player	Country	M	Career Span
34	Williams, J.P.R.	Wales	44	1969–81
32	Edwards, G.O.	Wales	45	1967–78
27	Davies, T.G.R.	Wales	38	1967–78
26	Jones, K.J.	Wales	41	1947–57
23	Davies, T.M.	Wales	31	1969–76
23	McBride, W.J.	Ireland	53	1962–75
23	Owen, R.M.	Wales	30	1901–12
23	Price, G.	Wales	35	1975–83
23	Rives, J-P.	France	35	1975–83
22	Gibson, C.M.H.	Ireland	56	1964–79
22	Kyle, J.W.	Ireland	42	1947–58
22	Trew, W.J.	Wales	26	1900–13
21	Bannerman, J.M.	Scotland	36	1921–29
21	Cove-Smith, R.	England	27	1921–29
21	Lowe, C.N.	England	24	1913–23
21	Martin, A.J.	Wales	28	1974–81
21	Slattery, J.F.	Ireland	48	1970–83
20	Bertranne, R.	France	37	1971–81
20	Davies, W.J.A.	England	21	1913–23
20	Paparemborde, R.	France	29	1976–83
20	Smith, I.S.	Scotland	31	1924–33
20	Stephenson, G.V.	Ireland	40	1920–30
20	Wakefield, W.W.	England	30	1920–27
20	Wheel, G.A.D.	Wales	27	1974–82

ENGLAND PLAYERS

Aarvold, C.D. 1928 Ww Iw Fw Sw; 1929 Ww Il Fw; 1931 Wd Sl Fl; 1932 Wl Iw Sw; 1933 Wl

Adams, A.A. 1910 Fw

Adey, G.J. 1976 Il Fl

Adkins, S.J. 1950 Iw Fl Sl; 1953 Ww Id Fw Sw

Agar, A.E. 1952 Wl Sw Iw Fw; 1953 Ww Id

Alderson, F.H.R. 1891 Ww Iw Sl; 1892 Ww Sw; 1893 Wl

Alexander, H. 1900 Iw Sd; 1901 Wl Il Sl; 1902 Wl Iw

Alexander, W. 1927 Fl

Allison, D.F. 1956 Wl Iw Sw Fl; 1957 Ww; 1958 Wd Sd

Allport, A. 1892 Ww; 1893 Iw; 1894 Ww Il Sl

Anderson, S. 1899 Il

Archer, H. 1909 Wl Iw

Armstrong, R. 1925 Ww

Arthur, T.G. 1966 Wl Id

Ashby, R.C. 1966 Id Fl

Ashcroft, A. 1956 Wl Iw Sw Fl; 1957 Ww Iw Fw Sw; 1958 Wd Iw Fw Sd; 1959 Iw Fd Sd

Ashford, W. 1897 Wl Il; 1898 Sd Ww

Ashworth, A. 1892 Iw

Askew, J.G. 1930 Ww Il Fw

Aslett, A.R. 1926 Wd Il Fw Sl; 1929 Sl Fw

Assinder, E.W. 1909 Wl

Aston, R.L. 1890 Sw Iw

Auty, J.R. 1935 Sl

Bainbridge, S.J. 1982 Fw Ww; 1983 Fl Wd Sl Il

Baker, D.G.S. 1955 Wl Id Fl Sw

Baker, E.M. 1895 Ww Iw Sl; 1896 Ww Il Sl; 1897 Wl

Baker, H.C. 1887 Wd

Bance, J.F. 1954 Sw

Barr, R.J. 1932 Wl Iw

Barrett, E.I.M. 1903 Sl

Barrington, T.J.M. 1931 Wd Il

Barrington-Ward, L.E. 1910 Ww Id Fw Sw

Barron, J.H. 1896 Sl; 1897 Wl Il

Bartlett, J.T. 1951 Wl

Bartlett, R.M. 1957 Ww Iw Fw Sw; 1958 Iw Fw Sd

Barton, J. 1967 Iw Fl Wl; 1972 Fl

Bateson, A.H. 1930 Ww Il Fw Sd

Baume, J.L. 1950 Sl

Baxter, J. 1900 Wl Iw Sd

Bazley, R.C. 1952 Iw Fw; 1953 Ww Id Fw Sw; 1955 Wl Id Fl Sw

Beaumont, W.B. 1975 Il; 1976 Wl Sl Il Fl; 1977 Sw Iw Fl Wl; 1978 Fl Wl Sw Iw; 1979 Sd Il Fw Wl; 1980 Iw Fw Ww Sw; 1981 Wl Sw Iw Fl; 1982 Sd

Bedford, H. 1890 Sw Iw

Bedford, L.L. 1931 Wd Il

Beer, I.D.S. 1955 Fl Sw

Beese, M.C. 1972 Wl Il Fl

Bell, F.J. 1900 Wl

Bell, H. 1884 Iw

Bell, P.J. 1968 Wd Id Fl Sw

Bell, R.W. 1900 Wl Iw Sd

Bendon, G.J. 1959 Wl Iw Fd Sd

Bennett, N.O. 1947 Ww Sw Fw; 1948 Wd Il Sl

Bennett, W.N. 1975 Sw; 1976 Sl (R); 1979 Sd Il Fw Wl

Bennetts, B.B. 1909 Wl

Berridge, M.J. 1949 Wl Il

Berry, H. 1910 Ww Id Fw Sw

Berry, J. 1891 Ww Iw Sl

Berry, J.T.W. 1939 Ww Il Sw

Birkett, J.G.G. 1906 Sw; 1907 Wl Sl; 1908 Wl Iw Sl; 1910 Ww Id Sw; 1911 Wl Fw Il Sw; 1912 Ww Iw Sl Fw

Bishop, C.C. 1927 Fl

Black, B.H. 1930 Ww Il Fw Sd; 1931 Wd Il Sl Fl; 1932 Sw; 1933 Wl

Blacklock, J.H. 1898 Il; 1899 Il

Blakeway, P.J. 1980 Iw Fw Ww Sw; 1981 Wl Sw Iw Fl; 1982 Il Fw Ww

Blakiston, A.F. 1920 Sw; 1921 Ww Iw Sw Fw; 1922 Wl; 1923 Sw Fw; 1924 Ww Iw Fw Sw; 1925 Ww Id Sl Fw

Bolton, R. 1933 Wl; 1936 Sw; 1937 Sw; 1938 Wl Iw

Bolton, W.N. 1882 Ww; 1883 Iw Sw; 1884 Ww Iw Sw; 1885 Iw; 1887 Il Sd

Bonaventura, M.S. 1931 Wd

Bond, A.M. 1979 Sd Il; 1980 Iw 1982 Il

Bonham-Carter, E. 1891 Sl

Bonsor, F. 1886 Ww Iw Sd; 1887 Wd Sd

Boobyer, B. 1950 Wl Iw Fl Sl; 1951 Wl Fl; 1952 Sw Iw Fw

Booth, L.A. 1933 Wl Iw Sl; 1934 Sw; 1935 Wd Iw Sl

Botting, I.J. 1950 Wl Iw

Boughton, H.J. 1935 Wd Iw Sl

Boyle, S.B. 1983 Wd Sl Il

Boylen, F. 1908 Wl Iw Sl

Bradby, M.S. 1922 Iw Fd

Bradley, R. 1903 Wl

Bradshaw, H. 1892 Sw; 1893 Wl Iw Sl; 1894 Ww Il Sl

Braithwaite-Exley, B. 1949 Wl

Brettargh, A.T. 1900 Wl; 1903 Il Sl; 1904 Wd Iw Sl; 1905 Il Sl

Briggs, A. 1892 Ww Iw Sw

Brinn, A. 1972 Wl Il Sl

Broadley, T. 1893 Wl Sl; 1894 Ww Il Sl; 1896 Sl

Bromet, W.E. 1891 Ww Iw; 1892 Ww Iw Sw; 1893 Wl Iw Sl; 1895 Ww Iw Sl; 1896 Il

Brook, P.W.P. 1930 Sd; 1931 Fl; 1936 Sw

Brooke, T.J. 1968 Fl Sw

Brophy, T.J. 1964 Il Fw Sl; 1965 Wl Il; 1966 Wl Id Fl

Brough, J.W. 1925 Ww

Brougham, H. 1912 Ww Iw Sl Fw

Brown, A.A. 1938 Sl

Brown, L.G. 1911 Wl Fw Il Sw; 1913 Ww Fw Iw Sw; 1914 Ww Iw Sw Fw; 1921 Ww Iw Sw Fw; 1922 Wl

Brown, T.W. 1928 Sw; 1929 Ww Il Sl Fw; 1932 Sw; 1933 Wl Iw Sl

Brunton, J. 1914 Ww Iw Sw

Brutton, E.R. 1886 Sd

Buckingham, R.A. 1927 Fl

Bucknall, A.L. 1970 Iw Wl Sl Fl; 1971 Wl Iw Fd Sl

Budworth, R.T.D. 1890 Wl; 1891 Ww Sl

Bull, A.G. 1914 Ww

Bullough, E. 1892 Ww Iw Sw
Bulpitt, M.P. 1970 Sl
Bunting, W.L. 1897 Il Sw; 1898 Il Sd Ww; 1899 Sl;
1900 Sd; 1901 Il Sl
Burland, D.W. 1931 Wd Il Fl; 1932 Iw Sw; 1933 Wl
Iw Sl
Burton, H.C. 1926 Wd
Burton, M.A. 1972 Wl Il Fl Sl; 1974 Fd Ww; 1975
Sw; 1976 Wl Sl Il Fl; 1978 Fl Wl
Butcher, W.V. 1903 Sl; 1904 Wd Iw Sl; 1905 Wl Il
Sl
Butler, A.G. 1937 Ww Iw
Butler, P.E. 1976 Fl
Butterfield, J. 1953 Fw Sw; 1954 Ww Iw Sw Fl;
1955 Wl Id Fl Sw; 1956 Wl Iw Sw Fl; 1957 Ww Iw
Fw Sw; 1958 Wd Iw Fw Sd; 1959 Wl Iw Fd Sd
Byrne, F.A. 1897 Wl
Byrne, J.F. 1894 Ww Il Sl; 1895 Iw Sl; 1896 Il; 1897
Wl Il Sw; 1898 Il Sd Ww; 1899 Il
Cain, J.J. 1950 Wl
Campbell, D.A. 1937 Ww Iw
Candler, P.L. 1935 Wd; 1936 Wd Il Sw; 1937 Ww
Iw Sw; 1938 Wl Sl
Cannell, L.B. 1948 Fl; 1949 Wl Il Fw Sw; 1950 Wl
Iw Fl Sl; 1952 Wl; 1953 Ww Id Fw; 1956 Iw Sw Fl;
1957 Ww Iw
Caplan, D.W.N. 1978 Sw Iw
Cardus, R.M. 1979 Fw Wl
Carey, G.M. 1895 Ww Iw Sl; 1896 Ww Il
Carleton, J. 1980 Iw Fw Ww Sw; 1981 Wl Sw Iw Fl;
1982 Sd Il Fw Ww; 1983 Fl Wd Sl Il
Carr, R.S.L. 1939 Ww Il Sw
Cartwright, V.H. 1903 Wl Il Sl; 1904 Wd Sl; 1905
Wl Il Sl; 1906 Wl Il Sw
Catcheside, H.C. 1924 Ww Iw Fw Sw; 1926 Wd Il;
1927 Iw Sl
Cattell, R.H.B. 1895 Ww Iw Sl; 1896 Ww Il Sl; 1900
Wl
Cave, W.T.C. 1905 Wl
Challis, R. 1957 Iw Fw Sw
Chambers, E.L. 1910 Ww Id
Chantrill, B.S. 1924 Ww Iw Fw Sw
Chapman, C.E. 1884 Ww
Chapman, F.E. 1910 Ww Id Fw Sw; 1912 Ww; 1914
Ww Iw
Cheesman, W.I. 1913 Ww Fw Iw
Christopherson, P. 1891 Ww Sl
Clarke, A.J. 1935 Wd Iw Sl; 1936 Wd Il
Clarke, S.J.S. 1963 Ww Id Fw Sw; 1964 Wd Il; 1965
Il Fw Sd
Clements, J.W. 1959 Iw Fd Sd
Cleveland, C.R. 1887 Wd Sd
Clibborn, W.G. 1886 Ww Iw Sd; 1887 Wd Il Sd
Coates, V.H.M. 1913 Ww Fw Iw Sw
Cobby, W. 1900 Wl
Cockerham, A. 1900 Wl
Colclough, M.J. 1978 Sw Iw; 1980 Fw Ww Sw; 1981
Wl Sw Iw Fl; 1982 Sd Il Fw Ww; 1983 Fl
Coley, E. 1929 Fw; 1932 Wl
Collins, P.J. 1952 Sw Iw Fw
Considine, S.G.U. 1925 Fw
Conway, G.S. 1920 Fw Iw Sw; 1921 Fw; 1922 Wl Iw
Fd Sw; 1923 Ww Iw Sw Fw; 1924 Ww Iw Fw Sw;
1927 Ww

Cook, J.G. 1937 Sw
Cook, P.W. 1965 Il Fw
Cooke, D.A. 1976 Wl Sl Il Fl
Cooke, D.H. 1981 Wl Sw Iw Fl
Cooke, P. 1939 Ww Il
Coop, T. 1892 Sw
Cooper, J.G. 1909 Wl
Cooper, M.J. 1973 Fw Sw; 1975 Fl Wl; 1976 Wl;
1977 Sw Iw Fl Wl
Cooper, S.F. 1900 Wl; 1902 Wl Iw; 1905 Wl Il Sl;
1907 Wl
Corbett, L.J. 1921 Fw; 1923 Ww Iw; 1924 Ww Iw
Fw Sw; 1925 Ww Id Sl Fw; 1927 Ww Iw Sl Fl
Corless, B.J. 1976 Il (R); 1977 Sw Iw Fl Wl; 1978 Fl
Wl Sw Iw
Cotton, F.E. 1971 Sl; 1973 Wl Fl Fw Sw; 1974 Sl Il;
1975 Il Fl Wl; 1976 Wl Sl Il Fl; 1977 Sw Iw Fl Wl;
1978 Sw Iw; 1980 Iw Fw Ww Sw; 1981 Wl
Coulman, M.J. 1967 Iw Fl Sw Wl; 1968 Wd Id Fl Sw
Coulson, T.J. 1927 Ww; 1928 Ww
Court, E.D. 1885 Ww
Cove-Smith, R. 1921 Sw Fw; 1922 Iw Fd Sw; 1923
Ww Iw Sw Fw; 1924 Ww Iw Fw Sw; 1925 Ww Id
Sl Fw; 1927 Ww Iw Sl Fl; 1928 Ww Iw Fw Sw;
1929 Ww Il
Coverdale, H. 1910 Fw; 1912 Iw Fw; 1920 Wl
Cowling, R.J. 1977 Sw Iw Fl Wl; 1978 Fl; 1979 Sd Il
Cowman, A.R. 1971 Sl; 1973 Wl Il
Cox, N.S. 1901 Sl
Cranmer, P. 1934 Ww Iw Sw; 1935 Wd Iw Sl; 1936
Wd Il Sw; 1937 Ww Iw Sw; 1938 Wl Iw Sl
Cridlan, A.G. 1935 Wd Iw Sl
Cumberlege, B.S. 1920 Wl Iw Sw; 1921 Ww Iw Sw
Fw; 1922 Wl
Cumming, D.C. 1925 Sl Fw
Currie, J.D. 1956 Wl Iw Sw Fl; 1957 Ww Iw Fw Sw;
1958 Wd Iw Fw Sd; 1959 Wl Iw Fd Sd; 1960 Ww
Iw Fd Sw; 1962 Wd Iw Fl
Cusworth, L. 1982 Fw Ww; 1983 Fl Wd
Dalton, T.J. 1969 Sw (R)
Danby, T. 1949 Wl
Daniell, J. 1899 Wl; 1900 Iw Sd; 1902 Iw Sw; 1904
Iw Sl
Darby, A.J.L. 1899 Il
Davey, J. 1908 Sl; 1909 Wl
Davey, R.F. 1931 Wd
Davidson, Jas 1897 Sw; 1898 Sd Ww; 1899 Il Sl
Davidson, Jos 1899 Wl Sl
Davies, G.H. 1981 Sw Iw Fl; 1982 Sd Il; 1983 Fl Wd
Sl
Davies, P.H. 1927 Iw
Davies, V.G. 1922 Wl
Davies, W.J.A. 1913 Ww Fw Iw Sw; 1914 Iw Sw
Fw; 1920 Fw Iw Sw; 1921 Ww Iw Sw Fw; 1922 Iw
Fd Sw; 1923 Ww Iw Sw Fw
Davies, W.P.C. 1953 Sw; 1954 Iw; 1955 Wl Id Fl
Sw; 1956 Wl; 1957 Fw Sw; 1958 Wd
Davis, A.M. 1963 Ww Id Sw; 1964 Wd Il Fw Sl;
1966 Wl; 1970 Iw Wl Sl
Day, H.L.V. 1920 Wl; 1922 Wl Fd; 1926 Sl
Dean, G.J. 1931 Il
Dee, J.M. 1962 Sd
Devitt, Sir T.G. 1926 Il Fl; 1928 Ww
Dewhurst, J.H. 1887 Wd Il Sd; 1890 Wl

Dibble, R. 1906 Sw; 1908 Wl Iw Sl; 1909 Wl Iw Sl; 1910 Sw; 1911 Wl Fw Sw; 1912 Ww Iw Sl

Dicks, J. 1934 Ww Iw Sw; 1935 Wd Iw Sl; 1936 Sw; 1937 Iw

Dillon, E.W. 1904 Wd Iw Sl; 1905 Wl

Dingle, A.J. 1913 Iw; 1914 Sw Fw

Dixon, P.J. 1972 Wl Il Fl Sl; 1973 Il Fw Sw; 1974 Sl Il Fd Ww; 1975 Il; 1976 Fl; 1977 Sw Iw Fl Wl; 1978 Fl Sw Iw

Dobbs, G.E.B. 1906 Wl Il

Doble, S.A. 1973 Wl

Dobson, D.D. 1902 Wl Iw Sw; 1903 Wl Il Sl

Dobson, T.H. 1895 Sl

Dodge, P.W. 1978 Wl Sw Iw; 1979 Sd Il Fw Wl; 1980 Ww Sw; 1981 Wl Sw Iw Fl; 1982 Sd Fw Ww; 1983 Fl Wd Sl Il

Donnelly, M.P. 1947 Il

Dovey, B.A. 1963 Ww Id

Dowson, A.O. 1899 Sl

Drake-Lee, N.J. 1963 Ww Id Fw Sw; 1964 Wd Il; 1965 Wl

Duckett, H. 1893 Iw Sl

Duckham, D.J. 1969 Il Fw Sw Wl; 1970 Iw Wl Sl Fl; 1971 Wl Iw Fd Sl; 1972 Wl Il Fl Sl; 1973 Wl Il Fw Sw; 1974 Sl Il Fd Ww; 1975 Il Fl Wl; 1976 Wl Sl

Dudgeon, H.W. 1897 Sw; 1898 Il Sd Ww; 1899 Wl Il Sl

Duncan, R.F.H. 1922 Iw Fd Sw

Dunkley, P.E. 1931 Il Sl; 1936 Wd Il Sw

Duthie, J. 1903 Wl

Dyson, J.W. 1890 Sw; 1892 Sw; 1893 Iw Sl

Ebdon, P.J. 1897 Wl Il

Eddison, J.H. 1912 Ww Iw Sl Fw

Edgar, C.S. 1901 Sl

Edwards, R. 1921 Ww Iw Sw Fw; 1922 Wl Fd; 1923 Ww; 1924 Ww Fw Sw

Elliot, C.H. 1886 Ww

Elliot, E.W. 1901 Wl Il Sl; 1904 Wd

Elliot, W. 1932 Iw Sw; 1933 Wl Iw Sl; 1934 Ww Iw

Elliott, A.E. 1894 Sl

Ellis, J. 1939 Sw

Emmott, C. 1892 Ww

Estcourt, N.S.D. 1955 Sw

Evans, E. 1950 Wl; 1951 Il Fl Sw; 1952 Wl Sw Iw Fw; 1953 Id Fw Sw; 1954 Ww Iw Fl; 1956 Wl Iw Sw Fl; 1957 Ww Iw Fw Sw; 1958 Wd Iw Fw Sd

Evans, G.W. 1972 Sl; 1973 Wl (R) Fw Sw; 1974 Sl Il Fd Ww

Evans, N.L. 1932 Wl Iw Sw; 1933 Wl Iw

Evanson, A.M. 1882 Ww; 1883 Iw Sw; 1884 Sw

Evershed, F. 1890 Wl Sw Iw; 1892 Ww Iw Sw; 1893 Wl Iw Sl

Eyres, W.C.T. 1927 Iw

Fagan, A.R.St L. 1887 Il

Fairbrother, K.E. 1969 Il Fw Sw Wl; 1970 Iw Wl Sl Fl; 1971 Wl Iw Fd

Faithfull, C.K.T. 1924 Iw; 1926 Fw Sl

Fallas, H. 1884 Iw

Fegan, J.H.C. 1895 Ww Iw Sl

Field, E. 1893 Wl Iw

Fielding, K.J. 1969 Il Fw Sw; 1970 Iw Fl; 1972 Wl Il Fl Sl

Finlan, J.F. 1967 Iw Fl Sw Wl; 1968 Wd Id; 1969 Il Fw Sw Wl; 1970 Fl

Finlinson, H.W. 1895 Ww Iw Sl

Firth, F. 1894 Ww Il Sl

Fletcher, N.C. 1901 Wl Il Sl; 1903 Sl

Fletcher, T. 1897 Wl

Fookes, E.F. 1896 Ww Il Sl; 1897 Wl Il Sw; 1898 Il Ww; 1899 Il Sl

Ford, P.J. 1964 Wd Il Fw Sl

Forrest, J.W. 1930 Ww Il Fw Sd; 1931 Wd Il Sl Fl; 1934 Iw Sw

Forrest, R. 1899 Wl; 1900 Sd; 1902 Iw Sw; 1903 Il Sl

Foulds, R.T. 1929 Ww Il

Fox, H.F. 1890 Wl Sw

Francis, T.E.S. 1926 Wd Il Fw Sl

Frankcom, G.P. 1965 Wl Il Fw Sd

Fraser, G. 1902 Ww Il Sl; 1903 Wl Il

Freakes, H.D. 1938 Wl; 1939 Ww Il

French, R.J. 1961 Wl Il Fd Sw

Fry, H.A. 1934 Ww Iw Sw

Fuller, H.G. 1882 Ww; 1883 Iw Sw; 1884 Ww

Gadney, B.C. 1932 Iw Sw; 1933 Iw Sl; 1934 Ww Iw Sw; 1935 Sl; 1936 Wd Il Sw; 1937 Sw; 1938 Wl

Gamlin, H.T. 1899 Wl Sl; 1900 Wl Iw Sd; 1901 Sl; 1902 Wl Iw Sw; 1903 Wl Il Sl; 1904 Wd Iw Sl

Gardner, E.R. 1921 Ww Iw Sw; 1922 Wl Iw Fd; 1923 Ww Iw Sw Fw

Gavins, M.N. 1961 Wl

Gay, D.J. 1968 Wd Id Fl Sw

Gent, D.R. 1906 Wl Il; 1910 Ww Id

George, J.T. 1947 Sw Fw; 1949 Il

Gerrard, R.A. 1932 Wl Iw Sw; 1933 Wl Iw Sl; 1934 Ww Iw Sw; 1936 Wd Il Sw

Gibbs, G.A. 1947 Fw; 1948 Il

Gibbs, J.C. 1925 Ww; 1926 Fw; 1927 Ww Iw Sl Fl

Gibbs, N. 1954 Sw Fl

Giblin, L.F. 1896 Ww Il; 1897 Sw

Gibson, C.O.P. 1901 Wl

Gibson, G.R. 1899 Wl; 1901 Sl

Gibson, T.A. 1905 Wl Sl

Gilbert, F.G. 1923 Ww Iw

Gilbert, R. 1908 Wl Iw Sl

Giles, J.L. 1935 Wd Iw; 1937 Ww Iw; 1938 Iw Sl

Glover, P.B. 1971 Fd

Godwin, H.O. 1959 Fd Sd; 1963 Sw; 1964 Il Fw Sl

Gordon-Smith, G.W. 1900 Wl Iw Sd

Gotley, A.L.H. 1910 Fw Sw; 1911 Wl Fw Il Sw

Graham, D. 1901 Wl

Gray, A. 1947 Ww Il Sw

Green, J. 1905 Il; 1906 Sw; 1907 Wl Il Sl

Greenwell, J.H. 1893 Wl Iw

Greenwood, J.E. 1912 Fw; 1913 Ww Fw Iw Sw; 1914 Ww Sw Fw; 1920 Wl Fw Iw Sw

Greenwood, J.R.H. 1966 Id Fl Sl; 1969 Il

Gregory, G.G. 1931 Il Sl Fl; 1932 Wl Iw Sw; 1933 Wl Iw Sl; 1934 Ww Iw Sw

Gregory, J.A. 1949 Wl

Grylls, W.M. 1905 Il

Guest, R.H. 1939 Ww Il Sw; 1947 Ww Il Sw Fw; 1948 Wd Il Sl; 1949 Fw Sw

Gummer, C.H.A. 1929 Fw

Gurdon, C. 1883 Sw; 1884 Ww Sw; 1885 Iw; 1886 Ww Iw Sd

Gurdon, E.T. 1882 Ww; 1883 Iw Sw; 1884 Ww Iw Sw; 1885 Ww Iw; 1886 Sd

Haigh, L. 1910 Ww Id Sw; 1911 Wl Fw Il Sw

Hale, P.M. 1970 Iw Wl
Hall, C. 1901 Il Sl
Hall, J. 1894 Ww Il Sl
Hall, N.M. 1947 Ww Il Sw Fw; 1949 Wl Il; 1952 Wl
   Sw Iw Fw; 1953 Ww Id Fw Sw; 1955 Wl Id
Hamilton-Hill, E.A. 1936 Wd Il
Hamilton-Wickes, R.H. 1924 Iw; 1925 Ww Id Sl
   Fw; 1926 Wd Il Sl; 1927 Ww
Hammett, E.D.G. 1920 Wl Fw Sw; 1921 Ww Iw Sw
   Fw; 1922 Wl
Hammond, C.E.L. 1905 Sl; 1906 Wl Il Sw; 1908 Wl
   Iw
Hancock, A.W. 1965 Fw Sd; 1966 Fl
Hancock, G.E. 1939 Ww Il Sw
Hancock, J.H. 1955 Wl Id
Hancock, P.F. 1886 Ww Iw; 1890 Wl
Hancock, P.S. 1904 Wd Iw Sl
Handford, F.G. 1909 Wl Iw Sl
Hands, R.H.M. 1910 Fw Sw
Hanley, J. 1927 Ww Sl Fl; 1928 Ww Iw Fw Sw
Hannaford, R.C. 1971 Wl Iw Fd
Hanvey, R.J. 1926 Wd Il Fw Sl
Harding, E.H. 1931 Il
Harding, V.S.J. 1961 Fd Sw; 1962 Wd Iw Fl Sd
Hardwick, P.F. 1902 Iw Sw; 1903 Wl Il Sl; 1904 Wd
   Iw Sl
Hardy, E.M.P. 1951 Il Fl Sw
Hare, W.H. 1974 Ww; 1978 Fl; 1980 Iw Fw Ww Sw;
   1981 Wl Sw; 1982 Fw Ww; 1983 Fl Wd Sl Il
Harper, C.H. 1899 Wl
Harris, S.W. 1920 Iw Sw
Harris, T.W. 1929 Sl; 1932 Iw
Harrison, A.C. 1931 Il Sl
Harrison, A.L. 1914 Iw Fw
Harrison, G. 1885 Ww Iw
Harrison, H.C. 1909 Sl; 1914 Iw Sw Fw
Hartley, B.C. 1901 Sl; 1902 Sw
Haslett, L.W. 1926 Il Fw
Hastings, G.W.D. 1955 Wl Id Fl Sw; 1957 Ww Iw
   Fw Sw; 1958 Wd Iw Fw Sd
Havelock, H. 1908 Wl Iw
Hawcridge, J.J. 1885 Ww Iw
Hayward, L.W. 1910 Id
Hazell, D.St G. 1955 Wl Id Fl Sw
Hearn, R.D. 1966 Fl Sl; 1967 Iw Fl Sw Wl
Heaton, J. 1935 Wd Iw Sl; 1939 Ww Il Sw; 1947 Il
   Sw Fw
Henderson, A.P. 1947 Ww Il Sw Fw; 1948 Il Sl Fl;
   1949 Wl Il
Henderson, R.S.F. 1882 Ww; 1883 Sw; 1884 Ww
   Sw; 1885 Ww
Heppell, W.G. 1903 Il
Herbert, A.J. 1958 Fw Sd; 1959 Wl Iw Fd Sd
Hesford, R. 1981 Sw (R); 1982 Sd Fw (R); 1983 Fl (R)
Hetherington, J.G.G. 1958 Iw; 1959 Wl Iw Fd Sd
Hewitt, E.N. 1951 Wl Il Fl
Hickson, J.L. 1887 Wd Il Sd; 1890 Wl Sw Iw
Higgins, R. 1954 Ww Iw Sw; 1955 Wl Id Fl Sw;
   1957 Ww Iw Fw Sw; 1959 Wl
Hignell, A.J. 1976 Wl Sl Il; 1977 Sw Iw Fl Wl; 1978
   Wl; 1979 Sd Il Fw Wl
Hill, B.A. 1903 Il Sl; 1904 Wd Iw; 1905 Wl; 1907 Wl
Hiller, R. 1968 Wd Id Fl Sw; 1969 Il Fw Sw Wl;
   1970 Iw Wl Sl; 1971 Iw Fd Sl; 1972 Wl Il

Hind, A.E. 1906 Wl
Hind, G.R. 1910 Sw; 1911 Il
Hobbs, R.F.A. 1899 Sl; 1903 Wl
Hobbs, R.G.S. 1932 Wl Iw Sw
Hodges, H.A. 1906 Wl Il
Hodgson, J.Mc D. 1932 Wl Iw Sw; 1934 Ww Iw;
   1936 Il
Hodgson, S.A.M. 1960 Ww Iw Fd Sw; 1961 Wl;
   1962 Wd Iw Fl Sd; 1964 Wd
Hofmeyr, M.B. 1950 Wl Fl Sl
Holford, G. 1920 Wl Fw
Holland, D. 1912 Ww Iw Sl
Holliday, T.E. 1923 Sw Fw; 1925 Id Sl Fw; 1926 Fw
   Sl
Holmes, C.B. 1947 Sw; 1948 Il Fl
Holmes, E. 1890 Sw Iw
Holmes, W.A. 1950 Wl Iw Fl Sl; 1951 Wl Il Fl Sw;
   1952 Sw Iw Fw; 1953 Ww Id Fw Sw
Holmes, W.B. 1949 Wl Il Fw Sw
Hook, W.G. 1951 Sw; 1952 Wl
Hooper, C.A. 1894 Ww Il Sl
Hopley, F.J.V. 1907 Wl; 1908 Iw
Hordern, P.C. 1931 Il Sl Fl; 1934 Ww
Horley, C.H. 1885 Iw
Horrocks-Taylor, J.P. 1958 Wd; 1961 Sw; 1962 Sd;
   1964 Wd
Horsfall, E.L. 1949 Wl
Horton, A.L. 1965 Wl Il Fw Sd; 1966 Fl Sl
Horton, J.P. 1978 Wl Sw Iw; 1980 Iw Fw Ww Sw;
   1981 Wl; 1983 Sl Il
Horton, N.E. 1969 Il Fw Sw Wl; 1971 Iw Fd Sl; 1974
   Sl; 1975 Wl; 1977 Sw Iw Fl Wl; 1978 Fl Wl; 1979
   Sd Il Fw Wl; 1980 Iw
Hosen, R.W. 1964 Fw Sl; 1967 Iw Fl Sw Wl
Hosking, G.R.d'A. 1949 Wl Il Fw Sw; 1950 Wl
Houghton, S. 1892 Iw; 1896 Ww
Howard, P.D. 1930 Ww Il Fw Sd; 1931 Wd Il Sl Fl
Hubbard, G.C. 1892 Ww Iw
Hubbard, J.C. 1930 Sd
Hudson, A. 1906 Wl Il; 1908 Wl Iw Sl; 1910 Fw
Hughes, G.E. 1896 Sl
Hulme, F.C. 1903 Wl Il; 1905 Wl Il
Hunt, J.T. 1884 Ww
Hurst, A.C.B. 1962 Sd
Huskisson, T.F. 1937 Ww Iw Sw; 1938 Wl Iw; 1939
   Ww Il Sw
Hutchinson, F. 1909 Iw Sl
Hutchinson, J.E. 1906 Il
Hyde, J.P. 1950 Fl Sl
Hynes, W.B. 1912 Fw
Ibbitson, E.D. 1909 Wl Iw Sl
Imrie, H.M. 1907 Il
Inglis, R.E. 1886 Ww Iw Sd
Irvin, S.H. 1905 Wl
Jackett, E.J. 1906 Wl Il Sw; 1907 Wl Il Sl; 1909 Wl
   Iw Sl
Jackson, B.S. 1970 Sl (R) Fl
Jackson, P.B. 1956 Wl Iw Fl; 1957 Ww Iw Fw Sw;
   1958 Wd Fw Sd; 1959 Wl Iw Fd Sd; 1961 Sw; 1963
   Ww Id Fw Sw
Jackson, W.J. 1894 Sl
Jacob, F. 1897 Wl Il Sw; 1898 Il Sd Ww; 1899 Wl Il
Jacob, H.P. 1924 Ww Iw Fw Sw; 1930 Fw
Jacob, P.G. 1898 Il

Jacobs, C.R. 1956 Wl Iw Sw Fl; 1957 Ww Iw Fw Sw; 1958 Wd Iw Fw Sd; 1960 Ww Iw Fd Sw; 1961 Wl Il Fd Sw; 1964 Wd Il Fw Sl

Jago, R.A. 1906 Wl Il; 1907 Wl Il

Janion, J.P.A.G. 1971 Wl Iw Fd Sl; 1972 Wl Sl

Jarman, J.W. 1900 Wl

Jeavons, N.C. 1981 Sw Iw Fl; 1982 Sd Il Fw Ww; 1983 Fl Wd Sl Il

Jeeps, R.E.G. 1956 Wl; 1957 Ww Iw Fw Sw; 1958 Wd Iw Fw Sd; 1959 Iw; 1960 Ww Iw Fd Sw; 1961 Wl Il Fd Sw; 1962 Wd Iw Fl Sd

Jeffery, G.L. 1886 Ww Iw Sd; 1887 Wd Il Sd

Jennins, C.R. 1967 Iw Fl

Jewitt, J. 1902 Wl

Johns, W.A. 1909 Wl Iw Sl; 1910 Ww Id Fw

Johnston, W.R. 1910 Ww Id Sw; 1912 Ww Iw Sl Fw; 1913 Ww Fw Iw Sw; 1914 Ww Iw Sw Fw

Jones, F.P. 1893 Sl

Jones, H.A. 1950 Wl Iw Fl

Jorden, A.M. 1970 Fl; 1973 Il Fw Sw; 1974 Fd; 1975 Wl Sw

Jowett, D. 1890 Sw Iw; 1891 Ww Iw Sl

Judd, P.E. 1962 Wd Iw Fl Sd; 1963 Sw; 1965 Il Fw Sd; 1966 Wl Id Fl Sl; 1967 Iw Fl Sw Wl

Keeling, J.H. 1948 Wd

Keen, B.W. 1968 Wd Id Fl Sw

Keeton, G.H. 1904 Wd Iw Sl

Kelly, G.A. 1947 Ww Il Sw; 1948 Wd

Kelly, T.S. 1906 Wl Il Sw; 1907 Wl Il Sl; 1908 Iw Sl

Kemble, A.T. 1885 Ww Iw; 1887 Il

Kemp, D.T. 1935 Wd

Kemp, T.A. 1937 Ww Iw; 1939 Sw; 1948 Wd

Kendall, P.D. 1901 Sl; 1902 Wl; 1903 Sl

Kendall-Carpenter, J.M.K. 1949 Il Fw Sw; 1950 Wl Iw Fl Sl; 1951 Il Fl Sw; 1952 Wl Sw Iw Fw; 1953 Ww Id Fw Sw; 1954 Ww Iw Fl

Kendrew, D.A. 1930 Ww Il; 1933 Iw Sl; 1934 Sw; 1935 Wd Iw; 1936 Wd Il

Kennedy, R.D. 1949 Il Fw Sw

Kent, C.P. 1977 Sw Iw Fl Wl; 1978 Fl (R)

Kent, T. 1891 Ww Iw Sl; 1892 Ww Iw Sw

Kershaw, C.A. 1920 Wl Fw Iw Sw; 1921 Ww Iw Sw Fw; 1922 Wl Iw Fd Sw; 1923 Ww Iw Sw Fw

Kewney, A.L. 1906 Wl Il Sw; 1909 Wl Iw Sl; 1911 Wl Fw Il Sw; 1912 Iw Sl

Key A. 1930 Il; 1933 Wl

Keyworth, M. 1976 Wl Sl Il

Kindersley, R.S. 1882 Ww; 1884 Sw; 1885 Ww

King, I. 1954 Ww Iw

King, J.A. 1911 Wl Fw Il Sw; 1912 Ww Iw Sl; 1913 Ww Fw Iw Sw

King, Q.E.M.A. 1921 Sw

Kingston, P. 1979 Il Fw Wl

Kitching, A.E. 1913 Iw

Kittermaster, H.J. 1925 Ww Id; 1926 Wd Il Fw Sl

Knight, P.M. 1972 Fl Sl

Knowles, E. 1896 Sl; 1897 Sw

Knowles, T.C. 1931 Sl

Krige, J.A. 1920 Wl

Labuschagne, N.A. 1953 Ww 1955 Wl Id Fl Sw

Lagden, R.O. 1911 Sw

Laird, H.C.C. 1927 Ww Iw Sl; 1928 Ww Iw Fw Sw; 1929 Ww Il

Lambert, D. 1908 Wl Sl; 1911 Wl Fw Il

Lampkowski, M.S. 1976 Wl Sl Il

Lapage, W.N. 1908 Wl Iw Sl

Larter, P.J. 1968 Wd Id Fl Sw; 1969 Il Fw Sw Wl; 1970 Iw Wl Sl Fl; 1971 Wl Iw Fd Sl; 1973 Wl

Law, D.E. 1927 Iw

Lawrie, P.W. 1910 Sw; 1911 Sw

Lawson, R.G. 1925 Id

Lawson, T.M. 1928 Ww

Le Fleming, J. 1887 Wd

Leadbetter, M.M. 1970 Fl

Leadbetter, V.H. 1954 Sw Fl

Leake, W.R.M. 1891 Ww Iw Sl

Leather, G. 1907 Il

Leslie-Jones, F.A. 1895 Ww Iw

Lewis, A.O. 1952 Wl Sw Iw Fw; 1953 Ww Id Fw Sw 1954 Fl

Leyland, R. 1935 Wd Iw Sl

Livesay, R.O'H. 1898 Ww; 1899 Wl

Lloyd, R.H. 1968 Wd Id Fl Sw

Locke, H.M. 1923 Sw Fw; 1924 Ww Fw Sw; 1925 Ww Id Sl Fw; 1927 Ww Iw Sl

Lockwood, R.E. 1887 Wd Il Sd; 1891 Ww Iw Sl; 1892 Ww Iw Sw; 1893 Wl Iw; 1894 Ww Il

Lohden, F.C. 1893 Wl

Longland, R.J. 1932 Sw; 1933 Wl Sl; 1934 Ww Iw Sw; 1935 Wd Iw Sl; 1936 Wd Il Sw; 1937 Ww Iw Sw; 1938 Wl Iw Sl

Lowe, C.N. 1913 Ww Fw Iw Sw; 1914 Ww Iw Sw Fw; 1920 Wl Fw Iw Sw; 1921 Ww Iw Sw Fw; 1922 Wl Iw Fd Sw; 1923 Ww Iw Sw Fw

Lowrie, F.W. 1890 Wl

Lowry, W.M. 1920 Fw

Luddington, W.G.E. 1923 Ww Iw Sw Fw; 1924 Ww Iw Fw Sw; 1925 Ww Id Sl Fw; 1926 Wd

Luxmoore, A.F.C.C. 1900 Sd; 1901 Wl

Luya, H.F. 1948 Wd Il Sl Fl; 1949 Wl

Lyon, G.H.d'O. 1908 Sl

MacIlwaine, A.H. 1912 Ww Iw Sl Fw; 1920 Iw

Mackie, O.G. 1897 Sw; 1898 Il

MacLennan, R.R.F. 1925 Id Sl Fw

Madge, R.J.P. 1948 Wd Il Sl

Malir, F.W.S. 1930 Ww Il Sd

Mangles, R.H. 1897 Wl Il

Manley, D.C. 1963 Ww Id Fw Sw

Mann, W.E. 1911 Wl Fw Il

Marques, R.W.D. 1956 Wl Iw Sw Fl; 1957 Ww Iw Fw Sw; 1958 Wd Iw Fw Sd; 1959 Wl Iw Fd Sd; 1960 Ww Iw Fd Sw; 1961 Wl

Marquis, J.C. 1900 Iw Sd

Marriott, C.J.B. 1884 Ww Iw Sw; 1886 Ww Iw Sd; 1887 Il

Marsden, G.H. 1900 Wl Iw Sd

Marsh, J.H. 1892 Iw

Marshall, H. 1893 Wl

Marshall, R.M. 1938 Iw Sl; 1939 Ww Il Sw

Martin, N.O. 1972 Fl (R)

Martindale, S.A. 1929 Fw

Massey, E.J. 1925 Ww Id Sl

Mathias, J.L. 1905 Wl Il Sl

Matters, J.C. 1899 Sl

Matthews, J.R.C. 1949 Fw Sw; 1950 Iw Fl Sl; 1952 Wl Sw Iw Fw

Maud, P. 1893 Wl Iw

Maxwell, A.W. 1976 Wl Sl Il Fl; 1978 Fl

Maxwell-Hyslop, J.E. 1922 Iw Fd Sw
Maynard, A.F. 1914 Ww Iw Sw
McCanlis, M.A. 1931 Wd Il
McFadyean, C.W. 1966 Id Fl Sl; 1967 Iw Fl Sw Wl; 1968 Wd Id
Meikle, G.W.C. 1934 Ww Iw Sw
Meikle, S.S.C. 1929 Sl
Mellish, F.W. 1920 Wl Fw Iw Sw; 1921 Ww Iw
Merriam, L.P.B. 1920 Wl Fw
Middleton, B.B. 1883 Iw
Middleton, J.A. 1922 Sw
Miles, J.H. 1903 Wl
Millett, H. 1920 Fw
Mills, S.G.F. 1983 Wd
Mills, W.A. 1906 Wl Il Sw; 1907 Wl Il Sl; 1908 Wl
Milman, D.L.K. 1937 Ww; 1938 Wl Iw Sl
Milton, C.H. 1906 Il
Milton, J.G. 1904 Wd Iw Sl; 1905 Sl; 1907 Il
Mitchell, F. 1895 Ww Iw Sl; 1896 Ww Il Sl
Mitchell, W.G. 1890 Wl Sw Iw; 1891 Ww Iw Sl; 1893 Sl
Mobbs, E.R. 1909 Wl Iw Sl; 1910 Id Fw
Moore, E.J. 1883 Iw Sw
Moore, N.H. 1904 Wd Iw Sl
Moore, P.B.C. 1951 Wl
Moore, W.K.T. 1947 Ww Il; 1949 Fw Sw; 1950 Iw Fl Sl
Mordell, R.J. 1978 Wl
Morfitt, S. 1894 Ww Il Sl; 1896 Ww Il Sl
Morgan, J.R. 1920 Wl
Morgan, W.G.D. 1960 Ww Iw Fd Sw; 1961 Wl Il Fd Sw
Morley, A.J. 1973 Wl Il; 1975 Sw
Morris, A.D.W. 1909 Wl
Morrison, P.H. 1890 Wl Sw Iw; 1891 Iw
Mortimer, W. 1899 Wl
Morton, H.J.S. 1909 Iw Sl; 1910 Ww Id
Moss, F. 1885 Ww Iw; 1886 Ww
Mycock, J. 1947 Ww Il Sw Fw
Myers, E. 1920 Iw Sw; 1921 Ww Iw; 1922 Wl Iw Fd Sw; 1923 Ww Iw Sw Fw; 1924 Ww Iw Fw Sw; 1925 Sl Fw
Myers, H. 1898 Il
Nanson, W.M.B. 1907 Wl
Neale, B.A. 1951 Il Fl Sw
Neale, M.E. 1912 Fw
Neary, A. 1971 Wl Iw Fd Sl; 1972 Wl Il Fl Sl; 1973 Wl Il Fw Sw; 1974 Sl Il Fd Ww; 1975 Il Fl Wl Sw; 1976 Wl Sl Il Fl; 1977 Iw; 1978 Fl (R); 1979 Sd Il Fw Wl; 1980 Iw Fw Ww Sw
Nelmes, B.G. 1978 Wl Sw Iw
Newbold, C.J. 1904 Wd Iw Sl; 1905 Wl Il Sl
Newman, S.C. 1947 Fw; 1948 Wd
Newton, A.W. 1907 Sl
Newton-Thompson, J.O. 1947 Sw Fw
Nichol, W. 1892 Ww Sw
Nicholas, P.L. 1902 Wl
Nicholson, B.E. 1938 Wl Iw
Nicholson, E.S. 1935 Wd Iw Sl; 1936 Wd
Nicholson, E.T. 1900 Wl Iw
Nicholson, T. 1893 Iw
Ninnes, B.F. 1971 Wl
Norman, D.J. 1932 Wl
North, E.G.H. 1891 Ww Iw Sl

Northmore, S. 1897 Il
Novak, M.J. 1970 Wl Sl Fl
Novis, A.L. 1929 Sl Fw; 1930 Ww Il Fw; 1933 Iw Sl
Oakes, R.F. 1897 Wl Il Sw; 1898 Il Sd Ww; 1899 Wl Sl
Oakley, F.E. 1913 Sw; 1914 Iw Sw Fw
Oakley, L.F.L. 1951 Wl
Obolensky, A. 1936 Wd Il Sw
Old, A.G.B. 1972 Wl Il Fl Sl; 1974 Sl Il Fd Ww; 1975 Il; 1976 Sl Il; 1978 Fl
Oldham, W.L. 1908 Sl
O'Neill, A. 1901 Wl Il Sl
Osborne, S.H. 1905 Sl
Oughtred, B. 1901 Sl; 1902 Wl Iw Sw; 1903 Wl Il
Owen, J.E. 1963 Ww Id Fw Sw; 1965 Wl Il Fw Sd; 1966 Id Fl Sl
Owen-Smith, H.G. 1934 Ww Iw Sw; 1936 Wd Il Sw; 1937 Ww Iw Sw
Page, J.J. 1971 Wl Iw Fd Sl; 1975 Sw
Pallant, J.N. 1967 Iw Fl Sw
Palmer, A.C. 1909 Iw Sl
Palmer, F.H. 1905 Wl
Palmer, G.V. 1928 Iw Fw Sw
Pargetter, T.A. 1962 Sd; 1963 Fw
Parker, G.W. 1938 Iw Sl
Parsons, E.J. 1939 Sw
Parsons, M.J. 1968 Wd Id Fl Sw
Patterson, W.M. 1961 Sw
Pattisson, R.M. 1883 Iw Sw
Payne, A.T. 1935 Iw Sl
Payne, C.M. 1964 Il Fw Sl; 1965 Il Fw Sd; 1966 Wl Id Fl Sl
Payne, J.H. 1882 Ww; 1883 Iw Sw; 1884 Iw; 1885 Ww Iw
Pearce, G.S. 1979 Sd Il Fw Wl; 1982 Sd; 1983 Fl Wd Sl Il
Peart, T.G.A.H. 1964 Fw Sl
Pease, F.E. 1887 Il
Percival, L.J. 1891 Iw; 1892 Iw; 1893 Sl
Periton, H.G. 1925 Ww; 1926 Wd Il Fw Sl; 1927 Ww Iw Sl Fl; 1928 Iw Fw Sw; 1929 Ww Il Sl Fw; 1930 Ww Il Fw Sd
Perry, D.G. 1963 Fw Sw; 1964 Wd Il; 1965 Wl Il Fw Sd; 1966 Wl Id Fl
Perry, S.V. 1947 Ww Il; 1948 Wd Il Sl Fl
Peters, J. 1906 Sw; 1907 Il Sl; 1908 Wl
Phillips, M.S. 1958 Iw Fw Sd; 1959 Wl Iw Fd Sd; 1960 Ww Iw Fd Sw; 1961 Wl; 1963 Ww Id Fw Sw; 1964 Wd Il Fw Sl
Pickering, A.S. 1907 Il
Pickering, R.D.A. 1967 Iw Fl Sw Wl; 1968 Fl Sw
Pickles, R.C.W. 1922 Iw Fd
Pierce, R. 1898 Il; 1903 Sl
Pilkington, W.N. 1898 Sd
Pillman, C.H. 1910 Ww Id Fw Sw; 1911 Wl Fw Il Sw; 1912 Ww Fw; 1913 Ww Fw Iw Sw; 1914 Ww Iw Sw
Pillman, R.L. 1914 Fw
Pinch, J. 1896 Ww Il; 1897 Sw
Pitman, I.J. 1922 Sw
Plummer, K.C. 1969 Wl; 1976 Sl Il Fl
Poole, F.O. 1895 Ww Iw Sl
Poole, R.W. 1896 Sl
Pope, E.B. 1931 Wd Sl Fl

Portus, G.V. 1908 Iw

Poulton, R.W. 1909 Iw Sl; 1910 Ww; 1911 Sw; 1912 Ww Iw Sl; 1913 Ww Fw Iw Sw; 1914 Ww Iw Sw Fw

Powell, D.L. 1966 Wl Id; 1969 Il Fw Sw Wl; 1971 Wl Iw Fd Sl

Pratten, W.E. 1927 Sl Fl

Preece, I. 1948 Il Sl Fl; 1949 Fw Sw; 1950 Wl Iw Fl Sl; 1951 Wl Il Fl

Preece, P.S. 1973 Wl Il Fw Sw; 1975 Il Fl Wl; 1976 Wl (R)

Prentice, F.D. 1928 Iw Fw Sw

Prescott, R.E. 1937 Ww Iw; 1938 Iw; 1939 Ww Il Sw

Preston, N.J. 1980 Iw Fw

Price, H.L. 1922 Iw Sw; 1923 Ww Iw

Price, J. 1961 Il

Price, T.W. 1948 Sl Fl; 1949 Wl Il Fw Sw

Prout, D.H. 1968 Wd Id

Pullin, J.V. 1966 Wl; 1968 Wd Id Fl Sw; 1969 Il Fw Sw Wl; 1970 Iw Wl Sl Fl; 1971 Wl Iw Fd Sl; 1972 Wl Il Fl Sl; 1973 Wl Il Fw Sw; 1974 Sl Il Fd Ww; 1975 Il Wl (R) Sw; 1976 Fl

Purdy, S.J. 1962 Sd

Pyke, J. 1892 Ww

Pym, J.A. 1912 Ww Iw Sl Fw

Quinn, J.P. 1954 Ww Iw Sw Fl

Rafter, M. 1977 Sw Fl Wl; 1978 Fl Wl Sw Iw; 1979 Sd Il Fw Wl; 1980 Ww (R); 1981 Wl

Ralston, C.W. 1972 Wl Il Fl Sl; 1973 Wl Il Fw Sw; 1974 Wl Il Fd Ww; 1975 Il Fl Wl Sw

Ramsden, H.E. 1898 Sd Ww

Ranson, J.M. 1964 Wd Il Fw Sl

Raphael, J.E. 1902 Wl Iw Sw; 1905 Wl Sl; 1906 Wl Sw

Redmond, G.F. 1970 Fl

Redwood, B.W. 1968 Wd Id

Reeve, J.S.R. 1929 Fw; 1930 Ww Il Fw Sd; 1931 Wd Il Sl

Regan, M. 1953 Ww Id Fw Sw; 1954 Ww Iw Sw Fl; 1956 Iw Sw Fl

Rew, H. 1929 Sl Fw; 1930 Fw Sd; 1931 Wd Sl Fl; 1934 Ww Iw Sw

Reynolds, F.J. 1937 Sw; 1938 Iw Sl

Reynolds, S. 1900 Wl Iw Sd; 1901 Il

Rhodes, J. 1896 Ww Il Sl

Richards, E.E. 1929 Sl Fw

Richards, J. 1891 Ww Iw Sl

Richards, S.B. 1965 Wl Il Fw Sd; 1967 Iw Fl Sw Wl

Richardson, J.V. 1928 Ww Iw Fw Sw

Rimmer, G. 1949 Wl Il; 1950 Wl; 1951 Wl Il Fl; 1952 Wl; 1954 Ww Iw Sw

Rimmer, L.I. 1961 Wl Il Fd Sw

Ripley, A.G. 1972 Wl Il Fl Sl; 1973 Wl Il Fw Sw; 1974 Sl Il Fd Ww; 1975 Il Fl Sw; 1976 Wl Sl

Risman, A.B.W. 1959 Wl Iw Fd Sd; 1961 Wl Il Fd

Ritson, J.A.S. 1910 Fw Sw; 1912 Fw; 1913 Ww Fw Iw Sw

Rittson-Thomas, G.C. 1951 Wl Il Fl

Robbins, P.G.D. 1956 Wl Iw Sw Fl; 1957 Ww Iw Fw Sw; 1958 Wd Iw Sd; 1960 Ww Iw Fd Sw; 1961 Wl; 1962 Sd

Roberts, A.D. 1911 Wl Fw Il Sw; 1912 Iw Sl Fw; 1914 Iw

Roberts, E.W. 1901 Wl Il; 1906 Wl Il; 1907 Sl

·Roberts, G.D. 1907 Sl; 1908 Wl

Roberts, J. 1960 Ww Iw Fd Sw; 1961 Wl Il Fd Sw; 1962 Wd Iw Fl Sd; 1963 Ww Id Fw Sw

Roberts, R.S. 1932 Iw

Roberts, S. 1887 Wd Il

Roberts, V.G. 1947 Fw; 1949 Wl Il Fw Sw; 1950 Iw Fl Sl; 1951 Wl Il Fl Sw; 1956 Wl Iw Sw Fl

Robertshaw, A.R. 1886 Ww Iw Sd; 1887 Wd Sd

Robinson, A. 1890 Wl Sw Iw

Robinson, E.F. 1954 Sw; 1961 Il Fd Sw

Robinson, G.C. 1897 Il Sw; 1898 Il; 1899 Wl; 1900 Iw Sd; 1901 Il Sl

Robinson, J.J. 1893 Sl; 1902 Wl Iw Sw

Robson, A. 1924 Ww Iw Fw Sw; 1926 Wd

Robson, M. 1930 Ww Il Fw Sd

Rogers, D.P. 1961 Il Fd Sw; 1962 Wd Iw Fl; 1963 Ww Id Fw Sw; 1964 Wd Il Fw Sl; 1965 Wl Il Fw Sd; 1966 Wl Id Fl Sl; 1967 Sw Wl; 1969 Il Fw Sw Wl

Rogers, J.H. 1890 Wl Sw Iw; 1891 Sl

Rogers, W.L.Y. 1905 Wl Il

Rollitt, D.M. 1967 Iw Fl Sw Wl; 1969 Il Fw Sw Wl; 1975 Sw

Roncoroni, A.D.S. 1933 Wl Iw Sl

Rose, W.M.H. 1981 Iw Fl; 1982 Sd Il

Rossborough, P.A. 1971 Wl; 1974 Sl Il; 1975 Il Fl

Rosser, D.W.A. 1965 Wl Il Fw Sd; 1966 Wl

Rotherham, Alan 1882 Ww; 1883 Sw; 1884 Ww Sw; 1885 Ww Iw; 1886 Ww Iw Sd; 1887 Wd Il Sd

Rotherham, Arthur 1898 Sd Ww; 1899 Wl Il Sl

Roughley, D.F.K. 1974 Sl Il

Rowell, R.E. 1964 Wd; 1965 Wl

Royds, P.M.R. 1898 Sd Ww; 1899 Wl

Rudd, E.L. 1965 Wl Il Sd; 1966 Wl Id Sl

Rutherford, D. 1960 Ww Iw Fd Sw; 1965 Wl Il Fw Sd; 1966 Wl Id Fl Sl

Ryalls, H.J. 1885 Ww Iw

Ryan, P.H. 1955 Wl Id

Sadler, E.H. 1933 Iw Sl

Sagar, J.W. 1901 Wl Il

Sample, C.H. 1884 Iw; 1885 Iw; 1886 Sd

Sanders, D.L. 1954 Ww Iw Sw Fl; 1956 Wl Iw Sw Fl

Sanders, F.W. 1923 Iw Sw Fw

Sandford, J.R.P. 1906 Il

Sangwin, R.D. 1964 Wd

Sargent, G.A.F. 1981 Iw(R)

Savage, K.F. 1966 Wl Id Fl Sl; 1967 Iw Fl Sw Wl; 1968 Wd Fl Sw

Saxby, L.E. 1932 Wl

Scholfield, J.A. 1911 Wl

Schwarz, R.O. 1899·Sl; 1901 Wl Il

Scorfield, E.S. 1910 Fw

Scott, C.T. 1900 Wl Iw; 1901 Wl Il

Scott, E.K. 1947 Ww; 1948 Wd Il Sl

Scott, F.S. 1907 Wl

Scott, H. 1955 Fl

Scott, J.P. 1978 Fl Wl Sw Iw; 1979 Sd (R) Il Fw Wl; 1980 Iw Fw Ww Sw; 1981 Wl Sw Iw Fl; 1982 Il Fw Ww; 1983 Fl Wd Sl Il

Scott, J.S.M. 1958 Fw

Scott, M.T. 1887 Il; 1890 Sw Iw

Seddon, R.L. 1887 Wd Il Sd

Sellar, K.A. 1927 Ww Iw Sl; 1928 Ww Iw Fw

Sever, H.S. 1936 Wd Il Sw; 1937 Ww Iw Sw; 1938 Wl Iw Sl

Shackleton, I.R. 1970 Iw Wl Sl

Sharp, R.A.W. 1960 Ww Iw Fd Sw; 1961 Il Fd; 1962 Wd Iw Fl; 1963 Ww Id Fw Sw

Shaw, C.H. 1906 Sw; 1907 Wl Il Sl

Shaw, F. 1898 Il

Shaw, J.F. 1898 Sd Ww

Sherriff, G.A. 1966 Sl

Shewring, H.E. 1905 Il; 1906 Wl Sw; 1907 Wl Il Sl

Shooter, J.H. 1899 Il Sl; 1900 Iw Sd

Shuttleworth, D.W. 1951 Sw; 1953 Sw

Sibree, H.J.H. 1909 Iw Sl

Silk, N. 1965 Wl Il Fw Sd

Simpson, C.P. 1965 Wl

Simpson, T. 1902 Sw; 1903 Wl Il Sl; 1904 Iw Sl; 1905 Il Sl; 1906 Sw

Sladen, G.M. 1929 Ww Il Sl

Slemen, M.A.C. 1976 Il Fl; 1977 Sw Iw Fl Wl; 1978 Fl Wl Sw Iw; 1979 Sd Il Fw Wl; 1980 Iw Fw Ww Sw; 1981 Wl Sw Iw Fl; 1982 Sd Il Fw Ww

Slocock, L.A.N. 1907 Wl Il Sl; 1908 Wl Iw Sl

Slow, C.F. 1934 Sw

Small, H.D. 1950 Wl Iw Fl Sl

Smallwood, A.M. 1920 Fw Iw; 1921 Ww Iw Sw Fw; 1922 Iw Sw; 1923 Ww Iw Sw Fw; 1925 Id Sl

Smart, C.E. 1979 Fw Wl; 1981 Sw Iw Fl; 1982 Sd Il Fw Ww; 1983 Fl Wd Sl Il

Smart, S. 1913 Ww Fw Iw Sw; 1914 Ww Iw Sw Fw; 1920 Wl Iw Sw

Smeddle, R.W. 1929 Ww Il Sl; 1931 Fl

Smith, C.C. 1901 Wl

Smith, D.F. 1910 Ww Id

Smith, J.V. 1950 Wl Iw Fl Sl

Smith, K. 1974 Fd Ww; 1975 Wl Sw

Smith, M.J.K. 1956 Wl

Smith, S.J. 1973 Il Fw Sw; 1974 Il Fd; 1975 Wl (R); 1976 Fl; 1977 Fl (R); 1980 Iw Fw Ww Sw; 1981 Wl Sw Iw Fl; 1982 Sd Il Fw Ww; 1983 Fl Wd Sl

Smith, S.R. 1959 Wl Fd Sd; 1964 Fw Sl

Smith, T. 1951 Wl

Soane, F. 1893 Sl; 1894 Ww Il Sl

Sobey, W.H. 1930 Ww Fw Sd; 1932 Wl

Solomon, B. 1910 Ww

Sparks, R.H.W. 1928 Iw Fw Sw; 1929 Ww Il Sl; 1931 Il Sl Fl

Speed, H. 1894 Ww Il Sl; 1896 Sl

Spence, F.W. 1890 Iw

Spencer, J. 1966 Wl

Spencer, J.S. 1969 Il Fw, Sw Wl; 1970 Iw Wl Sl Fl; 1971 Wl Iw Sl

Spong, R.S. 1929 Fw; 1930 Ww Il Fw Sd; 1931 Fl; 1932 Wl

Spooner, R.H. 1903 Wl

Springman, H.H. 1887 Sd

Spurling, N. 1886 Iw Sd; 1887 Wd

Squires, P.J. 1973 Fw Sw; 1974 Sl Il Fd Ww; 1975 Il Fl Wl Sw; 1976 Wl; 1977 Sw Iw Fl Wl; 1978 Fl Wl Sw Iw; 1979 Sd Il Fw Wl

Stafford, R.C. 1912 Ww Iw Sl Fw

Stanbury, E. 1926 Wd Il Sl; 1927 Ww Iw Sl Fl; 1928 Ww Iw Fw Sw; 1929 Ww Il Sl Fw

Standing, G. 1882 Ww; 1883 Iw

Stanger-Leathes, C.F. 1905 Il

Stark, K.J. 1927 Ww Iw Sl Fl; 1928 Ww Iw Fw Sw

Starks, A. 1896 Ww Il

Starmer-Smith, N.C. 1970 Iw Wl Sl Fl

Start, S.P. 1907 Sl

Steeds, J.H. 1949 Fw Sw; 1950 Iw Fl Sl

Steele-Bodger, M.R. 1947 Ww Il Sw Fw; 1948 Wd Il Sl Fl

Steinthal, F.E. 1913 Ww Fw

Stevens, C.B. 1970 Iw Wl Sl; 1972 Wl Il Fl Sl; 1973 Wl Il Fw Sw; 1974 Sl Il Fd Ww; 1975 Il Fl Wl Sw

Stirling, R.V. 1951 Wl Il Fl Sw; 1952 Wl Sw Iw Fw; 1953 Ww Id Fw Sw; 1954 Ww Iw Sw Fl

Stoddart, A.E. 1885 Ww Iw; 1886 Ww Iw Sd; 1890 Wl Iw; 1893 Wl Sl

Stoddart, W.B. 1897 Wl Il Sw

Stone, F.le S. 1914 Fw

Stoop, A.D. 1905 Sl; 1906 Sw; 1907 Wl; 1910 Ww Id Sw; 1911 Wl Fw Il Sw; 1912 Ww Sl

Stoop, F.M. 1910 Sw; 1911 Fw Il

Stout, F.M. 1897 Wl Il; 1898 Il Sd Ww; 1899 Il Sl; 1903 Sl; 1904 Wd Iw Sl; 1905 Wl Il Sl

Stout, P.W. 1898 Sd Ww; 1899 Wl Il Sl

Strong, E.L. 1884 Ww Iw Sw

Swarbrick, D.W. 1947 Ww Il Fw; 1948 Wd; 1949 Il

Swayne, D.H. 1931 Wd

Swayne, J.W.R. 1929 Ww

Swift, A.H. 1983 Fl Wd Sl

Syddall, J.P. 1982 Il

Sykes, A.R.V. 1914 Fw

Sykes, F.D. 1955 Fl Sw

Sykes, P.W. 1948 Fl; 1952 Sw Iw Fw; 1953 Ww Id Fw

Syrett, R.E. 1958 Wd Iw Fw; 1960 Ww Iw Fd Sw; 1962 Wd Iw Fl

Tallent, J.A. 1931 Sl Fl; 1932 Wl; 1935 Iw

Tanner, C.C. 1930 Sd; 1932 Wl Iw Sw

Tarr, F.N. 1909 Wl; 1913 Sw

Tatham, W.M. 1882 Ww; 1883 Iw Sw; 1884 Ww Iw Sw

Taylor, A.S. 1882 Ww; 1883 Iw; 1886 Ww Iw

Taylor, E.W. 1892 Iw; 1893 Iw; 1894 Ww Il Sl; 1895 Ww Iw Sl; 1896 Ww Il; 1897 Wl Il Sw; 1899 Il

Taylor, F. 1920 Fw Iw

Taylor, F.M. 1914 Ww

Taylor, J.T. 1897 Il; 1899 Il; 1900 Iw; 1901 Wl Il; 1902 Wl Iw Sw; 1903 Wl Il; 1905 Sl

Taylor, P.J. 1955 Wl Id; 1962 Wd Iw Fl Sd

Taylor, R.B. 1966 Wl; 1967 Iw Fl Sw Wl; 1969 Fw Sw Wl; 1970 Iw Wl Sl Fl; 1971 Sl

Taylor, W.J. 1928 Ww Iw Fw Sw

Teden, D.E. 1939 Ww Il Sw

Teggin, A. 1884 Iw; 1885 Ww; 1886 Iw Sd; 1887 Il Sd

Thomas, C. 1895 Ww Iw Sl; 1899 Il

Thompson, P.H. 1956 Wl Iw Sw Fl; 1957 Ww Iw Fw Sw; 1958 Wd Iw Fw Sd; 1959 Wl Iw Fd Sd

Thomson, G.T. 1882 Ww; 1883 Iw Sw; 1884 Iw Sw; 1885 Iw

Thomson, W.B. 1892 Ww; 1895 Ww Iw Sl

Thorne, J.D. 1963 Ww Id Fw

Tindall, V.R. 1951 Wl Il Fl Sw

Todd, A.F. 1900 Iw Sd

Toft, H.B. 1936 Sw; 1937 Ww Iw Sw; 1938 Wl Iw Sl; 1939 Ww Il Sw

Toothill, J.T. 1890 Sw Iw; 1891 Ww Iw; 1892 Ww Iw Sw; 1893 Wl Iw Sl; 1894 Ww Il
Tosswill, L.R. 1902 Wl Iw Sw
Towell, A.C. 1948 Fl; 1951 Sw
Travers, B.H. 1947 Ww Il; 1948 Wd; 1949 Fw Sw
Treadwell, W.T. 1966 Id Fl Sl
Trick, D.M. 1983 Il
Tristram, H.B. 1883 Sw; 1884 Ww Sw; 1885 Ww; 1887 Sd
Troop, C.L. 1933 Iw Sl
Tucker, J.S. 1922 Wl; 1925 Ww Id Sl Fw; 1926 Wd Il Fw Sl; 1927 Ww Iw Sl Fl; 1928 Ww Iw Fw Sw; 1929 Ww Il Fw; 1930 Ww Il Fw Sd; 1931 Wd
Tucker, W.E. 1926 Il; 1930 Ww Il
Tucker, W.E. 1894 Ww Il; 1895 Ww Iw Sl
Turquand-Young, D. 1928 Ww; 1929 Il Sl Fw
Turner, M.F. 1948 Sl Fl
Twynam, H.T. 1883 Iw; 1884 Ww Iw Sw
Underwood, A.M. 1962 Wd Iw Fl Sd; 1964 Il
Unwin, E.J. 1937 Sw 1938 Wl Iw Sl
Unwin, G.T. 1898 Sd
Uren, R. 1948 Il Sl Fl; 1950 Iw
Uttley, R.M. 1973 Il Fw Sw; 1974 Il Fd Ww; 1975 Fl Wl Sw; 1977 Sw Iw Fl Wl; 1979 Sd; 1980 Iw Fw Ww Sw
Valentine, J. 1890 Wl; 1896 Ww Il Sl
van Ryneveld, C.B. 1949 Wl Il Fw Sw
Varley, H. 1892 Sw
Vassall, H. 1882 Ww
Vassall, H.H. 1908 Iw
Vaughan, D.B. 1948 Wd Il Sl; 1949 Il Fw Sw; 1950 Wl
Vaughan-Jones, A. 1932 Iw Sw; 1933 Wl
Vickery, G. 1905 Il
Vivyan, E.J. 1901 Wl; 1904 Wd Iw Sl
Voyce, A.T. 1920 Iw Sw; 1921 Ww Iw Sw Fw; 1922 Wl Iw Fd Sw; 1923 Ww Iw Sw Fw; 1924 Ww Iw Fw Sw; 1925 Ww Id Sl Fw; 1926 Wd Il Fw Sl
Wackett, J.A.S. 1959 Wl Iw
Wade, C.G. 1882 Ww; 1883 Iw Sw; 1884 Ww Sw; 1885 Ww; 1886 Ww Iw
Wade, M.R. 1962 Wd Iw Fl
Wakefield, W.W. 1920 Wl Fw Iw Sw; 1921 Ww Iw Sw Fw; 1922 Wl Iw Fd Sw; 1923 Ww Iw Sw Fw; 1924 Ww Iw Fw Sw; 1925 Ww Id Sl Fw; 1926 Wd Il Fw Sl; 1927 Sl Fl
Walker, G.A. 1939 Ww Il
Walker, H.W. 1947 Ww Il Sw Fw; 1948 Wd Il Sl Fl
Wallen, J.N.S. 1927 Fl
Walton, E.J. 1901 Wl Il; 1902 Iw Sw
Walton, W. 1894 Sl
Ward, G. 1913 Ww Fw Sw; 1914 Ww Iw Sw
Ward, H. 1895 Ww
Ward, J.W. 1896 Ww Il Sl
Wardlow, C.S. 1971 Wl Iw Fd Sl
Warfield, P.J. 1973 Wl Il; 1975 Il Fl Sw
Warr, A.L. 1934 Ww Iw
Watkins, J.A. 1973 Wl; 1975 Fl Wl
Watkins, J.K. 1939 Ww Il Sw
Watson, F.B. 1908 Sl; 1909 Sl
Watson, J.H.D. 1914 Ww Sw Fw
Watt, D.E.J. 1967 Iw Fl Sw Wl
Webb, C.S.H. 1932 Wl Iw Sw; 1933 Wl Iw Sl; 1935 Sl; 1936 Wd Il Sw

Webb, J.W.G. 1926 Fw Sl; 1929 Sl
Webb, R.E. 1967 Sw Wl; 1968 Id Fl Sw; 1969 Il Fw Sw Wl; 1972 Il Fl
Webb, St L.H. 1959 Wl Iw Fd Sd
Webster, J.G. 1972 Wl Il; 1973 Wl; 1974 Sl Ww; 1975 Il Fl Wl
Wedge, T.G. 1909 Wl
Weighill, R.H.G. 1947 Sw Fw; 1948 Sl Fl
Wells, C.M. 1893 Sl; 1894 Ww Sl; 1896 Sl; 1897 Wl Sw
West, B.R. 1968 Wd Id Fl Sw; 1970 Iw Wl Sl
Weston, H.T.F. 1901 Sl
Weston, L.E. 1972 Fl Sl
Weston, M.P. 1960 Ww Iw Fd Sw; 1961 Wl Il Fd Sw; 1962 Wd Iw Fl; 1963 Ww Id Fw Sw; 1964 Wd Il Fw Sl; 1965 Fw Sd; 1966 Sl; 1968 Fl Sw
Weston, W.H. 1933 Iw Sl; 1934 Iw Sw; 1935 Wd Iw Sl; 1936 Wd Sw; 1937 Ww Iw Sw; 1938 Wl Iw Sl
Wheatley, A. 1937 Ww Iw Sw; 1938 Wl Sl
Wheatley, H.F. 1936 Il; 1937 Sw; 1938 Wl Sl; 1939 Ww Il Sw
Wheeler, P.J. 1975 Fl Wl; 1976 Wl Sl Il; 1977 Sw Iw Fl Wl; 1978 Fl Wl Sw Iw; 1979 Sd Il Fw Wl; 1980 Iw Fw Ww Sw; 1981 Wl Sw Iw Fl; 1982 Sd Il Fw Ww; 1983 Fl Sl Il
White, D.F. 1947 Ww Il Sw; 1948 Il Fl; 1951 Sw; 1952 Wl Sw Iw Fw; 1953 Ww Id Sw
Whiteley, E.C.P. 1931 Sl Fl
Whiteley, W. 1896 Ww
Whitley, H. 1929 Ww
Wigglesworth, H.J. 1884 Iw
Wightman, B.J. 1959 Wl; 1963 Ww Id
Wilkins, D.T. 1951 Wl Il Fl Sw; 1952 Wl Sw Iw Fw; 1953 Ww Id Fw Sw
Wilkinson, E. 1886 Ww Iw Sd; 1887 Wd Sd
Wilkinson, H. 1929 Ww Il Sl; 1930 Fw
Wilkinson, R.M. 1976 Wl Sl Il Fl
Willcocks, T.H. 1902 Wl
Willcox, J.G. 1961 Il Fd Sw; 1962 Wd Iw Fl Sd; 1963 Ww Id Fw Sw; 1964 Wd Il Fw Sl
William-Powlett, P.B.R.W. 1922 Sw
Williams, C.G. 1976 Fl
Williams, C.S. 1910 Fw
Williams, J.E. 1954 Fl; 1955 Wl Id Fl Sw; 1956 Iw Sw Fl; 1965 Wl
Williams, J.M. 1951 Il Sw
Williams, S.G. 1902 Wl Iw Sw; 1903 Il Sl; 1907 Il Sl
Williams, S.H. 1911 Wl Fw Il Sw
Williamson, R.H. 1908 Wl Iw Sl
Wilson, A.J. 1909 Iw
Wilson, C.E. 1898 Il
Wilson, D.S. 1953 Fw; 1954 Ww Iw Sw Fl; 1955 Fl Sw
Wilson, G.S. 1929 Ww Il
Wilson, K.J. 1963 Fw
Wilson, R.P. 1891 Ww Iw Sl
Wilson, W.C. 1907 Il Sl
Winn, C.E. 1952 Wl Sw Iw Fw; 1954 Ww Sw Fl
Winterbottom, P.J. 1982 Sd Il Fw Ww; 1983 Fl Wd Sl Il
Wintle, T.C. 1966 Sl; 1969 Il Fw Sw Wl
Winton, R.F.C. de 1893 Wl
Wodehouse, N.A. 1910 Fw; 1911 Wl Fw Il Sw; 1912 Ww Iw Sl Fw; 1913 Ww Fw Iw Sw

Wood, A. 1884 Iw
Wood, A.E. 1908 Wl Iw
Wood, G.W. 1914 Ww
Wood, R. 1894 Il
Wood, R.D. 1901 Il; 1903 Wl Il
Woodgate, E.E. 1952 Wl
Woodruff, C.G. 1951 Wl Il Fl Sw
Woods, S.M.J. 1890 Wl Sw Iw; 1891 Ww Iw Sl; 1892 Iw Sw; 1893 Wl Iw; 1895 Ww Iw Sl
Woods, T. 1908 Sl
Woods, T. 1920 Sw; 1921 Ww Iw Sw Fw
Woodward, C.R. 1980 Iw Fw Ww Sw; 1981 Wl Sw Iw Fl; 1982 Sd Il Fw Iw; 1983 Il
Woodward, J.E. 1952 Wl Sw; 1953 Ww Id Fw Sw; 1954 Ww Iw Sw Fl; 1955 Wl Id; 1956 Sw
Wooldridge, C.S. 1882 Ww; 1883 Iw Sw; 1884 Ww Iw Sw; 1885 Iw
Worton, J.R.B. 1926 Wd; 1927 Ww
Wrench, D.F.B. 1964 Fw Sl

Wright, C.C.G. 1909 Iw Sl
Wright, I.D. 1971 Wl Iw Fd Sl (R)
Wright, J.C. 1934 Ww
Wright, J.F. 1890 Wl
Wright, T.P. 1960 Ww Iw Fd Sw; 1961 Wl Il Fd Sw; 1962 Wd Iw Fl Sd
Wright, W.H.G. 1920 Wl Fw
Wyatt, D.M. 1976 Sl (R)
Yarranton, P.G. 1954 Ww Iw; 1955 Fl Sw
Yiend, W. 1892 Ww Iw Sw; 1893 Iw Sl
Young, A.T. 1924 Ww Iw Fw Sw; 1925 Fw; 1926 Il Fw Sl; 1927 Iw Sl Fl; 1928 Ww Iw Fw Sw; 1929 Il
Young, J.R.C. 1958 Iw; 1960 Ww Iw Fd Sw; 1961 Wl Il Fd
Young, M. 1977 Sw Iw Fl Wl; 1978 Fl Wl Sw Iw; 1979 Sd
Young, P.D. 1954 Ww Iw Sw Fl; 1955 Wl Id Fl Sw
Youngs, N.G. 1983 Il

FRANCE PLAYERS

Abadie, A. 1964 Iw
Abadie, A. 1968 Sw Iw
Aguerre, R. 1979 Sw
Aguirre, J-M. 1972 Sl; 1973 Ww Il; 1974 Iw Wd; 1976 Wl (R) Ew; 1977 Ww Ew Sw Iw; 1978 Ew Sw Iw Wl; 1979 Id Ww El Sw; 1980 Wl Iw
Albaladejo, P. 1954 Ew; 1960 Ww Iw; 1961 Sw Ed Ww Iw; 1962 Sw Ew Wl Iw; 1963 Sl Iw El Ww; 1964 Sl Wd Iw
Alvarez, A. 1947 Sw Iw Wl El; 1948 Il Sl Ww Ew; 1949 Iw El Ww; 1951 Sw Ew Ww
Ambert, A. 1930 Sw Iw El Wl
Amestoy, J.B. 1964 El
André, G. 1913 El Wl Il; 1914 Il Wl El
Anduran, J. 1910 Wl
Arcalis, R. 1950 Sl Id; 1951 Il Ew Ww
Aristouy, P. 1948 Sl; 1950 Sl Id Ew Wl
Arnal, J-M. 1914 Il Wl
Arnaudet, M. 1964 Iw; 1967 Ww
Arrieta, J. 1953 El Wl
Astre, R. 1972 Il; 1973 El (R); 1975 Ew Sw Il
Augé, J. 1929 Sl Wl
Augras, L. 1931 Iw Sl Wl
Averous, J-L. 1975 Sw Il; 1976 Iw Wl Ew; 1977 Ww Ew Sw Iw; 1978 Ew Sw Iw; 1980 El Sl
Azarete, J-L. 1969 Wd; 1970 Sw Iw Wl; 1971 Sw Id Ed; 1972 Ew Wl; 1973 Ww Il; 1974 Iw; 1975 Wl
Bader, E. 1927 Il Sl
Badin, C-F. 1973 Ww Il
Baillette, M. 1925 Il Sl; 1926 Wl; 1927 Il Wl; 1930 Sw Iw El; 1931 Iw Sl Ew
Ballarin, J. 1924 El; 1925 Sl
Baquet, J. 1921 Iw
Barrau, M. 1971 Sw Ed Wl; 1972 Ew Wl; 1973 Sw El Il; 1974 Iw Sl
Barrère, P. 1931 Wl
Barthe, E. 1925 Wl El
Barthe, J. 1955 Sw; 1956 Iw Wl Ew; 1957 Sl Il El Wl; 1958 Sl El Ww Iw; 1959 Sw Ed Ww
Bascou, P. 1914 El

Basquet, G. 1947 Sw Iw Wl El; 1948 Il Sl Ww Ew; 1949 Sl Iw El Ww; 1950 Sl Id Ew Wl; 1951 Sw Il Ew Ww; 1952 Sw Il Wl El
Bastiat, J-P. 1970 Sw Iw Wl; 1971 Sw Id; 1972 Sl; 1973 El; 1975 Wl; 1976 Sw Iw Wl Ew; 1977 Ww Ew Sw Iw; 1978 Ew Sw Iw Wl
Baudry, N. 1949 Sl Iw Ww
Baulon, R. 1954 Sw Wl Ew; 1955 Iw Ew Wl; 1956 Sl Iw Wl Ew; 1957 Sl Il
Bavozet, J. 1911 Sw El Wl
Bayard, J. 1923 Sl Wl El; 1924 Wl
Bayardon, J. 1964 Sl El
Beguet, L. 1922 Il; 1923 Sl Wl El Iw; 1924 Sw Il El
Behotéguy, A. 1923 El; 1924 Sw Il El Wl; 1926 El; 1927 Ew; 1928 Il El Ww; 1929 Sl Wl El; 1930 Wl
Behotéguy, H. 1923 Wl; 1928 Il El Ww
Belascain, C. 1978 Ew Sw Iw Wl; 1979 Id Ww El Sw; 1982 Wl El Sl Iw; 1983 Ew Sw Il Ww
Belletante, G. 1951 Il Ew Ww
Bénésis, R. 1969 Wd; 1970 Sw Iw Wl Ew; 1971 Sw Id Ed Wl; 1972 Sl Il Ew Wl; 1973 El Ww Il; 1974 Iw Wd Ed Sl
Berbizier, P. 1981 Sw Iw Ww Ew; 1982 Iw; 1983 Sw Il
Berejnoi, J-C. 1964 Sl Wd Iw; 1965 Sw Id El Ww; 1966 Sd Iw Ew Wl; 1967 Sl Ew Ww Iw
Berges, B. 1926 Il
Bergougnan, Y. 1947 Sw Iw Wl El; 1948 Sl Ww Ew; 1949 Sl El
Bernard, R. 1951 Sw Il Ew Ww
Bernon, J. 1922 Il; 1923 Sl
Berot, J-L. 1969 Sl Il; 1970 Ew; 1971 Sw Id Ed Wl; 1972 Sl Il Ew Wl; 1974 Iw
Bertrand, P. 1951 Il Ew Ww; 1953 Sw Il El Wl
Bertranne, R. 1971 Ed Wl; 1972 Sl Il; 1973 El; 1974 Iw Wd Ed Sl; 1975 Wl Ew Sw Il; 1976 Sw Iw Wl Ew; 1977 Ww Ew Sw Iw; 1978 Ew Sw Iw Wl; 1979 Id Ww El Sw; 1980 Wl El Sl Iw; 1981 Sw Iw Ww Ew
Besset, A. 1914 Wl El

Besset, E. 1924 Sw

Besson, M. 1924 Il; 1925 Il El; 1926 Sl Wl; 1927 Il

Besson, P. 1963 Sl Iw El

Bidart, L. 1953 Wl

Biémouret, J-P. 1969 El Wd; 1970 Iw Wl Ew; 1971 Wl; 1972 Ew Wl; 1973 Sw El Ww Il

Biénès, R. 1950 Sl Id Ew Wl; 1951 Sw Il Ew Ww; 1952 Sw Il Wl El; 1953 Sw Il El; 1954 Sw Iw Wl Ew; 1956 Sl Iw Wl Ew

Bigot, C. 1930 Sw El; 1931 Iw Sl

Bilbao, L. 1978 Iw; 1979 Id

Billac, E. 1920 Sl El Wl Iw; 1921 Sw Wl; 1922 Wl; 1923 El

Bioussa, A. 1924 Wl; 1925 Il Sl El; 1926 Sl Il El; 1928 El Ww; 1929 Il Sl Wl El; 1930 Sw Iw El Wl

Bioussa, C. 1913 Wl Il; 1914 Il

Biraben, M. 1920 Wl Iw; 1921 Sw Wl El Iw; 1922 Sd Ed Il

Blanco, S. 1981 Sw Ww Ew; 1982 Wl El Sl Iw; 1983 Ew Sw Il Ww

Boffelli, V. 1972 Sl Il; 1974 Iw Wd Ed Sl; 1975 Wl Sw Il

Bonal, J-M. 1968 Ew Ww; 1969 Sl Il El; 1970 Wl Ew

Bonamy, R. 1928 Il

Boniface, A. 1954 Iw Wl Ew; 1955 Sw Iw; 1956 Sl Iw Wl; 1957 Sl Il Wl; 1958 Sl El; 1959 Ed; 1962 Ew Wl Iw; 1963 Sl Iw El Ww; 1964 Sl El Wd; 1965 Ww; 1966 Sd Iw Ew Wl

Boniface, G. 1960 Ww Iw; 1961 Sw Ed Ww Iw; 1963 Sl Iw El Ww; 1964 Sl; 1965 Sw Id El Ww; 1966 Sd Iw Ew Wl

Bonnes, E. 1924 Wl

Bonnus, F. 1950 Sl Id Ew Wl

Borchard, G. 1911 Il

Borde, F. 1920 Iw; 1921 Sw Wl El; 1922 Sd Wl; 1923 Sl Iw; 1924 El; 1925 Il; 1926 El

Bordenave, L. 1948 Sl Ww Ew; 1949 Sl

Boubée, J. 1921 Sw El Iw; 1922 Ed Wl; 1923 El Iw; 1925 Sl

Boudreau, M. 1910 Wl Sl

Bouguyon, G. 1961 Ed Ww Iw

Bouquet, J. 1954 Sw; 1955 Ew; 1956 Sl Iw Wl Ew; 1957 Sl El Wl; 1958 Sl El; 1959 Sw Ww Il; 1960 Sw Ed Ww Iw; 1961 Sw Ed Ww Iw; 1962 Sw Ew Wl Iw

Bourdeu, J-R. 1952 Sw Il Wl El; 1953 Sw Il El

Bourgarel, R. 1970 Sw Iw Ew; 1971 Wl; 1973 Sw

Bousquet, A. 1921 El Iw

Bousquet, R. 1927 Il Sl Wl Ew; 1928 Wl El; 1930 Wl

Boyau, M. 1912 Il Sl Wl El; 1913 Wl Il

Branca, G. 1928 Sl; 1929 Il Sl

Bréjassou, R. 1952 Sw Il Wl El; 1953 El Wl; 1954 Sw Iw; 1955 Sw Iw Ew Wl

Bringeon, R. 1925 Wl

Brun, G. 1950 Ew Wl; 1951 Sw Ew Ww; 1952 Sw Il Wl El; 1953 El Wl

Bruneau, M. 1910 Wl El; 1913 El

Buchet, E. 1982 El

Buisson, H. 1931 Ew

Buonomo, Y. 1972 Il

Burgun, M. 1910 Wl Sl Il; 1911 Sw El; 1912 Il Sl; 1913 Sl El; 1914 El

Bustaffa, D. 1978 Wl; 1980 Wl El Sl

Buzy, E. 1947 Sw Iw Wl El; 1948 Il Sl Ww Ew; 1949 Sl Iw El Ww

Cabanier, J-M. 1964 Sl; 1965 Sw Id Ww; 1966 Sd Iw Ew Wl; 1967 Sl Ew Ww Iw; 1968 Sw Iw

Cadenat, J. 1910 Sl El; 1911 Wl Il; 1912 Wl El; 1913 Il

Cahuc, F. 1922 Sd

Camberabero, D. 1983 Ew Ww

Camberabero, G. 1967 Ew Ww Iw; 1968 Sw Ew Ww

Camberabero, L. 1965 Sw Id; 1966 Ew Wl; 1967 Ew Ww Iw; 1968 Sw Ew Ww

Cambré, T. 1920 El Wl Iw

Camel, A. 1928 Sl Il El Ww; 1929 Sl Wl El; 1930 Sw Iw El Wl

Camel, M. 1929 Wl El

Camicas, F. 1928 Sl Il El Ww; 1929 Il Sl Wl El

Camo, E. 1931 Iw Sl Wl Ew

Campaes, A. 1965 Ww; 1968 Sw Iw Ew Ww; 1969 Sl Wd

Cantoni, J. 1970 Wl; 1971 Sw Id Ed Wl; 1972 Sl Il; 1973 Sw Ww Il; 1975 Wl (R)

Capdouze, J. 1965 Sw Id El

Capmau, A. 1914 El

Carabignac, J. 1951 Sw Il; 1952 Wl El; 1953 Sw Il

Carbonne, P. 1927 Wl

Caron, L. 1947 El; 1948 Il Ww Ew; 1949 Sl Iw El Ww

Carpentier, M. 1980 El; 1981 Sw Iw; 1982 El Sl

Carrère, C. 1967 Sl Ew Ww Iw; 1968 Sw Iw Ew Ww; 1969 Sl Il; 1970 Sw Iw Wl Ew; 1971 Ed Wl

Carrère, J. 1956 Sl; 1957 El Wl; 1958 Sl; 1959 Il

Carrère, R. 1953 El

Casaux, L. 1959 Il; 1962 Sw

Cassayet, A. 1920 Sl El Wl; 1921 Wl El Iw; 1922 Sd Ed Wl; 1923 Sl Wl El Iw; 1924 Sw El Wl; 1925 Il Sl Wl; 1926 Sl Il El Wl; 1927 Il Sl Wl

Castets, J. 1923 Wl El Iw

Caujolle, J. 1913 El; 1914 Wl El

Caussade, A. 1979 Id Ww El; 1980 Wl El Sl; 1981 Sw (R) Iw

Caussarieu, G. 1929 Il

Cayrefourcq, E. 1921 El

Cazenave, A. 1927 Ew; 1928 Sl

Cazenave, F. 1950 Ew; 1952 Sw; 1954 Iw Wl Ew

Celaya, M. 1953 El Wl; 1954 Iw Ew; 1955 Sw Iw Ew Wl; 1956 Sl Iw Wl Ew; 1957 Sl Il El Wl; 1958 Sl El Ww; 1959 Sw Ed; 1960 Sw Ed Ww Iw; 1961 Sw Ed Ww Iw

Cester, E. 1966 Sd Iw Ew; 1967 Ww; 1968 Sw Iw Ew Ww; 1969 Sl Il El Wd; 1970 Sw Iw Wl Ew; 1973 Sw Ww Il; 1974 Iw Wd Ed Sl

Chapuy, L. 1926 Sl

Charpentier, G. 1911 El; 1912 Wl El

Chevallier, B. 1952 Sw Il Wl El; 1953 El Wl; 1954 Sw Iw Wl; 1955 Sw Iw Ew Wl; 1956 Sl Iw Wl Ew; 1957 Sl

Chilo, A. 1920 Sl Wl; 1925 Il

Cholley, G. 1975 Ew Sw Il; 1976 Sw Iw Wl Ew; 1977 Ww Ew Sw Iw; 1978 Ew Sw Iw Wl; 1979 Id Sw

Choy, J. 1930 Sw Iw El Wl; 1931 Iw

Clady, A. 1931 Iw Sl Ew

Clauzel, F. 1924 El Wl; 1925 Wl

Claverie, H. 1954 Wl

Clément, J. 1921 Sw Wl El; 1922 Sd Ed Wl Il; 1923 Sl Wl Iw

Clément, P. 1931 Wl

Clémente, M. 1980 Sl Iw
Cluchague, L. 1924 Sw; 1925 El
Codorniou, D. 1980 Wl El Sl Iw; 1981 Sw Ww Ew; 1983 Ew Sw Il Ww
Colombier, J. 1952 Wl El
Combe, J. 1910 Sl El Il; 1911 Sw
Communeau, M. 1910 Sl El Il; 1911 Sw El Il; 1912 Il Sl Wl El; 1913 El
Condom, J. 1983 Ew Sw Il Ww
Conil de Beyssac, J. 1912 Il Sl; 1914 Il Wl El
Constant, G. 1920 Wl
Coscoll, G. 1921 Sw Wl
Costes, F. 1979 El Sw; 1980 Wl Iw
Coulon, J. 1928 Sl
Crabos, R. 1920 Sl El Wl Iw; 1921 Sw Wl El Iw; 1922 Sd Ed Wl Il; 1923 Sl Iw; 1924 Sw Il
Crancee, R. 1961 Sw
Crauste, M. 1958 Sl El Ww Iw; 1959 Ed Ww Il; 1960 Sw Ed Ww Iw; 1961 Sw Ed Ww Iw; 1962 Sw Ew Wl Iw; 1963 Sl Iw El Ww; 1964 Sl El Wd Iw; 1965 Sw Id El Ww; 1966 Sd Iw Ew Wl
Crémaschi, M. 1982 Wl Sl
Danion. J. 1924 Il
Danos, P. 1958 Sl El Ww Iw; 1959 Sw Ed Ww Il; 1960 Sw Ed
Darrieussecq, A. 1973 El
Darrouy, C. 1957 Il El Wl; 1959 Ed; 1963 Sl Iw El Ww; 1964 El Wd Iw; 1965 Sw Id El; 1966 Sd Iw Ew Wl; 1967 Sl Ew Ww Iw
Daudignon, G. 1928 Sl
Dauga, B. 1964 Sl El Wd Iw; 1965 Sw Id El Ww; 1966 Sd Iw Ew Wl; 1967 Sl Ew Ww Iw; 1968 Sw Iw; 1969 Sl Il El; 1970 Sw Iw Wl Ew; 1971 Sw Id Ed Wl; 1972 Sl Il Wl
Dauger, J. 1953 Sw
De Gregorio, J. 1960 Sw Ed Ww Iw; 1961 Sw Ed Ww Iw; 1962 Sw Ew Wl; 1963 Sl Ww; 1964 El
Dedet, J. 1910 Sl El Il; 1911 Wl Il; 1912 Sl; 1913 El Il
Dedieu, P. 1963 El; 1964 Wd Iw; 1965 Sw Id El Ww
Delage, C. 1983 Sw Il
Descamps, P. 1911 Sw
Destarac, L. 1926 Sl Il El Wl; 1927 Wl Ew
Desvouges, R. 1914 Wl
Dintrans, P. 1980 El Sl Iw; 1981 Sw Iw Ww Ew; 1982 Wl El Sl Iw; 1983 Ew Ww
Dizabo, P. 1948 Sl Ew; 1949 Sl Iw El Ww; 1950 Sl Id
Domec, A. 1929 Wl
Domec, H. 1953 Wl; 1954 Sw Iw Wl Ew; 1955 Sw Iw Ew Wl; 1956 Iw Wl; 1958 El Ww Iw
Domenech, A. 1954 Wl Ew; 1955 Sw Iw Ew Wl; 1956 Sl Iw Wl Ew; 1957 Sl Il El Wl; 1958 Sl El; 1960 Sw Ed Ww Iw; 1961 Sw Ed Ww Iw; 1962 Sw Ew Wl Iw; 1963 Ww
Domercq, J. 1912 Il Sl
Dospital, P. 1980 Iw; 1981 Sw Iw Ww Ew; 1982 Iw; 1983 Ew Sw Il Ww
Dourthe, C. 1967 Sl Ew Ww Iw; 1968 Ww; 1969 Wd; 1972 Il; 1973 Sw El; 1974 Iw; 1975 Wl Ew Sw
Droitecourt, M. 1973 El; 1974 Ed Sl; 1976 Sw Iw Wl
Dubertrand, A. 1974 Iw Wd Ed; 1976 Sw
Dubois, D. 1971 Sw
Dubroca, D. 1982 El Sl
Duclos, A. 1931 Sl
Ducousso, J. 1925 Sl Wl El

Dufau, G. 1948 Il; 1949 Iw Ww; 1950 Sl Ew Wl; 1951 Sw Il Ew Ww; 1952 Wl; 1953 Sw Il El Wl; 1954 Sw Iw Wl Ew; 1955 Sw Iw Ew Wl; 1956 Sl Iw Wl; 1957 Sl Il Ew Wl
Dufau, J. 1912 Il Sl Wl El
Dufour, G. 1911 Wl
Duhard, Y. 1980 El
Duhau, J. 1928 Il; 1930 Iw; 1931 Iw Sl Wl
Dulaurans, C. 1926 Il; 1928 Sl, 1929 Wl
Dupont, C. 1923 Sl Wl Iw; 1924 Sw Il Wl; 1925 Sl; 1927 Ew; 1928 Ww; 1929 Il
Dupont, J.L. 1983 Sw
Dupouy, A. 1924 Wl
Duprat, B. 1966 Ew Wl; 1967 Sl Ew; 1968 Sw Iw; 1972 Ew Wl
Dupuy, J. 1956 Sl Iw Wl Ew; 1957 Sl Il El Wl; 1958 Sl El; 1959 Sw Ed Ww Il; 1960 Ww Iw; 1961 Sw Ed; 1962 Sw Ew Wl Iw; 1963 Ww; 1964 Sl
Dutour, F. 1911 El Il; 1912 Sl Wl El; 1913 Sl
Dutrain, H. 1947 El; 1949 Iw El Ww
Duval, R. 1911 El Wl Il
Echave, L. 1961 Sw
Erbani, D. 1983 Il Ww
Esponda, J-M. 1969 Sl Il (R) El
Estève, A. 1972 Il Ew Wl; 1973 Sw El Il; 1974 Iw Wd Ed Sl; 1975 Wl Ew
Estève, P. 1983 Ew Sw Il Ww
Etcheberry, J. 1923 Wl Iw; 1924 Sw Il El Wl; 1926 Sl Il El; 1927 Il Sl Wl
Etchenique, J-M. 1975 Ew
Etchepare, J. 1922 Il
Etcheverry, M. 1971 Sw Id
Eutrope, A. 1913 Il
Fabre, J. 1963 Sl Iw El Ww; 1964 Sl El
Fabre, M. 1982 Iw
Failliot, P. 1911 Sw Wl Il; 1912 Il Sl El; 1913 El Wl
Fargues, H. 1923 Iw
Faure, F. 1914 Il Wl El
Favre, G. 1913 El Wl
Ferrien, R. 1950 Sl Id Ew Wl
Fite, R. 1963 Ww
Forestier, A. 1912 Wl
Forgues, F. 1911 Sw El Wl; 1912 Il Wl El; 1913 Sl Wl; 1914 Il El
Fort, J. 1967 Ww Iw
Fourès, H. 1951 Sw Il Ew Ww
Fournet, F. 1950 Wl
Fouroux, J. 1974 Wd Ed; 1975 Wl; 1976 Sw Iw Wl Ew; 1977 Ww Ew Sw Iw
Franquenelle, A. 1911 Sw; 1913 Wl Il
Furcade, R. 1952 Sw
Gabernet, S. 1980 El Sl; 1981 Sw Iw Ww Ew; 1982 Iw
Gachassin, J. 1961 Sw Iw; 1964 Sl El Wd Iw; 1965 Sw Id El Ww; 1966 Sd Iw Ew Wl; 1967 Sl Ww Iw; 1968 Iw Ew; 1969 Sl Il
Galau, H. 1924 Sw Il El Wl
Galia, J. 1927 Ew; 1928 Sl Il El Ww; 1929 Il El; 1930 Sw Iw El Wl; 1931 Sl Wl Ew
Gallion, J. 1978 Ew Sw Iw Wl; 1979 Id Ww El Sw; 1980 Wl El Sl Iw
Galy, J. 1953 Wl
Gayraud, W. 1920 Iw
Gensanne, R. 1962 Sw Ew Wl Iw; 1963 Sl

Gérald, G. 1927 Ew 1928 Sl; 1929 Il Sl Wl El; 1930 Sw Iw El Wl; 1931 Iw Sl Ew

Gerintes, G. 1925 Il; 1926 Wl

Gonnet, C-A. 1921 El Iw; 1922 Ed Wl: 1924 Sw El; 1926 Sl Il El Wl; 1927 Il Sl Wl Ew

Got, R. 1920 Iw; 1921 Sw Wl; 1922 Sd Ed Wl Il; 1924 Il El Wl

Gourdon, J-F. 1974 Sl, 1975 Wl Ew Sw Il; 1976 Sw Iw Wl Ew; 1978 Ew Sw; 1979 Ww El Sw; 1980 Iw

Graciet, R. 1926 Il Wl; 1927 Sl; 1929 El

Graule, V. 1926 Il El Wl; 1927 Sl Wl

Greffe, M. 1968 Ww

Gruarin, A. 1964 Wd Iw; 1965 Sw Id El Ww; 1966 Sd Iw Ew Wl; 1967 Sl Ew Ww Iw; 1968 Sw Iw

Guélorguet, P. 1931 Ew

Guichemerre, A. 1920 El; 1921 El Iw; 1923 Sl

Guilbert, A. 1975 Ew Sw Il; 1979 Id Ww El

Guillemin, P. 1910 Wl Sl El Il; 1911 Sw El Wl

Haget, A. 1953 El; 1954 Iw Ew; 1955 Ew Wl; 1957 Il El

Haget, F. 1976 Sw; 1978 Sw Iw Wl; 1979 Id Ww El Sw; 1980 Wl Sl Iw

Haget, H. 1928 Sl

Halet, J. 1925 Sl Wl

Harize, D. 1977 Ww Ew Sw Iw

Hauc, J. 1928 El; 1929 Il Sl

Hauser, M. 1969 El

Hedembaigt, M. 1913 Sl; 1914 Wl

Herice, D. 1950 Id

Herrero, A. 1964 El Wd Iw; 1965 Sw Id El Ww; 1966 Wl; 1967 Sl Ew Iw

Herrero, B. 1983 Il

Hiquet, J-C. 1964 El

Hoche, M. 1957 Il El Wl

Houblain, H. 1910 Wl

Houdet, R. 1927 Sl Wl; 1928 Ww; 1929 Il Sl El; 1930 Sw El

Hourdebaigt, M. 1910 Wl Sl El Il

Hutin, R. 1927 Il Sl Wl

Iguinitz, E. 1914 El

Ihingoue, D. 1912 Il Sl

Imbernon, J-F. 1976 Iw Wl Ew; 1977 Ww Ew Sw Iw; 1978 Ew; 1979 Id; 1981 Sw Iw Ww Ew; 1982 Iw; 1983 Il Ww

Iraçabal, J. 1969 Sl Il Wd; 1970 Sw Iw Wl Ew; 1971 Wl; 1972 Ew Wl; 1973 Sw El Ww Il; 1974 Iw Wd Ed Sl

Jardel, J. 1928 Il El

Jauréguy, A. 1920 Sl El Wl Iw; 1922 Sd Wl; 1923 Sl Wl El Iw; 1924 Sw Wl; 1925 Il; 1926 Sl El Wl; 1927 Il Ew; 1928 Sl El Ww; 1929 Il Sl Wl

Jauréguy, P. 1913 Sl Wl Il

Jeangrand, H. 1921 Iw

Jeanjean, P. 1948 Il

Joinel, J-L. 1979 Id Ww El Sw; 1980 Wl El Sl Iw; 1981 Sw Iw Ww Ew; 1982 El Sl Iw; 1983 Ew Sw Il Ww

Jol, M. 1947 Sw Iw Wl El; 1949 Sl Iw El Ww

Junquas, L. 1947 Sw Iw Wl El; 1948 Sl Ww

Labadie, P. 1952 Sw Il Wl El; 1953 Sw Il; 1954 Sw Iw Wl Ew; 1955 Sw Iw Ew Wl; 1956 Iw; 1957 Il

Labarthete, R. 1952 Sw

Labazuy, A. 1952 Il; 1954 Sw Wl; 1956 Ew; 1958 Ww Iw; 1959 Sw Ed Ww

Laborde, C. 1965 El

Laborderie, M. de 1921 Iw; 1922 Il; 1925 Wl El

Lacans, P. 1981 Ww Ew; 1982 Wl

Lacaussade, R. 1948 Sl

Lacaze, C. 1962 Ew Wl Iw; 1963 Ww; 1964 Sl El; 1966 Sd Iw Ew Wl; 1967 Sl Ew; 1968 Sw Ew Ww; 1969 El

Lacaze, H. 1928 Il Ww; 1929 Il Wl

Lacaze, P. 1959 Sw Ed Ww Il

Lacazedieu, C. 1923 Wl Iw; 1928 Il; 1929 Sl

Lacoste, J. 1914 Il Wl El

Lacroix, P. 1960 Ww Iw; 1961 Sw Ed Ww Iw; 1962 Sw Ew Wl Iw; 1963 Sl Iw El Ww

Lafarge, Y. 1981 Iw (R)

Laffond, A. 1922 Ed

Laffont, H. 1926 Wl

Lafitte, R. 1910 Wl Sl

Lalande, M. 1923 Sl Wl Iw

Lane, G. 1910 Wl El; 1911 Sw Wl; 1912 Il Wl El; 1913 Sl

Laporte, G. 1981 Iw Ww Ew

Larribeau, L. 1912 Il Sl Wl El; 1913 Sl; 1914 Il El

Larrieu, J. 1920 Iw; 1921 Wl; 1923 Sl Wl El Iw

Larrue, H. 1960 Ww Iw

Lasâosa, P. 1950 Id; 1952 Sw Il El

Lassegue, J. 1947 Sw Iw Wl; 1948 Ww; 1949 Iw El Ww

Lasserre, J-C. 1964 Sl El Wd Iw; 1965 Ww; 1967 Sl

Lasserre, M. 1968 Ew Ww; 1969 Sl Il El; 1970 Ew; 1971 Ed Wl

Lasserre, R. 1914 Il Wl; 1920 Sl; 1921 Sw Wl Iw; 1922 Sd Ed Wl Il; 1923 Wl El; 1924 Sw Il

Laterrade, G. 1910 El Il; 1911 Sw El Il

Laudouar, J. 1962 Iw

Laugâ, P. 1950 Sl Id Ew Wl

Laurent, A. 1925 Sl Wl El; 1926 Wl

Laurent, J. 1920 Sl El Wl

Lavaud, P. 1914 Il Wl

Lavergne, P. 1950 Sl

Lavigne, B. 1920 El Wl

Lazies, H. 1956 Ew; 1957 Sl

Le Droff, J. 1964 Sl El; 1970 Ew; 1971 Sw Id

Legrain, M. 1910 Il; 1911 Sw El Wl Il; 1913 Sl El Wl Il; 1914 Il Wl

Lepatey, J. 1955 Sw Iw Ew Wl

Lepatey, L. 1924 Sw Il El

Lescarboura, J-P. 1982 Wl El Sl Iw

Lesieur, E. 1910 Sl El Il; 1911 El Il; 1912 Wl

Leuvielle, M. 1913 Sl El Wl; 1914 Wl El

Levasseur, R. 1925 Wl El

Lira, M. 1963 Iw El Ww; 1964 Wd Iw; 1965 Sw Id

Llary, R. 1926 Sl

Lobies, J. 1921 Sw Wl El

Lorieux, A. 1982 Wl

Loury, A. 1927 Ew; 1928 Sl Il

Lousteau, M. 1923 El

Lubin-Lebrère, M-F. 1914 Il El; 1920 Sl El Wl Iw; 1921 Sw; 1922 Sd Ed Wl; 1924 Wl; 1925 Il

Lubrano, A. 1973 Sw

Lux, J-P. 1967 Ew Ww Iw; 1968 Iw Ew; 1969 Sl Il El; 1970 Sw Iw Wl Ew; 1971 Sw Id Ed Wl; 1972 Sl Il Ew Wl; 1973 Sw El; 1974 Iw Wd Ed Sl; 1975 Wl

Magnanou, C. 1923 El; 1925 Wl El; 1926 Sl; 1929 Sl Wl; 1930 Sw Iw El Wl

Magnol, M. 1928 Sl; 1929 Sl Wl El
Majérus, R. 1928 Ww; 1929 Il Sl; 1930 Sw Iw El Wl
Maleig, A. 1979 Ww El; 1980 Wl El
Malmann, R. de 1910 El Il
Malquier, Y. 1979 Sw
Manoir, Y. du 1925 Il Sl Wl El; 1926 Sl; 1927 Il Sl
Mantoulan, C. 1959 Il
Marcet, J. 1925 Il Sl Wl El; 1926 Il El
Marchal, J-F. 1979 Sw; 1980 Wl Sl Iw
Marchand, R. 1920 Sl Wl
Marot, A. 1970 Sw Iw Wl
Marquesuzaâ, A. 1959 Sw Ed Ww; 1960 Sw Ed
Martin, C. 1910 Wl Sl
Martin, J-L. 1972 Sl Il
Martin, L. 1948 Il Sl Ww Ew; 1950 Sl
Martine, R. 1952 Sw Il; 1954 Sw Iw Wl Ew; 1955 Sw Iw Wl; 1958 Ww Iw; 1960 Sw Ed; 1961 Sw
Martinez, G. 1982 Wl El Sl; 1983 Ew Ww
Mas, F. 1963 Sl Iw El Ww
Maso, J. 1967 Sl; 1968 Sw Ww; 1969 Sl Il Wd; 1972 Ew Wl; 1973 Ww Il
Masse, A. 1910 Wl Sl El Il
Matheu, J. 1947 Sw Iw Wl El; 1948 Il Sl Ww Ew; 1949 Sl Iw El Ww; 1950 Ew Wl; 1951 Sw Il
Mauduy, G. 1958 Sl El; 1961 Ww
Mauran, J. 1952 Wl El; 1953 Il El
Mauriat, P. 1910 Wl Sl El Il; 1911 Sw El Wl Il; 1912 Il Sl; 1913 Sl Wl Il
Maury, A. 1925 Il Sl Wl El; 1926 Sl Il El
Maysonnié, J. 1910 Wl
Menrath, A. 1910 Wl
Menthiller, Y. 1964 Wd; 1965 El
Mericq, S. 1959 Il; 1960 Sw Ed Ww; 1961 Iw
Merquey, J. 1950 Sl Id Ew Wl
Mesny, P. 1981 Iw Ww (R); 1982 Iw
Meyer, S. 1960 Sw Ed
Miãs, L. 1951 Sw Il Ew Ww; 1952 Il Wl El; 1953 Sw Il Wl; 1954 Sw Iw Wl; 1958 Sl El Ww Iw; 1959 Sw Ww Il
Mir, J-H. 1968 Iw
Moga, A. 1947 Sw Iw Wl El; 1948 Il Sl Ww Ew; 1949 Sl Iw El Ww
Mommejat, B. 1958 Iw; 1959 Sw Ed Ww Il; 1960 Sw Ed Iw; 1962 Sw Ew Wl Iw; 1963 Sl Iw Ww
Moncla, F. 1957 Il El Wl; 1959 Sw Ed Ww Il; 1960 Sw Ed Ww Iw; 1961 Sw Ed Ww Iw
Monie, R. 1957 El
Monnier, R. 1911 Il; 1912 Sl
Monniot, M. 1912 Wl El
Montade, C. 1925 Il Sl Wl; 1926 Wl
Moraitis, B. 1969 El Wd
Morère, J. 1927 Ew; 1928 Sl
Mounicq, P. 1911 Sw El Wl Il; 1912 Il El; 1913 Sl El
Moureu, P. 1920 Iw; 1921 Wl El Iw; 1922 Sd Wl Il; 1923 Sl Wl El Iw; 1924 Sw Il El Wl; 1925 El
Muison, J. du 1910 Il
Namur, R. 1931 Ew
Noble, J-C. 1968 Ew Ww
Novès, G. 1978 Wl; 1979 Id Ww
Olive, D. 1951 Il; 1952 Il
Orso, J-C. 1983 Ew Sw
Paco, A. 1975 Wl Ew; 1976 Sw Iw Wl Ew; 1977 Ww Ew Sw Iw; 1978 Ew Sw Iw Wl; 1979 Id Ww El Sw; 1980 Wl

Palmié, M. 1976 Sw Iw Wl Ew; 1977 Ww Ew Sw Iw; 1978 Ew Sw Iw Wl
Paoli, R. 1911 Il; 1912 Il Sl
Paparemborde, R. 1976 Sw Iw Wl Ew; 1977 Ww Ew Sw Iw; 1978 Ew Sw Iw Wl; 1979 Id Ww El Sw; 1980 Wl El Sl; 1981 Sw Iw Ww Ew; 1982 Wl Iw; 1983 Ew Sw Il Ww
Pardo, L. 1924 Il El
Pardo, L. 1981 Sw Iw Ww Ew; 1982 Wl El Sl
Paries, L. 1970 Sw Iw Wl; 1975 Ew Sw Il
Pascalin, P. 1950 Id Ew Wl; 1951 Sw Il Ew Ww
Pascarel, J. 1912 Wl El; 1913 Sl El Il
Pascot, J. 1922 Sd Ed Il; 1923 Sl; 1926 Il
Pauthe, G. 1956 Ew
Pebeyre, E. 1947 Sw Iw Wl El
Pebeyre, M. 1970 Ew; 1971 Id; 1973 Ww
Pecune, J. 1974 Wd Ed Sl; 1976 Iw Wl Ew
Pedeutour, P. 1980 Iw
Pellissier, L. 1928 Il El Ww
Perrier, P. 1982 Wl El Sl Iw (R)
Petit, C. 1931 Wl
Peyroutou, G. Sw El
Phliponneau, J-F. 1973 Ww Il
Pierrot, G. 1914 Il Wl El
Pilon, J. 1949 El; 1950 Ew
Piqué, J. 1962 Sw; 1964 El Wd Iw; 1965 Sw Id El Ww
Piquemal, M. 1927 Il Sl; 1929 Il; 1930 Sw Iw El Wl
Piquiral, E. 1924 Sw Il El Wl; 1925 El; 1926 Sl Il El Wl; 1927 Il Sl Wl Ew; 1928 El
Piteu, R. 1921 Sw Wl El Iw; 1922 Sd Ed Wl Il; 1923 El; 1924 El; 1925 Il Wl El; 1926 El
Plantefol, A. 1968 Ew Ww; 1969 El Wd
Podevin, G. 1913 Wl Il
Pomathios, M. 1948 Il Sl Ww Ew; 1949 Sl Iw El Ww; 1950 Sl Id Wl; 1951 Sw Il Ew Ww; 1952 Wl El; 1953 Sw Il Wl; 1954 Sw
Pons, P. 1920 Sl El Wl; 1921 Sw Wl; 1922 Sd
Porra, M. 1931 Iw
Porthault, A. 1951 Sw Ew Ww; 1952 Il; 1953 Sw Il
Poydebasque, F. 1914 Il Wl
Prat, J. 1947 Sw Iw Wl El; 1948 Il Sl Ww Ew; 1949 Sl Iw El Ww; 1950 Sl Id Ew Wl; 1951 Sw Ew Ww; 1952 Sw Il Wl El; 1953 Sw Il El Wl; 1954 Sw Iw Wl Ew; 1955 Sw Iw Ew Wl
Prat, M. 1951 Il, 1952 Sw Il Wl El; 1953 Sw Il El; 1954 Iw Wl Ew; 1955 Sw Iw Ew Wl; 1956 Iw Wl; 1957 Sl Il Wl; 1958 Ww Iw
Prevost, A. 1927 Il Sl Wl
Princlary, J. 1947 Sw Iw Wl
Puech, L. 1920 Sl El Iw; 1921 El Iw
Puget, M. 1966 Sd Iw; 1969 El; 1970 Wl
Puig, A. 1926 Sl El
Quaglio, A. 1958 Sl El Ww Iw; 1959 Sw Ed Ww Il
Quilis, A. 1971 Id
Ramis, R. 1922 Ed Il; 1923 Wl
Rancoule, H. 1955 Ew Wl; 1958 Ww Iw; 1959 Sw Ww; 1960 Iw; 1961 Ed Ww; 1962 Sw Ew Wl Iw
Raymond, F. 1925 Sl; 1927 Wl; 1928 Il
Razat, J-P. 1963 Sl Iw
Rebujent, R. 1963 El
Revallier, D. 1981 Sw Iw Ww Ew; 1982 Wl Sl Iw
Revillon, J. 1926 Il El; 1927 Sl
Ribère, E. 1924 Il; 1925 Il Sl; 1926 Sl Il Wl; 1927 Il

Sl Wl Ew; 1928 Sl Il El Ww; 1929 Il El; 1930 Sw Iw El Wl; 1931 Iw Sl Wl Ew

Rives, J-P. 1975 Ew Sw Il; 1976 Sw Iw Wl Ew; 1977 Ww Ew Sw Iw; 1978 Ew Sw Iw Wl; 1979 Id Ww El Sw; 1980 Wl El Sl Iw; 1981 Sw Iw Ww Ew; 1982 Wl El Sl Iw; 1983 Ew Sw Il Ww

Rodrigo, M. 1931 Iw Wl

Rodriguez, L. 1982 Wl El Sl Iw; 1983 Ew Sw

Rogé, L. 1953 El Wl; 1954 Sw; 1955 Sw Iw; 1956 Wl Ew; 1957 Sl; 1960 Sw Ed

Rollet, J. 1963 Iw

Romero, H. 1962 Sw Ew Wl Id; 1963 El

Romeu, J-P. 1973 Sw El Ww Il; 1974 Wd Ed Sl; 1975 Wl; 1976 Sw Iw Wl Ew; 1977 Ww Ew Sw Iw

Roques, A. 1958 Ww Iw; 1959 Sw Ed Ww Il; 1960 Sw Ed Ww Iw; 1961 Sw Ed Ww Iw; 1962 Sw Ew Wl Iw; 1963 Sl

Roques, J-C. 1966 Sd Iw

Rouan, J-C. 1953 Sw Il

Roucaries, G. 1956 Sl

Rouffia, L. 1948 Il

Roujas, R. 1910 Il

Rousie, M. 1931 Sl

Rupert, J-J. 1964 Sl; 1965 El Ww; 1966 Sd Iw Ew Wl; 1968 Sw

Saisset, O. 1972 Sl Il; 1973 Sw El Ww Il; 1974 Iw; 1975 Wl

Salas, P. 1980 Wl El

Salinie, R. 1923 El

Sallefranque, M. 1982 Wl El Sl

Salut, J-P. 1967 Sl; 1968 Iw Ew; 1969 Il

Samatan, R. 1930 Sw Iw El Wl; 1931 Iw Sl Wl Ew

Sanac, A. 1953 Sw Il; 1954 Ew; 1957 Sl Il El Wl

Sangalli, F. 1975 Il; 1976 Sw; 1977 Ww Ew Sw Iw

Sarrade, R. 1929 Il

Saux, J-P. 1960 Ww; 1961 Ed Ww Iw; 1962 Sw Ew Wl Iw; 1963 Sl Iw El

Savy, M. 1931 Iw Sl Wl Ew

Sayrou, J. 1926 Wl; 1928 El Ww; 1929 Sl Wl El

Scohy, R. 1931 Sl Wl Ew

Sébedio, J. 1913 Sl El; 1914 Il; 1920 Sl Iw; 1922 Sd Ed; 1923 Sl

Sella, P. 1983 Ew Sw Il Ww

Semmartin, J. 1913 Wl Il

Senal, G. 1975 Wl

Sentilles, J. 1912 Wl El; 1913 Sl

Serin, L. 1928 El; 1929 Wl El; 1930 Sw Iw El Wl; 1931 Iw Wl Ew

Serre, P. 1920 Sl El

Servole, L. 1931 Iw Sl Wl Ew

Sicart, N. 1922 Il

Sillières, J. 1970 Sw Iw; 1971 Sw Id Ed; 1972 Ew Wl

Siman, M. 1948 Ew; 1949 Sl; 1950 Sl Id Ew Wl

Sitjar, M. 1964 Wd Iw; 1967 Ew Ww Iw

Skréla, J-C. 1972 Il (R) Ew Wl; 1973 Ww; 1974 Wd Ed Sl; 1975 Wl (R) Ew Sw Il; 1976 Sw Iw Wl Ew;

1977 Ww Ew Sw Iw; 1978 Ew Sw Iw Wl

Soro, R. 1947 Sw Iw Wl El; 1948 Il Sl Ww Ew; 1949 Sl Iw El Ww

Sorondo, M. 1947 Sw Iw Wl El; 1948 Il

Souich, C. du 1911 Wl Il

Soulié, E. 1920 El Iw; 1921 Sw El Iw; 1922 Ed Wl Il

Spanghero, C. 1971 Ed Wl; 1972 Sl Ew Wl; 1974 Iw Wd Ed Sl; 1975 Ew Sw Il

Spanghero, W. 1965 Sw Id El Ww; 1966 Sd Iw Ew Wl; 1967 Sl Ew; 1968 Sw Iw Ew Ww; 1969 Sl Il Wd; 1971 Ed Wl; 1972 Ew; 1973 Sw El Ww Il

Stener, G. 1956 Sl Iw Ew

Struxiano, P. 1913 Wl Il; 1920 Sl El Wl Iw

Sutra, G. 1969 Wd; 1970 Sw Iw

Swierczinski, C. 1969 El

Taffary, M. 1975 Wl Ew Sw Il

Taillantou, J. 1930 Iw Wl

Tarricq, P. 1958 Ww Iw

Tavernier, P. 1913 Il

Terreau, M. 1947 Sw Iw Wl El; 1948 Il Ww Ew; 1949 Sl; 1951 Sw

Theuriet, A. 1910 Sl; 1911 Wl; 1913 El

Thevenot, G. 1910 Wl El Il

Thierry, R. 1920 Sl El Wl

Thil, P. 1912 Wl El; 1913 Sl El Wl

Tignol, P. 1953 Sw Il

Torreilles, S. 1956 Sl

Trillo, J. 1968 Sw Iw; 1969 Il El Wd; 1970 Ew; 1971 Sw Id; 1972 Sl; 1973 Sw El

Triviaux, R. 1931 Ew

Ugartemendia, J-L. 1975 Sw Il

Vallot, E. 1912 Sl

Vannier, M. 1953 Wl; 1954 Sw Iw; 1955 Sw Iw Ew Wl; 1956 Sl Iw Wl Ew; 1957 Sl Il El Wl; 1958 Sl El Ww Iw; 1960 Sw Ed Ww Iw; 1961 Ed Ww Iw

Vaquer, F. 1921 Sw Wl; 1922 Wl

Vaquerin, A. 1972 Sl Il; 1973 Sw; 1974 Wd Ed Sl; 1975 Wl Ew Sw Il; 1979 Ww El; 1980 Sl Iw

Vareilles, C. 1910 Sl El

Varenne, F. 1952 Sw

Varvier, T. 1911 El Wl; 1912 Il

Vellat, E. 1927 Il Ew

Verger, A. 1927 Wl Ew; 1928 Il El Ww

Viard, G. 1969 Wd; 1970 Sw; 1971 Sw Id

Vigerie, M. 1931 Wl

Vigier, R. 1956 Sl Wl Ew; 1957 Sl El Wl; 1958 Sl El Ww Iw; 1959 Sw Ed Ww Il

Vignes, C. 1958 Sl El

Villepreux, P. 1967 Iw; 1968 Iw; 1969 Sl Il El Wd; 1970 Sw Iw Wl Ew; 1971 Sw Id Ed Wl; 1972 Sl Il Ew Wl

Viviès, B. 1978 Ew Sw Iw Wl: 1981 Sw

Wolff, J-P. 1982 El

Yachvili, M. 1968 Ew Ww; 1969 Sl Il; 1971 Ed

Zago, F. 1963 Iw El

IRELAND PLAYERS

Abraham, M. 1912 El Sw Ww; 1914 Wl

Adams, C. 1908 El; 1909 El; 1910 Fw; 1911 Ew Sw Wl Fw; 1912 Sw Ww; 1913 Wl Fw; 1914 Fw El Sw

Agar, R.D. 1947 Fl Ew Sw Wl; 1948 Fw; 1949 Sw Ww; 1950 Fd El Wl

Agnew, P.J. 1974 Fl (R)

Ahearn, T. 1899 Ew

Alexander, R. 1936 Ew Sw Wl; 1937 El Sw Ww; 1938 El Sl; 1939 Ew Sw Wl

Allen, C.E. 1900 El Sd Wl; 1901 Ew Sl Wl; 1903 Sl Wl; 1904 El Sl Ww; 1905 Ew Sw Wl; 1906 Ew Sl Ww; 1907 Sl Wl

Allen, G.G. 1896 Ew Sd Ww; 1897 Ew Sl; 1898 Ew Sl; 1899 Ew Ww

Allen, T.C. 1885 El

Allison, J.B. 1899 Ew Sw; 1900 El Sd Wl; 1901 Ew Sl Wl; 1902 El Sw Wl; 1903 Sl

Anderson, F.E. 1953 Fw Ed Sw Wl; 1954 Fl El Sw Wl; 1955 Fl Ed Sw Wl

Anderson, H.J. 1903 Ew Sl; 1906 Ew Sl

Andrews, H.W. 1889 Sl Ww

Arigho, J.E. 1928 Fw El Ww; 1929 Fw Ew Sl Wd; 1930 Fl Ew Sw Wl; 1931 Fl Ew Sw Wl

Armstrong, W.K. 1961 Ew

Aston, H.R. 1908 El Wl

Atkins, A.P. 1924 Fw

Atkinson, J.M. 1927 Fw

Bailey, A.H. 1934 Wl; 1935 El Sw Ww; 1936 Ew Sw Wl; 1937 El Sw Ww; 1938 El Sl

Bailey, N. 1952 El

Bardon, M.E. 1934 El

Barnes, R.J. 1933 Ww

Barr, A. 1898 Wl; 1899 Sw; 1901 Ew Sl

Beamish, C.E.St J. 1933 Ww Sl; 1934 Sl Wl; 1935 El Sw Ww; 1936 Ew Sw Wl; 1938 Wl

Beamish, G.R. 1925 Ed Sl Ww; 1928 Fw El Sw Ww; 1929 Fw Ew Sl Wd; 1930 Fl Sw Wl; 1931 Fl Ew Sw Wl; 1932 El Sw Ww; 1933 El Ww Sl

Beatty, W.J. 1910 Fw; 1912 Fw Ww

Becker, V. 1974 Fl Wd

Beckett, G.G.P. 1908 El Sw Wl

Bell, W.E. 1953 Fw Ed Sw Wl

Bennett, F. 1913 Sl

Berkery, P.J. 1954 Wl; 1955 Wl; 1956 Sw Ww; 1957 Fw El Sw Wl; 1958 El Sw

Bermingham, J.J. 1921 El Sw Wl Fl

Blackham, J.C. 1909 Sl Wl; 1910 Ed Sl Wl

Blake-Knox, S.E.F. 1976 Ew Sl; 1977 Fl (R)

Blayney, J. 1950 Sw

Bond, A.T.W. 1894 Sw Ww

Bornemann, W.W. 1960 El Sl Wl

Bowen, D. St J. 1977 Wl El Sl

Boyd, C.A. 1900 Sd; 1901 Sl Wl

Boyle, C.V. 1936 Ew Sw Wl; 1937 El Sw Ww; 1938 Wl; 1939 Wl

Brabazon, H.M. 1884 El; 1886 El

Bradley, M.J. 1920 Wl Fl; 1922 El Sl Wl Fw; 1923 El Sl Ww Fl; 1925 Fw Sl Ww; 1926 Fw Ew Sw Wl; 1927 Fw Ww

Bradshaw, G. 1903 Wl

Bradshaw, R.M. 1885 El Sl

Brady, A.M. 1966 Sl; 1968 Ed Sw Ww

Brady, J.A. 1976 Ew Sl

Brady, J.R. 1951 Sw Wd; 1953 Fw Ed Sw Wl; 1954 Wl; 1956 Ww; 1957 Fw El Sw Wl

Bramwell, T. 1928 Fw

Brennan, J.I. 1957 Sw Wl

Bresnihan, F.P.K. 1966 Ed Ww; 1967 El Sw Ww Fl; 1968 Fl Ed Sw Ww; 1969 Fw Ew Sw Wl; 1970 Fl El Sw Wl; 1971 Fd El Sw Wl

Brett, J.T. 1914 Wl

Brophy, N.H. 1957 Fw El; 1959 El Sw Wl Fw; 1960 Fl; 1961 Sl Wl; 1962 El Sl Wd; 1963 Ed Ww; 1967 El Sw Ww Fl

Brown, E.L. 1958 Fl

Brown, G.S. 1912 Sw Ww

Brown, W.H. 1899 Ew

Brown, W.J. 1970 Fl Sw Ww

Brown, W.S. 1893 Sd Wl; 1894 Ew Sw Ww

Browne, D. 1920 Fl

Browne, H.C. 1929 Ew Sl Wd

Browne, W.F. 1925 Ed Sl Ww; 1926 Sw Wl; 1927 Fw El Sw Ww; 1928 El Sw

Bruce, S.A.M. 1883 El Sl; 1884 El

Brunker, A.A. 1895 El Wl

Bryant, C.H. 1920 El Sl

Buchanan, A.McM. 1926 Ew Sw Wl; 1927 Sw Ww

Buchanan, J.B.W. 1884 El Sl

Buckley, J.H. 1973 Ew Sl

Bulger, L.Q. 1896 Ew Sd Ww; 1897 Ew Sl; 1898 Ew Sl Wl

Burges, J.H. 1950 Fd El

Burns, I.J. 1980 El (R)

Butler, L. 1960 Wl

Butler, N. 1920 El

Byers, R.M. 1928 Sw Ww; 1929 Ew Sl Wd

Byrne, E.M.J. 1977 Sl Fl; 1978 Fl Wl El

Byrne, F. 1962 Fl

Byrne, S.J. 1953 Sw Wl; 1955 Fl

Byron, W.G. 1896 Ew Sd Ww; 1897 Ew Sl; 1898 Ew Sl Wl; 1899 Ew Sw Ww

Caddell, E.D. 1904 Sl; 1905 Ew Sw Wl; 1906 Ew Sl Ww; 1907 Ew Sl; 1908 Sw Wl

Cagney, S.J. 1925 Ww; 1926 Fw Ew Sw Wl; 1927 Fw; 1928 El Sw Ww; 1929 Fw Ew Sl Wd

Callan, C.P. 1947 Fl Ew Sw Wl; 1948 Fw Ew Sw Ww; 1949 Fl Ew

Cameron, E.D. 1891 Sl Wl

Campbell, E.F. 1899 Sw Ww; 1900 El Wl

Campbell, S.B.B. 1911 Ew Sw Wl Fw; 1912 Fw El Sw Ww; 1913 El Sl Fw

Campbell, S.O. 1980 El Sw Fl Ww; 1981 Fl Wl El Sl; 1982 Ww Ew Sw Fl; 1983 Sw Fw Wl Ew

Canniffe, D.M. 1976 Wl Ew

Cantrell, J.L. 1976 Fl Wl Ew Sl; 1981 Sl

Carpendale, M.J. 1886 Sl; 1887 Wl; 1888 Ww Sl

Carroll, C. 1930 Fl

Carroll, R. 1947 Fl; 1950 Sw Wl

Casement, F. 1906 Ew Sl Ww

Casey, P.J. 1963 Fl Ed Sl Ww; 1964 Ew Sl Wl Fl; 1965 Fd Ew Sw

Casey, T.C. 1930 Sw; 1932 El

Chambers, J. 1886 El Sl; 1887 Ew Sl Wl

Chambers, R.R. 1951 Fw Ew Sw Wd; 1952 Fw Wl

Clarke, J.A.B. 1922 Sl Wl Fw; 1923 Fl; 1924 El Sl Ww

Clegg, R.J. 1973 Fw; 1975 Ew Sl Fw Wl

Clifford, T. 1949 · Fl Ew Sw Ww; 1950 Fd El Sw Wl; 1951 Fw Ew; 1952 Fw Sw Wl

Clinch, A.D. 1892 Sl; 1893 Wl; 1895 El Sl Wl; 1896 Ew Sd Ww; 1897 Ew Sl

Clinch, J.D. 1923 Ww; 1924 Fw El Sl Ww; 1925 Fw Ed Sl; 1926 Ew Sw Wl; 1927 Fw; 1928 Fw El Sw Ww; 1929 Fw Ew Sl Wd; 1930 Fl Ew Sw Wl; 1931 Fl Ew Sw Wl

Clune, J.J. 1913 Wl Fw; 1914 Fw El Wl

Coffey, J.J. 1900 El; 1901 Wl; 1902 El Sw Wl; 1903 Ew Sl Wl; 1905 Ew Sw Wl; 1906 Ew Sl Ww; 1907 Ew; 1908 Wl; 1910 Fw

Cogan, W. St J. 1907 Ew Sl

Collier, S.R. 1883 Sl

Collis, W.R.F. 1924 Fw Ww; 1925 Fw Ed Sl; 1926 Fw

Collis, W.S. 1884 Wl

Collopy, G. 1891 Sl; 1892 Sl

Collopy, R. 1923 El Sl Ww Fl; 1924 Fw El Sl Ww; 1925 Fw Ed Sl Ww

Collopy, W.P. 1914 Fw El Sw Wl; 1921 El Sw Wl Fl; 1922 El Sl Wl Fw; 1923 Sl Ww Fl; 1924 Fw El Sl Ww

Cook, H.G. 1884 Wl

Coote, P.B. 1933 Sl

Corcoran, J.C. 1948 Fw

Corken, T.S. 1937 El Sw Ww

Corley, H.H. 1902 El Sw Wl; 1903 Ew Sl Wl; 1904 El Sl

Cormac, H.S.T. 1921 El Sw Wl

Costello, P. 1960 Fl

Cotton, J. 1889 Ww

Coulter, H.H. 1920 El Sl Wl

Courtney, A.W. 1920 Sl Wl Fl; 1921 El Sw Wl Fl

Craig, R.G. 1938 Sl Wl

Crawford, E.C. 1885 El

Crawford, W.E. 1920 El Sl Wl Fl; 1921 El Sw Wl Fl; 1922 El Sl; 1923 El Sl Ww Fl; 1924 Fw El Ww; 1925 Fw Ed Sl Ww; 1926 Fw Ew Sw Wl; 1927 Fw El Sw Ww

Crean, T.J. 1894 Ew Sw Ww; 1895 El Sl Wl; 1896 Ew Sd Ww

Crichton, R.Y. 1920 El Sl Wl Fl; 1921 Fl; 1922 El; 1923 Ww Fl; 1924 Fw El Sl Ww; 1925 Ed Sl

Cromey, G.E. 1937 El Sw Ww; 1938 El Sl Wl; 1939 Ew Sw Wl

Crossan, K.D. 1982 Sw

Crowe, L. 1950 El Sw Wl

Crowe, M.P. 1929 Wd; 1930 Ew Sw Wl; 1931 Fl Sw Wl; 1932 Sw Ww; 1933 Ww Sl; 1934 El

Crowe, P. 1935 El; 1938 El

Cullen, T.J. 1949 Fl

Cullen, W.J. 1920 El

Culliton, M.G. 1959 El Sw Wl Fw; 1960 El Sl Wl Fl; 1961 Ew Sl Wl Fl; 1962 Sl Fl; 1964 Ew Sl Wl Fl

Cunningham, D.McC. 1923 El Sl Ww; 1925 Fw Ed Ww

Cunningham, M.J. 1955 Fl Ed Sl Wl; 1956 Fl Sw Ww

Cunningham, W.A. 1920 Wl; 1921 El Sw Wl Fl; 1922 El; 1923 Sl Ww

Curtis, A.B. 1950 Fd El Sw

Cussen, D.J. 1921 El Sw Wl Fl; 1922 El; 1923 El Sl Ww Fl; 1926 Fw Ew Sw Wl; 1927 Fw El

Daly, J.C. 1947 Fl Ew Sw Wl; 1948 Ew Sw Ww

Daly, M.J. 1938 El

Dargan, M. 1952 Sw Wl

Davidson, C.T. 1921 Fl

Davidson, I.G. 1899 Ew; 1900 Sd Wl; 1901 Ew Sl Wl; 1902 El Sw Wl

Davidson, J.C. 1969 Fw Ew Sw Wl

Davies, F.E. 1892 Sl Ww; 1893 El Sd Wl

Davis, J.L. 1898 Ew Sl

Davis, W.J.N. 1890 Sl Wd El; 1891 El Sl Wl; 1892 El Sl; 1895 Sl

Davison, W. 1887 Wl

Davy, E.O'D. 1925 Ww; 1926 Fw Ew Sw Wl; 1927 Fw El Sw Ww; 1928 Fw El Sw Ww; 1929 Fw Ew Sl Wd; 1930 Fl Ew Sw Wl; 1931 Fl Ew Sw Wl; 1932 El Sw Ww; 1933 El Ww Sl; 1934 El

Dawson, A.R. 1958 El Sw Wl Fl; 1959 El Sw Wl Fw; 1960 Fl; 1961 Ew Sl Wl Fl; 1962 Sl Fl Wd; 1963 Fl Ed Sl Ww; 1964 Ew Sl Fl

de Lacy, H. 1948 Ew Sw

Dean, P.M. 1982 Ww Ew Sw Fl

Deane, E.C. 1909 El

Deering, M. 1929 Wd

Deering, S.J. 1935 El Sw Ww; 1936 Ew Sw Wl; 1937 El Sw

Deering, S.M. 1974 Wd; 1976 Fl Wl Ew Sl; 1977 Wl El

Delaney, M.G. 1895 Wl

Dennison, J.P. 1973 Fw; 1975 Ew Sl

Dick, C.J. 1961 Wl Fl; 1962 Wd; 1963 Fl Ed Sl Ww

Dick, J.S. 1962 El

Dick, J.S. 1887 Ew Sl Wl

Dickson, J.A.N. 1920 El Wl Fl

Doherty, W.D. 1920 El Sl Wl; 1921 El Sw Wl Fl

Donaldson, J.A. 1958 El Sw Wl

Donovan, T.M. 1889 Sl

Dooley, J.F. 1959 El Sw Wl

Doran, B.R.W. 1900 Sd Wl; 1901 Ew Sl Wl; 1902 El Sw Wl

Doran, E.F. 1890 Sl Wd

Doran, G.P. 1899 Sw Ww; 1900 El Sd; 1902 Sw Wl; 1903 Wl; 1904 El

Douglas, A.C. 1923 Fl; 1924 El Sl; 1928 Sw

Dowse, J.C.A. 1914 Fw Sw Wl

Doyle, J.L. 1935 Ww

Doyle, M.G. 1965 Fd Ew Sw Wl; 1966 Fl Ed Sl Ww; 1967 El Sw Ww Fl; 1968 Fl Ed Sw Ww

Doyle, T.J. 1968 Ed Sw Ww

Duggan, A.T.A. 1964 Fl; 1966 Ww; 1967 Sw Ww; 1968 Fl Ed Sw Ww; 1969 Fw Ew Sw Wl; 1970 Fl El Sw Ww; 1971 Fd El Sw Wl

Duggan, W. 1920 Sl Wl

Duggan, W.P. 1975 Ew Sl Fl Wl; 1976 Fl Wl Sl; 1977 Wl El Sl Fl; 1978 Sw Fl Wl El; 1979 Ew Sd; 1980 El; 1981 Fl Wl El Sl; 1982 Ww Ew Sw; 1983 Sw Fw Wl Ew

Dunlop, R.W. 1889 Ww; 1890 Sl Wd El; 1891 El Sl Wl; 1892 El Sl; 1893 Wl; 1894 Ww

Dunn, P.E.F. 1923 Sl

Dunne, M.J. 1929 Fw Ew Sl; 1930 Fl Ew Sw Wl; 1932 El Sw Ww; 1933 El Ww Sl; 1934 El Sl Wl

Dwyer, P.J. 1962 Wd; 1963 Fl; 1964 Sl Wl

Edwards, R.W. 1904 Ww

Edwards, T. 1890 Sl Wd El; 1892 Ww; 1893 El

Edwards, W.V. 1912 Fw El

Egan, J.D. 1922 Sl

Egan, J.T. 1931 Fl Ew

Egan, M.S. 1893 El; 1895 Sl

Ekin, W. 1888 Ww Sl

Elliott, W.R.J. 1979 Sd

English, M.A.F. 1958 Wl Fl; 1959 El Sw Fw; 1960 El Sl; 1961 Sl Wl Fl; 1962 Fl Wd; 1963 Ed Sl Ww

Ensor, A.H. 1973 Wl Fw; 1974 Fl Wd Ew Sw; 1975

Ew Sl Fw Wl; 1976 Fl Wl Ew; 1977 Fl; 1978 Sw Fl Wl El

Entrican, J.C. 1931 Sw

Fagan, C. 1956 Fl El Sw

Farrell, J.L. 1926 Fw Ew Sw Wl; 1927 Fw El Sw Ww; 1928 Fw El Sw Ww; 1929 Fw Ew Sl Wd; 1930 Fl Ew Sw Wl; 1931 Fl Ew Sw Wl; 1932 El Sw Ww

Feddis, N. 1956 El

Feighery, C.F.P. 1972 Fw Ew

Feighery, T.A.O. 1977 Wl El

Ferris, J.H. 1900 El Sd Wl; 1901 Wl

Finlay, J.E. 1913 El Sl Wl; 1920 El Sl Wl

Finn, M.C. 1979 Ew; 1982 Ww Ew Sw Fl; 1983 Sw Fw Wl Ew

Finn, R. 1977 Fl

Fitzgerald, C.C. 1902 El; 1903 Ew Sl

Fitzgerald, C.F. 1980 El Sw Fl Ww; 1982 Ww Ew Sw Fl; 1983 Sw Fw Wl Ew

Fitzgerald, J. 1884 Wl

Fitzpatrick, M.P. 1978 Sw; 1980 Sw Fl Ww; 1981 Fl Wl El Sl

Fletcher, W.W. 1883 El

Flood, R.S. 1925 Ww

Flynn, M.K. 1959 Fw; 1960 Fl; 1962 El Sl Fl Wd; 1964 Ew Sl Wl Fl; 1965 Fd Ew Sw Wl; 1966 Fl Ed Sl; 1972 Fw Ew

Fogarty, T. 1891 Wl

Foley, B.O. 1976 Fl Ew; 1977 Wl (R); 1980 Fl Ww; 1981 Fl El Sl

Forbes, R.E. 1907 Ew

Forrest, A.J. 1883 El; 1885 Sl

Forrest, E.G. 1889 Sl Ww; 1890 Sl El; 1891 El; 1893 Sd; 1894 Ew Sw Ww; 1895 Wl; 1897 Ew Sl

Forrest, H. 1893 Sd Wl

Fortune, J.J. 1964 Ew

Foster, A.R. 1910 Ed Sl Fw; 1911 Ew Sw Wl Fw; 1912 Fw El Sw Ww; 1914 El Sw Wl; 1921 El Sw Wl

Franks, J.G. 1898 Ew Sl Wl

Frazer, E.F. 1891 Sl; 1892 Sl

Freear, A.E. 1901 Ew Sl Wl

Fulton, J. 1895 Sl Wl; 1896 Ew; 1897 Ew; 1898 Wl; 1899 Ew; 1900 Wl; 1901 Ew; 1902 El Sw Wl; 1903 Ew Sl Wl; 1904 El Sl

Gage, J.H. 1926 Sw Wl; 1927 Sw Ww

Galbraith, H.T. 1890 Wd

Ganly, J.B. 1927 Fw El Sw Ww; 1928 Fw El Sw Ww; 1929 Fw Sl; 1930 Fl

Gardiner, F. 1900 El Sd; 1901 Ew Wl; 1902 El Sw Wl; 1903 Ew Wl; 1904 El Sl Ww; 1906 Ew Sl Ww; 1907 Sl Wl; 1908 Sw Wl; 1909 El Sl

Gardiner, J.B. 1923 El Sl Ww Fl; 1924 Fw El Sl Ww; 1925 Fw Ed Sl Ww

Gardiner, S. 1893 El Sd

Gardiner, W. 1892 El Sl; 1893 El Sd Wl; 1894 Ew Sw Ww; 1895 El Sl Wl; 1896 Ew Sd Ww; 1897 Ew Sl; 1898 Wl

Garry, M.G. 1909 El Sl Wl; 1911 Ew Sw Wl

Gaston, J.T. 1954 Fl El Sw Wl; 1955 Wl; 1956 Fl El

Gavin, T.J. 1949 Fl Ew

Gibson, C.M.H. 1964 Ew Sl Wl Fl; 1965 Fd Ew Sw Wl; 1966 Fl Ed Sl Ww; 1967 El Sw Ww Fl; 1968 Ed Sw Ww; 1969 Ew Sw Wl; 1970 Fl El Sw Ww; 1971 Fd El Sw Wl; 1972 Fw Ew; 1973 Ew Sl Wl

Fw; 1974 Fl Wd Ew Sw; 1975 Ew Sl Fw Wl; 1976 Fl Wl Ew Sl; 1977 Wl El Sl Fl; 1978 Fl Wl El; 1979 Sd

Gibson, M.E. 1979 Fd Wl Ew Sd; 1981 Wl (R)

Gifford, H.P. 1890 Sl

Gillespie, J.C. 1922 Wl Fw

Gilpin, F.G. 1962 El Sl Fl

Glass, D.C. 1958 Fl; 1960 Wl; 1961 Wl

Glennon, J.J. 1980 El Sw

Godfrey, R.P. 1954 Sw Wl

Goodall, K.G. 1967 El Sw Ww Fl; 1968 Fl Ed Sw Ww; 1969 Fw Ew Sw; 1970 Fl El Sw Ww

Gordon, A. 1884 Sl

Grace, T.O. 1972 Fw Ew; 1973 Ew Sl Wl; 1974 Ew Sw; 1975 Ew Sl Fw Wl; 1976 Fl Wl Ew Sl; 1977 Wl El Sl Fl; 1978 Sw

Graham, R.I. 1911 Fw

Grant, E.L. 1971 Fd El Sw Wl

Grant, P.J. 1894 Sw Ww

Graves, C.R.A. 1934 El Sl Wl; 1935 El Sw Ww; 1936 Ew Sw Wl; 1937 El Sw; 1938 El Sl Wl

Gray, R.D. 1923 El Sl; 1925 Fw; 1926 Fw

Greene, E.H. 1884 Wl; 1885 El Sl; 1886 El

Greeves, T.J. 1907 Ew Sl Wl; 1909 Wl

Gregg, R.J. 1953 Fw Ed Sw Wl; 1954 Fl El Sw

Griffin, C.S. 1951 Fw Ew

Griffin, J.L. 1949 Sw Ww

Grimshaw, C. 1969 Ew (R)

Guerin, B.N. 1956 Sw

Gwynn, A.P. 1895 Wl

Gwynn, L.H. 1893 Sd; 1894 Ew Sw Ww; 1897 Sl; 1898 Ew Sl

Hakin, R.F. 1976 Wl Sl; 1977 Wl El Fl

Hall, R.O.N. 1884 Wl

Hall, W.H. 1923 El Sl Ww Fl; 1924 Fw Sl

Hallaran, C.F.G.T. 1921 El Sw Wl; 1922 El Sl Wl; 1923 El Fl; 1924 Fw El Sl Ww; 1925 Fw; 1926 Fw Ew

Halpin, T. 1909 Sl Wl; 1910 Ed Sl Wl; 1911 Ew Sw Wl Fw; 1912 Fw El Sw

Hamilton, A.J. 1884 Wl

Hamilton, R.L. 1926 Fw

Hamilton, R.W. 1893 Wl

Hamlet, G.T. 1902 El Sw Wl; 1903 Ew Sl Wl; 1904 Sl Ww; 1905 Ew Sw Wl; 1907 Ew Sl Wl; 1908 El Sw Wl; 1909 El Sl Wl; 1910 Ed Sl Fw; 1911 Ew Sw Wl Fw

Hanrahan, C.J. 1926 Sw Wl; 1927 El Sw Ww; 1928 Fw El Sw; 1929 Fw Ew Sl Wd; 1930 Fl Ew Sw Wl; 1931 Fl; 1932 Sw Ww

Hardy, G.G. 1962 Sl

Harman, G.R.A. 1899 Ew Ww

Harper, J. 1947 Fl Ew Sw

Harpur, T.G. 1908 El Sw Wl

Harvey, F.M.W. 1907 Wl; 1911 Fw

Harvey, G.A.D. 1903 Ew Sl; 1904 Ww; 1905 Ew Sw

Harvey, T.A. 1900 Wl; 1901 Sl Wl; 1902 El Sw Wl; 1903 Ew Wl

Headon, T.A. 1939 Sw Wl

Healey, P. 1901 Ew Sl Wl; 1902 El Sw Wl; 1903 Ew Sl Wl; 1904 Sl

Heffernan, M.R. 1911 Ew Sw Wl Fw

Hemphill, R. 1912 Fw El Sw Ww

Henderson, N.J. 1949 Sw Ww; 1950 Fd; 1951 Fw Ew Sw Wd; 1952 Fw Sw Wl El; 1953 Fw Ed Sw

Wl; 1954 Fl El Sw Wl; 1955 Fl Ed Sl Wl; 1956 Sw Ww; 1957 Fw El Sw Wl; 1958 El Sw Wl Fl; 1959 El Sw Wl Fw

Henebrey, G.J. 1906 Ew Sl Ww; 1909 Wl

Heron, A.G. 1901 Ew

Herrick, R.W. 1886 Sl

Heuston, F.S. 1883 El Sl

Hewitt, D. 1958 El Sw Fl; 1959 Sw Wl Fw; 1960 El Sl Wl Fl; 1961 Ew Sl Wl Fl; 1962 Sl Fl; 1965 Wl

Hewitt, F.S. 1924 Ww; 1925 Fw Ed Sl; 1926 Ew; 1927 El Sw Ww

Hewitt, T.R. 1924 Ww; 1925 Fw Ed Sl; 1926 Fw Ew Sw Wl

Hewitt, V.A. 1935 Sw Ww; 1936 Ew Sw Wl

Hewitt, W.J. 1954 El; 1956 Sw; 1959 Wl

Hickie, D.J. 1971 Fd El Sw Wl; 1972 Fw Ew

Higgins, J.A.D. 1947 Sw Wl; 1948 Fw Sw Ww

Higgins, W.W. 1884 El Sl

Hillary, M. 1952 El

Hingerty, D. 1947 Fl Ew Sw Wl

Hinton, W.P. 1907 Wl; 1908 El Sw Wl; 1909 El Sl; 1910 Ed Sl Wl Fw; 1911 Ew Sw Wl; 1912 Fw El Ww

Hipwell, M.L. 1962 El Sl; 1968 Fl; 1969 Fw (R) Sw (R) Wl; 1971 Fd El Sw Wl

Hobbs, T.H.M. 1884 Sl; 1885 El

Hogg, W. 1885 Sl

Holmes, G.W. 1913 El Sl

Holmes, L.J. 1889 Sl Ww

Hooks, K.J. 1981 Sl

Horan, A.K. 1920 El Wl

Houston, K.J. 1964 Sl Wl; 1965 Fd Ew

Hughes, R.W. 1883 El Sl; 1884 El Sl; 1885 El; 1886 El

Hunt, E.W.F.de V. 1930 Fl; 1932 El Sw Ww; 1933 El

Hunter, D.V. 1885 Sl

Hunter, L. 1968 Ww

Hunter, W.R. 1962 El Sl Fl Wd; 1963 Fl Ed Sl; 1966 Fl Ed Sl

Hutton, S.A. 1967 Sw Ww Fl

Irvine, H.A.S. 1901 Sl

Irwin, D.G. 1980 Fl Ww; 1981 Fl Wl El Sl; 1982 Ww; 1983 Sw Fw Wl Ew

Irwin, J.W.S. 1938 El Sl; 1939 Ew Sw Wl

Irwin, S.T. 1900 El Sd Wl; 1901 Ew Wl; 1902 El Sw Wl; 1903 Sl

Jack, H.W. 1914 Sw Wl; 1921 Wl

Jackson, A.R.V. 1911 Ew Sw Wl Fw; 1913 Wl Fw; 1914 Fw El Sw Wl

Jackson, F. 1923 El

Jameson, J.S. 1889 Sl Ww; 1891 Wl; 1892 El Ww; 1893 Sd

Jeffares, E.W. 1913 El Sl

Johnston, J. 1884 Sl; 1885 Sl; 1886 El; 1887 Ew Sl Wl

Johnston, M. 1884 El Sl; 1886 El

Johnston, R. 1893 El Wl

Johnston, R.W. 1890 Sl Wd El

Johnston, T.J. 1892 El Sl Ww; 1893 El Sd; 1895 El

Johnstone, W.E. 1884 Wl

Kavanagh, J.R. 1953 Fw Ed Sw Wl; 1954 Sw Wl; 1955 Fl Ed; 1956 El Sw Ww; 1957 Fw El Sw Wl; 1958 El Sw Wl; 1959 El Sw Wl Fw; 1960 El Sl Wl Fl; 1961 Ew Sl Wl Fl; 1962 Fl

Kavanagh, P. 1952 El; 1955 Wl

Keane, M.I. 1974 Fl Wd Ew Sw; 1975 Ew Sl Fw Wl; 1976 Fl Wl Ew Sl; 1977 Wl El Sl Fl; 1978 Sw Fl Wl El; 1979 Fd Wl Ew Sd; 1980 El Sw Fl Ww; 1981 Fl Wl El Sl; 1982 Ww Ew Sw Fl; 1983 Sw Fw Wl Ew

Kearney, R.K. 1982 Fl

Keeffe, E. 1947 Fl Ew Sw Wl; 1948 Fw

Kelly, J.C. 1962 Fl Wd; 1963 Fl Ed Sl Ww; 1964 Ew Sl Wl Fl

Kelly, S. 1954 Sw Wl; 1955 Sl; 1960 Wl Fl

Kelly, W. 1884 Sl

Kennedy, A.G. 1956 Fl

Kennedy, F.A. 1904 El Ww

Kennedy, H. 1938 Sl Wl

Kennedy, J.M. 1884 Wl

Kennedy, K.W. 1965 Fd Ew Sw Wl; 1966 Fl Ed Ww; 1967 El Sw Ww Fl; 1968 Fl; 1969 Fw Ew Sw Wl; 1970 Fl El Sw Ww; 1971 Fd El Sw Wl; 1972 Fw Ew; 1973 Ew Sl Wl Fw; 1974 Fl Wd Ew Sw; 1975 Fw Wl

Kennedy, T.J. 1979 Fd Wl Ew (R); 1980 El Sw Fl Ww

Keogh, F.S. 1964 Wl Fl

Kiely, M.D. 1962 Wd; 1963 Fl Ed Sl Ww

Kiernan, M.J. 1982 Ww (R) Ew Sw Fl; 1983 Sw Fw Wl Ew

Kiernan, T.J. 1960 El Sl Wl Fl; 1961 Ew Sl Wl Fl; 1962 El Wd; 1963 Fl Sl Ww; 1964 Ew Sl; 1965 Fd Ew Sw Wl; 1966 Fl Ed Sl Ww; 1967 El Sw Ww Fl; 1968 Fl Ed Sw Ww; 1969 Fw Ew Sw Wl; 1970 Fl El Sw Ww; 1971 Fd; 1972 Fw Ew; 1973 Ew Sl

Killeen, G.V. 1912 El Sw Ww; 1913 El Sl Wl Fw; 1914 El Sw Wl

King, H. 1883 El Sl

Knox, H.J. 1904 Ww; 1905 Ew Sw Wl; 1906 Ew Sl Ww; 1907 Wl; 1908 Sw

Kyle, J.W. 1947 Fl Ew Sw Wl; 1948 Fw Ew Sw Ww; 1949 Fl Ew Sw Ww; 1950 Fd El Sw Wl; 1951 Fw Ew Sw Wd; 1952 Fw Sw Wl El; 1953 Fw Ed Sw Wl; 1954 Fl; 1955 Fl Ed Wl; 1956 Fl El Sw Ww; 1957 Fw El Sw Wl; 1958 El Sw

L'Estrange, L.P.F. 1962 El

Lambert, N.H. 1934 Sl Wl

Lamont, R.A. 1965 Fd Ew; 1966 Fl Ed Sl Ww; 1970 Fl El Sw Ww

Landers, M.F. 1904 Ww; 1905 Ew Sw Wl

Lane, D. 1934 Sl Wl; 1935 El Sw

Lane, M.F. 1947 Wl; 1949 Fl Ew Sw Ww; 1950 Fd El Sw Wl; 1951 Fw Sw Wd; 1952 Fw Sw; 1953 Fw Ed

Lane, P. 1964 Wl

Langan, D.J. 1934 Wl

Lavery, P.J. 1974 Wd; 1976 Wl

Lawler, P.J. 1951 Sw; 1952 Fw Sw Wl El; 1953 Fw; 1954 El Sw; 1956 Fl El

Lawlor, P.J. 1935 El Sw Ww; 1937 El Sw Ww

Le Fanu, V.C. 1886 El Sl; 1887 Ew Wl; 1888 Sl; 1889 Ww; 1890 El; 1891 El; 1892 El Sl Ww

Leahy, M.W. 1964 Wl

Lee, S. 1891 El Sl Wl; 1892 El Sl Ww; 1893 El Sd Wl; 1894 Ew Sw Ww; 1895 El Wl; 1896 Ew Sd Ww; 1897 Ew; 1898 Ew

Lenihan, D.G. 1982 Ww Ew Sw Fl; 1983 Sw Fw Wl Ew

Levis, F.H. 1884 El

Lightfoot, E.J. 1931 Fl Ew Sw Wl; 1932 El Sw Ww; 1933 El Ww Sl

Lindsay, H. 1893 El Sd Wl; 1894 Ew Sw Ww; 1895 El; 1896 Ew Sd Ww; 1898 Ew Sl Wl

Little, T.J. 1898 Wl; 1899 Sw Ww; 1900 Sd Wl; 1901 Ew Sl

Lloyd, R.A. 1910 Ed Sl; 1911 Ew Sw Wl Fw; 1912 Fw El Sw Ww; 1913 El Sl Wl Fw; 1914 Fw El; 1920 El Fl

Lydon, C.T.J. 1956 Sw

Lyle, R.K. 1910 Wl Fw

Lyle, T.R. 1885 El Sl; 1886 El; 1887 Ew Sl

Lynch, J.F. 1971 Fd El Sw Wl; 1972 Fw Ew; 1973 Ew Sl Wl; 1974 Fl Wd Ew Sw

Lynch, L.M. 1956 Sw

Lytle, J.H. 1894 Ew Sw Ww; 1895 Wl; 1896 Ew Sd Ww; 1897 Ew Sl; 1898 Ew Sl; 1899 Sw

Lytle, J.N. 1889 Ww; 1890 El; 1891 El Sl; 1894 Ew Sw Ww

Lyttle, V.J. 1938 El; 1939 Ew Sw

Macaulay, J. 1887 Ew Sl

Macdonald, J.A. 1883 El Sl; 1884 El Sl

MacHale, S. 1965 Fd Ew Sw Wl; 1966 Fl Ed Sl Ww; 1967 Sw Ww Fl

Maclear, B. 1905 Ew Sw Wl; 1906 Ew Sl Ww; 1907 Ew Sl Wl

MacNeill, H.P. 1981 Fl Wl El Sl; 1982 Ww Ew Sw Fl; 1983 Sw Fw Wl Ew

Madden, M.N. 1955 Ed Sl Wl

Magee, J.T. 1895 El Sl

Magee, L.M. 1895 El Sl Wl; 1896 Ew Sd Ww; 1897 Ew Sl; 1898 Ew Sl Wl; 1899 Ew Sw Ww; 1900 El Sd Wl; 1901 Ew Sl Wl; 1902 El Sw Wl; 1903 Ew Sl Wl; 1904 Ww

Maguire, J.F. 1884 Sl

Mahoney, J.H. 1923 El

Malcolmson, G.L. 1936 Ew Sw Wl; 1937 El Sw Ww

Maloney, J. 1950 Sw

Marshall, B.D.E. 1963 Ed

Massey-Westropp, R.H. 1886 El

Mattsson, J. 1948 Ew

Mayne, R.B. 1937 Ww; 1938 El Wl; 1939 Ew Sw Wl

Mayne, R.H. 1888 Ww Sl

Mayne, T. 1921 El Sw Fl

Mays, K.M.A. 1973 Ew Sl Wl

McAllan, G.H. 1896 Sd Ww

McBride, W.J. 1962 El Sl Fl Wd; 1963 Fl Ed Sl Ww; 1964 Ew Sl Fl; 1965 Fd Ew Sw Wl; 1966 Fl Ed Sl Ww; 1967 El Sw Ww Fl; 1968 Fl Ed Sw Ww; 1969 Fw Ew Sw Wl; 1970 Fl El Sw Ww; 1971 Fd El Sw Wl; 1972 Fw Ew; 1973 Ew Sl Wl Fw; 1974 Fl Wd Ew Sw; 1975 Ew Sl Fw Wl

McCallan, B. 1960 El Sl

McCarten, R.J. 1961 Ew Wl Fl

McCarthy, J.S. 1948 Fw Ew Sw Ww; 1949 Fl Ew Sw Ww; 1950 Wl; 1951 Fw Ew Sw Wd; 1952 Fw Sw Wl El; 1953 Fw Ed Sw; 1954 Fl El Sw Wl; 1955 Fl Ed

McCarthy, T. 1898 Wl

McClelland, T.A. 1921 El Sw Wl Fl; 1922 El Wl Fw; 1923 El Sl Ww Fl; 1924 Fw El Sl Ww

McClenahan, R.O. 1923 El Sl Ww

McClinton, A.N. 1910 Wl Fw

McCombe, W.McM. 1968 Fl; 1975 Ew Sl Fw Wl

McConnell, A.A. 1948 Fw Ew Sw Ww; 1949 Fl Ew

McConnell, G.V. 1912 Fw El; 1913 Wl Fw

McConnell, J.W. 1913 Sl

McCormac, F.M. 1909 Wl; 1910 Wl Fw

McCormick, W.J. 1930 Ew

McCoull, H.C. 1895 El Sl Wl; 1899 Ew

McCracken, H. 1954 Wl

McDermott, S.J. 1955 Sl Wl

McDonnell, A.C. 1889 Ww; 1890 Sl Wd; 1891 El

McDowell, J.C. 1924 Fw

McFarland, B.A.T. 1920 Sl Wl Fl; 1922 Wl

McGann, B.J. 1969 Fw Ew Sw Wl; 1970 Fl El Sw Ww; 1971 Fd El Sw Wl; 1972 Fw Ew; 1973 Ew Sl Wl; 1976 Fl Wl Ew Sl

McGown, T.M.W. 1899 Ew Sw; 1901 Sl

McGrath, N.F. 1934 Wl

McGrath, P.J. 1965 Ew Sw Wl; 1966 Fl Ed Sl Ww

McGrath, R.J.M. 1977 Wl El Fl (R); 1982 Ww Ew Sw Fl; 1983 Sw Fw Wl Ew

McGrath, R.M. 1909 Sl

McGrath, T. 1956 Ww; 1958 Fl; 1960 El Sl Wl Fl

McGuire, E.P. 1963 Ed Sl Ww; 1964 Ew Sl Wl Fl

McIldowie, G. 1910 Ed Sl Wl

McIlrath, J.A. 1976 Fl; 1977 Wl El

McIlwaine, E.H. 1895 Sl Wl

McIlwaine, J.E. 1897 Ew Sl; 1898 Ew Sl Wl; 1899 Ew Ww

McIntosh, L.M. 1884 Sl

McIvor, C.V. 1912 Fw El Sw Ww; 1913 El Sl Fw

McKay, J.W. 1947 Fl Ew Sw Wl; 1948 Fw Ew Sw Ww; 1949 Fl Ew Sw Ww; 1950 Fd El Sw Wl; 1951 Fw Ew Sw Wd; 1952 Fw

McKee, W.D. 1948 Fw Ew Sw Ww; 1949 Fl Ew Sw Ww; 1950 Fd El

McKelvey, J.M. 1956 Fl El

McKibbin, A.R. 1977 Wl El Sl; 1978 Sw Fl Wl El; 1979 Fd Wl Ew Sd; 1980 El Sw

McKibbin, C.H. 1976 Sl (R)

McKibbin, D. 1950 Fd El Sw Wl; 1951 Fw Ew Sw Wd

McKibbin, H.R. 1938 Wl; 1939 Ew Sw Wl

McKinney, S.A. 1972 Fw Ew; 1973 Wl Fw; 1974 Fl Ew Sw; 1975 Ew Sl; 1976 Fl Wl Ew Sl; 1977 Wl El Sl; 1978 Sw (R) Fl Wl El

McLaughlin, J.H. 1887 Ew Sl; 1888 Ww Sl

McLean, R.E. 1883 El Sl; 1884 El Sl; 1885 El

McLennan, A.C. 1977 Fl; 1978 Sw Fl Wl El; 1979 Fd Wl Ew Sd; 1980 El Fl; 1981 Fl Wl El Sl

McLoughlin, G.A.J. 1979 Fd Wl Ew Sd; 1980 El; 1982 Ww Ew Sw Fl; 1983 Sw Fw Wl Ew

McLoughlin, R.J. 1962 El Sl Fl; 1963 Ed Sl Ww; 1964 Ew Sl; 1965 Fd Ew Sw Wl; 1966 Fl Ed Sl Ww; 1971 Fd El Sw Wl; 1972 Fw Ew; 1973 Ew Sl Wl Fw; 1974 Fl Wd Ew Sw; 1975 Ew Sl Fw Wl

McMahon, L.B. 1931 Ew; 1933 El; 1934 El; 1936 Ew Sw Wl; 1937 El Sw Ww; 1938 El Sl

McMaster, A.W. 1972 Fw Ew; 1973 Ew Sl Wl Fw; 1974 Fl Ew Sw; 1975 Fw Wl; 1976 Fl Wl

McMordie, J. 1886 Sl

McMorrow, A. 1951 Wd

McNamara, V. 1914 El Sw Wl

McNaughton, P.P. 1978 Sw Fl Wl El; 1979 Fd Wl Ew Sd; 1980 El Sw Fl Ww; 1981 Fl

McSweeney, D.A. 1955 Sl

McVicker, H. 1927 El Sw Ww; 1928 Fw

McVicker, J. 1924 Fw El Sl Ww; 1925 Fw Ed Sl

Ww; 1926 Fw Ew Sw Wl; 1927 Fw El Sw Ww; 1928 Ww; 1930 Fl
McVicker, S. 1922 El Sl Wl Fw
Meares, A.W.D. 1899 Sw Ww; 1900 El Wl
Megaw, J. 1934 Wl; 1938 El
Millar, A. 1883 El
Millar, H.J. 1904 Ww; 1905 Ew Sw Wl
Millar, S. 1958 Fl; 1959 El Sw Wl Fw; 1960 El Sl Wl Fl; 1961 Ew Sl Wl Fl; 1962 El Sl Fl; 1963 Fl Ed Sl Ww; 1964 Fl; 1968 Fl Ed Sw Ww; 1969 Fw Ew Sw Wl; 1970 Fl El Sw Ww
Millar, W.H.J. 1951 Ew Sw Wd; 1952 Sw Wl
Miller, F.H. 1886 Sl
Milliken, R.A. 1973 Ew Sl Wl Fw; 1974 Fl Wd Ew Sw; 1975 Ew Sl Fw Wl
Millin, T.J. 1925 Ww
Minch, J.B. 1913 El Sl; 1914 El Sw
Moffatt, J. 1888 Ww Sl; 1889 Sl; 1890 Sl Wd; 1891 Sl
Moffatt, J.E. 1904 Sl; 1905 Ew Sw Wl
Moffett, J.W. 1961 Ew Sl
Molloy, M.G. 1966 Fl Ed; 1967 El Sw Ww Fl; 1968 Fl Ed Sw Ww; 1969 Fw Ew Sw Wl; 1970 Fl El Sw Ww; 1971 Fd El Sw Wl; 1973 Fw
Moloney, J.J. 1972 Fw Ew; 1973 Ew Sl Wl Fw; 1974 Fl Wd Ew Sw; 1975 Ew Sl Fw Wl; 1976 Sl; 1978 Sw Fl Wl El; 1980 Sw Ww
Moloney, L.A. 1976 Wl (R) Sl; 1978 Sw (R)
Monteith, J.D.E. 1947 Ew Sw Wl
Montgomery, A. 1895 Sl
Montgomery, F.P. 1914 El Sw Wl
Montgomery, R. 1887 Ew Sl Wl; 1891 El; 1892 Ww
Moore, C.M. 1887 Sl; 1888 Ww Sl
Moore, D.F. 1883 El Sl; 1884 El Wl
Moore, F.W. 1884 Wl; 1885 El Sl; 1886 Sl
Moore, H. 1910 Sl; 1911 Wl Fw; 1912 Fw El Sw Ww
Moore, T.A.P. 1973 Ew Sl Wl Fw; 1974 Fl Wd Ew Sw
Moran, F.G. 1936 Ew; 1937 El Sw Ww; 1938 Sl Wl; 1939 Ew Sw Wl
Morgan, G.J. 1934 El Sl Wl; 1935 El Sw Ww; 1936 Ew Sw Wl; 1937 El Sw Ww; 1938 El Sl Wl; 1939 Ew Sw Wl
Moriarty, C.C.H. 1899 Ww
Moroney, J.C.M. 1968 Ww; 1969 Fw Ew Sw Wl
Moroney, T.A. 1964 Wl; 1967 El
Morphy, E.McG. 1908 El
Morris, D.P. 1931 Wl; 1932 El; 1935 El Sw Ww
Morrow, J.W.R. 1883 El Sl; 1884 El Wl; 1885 Sl; 1886 El Sl; 1888 Sl
Mortell, M. 1953 Fw Ed Sw Wl; 1954 Fl El Sw Wl
Morton, W.A. 1888 Sl
Moyers, L.W. 1884 Wl
Mulcahy, W.A. 1958 El Sw Wl Fl; 1959 El Sw Wl Fw; 1960 El Sl Wl; 1961 Ew Sl Wl; 1962 El Sl Fl Wd; 1963 Fl Ed Sl Ww; 1964 Ew Sl Wl Fl; 1965 Fd Ew Sw Wl
Mullan, B. 1947 Fl Ew Sw Wl; 1948 Fw Ew Sw Ww
Mullane, J.P. 1928 Ww; 1929 Fw
Mullen, K.D. 1947 Fl Ew Sw Wl; 1948 Fw Ew Sw Ww; 1949 Fl Ew Sw Ww; 1950 Fd El Sw Wl; 1951 Fw Ew Sw Wd; 1952 Fw Sw Wl
Mulligan, A.A. 1956 Fl El; 1957 Fw El Sw Wl; 1958 El Sw Fl; 1959 El Sw Wl Fw; 1960 El Sl Wl Fl; 1961 Wl Fl

Murphy, C.J. 1939 Ew Sw Wl; 1947 Fl Ew
Murphy, J.G.M.W. 1952 Sw Wl El; 1958 Wl
Murphy, J.J. 1982 Ww (R)
Murphy, N.A.A. 1958 El Sw Wl Fl; 1959 El Sw Wl Fw; 1960 El Sl Wl Fl; 1961 Ew Sl Wl; 1962 El; 1964 Ew Sl Wl Fl; 1965 Fd Ew Sw Wl; 1966 Fl Ed Sl Ww; 1967 El Sw Ww Fl; 1969 Fw Ew Sw Wl
Murphy, N.F. 1930 Ew Wl; 1931 Fl Ew Sw Wl; 1932 El Sw Ww; 1933 El
Murphy-O'Connor, J. 1954 El
Murray, J.B. 1963 Fl
Murray, P.F. 1927 Fw; 1929 Fw Ew Sl; 1930 Fl Ew Sw Wl; 1931 Fl Ew Sw Wl; 1932 El Sw Ww; 1933 El Ww Sl
Murtagh, C.W. 1977 Sl
Nash, L.C. 1889 Sl; 1890 Wd El; 1891 El Sl Wl
Neely, M.R. 1947 Fl Ew Sw Wl
Neill, H.J. 1885 El Sl; 1886 Sl; 1887 Ew Sl Wl; 1888 Ww Sl
Neill, J.McF. 1926 Fw
Nelson, J.E. 1948 Ew Sw Ww; 1949 Fl Ew Sw Ww; 1950 Fd El Sw Wl; 1951 Fw Ew Wd; 1954 Fl
Nelson, R. 1883 Sl; 1886 Sl
Nesdale, T.J. 1961 Fl
Nicholson, P.C. 1900 El Sd Wl
Norton, G.W. 1949 Fl Ew Sw Ww; 1950 Fd El Sw Wl; 1951 Fw Ew Sw
Notley, J.R. 1952 Fw Sw
O'Brien, B. 1893 Sd Wl
O'Brien, B.A.P. 1968 Fl Ed Sw
O'Brien, D.J. 1948 Ew Sw Ww; 1949 Fl Ew Sw Ww; 1950 Fd El Sw Wl; 1951 Fw Ew Sw Wd; 1952 Fw Sw Wl El
O'Brien, K.A. 1980 El
O'Brien-Butler, P.E. 1897 Sl; 1898 Ew Sl; 1899 Sw Ww; 1900 El
O'Callaghan, C.T. 1910 Wl Fw; 1911 Ew Sw Wl Fw; 1912 Fw
O'Callaghan, M.P. 1962 Wd; 1964 Ew Fl
O'Callaghan, P. 1967 El; 1968 Fl Ed Sw Ww; 1969 Fw Ew Sw Wl; 1970 Fl El Sw Ww; 1976 Fl Wl Ew Sl
O'Connell, P. 1913 Wl Fw; 1914 Fw El Sw Wl
O'Connell, W.J. 1955 Fl
O'Connor, H.S. 1957 Fw El Sw Wl
O'Connor, J. 1895 Sl
O'Connor, J.J. 1933 Sl; 1934 El Sl Wl; 1935 El Sw Ww; 1936 Sw Wl; 1938 Sl
O'Connor, P.J. 1887 Wl
O'Conor, J.H. 1890 Sl Wd El; 1891 El Sl; 1892 El Ww; 1893 El Sd; 1894 Ew Sw Ww; 1895 El; 1896 Ew Sd Ww
Odbert, R.V.M. 1928 Fw
O'Donnell, R.C. 1980 Sw Fl Ww
O'Donoghue, P.J. 1955 Fl Ed Sl Wl; 1956 Ww; 1957 Fw El; 1958 El Sw Wl
O'Driscoll, B.J. 1971 Fd (R) El Sw Wl
O'Driscoll, J.B. 1978 Sw; 1980 El Sw Fl Ww; 1981 Fl Wl El Sl; 1982 Ww Ew Sw Fl; 1983 Sw Fw Wl Ew
O'Flanagan, M. 1948 Sw
O'Hanlon, B. 1947 Ew Sw Wl; 1948 Fw Ew Sw Ww; 1949 Fl Ew Sw Ww; 1950 Fd
O'Leary, A. 1952 Sw Wl El
O'Loughlin, D.B. 1938 El Sl Wl; 1939 Ew Sw Wl

O'Meara, J.A. 1951 Fw Ew Sw Wd; 1952 Fw Sw Wl El; 1953 Fw Ed Sw Wl; 1954 Fl El Sw; 1955 Fl Ed; 1956 Sw Ww; 1958 Wl

O'Neill, H.O'H. 1930 Ew Sw Wl; 1933 El Ww Sl

O'Neill, J.B. 1920 Sl

O'Neill, W.A. 1952 El; 1953 Fw Ed Sw Wl

O'Reilly, A.J.F. 1955 Fl Ed Sl Wl; 1956 Fl El Sw Ww; 1957 Fw El Sw Wl; 1958 El Sw Wl Fl; 1959 El Sw Wl Fw; 1960 El; 1961 Ew Fl; 1963 Fl Sl Ww; 1970 El

O'Sullivan, J.M. 1884 Sl; 1887 Sl

O'Sullivan, P.J.A. 1957 Fw El Sw Wl; 1959 El Sw Wl Fw; 1961 Ew Sl; 1962 Fl Wd; 1963 Fl

O'Sullivan, W. 1895 Sl

Orr, P.A. 1976 Fl Wl Ew Sl; 1977 Wl El Sl Fl; 1978 Sw Fl Wl El; 1979 Fd Wl Ew Sd; 1980 El Sw Fl Ww; 1981 Fl Wl El Sl; 1982 Ww Ew Sw Fl; 1983 Sw Fw Wl Ew

Owens, R.H. 1922 El Sl

Parke, J.C. 1903 Wl; 1904 El Sl Ww; 1905 Wl; 1906 Ew Sl Ww; 1907 Ew Sl Wl; 1908 El Sw Wl; 1909 El Sl Wl

Parr, J.S. 1914 Fw El Sw Wl

Patterson, C.S. 1979 Fd Wl Ew Sd; 1980 El Sw Fl Ww

Patterson, R.d'A. 1912 Fw Sw Ww; 1913 El Sl Wl Fw

Payne, C.T. 1926 Ew; 1927 Fw El Sw; 1928 Fw El Sw Ww; 1929 Fw Ew Wd; 1930 Fl Ew Sw Wl

Pedlow, A.C. 1953 Wl; 1954 Fl El; 1955 Fl Ed Sl Wl; 1956 Fl El Sw Ww; 1957 Fw El Sw Wl; 1958 El Sw Wl Fl; 1959 El; 1960 El Sl Wl Fl; 1961 Sl; 1962 Wd; 1963 Fl

Pedlow, J. 1884 Wl

Pedlow, R. 1891 Wl

Pedlow, T.B. 1889 Sl Ww

Peel, T. 1892 El Sl Ww

Phipps, G.C. 1950 El Wl; 1952 Fw Wl El

Pike, T.O. 1927 El Sw Ww; 1928 Fw El Sw Ww

Pike, V.J. 1931 Ew Sw Wl; 1932 El Sw Ww; 1933 El Ww Sl; 1934 El Sl Wl

Pike, W.W. 1883 Sl

Pinion, G. 1909 El Sl Wl

Piper, O.J.S. 1909 El Sl Wl; 1910 Ed Sl Wl Fw

Polden, S.E. 1913 Wl Fw; 1914 Fw; 1920 Fl

Popham, I. 1922 Sl Wl Fw; 1923 Fl

Potterton, H.N. 1920 Wl

Pratt, R.H. 1933 El Ww Sl; 1934 El Sl

Price, A.H. 1920 Sl Fl

Pringle, J.C. 1902 Sw Wl

Purcell, N.M. 1921 El Sw Wl Fl

Purdon, W.B. 1906 Ew Sl Ww

Purser, F.C. 1898 Ew Sl Wl

Quinlan, S.V.J. 1956 Fl El Ww; 1958 Wl

Quinn, B.T. 1947 Fl

Quinn, F.P. 1981 Fl Wl El

Quinn, J.P. 1910 Ed Sl; 1911 Ew Sw Wl Fw; 1912 El Sw Ww; 1913 El Wl Fw; 1914 Fw El Sw

Quinn, K. 1947 Fl; 1953 Fw Ed Sw

Quinn, M.A.M. 1973 Fw; 1974 Fl Wd Ew Sw; 1977 Sl Fl

Quirke, J.T.M. 1962 El Sl; 1968 Sw

Rambaut, D.F. 1887 Ew Sl Wl; 1888 Ww

Rea, H.H. 1969 Fw

Read, H.M. 1910 Ed Sl; 1911 Ew Sw Wl Fw; 1912 Fw El Sw Ww; 1913 El Sl

Reardon, J.V. 1934 El Sl

Reid, C. 1899 Sw Ww; 1900 El; 1903 Wl

Reid, J.L. 1934 Sl Wl

Reid, P.J. 1948 Fw Ew Ww

Reid, T.E. 1953 Ed Sw Wl; 1954 Fl; 1955 Ed Sl; 1956 Fl El; 1957 Fw El Sw Wl

Reidy, C.J. 1937 Ww

Reidy, G.F. 1953 Wl; 1954 Fl El Sw Wl

Richey, H.A. 1889 Ww; 1890 Sl

Ridgeway, E.C. 1932 Sw Ww; 1935 El Sw Ww

Ringland, T.M. 1982 Ww Ew Fl; 1983 Sw Fw Wl Ew

Riordan, W.F. 1910 Ed

Ritchie, J.S. 1956 Fl El

Robb, C.G. 1904 El Sl Ww; 1906 Sl

Robbie, J.C. 1976 Fl; 1977 Sl Fl; 1981 Fl Wl El Sl

Robinson, T.T.H. 1904 El Sl; 1905 Ew Sw Wl; 1907 Ew Sl Wl

Roche, J. 1890 Sl Wd El; 1891 El Sl Wl; 1892 Ww

Roche, R.E. 1955 Ed Sl; 1957 Sw Wl

Roche, W.J. 1920 El Sl Fl

Roddy, P.J. 1920 Sl Fl

Roe, R. 1952 El; 1953 Fw Ed Sw Wl; 1954 Fl El Sw Wl; 1955 Fl Ed Sl Wl; 1956 Fl El Sw Ww; 1957 Fw El Sw Wl

Rooke, C.V. 1891 El Wl; 1892 Fl Sl Ww; 1893 El Sd Wl; 1894 Ew Sw Ww; 1895 El Sl Wl; 1896 Ew Sd Ww; 1897 Ew Sl

Ross, D.J. 1884 El; 1885 Sl; 1886 El Sl

Ross, G.R.P. 1955 Wl

Ross, J.F. 1886 Sl

Ross, J.P. 1885 El Sl; 1886 El Sl

Ross, N.G. 1927 Fw El

Ross, W.McC. 1932 El Sw Ww; 1933 El Ww Sl; 1934 El Sl

Russell, J. 1931 Fl Ew Sw Wl; 1933 El Ww Sl; 1934 El Sl Wl; 1935 El Sw Ww; 1936 Ew Sw Wl; 1937 El Sw

Rutherford, W.G. 1884 El Sl; 1885 El; 1886 El; 1888 Ww

Ryan, E. 1937 Ww; 1938 El Sl

Ryan, J. 1897 Ew; 1898 Ew Sl Wl; 1899 Ew Sw Ww; 1900 Sd Wl; 1901 Ew Sl Wl; 1902 El; 1904 El

Ryan, J.G. 1939 Ew Sw Wl

Ryan, M. 1897 Ew Sl; 1898 Ew Sl Wl; 1899 Ew Sw Ww; 1900 El Sd Wl; 1901 Ew Sl Wl; 1903 Ew; 1904 El Sl

Sayers, H.J.M. 1935 El Sw Ww; 1936 Ew Sw Wl; 1938 Wl; 1939 Ew Sw Wl

Schute, F.G. 1913 El Sl

Scott, D. 1961 Fl; 1962 Sl

Scott, R.D. 1967 El Fl; 1968 Fl Ed Sw

Scovell, R.H. 1883 El; 1884 El

Scriven, G. 1883 El Sl

Sealy, J. 1896 Ew Sd Ww; 1897 Sl; 1899 Ew Sw Ww; 1900 El Sd

Shanahan, T. 1885 El Sl; 1886 El; 1888 Ww Sl

Sheehan, M.D. 1932 El

Sherry, B.F. 1967 El Sw; 1968 Fl Ed

Sherry, M.J.A. 1975 Fw Wl

Siggins, J.A.E. 1931 Fl Ew Sw Wl; 1932 El Sw Ww; 1933 El Ww Sl; 1934 El Sl Wl; 1935 El Sw Ww; 1936 Ew Sw Wl; 1937 El Sw Ww

Slattery, J.F. 1970 Fl El Sw Ww; 1971 Fd El Sw Wl; 1972 Fw Ew; 1973 Ew Sl Wl Fw; 1974 Fl Wd Ew Sw; 1975 Ew Sl Fw Wl; 1977 Sl Fl; 1978 Sw Fl Wl El; 1979 Fd Wl Ew Sd; 1980 El Sw Fl Ww; 1981 Fl Wl El Sl; 1982 Ww Ew Sw Fl; 1983 Sw Fw Wl Ew

Smartt, F.N.B. 1908 El Sw; 1909 El

Smith, J.H. 1951 Fw Ew Sw Wd; 1952 Fw Sw Wl El; 1954 Fl Wl

Smith, R.E. 1892 El

Smithwick, F.F.S. 1898 Sl Wl

Smyth, J.T. 1920 Fl

Smyth, P.J. 1911 Ew Sw Fw

Smyth, R.S. 1903 Ew Sl; 1904 El

Smyth, T. 1908 El Sw Wl; 1909 El Sl Wl; 1910 Ed Sl Wl Fw; 1911 Ew Sw Wl; 1912 El

Smyth, W.S. 1910 Wl Fw; 1920 El

Solomons, B.A.H. 1908 El Sw Wl; 1909 El Sl Wl; 1910 Ed Sl Wl

Sparrow, W. 1893 Wl; 1894 Ew

Spring, D.E. 1978 Sw; 1979 Sd; 1980 Sw Fl Ww; 1981 Wl

Spring, R.M. 1979 Fd Wl Ew

Spunner, H.F. 1884 Wl

Stack, C.R.R. 1889 Sl

Steele, H.W. 1976 Ew; 1977 Fl; 1978 Fl Wl El; 1979 Fd Wl Ew

Stephenson, G.V. 1920 Fl; 1921 El Sw Wl Fl; 1922 El Sl Wl Fw; 1923 El Sl Ww Fl; 1924 Fw El Sl Ww; 1925 Fw Ed Sl Ww; 1926 Fw Ew Sw Wl; 1927 Fw El Sw Ww; 1928 Fw El Sw Ww; 1929 Fw Ew Wd; 1930 Fl Ew Sw Wl

Stephenson, H.W.V. 1922 Sl Wl Fw; 1924 Fw El Sl Ww; 1925 Fw Ed Sl Ww; 1928 El

Stevenson, J. 1889 Sl

Stevenson, J.B. 1958 El Sw Wl Fl

Stevenson, R. 1887 Ew Sl Wl; 1889 Sl Ww; 1890 Sl Wd El; 1891 Wl; 1892 Ww; 1893 El Sd Wl

Stevenson, T.H. 1895 El Wl; 1896 Ew Sd Ww; 1897 Ew Sl

Stewart, A.L. 1913 Wl Fw; 1914 Fw

Stewart, W.J. 1922 Fw; 1924 Sl; 1928 Fw El Sw Ww; 1929 Fw Ew Sl Wd

Stoker, E.W. 1888 Ww Sl

Stoker, F.O. 1886 Sl; 1888 Ww; 1889 Sl; 1891 Wl

Stokes, O.S. 1884 El

Stokes, P. 1913 El Sl; 1914 Fw; 1920 El Sl Wl Fl; 1921 El Sw Fl; 1922 Wl Fw

Stokes, R.D. 1891 Sl Wl

Strathdee, E. 1947 Ew Sw Wl; 1948 Fw Ww; 1949 Ew Sw Ww

Stuart, I.M.B. 1924 El Sl

Sugars, H.S. 1907 Sl

Sugden, M. 1925 Fw Ed Sl Ww; 1926 Fw Ew Sw Wl; 1927 El Sw Ww; 1928 Fw El Sw Ww; 1929 Fw Ew Sl Wd; 1930 Fl Ew Sw Wl; 1931 Fl Ew Sw Wl

Sullivan, D.B. 1922 El Sl Wl Fw

Sweeney, J.A. 1907 Ew Sl Wl

Symes, G.R. 1895 El

Synge, J.S. 1929 Sl

Taggart, T. 1887 Wl

Taylor, A.S. 1910 Ed Sl Wl; 1912 Fw

Taylor, D.R. 1903 Ew

Taylor, J. 1914 El Sw Wl

Taylor, J.W. 1883 El Sl

Tector, W.R. 1955 Fl Ed Sl

Tedford, A. 1902 El Sw Wl; 1903 Ew Sl Wl; 1904 El Sl Ww; 1905 Ew Sw Wl; 1906 Ew Sl Ww; 1907 Ew Sl Wl; 1908 El Sw Wl

Teehan, C. 1939 Ew Sw Wl

Thompson, C. 1907 Ew Sl; 1908 El Sw Wl; 1909 El Sl Wl; 1910 Ed Sl Wl Fw

Thompson, J.A. 1885 Sl

Thompson, J.K.S. 1921 Wl; 1922 El Sl Fw; 1923 El Sl Ww Fl

Thompson, R.H. 1952 Fw; 1954 Fl El Sw Wl; 1955 Fl Sl Wl; 1956 Ww

Thornhill, T. 1892 El Sl Ww; 1893 El

Thrift, H.B. 1904 Ww; 1905 Ew Sw Wl; 1906 Ew Ww; 1907 Ew Sl Wl; 1908 El Sw Wl; 1909 El Sl Wl

Tierney, D. 1938 Sl Wl; 1939 Ew

Tillie, C.R. 1887 Ew Sl; 1888 Ww Sl

Todd, A.W.P. 1913 Wl Fw; 1914 Fw

Torrens, J.D. 1938 Wl; 1939 Ew Sw Wl

Tucker, C.C. 1979 Fd Wl; 1980 Fl (R)

Tuke, B.B. 1890 El; 1891 El Sl; 1892 El; 1894 Ew Sw Ww; 1895 El Sl

Turley, N. 1962 El

Tyrrell, W. 1910 Fw; 1913 El Sl Wl Fw; 1914 Fw El Sw Wl

Uprichard, R.J.H. 1950 Sw Wl

Waide, S.L. 1932 El Sw Ww; 1933 El Ww

Waites, J. 1886 Sl; 1889 Ww; 1890 Sl Wd El; 1891 El

Waldron, O.C. 1966 Sl Ww

Walker, S. 1934 El Sl; 1935 El Sw Ww; 1936 Ew Sw Wl; 1937 El Sw Ww; 1938 El Sl Wl

Walkington, D.B. 1887 Ew Wl; 1888 Ww; 1890 Wd El; 1891 El Sl Wl

Wall, H. 1965 Sw Wl

Wallace, Jas 1904 El Sl

Wallace, Jos 1903 Sl Wl; 1904 El Sl Ww; 1905 Ew Sw Wl; 1906 Ww

Wallace, T.H. 1920 El Sl Wl

Wallis, A.K. 1892 El Sl Ww; 1893 El Wl

Wallis, T.G. 1921 Fl; 1922 El Sl Wl Fw

Wallis, W.A. 1883 Sl

Walmsley, G. 1894 Ew

Walpole, A. 1888 Sl

Walsh, E.J. 1887 Ew Sl Wl; 1892 El Sl Ww; 1893 El

Walsh, J.C. 1960 Sl; 1961 Ew Sl Fl; 1963 Ed Sl Ww; 1964 Ew Sl Wl Fl; 1965 Fd Sw Wl; 1966 Fl Sl Ww; 1967 El Sw Ww Fl

Ward, A.J.P. 1978 Sw Fl Wl El; 1979 Fd Wl Ew Sd; 1981 Wl El Sl; 1983 Ew (R)

Warren, J.P. 1883 El

Warren, R.G. 1884 Wl; 1885 El Sl; 1886 El; 1887 Ew Sl Wl; 1888 Ww Sl; 1889 Sl Ww; 1890 Sl Wd El

Wells, H.G. 1891 Sl Wl; 1894 Ew Sw

Wheeler, G.H. 1884 Sl; 1885 El

Wheeler, J.R. 1922 El Sl Wl Fw; 1924 El

Whelan, P.C. 1975 Ew Sl; 1977 Wl El Sl Fl; 1978 Sw Fl Wl El; 1979 Fd Wl Ew Sd; 1981 Fl Wl El

White, M. 1906 Ew Sl Ww; 1907 Ew Wl

Whitestone, A.M. 1883 Sl

Williamson, F.W. 1930 Ew Sw Wl

Wilson, F. 1977 Wl El Sl

Wilson, H.G. 1905 Ew Sw Wl; 1906 Ew Sl Ww;

1907 Ew Sl Wl; 1908 El Sw Wl; 1909 El Sl Wl; 1910 Wl

Withers, H.H.C. 1931 Fl Ew Sw Wl

Wood, B.G.M. 1954 El Sw; 1956 Fl El Sw Ww; 1957 Fw El Sw Wl; 1958 El Sw Wl Fl; 1959 El Sw Wl Fw; 1960 El Sl Wl Fl; 1961 Ew Sl Wl Fl

Wood, G.H. 1913 Wl; 1914 Fw

Woods, D.C. 1889 Sl

Wright, R.A. 1912 Sw

Yeates, R.A. 1889 Sl Ww

Young, G. 1913 El

Young, R.M. 1965 Fd Ew Sw Wl; 1966 Fl Ed Sl Ww; 1967 Ww Fl; 1968 Ww; 1969 Fw Ew Sw Wl; 1970 Fl El Sw Ww; 1971 Fd El Sw Wl

SCOTLAND PLAYERS

Abercrombie, C.H. 1910 Iw El; 1911 Fl Wl; 1913 Fw Wl

Abercrombie, J.G. 1949 Fw Ww Il; 1950 Fw Wl Il Ew

Agnew, W.C.C. 1930 Ww Il

Ainslie, T. 1883 Ww Iw El; 1884 Ww Iw El; 1885 Wd Iw

Aitchison, G.R. 1883 Iw

Aitchison, T.G. 1929 Wl Iw Ew

Aitken, A.I. 1889 Iw

Aitken, G.G. 1924 Ww Iw El; 1925 Fw Ww Iw Ew; 1929 Fw

Aitken, J. 1977 El Iw Fl; 1981 Fl Ww El Iw; 1982 Ed Il Fw Ww; 1983 Fl Wl Ew

Aitken, R. 1947 Wl

Allan, J.L. 1952 Fl Wl Il; 1953 Wl

Allan, J.L.F. 1957 Il El

Allan, J.W. 1927 Fw; 1928 Il; 1929 Fw Wl Iw Ew; 1930 Fl Ed; 1931 Fw Wl Il Ew; 1932 Wl Il; 1934 Iw El

Allan, R.C. 1969 Il

Allardice, W.D. 1948 Fw Wl Il; 1949 Fw Ww Il El

Anderson, A.H. 1894 Il

Anderson, D.G. 1889 Iw; 1890 Ww Iw El; 1891 Ww Ew; 1892 Ww El

Anderson, E. 1947 Il El

Angus, A.W. 1909 Wl; 1910 Fw Wl El; 1911 Wl Il; 1912 Fw Wl Il Ew; 1913 Fw Wl; 1914 El; 1920 Fw Ww Iw El

Arneil, R.J. 1968 Il El; 1969 Fw Wl Il El; 1970 Fl Wl Il Ew; 1971 Fl Wl Il Ew; 1972 Fw Wl Ew

Asher, A.G.G. 1884 Ww Iw El; 1885 Wd; 1886 Iw Ed

Auld, W. 1889 Ww; 1890 Ww

Bain, D.M. 1911 El; 1912 Fw Wl Ew; 1913 Fw Wl Iw El; 1914 Wl Il

Baird, G.R.T. 1982 Ed Il Fw Ww; 1983 Il Fl Wl Ew

Balfour, A. 1896 Wl Id Ew; 1897 El

Bannerman, J.M. 1921 Fl Ww Il El; 1922 Fd Wd Iw El; 1923 Fw Ww Iw El; 1924 Fl Ww Iw El; 1925 Fw Ww Iw Ew; 1926 Fw Ww Il Ew; 1927 Fw Ww Il Ew; 1928 Fw Wl Il El; 1929 Fw Wl Iw Ew

Barnes, I.A. 1972 Wl; 1974 Fw (R); 1975 El (R); 1977 Iw Fl Wl

Barrie, R.W. 1936 El

Bearne, K.R.F. 1960 Fl Wl

Beattie, J.A. 1929 Fw Wl; 1930 Ww; 1931 Fw Wl Il Ew; 1932 Wl Il El; 1933 Ww Ew Iw; 1934 Iw El; 1935 Wl Il Ew; 1936 Wl Il El

Beattie, J.R. 1980 Il Fw Wl El; 1981 Fl Ww El Iw; 1983 Fl Wl Ew

Bedell-Sivright, D.R. 1900 Wl; 1901 Ww Iw Ew; 1902 Wl Il El; 1903 Ww Iw; 1904 Wl Iw Ew; 1906 Wl Iw El; 1907 Ww Iw Ew; 1908 Wl Il

Bedell-Sivright, J.V. 1902 Wl

Bell, D.L. 1975 Iw Fl Ww El

Bell, J.A. 1901 Ww Iw Ew; 1902 Wl Il El

Bell, L.H.I. 1900 Ed; 1904 Wl Iw

Berkley, W.V. 1926 Fw; 1929 Fw Wl Iw

Berry, C.W. 1884 Iw El; 1885 Wd; 1887 Iw Ww Ed; 1888 Wl Iw

Bertram, D.M. 1922 Fd Wd Iw El; 1923 Fw Ww Iw El; 1924 Ww Iw El

Biggar, A.G. 1970 Fl Il Ew; 1971 Fl Wl Il Ew; 1972 Fw Wl

Biggar, M.A. 1975 Iw Fl Ww El; 1976 Wl Ew Iw; 1977 Iw Fl Wl; 1978 Il Fl Wl El; 1979 Wl Ed Id Fl; 1980 Il Fw Wl El

Bishop, J.M. 1893 Id

Bisset, A.A. 1904 Wl

Black, A.W. 1947 Fl Wl; 1948 Ew; 1950 Wl Il Ew

Black, W.P. 1948 Fw Wl Il Ew; 1951 El

Blackadder, W.F. 1938 Ew

Blaikie, C.F. 1963 Iw El; 1966 Ew; 1969 Fw Wl Il El

Blair, P.C.B. 1913 Fw Wl Iw El

Borthwick, J.B. 1938 Ww Iw

Boswell, J.D. 1889 Ww Iw; 1890 Ww Iw El; 1891 Ww Iw Ew; 1892 Ww Iw El; 1893 Id Ew; 1894 Il Ew

Bowie, T.C. 1913 Iw El; 1914 Il El

Boyd, G.M. 1926 Ew

Boyd, J.L. 1912 Ew

Boyle, A.C.W. 1963 Fw Wl Iw

Boyle, A.H.W. 1967 Fw; 1968 Fl Wl Il

Brash, J.C. 1961 El

Breakey, R.W. 1978 El

Brewster, A.K. 1977 El; 1980 Il Fw

Brown C.H.C. 1929 Ew

Brown, A.H. 1928 El; 1929 Fw Wl

Brown, A.R. 1971 Ew; 1972 Fw Wl Ew

Brown, D.I. 1933 Ww Ew Iw

Brown, G.L. 1970 Fl Wl (R) Il Ew; 1971 Fl Wl Il Ew; 1972 Fw Wl Ew; 1973 El (R); 1974 Wl Ew Il Fw; 1975 Iw Fl Ww El; 1976 Fl Wl Ew Iw

Brown, J.A. 1908 Wl Il

Brown, J.B. 1883 Ww Iw El; 1884 Ww Iw El; 1885 Iw; 1886 Ww Iw Ed

Brown, P.C. 1964 Fw Wl Iw Ew; 1965 Il Ed; 1969 Il El; 1970 Wl Ew; 1971 Fl Wl Il Ew; 1972 Fw Wl Ew; 1973 Fl Ww Iw El

Brown, T.G. 1929 Wl

Brown, W.S. 1883 Ww El

Browning, A. 1920 Iw; 1922 Fd Wd Iw; 1923 Ww Iw El

Bruce, C.R. 1947 Fl Wl Il El; 1949 Fw Ww Il El

Bruce, N.S. 1958 Fw Il Ed; 1959 Fl Ww Il Ed; 1960 Fl Wl Iw El; 1961 Fl Ww Iw El; 1962 Fl Ww Iw Ed; 1963 Fw Wl Iw El; 1964 Fw Wl Iw Ew

Bruce, R.M. 1948 Fw Wl Il

Bruce-Lockhart, J.H. 1913 Wl; 1920 El

Bruce-Lockhart, L. 1948 Ew; 1950 Fw Wl; 1953 Il El

Bruce-Lockhart, R.B. 1937 Il; 1939 Il El

Bryce, R.D.H. 1973 Iw(R)

Bryce, W.E. 1922 Wd Iw El; 1923 Fw Ww Iw El; 1924 Fl Ww Iw El

Brydon, W.R.C. 1939 Wl

Buchanan, F.G. 1910 Fw; 1911 Fl Wl

Buchanan, J.C.R. 1921 Ww Il El; 1922 Wd Iw El; 1923 Fw Ww Iw El; 1924 Fl Ww Iw El; 1925 Fw Iw

Bucher, A.M. 1897 El

Budge, G.M. 1950 Fw Wl Il Ew

Bullmore, H.H. 1902 Il

Burnet, W. 1912 Ew

Burnet, W.A. 1934 Wl; 1935 Wl Il Ew; 1936 Wl Il El

Burnett, J.N. 1980 Il Fw Wl El

Burrell, G. 1950 Fw Wl Il

Cairns, A.G. 1903 Ww Iw Ew; 1904 Wl Iw Ew; 1905 Wl Il Ew; 1906 Wl Iw El

Calder, J.H. 1981 Fl Ww El Iw; 1982 Ed Il Fw Ww; 1983 Il Fl Wl Ew

Cameron, A. 1948 W1; 1950 Il Ew; 1951 Fl Ww Il El; 1953 Il El; 1955 Fl Ww Iw El; 1956 Fw Wl Il

Cameron, A.D. 1951 Fl; 1954 Fl Wl

Cameron, A.W. 1887 Ww; 1893 Wl; 1894 Il

Cameron, D. 1953 Il El; 1954 Fl Il El

Cameron, N.W. 1952 El; 1953 Fl Wl

Campbell, G.T. 1892 Ww Iw El; 1893 Id Ew; 1894 Wl Il Ew; 1895 Ww Iw Ew; 1896 Wl Id Ew; 1897 Iw; 1899 Il; 1900 Ed

Campbell, H.H. 1947 Il El; 1948 Il Ew

Campbell, J.A. 1900 Id

Campbell, N.M. 1956 Fw Wl

Campbell-Lamerton, M.J. 1961 Fl Ww Iw; 1962 Fl Ww Iw Ed; 1963 Fw Wl Iw El; 1964 Iw Ew; 1965 Fl Wl Il Ed; 1966 Fd Wl Iw Ew

Carmichael, A.B. 1967 Il; 1968 Fl Wl Il El; 1969 Fw Wl Il El; 1970 Fl Wl Il Ew; 1971 Fl Wl Il Ew; 1972 Fw Wl Ew; 1973 Fl Ww Iw El; 1974 Wl Ew Il Fw; 1975 Iw Fl Ww El; 1976 Fl Wl Ew Iw; 1977 El Iw (R) Fl Wl; 1978 Il

Carmichael, J.H. 1921 Fl Ww Il

Cassels, D.Y. 1883 Ww Iw El

Cawkwell, G.L. 1947 Fl

Chambers, H.F.T. 1888 Wl Iw; 1889 Ww Iw

Charters, R.G. 1955 Ww Iw El

Chisholm, D.H. 1964 Iw Ew; 1965 Ed; 1966 Fd Iw Ew; 1967 Fw Ww; 1968 Fl Wl Il

Chisholm, R.W.T. 1955 Iw El; 1956 Fw Wl Il El; 1958 Fw Wl Il

Church, W.O. 1906 Wl

Clark, R.L. 1972 Fw Wl Ew; 1973 Fl Ww Iw El

Clauss, P.R. 1891 Ww Iw Ew; 1892 Ww El; 1895 Iw

Clay, A.T. 1886 Ww Iw Ed; 1887 Iw Ww Ed; 1888 Wl

Coltman, S. 1948 Il; 1949 Fw Ww Il El

Connell, G.C. 1968 El; 1969 Fw El; 1970 Fl

Cooper, M.McG. 1936 Wl Il

Cordial, I.F. 1952 Fl Wl Il El

Cotter, J.L. 1934 Iw El

Cottington, G.S. 1934 Iw El; 1935 Wl Il; 1936 El

Coughtrie, S. 1959 Fl Ww Il Ed; 1962 Ww Iw Ed; 1963 Fw Wl Iw El

Couper, J.H. 1896 Wl Id; 1899 Il

Coutts, F.H. 1947 Wl Il El

Coutts, I.D.F. 1951 Fl; 1952 El

Cowan, R.C. 1961 Fl; 1962 Fl Ww Iw Ed

Cowie, W.L.K. 1953 El

Cownie, W.B. 1893 Wl Id Ew; 1894 Wl Il Ew; 1895 Ww Iw Ew

Crabbie, G.E. 1904 Wl

Crabbie, J.E. 1900 Wl; 1902 Il; 1903 Ww Iw; 1904 Ew; 1905 Wl

Craig, J.B. 1939 Wl

Cranston, A.G. 1976 Wl Ew Iw; 1977 El Wl; 1978 Fl (R) Wl El

Crawford, J.A. 1934 Iw

Crawford, W.H. 1938 Ww Iw Ew; 1939 Wl El

Crichton-Miller, D. 1931 Wl Il Ew

Crole, G.B. 1920 Fw Ww Iw El

Cumming, R.S. 1921 Fl Ww

Cunningham, G. 1908 Wl Il; 1909 Wl Ew; 1910 Fw Iw El; 1911 El

Cunningham, R.F. 1979 Wl Ed

Currie, L.R. 1948 Fw Wl Il; 1949 Fw Ww Il El

Cuthbertson, W. 1980 Il; 1981 Ww El Iw; 1982 Ed Il Fw Ww; 1983 Il Fl Wl

Dalgleish, A. 1890 Ww El; 1891 Ww Iw; 1892 Ww; 1893 Wl; 1894 Wl Il

Dalgleish, K.J. 1951 Il El: 1953 Fl Wl

Dallas, J.D. 1903 Ew

Davidson, J.A. 1959 Ed; 1960 Iw El

Davidson, J.N.G. 1952 Fl Wl Il El; 1953 Fl Wl; 1954 Fl

Davidson, R.S. 1893 Ew

Davies, D.S. 1922 Fd Wd Iw El; 1923 Fw Ww Iw El; 1924 Fl El; 1925 Ww Iw Ew; 1926 Fw Ww Il Ew; 1927 Fw Ww Il

Dawson, J.C. 1948 Fw Wl; 1949 Fw Ww Il; 1950 Fw Wl Il Ew; 1951 Fl Ww Il El; 1952 Fl Wl Il El; 1953 El

Deans, C.T. 1978 Fl Wl El; 1979 Wl Ed Id Fl; 1980 Il Fw; 1981 Fl Ww El Iw; 1982 Ed Il Fw Ww; 1983 Il Fl Wl Ew

Deans, D.T. 1968 El

Deas, D.W. 1947 Fl Wl

Dick, L.G. 1972 Wl (R) Ew; 1974 Wl Ew Il Fw; 1975 Iw Fl Ww El; 1976 Fl; 1977 El

Dick, R.C.S. 1934 Wl Iw El; 1935 Wl Il Ew; 1936 Wl Il El; 1937 Ww; 1938 Ww Iw Ew

Dickson, G. 1979 Wl Ed Id Fl; 1980 Wl; 1981 Fl; 1982 Ww (R)

Dickson, M.R. 1905 Il

Dickson, W.M. 1912 Fw Wl Ew; 1913 Fw Wl Iw

Dobson, J. 1911 El; 1912 Fw Wl Il Ew

Dobson, J.D. 1910 Iw

Dobson, W.G. 1922 Wd Iw El

Docherty, J.T. 1955 Fl Ww; 1956 El; 1958 Fw Wl Il Ed

Dods, F.P. 1901 Iw

Dods, J.H. 1895 Ww Iw Ew; 1896 Wl Id Ew; 1897 Iw El

Gracie, A.L. 1921 Fl Ww Il El; 1922 Fd Wd Iw El; 1923 Fw Ww Iw El; 1924 Fl
Graham, I.N. 1939 Il El
Graham, J. 1926 Il Ew; 1927 Fw Ww Il Ew; 1928 Fw Wl Il El; 1930 Il Ed; 1932 Wl
Grant, D. 1965 Fl Ed; 1966 Fd Wl Iw Ew; 1967 Fw Ww Il El; 1968 Fl
Grant, D.M. 1911 Wl Il
Grant, M.L. 1955 Fl; 1956 Fw Wl; 1957 Fw
Grant, T.O. 1960 Iw El; 1964 Fw Wl
Gray, D. 1978 El; 1979 Id Fl; 1980 Il Fw Wl El; 1981 Fl
Gray, G.L. 1937 Ww Il El
Gray, T. 1950 Ew; 1951 Fl El
Greenlees, H.D. 1928 Fw Wl; 1929 Iw Ew; 1930 Ed
Greenlees, J.R.C. 1900 Id; 1902 Wl Il El; 1903 Ww Iw Ew
Greenwood, J.T. 1952 Fl; 1955 Fl Ww Iw El; 1956 Fw Wl Il El; 1957 Fw Ww El; 1958 Fw Wl Il Ed; 1959 Fl Ww Il
Greig, A. 1911 Il
Greig, L.L. 1907 Ww; 1908 Wl Il
Greig, R.C. 1893 Wl; 1897 Iw
Grieve, C.F. 1935 Wl; 1936 El
Grieve, R.M. 1935 Wl Il Ew; 1936 Wl Il El
Gunn, A.W. 1912 Fw Wl Il; 1913 Fw
Hamilton, A.S. 1914 Wl; 1920 Fw
Hannah, R.S.M. 1971 Il
Harrower, P.R. 1885 Wd
Hart, T.M. 1930 Ww Il
Harvey, L. 1899 Il
Hastie, A.J. 1961 Ww Iw El; 1964 Iw Ew; 1965 Ed; 1966 Fd Wl Iw Ew; 1967 Fw Ww Il; 1968 Fl Wl
Hastie, I.R. 1955 Fl; 1958 Fw Ed; 1959 Fl Ww Il
Hastie, J.D.H. 1938 Ww Iw Ew
Hay, B.H. 1976 Fl; 1978 Il Fl Wl El; 1979 Wl Ed Id Fl; 1980 Il Fw Wl El; 1981 Fl Ww El Iw
Hegarty, C.B. 1978 Il Fl Wl El
Hegarty, J.J. 1951 Fl; 1953 Fl Wl Il El; 1955 Fl
Henderson, B.C. 1963 El; 1964 Fw Iw Ew; 1965 Fl Wl Il Ed; 1966 Fd Wl Iw Ew
Henderson, F.W. 1900 Wl Id
Henderson, I.C. 1939 Il El; 1947 Fl Wl El; 1948 Il Ew
Henderson, J.H. 1953 Fl Wl Il El; 1954 Fl Il El Wl
Henderson, J.M. 1933 Ww Ew Iw
Henderson, J.Y.M. 1911 El
Henderson, M.M. 1937 Ww Il El
Henderson, N.F. 1892 Iw
Henderson, R.G. 1924 Iw El
Hendrie, K.G.P. 1924 Fl Sw Iw
Hendry, T.L. 1893 Wl Id Ew; 1895 Iw
Henriksen, E.H. 1953 Il
Hepburn, D.P. 1948 Fw Wl Il Ew; 1949 Fw Ww Il El
Hill, C.C.P. 1912 Fw Il
Hinshelwood, A.J.W. 1966 Fd Iwl Iw Ew; 1967 Fw Ww Il El; 1968 Fl Wl Il El; 1969 Fw Wl Il; 1970 Fl Wl
Hodgson, C.G. 1968 Il El
Hogg, C.G. 1978 Fl (R) Wl (R)
Holms, W.F. 1886 Ww Ed; 1887 Iw Ed; 1889 Ww Iw
Horsburgh, G.B. 1937 Ww Il El; 1938 Ww Iw Ew; 1939 Wl Il El

Howie, D.D. 1912 Fw Wl Il Ew; 1913 Fw Wl
Howie, R.A. 1924 Fl Ww Iw El; 1925 Ww Iw Ew
Hoyer-Miller, G.C. 1953 Il
Huggan, J.L. 1914 El
Hume, J. 1912 Fw; 1920 Fw; 1921 Fl Ww Il El; 1922 Fd
Hume, J.W.G. 1928 Il; 1930 Fl
Hunter, J.M. 1947 Fl
Hunter, M.D. 1974 Fw
Hunter, W.J. 1964 Fw Wl; 1967 Fw Ww Il El
Hutchison, W.R. 1911 El
Hutton, A.H.M. 1932 Il
Hutton, J.E. 1930 Ed; 1931 Fw
Inglis, H.M. 1951 Fl Ww Il El; 1952 Wl Il
Inglis, J.M. 1952 El
Inglis, W.M. 1937 Ww Il El; 1938 Ww Iw Ew
Innes, J.R.S. 1939 Wl Il El; 1948 Fw Wl Il Ew
Ireland, J.C.H. 1925 Ww Iw Ew; 1926 Fw Ww Il Ew; 1927 Fw Ww Il Ew
Irvine, A.R. 1973 Fl Ww Iw El; 1974 Wl Ew Il Fw; 1975 Iw Fl Ww El; 1976 Fl Wl Ew Iw; 1977 El Iw Fl Wl; 1978 Il Fl El; 1979 Wl Ed Id Fl; 1980 Il Fw Wl El; 1981 Fl Ww El Iw; 1982 Ed Il Fw Ww
Irvine, T.W. 1885 Iw; 1886 Ww Iw Ed; 1887 Iw Ww Ed; 1888 Wl Iw; 1889 Iw
Jackson, K.L.T. 1933 Ww Ew Iw; 1934 Wl
Jackson, T.G.H. 1947 Fl Wl El; 1948 Fw Wl Il Ew; 1949 Fw Ww Il El
Jackson, W.D. 1964 Iw; 1965 Ed; 1969 Fw Wl Il El
Jamieson, J. 1883 Ww Iw El; 1884 Ww Iw El; 1885 Wd Iw
Johnston, D.I. 1980 Il Fw Wl El; 1982 Ed Il Fw Ww; 1983 Il Fl Wl
Johnston, J. 1952 Fl Wl Il El
Johnston, W.C. 1922 Fd
Johnston, W.G.S. 1935 Wl Il; 1937 Ww Il El
Keith, G.J. 1968 Fl Wl
Keller, D.H. 1949 Fw Ww Il El; 1950 Fw Wl Il
Kelly, R.F. 1928 Fw Wl El
Kemp, J.W.Y. 1954 Wl; 1955 Fl Ww Iw El; 1956 Fw Wl Il El; 1957 Fw Ww Il El; 1958 Fw Wl Il Ed; 1959 Fl Ww Il Ed; 1960 Fl Wl Iw El
Kennedy, F. 1920 Fw Ww Iw El; 1921 El
Kennedy, N. 1903 Ww Iw Ew
Ker, H.T. 1887 Iw Ww Ed; 1888 Iw; 1889 Ww; 1890 Iw El
Kerr, D.S. 1923 Fw Ww; 1924 Fl; 1926 Il Ew; 1927 Ww Il Ew; 1928 Il El
Kerr, G.C. 1898 Iw Ed; 1899 Il Ww Ew; 1900 Wl Id Ed
Kerr, J.M. 1936 Il El; 1937 Ww Il
Kerr, W. 1953 El
Kidston, D.W. 1883 Ww El
Kilgour, I.J. 1921 Fl
King, J.H.F. 1953 Fl Wl El; 1954 El
Kininmonth, P.W. 1949 Fw Ww Il El; 1950 Fw Wl Il Ew; 1951 Fl Ww Il El; 1952 Fl Wl Il; 1954 Fl Il El Wl
Kinnear, R.M. 1926 Fw Ww Il
Knox, J. 1903 Ww Iw Ew
Kyle, W.E. 1902 Wl Il El; 1903 Ww Iw Ew; 1904 Wl Iw Ew; 1905 Wl Il Ew; 1906 Wl Iw El; 1908 Ew; 1909 Wl Iw Ew; 1910 Wl
Laidlaw, A.S. 1897 Iw

Laidlaw, F.A.L. 1965 Fl Wl Il Ed; 1966 Fd Wl Iw Ew; 1967 Fw Ww Il El; 1968 Fl Wl Il; 1969 Fw Wl Il El; 1970 Fl Wl Il Ew; 1971 Fl Wl Il

Laidlaw, R.J. 1980 Il Fw Wl El; 1981 Fl Ww El Iw; 1982 Ed Il Fw Ww; 1983 Il Fl Wl Ew

Laing, A.D. 1914 Wl Il El; 1920 Fw Ww Iw; 1921 Fl

Lambie, I.K. 1979 Wl Ed

Lambie, L.B. 1934 Wl Iw El; 1935 Wl Il Ew

Lamond, G.A.W. 1899 Ww Ew; 1905 Ew

Langrish, R.W. 1930 Fl; 1931 Fw Wl Il

Lauder, W. 1969 Il El; 1970 Fl Wl Il; 1973 Fl; 1974 Wl Ew Il Fw; 1975 Iw Fl; 1976 Fl 1977 El

Laughland, I.H.P. 1959 Fl; 1960 Fl Wl Iw El; 1961 Ww Iw El; 1962 Fl Ww Iw Ed; 1963 Fw Wl Iw; 1964 Fw Wl Iw Ew; 1965 Fl Wl Il Ed; 1966 Fd Wl Iw Ew; 1967 El

Lawrie, J.R. 1922 Fd Wd Iw El; 1923 Fw Ww Iw El; 1924 Ww Iw El

Lawrie, K.G. 1980 Fw (R) Wl El

Lawson, A.J.M. 1972 Fw (R) Ew; 1973 Fl; 1974 Wl Ew; 1976 Ew Iw; 1977 El; 1979 Wl Ed Id Fl; 1980 Wl (R)

Lawther, T.H.B. 1932 Wl

Ledingham, G.A. 1913 Fw

Lees, J.B. 1947 Il; 1948 Fw Wl Ew

Leggatt, H.T.O. 1891 Ww Iw Ew; 1892 Ww Iw; 1893 Wl Ew; 1894 Il Ew

Lely, W.G. 1909 Iw

Leslie, D.G. 1975 Iw Fl Ww El; 1976 Fl Wl Ew Iw; 1980 El; 1981 Ww El Iw; 1982 Ed; 1983 Il Fl Wl Ew

Liddell, E.H. 1922 Fd Wd Iw; 1923 Fw Ww Iw El

Lind, H. 1928 Il; 1931 Fw Wl Il Ew; 1932 Wl El; 1933 Ww Ew Iw; 1934 Wl Iw El; 1935 Il; 1936 El

Lindsay, A.B. 1910 Iw; 1911 Il

Lindsay, G.C. 1884 Ww; 1887 Ww Ed

Lindsay-Watson, R.H. 1909 Iw

Little, A.W. 1905 Wl

Logan, W.R. 1931 Ew; 1932 Wl Il; 1933 Ww Ew Iw; 1934 Wl Iw El; 1935 Wl Il Ew; 1936 Wl Il El; 1937 Ww Il El

Lorraine, H.D.B. 1933 Ww Ew Iw

Loudoun-Shand, E.G. 1913 El

Lowe, J.D. 1934 Wl

Lumsden, I.J.M. 1947 Fl Wl; 1949 Fw Ww Il El

Lyall, G.G. 1948 Fw Wl Il Ew

Mabon, J.T. 1898 Iw Ed; 1899 Il; 1900 Id

MacCallum, J.C. 1905 Ew; 1906 Wl Iw El; 1907 Ww Iw Ew; 1908 Wl Il Ew; 1909 Wl Iw Ew; 1910 Fw Wl Iw El; 1911 Fl Il El; 1912 Fw Wl Il Ew

Macdonald, D.C. 1953 Fl Wl; 1958 Il Ed

Macdonald, D.S.M. 1977 El Iw Fl Wl; 1978 Il Wl El

Macdonald, J.D. 1966 Fd Wl Iw Ew; 1967 Fw Ww Il El

Macdonald, J.M. 1911 Wl

Macdonald, J.S. 1903 Ew; 1904 Wl Iw Ew; 1905 Wl

Macdonald, K.R. 1956 Fw Wl Il; 1957 Ww Il El

Macdonald, R. 1950 Fw Wl Il Ew

Macdonald, W.A. 1889 Ww; 1892 Iw El

Macdonald, W.G. 1969 Il (R)

Macdougall, J.B. 1913 Fw; 1914 Il; 1921 Fl Il El

MacEwan, N.A. 1971 Fl Wl Il Ew; 1972 Fw Wl Ew; 1973 Fl Ww Iw El; 1974 Wl Ew Il Fw; 1975 Ww El

MacEwan, R.K.G. 1954 Fl Il Wl; 1956 Fw Wl Il El; 1957 Fw Ww Il El; 1958 Wl

Macfarlan, D.J. 1883 Ww; 1884 Ww Iw El; 1886 Ww Iw; 1887 Iw; 1888 Iw

MacGregor, D.G. 1907 Ww Iw Ew

MacGregor, G. 1890 Ww Iw El; 1891 Ww Iw Ew; 1893 Wl Id Ew; 1894 Wl Il Ew; 1896 Ew

MacGregor, I.A.A. 1955 Iw El; 1956 Fw Wl Il El; 1957 Fw Ww Il

MacIntyre, I. 1890 Ww Iw El; 1891 Ww Iw Ew

Mackay, E.B. 1920 Ww; 1922 El

Mackenzie, C.J.G. 1921 El

Mackenzie, D.D. 1947 Wl Il El; 1948 Fw Wl Il

Mackenzie, D.K.A. 1939 Il El

Mackenzie, J.M. 1909 Wl Iw Ew; 1910 Wl Iw El; 1911 Wl Il

Mackie, G.Y. 1976 Fl Wl; 1978 Fl

MacKinnon, A. 1898 Iw Ed; 1899 Il Ww Ew; 1900 Ed

Mackintosh, C.E.W.C. 1924 Fl

Mackintosh, H.S. 1929 Fw Wl Iw Ew; 1930 Fl Ww Il Ed; 1931 Fw Wl Il Ew; 1932 Wl Il El

MacLachlan, L.P. 1954 Il El Wl

Maclagan, W.E. 1883 Ww Iw El; 1884 Ww Iw El; 1885 Wd Iw; 1887 Iw Ww Ed; 1888 Wl Iw; 1890 Ww Iw El

MacLennan, W.D. 1947 Fl Il

Macleod, D.A. 1886 Iw Ed

MacLeod, K.G. 1906 Wl Iw El; 1907 Ww Iw Ew; 1908 Il Ew

MacLeod, L.M. 1904 Wl Iw Ew; 1905 Wl Il

Macleod, W.M. 1886 Ww Iw

Macmillan, R.G. 1887 Iw Ww Ed; 1890 Ww Iw El; 1891 Ww Ew; 1892 Ww Iw El; 1893 Wl Ew; 1894 Wl Il Ew; 1895 Ww Iw Ew; 1897 Iw El

MacMyn, D.J. 1925 Fw Ww Iw Ew; 1926 Fw Ww Il Ew; 1927 Ew; 1928 Fw

Macphail, J.A.R. 1949 El

Macpherson, D.G. 1910 Iw El

Macpherson, G.P.S. 1922 Fd Wd Iw El; 1924 Ww El; 1925 Fw Ww Ew; 1927 Fw Ww Il Ew; 1928 Fw Wl El; 1929 Iw Ew; 1930 Fl Ww Il Ed; 1931 Wl Ew; 1932 El

Macpherson, N.C. 1920 Ww Iw El; 1921 Fl El; 1923 Iw El

Macrae, D.J. 1937 Ww Il El; 1938 Ww Iw Ew; 1939 Wl Il El

Madsen, D.F. 1974 Wl Ew Il Fw; 1975 Iw Fl Ww El; 1976 Fl; 1977 El Iw Fl Wl; 1978 Il

Mair, N.G.R. 1951 Fl Ww Il El

Maitland, G. 1885 Wd Iw

Maitland, R. 1884 Ww; 1885 Wd

Malcolm, A.G. 1888 Iw

Marsh, J. 1889 Ww Iw

Marshall, J.C. 1954 Fl Il El Wl

Marshall, K.W. 1934 Wl Iw El; 1935 Wl Il Ew; 1936 Wl; 1937 El

Martin, H. 1908 Wl Il Ew; 1909 Wl Ew

Maxwell, G.H.H.P. 1913 Iw El; 1914 Wl Il El; 1920 Ww El; 1921 Fl Ww Il El; 1922 Fd El

Maxwell, J.M. 1957 Il

McArthur, J.P. 1932 El

McClung, T. 1956 Il El; 1957 Ww Il El; 1959 Fl Ww Il; 1960 Wl

McCowan, D. 1883 Iw El; 1884 Iw El

McCowat, R.H. 1905 Il

McCrae, I.G. 1967 El; 1968 Il; 1969 Fw (R) Wl; 1972 Fw

McCrow, J.W.S. 1921 Il

McEwan, M.C. 1886 Ed; 1887 Iw Ww Ed; 1888 Wl Iw; 1889 Ww Iw; 1890 Ww Iw El; 1891 Ww Iw Ew; 1892 El

McEwan, W.M.C. 1894 Wl Ew; 1895 Ww Ew; 1896 Wl Id Ew; 1897 Iw El; 1898 Iw Ed; 1899 Il Ww Ew; 1900 Wl Ed

McGeechan, I.R. 1973 Fl Ww Iw El; 1974 Wl Ew Il Fw; 1975 Iw Fl Ww El; 1976 Fl Wl Ew Iw; 1977 El Iw Fl Wl; 1978 Il Fl Wl; 1979 Wl Ed Id Fl

McGlashen, T.P.L. 1947 Fl Il El; 1954 Fl Il El Wl

McGregor, J.R. 1909 Iw

McGuinness, G.M. 1983 Il

McHarg, A.F. 1968 Il El; 1969 Fw Wl Il El; 1971 Fl Wl Il Ew; 1972 Fw Ew; 1973 Fl Ww Iw El; 1974 Wl Ew Il Fw; 1975 Iw Fl Ww El; 1976 Fl Wl Ew Iw; 1977 El Iw Fl Wl; 1978 Il Fl Wl; 1979 Wl Ed

McIndoe, F. 1886 Ww Iw

McKeating, E. 1957 Fw Ww; 1961 Ww Iw El

McKendrick, J.G. 1889 Iw

McLaren, D.A. 1931 Fw

McLaren, E. 1923 Fw Ww Iw El; 1924 Fl

McLauchlan, J. 1969 El; 1970 Fl Wl; 1971 Fl Wl Il Ew; 1972 Fw Wl Ew; 1973 Fl Ww Iw El; 1974 Wl Ew Il Fw; 1975 Iw Fl Ww El; 1976 Fl Wl Ew Iw; 1977 Wl; 1978 Il Fl Wl El; 1979 Wl Ed Id Fl

McLean, D.I. 1947 Il El

McLeod, H.F. 1954 Fl Il El Wl; 1955 Fl Ww Iw El; 1956 Fw Wl Il El; 1957 Fw Ww Il El; 1958 Fw Wl Il Ed; 1959 Fl Ww Il Ed; 1960 Fl Wl Iw El; 1961 Fl Ww Iw El; 1962 Fl Ww Iw Ed

McMillan, K.H.D. 1953 Fl Wl Il El

McNeil, A.S.B. 1935 Il

McPartlin, J.J. 1960 Fl Wl; 1962 Fl Ww Iw Ed.

McQueen, S.B. 1923 Fw Ww Iw El

Melville, C.L. 1937 Ww Il El

Menzies, H.F. 1893 Wl Id; 1894 Wl Ew

Methuen, A. 1889 Ww Iw

Michie, E.J.S. 1954 Fl Il El; 1955 Ww Iw El; 1956 Fw Wl Il El; 1957 Fw Ww Il El

Millar, J.N. 1892 Ww Iw El; 1893 Wl; 1895 Iw Ew

Millar, R.K. 1924 Iw

Millican, J.G. 1973 Ww Iw El

Milne, C.J.B. 1886 Ww Iw Ed

Milne, I.G. 1979 Id Fl; 1980 Il Fw; 1982 Ed Il Fw Ww; 1983 Il Fl Wl Ew

Milne, W.M. 1904 Iw Ew; 1905 Wl Il

Milroy, E. 1910 Wl; 1911 El; 1912 Wl Il Ew; 1913 Fw Wl Iw El; 1914 Il El

Mitchell, G.W.E. 1968 Fl Wl

Mitchell, J.G. 1885 Wd Iw

Monteith, H.G. 1905 Ew; 1906 Wl Iw El; 1907 Ww Iw; 1908 Ew

Monypenny, D.B. 1899 Il Ww Ew

Moodie, A.R. 1909 Ew; 1910 Fw; 1911 Fl

Morgan, D.W. 1973 Ww Iw El; 1974 Il Fw; 1975 Iw Fl Ww El; 1976 Fl Wl; 1977 Iw Fl Wl; 1978 Il Fl Wl El

Morrison, M.C. 1896 Wl Id Ew; 1897 Iw El; 1898 Iw Ed; 1899 Il Ww Ew; 1900 Wl Ed; 1901 Ww Iw Ew; 1902 Wl Il El; 1903 Ww Iw; 1904 Wl Iw Ew

Morrison, R.H. 1886 Ww Iw Ed

Morrison, W.H. 1900 Wl

Morton, D.S. 1887 Iw Ww Ed; 1888 Wl Iw; 1889 Ww Iw; 1890 Iw El

Mowat, J.G. 1883 Ww El

Muir, D.E. 1950 Fw Wl Il Ew; 1952 Wl Il El

Munnoch, N.M. 1952 Fl Wl Il

Munro, P. 1905 Wl Il Ew; 1906 Wl Iw El; 1907 Iw Ew; 1911 Fl Wl Il

Munro, S. 1980 Il Fw; 1981 Fl Ww El Iw

Munro, W.H. 1947 Il El

Murdoch, W.C.W. 1935 Ew; 1936 Wl Il; 1939 El; 1948 Fw Wl Il Ew

Murray, G.M. 1921 Il; 1926 Ww

Murray, H.M. 1936 Wl Il

Murray, R.O. 1935 Wl Ew

Murray, W.A.K. 1920 Fw Iw; 1921 Fl

Neill, J.B. 1963 El; 1964 Fw Wl Iw Ew; 1965 Fl

Neill, R.M. 1901 Ew; 1902 Il

Neilson, G.T. 1891 Ww Iw Ew; 1892 Ww El; 1893 Wl; 1894 Wl Il; 1895 Ww Iw Ew; 1896 Wl Id Ew

Neilson, R.T. 1898 Iw Ed; 1899 Il Ww; 1900 Id Ed

Neilson, W. 1891 Ww Ew; 1892 Ww Iw El; 1893 Id Ew; 1894 Ew; 1895 Ww Iw Ew; 1896 Id; 1897 Iw El

Neilson, W.G. 1894 Ew

Nelson, J.B. 1925 Fw Ww Iw Ew; 1926 Fw Ww Il Ew; 1927 Fw Ww Il Ew; 1928 Il El; 1929 Fw Wl Iw Ew; 1930 Fl Ww Il Ed; 1931 Fw Wl Il

Nelson, T.A. 1898 Ed

Nichol, J.A. 1955 Ww Iw El

Nimmo, C.S. 1920 El

Ogilvy, C. 1911 Il El; 1912 Il

Orr, C.E. 1887 Iw Ww Ed; 1888 Wl Iw; 1889 Ww Iw; 1890 Ww Iw El; 1891 Ww Iw Ew; 1892 Ww Iw El

Orr, H.J. 1903 Ww Iw Ew; 1904 Wl Iw

Orr, J.E. 1889 Iw; 1890 Ww Iw El; 1891 Ww Iw Ew; 1892 Ww Iw El; 1893 Id Ew

Orr, J.H. 1947 Fl Wl

Osler, F.L. 1911 Fl Wl

Park, J. 1934 Wl

Paterson, D.S. 1970 Il Ew; 1971 Fl Wl Il Ew; 1972 Wl

Paterson, J.R. 1925 Fw Ww Iw Ew; 1926 Fw Ww Il Ew; 1927 Fw Ww Il Ew; 1928 Fw Wl Il El; 1929 Fw Wl Iw Ew

Patterson, D. 1896 Ww

Pattullo, G.L. 1920 Fw Ww Iw El

Paxton, I.A.M. 1982 Ed Il Fw Ww; 1983 Il Ew

Paxton, R.E. 1982 Il

Pearson, J. 1909 Iw Ew; 1910 Fw Wl Iw El; 1911 Fl; 1912 Fw Wl; 1913 Iw El

Pender, I.M. 1914 El

Pender, N.E.K. 1977 Iw; 1978 Fl Wl El

Penman, W.M. 1939 Il

Peterkin, W.A. 1883 Iw; 1884 Ww Iw El; 1885 Wd Iw

Pollock, J.A. 1982 Ww; 1983 Ew

Polson, A.H. 1930 Ed

Purdie, W. 1939 Wl Il El

Purves, A.B.H.L. 1906 Wl Iw El; 1907 Ww Iw Ew; 1908 Wl Il Ew

Purves, W.D.C.L. 1912 Fw Wl Il; 1913 Iw El

Rea, C.W.W. 1969 Fw Wl Il; 1970 Fl Wl Il; 1971 Fl Wl Ew

Reid, C. 1883 Ww Iw El; 1884 Ww Iw El; 1885 Wd Iw; 1886 Ww Iw Ed; 1887 Iw Ww Ed; 1888 Wl Iw

Reid, J.M. 1898 Iw Ed; 1899 Il

Reid, M.F. 1883 Iw El

Reid-Kerr, J. 1909 Ew

Relph, W.K.L. 1955 Fl Ww Iw El

Renwick, J.M. 1972 Fw Wl Ew; 1973 Fl; 1974 Wl Ew Il Fw; 1975 Iw Fl Ww El; 1976 Fl Wl Ew (R); 1977 Iw Fl Wl; 1978 Il Fl Wl El; 1979 Wl Ed Id Fl; 1980 Il Fw Wl El; 1981 Fl Ww El Iw; 1982 Ed Il Fw Ww; 1983 Il Fl Wl Ew.

Renwick, W.N. 1938 Ew; 1939 Wl

Ritchie, G.F. 1932 El

Ritchie, J.M. 1933 Ww Ew Iw; 1934 Wl Iw El

Ritchie, W.T. 1905 Il Ew

Robb, G.H. 1885 Wd

Roberts, G. 1938 Ww Iw Ew; 1939 Wl El

Robertson, A.W. 1897 El

Robertson, D.D. 1893 Wl

Robertson, I. 1968 El; 1969 El; 1970 Fl Wl Il Ew

Robertson, I.P.M. 1910 Fw

Robertson, J. 1908 Ew

Robertson, K.W. 1979 Wl Ed Id Fl; 1980 Wl El; 1981 Fl Ww El Iw; 1982 Ed Il Fw; 1983 Il Fl Wl Ew

Robertson, L. 1908 Ew; 1911 Wl; 1912 Wl Il Ew; 1913 Wl Iw El

Robertson, M.A. 1958 Fw

Robertson, R.D. 1912 Fw

Robson, A. 1954 Fl; 1955 Fl Ww Iw El; 1956 Fw Wl Il El; 1957 Fw Ww Il El; 1958 Wl Il Ed; 1959 Fl Ww Il Ed; 1960 Fl

Rodd, J.A.T. 1958 Fw Wl Il Ed; 1960 Fl Wl; 1962 Fl; 1964 Fw Wl; 1965 Fl Wl Il

Rogerson, J. 1894 Wl

Roland, E.T. 1884 Iw El

Rollo, D.M.D. 1959 Ed; 1960 Fl Wl Iw El; 1961 Fl Ww Iw El; 1962 Fl Ww Ed; 1963 Fw Wl Iw El; 1964 Fw Wl Iw Ew; 1965 Fl Wl Il Ed; 1966 Fd Wl Iw Ew; 1967 Fw Ww El; 1968 Fl Wl Il

Rose, D.M. 1951 Fl Ww Il El; 1953 Fl Wl

Ross, A. 1924 Fl Ww

Ross, A. 1905 Wl Il Ew; 1909 Wl Iw

Ross, A.R. 1911 Wl; 1914 Wl Il El

Ross, E.J. 1904 Wl

Ross, G.T. 1954 Il El Wl

Ross, I.A. 1951 Fl Ww Il El

Ross, J. 1901 Ww Iw Ew; 1902 Wl; 1903 Ew

Ross, K.I. 1961 Ww Iw El; 1962 Fl Ww Iw Ed; 1963 Fw Wl El

Ross, W.A. 1937 Ww El

Rottenburg, H. 1899 Ww Ew; 1900 Wl Id Ed

Roughead, W.N. 1928 Fw Wl Il El; 1930 Il Ed; 1931 Fw Wl Il Ew; 1932 Wl

Rowan, N.A. 1980 Wl El; 1981 Fl Ww El Iw

Rowand, R. 1930 Fl Ww; 1932 El; 1933 Ww Ew Iw; 1934 Wl

Roy, A. 1938 Ww Iw Ew; 1939 Wl Il El

Russell, W.L. 1906 Wl Iw El

Rutherford, J.Y. 1979 Wl Ed Id Fl; 1980 Il Fw El; 1981 Fl Ww El Iw; 1982 Ed Il Fw Ww; 1983 Ew

Sampson, R.W.F. 1939 Wl; 1947 Wl

Sanderson, G.A. 1907 Ww Iw Ew; 1908 Il

Schulze, D.G. 1905 Ew; 1907 Iw Ew; 1908 Wl Il Ew; 1909 Wl Iw Ew; 1910 Wl Iw El; 1911 Wl

Scobie, R.M. 1914 Wl Il El

Scotland, K.J.F. 1957 Fw Ww Il El; 1958 Ed; 1959 Fl Ww Il Ed; 1960 Fl Wl Iw El; 1961 Fl Ww Iw El; 1962 Fl Ww Iw Ed; 1963 Fw Wl Iw El; 1965 Fl

Scott, D.M. 1950 Il Ew; 1951 Ww Il El; 1952 Fl Wl Il; 1953 Fl

Scott, J.M.B. 1907 Ew; 1908 Wl Il Ew; 1909 Wl Iw Ew; 1910 Fw Wl Iw El; 1911 Fl Wl Il; 1912 Wl Il Ew; 1913 Wl Iw El

Scott, J.S. 1950 Ew

Scott, J.W. 1925 Fw Ww Iw Ew; 1926 Fw Ww Il Ew; 1927; Fw Ww Il Ew; 1928 Fw Wl El; 1929 Ew; 1930 Fl

Scott, R. 1898 Iw; 1900 Id Ed

Scott, T. 1896 Wl; 1897 Iw El; 1898 Iw Ed; 1899 Il Ww Ew; 1900 Wl Id Ed

Scott, T.M. 1893 Ew; 1895 Ww Iw Ew; 1896 Wl Ew; 1897 Iw El; 1898 Iw Ed; 1900 Wl Id

Scott, W.P. 1900 Id Ed; 1902 Il El; 1903 Ww Iw Ew; 1904 Wl Iw Ew; 1905 Wl Il Ew; 1906 Wl Iw El; 1907 Ww Iw Ew

Scoular, J.G. 1906 Wl Iw El

Selby, J.A.R. 1920 Ww Iw

Shackleton, J.A.P. 1959 Ed; 1963 Fw Wl; 1964 Wl; 1965 Il

Sharp, G. 1960 Fl; 1964 Fw Wl

Shaw, G.D. 1936 Wl; 1937 Ww Il El; 1939 Il

Shaw, I. 1937 Il

Shaw, J.N. 1921 Ww Il

Shaw, R.W. 1934 Wl Iw El; 1935 Wl Il Ew; 1936 Wl Il El; 1937 Ww Il El; 1938 Ww Iw Ew; 1939 Wl Il El

Shedden, D. 1973 Fl Ww Iw El; 1976 Wl Ew Iw; 1977 Iw Fl Wl; 1978 Il Fl Wl

Shillinglaw, R.B. 1960 Iw El; 1961 Fl

Simmers, B.M. 1965 Fl Wl; 1967 Fw Ww Il; 1971 Fl (R)

Simmers, W.M. 1926 Ww Il Ew; 1927 Fw Ww Il Ew; 1928 Fw Wl Il El; 1929 Fw Wl Iw Ew; 1930 Fl Ww Il Ed; 1931 Fw Wl Il Ew; 1932 Wl Il El

Simpson, J.W. 1893 Id Ew; 1894 Wl Il Ew; 1895 Ww Iw Ew; 1896 Wl Id; 1897 El; 1899 Ww Ew

Simpson, R.S. 1923 Iw

Simson, E.D. 1902 El; 1903 Ww Iw Ew; 1904 Wl Iw Ew; 1905 Wl Il Ew; 1906 Wl Iw El; 1907 Ww Iw Ew

Simson, J.T. 1909 Wl Iw Ew; 1910 Fw Wl; 1911 Il

Simson, R.F. 1911 El

Sloan, A.T. 1914 Wl; 1920 Fw Ww Iw El; 1921 Fl Ww Il El

Sloan, D.A. 1950 Fw Wl Ew; 1951 Ww Il El; 1953 Fl

Sloan, T. 1906 Wl; 1907 Ww Ew; 1908 Wl; 1909 Iw

Smeaton, P.W. 1883 Iw El

Smith, A.R. 1895 Ww Iw Ew; 1896 Wl Id; 1897 Iw El; 1898 Iw Ed; 1900 Id Ed

Smith, A.R. 1955 Ww Iw El; 1956 Fw Wl Il El; 1957 Fw Ww Il El; 1958 Fw Wl Il; 1959 Fl Ww Il Ed; 1960 Fl Wl Iw El; 1961 Fl Ww Iw El; 1962 Fl Ww Iw Ed

Smith, D.W.C. 1949 Fw Ww Il El; 1950 Fw Wl Il; 1953 Il

Smith, G.K. 1957 Il El; 1958 Fw Wl; 1959 Fl Ww Il Ed; 1960 Fl Wl Iw El; 1961 Fl Ww Iw El

Smith, H.O. 1895 Ww; 1896 Wl Id Ew; 1898 Iw Ed; 1899 Il Ww Ew; 1900 Ed; 1902 El

Smith, I.S. 1924 Ww Iw El; 1925 Fw Ww Iw Ew; 1926 Fw Ww Il Ew; 1927 Fw Il Ew; 1929 Fw Wl Iw Ew; 1930 Fl Ww Il; 1931 Fw Wl Il Ew; 1932 Wl Il El; 1933 Ww Ew Iw

Smith, I.S.G. 1970 Fl Wl Il Ew; 1971 Fl Wl Il

Smith, M.A. 1970 Wl Il Ew

Smith, R.T. 1929 Fw Wl Iw Ew; 1930 Fl Ww Il

Smith, T.J. 1983 Ew

Somerville, D. 1883 Ww Iw El; 1884 Ww

Spence, K.M. 1953 Il

Spencer, E. 1898 Iw

Spiers, L.M. 1907 Ww Iw Ew; 1908 Wl Il Ew; 1910 Fw Wl El

Stagg, P.K. 1965 Fl Wl Ed; 1966 Fd Wl Iw Ew; 1967 Fw Ww Il El; 1968 Fl Wl Il El; 1969 Fw Wl Il (R); 1970 Fl Wl Il Ew

Steele, W.C.C. 1969 El; 1971 Fl Wl Il Ew; 1972 Fw Wl Ew; 1973 Fl Ww Iw El; 1975 Iw Fl Ww El; 1976 Wl Ew Iw; 1977 El

Stephen, A.E. 1885 Wd; 1886 Iw

Steven, R. 1962 Iw

Stevenson, A.K. 1922 Fd; 1923 Fw Ww El

Stevenson, A.M. 1911 Fl

Stevenson, G.D. 1956 El; 1957 Fw; 1958 Fw Wl Il Ed; 1959 Ww Il Ed; 1960 Wl Iw El; 1961 Fl Ww Iw El, 1963 Fw Wl Iw; 1964 Ew 1965 Fl

Stevenson, H.J. 1888 Wl Iw; 1889 Ww Iw; 1890 Ww Iw El; 1891 Ww Iw Ew; 1892 Ww Iw El; 1893 Id Ew

Stevenson, L.E. 1888 Wl

Stevenson, R.C. 1910 Fw Iw El; 1911 Fl Wl Il

Stevenson, R.C. 1897 Iw El; 1898 Ed; 1899 Il Ww Ew

Stevenson, W.H. 1925 Fw

Stewart, A.M. 1914 Wl

Stewart, C.E.B. 1960 Wl; 1961 Fl

Stewart, J. 1930 Fl

Stewart, J.L. 1921 Il

Stewart, M.S. 1932 Wl Il; 1933 Ww Ew Iw; 1934 Wl Iw El

Stewart, W.A. 1913 Fw Wl Iw; 1914 Wl

Steyn, S.S.L. 1911 El; 1912 Il

Strachan, G.M. 1973 Ww Iw El

Stronach, R.S. 1901 Ww Ew; 1905 Wl Il Ew

Stuart, C.D. 1909 Iw; 1910 Fw Wl Iw El; 1911 Il El

Stuart, L.M. 1923 Fw Ww Iw El; 1924 Fl; 1928 El; 1930 Il Ed

Suddon, N. 1965 Wl Il Ed; 1968 El; 1969 Fw Wl Il; 1970 Il Ew

Sutherland, W.R. 1910 Wl El; 1911 Fl El; 1912 Fw Wl Ew; 1913 Fw Wl Iw El; 1914 Wl

Swan, J.S. 1953 El; 1954 Fl Il El Wl; 1955 Fl Ww Iw El; 1956 Fw Wl Il El; 1957 Fw Ww; 1958 Fw

Swan, M.W. 1958 Fw Wl Il Ed; 1959 Fl Ww Il

Sweet, J.B. 1913 El; 1914 Il

Symington, A.W. 1914 Wl El

Tait, J.G. 1885 Iw

Tait, P.W. 1935 Ew

Taylor, E.G. 1927 Ww

Taylor, R.C. 1951 Ww Il El

Telfer, C.M. 1969 Fw Wl Il El; 1972 Fw Wl Ew; 1973 Ww Iw El; 1974 Wl Ew Il; 1976 Fl

Telfer, J.W. 1964 Fw Wl Iw Ew; 1965 Fl Wl Il; 1966 Fd Wl Iw Ew; 1967 Ww Il El; 1968 El; 1969 Fw Wl Il El; 1970 Fl Wl Il

ten Bos, F.H. 1959 Ed; 1960 Fl Wl; 1961 Fl Ww Iw El; 1962 Fl Ww Iw Ed; 1963 Fw Wl Iw El

Tennent, J.M. 1909 Wl Iw Ew; 1910 Fw Wl El

Thom, D.A. 1934 Wl; 1935 Wl Il Ew

Thom, G. 1920 Fw Ww Iw El

Thom, J.R. 1933 Ww Ew Iw

Thomson, A.E. 1921 Fl Ww El

Thomson, A.M. 1949 Il

Thomson, B.E. 1953 Fl Wl Il

Thomson, I.H.M. 1951 Ww Il; 1952 Fl Wl Il; 1953 Il El

Thomson, R.H. 1960 Iw El; 1961 Fl Ww Iw El; 1963 Fw Wl Iw El; 1964 Fw Wl

Thomson, W.J. 1899 Ww Ew; 1900 Wl

Timms, A.B. 1896 Wl; 1900 Wl Id; 1901 Ww Iw Ew; 1902 Wl El; 1903 Ww Ew; 1904 Iw Ew; 1905 Il Ew

Tod, H.B. 1911 Fl

Tod, J. 1884 Ww Iw El; 1885 Wd Iw; 1886 Ww Iw Ed

Tolmie, J.M. 1922 El

Tomes, A.J. 1976 Ew lw; 1977 El; 1978 Il Fl Wl El; 1979 Wl Ed Id Fl; 1980 Fw Wl El; 1981 Fl Ww El Iw; 1982 Ed Il Fw Ww; 1983 Il Fl Wl

Turk, A.S. 1971 Ew

Turnbull, F.O. 1951 Fl

Turnbull, G.O. 1896 Id Ew; 1897 Iw El; 1904 Wl

Turnbull, P. 1901 Ww Iw Ew; 1902 Wl Il El

Turner, F.H. 1911 Fl Wl Il El; 1912 Fw Wl Il Ew; 1913 Fw Wl Iw El; 1914 Il El

Turner, J.W.C. 1966 Wl; 1967 Fw Ww Il El; 1968 Fl Wl Il El; 1969 Fw; 1970 Ew; 1971 Fl Wl Il Ew

Usher, C.M. 1912 Ew; 1913 Fw Wl Iw El; 1914 El; 1920 Fw Ww Iw El; 1921 Ww El; 1922 Fd Wd Iw El

Valentine, A.R. 1953 Fl Wl Il

Valentine, D.D. 1947 Il El

Veitch, J.P. 1883 Iw; 1884 Ww Iw El; 1885 Iw; 1886 Ed

Waddell, G.H. 1957 El; 1958 Fw Wl Il Ed; 1959 Fl Ww Il Ed; 1960 Iw El; 1961 Fl; 1962 Fl Ww Iw Ed

Waddell, H. 1924 Fl Ww Iw El; 1925 Iw Ew; 1926 Fw Ww Il Ew; 1927 Fw Ww Il Ew; 1930 Ww

Wade, A.L. 1908 Ew

Walker, A. 1883 Ww Iw El

Walker, A.W. 1931 Fw Wl Il Ew; 1932 Il

Walker, J.G. 1883 Ww

Walker, M. 1952 Fl

Wallace, A.C. 1923 Fw; 1924 Fl Ww El; 1925 Fw Ww Iw Ew; 1926 Fw

Wallace, W.M. 1913 El; 1914 Wl Il El

Walls, W.A. 1883 Ww Iw El; 1884 Ww Iw El; 1886 Ww Iw Ed

Walter, M.W. 1906 Iw El; 1907 Ww Iw; 1908 Wl Il; 1910 Iw

Warren, J.R. 1914 Il

Warren, R.C. 1922 Wd Iw; 1930 Ww Il Ed

Waters, F.H. 1930 Fl Ww Il Ed; 1932 Wl Il

Waters, J.A. 1933 Ww Ew Iw; 1934 Wl Iw El; 1935 Wl Il Ew; 1936 Wl Il El; 1937 Ww Il El

Waters, J.B. 1904 Iw Ew

Watherston, J.G. 1934 Iw El

Watherston, W.R.A. 1963 Fw Wl Iw

Watson, W.S. 1974 Wl Ew Il Fw; 1977 Iw Fl Wl; 1979 Id Fl

Watt, A.G.M. 1947 Fl Wl Il; 1948 Fw Wl
Weatherstone, T.G. 1952 El; 1953 Il El; 1954 Fl Il El Wl; 1955 Fl; 1958 Wl Il Ed; 1959 Ww Il Ed
Welsh, R. 1895 Ww Iw Ew; 1896 Wl
Welsh, R.B. 1967 Il El
Welsh, W.B. 1928 Fw Wl Il; 1929 Iw Ew; 1930 Fl Ww Il Ed; 1931 Fw Wl Il Ew; 1932 Wl Il El; 1933 Ww Ew Iw
Welsh, W.H. 1900 Id Ed; 1901 Ww Iw Ew; 1902 Wl Il El
Wemyss, A. 1914 Wl Il; 1920 Fw El; 1922 Fd Wd Iw
West, L. 1903 Ww Iw Ew; 1905 Il Ew; 1906 Wl Iw El
Weston, V.G. 1936 Il El
White, D.B. 1982 Fw Ww
White, D.M. 1963 Fw Wl Iw El
White, T.B. 1888 Wl Iw; 1889 Ww
Whitworth, R.J.E. 1936 Il
Whyte, D.J. 1965 Wl Il Ed; 1966 Fd Wl Iw Ew; 1967 Fw Ww Il El
Will, J.G. 1912 Fw Wl Il Ew; 1914 Wl Il El
Wilson, A.W. 1931 Fw Il Ew
Wilson, G.A. 1949 Fw Ww El
Wilson, G.R. 1886 Ed; 1890 Ww Iw El; 1891 Iw

Wilson, J.H. 1953 Il
Wilson, J.S. 1908 Il; 1909 Wl
Wilson, J.S. 1931 Fw Wl Il Ew; 1932 El
Wilson, R. 1976 Ew Iw; 1977 El Iw Fl; 1978 Il Fl; 1983 Il
Wilson, R.L. 1951 Fl Ww Il El; 1953 Fl Wl El
Wilson, S. 1964 Fw Wl Iw Ew; 1965 Wl Il Ed; 1966 Fd Wl Iw; 1967 Fw Ww Il El; 1968 Fl Wl Il El
Wood, G. 1931 Wl Il; 1932 Wl Il El
Woodburn, J.C. 1892 Iw
Woodrow, A.N. 1887 Iw Ww Ed
Wotherspoon, W. 1891 Iw: 1892 Iw; 1893 Wl Ew; 1894 Wl Il Ew
Wright, F.A. 1932 El
Wright, H.B. 1894 Wl
Wright, K.M. 1929 Fw Wl Iw Ew
Wright, R.W.J. 1973 Fl
Wright, S.T.H. 1949 El
Young, E.T. 1914 El
Young, R.G. 1970 Wl
Young, T.E.B. 1911 Fl
Young, W.B. 1937 Ww Il El; 1938 Ww Iw Ew; 1939 Wl Il El; 1948 Ew

WALES PLAYERS

Ackerman, R.A. 1981 Ew Sl; 1982 Il Fw El Sl; 1983 Sw Iw Fl
Alexander, E.P. 1885 Sd; 1886 El Sl; 1887 Ed Iw
Alexander, W.H. 1898 Iw El; 1899 Ew Sl Il; 1901 Sl Iw
Allen, C.P. 1884 El Sl
Andrews, F. 1913 El Sw Iw
Andrews, F.G. 1884 El Sl
Andrews, G.E. 1926 Ed Sl; 1927 El Fw Il
Anthony, L. 1948 Ed Sw Fl
Arnold, W. 1903 Sl
Arthur, C.S. 1888 Il; 1891 El
Arthur, T. 1927 Sl Fw Il; 1929 El Sw Fw Id; 1930 El Sl Iw Fw; 1931 Ed Sw Fw Iw; 1933 Ew Sl
Ashton, C. 1959 Ew Sl Iw; 1960 El Sw Iw; 1962 Id
Attewell, L. 1921 El Sl Fw
Badger, O. 1895 El Sl Iw; 1896 El
Baker Jones, P. 1921 Sl
Baker Jones, T. 1882 El; 1883 Sl; 1884 Sl; 1885 El Sd
Baker, A. 1921 Iw; 1923 El Sl Fw Il
Baker, A.M. 1909 Sw; 1910 Sw
Bancroft, J. 1909 Ew Sw Iw; 1910 Fw El Sw Iw; 1911 Ew Fw Iw; 1912 El Sw Il; 1913 Iw; 1914 El Sw Fw
Bancroft, W.J. 1890 Sl Ew Id; 1891 El Sl Iw; 1892 El Sl Il; 1893 Ew Sw Iw; 1894 El Sw Il; 1895 El Sl Iw; 1896 El Sw Il; 1897 Ew; 1898 Iw El; 1899 Ew Sl Il; 1900 Ew Sw Iw; 1901 Ew Sl Iw
Barlow, T. M. 1884 Iw
Barrell, R. 1929 Sw Fw Id; 1933 Il
Bartlett, J.D. 1927 Sl; 1928 El Sw
Bassett, A. 1934 Iw; 1935 Ed Sw Il; 1938 Ew Sl
Bassett, J. 1929 El Sw Fw Id; 1930 El Sl Iw; 1931 Ed Sw Fw Iw; 1932 Ew Sw Il
Bayliss, G. 1933 Sl
Bebb, D.I.E. 1959 Ew Sl Iw Fl; 1960 El Sw Iw Fl;

1961 Ew Sl Iw Fl; 1962 Ed Sl Fw Id; 1963 El Fl; 1964 Ed Sw Fd; 1965 Ew Sw Iw Fl; 1966 Fw; 1967 Sl Il Fl Ew
Beckingham, G. 1953 El Sw; 1958 Fl
Bennett, I. 1937 Il
Bennett, P. 1969 Fd (R); 1970 Sw Fw; 1972 Sw (R); 1973 Ew Sl Iw Fl; 1974 Sw Id Fd El; 1975 Sl (R) Iw; 1976 Ew Sw Iw Fw; 1977 Iw Fl Ew Sw; 1978 Ew Sw Iw Fw
Bennett, P. 1891 El Sl; 1892 Sl Il
Bergiers, R.T.E. 1972 Ew Sw Fw; 1973 Ew Sl Iw Fl; 1974 El; 1975 Iw
Bevan, G.W. 1947 El
Bevan, J.C. 1971 Ew Sw Iw Fw; 1972 Ew Sw Fw; 1973 Ew Sl
Bevan, J.D. 1975 Fw Ew Sl
Bevan, S. 1904 Il
Beynon, B. 1920 Ew Sl
Beynon, E. 1925 Fw Il
Biggs, N. 1889 Il; 1892 Il; 1893 Ew Sw Iw; 1894 El Il
Biggs, S. 1895 El Sl; 1896 Sw; 1897 Ew; 1898 Iw El; 1899 Sl Il; 1900 Iw
Birch, J. 1911 Sw Fw
Birt, F.W. 1911 Ew Sw; 1912 El Sw Il; 1913 El
Bishop, E.H. 1889 Sl
Blackmore, J. 1909 Ew
Blake, J. 1899 Ew Sl Il; 1900 Ew Sw Iw; 1901 Ew Sl Iw
Blakemore, R.E. 1947 El
Bland, A.F. 1887 Ed Sl Iw; 1888 Sw Il; 1890 Sl Ew Id
Blyth, L. 1952 Ew Sw
Blyth, W.R. 1974 El; 1975 Sl (R); 1980 Fw El Sw Il
Boon, R.W. 1930 Sl Fw; 1931 Ed Sw Fw Iw; 1932 Ew Sw Il; 1933 Ew Il
Booth, J. 1898 Iw

Boots, G. 1898 Iw El; 1899 Il; 1900 Ew Sw Iw; 1901 Ew Sl Iw; 1902 Ew Sw Iw; 1903 Ew Sl Iw; 1904 Ed

Boucher, A.W. 1892 El Sl Il; 1893 Ew Sw Iw; 1894 El; 1895 El Sl Iw; 1896 El Il; 1897 Ew

Bowcott, H.M. 1929 Sw Fw Id; 1930 El; 1931 Ed Sw; 1933 Ew Il

Bowdler, F.A. 1928 El Sw Il Fl; 1929 El Sw Fw Id; 1930 El; 1932 Ew Sw Il; 1933 Il

Bowen, C. 1896 El Sw Il; 1897 Ew

Bowen, D.H. 1882 El; 1886 El Sl; 1887 Ed

Bowen, G.E. 1887 Sl Iw; 1888 Sw Il

Bowen, W. 1886 El Sl; 1887 Ed Sl Iw; 1889 Sl Il; 1890 Sl Ew Id; 1891 El Sl

Bowen, W. 1921 Sl Fw; 1922 Ew Sd Iw Fw

Brace, D.O. 1956 Ew Sw Il Fw; 1957 El; 1960 Sw Iw Fl; 1961 Iw

Braddock, K.J. 1967 Sl Il

Bradshaw, K. 1964 Ed Sw Iw Fd; 1966 Ew Sw Il Fw

Brewer, T.J. 1950 Ew; 1955 Ew Sl

Brice, A. 1899 Ew Sl Il; 1900 Ew Sw Iw; 1901 Ew Sl Iw; 1902 Ew Sw Iw; 1903 Ew Sl Iw; 1904 Ed Sw Il

Britton, G.R. 1961 Sl

Broderick, W.R.B. 1884 Iw

Broughton, A.E. 1929 Sw

Brown, A. 1921 Iw

Brown, J. 1925 Il

Brown J. 1907 Ew Sl Iw; 1908 Ew Sw; 1909 Ew

Burcher, D.H. 1977 Iw Fl Ew Sw

Burgess, R.C. 1977 Iw Fl Ew Sw; 1981 Iw Fl; 1982 Fw El Sl

Burnett, R. 1953 El

Burns, J. 1927 Fw Il

Bush, P.F. 1906 Ew; 1907 Iw; 1908 Ew Sw; 1910 Sw Iw

Butler, E.T. 1980 Fw El Sw Il; 1982 Sl; 1983 Ed Sw Iw Fl

Cale, W.R. 1949 Ew Sl Il; 1950 Ew Sw Iw Fw

Cattell, A. 1882 El; 1883 Sl

Challinor, C. 1939 El

Clapp, T.J.S. 1882 El; 1883 Sl; 1884 El Sl Iw; 1885 El Sd; 1886 Sl; 1887 Ed Sl Iw; 1888 Sw Il

Clare, J. 1882 El

Clark, S.S. 1887 Iw

Cleaver, W.B. 1947 El Sw Fw Iw; 1948 Ed Sw Fl Il; 1949 Il; 1950 Ew Sw Iw Fw

Clegg, B.G. 1979 Fl

Clement, W.H. 1937 El Sl Il; 1938 Ew Sl Iw

Cobner, T.J. 1974 Sw Id Fd El; 1975 Fw Ew Sl Iw; 1976 Ew Sw; 1977 Fl Ew Sw; 1978 Ew Sw Iw Fw

Coldrick, A.P. 1911 Ew Sw Iw; 1912 El Sw Fw

Coleman, E. 1949 Ew Sl Il

Coles, F.C. 1960 Sw Iw Fl

Collins, J.R. 1958 Ed Sw Fl; 1959 Ew Sl Iw Fl; 1960 El; 1961 Fl

Collins, T. 1923 Il

Conway-Rees, J. 1892 Sl; 1893 Ew; 1894 El

Cook, T. 1949 Sl Il

Cope, W. 1896 Sw

Cornish, F.H. 1897 Ew; 1898 Iw El; 1899 Il

Cornish, R.A. 1923 El Sl; 1924 El; 1925 El Sl Fw; 1926 Ed Sl Iw Fw

Coslett, K. 1962 Ed Sl Fw

Cowey, B.T.V. 1934 El Sw Iw; 1935 Ed

Cresswell, B. 1960 El Sw Iw Fl

Cummins, W. 1922 Ew Sd Iw Fw

Cunningham, L.J. 1960 El Sw Iw Fl; 1962 Ed Sl Fw Id; 1964 Ed Sw Iw Fd

Dacey, M. 1983 Ed Sw Iw Fl

Daniel, D.J. 1891 Sl; 1894 El Sw Il; 1898 Iw El; 1899 Ew Il

Daniel, L.T.D. 1970 Sw

Daniels, P.C.T. 1982 Il

Dauncey, F.H. 1896 El Sw Il

Davey, E.C. 1930 Fw; 1931 Ed Sw Fw Iw; 1932 Ew Sw Il; 1933 Ew Sl; 1934 El Sw Iw; 1935 Ed Sw Il; 1936 Sw; 1937 El Il; 1938 Ew Iw

David, R.J. 1907 Iw

David, T.P. 1973 Fl; 1976 Iw Fw

Davidge, G.D. 1959 Fl; 1960 Sw Iw Fl; 1961 Ew Sl Iw; 1962 Fw

Davies, A.C. 1889 Il

Davies, B. 1895 El; 1896 El

Davies, C. 1947 Sw Fw Iw; 1948 Ed Sw Fl Il; 1949 Fl; 1950 Ew Sw Iw Fw; 1951 Ew Sl Id

Davies, C.H.A. 1957 Iw; 1958 Ed Sw Iw; 1961 Ew

Davies, C.L. 1956 Ew Sw Il

Davies, C.R. 1934 El

Davies, D. 1921 Iw; 1925 Il

Davies, D.B. 1907 Ew

Davies, D.B. 1962 Id; 1963 El Sw

Davies, D.G. 1923 El Sl

Davies, D.H. 1904 Sw

Davies, D.H. 1924 El

Davies, D.I. 1939 El

Davies, D.J. 1962 Id

Davies, D.M. 1950 Ew Sw Iw Fw; 1951 Ew Sl Id Fl; 1952 Ew Sw Iw Fw; 1953 Iw Fw; 1954 El

Davies, E. 1948 Il

Davies, E.G. 1912 El Fw

Davies, G. 1947 Sw; 1948 Ed Sw Fl Il; 1949 Ew Sl Fl; 1951 Ew Sl

Davies, G. 1928 Fl; 1929 El; 1930 Sl

Davies, G. 1921 Fw Iw; 1925 Fw

Davies, G. 1900 Ew Sw Iw; 1901 Ew Sl Iw; 1905 Ew Sw Iw

Davies, H. 1912 El Sw

Davies, H. 1898 Iw El; 1901 Sl Iw

Davies, H. 1939 Sw Iw; 1947 El Sw Fw Iw

Davies, H.J. 1924 Sl

Davies, H.J. 1959 Ew Sl

Davies, I.T. 1914 Sw Fw Iw

Davies, Revd J.A. 1913 Sw Fw Iw; 1914 El Sw Fw Iw

Davies, J.H. 1923 Il

Davies, L. 1939 Sw Iw

Davies, L. 1954 Fw Sw; 1955 Iw

Davies, L. 1966 Ew Sw Il

Davies, M. 1982 Il

Davies, M.J. 1939 Sw Iw

Davies, N.G. 1955 Ew

Davies, R.H. 1957 Sl Iw Fw; 1962 Ed Sl

Davies, S. 1923 Il

Davies, T.G.R. 1967 Sl Il Fl Ew; 1968 Ed Sw; 1969 Sw Iw Fd; 1971 Ew Sw Iw Fw; 1972 Ew Sw Fw; 1973 Ew Sl Iw Fl; 1974 Sw Fd El; 1975 Fw Ew Sl Iw; 1976 Ew Sw Iw Fw; 1977 Iw Fl Ew Sw; 1978 Ew Sw Iw

Davies, T.J. 1953 El Sw Iw Fw; 1957 El Sl Iw Fw; 1958 Ed Sw Fl; 1959 Ew Sl Iw Fl; 1960 El; 1961 Ew Sl Fl

Gray, A.J. 1968 Ed Sw
Greenslade, D. 1962 Sl
Griffin, Dr A. 1883 Sl
Griffiths, C. 1979 Ew (R)
Griffiths, D. 1889 Il
Griffiths, G. 1889 Il
Griffiths, G.M. 1953 El Sw Iw Fw; 1954 Iw Fw Sw;
 1955 Iw Fw; 1957 El Sl
Griffiths, V.M. 1924 Sl Il Fw
Gronow, B. 1910 Fw El Sw Iw
Gwilliam, J.A. 1948 Il; 1949 Ew Sl Il Fl; 1950 Ew Sw
 Iw Fw; 1951 Ew Sl Id; 1952 Ew Sw Iw Fw; 1953 El
 Iw Fw; 1954 El
Gwynn, D. 1882 El; 1887 Sl; 1890 Ew Id; 1891 El Sl
Gwynn, W.H. 1884 El Sl Iw; 1885 El Sd
Hall, I. 1970 Sw Ew; 1971 Sw; 1974 Sw Id Fd
Hancock, F.E. 1884 Iw; 1885 El Sd; 1886 Sl
Hannan, J. 1889 Sl Il; 1890 Sl Ew Id; 1891 El; 1892
 El Sl Il; 1893 Ew Sw Iw; 1894 El Sw Il; 1895 El Sl
 Iw
Harding, A.F. 1902 Ew Sw Iw; 1903 Ew Sl Iw; 1904
 Ed Sw Il; 1905 Ew Sw Iw; 1906 Ew Sw Il; 1907 Iw;
 1908 Ew Sw
Harding, G.F. 1882 El; 1883 Sl
Harding, T. 1889 Sl Il
Harding, W.R. 1923 El Sl Fw Il; 1924 Il Fw; 1925 Fw
 Il; 1926 Ed Iw Fw; 1927 El Sl Fw Il; 1928 El
Harris, D.J.E. 1959 Iw Fl; 1960 Sw Iw Fl; 1961 Ew Sl
Hathway, G. 1924 Il Fw
Hawkins, F. 1912 Il Fw
Hayward, D. 1949 Ew Fl; 1950 Ew Sw Iw Fw; 1951
 Ew Sl Id Fl; 1952 Ew Sw Iw Fw
Hayward, D.J. 1963 El; 1964 Sw Iw Fd
Hayward, G. 1908 Sw Iw; 1909 Ew
Hellings, R. 1897 Ew; 1898 Iw El; 1899 Sl Il; 1900
 Ew Iw; 1901 Ew Sl
Herrera, R.C. 1925 Sl Fw Il; 1926 Ed Sl Iw Fw; 1927
 El
Hiams, H. 1912 Il Fw
Hickman, A. 1930 El; 1933 Sl
Hiddlestone, D. 1922 Ew Sd Iw Fw
Hill, A.F. 1885 Sd; 1886 El Sl; 1888 Sw Il; 1889 Sl;
 1890 Sl Id; 1893 Ew Sw Iw; 1894 El Sw Il
Hirst, G.L. 1912 Sw; 1913 Sw; 1914 El Sw Fw Iw
Hinam, S. 1925 Il; 1926 Ed Sl Iw Fw
Hinton, J.T. 1884 Iw
Hodder, W. 1921 El Sl Fw
Hodges, J.J. 1899 Ew Sl Il; 1900 Ew Sw Iw; 1901
 Ew Sl; 1902 Ew Sw Iw; 1903 Ew Sl Iw; 1904 Ed
 Sw; 1905 Ew Sw Iw; 1906 Ew Sw Il
Hodgson, G.T.R. 1962 Id; 1963 El Sw Il Fl; 1964 Ed
 Sw Iw Fd; 1966 Sw Il Fw; 1967 Il
Hollindale, B. 1913 El
Hollingdale, T. 1928 El Sw Il Fl; 1930 El
Holmes, T.D. 1979 Sw Iw Fl Ew; 1980 Fw El Sw Il;
 1982 Il Fw El; 1983 Ed Sw Iw Fl
Hopkin, W.H. 1937 Sl
Hopkins, P.L. 1909 Ew Iw; 1910 El
Hopkins, R. 1970 Ew (R)
Hopkins, T. 1926 Ed Sl Iw Fw
Hopkins, W.J. 1925 El Sl
Howells, B. 1934 El
Howells, G. 1957 El Sl Iw Fw
Howells, W.H. 1888 Sw Il

Hughes, D. 1970 Sw Ew Il
Hughes, G. 1934 El Sw Iw
Hughes, H. 1887 Sl 1889 Sl
Hughes, K. 1970 Il; 1974 Sw
Hullin, W.G. 1967 Sl
Hurrell, J.E. 1959 Fl
Hutchinson, F. 1894 Il; 1896 Sw Il
Huxtable, R. 1920 Fw Iw
Huzzey, H.V.P. 1898 Iw El; 1899 Ew Sl Il
Hybart, A.J. 1887 Ed
Ingledew, H.M. 1890 Id; 1891 El Sl
Isaacs, I. 1933 Ew Sl
Jackson, T.H. 1895 El
James, B. 1968 Ed
James, C.R. 1958 Fl
James, D. 1891 Iw; 1892 Sl Il; 1899 Ew
James, D.R. 1931 Fw Iw
James, E. 1890 Sl; 1891 Iw; 1892 Sl Il; 1899 Ew
James, M. 1948 Ed Sw Fl Il
James, T.O. 1935 Il; 1937 Sl
James, W.J. 1983 Ed Sw Iw Fl
James, W.P. 1925 El Sl
Jarman, H. 1910 El Sw Iw; 1911 Ew
Jarrett, K.S. 1967 Ew; 1968 Ed Sw; 1969 Sw Iw Fd
 Ew
Jenkins, A. 1920 Ew Sl Fw Iw; 1921 Sl Fw; 1922
 Fw; 1923 El Sl Fw Il; 1928 Sw Il
Jenkins, A.M. 1895 Iw; 1896 El
Jenkins, D.M. 1926 Ed Sl Iw Fw
Jenkins, D.R. 1929 El
Jenkins, E. 1910 Sw Iw
Jenkins, E.M. 1927 Sl Fw Il; 1928 El Sw Il Fl; 1929
 Fw; 1930 El Sl Iw Fw; 1931 Ed Sw Fw Iw; 1932 Ew
 Sw Il
Jenkins, L. 1923 Sl Fw
Jenkins, L.H. 1954 Iw; 1956 Ew Sw Il Fw
Jenkins, V.G.J. 1933 Ew Il; 1934 Sw Iw; 1935 Ed
 Sw; 1936 Ed Sw Iw; 1937 El; 1938 Ew Sl; 1939 El
Jenkins, W. 1912 Il Fw; 1913 Sw Iw
John, A. 1925 Il; 1928 El Sw Il
John, B. 1967 Sl; 1968 Ed Sw Il Fl; 1969 Sw Iw Fd
 Ew; 1970 Sw Ew Il; 1971 Ew Sw Iw Fw; 1972 Ew
 Sw Fw
John, D.E. 1923 Fw Il; 1928 El Sw Il
John, E.R. 1950 Ew Sw Iw Fw; 1951 Ew Sl Id Fl;
 1952 Ew Sw Iw Fw; 1953 El Sw Iw Fw; 1954 El
John, G. 1954 El Fw
John, J.H. 1926 Ed Sl Iw Fw; 1927 El Sl Fw Il
Johnson, T. 1921 El Fw Iw; 1923 El Sl Fw; 1924 El
 Sl; 1925 El Sl Fw
Johnson, W.D. 1953 El
Jones, A. 1934 Sw Iw
Jones, A.H. 1933 Ew Sl
Jones, B. Lewis 1950 Ew Sw Iw Fw; 1951 Ew Sl;
 1952 Ew Iw Fw
Jones, B.J. 1960 Iw Fl
Jones, Bob 1901 Iw
Jones, Bobby 1926 Ed Sl Fw
Jones, C.W. 1934 El Sw Iw; 1935 Ed Sw Il; 1936 Ed
 Sw Iw; 1938 Ew Sl Iw
Jones, C.W. 1920 Ew Sl Fw
Jones, D. 1948 Ed
Jones, D. 1897 Ew
Jones, D. 1902 Ew Sw Iw; 1903 Ew Sl Iw; 1905 Ew
 Sw Iw; 1906 Ew Sw

Powell, R.W. 1888 Sw Il

Powell, W.C. 1926 Sl Iw Fw; 1927 El Fw Il; 1928 Sw Il Fl; 1929 El Sw Fw Id; 1930 Sl Iw Fw; 1931 Ed Sw Fw Iw; 1932 Ew Sw Il; 1935 Ed Sw Il

Powell, W.J. 1920 Ew Sl Fw Iw

Price, B. 1961 Iw Fl; 1962 Ed Sl; 1963 El Sw Fl; 1964 Ed Sw Iw Fd; 1965 Ew Sw Iw Fl; 1966 Ew Sw Il Fw; 1967 Sl Il Fl Ew; 1969 Sw Iw Fd

Price, G. 1975 Fw Ew Sl Iw; 1976 Ew Sw Iw Fw; 1977 Iw Fl Ew Sw; 1978 Ew Sw Iw Fw; 1979 Sw Iw Fl Ew; 1980 Fw El Sw Il; 1981 Ew Sl Iw Fl; 1982 Il Fw El Sl; 1983 Ed Iw Fl

Price, M.J. 1959 Ew Sl Iw Fl; 1960 El Sw Iw Fl; 1962 Ed

Price, R.E. 1939 Sw Iw

Price, T.G. 1965 Ew Sw Iw Fl; 1966 Ew; 1967 Sl Fl

Priday, A.J. 1958 Iw; 1961 Iw

Pritchard, C. 1928 El Sw Il Fl; 1929 El Sw Fw Id

Pritchard, C.C. 1904 Sw Il; 1906 Ew Sw

Pritchard, C.M. 1904 Il; 1905 Ew Sw; 1906 Ew Sw Il; 1907 Ew Sl Iw; 1908 Ew; 1910 Fw El

Prosser, D.R. 1934 Sw Iw

Prosser, G. 1934 El Sw Iw

Prosser, J. 1921 Iw

Prosser, R. 1956 Sw Fw; 1957 El Sl Iw Fw; 1958 Ed Sw Iw Fl; 1959 Ew Sl Iw Fl; 1960 El Sw Iw Fl; 1961 Iw Fl

Prothero, G.J. 1964 Sw Iw Fd; 1965 Ew Sw Id Fl; 1966 Ew Sw Il Fw

Pryce-Jenkins, T.J. 1888 Sw Il

Pugh, C. 1924 Wl Sl Il Fw; 1925 El Sl

Pugsley, J. 1910 El Sw Iw; 1911 Ew Sw Fw Iw

Pullman, J. 1910 Fw

Purdon, F.J. 1882 El; 1883 Sl

Quinnell, D.L. 1972 Fw (R); 1973 Ew Sl; 1974 Sw Fd; 1975 Ew (R); 1977 Iw (R) Fl Ew Sw; 1978 Ew Sw Iw Fw; 1979 Sw Iw Fl Ew

Radford, W.J. 1923 Il

Ralph, A.R. 1931 Fw Iw; 1932 Ew Sw Il

Ramsey, S.H. 1896 El; 1904 Ed

Randell, R. 1924 Il Fw

Raybould, W.H. 1967 Sl Il Fl Ew; 1968 Il Fl; 1970 Ew Il Fw (R)

Rees, A. 1962 Ed Sl Fw

Rees, A.M. 1934 El; 1935 Ed Sw Il; 1936 Ed Sw Iw; 1937 El Sl Il; 1938 Ew Sl

Rees, B.I. 1967 Sl Il Fl

Rees, C.F.W. 1974 Id; 1981 Fl; 1982 Il Fw El Sl; 1983 Ed Sw Iw Fl

Rees, D. 1968 Sw Il Fl

Rees, D. 1900 Ew; 1903 Ew Sl; 1905 Ew Sw

Rees, H. 1937 Sl Il; 1938 Ew Sl Iw

Rees, H.E. 1979 Sw Iw Fl Ew; 1980 Fw El Sw Il; 1983 Ed Sw Iw Fl

Rees, J. 1920 Ew Sl Fw Iw; 1921 El Sl Iw; 1922 Ew; 1923 El Fw Il; 1924 El

Rees, J.I. 1934 El Sw Iw; 1935 Sw; 1936 Ed Sw Iw; 1937 El Sl Il; 1938 Ew Sl Iw

Rees, L. 1933 Il

Rees, P. 1947 Fw Iw

Rees, P.M. 1961 Ew Sl Iw; 1964 Iw

Rees, T.E. 1926 Iw Fw; 1928 El

Rees, T.J. 1935 Sw Il; 1936 Ed Sw Iw; 1937 El Sl

Rees-Jones, G.R. 1934 El Sw; 1935 Il; 1936 Ed

Reeves, F. 1920 Fw Iw; 1921 El

Rhapps, J. 1897 Ew

Rice-Evans, W. 1890 Sl; 1891 El Sl

Richards, B. 1960 Fl

Richards, C. 1922 Ew Sd Iw Fw; 1924 Il

Richards, D.S. 1979 Fl Ew; 1980 Fw El Sw Il; 1981 Ew Sl Iw Fl; 1982 Il Fw; 1983 Ed Sw Iw

Richards, E.S. 1885 El; 1887 Sl

Richards, G. 1927 Sl

Richards, I. 1925 El Sl Fw

Richards, K.H.L. 1961 Ew Sl Iw Fl

Richards, M.C.R. 1968 Il Fl; 1969 Sw Iw Fd Ew

Richards, R. 1956 Fw

Richards, R. 1913 Sw Fw Iw

Richards, T.L. 1923 Il

Richardson, S.J. 1979 Ew

Rickards, A.R. 1924 Fw

Ring, J. 1921 El

Ring, M.G. 1983 Ed

Ringer, P. 1979 Sw Iw Fl Ew; 1980 Fw El

Roberts, C. 1958 Iw Fl

Roberts, D.E.A. 1930 El

Roberts, E. 1886 El; 1887 Iw

Roberts, E.J. 1888 Sw Il; 1889 Il

Roberts, H.M. 1961 Ew Sl Iw Fl; 1962 Sl Fw; 1963 Il

Roberts, J. 1927 El Sl Fw Il; 1928 El Sw Il Fl; 1929 El Sw Fw Id

Roberts, M.G. 1971 Ew Sw Iw Fw; 1973 Iw Fl; 1975 Sl; 1979 Ew

Roberts, T. 1921 Sl Fw Iw; 1922 Ew Sd Iw Fw; 1923 El Sl

Roberts, W. 1929 El

Robins, J.D. 1950 Ew Sw Iw Fw; 1951 Ew Sl Id Fl; 1953 El Iw Fw

Robins, R.J. 1953 Sw; 1954 Fw Sw; 1955 Ew Sl Iw Fw; 1956 Ew Fw; 1957 El Sl Iw Fw

Robinson, I.R. 1974 Fd El

Rocyn-Jones, D.N. 1925 Il

Roderick, W.R.B. 1884 Iw

Rosser, M.A. 1924 Sl Fw

Rowlands, C.E. 1926 Iw

Rowlands, D.C.T. 1963 El Sw Il Fl; 1964 Ed Sw Iw Fd; 1965 Ew Sw Iw Fl

Rowlands, G. 1954 El Fw; 1956 Fw

Rowlands, J. 1885 El

Rowlands, K.A. 1962 Fw Id; 1963 Il; 1965 Iw Fl

Rowles, G.R. 1892 El

Samuel, D. 1891 Iw; 1893 Iw

Samuel, F. 1922 Sd Iw Fw

Samuel, J. 1891 Iw

Scourfield, T. 1930 Fw

Scrine, F. 1899 Ew Sl; 1901 Iw

Shanklin, J.L. 1970 Fw; 1973 Iw Fl

Shaw, G. 1973 Ew Sl Iw Fl; 1974 Sw Id Fd El; 1977 Iw Fl

Shea, J. 1920 Ew Sl; 1921 El

Simpson, H.J. 1884 El Sl Iw

Skrimshire, R.T. 1899 Ew Sl Il

Skym, A. 1928 El Sw Il Fl; 1930 El Sl Iw Fw; 1931 Ed Sw Fw Iw; 1932 Ew Sw Il; 1933 Ew Sl Il; 1935 Ed

Smith, J.S. 1884 El Iw; 1885 El

Sparks, B. 1954 Iw; 1955 Ew Fw; 1956 Ew Sw Il; 1957 Sl

Spiller, W. 1910 Sw Iw; 1911 Ew Sw Fw Iw; 1912 El Fw; 1913 El

Squire, J. 1977 Iw Fl; 1978 Ew Sw Iw Fw; 1979 Sw Iw Fl Ew; 1980 Fw El Sw Il; 1981 Ew Sl Iw Fl; 1982 Il Fw El; 1983 Ed Sw Iw Fl

Stadden, W.H. 1884 Iw; 1886 El Sl; 1887 Iw; 1888 Sw; 1890 Sl Ew

Stephens, G. 1912 El Sw Il Fw; 1913 El Sw Fw Iw

Stephens, I. 1981 Ew Sl Iw Fl; 1982 Il Fw El Sl

Stephens, Revd J.G. 1922 Ew Sd Iw Fw

Stephens, J.R.G. 1947 El Sw Fw Iw; 1948 Il; 1949 Sl Il Fl; 1951 Fl; 1952 Ew Sw Iw Fw; 1953 El Sw Iw Fw; 1954 El Iw; 1955 Ew Sl Iw Fw; 1956 Sw Il Fw; 1957 El Sl Iw Fw

Stock, A.R. 1924 Fw; 1926 Ed Sl

Stone, P. 1949 Fl

Strand-Jones, J. 1902 Ew Sw Iw; 1903 Ew Sl

Sutton, S. 1982 Fw El

Sweet-Escott, R.B. 1891 Sl; 1894 Il; 1895 Iw

Tamplin, W.E. 1947 Sw Fw Iw; 1948 Ed Sw Fl

Tanner, H. 1936 Ed Sw Iw; 1937 El Sl Il; 1938 Ew Sl Iw; 1939 El Sw Iw; 1947 El Sw Fw Iw; 1948 Ed Sw Fl Il; 1949 Ew Sl Il Fl

Taylor, A.R. 1937 Il; 1938 Iw; 1939 El

Taylor, C.G. 1884 El Sl Iw; 1885 El Sd; 1886 El Sl; 1887 Ed Iw

Taylor, J. 1967 Sl Il Fl Ew; 1968 Il Fl; 1969 Sw Iw Fd Ew; 1970 Fw; 1971 Ew Sw Iw Fw; 1972 Ew Sw Fw; 1973 Ew Sl Iw Fl

Thomas, A. 1964 Ed

Thomas, A.G. 1952 Ew Sw Iw Fw; 1953 Sw Iw Fw; 1954 El Iw Fw; 1955 Sl Iw Fw

Thomas, B.E. 1963 El Sw Il Fl; 1964 Ed Sw Iw Fd; 1965 Ew; 1966 Ew Sw Il; 1969 Sw Iw Fd Ew

Thomas, C. 1925 El Sl

Thomas, C.J. 1888 Il; 1889 Sl Il; 1890 Sl Ew Id; 1891 El Iw

Thomas, D. 1954 Iw

Thomas, D. 1961 Iw

Thomas, D. 1930 Sl Iw; 1932 Ew Sw Il; 1933 Ew Sl; 1934 El; 1935 Ed Sw Il

Thomas, D.J. 1904 Ed; 1910 El Sw Iw; 1911 Ew Sw Fw Iw; 1912 El

Thomas, D.L. 1937 El

Thomas, E. 1904 Sw Il; 1909 Sw Iw; 1910 Fw

Thomas, G. 1890 Id; 1891 Sl

Thomas, G. 1923 El Sl Fw Il

Thomas, H. 1912 Fw

Thomas, H. 1936 Ed Sw Iw; 1937 El Sl Il

Thomas, H.W. 1913 El

Thomas, I. 1924 El

Thomas, L.C. 1885 El Sd

Thomas, M.C. 1949 Fl; 1950 Ew Sw Iw Fw; 1951 Ew Sl Id Fl; 1952 Ew Sw Iw Fw; 1953 El; 1956 Ew Sw Il Fw; 1957 El Sl; 1958 Ed Sw Iw Fl; 1959 Iw Fl

Thomas, M.G. 1921 Sl Fw Iw; 1923 Fw; 1924 El

Thomas, R. 1908 Iw; 1909 Sw

Thomas, R. 1900 Ew Sw Iw; 1901 Ew

Thomas, R. 1909 Iw; 1911 Sw Fw; 1912 El Sw; 1913 El

Thomas, R.C.C. 1949 Fl; 1952 Iw Fw; 1953 Sw Iw Fw; 1954 El Iw Fw Sw; 1955 Sl Iw; 1956 Ew Sw Il; 1957 El; 1958 Ed Sw Iw Fl; 1959 Ew Sl Iw Fl

Thomas, R.L. 1889 Sl Il; 1890 Id; 1891 El Sl Iw; 1892 El

Thomas, S. 1890 Sl Ew; 1891 Iw

Thomas, W. 1927 El Sl Fw Il; 1929 El; 1931 Ed Sw; 1932 Ew Sw Il; 1933 Ew Sl Il

Thomas, W.Ll. 1894 Sw; 1895 El Iw

Thomas, W.D. 1968 Sw Il Fl; 1969 Ew; 1970 Sw Ew Il Fw; 1971 Ew Sw Iw Fw; 1972 Ew Sw Fw; 1973 Ew Sl Iw Fl; 1974 El

Thomas, W.H. 1885 Sd; 1886 El Sl; 1887 Ed Sl; 1888 Sw Il; 1890 Ew Id; 1891 Sl Iw

Thomas, W.J. 1961 Fl; 1963 Fl

Thomas, W.T. 1930 El

Thompson, J. 1923 El

Towers, W.H. 1887 Iw

Travers, G. 1903 Ew Sl Iw; 1905 Ew Sw Iw; 1906 Ew Sw Il; 1907 Ew Sl Iw; 1908 Ew Sw Iw; 1909 Ew Sw Iw; 1911 Sw Fw Iw

Travers, W.H. 1937 Sl Il; 1938 Ew Sl Iw; 1939 El Sw Iw; 1949 Ew Sl Il Fl

Treharne, E. 1882 El

Trew, W.J. 1900 Ew Sw Iw; 1901 Ew Sl; 1903 Sl; 1905 Sw; 1906 Sw; 1907 Ew Sl; 1908 Ew Sw Iw; 1909 Ew Sw Iw; 1910 Fw El Sw; 1911 Ew Sw Fw Iw; 1912 Sw; 1913 Sw Fw

Trott, R.F. 1948 Ed Sw Fl Il; 1949 Ew Sl Il Fl

Truman, H. 1934 El; 1935 Ed

Trump, L. 1912 El Sw Il Fw

Turnbull, B.R. 1925 Il; 1927 El Sl; 1928 El Fl; 1930 Sl

Turnbull, M.J. 1933 Ew Il

Uzzell, H. 1912 El Sw Il Fw; 1913 Sw Fw Iw; 1914 El Sw Fw Iw; 1920 Ew Sl Fw Iw

Uzzell, J.R. 1965 Ew Sw Iw Fl

Vickery, W. 1938 Ew Sl Iw; 1939 El

Vile, T.H. 1908 Ew Sw; 1910 Iw; 1912 Il Fw; 1913 El; 1921 Sl

Waldron, R. 1965 Ew Sw Iw Fl

Waller, P.D. 1909 Ew Sw Iw; 1910 Fw

Walters, D. 1902 Ew

Wanbon, R. 1968 Ed

Ward, W. 1934 Sw Iw

Warlow, J. 1962 Id

Watkins, D. 1963 El Sw Il Fl; 1964 Ed Sw Iw Fd; 1965 Ew Sw Iw Fl; 1966 Ew Sw Il Fw; 1967 Il Fl Ew

Watkins, E. 1926 Sl Iw Fw

Watkins, E. 1924 Wl Sl Il Fw

Watkins, E. 1937 Sl Il; 1938 Ew Sl Iw; 1939 El Sw

Watkins, H. 1904 Sw Il; 1905 Ew Sw Iw; 1906 Ew

Watkins, S.J. 1964 Sw Iw Fd; 1965 Ew Sw Iw Fl; 1966 Ew Sw Il Fw; 1967 Sl Il Fl Ew; 1968 Ed Sw; 1969 Sw Iw Fd Ew; 1970 Ew Il

Watkins, W. 1959 Fl

Watts, D. 1914 El Sw Fw Iw

Watts, J. 1907 Ew Sl Iw; 1908 Ew Sw Iw; 1909 Sw Iw

Watts, W. 1914 El

Watts, W.H. 1892 El Sl Il; 1893 Ew Sw Iw; 1894 El Sw Il; 1895 El Iw; 1896 El

Weaver, D. 1964 Ed

Webb, J. 1907 Sl; 1908 Ew Sw Iw; 1909 Ew Sw Iw; 1910 Fw El Sw Iw; 1911 Ew Sw Fw Iw; 1912 El Sw

Webb, J.E. 1889 Sl

Wells, G.T. 1955 Ew Sl; 1957 Iw Fw; 1958 Ed Sw

Westacott, D. 1906 Il

Wetter, H. 1913 El